Quality Management
Handbook

QUALITY AND RELIABILITY

A Series Edited by

Edward G. Schilling
Center for Quality and Applied Statistics
Rochester Institute of Technology
Rochester, New York

Other volumes in preparation

Quality Management Handbook

Edited by

LOREN WALSH
RALPH WURSTER
RAYMOND J. KIMBER

Hitchcock Publishing Company
Wheaton, Illinois

MARCEL DEKKER INC.
ASQC QUALITY PRESS

New York and Basel
Milwaukee, Wisconsin

Library of Congress Cataloging-in-Publication Data
Main entry under title:

Quality management handbook.

Includes index.
1. Quality control—Handbooks, manuals, etc.
I. Walsh, Loren. II. Wurster, Ralph, [date]
III. Kimber, Raymond J., [date]
TS156.Q3Q37 1985   658.5'62   85-29354
ISBN 0-8247-7438-8

MARCEL DEKKER, INC.
270 Madison Avenue, New York, New York 10016

Current printing (last digit):
10 9 8 7 6 5 4 3 2 1

PRINTED IN THE UNITED STATES OF AMERICA

FOREWORD

Quality used to be the sole responsibility of the Quality Professional and confined to the manufacturing floor. Now we see a company-wide concern with quality and recognize that it is affected by every member of the organization. Quality is the broadest of all management functions. What used to be considered a technical subject has now become a management subject. Passing through this transition has been difficult because everyone didn't have the same comprehension of what was involved; they couldn't communicate.

That is why I am so delighted with the *Quality Management Handbook*. It covers all the aspects that managers need to deal with and also provides support for the professional. The authors have been carefully selected for their understanding of the overall subject of Quality Management, as well as the specific functions they are dealing with. We reside in an era where quality has become an absolute necessity instead of an added characteristic. It is the price of admission to a market, not something that can be viewed as extra. Running an organization to make that happen requires management participation. During my years in the quality business I have seen a great many changes in the material available to those who were involved in making quality happen—beginning with vague government specifications that urged control of "nonconforming material" by means of statistical tables that could be used by a few skilled people, and into the emerging philosophy that came with the recognition that quality was something that could actually be caused.

This handbook is an attempt to bring together a great deal of what is known today about how to make quality happen. All of the authors do not agree with each other completely and that speaks for the honesty of the book. Controversy and discussion lead to growth. These people are writing from experience and information: together they have produced a startling collection of quality know-how.

The handbook is meant to be used as reference, but I think it should be read in depth as well. Each chapter contains some information that the reader does not now possess; at least, I know that is true in my case. Looking through it will lead the reader to questions that the book can help to answer, and that may institute the development of a clearer understanding of the philosophy of Quality Management.

Philip Crosby

PREFACE

It was not very long ago that quality was considered something that was added to a product or service—usually by a group or department called quality control or quality assurance or, perhaps, inspection. It was assumed that, like any other service function, the addition of quality cost money. It was also assumed by many that the lowest possible price for a product or service would be realized without this added frill.

Further, because this addition to the product or service was provided by the "quality" department, that department was then responsible for quality. It seemed straightforward. If the paint department was responsible for putting on paint, the quality department was responsible for adding quality. Many production, sales, and engineering managers (and other company executives)—and nearly all the quality department managers—honestly believed that quality was the responsibility of the quality department. Unfortunately, as Phil Crosby put it, "Quality managers proudly stood up and announced that they personally were responsible for quality in a particular operation. Just as regularly, and not so proudly, they were sent down in flames when they were unable to solve all of the quality problems of the company." (Crosby's book *Quality Is Free* was one of the first to shatter the myth that quality managers were responsible for product quality.)

In recent times, thanks largely to Crosby, W. Edwards Deming, and a few others, the concept that quality must be designed and built into a product or service—that it cannot be added like an accessory—began to grow and even flourish.

But if quality is supposed to be designed and built into the product or service, not added to it by the quality department, who then is responsible for it? The answer, again provided by Crosby and Deming: management is. Since management (and in particular, upper management) collectively is now responsible for quality, *all* managers are quality managers—including, of course, the manager of the quality department. Does that mean that the marketing manager or the comptroller is responsible for quality? The answer is, absolutely. And so are the chief engineer, and the purchasing manager and the millwright foreman responsible for quality.

Thus was born the necessity for the *Quality Management Handbook*, a book for all managers because all managers are now quality managers. The *Quality Management Handbook* was created as a handy desk reference. It has been written primarily for—but is certainly not limited to—managers and other executives who now must have at least a handshake understanding of the technology of quality.

By and large, this book does not contain heavy mathematics or engineering terminology; those subjects are thoroughly covered in books on math and engineering. The *Quality Management Handbook*, instead, is intended to be used as a first reference—much like an encyclopedia. Most chapters contain a bibliography and/or an additional reading list for those who would like to further pursue their knowledge of a topic. We believe that this book contains, in one volume, a wealth of knowledge and information, much of which is unavailable in other books.

No work of this extent could be completed by one or even several people. The editors were assisted by many people and our thanks is hardly sufficient to repay their efforts. To the authors of the chapters included here—the people who really made this book possible—is owed an overwhelming debt of gratitude. They gave of their time and knowledge, and then their patience while it was all being put together. Special thanks are also due Shirley Sustman, Annette Mola, Candi Loftus, Lisbeth Schar, Arlene Bartolini, Bev Morris, Joan Wilder, and Charlie Doyle. We are indebted to them.

Loren Walsh
Ralph Wurster
Raymond J. Kimber

CONTENTS

CONTRIBUTORS

Dan D. Ashcraft   Oklahoma State University, Stillwater, Oklahoma

Charles A. Aubrey, II   Bank One Corporation, Columbus, Ohio

Quality Assurance Group, Electronics Division   Allen-Bradley Company, Milwaukee, Wisconsin

Harold S. Balaban   Advanced Research and Development Group, Aeronautical Radio, Inc., Annapolis, Maryland

Douglas A. Blakeslee   Eaton Corporation, Danbury, Connecticut

Carl C. Blau   NCR Corporation, Dayton, Ohio

William E. Blouch   Loyola College in Maryland, Baltimore, Maryland

Keith Burbridge   BFH Parametrics, Mountain View, California

William Cash   Unitek Corporation, Monrovia, California

William A. Chapman   NCR Corporation, Dayton, Ohio

Charles A. Cianfrani   Fischer & Porter Company, Warminster, Pennsylvania

Joseph J. Cieplak   Acco Industries, Inc., Bridgeport, Connecticut

Robert E. Cole*   University of Michigan, Ann Arbor, Michigan

---

*Present affiliation: Wilson Center, Washington, D.C.

Philip B. Crosby   Philip Crosby Associates, Inc., Winter Park, Florida

Ralph Deaghn   Packer Engineering, Naperville, Illinois

Anthony DeBellis   Acco Industries, Inc., Bridgeport, Connecticut

Eugene W. Ellis   Eugene W. Ellis, Associates, Sanford, North Carolina

Norbert L. Enrick   Kent State University, Kent, Ohio

Ralph A. Evans   Evans Associates, Durham, North Carolina

Donald F. Faw   NCR Corporation, Dayton, Ohio

David L. Field   Consultant, Lake Bluff, Illinois

Lowell W. Foster   Lowell W. Foster Associates, Inc., Minneapolis, Minnesota

Robert W. Grenier   Weil-McLain Co., Michigan City, Indiana

John T. Hagan   International Telephone and Telegraph Corporation, New York, New York

John J. Heldt   FLR Consulting Services, San Jose, California

Spencer Hutchens, Jr.   Intertek Services Corporation, Rolling Hills, California

Roger G. Langevin   Argyle Associates, Inc., New Canaan, Connecticut

Ronald A. Lavoie   Federal Products Corporation, Providence, Rhode Island

Jay Leek   Philip Crosby Associates, Inc., Winter Park, Florida

Cal S. McCamy   Macbeth Division of Kollmorgen Corporation, Newburgh, New York

Paul J. Mikelonis   General Casting Corporation, Waukesha, Wisconsin

Richard Y. Moss   Hewlett-Packard Company, Palo Alto, California

Ben A. Murray   Ben Murray Associates, New York, New York

James A. Nelson   Buehler Limited, Lake Bluff, Illinois

Kenneth Packer   Packer Engineering, Naperville, Illinois

David Pettigrew   Consultant, LaGrange, Illinois

George O. Rice   Rockwell International, Anaheim, California

William Schleicher   Hitchcock Publishing Co., Wheaton, Illinois

Frank Sliwak   Consultant, Cassleberry, Florida

Martin Smith   Dyna Pak Corporation, Stanhope, New Jersey

Frank H. Squires   Squires Associates, Los Angeles, California

Mae-Goodwin Tarver   Quest Associates Ltd., Park Forest, Illinois

Jon Turino   Logical Solutions, Inc., Campbell, California

Robert W. Vincent   Philip Crosby Associates, Inc., Winter Park, Florida

Darrell Ward   Consultant, West Chicago, Illinois

Kermit F. Wasmuth*   Martin Marietta Corporation, Orlando, Florida

Lewis E. Zwissler   Management Analysis Company, San Diego, California

_____

*Present affiliation: Consultant, Katy, Texas

Quality Management
Handbook

1

MANAGEMENT AND POLICY

PHILIP B. CROSBY

Philip Crosby Associates, Inc.
Winter Park, Florida

I. INTRODUCTION

Quality management is the system of establishing defect prevention actions and attitudes within a company or organization on a permanent basis for the purpose of assuring conforming products or services. Quality management includes conducting measurement and appraisal activities such as inspection and test, standard control, software evaluation, product qualification, and more. The basic concepts of quality management—as they relate to a company—were derived from quality control as it relates to a process.

II. QUALITY CONTROL

Quality control is concerned with observing a process, identifying the variable characteristics of its content, and then tracking these variables through scientifically devised statistical methods. The measurement of the variables, while they are being accomplished, permits holding the process to its specified performance limits. This prevents defects from occurring; or at least finds them at the earliest possible moment.

III. QUALITY MANAGEMENT

Quality management treats the company as a process and the various management systems within that process as the variables that require measurement and control. However, each of these variables is devised and conducted by a group of individuals, whereas in quality control the variables are accomplished by a chemical or physical process. That is why quality management requires an understanding of the way the whole company operates. It also requires a comprehension of the company goals, which are not spelled out on a process plan or blueprint; a familiarity with other functional management systems, such as marketing, engineering, finance, and purchasing; and a willingness to spend time helping other functions measure and control their own operating characteristics.

Quality control is thing and process oriented; quality management is people and system oriented. The purpose of quality management is to make the company run more smoothly and more profitably by preventing problems. It also serves as the key element in solving those difficulties that do escape the prevention system. In many ways quality management serves as a catalyst— bringing together activities with a common purpose and different methods.

Quality management must report organizationally in such a way that it is free of control by those whom it is measuring and assisting. In most cases this means that it should be working for the chief executive officer. It should never be part of operations because this is only a small part of its activities.

IV. QUALITY ENGINEERING

Quality engineering is a major element contained within the quality management function. It is responsible for activities within other departments and particularly involved with establishing their internal quality control programs. Quality engineering assists the appraisal function in establishing acceptance methods and procedures, conducts failure analysis, and reports results and needs for corrective action.

A. Purchasing

Quality engineering assists purchasing in vendor selection, prepares the buyer rating results, and trains supplier personnel in quality concepts and techniques. It determines the need for source control or inspection and sets up the appraisal plan for products or services in conjunction with purchasing.

B. Engineering

A major role of quality engineering is to help arrange design reviews, product qualification, life testing, and other objective performance measurements oriented to prevention. It provides engineering with data concerning manufacturing and customer experience with products.

C. Marketing and Sales

Marketing depends on quality engineering to provide product performance data to assist in the selling of the product, conduct quality seminars for the customers, and handle consumer affairs activities. Quality engineers share results with marketing concerning specific causes of complaints and ways of preventing them. They also provide experience data to assist in developing new specifications.

D. Comptroller

Quality engineering assists the comptroller in identifying the characteristics of the cost of quality within both product and service areas. Another responsibility would be to devise quality control programs to evaluate clerical accuracy.

E. Manufacturing

In the manufacturing area, quality engineering determines appraisal activities for each product and process, assists in selecting test equipment and devising sampling techniques, and conducts quality orientation for manufacturing personnel.

F. Administration

Quality engineering arranges new employee orientation programs in cooperation with personnel and conducts company-wide quality awareness activities. It also provides measurement guidance for internal programs.

G. Top Management

Top management is furnished quality status information showing areas where problems are occurring and listing specific causes, responsibilities, and actions under way. Quality engineering also provides continuing status charts visible in work areas (both white and blue collar) and gives smaller, desk-size copies to key management personnel.

V. QUALITY DEPARTMENT ACTIVITIES

A. Appraisal Operations

The inspection and test functions—ranging from suppliers' plants, through receiving, in-process, assembly, clerical, engineering, field, and wherever applicable—for the company should be designed specifically by quality engineering. No appraisal activities should be conducted by chance; all must be part of the overall concept of treating the company as one large process that continually needs to be measured.

B. Failure Analysis

This is one of the most important jobs in the quality engineering task list. Analysis must be conducted primarily to determine the integrity of the overall quality management system, as well as getting the specific problem surfaced and resolved.

C. Appraisal

All appraisal functions having to do with the acceptance of the company's products or services must be accomplished by the quality department. In turn, quality engineering assumes responsibility for training and leadership of the personnel involved. The data generated by appraisal are the quality department's most significant product. It is these data that form the prevention strategy for the company; they also tell, on a continuing basis, a clear story of the status of the output.

D. Consumer Affairs

Customers with complaints need someone to talk with who is on their side. This function must be carefully oriented to think in customer's terms. All complaints must be handled within two working days and all departments that caused the problems must take corrective action immediately.

E. Quality Education

Administering the professional and other employee training necessary to maintain the competence of the quality function itself and the awareness of other departments is a key function. Actual training will be accomplished by quality management's functional personnel, but quality education must provide the spark and coordination.

F. Product Safety

The handling of product safety problems must be assigned to special teams consisting of quality engineers, lawyers, and appropriate specialists. Quality must chair this team.

G. Environmental Quality

This function is the liaison between the regulatory agencies and the company to make certain that all regulations are known and met. It must conduct continual self-audits within the company and manage the environmental quality function policies.

VI. STRATEGY OF QUALITY MANAGEMENT

Installing a quality management system in a company is a never-ending, long-range effort. There are six phases of evolution. They are listed in sequence, yet all of them occur in parallel since a company is a growing entity with new members coming and old members leaving on a regular basis. Each person must be taken through these phases in some manner; otherwise, he or she will not be in step with the remainder of the company.

A. Comprehension

There must be a solid understanding of what quality is all about, how the company feels about it, and a recognition that the goal is to "do things right the first time." In the case of management, this is the stage when it decides there has to be a better way of reaching its goals than continuing with the waste that faces it. All members of the company are included in the orientation.

B. Commitment

Everyone must in some way signify that they understand the quality concepts, agree with the goals, and will do their best to participate. The method of accomplishing this depends on the personality of the individual company. Some companies form a "quality club," some just request a show of hands, some sign pledges, some take group photos. No one way is best. However, the strategist should recognize that the step cannot be ignored. If the commitment is not registered as a conscious act, it will not be remembered.

C. Competence

Committed people who understand what has to be done will want to put their own houses in order. This is where the functional department can begin its own internal quality control programs with the assistance of the quality management function. Also, it is very important that quality function assures that all its activities are accomplished with the maximum effectiveness. There is a significant responsibility and burden in leading a quality improvement program—you must always work harder than anyone else in getting things right the first time. Zero defects has to be the performance standard of the quality department at all times.

D. Communication

Quality awareness activities expose the desire on the part of employees (of all levels) to have their problems heard. It is best to reach out early and ask to hear the problems rather than wait to be approached. Error-cause identification programs, group meetings, and discussions are very helpful and practical, particularly when set up on a continual basis. Professionally designed and marketed programs such as Buck-A-Day* provide employees with an interesting program that will improve morale and communications. They will also save the company money. An important part of the communication phase is that you must be ready to continue to work at it for a long time.

E. Correction

When people contribute ideas and participate, management must be ready to do something. Most of the problems that occur in a company can be corrected only by management. When employees see that management is really taking action, they will believe that management is serious about the whole business of defect prevention. Corrective action should be organized through natural interfaces and a methodical listing of problems taken to the proper activities for correction. Follow-through should be in a disciplined manner. Employees who list items must be notified immediately that their input has been received and be told of the disposition of the items.

F. Continuance

As noted, the phases must be conducted on a continuing basis. However, this will not happen unless they are scheduled exactly and someone is responsible for continuing and conducting them. Planned acts range from a visit to a new executive in the manner of "welcome wagon," to the orientation of new employees as they join the company (not after they have been there for a while), and to the recommitment of the entire population to quality improvement on an annual basis.

G. Policies

A company management must state clearly its method of operating if it wants its employees to understand and implement it. The six C's apply to running

---

*Copyright Industrial Motivation, Inc., 331 Madison Avenue, New York.

a company, as well as to installing a defect prevention quality program. Managers of all functions and professions traditionally blame their senior management for not supporting them or for not providing the proper leadership. In reality, individual managers must make certain that the policies necessary to their functions exist and that everyone understands them.

In quality management there are three key policies that have to exist to smooth the way for installing the company-wide program.

1. The company management must state its standards concerning the subject of quality. The policy should be couched in words typically used within the company, but the policy should state these things:

> It is the intent of the X Company and its management that all products and services supplied by this company will conform exactly to the specifications and advertisements our customers have used to purchase from us. The quality department is responsible for assuring that all products or services received by the company meet this requirement and for reporting any differences immediately so that corrective action can take place.
>
> Quality means conformance to the requirements. Our standard is zero defects, which means "do it right the first time." Our performance measurement is the cost of quality, which is the expense of doing things wrong. The comptroller reports the cost of quality.
>
> Each department will conduct its own internal, continual quality improvement program (with support from the quality department) to guarantee its ability to meet these standards, and each employee is expected to do everything he or she can to help all of us accomplish this necessary goal. Communication programs will be conducted continually to assure that each of us can hear the other on this subject.

2. The management must clearly state the organizational responsibility and reporting relationship of the quality department. The department itself must issue an operating policy concerning all the activities that take place within it.

> The company quality department must always be organizationally independent of those operations it is charged with measuring. For that reason the quality director will report to the chief executive officer.
>
> The quality department will assist other departments in devising and conducting the appropriate internal quality control programs, and will conduct company-wide quality awareness functions.
>
> In addition, the department will perform all appraisal activities, report the results, and conduct corrective action systems. Quality engineering, consumer affairs, environmental quality, product safety, reliability, and other appropriate functions shall be included in the department's responsibility.

3. The management policy must state what it means by requiring other departments to:

> Conduct appropriate internal quality control programs in their operation. This means a "spelling out of how those departments can identify the necessary actions to develop Comprehension (rewriting the quality logic so that it fits the terms of their professions); Commitment (deciding to do some reviews and inspection inside); Competence (conducting internal audits

with the support of quality engineering); Communication (conducting quality awareness and error cause removal or Make Certain activities); Correction (setting up an action team); and Continuance (having their own quality improvement team to review status continually).

The astute quality department will supply guidelines to other functions—
which they will be delighted to receive—concerning some actions to be taken
and methods of measuring nonhardware activities. All of these policies, and
the procedures necessary to implement them, should be included in the company
quality manual.

Quality management and the defect prevention system it creates must be
treated as a living system requiring continual nourishment and attention. The
quality department does not need to be large in terms of numbers of people or
budget. It needs only to be large in terms of action and strategy.

FURTHER READING

Crosby, P. B., *The Art of Getting Your Own Sweet Way*, McGraw-Hill, New
York, 1972. Paperback: Hawthorne Books.
Crosby, P. B., *Cutting the Cost of Quality*, Farnsworth, Boston, 1967.
Crosby, P. B., *Quality Is Free*, McGraw-Hill, New York, 1979. Paperback:
New American Library Mentor Series.
Crosby, P. B., *Strategy of Situation Management*, Farnsworth, Boston, 1969.

2

ORGANIZATION AND PLANNING

KERMIT F. WASMUTH*

Martin Marietta Corporation
Orlando, Florida

I. INTRODUCTION

The organization of the quality function is the second most important element in building an effective quality system. The first is the recognition by the general management that the quality task is a vital cog in the machinery of production, and one that deserves a clear commitment for support. Essential to this support is a well-defined management policy identifying the quality role. All too frequently this role is either obscurely stated or not defined at all. In today's complex industrial world a quality system can take many forms, depending on a myriad of influencing factors. It is imperative that in every case the organization should be structured around a statement of company policy which clearly defines the authority, responsibility, and accountability of the executive leading the quality effort. There must be no doubt as to the scope of this task.

II. QUALITY CHARTER

For a small company the statement of quality policy can be as simple as the following:

> The quality manager (or chief inspector) reports directly to the plant manager and is responsible to determine by sufficient inspection that the company products conform to all pertinent company/customer specifications and drawings. Products deviating from specifications will be withheld from shipment and will be reviewed jointly by the plant manager and the quality manager for disposal and corrective action.

Such a statement clearly identifies that quality is an independent function and that the task is limited to one of inspection and the accumulation of defect

---

Present affiliation: Consultant, Katy, Texas.

data for review. Inasmuch as no mention is made of the accumulation of historical data, it must be assumed that none is required.

At the other end of the spectrum the statement of responsibility, accountability, and authority for the quality manager of a very large corporation can be extensive and detailed; for example:

Under the policy guidance of the vice president and general manager, responsibility, accountability, and authority is vested in the director/manager of quality as follows:

Responsibility:

1. Plan, control, direct, develop, and evaluate the operations of the functional departments assigned to his or her area
   a. Quality assurance, which includes:
      Product assurance
      Quality audit
      Laboratories
   b. Quality control, which includes:
      Internal quality control
      Supplier quality control
   c. Quality program management
2. Ensure that products delivered to customers meet all standards of quality contained in contracts and specifications.
3. Ensure that operations or processes affecting quality standards and performance are tested, audited, and evaluated.
4. Ensure that program areas are supported and assisted in terms of systems, techniques, and trained personnel necessary to enable such programs to meet quality standards and requirements.
5. Examine quality policies, instructions, and procedures to ensure that they are effective, appropriate, and congruent with the accomplishment of division objectives.
6. Establish a work environment that ensures the development and effective utilization of personnel and the proper combining of resources necessary to carry out quality programs and meet objectives.
7. Maintain a continuing liaison with customer personnel and agencies which generates a positive understanding of quality systems and commitment.
8. Communicate division goals; develop and disseminate concise statements of the quality groups tasks and standards of performance, and evaluate results against these standards.

Accountability:

1. Products delivered to customers meeting all specified standards of quality contained in contracts and specifications.
2. Achievement of required quality at cost within limits of allocated funds.
3. The performance, morale, and motivation of assigned personnel.
4. The integration of his assigned functional departments with the remainder of the division.
5. Prepare data that identify for management trends in hardware quality, costs related to scrap and production errors, and overall cost of the quality function.

Authority:

1. The supervision, administration, and execution of programs, policies, and functions assigned, so as to ensure the division's capability of attaining its profit and long-range commitments.
2. Develop and maintain systems, controls, and techniques which provide for the timely detection, solution, and elimination of quality problems and their causes.
3. Approve program personnel certification board requirements.

Whatever the dimensions of the task—if it is clearly defined—both the quality organization and the rest of the production operation understand what the quality department is required to do.

An equally important element in organizing for quality is the recognition that the production of a quality product is the responsibility of every division of the company involved in the production process: engineering, manufacturing, material handling, and purchasing, as well as quality. This responsibility begins at the point of initial design and continues throughout the life of the product. All company divisions must keep the requirement for quality basic in their activities. Only by working as a team can the goal of a product that delivers ultimate customer satisfaction at the lowest cost be achieved.

III. THE BASIC QUALITY TASK

An understanding of the basic task to be accomplished is fundamental to developing an organization. Although there are many variations of emphasis, the fundamental tasks of the quality organization can be identified as follows:

1. *The prevention of defects through analysis of requirements*: It is axiomatic that elimination of potential problems before production begins will result in lower cost and a better-quality product. Unaccountably, this is an area all too frequently ignored. The inclusion of manufacturing and quality personnel in the early review of preliminary designs can reap handsome rewards by way of a more realistic tolerancing, dimensioning for easier machining, elimination of difficult assembly processes, better understanding of test requirements, and so on.

Quality reviews at this stage can establish the proper sequencing of inspection requirements, eliminating unnecessary inspections which make no real contribution to product quality. The review will also pinpoint similarities in design to past products which have suffered from failures or defects. Early identification of such problems can lead to corrections or changes that will eliminate the probability of recurrence.

2. *Control of the manufacturing and test operations*: To achieve product quality it is necessary to be certain that every manufacturing action is performed according to predetermined standards and instructions. There is no substitute for the discipline that ensures this control. In theory it makes no difference who exercises such control. The factory workers who are properly motivated can be just as effective in controlling their output as the inspector who normally checks their work. This is equally true for all other functions involved in product manufacture.

In real life, however, the practicalities of meeting cost and schedule commitments generally mitigate against production personnel being an effective force for sustained and improved quality. It falls to the quality organization to exercise this control or restraining activity. It is incumbent that they be equipped both mentally and technically to accept the responsibility. Failure to do an effective job has sometimes been due to the reluctance of quality management to accept the fact that the company really meant for them to control the production operation to the degree necessary to produce satisfactory hardware.

3. *Detection of defectives in the hardware*: Detection of hardware and test errors is the traditional role of the inspection force within the quality organization. The effectiveness of this function has a marked effect on overall control of the product.

4. *Corrective action to prevent repetition of mistakes*: Repetitive mistakes are costly, interfere with schedules, and are unnecessary. Every company, however small, must have a system to recognize repetitive problems and eliminate their cause. It is important to recognize that the elimination of some problems may be so costly as to prohibit any constructive action. A conscious decision to take no action must be carefully weighed against the possible results of such a decision.

5. *Planning for a more effective operation*: One of the more noticeable shortcomings in many quality organizations is the absence of effort directed toward the future needs of the division. All too frequently the planning effort is concentrated on today's problems, with little thought given to future developments. Clearly, a function of quality is to provide expertise to consider possible changes or modifications in order to be more effective and meet future challenges.

IV. ORGANIZATIONAL CONCEPTS

At the outset it should be recognized that there are no absolutes with respect to the manner in which the quality function is organized. The basic tasks of quality must be satisfied in some manner, but the organization required is dependent on a variety of factors. It should be developed to fit the job at hand: what is required for complex mechanical hardware is patently different from that required for a supplier of simple parts, a chemical processing concern, or a supplier of services.

The opening paragraph of this chapter identified the need for a commitment by management; a definition of the quality charter—what, precisely, does the management expect from the quality group? The size of the task has a marked influence on the nature of the ultimate organization. The most effective group is one that accomplishes its task with a minimum of organizational requirements.

There is also no common agreement with respect to what the organization for quality is called. Quality Control, Quality Division, Quality Assurance, Product Assurance, and Quality and Reliability Assurance are all titles that appear on company organization charts, and it matters little what the organization is called as long as its charter is properly defined. Quality assurance, for example, has been used to designate a total, complex quality organization; a small audit group in such an organization; a group responsible for all non-inspection quality tasks; and a separate organization independently auditing and reviewing all aspects of quality within a company.

The specific task requirements may also influence the basic approach to organization. A limited responsibility may be best served by a quality assurance group acting in a staff capacity as mentioned above. Some large organizations consider it desirable to monitor the quality function by having a group of operating executives act as a quality committee, or quality council, establishing basic policy and ensuring that such policy is communicated to the operating divisions. The important factor is to recognize the scope of the work and to organize for it. It is also necessary to recognize that flexibility and the ability to change must be allowed for in the structure.

In every company there are built-in constraints that can have an effect on how a task is organized, and these constraints must be recognized and taken into consideration. Identified below are a number of such constraints with a short paragraph outlining their effect. These are by no means all that could be developed, nor are they examined in detail. Rather, they are indicators of real-life situations that must be faced in the development of a good quality organization. Organizational theorists sometimes choose to ignore these constraints, but they are real and must be a consideration in any organizing effort.

1. *Company operational and organizational guidelines*: Every company has developed over its history certain guidelines relating to how it organizes and operates. Usually, but not always, these are written down in the form of policy or standard practice manuals. Although these are not necessarily inviolate, the wise manager will find it prudent to stay within these guidelines unless they prevent the proper accomplishment of the quality objective.

2. *Management style*: Over the years, most companies develop a management "style." This style or attitude is reflected in the way the management team operates, both within the organization and in the marketplace. For example; some companies are highly disciplined, outlining in written procedures all possible situations and following the procedures to the letter. At the other end of the spectrum is the laissez-faire approach; nothing very formal, each executive doing his or her own thing and keeping in touch with peers in the organization. In some organizations nothing gets done unless the top executive personally decides. This is not the place to comment on the merits of the various styles but only to point out that the company style must be considered in organizing for quality. It would be unrealistic to propose a highly formalized procedural system in a company where day-to-day problems are attacked by informal meetings of management. This is not to say that quality discipline should be ignored, but it must be organized in a manner that will fit the ongoing style. Traumatic changes can occur when a new chief executive arrives who operates with a completely different organizational style.

3. *Customer influences*: More frequently than not, the quality organization is dictated/affected by requirements of the customer. This may come from specifications, process controls, or even certain administrative actions required in order to do business. This is particularly true for companies having contracts with government agencies, each of which has its own special set of requirements or regulations. One of the quality manager's more difficult tasks is to develop an understanding in all levels of management (outside the quality organization) that these customer requirements are real and must be satisfied. Unfortunately, requirements of different customers are sometimes divergent to the point where multiple systems may be required. The challenge is to meet the intent of the requirements with the minimum disruption of the normal quality system. Quality costs can become exaggerated if the organization is expanded to cover every eventuality. This problem has always been particularly acute for those companies that act as subcontractors to a variety of other manufacturing concerns. Those who have a sound quality system based on well-established controls are usually able to negotiate an agreement substituting their procedures for the customer's requirements.

4. *Company size*: It would seem to go without saying that the size of the company itself has a marked effect on the quality organization. Although the basic quality task must be accomplished, the function has to fit into the framework of the overall organization. Large organizations have the facilities and finances to maintain systems and records, which, although desirable, may be well beyond the means of a smaller company. Conversely, a pitfall of some quality management teams is the urge to expand and grow simply because the company is large. Size and number of systems are not the measure of a superior quality operation—effectiveness is!

5. *Diversity and complexity of product line*: The diversity and complexity of the company product line have a strong influence on the development of the quality organizational structure. An organization that is suitable for the manufacture of a few, large, highly sophisticated, and individually costly articles may not resemble at all that required to produce volume deliveries of small, diverse, highly precise parts from automatic machinery. It is erroneous to conclude that any given quality system or technique, however successful in the past, is necessarily useful when the manufacturing product line changes radically or becomes completely different. As has been mentioned previously, the quality system must adapt itself to the evniroment in which it operates. The quality control system that is unable to change with product-line variations will eventually have to bear either the stigma of unnecessary cost or the failure to produce satisfactory hardware.

It is true that the same type of controls are often a requirement for entirely different products. It does not follow, however, that the technique of application must be the same. Indeed, the technique may be so radically different as to require a different organizational pattern. For example, precision castings for a space vehicle may have the same tolerance requirements as those for an engine block on an automotive assembly line. Automatic gaging would be prohibitively costly in the case of the space vehicle where the few castings involved would probably be checked individually by a highly skilled inspector, either by actual layout on a surface plate, or through the use of an inspection measuring machine. The automotive assembly line would probably have automatic gaging equipment built into the assembly line, which would be monitored by less-skilled checkers or by the production personnel. Both methods achieve the same end but through different techniques and a different organizational alignment.

6. *Stability of the product line*: Product stability can also have an influence on organizational structure. A product line that is relatively the same from year to year can generate economies, both in the use of personnel and selection of the most useful and economic equipment. Less supervision, more use of production checking data instead of direct inspection, and elimination of formal corrective action teams are ready candidates for system improvement in a stable manufacturing environment.

Improvements such as the above cannot be achieved when the product line changes frequently. A different structure is required to identify problems as they occur and to take the required action to correct them. The manager of the quality function must be alert to recognize when a change in product requires a change in the quality system.

7. *Financial stability*: Quality is a part of the business aspect of every company and its operation is dependent on the overall profitability of the concern. Quality managers cannot ignore, as some would have us believe, the cost of doing business and the financial stability of the entire organization. Quality managers should get their fair share of the money but must recognize

that the program has to be developed to fit the funds available. If risk taking is involved, the risks should be clearly identified to the company management.

8. *Availability of personnel*: The organization must always be formulated around the requirements of the task at hand. It would be unrealistic, however, not to recognize that the availability of certain key personnel may affect the formation of the ideal organization. Lack of certain skills in quantity may make it necessary for supervisory personnel to head more than one element where normally a separate grouping would be preferable. This can be true in lower-level technical assignments, where either cost or inability to hire creates a necessity for doubling up of responsibility. This may end up being cost-effective but usually involves the risk of missing some important element in the inspection cycle.

V. QUALITY FUNCTIONS TO BE CONSIDERED IN ORGANIZATIONAL PLANNING

The spectrum of functions that have been assigned to the quality organization is very broad. Some of these functions are universally accepted as a part of the quality role, whereas others are considered by many managements as being outside their conception of the quality charter. The following paragraphs identify the tasks that can be considered as part of the quality charter in the broadest sense. It should not be assumed that every organization must involve itself with each of these activities. The basic premise still holds that the organization should fit the job at hand, and cover only those tasks necessary to produce a quality product. Every production environment has need for different controls, and the quality charter should be structured around those needs, not to a list of possible functions. The general management of the company should be made aware of all of the possible quality tasks in order to support and, indeed, demand the controls required. Further, the paragraphs below are intended only as a brief outline of the principal elements of the function. Specific methodologies for the various tasks are covered in other chapters.

1. *Product design reviews*: Earlier, a basic quality function was identified as being the prevention of defects through analysis of requirements. Inclusion of quality engineers in the design review process at the earliest possible time is the medium for accomplishing this objective. Where formal design reviews do not exist, or where products are manufactured from another company's design, the quality engineers should still begin to critique the design as early as possible. This review should emphasize ease of manufacture and inspection, required process controls, similarity to past products which developed defects, and consideration of tolerancing problems in manufacture and assembly. It is not the responsibility of quality personnel to be the design checking function of the engineering department. Although glaring design deficiencies should not be allowed to develop without comment, the quality critique should be limited to matters that affect the manufacture and quality of the product. The danger in design reviews results from quality engineers frequently wishing to instruct the engineering department on how to design the product in its entirety.

2. *Quality planning*: Every quality organization should have a planning function, however small. In very small operations it may be part of the department head's duties, but it must exist for quality to survive. The many aspects of quality planning are diverse and will be covered in detail later in this chapter.

3. *Purchase order review*: The review by the quality group of all purchase orders for production materials is similar to the requirement for design review. History shows that purchased material is usually subject to more problems and uncompensated cost losses than that produced in-house. A considerable portion of these problems are the result of incomplete communication between the supplier and the company. Inasmuch as the department usually involved in stopping the flow of incoming material is the quality organization, it is imperative that they be represented as the order is placed. A review of purchase orders prior to release tends to minimize rejections by ensuring (a) that the proper specifications have been included, (b) that the necessary documentation has been requested, (c) that any additional inspection requirements are clearly stated, and (d) that the supplier selected is a satisfactory source and has been approved by the quality department.

This requirement for review must be organized as a function of volume. The quality group must make certain that the flow of the documentation through the division does not impede the placement of orders. The quality function can be handled by a single individual or a group, depending on the volume to be processed. In large organizations where the purchase order system is computerized, the quality input can be made a part of the system and input fed into the purchase order through a terminal located in the quality area.

4. *Supplier control*: A large part of the dollar cost of many manufactured products is spent in the plants of suppliers: in some companies it is actually a majority of the total cost. Many of these companies, however, spend virtually no money in the control of this supplier effort. The role of evaluating and checking the performance of these suppliers falls largely to the quality organization. A separate quality function dedicated to ensuring that the suppliers are attempting to meet all the requirements of the contract can result in significant savings. This is reflected principally in the elimination of defectives found in receiving inspection or even later in the production cycle where delay can be more costly than the actual part. This identifiable quality function is one of the most undervalued, and often unused, tools in the quality system.

5. *Receiving inspection*: This group is charged with determining that the parts and materials received from suppliers do, in fact, meet the requirements of the purchase order, including the receipt of proper documentation. The tasks vary from simple inspections to highly sophisticated tests using the most modern computerized techniques. The receiving inspection group also develops historical records of supplier performance for use in the placement of future orders. Some companies include purhcase order review (previously identified) as part of the receiving inspection function.

6. *Stores inspection and control*: Parts and materials need to be well controlled once they are manufactured or received from suppliers. It is the responsibility of Quality to determine that the system devised by the company for this control is being followed and that different materials and parts are not mixed together or issued incorrectly. Depending on company size, this task can either be a separate function or an added responsibility of another segment of Quality (i.e., receiving inspection, production inspection).

7. *Tool and fixture inspection*: The majority of manufacturing operations employ the use of specially manufactured tools and assembly fixtures. To minimize future rejection of hardware, the quality organization should be required to inspect such tools for adherence to the tool drawings and to inspect the first production lot for adherence to the engineering specifications prior to release of the tools for production.

✗ 8. *Product inspection*: Product inspection is the day-to-day chore of sorting the good from the bad. The inspection force is divided generally into three groups.

  a. *Fabricated parts*: All the piece-part hardware and the processes that produce them are controlled and inspected. This may be accomplished by sampling during a production run, by lot inspection prior to moving to the next production station, or at the end of the production of the finished article. Depending on the repeatability of the production equipment and the experience of the work force, this inspection can be very intense or simply an occasional check on a proven process.

  b. *Subassembly inspection*: As individual parts are assembled into larger components or subassemblies, a further check is required to ensure conformance as well as completeness. Frequently, a part of subassembly inspection involves test routines where operating components have been installed. Here again it should be recognized that the earlier problems are discovered, the lower will be the ultimate cost.

  c. *Final assembly*: The last critical inspection takes place during and after the final completion of the hardware. The degree to which this is emphasized has a relationship to the inspections and tests accomplished prior to this point; where subassembly inspections has been minimal, final inspection must be rigorous and all-inclusive. A system built on a heavy inspection and test cycle prior to final assembly may require only a rigorous final test. The variations in philosophy are limitless with respect to the degree of inspection at various stations. The true test is the production of satisfactory hardware with minimum losses due to bad hardware.

✗ 9. *Test control*: The role of the quality group with respect to the test function varies widely from industry to industry and from company to company. Each method has its strong adherents and it is sufficient to say that with the right management environment any of them can be successful. Some of the most widely recognized methods for quality monitoring and control are outlined briefly below.

  a. *Quality operation of the test department*: In this system the quality division is directly responsible to write test procedures, design the test equipment, and run the actual tests as an independent agency.

  b. *Direct control of test by monitoring all phases*: The quality group is responsible to review and approve test procedures written by others, verify that the test setups are in conformance with the approved procedures, monitor the testing as it is being performed, and certify the test results as being acceptable. Their responsibility involves stopping the testing at any point where the results are not in accordance with procedures or specifications.

  c. *Monitoring of tests written and performed by other departments*: In this system the quality role is limited to observing the tests as performed by a test organization and certifying that the results match the written procedures.

  d. *Minimum role*: The minimum role that quality personnel can perform in the test area is to verify that written procedures exist, that they are being followed, and that a spotcheck of the test results indicates compliance to the requirements.

The gamut of quality participation actually involves combinations of systems outlined above. Again, the objective is to be certain that for the product involved, sufficient independent quality control is exercised to ensure satisfactory hardware.

10. *Final acceptance*: Final acceptance of the product prior to delivery is a basic quality task. Organizationally, this can take different forms: a part of a test; the last inspection station; or in the case of alrge complicated items, a final review of product and paperwork in a separate department.

11. *Customer interface*: The customer interface that pertains particularly to the quality organization is the one that has to do with those who make acceptance for the customer. The quality department, having the records and history of the product, as well as the customer's spectifications, is charged with the task of interfacing with the customer to assure acceptance of the hardware. One of the pitfalls that some companies make for themselves is the mistake of having salespeople attempt to "sell" the customer the finished product, and then try to explain any questionable items. Not only does this not satisfy the customer, it frequently generates a general distrust of the producer's intentions. Quality personnel are best equipped to handle this sensitive interface.

12. *Process control*: The control of the basic processes used in the production of hardware and other products is fundamental to achieving an acceptable end result. Heat treatment, chemical processing, batch mixing, surface preparation, and protection are examples of the types of processing that must be rigorously controlled if rejection costs are to be kept within bounds. In the nonhardware industries, such as petroleum, medicines, and foodstuffs, process control is the only real control prior to sampling the final product. The staffing of the process control function is dependent on the number and type of processes involved. Where it fits organizationally within the quality group is determined by its size relationship to other quality operations.

13. *Laboratory operations*: All quality organizations do not need the services of a full-time laboratory, but most need some laboratory work performed on a routine basis. Chemical and physical analysis of materials, process control checks, requirements for x-ray, and so on, are all laboratory operations essential to good quality control. These services may be obtained in a more cost-effective manner by the use of outside laboratory facilities. Where the work is sufficiently extensive to justify an in-house quality laboratory, it is often expanded to include process control, calibration, and basic measurement standards.

14. *Calibration of equipment*: Calibration of equipment presumes the existence of nonproduction use standards to which the day-to-day working equipment can be compared and adjusted. These working standards must, in turn, be regularly checked against master standards, usually traceable to the U.S. Bureau of Standards. The services of special laboratories for this service are often employed in preference to developing an in-house capability. The use of these special laboratories is a perfectly satisfactory method of maintaining calibration as long as the system employed is under the control of some element of the quality organization. As mentioned previously, where a quality laboratory exists, calibration, or at least the maintenance of standards, is often an element of the laboratory organization. Organizing for the calibration function must encompass all equipments used throughout the operation—developmental equipment as well as production. A common mistake is to assume that engineering equipment used for product development does not need the rigorous calibration requirements that production equipment requires. It is impossible to develop products that will perform according to the specifications if

the equipment used in development is not held to the same requirements that the production force will use. Those engaged in government contracting are subjected to very rigorous controls in the area of calibration. Much of the success of many of our national programs can be traced to adherence to these standards.

15. *Certification of operators*: In the somewhat distant past the journeyman machinist, welder, and so on, was exceedingly well trained, having served a long apprenticeship. Today when many critical production operations are, or can be, in the hands of newly trained semiskilled employees, a minimum level of proficiency must be obtained before new employees are allowed to proceed on their own. The practice of ensuring this skill level by a mandatory training and certification program is becoming increasingly common among companies anxious to protect their reputation and their profits. After classroom training, on-the-job experience, and testing (both written and manual demonstration) the employee is "certified" capable of doing the work assigned. Achieving this certification may take only a few hours or several weeks, depending on the assignment.

The quality organization should be responsible for monitoring this program, issuing the evidence of certification, and systematically checking for violations of the prescribed rules. In some companies the quality organization has been given the responsibility for the testing as well.

16. *Corrective action*: Corrective action is the quality function designed to review discrepancies, determine their cause, and ensure that a solution to the problem is implemented. Corrective action is more than finding a solution— corrective action is not complete until the solution has been implemented into the system. The solution may affect various divisions of a company: engineering, manufacturing, quality, purchasing, and so on. Repetition of mistakes represents an unnecessary loss of production dollars that fast, accurate, and complete corrective action can minimize.

Organizing for corrective action can be as simple as assigning the responsibility to an area quality supervisor. In the smaller company this supervisor is the one relatively unbiased person who has access to all the information pertaining to the problem.

Large organizations find corrective action to be most effective when it is set up as a separate group within the quality structure. This group has its own staff of engineers to analyze problems and seek permanent solutions. Frequently, special projects within a company have quality corrective action engineers assigned directly to the project.

17. *Statistical analysis and data reporting*: Adequate records are paramount in any quality system. The "build history" of a product is often required to prove exactly what actions took place during manufacture or processing. Such records are usually the output of the planning operation.

Equally important is the gathering and analysis of statistical data relating to the production output from the viewpoint of the quality management. The availability of computer storage and printout has increased enormously the ability of quality personnel to produce data. These data can include every aspect of the quality function. Receiving inspection reports, process and manufacturing trend data, repetitive nonconformances, test yields, and so on, must be produced in a form that when reviewed by other than quality personnel is understandable and complete. Data are useful only when their meaning is clear and leads to some constructive action. It is a common fault of programmers to load data into the system that will never be retrieved for use. Only that information required for regular management use should become a part of the permanent data base.

✕ 18. *Audits*: Audit of the quality function—indeed, of the entire manufacturing process—is a historical element of the quality system. The degree
of responsibility given to the quality audit function varies with respect to
the size of the company, the historical performance of the product in the marketplace, and the desire of the company management to have independent reviews of the performance of the manufacturing operation. Some companies
extend the audit function in areas other than those closely related to manufacturing on the premise that such audits identify problems that might otherwise go unnoticed, and can be wasteful of both time and money. In some companies quality audits are considered an important enough element to warrant
an independent unit reporting directly to the quality manager. Usually, they
are considered to be a part of the quality engineering function, separated
specifically from the "hands-on" elements of quality control.

19. *Administration*: The administrative element of the quality organization
is charged with the responsibility for writing and issuing quality procedures;
developing hiring and training plans; preparation and control of the quality
budget; and frequently has the added responsibility of some elements identified previously, such as data accumulation and certification of operators. In
organizations where such elements represent few actual personnel, the administration department offers the leadership capability that can be used to minimize supervisory overhead. Most often the administrative department manager
reports directly to the top quality executive.

20. *Facilities acquisition*: The acquisition of the necessary facilities for
the quality operation is an increasingly important element of developing a quality system. The equipment available has become more diverse and in some
cases very sophisticated. Selection of such equipment requires more detailed
analysis, both from the standpoint of application as well as cost-effectiveness.
Where and how this analysis should be performed is not as important as the
concept that the quality organization is a part of the approval cycle. In smaller
companies the details of selection and ordering are often done by a separate
facilities group with the head of Quality approving the package and suggesting revisions. Larger organizations, where considerable quantities of equip-
ment/tools are to be ordered, require a group of quality engineers who review
requirements, search for acceptable equipment, evaluate the alternatives for
cost-effectiveness, and make the ultimate selection for presentation to the
management facility control group. Where such a quality function is required,
it is also frequently a part of the administration department.

21. *Advanced quality technology*: In today's rapidly changing engineering
and manufacturing environment it is incumbent on the quality department to
keep abreast of these techniques and to determine what new quality methods
are required. In recent years many larger organizations have funded separate
quality research programs to advance the state of the art in measurement techniques, process control, computer applications, and defect detection. Although
this has not been as widespread as desirable, it recognizes that quality must
be a part of the development process and not be left in a "catch-up" posture.
It should be an organizational entity, usually a part of quality engineering or
the quality laboratory, that must be considered in the development of the
system.

22. *Additional responsibilities*: Some managements have seen fit to
strengthen the quality role by assigning tasks not traditionally accepted as a
basic quality function, although they do have a bearing on the customers'
evaluation of the company as a producer of satisfactory hardware. In the
formulation of a total quality system the following elements should be reviewed
to make a determination as to the best organizational assignment.

a. *Reliability*: Reliability studies, projections, and analysis have, for the most part, been a traditional element of the engineering department. Recent history indicates that this role, at least in part, is being assigned as a quality function, particularly with respect to reliability assurance, the degree to which the product meets the predicted reliability.

b. *Safety*: Safety, particularly as relating to the design and manufacture of the product, is also being assigned to the quality organization. The independent and impartial assessment that can be made by Quality is the principal reason for this approach by top management. Safety has become such an important part of the manufacturing scene that an impartial review is mandatory.

c. *Product liability*: Although safety and product liability go hand in hand, it is not mandatory that they be assigned to the same personnel. We must remember that we are considering product liability and safety in terms of design, manufacture, and use, not in terms of the legal aspects that prevail once a product liability suit is instigated. Safety, for example, might respond to a problem regarding assembly practices with the plant which would have no affect whatever on the ultimate use by the customer. Product liability, on the other hand, may be concerned with an ultimate fatique failure, one which never could occur during manufacture and test.

d. *Field service reporting*: Reporting of field service usage, including warranty claims, is a certain indicator of the reliability and usability of the product. Failure to analyze these reports and compare them to in-house failure rates can lead to catastrophic warranty and reshipment costs. The quality department is the keeper of the in-house failure history. Some organizations have simplified their handling and correction of field failures by making them a responsibility of the quality organization.

e. *Configuration management*: In more complex products where changes to the design are to be expected, the configuration management system must be accurate and timely to preclude delivery of incorrect material and to ensure updating of hardware with a minimum cost impact. Before the general use of computers to maintain and update configuration data, it was usually the responsibility of the quality department to manage configuration control by means of a manual system. Although the computer has simplified this task so that the inputs can more readily be matched against the hardware, some companies still look to the quality department to operate and manage the system.

VI. TYPES OF ORGANIZATION

We have defined the basic quality task, discussed some organizational concepts with regard to quality, and outlined the functions that must be considered when developing a quality system. The form of the organization can now be considered. It must be emphasized that all the elements previously identified are not a requirement for every organization. Only the larger and more diversified company would need them all. In developing the organization all functions must be considered, however, and a conscious decision made with respect to each one. To overlook or disregard an obvious need can only lead to catastrophy.

There are certain fundamental organizational patterns that should be considered when putting the quality group together. As mentioned previously, company policy and tradition often have an impact on the structure of any organization. An adequate quality system can be developed irrespective of the basic format employed.

A. Staff Versus Line Function

An important philosophical concept concerning organizing a quality group is the determination of its role as either an operating department in the line organization or as a quality assurance group operating in a staff position reporting to the chief operating executive. A staff group has the ability to move freely outside the normal operating environment, monitoring the results of the system and reporting its findings to management. In such a setting the inspection work is usually performed by personnel reporting to an inspection chief. Other functions relating to the quality system may be assigned to departments within the manufacturing or engineering organizations. A major disadvantage of this type of staff assignment is that the group is often not empowered to do other than report the situation. The group must achieve corrective action by discussion and persuasion, with the chief operating executive as the final arbiter. In the absence of any operational authority there arises a normal reluctance to force many problems to their ultimate solution, the result being that proper corrective action is never pushed to a conclusion. There is the tendency to become more interested in finding fault than in eliminating troublesome company problems. This attitude can develop when the quality assurance group is made to feel like "outsiders" and not part of the team. There are, of course, companies that empower the quality staff to enforce corrective action by literally stopping the work effort if necessary. Such actions can be successful only where the quality staff is exceptionally well qualified and respected.

Examples of the quality staff organization are shown in Figs. 1 and 2. In Fig. 1 the production division is responsible for the direct inspection function and the engineering department takes care of the laboratory and calibration requirements. Figure 2 is a different arrangment of the same staff concept, with inspection being a separate entity.

When the quality function is established as a part of the operational line organization the quality department manager should report to the same management level as those in charge of manufacturing, engineering, and material. As an operating executive the quality manager has the responsibility not only to assure that acceptable hardware is delivered to the customer but also to minimize operational costs through rapid and responsive corrective action and preventive quality control. The form of the organization may vary, as we shall see, but the focus should be on implementing the controls necessary to carry out the established quality role.

B. Small Versus Large Companies

The problem of the smaller company is to achieve the proper result with resources that are limited by comparison to larger organizations. Personnel must be selected who are capable of doing more than one function. Specialists are a luxury that can seldom be justified. Once the quality charter has been identified and agreement reached relative to the scope of activities to be pursued, the work must be organized in as simple a manner as possible. Smaller

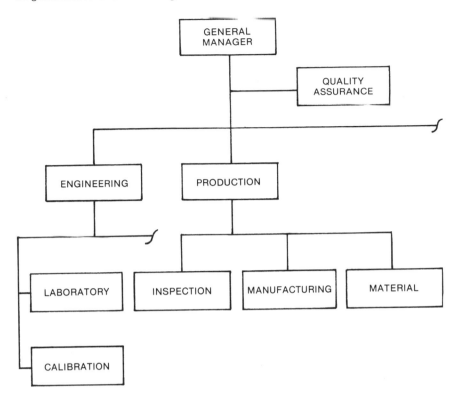

FIGURE 1   In this organizational configuration, the production division is responsible for the inspection function and the engineering group is responsible for laboratory and calibration functions. All functions report to the general manager.

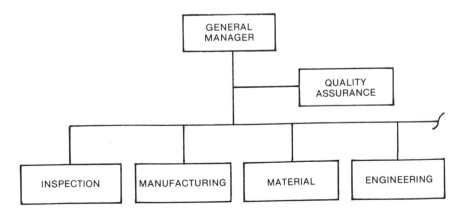

FIGURE 2   In this example, the inspection function is performed by a separate group which reports to the general manager.

companies tend to adopt the horizontal form of organization, with all the principal supervisors reporting directly to the department head. This simplifies communication and allows for rapid top-level decision making.

As a case in point, consider a shop whose output is relatively straightforward sheet metal and machine shop detail parts. The quality task has been described as:

1. Inspection, including raw materials
2. Collection of data regarding shop defects and losses
3. Process control of certain chemical operations, such as cleaning, painting, and chemical finishing
4. Monitoring customer complaints

Such an organization could be organized as shown in Fig. 3.

A more effective alignment would be to have a strong supervisor over all of the inspection effort, with all the other functions continuing to report to the quality manager (see Fig. 4). Such an arrangement would still give the manager instant access to problem areas from both plant and customer, and at the same time minimize the number of upper-level supervisors required.

As the organization increases in both size and complexity of function, the need develops to reduce the span of control of the upper-level supervision. (Span of control relates to the number of different organizational elements for which a given supervisor is responsible.) The organization tends to change from a horizontal orientation to a more vertical alignment (see Figs. 5 and 6). This allows the department manager to devote time to those matters which he or she considers important to the well-being of the department and the company. It presumes more highly qualified leaders reporting directly to the manager: supervisors who are expert in their particular discipline and capable of making decisions regarding their part of the operation.

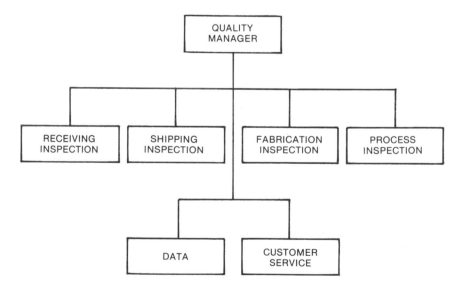

FIGURE 3   Horizontal reporting, where each group supervisor reports to the same quality manager, is typical in the smaller shop.

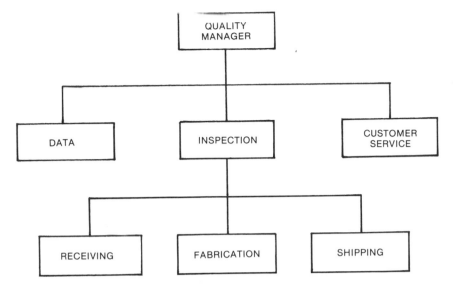

FIGURE 4   A modified form of horizontal reporting puts all inspection functions under a single strong supervisor.

No set rules govern the choice of organization but in a quality group it is particularly important that sufficient leadership be available to respond quickly to problems that affect the production process. There is an ever-present danger in a very extended horizontal arrangement that problems may get set aside because of the press of other business demanding the attention of the top decision maker. As has been stated previously, the best organization is one that gets the job done effectively, at minimum cost, recognizing that cost sometimes gives way to certain preferences in organizational concepts. What cannot be allowed to suffer is effectiveness.

The large organization has the need for specialists in many of the quality disciplines. The generalist who has broad knowledge and responsibility appears higher and higher in the organization and his or her skills are managerial as contrasted to technical.

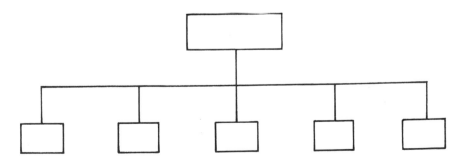

FIGURE 5   Horizontal reporting is typical in the smaller organization. Blocks are meant to be general. No labels are needed.

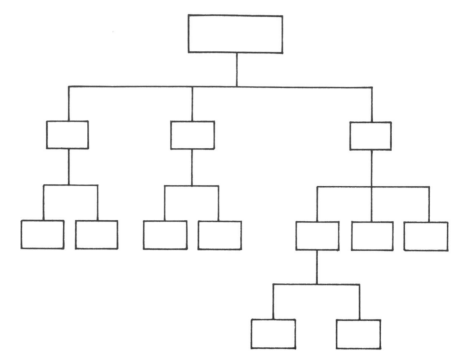

FIGURE 6   As an organization becomes larger and more complex, vertical reporting becomes more typical.

In a very large corporation that is involved with the majority of the functions outlined as the quality task, the organizational possibilities are endless. Certain real-life situations tend to establish patterns: for example, grouping of similar activities, such as receiving inspection, source inspection, and control of stores. These are not only related but are often physically located in proximity to one another. The ability to share equipment and space may also dictate an organizational alignment. If the quality laboratories and receiving inspection are close together, a sharing of equipment offer substantial savings. Some companies require that very expensive equipment (i.e., electronic test gear) be shared between divisions, such as quality and engineering. These considerations should be uppermost in the mind of the quality executive when planning an organization.

An organization for such a large company might take the form shown in Fig. 7. Another grouping of the same functions is shown in Fig. 8. The second plan reduces the number of people reporting to the quality executive from eight to five; it raises the quality audit to a more important level, reporting to the director; all the projects are consolidated under one project manager; and the inspection and test group now has responsibility for all inspection, including source and receiving. The large company with more personnel available has a better opportunity to match skills with job requirements and to organize around the elements of the job, whereas the smaller company may have to organize more around the available talent.

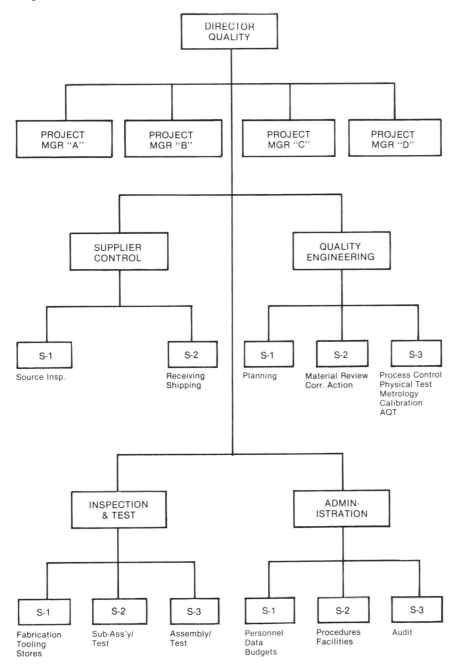

FIGURE 7 In a large organization, similar activities are often grouped. In addition, more and more specialists are needed. The generalist moves higher in the organization and that person's skills are used in a managerial rather than a technical way.

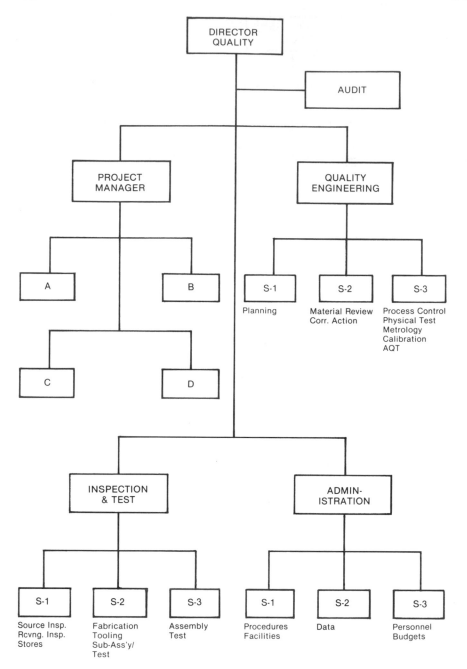

FIGURE 8   A modified version of Fig. 7 reduces the number of groups that report to the head of the organization, and places some of those groups under a supervisor or manager.

C. Multidivisional or International Corporations

Many multidivisional or internationally oriented corporations have a headquarters staff group for quality. A vice-president or director of quality reporting to the chief operating executive is responsible for corporate wide activities in the quality field. These responsibilities generally include:

1. Development of general policies, objectives, and standards
2. Preparation of basic training criteria
3. Consulting and audit service to the divisions
4. Review of capital equipment requirements
5. Preparation of reports to top management
6. Representing the corporation in interchanges with government and industry groups

It must be noted that the responsibility of such a quality executive is frequently not supported by the authority necessary to achieve the objective. Different product mixes, the degree of autonomy of the individual division managers, and even cultural differences in the case of multinational corporations mitigate against much real achievement by a headquarter's staff unless the chief executive is constantly and pointedly supportive. Even with such support the quality headquarter's staff personnel must be persuasive and tactful if they are to obtain the necessary cooperation from the divisions.

D. The Final Organization

It must now be clear that there is no "best" way to organize the quality function. The definition of the quality role identifies the scope of the job and the elements needed to satsify that role. The organizational framework to support that role must be tailored for every company, keeping in mind the various influences that have been described. It is particularly important that the organization be oriented toward those elements that have the greatest impact on the ultimate worthiness of the product and the cost to produce it.

Several alternative organizations have been suggested, but they should not constitute a boundary, only a basis for further development. The quality executive should be ever mindful that "large" is not synonymous with excellence and that every organization should be no larger than necessary to accomplish the assigned quality role.

VII. QUALITY PLANNING

Quality planning can be defined as the sum of those actions taken in preparation for the accomplishment of the assigned quality task. In the early stages of the development of inspection systems it was usually limited to planning where inspection points were to be identified within the production cycle. Planning now involves a myriad of tasks, depending on the size and complexity of the production operation. The development of the organizational structure determines to a considerable degree how much planning is required and who must do it. Wherever there is a requirement for a quality task there must be a plan to accomplish it. Someone in the quality department must develop and identify the steps and actions to be taken. The scope of the quality planning effort is therefore similar to the basic role identified in the quality charter. The number and type of plans required become a function of the complexity of the work effort and the experience of the work force. The requirement for detailed planning usually increases in proportion to complexity of product or system, lack of experience in the work force, and the amount of customer regulation imposed. Conversely, plans can simplified when the products or system are less complex: where the personnel are highly qualified and the amount of customer regulations are minimal. In the real world, where these factors may vary from department to department, it is necessary to be certain that the plan prepared recognizes the conditions that exist.

Quality planning can be classified as administrative (nonhardware) plans, having to do with the operational and business aspects of the system; and product-oriented plans, which relate to the activities involved in producing the product.

A. Administrative Planning

Administrative planning begins with the preparation of the overall quality program plan for the company. It is a reflection of the basic quality charter agreed to between the chief operating executive and the quality manager. In many cases it is one and the same. Other administrative plans are:

1. *Policy and procedures manual*: A quality policy and procedures manual is the resources document for all additional planning, as it contains the guidelines for the entire quality activity. The procedures themselves are often the actual step-by-step plan of operation for certain tasks, particularly ones that are repetitious and unlikely to change suddenly. The manual is the framework on which the rest of the quality plans can be overlaid.

2. *Special program plans*: The customer/company program leadership may require that special quality plans be developed. Such plans usually describe special paperwork and reporting systems, but they may also dictate the manner in which certain inspections or tests are to be accomplished. These controls may be more stringent than normal or they may call for a relaxation of some existing controls. Such plans are usually developed by the quality personnel assigned to the program. They must be carefully controlled in order that the personnel working on the shop floor will not be confused by the exceptions to the normal procedures.

3. *Planning for audits*: The audit group, regardless of size, must develop audit plans and schedules in order to have a consistency of approach and reporting within the company. Audit plans must be sufficiently detailed and clear that changes in the audit personnel will not affect the efficiency of the audit program.

4. *Personnel planning*: Every organization must have well-identified requirements for the number and type of personnel required for the year ahead, with acquisition requirements by the month. The employment department must be given adequate time to hire the proper personnel. When ample numbers of qualified people are not available in the area, a training plan and schedule will also be required. Even in the smaller company where personnel acquisition is handled personally by the quality manager, a plan must be made to indicate when additional personnel are needed.

5. *Equipment acquisition*: Equipment acquisition is similar to personnel acquisition in that it requires a plan that indicates month by month the new equipment required, the justification for its use, estimated lead time, and cost. Irrespective of the approval cycle for such equipment, the quality department is responsible for planning to meet its needs and for justifying the expenditure of the capital dollars.

6. *Other administrative plans*: Depending on the size of the organization and the charter given the quality department, many other plans of an administrative nature may be required, such as:

a. Long-range forecasts of personnel, equipment, and space
b. Accumulation of cost data by work center/department
c. Plan for the accumulation, storage, and retrieval of nonconformance and yield data
d. Plan for the training and certification of employees in certain critical manufacturing and test skills

B. Product-Oriented Planning

All of processing or manufacturing work effort is controlled by some type of written plan or instruction. Such plans may be written by a singular group within the manufacturing organization, or they may be distributed to a number of different elements, such as tool engineering, manufacturing engineering, manufacturing test, or in the case of test design and planning, may come from the engineering organization.

In every case the quality group must be a part of the team developing the plans to ensure that the product will meet the requirements of the contract. Insertion of specific inspection points in the processing and test cycle must be a part of every manufacturing plan. In some instances a special inspection plan must be developed separately from the manufacturing information for quality personnel to assure proper conformance.

In addition to those plans generated for use by production personnel the quality department develops other plans relating to the product.

1. *Supplier plans*: An overall methodology for the approval and control of suppliers to the company is usually contained in the quality procedures manual. In addition, specific instructions/inspections are frequently required. These should be transmitted to the supplier as a part of the purchase order.

2. *Receiving inspection*: The quality department must develop the inspection/test plans for the multitude of parts and equipment that are received by the company from outside sources. These plans must recognize what has taken place at the plant of the supplier and what subsequent inspections will be done during the in-house processing cycle.

3. *Laboratory and calibration*: The amount of laboratory testing and the general rules for the maintenance of standards and calibration of equipment are usually contained in the quality procedures manual. Individual calibration and laboratory testing procedures must be separately planned and maintained in a current file in the work area. In an organization with much diverse equipment, this can be a very heavy planning load. Although some calibrations can be done by the use of the equipment manufacturers' manuals, the planners must be certain they meet the requirements of in-plant usage.

4. *Process control*: Plans for the control of special processes used during the production process are an extremely important part of the quality control operation. Heat treatment, metal finishing, batch control, and chemical formulation are examples of processes that must have well-written plans for each step of the process and an indication of what physical action the quality group must take to ensure a successful result.

5. *Planning for inspection*: The actual inspection of parts, components, and assemblies is the original and traditional function of a quality organization. The plans associated with this effort range from the very simple (such as a

dimensional checkoff card) to an extensive step-by-step document outlining in detail the plan for acceptance of the product. There is no substitute for the planning required to assure a satisfactory product. As in all aspects of quality control, it is possible to overemphasize the planning of inspection points and produce more paper than product. The mark of the proficient quality planner is to cover every important element without inserting unnecessary checkpoints that are unproductive in terms of product use.

The inspection planner must work closely with those planning the test procedures when tests are required. Frequently, the test and inspection planner may be the same quality engineer.

6. *Planning for test*: Testing of many products has become the major element in the proof of acceptability and usability. Testing covers an extreme breadth of activity, from simple tension tests of material samples to hours-long runs of equipment undergoing changing environmental conditions. Organizationally, the quality group may not be the leaders in the formulation of test plans and the development of test equipment. The quality organization in all cases must have competent personnel reviewing and approving both plans and equipment. In some cases the level of testing required at receiving inspection may be so sophisticated that a special quality engineering group may be required to write the test plans, set up the equipment, and monitor, if not run, the tests.

VIII. ORGANIZATION OF THE PLANNING FUNCTION

The manner in which planning for the quality operation is organized is similar to that of the overall quality organization in that it depends on the scope and size of the assigned quality task. The most effective planning operation is one that gives the quality department all the necessary tools (i.e., direction, documentation, and equipment) at a reasonable administrative cost. In some small companies the planning can be accomplished by consultation between the inspectors and the supervisors, with the ultimate plans being produced on simple inspection forms. As the size of the company grows and the complexity of the products increase, the need for specialized planners becomes a necessity. Where these special planners should report organizationally becomes an administrative decision of the quality manager, as there is no clear pattern historically.

A. Central Versus Decentralized Planning

Centralized planning implies that all planning is performed by one group. Such an approach is not practical because of differences in both disciplines and physical location. It is, however, possible to group large segments of the various planning operations into one or two central operations, usually with substantial savings in efficiency and cost. For example, all inspection and test type planning could be located in one area adjacent to the corresponding manufacturing planning organization. This could include piece-parts inspection, process control, subassembly and assembly inspection, and all associated test operations. In addition to probable cost savings in the number of personnel required, such a central planning group would ensure uniformity of inspection between different products and programs. The preparation of receiving inspection plans could also be a function of such a group. Similarly, all administration planning could be grouped together, either as a part of the quality engineering function, or as the responsibility of a quality administrator reporting directly to the department head. As the responsibilities and size of the quality function increase, it is doubly important that the control of the business aspects of the department be grouped together and monitored closely.

Some quality planning, such as laboratory and calibration work, are most effectively handled in the functional areas involved, where the personnel are specialists and are working with the equipment daily. Some corporations, particularly those with several large, important, and nonsimilar programs, prefer to decentralize a large part of the inspection, test, and administrative planning and have it done within the confines of the quality program staff. The peculiar requirements of each program may differ to such a degree that special instructions are required. This may even be reflected in plans for receiving inspection. Program funding restrictions usually prohibit the use of specialists in every discipline, so the program planner has to be more versatile and qualified to plan a variety of inspection requirements. Certainly this approach is proper for cases where the requirements differ extensively from the rest of the plant operation, but the quality department head must be ever watchful to be certain that the need for decentralization is real. The tendency for overall program management to want everything under its control does not necessarily lead to the most efficient quality effort.

Planning for the quality group's participation in extensive test programs frequently requires a special test group with a preponderance of highly qualified engineering personnel. Where the role of the quality organization is to approve the test plan and equipment and to monitor the test itself, the quality personnel must be located in close proximity to the engineers responsible for the initial planning. In companies where the engineering department is heavily involved in the test program, their quality department counterparts must have the same level of technical expertise as those planning the operation.

B. Skill Requirements For Planners

All skilled quality personnel do not make good planners, even though their technical capability may be very high. It requires a special talent and disposition to do a good planning job, day after day. Some employees are temperamentally unsuited for the task because of its confining nature, and planners must be selected by temperament as well as technical ability. A checklist of planner prerequisites would include:

1. An understanding of the technical process
2. The ability to recognize what elements are truly important
3. The ability to use simple language and terminology in order to help the inspector to understand the requirements
4. An understanding of the interrelationships that exist on the production line so as not to create unnecessary delays
5. The ability to foresee "what if" situations in order to have a recovery plan available
6. A personality that can accept and work under the pressure of constant changes in plans and requirements

Organization and planning are the keys to success in quality control. They both begin with the establishment of the quality role by management. The development of the organization to fit the task also establishes the basic parameters of the planning required. Organizational development or improvement should not be used as an excuse for growth. Organization implies an orderly approach to a defined goal, which is achieved by the use of intelligent planning. Excesses in either organization or planning are both costly and ineffective.

FURTHER READING

Cox, A., *The Cox Report on the American Corporation*, Delacorte Press, New York, 1982.

Drucker, P. F., *Management—Tasks, Responsibilities, Practices*, Harper & Row, New York, 1973.

Greenwalt, C. H., *The Uncommon Man*, McGraw-Hill, New York, 1959.

Harrison, R., "Understanding Your Organization's Character," in *On Management*, Harvard Business Review, eds., Harper & Row, New York, 1975.

March, J. G. and H. A. Simon, *Organization*, Wiley, New York, 1966.

3

ASSET MANAGEMENT

JAY LEEK

Philip Crosby Associates, Inc.
Winter Park, Florida

I. INTRODUCTION

Within the structures of business management, there are many systems and procedures developed to perform line functions. These line or direct functions range from marketing to design and production. Additionally, there are staff or support functions that assist the line functions. One of the support systems is asset management. Support systems for the management of assets are complex, because they are designed to interface with many other facets of business management. The assets discussed in this chapter are sometimes referred to as capital equipment, measuring equipment, and/or instrumentation used by engineering, manufacturing, and quality organizations to measure, assess, and evaluate processes and products. The purhcasing process related to these assets requires careful planning. Asset management may be defined as the planning acquisition and control of capital equipment.

II. ORGANIZATION

Organization for the management of assets can be accomplished by a centralized or decentralized system. The elements affecting the determination of which system is used should be product lines, company size, product sophistication, process complexity, and company policy regarding rental agreements versus purchases.

Decentralized asset management typically lends itself to smaller companies with less complex processes and to those that prefer rental agreements to purchases. (The company policy in this regard is usually based on tax advantages.) In a smaller company, the volume of assets is much less and control can be handled by individual departments, so planning, acquisition, and control of these assets are less formal, with little documentation required.

In the centralized form of asset management, each company organization submits its requirements through one group. This group has the responsibility for administering the asset management system. It may also have the responsibility for implementing the planning function of capital assets and for controlling these assets after purchase. Such planning, administration, and control require cooperation and coordination from all company organizations.

As a service organization, the quality assurance group works closely with the operational and service organizations within a company, and therefore should be the prime contender for handling assets management. They must stay abreast of technological changes and be able to assess requests for new or additional equipment. This may not be true in all organizations, but responsibilities can be adjusted. However, experience shows that asset management is best operated in a centralized control form for inventory control and consolidation of annual capital planning.

The remainder of this chapter describes and discusses the planning, acquisition, and control of capital equipment. Covered are capital equipment/assets relative to the long- and short-range plan, justification, acquisition, utilization, and how to plan equipment and when and why to plan for it. Also covered are the acquisition process, the benefits received from proper justification and processing requests for approval to purchase capital assets, the proper control of assets, and the advantages received from proper and well-coordinated controls. A note of caution here. The system described is not the only system of asset management; many systems will work in the right environment, with the right people to maintain the proper disciplines. The system described in the ensuing chapter is an operating system and is offered as an effective method of asset management.

III. PLANNING

Planning is one of, if not the most important, problem faced in asset management. Sound, logical, well-thought-out planning can be a direct road to successful operation; on the other hand, poor planning invariably results in disorganization and failure. There is no simple formula to establish criteria for good planning. It is a matter of optimizing the critical path to accomplish the task, then considering alternative methods to accomplish the same end. When establishing the critical path, set milestones and alternative paths for each. Then if the optimum path encounters an obstacle, it is only necessary to return to the last major milestone and select an alternative. The return on the investment of time spent in good planning is realized in effective and efficient achievement of the intended goals.

In asset management there are essentially two types of planning necessary: long range, sometimes referred to as strategic and short range, sometimes called tactical. Strategic planning generally covers 5 years. It should be understood, however, that the longer the time frame, the less detailed and accurate planning becomes. Each year the plan is updated, bringing more reality to the current year.

In long-range planning, adjustments can be made to the plan with ample time to return to the original path or to set up a different task to arrive at the desired point. The original goal is never lost, yet can be examined from several angles before execution. On the other hand, short-range or tactical planning is sensitive and responsive to changes, but has limited options. The objectives and milestones of the short-range plan typically covers the next 12 months, and because of reaction time affords less opportunity to effect corrective actions on the path to overall achievement of the objectives.

A. Long Range Planning

Generally, the purpose of a long-range plan (LRP) is to provide a strategic route and timetable for the company to acquire new business sales and revenue for an extended period. The LRP varies from company to company but typically covers 5 years, with the first year representing a relative firm picture and the last year of the plan being less precise. In the LRP the company's executives develop and communicate a consolidated program for business growth or for sustaining existing levels. Through this planning, all of the aspects of the business are examined in detail. Just as the number of years the plan covers vary, so can the contents vary.

An element critical to the plan's effectiveness is capital expenditures. Decisions on capital planning are complex and are best discussed with the various operating organizations. When the LRP is established, it is essential that each organization be given the opportunity to project and communicate their capital requirements. At the beginning of a financial year, the organization that has the responsibility for capital plan administration provides each operating organization with a detailed review of the business philosophy, product mix, and baseline for the years covered by the LRP. The various year's planning is reviewed individually and collectively to assure continuity of requirements and business interfaces among contributing organizations. As mentioned, the amount of detail planning should decrease for each year, with the plan's earlier years having more detail provided than the latter years.

The Plan

Figures 1 and 2 show typical forms used in an operating system to document the asset management planning operation. In using these forms, each organization provides consistent information to communicate the objectives of the planned acquisition. Figure 1 is the worksheet referenced and Fig. 2 is a summary of the information provided on the worksheets. The instructions to complete Fig. 2 are provided in Fig. 3.

The business profile, outlining objectives and milestones, is provided to the operating organizations. Each organization then establishes supporting objectives within its own area of responsibility. These supporting objectives are documented in the justification block of the planning worksheet (Fig. 2) and become the basis for the selection of capital equipment. When that has been done, the equipment description is provided in the description block. Typically, planning for the latter years is difficult with regard to the details regarding the equipment needed. In this case a logical generic description is provided; then in the following years additional information is provided as details become available. The same situation holds for cost identification. If the specific equipment is known, obtaining a quotation is often of little value when it is time to purchase. In estimating costs, however, projections should be as accurate as possible.

Two remaining items significant in long-range planning are priority and need codes. These items signify to the reviewer the application planned. There may be certain information known only to senior company executives, such as program risks or the probability of success for a new product line. In such cases the decision to consider acquisition relative to particular programs may be deferred.

The information on the worksheet (Fig. 1) is summarized on the capital asset planning form (Fig. 2), thus yielding a planning sheet for each organization. At this point, finalization of the LRP may differ from one company to

ORGN. NO.	ORGN. TITLE		ITEM	
NEED DATE (Month 1 Yr. — Installed)		EST. LEAD TIME (Days)		ESTIMATED COST
PRIORITY CODE		NEED CODE		
PROGRAM				EQUIP.
				INSTALL.
ESTIMATED UTILIZATION (%)		SPAN TIME OF USE (Months)		TOTAL

DESCRIPTION

JUSTIFICATION

REQUEST APPROVALS	REQUESTER	DATE	DEPT. MGR.	DATE
FINAL APPROVAL	REQUESTER	DATE	DEPT. MGR.	DATE

FIGURE 1   Capital assets planning worksheet.

ORGANIZATION NO.			ORGANIZATION NAME						SHEET OF		
BUDGET LINE CODE	NEED CODE	PRODUCT LINE CODE	ITEM DESCRIPTION	YEAR	PRIOR. CODE	EQUIPMENT COSTS	NEW INST. COSTS	TOTAL COSTS	AUTHORITY FOR EXPENDITURE		
									NUMBER	AMOUNT	DATE

NORTHROP

FIGURE 2 Capital assets planning.

BLOCK NO.	DESCRIPTION
1	Consecutive numbers for each item (1, 2, 3, etc.).
2	Capital Asset Need Code:
	1. Code 1 - Firm Business
	2. Code 2 - Planned Business
	3. Code 3 - Potential Business
3	Product Line Code (Examples):
	1. Product Line A
	2. Product Line B
	3. Etcetera
4	Item Description (Make, Model, etc.).
5	Calendar year for which request is made (use last 2 digits, e.g., 81).
6	Capital Asset Priority (see Definitions).
7	Costs in thousands (e.g., 1918.4.).
8	To be completed during AFE* processing.

* Authority for Expenditure.

FIGURE 3

the next. For a company that is structured vertically, it may be advantageous to summarize the plans on a single capital asset planning sheet at predetermined levels, to afford a logical review. For horizontally structured companies, each operating organization may submit plans independent of the others. In a horizontally structured organization the individual plans can be summarized on a single planning sheet. Once completed, the capital plan can be included in the other portions of the company's long-range plan. Each year, as the LRP is updated, the capital plan can also be reviewed and updated. The plan is a tool to aid management in executing the rigorous task of operating a business.

Standardization

In developing the asset management system, it is important that the goals of the LRP be kept in mind. For example, equipment should not be chosen arbitrarily, without careful thought being given to how, where, how frequent, and by whom the equipment is to be used. Considerations related to equipment utilization and standardization should also become a part of the LRP. Standardization of equipment is influenced by many facets of business performance. If any of these are overlooked, a "white elephant" may be purchased, resulting in an additional, unpredictable expenditure to make the device usable. Elements requiring standardization include:

Facilities
User experience level
Maintenance capability
Calibration sophistication
Spare-parts inventory

Facilities

When considering standardization relative to facilities, consideration should be given to the physical constraints and utilities. When considering the acquisition of large equipment, space becomes a major factor. If two organizations are planning major installations simultaneously, they should either be closely coordinated or prioritized to accommodate one or the other. If there is a section in the LRP identifying floor space, appropriate mention should be made to alert others to the need for expanded or new facilities. The utilities requirements for a planned acquisition may not present a problem unless there is excessive demand (i.e., electric, gas, water, air) to the extent that a major modification is required. In this event, additional planning should be accomplished at the earliest date.

User Experience Level

The second element of standardization is the users' experience level. With the installation of new equipment, it is frequently necessary to consult the manufacturer and obtain recommendations relative to required operator experience level as well as available training. Typically, large equipment manufacturers support training; however, the level of prerequisite knowledge may differ. In any event, it may be necessary to make additional investments to assure adequate operator training.

Maintenance Capability

Considerations similar to those for the operator, should be given to maintenance training. If offered, a manufacturer may provide maintenance training for several years, after which it is necessary to be self-sustaining or to purchase a service contract. These decisions have an impact on the life-cycle cost of the acquisition and if not considered may cause extensive recurring costs. It is good asset management to acquire as few unique or special devices as possible.

Calibration Sophistication

If the manufacturing department plans the acquisition of automated process equipment requiring calibration accuracy not presently available within the facility, additional planning is necessary by the support organization responsible for calibration. Major process equipment typically does not lend itself to calibration outside the facility; therefore, the capability should be available within the company. In meeting these requirements for calibration, additional acquisitions by the support organizations may be necessary.

Spare-Parts Inventory

The last element involved in standardization is the spare-parts inventory. It would be convenient and inexpensive to stock only one set of spares to cover all possible requirements; that is utopia, however, and in reality never happens. Therefore, when considering a new acquisition an attempt should be made to maximize the use of existing inventory. This is not to say that a new equipment purchase should be denied because the present level of spares is inadequate.

The purpose of standardization planning is to facilitate growth in capability and technology. Communicate the needs through the capital plan portion of the LRP, in a fashion that support functions can do the same level of planning. This results in a coordinated goal-oriented approach to solving company growth problems. Standardization is attained through a concentrated effort of communicating intent in the LRP. When an item first appears on the LRP it may simply state that "to meet process rate requirements it is necessary to automate subassembly and final assembly test." It is estimated that existing utilities and calibration capabilities will suffice. Floor space requirements are estimated at 300 to 400 ft^2. This type of entry can be expanded each year as the plan matures until the equipment is placed on order.

B. Short-Range Planning

Updating the LRP

As pointed out in Sec. III.A, the LRP is a means of communicating the intent of implementing the requirements of the company. When it comes to planning the following year's activities, it is no longer a matter of communicating intent, but a matter of identifying and implementing reality.

The forms used (Figs. 1 and 2) are essentially an extension of broader material found in the LRP. The forms are used in identifying capital equipment requirements for the 5-year plan, and as stated earlier, the SRP provides the detail necessary to support the more immediate acquisitions. After having an objective materialize over a period of years, it should not be difficult to identify the current requirements and then execute its implementation.

Utilization

As standardization was a major consideration for long-range planning of capital equipment, utilization becomes critical when finalizing the SRP or tactical plan. Planning for utilization becomes critical in the short-range plan because this information provides the final justification for the purchase and demonstrates how the new equipment is to work for the company: how the acquisition will create a "return on investment" (ROI). Utilization is assuring that the equipment will be in service and in use a maximum amount of time to obtain the greatest return on investment. In some instances a decision to lease the equipment for a limited usage might prove to be the best economic choice. These options should always be considered prior to acquisition by purchase if utilization proves uneconomical.

Utilization of a standard test instrument need not be 100%, nor need it be utilized through its full service life. Standard electrical/electronic instrumentation typically has a useful service life of 5 to 7 years, whereas mechanical devices have a considerably longer service life. If a user requests a device and identifies only a 2- or 3-year need, upon completion of this period the device will be returned to inventory and utilized elsewhere later. Another type of limited need is a requirement of only 8 to 10 hours of use per week; it does not mean that the acquisition would not be economical; instead, it could be made available the remainder of the time for others to use unless it is dedicated to a special station, in which case economics would prevail.

C. Scheduling

Scheduling the acquisition of assets is another function of the asset management process. The heading need date of Figs. 1 and 2 is the date that must be met for the commitments of the program to be satisfied considering the equipment manufacturer's lead time, installation, and startup problems. It may be necessary to order instrumentation 12 to 18 months in advance to allow for delays. Predictable delays can be exemplified when considering the acquisition of a computer-controlled test station and the time required for writing and verifying programs. Buying this type of equipment at the time it is needed is shortsighted and should be avoided. Since predictable delays must be considered when establishing need dates, it is also necessary to examine other possible contingencies. In doing this, the date identified on the acquisition form presents as small a risk as possible. There should be coordination with the equipment suppliers to determine the best delivery information.

IV. ACQUISITION

The acquisition process can be difficult. It contains the same problems as those other processes and is generally difficult to monitor. The process contains three elements: justification, document processing, and receipt. The justification discussed here is a part of the documentation prepared for acquisition. Since it is the most important phase of the acquisition process (i.e., convincing management of the need), considerable attention has been given to this subject.

A. Justification

Before discussing the details of justifying capital equipment, there is a general consideration worthy of mention. When a person determines that a new piece of equipment is needed, there usually is good justification. But there is often difficulty in communicating this justification to those responsible for approval and acquisition. In many cases the equipment is so directly related to the person's duties that justification for the equipment becomes a defense of the job. This sometimes breeds resentment and a resistance to preparing effective justification because of pride. Too often it is said: "Isn't it enough that I say I need the equipment—doesn't my judgment mean anything?" Of course it does, and astute management takes the requestor's experience and judgment into consideration. No requestor should fear embarrassment or castigation for making a sincere request. Management does not challenge the need. Rather, they weigh the degree of need for one request with all others to arrive at a total equipment requirement consistent with available funds and company objectives. The advice to requesting and using organizations in this regard is to be objective and impersonal. Another person or department which was objective and impersonal may get the dollars for an item of lesser need simply because management was given more meaningful facts for review.

Justification for control equipments usually fall into the following categories: (1) must have, (2) needed, and (3) desired. The amount of effort and detail put into justification varies for each of these categories. However, it is wise to cover all the points listed below which are applicable to the case. It should not be assumed that management is aware of the facts relative to an acquisition. Present tham all. Many justifications for urgent items encounter difficulties with management if the "must" characteristics of the equipment is not clearly and decisively established. The points to be considered in a complete and sound justification are listed below and then discussed in detail.

Description versus justification
Listing of specific facts
Effect on work if not obtained
Amount of usage
If unique, who designated or prepared specifications? Who will operate?
Growth potential
Analysis of total cost
Intangible benefits

Description versus Justification

Give a complete, detailed description of the item desired and what it does. Catalog or vendors' numbers (e.g., C-210 and B-300) may be clear to the requestor but may not be to management. A short, clear statement describing the function is appreciated by a busy executive. The requestor may know what an "exciter" does, but if mention is not made of vibration, for example, the general manager or finance manager may not know what the item is for or, even worse, assume that it is for a different function.

Also, a description should not be used as the justification: This is the most common failing of equipment justifications. Much detail is often given regarding the type of test to be performed or measurement to be taken in a justification statement. For a complete justification, the reason the test is to be performed or measurement taken should be provided. An example of this is a detailed description of the capability of a vibration system to perform up to 3 kHz whereas the present equipment provides vibration to only 2 kHz. So far, so good, but the most important information is the explanation of why the 3 kHz is needed—new specification, contract change, design trend, and so on. As noted, this is the most common failing in justification preparation.

Listing of Specific Facts

The word "more" should be avoided in a justification. Examples of this are *more* accurate, *more* complete, *more* sensitive, *more* range, *more* economical. This is practically meaningless to top management and may offend them by giving the impression that vague facts are being forced on them. If the equipment wanted is *more* accurate, give the details. For example, old equipment may be accurate to only 1% and the equipment desired is 0.1% accurate. Then follow up with a reason for greater accuracy. The same applies to comparable characteristics, such as sensitivity, range, completeness, and economy. Economic parameters should be substantial by providing actual and estimated costs and anticipated savings. Get help on this score from financial specialists if it is felt that one person cannot do a complete job.

Effect on Work If Not Obtained

If the effect on work is not treated in the justification, an astute general manager will ask it during the review. Justification must be available or the case will probably die on the spot. If there is no significant effect on the work, the only result may be embarrassment at taking up time in preparing, presenting, and reviewing a justification for an unneeded acquisition. The effects of not obtaining the desired equipment have been assessed and should be covered in detail. All the positive reasons given may not be as strong as the negative effects on nonacquisition, such as nonperformance on a specification requirement, requiring customer waiver or outside subcontract, product liability exposure, inefficient or uneconomical operation involving schedule slippage or cost overruns, loss of competitive position, and acquiring the reputation of being behind the state of the art. The decision to acquire new equipment should be based not only on what the equipment will do, but also on the penalties that may result if the equipment is not acquired.

Amount of Usage

Be factual when identifying the usage of the proposed equipment. This is similar in financial analysis to return on investment. Indicate the planned work that is firm and that which is anticipated. Utilization (as discussed in Sec. III.B.2) for most equipment is the *total* time it is "tied up" on a job, including setup, calibration, running time, holding time for quick-look review of data, and teardown time. Management may think only in terms of running time; 10% running time for a vibration system may represent 100% utilization, but if this is not thoroughly explained, management may interpret this to mean that the equipment will be idle 90% of the time.

If Unique, Who Designed or Prepared Specifications?

If the equipment being requested is pushing the state of the art, management should be convinced that the technical homework has been done. There is a natural reluctance on the part of management to invest large funds in an untried item. Be sure, therefore, that a coordinated input is received from specialists within the organization or from outside consultants if necessary. Many justifications fall into stormy waters when management determines that the experts available within the organization have not been consulted on a developmental acquisition. Encourage competent people to review the design, specifications, or requirements. Identify the areas of technical risk. For unique facilities identify the operational features. Are personnel trained to operate the equipment? If so, they should be identified. If not, discuss the detailed plans that have been developed to achieve this capability: for example, have the vendor train the personnel; send personnel to appropriate training classes; or hire a consultant to operate and train people on the job. Such training requires funds and time. Management should be made aware of this and their approval requested.

Growth Potential

Before management gives its approval to spend a large amount of money, they generally want some assurance that there is little likelihood for a near-term repeat performance. Consult marketing or advanced systems organizations. Determine the trends that might affect this acquisition. Are the items being tested getting bigger, specifications getting tighter, acceptance quality level increasing, frequencies getting higher? If this help is unavailable within the company, do some independent research or seek help outside the company. Acquiring growth potential in a facility may increase its current cost, but it may be good business since costs are continually on the rise. Buying tomorrow's capability today may save money and obtain a favorable competitive position. It is easier to win business with capability than with statements of intent to acquire it.

Analysis of Total Cost

One of the pitfalls many equipment justifications encounter is an incomplete listing of an item's cost. The purchase price is only a part. What about the maintenance and operating cost? Make sure that equipment listed is acceptable to the standardization committee within the company (see Sec. III.A), and whenever possible, assure minimizing life-cycle costs. If these costs are anticipated to be lower than those of similar existing equipment, describe the cost saving. It should help to sell the case. If maintenance and operating costs are going to be higher, describe, explain, and justify these higher costs. It is better to do it now. Otherwise, a critical general manager may bring this out during a review of your justification, and your integrity may be challenged. Even if the equipment is acquired, the higher maintenance and operating costs will not go away. If the costs are high, trouble may result even though the high cost may be justified, since the initiator will be explaining things after the fact. Also, management may feel that there has been a deliberate withholding of information which they should have had to make a proper and complete assessment of the request.

Intangible Benefits

This is the icing on the cake. Include such things as enhancement of company image, attractiveness to technical applicants, meeting customer's unusual requirements, beneficial effects on employee morale, and stress unusual or unique characteristics, such as first of a kind, largest, most accurate, most productive, or most sensitive. Know management and use what appeals to them. If the requestor has done a thorough and complete job on items 1 through 7, no "selling" is required. However, remember that top management looks at a broad base, and these types of intangibles enhance a broadened overview.

The essentials of a good justification, when reviewed, seem simple and straightforward. If there is a magic formula, it is simple "give management *all* the facts" and success will be more frequent.

B. Documentation Process

The documentation process should be properly coordinated and closely monitored. The process described, although complex, has been effectively implemented. The system described may need tailoring depending on a company's organization. Achieving the goals of asset management and providing control is of significancs; the system ultimately implemented is not.

To begin with, the short-range plan, once approved, becomes the source of the majority of information necessary to complete the form and initiate the request for acquisition approval. Considering the forms discussed previously (Figs. 1 and 2), there are two ways of initiating a request. The first is controlled by the administrator. The administrator disassembles the capital plan (previously assembled by organization/department) and reassembles it according to need dates (as explained earlier, this considers manufacturers' lead times). Thereafter, at the beginning of each month, the administrator initiates the acquisition request form and returns it to the user for signature and further processing. Processing in this fashion, however, does not allow for program slips or changing requirements; it assumes that the plan was accurate. The second system is to allow the initiator to execute the plan and order what is needed when it is needed as long as it stays within the initial plan.

Figure 4 shows the form used to document the "authority for expenditure." The form serves to collect the information leading to the final decision to make the acquisition. The first page of the form provides:

PAGE 1 OF 2

ITEM NO.	QTY	PART/MODEL NO.	DESCRIPTION	UNIT COST	TOTAL COST

1. BUDGET LINE ITEM 2. DATE PREPARED 3. PURCHASE ORDER NO. 4. SHIP TO PLANT 5. AFE NO.
6. REQUESTED BY 7. PHONE EXT 8. ORGANIZATION TITLE 9. ORGN NO. 10. DATE REQUIRED
11. VENDOR ADDRESS CITY / STATE 12. NO. BIDS REC'D

13. INCLUDE ALL SUPPLIES, SERVICES, REQUIREMENTS AND INSTALLATION COSTS

14. REASON FOR EXPENDITURE

15. SAVINGS/PAYBACK ACCOMPLISHED BY REASON OF EXPENDITURE

DISTRIBUTION: **WHITE**—ACCOUNTS PAYABLE; **GREEN**—PURCHASING; **YELLOW & PINK**—PROPERTY ADMINISTRATION; **GOLD**—REQUESTING ORGANIZATION

FIGURE 4 Authority for expenditure.

1. Requesting organization
2. Manufacture supplying the equipment
3. Description and cost of the equipment
4. Justification
5. Alternative action

The reviewer is provided with the rationale necessary to support the acquisition. The second page provides:

1. Disposition of equipment being replaced (if applicable)
2. Cost considerations

PAGE 2 OF 2

17. AFE NO.

16. EXISTING ASSETS REPLACED AS A RESULT OF EXPENDITURE (INDICATE BY NAME AND ASSET NUMBER)

18. ALTERNATE ACTION

19. COMMENTARY

20. APPROVALS	DATE
a. ORIGINATOR	
b. SECTION MANAGER	
c. DEPARTMENT MANAGER	
d. LABORATORY SERVICES	
e. FACILITIES	
f. PROPERTY ADMINISTRATION	
g. FINANCIAL MANAGEMENT	
h. VICE PRESIDENT & GENERAL MANAGER	

CORPORATE APPROVALS	DATE
DIRECTOR, FACILITIES DEPARTMENT	
PROPERTY ADMINISTRATION	

21. ACCOUNT NO. ORG. NO.

a. ☐ LEASE

b. ☐ EXPENSE

22. ACCOUNT NO. ORG. NO.

☐ CAPITAL ASSET

a. ☐ NEW ☐ USED USEFUL LIFE: YEARS

b. COMSUMPTION PATTERN: ☐ STRAIGHT LINE ☐ DECLINING BALANCE

c. ESTIMATED SALVAGE (RESIDUAL) VALUE AT END OF USEFUL LIFE: ____________ % OF ORIGINAL COST

23. ☐ ASSET ☐ EXPENSE

	TOTAL DSD	ORG.
a. AMOUNT IN 19____BUDGET	$	$
b. TOTAL COMMITTED/INCLUDING THIS REQUEST	$	$
c. BUDGETED BALANCE AVAILABLE	$	$

DISTRIBUTION: **WHITE**—ACCOUNTS PAYABLE; **GREEN**—PURCHASING; **YELLOW & PINK**—PROPERTY ADMINISTRATION; **GOLD**—REQUESTING ORGANIZATION

FIGURE 4 (Continued)

3. Commentary (additional, intangible benefits received as a result of this acquisition)
4. Approval signatures

Regardless of the system used, once the requirement is verified, the request for acquisition form is signed by the initiator. The missing element then is control, which is discussed in Sec. V. Having obtained the initiator's signature, the document is next submitted to appropriate levels of management for review and approval. It should be noted that this is the last time that these managers will have an opportunity to review the document for administrative and technical details before the final review by senior approval authority reviews or challenges it. After the department manager has completed his or her review, the request is returned to the administrator for approval and entry into budget commitments. Recording the commitment assures a continuous status of capital asset commitments for reporting to upper management.

The document is then forwarded to the financial organization and to the company's chief executive officer for final review and approval. The flow described above is shown in Fig. 5. Typically, the form is multicopy, and after the order is placed, the form is distributed to persons in the approval loop.

C. Receipt/Inspection

Once the equipment has been received, it is necessary to assure its operating condition. The equipment may be delivered to the intended user, who in conjunction with the group charged with maintenance and calibration, performs functional testing, exercising all parameters of the equipment. When exotic or state-of-the-art equipment is involved, the equipment should be exercised to the manufacturer's specifications to preclude problems after the warranty expires. Many equipment manufacturers will install and test newly delivered systems at no additional cost. The user organization and those with maintenance responsibility should avail themselves of this service when available from the manufacturer.

The organization having responsibility for maintenance and calibration normally is equipped to exercise equipment of a routine nature to the fullest extent of the manufacturer's specification. As part of the asset management systems, newly purchased equipment should be calibrated and certified prior to use. This receiving inspection/certification serves a dual purpose; it assures that equipment is not damaged in transit or contains latent defects at the time of receipt, and calibration assures accuracy of measurements.

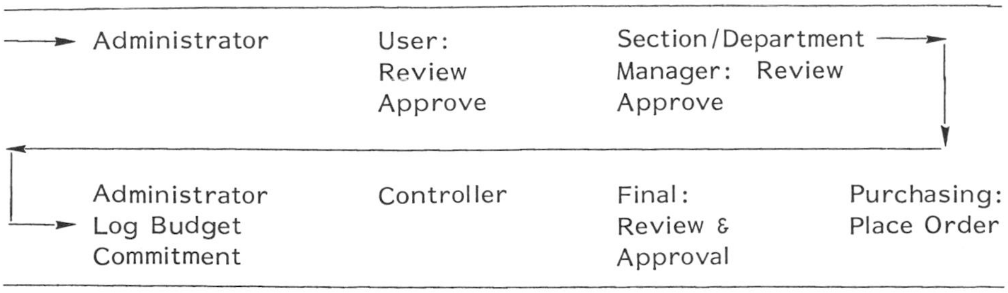

Administrator →	User: Review Approve	Section/Department → Manager: Review Approve	
Administrator Log Budget Commitment	Controller	Final: Review & Approval	Purchasing: Place Order

FIGURE 5 Approval Flow Chart

V. CONTROL

Once the equipment has been received, inspected, and calibrated, it is necessary to assure that proper systems exist to control it through its life cycle.
The management control system to be discussed includes:

1. Custodial control
2. Maintenance and calibration
3. Inventory
4. Training
5. Spare parts
6. Budgetary
7. Equipment disposition

To facilitate a management control system, a series of asset identification
numbers is generated and issued for each piece of equipment and a log maintained by a central "property administrator." The asset numbering system
need only provide that each piece of equipment have its own identifier. Frequently, there is more than one piece of a given type of equipment within a
facility and the equipment serial numbers are generally small and often internal,
requiring disassembly to locate. Using a unique numbering system facilitates
affixing the number externally on the equipment and results in a uniform,
easily monitored, identification system.

A. Custodial Control

Once the system of identification is established, someone must be charged with
the responsibility for "care and feeding" after the equipment is put into use.
Within the plant or facility one person from each operating department should
be assigned responsibility as equipment custodian. Departments can be combined if small. The equipment custodian is responsible for the continuous
status of the equipment, including where it is being used, assuring proper
operating condition and calibration requirements. (The calibration cycle is
discussed below.)
    When equipment is assigned to area custodians, they sign the "asset trans-
fer" (Fig. 6). This acknowledgment signifies that the custodian accepts responsibility for the equipment, is aware of its intended use, and is aware of
the calibration schedule that has been established. Figure 6 shows a sample
form with asset number, issuing activity, recipient, equipment description
(serial number is optional), and calibration cycle. The content or information
on the form should be provided to meet individual system requirements. The
information contained on this receipt document becomes a part of the property
administration log, where the central control documents are maintained for the
asset inventory system.

B. Maintenance and Calibration

The next element of control is maintenance and calibration. Systems and organizational responsibilities established to perform this function range from
very basic to very elaborate. This control is necessary to cycle the equipment
periodically for calibration and maintenance. This periodic cycling is documented through updating of an "equipment history record" (EHR; Fig. 7).

DIV.				ASSET NUMBER			TO-ORGN. NO.				CUSTODIAN			CODE
1	2	3	4	5	6	7	8	9	10	11	12	13	14	80

REL-DATE			MIL	DSD	FROM ORG. NO.		CUSTODIAN	
MONTH		YEAR						

				SERIAL NO.
				MODEL NO.
65	66	67	68	

DESCRIPTION

DATE ISSUED / / 19	ISSUED BY:
DATE RECEIVED / / 19	RECEIVED BY:

REMARKS:

FIGURE 6   Asset transfer ticket.

This EHR becomes the document to maintain a history or fingerprint describing both routine and significant events, including required maintenance throughout its service life. The calibration results may be shown in terms of attribute data; however, maintaining variable data allows statistical analysis to predict maintenance requirements, wear-out, calibration frequencies, and so on. More specifically, if the measurement is correct and within its tolerance limitations, it suffices to say "No cal. required;" however, if the measurement is beyond its tolerance limits or variable data are maintained, the specific measurement and action taken to correct it should be entered on the EHR. Again the variable data taken are necessary for proper assessment of equipment stability and therefore become an important consideration in determining succeeding calibration cycles. For additional information regarding calibration or metrology systems, refer to Chapter 28.

C. Inventory

One of the most effective tools in asset management is "inventory control." This refers not only to equipment in storage, but also to equipment in use within the facility. An effective inventory is usually necessary and should be dynamic in nature. When a department makes a request for new equipment, it would be simple enough to buy the new equipment at the least price with the best delivery; conversely, effective asset management comes from being able to research inventory and find an instrument with the same or similar capability. Should such equipment be available from inventory, arrangements can be made either to loan it to accomplish the task, or to issue it permanently. If the equipment is available under the custodial control of another department and utilization there is low, a sharing arrangement or a transfer may be arranged. Moving equipment between departments is generally not an easy task. However, once managers become familiar with the practice of a dynamic inventory, they usually cooperate; the important point here is that a dynamic inventory is a two-way street. This is not to say that once the initial equipment has been purchased, further acquisitions are not necessary—quite the opposite.

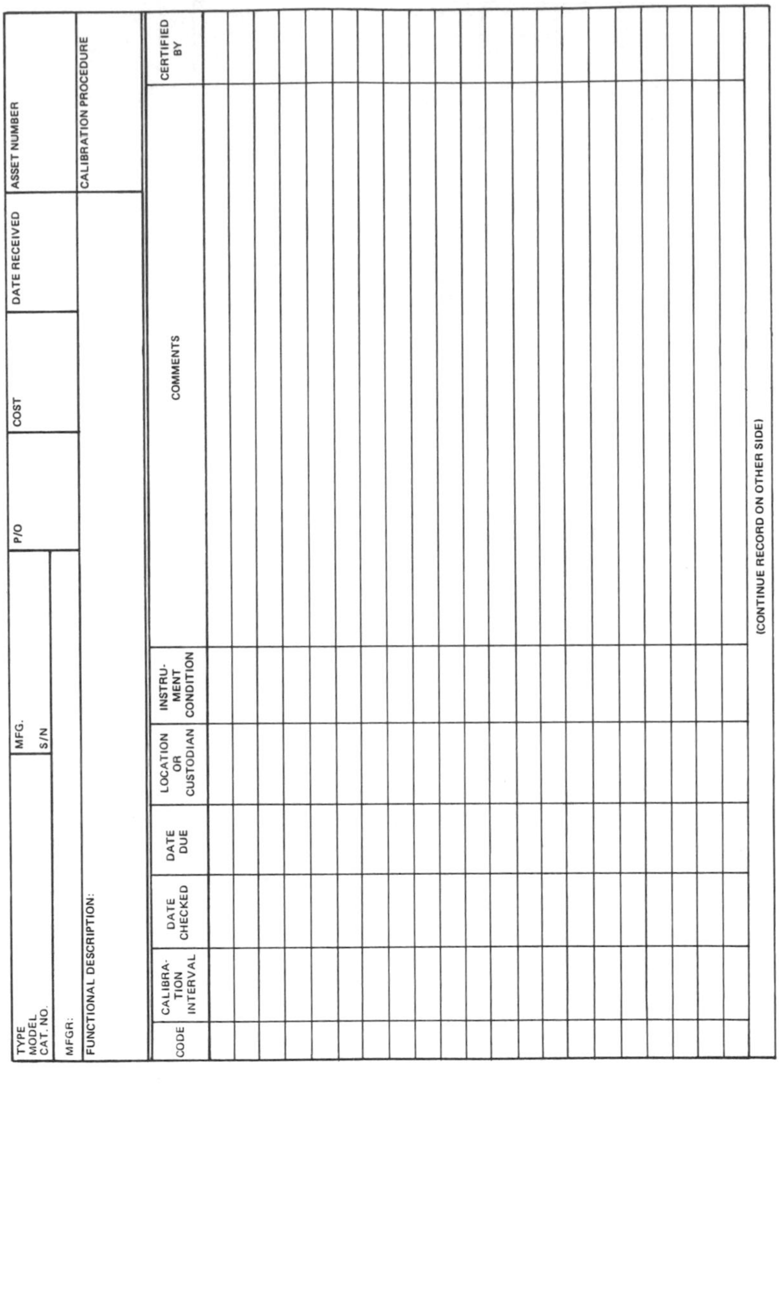

TYPE MODEL CAT. NO.	MFG.	P/O	COST	DATE RECEIVED	ASSET NUMBER
MFGR:	S/N				
FUNCTIONAL DESCRIPTION:					CALIBRATION PROCEDURE

CODE	CALIBRATION INTERVAL	DATE CHECKED	DATE DUE	LOCATION OR CUSTODIAN	INSTRUMENT CONDITION	COMMENTS	CERTIFIED BY

(CONTINUE RECORD ON OTHER SIDE)

FIGURE 7 Equipment history record.

Equipment lives out its useful life, gets damaged beyond economical repair, does not meet new requirements, or there is not enough to go around. Any of these reasons constitutes the need for acquisition. The important point to remember is to check inventory before making a financial commitment; the cost savings can be put to use in other areas.

D. Training

The next element of control is training for both equipment operation and maintenance. Training can be of a generic type, such as electronics or mechanics; of a specific type, such as meters, coordinate measurement systems, and differential gage systems; or operator training, as described by the manufacturer. Manufacturer's training can be performed either in-house or at the manufacturer's facilities and in-house combined. Again, it is very important to consider training when computing the cost of an acquisition; if not, the group may end up with equipment it can neither operate nor maintain.

E. Spare Parts

The next points concern the control of spare-parts inventory. Deciding on quantity and type of spares begins with establishing a "spares policy." That is, spares must coincide with the maintenance policy: maintaining the equipment, purchasing a service contract, or somewhere in between. Once the policy is established, it should remain constant across all equipment. By remaining consistent, other departments will learn what to expect and will have a better understanding of what is necessary to keep their equipment in top operating condition.

F. Budgetary

Budgetary controls are usually established and tailored to a specific operating practice of a company and therefore are too detailed and varied to be discussed here. The point to be made, however, is that once the annual "capital budget" has been established, it is essential that it be controlled in a manner similar to the assets themselves. The group with the responsibility for equipment inventory control, standardization, maintenance and calibration, and spares is best equipped to oversee the budgetary control of capital equipment. Information relating to basic price, option cost, deliveries, and rental costs makes this organization a natural focal point which can provide timely, accurate data as to status. Again, the critical point is "consistency." If each department is handling its own controls, the entire system can be unwieldly. On the other hand, if a central department has this responsibility, the total system becomes much more effective.

G. Equipment Disposition

The final element of control is that of equipment disposition after it has completed its useful life or when it is damaged beyond repair. The first decision to be made is whether to replace the equipment, and if so, whether it be the same type or an improved model. Essentially, the planning phase of the acquisition process begins at this point. However, in a working system of asset management, the planning would have been completed and, in fact, would have predicted the end-of-life condition. If the asset is damaged beyond repair, the equipment should be scrapped and, where possible, component parts that may be usable as spares should be salvaged. If, the equipment is still operational but no longer possesses the accuracy or stability necessary to support its intended use, the asset should be sold or disposed of in any manner the company elects. The point here is that once the device has completed its useful life, it should be removed from inventory. Carrying it on the inventory is of no value and adds unnecessarily to the controls required.

4

MANAGEMENT COMMUNICATION

MARTIN SMITH

Dyna Pak Corporation
Stanhope, New Jersey

I. INTRODUCTION

One of the major problems confronting quality professionals today is that of opening up and maintaining effective communication links with various levels of management. Too often, for example, the same quality performance report is issued to everybody, from the first-line supervisor through the president. Results are generally predictable. The president needs summary information, contrasting goals, and actual results. The supervisor needs details relating to performance by operator, shift, and machine. Issuing the same report to both persons is self-defeating; only one level will be able to use the information. The astute quality professional will therefore provide each level of management with the information best suited to convey results, highlighting areas in need of attention so that each level will be able to act and to take corrective action.

The entire structure of communications between quality assurance and management is vital to the success of the quality program. The best quality program available can only be as potent as the ability of company management to have the information it needs to make things happen. Without this vital communication network, quality will falter.

There are certain ways to establish effective communication links within the company which will enhance the quality information flow. The first of these is concerned with the relationship of quality assurance to top management.

II. QUALITY ASSURANCE AND TOP MANAGEMENT

"Top management must commit itself to achieving quality or it will never happen." These are good words but they are meaningless without tangible methods for top management to demonstrate that support. It is simply not enough to have the president tell the staff that he or she wants quality. The mechanism must be established which sets quality goals and then measures progress against those goals.

Nothing is as hard to achieve as quality without the active involvement of top management. Quality must be planned, measured, and controlled in similar fashion to sales, costs, productivity, and other company needs. Quality just will not happen by itself; it needs the full thrust of management commitment, not just well-intentioned statements.

There are four very practical tools that can make that top management commitment a reality:

1. A quality policy
2. A company quality plan
3. A quality board
4. A quality assurance reporting relationships

A. Quality Policy

The first step is to think through exactly what top management expects from the quality function. This should include the expected level of involvement in different areas of the company. The quality policy answers such questions as:

1. "Should our product be the best in the industry, or should it merely be competitive?" Where, in fact, do we want it to be? (Each of these positions demands a certain price which individual companies must recognize.)
2. "Are quality practices and techniques to extend to design and service, or do we want to confine quality assurance to manufacturing?"
3. "To which management level should quality assurance report?"
4. "What level of costs are acceptable in achieving the quality program?"
5. "How will customer quality needs be satisfied in after-sales service? How flexible should the company be in settling customer claims for substandard quality?"
6. "What degree of control should be exercised over vendors?"

Stating the Policy

Effective company quality policies can generally be expressed in just a few pages. The policy is not designed to include quality methodologies and techniques—it simply sets the stage for achievement of the quality program. A typical quality policy for a capital goods manufacturer is shown in Fig. 1.

Notice that in the first paragraph the company specifically states its desire to be "among the leaders in the industry." This clearly indicates the company's desire to have its products above the average competitive level, but does not lock it in to beat *all* its competitors. That allows the company to produce a first-class product, but does not require the company to incur the extra costs necessary to move ahead of all competitors.

Notice also that the criteria for competitive quality rest in the customer's eyes through the words "judged by our customers." Nothing could be clearer. The success of the company's quality efforts has been given a definitive measurement that can be checked by customer surveys.

The second paragraph describes the level of service to the customer without leaving room for doubt. There are no ambiguities. Customer claims are to be settled within time spans indicated in customer contracts.

The third and fourth paragraphs establish the organizational relationships that quality assurance has with other company components and places control of quality in the hands of the general manager.

QUALITY GOODS, INC.

QUALITY POLICY

Policy statement

1. It is the policy of Quality Goods, Inc. to deliver products whose performance quality is judged by our customers to be among the leaders in the industry.

2. Our goal is to provide the proper environment in which product quality meets or exceeds contractual obligations with our customers, and which gives the necessary service level to customers to fulfill the intended function of our products for a period of time to satisfy customer requirements. Customer claims for defective workmanship will be evaluated and settled within the time limits expressed in individual contracts.

3. It will be the responsibility of company general managers, in cooperation with their respective quality assurance managers, to establish an effective quality function which achieves the company's quality program.

4. To assure effectiveness of the quality program in the most objective manner possible, each quality assurance manager will report directly to the general manager of the operating unit and be placed at the same organizational level of manufacturing, engineering, materials and marketing.

5. Final product acceptance decisions, based on company quality requirements and specifications, are the sole responsibility of each unit's general manager.

6. Quality programs are intended for application to all functional areas (marketing, engineering, materials, and manufacturing) involved with shipping and servicing specified quality products for customers.

7. Quality programs will be achieved within specified quality cost budgets established by unit general managers which have been approved by the company president.

Reference Procedures

QA 202	Quality Board Responsibilities
QA 203	The Company Quality Plan
QA 300	Cost of Quality Reporting
QA 315	Vendor Quality
QA 402	Design Quality and Reliability
QA 403	Pre-Production Quality
QA 500	Product and Process Quality
QA 600	Quality Information Systems
QA 703	Field Service Quality
QA 805	Quality Measurement Systems
QA 830	Quality Surveys
QA 900	Quality Training

FIGURE 1 Quality policy statement.

The fifth paragraph places responsibility for shipped quality on the shoulders of the general manager, where it must be to assure achievement of quality policy.

The sixth paragraph assures that quality will be applied to such functional company components as manufacturing, purchasing, warehousing, design, and service.

The last paragraph establishes the necessity for achieving the quality program goals within financial boundaries consistent with company cost goals. In practice, cost-of-quality goals are established based on those tasks necessary for meeting company quality policy.

Finally, references are made to specific procedures designed to assurance compliance to the policy.

B. The Company Quality Plan

While quality *policy* is the formalized commitment of management to quality, the company quality *plan* is a detailed expression of how that policy will be achieved. The quality plan is normally the creation of the quality assurance manager with the blessing of the general manager. It describes quantifiable quality goals (cost of quality, warranty, etc.) and supports those goals with specific plans of action.

The quality plan is similar to a general's tactical plan in a combat zone. The tactical plan (quality plan) is an extension of military strategy (quality policy) and is an expression of how that strategy will be achieved. As such, the quality plan should encompass all aspects of the quality program from design, through manufacturing, and into service.

The time span of the quality plan is flexible and should reflect the period of time it takes to accomplish major tasks. Three years is typical; 5 years is not unusual.

Figure 2 is a page from the quality plan of the same capital-goods manufacturer discussed earlier. Notice that very definitive problems (sometimes called "opportunities") are described together with a plan of action to respond to the problem/opportunity. Specific people are assigned to assure completion of the tasks by stated completion dates. Similarly, component plans of action are written for manufacturing, materials, and marketing. A list of plans of action are, of course, dependent on those problems unique to the company and areas of improvement which will result in lowered scrap, rework, and warranty charges.

Each contributing manager should approve his or her section of the plan, and the final quality plan should then be approved by the unit general manager. This will assure that the plan is workable and gains management support. Progress *must* be reviewed periodically against scheduled completion dates by the quality assurance manager. The quality assurance manager and general manager must insist that "behind-schedule" items be brought up to date or the tasks will not be completed.

C. The Quality Board

Once a quality policy has been adopted and the quality plan approved by top management, execution of the plan starts. Unfortunately, it is during the crucial state of execution that many quality programs fail to deliver.

The fault for that can be laid at many doorsteps, but frequently the problem arises because top management thinks the quality program is now on "automatic."

QUALITY GOODS, INC.

QUALITY PLAN

1983-1985

Section #6: Engineering Quality Systems

Problem/Opportunity	Plan of Action	Person(s) Assigned	Time Frame
There is no pre-production quality planning resulting in excess scrap/rework and warranty problems.	Develop a procedure which includes design review, reliability predictions, life-cycle testing, etc.	Director of Engineering, Manager of Quality Engineering	10/83
Quality characteristics are not specified on engineering drawings which creates confusion in manufacturing as to which characteristics are most important.	Identify quality characteristics by critical - major - minor categories on engineering drawings.	Manager Design Engineering, Quality Manufacturing	1/84
There are constant errors made in manufacturing due to specification of wrong parts.	Define bill-of-materials system.	Director of Engineering, Manager Manufacturing Engineering, Manager Quality	3/84

FIGURE 2   Portion of a quality plan.

They often believe that a quality policy and quality plan are all that are needed to make things happen.

But the successful execution of quality plans is much the same as the successful execution of plans aimed at productivity, costs, and other critical company needs. Plans are simply not enough to get the job done. Controls and follow-up are the remaining prime ingredients.

The quality board is a proven way to keep top management in constant touch with progress—or lack of progress—of the quality plan. It opens doors of communication with company-wide management and provides an opportunity for the quality assurance manager to keep programs on track.

The quality board should have the responsibility to support the implementation of the quality plan and to provide continuing direction for the company's quality programs. Other subjects for discussion can range from policy matters to the handling of major company problems and any other matters essential to successful accomplishment of the quality policy.

Typically, the board would be composed of the directors of quality assurance, manufacturing, engineering, and marketing, with the general manager as chairman. By placing charimanship of the committee in the hands of the general manager, the quality board is assured of a "balanced" look at the issues presented. Since the general manager is the person vested with primary responsibility for achievement of quality goals, it makes good sense to have him or her run the top quality committee of the company.

D. Quality Assurance Reporting Relationships

The final major ingredient of effective communications with top management involves organization. If quality assurance reports to anybody other than the general manager, communications will be hampered. There is no contesting the fact that the quality message will not come across as clearly; it will be filtered through the eyes and ears of another manager (typically of manufacturing or engineering), who has several other balls to juggle. The message the quality assurance manager wants to get across is bound to be difused and weakened.

Another strong argument can be made for a direct reporting relationship of quality assurance to the general manager. It is simply human nature to expect the general manager to place more emphasis on those functions reporting directly to him or her. Should quality assurance be relocated to a lower management level, the quality program will just not receive the time and attention it demands to assure its contribution to profitability. If the general manager is going to be held responsible for attainment of quality goals, he or she must have direct access to the quality function, and it must be placed on a level that assures its objectivity. That objectivity can be misplaced if quality assurance reports to an organizational component (such as engineering or manufacturing) which has other primary goals.

III. REPORTING TECHNIQUES

While one of the historic problems of quality assurance has been communications with top management, another concern has been reporting techniques. What information needs to be reported to control quality, how often, and how should it be presented? Getting the right answers to those questions has caused many a headache for quality professionals.

Too often, either too much or too little information has been supplied by quality assurance. Failure to utilize some basic principles of control reporting has, in essence, shut a communications door, a door that quality assurance needs open.

Improvement in reporting techniques can be obtained through a study of:

The selection of information needed to control operations
How to present that information
Reporting that information to different organization levels

A. Selecting the Information to Report

Other than special reports, there are three basic and essential performance reports: (1) cost of quality, (2) lot acceptance rates, and (3) process average defective.

Cost of Quality

Cost of quality (COQ) is a valuable tool in the quality practitioner's kit. It allows him or her to communicate with all company levels and functions regarding just how well the quality program is progressing. It is expressed in costs, and costs are universally understood. If a company does not use COQ, its quality manager is at a severe disadvantage. His or her claims to accomplishments will probably be subjective, and subjective claims are usually challenged. COQ—a quantifiable measure—removes all the subjectivity.

When starting a COQ program, the quality assurance manager may need to gather the numbers personally to show people how it is done. When the COQ report gets off the ground, however, it is best to have it published by the finance department. That will lend the numbers respectability; they will remain unquestioned. A quality assurance manager who publishes his or her own numbers is always suspect in others' eyes.

Lot Acceptance Rate

The lot acceptance rate is a measure of importance in any business or industry where parts can be measured in discrete numbers. It is a number of significance to the production facility (and that could be a clerical station as well as a manufacturing operation). The lot acceptance rate tells production people how much work must be sorted to cull defective parts. It is, therefore, a rough measure of their labor costs for defective work, as well as an indication of the scrap and rework problems being experienced. If, for example, a machine shop processes 1000 lots during the week, and if the lot rejection rate is 10%, manufacturing then knows that it will incur excess labor costs for 100 lots to sort out defective work. The lot acceptance rate is a prime method of communication with manufacturing management because they will understand the penalty incurred for poor quality. The manufacturing manager will probably know within 5% the costs that are being absorbed because the manager's staff did not pay close attention to the quality aspects of their jobs. Sorting should be both handled and charged to manufacturing so that they are penalized for poor-quality work. If sorting is performed by quality assurance, manufacturing will not pay close attention to quality, and the lot acceptance rate criterion will lose much of its meaning.

Process Average Defective

The process average defective is a measurement of how well the process is turning out acceptable quality products. Thus it is a measurement of great significance to the quality practitioner as well as the manufacturing engineer and product engineer. It is an indication of where they must concentrate their energies.

The process average defective is based on the number of samples measured by inspectors (or operators). It is explained as follows:

Week: 4/10/83
Dept.: Drilling

Samples inspected: 500
Samples rejected: 25
Process average defective: 5%

In this example, inspectors in the drilling department of a machinery manufacturer sample inspected 500 parts during the week and found 25 pieces defective. Dividing the 25 defective pieces by the 500 sampled pieces and multiplying × 100 results in a process average defective of 5%. The process is therefore producing 95% acceptable parts (assuming, of course, use of valid sampling plans and random selection procedures).

This figure is useful to the manufacturing engineer because it relates the adequacy of tools, gages, and fixtures, and demonstrates over a period of time the condition of the equipment. The product engineer is similarly interested because it demonstrates the effectiveness of the design and the adequacy of the tolerances. The quality engineer will also watch the process average defective so as to reduce scrap and rework on those processes exhibiting high defect rates.

B. How to Present the Information

One basic rule should govern the presentation of quality information aimed at getting corrective action: Keep it simple. Reports should be easily understood by all levels of the organization, and information presented should not be cluttered with peripheral information. It is helpful to present information in graphical form so that trends can be quickly detected.

Figure 3 is a monthly lot rejection report for Quality Goods' machine shop. The top left-hand side of the report displays the salient numbers: current monthly performance, year-to-date performance, and the previous year's average. What could be simpler? At a glance the reader can compare current performance with last year's rate to see if any improvement has been made.

The next section displays the graph. It is apparent that lot rejections have stabilized somewhat during the year and that every month was below the previous year's average (1982 $\bar{x}$). Again, the simplicity of the salient numbers and the graph provide for good communications. It would be difficult to misinterpret their meaning.

The final section of the lot rejection report for the machine shop shows the top defects and top causes of defects for the month. Notice that the top two defects for November accounted for 75% of the rejections and that the top two causes constituted 85% of the causes for rejection.

What could be simpler? The entire report can *easily* be interpreted by anybody from machine operator to company president, yet all the information needed to generate action is present. From the report you can see where you have been, where you are now, and where you are heading. You can also see the top problems and their causes. Communication is instant and clear.

C. Management Reports

The larger a company becomes, or the more complex its operations are, the greater the need to present succeeding levels of the company organization with differing amounts of reporting detail. Since the purpose of reporting is for control and improvement, the president will need summary information of all operations and the production supervisor will need detailed information of his or her operation alone. Figure 3 is a good example of the kind of information

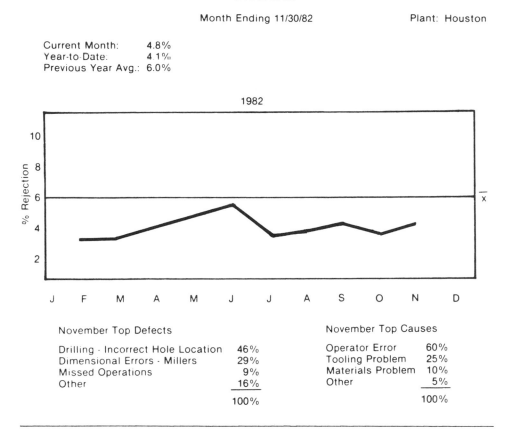

MACHINE SHOP

Month Ending 11/30/82   Plant: Houston

Current Month: 4.8%
Year-to-Date.   4.1%
Previous Year Avg.: 6.0%

1982

November Top Defects		November Top Causes	
Drilling - Incorrect Hole Location	46%	Operator Error	60%
Dimensional Errors - Millers	29%	Tooling Problem	25%
Missed Operations	9%	Materials Problem	10%
Other	16%	Other	5%
	100%		100%

FIGURE 3   Quality Goods, Inc., lot rejection rates.

the production manager needs to control the shop's quality performance. The machine shop supervisor, on the other hand, will need the same information as shown, but applied to his or her individual sections. The machine shop supervisor will also need specific listings of quality performance by operator and by machine. That level of detail allows zeroing-in on problem people and equipment. Pareto information by part number will also help focus on major quality problems.

Normally, summary reports for general managers will take the form shown in Fig. 4. Section A of the report summarizes quality performance for all of the individual plants of Quality Goods, Inc., and shows the total plant average. Although this report is issued monthly, many companies prefer to have weekly reports. The shorter the time interval of control reports, the faster the response in correcting problems. A good example is the November 12.5% lot rejection rate for the Pittsburgh plant. If this report had been issued weekly it would have received prompt management attention and quite possibly the rate would have been lower by the time the month ended.

Section B of the report explains the problems, solutions, and opportunities in quality performance. Note the explanation for the problems found at the

QUALITY GOODS, INC.

QUALITY PERFORMANCE

Month Ending 11/30/80

A. Summary of Month & YTD

Plant Location	Lot Rejection %			Avg.	Process Defective %	
	Nov.	YTD	82	Nov.	YTD	82
Houston	7.4	8.2	7.7	3.4	2.9	3.9
Pittsburgh	12.5	6.5	7.3	5.7	2.8	3.6
Los Angeles	4.5	7.1	8.4	4.2	3.3	3.7
All Plant Avg.	7.8	7.3	7.8	4.4	3.0	3.7

B. Outstanding Problems, Solutions, Opportunities

1. Heavy rejection rate at Pittsburgh - assembly and
    automatic screen machines. New station fixtures now
    being installed at assembly and screw machines now
    in planned maintenance overhaul.

2. The new preventive action program aimed at reducing scrap
    and refinish has just completed its third month at Los
    Angeles, and the results have been encouraging. Lot
    rejections were down to 4.5%, the lowest rejection rate
    ever.

FIGURE 4   General manager's summary report.

Pittsburgh plant, as well as an explanation of the low 4.5% November lot rejection rate at Los Angeles.

A refinement to this report could include lot rejection and process average
defective goals by plant. Some general managers prefer to issue specific goals,
whereas others use the previous year's average as a base and ask for a lower
rate. It all depends on the extent of the quality problems as well as the "gold
mines" available.

IV. COMMUNICATION FOR PREVENTIVE ACTION

Quality assurance is bombarded with multitudes of problems but should not
surrender to the impulse to spend its time dashing around madly putting out
all the fires. Quality assurance *must* always take the lead, steering other
departments along the path of problem resolution and problem prevention.

Nobody else is going to do it, at least not to the extent that quality assurance will. Putting out fires is not enough. The fire will come back.

Preventive action always starts with identification of areas of opportunity (the major, high-cost quality problems). The action must be organized to attack the problems successfully. This organization usually involves a focusing of efforts on (1) customer quality problems; and (2) the costs of scrap, rework, and sorting of products in-house.

A. Customer Quality Problems

These problems involve complaints, warranty, retrofits, upgrades, and any other mechanism by which customers express their dissatisfaction with quality. It should be noted that many times customers and the company may look upon quality standards differently. Shoddy quality can mean different things to customers than to a company. If, for example, a trend in customer complaints is noted for paint problems (sags, runs, thickness, peeling), a peek at company specifications might show some latitude for quality acceptance—an obvious dichotomy with customer expectations. Yet these type of differences tend to occur frequently, if only because specifications are dynamic. Specifications can change for many reasons; notably for cost reduction, but specification changes may overlook potential customer complaints.

Some method, therefore, needs to be devised to look at outgoing products with "customer eyes." The product audit, which provides management with an indication of the outgoing quality level, is probably one of the best methods. It is composed of quality characteristics obtained from marketing's field service and quality assurance (Fig. 5). Those characteristics are a reflection of what must be controlled to assure customer satisfaction. As such, they are not derived from product specifications. Where the two do not mesh, quality assurance, marketing, and engineering jointly decide what specification changes are necessary to agree with customer expectations for the product.

Product audits are taken randomly by quality assurance. As shown in Fig. 5, each quality characteristic is rated as critical, major, or minor and assigned a possible point value. Those point values are explained on the lower third of the form.

The product auditor evaluates the product selected and assigns earned points based on what type of job was done. The auditor can assign portions of the possible point total if, in his or her judgment, some of the job was done correctly. The actual rating is made characteristic by characteristic on the middle section of the form.

A final point total is tabulated and shown opposite "actual points" on the top of the form. This total is divided by the "possible points" total and multiplied by 100 to arrive at the rating. In this example the rating was 93%.

The product audit is a workable device to communicate outgoing quality levels with management people and operators alike. It alerts the organization to the needs and desires of customers. The product audit is an effective tool for corrective action.

Since the product audit is an in-house tool, quality problems found by customers must be handled differently. There are numerous methods for investigation, compilation, and reporting of customer quality problems. One of the major roadblocks to resolving these problems and invoking preventive action occurs because of this sheer mass and a lack of organization in attacking the problems.

QUALITY GOODS, INC.

PRODUCT AUDIT

Plant: L.A.   Date: 10-15   Auditor: L. Jones

Machine Audited: 4021-R   Possible Points: 470

Customer: RLF   Actual Points: 435   Rating: 93%

Quality Characteristic	Possible Points	Actual Points
Control Unit Tension Device	100	100
Control Unit Actuator	50	40
Control Unit Gear Train	100	100
Automatic Lubricator	50	50
Cosmetics - Paint	50	25
Cosmetics - Sheet Metal Finish	10	10
Cosmetics - Welds	50	50
Support Block Positioner	10	10
Turnaround Device	50	50
Total Points:		435

Critical (100 points) - Could cause personal injury, result in machine downtime of 48 hours or more, or result in warranty claims over $500.

Major (50 points) - Could cause machine downtime under 48 hours, result in warranty claims under $500, or crerate customer dissatisfaction with cosmetics.

Minor (10 points) - Minor defects in cosmetics or workmanship not resuling in warranty claims or machine downtime.

FIGURE 5   Quality characteristic ratings.

There are two basic methods of handling customer quality problems. One involves use of a small group of marketing, manufacturing, product engineering, and quality assurance representatives. Their purpose is not to solve the problems, but to assign priorities for corrective action to the functional departments bearing responsibility. This method assures not only good communications regarding customer complaints, but also a total business approach to the problem resolution. It will, in other words, allow the company to deal with the most pressing problems first, and handle the balance in a descending order of importance.

The other method assigns quality engineers to product lines, allowing them to assign priorities for corrective action, investigate and analyze customer complaints, and work with the functional departments for corrective action.

B. Internal Failures

There are also several different professional approaches from which to select when combating scrap, rework, and sorting costs incurred in manufacturing. Either the team approach or the quality engineer approach mentioned earlier is feasible. In companies with extensive failure costs, both approaches are utilized successfully. The team approach should focus on specific manufacturing engineering, quality assurance, and materials. Either method will generate results and open up communication channels for preventive action techniques.

5

MOTIVATION

WILLIAM CASH

Unitek Corporation
Monrovia, California

I. BRIEF HISTORY OF MOTIVATION

The earliest speculations concerning motivation stemmed primarily from the instinct theory and the philosophical nature of human beings. Early thoughts on the subject from philosophers and theologians indicated a belief that the fundamental difference between animals and *Homo sapiens* was our ability to rise above the baser instincts of animals to some higher level of moral and ethical behavior. Animals behavior is based on instinct, whereas that of human beings arises from our ability to think, reason, and know right from wrong.

The field of psychology was developed to explore human and animal motivation, both from the psychoanalytical approach begun by Sigmund Freud and from a more experimental or scientific approach. Developing along parallel lines, each area of psychology began to address the basic question of what motivation is and how motivation in animals differs from that in human beings.

As bodies of knowledge and methodologies developed, schools of thought began to branch out in each major area. Those in the scientific or experimental areas, often referred to as "rat psychologists," extended their findings to human beings by exploring the reactions of animals in controlled environments. Experimental psychologists began to develop entirely new areas of investigation, and we soon had "personality," "social," "industrial," and "abnormal" psychologists. Each of these disciplines looked at motivation in different settings and circumstances.

The psychoanalytical school of investigation developed more slowly because its primary method of exploring human motivation was by interview, observation, and general self-reports. Humanistic and clinical psychology, sometimes referred to as the "touchy-feely" group, felt that the best way to study human behavior was to work directly with subjects in long and involved investigations. The more scientific schools emphasized the rigors of their methodology, whereas the humanists relied more on extensive observation.

The more recent school of behaviorism, made popular by B. F. Skinner, has probably caused more breakthroughs in the application of many theories than has almost any other approach. The major difference between the earlier schools of thought and behaviorism is the focus on what is said or done (observable behavior), as opposed to the psychoanalytical or humanistic school, which explores or tries to guess at what motivates such behavior.

Early in the study of human beings it was believed that we were born with certain motivations built in. The combinations of instincts were different in each human being, which it was thought accounted for the differences in our behavior. Modern psychologists view this internal motivation as being in the form of drives. To accomplish these internal motivational goals, the drives within us must be reduced in some way. By reaching such goals, we satisfy ourselves and thus reduce these drives. The drive to accomplish a goal may be linked to the goals that are available, the paths open to a person to achieve the goals, and to the strength of the drive itself.

For example, one quality control manager gets a college degree in microbiology because she wants to be the first in her family to graduate from college. Another manager won a scholarship in the sciences in high school, and simply fell into biology, but after the first two courses, decided to be the best-darn biology major at USC.* The first manager was aiming at one goal, to be the first to graduate from college in her family, and of the paths available to get to that goal, she did not necessarily choose the easiest one. The second manager, after finding himself on a particular path toward the goal of a degree in the sciences, not only narrowed his goals to the biological area of science, but set a standard of excellence for himself. This leads us to one clear-cut conclusion which today is accepted by more and more students of human behavior: Motivation is learned behavior. Taken one step further: All behavior is learned. We must recognize, however, that nutrition, environment, culture, language, economic status, and physical capacity (or lack of it) all contribute to our individual abilities to learn certain behavior and to grow as adults. Philosophically, we may be created equal, but we are certainly not born equal. There are factors within us which motivate us, and barriers outside us, whether real or imaginary, which hinder, delay, or demotivate us. Before exploring some basic principles of motivation that can be used on the job, it is crucial for our understanding of this highly complex area of human behavior to explore some theories. Just as understanding theories is essential in the scientific disciplines to which you are committed, so is this area. These theories are absolutely fundamental to an understanding of your own motivation and that of your employees.

II. BASIC THEORIES OF MOTIVATION

A. Maslow's Hierarchy of Needs

The most commonly quoted theory of human motivation, and perhaps the easiest to understand, is Abraham Maslow's hierarchy of needs [1]. Maslow's theory is in itself a brief summary of modern psychological history beginning with the biological basis of motivations and continuing up to a higher order of motivation: self-actualization. His theory reflects a certain belief in the human desire to rise above the basic needs and grow. The assumption of growth is the key to his theory. Let's explore briefly Maslow's model of motivation that explains our concern for growth and self-enhancement, leading to self-actualization (Fig. 1).

----

*
 They both accomplished their goals, but came to them from two very distinct directions.

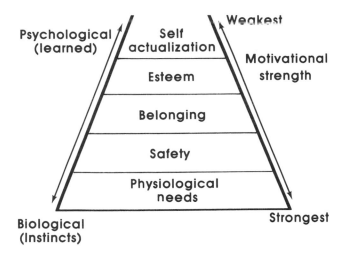

FIGURE 1   Maslow's hierarchy of needs.

The model is a simple linear explanation of what causes us to be motivated. We have the need for food, water, and sex, so we do what is necessary to satisfy those basic needs. Once those are satisfied, we can then move on to clothing, shelter, and security, which constitute the next level of motivation. Once those levels have been satisfied, we are motivated to seek the next level of satisfaction, which is the belonging or love need. This desire to be loved and to love and have an emotional investment in others is the next step in the hierarchy. Once we feel loved, needed, and wanted, we are concerned about our self-esteem, image, respect of others, and the admiration or prestige given to us by our peers, subordinates, managers, family, and friends.

Self-actualization, a concept that has been greatly expanded by the noted psychologist Carl Rogers [2], is not only hard to define, but perhaps harder to explain. Self-actualization is akin to striving for the ultimate self-growth: personal accomplishment or achievement, or the maximization of our total human potential. It is a self-selection of excellence.

As with any theory, there are several basic problems with Maslow's, one of which that it is perhaps too simple. Unfortunately, much of what motivates us is a group of complex variables, not a nice neat chain of events in which first this happens, which causes this effect, then another, and so on. In Maslow's simple chain, much is lost. It is difficult to use the theory as an analytical tool. In an industrialized society such as the United States, roughly 70 to 80% of the population has its physiological, safety, and belonging needs satisfied to some degree. Probably 5 to 10% of the population consistently reaches a level of satisfaction as self-actualizers. This does not mean that we, as a society, do not have starving people, alienated citizens, and bored and dissatisfied workers. Obviously, the higher you move up the hierarchy, the more difficult it is to decide what is satisfying to whom and for how long. This whole concept of satisfaction and dissatisfaction was addressed in a more specific fashion by Frederick Herzberg.

B. Herzberg's Two-Factor Theory

It was natural to assume that some factors in the work setting were highly
satisfactory to workers and that others were not. In Herzberg's [3] early
research involving some 200 engineers and accountants, he discovered that
there were factors that were satisfying to employees on the job, but which
were not the opposite of dissatisfying factors. The two-factor theory means
that employees may be dissatisfied by the level of an item but may not be motivated by more of that item.* Herzberg labeled these two continuums "motivators" and "hygiene factors."

Hygiene or maintenance factors are those elements that kept employees
satisfied on the job, such as good supervision, company policy and procedures,
salary, the job itself, security, and working conditions. Employees are not
necessarily motivated except for a very short period of time by a raise or a
new boss, but if the boss were a very difficult person and no one received a
raise, the employees could be very dissatisfied. Those elements in the work
setting that are seen as motivators include the work itself, growth, achievement, recognition, advancement, and responsibility.

There are essentially two common criticisms of Herzberg's theory. First,
the methods of research used in interviews and questionnaires is not the best
way to identify motivators and dissatisfiers on the job. The other criticism is
that Herzberg's theory is, again, just too simple.

From a practical point of view the theory is most useful in redesigning jobs
with more responsibility, interpersonal relationship, and growth opportunity
through advancement. Many of the satisfiers have been used in the recent
wave of job enrichment, job enlargement, and quality-of-work-life movements.
Although it has some application to large work forces, the theory is still not
entirely useful in identifying specific motivation profiles of individuals or their
motivation patterns.

C. David McClelland's Achievement, Affiliation,
Power Theory

McClelland [4] and Atkinson, reflecting the influence of others, focused exclusively on the motivations of the individual, using as their primary research
tool the thematic apperception test (TAT). The TAT, designed by Henry A.
Murray, [5] requires that the subject write a story about several pictures which
he or she is shown. These stories are then analyzed and interpreted by a
trained psychologist.

The most interesting result of the McClelland et al. research is that this
research made a break with the traditionally biological-based motives. Using
a long-term longitudinal study, McClelland was able to identify three basic
needs. The need to achieve, normally shown as "n-Ach," is essentially a
person's desire to achieve a goal for positive reasons and to avoid negative
consequences.

After long and exhaustive research, McClelland established two other needs:
power and affiliation. Affiliation is somewhat biologically based, but the need
for power is simply the desire to have an impact. Affiliation is the need for
close interpersonal relationships or contact. McClelland's research indicates

---

*
 If we did not pay employees, they would be dissatisfied, but giving employees a raise is not necessarily the best way to motivate them.

that we all have these needs. The real concern then becomes to identify the dominant motive and the motive profile.* Here are some typical motive profiles based on the work of McClelland and his associates (Fig. 2).

The motivation of most salespeople is to sell the products or services they represent; this cannot be done at the expense of the customer. Therefore, salespersonnel must have a reasonable ability to get along with customers while balancing this against the need to have impact on, or sell to, the customers. The salesperson's needs are perhaps greater than the customer's needs to upgrade services or products. Although most salespeople have the desire to sell, they must do so in a way that is not offensive; hence to some extent, they must be able to affiliate with their customers. Good salespersons must also have impact to make the sales, quotes, and contacts that are necessary if they are to be successful in their profession. While the dominant motive may be achievement, the typical salesperson must be able to relate to customers and while retaining enough influence to get the job done.

Power—the desire to have an impact on others, to be approached for advice and to offer it, to be a mover and a shaker—is the next of McClelland's needs. Power can be seen both as a positive force for good or as a negative force for bad. Recognizing that power over others and over resources can be misused, we will discuss the concept of power as a positive force. The desire to influence, to have impact, or to be in charge are all part of the need for power.

Teaching is a power position. Seldom, if ever, do teachers enter the field for money or to attain financial goals, although many do attain such goals. Most teachers have a strong desire to have an impact on their students. College professors, especially, have the type of power which, in some cases, determines if a student will pass or fail. This does not mean that professors are devoid of achievement needs or affiliation needs, but if

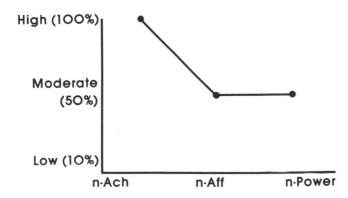

FIGURE 2   Achievement, affiliation, and power profile of a "typical" salesperson.

McBer and Company, 137 Newbury Street, Boston, MA, 02116, provides a training program that enables you to identify motive profiles.

accomplishment or achievement is measured in money, most teachers do not enter the field for that reason. Even if achievement is measured by the number of articles written, papers or books published, or grants received, such achievement is attained by only 10% or less of the people in the teaching profession. A typical profile of someone high in power, such as a teacher, might look as shown in Fig. 3.

Affiliation is the desire for close interpersonal relationships and can be seen in such professions as social workers, nurses, and ministers. People who have the desire to aid and assist others as basic goals are usually attracted to these professions.

The real problems arise when a person with one set of motivations is needed and the person involved has another. Jobs themselves have certain motivational patterns that require certain types of people. Suppose that you are a quality control supervisor in a job that requires someone with a high achievement motivation and a desire to have an impact on the production people. The work motive profile is the solid line and your motive profile is shown by the dashes. What types of difficulty would you have? (See Fig. 4.)

Assume that the job requires precise thinking, the ability to work alone, judgment, decisiveness, and adherence to a number of corporate and governmental standards (such as GMP and GLP).* If the product does not meet the standards, the quality control supervisor must shut down the line. If in this job we placed a person who has a high need for affiliation, which could mean that this person is friendly, outgoing, easy to talk to, is constantly being reminded about sloppy, inaccurate work habits, and has trouble making a decision, the result is a poor job/person fit.

McClelland's approach is probably the most useful concept and can easily be learned. An achievement-oriented person could be described as someone with a need to have the lowest rejection rate in the plant, the closest adherence to delivered product as possible, and the fewest customer complaints. Outside the plant this person might have the best first-serve percentage in tennis and/or the lowest golf score. We all need to achieve at a variety of goals or tasks both at work and in our personal lives. Affiliation, to be "in" with the rest of your working group, to have friends in production, to be liked by employees on the line, to be loved, and to like and enjoy the company of

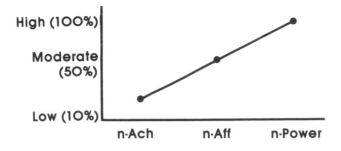

FIGURE 3   Achievement, affiliation, and power profile of a "typical" teacher.

*
GMP and GLP stands for good manufacturing practices and good laboratory practices.

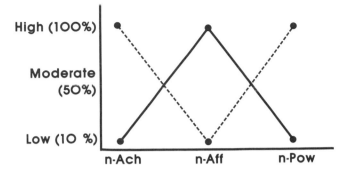

FIGURE 4   Conflicts may occur if the job needs (solid line) are not matched by the individual's needs (dashed line).

others at work and at home are some characteristics of an affiliation-oriented person.

A power-oriented person would be inclined to seek out nomination for an important committee, to be the one the plant manager calls in for advice, to be asked to write an article for a magazine, and to be elected person-of-the-year by the local chamber of commerce. Achievement, affiliation, and power are needs we all have, which helps to make McClelland's theory the easiest to understand and use.

D.   Two More Motivation Theories

The first of two other theories that deserve brief mention among the many that exist is the approach suggested by Vroom [6] and Porter and Lawler [7]. Vroom sees motivation as being made up of certain expectations and the force of "valence" to achieve those expectations. Valence × expectancy = motivation and the resultant behavior.* If you want anything badly enough, you will find a path to that goal which, to some degree, will be satisfying to you. The desire and path motivate you to behave in such a way as to accomplish, to some degree, what you want to accomplish.

Porter and Lawler have directed their attention to the job content and the degree of job satisfaction or rewards gained from the job—the amount of effort an employee puts forth in terms of ability and how he or she see the job. Once the employee begins to perform the job, there are rewards for that perform-ance, such as pay or compliments. If these rewards are seen as equitable and fair, satisfaction results and the cycle begins anew. The real question is: "Am I getting a just or fair reward and the accompanying satisfaction?"

E.   A Comparison of the Big Three

The three major theorists—Maslow, Herzberg, and McClelland—together with Vroom and Porter and Lawler give us much to think about when we ask: "What makes people behave the way they do?" Although it is dangerous and sometimes

---

* Valence is the weight or strength of desire to achieve the goal or the expecta-tion, and these two forces equal motivation.

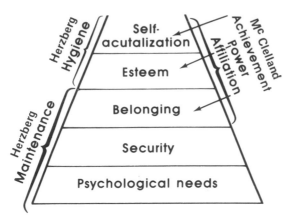

FIGURE 5   Comparison of the theoretical profiles of Maslow, McClelland, and Herzberg.

misleading to compare various theories, we have done this for the three major theorists in Fig. 5.

Now that we have established that motivation is highly complex and that there are many theories to explain our behavior, let's begin to take some of that knowledge and address more practical questions.

III. THE QUALITY MANAGER AS A MOTIVATOR

To better understand yourself and others, we need to explore some basic elements of motivation. The four basic areas we need to be concerned about are personality, values, goals, and perception, which mix to form motivation. For our purposes, motivation is learned behavior which is directed toward a goal that is sometimes known and sometimes unknown. First, we examine the components that comprise motivation, and then we discuss the definition in more detail (Fig. 6).

Your personality, which is simply how you treat others, is made up of a number of complex happenings in which you may be consciously or unconsciously engaged. We know that nutrition affects how the brain and body develops, but we cannot know how other cultural and situational variables affect the growth and development of each human being. Your value system, which you have developed, interacts with your personality and to a large extent determines how you see the world and what goals you set for yourself. Your personality is the manner in which you behave (say and do) toward others, and your value systems are the internal justification for such behavior. Value systems add a degree of importance to our personality and are determined at a young age.

Goals may be as elementary as avoiding the mean dog down the street or completing high school, buying a car, marrying rich, or writing a chapter on motivation. Multiplication signs are needed to indicate that what we are and

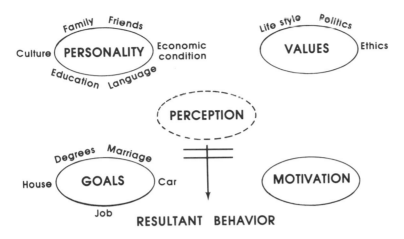

FIGURE 6   The components of motivation.

what we are not are not simply additive, but interactive—so much so that it
makes personality, values, and goals difficult to separate.

Our value systems, and to some extent our personality, can be seen in the
goals that we select. The desire to reach these goals and the strength of the
desire constitute motivation. Motivation, for the most part, is internal. Once
we have decided that a goal is worth trying for, we examine our choices or
ways of attaining the goal. Several problems can occur to prevent or stifle
our motivation.

There may be only one goal—a supervisory or management position—but
many people may want the same goal. Often, the world outside does not recognize or cooperate with us. The extent to which we allow this interference
to demotivate or discourage us says something about our personality and value
system. Motivation, the desire to achieve the goal, may not be there. We may
not be willing to pay the price. Competition can be demotivating and create
goal conflicts within us. Goal conflict can be another motivational problem.
We want to finish our degree, but working and making money keep us in a
state of indecision, so we do a mediocre job at work and never enroll in night
school. Suppose that we wanted to get promoted, and promotions are based
on who drinks with whom, or who plays golf with whom. Not only don't we
drink, but we can't stand golf! Such conflicts may produce serious problems.
The other common problem is that motivation, or the goal itself, may be too
high or too low. Goals that are impossible to obtain or too easy to achieve
seldom motivate us for long.

Once again, let's look at the definition of motivation. It is learned behavior
that is directed toward a goal or goals which are sometime known and sometimes unknown. It is the firm position of this author that behavior is learned.
We may not remember the precise set of circumstances or variables from which
we acquired the behavior, but we did learn it somewhere. The most obvious
example is to watch children as they behave like their mothers, fathers, brothers, or sisters. These learned behaviors constitute a huge repertoire of behavior which we direct toward a goal or goals. The goal or goals may be known
to us, and then again, may not. Often when asked, "Why did you do that?"
we have no real answer. I'm not talking about those situations in which we

want to cover up, lie, or deceive ourselves. Whether or not we have consciously selected a goal to be achieved, the behavior exhibited is typically
goal directed.

The real question of the manager is: "Can you motivate others?" The
answer is: "Yes and no." We hear that a particular person is a spark plug,
motivator, a leader, or a role model for others. Many evangelists rely on
this approach to motivate. They are able to stir such basic emotions as fear,
love, and sympathy. Sales meetings which end up in pep talks, the company
song, or other so-called motivational techniques are effective for a short period. This temporal effect may wear off within minutes, or within days, unless we internalize the message and become self-motivated to sell better. When
we have internalized the motivational message, we begin to set goals for ourselves and try to decide how we can best go about reaching those goals. Having a talk with your employees and encouraging them to do a better job may be
a nice thing to do, but do not expect it to have a long lasting effect. Yes,
we can have some short-range effects on others—and longer-range effects if
they internalize the message or goal within themselves.

Can you motivate yourself? Yes. Theorists and practitioners agree that
the strongest and most persistent kind of motivation is self-motivation. Setting reachable goals, selecting appropriate behavior, and making steady progress toward your goals can enable you to strengthen your motivation. Internal
motivation is the strongest and most effective kind of motivation. Once again,
selection of the goal can be a key, together with the alternative avenues of
getting to that goal. You can assist and aid your employees by helping them
set goals, provide an atmosphere conductive to productive work, and aid them
in being successful at attaining their individual goals. You have heard that
you can grow up to be president of the United States, but the probability of
such an event occurring is very slim; so you realize from the start that achieving such a goal may be impractical. Getting a master's degree in chemistry
after being out of school for 18 years may present unique problems. You may
need to polish up your skills and talk with some professors before you enroll
in the first course. Then, do you attend classes full-time, quit your job, go
on weekends or evenings, or choose some other alternative? Will the company
assist you through their educational assistance program? Can you pay for the
courses on your own? Can you deduct the cost from your income tax? Do you
take the money out of your savings?

Making progress toward a goal can motivate you even further. One way to
increase your motivation is to set milestones and mark your progress as you
go. Going back to school for a degree might be easier if you take two courses
at night rather than looking at the entire goal. Breaking the goal down into
small chunks or bits may make progress seem easier and more meaningful.

A better question than "Can I motivate myself or others?" is "How can I
provide an environment to permit my employees to motivate themselves and
others?" "What can I do to reinforce appropriate behavior?"

A. Critical Motivation Factors

Overt signs of enthusiasm or a constant positive expression on the part of an
employee are not necessarily indicators of motivation. Just as no person can
be expected to work every hour or minute on the job, we should not expect
permanent smiles on our employees' faces; identifying whether a person is
motivated or not is a very difficult task at best. There are some people who
have, as part of their basic personality, the type of charismatic leadership

which makes others want to work for them. We have all worked for, or been taught by, someone whom we admired or wanted to be like. Although not every manager or supervisor can be such a person, there are some basic assumptions or principles of motivation that can help managers to understand and provide knowledge on which to base attempts to motivate. Some of these principles were discussed earlier. Once you understand these basic principles, you may be better able to select and place people in appropriate jobs, redesign the work to include more motivating factors, or—the most difficult task of all—actually change the behavior of others.

B. Basic Principles of Motivation

1. Motivation is internal. There are certainly factors outside a person which can enhance or motivate. However, the person must decide what is and what is not motivational to him or her.

2. Most goals are self-defined and often self-limiting. The boss may want an employee to become the best chemist in the department, but all the prodding in the world may not motivate the employee unless that is the person's desired goal.

3. Goals external to an employee must be challenging, achievable, and desirable. Motivation requires the expenditure of ourselves and energy to risk sacrifices to obtain goals. The desirability of the goal is important, but so is the achievability of the level of challenge it provides. A more direct way of saying it is: "What do you want?"; "How badly do you want it?"; "What is the probability of you achieving it?" We simply cannot will something into being. Ability, IQ, and opportunities all play a part in achieving any goal. Setting a goal by or for one of your employees without taking into account his or her desires, needs, and objects is wasted effort.

4. Motivation and behavior are learned. People are not born a certain way; they are, however, often creatures of habit. Often, motivation means teaching people new behavior patterns. Barring physical or mental limitations, people can learn new behavior or be shown new ways of doing things and of accomplishing their goals.

5. Because behavior is learned, it can be changed. First, it can be changed by experiencing a dramatic or traumatic life incident, such as a divorce, death, being fired from a good job, or other experience which causes a person to alter his or her behavior. The second way of changing behavior is through a conscious effort: identifying what needs to be changed, altering the cognative network, changing the way we think about our behavior, trying the new behavior, and receiving the kind of reinforcement that encourages us to continue the new behavior. The third way is to alter surface behavior or simply to change some small things without undergoing the deeper thought and behavior change necessary. The fourth way is to appear as if you have changed, when in fact you have simply learned to cope or behave in such a way as to fool those around you. Behavior can be changed, but it requires considerable effort on the part of the person doing the changing and reinforcement on the part of the person who sees and wants the change to take place.

6. Behavior involves a degree of risk. For every behavior we engage in, there is a risk to be taken, a price to be paid, and a benefit to be derived. Moving to a new job may be highly risky to one person and not at all risky to another. There is often a fear of loss as well as a fear of gain. "If I leave teaching to go into industry and quality work and I don't make it, I will have lost tenure and my professorship." "But if I don't take this industry offer,

I may be here for another 30 years with one more promotion to go." We must define for ourselves what is risk and what is not.

7. Motivation is individually specific, and therefore the selection of goals and the need to accomplish them may vary from person to person.

8. The inability to select an appropriate goal may be every bit as distressing as having a path to a clearly defined goal frustrated. The old question "What do you want to be when you grow up?" is a good illustration. We seldom expect the revelations of a 7-year-old to be as accurate as those of a 17-, 27-, or 37-year-old. Typically, the longer a person waits to select goals for life, the more frustrating the selection process. The probability of frustration to reach that goal increases.

9. There is always more than one path to a goal. The ability to perceive the various paths and consider alternatives may assist us in staying motivated when things get rough. We may have chosen to obtain a college degree as a goal, but immediately after high school we join the service, get married, start our own business, and finally end up going to school at night and on weekends.

10. When the particular path we have chosen is blocked toward our goal and frustration results, the selection of an alternative is critical if we are to maintain our motivation to achieve that goal. As manager, the success of your counseling may be reflected in your ability to assist employees in selecting the alternatives.

11. The strength or desire to achieve a goal is a result of whether we see the goal as achievable. Achieveability and other reinforcers give a person an impetus to continue toward the goal.

12. One way of making a goal more achievable is to break it down into smaller, achievable steps. Obtaining a Ph.D. in biochemistry may be much easier if we begin by getting accepted by the school. Completing the general requirements may be the next step, long before we even get into our major.

13. Motivation is complex. Telling employees that they are not motivated or telling them they should be is about as effective as saying to someone who is obviously furious: "Say, you're mad, aren't you?" Knowledge of yourself, your employees, and the situation can aid you in providing the climate in which a person can motivate himself or herself. Seldom will you know all the factors that go into motivating your employees.

14. Motivation is influenced by outside variables. The old idea that when you leave for work you leave your home problems home, and when you leave work, you leave your work problems at work, is just that—an old idea. Idealistically, we should be able to make that separation, but practically, we cannot. What happens at home does influence what happens at work, and the degree to which it affects a person depends on the individual.

15. Motivation can best be identified by what a person says or does. Your safest bet as a manager is not to attempt to guess at the motivation of each employee, but rather to observe the behavior, remembering that some of the behavior may be influenced by you, the work being done, the other workers, and the conditions under which the employee works.

16. Usually, the closer you get to a goal, the stronger the motivation to achieve the goal; this depends a great deal on the difficulty of achievement and the importance the person places on the goal.

17. Typically, positive expectations create positive results when a person possesses skills and knowledge to reach the goal. Just saying "I know you can do it" is not enough. But providing the person with the skills, practice, and feedback together with the positive expectation can greatly enhance the chances for achievement. The way you assign work often gives away your expectations.

18. Motivation can be influenced by positive and negative reinforcement and feedback. Positive reinforcement for appropriate behavior will encourage a person to continue that behavior. Negative reinforcement will discourage someone from behaving in an appropriate way. Feedback is nothing more than a knowledge of results; therefore, letting someone know how he or she did or did not perform can influence the person's performance.

19. Reinforcement and feedback should be as immediate as possible. The closer the reinforcement and feedback to the event or behavior, the greater the influence on the behavior.

20. To be effective, positive reinforcement, especially when attempting to change behavior, must be continuous.

In motivating yourself and others you must ask yourself: "What is it that I want to accomplish, and how far away from perfection can I be and still be satisfied with what I have accomplished?"

Keeping these basic principles in mind, here are some questions you need to direct to yourself when you are considering the broad issue of how to motivate your employees.

C. Questions to Ask Yourself About Motivation

1. How well does the job/person fit in my department?
   a. Have I selected the appropriate persons?
   b. Have I placed these people into appropriate jobs?
2. What kind of climate (work setting) have I created which will allow the motivation of my employees to emerge?
3. What kind of reinforcer am I?
   a. When a job is well done do I say "Good job?"
   b. Do I have positive expectations of my employees?
   c. How often do I relieve frustrations by assisting my employees in accomplishing their goals and work goals?
4. When providing feedback to my employees on their work, am I:
   a. Specific rather than general?
   b. Asking for improvements in one or two areas and not overloading them with information?
   c. Expressing myself in terms of more or less rather than either/or?
   d. Willing to coach them and, where appropriate, show them how?
5. Do employees who work for me know:
   a. What the standards of performance are?
   b. That they are allowed freedom in selecting (wherever possible) the method for doing their job?
   c. That mistakes and errors are not fatal but treated as problems to be solved?
   d. That they may contribute their ideas to improve the operation?
6. When I select employees, I look for the qualifications that best fit the positions available.
7. When and where possible, I make myself available to employees for discussions about their careers.
8. When assigning work, I attempt to provide growth and learning opportunities for those who want such opportunities.
9. When there is a slip in performance, I immediately consult with the employee and establish a procedure for getting the performance up to standard.

10. Recognizing that in the quality function conflict may be a result of doing our work well, I encourage my employees to attempt to resolve the conflict constructively.
11. Am I reasonably consistent in what I say and what I do toward my employees?
12. Do I allow my employees and myself to be human?
     a. Respect their rights and mine to be angry, happy, sad, or quiet?
     b. Respect their right of privacy and confidentiality?

IV. CONCLUSION

There are no simple ways to motivate others. If a formula existed to motivate others, it would make the job of managing human beings at least manageable. One of the biggest obstacles to overcome as a manager with a technical background is the ability to work with and through others. The more you can enhance your people skills, the better manager you can be.

In this chapter we have discussed the history of motivation and several major theories. The model of motivation can give us greater insight into how several complex factors influence our behavior and motivation. Finally, we discussed some principles of motivation and provided a checklist for examining ourselves as motivators. Applying any knowledge is, at best, difficult. If you can further understand yourself and your employees, the probabilities of your being a successful manager are high.

REFERENCES

1. A. H. Maslow, *Motivation and Personality*, Harper & Row, New York, 1954.
2. C. R. Rogers, *On Becoming a Person*, Houghton Mifflin, Boston, 1961.
3. F. B. Herzberg, B. Mausner, and B. Snyderman, *The Motivation to Work*, Wiley, New York, 1959.
4. D. McClelland, *The Achieving Society*, D. Van Nostrand, Princeton, N.J., 1961.
5. H. A. Murray, *Explorations in Personality*, Oxford University Press, New York, 1938.
6. V. Vroom, *Work and Motivation*, Wiley, New York, 1964.
7. E. E. Lawler III and L. W. Porter, "Antecedent Job Attitudes of Effective Managerial Performance," *Organizational Behavior and Human Performance*, Vol. 2, 1967, pp. 122—142.

FURTHER READING

Allport, G. W., *Pattern and Growth in Personality*, Holt, Rinehart and Winston, New York, 1961.
Arkes, H. R., and J. P. Garske, *Psychological Theories of Motivation*, Brooks/ Cole, Monterey, Calif, 1977.
Atkinson, J. W., *An Introduction to Motivation*, Van Nostrand Reinhold, New York, 1964.

Birney, R. C., H. Burdick, and R. C. Teevan, *Fear of Failure Motivation*, Wiley, New York, 1969.

Festinger, L. A., *A Theory of Cognitive Dissonance*, Row Peterson, Evanston, Ill., 1957.

Heckhausen, H., *The Anatomy of Achievement Motivation*, Academic Press, New York, 1967.

Klein, G. S., *Perception, Motives, and Personality*, Alfred A. Knopf, New York, 1970.

Maslow, A. H., *Toward a Psychology of Being*, 2nd ed, Viking, New York, 1971.

McClelland, D. C., and D. G. Winter, *Motivating Economic Achievement*, The Free Press, New York, 1969.

Rogers, C. R., *Freedom to Learn*, Charles E. Merrill, Columbus, Ohio, 1969.

Skinner, B. F., *Science and Human Behavior*, Macmillan, New York, 1953.

Weiner, B., *Theories of Motivation: From Mechanism to Cognition*, Rand McNally, Chicago, 1972.

6

QUALITY CIRCLES

ROBERT E. COLE*

University of Michigan
Ann Arbor, Michigan

I. INTRODUCTION

The evolution of quality control circles in Japan represents perhaps the most innovative personnel utilization strategy in postwar Japanese industry. From its small beginnings in the early 1960s, small-group participative problem-solving teams have become the norm in the large-scale manufacturing sector. They are now spreading to the service sector and nonproduction areas in manufacturing as well. These developments have not escaped the attention of American managers.

By mid-1982 an estimated 1000 American firms had adopted, at least on an experimental basis, some version of quality control circles. The recently established International Association of Quality Circles had over 2700 members, and the Americal Society for Quality Control was reevaluating its role so that it would be able to provide services in this area.

What are quality control (QC) circles? A QC circle is a relatively autonomous problem-solving group, composed of a small number of people (ideally 10) employed in the same workshop. The circles are usually led by a first-line supervisor or a senior worker. According to a recent survey by the Union of Japanese Scientists and Engineers, the circles meet on the average of 1 hour, two or three times a month. Seventy percent of the firms hold circle meetings on regular paid time, with the rest being held before or after working hours. Of those holding meetings before or after regular working hours, 70% pay some sort of allowance, with about half of those paying overtime rates.

The QC circles are, in principle, "spontaneously" formed study groups that concentrate on solving job-related quality problems. These problems are broadly conceived as improving methods of production as part of company-wide efforts. The most typical areas of operation for the circles, in order of their prominence, are cost reduction, quality improvements, improvement of

---

*Present affiliation: Wilson Center, 1000 Jefferson Drive S.W., Washington, D.C.

tooling, upgrading of skill, and safety. More specifically, this may include such issues as reduction of defects, scrap reduction, decreased downtime, improved work standards, and removal of safety hazards.

At each circle meeting, all members are given assignments which they are expected to complete using both company and noncompany time. These assignments involve firsthand observation of specific practices at the workshop and the collection and analysis of data. The three most commonly used techniques are Pareto diagrams, cause-and-effect diagrams, and graphs. At the QC circle meeting, the brainstorming approach operates. Each member is expected to participate and put forward his or her ideas. No idea is criticized and members are encouraged to give their opinions no matter how outlandish they might seem. Selection of study themes and the timetable for achieving them are usually set by the circle members themselves; Pareto diagrams are often used to facilitate this process. However, in many companies, management clearly "encourages" the selection of certain themes in as subtle a fashion as possible.

QC circles emerged out of a long process during which industrial leaders sought to upgrade the quality of Japanese products. Exports were seen as the lifeblood of the national economy, and these leaders saw the upgrading of quality as imperative to ensuring the restoration and expansion of a devastated economy. The circles evolved at the end of a long chain of events designed to improve quality through the introduction of statistical quality control and later, total quality control practices.

It is well known that the principal instrument of this concerted effort was the Union of Japanese Scientists and Engineers (JUSE), established in 1946. JUSE played the major role in leading, coordinating, and providing educational and training materials and programs to facilitate the development of circle activity. It is less well known that JUSE's efforts were actively supported at an early date by Keidanren, the most powerful business federation in Japan. Since shortly after its founding, the chairman of JUSE has either been the chairman of Keidanren or a former chairman. Ishikawa Kaoru, who has provided much of the intellectual leadership for JUSE, is the son of the first man to sit simultaneously as chairman of JUSE and as chairman of Keidanren. These linkages have provided a powerful legitimation and support for JUSE activities, which has facilitated the achievement of their quality objectives. Japan's rise to a position of world leadership in quality cannot be understood without a recognition of this background.

II. QUALITY PRACTICES

The story of how key American advisors stimulated the development of quality practices in Japan has been told many times and we need not review these developments in great detail. U.S. occupation officials encouraged the teaching of wartime industrial standards as a means of restoring basic industries such as communications. As part of this effort, American statisticians and QC experts came to Japan to work with the Japanese. Especially notable is the visit of W. Edwards Deming for an 8-day seminar in July 1950 designed to teach Japanese engineers statistical methods of quality control. The seminar had a major impact.

In 1954, Joseph Juran arrived to teach quality control as a management tool with stress on total quality control. Before long, the statistical concepts and techniques spread from management to supervisors and eventually to workers through the mechanism of QC circles.

In analyzing these developments, two common misunderstandings often develop. First, it is assumed that the Japanese have simply carried out the quality principles developed in the United States; and second, it is assumed that the Japanese knew exactly where they were going. Although QC circles are consistent with the ideas of total quality control stressed by American experts, the Americans did not anticipate the spread of quality control practices to production workers in problem-solving groups. Indeed, the Japanese leaders of the quality movement did not anticipate this outcome themselves. To some extent, JUSE was in the position in the early 1960s of trying to rush to the head of the parade to assume leadership of an explosive movement.

The Japanese gave a simple yet profound twist to the original ideas propagated by the Western experts. Quality control shifted from being the prerogative of the minority of engineers with limited shop experience to being the responsibility of each employee. Instead of adding additional layers of inspectors and reliability assurance personnel when quality problems arise as is customary in many U.S. firms, each worker, in concert with his or her workmates, is expected to take responsibility for solving quality problems. Self-inspection plays a major role in this approach.

Third, the Japanese like to downplay their knowledge of statistical quality control prior to the arrival of their American instructors. This is a charming cultural trait, but it gives the Americans a rather distorted view of their responsibility for current outcomes. Many of the early postwar Japanese leaders of quality control were engineers who had worked in the wartime aircraft industry. The high quality of Japanese airplanes and the industry's good repair capability suggests considerable knowledge of quality control practices.

Finally, there was within Japan a prewar and wartime tradition of employee training and group meetings of production workers to solve problems. QC circles represent a formalization of these traditions, combined with a new problem-solving methodology. This inheritance certainly facilitated the acceptance of QC circles by both managers and workers. The point of reciting this history is to stress the way in which American ideas on quality control were adapted to indigenous Japanese cultural, social, political, and economic conditions. Let me also suggest that Americans seeking now to borrow Japanese quality control circles will also have to adapt them to the indigenous cultural, social, political, and economic conditions prevailing in the United States. This is a theme to which we shall return below.

III. STUDY PROCESS

QC circles have captured the attention of many people because they serve as a remarkable vehicle for accomplishing a variety of objectives. Let us consider four aspects of their performance. First, the QC circle is not a response to specific problems. Rather, it is a continuous study process that operates in the workshop. That is, it functions as monitoring behavior that scans the environment for opportunities, does not wait to be activated by a problem, and does not stop its activities when a problem has been found and solved. This is a rare quality in organizations and one that can be a remarkable asset. While some organizations are accustomed to having a few elite officials function in this fashion, until QC circles we have not contemplated the possibility of having large numbers of employees performing this function. The potential for a fuller utilization of human resources is clear.

Second, as noted by Juran, most motivational schemes assume that workers know how to raise productivity and improve quality but that they are holding back for no justifiable reason. Operator indifference or even sabotage are the normal problems that management thinks it faces. Close supervision and/ or financial incentives are the common response. The QC circle, to the contrary, starts with the assumption that the causes of poor quality performance are not known by either management or workers. It further assumes that analysis is needed to discover and remedy these causes. A corollary of this assumption is that you must provide participants with the tools and the training necessary to discover causes and to remedy them. To be sure, sometimes the causes of problems are indeed known by management and/or labor. But the beauty of the QC circle assumption—that the cause is unknown—is that it avoids trying to fix blame for problems and instead focuses attention on the problem-solving process itself.

Third, even if the solutions arrived at by workers are not better than those arrived at by technical personnel—although they often clearly are—we can anticipate that workers will implement enthusiastically solutions to problems which they themselves have solved. In contrast, employees respond with much less enthusiasm when management has defined both the problem and the solution with no input allowed for the employees. This is certainly the most fundamental of motivational principles: you carry out with enthusiasm policies where you have been part of the problem-defining and problem-solving process.

Finally, QC circles are hardly a panacea for solving all management and worker problems. What the QC circles does is to provide a vehicle for unlocking the potential for worker contribution to the organization. It is a vehicle for allowing the worker a sense of dignity, a sense of fuller participation in the organization, and an opportunity to develop his or her skills. At the same time, it contributes to high-priority organizational goals, such as raising productivity and improving quality. It is not the only vehicle for these purposes; many of these gains may be achieved by alternative methods. What is important is that some vehicle exists.

IV. OBSERVATIONS

Some final observations on the evaluation of the Japanese experience are in order before turning to the QC circle experience in the United States. We are increasingly cultivating a myth of Japanese invincibility in this country. QC circles are being touted by some as a major factor in Japan's productivity and quality achievements. It seems sometimes the Japanese can do no wrong. Such a distorted image will not help us achieve the realistic assessment of Japanese practices necessary for us to learn from them.

First, the QC circles are only partly responsible for the achievements made by the Japanese in proving product quality. A variety of other practices have been critical.

Second, the Japanese have a good many problems in the operation of their QC circles. A common estimate of officials in the *most successful* companies is that one-third of the circles are making major contributions, one-third are functioning in some fashion, and one-third exist little more than on paper. A JUSE report (1980) indicates that of the companies JUSE surveyed, as many as 48% fell into the following categories:

Approximately one-half of their circles were active (32%).
A few of their circles were active (14%).
Their circles were nonactive or offered no comment (2%).

Moreover, the JUSE sample of 508 companies was undoubtedly biased toward those companies with more successful programs. Think what the performance must be like in the worst companies. Finally, even in companies that reported all, or nearly all of their circles as active (the remaining 52% of the sample), one may wonder just what constitutes an active circle. We cannot assume that active circles are contributing circles. What, then, are some of the problems faced by Japanese circles? For all the emphasis on spontaneity and bottom-up initiative in QC circles, there is a great deal of top-down control in many Japanese companies. Survey data show that workers often see small-group participative activities as a burden imposed by management rather than their own program. Many companies have quotas of suggestions imposed on their circles. In short, QC circles in Japan often take on a coercive aspect which is hardly conductive to motivating workers to come up with innovative behavior.

A related problem is that whereas in theory there is equal emphasis on the development of worker potential and productivity, in practice the emphasis on productivity has played a prominent role. That often leads workers to question the benefits which the circles have for them. Moreover, the unions have not been very involved in QC circle activities, so that management has been free to emphasize short-term productivity goals at the expense of worker development. Finally, as the QC circle movement has developed, there is a routinization of the original spontaneity. The circles become more of a regular feature in a bureaucratic organization. Under these conditions, participation in the circles tends to turn into ritualistic behavior. Workers often just go through the motions to keep management "off their back."

These comments are not intended to diminish Japanese achievements. These achievements have been substantial. For example, any company which can say that they have 90% of their production workers in circles, and that one-thrid of these workers are making significant contributions, is a company that has accomplished a great deal. Japanese management is clearly on the right track. They may be far from perfect, but they do work very hard on improvement.

V. CIRCLES IN AMERICA

Finally, let us consider briefly some observations on QC circles in American firms. The number of firms adopting QC circles is growing at an exponential rate. In keeping with this growth, the number of consultant firms claiming to be capable of implementing circle activities is also growing at an exponential rate. There is no doubt that there will be many failures in the next few years. This is not to say that circles cannot have a lasting impact. What are some of the problems being encountered? My observations are based on tracking a number of companies involved in these efforts. Some of the problems that emerge are:

1. *Unrealistic expectations*: Many companies seem to be assuming that QC circles can singlehandedly improve product quality, productivity, worker morale, and union relations. Such expectations are naive. Circles do have a contribution to make in these areas but only in conjunction with a wide range of other policy changes.

2. *Failure to institutionalize circle activity*: In many companies, circles are just another staff program and programs have beginnings and ends. For circles to become standard operating procedure, line responsibility for their activities must be achieved. But too often this has not developed. Facilitators often assume so much ownership of the program that managerial and worker commitment and responsibility for circle success is significantly reduced.

3. *Top-management support*: In those companies adopting circles, top management is ordinarily enthusiastic at the initial stages. As experience with the circles grows, however, those committed to circle success realize that there are many company policies and reward systems that will suffocate circle activity unless they are changed. But top management is often not prepared for such changes. They seem to operate on the view that QC circles can simply be set up and then you can walk away from them. This lack of follow-through commitment by top management will kill many programs.

4. *Middle-management resistance*: In most companies, the major initial problem encountered is the resistance of middle management. They often see circles as a threat to their own power and authority, and not incorrectly so. Often, they are bypassed in setting up the circles and then expected to co-operate in their operation. What is required is prior training of middle management with the goal being to show them that the circles can help achieve their existing objectives. This can be a long process.

5. *Quick payback*: Management often expects circles to demonstrate quick payback and installs elaborate measurement systems to capture such payback. When it is not forthcoming, they lose their enthusiasm rather quickly. QC circles, however, require time to develop and mature. Many of their achievements, such as preventive problem solving and worker cooperation in implementation of suggestions, are not captured by conventional measurement systems. It is interesting to note that the Japanese are much more relaxed about measurement of circle activity rather than measuring circle performance through their existing audit systems.

6. *Union involvement*: In unionized firms, many companies fail to involve unions fully in QC circle activities. Without such involvement, unions tend to be quite suspicious of circle activity as just another management con game. The unions have numerous ways of killing QC circle activity.

7. *Heavy reliance on outside consultants*: There are now a large number of both good and bad consultants offering advice on QC circles. Management has great difficulty in separating the incompetents from those with the "real goods." Moreover, consultants do not like to talk about failure. It is bad for business. We lack the existence of a nonprofit association such as JUSE which is capable of collecting, standardizing, and feeding back to companies the information on "best practice." Until we develop this capability, the probability of failure will be higher than it might otherwise be.

These are some of the major problems being encountered. They are by no means the only ones.

VI. CONTRIBUTION

QC circles do have a significant contribution to make in enhancing quality and productivity while contributing to worker development and worker participation in decision making. Whether this potential will be realized in the United States remains to be seen. We will need to adapt Japanese practices to our own needs and environment just as the Japanese have adapted ours.

FURTHER READING

Cole, R. E., *Work, Mobility, and Participation: A Comparative Study of American and Japanese Industry*, University of California Press, Berkeley, Calif., 1979.

Gibson, P., *Quality Circles: An Approach to Productivity Improvement*, Pergamon Press, Elmsford, N.Y., 1983.

Gryna, F., *Quality Circles: A Team Approach to Problem Solving*, American Management Association (AMACOM), New York, 1982.

Ingle, S., *Quality Circle Master Guide*, Prentice-Hall, Englewood Cliffs, N.J., 1981.

International Association of Quality Circles, *QC Sources, Selected Writing on Quality Circles*, IAQC, 1984.

Japanese Union of Scientists and Engineers, *QC Circle Koryu, General Principles of the QC Circle*, JUSE, Tokyo.

Mohr, W., and H. Mohr, *Quality Circles: Changing Images of People at Work*, Addison-Wesley, Reading, Mass., 1983.

Thompson, P., *Quality Circles: How to Make Them Work in America*, American Management Association (AMACOM), New York, 1983.

7

QUALITY COSTS

JOHN T. HAGAN

International Telephone and Telegraph Corporation
New York, New York

I. QUALITY COST SYSTEM CONCEPT

In spite of the obvious benefits that a well-organized quality program can logically provide, its real value will ultimately be determined by its ability to contribute to improved customer satisfaction and to cold, hard profits. That is the real-life business environment in which quality management faces its day-to-day existence, and is the principal reason why "quality costs" or the "cost of quality" should become an integral part of an effective quality management system.

The first step in developing the concept of quality costs is to establish a clear picture of the difference between "quality costs" and the "cost of quality management." Make sure that management does not see quality costs as the expenses of the quality function, particularly if the quality organization is seen as a drag on income (see Fig. 1). Fundamentally, each time that an employee must redo any part of his or her work, regardless of who is responsible, the cost of quality is increased. The most obvious source is the reworking of a manufactured article, the retesting of an assembly, or the rebuilding of a tool because it was originally unacceptable. Other sources are less obvious: the repurchasing of parts and the rewriting of engineering or contract agreements fall into this category.

Unfortunately, many such costs are overlooked or unrecognized simply because accounting systems ordinarily are not designed to identify them. It is for this specific reason that the technology or system of quality costs was created. It was designed to recognize the cost of "doing things over" as a significant addition to the cost of quality management, and to show them collectively as an otherwise hidden opportunity for profit improvement.

When the cost of quality is not viewed in this manner, it is easy to understand why top management is sensitive only to overall costs and schedules, and quality management is viewed merely as an overhead expense. The real effect of quality on schedules and overall costs is not quantified. If the hidden but true costs of quality are rising (or are tolerated at too high a level), they will adversely affect both the competitiveness and the profitability of a

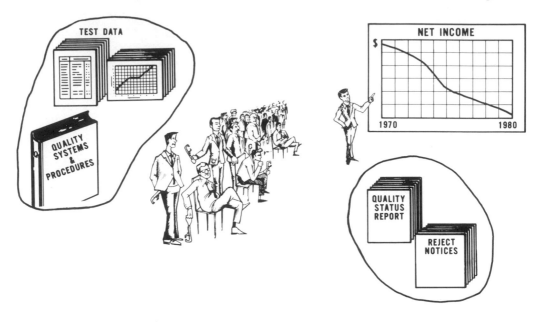

FIGURE 1   Cost of quality: as management sees it.

company, and it would not be uncommon for this condition to exist without top
management's awareness.

A clear understanding and use of a quality cost system offers a company
the opportunity to prevent serious trouble. Simply stated, quality costs are
a measure of all costs associated with the achievement of product quality
(*product quality* can be defined as conformance to all product requirements
established by a company and its contracts with customers and society). Specifically, quality costs are a total of (1) the costs of *appraising* product for
conformance to requirements, (2) the costs incurred by *failure* to meet product
requirements, and (3) the investment costs of *preventing* product failures.
Table 1 shows a general description of the kinds of activities that make up
these prevention, appraisal, and failure costs. Table 2 is a quality cost matrix
which shows how quality costs are related to specific phases of product life.
(*Note*: If there is an installation or maintenance phase subsequent to manufacturing, additional lines can be added to the matrix to show these phases.)

The strategy for using quality costs is quite simple: (1) make a direct
attack on failure costs and try to reduce them to zero, (2) reduce appraisal
costs according to results achieved, and (3) invest in prevention activities to
the extent necessary to maintain and improve your accomplishments. This
strategy is based on the premises that (1) for each failure there is an *assignable cause*; (2) causes are *discoverable* and *preventable*; and (3) prevention
is *always cheaper* (see Fig. 2 for example of a typical improvement opportunity
and Fig. 3 for an actual case history).

Quality costs are reduced through proper analysis of "cause and effect."
As failures are revealed through appraisal actions, they should be examined
for assignable cause and eliminated through effective corrective action. The
further along in the process that a "failure" is discovered (i.e., the nearer
end-product use by the customer), the more expensive it is to correct. As

TABLE 1   Quality Costs: General Description

PREVENTION COSTS	The Cost of all activities specifically designed to prevent defects in design, purchased materials and deliverable products. Includes activities accomplished prior to and during design, purchasing and manufacturing to assure that acceptable results will be achieved in each case. Examples are design reviews, vendor capability surveys and process capability studies.
APPRAISAL COSTS	Costs incurred in the conduct of appraisals (inspections and tests) of design, purchased materials and manufactured products to determine compliance with established requirements. Requirements include marketing specifications, product and process specifications, engineering drawings, company procedures, operating instructions, professional or industry standards, government regulations, and any other document that can affect the definition of product.
FAILURE COSTS	Costs required to evaluate, disposition and either correct or replace defective product, tools and associated product documents. Includes both material and labor costs, with full burden for all direct labor involved.

failure costs are reduced, appraisal efforts can usually also be reduced (in a statistically sound manner). The knowledge gained from this improvement can then be applied, through prevention activities, to all new work. When the level of prevention produces a minimum of appraisal and failure costs, a state of "quality control" is said to exist.

As straightforward as this approach may seem, it cannot work unless there is first, a basic quality measurement system which clearly identifies the correctable elements of failure that represent the potential for cost improvement. Such a system is designed to utilize the data from significant inspections, tests, and process control measurements as a measure of company performance and a source for determining cost-reduction projects. This measurement is a basic and important role of quality management. The potential for improvement can be determined only by a system of accurate and dependable measurement and analysis.

As a minimum, the results of important quality measurements in key operating areas (i.e., receiving inspection, fabrication, processing, assembly, test, etc.) should be collected and plotted. The frequency of plotting can be daily, weekly, or monthly—depending to a large degree on the sensitivity of the measurements. Whether these measures are reported as "percent defective," "defects per unit," or other, the costs associated with these defects are "failure" costs. Therefore, each improvement in measure of performance results in a direct reduction of these failure costs. Reduction of these costs is the prime target of the quality cost system (see Fig. 4).

Since every dollar of quality cost saved will have a positive effect on profits, the value of clearly identifying and using quality costs should be obvious, and minimizing quality costs should be a prime company objective. Achieving such an objective, however, has some built-in problems: (1) there are many variations in accounting systems, (2) quality cost definitions can get very detailed,

TABLE 2   Quality Cost Matrix

	PREVENTION	APPRAISAL	FAILURE
DESIGN	DESIGN REVIEW	QUALIFICATION TEST	REDESIGN
PURCHASING	VENDOR EVALUATIONS	RECEIVING INSPECTION	VENDOR REJECTS
MANUFACTURING PLANNING	PROCESS CAPABILITY STUDIES	EQUIPMENT CALIBRATION	TOOLING REWORK
PRODUCTION	OPERATOR TRAINING PLANS	PRODUCT INSPECTION & TEST	SCRAP, REWORK & WARRANTY

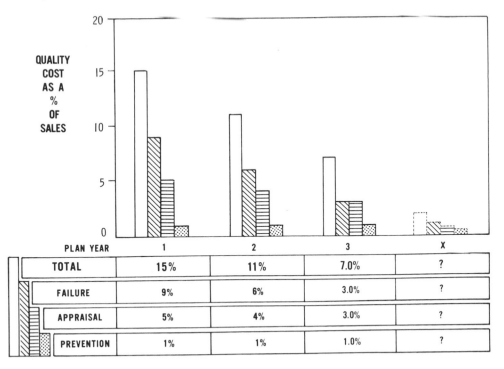

PLAN YEAR	1	2	3	X
TOTAL	15%	11%	7.0%	?
FAILURE	9%	6%	3.0%	?
APPRAISAL	5%	4%	3.0%	?
PREVENTION	1%	1%	1.0%	?

FIGURE 2   Possible performance improvement.

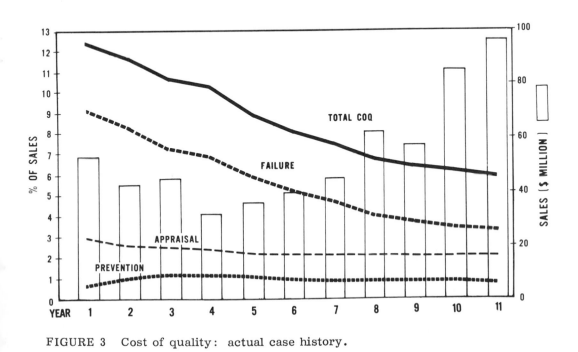

FIGURE 3   Cost of quality: actual case history.

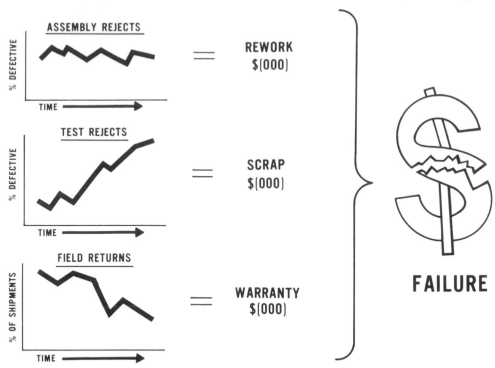

FIGURE 4   Cost of defects.

(3) there are as many ways to bury costs in industry as there are people with imagination, and (4) accurately exposing failure costs may limit the flexibilities that operating departments often claim to need.

Identifying and collecting quality costs must be comprehensive if the system is to be effective, but it also has to be practical. The company that understands this will make its quality cost system an asset. The collection and reporting of quality costs should not be any more detailed than the basic company cost accounting system. When large quality costs are incurred but are not totally identified within the cost accounting system (e.g., scrap or rework costs), estimates should be used until the system can be adjusted. This is necessary in order that a reasonable picture of total quality costs be portrayed and important management actions not be overlooked.

It is essential that both the detailed definitions and the responsibility for quality cost compilation and reporting be a function of the comptroller's office. A comptroller's procedure for quality costs should provide definitions or estimates and location of quality costs within the company manual of accounts. It will also define which cost elements require the addition of associated labor benefits, full burden, or allocated costs in order to portray accurately "total cost to the company." Holding the comptroller responsible for quality cost measurement will establish three important standards for the overall program: (1) it will keep collection costs within the practical limits; (2) it will provide the stamp of financial validity to the program; and (3) it will provide the opportunity for effective teamwork to develop between the comptroller and the quality organization.

In developing the details of a quality cost system, there are two important criteria to remember. First, recognize that quality costs are a tool to justify improvement actions (and measure their effectiveness), and second, the inclusion of insignificant details (individually less than 2% of total quality costs) is not essential to effective use of the system. If all major costs are captured and utilized, the objectives of quality cost improvement can be justified and accomplished. Consistency and integrity will pay off. Comparisons with others are meaningless. It is the incremental change in quality costs consistently measured that counts—*not* how you measure them.

II. QUALITY COST DEFINITIONS

The following detailed definitions of quality costs are the author's. There are many other, equally valuable approaches (e.g., ASQC's pamphlet, *Quality Costs—What and How*). The author's approach attempts to relate each element of quality cost to specific elements of the quality management system.

1. *Prevention Costs*
    a. *Product design*: Costs incurred in the quality control of new product design developments or major design changes prior to the release of engineering drawings.
        (1) *Design reviews*: The total cost (including planning) of all design reviews conducted prior to the release of design documents for the fabrication of prototypes or pilot models. These reviews should maximize initial conformance to the required characteristics of the design with regard to function, reliability safety, configuration, producibility, serviceability, maintainability, and product cost.
        (2) *Design checking and support*: The cost of engineering drawing checkers, reliability, components, and materials engineers as applicable to the prevention of design deficiencies.
    b. *Purchasing*: Costs incurred in the quality control of vendor-supplied parts, materials, and processes, prior to the finalization of purchase order commitments.
        (1) *Supplier reviews*: The cost of reviewing and evaluating suppliers' capabilities to meet company requirements.
        (2) *Supplier rating*: The cost of developing and maintaining a supplier rating system based on actual performance to established requirements.
        (3) *Purchase order technical data reviews*: The cost for reviews of purchase order technical data (usually by quality personnel) to assure its ability to communicate, clearly and completely, purchased product technical and quality requirements to respective suppliers.
        (4) *Supplier quality planning*: The total cost of planning for the incoming and source inspections and tests necessary to determine acceptance of supplier products. Includes the preparation of necessary documents and development costs for inspection and test equipment.
    c. *Quality planning*: Cost incurred in the evaluation of manufacturing plans and in the development and integration of quality plans.

(1) *Manufacturing process evaluations*: The cost of activities established for the purpose of evaluating new manufacturing machinery, fabrication equipment, processes, and tools to assure their capability for initially and consistently performing within required limits.

(2) *Inspection and test planning*: The total cost for development of necessary product inspection and test plans, documentation systems, and workmanship standards. Includes development costs for new or special-quality programs, acceptance gages, and product test equipment.

d. *Quality administration*: Costs incurred in the overall administration of the quality management function.

(1) *Administrative labor*: Compensation costs for all quality personnel (e.g., managers and directors, supervisors, and clerical) who are 100% administrative.

(2) *Administrative expenses*: All other costs and expenses charged to or allocated to the quality management function and not specifically covered elsewhere in this report.

e. *Quality training*: Costs incurred in the development and implementation of formal training programs for the purpose of preventing errors. Includes the total cost (course preparation, instruction, and necessary materials) of quality improvement programs, new employee quality orientations, and other programs designed to provide:

(1) Inspector and operator training in new manufacturing methods, processes, or workmanship standards.

(2) Tester training in new product designs and testing procedures.

(3) Training required by new or revised company procedures affecting the control of quality.

This item is specifically not intended to include any portion of the the basic apprentice or skill training necessary to be qualified for individual assignments throughout the company.

f. *Quality audits*: The cost of quality audits specifically performed to measure the effectiveness of quality system performance. Includes audits applied to areas (e.g., handling, order writing, etc.) that are not normally included as part of the appraisal system and product audits over and above the normal appraisal system (e.g., finished goods ready for delivery).

2. *Appraisal costs*

a. *Product design/qualification tests*: Costs incurred in the qualification testing of new products or major changes to existing products. Includes costs for the inspection and test of qualification units under ambient conditions and the extremes of environmental parameters. Qualification inspections and tests are usually conducted to verify that all design requirements have been met or, when failures occur, to identify clearly where redesign efforts are required. Qualification may be performed on prototype units, pilot runs, or the initial production run of new products.

b. *Supplier product inspection and test*: Costs incurred in providing appraisal of supplier's products for conformance to requirements.

(1) *Routine inspections and tests*: Total costs for the normal or routine incoming inspection and test of purchased materials,

products, or processes. These costs represent the continuing normal cost of purchased goods inspection and test.

(2) *Qualification of supplier product*: The cost of additional inspection and test (including environmental tests) required to qualify the release of production quantities of purchased goods. These costs may be repeated periodically. They typically apply to the following situations:

(a) First article inspection (detailed inspection and key environmental tests) on a sample of the first production buy of new components or material.

(b) Qualification test or first article inspection for second and third sources of previously qualified end-product components.

(c) First article inspection of the initial supply of customer furnished parts.

(d) First article inspection of the initial purchased quantity of goods for resale.

(3) *Source inspections, tests, and control programs*: All company-incurred costs (including travel) for the conduct of any of the activities described in items (1) and (2) at the vendor's plant or at an independent test laboratory. This item will normally include product acceptance costs associated with direct shipments from vendor to customer or to installation sites.

c. *In-process and final inspection and test*: Costs incurred for all in-process and final inspection and acceptance tests of manufactured products.

(1) *Planned inspections and tests*: The cost of all planned inspections and tests conducted on manufactured product at selected points throughout the manufacturing process, including the total cost of destructive test samples (does not include sorting of rejected lots of material or product).

(2) *Setup inspections*: The cost of all setup or first-piece inspections utilized to assure that each combination of machine and tool is properly adjusted to produce acceptable products before the start of each production lot.

(3) *Special tests (production)*: The cost of all nonroutine inspections and tests conducted on manufactured product as a part of the acceptance plan. These costs will normally include periodic sampling of sensitive product for more detailed and extensive inspections and tests to assure continued conformance to critical environmental requirements.

(4) *Process control measurements*: The cost of all inspections, tests, and measurements conducted on product processing equipment and/or materials (e.g., plating tank temperature and chemical content) to assure their conformance to preestablished standards. Includes adjustments made to maintain continued acceptable results.

(5) *Laboratory support*: The total cost of any laboratory tests required in support of inspection and test plans.

(6) *Miscellaneous inspections*: The cost of all inspections not covered elsewhere (e.g., stores, packaging, and shipping activities).

(7) *Depreciation allowances*:   Total depreciation allowances for
all capitalized inspection or test equipment.
d. *Maintenance and calibration*:   Costs incurred in the maintenance
and calibration of acceptance inspection and test equipment.
(1) *Maintenance and calibration labor*:   The cost of all inspections,
calibration, maintenance, and control of measurement equipment, instruments, and gages used for the inspection and
test of product and manufacturing processes.
(2) *Measurement equipment expenses*:   The procurement or manufacturing cost of all inspection and test equipment and gages
that are not capitalized.
3. *Failure Costs*
a. *Design failure costs*:   Costs incurred due to initial design
inadequacies.
(1) *Engineering corrective action*:   After initial release of design
to production, the total cost of all problem investigation and
redesign efforts (including requalification as necessary) except as directed by and billed to the customer.
(2) *Rework due to design changes*:   The cost of all rework
(materials, labor, and burden) specifically required as part
of the implementation plan (effectivity) for engineering
changes.
(3) *Scrap due to design changes*:   The cost of all scrap (materials, labor, and burden) required as a part of the implementation plan (effectivity) for engineering changes.
b. *Supplier product rejects*:   Cost incurred due to purchased item
rejects.
(1) *Disposition costs*:   The cost to disposition or sort incoming
inspection rejects.   Includes the cost of reject documentation,
review and evaluation, disposition orders, handling, and
transportation (except as charged to the supplier).
(2) *Replacement costs*:   The added cost of replacement for all
items rejected and returned to the supplier.   Includes additional transportation and expediting costs when not paid for
by the supplier.
(3) *Correction action plans*:   The cost of company-sponsored
failure analyses and investigations into the cause of supplier
rejects and determination of necessary corrective actions.
Includes the cost of visits to supplier plants for this specific
purpose and the cost to provide added inspection protection
while the problem is being resolved.
c. *Material review and corrective action*:   Costs incurred in the review and disposition of nonconforming manufactured products and
the corrective actions necessary to prevent recurrence.
(1) *Disposition costs*:   All costs incurred in the review and disposition of nonconforming manufactured product, in the analysis of quality data to determine significant items for correction action (Pareto principle), and in the investigation of
these to determine cause.
(2) *Failure analysis costs*:   The cost of failure analyses conducted
or obtained in support of defect cause identification.
(3) *Investigation support costs*:   The additional cost of special
runs of product or controlled lots of material (designed

experiments) conducted specifically to obtain information useful to the determination of the cause of a particular defect.

    (4) *Manufacturing corrective actions*: The actual cost of manufacturing corrective actions taken to remove or eliminate the causes of nonconformances identified for correction. This item will normally include such activities as rewriting operator instructions, redevelopment of specific manufacturing processes or flow procedures, redesign or modification of tooling, and the development and implementation of specific training needs.

d. *Rework*: The total cost (labor, material, and overhead) of reworking defective product.

    (1) *Manufactured product rework*: The total cost (material, labor, and burden) of all rework or repairs done to manufactured product as required by specific work order, personal assignment, or as a planned part of the standard manufacturing operation. Does not include rework due to design change [see item 3.a(2)].

    (2) *Reinspection and retest*: That portion of inspection and test labor that is incurred because of rejects (includes documentation of rejects, fault finding in test, and inspection and test after rework) and sorting of defective lots.

    (3) *Supplier product rework*: The total cost of supplier product repairs not billed to suppliers. Also includes any added production costs necessitated by the decision to use material that is less than totally conforming.

e. *Scrap*: The total cost (material, labor, and overhead) of defective product that cannot be reworked to conform to requirements.

    (1) *Product spoilage*: Product spoilage is considered as material or product which, because of irreparability or uneconomical rework cost, is discarded (scrapped). This item includes the total cost (material, labor, and burden) of all such material and product, regardless of whether it is accounted for on scrap tickets, counted as planned or unplanned yield losses, or simply discarded on the manufacturing floor. Does not include scrap due to design change [see item 3.a(3)].

    (2) *Substandard product costs*: Total amount of selling costs and price differential required to sell nonconforming or off-grade products.

    (3) *Material losses*: Scrap is also intended to cover the cost of material or parts shortages due to damage, theft, and other (perhaps unknown) reasons. A measure of these costs may be obtained from a periodic review of inventory adjustments.

    (4) *Labor losses*: When direct productive labor is lost for reasons of product defects, regardless of cause, these losses are the equivalent of scrap, except that there are no concurrent material losses. Typical losses are caused by machine shutdowns and reset-up or line stoppages due to defective material being produced or defective raw material being supplied.

f. *External failure costs*: All costs incurred due to product defects or suspected defects after delivery to customer.

    (1) *Complaint investigations*: The total cost of investigating and resolving individual customer complaints.

(2) *Returned goods/field service*: The total cost of evaluating and repairing or replacing defective goods after delivery or acceptance by the customer. This includes the full cost of any necessary recall activity. It does not include repairs accomplished as part of a maintenance or modification contract.

(3) *Retrofit costs*: Costs to correct nonconformance to the required engineering drawing issue (configuration or change level) or to update product to a mandatory new design change level.

(4) *Warranty claims*: The total cost of additional claims paid to the customer to cover legitimate expenses, such as repair costs to remove the defective hardware from their system.

(5) *Liability costs*: Company-paid costs due to product liability claims, including the cost of product liability insurance.

(6) *Penalties*: Cost of penalties due to less than full product performance.

TABLE 3   Quality Cost Report

QUALITY COST REPORT
FOR THE MONTH ENDING _____

(In Thousands of U.S. Dollars)

DESCRIPTION	CURRENT MONTH			YEAR TO DATE		
	QUALITY COSTS	AS A PERCENT OF		QUALITY COSTS	AS A PERCENT OF	
		SALES	OTHER		SALES	OTHER
1 PREVENTION COSTS						
1.1 Product Design						
1.2 Purchasing						
1.3 Quality Planning						
1.4 Quality Administration						
1.5 Quality Training						
1.6 Quality Audits						
TOTAL PREVENTION COSTS						
PREVENTION TARGETS						
2 APPRAISAL COSTS						
2.1 Product Qualification Tests						
2.2 Supplier Product Inspection and Test						
2.3 In Process and Final Inspection and Test						
2.4 Maintenance and Calibration						
TOTAL APPRAISAL COSTS						
APPRAISAL TARGETS						
3 FAILURE COSTS						
3.1 Design Failure Costs						
3.2 Supplier Product Rejects						
3.3 Material Review and Corrective Action						
3.4 Rework						
3.5 Scrap						
3.6 External Failure Costs						
TOTAL FAILURE COSTS						
FAILURE TARGETS						
TOTAL QUALITY COSTS						
TOTAL QUALITY TARGETS						

MEMO DATA	CURRENT MONTH		YEAR TO DATE		FULL YEAR	
	BUDGET	ACTUAL	BUDGET	ACTUAL	BUDGET	ACTUAL
Net Sales						
Other Base (Specify)						

In developing the details of a quality cost system, it is important that the quality manager and the comptroller work together. It is the responsibility of the quality manager to expalin quality costs to the comptroller. Do not expect the comptroller to know anything about it.

Since the costs involved may be incurred by any department, function, or cost center, a customized internal quality cost procedure is usually required. This procedure will describe the sources of data to be reported from the accounts ledgers in terms of existing account, department, and cost center codes. It will describe how any required estimates are to be prepared and where to use associated labor benefits, allocated costs, and labor burdens. It will also provide the parameter against which quality costs are compared. For long-range trend analyses, net sales is the parameter most often used. For short-range actions, parameters such as factory costs, standard input to inventory, or value added may be more useful because they are directly related to quality costs as they are *incurred* and *reported* (see Table 3 for a sample quality cost report).

III. QUALITY COST SYSTEM IMPLEMENTATION

Implementation of the quality cost system requires the participation and support of top management. Convincing top management to take an active role is clearly the job of the quality manager. He or she must be made to recognize that unless total quality costs are realistically established, it is difficult to determine the amount of quality management effort that is really necessary. Additional quality efforts may appear to be just adding costs without having specific cost objectives against which to measure effectiveness.

The proper balance is to establish the quality management effort at the level necessary to reduce the total cost of quality and then, as progress is achieved, adjust it to where total quality costs are at the lowest attainable level. This approach prevents unheeded growth in quality costs and creates an improved quality reputation. The top management that understands this will certainly support your program.

Once the quality cost system is accepted and installed, it should be used to justify and support improvement in each major area of product activity. Quality costs should be established for each major product line or cost center within the manufacturing operation. Each individual area can then look at the improvement potential that exists and establish meaningful goals. It is at this stage that the quality cost system becomes an integral part of quality measurement and becomes coupled with the identification and elimination of the causes of defects. This brings you full circle to the analysis of basic quality data (inspection and test results) to identify specific problems for investigation and corrective action.

There are many methods for the analysis of quality data, but it also takes knowledge of the products and processes involved. Some knowledge of basic statistics is useful but more important is an inquisitive desire to find and eliminate the causes of defects. Once a cause in need of correction is identified, the action necessary must be carefully determined, and it must be individually justified on the basis of an equitable cost trade-off (e.g., a $500 per week rework problem versus a $5000 solution). At this point, experience in measuring quality costs will be invaluable in estimating the payback for individual corrective action investments. Cost-benefit justification of corrective action is a continuing part of the program.

It is important to recognize that the generation of errors and defects is not limited to manufacturing operators. Errors that result in scrap and rework are often caused by product and process design engineers, by the designers and fabricators of tools, by those who determine machine capabilities, and by those who provide the written instructions for the operator. Also, errors that affect product can be caused by a calibration technician, a maintenance worker and even a material handler, who can put the parts in the wrong bin or deliver product for processing out of sequence to the manufacturing plan. Clearly, almost anyone within the total operation can contribute to failure costs. Effective corrective action, therefore, can and will take many avenues throughout the operating organizations.

Some problems have fairly obvious solutions. They can usually be fixed immediately (e.g., replacement of a worn bearing or a worn tool). Others are more insidious (such as a marginal condition in design or processing) and are almost never discovered and corrected without the benefit of a well-organized and formal approach. Marginal conditions usually result in problems that can easily become lost in the accepted cost of doing business. Having an organized corrective action system justified by quality costs will surface such problems for management's visibility and action. The true value of corrective action is that you only have to pay for it once, whereas failure to take corrective action may be paid for over and over again.

One mission of quality management is to convince top management of the long-range effects of total quality costs on profits and the quality reputation of the company. Management must believe that quality is just as important in the overall business plan as are schedules and costs. A businesslike concept of quality management (based on quality costs) can lead to improved overall performance, reputation, and profits.

Implementation of a cost-oriented quality management system will not automatically lead to utopia. The demands of quality, cost, and schedule will still have to be balanced, or managed, through periods of changing business demands and new technologies. The difference, where it occurs, will be in the greater utilization and contribution of the quality management function.

ACKNOWLEDGMENTS

Portions of this chapter have been adapted, by permission of the publishers, from *A Management Role for Quality Control*, by John T. Hagan, © 1968 by American Management Association, Inc., pp. 230–239, all rights reserved; and *Quality Costs at Work*, by John T. Hagan, © 1973 American Society for Quality Control, Inc.

FURTHER READING

American Society for Quality Control, *Guide for Managing Vendor Quality Costs*, ASQC, Milwaukee, Wis.

American Society for Quality Control, *Guide for Reducing Quality Costs*, ASQC, Milwaukee, Wis.

American Society for Quality Control, *Quality Costs—What and How*, ASQC, Milwaukee, Wis.

Groocock, J. M., *The Cost of Quality*, Pitman, Marshfield, Mass., 1974.

Juran, J. M., and F. M. Gryna, *Quality Planning and Analysis*, McGraw-Hill, New York, 1970.

Morgan, D. E., and W. G. Ireson, *A Guide to Quality Cost Analysis*, Technical Report 8, Office of Assistant Secretary of Defense, Washington D.C., 1967.

Research Institute of America, "Holding Down Cost by Improving Your Quality Control," Staff Recommendation, File 33, April 14, 1975.

8

SYSTEMS APPROACH TO QUALITY COSTS

WILLIAM E. BLOUCH

Loyola College in Maryland
Baltimore, Maryland

I. INTRODUCTION

The design of business information systems has undergone a startling transformation over the last few decades. We have gone from centralized custodial accounting systems to integrated management information systems. Currently we are experiencing a trend that is moving toward on-line real-time
systems that provide immediate data transmission into the system and feedback
that is received in sufficient time to change or control the operating environment. The use of microprocessors, microcomputers, and minicomputers has
spurred developments in this area. These on-line real-time systems can be
centralized. However, there is an emphasis on getting computer power to the
lower levels of an organization where it is needed. As a result, many organizations are moving in the direction of simpler and easier-to-use decentralized
systems called *distributed processing systems*, which Thierauf defines as "an
approach to placing low-cost computer power, starting at the various points
of data entry, and linking these points, where deemed necessary, with a centralized computer via a distributed communications network" [1].

Such systems can be programmed to react very quickly to user's needs.
These on-line real-time systems attempt to establish a total systems approach
for an organization by integrating all functional areas. Also, these systems
are capable of utilizing complex mathematical models that call for operations
research techniques, enabling management to solve problems that either pertain to one specific operational area or problems that cut across functional
areas.

Much has been written about the various methods used by manufacturers
to keep track of inventory costs for determining income. Among others, these
methods include job order costing or process costing. Of course, standard
costs may be used in combination with either job order or process costing to
accumulate costs of production. Each of these systems provides a product
cost for inventory on a physical measure basis by accumulating and allocating
costs to units produced during a period. Unfortunately, these systems are
still relatively unsophisticated. Managers could make their systems much more
effective by applying new technologies that are now available to them.

Managers are constantly concerned about increased costs that reduce profits. Subordinates are forever being told to trim budgets. Quality costs have
often been neglected when cost control is discussed. Renowned experts have
stated that as much as 20% of the cost of all manufacturing in the United States
can be attributed to costs of quality (inspection, repair, complaints, redesign
needs, rework, between-process reallocation of control, etc.). Nevertheless,
managers often fail to consider controlling quality costs as a means of increasing profitability. Quality costs must be reduced to acceptable, budgeted levels.
This cost reduction must take place within the broader quality control system.
Pleasing customers may be a frustrating exercise if costs are so high that you
either lose money or pass the loss on to customers through higher prices.
Unfortunately, managers are sometimes unaware of true quality costs either
because there is no quality cost reporting or because all quality costs are not
tabulated. The technology exists for managers to deal adequately with tabulating, reporting, and controlling all quality costs within their costing subsystem. A total systems approach is important. Quality control programs will
work only where there is cooperation among all parties involved. This includes
everyone from design engineers and production personnel to people from accounting, marketing, and sales.

II. QUALITY CONTROL PROGRAMS

A system of quality control is concerned with product design quality as well as
processing and performance quality [2]. Adequate control must be maintained
throughout the entire process. Management, utilizing an on-line real-time
system, can constantly monitor manufacturing operations. Less scrap, rework,
repair, and so on, will lower material and processing costs as well as increase
productivity. Managers, utilizing a quality control program, have more control over products moving from process to process.

A quality control program can be set up as illustrated in Fig. 1. Cost control begins in step 1 of Fig. 1. To remain competitive, management must choose
the lowest-cost materials and processing methods that are still consistent with
the degree of quality desired. Much cooperation is needed between designers,
production, and marketing personnel. Situations often exist whereby management can increase sales, and therefore profits, by improving product quality.
Unless marketing and sales personnel convey this information back to appropriate design and production people, the company may not be maximizing profits. Figure 2 shows an example of this situation.

Product A in Fig. 2 is a manufactured product with liberal tolerances and
poor process control. Product B is the same product with tightened tolerances
and improved process control. Even though it costs less to make a product A,
product B is a better product, more dependable, has a wider range or applicability, and therefore sells many more units. As one can see, product A costs
$60 per unit to manufacture, whereas product B costs $80. However, net income for product B is higher due to the increased number of items sold. Obviously, management must have timely information to determine whether the
product is being produced to much narrower specifications and tolerance limits
than needed. An on-line, real-time system can provide a production manager
with allowable variances of specifications and tolerances for any particular
customer. Information about the quality needs of customers can be set up
within the system and be readily available. Management can also extract related cost data from the system so that proper decisions can be made.

Step 1   SPECIFICATION REVIEWS

Analyses of specifications which define the product intended to serve customer demand.

Purpose: Assure accurate, current and complete specifications, which clearly describe the product needed.

Step 2a   PROCESS FLOW CHARTS

Outlines of production lines in schematic form.

Purpose: Identify the operations through which materials will flow.

Step 2b   OPERATION DESCRIPTIONS OR PROCESS SPECIFICATIONS

Descriptions or specifications and tolerance regarding methods, procedures, settings and adjustment of each operation or process.

Purpose: Lay down the basic quality requirements for each operation or process.

Step 3   QUALITY AUDITS

Inspections, tests and measurements of product quality.

Purpose: Assure that standards, specifications and tolerances are maintained.

Step 4   QUALITY HISTORIES AND CORRECTIVE FEEDBACK

Analysis of quality performance as a basis for corrective action.

Purpose: Identify areas where long-term quality problems exist and require remedy.

IN SUM   Step 1: States what the system is required to produce.
          Step 2: Shows how the product is to be manufactured.
          Step 3: Measures actual performance.
          Step 4: Provides the corrective feedback loop.

FIGURE 1   Major steps of quality control program. (From Ref. 3.)

	Product A	Product B
Sales (units)	1,000	4,000
Sales (dollars)	$100,000	$480,000
Less Cost of Goods Sold	60,000	320,000
Gross Profit	40,000	160,000
Less Operating Expenses	30,000	30,000
Net Income (before taxes)	$ 10,000	$130,000

FIGURE 2   Sales analysis.

Step 2 of Fig. 1 calls for a quality plan that will indicate immediately any faulty operations and the proper procedures for correcting the problem. Faulty operations result in excessive scrap and rework costs. The quality plan should specify the procedures for inspection and testing both during processing and in final inspection so that any problems are discovered at the earliest possible point.

In some cases, testing and inspection can be expensive. Step 3 of Fig. 1 concerns itself with actively conducting these tests and inspections. Management must make use of mathematical and statistical models to a much larger extent than has actually been done in the past. For example, determining appropriate sample sizes for testing and inspection purposes can greatly decrease costs for these activities. This is particularly true if management is dealing with sample sizes that are larger than needed. Statistical methods can be applied to determine optimum sample sizes. This is extremely beneficial in the testing situation that calls for the product to be destroyed. However, accountants have been very slow in combining statistical and mathematical techniques with costing systems.

Step 4 of Fig. 1 is also important. It demands a system that allows management to utilize historical quality performance and cost information as a basis for corrective action. This historical information is the feedback that management needs for proper control of the production process. This feedback must be available in a timely manner. It can take a number of forms. Lester et al. advocate the use of two basic feedback tools: the quality performance record and the defect frequency record [3, pp. 108—110]. These tools could readily be incorporated into most quality control systems with a minimum amount of difficulty.

III. MANUFACTURING COSTING PROCEDURES

Cost accounting procedures for dealing with quality control problems such as scrap, spoiled items, defective items, and so on, are often unsophisticated. Take scrap, for example. Frequently, firms account for scrap only when it is sold. At that time all they record is any income that may be received from the sale of such items. Although managers are aware that they should keep scrap to a minimum, they are not sure how costly it is. Often, no effort is made to inventory scrap.

Spoilage may be normal in a manufacturing process. In this case its cost is usually considered in determining a factory overhead rate. Therefore, it is distributed to the production that was completed during the period. If abnormal spoilage occurs, the quality control system must be able to pick this up and report it immediately to management. One way of dealing with this is to establish normal spoilage rates and amounts for the different types of materials used. Actual rates and amounts for departments are compared against norms and variances reported to management in a timely manner so that corrective action can be taken. These normal levels are easily used within a standard costing framework.

Some companies find that defective work may occur on a regular basis and they build this additional cost into their projected factory overhead costs and in the resulting factory overhead rate. Again, management should monitor the number of defects and compare normal amounts with the actual number of defects to maintain effective cost control.

To illustrate how a manufacturer might institute a standard cost system and account for scrap, rework, and so on, let's use the data given in Fig. 3. Super Surf Boards manufactures a single, uniform product. They have just switched from an actual cost system to a standard cost system. The standard costs for one surf board and some additional information are given in Fig. 3.

Factory overhead is applied on the basis of standard direct labor hours, by using rates established at the beginning of the year. Normal production is 6500 units per month. During the month of October 6000 units were produced and there was no beginning or ending work-in-process inventory.

The surf boards are manufactured from fiberglass that is molded and then finished. Finishing includes trimming any excess fiberglass, checking all specifications, and polishing the surf board. The standards for materials include a small allowance for scrap. Also, management has built into its factory overhead application rate ($3 per direct labor hour) an estimate for all the indirect labor that is related to production. This includes the production supervisor's salary and the salary of quality control checkers. Also included is an allowance for defective boards that may be produced. Defective boards may be cracked, not properly formed, or not meet other specifications.

The standard costing system would have yielded the actual costs of production as well as the standard costs for units processed during October. This costing system should also analyze the differences between actual costs and standard costs. These differences are usually analyzed in the form of variances that relate to each of the three main elements of the production process (direct materials, direct labor, and factory overhead).

Setting standards costs for materials involved determining the quality of material that should have been used in making a finished surf board and the price that should have been paid in purchasing this material. Typically, any differences between actual cost and standard costs of materials are broken down into two variances. These are the material price variance and the material quantity variance. These variances can be calculated from the data shown in Fig. 4.

Figure 4 shows that materials were purchased at a price less than the standard cost. Even though this gives a favorable price variance, quality

---

Direct material: 30 lbs. at $1.00 per lb $30.00
Direct labor: 1 hour at $4.50 . . . .   4.50
Factory overhead: 1 hour at $3.00 . . . .   3.00
    Variable (1 hour at $1.00)
    Fixed (1 hour at $2.00)
                      Total $37.50

Other Data:
    Material purchased: 300,000 lbs.
    Material used in production: 200,000 lbs.
    Direct labor: 6,500 hours at a total cost of $27,950
    Variable overhead cost incurred: $8,750
    Fixed overhead incurred: $13,000

FIGURE 3   Surf board standard costs.

Material Price Variance:

Actual quantity of material purchased × Actual cost per lb.

300,000 lbs. × $.95 = $285,000

Actual quantity of material purchased × Standard cost per lb.

300,000 lbs. × $1.00 = 300,000

$15,000 Favorable Price Variance

Material Quantity Variance:

Actual quantity of materials used × Standard cost per lb.

200,000 lbs. × $1.00 = $200,000

Standard quantity of materials allowed × Standard cost per lb. for actual production

6,000 units × 30 lbs. per unit × $1.00 = 180,000

$18,000 Unfavorable Quantity Variance

Excess of Actual over Standard (Unfavorable)

$ 3,000

FIGURE 4   Materials variances.

control must be sure that the materials purchased were not of inferior quality. The material quantity variance is unfavorable. More materials were
used than should have been used. This also calls for an investigation to
determine the cause of this unfavorable variance. Perhaps Super Surf
Boards wasted materials or had an unusually high number of defective items.

Labor costs are also broken down into the two variances. Like materials,
standards costs for labor are based on the hours of labor that should be
used in making one finished surf board and the labor rate that should be
paid. Any difference between actual costs for labor and standard costs are
shown in two labor variances: the labor rate variance and the labor efficiency variance. These variances are calculated in Fig. 5. These variances
should also be investigated. Perhaps Super Surf Boards wasted materials
or had an unusually high number of defective items.

Although the labor rate variance is favorable, it might be wise to determine the cause. Maybe the $4.50 per hour standard labor cost was in an-
ticipation of a labor cost increase attributable to a new union labor contract.
Perhaps the actual increase in labor costs was not as high as anticipated.
Taking another approach, maybe the favorable rate variance resulted from
using lower-rated, less skilled employees in the production process. If
these people do not possess the necessary skills, this situation could prove
very costly if it continues in the future. The labor efficiency variance is
unfavorable. This indicates that more labor hours were used than should
have been used. If management did use underqualified personnel in the
production process, this might explain why 500 more hours of labor were
incurred in excess of standard hours for the month. Maybe the unfavorable
variance was due to other reasons. Perhaps more labor hours were needed
because the material was of an inferior quality and labor had to spend more
time in production. Again, quality control would be very interested in this
situation.

Calculation of differences between standard factory overhead and actual
factory overhead is somewhat more complicated than it was for direct materials and direct labor. This is due to the fact that factory overhead is made
up of many elements. These elements consist of fixed costs (i.e., factory
rent, production supervisor's salary, etc.) as well as variable costs (i.e.,
electric costs, indirect materials, etc.). As a result, the analysis of the
factory overhead variances is a complicated task. There are a number of
approaches taken. These include the two-variance, three-variance, or four-
variance analyses. Each of these methods tries to isolate causes for any
variances that exist between actual and standard overhead costs and guide
management toward any corrective action that may be needed. Even though
the four-variance method is the most complete, the two-variance approach
is the most frequently used in practice.

The two-variance analysis looks at the controllable variance and the volume variance. These are calculated from data in Fig. 6. The unfavorable
controllable variance is due to the fact that actual variable overhead was
greater than anticipated. The volume variance is unfavorable because total
fixed factory overhead was underapplied to production. This resulted because the factory overhead rate is based on normal production and they
produced at a level short of normal production. This indicated a loss due
to idle capacity.

In addition to the normal factory overhead variances that are reported,
management might want to look very closely at a few select components of
overhead. In our example, factory overhead was applied to production at

Labor Rate Variance:

Actual labor hours incurred   x   Actual hourly rate

6,500 hours   x $4.30   = $27,950

                                       $1,300 Favorable Labor Rate Variance

Actual labor hours incurred   x   Standard hourly rate

6,500 hours   x $4.50   =   29,250

Labor Efficiency Variance:

Actual labor hours incurred   x   Standard hourly rate

6,500 hours   x $4.50   = $29,250

                                       $2,250 Unfavorable Labor Efficiency Variance

Standard hours allowed for actual production   x   Standard hourly rate

6,000 hours   x $4.50   =   27,000

Excess of Actual over Standard Cost (Unfavorable) $ 950

FIGURE 5   Labor variances.

Controllable Variance:

Actual factory overhead incurred (Fixed + Variable) $21,750

Budgeted factory overhead for actual level of production:

    Fixed: (Based on normal production) $13,000

    Variable: (6,000 units x $1.00)   6,000

                                $19,000

$2,750 Unfavorable Controllable Variance

Volume Variance:

Budget factory overhead for actual level of production (see above) $19,000

Standard factory overhead allowed for actual production (6,000 units x $3.00 per unit) $18,000

$1,000 Unfavorable Volume Variance

Excess of Actual over Standard (Unfavorable) $3,750

FIGURE 6 Overhead variances.

| | Standard | | | | |
	Variable	Fixed	Total	Actual	Difference
Set-up costs	$ .06	$ 30,000	$ 34,680	$ 35,000	(320)
Rework time	.15	0	11,700	10,000	1,700
Inspection time	.09	20,000	27,020	27,100	(80)
All other	.70	160,000	160,600	162,600	(2,000)
TOTAL	$1.00	$156,000	$234,000	$234,700	(700)

FIGURE 7   Standard factory overhead costs per unit.

$3 per hour ($1 variable and $2 fixed). Production personnel and quality control personnel might request reports dealing with rework costs, setup costs, inspection costs, and so on. Standards for these items could be broken out from the total factory overhead standards. Figure 7 illustrates this. The actual cost figures could be extracted from the data in the system. Any differences between actual and standard costs should be evaluated by appropriate quality control personnel.

In most process costing systems, all the variances discussed are reported to the responsible personnel together with normal production cost information. Many times, however, this information comes too late. Production managers, quality control supervisors and others need the information on a more timely basis so that adjustments can be made at once before any more faulty units are processed or costs get out of control. An on-line real-time system can be very beneficial at this point. Information can be obtained from the system as it is needed and adjustments made at that time. At the

Department	Items Produced	Scrapped	% Scrap	Scrap Cost	Reason
Cutting	3,500	170	4.9	$680	Tooling defects
Finishing	2,200	30	1.4	180	Poor Workmanship
				$860	

Department Summary:	Cutting	Finishing	Total
Total Scrap for Week	$ 680	$ 180	$ 860
Scrap Cost Year-to-Date	$ 9,675	$ 2,325	$12,000
Predetermined Scrap Allow. for year	$30,000	$10,000	$40,000

FIGURE 8   Scrap report for week ending March 14, 1980.

	Month/ Year	Units Produced	% Scrap	Average Scrap Cost Per Unit	Total Scrap Costs	Scrap as % Prod. Costs
Current Month:	Feb. 1980	300,000	1.5	$.35	$1,575	1.05
Last Month:	Jan. 1980	300,000	2.0	$.35	$2,100	1.40
Previous Month:	Dec. 1979	280,000	1.8	$.29	$1,462	1.04

FIGURE 9   Three-month scrap summary.

very least, the system should be capable of generating reports about scrap loss or losses due to defective items. For example, scrap reports can be generated that keep track of scrap resulting from current production as well as year-to-date figures. Figure 8 illustrates one approach to this type of report for a company that has two departments.

Although Fig. 8 is a weekly scrap report, there is no reason that management cannot utilize daily reports if they are needed and the information is available. Emphasis should be on cost savings by reducing scrap losses. Management may also be interested in comparing scrap losses in the current period with the losses incurred in a previous period.

Figure 9 illustrates one form this report might take. It is only when management becomes aware of problems involving increasing scrap costs (or any other costs) that they are prompted to take necessary corrective action. Reports of this information should be designed so that management and production personnel are readily alerted about any increasing cost trends that may be developing unnecessarily.

IV. FORMULATING COSTS OF QUALITY

Thus far we have assumed that quality costs can be gathered by the system. An organization must have a systematic approach for doing this. Quality costs can be broken down a number of ways. One approach is to classify these costs in the following categories [3, p. 198]:

1. Costs of prevention of off-standard quality
2. Cost of appraisal of quality status in the plant
3. Cost of in-house failures
4. Cost of customer complaints

These categories cover all costs associated with administering an effective quality control program. In addition, in-house failures can be measured by the amount of cost of scrap, repairs, and related losses. Costs of customer complaints are losses due to canceled orders, price adjustments for inferior quality of finished items, or even loss of customers. Figure 10 is a list of items that prove helpful for collecting relevant data on costs of quality for the categories given above. Cost accountants, engineers, time-study managers, and production personnel can generate cost estimates of these figures. These estimates should be entered and used within the costing system. However,

Prevention Elements

>   Gage and test equipment design
>   New product reviews
>   Preparation of quality plans
>   Station control
>   Inspection and testing standards for incoming materials and components
>   Management of the quality control effort
>   Inspection specifications and standards for manufactured product

Appraisal Elements

>   Materials and labor for testing and inspection of incoming lots
>   In-process inspection labor
>   Final inspection labor and materials
>   Quality audits
>   Preparation and review of test and inspection reports
>   Calibration of test equipment
>   Life testing of product

In-House Failures

>   Scrap, representing waste of materials, energy and labor (but not
>   including obsolete material scrapped)
>   Rework to convert defectives to acceptable quality
>   Defective materials and components purchased for which the vendor
>   is not charged back
>   Engineering effort to salvage or release nonconforming products,
>   components or materials
>   Lost profits and holding costs for defective items that must be
>   sold as seconds, substandards or down-graded products

Customer Complaints and Dissatisfaction

>   Response to complaints -- requiring the shipping back of unacceptable
>   product, engineering and sales effort, and expenses in meeting with
>   customers and seeking satisfactory accommodations, replacement of
>   defective items
>   Materials and labor, engineering and sales expenses involved in the
>   repair of defectives
>   Rejection of product by customer
>   Removal from customer's "approved vendor list" because of repeated
>   failure to meet quality standards; loss of market share from
>   excessive customer dissatisfaction incidents
>   Product liability law suits and related problems, whose incidence has
>   been increasing annually

FIGURE 10   Items helpful for collecting data on quality costs. (From Ref. 3, pp. 199–200.)

Job Title	No.	Total, $	Defects Prevention, $	Defects Appraisal, $
Quality Control Manager	1	20,000	20,000	–
Process Engineer	2	30,000	24,000	6,000
Process Technicians	2	20,000	–	20,000
Incoming Materials Inspector	1	12,000	–	12,000
Secretary-Analyst	1	8,000	8,000	–
Chief Inspector	1	10,000	5,000	5,000
Total	8	100,000	57,000	43,000

FIGURE 11   Annual costs of proposed quality control organization.

having the estimated costs available is not enough. Actual quality costs
should be compared to estimated figures and any differences handled accordingly by the responsible management personnel.

Lester prepared a proposed quality cost-reduction program for the Hawley-
Lynch Company [3, pp. 245–250]. Using cost factors, they developed projections for the quality control costs for the current year as well as a number
of years in the future. These costs are given in Figs. 11 and 12. The costs

Categories	Current	1 Year	Projected 2 Years	3 Years
Preventive Cost, $				
QC Supervisor	10,000	–	–	–
QC Manager	–	20,000	20,000	20,000
Secretary-Analyst	–	8,000	8,000	8,000
Chief Inspector	–	5,000	5,000	5,000
Design of Gages & Test Equip.	50,000	50,000	50,000	50,000
All Other	–	10,000	10,000	10,000
Total Preventive	60,000	93,000	93,000	93,000
Percent of Sales	0.300	0.465	0.465	0.465
Appraisal Cost, $				
Process Engineer	–	6,000	6,000	6,000
Process Technicians	–	20,000	20,000	20,000
Chief Inspector	–	5,000	5,000	5,000
In-coming Materials Inspection	–	13,000	12,000	12,000
In-process Inspection	65,000	125,000	117,000	110,000
Final Inspection	100,000	192,000	180,000	169,000
All Other	5,000	10,000	10,000	10,000
Total Appraisal	170,000	371,000	350,000	332,000
Percent of Sales	0.850	1.852	1.756	1.661
In-house Failure Cost, $	2,000,000	2,000,000	1,500,000	750,000
Percent of Sales	10.00	10.00	7.50	3.75
Customer Complaint Cost, $	1,000,000	500,000	250,000	250,000
Percent of Sales	5.00	2.50	1.25	1.25

FIGURE 12   Current and projected quality costs.

Categories	Current Percent	Projected Percent		
		Year 1	Year 2	Year 3
Prevention	0.300	0.465	0.465	0.465
Appraisal	0.850	1.852	1.756	1.661
In-house Failures	10.000	10.000	7.500	3.750
Customer Complaints	5.000	2.500	1.250	1.250
Total	16.150	14.817	10.971	7.126
Costs Reductions		1.333	5.179	9.024
Savings Based on $20,000,000 Sales		$266,600	$1,035,800	$1,804,800

FIGURE 13   Current and projected quality costs as a percent of sales billed.

are given as a percentage of sales in Fig. 13, and the cost savings are high-
lighted in anticipation of top management more readily accepting and supporting the proposed quality control program. Timely updates of current costs
as well as updated projections of future costs should be mandatory in this
system. Management must compare budgeted current expenditures with actual
quality control costs and determine the cause of any variances that might result.

Categories	Current	1 Year	Projected 2 Years	3 Years
Preventive Cost, $				
QC Supervisor	10,000	–	–	–
QC Manager	–	20,000	20,000	20,000
Secretary-Analyst	–	8,000	8,000	8,000
Chief Inspector	–	5,000	5,000	5,000
Design of Gages & Test Equip.	50,000	50,000	50,000	50,000
All Other	–	10,000	10,000	10,000
Total Preventive	60,000	93,000	93,000	93,000
Percent of Production Costs	.46	.72	.72	.72
Appraisal Cost, $				
Process Engineer	–	6,000	6,000	6,000
Process Technicians	–	20,000	20,000	20,000
Chief Inspector	–	5,000	5,000	5,000
In-coming Materials Inspection	–	13,000	12,000	12,000
In-process Inspection	65,000	125,000	117,000	110,000
Final Inspection	100,000	192,000	180,000	169,000
All Other	5,000	10,000	10,000	10,000
Total Appraisal	170,000	371,000	350,000	332,000
Percent of Production Costs	1.31	2.85	2.69	2.55
In-house Failure Cost, $	2,000,000	2,000,000	1,500,000	750,000
Percent of Production Costs	15.38	15.38	11.54	5.77
Customer Complaint Cost, $	1,000,000	500,000	250,000	250,000
Percent of Production Costs	7.69	3.85	1.92	1.92

FIGURE 14   Current and projected quality costs.

Categories	Current Percent	Projected Percent		
		Year 1	Year 2	Year 3
Prevention	.46	.72	.72	.72
Appraisal	1.31	2.85	2.69	2.55
In-house Failures	15.38	15.38	11.54	5.77
Customer Complaints	7.69	3.85	1.92	1.92
Total	24.84	22.80	16.87	10.92
Costs Reduction		2.04	7.97	13.88
Savings Based on $13,000,000 Production Costs		$265,200	$1,036,100	$1,804,400

FIGURE 15   Current and projected quality costs as a percent of production costs.

Production supervisors might be more interested in having quality costs reported as a percentage of the costs of units produced [3, p. 201].

Figures 14 and 15 show the data based on a percentage of production costs. Perhaps the production manager may be interested in only select data (i.e., in-house failures or results of appraisal costs). Rather than doing this on a yearly basis, monthly or weekly basis would provide better feedback for management control. With the proper information system, all data can easily be obtained from the system and will be useful in management decision making.

V. CONCLUSION

As we move toward more computerized organizations, the growth and survival of these organizations will greatly depend on the effective use of data in major functional areas where planning decisions are made. Controlling quality costs can help manufacturing organizations greatly decrease their production costs while increasing the quality of their products. While an on-line real-time system can provide immediate feedback for assessing quality control and related costs, an effective quality control program may be instituted in many other types of systems. Regardless of the type of system, it is important to have the cooperation of all people. This cooperation must come from top management as well as designers, production, accounting, marketing, and sales personnel. The cost of any quality control system must be more than offset by the benefits derived for it to be practical. Only by recognizing and tabulating quality costs can management effectively control such costs, thereby increasing profits and providing consumers with better, more reliable products.

REFERENCES

1. R. J. Thierauf, *Distributed Processing Systems*, Prentice-Hall, Englewood Cliffs, N.J., 1978, p. 52.
2. R. S. Polemene, "The Operational Audit of Quality Control," *The Internal Auditor*, January—February, 1975, p. 39.
3. R. H. Lester, N. L. Enrick, and H. E. Mottley, *Quality Control for Profit*, Industrial Press, New York, 1977, p. 32.

FURTHER READING

Garrison, R. H., *Managerial Accounting*, 3rd ed., Business Publications,
    Plano, Tex., 1982.
Horngren, C. T., *Cost Accounting: A Managerial Emphasis*, 5th ed.,
    Prentice Hall, Englewood Cliffs, N.J., 1982.
Lynch, R. M., and R. W. Williamson, *Accounting for Management Planning
    and Control*, 3rd ed., McGraw-Hill, New York, 1983.
Morse, W. J., J. R. Davis, and A. L. Hartgraves, *Management Accounting*,
    Addison-Wesley, Reading, Mass., 1984.
Rayburn, L. G., *Principles of Cost Accounting with Managerial Applications*,
    Richard D. Irwin, Homewood, Ill., 1979.

9

LIFE-CYCLE COSTS

H. K. BURBRIDGE

BFH Parametrics
Mountain View, California

I. INTRODUCTION

In the year 1957 *Sputnik* burst upon an astounded world. The USSR had beaten the United States into space. Taking stock of our resources, we began an all-out effort to catch up. Subminiaturization of rocketry and space subsystems was a necessity since we lacked the booster efficiency to deliver weighty payloads into orbit.

In 1958 the National Aeronautics and Space Administration (NASA) was created to mount the effort needed for the *Apollo* series. The ultimate in system performance was demanded and achieved in a climate of "expense is no object." During the same time the military services faced the task of providing more sophisticated weapon systems to the service arms. The criterion was again technical excellence of performance regardless of price.

In the 1970s the nation awakened by degrees to the fact that the purse was not bottomless. The military and NASA both recognized that excellence without regard to cost could no longer be sustained. Congressional appropriations had not increased significantly, but the cost of new hardware had.

Prices for labor and materials climbed while the need for new systems increased, and something had to give. A new term, "cost effectiveness," meant "a system that will do the job, at an affordable price." The proponents of this new philosophy worked to change all the ground rules. Now planners were required to purchase only sufficient performance to accomplish the system end function. The objective was to match a reasonable purchase price to the performance plateau envisioned. Thus was born design to cost (DTC).

The government purchaser now espoused a policy that commercial industry had pursued for many years. Offer a product for sale at a marketable price that will perform its end function efficiently throughout its useful life. One does not stay in business very long without following this policy!

The government's first step was to form a body of policy and documentation to tell those who must do it how it must be done. Design to cost, and its companion, life-cycle cost (LCC), were no exception to this rule. Very rapidly both terms became widespread in government circles and began to appear in government new-business solicitations. Although these two terms are complementary, there is a fundamental difference.

II. DESIGN TO COST

The government customer sets bounds on the cost involved in the design of
new systems. These bounds take the form of goals or objectives in one or
more variations. Essentially, a design-to-cost (DTC) requirement is formulated from one or a series of affordability studies conducted by the government. These studies seek to answer the question: What new starts can be
undertaken by the government, at a tolerable price, within the budget allocated
for new business/new systems acquisition?

Design to cost covers the research, development, test, and evaluation
(RDT&E) phase of new contracts, and may extend through the full-scale development (FSD) phase. RDT&E may be considered to encompass the varifica-
tion of a given design when translated into a system or systems. FSD begins
at that point in system maturation where one or more system prototypes become available for evaluation under field operating conditions. During this
phase, processes are explored and finalized. This would include such processes as verification of human-machine interface, demonstration of the maintenance concepts, the logistic support system, and other variables associated
with system field deployment.

DTC differs from LCC in that it is capable of being tracked. The progress
of stated objectives as realized are related by a cost accumulation process.
Hence DTC requirements are contract deliverable reports list (CDRL) items
that must be reported on a scheduled basis. Incentive payments for contract
compliance are based on the achievement of goals. LCC does not, however,
form part of contract compliance.

LCC is a forecast of the cost to support a system throughout the operations
and maintenance (O&M) phase of a program. O&M covers the operation, maintenance, and repair of new systems, and in addition the costs of test and
handling equipment, spares, and logistic support. In some cases the retire-
ment cost involved in replacing the systems may be included. The accumulation of cost involved in the several phases—RDT&E, FSD, and O&M—represents the cost of ownership to the government.

III. LIFE-CYCLE COST

The accuracy of LCC is a direct function of a number of parameters governing
the system. LCC depends on complex trades, among which are:

    Reliability/failure rate of system
    Maintenance policy, if applicable
    Sparing requirements and logistic support plan
    Deployment policy, duty cycle, and availability requirements
    Warranty structure, if applicable
    System retirement/replacement plan

The Department of Defense (DoD) has published representative cost values
illustrative of cost of owning systems by program phase. These are depicted
frequently as bar charts (Fig. 1). Those government-released documents
which may be considered in a formulation of a body of policy are listed in the
References [1—6]. This list plus a number of other documents forms the
hierarchy of government directives that is confronted when dealing with DTC.

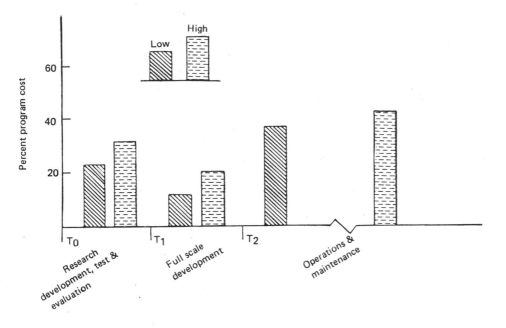

FIGURE 1   Representative costs of owning systems by program phase.

Before government policymakers could deal with the process of DTC, they faced doing something about the extremely high cost of the O&M phase of system ownership. The bar chart (Fig. 1) shows that for the average maintainable military system deployed in field use, the cost of operating and maintaining it can run from 40 to 55% of the total cost of ownership. Obviously, something needed to be done about LCC in, and during, the RDT&E phase of system development.

Government documents reveal the changes in military mind-set as they considered the problems. The joint design to cost guide [6], which is 55 pages in length, is binding on all military services and the contractors who provide systems and subordinate hardware to the DoD. The total thrust is toward cost-effectiveness and effectiveness that involves money—which is what it is all about.

IV. MONEY

How far will $20 go in the local grocery store? The answer is, not very far. A decade ago, $20 would buy a great deal more than it will today. Why? Money has its own dynamism and its fluctuations can be quite extreme. When planning for the purchase of new systems, the government allows for the changing value of money. Table 1 deals with inflation in the world marketplace.

The R values (Table 1) refer to calendar years; for example, R 46 denotes the rate of inflation applicable during the year 1946. Similarly, R 25 forecasts the rate of inflation expected during the year 2025. In 1946 the inflation rate was a mere 3.2%, while in 1979 the rate advanced to 11.7%. What more dramatic illustration could one have of the changing value of money?

TABLE 1   Current System Values

INFLATION RATE FACTORS (1946 - 2025)

R46 = .032	R47 = .032	R48 = .034	R49 = .034	R50 = .033
R51 = .032	R52 = .035	R53 = .035	R54 = .036	R55 = .036
R56 = .037	R57 = .037	R58 = .038	R59 = .039	R60 = .040
R61 = .038	R62 = .041	R63 = .045	R64 = .050	R65 = .052
R66 = .053	R67 = .053	R68 = .054	R69 = .054	R70 = .053
R71 = .054	R72 = .055	R73 = .055	R74 = .067	R75 = .097
R76 = .080	R77 = .076	R78 = .079	R79 = .117	R80 = .139
R81 = .111	R82 = .116	R83 = .102	R84 = .092	R85 = .093
R86 = .093	R87 = .093	R88 = .093	R89 = .093	R90 = .093
R91 = .093	R92 = .093	R93 = .093	R94 = .093	R95 = .093
R96 = .093	R97 = .093	R98 = .093	R99 = .093	R00 = .093
R01 = .093	R02 = .093	R03 = .093	R04 = .093	R05 = .093
R06 = .093	R07 = .093	R08 = .093	R09 = .093	R10 = .093
R11 = .093	R12 = .093	R13 = .093	R14 = .093	R15 = .093
R16 = .093	R17 = .093	R18 = .093	R19 = .093	R20 = .093
R21 = .093	R22 = .093	R23 = .093	R24 = .093	R25 = .093

TABLE 2 June 1980 NASA Comptroller Indices

	TO FY 1971	TO FY 1972	TO FY 1973	TO FY 1974	TO FY 1975	TO FY 1976	TO FY TP	TO FY 1977	TO FY 1978	TO FY 1979	TO FY 1980	TO FY 1981	TO FY 1982	TO FY 1983	TO FY 1984	TO FY 1985	TO FY 1986	TO FY 1987	TO FY 1988
FROM FY 1971	1.000	1.057	1.118	1.198	1.327	1.447	1.477	1.602	1.727	1.892	2.110	2.369	2.636	2.882	3.141	3.424	3.733	4.068	4.430
FROM FY 1972	.946	1.000	1.058	1.133	1.255	1.369	1.397	1.516	1.634	1.790	1.996	2.241	2.488	2.727	2.972	3.231	3.531	3.849	4.151
FROM FY 1973	.894	.945	1.000	1.072	1.187	1.294	1.321	1.433	1.546	1.692	1.887	2.119	2.352	2.578	2.809	3.063	3.338	3.639	3.926
FROM FY 1974	.835	.882	.933	1.000	1.108	1.208	1.233	1.337	1.443	1.579	1.761	1.977	2.195	2.406	2.622	2.858	3.116	3.396	3.698
FROM FY 1975	.754	.797	.843	.903	1.000	1.090	1.113	1.207	1.301	1.426	1.590	1.785	1.983	2.172	2.367	2.580	2.812	3.066	3.338
FROM FY 1976	.691	.730	.773	.828	.917	1.000	1.021	1.107	1.194	1.308	1.458	1.637	1.818	1.992	2.171	2.366	2.579	2.811	3.053
FROM FY TP	.677	.716	.757	.811	.898	.980	1.000	1.085	1.169	1.281	1.429	1.604	1.781	1.951	2.127	2.318	2.527	2.754	2.999
FROM FY 1977	.624	.660	.698	.748	.828	.903	.922	1.000	1.078	1.181	1.317	1.479	1.642	1.799	1.961	2.137	2.330	2.539	2.765
FROM FY 1978	.579	.612	.647	.694	.768	.838	.855	.928	1.000	1.096	1.222	1.378	1.523	1.669	1.819	1.983	2.161	2.366	2.556
FROM FY 1979	.529	.569	.591	.633	.701	.765	.781	.847	.913	1.000	1.115	1.252	1.380	1.523	1.663	1.810	1.973	2.150	2.341
FROM FY 1980	.474	.501	.530	.568	.629	.686	.700	.759	.818	.897	1.000	1.123	1.246	1.366	1.489	1.623	1.769	1.928	2.098
FROM FY 1981	.422	.446	.472	.506	.560	.611	.623	.676	.728	.799	.891	1.000	1.110	1.217	1.326	1.445	1.575	1.717	1.870
FROM FY 1982	.380	.402	.425	.455	.505	.550	.562	.609	.657	.719	.802	.901	1.000	1.096	1.194	1.302	1.419	1.547	1.684
FROM FY 1983	.347	.367	.388	.416	.460	.502	.512	.556	.599	.656	.732	.822	.913	1.000	1.090	1.188	1.295	1.412	1.537
FROM FY 1984	.318	.337	.356	.381	.422	.461	.470	.510	.550	.602	.672	.754	.837	.918	1.000	1.090	1.188	1.295	1.410
FROM FY 1985	.292	.309	.327	.350	.388	.423	.431	.468	.504	.553	.616	.692	.768	.842	.917	1.000	1.090	1.188	1.294
FROM FY 1986	.268	.283	.300	.321	.356	.388	.396	.429	.463	.507	.565	.635	.705	.772	.842	.917	1.000	1.090	1.187
FROM FY 1987	.246	.260	.276	.294	.326	.356	.363	.394	.425	.465	.519	.582	.647	.708	.772	.842	.917	1.000	1.089
FROM FY 1988	.226	.239	.253	.270	.300	.327	.333	.356	.390	.427	.476	.535	.594	.651	.709	.773	.842	.918	1.000

Table 2 differs slightly from Table 1 and goes by periods from fiscal year 1971 to fiscal year 1988. Selecting values at random, goods and services obtained for a dollar in 1971 require 2.369 dollars in fiscal year 1981. Viewing the information another way, one may infer that a 1971 dollar would buy only 42.2 cents worth of goods in a 1981 market. Expressed in yet another manner—versus a 1971 standard—a 1981 dollar is worth only 41 cents.

All these factors must be taken into consideration by government and industry when planning procurement of systems. Nor is the planning for the dynamics of money restricted to the government alone. Such planning must form a basic part of every business and every household when dealing with the vending and purchase of goods and services.

V. SOLVING THE PROBLEMS

The entire discipline of DTC/LCC (or simply DTLCC) bristled with problems to be solved. Many of these required parallel solutions. Some of these problems were how to:

Estimate the cost of systems not yet designed
Set DTC goals and objectives
Forecast LCC values

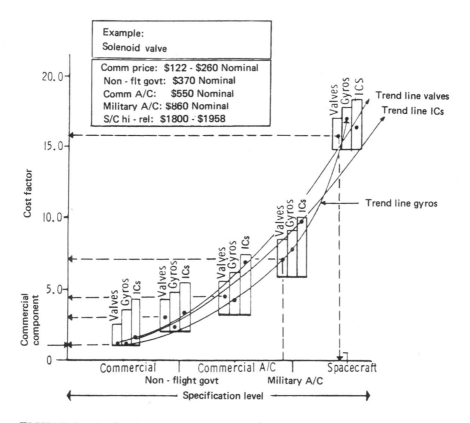

FIGURE 2   Estimated component cost factor versus specification level (supplier impact on specifications).

Provide rapid answers to these questions
Inject credibility into the answers
Cope with the dynamism of money
Standardize on the methodology undergirding the solutions

At this point, statisticians, applied mathematicians, and economists got into the act. It has been known for many years that relationships exist among the physical descriptors, performance measures, the other variables of systems, and the cost to obtain such systems in the form of hardware. Relationships of this type are known as cost estimating relationships (CERs). For instance, there is a relationship between the cost of many hardware items and their weights. Similarly, there is a relationship between reliability figures of merit and the hardware to which they apply. Other variables, such as the cost impact of the imposition of military specifications on a system, can also be represented by a CER.

Initially, CERs merely furnished a graphical representation of cost related to some other measure of system significance. What was needed was a means to interrelate all the CERs to describe a system in terms of performance versus the cost to obtain that performance. This evolved rather rapidly, although many contend that "like Topsy, it just growed." Today, the means have become a rigorous discipline known as parametric analysis.

In Fig. 2 a CER with trend lines shows the relationship of government requirements on an item of hardware versus the cost increments. The lowest cost is the commercial price; the highest cost is for a high-reliability item for use in a spacecraft.

VI. PARAMETRICS

Parametric analysis is a valuable tool for the preparation of credible cost estimates for new business proposals. A major advantage of the discipline is the ability to evolve rational cost values from parametric cost models when comparatively little is known about systems. This occurs in the early design concept phase of acquisition activity on the part of the customer.

A parametric cost model makes use of the relationships among systems performance measures, systems physical descriptors, and the cost required to obtain a given level of performance from the hardware and software. Interactive sets of equations are constructed to relate measures of performance to cost. This is done by employing cost estimating relationships (CERs) as a point of departure for the equation set. A CER is a simple device usually in graphic form, displaying the relationship of cost to some measure pertinent to the operation of the system.

Should a domestic washing machine, for example, be purchased from a mail-order house? The price will be quoted, as will the weight and the cost to ship it from the vendor to the customer. Obviously, a relationship exists between the measurable parameter of weight and the dollar value of the salable article. Expressed in other terms, the machine costs so much per pound of weight, much as a pound of potatoes costs some varying dollar value.

Expanding the example, the price of potatoes per pound is set on the basis of the interaction among a number of variables. These variables include the cost of labor to plant and harvest the crop, the price of fertilizers and pesticides, the price of farm machinery employed in their cultivation, the amount of crop yield per annum, and environmental factors such as sun and rain.

The fixed costs incurred are those such as buildings, rental of land if applicable, fringe benefits for labor, and some reasonable return on investment for the producer (profit).

In the case of the washing machine, the price represents a cumulative value comprising the cost to design and develop the device, the cost to translate the design into operable hardware, the cost to test and verify its operation, the cost to the manufacturer of doing business, often known as burden, and again some reasonable return on investment. All the values in the example have been determined over a period of time by empirical methods, and these values, verified by experience in the marketplace, constitute the data base for the CERs to construct parametric models.

As CERs are graphic tools, translation methods are needed to convert them into more readily handled equations and sets of interactive equations known as algorithms. These make analogies among real relationships, frequently logarithmic in nature. Among these relationships expressed mathematically are the engineering complexity of design and development, the hardware manufacturing complexity, the schedule, the types of materials, and many others. Additional algorithms treat the burden for the task, the fee, and the size of the articles to be produced, and further subdivisions of complexity treat structural items as opposed to electronic items.

For software, other variables are considered, among which are the level of language to be used, the skill mix of the personnel creating the software, the number of lines of code, the number of executable instructions, and many other descriptors applicable to the required design and evolution of the software packages.

A. Parametric Cost Analysis

Several available cost models have a DTC subroutine such as the user-leased RCA programmed review of information for cost estimation (PRICE) model. As the models operate on the basis of overlaid CERs and algorithms, variables such as the cost to achieve an increment in reliability can be assessed rapidly. Similarly, changes in the weight of system components can be assessed in terms of cost impact, as can changes in:

Materials
Manufacturing processes
Number and type of electronic parts
Program schedule
Number of breadboards, brass-boards
Prototypes
Test iterations

Cost analyses can rapidly reflect the compromises among several design alternatives and delta values obtained candidate versus candidate.

This process leads to the selection of a design baseline. Once the baseline is evolved, a cost file can be created and changed by a process known as NAMELIST to reflect subsequent changes to the baseline. Further, the cost of such changes can be accumulated and reflected periodically in progress reports to the customer as progress toward the achievement of DTC objectives.

B. Validity of Parametric Estimates

As with the design process, there is a maturation in cost estimating directly proportional to the state of design progress. The early estimates, based on the imperfect or incomplete definition of the design, are considered as "sizing" estimates of cost. As the design matures and more detailed information becomes available, the cost-estimates output from the modeling process becomes more reliable. Depicted graphically, the cost estimates produced at specific schedule points in a program (Fig. 3) closely resemble a classic "tolerance funnel."

There is one major advantage of employing parametric cost estimating models to assess design-to-cost and life-cycle-cost effects on programs. Such models, while delivering answers in near real time, are also capable of accepting all the input variables and handling them either singly or simultaneously. The method of handling DTC differs from LCC in that DTC deals with design variables and LCC deals with the variables encountered by the system in field service. Figures 4 and 5 depict the information flow as it is processed by parametric models and shows the respective outputs for both forms of analysis.

C. The Reliability/Quality Challenge

The path from a reliability figure of merit of 0.9 to 0.999 is long and difficult. Not only is it difficult from a technological viewpoint, but also from a budgetary standpoint. In Fig. 6 note that while cost, depicted by the ordinate of the graph, is dimensionless, the dollar value ascends almost vertically the nearer one gets to the theoretical figure of unity on the abscissa.

Again, parametric models come to the rescue of the engineer who must design to cost. As a rule, such models possess algorithms that take into account the reliability variable and its impact on system and subordinate hardware cost. Obviously, during the trade study analysis phase of design the engineer can

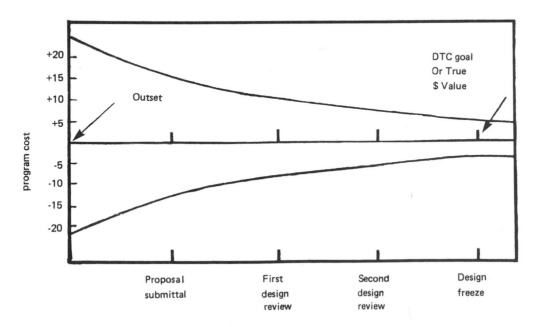

FIGURE 3   Tolerance funnel (dollars).

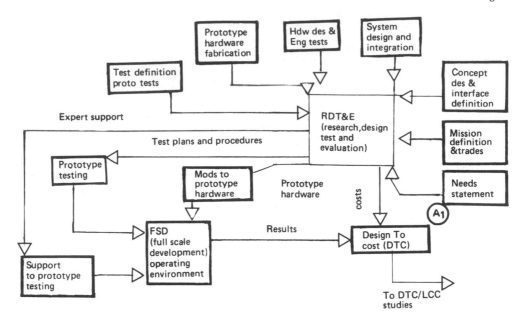

FIGURE 4   Parametrics support to design to cost.

easily determine the cost penalty imposed per percentage-point increment of
reliability enhancement to a design. Again, these algorithms have been developed from a complex series of CERs, developed to accommodate parallel,
standby, phantom, graceful degradation, and other modes of redundancy.

   Once more the answers are available to either the engineer or the cost
analyst in near real time. This means that both are working "smart" rather

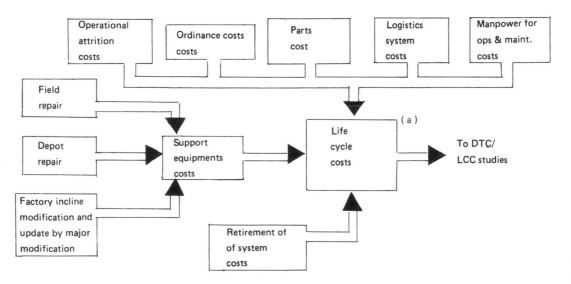

FIGURE 5   Parametric support to life-cycle cost analysis.

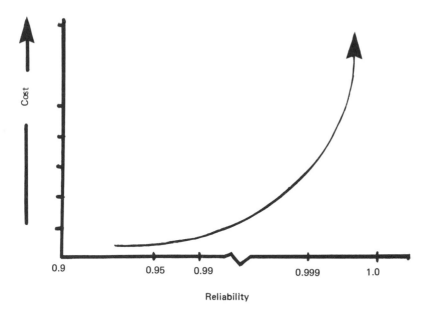

FIGURE 6   Cost estimating relationship: reliability versus cost.

than just plain "hard." Similarly, these techniques of analysis can be applied
to the overall field of quality assurance, although the state of the art is not
so far advanced.

D. Quality and Parametrics

Quality organizations ideally should report to the highest levels of management
allocating the quality assurance budgets. In the past, the quality assurance
discipline, involving the broadly based subordinate disciplines of quality engineering, quality test, and inspection, derived its budget as a percentage of
manufacturing costs. This contrasts with reliability engineering in that reliability, considered to be another parameter of design, derived its operating
budget from engineering. Although the quality funding source is by no means
invariably expressed as a percentage of manufacturing costs, the practice is
sufficiently widespread to lend truth to such a generalization. Today, in the
climate of cost-effectiveness, both military and commercial, no longer can quality assurance budgetary considerations be based so loosely.

Figure 7 illustrates one of the numerous methods by which parametric analysis can assist in evolving credible costs for the overall quality function. If
there is one thing that a modern quality assurance operation does well, it is
keeping accurate, voluminous, and timely statistical records and pertinent
data. Most quality managers can estimate quite accurately the stepwise costs
of the quality operation with which they are involved daily, and justify these
dollar values against an operating budget. Less common, however, is the case
where quality funding is allocated from the outset of a new task by machine-
manipulated methods. Figure 7 also illustrates the process mode leading to the
construction of a parametric model to handle quality information of several
sorts and evolve dollar outcomes per process. The figure is by no means complete, and numerous variations on the general theme are not only possible,

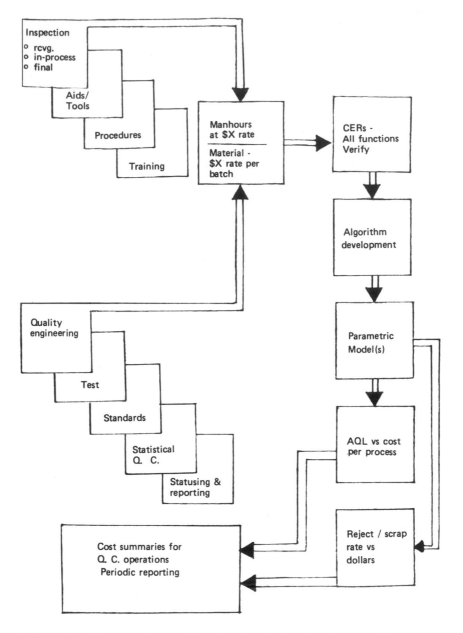

FIGURE 7   Parametric model: flowchart showing the quality versus cost
process.

but necessary. In many cases it should be possible to develop suitable algorithms without the intervening step of generating CERs. However, the CER is a valuable tool as a stand-alone, and these days with CADAM and computer graphics, CERs can be constructed very rapidly.

VII. QUALITY EFFECT ON DTLCC

In the DTC phase, the quality role does not change markedly from what is has been traditionally. Quality still remains the arbiter of whether or not the hardware built meets and/or exceeds the design specifications. All the inspection processes are still needed, as are all the quality engineering functions. The axion "quality must be built into the design" is still as true as ever.

Perhaps the greatest impact on the quality process occurs when the product is deployed in field service, in other words, the O&M phase contributing to the LCC. If the quality is poor, the field-failure rate of the system product or device will be high. Similarly, the reliability of the product in the field will be markedly lower than the inherent reliability of the design.

Rapid feedback of field failures, associated quality problems, and field product performance information in general are vital elements. This information is needed if the O&M costs within the LCC envelope are to remain substantially as forecast. As these data come to hand, the parametric model can be pressed into service to provide rapid outputs of cost increases due to unforeseen field mortality. At the same time, costs for redesign, production quick fixes, and other remedial activity can be forecast and brought forward to management for refunding decisions. The O&M phase contributes the major portion of the total cost of ownership to the military and commercial customer purchasing maintainable systems. For this reason, accurate multiple forecasts of LCC must be ongoing, and must be provided with valid performance information feedback.

Much has been left unsaid; much remains yet to be researched and formalized. From the early steps in DTLCC the military and commercial producers of systems have of necessity entered into a symbiotic relationship with the parametric model and the digital computer. Parametric modeling for DTLCC and all phases of research development and manufacture of new systems is here today and constitutes the wave of the future. It may well be that the wave is but one of many in a stormy sea where costs must be held down and performance brought up to an acceptable level at an affordable cost. New techniques are evolving almost daily to relate performance variables one to another. New parameters and their relationships are being evolved and applied to the DTLCC process. Of these, cost is but another parameter among many, but perhaps the single most important one of the entire set. The watchword of yesteryear throughout the military community was quality at any price. The watchword today is acceptable quality at any price the customer can afford.

REFERENCES

1. DoD directive 500C.1, "Acquisition of Major Defense Systems," December 22, 1975.
2. Deputy Secretary of Defense memorandum for secretaries of the military departments and DSARC principals, "Design to Cost Objectives on DSARC Programs," June 18, 1973.

3. Deputy Secretary of Defense memorandum for secretaries of the military departments, "Application of Design to Cost Management Principles to Subsystems and Other Than Major Weapon Systems," May 24, 1974.

4. DoD 7110-1-M, "Department of Defense Budget Guidance Manual," June 15, 1973.

5. DoD Instruction 5000.2, "Decision Coordinating Paper (DCP) and the Defense Systems Acquisition Review Council (DSARC)," January 21, 1975.

6. Joint design to cost guide (AMC 700-6, NAVMAT P5242, ALFCP/AFSCP 800-19), "A Conceptual Approach for Major Weapon System Acquisition," October 3, 1973.

10

STATISTICS WITHOUT MATH

EUGENE W. ELLIS

Eugene W. Ellis, Associates
Sanford, North Carolina

To exist in today's competitive environment, industry must upgrade quality and decrease costs. Unfortunately, most companies, especially those in the United States, have the mistaken belief that improved quality must always be associated with increased costs. The basis of such a belief is the assumption that quality can only be improved by performing additional inspection after production to sort out all scrap and items that require rework. Without a doubt, such inspection, plus the rework and scrap involved, does create additional nonproductive costs in order to upgrade quality.

Many companies, however, especially those in Japan, have proven that it is possible to improve quality while *decreasing* costs. Such a program is achieved by discarding the old additional-inspection assumption and replacing it with a statistical process control system that "produces all things right the first time." Under such a "make it right" system, rework and scrap plus their costs are eliminated and inspection is not needed to look for rework and scrap items that do not exist. The utopia of improving quality while decreasing costs can thus be achieved.

Unfortunately, however, very few successful process control programs exist in the United States. It is felt that this lack of success is due directly to the training that has been performed for most programs. In most cases, the training has been performed by statistical experts and the emphasis has been on the use of complex sounding statistical/mathematical terms. Such terms simply "turn off" management and production workers, and thus the attempted process control system quickly fails. Experience shows that when the proposed program is presented using statistical logic but not statistical terms, instead of being turned off, production workers are actually enthusiastic because they can see that statistical process control is a most logical operation mode.

Statistical application in industry actually involves three separate functions. These functions are data analysis, statistical sampling, and process control. Trained statisticians are needed for the data analysis and statistical sampling functions, but only statistical logic, without the need of statistical terms, is needed for process control. Separating process control logic from the data analysis and statistical sampling functions eliminates the need for the use of statistical terms. In addition, by using nomographs for most necessary mathematical calculations, a successful statistical process control program can exist

without the need of complex-sounding statistical terms. Also, when a successful process control system does exist, the requirements for most data analysis
and statistical sampling functions are eliminated.

Basic statistical logic indicates that in every process there are an infinite
number of factors that can affect—to various degrees—the final product.
Usually, only a few of these factors have any significant effect on the final
product, and controls are established for these factors (e.g., operator's adjustments, speed of process, etc.). However, a great many other factors
which are felt to have only an insignificant effect on the final product also
exist and these are usually not controlled and often not even identified (e.g.,
meshing of gears of a machine in the process, variations in item placement
within a fixture, etc.). Because these factors are not controlled, they have
a random effect (no matter how small) from item to item in the process (see
Fig. 1).

Although the noncontrolled factors individually have very little effect on
the final product, there are so many of them that collectively they do prevent
all items in the process from being produced identically. However, because
the noncontrolled factors are operating independently and in a random manner
(*plus* effect on some pieces, *minus* effect on others), they have a tendency to
"average out," and thus most items are produced at or near the target point

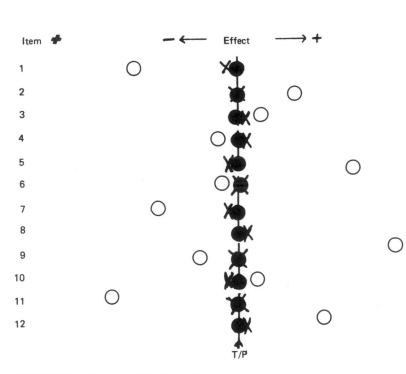

FIGURE 1   Factor effect on final product.

as established by the significant factors being controlled. But not all noncontrolled effects will average out, so some items will vary to different degrees
than others from the target point.

This central tendency and spread caused by the noncontrolled factors can
be visibly identified when a series of items produced by the process are measured and plotted as a histogram. A histogram plot represents the "population"
of items being produced by the process, as shown in Fig. 2. The target point
and spread of the population will remain consistent provided that the controls
on the significant factors are constant and no new noncontrolled factors are
added to the process.

The recognition that each process produces a consistent population of items
rather than just a series of individual items is the basic statistical logic needed
for a successful process control program. When the concept of a population is
understood, it is logical that if the limits of the spread of the population are
controlled to within requirements, the process will produce only confirming
items.

Examination of the ideal population (see Fig. 3) indicates that a successful
process control system exists because the target point of the population is
held at or near nominal and the spread of the population is less than the width
of the tolerance requirements. All other situations produce nonconforming
items and costly inspection, rework, and scrap.

As the population's target point is the result of the controls established on
selected significant factors, any shift problem can only be due to errors in the
established control points (see Fig. 4). As the population's spread is the result of the random variations of the noncontrolled factors in the process, any
spread problem can be caused only by significant factors being in the process
that have not been identified and are not under control (see Fig. 5).

It should be noted that often a noncontrolled spread factor can exist at a
designated control point because the designated control point cannot be exactly
established (see Fig. 6). A common example of this situation is an operation
using a visual gage setting and adjustment at the approximate control point
rather than at the exact control point established.

For a successful process control system, the first and most important step
is the identification of the population's target point and spread limits. The
spread and target (S/T) worksheet is an excellent tool for such a determination. Construction of the S/T worksheet is simple. Select a minimum of 25
representative items from the process and measure the final product. The
S/T worksheet is used as follows:

1. Select the cell boundaries/cell midpoint so that the spread of plotted
   data will cover 6 to 16 cells (keep the cell width consistent).
2. Record the data as a count of one each in the appropriate tally block.
3. Count the number of tallies in each block and record the total in the
   appropriate frequency block. Record the total of all tallies in sum
   block. Record twice the sum in the "2 × sum" block.
4. For each cell, add the accumulated frequency and the frequency of the
   cell above to the frequency of the appropriate cell and record the total
   as the accumulated frequency of the appropriate cell. (on the first
   tally cell at the top, the accumulated frequency will be equal to frequency, as the accumulated frequency and frequency of the cell above
   are both zero.) If no addition error is made, the last accumulated
   frequency figure will equal 2 × sum.

PRODUCTION MEASUREMENT RECORD

PART NO. 12345   DIMENSION 1.530-1.540   OPERATION NO. _____

TALLY

GAGE DIVISIONS	1	2	3	4	5	6	7	8	9	10	11	12	13	14	15	16	17	18	19	20	21	22	23	TOTAL
1.543 (MAX.)	X																							1
1.542	X	X																						2
1.541	X	X																						
1.540	X	X	X	X	X	X	X																	7
1.539	X	X	X	X	X	X	X	X	X	X	X	X	X											13
1.538	X	X	X	X	X	X	X	X	X	X	X	X	X	X	X									15
1.537	X	X	X	X	X	X	X	X																8
1.536	X	X	X																					3
1.535	X																							1
1.534																								
1.533																								
1.532																								
1.531																								
1.530 (MIN.)																								

FIGURE 2   Histogram plot.

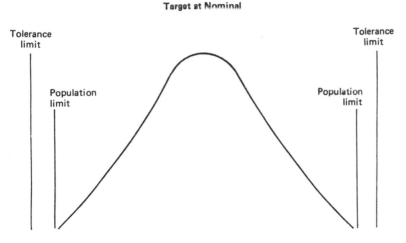

FIGURE 3   Ideal target at nominal.

5. For each cell, divide the accumulated frequency by 2 × sum and multiply the result by 100. Record the answer in the "% over" column. (Note that 25-, 50-, or 100-piece samples make this calculation very simple.)

6. On the grid, match each cell's horizontal line with the "% over" vertical line that corresponds to the "% over" figure. Plot a circle on the grid for all "% over" amounts less than 10 or greater than 90. Plot X's for "% over" amounts 10 to 90.

7. Fit a straight line through the X points on the grid and draw a line across the grid. If the X points do not create a reasonable straight line, the data are not applicable for analysis.

8. The target of the population is the horizontal cell boundaries/cell midpoint point, which corresponds to the intersection of the drawn diagonal straight line and the "50% over" vertical line.

9. Determine the points where the diagonal straight line crosses the left cell and right cell vertical lines on the edge of the grid and record the points in the left cell and right cell blocks. Subtract the right cell point from the left cell point and record as "difference."

10. The total spread extent is the difference times the established cell width. The percent of tolerance is the extent divided by the total tolerance.

11. Determine the percent over or the percent under for any selected point by locating the point on the cell boundaries/cell midpoint scale and project horizontally to the fitted straight line and then vertically upward to the "% over" scale or vertically downward to the "% under" scale.

12. For a visual picture of the population, project horizontally from the intersection on the grid of the straight line and the leftmost vertical A line to the A line in the tally area and place a slash mark on the tally area line. Repeat for vertical lines B, C, D, E, F, and G, matching them with their corresponding tally lines. Draw a line connecting

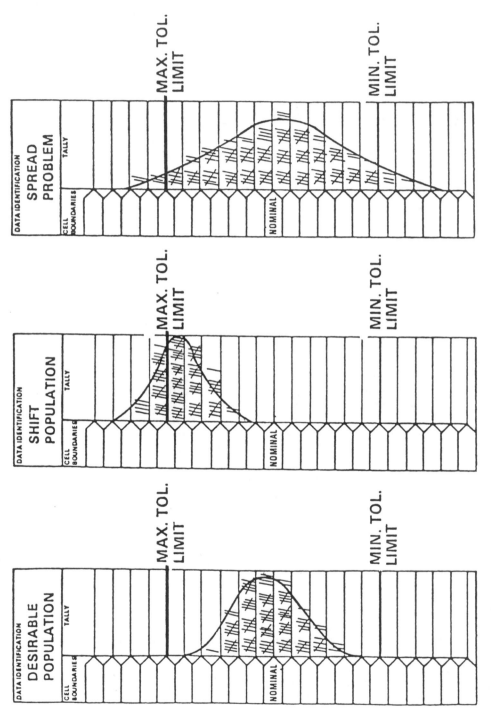

FIGURE 4   Shift and spread problems produce nonconforming items.

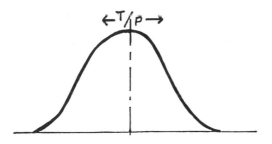

"Target" or center point of final population
caused by the established control points
of the identified significant factors

FIGURE 5   Control factors establish target
point.

the slash marks for a picture of population. When issuing process
reports such a picture is often very useful.

A fitted straight diagonal line across the grid indicates that the process is
operating in a normal manner. If the X points on the grid form a smooth curve
rather than a straight line, it is often an indication that one side of the population is being constrained. When such a situation exists, data transformation
(the square or the square root of the basic data) will usually result in a
straight line.

If tally points appear above or below where the fitted straight line passes
the edges of the grid, it is an indication that such data are from a different
population (different control points) than the population being studied. The
existence of such points questions the consistency of the process.

Visual examination of the S/T worksheet often indicates unexpected variations in the process. For example, a normal process will always have approximately equally spread tails on both sides of the target point. If one of these

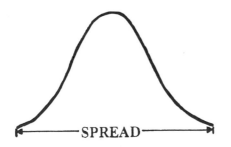

"Spread" within final population caused
by the random fluctuations of the
non-controlled factors

FIGURE 6   Noncontrolled factors cause
spread.

DATA IDENTIFICATION

P/N 23456
1.530 - 1.540 Dimension

PREPARED BY:

DATE:

CELL BOUNDARIES AB C D E F G	CELL MID POINT	FREQ.	ACCUM. FREQ.	% OVER
1.5425	1.542			
1.5415	1.541	1	1	1
1.5405	1.540	2	4	4
1.5395	1.539	7	13	13
1.5385	1.538	13	33	33
1.5375	1.537	15	61	61
1.5365	1.536	8	84	84
1.5355	1.535	3	95	95
1.5345	1.534	1	99	99
1.5335	1.533		106	100
1.5325	1.532			
1.5315	1.531			
1.5305	1.530			
1.5295				

SUM: 50   SUM: 100   %X SUM

MAX. TOL.

MIN. TOL.

LEFT CELL	15.6
RIGHT CELL	7.0
(MINUS) DIFFERENCE (EQUALS)	8.6

50% Over Point	= TARGET
1.5373	(EQUALS)

X. (TIMES)

CELL WIDTH
.001

= (EQUALS)

% OVER SPEC.	3
% UNDER SPEC.	0

Total Spread

EXTENT	% OF TOLERANCE
.0086	86

tails is cut off and does not exist, it is an indication that something not random is being done to the process, as tails will always exist in a normal process under control.

In a metal-working operation, a cutoff condition on the rework side of tolerance often indicates that the operator is taking time to inspect the work and is performing rework on those items that are outside tolerance. Such an operation creates nonproductive costs.

If the S/T worksheet indicates that the target point of the process is near nominal and the spread of the population is 80% or less than requirements, an "ideal" population exists. An ideal population will consistently produce all items to requirements provided that the target point is held near nominal and excessive spread does not suddenly happen.

It should be noted that personnel not completely familiar with statistical process control logic often fear that even when an ideal population exists, a "stray" item far outside the population limits might be produced. As such an item must be from a population with a different target point, and the designated controls establish the population's target point, such an item can be produced only when there has been a significant variation in an established control point. Such a variation is usually easily identified by the operation, and items produced under such a variation of control point should be removed from regular production.

However, even when an ideal population exists, it is necessary periodically to check the process to assure that neither the target point nor the spread of the process has changed significantly. The target control (T/C) sheet, shown in Fig. 8, is an ideal tool for this purpose. The instructions for use of the T/C sheet are as follows:

1. In the blocks on the left of the color area, record, as indicated, maximum tolerance point, half maximum tolerance point, nominal tolerance point, half minimum tolerance point, and minimum tolerance point. The green band area of the sheet is between the half tolerance points and the red area is outside the maximum and minimum tolerance points.
2. After setting up the process, measure and plot with circles the successive items produced.
3. Adjust the target point controls if two items within five are in the yellow band on the same side of the green band or if one item is in the red band.
4. Advance to the machine operation mode when five pieces in a row are in the green band.
5. Machine operation mode:
   a. Select a measurement frequency so that at least 20 items will be plotted prior to a necessary adjustment. (Be conservative at first and increase the frequency of checks as experience warrants.)
   b. Measure the item at the indicated frequency and if the measurement falls in:
      (1) The green band - Do not adjust and continue frequency measurement.
      (2) The yellow band - Measure the next piece. If this measurement is in:

FIGURE 7 Spread and target worksheet.

MACHINE _____ OPERATION _____ PART NUMBER _____

DEPARTMENT _____ SHIFT _____ DATE _____ SHEET NO. _____

MACHINE SET UP: (Record with 0)

Set machine and plot succesive measurement or one piece per load.

Make an adjustment if 2 within FIVE, pieces are in yellow on the same side of green or one is in the red.

Restudy spread if, with same adjustment, 2 within five are in yellow but on opposite sides of green.

Go to MACHINE OPERATION made when FIVE pieces in a row are in the green.

MACHINE OPERATION: (Record with check)

Plot a part measurement after every _____ part.*

If the measurement is in the:

Green   -Do not adjust and continue MACHINE OPERATION.
Red   -Adjust.
Yellow   -Measure next piece. If measurement is in the:
     Green   -Do not adjust and continue MACHINE OPERATION.
     Yellow   -On the same side as previous piece - ADJUST.
     Yellow   -On opposite side of previous piece - STOP.
           and restudy spread.
     Red   -ADJUST.

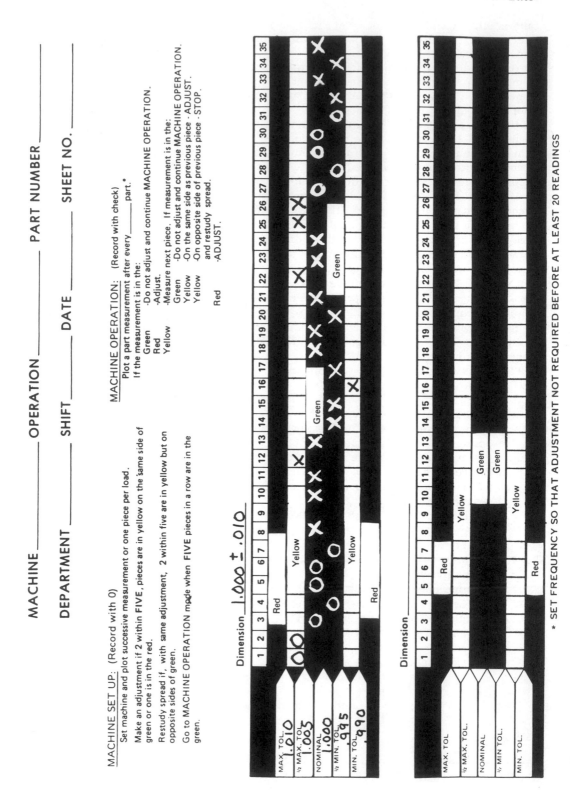

Dimension 1.000 ± .010

MAX. TOL. 1.010
½ MAX. TOL. 1.005
NOMINAL 1.000
½ MIN TOL. .995
MIN. TOL. .990

Dimension

MAX. TOL
½ MAX. TOL.
NOMINAL
½ MIN TOL.
MIN. TOL.

* SET FREQUENCY SO THAT ADJUSTMENT NOT REQUIRED BEFORE AT LEAST 20 READINGS

       (a)   The green band: Do not adjust—continue frequency measurement.

       (b)   The yellow band on the same side of nominal: Adjust.

       (c)   The yellow band on the opposite side of nominal: Stop the process and correct the spread situation.

       (d)   The red band: Adjust.

    (3)   The red band adjust.

The T/C sheet is not only an excellent method for process control but also furnishes documentary evidence that the process operated in control for the period indicated on the T/C worksheet. Such evidence is often very important in today's legal environment.

The target control sheet also eliminates many operator adjustments that are unnecessary and can cause nonconformance with the product. For example, if the operator does not recognize that the process produces a population with a spread that is not operator controlled, he or she can measure an item produced near tolerance and assume that a displaced target point exists. To correct the situation the operator makes an adjustment to the process which can actually cause the population to shift and produce nonconforming items. Actually, the near-tolerance item could be part of the spread in a population correctly centered. A decision-making format to adjust or not to adjust is shown in Fig. 9.

Unnecessary process adjustments can increase the spread of the process as well as causing nonconformances to exist. The target control sheet eliminates excessive adjustments and is also a control that the spread of the process has not increased significantly. This control is achieved by the requirement that the process has to be reexamined when two successive yellow band items, each on a different side of the green band area, are found.

When the S/T worksheet indicates that the spread of the population is greater than 80% of tolerance requirements, a spread problem exists. To correct a spread problem, additional factors not currently controlled must be identified and placed under control (see Fig. 10). It should be noted that inexactness in setting current controls could be the factor needing better control (e.g., an operator setting a control approximately instead of exactly).

An examination of the process usually reveals several possible significant candidates that are not being controlled. The inherent spread worksheet is a tool to determine the effect of controlling an additional factor when it is not convenient to control the factor exactly for the series of at least 25 items needed for a S/T worksheet determination.

Use for analysis the four-piece, three-piece, or two-piece inherent spread worksheet, depending on whether it is more convenient to control four, three, or two successive items at a time (the higher the number of items being controlled, the more precise are the results) (see Fig. 11). The instructions for the inherent spread worksheets are as follows:

1.   While holding the selected factor as nearly constant as possible, produce four, three, or two successive items.

2.   Measure the items and record the measurements on the horizontal line 1 in the data area of the inherent spread worksheet selected.

FIGURE 8   Target control sheet.

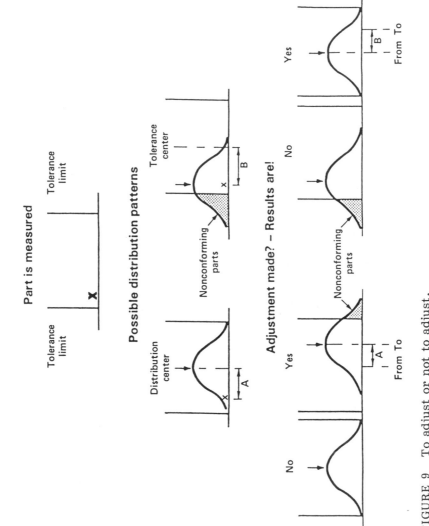

FIGURE 9   To adjust or not to adjust.

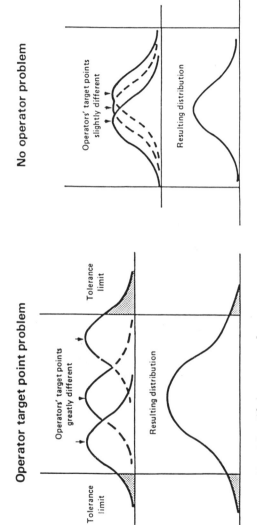

FIGURE 10 Identifying spread.

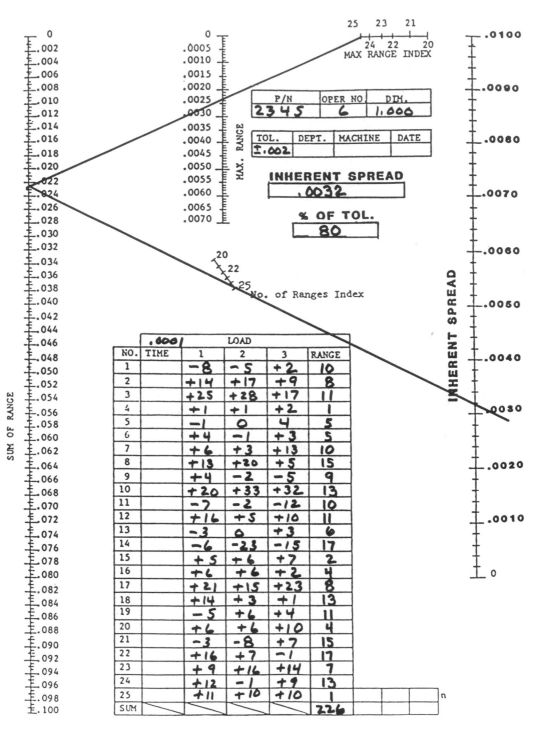

FIGURE 11   Inherent spread worksheet.

3. Repeat steps 1 and 2 for 24 additional time intervals and record the data on horizontal lines 2 to 25. Note that the control on the factor selected can vary between the different sets of time-interval readings but must be constant during the items produced in a set.

4. Determine, for each set of readings, the difference between the largest and the smallest reading within the set and record result in appropriate range block.

5. Add and record the sum of the 25 range blocks.

6. Indicate this sum on the sum of ranges scale and draw a straight line to the maximum expected range index number that corresponds to the number of individual ranges involved.

7. Eliminate any individual range that is greater than the amount indicated by where the straight line crosses the maximum range scale. If a range is eliminated, recalculate a new sum of ranges.

8. Indicate the final sum of ranges on the sum of ranges scale and draw straight line to the number of ranges index point that corresponds to the number of ranges in the sum of ranges. Extend the straight line through the inherent spread scale. The reading on the inherent spread scale is the inherent spread of the process if the selected factor was held constant.

If difficulty exists in identifying factors that might need control in the process, a "fishbone" diagram can be significant aid. To establish such a diagram:

1. Draw a long straight horizontal line to represent the process.

2. Establish a branch arrow to the horizontal line for each major contributor to the process and label each arrow.

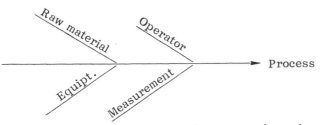

3. For each major contributor to the process branch arrow, establish branch arrows representing each significant factor of that function.

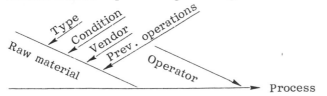

4. If necessary, establish smaller twigs to each significant factor's branch arrows, representing factors contributing to the significant factor involved.

The fishbone diagram creates a systematic analysis of all factors that contribute to a process and therefore can be very valuable in identifying factors that could have an important effect on the final product.

In analyzing a process, a special situation exists when the process produces only one item per run. Using statistical logic, it is recognized that the process itself can produce a population of items with a center point with a spread around the center point, and the single item produced must be part of that process population. Therefore, the single item itself could vary from its target point in relationship to the inherent spread of the process. The single-item worksheet is an excellent tool for determining the inherent spread of a single-item process when a series of similar single runs are produced by the same basic process (see Fig. 12).

1. For each of 25 different items produced one piece at a time on the basic process (e.g., different diameters on different pieces produced by the same basic Bridgeport Machine operation), record the part number, the requirement original target point, and a measurement after the first target point attempt.
2. Determine the difference between the target point and the resulting measurement. Record the difference as plus or minus.
3. Plot the 25 plus and minus differences on a S/T worksheet. If any individual readings are outside the indicated spread, eliminate these readings and replot.
4. The spread as indicated on the S/T worksheet is the inherent spread of the process. Expected variation of an individual item from its target point can be up to 50% of the indicated spread. (Example: If the S/T spread is 18 units, an individual piece to be produced by the process can vary up to ±9 units from the target point selected.)

If after an inherent spread analysis it is determined that it is not economically feasible to decrease a process inherent spread to at least 80% of requirements (e.g., new expensive equipment would be needed), contact the design engineering personnel for possible relaxation of the tolerance so that the economical 80% spread requirement can be achieved (see Fig. 13). If the tolerance width is increased to 125% of the minimum economically feasible spread, the 80% of tolerance requirement for the spread will be achieved. In almost all instances, the design engineers—if also trained in statistical logic—will agree to a reasonably extended tolerancing because they realize that such an extension will be to their advantage. (A successful process control program requires maximum cooperation between design engineering and manufacturing.)

In most industries a basic conflict usually exists between design engineering and manufacturing. The design engineer determines a desired requirement and then as a concession to manufacturing allows a tolerance around that desired requirement, although the desired requirement is always preferred. Manufacturing, on the other hand, usually considers all items within the tolerance limits equally good and therefore does not necessarily try to make all items at or near the desired requirement. This situation is especially true when the spread of the process is greater than the tolerance width because to prevent producing scrap items, manufacturing will target the process to the rework side of requirements (see Fig. 14). (Each item can be inspected and those outside requirements can be reworked back into requirements.) Such a rework technique has three serious drawbacks:

1. The 100% inspection and the rework operation are nonproductive costs.
2. Experience shows that isolated secondary rework operations often produce scrap which may or may not be identified.

EQUIPMENT <u>BRIDGEPORT</u>   OPERATION <u>DIA.</u>   DATE____

PART NUMBER	REQUIREMENT	TARGET POINT	MEASUREMENT	DIFFERENCE
12345	1.0000 ± .002	1.0000	1.0002	+ 2
43217	1.5000 ± .003	1.5000	1.4996	− 4
ETC.	ETC.	2.4000	2.4000	0
		.5000	.5009	+ 9
		3.2000	3.2001	+ 1
		1.0000	.9998	− 2
		2.0000	1.9996	− 4
		3.0000	3.0005	+ 5
		1.5000	1.5002	+ 2
		1.0000	1.0000	0
		.7500	.7503	+ 3
		.8750	.8754	+ 4
		1.0000	1.0002	+ 2
		2.0000	1.9998	− 2
		1.0000	1.0001	+ 1
		1.5000	1.5004	+ 4
		3.5000	3.5003	+ 3
		.7500	.7502	+ 2
		1.0000	.9995	− 5
		1.0000	1.0004	+ 4
		2.0000	2.0003	+ 3
		.8000	.8001	+ 1
		1.5000	1.5006	+ 6
		.9000	.8998	− 2
		1.4000	1.4000	0

Instructions:
1. For DIFFERENCE subtract Measurement from TARGET POINT and record as plus or minus. All measurements must be result of first target point attempt. Do not record rework measurements.
2. Plot plus and minus differences on Spread & Target Worksheet. If individual readings are outside of indicated spread, eliminate such readings and replot. Final spread on Worksheet is inherent spread of involved operation.

FIGURE 12   Single-item worksheet.

EQUIPMENT CAPABILITY (SINGLE ITEM)

DATA IDENTIFICATION

PREPARED BY:

DATE:

CELL BOUNDARIES	TALLY	CELL MID POINT	FREQ.	ACCUM. FREQ.	% OVER
+11.5					
+9.5	I		1	1	2
+7.5	I		1	3	6
+5.5	IIII		4	8	16
+3.5	IIIII II		7	19	38
+1.5	IIIII I		6	32	64
−0.5	III		3	41	82
−2.5	II		2	46	92
−4.5	I		1	49	98
−6.5				50	
−8.5					
−10.5					
	SUM 25		SUM 25	50	2X SUM

LEFT CELL	15.0	50% Over Point
RIGHT CELL	6.0	+.00015 = TARGET
(MINUS)		(EQUALS)
DIFFERENCE	9.0	CELL WIDTH .0002
(EQUALS)		

X (TIMES) = (EQUALS)

EXTENT .0018" Total Spread

% OVER SPEC.   % OVER SPEC.
% UNDER SPEC.   % UNDER SPEC.

% OF TOLERANCE

PERCENT OVER

PERCENT UNDER

Design engineer's desired dimension

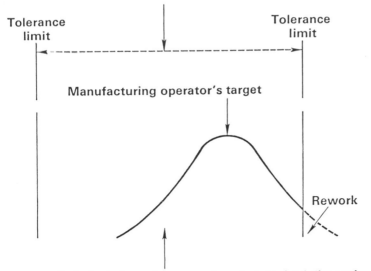

FIGURE 14 Target for rework.

3. Even if the inspection and rework operation is successful and no scrap items are produced, the targeting point near the rework side of tolerance produces the majority of conforming items near the extreme of tolerance rather than at the desired requirement (see Fig. 15).

Design engineers who understand statistical logic recognize the three drawbacks associated with too-narrow tolerances. In addition, they recognize that with compatible sufficiently wide tolerances, only the few items in the tails of the process populations will be near the tolerance limits. The majority of the items will be at or near the desired requirement provided that manufacturing has successful process control of the operations (a population targeted at or near nominal and spread less than 80% of tolerance).

Because extending a tolerance is a much more economical mode of operation, plus the fact that additional items will be produced near the desired requirement with only a few produced in the extended area, most design engineers are willing to increase tolerances as necessary if assured that the items will be manufactured in a statistical process control environment (see Fig. 16). Such an environment exists when manufacturing and design engineers work together under statistical logical concepts. However, if the design engineers desire additional assurance, they can require that "85% of all items produced must be in the middle half of tolerance." Because 87% of items in a population are within the middle half of a population's spread, a statistical process control system is required to achieve such a requirement economically.

FIGURE 13 Spread and target worksheet.

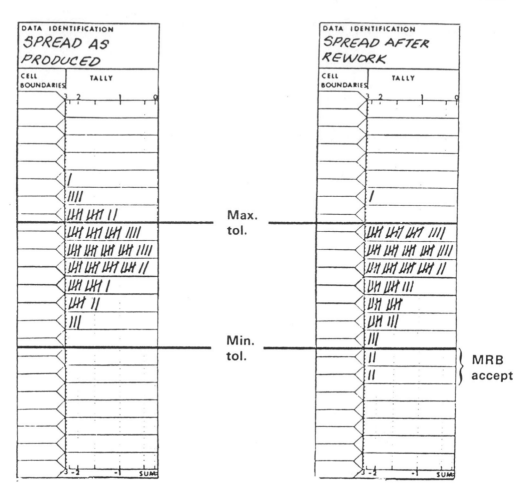

FIGURE 15   Population after rework.

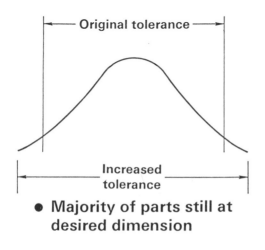

FIGURE 16   Population after increased tolerance.

CONCLUSION

The steps for establishing a successful process control program are:

1. Recognize that processes produce populations rather than individual items.
2. Establish a picture of the population.
3. If a shift problem exists, revise the established controls to correct the situation.
4. If a spread problem exists, select additional factors for control.
5. If it is not economically feasible to decrease spread to 80% or less of tolerance, ask the design engineers for an increased tolerance.
6. When an ideal population exists, use a target control worksheet for assurance that only conforming items are being produced.

A successful process control operation produces only confirming items. Excessive nonproductive inspection costs, rework costs, and scrap costs are eliminated. Quality can be achieved while decreasing costs when statistical logic is used.

11

PARETO ANALYSIS

FRANK H. SQUIRES

Squires Associates
Los Angeles, California

I. INTRODUCTION

The Pareto method of analysis may be the most valuable statistical tool in the armory of the quality engineer. In situations where it is applicable, and where it has not yet been applied, it is capable of producing substantial, even spectacular quality improvement almost overnight.

Pareto (1848—1923) was an Italian economist who, in the course of his studies, took note of the extreme maldistribution of incomes. He observed that the distribution of large incomes is confined to a few, whereas the small incomes are distributed among many.

It did not require an economist to make this simple observation; it could have been made by any intelligent layperson in ancient Babylon or modern America, but it seemed to Pareto that incomes were distributed in conformance with a general principle of maldistribution. He propounded a law which asserts, in effect, that while many may get, a few will get the most. More generally, while many (articles or individuals) may vary, a few will vary the most. For example:

1. "Only 10 to 20% of all juvenile delinquents account for at least 50% of all violent delinquent crimes"[1].
2. A study of medical malpractice conducted by the Rand Corporation found extreme maldistribution in malpractice. The sample taken consisted of 8000 doctors practicing over a 4-year period in the Los Angeles area. All 8000 being insured by one company, the data revealed that 46 doctors accounted for 10% of the claims. Less than 1% of the doctors were responsible for 10% of claims! The maldistribution was even more extreme in the matter of claims paid; the same 46 doctors were responsible for 30% of claims paid [2].
3. "Although there are some 15,000 brokers in the country, 100 to 200 of them do 95% of the total business" [3].

None of the above was referred to as what might be called a Pareto maldistribution, but that is what each of them is. Once the idea of maldistribution in human behavior—and in the incidence of defects in manufactured articles—has been grasped, it is possible to find almost daily examples in the press and in magazines. Our particular interest is in the maldistribution of types of defect in the manufacture of industrial products.

II. THE 10/90 LAW

Pareto's law has been popularized as the 10/90 law, according to which 10% of the types of defect that occur can be expected to account for 90% of the total defects. The few worst offenders, the 10%, have been named the "vital few," while the remainder have been categorized as the "trivial many." The goal of the Pareto method of inspection and analysis is to identify the vital few so that massive corrective action may be applied where it will do the most good, most quickly.

As an example, let Electronics Unlimited be manufacturing a transceiver, an assembly with many quality characteristics. It is the end of the month; management is holding the customary postmortem. There is particular anguish at the appalling number of defects generated during assembly: a total of 8000 defects for only 2000 completed units. Nice round numbers like these do not occur in practice but they will do for our purpose.

Management wants to know what is to be done about it. Production assures them that they are working vigorously at the problem; they are doing their best.

"I'm sure you're doing your best, but we have had numbers something like this for the last few months. What can we do to make a really substantial reduction? What's your plan?"

Production promises to continue its search for the causes of the many defects, but with more hope than assurance of success. It is not a new situation; as the president said, it has been bugging them for the last few months, ever since they had upped production to 2000 units a month. Actually, the defect problem is at an impasse.

Then the quality manager, fresh from a seminar, speaks up. "Let's try Pareto."

"Pareto! Who or what is Pareto?"

The quality manager explains the 10/90 law. It sounds a bit far out, but management agrees to give it a try. It is the more acceptable because the quality manager does not propose any additional expense, just a better use of existing resources.

Quality assurance makes the following preparations:

1. Compute the pre-Pareto average quality level. This is known already in our example: an average 4 defects per unit (8000/2000). In cases where it is not known, an effort must be made to arrive, at the least, at an estimate. Management, shop supervision, and the operators will all want to know what this new system has done for them. It seems obvious that when an effort at quality improvement is programmed, the starting condition should be known so that the improvement may be measured; yet such a necessary provision is overlooked all too frequently.
2. Code the defects; otherwise, the records will be confused by the propensity of inspectors to describe the same defect differently. Let us assume that quality assurance and production agree on 16 types of defect, numbered 1 through 16.

3. Compute the average cost of a rework. There will be a substantial reduction in rework cost. Unless steps are taken to record these savings, knowledge of them will be lost. Money not spent by production on rework is not recorded! Many quality improvement programs have failed to collect the recognition they have earned because of the failure to set up records of savings attributable to the program. The savings are typically a reduction in production costs; they do not appear in cost accounting records, except negatively by their absence.
4. Design an inspection tally sheet (see Fig. 1).
5. Design a Pareto worksheet (see Fig. 2).
6. Design a Pareto array (see Fig. 3).

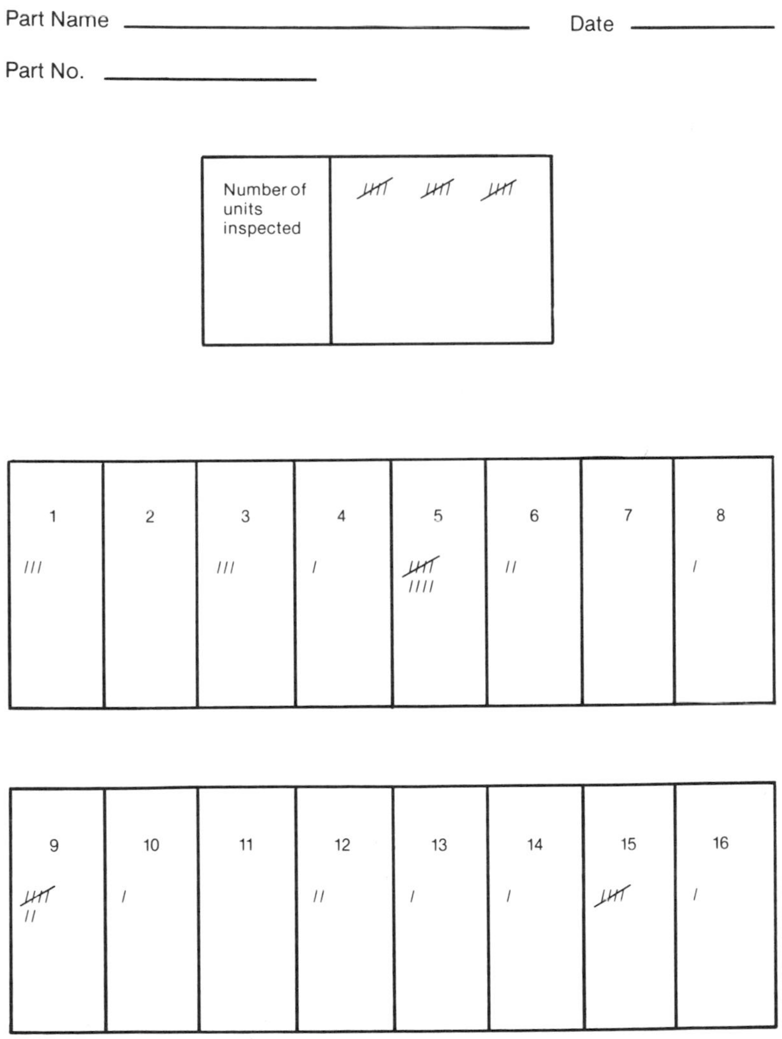

Part Name _____   Date _____

Part No. _____

Number of units inspected	⊥⊦⊤ ⊥⊦⊤ ⊥⊦⊤

1	2	3	4	5	6	7	8
///		///	/	⊥⊦⊤ ////	//		/

9	10	11	12	13	14	15	16
⊥⊦⊤ //	/		//	/	/	⊥⊦⊤	/

FIGURE 1   Inspection tally sheet (Pareto analysis).

Part Name _____   Date _____

Part No. _____

DEFECT by CODE No.	FREQUENCY	% of 8,000
1	640	8%
2	160	2%
3	80	1%
4	320	4%
5	2480	31%
6	160	2%
7	80	1%
8	80	1%
9	1920	24%
10	80	1%
11	80	1%
12	160	2%
13	80	1%
14	80	1%
15	1520	19%
16	80	1%
	8000	100%

FIGURE 2   Pareto analysis worksheet.

Preparations should include seminars for production supervisors, inspectors, and such members of management as may wish to "audit" the proceedings. The defect code should be blown up to poster size and displayed in the assembly area.

Right! It's the first day of the new month. The system goes into effect. Actually, nothing much will change; the defect code will be on display; the inspectors will be using the new tally sheets; everything else will go on as before. The main task in the first month is the collection of data.

Part Name ━━━━ ━━━━━ Date ━━━━━

Part No. ━━━━━━━━

DEFECT by CODE No.	FREQUENCY	% of 8000
5	2480	31%
9	1920	24%
15	1520	19%
1	640	8%
4	320	4%
2	160	2%
6	160	2%
12	160	2%
3	80	1%
16	80	1%
	8000	100%

FIGURE 3   Pareto array.

A. Use of the Tally Sheet

A given sheet is to be used only at one inspection station and only for one shift. It does not "travel" with the unit to the next station. Tally sheets are to be collected by quality engineers at the end of each shift for safekeeping.

Although it would be preferable that customary routine should be followed during the first month of data collecting, it is possible that production supervisors will react to the scores on the tally sheets. An inspection tally sheet at a particular station may look like Fig. 1. It is obvious that tallies are already stacking up on defect codes 5, 9, and 15. As a consequence, there will

be some "nibbling" at defects by corrective action during the month, as distinct from the massive assault that will be planned when the total score is in
and has been analyzed. This will have to be tolerated since, on principle, it
would be inadvisable to instruct supervisors to disregard obvious corrective
action. It will affect the anticipated results, but only slightly since such spor-
adic action can have only a limited effect. We are going to assume that the
numbers remain the same and that at the end of the month we are confronted
again with 8000 defects found and corrected on 2000 units.

A note on counting. The electronic product taken as an example is generally assembled by a line of operators with inspection stations interspersed.
As a consequence, each unit is counted at each inspection station and may be
counted more than once at one or more stations as the units are sent back for
rework. The end-of-the-month count on units is of finished units, fully signed
off by inspection. All defects on all tally sheets are counted. This will mean
that defects found on partially finished units left over from the previous month
will be counted in, but not defects found on partially assembled units in
the current month. It averages out in the long run and simplifies counting.

B. Month-End Pareto Analysis

The quality engineers, preferably a team of two, make the Pareto analysis:

1. Check the count of completed units with production control. A total
    of 2000 is agreed on.
2. Confirm that all the inspection tally sheets are in. Incidentally, these
    are mere tally sheets; the cause for rejection in each case will have been
    written on a tag attached to the rejected unit.
3. Transfer tallies from the inspection sheets to the Pareto worksheet.
    The frequency of occurrence of each of the 16 types of defect is en-
    tered; frequencies are summed to provide the total of 8000 defects;
    each frequency is transformed into a percentage of the total of 8000.
    Figure 2 represents the completed worksheet. Although these numbers
    have been fabricated for this example, they approximate numbers
    obtained from a similar product.
4. Transfer the scores to the Pareto array, placing them in rank order
    with the largest score in first place. Figure 3 represents a typical
    Pareto maldistribution. Only 3 of 16 types of defects are responsible
    for 74% of all defects. The "vital few" have been exposed. They are
    defect codes 5, 9, and 15.

C. The Presentation

Quality assurance is now in a position to demonstrate the maldistribution, which
it had assured management and production would occur. The opportunity for
an impressive "media" event should not be thrown away. Do not circulate
information of such a unique and startling character by means of the prosaic
interoffice memorandum.

Prepare a poster-size array with defect descriptions replacing the code numbers. Call a conference of managers and supervisors. Try to get the person
at the apex of the organizational pyramid; the first sight of a Pareto array is a
unique event in anybody's life. Unveil the array. Make no comment. It will
speak for itself!

The impact on management of the first presentation will determine to a considerable degree the support provided for the corrective action that is so clearly indicated. In this, as in every other application of quality assurance technology, the support of management is crucial.

D. Corrective Action

A campaign of corrective action can now be planned, guided by exact knowledge of the identity and magnitude of the maldistribution of defects. It is as though we knew the exact disposition and numbers of the enemy's forces. The Pareto does for industrial management what the breaking of the Japanese code did for U.S. commanders in World War II.

The search for the causes of defect codes 5, 9, and 15 is likely to take us into the areas of activity of several departments. A task force should be formed, composed of persons from quality assurance, operating production, production control, and engineering design. Their first task will be to categorize the probable causes of the defects coded 5, 9, and 15.

Are the defects, or any one of them, caused by sheer lack of manual skill on the part of the operators? If so, plans for retraining can be made and put into effect.

Are the defects caused by an apparent lack of motivation in the operators? If so, is it due to some malquality in first-line supervision? Or is it due to the nature of the small segments of work performed by individual operators, perhaps a seeming triviality which makes no demand on the intelligence? If the latter, the task force may be well advised to go back to Herzberg's *Work and the Nature of Man* [4].

If, on the contrary, the lack of motivation is more a matter of confusion caused by a complexity that the operators do not understand, the designers can be called upon to conduct short instructional sessions. It is, or should be, a prime requirement of good supervision that operators understand their tasks and the purpose and significance of them to the end product.

Are the defects caused by inadequate work instructions, or by ambiguities in the schematic diagrams used by assembly? If so, appropriate action can be taken.

When the causes for defects have been categorized as to worker or management responsibility, the costs of proposed corrective action must be weighed and considered. While the finer points of corrective action planning are being worked on, the shop will continue assembling units. There will be a spontaneous reaction to these first revelations of Pareto; the information alone is a powerful motivator (see below). Although task force plans may subsequently change the direction of some phases of the spontaneous effort, the effort itself should receive full technical and moral support from members of the task force.

III. THE PARETO ARRAY AS MOTIVATOR

The Pareto array is a potent motivator. It presents line workers with a picture of the defect situation so startlingly clear that it inspires in them an irresistible impulse to participate in the plans for corrective action. Management earnestly desires "participation" and the motivation within the line workers to participate. Nothing does it so well as the Pareto. Do not waste the opportunity.

Assemble the line workers in a conference room. Use the blown-up array with the defect descriptions. Let the presentation be made jointly by one member each from production and quality assurance. Their rank is important. They must not be so high up that they are unknown to the line workers; they must be persons to whom the assemblers can talk freely while still knowing that they have enough authority to get done what is agreed upon.

There will be plenty of suggestions. Keep a record of all of them; indeed, suggestions may be put up on a blackboard and tallied as certain suggestions are repeated. A Pareto maldistribution of suggestions may occur to the amusement and interest of the group of operators and managers.

A. The Production Quality Statistic

Month by month the disproportionate contribution made by the vital few will diminish. Total defects will be reduced as a consequence, and so will average defects per accepted unit. This statistic—average defects per unit—is not a measure of product quality; the defects are all corrected. But it is a measure of the ability of production to achieve quality standards. As such, it should be displayed so that production may see what improvement has been made, and take satsifaction in it.

For this purpose a chart should be prepared on which average defects per unit are plotted against time in months. It, too, should be blown up to poster size and hung where everyone in the assembly area can see it. It should be simple as billboard posters are simple—conveying a single message, comprehensible at a glance.

The chart, showing average defects per unit versus time in months, may be called the progress chart. In addition to indicating the improvement in the production effort, it serves a second important function. In time, perhaps in 8 months or so, the descending curve will flatten out. When it has remained constant for several months with only slight perturbations, it is an indication that the system has stabilized.

The "system" is the product and the forces endeavoring to bring it into the ideal zero-defects condition. The "forces" are management's skill in planning, the dexterity of the operators, the acuity of the inspectors, and the efficacy of quality assurance technology—in this case the application of the Pareto principle. The leveling off of the progress curve indicates that the existing combination has pushed the defect rate down as far as it is able.

Let us say that the curve has leveled off at 0.4 defect per unit. This is as far as the Pareto-driven effort will go, that is, the effort powered only by the Pareto system and not involving any additional expenditure on equipment or personnel. Management may now decide whether to "live with" the average of 0.4 defect per unit or make an effort to reduce it still further. If the latter, a radical change or changes will have to be made. It may not be worth it, but that is an additional advantage of the Pareto system—it presents management with results which indicate clearly that a choice must be made. The choice, of course, may be not to change.

If in our hypothetical case the latter course is agreed on, do not relax in the collection and analysis of data. Least of all, do not stop plotting the monthly average defects per unit.

B. The Trivial Many

As the months succeed one another and as the high scores of the vital few are cut down to size, there will be a tendency to apply the same forceful procedure to the trivial many. Don't! Or, at least, be careful; it is easy to run into a condition of diminishing returns.

C. Pareto-Promoted Cost Reduction

Let us assume that the average cost of rework in the assembly area was found to be $5. Now we are at the end of the second month; production has concentrated on correcting the causes of defects 5, 9, and 15. Total defects are down by 500. The savings are, then, $2500. This is money not spent on 500 reworks which we assume would have been necessary had the Pareto system not been installed. It does not appear in cost accounting records. Cost accounting is busy enough keeping a record of money spent without worrying about money not spent.

Quality assurance should circulate this information for everyone's gratification. It would be an excellent occasion for congratulations to production.

Let us assume that we are now at the end of the third month of Pareto. Total defects are down by a further 300. The savings are not computed from the previous month, but from the starting month's figure of 8000 reworks at $5 each. Hence the saving for the third month is $4000 (800 defect reworks at $5 each).

It is essential for the success of any quality improvement program—Pareto or otherwise—that the quality assurance staff devise a method of demonstrating the dollar benefit to the company, since it so frequently is a reduction of production expense not recorded by orthodox methods of cost accounting.

IV. OTHER APPLICATIONS

The possible applications of Pareto are almost without number. The principle may be applied in any situation comprised of articles or persons subject to the expectation that each will conform to prescribed quality standards.

A. Absenteeism

Absenteeism is becoming more prevalent. Why it should be so is a difficult question to answer, but the Pareto may help you to minimize it. In a hypothetical example, consider a section of 20 workers. In a month of 20 days, 400 operator days should be provided. However, in the month considered there were 32 days of absence distributed among the whole group—an absentee rate of 8%.

A few persons are the worst offenders; they have been spoken to on several occasions. But how much worse are they? In Pareto terms, the maldistribution magnitude for being late among the 20 people is unknown.

The daily attendance records for the month are consulted. The record for each person is established and days late for each is expressed as a percentage of the total of 400 workdays. The results are arranged as shown in Fig. 4.

There are the worst offenders: Jack, Charlotte, and Jane. We anticipated that these three would be somewhere near the top, but not for one second would we have guessed that between them they would account for 63% of all absences.

Confronted by these results, we may feel that we have been too tolerant—especially in the case of Jack. The extreme disproportion may be as much of a surprise to Jack, Charlotte, and Jane. None see their own misbehaviour too clearly. Indeed, these three may be shocked into an attempt to better attendance when shown the Pareto breakdown. Should it be posted in the work area? It might have a salutary effect, not only by showing relative attendance, but also by the demonstration of the ability of management to present such information in a manner so immediately comprehensible.

<u>Absentee Report</u>

Working days in month....20

Personnel................20

Total work days.........400

Total days absent........32

Absentee rate............8%

Name	Days Absent	% of 32
Jack	9	28%
Charlotte	6	19
Jane	5	16
William	2	6
Violet	2	6
Candice	2	6
Aloysius	2	6
Juan	1	3
Kim	1	3
Alice	1	3
Ronald	1	3
	32	99%

Jack, Charlotte and Jane account for 63% of

all absences, although they are only 3 out

of 20. A typical Pareto maldistribution.

FIGURE 4

B. Suppliers

Large corporations have many suppliers. Among many suppliers, there are
bound to be a few who cause a disproportionate amount of trouble by virtue
of poor quality or late deliveries or both. What may be done about late
deliveries?

Design a log for use at the receiving dock. As each lot arrives enter supplier's name, part name and number, quantity. Enter a score of 0 (zero) for
delivery arriving on the day promised, a score of minus 1, 5, or whatever for
days early, a score of plus 1, 10, or whatever for days late.

At the end of the month, compute average days late per lot for each supplier. Present the results in a Pareto array. To arrive at comparative performance, present each average as a percentage of the sum of the averages.

The total of days late for each supplier might be presented as a percentage of the sum of all days late. But this will not do because suppliers provide different numbers of lots. Should poor deliveries be compensated by early deliveries? No, because what we require is delivery on time. Early deliveries might cause a warehousing problem. Action to be taken will have to be suited to circumstances; the worst supplier in terms of delivery may be a sole supplier! But it is well to let suppliers to whom we address complaints know that we are talking from numbers and not from a mere impression.

C. Customer Accounts

A company will surely know which are its best accounts, but unless it runs a Pareto distribution of dollar sales it is unlikely that it will know exactly how few contribute so much. The knowledge is important in that it should dictate priorities in the assignment of salespeople and engineers.

D. Equipment

In a large shop there is bound to be a maldistribution of downtime among the various pieces of manufacturing equipment. Shop supervisors and production control people are likely to know which machines are down the most, but unless Pareto-style records have been kept and analyzed, the extent of the maldistribution will not be known. When not known, maldistributions are almost always underestimated, leaving planners with too optimistic an outlook.

In a particular case, 18 presses were engaged in the mass production of plastic parts, three shifts daily, each day of the month. In a month of 30 days there were available, or should have been, 12,960 machine hours (30 times 24 times 18).

It was explained to management and the people in the shop what was going to be done. They were invited to guess which machines were the worst on downtime and what percentage of total downtime they were accountable for. They were right on the machines, but woefully short on the percentages.

All that was required was a simple log recording unscheduled downtime in hours. It was found that 2 of 18 presses were responsible for 67% of the unscheduled downtime. It was a shock. It prompted the expenditure of a considerable sum on repairs, a sum quickly recovered when the machines went back on line.

E. Decision Making

There is much advice on decision making given in current management literature. Yet only rarely does one find any reference to the Pareto system, or to "10/90," or to the "vital few." Nevertheless, the Pareto principle of maldistribution and the method of measuring it is a superior decision-making aid. It should be in the kit of procedures of every decision maker.

Quantity, cost, and quality are the three major concerns of management. (All are quantifiable; quality is the relative absence of defects.) All are composed of many elements or characteristics subject to maldistribution. All need Pareto.

Who was the man whose name has become a household word in quality assurance? Vilfredo Frederico Damaso Pareto, the son of a Genoese nobleman, was born in Paris in 1848. His father, a fiery advocate of a united Italy, had fled Genoa to save his head from those opposed to unification. The family returned to Italy in 1858. Unification was on the way; a united Italy came into being in 1861 except that it did not include Rome. Italy annexed it in 1870.

Vilfredo studied engineering and was awarded a doctorate in 1869. He practiced engineering and occupied several important posts, including general manager of Italian Iron Works. Industrial experience and the social unrest of the times turned his mind to economics and sociology. By the early 1890s he was well known as an economist. His stature in this field is evidenced by his inclusion in *Ten Great Economists* by Joseph A. Schumpeter [5]. By this time, the early 1890s, he was in trouble with the authorities. His father had agitated for unification; Vilfredo was loud in condemnation of the government of a united Italy. Schumpeter writes: "He saw nothing but incompetence and corruption. He fought with impartial fury the governments which succeeded one another." He went so far that he became known as an "ultraliberal." In those days it meant an uncompromising advocate of laissez-faire, the exact opposite of the sense in which we use it now to indicate an opponent of what is left of laissez-faire. He had made up his mind that he must get out of Italy and had decided on Switzerland, when he was offered the chair of economics in the faculty of law at Lausanne University.

He succeeded Leon Walrus (another of Joseph Schumpeter's Ten Great Economists). The analytical economics he developed were built on foundations laid by Walrus [6]. It is interesting that his work on a particular theory of value, coupled with F. Y. Edgeworth's development of indifference curve analysis, is said to have been "the foundation upon which modern welfare economics is based" [6].

But in contrast, he was also claimed by Mussolini as a contributor to the theory of Fascism. This was work Pareto did on elites. He had observed that in the Italy of his time, and in the history generally, regardless of which party or which class was in power, the rulers were an elite minority within the party or class. Pareto spoke somewhat humorously of the "circulation of elites" as though it were a political principle [5]. Mussolini conferred senatorial rank on Pareto, but he would have none of it; he was happy to see some order restored, but he deplored the methods.

It was from some work he did on the maldistribution of incomes that we get our theory of industrial maldistribution. His studies led him to "postulate what became known as Pareto's law, that whatever the political or taxation conditions, income will be distributed in the same way in all countries. He noted that the distribution of incomes is heavily concentrated among the lower income groups, and asserted that the number of incomes fell proportionately with the size of income [6]. The source adds: "Pareto's law has not, in fact, proved valid in its strict sense." This is in reference to the distribution of incomes; the comment does not invalidate our use of Pareto's law as it applies to the industrial situation; we are not looking for exactitude.

Knowledge of this fascinating person might have been confined to students of economics theory were it not for the fortunate recognition by J. M. Juran [7, 8] of the applicability of the principle of income maldistribution to the industrial quality scene.

To summarize: Look for maldistribution wherever articles and/or people are many, and where the circumstances dictate conformance to prescribed standards of quality or to acceptable modes of conduct.

REFERENCES

1. Paul Strasburg, Associate Director, Vera Institute of Justice, quoted in the September 1978 issue of *Psychology Today*.
2. RAND Corporation, reported in *Psychology Today*, September 1978.
3. J. C. Goulden, *The Million Dollar Lawyers*, Putnam, New York, 1977.
4. F. Herzberg, *Work and the Nature of Man*, World Publishers, Chicago, 1966.
5. J. A. Schumpeter, *Ten Great Economists*, Oxford University Press, New York, 1951.
6. Bannock, Baxter, and Rees, eds., *The Penguin Dictionary of Economics*, Viking Penguin, New York, 1972.
7. J. M. Juran et al., "Pareto, Lorenz, Cournot, and Bernoulli," *Industrial Quality Control*, October 1960.
8. J. M. Juran, "Universals in Management Planning and Controlling," *The Management Review*, 1954, pp. 748–761.

FURTHER READING

Dodge, H. F., and H. G. Romig, *Sampling Inspection Tables*, 2nd ed., Wiley, New York, 1967.

Grant, E. L., and R. S. Leavenworth, *Statistical Quality Control*, 5th ed., McGraw–Hill, New York, 1980.

Ishikawa, K., *Guide to Quality Control*, Asian Productivity Organisation, Tokyo, 1976.

Juran, J. M., Editor-in-Chief, *Quality Control Handbook*, 3rd ed., McGraw–Hill, New York, 1974.

Peach, P., *Quality Control for Management*, Prentice–Hall, Englewood Cliffs, N.J., 1964.

Shewhart, W. A., *Economic Control of Quality of Manufactured Product*, D. Van Nostrand Company, Princeton, N.J., 1931.

Shewhart, W. A., in *Statistical Method from the Viewpoint of Quality Control*, W. E. Deming, ed., Lancaster Press, Lancaster, Pa., 1945 reprint.

12

PROCESS CAPABILITY STUDIES

MAE-GOODWIN TARVER

Quest Associates Ltd.
Park Forest, Illinois

I. INTRODUCTION

A. Definitions

Process: The combination of Men, Machines, and Materials used to manufacture or fabricate a product [1].

Capability: The capacity or ability to reproduce product characteristics
  such as mass, dimension, or the presence, absence, or degree of a
  quality attribute.

Process capability study: The systematic study of a process to determine
  its ability to meet specifications or tolerance limits under normal operating conditions (NOC).

Normal operating conditions (NOC): Conditions that occur when a plant or
  manufacturing process is operating under approved instructions, using
  specified raw materials, and trained, experienced operators; it includes
  different operators, different lots of raw materials or components, tool
  wear, or other factors that may be affected by time.

Machine capability study: The systematic study of a machine under somewhat controlled conditions to determine its inherent variation; machine
  adjustments are not made, usually a single operator is used, and a single
  lot of raw material or components is used [2]. For this reason, machine
  capability studies are usually confined to equipment development shops.

Natural tolerance: The inherent or natural variation of a process when it
  is in a steady state (state of control); numerically, it is expressed as
  ±3 standard deviations or ±3σ.

B. Purpose of Capability Studies

To keep satisfied customers, producers must meet customer quality requirements. A very important requirement is that significant quality characteristics
be held within specified tolerance limits. The major purpose of process capability studies, therefore, is to discover whether a process is in a steady state
(state of control), and if it is, whether the product will meet the customer's
quality requirements.

It is also important to note that process performance is not the same as process capability [3]. Process capability means that only "natural" or inherent variation is introduced into the process by extraneous (and sometimes uncontrolled) factors such as humidity, temperature, and so on.

When a process is in a steady state, no extraneous factors are "rocking" the process; only "natural" process variation is present. When this state of control is encountered, the observed process variation is considered to be *economically* irreducible under the current operating conditions of the process.

C. Scope of the Method

Process capability studies have a wide range of application in industry. Problems in almost all industries will fall into one or more of the following categories:

1. *Quality*: too many defective units being produced
2. *Cost*: excessive scrap, rework, or repair, low yields, and so on
3. *Lack of information*: process trends, effect of new materials, methods, tooling, and so on
4. *Engineering problems*: design, specifications, quotations, and so on

The concept of analyzing process variation can be used to solve problems in all industries. The exact method used for this purpose, however, will be industry dependent. For example, high-speed, continuous operations are easily studied using the control chart system because groups of samples can be drawn from the process under normal operating conditions over a long period of time. Job-shop operations, on the other hand, run one product line for a short period of time and then change over to another product line. The usual control chart may not be appropriate for such operations. Special methods for analyzing process variation must also be used for the process industries because they produce relatively homogeneous liquids, slurries, and pulps. Multiple samples per time period may not be appropriate under these circumstances.

D. Questions Answered by Capability Studies

The information obtained from each study must answer the following questions [3, 4]:

Was the process in a state of control during the study?
Does the process meet the specified tolerance? If not, can it do so by centering the process average on the nominal value?
Is the process inherently capable of meeting the specified tolerance? If not, is it economically feasible to reduce the process spread?

All capability studies must be carefully planned to answer the foregoing questions. Data must be collected in a systematic manner to answer them; otherwise, invalid information will result.

E. Short-Run Versus Long-Run Studies

There are two generally used methods for collecting information from continuous processes: (1) short-run capability studies, where a large number of consecutive product units are drawn; and (2) long-run studies, where samples are drawn from the process over a long period of time, a small number of product units appearing in each sample. The first method gives an instantaneous picture (or snapshot) of process variation and that will probably be the smallest variation which can be expected from the process. The second method gives a much more accurate picture of process variability since it exposes the process to factors that may disturb its stability and can result in increased process variation. Examples of each, together with their advantages and disadvantages, will be discussed in subsequent sections of this chapter.

Regardless of the type of capability study to be run, four steps are required [3]:

1. *Collecting data*: determining how many sample units are needed and the frequency of sampling
2. *Plotting the data*: using histograms or control charts
3. *Interpreting data patterns*: diagnosing any indicated quality problems
4. *Isolating and removing assignable causes*: uncovering the inherent process variation

II. SHORT-RUN CAPABILITY STUDIES

A. Planning the Study

Draw consecutive sample units from the production stream whenever possible. If the sample size selected is too large to assure consecutive product units, draw them a few at a time over as short a time period as possible. The sampling frequency must be short enough to prevent "assignable causes" from enlarging the natural variation of the process under study. Some authors recommend tying a sample size to the production rate as follows [2, 5]:

1. If the process is running at 200 units per hour or more, sample 200 consecutive units.
2. If the process is running less than 200 units per hour, sample the equivalent of 1 hour's production but never less than 50 product units.

There is, however, a second way of selecting an appropriate sample size. For example, if you wish to have 95% assurance of including at least 95% of the possible product measurements within the *maximum* and *minimum* values found in the sample, Table 1 shows that at least 93 sample units are required. For this reason, 100 sample units were drawn from the process in the example shown for the short-run studies.

B. Example of a Short-Run Study

The short-run capability study will be illustrated using a blow-molding process for plastic bottles. The quality characteristic under discussion is the lip outside diameter (OD). A special type of closure will not fit properly if this dimension is too large or too small. The specification for this dimension had tentatively been set by the designer at 0.825 ± 0.014 in. One hundred consecutive bottles were sampled from mold 9 and the lip OD was measured on each of the samples. The "raw" data are shown in Fig. 1. Table 2 (p. 184) illustrates a method for calculating the number of cells and the cell width for frequency distributions. Using these methods, a frequency distribution compiled from the raw data of Fig. 1 is shown in Fig. 2, and the histogram (together with the *tentative* specification limits) is shown in Fig. 3. In Fig. 3 note that a small part of the last step lies above the upper specification limit.

TABLE 1   Selection of Sample Size for Short-run Capability Studies*

X% of Measurements Within Sample MAX and MIN	Number of Samples Required to Include at Least X% of Measurements within Sample Extremes with this Assurance (B)			
	99.7%	99%	95%	90%
99.7%	3100	2460	1757	1439
99	834	662	473	387
95	163	130	93	76
90	80	63	45	37
85	52	41	29	24

*Note: This table was calculated using the concepts given in Reference 6 and the Chi-square formula given in Reference 7.

Figure 4 shows the lip OD cumulative frequencies (from Fig. 2) plotted on normal probability paper. A straight line was eye-fitted to these plotted points between the 10 to 90% section of the graph. Because all of the points cluster closely about this line of best fit, for practical purposes the OD dimension data are considered to be normally distributed.*

Based on this assumption of normality, the long-run percentage of bottles expected to be outside the *tentative* specification limits for lip OD is calculated as follows, using information from Figs. 1 and 2:

Step 1:

$$K_H = \frac{\text{max. spec.} - \bar{X}}{S} = \frac{0.839 - 0.8254}{0.0049} = +2.78$$

$$K_L = \frac{\text{min. spec.} - \bar{X}}{S} = \frac{0.811 - 0.8254}{0.0049} = -2.94$$

Step 2: Look up in Grant and Leavenworth [9] (or any other table of the cumulative areas under the normal curve) the equivalent areas (E.A.) for +2.78 and for −2.94 [9]. You will get

$$K_H \approx 0.9973$$

$$K_L \approx 0.0016$$

Step 3:

% Inside spec. = $100(K_H$ E.A. $- K_L$ E.A.$) = 100(0.9973 - 0.0016 = 99.57\%$

Step 4:

% Outside spec. = $100 - \%$ inside $= 100 - 99.57 = 0.43\%$

---

*A more exact statistical method for this purpose is the chi-square goodness-of-fit test.

QUALITY CHARACTERISTIC *LIP OD (INCHES)* PART NO. ~~O 5-~~ ~~om~~
PLANT NO. *1400* LINE NO. *1A* DATE *4/9/80* NO. SAMPLES *100*
COMMENTS *MOLD #9 — LIP DROOP* INSPECTOR *Mary Doe*
SAMPLE SIZE (N) *100 BOTTLES*
MAX MEASUREMENT *0.838* MIN MEASUREMENT *0.814 in* RANGE *0.024 in*

1	0.822	0.823	0.820	0.824		
2	.818	* .838	.826	.824		
3	.820	.835	.816	.828		
4	.834	.826	.831	.816		
5	.819	.827	.826	.822		
6	.826	.825	.832	.833		
7	.816	.829	.819	.833		
8	.828	.824	.820	.817		
9	.833	.823	.827	.819		
10	* .814	.832	.830	.829		
11	.824	.822	.832	.827		
12	.823	.825	.821	.824		
13	.826	.825	.829	.833		
14	.823	.823	.827	.825		
15	.826	.829	.825	.826		
16	.823	.825	.828	.828		
17	.821	.817	.816	.819		
18	.825	.825	.825	.822		
19	.827	.824	.825	.827		
20	.827	.825	.820	.824		
21	.826	.822	.835	.834		
22	.818	.831	.824	.830		
23	.829	.822	.824	.830		
24	.826	.828	.831	.824		
25	.833	.820	.835	.823		

SPECIFICATIONS 0.825 ± 0.014 inch

FIGURE 1   Short-run capability study: process data sheet.

In addition to the information above, Juran suggests calculating a capability index (CI) [1]:

$$CI = \frac{6\sigma \text{ spread of process}}{\text{specification spread*}}$$

$$CI = \frac{0.0296}{0.028} = 1.06$$

---

*Juran's ratio is the inverse of this one.

NAME John Doe   DATE 5/5/80

DISTRIBUTION Mold #9 - LIP OD

CELL NO.	CELL BOUNDARIES LOWER	UPPER	CELL MID-PT.	TALLY OF OBSERVATIONS ++++ = 5	(1) d	(2) f	(3) Σfd	(4) Σfd²	% REL. f	% CUM. f
1	0.8125	.8155	0.814			-4	1	-4	16	1%	1%
2	.8155	.8185	.817	++++ |||	-3	8	-24	72	8	9
3	.8185	.8215	.820	++++ ++++		-2	11	-22	44	11	20
4	.8215	.8245	.823	++++ ++++ ++++ ++++ ++++	-1	23	-23	23	23	43
5	.8245	.8275	.826	++++ ++++ ++++ ++++ ++++ ||	0	27	0	0	27	70
6	.8275	.8305	.829	++++ ++++ |||	1	13	13	13	13	83
7	.8305	.8335	.832	++++ ++++		2	11	22	44	11	94
8	.8335	.8365	.835	++++		3	5	15	45	5	99
9	.8365	.8395	.838			4	1	4	16	1	100
						100	-19	273		
						Σf=N	Σfd	Σfd²		

(subtotals in Σfd column: -75, +54)

m = Cell Interval = 0.003

C = Assumed center = 0.826

$$\bar{X} = C + m\left(\frac{\Sigma fd}{N}\right) = 0.826 + 0.003\left(\frac{-19}{100}\right) = 0.826 - 0.00057 = 0.8254 \text{ in.}$$

$$S = m\sqrt{\frac{\Sigma fd^2 - \frac{(\Sigma fd)^2}{N}}{N-1}} = 0.003\sqrt{\frac{273 - \frac{(-19)^2}{100}}{100-1}} = 0.003\sqrt{\frac{273 - 3.61}{99}} = 0.003 \times \sqrt{2.7211} =$$

$$0.003 \times 1.6496 = 0.0049$$

Natural Tolerance (Process Capability) = $\pm 3\sigma = \pm 3(0.0049) = \pm 0.0148$

Limits for Individual Units = $\bar{X} \pm 3\sigma = 0.8254 \pm 0.0148 = 0.811 - 0.840$ (Rounded)

FIGURE 2   Short-run capability study: frequency distribution of data.

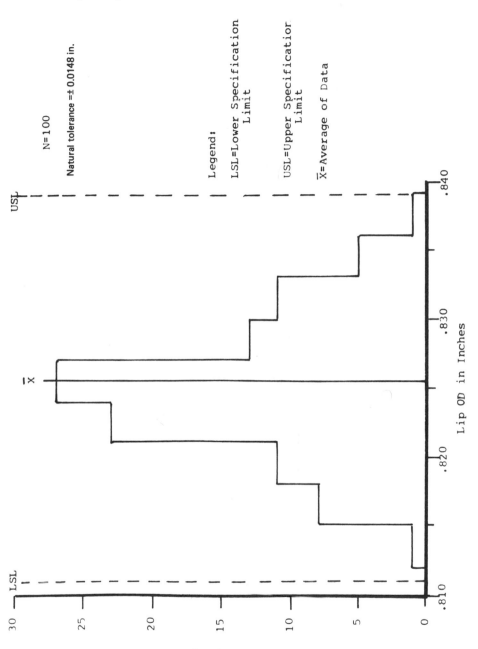

FIGURE 3   Histogram of lip OD data.

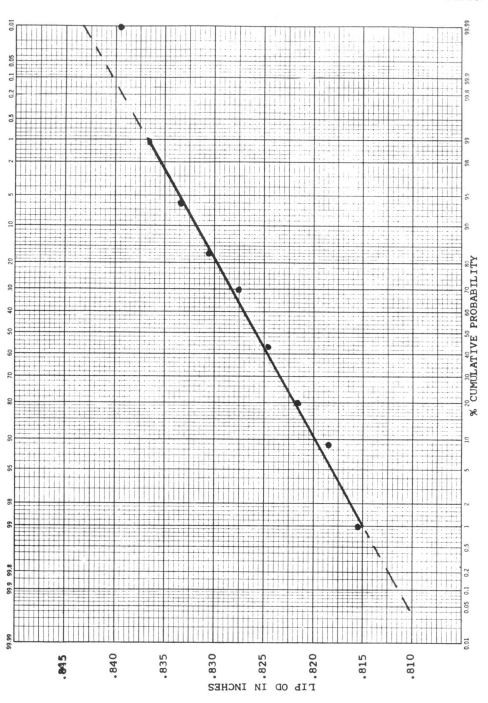

FIGURE 4   Normal probability plot: lip OD.

The interpretation of the capability index is as follows:

CI	Comments
0.75	Excellent process; material substitutions can be made when necessary; quality control cost will be low.
Above 0.75 but less than 1.00	Process okay; be cautious about material substitutions; tight quality control required usually.
Above 1.00	Process not adequate for specification band; reduce variation or widen specifications

The capability index in this example was 1.06; one of two decisions must be made before proceeding to a long-run capability study:

1. Work on the process to reduce its variation.
2. Widen the tentative specification limits.

The cost-effective solution, in this instance, was to widen the tentative specification limits from ±0.014 to ±0.018, a change of about 1.6σ. This was less costly than repairing molds or making new ones, since the specifications were tentative and were based only on designer experience.

III. LONG-RUN CAPABILITY STUDIES

A. Planning the Study

This type of capability study must be run over a long enough period of time to include the effects of different operators, different lots of materials or components, and so on. The information resulting from a long-run capability study can be used for many purposes:

1. Establishing setup procedures
2. Appraising the adequacy of product specifications
3. Troubleshooting process problems
4. Improving the process by eliminating assignable causes of variation

In planning long-run studies, the first questions that must be asked are: (1) Are the measurements reliable? and (2) How many sample units are required per subgroup? It is also assumed at this point that the measurements are variables data (dimensions, mass, etc.) and that process variation is much greater than that of the measuring process.

The number of samples per subgroup depends on the size of the shift from the process average that you wish to detect. The information shown in Table 3 is a guide for selecting subgroup size. A subgroup size of five sample units is often used for convenience, but its use is not obligatory. The cost of obtaining and inspecting each sample unit must also be considered. If these costs are very high, fewer samples per subgroup are used.

At least 20 to 25 subgroups are selected from the process. The frequency of sampling subgroups depends on how rapidly the process average shifts. A process whose average changes rapidly must be sampled more frequently than a process whose average changes slowly. The frequency of sampling is

TABLE 2   Guidelines for Forming a Frequency Distribution—
Variables Data

Guidelines	Example (From Fig. 1)
1. Calculate RANGE of the data: $R = MAX - MIN$	1. $R = 0.838 - 0.814 = \underline{0.024}$

2. Calculate the ideal number of cells [8] :
 	
    $K = 1 + 3.322 \ (Log_{10} N)$
	2. $K = 1 + 3.322 \ (Log_{10} \ \overline{100}) =$
	
	     $1 + 3.322 \ (2) \quad \underline{8}$

3. Calculate the cell width, m: $m = R/K$	3. $m = 0.024/8 = \underline{0.003}$

4. Decide upon cell boundaries of <u>first</u> cell	4. a. MIN = $\underline{0.314}$
	
	     b. Lower cell limit =
	        $0.814 - (0.003/2) =$
	        $0.814 - 0.0015 = \underline{0.8125}$

a. First cell midpoint is <u>near</u> the <u>MIN</u> measurement.	Upper cell limit =
b. Locate cell boundaries to prevent a measurement from falling <u>exactly</u> upon them.	$0.8125 + 0.003 = 0.8155$

usually every hour or two when the process is a typical continuous process.
Unless final inspection is considered to be part of the process, obtain the subgroups before this operation.

A "log" must be kept of all process adjustments and unusual occurrences,
such as line downtime, material or supplier changes, and so on, during the
time the study is run. These occurrences, although they may not seem important at the time, affect one's interpretation of the study results.

Although it is possible to run process capability studies using attributes
(fraction defective or numbers of defects) rather than variables (dimension,
mass, etc.), this is not generally recommended because [3]:

1. Studies based on attribute data cannot differentiate among out-of-control
   results caused by a shift in the process average, a change in the product specification, or excessive process variation causing more product
   to fall outside the limits (nonconforming product).
2. To achieve the same sensitivity as variable measurements, larger sample
   sizes must be used; hence sampling and inspection costs will be higher.

For process capability studies, when sampling from single-station processes,
it is customary to draw consecutive sample units at each time period. However,
sampling from processes containing multistation equipment is much more complex. Strictly speaking, each independent station is a separate process, but
if 12, 24, 48, or more independent stations are present, it may not be cost-
effective to run that number of concurrent capability studies.

One way to solve this problem is to select a representative station and to
study *only* this one. Practically, this may not be feasible since it is difficult
in a high-speed process to identify the station from which a particular sample
unit comes. If the product, as it is made, is identified with station numbers
or letters, one station is easily sampled.

If the sample units cannot be easily identified by station, it is a generally accepted practice to sample the subgroup units *at random* from the output of the process. In this case the "inherent" process variation is a mixture of within-station and between-station variation and the two sources cannot be separated unless the numerical value of one of these sources has been calculated from past data. A second problem is that a sample size is often selected which is an "even" function of the number of stations. For example, if there are 12 independent stations, a subgroup size of 2, 3, 4, or 6 is not recommended, but one containing 5, 7, or 9 product units is recommended because these will discourage false cyclical data patterns. Just as in the short-run capability studies, great care must be taken to assure that normal operating conditions (NOC) are maintained throughout the capability study. Any departures from NOC must be noted in the log.

B. Example of a Long-Run Process Capability Study: Precision Industry

A staking operation was required in the process of riveting a metal tongue to a flat surface during the fabrication of Francis Widgets. The rivet head height after staking was a critical quality characteristic. If rivet heights were too low, the tongue would be detached when an 8-lb pull was applied; if the height were too high, the head would not be broad enough to retain the metal tongue when this force was applied.

A capability study was run to investigate the quality characteristics of this staking operation before customer complaints became excessive. Based on pre-production runs, the quality control specification for rivet head height was set at 74 ± 6 thousandths of an inch. In this capability study it was important to detect a shift of 3σ units in either direction from the specification nominal (or midpoint) with a high degree of assurance *if* a shift occurred. Referring to Table 3, this meant that three consecutive riveted assemblies must be sampled at each time period. Because considerable line downtime had occurred in the past, a sampling frequency of 30 minutes was specified for the study.

The data resulting from this capability study are shown in Fig. 5 and the capability study control charts for subgroup averages and ranges are shown in Fig. 6. The limits for these charts were calculated from the factors shown in Table 4 by the methods given in Grant and Leavenworth [9]. In Fig. 6, all the plotted points are within the range and the average chart limits. This is the first condition for a controlled or steady-state process: the absence of excessive time-to-time variation when chart limits are calculated from capability study data [10]. The second condition for a controlled process is that data points plotted on control charts must vary in a random manner about their centerlines. This means that plotted points must not show the presence of trends, periodic fluctuations, or discontinuities [11]. If the plotted points show any of these effects, assignable causes of variation are present in the process *even though all the plotted points are inside control chart limits*. If *any one* of these two conditions for control is *not* met, assignable causes must be identified and removed before calculating the *natural tolerance or inherent capability* of the process, because a statement process of capability implies that the process is in a steady state.

A simple test for detecting nonrandom data patterns on control charts is the runs test. This test determines whether the distribution of plotted points *above and below* the control chart centerline follows a random pattern. The median value of individual measurements is frequently used for this purpose

TABLE 3   Selection of Subgroup Size for Long-run Capability Studies—
Variables Measurements*

To Detect This Shift In Either Direction From the Process Average ($\overline{X}'$)	Use the Following Subgroup Size
1.00 Sigma	23
1.25 "	15
1.50 "	10
1.75 "	8
2.00 "	6
2.25 "	5
2.50 "	4
2.75 "	3
3.00 "	3
3.25 "	2

*
α = Risk of detecting a *false* difference above or below the process
  average = 0.025

β = Risk of overlooking a *true* difference above or below the process
  average = 0.10

$$n = (K_{\alpha/2} + K_\beta)^2/(D)^2$$

n = Subgroup size

$K_{\alpha/2}$ = Normal Deviate associated with $\alpha/2$

$K\beta$ = Normal Deviate associated with β

$D = (\overline{X} - \overline{X}')/S$

since it is that value (regardless of distribution shape) which divides the data exactly in half. If it is an *average chart*, we can safely use the control chart centerline for this purpose even though individual measurements are not normally distributed.*

Runs above and below control chart centerlines are defined as *one or more sequential points* lying on one side of the line. For example, in Fig. 6, the *first two* points plotted on the average chart constitute the *first run*, while the *first* point plotted on the range chart is its *first run*. If every two *consecutive* points are connected by a straight line, it is very easy to count the total number of runs: count the number of times the *connecting* lines cross the centerline and add one to the total number of crossings.

In Fig. 6, we count 9 runs for the range chart and 14 runs for the average chart. Entering Table 5 with 21 plotted points, we see that the limits of runs for 21 points are 6 to 15. Since the actual numbers for both charts are within these limits (the number of runs on the average chart misses the upper limit

---

*The central limit theorem is a great comfort to those who have little faith in the normality of industrial measurements.

DIMENSIONAL CONTROL RECORD

PRODUCT _FRAMIS — WIDGET_ CODE _7857_   PLANT _# 75_

OPERATION _RIVET STAKING_ LINE NO. _7_   MACHINE _7A_

DATE _6/29/70_ SHIFT _1 + 2_   OPERATOR _JDL + KR_ INSPECTOR _JD + MS_

SAMPLE IDENTIFICATION

MEAS. NO.	AM 7:30	7:55	8:30	9:10	9:25	10:00	10:30	11:05	*NOON 12:00	PM 12:45	1:15	1:35
1	72	70	75	70	74	72	70	74	73	75	72	72
2	70	72	70	74	72	73	70	74	73	70	74	74
3	72	73	75	70	74	73	72	75	70	70	76	70
4												
5												
TOTAL	214	215	220	214	220	218	212	223	216	215	222	216
AVG.	71.3	71.7	73.3	71.3	73.3	71.7	70.7	74.3	72.0	71.7	74.0	72.0
RANGE	2	3	5	4	2	1	2	1	3	5	4	4

MEAS. NO.	PM 2:00	2:25	2:55	3:30	3:55	4:30	5:00	* 5:25	6:00
1	74	75	72	74	74	73	72	72	72
2	72	70	73	77	74	75	70	76	73
3	76	70	73	74	75	75	72	75	74
4									
5									
TOTAL	222	215	218	225	223	223	214	223	219
AVG.	74.0	71.6	72.6	75.0	74.3	74.3	71.3	74.3	73.0
RANGE	4	5	1	3	1	2	2	4	2

COMMENTS * LINE DOWN — STUCK METAL

HT. OF RIVET HEAD (IN 1000 THS OF AN INCH)

Specification: Rivet Head Height after Staking : 74 ± 6 thousandths

See Table 4 for Control Chart Factors

GRAND AVG.= $\dfrac{\text{Sum of Totals}}{\text{Total No. Meas.}}$ = _4587/63_ = _72.81_ = $\bar{\bar{X}}$

AVERAGE RANGE= $\dfrac{\text{Sum of Ranges}}{\text{Total No. Groups}}$ = _60/21_ = _2.86_ = $\bar{R}$

FIGURE 5 Long-run capability study: rivet-staking dimensional control record.

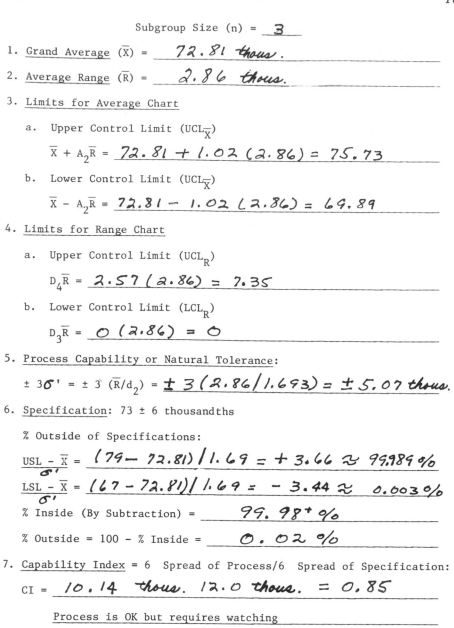

Subgroup Size (n) = __3__

1. <u>Grand Average</u> ($\overline{X}$) = __72.81 thous.__

2. <u>Average Range</u> ($\overline{R}$) = __2.86 thous.__

3. <u>Limits for Average Chart</u>

    a. Upper Control Limit ($UCL_{\overline{X}}$)

        $\overline{X} + A_2\overline{R}$ = __72.81 + 1.02 (2.86) = 75.73__

    b. Lower Control Limit ($UCL_{\overline{X}}$)

        $\overline{X} - A_2\overline{R}$ = __72.81 − 1.02 (2.86) = 69.89__

4. <u>Limits for Range Chart</u>

    a. Upper Control Limit (UCL_R)

        $D_4\overline{R}$ = __2.57 (2.86) = 7.35__

    b. Lower Control Limit (LCL_R)

        $D_3\overline{R}$ = __0 (2.86) = 0__

5. <u>Process Capability or Natural Tolerance</u>:

    $\pm 3\sigma' = \pm 3\ (\overline{R}/d_2)$ = __± 3 (2.86/1.693) = ± 5.07 thous.__

6. <u>Specification</u>: 73 ± 6 thousandths

    % Outside of Specifications:

    $\dfrac{USL - \overline{X}}{\sigma'}$ = __(79 − 72.81)/1.69 = + 3.66 ≈ 99.989 %__

    $\dfrac{LSL - \overline{X}}{\sigma'}$ = __(67 − 72.81)/1.69 = − 3.44 ≈ 0.003 %__

    % Inside (By Subtraction) = __99.98+ %__

    % Outside = 100 − % Inside = __0.02 %__

7. <u>Capability Index</u> = 6 Spread of Process/6 Spread of Specification:

    CI = __10.14 thous. 12.0 thous. = 0.85__

    <u>Process is OK but requires watching</u>

FIGURE 5 (Continued)

by one), there is no *strong* evidence that systematic process disturbances occurred during this capability study. To obtain additional information about the random distribution of points about control chart centerlines, we also examine the *length* of runs on either side of the line. An article by Frederick

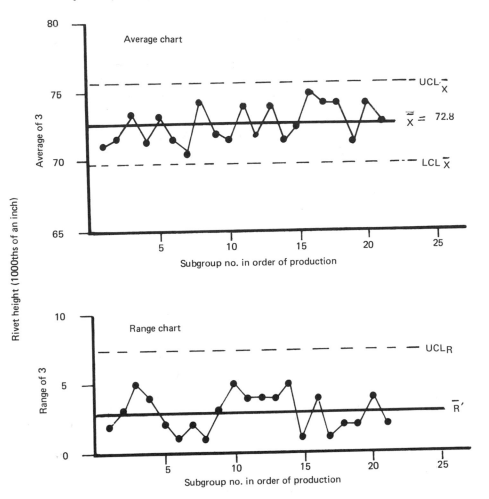

FIGURE 6   Control charts: final height of rivet head, subgroup size (n) = 3.

Mosteller in 1941 gave the 95% limiting values for *lengths* of runs. A summary of this information is as follows [11]:

Number of plotted points	Maximum run length about ξ
10—14	5 successive points
15—19	6 successive points
20—29	7 successive points
30—35	8 successive points

In addition, Western Electric's *SQC Handbook* recommends the following criteria for judging out-of-control conditions for *average charts* [12]:

1. If two out of three successive points fall at or outside the 2σ limits, assignable causes of variation are very likely to be present.
2. If four out of five successive points fall at or outside the 1σ limits, assignable causes of variation are likely to be present

For similar criteria for range charts, consult the Western Electric reference.

In our rivet height capability study (see Fig. 6), the longest run on the range chart contains six points (it misses its limit by one), while the longest run on the average chart is only three points. On the average chart, only two plotted points are at or beyond the 2σ limits (one point above and one point below the centerline). Again, there is no *strong* evidence of systematic process disturbances. We may therefore calculate the natural tolerance (process capability) of the rivet heights.

The *natural tolerance* of the rivet heights was ±5.1 thousandths (see the calculation sheet for Fig. 5), while the *specification tolerance* was ±6.0 thousandths. Comparing these two values, we obtain a *capability index* of 0.85, which is somewhat larger than the *ideal* ratio of 0.75. The significance of this difference is evaluated by plotting the capability study data against control chart limits calculated from the rivet-staking specifications [13]. These plots are shown in Fig. 7. Although the process average was below the specification nominal (72.8 versus 74 thousandths), none of the plotted points were outside the 3σ limits of the average and range charts. If the rivet-staking process average is adjusted to the 74-thousandths nominal value, the process is very capable of staying within the specification limits.

C. Example of a Long-Run Capability Study: Process Industry

Process industries have unique characteristics: (1) they modify raw materials by biological, chemical, or physical processes to make the final product; (2) samples taken during processing often have different chemical compositions and quality characteristics from those of the finished product; and (3) processes making the finished products are usually technically complex, requiring highly skilled plant personnel. Some examples of process industries are pulp and paper processes, pharmaceuticals, processing of raw materials to form resins and plastic materials, and food processing or packaging.

Capability studies of these processes sometimes require special types of control charts. When, for example, a critical quality characteristic is the percent solids in a homogeneous organic slurry, *one sample* of slurry is representative of the batch if it is drawn as the batch is continuously stirred in a large tank. Control charts for individual measurements are notoriously insensitive to small process disturbances; hence Cowden suggests using moving-average and moving-range charts for this type of process [14].

A second type of process industry exists which combines both precision industry and process industry functions. When this combination occurs, capability studies are run in the usual way and the data are plotted using traditional control charts. An example of this process-precision combination is found in the food industry (e.g., capability studies of filling equipment) (see Fig. 8) [15]. Note that the range chart is not out of control, indicating that the filling equipment is inherently *capable* of filling within ±1.09 g. The average net weights, however, are very much out of control. A log kept

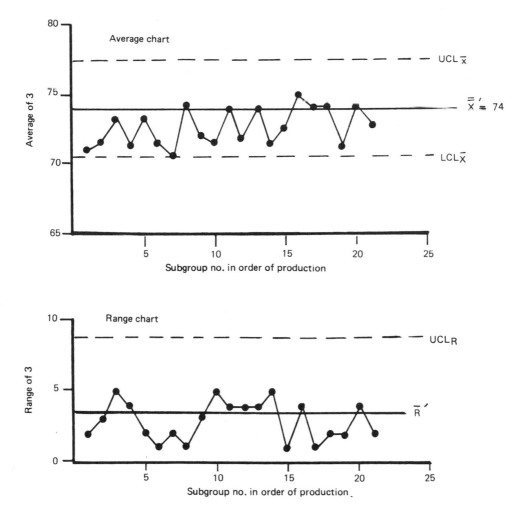

FIGURE 7   Data from Fig. 6 plotted against control chart limits.

during this study showed that the 3.3 hours of downtime could be "Paretoized" as follows:

Unit operation	Percent of total downtime
Freezer	28.8
Time-feed problems	21.7
Caser	19.6
Miscellaneous	12.6
Seamer	12.2
Filler	5.1
Total	100

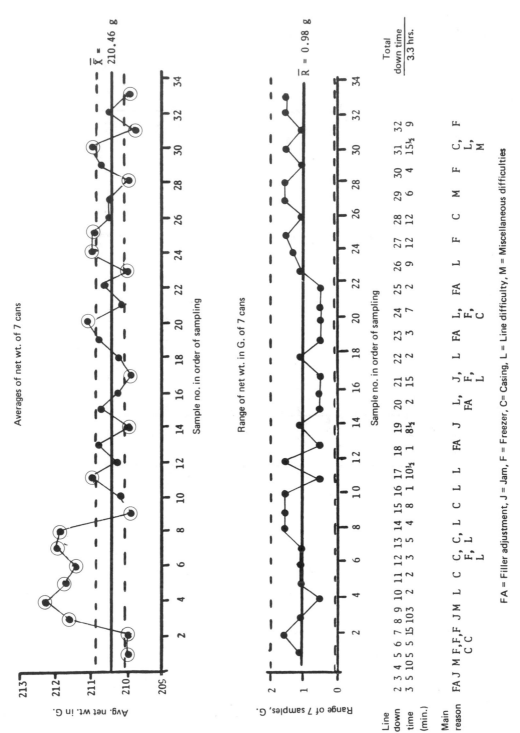

FIGURE 8   Filler control charts.

TABLE 4   Factors for X-Bar and R Charts

Chart for	Central Line	Chart Limits
Averages (X-bar)	$\overline{\overline{X}}$	$\overline{\overline{X}} \pm A_2\ (\overline{R})$
Ranges (R)	$\overline{R}$	$D_3 R$ and $D_4\overline{R}$
Process Capability	—	$\pm 3\sigma' = \pm 3\ (\overline{R}/d_2)$

Number of Sample Units	Multipliers for Chart Limits and Process Capability			
	A_2	D_3	D_4	d_2
2	1.880	0	3.267	1.128
3	1.023	0	2.575	1.693
4	0.729	0	2.282	2.059
5	0.577	0	2.115	2.326
6	0.483	0	2.004	2.534
7	0.419	0.076	1.924	2.704
8	0.373	0.136	1.864	2.847
9	0.337	0.184	1.816	2.970
10	0.308	0.223	1.777	3.078

*ASTM *Manual on Quality Control of Materials*. (January, 1951) has very extensive tables of Control Chart factors.

Obviously, the unit operation studied (filling equipment) was a minor cause of the quality problems in this process. To control filling operations effectively, other operations must be brought under control.

IV.   INTERPRETING CONTROL CHART PATTERNS IN CAPABILITY STUDIES [16]

A. Cycles

Cycles are short trends that repeat the pattern over a long enough period of time—processing variables come and go at somewhat regular intervals of time. The causes of cycles are as follows:

Average chart	Range chart
Temperature, humidity	Operator fatigue
Eccentricity	Maintenance
Differences in gages	Day shift/night shift
Worn threads	Tool wear

B. Gradual Change in Level

Some process element originally affects only a few pieces, but the number affected increases with time. The process may settle down to new level.

TABLE 5   Number and Length of Runs on Either Side of Control Chart
Centerline (95% Confidence Limits)*

No. of plotted points	Excessive fluctuation	Insufficient fluctuation
	If no. of runs > the no. given below	If no. of runs < the no. given below
10	9	2
11	9	3
12	10	3
13	11	3
14	12	3
15	12	4
16	13	4
17	13	5
18	14	5
19	15	5
20	15	6
25	18	8
30	21	10
35	24	12
40	27	14
45	30	16
50	33	18

*This chart is based upon the binomial distribution: $p = 0.50$ and $n =$ number of plotted points.

NOTE: 1. *Too few* runs (insufficient fluctuation) reflect trends, discontinuities, or long-term periodicity.
2. *Too many* runs (excessive fluctuation) reflect "mixtures," over-adjustment of the process, or short-term periodicity.

Average chart	Range chart
Gradual introduction of new materials, etc.	Better fixtures, better methods, greater skill of operators

C.   Sudden Shift in Level

Shifts in process levels are characterized by a strong change in one direction—a number of points appear on only one side of the centerline.

Average chart	Range chart
New operator	New operator
New inspector	New equipment
New machine	Changes in material

D. Trends

Trends are characterized by a strong movement of data, up or down.

Average chart	Range chart
Tool wear	Increasing trends
Deterioration of stored solutions	Tool wear
Aging of materials	
Seasonal effects	
Changes in standards	

E. Freaks

Freaks are defined as a single unit or group of units that differ greatly from others.

Average chart	Range chart
Wrong settings	Accidental damage
Error in measuring	Incomplete operation
Incomplete operation	Breakdown of operations

F. Groups or Bunches

A group is a clustering together of similar measurements.

Average chart	Range chart
Measuring problems	Freaks in data
Change in calibration	Mixture of distributions

G. Instability

Process instability means that erratic data fluctuations occur which are too wide for control limits.

Average chart	Range chart
Overadjustment of machine	Untrained operators
Carelessness of operator	Mixture of material
Differences in test pieces	Machine needs repairing
	Assemblies off center

H. Mixtures

Average chart	Range chart
Affects this chart more frequently	Different lots of material
Is a combination of two different differences in gages levels— different lots of material	

REFERENCES

1. J. M. Juran, Editor-in Chief, *Quality Control Handbook*, 3rd ed., McGraw-Hill, New York, 1974, Sec. 9.
2. H. C. Charbonneau and G. L. Webster, *Industrial Quality Control*, Prentice-Hall, Englewood Cliffs, N.J., 1978.
3. Western Electric Company, *Statistical Quality Control Handbook*, 2nd ed., Mack Printing Company, Easton, Pa. (4th printing, 1970), Sec. II, Pts. A and F.
4. The Bendix Corporation, Kansas City, Mo., *Capability Study Handbook (G-42)*, revised June 1968, prepared by SQC Dept. 416.
5. "Shortcuts for Machine Capability Studies," *Quality Management and Engineering*, February 1972.
6. J. W. Tukey, "Non-parametric Estimation II, Statistically Equivalent Blocks and Tolerance Regions—The Continuous Case," *Annals of Mathematical Statistics*, Vol. 18, 1947, pp. 529–539.
7. H. Scheffé and J. W. Tukey, *Annals of Mathematical Statistics*, Vol. 15, 1944, p. 217.
8. H. Arkin and R. R. Colton, *Statistical Methods*, 5th ed., Barnes & Noble Books, New York, 1970, p. 3, footnote 2.
9. E. L. Grant and R. S. Leavenworth, *Statistical Quality Control*, 5th ed., McGraw-Hill, New York, 1972.
10 C. A. Bennett and N. L. Franklin, *Statistical Analysis in Chemistry and the Chemical Industry*, Wiley, New York, 1954, Chap. 11, pp. 663–677.
11. F. Mosteller, "Note on Application of Runs to Quality Control Charts," *Annals of Mathematical Statistics* V. XII (1941) p. 232.
12. Western Electric Company, Inc., *Statistical Quality Control Handbook*, (2nd ed.), Mack Printing Company, Easton, Pa. (1958), pp. 25–27.
13. ASTM Manual on Quality Control of Materials, ASTM, Philadelphia, Pa. (Jan. 1951), p. 72.
14. D. J. Cowden, *Statistical Methods in Quality Control*, Prentice-Hall, Englewood Cliffs, N.J. (1957), pp. 342–345.
15. M–G. Tarver, "Systematic Process Analysis," *Quality Progress*, V. VII, No. 9, (Sept. 1974), pp. 28–32.
16. Western Electric SQC Handbook, Mack Printing Company, Easton, Pa. (1956), pp. 149–162.

13

RELIABILITY, ACCESSIBILITY, AND MAINTAINABILITY

RALPH A. EVANS

Evans Associates
Durham, North Carolina

I. CONCEPTS

A. Reliability

The word *reliability* refers to the concept of being able to depend (rely) on a product. That is, a product is reliable if users can, in their own jobs for their own purposes, rely on it. The concept becomes cloudy when product misuse or partial use is considered, although the user is rarely sympathetic to pedantic arguments about what is, or is not, misuse. The word has many definitions and variations, each of which is useful in a specific situation.

The word can be used as an adjective:

Reliability engineering: the set of engineering tasks performed to ensure achieving the desired level of reliability
Reliability program: includes reliability engineering and is the complete set of tasks (design, testing, management, purchasing, quality, manufacturing, etc.) to ensure achieving the desired level of reliability
Reliability measure: a quantitative measure of reliability

The word can also be used as a noun:

Reliability: the concept referred to in the first paragraph
Reliability: the probability that a system will successfully complete its mission, given that the system was in proper condition at the beginning (in practice, this definition must be extended to define the other terms therein).

The word is often used loosely and ambiguously to mean any or all of the above, or almost whatever the user wishes it to mean. In the 1950s the word included many activities that now have separate names, such as maintainability. Thus care must be used in reading the literature to interpret the author's meaning according to the context. An example of the use of *reliability* is: "The mission reliability of a transit-car propulsion system is 95%, where the user (system manager) wants the transit-car to complete a specific mission successfully (e.g., not fail during a 1-day run during the winter with high passenger traffic)."

When the simple concept of reliability is applied to a product, the product is often assumed to be in either of two states: up or down. When the product is up, it is usable; when it is down it is not usable and is in some stage of maintenance. Although not adequate for all products, the assumption of two states simplifies any analysis.

Reliability of a product is strongly affected by all activities throughout the life cycle, from system concept and definition, through design, production, field use, and maintenance. The design/development phase is often stressed because so many opportunities for good reliability can be irretrievably lost there.

Most reliability literature in the 1950s and 1960s was written by statisticians and design engineers. Thus they tended to stress the importance of their own activities, often at the expense of other equally important activities during the acquisition and use phases. For example, the old reliability literature stated that a product reached its peak of reliability just when it left the designer, and then everyone proceeded to degrade the reliability. That peak reliability was often misleadingly called *inherent reliability*.

Designs do not in themselves possess the characteristic of reliability—only the product has it. All designs are incomplete because they rely on others to use skill in building the product. In practice, inherent reliability only counted those failures that an imaginative, intelligent, aggressive, and able designer could not blame on someone else. Statisticians seemed to believe, erroneously, that the reliability discipline was a subset of statistics. Thus many books and articles on "reliability" dwelt largely with statistical equations and concepts. The reliability discipline does often profitably use the language of statistics, just as engineering often uses the language of mathematics.

B. Maintainability

The word *maintainability* refers to the concept of being able easily to restore a product to service (maintain it). That is, a product is maintainable if users can, in their own jobs for their own purposes, easily restore the product to service (i.e., convert it from a down condition to an up condition). Maintainability is distinguished from maintenance; *maintenance* is a physical act of maintaining a product. Like reliability, maintainability has many specific definitions and variations, each of which is useful in a specific situation.

An example of *maintainability* used as a noun is: maintainability is the probability that a system will be maintained in, or restored to, a specified condition within a given period of time, when maintenance is performed in accord with prescribed procedures and resources. (In practice, this definition must be extended to define the other terms therein.)

If is often useful to distinguish among three levels of maintenance:

1. At the scene, where the product or system is restored to some kind of usefulness by replacing an offending part
2. In a shop where the offending part has been taken for repair
3. At the factory or special depot where an offending part is rebuilt

Some kinds of failures are not noticeable by the user, but will still require maintenance. For example, if a propulsion system fails on one axle of a transit

car, the train could proceed on schedule and the riders will never know that a
part failure occurred.

An example of the use of the word *maintainability* is: "The maintainability
for repairing certain engine faults in an automobile at the shop within 6 hours
is 95% if an appointment is made ahead of time." Maintainability is strongly
affected by the logistic system, skills and attitudes of maintenance personnel,
the overall system operating management philosophy, and the design of the
item.

C. System Effectiveness

The term *system effectiveness* refers to any general measure of user satisfaction for a complicated system. Simple assumptions, such as the system being
either up or down, are usually completely inadequate for a complicated system.
Thus reliability and maintainability by themselves are generally inadequate
measures of user satisfaction for complicated systems such as a fleet of telephone service trucks, a rail transit system, or a hospital. Complicated systems rarely have a single simple measure of user satisfaction, but involve many
types and degrees of satisfaction.

There are several levels of users who must be satisfied with a product (the
actual list varies with the kind of product):

Owner
Manager
Clerk or operator
Customer served by the clerk or operator

It is important not to let the ambiguity in the words *user* or *customer* confuse the concept of user satisfaction. The higher on the user list one goes,
the more likely are economic considerations to be important in user satisfaction,
for example, life-cycle cost. Such costs can be extremely important to many
users and can affect the very fabric of our society. For example, the life-
cycle cost of an electric utility is important to everyone. The lower on the
user list one goes, the more likely are reliability, availability, and ease of use
to be important. It is up to each user to define the important measures of
system effectiveness.

D. Availability

The word *availability* refers to the concept of whether an item will be ready
(available) when it is needed. Like reliability, this word has many specific
definitions and variations, each of which is useful in a specific situation. An
example is the fraction of the time that a condensate feed pump at a generator
station is actually working. Availability is determined by the reliability, maintainability, and support system. It is often necessary to be concerned about
availability—irrespective of the trade-offs made between reliability and
maintainability.

An example of *availability* used as a noun is: *Steady-state field availability*
is the long-run fraction of time that a system is up under actual field conditions (in practice, this definition must be extended to define the other terms
therein). For a system that is either up or down, the steady-state availability
is the ratio of "mean uptime" to "mean uptime plus mean downtime."

E. R&M and RAM

R&M stands for reliability and maintainability. RAM is the acronym given to reliability, availability, and maintainability. Both are often used very loosely to mean what the user wishes at the moment.

F. R&M Program Needs

The root of the entire "reliability problem" is that there is no "reliability meter" or "life meter" which can be attached to a product to read its remaining life. Lives of nominally alike products differ widely—by as much as a factor of 10. The factors that affect life are not all known exactly. Thus many reliability engineering tasks are done for insurance, and no one can say in advance which will have been the effective ones and which could have been done without.

The old engineering rules of thumb and folklore are not enough to produce the desired degrees of R&M. When R&M are not specified and controlled, the R&M goals or requirements just will not be met. The reason we know that these statements are true is that they reflect real history. High R&M must be de-signed-in and then built-in. An item with high R&M cannot be bought like a keg of nails. The buyer must constantly monitor the supplier to be sure that:

The right R&M activities are done at the right time
Those activities affect the design and manufacture of the product

The need for a special R&M program is not based on sophisticated theory, but on the practical realization that without an effective program, high R&M is just simply not achieved—it is an unfortunate fact of life. Many other spe-cialty disciplines compete with R&M for project resources (money, calendar time, people), and all have good reason to. But if the product is not reliable, all the other specialty disciplines are wasted.

G. Quality of Conformance

The word *quality* is used in two quite different senses, quality of *per*formance and quality of *con*formance. Quality of performance indicates the number, kinds, and degrees of performance characteristics, such as in the difference between an old Volkswagen "bug" and a new Mercedes. Both cars can be ex-actly what they are supposed to be, and users of both can be quite satisfied. But the two products do differ in their qualities of performance.

There are four stages in describing quality of conformance:

1. User needs and desires
2. Formal statement of user requirements
3. Design documents (drawings, etc.)
4. Product

Performance characteristics are stated in the first two stages; they are the qualities of performance. R&M are performance characteristics just like range of a radar, ease of handling of a car, power of a microwave oven, and audio distortion in a radio. Quality of conformance requires that each stage conform reasonably to the previous stage. Because it is often difficult to know whether such conformance exists, and because there are always many interface and interpretation difficulties, quality of conformance also requires overall con-formance; that is, the product must conform to user needs and desires.

H. R&M Program Effectiveness

Management is the biggest bottleneck in achieving high R&M—management simply does not commit the resources (money, calendar time, people) to the program and then keep them committed when the usual conflicts arise among schedule, quality (of conformance), and cost. Each management decision to omit or delay a part of the program, when viewed narrowly with its own constraints, seems reasonable. But the overall result is to design and manufacture a product that does not have the desired R&M.

R&M activities, when performed, must make a difference to the product. That is, some group within the company—design engineering, production engineering, quality control, purchasing, and/or shipping—must do something different because of the results of the R&M tasks. R&M programs in the 1950s and 1960s had justified reputations as numbers games, because they were performed in a vacuum—rarely did anyone use the results.

The Department of Defense (DoD) has policies on program acquisition phases, such as conceptual, validation, full-scale development, and production and deployment. The DoD literature states the kind and degree of R&M tasks that ought to be done in each phase. The commercial and industrial world has similar ideas and policies. But in the real world of limited resources (DoD or not, it makes no difference) there are only three program phases with respect to R&M: not worried, get worried, get serious. The "not worried" phase involves good intentions for the R&M program, negligible commitment of resources to that program, and even less implementation of the R&M task results. The "not worried" phase usually lasts until the product exhibits bad R&M characteristics in the field. Then the "get worried" phase begins amid sound and fury in the executive suite. Finally, the "get serious" phase is implemented wherein the R&M effort gets the resources it needs. That is why this discussion of R&M program effectiveness begins (and ends) by stating that management is the biggest bottleneck in achieving high R&M.

I. One-Basket Projects

A one-basket project is a project in which "all your eggs are in one basket." In a one-basket project there are rarely realistic alternatives to accepting the output of the project, almost regardless of how poor that output is. Large systems, such as a new weapon system for the army, a rapid transit system, or a new electric power generating station, are often one-basket. The reasons for a project's being one-basket are social, political, economic, and/or strategic. The project personnel know when a project is one-basket; thus the user must acknowledge its existence and plan the acquisition strategy accordingly. When there are competitive developers, the projects are almost never one-basket.

II. MANAGEMENT

A. Control

Control is an essential management activity. It is often exercised poorly in an R&M program; thus it is important to understand how control works. Controlling anything is not a trivial matter, whether it is a project, a production process a machine, a person, and so on. Many of the concepts in controlling people and groups apply as well to inanimate processes. When striving for high reliability and maintainability it is all too easy to concentrate on only one step of the control process, such as motivation, and thus be ineffective or counterproductive.

The following four steps apply to any situation:

1. Know what is supposed to be done.
2. Know what is being done.
3. Take corrective action as required.
    a. Know what kind of corrective action to take.
    b. Have the resources (power, physical tools, administrative force, mental capability, calendar time, money, etc.) to implement that knowledge.
    c. Have the motivation (incentive) to take the action.
4. Assess the adequacy of the corrective action (and repeat these steps as necessary).

The first two steps are straightforward, although not trivial. Take corrective action as required is often the most difficult step. Thus it is explained in more detail.

Know what kind of corrective action to take. Very often there is no clear-cut, accurate-enough, agreed-upon conceptual model for the process or system. In the absence of such a model, everyone argues about what to do. Many political arguments are of this variety. Hidden disagreements with the results of the first two steps can surface at this substep and complicate the situation. It is important to separate (and agree upon the separation) fact, reasonable engineering judgment, and unsupported guesses. This substep can involve considerable research and development.

Have the resources to implement that knowledge. This substep often limits what is done. In physical systems there must be adequate torque, power, energy, voltage, and so on, to do physically what is called for. In organizations one needs the administrative power to compel other people to take the needed action. Those other people must then have the resources to implement the orders.

Have the motivation (incentive) to take the action. This was the essence of the early zero-defects programs and other motivational activities. Many of them had only transient success because they failed to consider the other substeps and steps. Managers sometimes attempt to apply pressure to subordinates, in the form of rewards or punishments, without supplying the knowledge and resources. Such pressures usually fail and can do more harm than good.

B. User and Producer

There are two separate managements involved, the management of the users and the management of the producer. Both must cooperate for high R&M requirements to be met. Even if both managements are within the same company, they must be considered separately because their budgets and resources will usually be separate.

Often, there are more difficulties when the two managements are different groups of one company. The difficulties arise because the two groups are not dealing at arm's length with each other. An outside contractor can be fired (if he or she is not too far into a one-basket project); a sister group can rarely, if ever, be fired for any reason. They have little incentive to cooperate fully with each other because each management has its own budgets and other constraints as if they were separate companies. The remainder of this discussion presumes that these two groups are cooperating well, and treats them as one management.

C. Formal Statement of User Requirements

The several levels of users must be questioned so that their needs and desires can be identified. Many of these needs and desires will be measures of system effectiveness. The needs and desires will not be uniform between, or even within, the various levels, nor will any one person's needs and desires necessarily be logically consistent. Finding these needs and desires is an important, resource-consuming step in acquiring any system, and often is neglected in the mistaken belief that it is not cost-effective. Making sense out of all this information is a difficult but necessary task.

After the user's needs and desires are collected, they must be reduced to a logically consistent, achievable, affordable set of formal performance requirements. These requirements will include some measures of system effectiveness which are related to reliability and maintainability (e.g., almost any measure that must be sustained over a period of time).

The performance requirements of the system must be allocated (broken down) to subsystems. Many of the allocations will be directly in terms of reliability, availability, and/or maintainability of the subsystems. Often, trade-offs can be made among those three characteristics of a subsystem. A formal, quantitative statement of R&M requirements is necessary if high reliability and maintainability are to be achieved.

Some system performance requirements will not translate directly into subsystem performance requirements, but must be adapted. For example, the formal user requirement might be a maximum of 2% per month actual service calls by the users. This has to be translated into numbers that are more easily measured or calculated in the laboratory, and will consider such things as a corresponding failure rate at maximum ambient temperature, extremes of line voltage, and a reference duty cycle for the equipment.

At this point in the project, it is necessary to decide whether a high R&M program is called for or not. For that, the criterion for high reliability and maintainability is needed. A very simple, accurate criterion is: High reliability and maintainability will not result from the usual R&M efforts (if any) of the company. Considerable honesty and self-appraisal is needed because rarely will a design group admit that its output does not produce adequately high reliability and maintainability. Generally, the required reliability and maintainability should be compared with the reliability and maintainability actually experienced in the field. The quality assurance group is usually the one most able to make that comparison and the resulting judgment. If there is a quantitative requirement, a high R&M program is necessary to achieve it.

Resources are limited, even at the very beginning of a project. As the project progresses, trade-offs will have to be made between quality (of conformance), schedule, and cost. It happens in virtually every project. Therefore, priorities have to be established among the performance requirements. One of the functions of each level of management is to give its rationale for trade-offs of quality, schedule, and cost to the next-lower level of management. If reliability and maintainability are very far down on the priority list, they might as well not be on the list at all. It is just too easy for a project manager to find reasons to take resources away from R&M programs. Thus reliability and maintainability must be among the top three performance requirements for any subsystem. After all, there is really not much user need for a system that does not work.

D. Contractual R&M Requirements

Contractual R&M requirements are not easy to fill. The necessary resources to fill them will be much more than an inexperienced management presumes (at least several times as much). A buyer who offers (1) a technical data package (set of fabrication drawings, etc.), and (2) assurances that when the item is produced thereto it will meet the R&M requirements, is not to be believed. Contract provisions for quantitative R&M requirements are innocous looking, and the engineering design group is likely to be overly optimistic about meeting those requirements. Quality assurance provisions, such as R&M acceptance or demonstration tests, can look very innocent, but be deadly.

Management that is inexperienced in handling formal R&M requirements can bring on painful contract nonperformance and disastrous litigation surrounding that nonperformance. To avoid those catastrophes it is well to hire an experienced person full time or as a consultant. Even with experienced advisors, a first such contract should be taken *only* on a cost-reimbursement basis.

E. R&M Program Plans

There should be a separate plan and allocated resources for the reliability program and for the maintainability program. If the reliability and maintainability programs are lumped together, the reliability program tends to get the lion's share. If either the program plan or resources for executing it are missing, there will be no program. Excellent source materials for these programs are found in the revised U.S. Military Standards cited in Refs. 1 and 2. They contain much valuable discussion of the reasons for the program tasks.

The program plan (for either reliability or maintainability) must include at least the following items:

A description of how the program will be conducted to meet the requirements of the statement of work.

Identification of each task in the program.

The procedures to evaluate the status and control of each task, and identification of the organizational unit with the authority and responsibility for executing it.

Description of (1) the interrelationships of R&M tasks, and (2) how they relate to other system-oriented tasks. The descriptions must include the procedures to assure that R&M task results and data are integrated with each other and with logistic support.

A schedule and milestones for each of the tasks.

Identification of known R&M problems, an assessment of their impact on meeting the R&M requirements, and their proposed solutions.

The method by which R&M requirements are disseminated to design engineers.

Description of the management structure, including relationships between line, staff, service, and policy organizations.

Sources of R&M design guidelines to be used.

Description of how R&M task results and data will be integrated into the
design and other project activities.

F. Program Reviews

These are peer working reviews, rather than impressive shows whose purpose
is to impress top management and the customer with how well things are going
and great they will be. The purpose of these program reviews is to catch sins
of omission or commission as early as possible. These reviews are scheduled
at appropriate project milestones, such as the following:

When the formal statement of user requirements is complete

When a working model has been demonstrated

When all technical risks have been eliminated, the drawings and associated
documents are complete, and the design is ready to turn over to
production

When some field experience has been acquired

G. Early Configuration Management

In any large company, and even in some small ones, different people and
groups gradually go their own ways. Assumptions or changes made by one
group are not reviewed by, or force fed to, all groups. It is often difficult
to get anyone to admit that this goes on, but it does. The difficulty is directly
analogous to being sure that everyone in the shop is using the latest production drawings. The quality engineering group is often charged with the responsibility to ensure that all groups are using the same set of assumptions
and that all of them are traceable to the formal statement of user requirements.
Everyone must play from the same sheet of music.

H. Failure Reporting, Analysis, and Corrective Action System (FRACAS)

The task is reasonably self-explanatory. Its purpose is to establish (1) a
closed-loop failure reporting system, (2) procedures for analyzing failures to
determine their cause, and (3) documentation for recording the corrective
action. Oversight and implementation must be someone's explicit responsibility.
Often the quality assurance group is in charge of this task. FRACAS can get
out of hand unless some judgment is used about which failures to analyze.

There are three levels of corrective action:

1. The "Band-Aid" approach, wherein the failed item is restored as
   necessary.
2. The design or production fix and/or field retrofit, wherein the cause
   of the offense is eliminated from other product.
3. Changes in the management system, wherein the situation that allowed
   the poor design or production to happen is eliminated.

The first two levels of corrective action are the usual ones. The third level
can be the most cost-effective.

I. Incentives

With due regard to the subparagraph on control, the design engineering and manufacturing groups must have incentives to design and manufacture products with the required degree of reliability and maintainability. In particular, all incentives for them to design or produce poor material should be removed. For example, nonconforming material should not count toward a production quota, and the performance rating of the design group should be heavily weighted by the degree to which the R&M requirements are achieved.

With the proper set of incentives, each group will be asking for R&M engineering assistance. If they are not asking for it, their incentives are not chosen wisely.

III. DESIGN

In principle, many of the R&M tasks are done for the benefit of the design group. In practice, it is all too easy for the design group to ignore the results from the R&M engineering tasks. A common example occurs when the reliability engineers show that special high-reliability parts must be used to satisfy the reliability requirement. Very often, the designers have ignored that output and specified ordinary parts—and believed that the reliability engineering task was related only to satisfying a silly statement of work.

A large part of the reliability effort by the design group involves greater attention to detail such as making all the stress calculations (e.g., temperature, power, current, and voltage for all electronic parts; physical stresses and environments for mechanical parts). Designers like to think they "do all the arithmetic" anyway, but they do not. Computer programs are available for many computers to take the drudgery out of the calculations.

A traditional maxim is the KISS system (Keep It Simple, Stupid). In some cases, more parts can reduce degradation failures (e.g., negative feedback in an electronic amplifier) and thus increase reliability. But in many cases a "Rube Goldberg" approach will send reliability into a nosedive.

Early configuration management is important. All analyses are based on associated assumptions about the system. The assumptions the design group makes about the system must be the same as those that other groups, especially R&M engineering, are making.

There is always a tension between using new parts and techniques to improve performance, and using the old tried-and-true materials and processes for high reliability. There is no easy answer here, but sadder, wiser users would gladly trade many of the new unreliable features for something that always worked. "If it isn't there, it can't fail."

A new design is often very carefully analyzed. But a fix on that design is made without the same careful analysis. Many fixes introduce new difficulties, sometimes much worse than the original one the fix was intended to cure. "The cure can be worse than the disease."

If a system is obsolescent, it is often wise not to try to correct a known, understood failure mode. The cure is likely to introduce new difficulties because not enough resources could be devoted to checking it out thoroughly. Operating and repair personnel are familiar with the old failure mode and have learned how to live with it.

It is common to trade off reliability against maintainability. Examples include using sockets for integrated circuits versus soldering them in place, using one large printed circuit board instead of several small ones, or using rivets rather than bolts and nuts and lockwashers. Forced air cooling seems good, except then the product has no better reliability than the forced-air cooling system. Care must be exercised that fabrication methods introduced to improve maintainability are not eliminated by manufacturing because they are too expensive.

Preventive maintenance looks much better on the drawing board than it does in the field. Not all preventive maintenance is done perfectly, and when it is done badly it can be much worse than no preventive maintenance at all. For example, in a nuclear power station, checks on the safety system are made by opening and/or closing valves. After the check, the valves are supposed to be returned to their original positions. Not doing so has caused severe difficulties. For most electronic equipment, no preventive maintenance should be allowed which requires accessing the inside of the equipment.

R&M growth is an essential part of the design process. There are two parts to R&M growth: "analyze and fix" and "test, analyze, and fix." The first part is much cheaper than the second. Most of the input comes from "doing all the arithmetic" on the design, the remainder comes from R&M engineering tasks. Designers tend to be success oriented. Someone who is failure oriented must go over the designs and ask, "How can it fail?", not "How can it succeed?" Or ask: "How can this extra gadget or service go wrong and what harm can it do?"

Human factors for the operators and service people are important considerations for any design group. Not only can people do things right, but they can do things wrong. People are as much a part of the system as are the hardware and software, and they can have a tremendous impact on system R&M.

Designers are people. They know what is important by what the managers always complain about or ask about. Those are not necessarily the same things that managers write memos about. If R&M is to have a high priority for designers, it must also have just as high priority for their managers.

IV. QUALITY

The relationship of reliability and quality has been questioned ever since formal reliability concepts were introduced. One difficulty arises because of the dual meanings of quality. Reliability is a quality of performance and thus is a subset of "quality." Quality of conformance is essential to achieve high reliability; thus "quality" is a subset of reliability. Once the sophomoric play on words is over, there need be no rivalry between "quality" and "reliability," and people can settle down to making better products.

Often an umbrella group, called product assurance, has quality assurance and R&M engineering under its wing. Quality assurance is broken down into quality control and quality engineering. Quality control is the inspection function. Quality engineering implements the engineering tasks that assure the several kinds of quality of conformance. It has four elements:

1. Planning for quality and quality control before the item is made
2. Information flow concerning quality
3. Critical reviews of projects so that quality difficulties are made visible
4. Evaluating project risks with regard to quality

The quality engineering group will help the R&M engineers decide how everyone will be sure that everything will actually have the characteristics that were planned as being necessary to achieve the required field R&M. "Everything" includes the materials coming into the plant, the in-process material flow, the internal processes, and the outgoing products. In particular, the quality engineers and the R&M engineers have to agree on the quality characteristics of materials, processes, and products. A quality characteristic is anything that will be checked to assure conformance of a product with its requirements. Choosing quality characteristics, sampling methods, and test and measurement techniques should not be left to the whim or inadequate knowledge of the inspector, but should be done by the quality engineering group in coordination with product engineering, design engineering, R&M engineering, and purchasing.

The quality engineering group will usually be the ones to ensure the early configuration control on a project. Early configuration control refers to (1) traceability of all requirements to the formal statement of user requirements, and (2) agreement among all users of extensions, adaptations, and allocations of those requirements.

In some companies, many of the tests are either performed or monitored by the quality assurance group. Acceptance or demonstration testing (to prove that the product does indeed have the desired R&M characteristics) is very complicated to plan, execute, and referee because so much hinges on the outcome. MIL-STD-785B (and references therein) provides much information on this topic. The following list shows things that must be specified and agreed upon by buyer and seller before the tests are run.

Mission profile—what the equipment will be used to do

Environmental profile—the kinds of weather, voltages, corrosive atmospheres, etc.

Operator and maintainer skill and attitude profiles

Detailed definitions of what is and what is not a failure, and how partial failures will be treated

Relevance and chargeability of each and every failure

Details of carrying out the test

Composition of an arbitration board to resolve arguments about failure definition, relevance, and chargeability, and about unexpected events during the test

Allowable history of test units (how representative they are of production units)

Permissible preventive maintenance

The statistical stopping boundary (number of failures versus total test time) for the test and the implied operating characteristics of that boundary

If the test is failed, or conditionally passed, how the retest will be handled when the item has been modified

Handling the foregoing testing problems requires appreciable familiarity with the item under test and its behavior in the field, as well as with statistical risks. It is no place for raw recruits or nice guys—there is too much at stake and the other side will have its experts there. Occasionally, the test will be run as part of the buyer's early use of the product. In that case, the seller has even more reason to watch things carefully. For example, do the buyer's operators want the test to succeed, or do they believe that the new products will threaten their jobs in some way?

On one-basket contracts the item will often be conditionally accepted even if it nominally fails the test. That process is accompanied by an appreciable amount of negotiation and double-talk on both sides.

Routine life tests on small samples of production units are often run to ensure that nothing has gotten out of control. Because they are internal tests, most of the difficulties above rarely apply.

The quality engineering group often handles the failure reporting, analysis, and corrective action system. It is a vital part of the R&M effort. Because conformance is the life blood of the quality engineering group, it will often be responsible for the database of failure information. One of the elements of early configuration control is having the database (and input information) organized in such a way that the data can be used to evaluate any subsystem R&M requirements as well as the system requirements. This compatibility is not easy to arrange, and must be considered in all extensions, adaptations, and allocations of R&M requirements. For example, if the system requirement is that there be no more than 2% customer complaints per month, how does the database handle a test failure that does not result in a customer complaint (because the failure is not self-announcing)?

Adequate resources (money, calendar time, people) must be available for the quality assurance group, and they must be aggressive in performing their duties. Otherwise, the entire R&M effort will be wasted.

V. PURCHASING

The mission of the purchasing department is to buy what is on the purchase requisition at the best possible combination of cost, schedule, and conformance-quality. There should be some way that requisitioners can make known their priorities with respect to cost, schedule, and conformance quality, and have the purchasing department abide by them. If the mission of the purchasing department is something less, the R&M effort is in trouble.

Many difficulties with purchased parts are unfairly laid on the purchasing department. If a need is not on the purchase request, the purchasing department does not know about it. If they do not know about it, they cannot consider it.

Often the situation is not as simple as stated above. Then the quality and R&M engineers must work with the purchasing department to ensure that adequate, useful records of cost, schedule, and conformance quality are kept on suppliers. Simpler rating schemes are easier to use (both for data in and data out) than complicated ones. The simpler schemes are usually quite adequate. Complicated schemes tend to have many hidden assumptions about relative priorities; they can give very arbitrary, precise answers to queries, but those answers do not necessarily reflect an accurate, useful picture of the real world.

When an inventory management system is computerized and includes the writing of purchase orders, the purchasing situation becomes very hazardous for quality unless there is a clear, easy path for the R&M and quality engineers to affect (1) the database which the program accesses, and (2) the basic rules of the program itself. The product assurance group will have to monitor such an inventory system very closely to be sure that the system is behaving in a way to assure high conformance quality.

When a purchasing department is called on to purchase a system or subsystem that must be developed, rather than parts which are bought off the

shelf, they must work very closely with the quality and R&M engineering
groups to ensure that reliability and maintainability have been considered
adequately in the product specifications, including any conformance testing
to be done. Putting R&M performance requirements in a specification can be
very expensive because the seller will have to undergo some kind of development or assurance program. A fabrication specification (i.e., using a technical data package) is much cheaper and can be effective if it has been adequately tested during previous buys.

Unresolvable disputes can arise between the purchasing department and
the R&M or quality engineering groups when the relative function of any of
them is called into question. Such disputes must be settled by higher management, who controls both groups. At the least, the functions of the groups
should be put in writing for future reference.

VI. MANUFACTURING

The traditional designer's point of view, which has found its way into the reliability literature, is that product reliability is a maximum when the design
leaves the design group. From there on in, all anyone can do is make it worse.
Naturally, manufacturing and quality engineers disagree strongly with that
notion.

Manufacturing engineers have (1) long believed that designers do not give
enough thought to economical producibility, and (2) long used the practice of
changing the design for better producibility. Many designers have never
worked in a manufacturing environment and so do not understand it. From
the viewpoint of reliability and maintainability, the manufacturing engineers
must work closely with quality and R&M engineers on any changes to the design to be sure that changes at worst do not degrade reliability or maintainability of the product.

Product made according to early designs has bad reliability and maintainability. That bad reliability and maintainability are improved by the process
known as R&M growth. R&M growth continues during all of the testing period
and often on into the manufacturing process. Even during early field use,
changes are made to enhance the reliability and maintainability of the product.
The changes are to the design or to manufacturing methods. In a high R&M
project, the manufacturing methods must be well documented so that quality
control can check that what is being done, ought to be done. When print and
practice disagree, one or both are changed until they do agree.

Because designs are incomplete and because reliability and maintainability
are made to grow, the concepts of inherent R&M or design R&M are misleading
at best. They imply that the design, which is nothing but a collection of words
and symbols on paper, has a reliability and a maintainability. That is not true
at all (although documents of course are themselves maintained). The drawings (and associated documents) do not possess such characteristics; only the
product does. Also, the design documents do not uniquely determine the product. It is very difficult to generate a set of design documents (often called a
technical data package) which (1) are complete and accurate enough to be used
as a fabrication specification, and (2) when followed, will result in a product
of the desired reliability and maintainability. Concepts such as inherent R&M
and design R&M wrongly direct attention away from the need for R&M growth
and for coordinated manufacturing practices.

It is conventional wisdom that performance specifications are often superior to fabrication specifications. The first tells what the resulting product must do (perform); the second tells how to make it (fabrication). The superiority is only partly and sometimes true. Performance specifications that involve reliability and maintainability are often very expensive to implement and can involve a development program. Sooner or later someone needs to prepare a fabrication specification for the manufacturing group to use.

The design, quality, R&M, purchasing, and manufacturing groups must all get together on the release of design documents for production. This is especially true for the requirements on purchased parts and on manufacturing processes. Everyone needs to be playing from the same sheet of music. For high R&M, configuration control needs to be in full operation. Material review boards and engineering change proposals need to be watched very carefully to ensure that reliability and maintainability will not be degraded unwittingly by a change to a different part or process—sometimes even when the change is supposedly for the better. In principle, *any* change whatsoever is a design change and ought to be analyzed as carefully as the original design. In practice, a great amount of engineering judgment is used instead of that analysis. That engineering judgment needs to have the inputs from quality and R&M engineers as well as from design and manufacturing engineers. The question is: Who has the burden of proof—those who want the change or those who question the change? Very often, the burden of proof is too heavy for anyone to carry.

Two critical times for reliability are when a production line is starting up or closing down. During startup people are learning what to do, and substituting for parts and materials that are not yet in house. During a close-down the best people are transferred to other production lines, and less overall care is given to the line that is closing down. Again people are substituting for parts and materials that are no longer in house and which there is no point in trying to get.

The manufacturing superintendent must have the proper incentives to produce high-conformance-quality product. These incentives must come from his or her manager. Manufacturing and shop superintendents are people. They know what is important by what their managers always complain about or ask about. Those are not necessarily the same things that managers write memos about. If R&M is to have a high priority for the manufacturing group, it must also have just as high priority for their managers and it must be reflected in any financial incentives. An end-of-month or end-of-quarter push to get product out of the door is not conducive to good quality.

VII. RELIABILITY AND SAFETY

A. Introduction to Design Techniques

The main functions of a reliability and safety program, in approximate order of priority, are:

to identify important failure modes and failure situations
eliminate identified important failure modes without introducing new ones
mitigate the consequences of identified important failure modes
eliminate or mitigate important failure situations
organize knowledge about failures to facilitate the foregoing actions

There are two general ways of implementing these functions:

1. Analyze and fix
2. Test, analyze, and fix

The first is cheaper and is usually part of the early design stage. The second is more expensive and is usually done when the first step has gone as far as it economically can; it is also used to verify (check) the early analysis. All but the last function are engineering (rather than statistical) and involve the blood, sweat, and tears common to most good engineering tasks. Statistics is used in the last function and is often a good way of communicating some of that knowledge about failures.

Good reliability and safety do not spring full blown from the early design stage. Rather, an aggressive reliability and safety program with adequate resources results in a gradual growth of the reliability and safety of the product. The program and growth period can extend from early design through field use. Reliability and safety are made to grow in the following ways:

Improving the overall design concept
Improving the reliability of individual components
Improving the local environment (e.g., temperature, shock, vibration, actions of operators and maintainers) of components and subsystems
Using redundancy and repair

Reliability and safety engineers use several kinds of diagrams of a system in their analyses. There is often considerable confusion about those diagrams, especially among theorists who work only with symbols rather than with actual product. It is convenient to use three classes of diagrams:

1. Physical diagram (e.g., wiring and piping diagrams; shows the actual physical location of system components)
2. Functional (flow) diagram (shows the flow of material or signals through the several system functions)
3. Logic diagram (shows the logical—usually good versus bad—relationships between logic states corresponding to system elements)

Often, the logic and functional diagrams look similar because (1) they both use blocks with names of system elements in the blocks, and (2) lines are used to connect the blocks. Often similar terms are used to describe relationships in logic and functional diagrams (e.g., series and parallel). These similarities often confuse theorists, who then confuse engineers while teaching them about logic diagrams. Engineers should always label the diagram according to its class, and insist that theorists do the same.

B. Organization of Action About Actual Failures

The handling and action concerning actual failures has three elements:

1. Data collection system
2. Analysis of failed item
3. Corrective action

The data collection system is often the most difficult element because (1) it usually involves dealing with people for whom your problem (getting good information) has a very low priority, and (2) much of the information will be unobtainable. Step 1 is to gain control of the physical system or location that failed. Step 2 is to get a copy of (1) the original failure reports by the operators, observers (if any), and repairers; and (2) any code sheets to decipher the failure report forms. In many cases there is only one report. If it is handwritten, it might well not be legible.

The next steps are done in any reasonable order, although it is often impossible to succeed at them. Interviews with anyone involved might help to supplement the recorded data. The actual system configuration (in as much detail as feasible) should be determined so that everyone will know exactly what it was that failed: for example, not just an automobile, but the brand, model, body, engine size, accessories, date of manufacture, and so on. The actual failure situation (in as much detail as feasible) should also be determined so that everyone will know the exact circumstances in which the failure occurred: for example, not just a car accident, but the kind of road, condition of road surface, weather before and during the accident, speeds and positions of all vehicles involved, who was driving, physiological and psychological condition of the driver, and so on.

All of the information gained so far is subject to tremendous human factors difficulties. The difficulties range from outright lies and fraud, through misrepresentation and dissembling, ignorance, and remembering wrongly. Somehow, it needs to be put into a database. The database needs to allow for all the human frailities that can turn otherwise good input into garbage. But few databases can do that. Thus more human factors enter the situation in the form of the restrictions and dichotomies forced on the analyst (or even on the input clerk) by the design of the database. Naturally, all these difficulties reflect themselves in the output of databases.

One way out of some of the documentation difficulties is to investigate only a few incidents in depth. More resources can be devoted to each incident, thus giving more accurate information about the incident. The statistical uncertainties introduced by sampling are usually small compared to the improved integrity of the input to the database.

The analysis of the failed item begins with studying the system to find the item that failed first and the circumstances that caused the first item to fail. If mechanical, electrical, or thermal violence accompanied the incident, it might not be possible to isolate the first failure. If software and hardware are involved, it might be impossible to tell which was at fault. If the fault was intermittent and the incident transitory, it is virtually hopeless to go further.

Once the failure has been isolated to a component, such as an integrated circuit, a torsion bar, or a burst hydraulic line, the physical failure analysis can begin. The analysis and verification steps should be thought out and recorded before physical analysis begins. The nondestructive tests always come first. Once an hypothesis is formed about the failure, the failure should be duplicated in the laboratory if feasible, to verify that the hypothesis is correct.

C. Reliability and Safety Growth

Reliability and safety growth is:

A management activity
An engineering activity
A statistical activity

The management activity consists of:

Including growth in the original program plan
Providing resources (money, time, people) to implement the plan
Providing the information flow about failures
Evaluating reliability and safety program reports to change priorities for
the ongoing program

Growth testing consists largely of accelerated tests whose intent is to provoke failures. If the observed failure mode can reasonably occur in practice, it is a candidate for elimination or amelioration.
The statistical activity involves:

Creating statistical models for accelerated testing and growth
Applying the models to test data, including calculating the uncertainties
Assisting engineers and managers in evaluating the meaning of the statistical
results

D. Organization of Knowledge About Potential Failures

Synthesizing the knowledge is an engineering activity that uses the mathematical language of logic and probability. Analyzing the knowledge so generated can be qualitative (little mathematics) or quantitative (all mathematics) and either way will usually involve computers for systems that contain more than 10 or so components. The books cited in Refs. 3 to 9 treat these topics, as do many others. Regardless of the titles, most of them deal with mathematics rather than with engineering. The *IEEE Transactions on Reliability* publishes several book reviews in each issue—it is a good way to keep up on the current books in the product assurance area. Several conferences have also been held on this general topic, and proceedings published [10—14].
    Failure modes, effects, and criticality analysis (FMECA) is one of the earliest developed and most popular methods of organizing knowledge about potential failures. In its early days, it did not contain the word *criticality* and was known simply as FMEA. The procedure is simple and easily learned. The FMECA is usually put on an oversize sheet of paper. Each sheet is labeled with the subsystem name and its unique description. Each element of the subsystem is put on a separate line. The line begins with the name and unique description of the element. The next column contains the failure modes; each failure mode is put on a separate line. The next column contains the effect (on the subsystem, or higher level) of that failure mode. The final column is some measure of criticality of the failure effect. A common set of measures uses the numbers 0 to 4; 0 means no effect, 4 means the worst possible effect. The words "critical (4), major (3), minor (2), trivial (1), none (0)" are often used instead of the numbers. Many people add more columns (which is why the paper is oversize) such as (1) a measure of the probability of failure, (2) the cause of the failure mode, and (3) the proposed action to eliminate the failure mode or to ameliorate its effect.
    The subsystem can be at any level of the system structure, from the system itself down to a subassembly. There is no single right way to do a FMECA; if it is useful (organizes knowledge well), it is good. Figure 1 is an example of FMECA.
    There are several techniques for developing logic diagrams. Their source material is:

FAILURE MODE & EFFECTS ANALYSIS

PRODUCT ___Steam Iron___ DONE BY _____ _____

DRAWING # HSSF44 REV A CKD BY _____ _____

CODE

CRITICALITY (CRIT)
C · Safety Hazard
MA · Major Fault · Requires Prompt Service
MN · Minor Fault · May Require Future Service
I · Insignificant

RELATIVE PROBABILITY OF OCCURRENCE (PROB)
H · High
M · Moderate
L · Low
U · Unlikely

ITEM	LINE/ PART NO	DESCRIPTION	FUNCTION OF PART	MODE OF FAILURE	EFFECT ON SYSTEM	CRIT	PROB	REMARKS	ACTION/ RESPONSIBILITY
1	8930	Plug	2 Wire Electrical Plug	Short	No heat or steam	MA	L		
				Open	No heat or steam	MA	L		
2	270931	Cord	Power from outlet to iron	Short	No heat or steam	MA	L		
				Open	No heat or steam	MA	L		
				Insulation Fail	Presents shock hazard	C	L	Lack info on Insulation heat resistance	Check insulation specs vs industry and Fed Safety standards. R. Jones due next Design Review
3	9942	Handle	Hold iron, support in upright position	Cracked, broken	Operator inconvenience to unusable	MN MA	L L		
4	12877	Upper Cover	Mount handle, plate, water indicator, bolt to lower plate	Tarnished finish	None on operation	MN	L		
18	25303	Bimetal Strip	Sense heat, open & close heat element circuit	Fail Open	No heat, no steam	MA	L		
				Fail Closed	Iron too hot. Surface remains at max temp of 350°F	MA	M		Prepare test plan for running life test on Bimetal Strip. S. Harris Due next Design Review
19	74903	Rivet	Carries current for heating element	Loose, burned surface	Low Heat	MA	L		
20	60872	Base Plate	Hot ironing surface mount for components, channels for steam	Tarnish	None on operation	I	H		
				Stripped Threads loose connection	Noise	MN	L		
					Shock Hazard	C	L		Determine cost of adding lock washer. L. Smith Due next Design Review
				Clogged	Decreased amount of steam	MA	H		
21	63923	Pressure Plug	Blow out due to overpressure	Not blow out at pressure limit	Burn hazard	C	L		a) Check field data for past history. R. Jones b) Draft test plan to check pressure plug. S. Harris c) QC establish sampling plan and inspection for plugs. N. Roberts All due next Design Review

FIGURE 1 Failure mode and effects analysis work sheet. (With the kind permission of Westinghouse Electric Corp. From "A Guide for the FMEA/FTA." Note: These are representative FMEA's/FTA's and do not necessarily represent products currently made.)

Observations on the physical processes and systems themselves
Physical diagrams
Functional (flow) diagrams
Conceptual breakdown of the system in any other useful way (e.g., thermal, mechanical, electrical, hydraulic descriptions)
Lists of failure modes

Most diagrams and their analyses are considerably simplified if modules can be identified and used in the diagrams. Each module then has its own diagram. A module is a collection of:

Events on a logic diagram, or
Functions on a functional (flow) diagram

such that their effects are entirely confined to the module. Then the module
can be used in the diagram in place of the collection.

The five most common, popular, or useful diagrams are listed below.

1. *Ishikawa fishbone diagram*: Also called Ishikawa diagram or fishbone
diagram; Kaoru Ishikawa is credited with orginating the concept. An example
is shown in Fig. 2. This is a qualitative technique. There are only a few
rules for drawing the diagram.

    a. Effects are horizontal lines. The spine is the main effect of concern.

    b. Causes are slanting vertical lines. Their ordering and location have
no importance.

    c. Each cause is, in itself, an effect and thus can have its own causes.

    d. The diagram should not become too complicated. If there is too much
information, begin a new chart using one of the subeffects as a new
spine on a new diagram.

The diagram can be created as a group effort. Success has been reported
in putting such a diagram on the shop floor to describe a manufacturing process, and having workers add to it as they discover important points. The
Ishikawa fishbone diagram can serve as a useful input to other logic diagrams.
It deserves to become more widely known and used.

2. *Reliability block diagrams*: This is the original logic diagram used by
reliability theoreticians. It is similar to a signal-flow graph. The following
rules govern creation of the diagram.

    a. The system is divided into modules.

    b. The system and each module have exactly two states (good or bad).
If more than two states are needed to describe module or system behavior (e.g., good, fail-safe, fail-unsafe), separate diagrams must be
drawn so that this rule is fulfilled. If that is not feasible, then strictly
speaking, a reliability block diagram cannot be drawn for the system,
and a functional diagram is usually used with other methods of analysis.
Extreme care must be used not to confuse the functional and logic diagrams, or wrong answers can result.

    c. The diagram is constructed so that flow through any set of blocks from
beginning to end is interpreted as "the system is good;" else, the system is bad.

The two most common constructions are *series* and *parallel*. A series system is good if and only if all its elements are good (Fig. 3). A parallel system
is bad if and only if all its elements are bad (Fig. 4). Many reliability block
diagrams can be composed of modules which are either in series or parallel
and which themselves contain only series or parallel submodules; Fig. 5 is an
example of such a diagram. (A discussion of the analysis of these diagrams is
included in this chapter.)

The most common error made in analysis is assuming erroneously that failure events for each block are statistically independent. The most common
reason for statistical dependence is common partial causes for the failure events
(e.g., environments such as flood, heat, cold, shock, and vibration). For
example, if the probability of burning up one astronaut in an oxygen atmosphere is P, what is the probability of burning up three astronauts in an oxygen

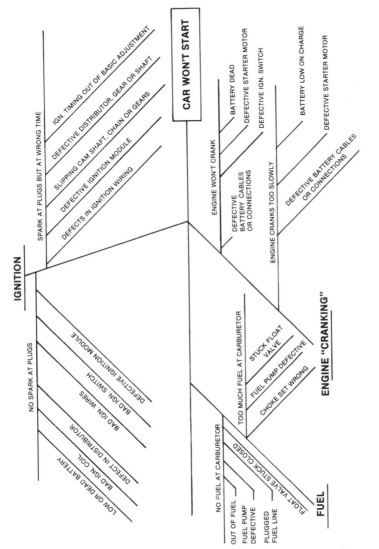

FIGURE 2 Fishbone diagram (Ishikawa cuase and effect diagram).

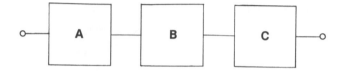

FIGURE 3   Components or assemblies in series.

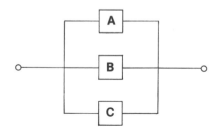

FIGURE 4   Components or assemblies in parallel.

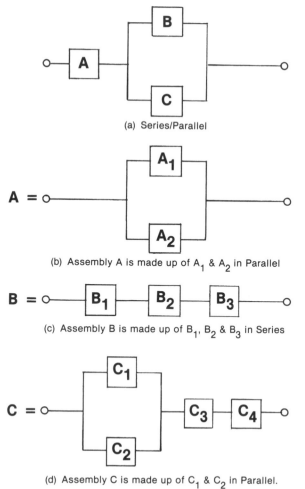

(a) Series/Parallel

(b) Assembly A is made up of A_1 & A_2 in Parallel

(c) Assembly B is made up of B_1, B_2 & B_3 in Series

(d) Assembly C is made up of C_1 & C_2 in Parallel.
The resulting Assembly is in Series with C_3 & C_4.

FIGURE 5   Assemblies in series parallel.

atmosphere? The answer lies in the fact that three astronauts did burn up in an oxygen atmosphere; the horrible burn-up catastrophes were not statistically independent—they had a common cause.

It is feasible and sometimes quite desirable to have separate diagrams for different classes of being bad (failure effects). Examples of classes of failure effects are (a) cause customer complaint, (b) non-self-announcing fail-safe, and (c) non-self-announcing fail-unsafe. As long as no logic errors are made, there are no rules at all which prohibit one from being as creatively useful as possible in drawing the diagrams.

3. *Fault trees (analysis and synthesis)*: A good discussion of several points of view about fault trees is given in Ref. 15. The fault tree itself is a collection of events and logical gates such that the output of the gate results if and only if the input events to the gate, when combined according to the logic rules for that gate type, cause the output event. For example, the output event for a logical AND gate results if and only if all the input events are present. Figure 6 shows the common symbols used for gates and events. Other gate symbols can be used if their logic is clearly and uniquely defined. The tree is drawn upside down (in the United States), with its root (top event) at the top; Fig. 7 is an example fault tree. Top events are unwanted events (failures or failure effects). The tree is developed by looking at each event locally and seeing how it could be caused. The development stops when the undeveloped events are sufficiently well understood that further development (for the purpose of the particular fault tree) is not needed; there are no arbitrary rules. Similarly, there are no rules for the number of top events or what they should be.

A limiting factor in developing a fault tree is that each event situation must be quantized; the most common quantization is two states. For example, a valve is usually considered to be either open or closed, either leaking or not leaking, and so on. But real components and systems have degrees of behavior. Valves can be partly closed, or have a small leak. There is no logic reason why several states cannot be used. But if they are, the fault tree becomes much more complicated, and the necessary database is not available for quantitative analysis.

Any conceptual model is an abstraction and simplification of the real world. The more simpleminded the model, the easier it is to work with, but the less well it represents reality. But it is not difficult to generate models that can not be solved with present tools. In generating fault trees, there are at least three different kinds of system representation that are used (either implicitly or explicitly) as inputs: (a) one-parameter (flow or potential), (b) two-parameter (flow and potential), and (c) mixtures of the two. In one-parameter system representation, the flow or potential methods are logically equivalent. They run into difficulty with things like check valves, whose flow versus potential relation depends on the direction of flow, burst pipes, or electrical ground fault. Separate fault trees have to be developed for each condition. The potential and flow methods respectively are described in Refs. 16 and 17. The two-parameter (flow and potential) method is described in Ref. 18.

The Lapp-Powers fault-tree synthesis algorithm [19] is a mixture of one-parameter and two-parameter methods, although it is more like combining two one-parameter descriptions. One first prepares a particular kind of directed graph (digraph) of the system from the physical and functional diagrams of the system. The digraph allows five conditions of "flow" from one node to another (*high* in either direction, *low* in either direction, *zero*). From this digraph, semiautomated methods can be used to construct the fault tree. The

FAULT TREE ANALYSIS LOGIC SYMBOLS

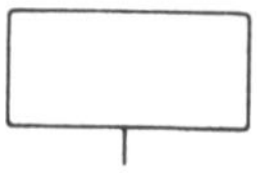

The RECTANGLE identifies an event, usually a malfunction, that results from the combination of fault events through the logic gates.

The AND GATE describes the logical operation whereby the coexistence of all input events is required to produce the output event.

The OR GATE defines the situation whereby the output event will exist if any or all of the input events are present.

The CIRCLE describes a basic fault event that requires no further development. This category includes component failures whose frequency and/or mode of failure are derived or known.

The DIAMOND describes a fault event that is considered basic in a given fault tree; however, the causes of the event have not been developed, either because the event is of insufficient consequence or the necessary information is unavailable.

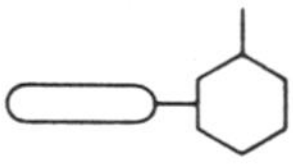

The INHIBIT GATE describes a causal relationship between one fault and another. The input event directly produces the output event if the indicated condition is satisfied.

The HOUSE indicates an event that is normally expected to occur.

The TRIANGLE indicates a transfer symbol. A line from the apex of the triangle denotes a transfer in and a line from the side denotes a transfer out.

FIGURE 6   Fault tree analysis logic symbols. (With the kind permission of Westinghouse Electric Corp. From "A Guide for the FMEA/FTA." Note: These are representative FMEA's/FTA's and do not necessarily represent products currently made.)

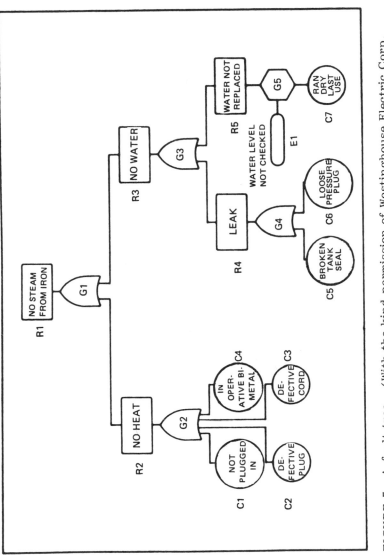

FIGURE 7   A fault tree. (With the kind permission of Westinghouse Electric Corp. From "A Guide for the FMEA/FTA." Note: These are representative FMEA's/FTA's and do not necessarily represent products currently made.)

technique has been particularly fruitful in describing processes. A "simple" nitric acid cooler with temperature feedback and pump-shutdown feedforward loops was used to illustrate the method. Ever since, experts have been arguing over the validity of the model for the process (many of those arguments appear in subsequent issues of the *IEEE Transactions on Reliability*). The arguments demonstrate that reducing a physical system to mathematics is neither trivial nor unique.

The main difficulty in quantitative analysis is similar to that for reliability block diagrams. The most common error made in analysis is erroneously assuming that failure events for each block are statistically independent. Statistical dependence arises largely in two ways: (a) some events can have a common partial cause, and (b) some events are mutually exclusive (e.g., valve open, valve closed).

4. *Cause-consequence charts*: This is a combination of a fault tree (although the Danes, who invented these charts, draw the root at the bottom) and then an expansion of the "top event" into a tree of consequences. Semiautomatic methods are available for generating these charts; they tend to use the two-parameter description of a system. Cause-consequence charts are described in Refs. 18 and 20 to 22. There is nothing inherent in this method that makes accounting for statistical dependence any easier than in reliability block diagrams or in fault trees.

5. *Schematic diagram*: Any schematic diagram is a diagram that implies a set of equations which connect the parts of the diagram. Thus given a schematic diagram, one has in principle a set of equations for the system. If that set of equations exists, it can be solved for the effect of variations in the parameters on the output of the system. The two most popular methods are worst-case analysis and parameter-variation analysis.

In worst-case analysis, all parameters are presumed to have limits of variation that will not be exceeded. All parameters are set at the values that produce the lowest output, and then at the values that produce the highest output. The resulting two extremes of output are the worst cases. The analysis is regarded by many people as being overly pessimistic and by others as being rather realistic. It is generally worth doing even if the results are used only approximately.

In parameter variations analysis, the equation is linearized by a Taylor's series. Each coefficient (in the Taylor's series) is multiplied by the standard deviation of the parameter involved in generating that coefficient; then the result is squared. All such terms are added and give the square of the standard deviation of the output. Often three standard deviations either side of nominal is regarded as the approximate practical limits of the variation. If analytic differentiation is not feasible, numerical differentiation can be used.

These techniques work only on rather small assemblies or subsystems because (a) the equations become too complicated to solve for larger systems, and (b) often the equations for larger systems are not even known—and if they were, many of the parameters in them might not be known. Thus the results are often used as an input to a FMECA or fault tree synthesis for the larger system.

E. Critical Items and Situations

A major reliability and safety function is to identify those items or situations which are high risk. For exmaple, a component might be used near its electrical and temperature limits because no other component is available. That component is a critical item. An example of a critical situation is a pervasive high-vibration or high-temperature condition is a subsystem.

Critical items and situations should be brought promptly and clearly to the attention of management so that they can be monitored. When the reliability or safety risk is too high, design or fabrication changes should be made. A formal procedure in reliability and safety reports needs to be arranged so that such conditions are highly visible to management

F. Budgeting

An allowed number of failures (e.g., 5% per year) is presumed to be given to a system. To design the subsystems, that allowance of 5% per year needs to be allocated to the subsystems. The allocation should be such that the critical resources (money, calendar time, people) consumed are minimized. Usually, only one or two of the resources will be critical. For example, if calendar time and people are in short supply, they will be used up before the money runs out. To allocate the allowance to subsystems, some idea of a reasonable number of failures for each subsystem has to be obtained.

This procedure is directly analogous to money budgeting at home. A certain amount of money is available. First one often calculates roughly how much money is desired for each item, such as food, clothing, housing, and savings; that is a projection. The total is usually too much for the available supply. Then the supply is usually allocated roughly to each item; that is an allocation. The fit is usually not too good. Then a give and take occurs until the amount of suffering is equalized in some way. When the process is completed, some assumptions will probably have been made, for example, no new clothes for this year for a family member or an inexpensive vacation for the family. This set of assumptions must be recorded because it is the basis of the fit. Budgeting can always be done, no matter how large or how small the available supply of money; thus no one is surprised that there is a fit. The thing that makes people happy or upset is those assumptions.

Budgeting for failures is exactly the same procedure. The projection of number of failures needed for each subsystem is based in some way on previous experience, either with similar subsystems or with the components of the subsystems. Usually, the projected total will exceed the supply, and the cut and try will begin. It is the assumptions made during the projections that are important. For example, if high-reliability parts are needed to meet the budget, that constraint must be very visible and must be communicated clearly to the design engineers.

Once the budget is established for each subsystem, the budgeting process goes down deeper into sub-subsystems and on down to components. The budgeting principles remain the same at each level. It is common for there to be several kinds of failures, each with its own budget. For example, the budgets could be 5% per year for safe failures and 0.1% per year for unsafe failures. In addition to failures, other things must be budgeted, such as development cost, weight, volume, power dissipation, unit production cost, and available people. The final budgets for everything must be compatible, have compatible assumptions, and be made clear to everyone concerned. Those assumptions will drastically affect the design process.

The word *prediction* is often used instead of the word *projection*. Thus one sees and hears the phrase *reliability prediction*. The word *prediction* is used in its probability sense of calculating the probability of an event from the probabilities of the subevents that comprise the event. For example, the probability of throwing a seven with a pair of fair dice is predicted (from the probabilities of occurrence of each of the faces) to be 6/36. Unfortunately, the word has other more usual meanings, so it is wise to avoid using the word to refer to the budgeting process.

The more experience with similar systems one has, the more complicated and exact the budgeting procedure can be. Usually, a database will be used during at least part of the budgeting. Most databases are not as good as their users would like to think those databases are. It is extremely difficult to get good field failure data to put into a database. A source of continual confusion in reliability work is the distinction between a failure and a removal, or between a failure and a customer complaint. A rule of thumb says that in the field there will be about two removals for each failure. Not all removed elements are failures, nor do all failures result in a removal. Similar considerations hold for the distinction between a failure and a customer complaint. It behooves everyone in the budgeting procedure to be very careful that the words are used carefully and properly in the requirements given, and in the budgets prepared.

The presumption in the budgeting process is that failures are allocated to subsystems by simple addition. This presumption implicitly assumes that the subsystems are in series (on the reliability block diagram) — which they usually are, or can be adjusted to be. If they are not thus in series, the calculations become very much more complicated; for example, the mission time must be considered.

G. Assessment

Assessment is the process by which data from tests and the field are used in a reliability model to calculate the observed reliability of a system. The observed values are then usually compared to the budgeted values. Very often, the field data are incomplete; that is, the operating temperatures, voltages, duty cycles, mechanical environment, failure environment, failure confirmation, and detailed service environment are unknown within rather wide limits. In some cases the types of data on the system are not in a form that matches anything in the system reliability model. These unknowns mean that the database into which the observations are to be put is incomplete and/or innaccurate. There is no good remedy for the difficulties. A good approach is to select a few equipments and sites and then investigate those user complaints in depth with specially trained people.

A good data collection system is essential no matter what approach is used. Suitable forms must be available for those who service the equipment and must be easy to fill out properly. The information on the forms is then gone over by trained people and entered into the database. Where feasible, the repairer can enter the information directly into the computer. The information can still be reviewed by trained people before it is allowed to enter the database. If forms and procedures are too complicated, people will not fill them out conscientiously. If they are too simple, there will not be enough useful information for corrective action.

Companies that do have good databases have invested tremendous resources (money, calendar time, people) in them. All the caveats about quality control and administration of databases apply to reliability and safety databases. Garbage in rarely averages out to anything but garbage out.

H. Classification of Failures

Classifying failures can be important for a variety of reasons. The classification, especially an implicit classification, affects how one looks at a failure.

Failure Mode Versus Failure Mechanism

The concepts of failure mode and failure mechanism are often used. Failure mode is the observable behavior of an item when it fails (e.g., the failure modes of an electric motor might be classified as bearing seizure, bearing wearout, winding short, winding open, overheating). Failure mechanism is the cause (in the item) of the observed failure mode. It is "one level down" from the failure mode. The distinction between failure mode and failure mechanism is arbitrary and depends on the level at which observations are made. For example, a failure mode of a radar is antenna failure; the failure mechanism might be motor failure. If the motor is observed, the failure mode might be bearing seizure and the failure mechanism might be loss of lubrication. If the bearing is observed, its failure mode would be loss of lubrication, and the failure mechanism might be seal failure. If the seal is observed, ... Thus the distinction between failure mode and failure mechanism depends on the subsystem level being observed.

Failure Models

There are three common simple conceptual models for failure.

1. *Damage-endurance*: The item accumulates damage until the endurance is reached, at which time the item fails. Up to that time, the item operates satisfactorily. The usual, tractable assumption is that damage accumulation is linear for constant severity level.
2. *Stress-strength*: The item is subjected to stresses. If the stress is less than the strength, the item is good as new. If the stress exceeds the strength, the item fails. Repeated applications of stress that is below the strength do no damage.
3. *Challenge-response*: The item contains many elements, some of which are rarely challenged during operation. The elements are either good or bad. If a bad element is challenged, the system response is to fail. If a bad element is not challenged, the system works satisfactorily. This model implies that system failure depends on system history. It is often difficult to distinguish between hardware and software failures when system failure is of this type. Virtually all software failures have this model.

Perception of Failure Consequences

Users views' of failure depend on what type of user is involved. For example, if a traction motor on a transit car fails but the train keeps running, a customer, clerk/operator, manager, or owner will perceive the failure consequence differently. The maintenance organization has its own perception of failure. Concerned bystanders might be interested in personal safety or the environment; their reactions can be different from all the rest.

Failure consequences can be virtually harmless, as when a cigarette lighter in a car fails, or can be catastrophic, as when a hoist chain fails, or somewhere in between.

Responsibility for Failure

Not all failures are relevant to a reliability test (e.g., a tree falling on a car is not a relevant failure for the automaker). Nor are all relevant failures chargeable to the producer (e.g., driving a passenger car 1000 miles at high speeds in low gear will cause the transmission and perhaps the engine to fail or severely degrade). Different kinds of responsibility are:

> Covered by warranty or not
> User, maintainer, or manufacturer (some failures are induced by the maintenance process)
> Design or production (important for legal liability, or for corrective action)
> Proper use, foreseeable misuse, unforeseeable misuse (important for liability)
> Placing blame or locating area for profitable corrective action

Announcement of Failure

Some failures announce themselves all too rudely (e.g., a tire blowout). Other failures become evident only when one attempts to use the function (e.g., a brake failure). There are important safety and maintenance consequences of the degree of self-announcement of a failure. Some failures announce themselves differently to different users. For example, if a traction motor fails on a transit car, the operator might know it immediately, whereas a passenger might never know it. Failures in a rarely used safety system are almost never self-announcing and thus can be dangerous.

If impending failure is announced in a fairly harmless way, the user is often much more satisfied than if failure is sudden and complete. Impending failures which are self-announcing can be entirely so or make themselves known only upon a test. Most aircraft engines are repaired "on condition," that is, when an impending failure makes itself known, usually by means of a special test.

Degree of Malfunction

Even though much simple reliability theory presumes that items are either good or bad, there are degrees of malfunction, such as minor degradation, noticeable degradation, and complete failure. If an item has several functions, some of them can fail without impairing the others.

Relative Severity of Different Failure Modes

Not all failure modes are equally undesirable. Some failure modes have worse effects than others. The most common classification is fail-safe and fail-unsafe. An example is duds (fail safe) and prematures (explodes before it leaves the scene) in artillery shells. Many safety systems are designed to force failures to be fail-safe. But if the safety system itself is unreliable, many safe failures are introduced to eliminate a few unsafe failures; when carried to an extreme, the system is so unreliable it is of no use whatsoever.

An example is legal efforts to eliminate some death causes, such as cancer. Rarely do legislators concern themselves with trade-offs against other death causes.

I. Redundancy Versus Replication

Redundancy is the provision of alternative methods of accomplishing a task. Not all replication is redundancy. The biggest complication arises when there are degrees of undesirability of failure modes, such as fail-safe versus fail-unsafe. When an attempt is made to decrease the probability of one kind of failure mode by adding equipment, the probability of some other failure mode is increased.

For example, a safety element is replicated for a total of three statistically independent elements in the safety subsystem. If the three elements are in logic parallel (the safety subsystem fails unsafe if and only if all three elements fail) for the unsafe failure mode, the probability of the unsafe failure mode is appreciably reduced. However, the three elements are in logic series (the safety subsystem fails safe if and only if any of its three elements fails) with the system for the safe failure mode. This complication illustrates the need to distinguish between a functional diagram and a logic diagram for a system. A system can have many logic diagrams.

Another example is relay contacts. If the contacts are put physically in parallel, the failure mode of "staying open when it should not" has its probability of occurrence reduced, whereas the failure mode of "staying closed when it should not" has its probability of occurrence increased.

Much elementary reliability literature does not explain this complication. It can be very important in practical systems. For example, historical anecdote refers to the "popsicle stick" phenomenon in early research nuclear reactors. The safety subsystems contained many relays, but were very unreliable (perhaps because of their design requirements). The relays were closing because the safety subsystems themselves were failing, rather than because the reactor itself was in trouble. Thus operators would put popsicle sticks between the contacts of the safety relays so that the system could be brought on line. This example also illustrates the importance of considering all the human factors in a system when assessing its safety.

The failure events of replicated elements often are not statistically independent but have a common partial cause of failure. The causes can be as subtle as silver migration in all the elements due to high humidity, or as obvious as an earthquake. The nominal benefits of redundancy are not fully obtained unless the failure events are fully statistically independent.

J. Trade-offs

During the design and manufacture of a product it is often necessary or desirable to trade off one characteristic against another. Some examples are given here.

1. *Operational reliability versus maintainability*: Some construction methods have good reliability and poor maintainability, and vice versa. The designer must choose a good combination.
2. *Operational reliability versus safety*: Adding safety equipment often decreases the operational reliability.
3. *One failure mode versus another*: A failure mode that is self-announcing is generally preferred to one that is not. A failure mode that signals impending failure is generally preferred to one that does not. A failure mode that allows partial operation (being able to limp home) is generally preferred to one that does not.
4. When human factors are concerned, preventive maintenance can degrade subsequent reliability more than no preventive maintenance.

Not everything a designer does involves difficult trade-offs, but many of them do. Good organization of knowledge about potential failures can help in the analysis to see whether trade-offs are involved in a design consideration.

K. Parts Program

An effective parts program should accomplish two important things.

1. *Set application guidelines and/or requirements for all kinds of parts*:
    For example, safety factors for maximum power dissipation or voltage
    for semiconductors, and safety factors for maximum mechanical stress
    on metal parts. In general, the burden of proof should be on the de-
    signer who wants to deviate from the application factors.
2. *Standardize on a relatively few part types and sizes*: This allows better
    logistics and better quality assurance for those parts. Designers tend
    not to be in favor of this restriction on them, but it is virtually always
    best for the system. In general, the burden of proof should be on the
    designer who wants to deviate from the standardization.

L. Acceptance Testing

Acceptance testing is discussed elsewhere in this chapter. It is too easy to
concentrate on the statistical part of the test and forget about the more important engineering and management elements of the test.

M. Nonuse Effects

Procedures should be established, maintained, and implemented to determine
the effects (on reliability) of storage, handling, packaging, transportation,
maintenance, and repeated exposure to functional testing. If any of them are
determined to be detrimental, the bad effects must be alleviated by design,
manufacturing, inspection, or other changes.

N. Task Effectiveness

None of the reliability and safety tasks will be effective unless the "product
knows about it." The results of those tasks must make a difference to someone—management, design, production, quality, purchasing, or shipping.
The difficulty of being done in isolation has plagued the reliability and safety
effort for decades. The best solution to the problem is for an affected group
to have the incentive to want the tasks done and thus to ask the reliability
and safety groups for their help. It is up to management to provide that
incentive.

VIII. MAINTAINABILITY AND SUPPORT

A. Introduction to Design Techniques

The main functions of a maintainability and support program, in approximate
order of priority, are:

To identify important causes of poor maintenance or excessive downtime
To eliminate identified important causes of poor maintenance or excessive
    downtime without introducing new ones
To provide a suitable support program (people and material)
To organize knowledge about maintenance difficulties to facilitate the fore-
    going actions

There are two general ways of implementing these functions:

1. Analyze and fix
2. Test, analyze, and fix

The first is cheaper and is usually part of the entire design stage. The second is more expensive and is usually done when the first step has gone as far as it economically can; it is also used to patch inadequate results of the first step. Identifying and eliminating causes of poor maintenance is a "blood, sweat, and tears" engineering task. Providing a suitable support function requires much planning and practical experience; the practical experience helps to generate feasible, comprehensive plans.

Planning the support function can be a tremendous task involving many people. It is relatively easy to decide in general what *ought* to happen. Planning so that the details *will* happen is very tedious and difficult. The theory tends to be useful only on a general level because the data (as opposed to intelligent guessing) needed for detailed theory do not exist. The overall support problem has a tremendous number of variables. To achieve a cost-effective solution to the problem, some kind of optimization needs to be done. But optimization techniques that are useful in the presence of great uncertainties in the parameters of the model are not availalbe. Most of the rest of this paragraph deals with maintainability rather than logistics. (See Refs. 23 to 26 for several books on logistics.)

B. Support Alternatives

The first alternative is whether or not to plan explicitly for support. If the item itself is cheaper to buy than to repair, support reduces to selling more items. Many electrical home appliances and power tools fall into this category. The remainder of this discussion presumes that it has been decided to plan for support. It is not feasible to state an order in which the following facets must be considered and decided upon. Usually, tentative decisions are made, then the entire situation is assessed repeatedly until the total support system is satisfactory.

1. *Work-breakdown structure*: The breakdown of a system into subsystems, sub-subsystems, . . . , assemblies, subassemblies, . . . , elementary components is called the work-breakdown structure. It is part of the design of a system. Generally, a repairer is presumed to approach a system at the top of the work-breakdown structure and proceed downward by progressively isolating the trouble. The troubleshooting stops when the trouble can be fixed.

2. *Sources of support*: Repair can be done by (a) a formal company organization such as the telephone companies use, (b) independent franchised companies such as many automobile dealerships, or (c) independent companies such as many automobile repair shops. Repair parts can also be provided by the original manufacturer or independent companies. For some large specialized systems (e.g., nuclear power plants or computers) large companies often set up special divisions to handle system support.

3. *Levels of support*: The three usual levels of support are discussed in Sec. I.B. Level 1 is the scene of the malfunction, level 2 is a repair shop, and level 3 is the factory or similar depot capable of complicated overhauls and service.

4. *Maintenance actions*: Repair and throwaway are the only two possible types of maintenance actions. At some level of the work-breakdown structure the only possible type of maintenance is throwaway (e.g., burned-out transistor). A decision must be made for every part of every system concerning the work-breakdown-structure level at which throwaway maintenance is to take place.

5. *Maintenance concept*: The maintenance concept deals with the work-breakdown-structure level at which malfunctions are detected, how they are detected (testing), and how decisions are made about which element to replace (diagnosis). The concept need not go into details, but rather provides a policy within which details are worked out as part of the support system. There are several test philosophies: built-in test equipment (BITE), automated test equipment (ATE), specialized test equipment, and general test equipment. The maintenance concept strongly affects logistics and costs.

6. *Test and diagnosis*: Once the maintenance concept has been established, the details of test and diagnosis must be worked out. An important consideration is "ease of support" versus "cost and complexity of tests and test equipment." Costs include costs of personnel acquisition and their training. The test equipment itself needs to be very reliable, especially with respect to non-self-announcing failures that cause wrong answers during the test. It is extremely difficult to choose tests such that an item passes the test if and only if the item works in the field. If there is built-in test equipment, the quality control effort during manufacturing can use it, as an added bonus.

7. *Modularity and commonality*: An equipment module usually provides a complete function at some level of the work-breakdown structure, and is usually replaceable as a module. If modules occur at too low a level, too many of them are needed, and isolation of a fault is difficult. If modules occur at too high a level, there is little if any commonality among them (and among other modules for similar equipment). Commonality is often called standardization. Most of its benefits are indirect; that is, the people who must design commonality into a system get all the work and few of the benefits. Thus they have a tendency to dislike it.

8. *Cannibalization*: Cannibalization involves obtaining a repair part from another system rather than from a repair-part inventory. For many kinds of systems it is a very convenient source of repair parts. But cannibalized repair parts are the most expensive repair parts there are. If cannibalization is likely to be practiced, it should be recognized and planned for.

9. *Repair parts*: Putting a part into a logistic system is usually very expensive. Anyone who has occasion to pay for repair parts knows that their cost seems exhorbitant. Designers often underestimate the logistic-system costs involved in adding another part to the system.

10. *Maintenance load*: All failures, regardless of relevance or chargeability, have to be fixed by the owner. All component failures, even if they do not cause noticeable system degradation, have to be fixed. Some people mistakenly believe that if customers are not inconvenienced, there are no failures to fix. The maintenance work load is easy to underestimate, at all maintenance levels.

C. Organization of Action About Actual Deficiencies

The data collection system itself needs to be integrated with other data systems, such as the one for handling the failures themselves. This portion of the data system, however, deals not with the actual failures, but with maintenance times and difficulties. The corrective action similarly deals not with the failure itself, but with its repair. The data collection system is used as a means for identifying maintainability design difficulties and errors and ini tiating corrective action. Corrective action can involve changes to (1) fault detection and isolation methods (both hardware and software), (2) packaging methods, and so on.

The database should be capable of supplying information on (1) logistics and support adequacy; (2) adequacy of support resources such as technical manuals, test equipment, and training; (3) personnel requirements; (4) maintainability deficiencies; (5) repair-time histories for use in projection ("prediction") and assessment; (6) compliance with maintainability requirements; and (7) effectiveness of, and resources consumed in, preventive maintenance.

All the database difficulties mentioned earlier in this chapter apply as well to the maintainability portion of the database.

D. Maintainability and Support Growth

Maintainability and support growth is:

A management activity
An engineering activity
A mathematical modeling activity

The management activity consists of:

Including growth in the original program plan
Providing resources (money, time, people) to implement the plan
Providing information flow about maintenance actions
Evaluating maintainability and support program reports to change priorities
   for the ongoing program

Growth testing consists largely of testing with actual mockups and with as complete "walk-throughs" as feasible. A mock-up is a simulated piece of equipment which can be used to check physical accessability, room to do things that are supposed to be done, and other ergonomic (human physiology) factors. For example, can the repairer actually fit into the space available? Can a repairer actually get a wrench into the desired space and then turn the bolt or nut? Will a rack actually pull out into the passageway? A walk-through can be mental and/or physical, and can use a physical model for clarity. Every detail of a maintenance action is then gone through in simulated form. There can be no handwaving to indicate how something is done or how something will get to where it is supposed to be. Physical models of large systems (e.g., an electric power generating station) can help the engineers and architects see how many different things they have unwittingly decided to put in one place. It is impossible to visualize all these things from the drawings.

Computerized models of the entire system, including logistics, are often part of a walk-through. By assigning probability distributions to failure times, maintenance times, other downtimes, modules removed during maintenance, and so on, Monte Carlo simulation programs can go through many months or years of system use. Some such models can take many worker-months or even worker-years to prepare and check out. The models can be incredibly detailed and include such things as (1) the several levels of maintenance, (2) fault isolation, (3) delays of all kinds, (4) personnel skill levels, and (5) test equipment adequacy. The more complicated the system, the more essential is a good model for it, and the more expensive that model is. Very simple items (e.g., a microcomputer) probably do not require a formal model at all.

E. Organization of Knowledge About Potential Maintenance Activities

Generally, this knowledge builds on that which has been gathered for reliability and safe activities. For example, a failure modes and effects analysis supplies valuable information on failure symptoms that can be used in diagnosis. Human factors information must be integrated with maintenance activities. For example, maintenance-induced failures (sins of both omission and commission) can be a very real cause of system unreliability and even catastrophe. Many of the models mentioned in the previous subparagraph are used to store this kind of knowledge.

The owner is interested in all failures and malfunctions, and symptoms thereof, whether true or false. Everything that goes wrong with the system, or apparently goes wrong with it, must be investigated and fixed regardless of whose fault it is. All efforts of repairers and their results (whether good or bad, right or wrong, wise or foolish), at all maintenance levels, must be paid for by the owner. This is a fact often overlooked by a buyer as well as the developer/seller of the system. The buck stops at the owner. This makes the maintenance activity incredibly more expensive than predicted by simple-minded failure/repair models.

Excellent maintainability can have unforeseen by-products. For example, some aircraft electronic equipment was so easy to diagnose, repair, and get at that repairers would cannibalize needed equipment from good, nearby aircraft rather than taking the time to go to the storeroom to get a repair part. Thus many aircraft were down because of the cannibalization (cannibalization is rarely reported by anyone). The result of excellent maintainability was a lower fraction of system readiness rather than a higher one. It is imperative that all knowledge about maintenance activities be organized and made readily available to designers and logisticians.

It is conventional wisdom to say that money can be saved by reducing maintenance needs. But if union rules, safety rules, or some other rules require a maintenance crew of a certain size, no money can be saved by reducing the maintenance load. Attention to detail is a prime requisite for intelligent decisions and actions.

F. Design Criteria

The following kinds of design criteria are necessary.

Checklists
Interchangeability requirements
Limited numbers of parts and sizes
Limited kinds of tools, accessories, test equipment, and support equipment
Proper ergonomic (human physiology) constraints on repairers
Limited repairer numbers, skills, and education
Accessibility of parts, test points, adjustments, and connections
Nondestructive inspection access panels
Test by visual methods only, without disassembly
Handling, mobility, and transportability
Logistic support coordination with other activities

G. Budgeting

The budgeting is more complicated than for failures because maintenance times
or rates do not simply add. Nevertheless, the system maintainability must be
allocated downward and projected ("predicted") upward until the results agree.
As with failure budgeting, achieving the budget is not the important thing (it
can always be done). The important thing is all the assumptions that had to
be made for the successful budget. Those assumptions become further constraints on design and maintainability. The maintainability model is essential
for the budgeting activity in analogy to the reliability model and failure
allowances.

H. Maintenance Analysis

Some books on this topic, in addition to the ones given earlier in this Section,
are cited in Refs. 24, 27, and 28. The following material is needed for the
analysis.

> Mean times to repair and/or restore at all maintenance levels
> Maintenance worker-hours as a function of maintenance task, flight hours,
>   operating time, and so on, for all maintenance levels
> False-alarm rates
> Proportion of faults that are detectable for all maintenance levels (include
>   built-in and external test and diagnosis)
> Levels of isolation during diagnosis at all work-breakdown-structure levels
>   for each level of maintenance
> Mixes of built-in, external, and manual test possible at all maintenance
>   levels and their associated software and technical costs, required skill
>   levels, personnel levels, and acquisition costs
> Producibility considerations
> All associated maintainability and life-cycle cost models
> Plans for performing corrective or preventive maintenance ahead of
>   schedule whenever the system is down (For large systems where down-
>   time is incredibly expensive, such as an electric power plant, this kind
>   of planning can pay for itself many times over.)

I. Maintenance Contracts and Reliability
Improvement Warranties

A maintenance contract is simply a contract to perform maintenance on a system for a stated period of time and for a stated cost. There are many varieties
and they can be built in to rental or leasing agreements. They are usually
purchased by (1) relatively small users as insurance policies against excessive
repair costs, or (2) larger users who believe they have better ways to invest
their resources than in running their own repair services. The contract can
be with the original seller or a third party.

A reliability improvement warranty (RIW) has some characteristics of a
maintenance contract and must include maintenance. But the period of time
covered by the contract and who the contractor is must meet certain requirements. The contractor must be one who can change the design and physically
make changes to the equipment. The period of time is such that the average
item will have returned to the contractor several times if the equipment reliability is not improved. Under these conditions the contractor has considerable financial incentive to change the design and modify the equipment as it
comes back so that it will not come back again. The contractor can make a

profit because the original contract price is paid regardless of what is done. The owner benefits from reduced downtime and associated costs.

J. Acceptance Testing

The same engineering and management caveats hold for maintainability acceptance tests as for reliability acceptance tests. The maintainability tests are more complicated statistically because the maintenance time is assumed to be distributed lognormally instead of exponentially.

K. Task Effectiveness

As for reliability tasks, maintainability tasks are useless unless their results are applied by design, manufacturing, repair service, and logistic groups. Ensuring that the task results are used is a management job. If they are not applied, management has wasted its resources and done a bad job. When things are done poorly, the blame goes squarely on the management.

IX. PRODUCT LIABILITY

Product liability is:

> A legal response to an unsafe failure
> A management problem
> An engineering problem
> A record-keeping problem
> A loss control problem
> A legal problem

Some products are designed or manufactured so that they are unconscionably unsafe. Some plaintiffs and their lawyers unconscionably and fraudulently misuse the product liability justice system. But there are a great many people on both sides who, in good faith, believe they are right. This section is not intended to give legal advice, nor should any such advice be inferred by the reader.

The law is what the highest court to rule on the case says it is. Laws vary from state to state and from time to time. It is convenient to think of two types of law: statute law and common (case) law. Examples of statute law are speed limits, the Uniform Commercial Code (UCC), and pollution restrictions. Statute law changes only when an arm of government changes the statute. Common law reflects what the courts regard as reasonable and just, usually in the absence of specific statutes. Most product liability suits are brought under common law, although some states have covered, or are considering covering, some of the area by statute law.

A tort, as opposed to a contract violation, is a wrong (of omission or commission) which results in injury. Strict liability in tort (as opposed to negligence) is a relatively recent development in common law by the courts and attempts to cut through legal technicalities so that a relatively helpless consumer can obtain suitable redress from a powerful manufacturer for injuries caused by the manufacturer's product. Roughly speaking, under the doctrine of strict liability in tort, a seller of a defective and unreasonably dangerous product is subject to liability for any harm the product causes, regardless of (1) seller's due care or contractual obligations, or (2) the user's reasonable misuse. This has come to be known as product liability. Unfortunately, the word *reasonable* is difficult to define in general.

Courts generally distinguish between a design defect in which all articles have nominally the same characteristics, a production defect in which the defective article does not conform to the design, and a warning and/or instruction defect. Foreseeable misuse must be considered during the design. This covers misuse during shipping, storage, and handling before the product gets in the hands of the user, as well as afterward. Again, the foreseeable misuse element removes legal technicalities that a seller could otherwise hide behind. For example, opening a paint can with a screwdriver would be considered misuse by the seller (if someone were hurt in the process). But it is *foreseeable* misuse because probably more paint cans are opened with screwdrivers than any other tool.

Design reviews of the product should consider safety and product liability. Advertising and marketing campaigns should be carefully reviewed by engineers and attorneys to be sure that the customer is not being encouraged to use the product unsafely. In product liability cases the courts are very likely to decide that any advertisement or claim is part of an express warranty or an instruction for use. Designers are allowed to make *reasonable* trade-offs of safety versus other characteristics; but *reasonable* must be defined in each case by the court (and jury). Many people believe that keeping good records of all engineering decisions is a big help in demonstrating the reasonableness of design decisions. But others are wary of records that show any trade-off of safety for something else. Incriminating evidence should never be generated, much less kept. Disclosure rules essentially give the plaintiff the right to see almost any of the seller's or manufacturer's documents.

Probably the best defense against product liability suits is for management to set strong safety requirements and then for the design group to make the product safer to meet those requirements. That is certainly one of the intents of the law. A safety requirement is an additional burden on the design engineer, manufacturing engineer, purchasing group, and quality assurance group. But it can pay for itself. Engineers tend to get discouraged when they read horror stories about unfounded, large product liability awards. But those awards, and the incentives they represent, are facts of life which should not be ignored.

Many companies are including product liability in a general loss control department. All major groups within the company, including the legal department, should be involved. The insurance carrier ought to be an advisor to the department.

In personal injury situations, there is no corporate shield to protect a negligent engineer or manager from criminal punishment by the courts. Engineers who believe they are being put in an untenable position by their management (being ordered to design or manufacture an unreasonably unsafe product) should consult an attorney.

Each company should have a group that is responsible for handling any complaints which could turn into a product liability suit. Two important techniques are:

1. Treat the complainant courteously and helpfully; discourteous treatment can cause the complainant to seek revenge. Be prepared to make the product right again if at all feasible, perhaps by exchanging the allegedly faulty product for a new one. Turn a potential plaintiff into a satisfied customer.

2. Gain physical posession of the allegedly faulty product (perhaps by exchanging it for a new one). Preserve it carefully. If there is litigation, the plaintiff has a legal right to inspect it.

See Refs. 29 to 32 for good books on this topic. The first one is very easy to read.

X. PROBABILITY AND STATISTICS: CONCEPTS AND MODELS

This is a brief summary of some concepts and models that are useful in reliability and maintainability engineering. Some of the concepts were originally developed for describing human groups and the terminology persists even though it is applied to inanimate objects.

A. Simple Systems

A population is a group of items that can be lumped together for any reason. Usually, the reason for lumping them together is that they presumably share many properties in common (e.g., they were all made on the same production line from the same drawings). In most circumstances the population is presumed to be very large. Even if only a few items are actually available, many could conceivably have been available. In reliability and maintainability, typical characteristics are time to failure (life), time to repair, stress, strength, damage, endurance.

1. *Failure rate of a population* (where the characteristic of concern is *life*): The failure rate is the relative rate at which living items die; it is often a function of age. For example, consider 2-year-old children living in the United States. About 1 per 1000 of them will die each year. For 6-year-olds, about 0.5 per 1000 will die each year. For 10-year-olds, the death rate reaches a minimum of about 0.4 per 1000 each year. At 18 years, the death rate has climbed to 1 per 1000 each year; at 35 it is up to about 2 per 1000 each year; at 43 it has doubled to 4 per 1000 each year; and at 70 it is about 40 per 1000 each year. The death rate considers only those then alive; it does not begin with a large group, say 100,000, and then say how many of those will die each year. Failure rate is an instantaneous rate, like car speed shown on a speedometer. If you are going 60 miles per hour at any instant, that does not necessarily mean that during the next hour you will go 60 miles. Failure rate can have several different units. For systems used in the field, "percent per month" or "percent per 1000 hours" is an easily understandable unit for failure rate and is often used and understood by reliability engineers and managers alike. For very reliable components, failure rate is often expressed in relative fraction per 10^9 hours.

2. *Hazard rate of a population*: The general term corresponding to failure rate. For example, it could give the relative rate at which items, under repair, finish their repair. Failure rate is a special case of hazard rate.

3. *Mean time to failure* (MTTF): The arithmetic average of lifetimes of units. It is often used, but can be very misleading when there are many short-lived items and only a few very long lived items. For example, in some common populations about 63% of the items will have lives shorter than the mean life, and about 40% will have lives less than one-half the mean. Another disadvantage of MTTF is that unreal assumptions are often made about very long lived items. For example, if a component were to have a constant failure rate (forever) of 10 per 10^9 hours, its mean life would be about 100,000 years.

Although the mathematics is accurate, the physics is not. Obviously, the chances of the failure rate's remaining constant for that long is nil. Thus, unless all lives tend to be similar, the use of MTTF is unwise.

4. *Survival fraction (reliability)*: The fraction of an original population which survives longer than any given time. A pair of them, one for a small fraction, one for a large fraction, are often used. For example, one might state that 90% of a fixed group of items will live at least 5 months and that only 10% will live at least 15 months.

5. *Constant failure (hazard) rate*: A mathematically tractable assumption that does not do too much violence to many kinds of data. Therefore, it is often used to describe lives of real items during a reasonably long portion of their lives.

6. *Bathtub curve*: This curve results when failure rate is plotted on a vertical axis against age on the horizontal axis. This curve represents human mortality quite well. In early life the failure rate tends to be high and decreasing (infant mortality); during a long period after that the failure rate tends to stay more or less constant (say within a factor of 2); finally, the failure rate begins an inexorable steeper and steeper climb (old age, wear-out). The curve looks something like a bathtub, whence the name. This explanation deals with items that are born, live, and die; items that can die and be reborn (repaired) are covered later. There is no law of nature which says that everything must have a bathtub curve, but many real things do.

7. *Statistical independence of events*: One of the most important concepts in reliability analysis. Two events (say A and B) are statistically independent if and only if the probability of A, given that B did occur, is exactly the same as the probability of A, given that B did not occur. For example, suppose that event A is "a person is carrying an umbrella" and event B is "it is raining." Obviously, the probability of "a person is carrying an umbrella," given that "it is raining," is quite different from the probability of "a person is carrying an umbrella," given that "it is not raining." Thus the two events, A and B, are not statistically independent; that is, they are statistically dependent. There are other equivalent definitions of statistical independence, the most common of which is that the probability of the joint event of A and B is the product of their individual probabilities if and only if A and B are statistically independent. The reasons that statistical independence is such a common assumption are that (a) it is tractable, and (b) there are rarely enough data on the details of any statistical dependence. Two reasonably tractable situations in which events are not statistically independent are: (a) the events have a common cause or partial cause (e.g., the weather), and (b) the events are mutually exclusive (e.g., raining and not-raining are mutually exclusive).

8. *Chain rule*: The name given to finding the probability of failure of a logic-series system composed of statistically independent elements. A logic-series system fails if and only if at least one of its elements fails. Thus the probability of system failure is the product of probabilities of failure of its elements. As an example, suppose that there are n elements, all nominally alike, and all having the same probability of success, p. Then the system probability of success is

$$R = p^n$$

Some sample calculations show the strong effect of n.

$p = 0.9$, $n = 10$; then $R = 0.35$ (not too good).
$p = 0.99$, $n = 100$; then $R = 0.37$ (not too good).

p = 0.9999, n = 10,000; then R = 0.37 (not good at all, considering the excellent reliability of the components).

p = 0.99, n = 300; then R = 0.05.

R = 0.99, n = 1000; then p = 0.99999 (a very high requirement).

The examples show that even with rather reliable components, large systems can have low probabilities of success. Thus for complex systems a strong reliability program is necessary.

9. *Poisson process*: This process represents a continuing situation where *events* occur at particular time instants. An example is a complex system where the events are failure/repair actions. The repair is assumed to be instantaneous, or the time clock can be assumed to stop at the instant of failure and resume when repair is completed. If a mark (for each event) is placed on the time axis, the Poisson (pronounced pwah-ssohn) process will show marks randomly distributed on the axis. The failure intensity (corresponds to the failure rate for nonrepairable items) is a constant. The term *failure intensity* (for a process) is deliberately chosen to be different from *failure rate* (for a population of items) to avoid confusion between the two concepts (see Table 1). The Poisson process is used as a model for many complex repairable systems.

10. *Mean time between failures* (MTBF): The average of times between events for a Poisson process (it actually applies mathematically to any process, but is a useful measure only for a homogeneous Poisson process) where the events are failures. MTBF suffers from the same difficulties as MTTF.

11. *Nonhomogeneous Poisson process*: This process is similar to the Poisson process except that the failure intensity can be a function of absolute time, that is, of time measured from an instant of clock time rather than from say the most recent failure (event). The bathtub curve (failure intensity versus age) is an example of a nonhomogeneous Poisson process and can represent the behavior of some real systems.

12. *Markov models*: These models are often used to represent systems which need more complicated descriptions than a Poisson process. The most common kind of Markov model uses the concept of *system states* and *transitions* between states. For example, system state might be given by the states (good, degraded, waiting for repair, in repair) of each of its subsystems. Transitions between states occur when a subsystem goes from one of its states to another, for example, goes from *in repair* to *good* by being repaired. The most common assumption about transition rates is that the instantaneous transition rate (e.g., failure rate) is a constant. It is reasonably straightforward to set up the transition equations and solve them by Laplace transforms.

It is best to learn probability and statistics from professional books on the topic rather than from articles in a trade journal or even from some engineering books. See Ref. 33 for a good elementary book on probability and statistics.

A word of caution for those about to embark on using this kind of mathematics: *Perfect arithmetic is cheap. Good engineering is much tougher to find.* That is, it is all too easy to fit mathematical models to some data. Extrapolating those models to regions outside the envelope of the data is futile, misleading, and usually very poor engineering. It is just as effective, and more fun, to throw darts at the executive decision dart board.

B. Complex Models

Many systems, such as computer networks and logistic support for a commercial aircraft, are so complicated that they need special kinds of models. Signal-flow graphs, fault trees, procedural models, and networks are examples of models used to represent such systems. A procedural model is a combination of many

TABLE 1   Upper and Lower Confidence Level Limits for Constant Failure Rate Situations

LCL = Lower statistical Confidence Limit
UCL = Upper statistical Confidence Limit
r.v. = random variable

The body of the table gives LCL and UCL for the mean. It applies when the failure rate or the failure intensity is constant:
Gamma (exponential) distribution - number of failures is fixed, total test time is a r.v.
Poisson distribution - number of failures is a r.v., total test time is fixed.

The 1-sided statistical confidence levels are given at the top of the seven columns so marked. The number of failures, r, is given in the leftmost column.

If the r.v. is discrete (viz., r is a r.v.), then also calculate the LCL and UCL using "r+1". The true LCL and UCL lie somewhere between the values found using r and using r+1. (The row for r=0 is never of any help.) Statisticians usually take the most pessimistic values, although there are randomizing techniques which (on the average) give the exact, statistical confidence levels.

r	2.5%	5.0%	10.0%	50.0%	90.0%	95.0%	97.5%
0	0.0	0.0	0.0	0.0	0.0	0.0	0.0
1	0.0253	0.0513	0.105	0.693	2.30	3.00	3.69
2	0.242	0.355	0.532	1.68	3.89	4.74	5.57
3	0.619	0.818	1.10	2.67	5.32	6.30	7.22
4	1.09	1.37	1.74	3.67	6.63	7.75	8.77
5	1.62	1.97	2.43	4.67	7.99	9.15	10.2
6	2.20	2.61	3.15	5.67	9.27	10.5	11.7
7	2.81	3.29	3.89	6.67	10.5	11.8	13.1
8	3.45	3.98	4.66	7.67	11.8	13.1	14.4
9	4.12	4.70	5.43	8.67	13.0	14.4	15.8
10	4.80	5.43	6.22	9.67	14.2	15.7	17.1
11	5.49	6.17	7.02	10.7	15.4	17.0	18.4
12	6.20	6.92	7.83	11.7	16.6	18.2	19.7
13	6.92	7.69	8.65	12.7	17.8	19.4	21.0
14	7.65	8.46	9.47	13.7	19.0	20.7	22.2
15	8.40	9.25	10.3	14.7	20.1	21.9	23.5
16	9.14	10.0	11.1	15.7	21.3	23.1	24.7
17	9.90	10.8	12.0	16.7	22.4	24.3	26.0
18	10.7	11.6	12.8	17.7	23.6	25.5	27.2
19	11.4	12.4	13.7	18.7	24.8	26.7	28.4
20	12.2	13.3	14.5	19.7	25.9	27.9	29.7
25	16.2	17.4	18.8	24.7	31.6	33.8	35.7
30	20.2	21.6	23.2	29.7	37.2	39.5	41.6
35	24.4	25.9	27.7	34.7	42.8	45.3	47.5
40	28.6	30.2	32.1	39.7	48.3	50.9	53.3
45	32.8	34.6	36.6	44.7	53.8	56.6	59.1
50	37.1	39.0	41.2	49.7	59.2	62.2	64.8

TABLE 1   (Continued)

For r = 20 or more, use linear interpolation as needed.

To find the LCL or UCL for the failure rate or the failure intensity, divide "the corresponding LCL or UCL for the mean" by the total test time.

Examples

1. Problem. The failure intensity is constant; the test is stopped at the 5-th failure; the total test time is 4,700 hours. Find the 5% LCL and 95% UCL for the failure intensity.

   Solution. For the mean: the LCL = 1.97 and UCL = 9.15.
   For the failure intensity: the LCL = 41.9% per 1000 hours and UCL = 195% per 1000 hours.
   The statistical confidence level for the interval is 95% - 5% = 90%.

2. Problem. The failure rate is constant; the test is stopped at 119,220 hours of total test time; the number of failures is 7. Find the 90% UCL for the failure rate.

   Solution. For the mean: the UCL is between 10.5 and 11.8.
   For the failure rate: the UCL is between 8.81% per 1000 hours and 9.90% per 1000 hours.

---

small models each of which gives a local procedure for any local situation. That is, the model chooses simple mathematics to represent each situation, such as failure of an item, shipping time for a repair part, waiting time for a repair service, and goodness of a repair. The model then runs through time and sees what happens, taking each thing as it randomly comes, just as in real life. The complexity comes in the interactions rather than in the local model for each local situation. Many of the models are proprietary because hundreds of thousands (perhaps millions) of dollars can be spent in developing them and their associated computer programs. Publications such as U.S. government reports, *IEEE Transactions on Reliability*, *Proceedings of the Annual Reliability and Maintainability Symposium*, and journals of other professional societies do contain articles on these kinds of models.

Computer programs are available for analyzing fault trees, reliability of networks, and other complicated systems. Finding good data to put into any of these models can be very difficult. Optimizing the behavior of such models is usually futile because the uncertainties in the parameters of the models are large enough to affect strongly the answers one gets.

C. Inferential Statistics

One of the main uses of statistical theory in reliability engineering is too infer something about the parameters of a model, given the actual experimental data. For example, if a process generated 4 failures in 120 hours of total test time (test time of all good and bad units added together), what can be said about the unknown true failure intensity of the process? Before the question can be answered, more must be known about the test situation and the model.

The most common meaning of probability in reliability is as relative frequencies (e.g., the relative frequency of each face showing on a fair throw of a fair die is 1/6). To talk meaningfully of relative frequencies, it must be clear exactly what is to have the relative frequency. In particular, a test must have a stopping boundary. A common such boundary in a life test is to stop when a particular number of failures or a particular total test time has been reached (whichever comes first). If the test is stopped whenever the boss has a whim or some other reason to stop the test, it cannot be analyzed by relative frequencies because the behavior of "the relative frequencies of the boss's whims during a life test" are not known very well.

Statistical estimates from test data will vary from test to test because the test data are different. An example is the behavior of any three fair rolls of a pair of fair dice. A competent applied statistician should be consulted to help plan the test and analyze the test data. The cost of that help is usually very small compared to the cost of the physical test.

There are two kinds of estimates: point and interval. A point estimate is a single number and is usually misleading because that number can be calculated very precisely but still be very far from the true value. For example, on the foregoing life test (4 failures in 120 hours), a point estimate of the constant failure intensity is 4 failures per 120 hours = 3.333% per hour—which looks very accurate. An interval estimate, however, gives an idea of the uncertainties involved. Assume that the test boundary was "stop at the fourth failure or at 500 hours, whichever comes first." The fourth failure came first. An interval estimate for the constant failure intensity is: The 80% statistical confidence limits are 1.5 to 5.5% per hour. The exact meaning of the statement is that 80% of the time such statements are made (i.e., the statistical confidence level), the interval between the limits will cover the true value. A table for statistical confidence limits for a Poisson process is shown; the statistical confidence level is obtained by subtracting the two percentages at the tops of the columns used. Usually, the two percentages are taken such that their sum is 1 (e.g., 5% and 95%). Statistical confidence intervals can be used as measures of uncertainty in the estimates. The larger the statistical confidence level (for a given set of data), the wider the interval becomes. Statistical confidence has little to do with engineering confidence, and the two should always be distinguished from each other.

Statistical significance refers to the results of a hypothesis test. The most common hypothesis tests (in reliability engineering) occur in acceptance sampling for quality control. Statistical significance is evaluated in the following way. Assume that the true value (of a population parameter, such as *true fraction nonconforming*) is the value in your hypothesis; this is called the *null hypothesis* because a null difference is being assumed. Then calculate the tail probability of getting worse test data than the ones you got on a test. That tail probability is called the statistical significance. If the statistical significance is small (e.g., less than 5%), the test data are considered very unlikely to have come from the hypothesized value. Otherwise, it is considered reasonable to act as if the hypothesized value is true; that is, the result is not statistically significant. Large values of tail probability often can arise from any of several hypotheses; thus the particular accepted hypothesis is not taken as being uniquely true. Statistical significance has little to do with engineering significance. One can exist without the other. In fact, it is always possible to take so few data that virtually any hypothesis will be statistically significant, or to take so many data that virtually no hypothesis will be statistically significant. For example, suppose that the average difference in yield between two manufacutring processes was 1% and was statistically significant. The chances are that the difference would be of no engineering significance (importance) whatsoever. On the other hand, the true difference between the average yields could be 20%, yet show up as not statistically significant because not enough data were taken.

Whenever a statistician (in a book, report, or verbally) uses words that sound familiar but which might have a special meaning, find out exactly what that special meaning is.

D. Bayesian Statistics

The mathematics of probability can be used to represent things other than relative frequency. It can, for example, represent degree of belief (subjective probability). The name of Bayes is given to this use of probability. For example, one could say that his degree of belief that a 7 will result from a throw of the dice is 20%—slightly different from the usual 6/36. Everyone uses degree of belief somewhat, although a prudent person adjusts his or her degree of belief to be the relative frequencies when they are known. For example, the outcomes of a fair throw of fair dice are well known; thus relative frequencies are used to describe those outcomes. But for a particular game, whether "the dice and throws are fair" or not is a matter of degree of belief.

A term often used with Bayesian probability is *prior probability*. It is the set of probabilities assigned to events before an experiment (test) is run. A corresponding term is *posterior probability*. It is the set of probabilities assigned to events after an experiment or test is run. A well-known, non-controversial probability formula is used to convert prior probabilities to posterior probabilities. Any controversies in the use of Bayesian methods arise in applying the concepts, not in the mathematics itself. The posterior probabilities from one experiment become the prior probabilities for the next experiment. People argue about the real meaning of Bayes probability, and there is no unique authority available to settle the argument.

There are three main uses of probability that are called Bayes:

1. Degree of belief
2. Use of prior probabilities
3. Decision theory using prior probabilities

It is useful to define a *Bayes-rational* person as one whose posterior degrees of belief are those calculated from the test results and his or her prior degrees of belief. Psychologists who have run experiments find that few people are actually Bayes rational. One of the reasons that people are not Bayes rational is that they do not understand the consequences of their prior degrees of belief.

If anyone chooses to use degrees of belief as prior probability, the following procedure should be followed when choosing a set of prior degrees of belief.

1. Choose a tentative set of prior degrees of belief.
2. Simulate various widely different test outcomes.
3. Calculate the set of posterior degrees of belief, for each test outcome, using the Bayes formula.
4. For each simulation, decide whether that is what you really do believe after seeing the simulated test data.
5. Revise the set of prior degrees of belief and go back to step 2. Continue until you are a Bayes-rational person.

The practical effect of this process is that a person becomes much less opinionated in his or her set of prior degrees of belief than the person was before the process of simulation.

There is much misuse of Bayesian statistics wherein the degrees of belief are extremely concentrated at very optimistic values of, say, failure rate. Then a few tests can be run, and if there are no failures, the person presumes that his or her posterior degrees of belief represent objective relative frequencies.

A conceptual difficulty in probability as degree of belief is that the true value of a parameter (e.g., a failure rate) is a random variable. But the term *random variable* does not mean that the true parameter is a random variable in the relative frequency sense. All it really means is that there is a probability distribution associated with the parameter (i.e., the degree of belief).

E. KISS Technique

KISS stands for Keep It Simple, Stupid. That is excellent advice in choosing probabilistic models for reliability and maintainability analyses. It is easy to get involved in complicated mathematics and to believe that something is really being accomplished. Rarely are there enough data to support even the simplest models, and it is impossible to verify the assumptions in more complicated models.

Reliability-statistics courses often stress fitting test data to a probability distribution such as Weibull or lognormal. The arithmetic can be done perfectly (and usually is), but the results do not really mean much. Almost any distribution can be used to interpolate well within the region of the data, but none of them can be used to extrapolate wisely very far outside the region of the data. The extrapolation arithmetic can be done with all the precision available to modern computers, but the model probably does not fit very well, even if physical analogies have been used to develop the model. If anyone persists in extrapolating very far, the minimum that must be done is to make an interval estimate of the extrapolation, not a point estimate.

XI. SOFTWARE

It is widely agreed that much computer software has many difficulties and does not satisfy user needs. What to call that dissatisfaction is very controversial. Part of the controversy arises from a misunderstanding of the nature of hardware reliability. The most familiar model of failure for hardware is degradation, whereby damage accumulates monotonically until the endurance is reached, at which instant failure occurs. Everyone agrees that software does not behave like that (if one ignores very rare difficulties with hardware); and even if it did, it could be instantly restored to like-new condition by reloading a master file.

There are three common simple conceptual models for failures:

1. Damage-endurance
2. Stress-strength
3. Challenge-response

The damage-endurance model does not apply. Most failures of computer software are of the challenge-response type; they have the following characteristics. The software contains many elements, some of which are rarely challenged (used) during operation. The elements are either good or bad.

If a bad element is challenged, the system response is to fail. If a bad element is not challenged, the system works satisfactorily. This model implies that system failure depends on system history. Occasionally, the stress-strength model applies, and then usually with regard to system overloads.

The major difficulty with computer software is not the bugs in the software itself, but with the inadequacy of the formal statement of user requirements. Do not be in a hurry to begin writing computer code. Two good books on system analysis are cited in Refs. 34 and 35.

A major element of structured analysis is the gradual transforming of a dirty problem (relatively undefined and unstructured) into a sequence of cleaner problems (relatively well defined and well structured). The users begin with a rather large dirty problem (e.g., "solve my accounting mess" or "build me a nice new shiny rapid transit system that never fails and gives everyone a seat"). Structured analysis is the process by which the analyst and the users find out together what feasible things are meant by "solve my accounting mess" and structure their findings so that those findings are understandable by everyone involved. Structure is a method of organization by which the relation of elements to each other and to the objectives are well defined and easily understandable by those who need to know. One of the great benefits of the emphasis on structure by system analysis and software experts is the caveat to analysts and programmers: It is not enough to be right, the program must also be readily understandable (easy to see the right meaning, hard to see a wrong meaning). In the early stages of analysis, it is better to be clear than to be right. For if one is clear, then right or wrong is obvious. But if one is not clear, who knows right from wrong?

If the analysis has been structured well, that structure will serve as a skeleton structure for the programming group. Having both groups use the same structure makes it easier to see if the actual program is implementing the formal statement of user requirements. The structure serves as a basis for program modules. Modules are not a random partitioning of a program, but a partitioning to aid in understanding, to make it easy to do the right thing, and to make it hard to do a wrong thing. A structured program will be partitioned into modules. Good modules are relatively independent of each other. A good discussion of modularization can be found in Ref. 36.

The two goals of module independence are maximizing the relationships within a module (called module strength) and minimizing the relationships among modules (called module coupling). The highest module strength comes from a module that performs a specific single function. The lowest module strength comes from a module that performs many unrelated functions. Module coupling is minimized by eliminating relationships between modules where feasible, and by weaking the necessary relationships.

Modules should be of a reasonable size, say between 10 and 100 statements. Having a module fit on one page is highly desirable just for human convenience. There is no need to use a shoehorn to fill this guideline, but other things being equal, opt for no more than one page.

Flexibility is the goal of having reasonably sized, independent modules. One thing is constant in the world of computer programs—user needs will change. Most users do not know what they really want until they see and use it. That is why physical models of buildings and systems are so popular. But models of computer programs are not feasible. When buyers actually begin to use the programs, their priorities and perceptions of their needs change. Then they want the programs to change to reflect those needs. Another reason for changes is from external causes such as new postal ZIP codes, new laws and regulations, or mandates from on high. The third reason for changes is that bugs are discovered in the program.

People might argue about the concept of reliability for software, but no one argues about the concept and need for maintainability. One interesting facet of of maintainability is documentation. At one time, people felt that a code must contain many comments and that flowcharts should be drawn for everything. Now people are having second thoughts. Consider the statement: A good program is its own documentation. Whenever there are multiple descriptions of anything, programs included, discrepancies can exist. An excellent booklet on programming style, written for experienced programmers, is *The Elements of Programming Style* [37]. All programmers who have ever outsmarted themselves on a computer ought to have a copy—it is fun to read and the message is deep.

Programs need to be tested. Testing is an art, not a science. Testing is the running of programs for the purpose of finding errors; there is one exception—it is reassuring to run the first test with input that ought to run easily and well. Testing any nontrivial program has two fundamental time limitations:

1. It is impossible in a lifetime to run all possible input data.
2. It is impossible in a lifetime to run all possible program paths.

All real tests are a compromise between these two limitations and the resources available (money, calendar time, people). See Ref. 38 for a useful book on testing.

When writing code there is a temptation to outguess the compiler and to try to squeeze the last bit of efficiency and speed out of the computer. Don't do it—for two reasons:

1. Spend the time trying to find a better algorithm. Better algorithms can do 10 times as much good as fiddling with code.
2. If you must fiddle with code, let the computer tell you where it is spending its time. Don't guess; know

There are models for software bugs and their removal rates. Most of them apply to large systems and to people with lots of money to spend. The *IEEE Transactions on Reliability* publishes many papers on this topic; the 1980 August issue was devoted almost entirely to it. Other journals as well are concerned with statistical models of program quality and reliability. As with hardware reliability, it is more important to "seek and destroy" failure modes and to use good design practices than it is to spend too much time on statistical analyses.

XII. HUMAN FACTORS

Human factors are responsible for most failures everywhere. Even hardware failures have their roots in someone's sins of omission or commission (a system analyst, a designer, a production worker). In actual system operation it is often the actions of operators or repairers that are responsible for catastrophes. Of course, people also do many things that machines cannot do, and even prevent many system catastrophes. The idea, then, is to design the system so that machines and people each do "their own thing."

The two most important guidelines in any process or system involving people are the following:

1. Make it easy to do the right thing, and hard to do the wrong thing.
2. Concentrate on corrective action, not blame.

Automobile accidents are a good example of the blame versus corrective action problem. People are a major portion of the reason for road and car accidents. Should we get rid of the "nut behind the wheel" or should we fool-proof our cars? One of the churches teaches: "Avoid the occasion of sin!" Similarly, the most effective way to reduce human failures is to avoid their occasion, not to reform people by education, training, threats, or altertization. Make it easy to do the right thing, and hard to do the wrong thing.

It is convenient to divide human factors into four areas: anthropometric constraints, physiological constraints, pyschological constraints, skill and/or knowledge constraints. Anthropometry deals with the bodily measurements of people: how tall they are, how far they can reach, and so on. Information in this category is reasonably common (see Ref. 39). Physiology deals with the amount of force a person can exert, how tired one becomes, being hung-over when coming to work on Monday morning, and so on (see Ref. 40).

Pyschology deals with attention spans, reactions to stimulii, emotions, attitudes, and so on. This is a difficult subject because there is less than universal agreement among professionals and because elements of the culture and subculture one comes from are so important in determining pyschological factors. Beware of pat answers that purport to show what *all* people want or how *all* people will react. It is tempting to look inward and say: "Other people are like me" (or, more accurately, "my perception of me"). That is only partly true, and then only in a general way. Beware of priority lists, based on answers to questionnaires, of peoples goals in life and what they consider as rewards. Any experiments on incentives (minus and plus) should be first on a small scale, and proceed outward very slowly. It is not always easy to know the reason for success in experiments with people. The "Hawthorne experiments" showed that many years ago (see Ref. 41). Very useful information on this as well as other human factors areas can be found in Swain and Guttman [42]. The book also has many useful references. The authors have done good pioneering work in this field. Some of their comclusions will surprise you. Read their work and find out.

Knowledge and skills are needed for performing any job and can be bottle-necks for anyone at any time. Where these are bottlenecks, education and training are called for. An example is good work instructions in a manufacturing plant. The instructions must match the skill levels and attitudes of the workers. Design engineers and managers are important in this category. Both of these groups often lack important human factors information.

Almost everyone is an expert on people, after all, because everyone has lots of practical experience. The subject should always be approached with a certain amount of humility. Experts with all the answers often do not allow any questions. The people who are responsible for making nuclear weapons (e.g., Sandia Laboratories) are in the position where they cannot make critical mistakes. They do not have the luxury of being able to place blame for a catastrophe. They have to take preventive or corrective action before anything catastrophic happens. So listen to them. Make it easy to do the right thing, and hard to do the wrong thing. Concentrate on corrective action, not blame.

ACKNOWLEDGMENT

Several illustrations in this chapter were taken from MB-3350-B, *A Guideline for the FMEA/FTA*, with the kind permission of Westinghouse Electric Corporation.

REFERENCES

1. MIL-STD-785B, *Reliability Program for Systems and Equipment Development and Production*, September 15, 1980 (or a later version).
2. MIL-STD-470A, *Maintainability Program for Systems and Equipment Development and Production*, 1981 (or a later version).
3. M. L. Shooman, *Probabilistic Reliability: An Engineering Approach*, McGraw-Hill, New York, 1968.
4. A. E. Green and A. J. Bourne, *Reliability Technology*, Wiley-Interscience, New York, 1972.
5. R. E. Barlow and F. Proschan, *Statistical Theory of Reliability and Life Testing*, Hold, Rinehart and Winston, New York, 1975.
6. D. K. Lloyd and M. Lipow, *Reliability: Management, Methods, and Mathematics*, 2nd ed., published by the authors, 1976.
7. P. D. T. O'Connor, *Practical Reliability Engineering*, Heyden, London, 1981.
8. B. S. Dhillon and C. Singh, *Engineering Reliability*, Wiley-Interscience, New York, 1981.
9. E. J. Henley and H. Kumamoto, *Reliability Engineering and Risk Assessment*, Prentice-Hall, Englewood Cliffs, N.J., 1981.
10. E. J. Henley and J. W. Lynn, eds., *Generic Techniques in System Reliability Assessment* (July 1973 conference), Noordhoff, Alphen aan den Rijn, The Netherlands, 1976.
11. R. E. Barlow, J. B. Fussell, and N. D. Singpurwalla, eds., *Reliability and Fault Tree Analysis* (September 1974 conference), SIAM, Philadelphia, 1975.
12. J. B. Fussell and G. R. Burdick, eds., *Nuclear System Reliability Engineering and Risk Assessment* (June 1977 conference), SIAM, Philadelphia, 1977.
13. G. Apostolakis, S. Garribba, and G. Volta, eds., *Synthesis and Analysis Methods for Safety and Reliability Studies* (July 1978 conference), Plenum, New York, 1980.
14. MB-3350-B, *A Guideline for the FMEA/FTA*, Westinghouse Corporate Product Integrity, 1977.
15. J. B. Fussell, G. J. Powers, and R. G. Bennetts, "Fault Trees—A State of the Art Discussion," *IEEE Transactions on Reliability*, Vol. R-23, April 1974, pp. 51–55.
16. J. S. Wu., S. L. Salem, and G. E. Apostolakis, "The Use of Decision Tables in the Systematic Construction of Fault Trees," in *Nuclear System Reliability Engineering and Risk Assessment*, J. B. Fussell and G. R. Burdick, eds. (June 1977 conference), SIAM, Philadelphia, 1977, pp. 800–824.
17. J. B. Fussell, "Computer Aided Fault Tree Construction for Electrical Systems," in *Reliability and Fault Tree Analysis*, R. E. Barlow, J. B. Fussell, and N. D. Singpurwalla, eds. (September 1974 conference), SIAM, Philadelphia, 1975, pp. 37–56.

18. J. R. Taylor and E. Hollo, "Experience with Algorithms for Automatic Failure Analysis," in *Nuclear System Reliability Engineering and Risk Assessment*, J. B. Fussell and G. R. Burdick, eds. (June 1977 conference), SIAM, Philadelphia, 1977, pp. 759–777.

19. S. A. Lapp and G. J. Powers, "Computer-Aided Synthesis of Fault-Trees," *IEEE Transactions on Reliability*, Vol. R-26, April 1977, pp. 2–13.

20. D. Nielsen, "Use of Cause-Consequence Charts in Practical System Analysis," in *Reliability and Fault Tree Analysis*, R. E. Barlow, J. B. Fussell, and N. D. Singpurwalla, eds. (September 1974 conference), SIAM, Philadelphia, 1975, pp. 849–880.

21. J. R. Taylor, "Sequential Effects in Failure Mode Analysis," in *Nuclear System Reliability Engineering and Risk Assessment*, J. B. Fussell and G. R. Burdick, eds. (June 1977 conference), SIAM, Philadelphia, 1977, pp. 881–894.

22. D. S. Nielsen, O. Platz, and B. Runge, "A Cause-Consequence Chart of a Redundant Protection System," *IEEE Transactions on Reliability*, Vol. R-24, April 1975, pp. 8–13.

23. B. S. Blanchard, *Logistics Engineering and Management*, Prentice-Hall, Englewood Cliffs, N.J., 1974.

24. B. S. Blanchard and E. E. Lowery, *Maintainability—Principles and Practices*, McGraw-Hill, New York, 1969.

25. G. Davis and S. Brown, *Logistics Management*, Lexington Books, Lexington, Mass., 1974.

26. J. L. Heskett, R. Ivie, and N. Glaskowsky, *Business Logistics, Management of Physical Supply and Distribution*, Ronald Press, New York, 1973.

27. D. Cunningham and W. Cox, *Applied Maintainability*, Wiley, New York, 1972.

28. A. K. S. Jardine, *Maintenance, Replacement and Reliability*, Halstead Press, New York, 1973.

29. J. F. Thorpe and W. H. Middendorf, *What Every Engineer Should Know About Product Liability*, Marcel Dekker, New York, 1979.

30. J. Kolb and S. S. Ross, *Product Safety and Liability*, McGraw-Hill, New York, 1980.

31. A. S. Weinstein, A. D. Twerski, H. R. Piehler, and W. A. Donaher, *Product Liability and the Reasonably Safe Product*, Wiley-Interscience, New York, 1978.

32. I. Gray, A. L. Bases, C. H. Martin, and A. Sternberg, *Product Liability: A Management Response*, AMACOM, New York, 1975.

33. I. Miller and J. Freund, *Probability and Statistics for Engineers*, Prentice-Hall, Englewood Cliffs, N.J., 1977.

34. C. Gane and T. Sarson, *Structured Systems Analysis: Tools and Techniques*, Improved System Technologies, 1977.

35. T. DeMarco, *Structured Analysis and System Specification*, Yourdon Press, New York, 1978.

36. G. J. Myers, *Composite/Structured Design*, Van Nostrand Reinhold, New York, 1978.

37. B. W. Kernighan and P. J. Plauger, *The Elements of Programming Style*, McGraw-Hill, New York, 1974.

38. G. J. Myers, *The Art of Software Testing*, Wiley-Interscience, New York, 1979.

30. J. Croney, *Anthropometry*, Van Nostrand Reinhold, New York, 1981.

40. MIL-STD-1472, *Human Engineering Design Criteria for Military Systems, Equipment, and Facilities.*

41. W. J. Dickson and F. J. Roethlisberger, *Counseling in an Organization—A Sequel to the Hawthorne Researches*, Harvard University Press, Cambridge, Mass., 1966.

42. A. D. Swain and H. E. Guttmann, *Handbook of Human Reliability Analysis with Emphasis on Nuclear Power Plant Applications*, (NUREG/CR-1278), Sandia Laboratories, 1980.

14

PLANNED PRODUCTION EXPERIMENTS

NORBERT L. ENRICK

Kent State University
Kent, Ohio

I. THE COMPETITIVE NEED FOR PLANNED PRODUCTION EXPERIMENTS

Modern manufacturing management is concerned with the need to develop new products and processes which will create output that:

Is highly marketable in terms of quality/cost and quality/price ratios
Meets adequate safety requirements
Is highly reliable, particularly when new space-age applications are involved

Planned experiments in production are carried out to discover optimal designs, efficient processing arrangements, the most suitable raw materials and component parts, and appropriate testing to assure quality and reliability.
The future of a firm depends on the success of such activities to assure:

Continued ability to come up with new, marketable products
Low-enough materials and processing costs to permit product pricing in a competitive way
Avoidance of waste of materials, scrap, energy consumption, and other costly or scarce resources

A. Illustrative Examples

Successful applications of planned production experiments abound. For example:

1. Through designed experiments, a manufacturer of pressure vessels uncovered sources in processing of undue rejections and scrap. A reduction of scrap losses from 12% to 3% was made possible over a span of about a year's continued experiments.
2. A producer of electric transmission cable ceramics applied design experiments to:
   a. Develop a superior and yet lower-materials-cost glaze
   b. Reduce scrap from 8% to 2%

    c.   Economize 25% on natural gas consumption in the kiln heat treat-
        ment by redesigning the kiln loading
    d.   Economize an additional 20% on natural gas consumption in the kiln
        by discovering a heating cycle that despite lower treatment time,
        gave adequate strength insulators
    An unexpected payoff was increased electric utility demand for the
    better quality product, as well as higher efficiency of production as a
    result of the saved energy and the reduction in scrap.

3.   A spinner and weaver of natural fiber textile products learned, through
    designed experiments, the interacting effect of fiber properties (fine-
    ness, length, strength) and process settings (roll distances, tension
    settings, twist applications, and lubricating additives). Based on this
    knowledge, he was able to purhcase less expensive, lower-grade raw
    stock but nevertheless to spin it into superior-quality yarn and pre-
    mium (price-added) fabric. He thus assured himself of a plentiful
    supply (of lower-grade fibers not usually desired by others), a good
    customer following (reliable, superior quality), and additional profit-
    ability as a base for expansion.

In this chapter we (1) show the basic methods of planned production experiments, and (2) demonstrate their application to product yield improvement,
product quality and reliability enhancement, and cost-analytical decisions.

II. RANDOMIZATION, REPLICATION, AND BALANCE

Well-designed experiments that yield useful information are in conformity with
the principles of randomized, replicated, and balanced design. The purpose
of randomization is to assure that there is no bias in choosing the sample
pieces to be tested. For example, in Fig. 1 in the upper left, pieces have
been taken from just one corner. They may represent a special condition
(operator, machine, materials) and thus misrepresent the production lot as a
whole. In the lower right, pieces have been randomly selected from all over
the lot, thus more truly representing the entire situation.

Everyone knows that obtaining one result is not enough. Therefore, it is
usually necessary to run at least two experiments. This is called *replication*
(see Fig. 1b). If there were three experiments, we say that the replication
is 3. If there were 10 experiments, the replication is 10.

Replication helps the experimenter by (1) providing more information than
a single run, and (2) permitting determination of the amount of "experimental
error" present in the study. "Error" is part of all experimenting. It is not
a result of "mistakes," but rather represents the inherent fluctuations or
variations in materials, machine running conditions (vibration, humidity,
temperature, etc.), and testing. From the replication, an estimate of the
magnitude of this fluctuation, variation, or "error" can be obtained and is a
valuable criterion for judging experiment findings.

Suppose that we want to test the effect of metal tensions versus plastic
tensions on the quality of electrical coils (see Fig. 1c). The wrong way would
be to put the metal tensions on one side of the machine and the plastic tensions
on the other (see the upper half of the diagram). Why? Because inevitably
there will be some wear in the bearing end of the machine. This will work on
the shaft and produce different quality on the bearing half, as against the

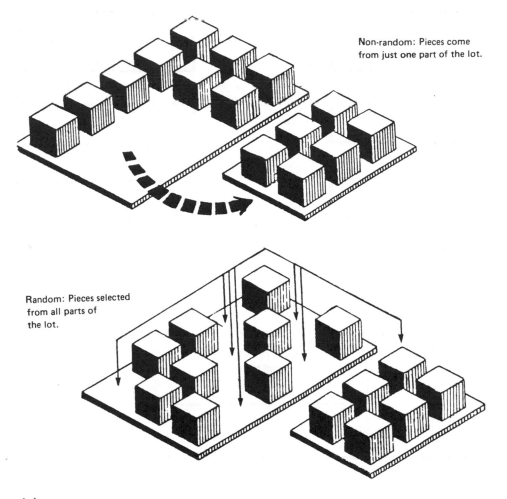

Non-random: Pieces come from just one part of the lot.

Random: Pieces selected from all parts of the lot.

(a)

FIGURE 1   (a) Randomization avoids possible bias in sampling; (b) replication; (c) how to balance an experiment; (d) balanced, replicated, and randomized experiment.

motor half. Thus the effects of bearing and metal tensions versus motor side and plastic tensions are *confounded*. That is, if metal tensions turn out not as good as plastic, we do not know whether that is really due to the metal or whether it is due to the fact that this is the bearing side of the machine (which is not as good a side as the motor side). Even if there were a perfect bearing and shaft, there still could be misalignment of the tension bar.

The right way is a proper, balanced design as shown in the lower half of the diagram: metal and plastic tensions are interspersed, so that the bearing side and the motor side now have equal effect: they are balanced.

An experiment combining replication, randomization, and balance is shown in Fig. 1d. The purpose of the experiment was to save on gas by trying a new heat treatment B (using less energy) against the established method A.

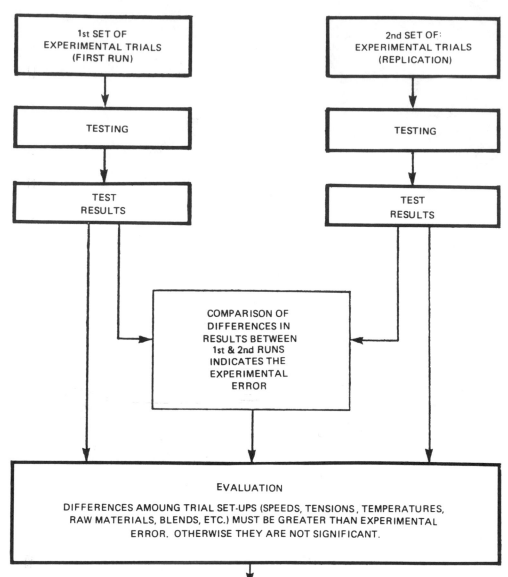

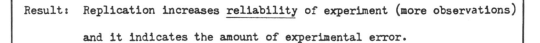

(b)

FIGURE 1   (Continued)

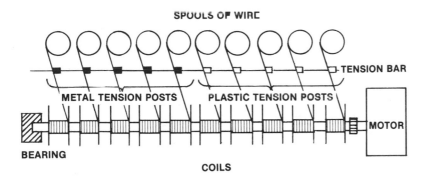

Not balanced: Metal posts are on bearing end, plastic posts are on motor end. Effect of machine sides is thus confounded with metal and plastic.

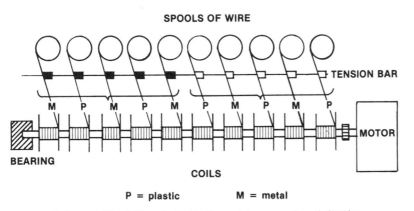

P = plastic   M = metal

Balanced: Metal M and plastic P are interspersed, and thereby balance out the effect of machine side (motor v. bearing end).

(c)

FIGURE 1   (Continued)

For each method, the output would be tested for quality. If there is no loss in quality, the energy-saving method B should be put into plant practice. The experiment is *replicated* because there are two runs. It is *balanced*, because from each run the same number of sample pieces are selected for test. It is *randomized* because the pieces are chosen at random from each output. In all good experiments equal attention is given to each of the principal requirements of replication, randomization, and balance.

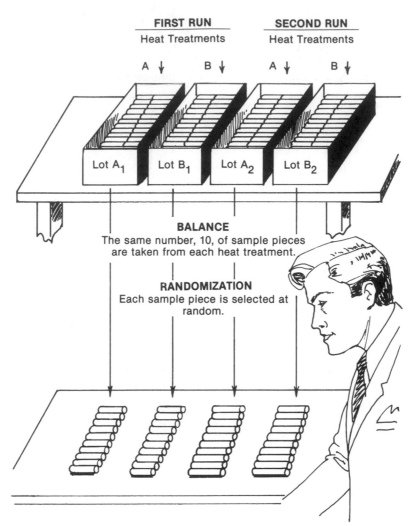

(d)

FIGURE 1   (Continued)

III. INTERACTION

Interaction is "the differential effect of one factor at various levels of another."
In plain English, an experimental study shows interaction effects when the
curves are not parallel.

   Figure 2a shows interaction. Tool life depends on both type of tool used
(carbide versus ceramic) and cutting speed. At slow speeds, carbide life is
longer; at high speeds ceramic tool life is longer. It is important to know
this so that we can use the best tool for each application.

   Figure 2b shows no interaction: No matter what tool is used, in this example ceramic always has less life than tungsten carbide. (This is not the

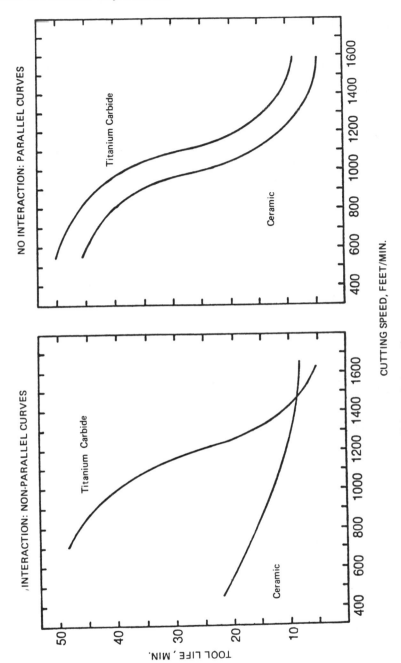

FIGURE 2   (a) Interaction versus (b) no interaction.

true situation, and part b of the graph is given merely to illustrate the "no interaction" case.)

   Note: The knowledge of interaction, where it is exists, is important, because it helps us select the best conditions for operating so as to achieve goals. Examples of such goals are cost reduction, quality improvement, waste minimization, energy savings, and the like. Most people who have not experimented seem to think that the world is primarily "noninteraction." Such a world would be simpler, because when everything is parallel, we can generalize more easily. In practice, however, there is interaction, generalizations are usually wrong, and opportunities for cost savings and profitability arise to those who know and capitalize on interaction effects. Knowing interactions is thus an important value of running well-designed experiments.

IV. MEASURING VARIABILITY

We can measure the amount of variation due to experimental error from the variation in the replication of the experiment. Figure 3 shows measurement of variability for an experiment with a replication of 4. The variance, in effect, is computed as shown. It represents the deviations of each test result from the arithmetic mean (average), squared, and then divided by n − 1. Here n is the number of tests or observations in the experiment (4 in our example).

(Example of 4 Sample Pieces Tested for Tensile Strength in Kilogram, k)

Strength, Y	Average Strength, $\bar{Y}$	Deviation from Average $Y - \bar{Y}$	Squared Deviation $(Y - \bar{Y})^2$
7	6	+1	1
4	6	−2	4
6	6	0	0
7	6	+1	1
Sums: 24		0	6

Arithmetic Mean, $\bar{Y}$ = (Sum of Y)/(No. of Tests, n)

= $\Sigma\ Y/N$ = 24/4 = 6

*Variance, s^2 = (Sum of Squared Deviations)/(n − 1)

= $\Sigma\ (Y - \bar{Y})/(4 - 1)$ = 6/3 = 2

*Standard Deviation = $\sqrt{s^2} = \sqrt{2}$ = 1.41

*Coefficient of Variation, $V\% = 100 \times s/\bar{Y} = 100 \times 1.41/6 = 23.5$

*These are the 3 most important measures of variability.

Σ = Sum of

FIGURE 3 How to measure variability.

The subtraction of 1, to get n − 1, represents an application of "degrees of freedom," to be discussed shortly. The *variance* is shown by s^2. Taking the square root yields the *standard deviation*, s.

In practice, the variance is calculated by means of a shortcut formula, as given in Fig. 4. But unless you understand the longer, regular method first, you will not understand the important fact that the variance is the deviations, squared, divided by n − 1. The variance thus measures the degree to which individual observations disperse themselves around the average. The particular way of calculating the variance and standard deviation are based on mathematical statistical foundations that have been shown in practice to serve well in analyzing data.

A. Degrees of Freedom

This is a special term, the "one less value." We have just seen its use in the calculation of the standard deviation, s, and the variance, s^2. The sample consisted of four pieces, yet the sum of the squared deviations was divided by 4 − 1 to obtain variance.

The use of degrees of freedom involves mathematical statistical foundations whose derivation is beyond the scope of this chapter. We will merely learn how to apply it.

Figure 5 brings a nonmathematical, intuitive explanation of why degrees of freedom is what it is, that is, why it is the "one less value." No matter how many shells there are in that example, we never need to lift more than that number of shells, less one, to find the location of the pea.

B. One-Factor Experiments: A Practical Case

Having laid the basic foundation and concepts, we are ready to look at a simple experiment, as in Fig. 6. The following is relevant:

Strength, Y	Y^2	
7	49	$s^2 = \dfrac{\Sigma Y^2 - (\Sigma Y)^2/n}{n-1}$
4	16	
6	36	$= \dfrac{150 - (24)^2/4}{4-1}$
7	49	
		$= \dfrac{150 - 576/4}{3}$
Sums: 24	150	
		$= \dfrac{150 - 144}{3} = \dfrac{6}{3} = 2*$

*This agrees with the method shown just before this.

s = 1.41 as before

FIGURE 4   How to measure variability: shortcut method.

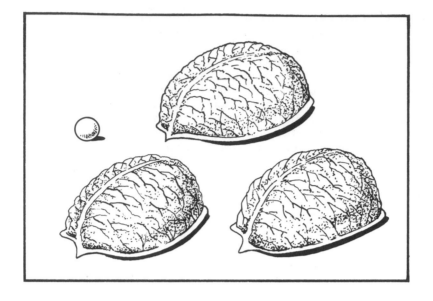

DEGREES OF FREEDOM

The "One-Less Value"

FIRST EXAMPLE: A sample consists of n = 5 pieces.
                    Degrees of Freedom is n - 1 = 4 pieces.

SECOND EXAMPLE: An experiment factor consists of three additives, such as
                    "low concentration," "high concentration" and "medium
                    concentration" of an emulsifier. The degrees of freedom is
                    3 - 1 = 2.

EXPLANATION: The Degrees of Freedom approach has its basis similar to
                    the pea-and-shell game, above. There are 3 shells, and thus
                    a maximum of 3 - 1 = 2 shells need be lifted to find the
                    pea. If there had been 10 shells, the maximum would have
                    been 10 - 1 = 9.

FIGURE 5   Degrees of freedom: the "one-less value."

1. *Purpose*: To investigate the effect of processing speed (low and high)
   on process yield. (Yield is the proportion of usable output per input.
   For example, in a casting process, if 200 lb is melted and poured and
   after trimming and waste 195 lb of castings are produced, the yield is
   $100 \times 195/200 = 97.5\%$.)
2. *Simplicity*: Instead of showing each yield, such as 97.5%, fully, we
   show "90% plus the percent shown." This gives us smaller figures with
   which to work. Instead of 97.5, for example, we now work with 7.5.
   Later we can restore the 90 to the final outcomes and results. For
   example, for the upper right-hand entry, the 5 is really 95 (or 95.0),
   in percent yield.
3. *This is a one-factor experiment*: The factor is speeds.
4. *The experiment levels are 2*: The two levels are "low speed" and "high
   speed." Had we had "low speed," "medium speed," and "high speed,"

Factor is "Machine Speeds" at Two Levels (Low and High). There
Are Four Trials (Replication r = 4).

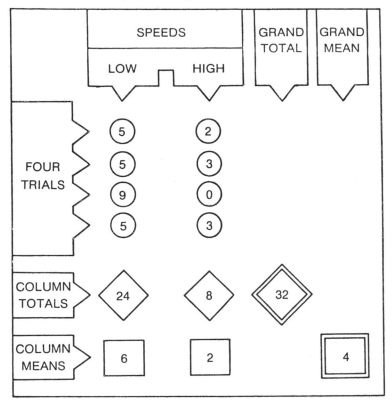

FIGURE 6 One factor experiment. Data are in terms of yield percent + 90
percent. For example, for Low Speed, first trial, the yield is 5 + 90 = 95
percent.

we would have had three levels. Had we had, for example, 100, 110,
120, and 130 ft/min, there would then have been four levels.
5. *Replication*: There are four trials per level, so the replication is 4.

In real life, we might investigate more than just speed as a factor. But
the purpose remains: to improve operations by looking at other factors that
affect yield. Higher yield means valuable savings in materials. Less scrap
saves not only costs but also energy (since a scrapped unit has used energy
but must be remelted and again consume energy before it can become useful
output).

Experimental Error Variance

The calculation of the error variance is accomplished, as shown in Fig. 7, by
applying our deviations-squared approach to each speed (low and high) separately. For low speeds, for example:

	Low Speed			High Speed		
	Y	$Y - \bar{Y}$	$(Y - \bar{Y})^2$	Y	$Y - \bar{Y}$	$(Y - \bar{Y})^2$
	5	−1	1	2	0	0
	5	−1	1	3	+1	1
	9	+3	9	0	−2	4
	5	−1	1	3	+1	1
Sums	24	0	12*	8	0	6*

Arithmetic Mean, $\bar{Y}$ 6   2
  $= \Sigma Y/n = 24/4$ and $8/4$

Variance, s^2_{error} for each speed   4   2
  $= \Sigma(Y - \bar{Y})^2/DF = 12/3$ and $6/3$

Experimental Error for Entire Experiment, s^2_{error} = error variance

$$= \frac{s^2_{\text{low speed error}} + s^2_{\text{high speed error}}}{\text{No. of variances}}$$

$$= (4 + 2)/2 = 3$$

The experimental error standard deviation is thus $\sqrt{3} = 1.73$

NOTE THAT THE EXPERIMENTAL ERROR VARIANCE IS ALSO CALLED
EXPERIMENTAL ERROR MEAN SQUARE OR JUST ERROR MEAN SQUARE, MSE

*This sum, $\Sigma(Y - \bar{Y})^2$ is also known as the Error Sum of Squares, SSE.

FIGURE 7   Calculation of experimental error variance.

1.   The deviations are −1, −1, 3, and −1, which are squared 1, 1, 9, and
     1, and sum to 12. This is known as the *sum of squares*, SS.
2.   The degrees of freedom, df = 4 − 1 = 3.
3.   SS/df = variance, s^2. In this case, 12/3 = 4.

For high speeds, $s^2 = 2$. Therefore, the average error variance of the two
speeds combined is simply $(4 + 2)/2 = 3$. The error standard deviation is now
$\sqrt{3} = 1.73$.

As an alternative procedure, we could have simply added the two sums of
squares, 12 + 6 = 18, divided by df = 3 to obtain 6, and averaged (by dividing
by 2 for the two SS values) to obtain 6/2 = 3 for the average error variance,
s^2. This second procedure is somewhat less obvious to understand than the
first one, but does save some steps and is thus preferred in practice.

The error variance just found is often called, alternatively, error mean
square, MSE (mean square of the error term). We must know both names because they are used interchangeably in the literature.

Between-Level Mean Square

To analyze experiment results properly, we must also determine another type of variance. This one is, however, always called a "mean square." In particular, it is the mean square of the difference between the averages obtained by the various levels of the experiment. Briefly, it is called the between-level mean square or simply mean square between, MSB. To find MSB, proceed as in Fig. 8:

1. For each of the individual observations per speed level, substitute its arithmetic mean. Thus the low-speed mean was 6, and we enter four of these 6's.
2. The grand mean is 4. Now, find the deviations, $6 - 4 = 2$, four times. Square these to obtain four 4's, which total to 16.
3. There are parallel steps for the high-speed group. Again, SS = 16. The two combined give a total SSB = 16 + 16 = 32.
4. The degrees of freedom, DF, is $2 - 1 = 1$. Note that there are two levels, so that df = $2 - 1 = 1$. Had there been five levels, df would have been $5 - 1 = 4$.
5. Dividing SSB/df = MSB = 32/1 = 32.

The difference among the two means (low speed and high speed) is significant only if its mean square is sufficiently greater than the error mean square

---

(Machine Speed vs. Process Yield Experiment. The Mean Square Obtained is for the Differences Between the Levels of Speed, Low and High.)

Step 1: For each Y, substitute the corresponding $\overline{Y}$. The low-speed arithmethic mean is 6, the high-speed arithmetic mean is 2. Then find the deviations from the Grand Mean, 4, square the deviations and sum. This is the Between Level Sum of Squares, SSB. This is sho shown below.

	Low Speed			High Speed		
Y	$\overline{Y} - \overline{\overline{Y}}$	$(\overline{Y} - \overline{\overline{Y}})^2$	Y	$\overline{Y} - \overline{\overline{Y}}$	$(\overline{Y} - \overline{\overline{Y}})^2$	TOTAL
6	+2	4	2	−2	4	
6	+2	4	2	−2	4	
6	+2	4	2	−2	4	
6	+2	4	2	−2	4	

Sum of Squares, SSB   16   16   32

Step 2: There are two levels. Hence the DF is $2 - 1 = 1$ Degree of Freedom.
Step 3: Find the Between-Level Meansquare from the division MSB = SSB/DF = 32/1 = 32.

Result: The Between-Speed Mean Square is 32. The prior Error Variance, also known as the Error Mean Square, is 3.

FIGURE 8   How to calculate between-level mean square, MSB.

to rule out chance fluctuations of sampling, testing, and inherent processing and materials variability as a possible cause of these differences.

We will next test for significance.

How to Test for Significance

As noted, we can say that the difference in effects among speeds is significant only if it is greater than could have been reasonably expected from experimental error variations. The standard procedure for testing is simple and follows the steps shown in Fig. 9.

Table of F Values for Significance Testing

This table is used, as was shown, in the significance test. Figure 10 is for a 5% risk of error: the risk of saying (erroneously) that an effect is significant when, in fact, it is not. A 5% risk obviously entails a 100% − 5% = 95% confidence level of being assured of a correct decision. The following other pairs of risk and confidence-level F tables can be found in most books on statistics: 10% and 90%; 2.5% and 97.5%; and 1% and 99%. For most practical purposes, the 5% and 95% pair is used most.

Unfortunately, no well-established criteria exist for judging which type of risk-confidence pair is most suited for a particular situation. In general, if a firm is considering expensive new equipment, before purchasing it, the firm will wish to be assured at the smallest practical risk level. Hence, the 1%−99% pair, or better, would be desired. On the other hand, if a good potential gain at little cost is obtainable, a 10%−90% pair may be acceptable.

At any time, when management is dissatisfied with the risk-confidence pair (as not being good enough), it can always authorize (at a cost) more testing and experimenting. The costs involved, however, are not only in monetary terms, but also in time (which may be at a premium) and in materials (which may be scarce until mass output can be arranged).

Is the difference between the 2 means significant or could it be just experimental error variation?

Step 1:   Form the ratio

$$F = \frac{\text{Mean-Square Between}}{\text{Error Mean Square}} = \text{MSB}/\text{MSE} = 32/3 = 10.7$$

Step 2:   The numerator MSB has 1 DF (Degree of Freedom), the denominator MSE has 7. (See prior Figure.) Therefore, the F-table (see next Figure) says we need a minimum F of 5.59 for significance.

Step 3:   Since the actual F-ratio, 10.7, exceeds this 5.59, the differences are significant.

NOTE: If, in Step 1, F had been below 5.59 there would not have been significance.

This F-table is for 5% risk of error, 95% confidence. It is the most widely used. Occasionally, other tables, for 10% and 90% or for 1% and 99% are needed.

FIGURE 9   How to do significance testing.

Five % Risk, 95 Percent Confidence Level

Degrees freedom for denominator	Degrees freedom for numerator											
	1	2	3	4	5	6	8	10	15	30	60	120
1	161	200	216	225	230	234	239	242	246	250	252	253
2	18.5	19.0	19.2	19.2	19.3	19.3	19.4	19.4	19.4	19.5	19.5	19.5
3	10.1	9.6	9.3	9.1	9.0	8.9	8.8	8.8	8.7	8.6	8.6	8.5
4	7.7	6.9	6.6	6.4	6.3	6.2	6.0	6.0	5.9	5.7	5.7	5.7
5	6.6	5.8	5.4	5.2	5.1	5.0	4.8	4.7	4.6	4.5	4.4	4.4
6	6.0	5.1	4.8	4.5	4.4	4.3	4.1	4.1	4.0	3.8	3.7	3.7
7	5.6	4.7	4.3	4.1	4.0	3.9	3.7	3.6	3.5	3.4	3.3	3.3
8	5.3	4.5	4.1	3.8	3.7	3.6	3.4	3.3	3.2	3.1	3.0	3.0
10	5.0	4.1	3.7	3.5	3.3	3.2	3.1	3.0	2.8	2.7	2.6	2.6
12	4.7	3.9	3.5	3.3	3.1	3.0	2.8	2.8	2.6	2.5	2.4	2.3
15	4.5	3.7	3.3	3.1	3.0	2.8	2.6	2.5	2.4	2.2	2.2	2.1
20	4.4	3.5	3.1	2.9	2.7	2.6	2.4	2.3	2.2	2.0	1.9	1.9
25	4.2	3.4	3.0	2.8	2.6	2.5	2.3	2.2	2.1	1.9	1.8	1.8
30	4.2	3.3	2.9	2.7	2.5	2.4	2.3	2.2	2.0	1.8	1.7	1.7
40	4.1	3.2	2.8	2.6	2.5	2.3	2.2	2.1	1.9	1.7	1.6	1.5
60	4.0	3.2	2.8	2.5	2.4	2.3	2.0	1.9	1.8	1.6	1.5	1.4
120	3.9	3.1	2.7	2.4	2.3	2.2	2.0	1.8	1.7	1.5	1.4	1.3

Example: Given $MS_{between}$ = 32 with DF = 1 and MS_{error} = 3 with DF = 7. Then, the observed F-ratio is 32/3 = 10.7. The tabular F-value is (For Numerator-DF = 3 and Denominator-DF = 7) is 4.3. Since the observed F-ratio is greater (at 10.7) than the tabular minimum F needed for significance, therefore the observed differences among the means are significant at the 95 percent level of confidence.

FIGURE 10   Table of F values for significance testing (5% risk, 95% confidence level).

C. Two-Factor Replicated Experiment

The previous example, although realistic, was quite simple. A more normal situation is when more than one factor is under investigation, as shown in Fig. 11. Interest is still in process yield (at 90% plus the percent shown), but instead of just looking at speeds, we examine an additional factor, the settings of the equipment. We now have:

1. Two sets of averages (arithmetic means): one for settings, one for speeds.
2. The replication is 2.
3. The grand mean is 4.0.

Calculation of Experimental Error Variance for a Two-Factor Replicated Experiment

The procedures, shown in Fig. 12, are parallel to the method already shown.

1. For each set (or "cell") the replication is 2.
2. The average for the first set is 7. Hence the deviations, +2 and −2, when squared, yield 4 + 4 = 8.
3. The degrees of freedom, df = 2 − 1 = 1.

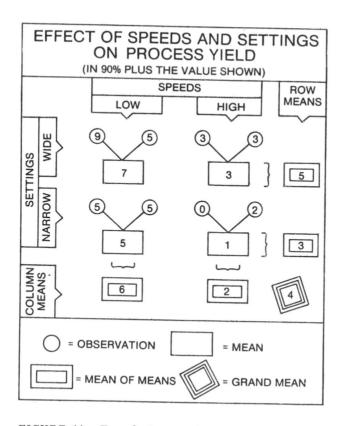

FIGURE 11   Two-factor replicated experiments. Factors are speeds and settings. Replication is 2.

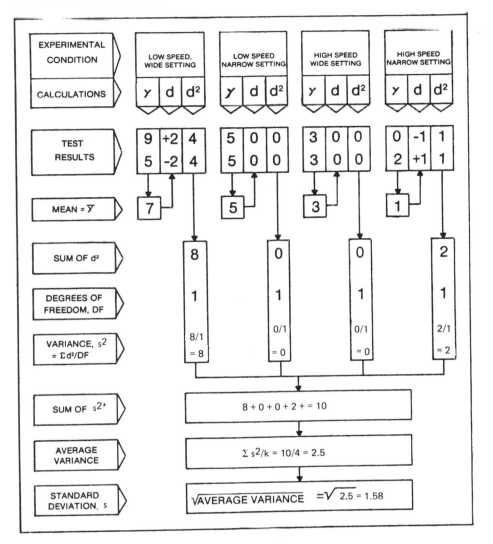

Notes: Y = individual observation. $Y - \bar{Y}$ = d = difference. Degrees of freedom, DF = $r - 1 = 2 - 1 = 1$, where r is the number of replications, k is the number of variances summed.

FIGURE 12 Calculation of experimental error variance and standard deviation.

4. The variance is now $8/1 = 8$.
5. Obtain all other error variances similarly. Average them, and find $s_{error}^2 = 2.5$. This is also known as error mean square, MSE.

We can again find MSB, this time one MSB for speeds and one MSB for settings, from the F ratio and test significance. But a more recently developed approach, using decision lines, which is gaining favor, is shown next.

Decision lines take the place of significance testing. The method for calculating decision lines is shown in Fig. 13. An experimentally observed average is significant if it falls outside these lines (see Fig. 15). The calculations proceed as in Fig. 14:

1. Gather data found in the preceding steps for the speeds-settings experiment.
2. Apply these to the formula shown for decision lines.
3. Refer to Fig. 14 for the appropriate factor h_d.
4. Enter your findings. In this example, the decision lines are 92.4 for the lower line and 95.6 for the upper line.

Factors h_d for Decision Lines

These factors, shown in Fig. 14, calculated by N. L. Enrick on the basis of tables and relationships given by Lloyd S. Nelson [1], are used as shown in Fig. 12.

Decision Line Chart

The arithmetic means and decision lines of the speeds-settings experiment are now plotted in Fig. 15. It is noted at a glance that only the difference between

---

STEP 1: GATHER THE DATA ALREADY FOUND:

$s = 1.58$, $\bar{\bar{Y}} = 4$, DF associated with $s = 4(2-1) = 4$, $n = 8$, h_d for the $k = 2$ speed means $= k = 2$ setting means is 2.78. h_d for the $k = 4$ speed-setting interaction means is 7.74.

STEP 2: APPLY THE FORMULA FOR DECISION LINES, dl:

$dl = \bar{\bar{Y}} \pm h_d(s)/\sqrt{n}\ = 94 \pm h_d(1.58)/\sqrt{8}$
    $= 94 \pm h_d(.559)$
    $= 94 \pm 1.6$ for speeds and for settings
    $= 94 \pm 4.2$ for speed-setting interactions.
Note that h_d varies because k varies ($k = 2$, $k = 4$).

STEP 3: PLOT THE DECISION LINES.

Any average falling outside the lines indicates a significant deviation from the Grand Mean, 94 percent yield, at the 95 percent confidence (5 percent risk) level.

NOTE: DECISION LINES AND MEANS ARE PLOTTED IN FIG. 15.

FIGURE 13   How to calculate decision lines.

(LINES ARE AT 95 PERCENT CONFIDENCE, 5 PERCENT RISK LEVELS)

Degrees Freedom, D.F.	Number k of Means Under Comparison																	
	2	3	4	5	6	7	8	9	10	12	14	16	18	20	24	30	40	60
2	4.30																	
3	3.18	6.73																
4	2.78	5.60	7.47															
5	2.57	4.99	6.60	8.06														
6	2.45	4.65	6.10	7.42	8.63													
7	2.36	4.43	5.79	7.00	8.14	9.01												
8	2.31	4.27	5.56	6.72	7.78	8.70	9.74											
9	2.26	4.14	5.39	6.50	7.51	8.45	9.39	10.24										
10	2.23	4.06	5.27	6.24	7.34	8.25	9.13	9.96	10.74									
11	2.20	3.99	5.16	6.22	7.18	8.06	8.92	9.73	10.50									
12	2.18	3.93	5.08	6.10	7.04	7.94	8.78	9.53	10.29	11.71								
14	2.15	3.85	4.95	5.96	6.86	7.72	8.49	9.25	9.99	11.34	12.58							
16	7.12	3.76	4.87	5.84	6.73	7.54	8.33	9.05	9.85	11.08	12.29	13.44						
18	2.10	3.73	4.80	5.76	6.62	7.42	8.18	8.91	9.60	10.87	12.08	13.21	14.27					
20	2.09	3.69	4.76	5.70	6.55	7.55	8.10	8.80	9.45	10.71	11.90	13.01	14.05	15.52				
24	2.06	3.63	4.68	5.60	6.44	7.20	7.94	8.63	9.27	10.51	11.65	12.70	13.73	14.73	16.55			
30	2.04	3.59	4.61	5.50	6.31	7.08	7.78	8.46	9.09	10.28	11.39	12.43	13.44	14.38	16.16	18.58		
60	2.00	3.48	4.47	5.32	6.10	6.83	7.49	8.14	8.73	9.88	10.92	12.08	12.86	13.77	15.44	17.72	21.17	27.04
120	1.98	3.44	4.39	5.24	5.99	6.71	7.36	7.98	8.58	9.68	10.71	11.93	12.58	13.47	15.11	17.34	20.67	26.35
Inf.	1.96	3.38	4.33	5.16	5.90	6.59	7.22	7.83	8.43	9.52	10.49	11.46	12.33	13.16	14.77	16.91	20.17	25.66

Source: Based on tables and relations developed in Nelson, LLoyd S. "Factors for the Analysis of Means," *J. of Quality Technology 6*, 4:175–181. Oct. 1974.

FIGURE 14 Factors h_d for decision lines (lines are at 95% confidence, 5% risk levels).

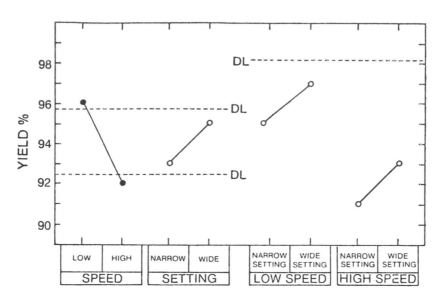

FIGURE 15   Speeds and settings experiment: averages and decision lines.

low and high speeds is significant. All other arithmetic means (or averages),
by failing to fall outside the decision limits, are not significantly different.

The decision to call a difference "significant," and to base management
action on this finding, is founded on a 5%-risk, 95%-confidence level pair in
this example. As in the case of the F tables, other risk-confidence pair
tables may be used. The 5%–95% pair is, however, the most widely, practically applicable.

D. Cost-Quality Decision Line Analysis, Multivariate Experiment

A decision line chart for a multivariate experiment involving quality-cost relations appears in Fig. 16. It involved the following:

1. *Purpose*: To investigate the effect on cost and quality of an electric
    switching device of these variables:
    a. Five wire slacks, in 0.01-in. increments
    b. Three wire sizes (gages 24 to 20)
    c. Two stranding methods (seven strands versus nine strands)
2. *Method*: From the replication of the experiment, the experiment error
    variance, MSE, was found. Then, using factors h_d of Fig. 15, the
    decision lines are established.
3. *Result*: The quality, in terms of number of action cycles (in hundreds)
    until device failure, are plotted against experimental conditions and
    relative costs, together with the decision line.

We note that the following yielded highest quality: slack 12, size 22, and
nine strands. Someone might now think that almost as good quality at much
less cost is obtainable for slack 12, size 22, and seven strands. But caution
must be advised. This point is inside the decision limits and thus is not

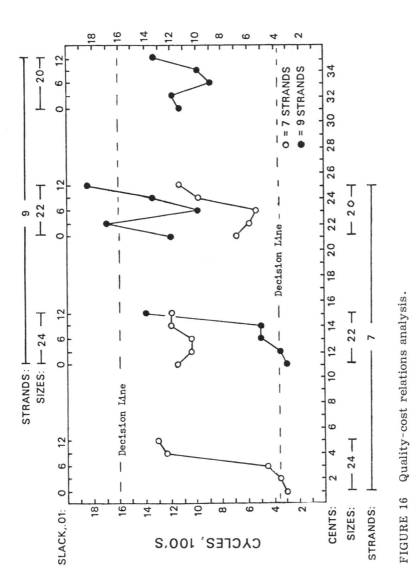

FIGURE 16 Quality-cost relations analysis.

significantly different from the grand average of only 9700 cycles of life. The same caution applies also to slack 12, size 24, nine strands.

The decision lines thus serve the important purpose of showing which test results are or are not significantly different from the grand mean. Only those that are will merit consideration as regards quality-cost relations and eventual manufacturing-marketing decisions.

APPENDIX A: CALCULATION OF MEAN SQUARES FOR SPEEDS-SETTINGS EXPERIMENT

For the two-factor replicated experiment on the effect of speeds and settings on process yield (percent), we used the decision line approach. Any points (arithmetic means) falling outside decision lines indicate significant deviation from the grand average of the experiment. A more traditional approach is by way of mean squares and the F ratio.

A. Experiment Totals

The experiment design, test results (experiment observations), and totals (for speeds and settings) appear in Fig. 17. The totals are needed for the calculation of mean squares. The entire approach of finding mean squares and F ratios is knows as "analysis of variance," "variance analysis," or ANOVA.

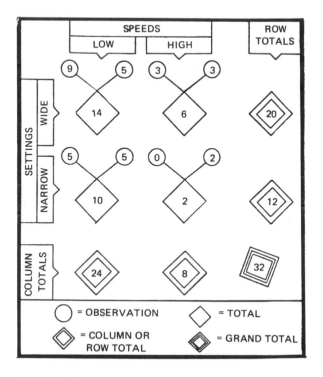

FIGURE 17   Speeds and settings process yield totals for columns, rows, and overall.

B. Worksheet

The process of finding mean squares is parallel to the method of Figs. 9 and 10, except that we add a column for "between-settings" effects, as shown in Fig. 18.

APPENDIX B: CALCULATION OF DECISION LINES FOR
STRAND-SLACK-SIZE EXPERIMENT FOR
QUALITY-COST RELATIONS

1. The experiment data, in terms of activation cycles until failure (in hundreds of cycles) are as follows:

		Wire gage size								
		24			22			20		
Number of strands	Wire slack (in. × 10^{-2})	Run 1	Run 2	Range	Run 1	Run 2	Range	Run 1	Run 2	Range
7	0	2	4	2	14	9	5	6	8	
7	3	5	2	3	6	15	9	5	7	2
7	6	6	3	3	14	7	7	6	5	1
7	9	9	16	7	12	12	0	8	12	4
7	12	14	12	2	10	14	4	12	11	1
9	0	3	3	0	10	14	4	12	11	1
9	3	2	5	3	17	17	0	16	8	8
9	6	5	5	0	10	10	0	10	8	2
9	9	6	4	2	16	11	5	13	7	6
9	12	13	15	2	20	17	3	12	15	3

2. The range R above represents in each case the difference between run 1 and run 2. In this special situation, when the replication is 2, based on two runs, a special simplified calculation of the experimental error variance is possible, based on

$$s^2_{error} = \frac{(\text{sum of ranges})^2}{\text{total number of observations}}$$

3. Squaring the ranges, we obtain 2^2, 3^2, 3^2, . . ., 2^2, 6^2, and 3^2 for all 30 R's. These squares add to $4 + 9 + 9 + \cdots + 4 + 36 + 9 = 453$. There is a total N of 60 observations.

4. Now, with $\Sigma R^2 = 453$ and N = 60, the estimated error variance is s^2_{error} = 453/60 = 7.55 and s_{error} = 2.748.

5. For plotting purposes, we now need the various arithmetic means and the grand mean, 9.7, as per the following calculations:

Sources of Variation

Steps	(1) Speeds	(2) Speeds	(3) Interaction	(4) Error	(5) Total**
a. Square the totals from the original data sheet.	$(24)^2$, $(8)^2$	$(20)^2$, $(12)^2$	$(14)^2$, $(10)^2$, $(6)^2$, $(2)^2$		$(9)^2$, $(5)^2$, $(3)^2$, $(3)^2$, $(5)^2$, $(5)^2$, $(0)^2$, $(2)^2$
b. Sum of a	640	544	336	178	178
c. No. of tests per each entry in a	4	4	2	1	1
d. b/c	160	136	168	178	178
e. Correction factor, C*	128	128	128	128	128
f. Sum of squares, SS	$d_1 - C = 32$	$d_2 - C = 8$	$d_3 - C - f_1 - f_2 = 0$	10	$d_5 - C = 50$
g. Degrees Freedom, DF	$2 - 1 = 1$	$2 - 1 = 1$	$(2-1)(2-1) = 1$	$4(2-1) = 4$	$8 - 1 = 7$

274

h. Meansquare f/g	32	8	0	2.5	—
i. F-ratio, h/h_4	$32/2.5 = 12.8$	$8/2.5 = 3.2$	0	—	—
j. Significance, %	97.5	Nil	None	—	—
k. Estimated Variance Component	$h_1 - h_4/c_1$ $\dfrac{32 - 2.5}{4} = 7.4$	$(h_2 - h_4)/c_2$ $\dfrac{8 - 2.5}{4} = 1.4$	$(h_3 - h_4)/c_3$ 0 0	h_4 2.5 2.5	row total: 11.3
l. k as a % of total	$7.4/11.3 = 65.5$	$1.4/11.3 = 12.4$	0	$2.5/11.3 = 22.1$	100

*Correction Factor, $C = $ (Grand Total)^2/(No. of Tests) $= (32)^2/8$. The entries in d are sometimes called "Gross Sum of Squares" so that the entries in f then would be called "Net Sum of Squares."

**Under row a each entry is the individual test or observation. Rows a to g under "Total" serve primarily as a check of calculations: Cols (1) + (2) + (3) + (4) = (5).

FIGURE 18 Worksheet for two-factor replicated variance analysis.

Number of strands	Wire slack (in. $\times 10^{-2}$)	Wire gage size			Slack mean	Group mean	Grand mean
		24	22	20			
7	0	3.0	11.5	7.0	7.2		
7	3	3.5	10.5	6.0	6.7		
7	6	4.5	10.5	5.5	6.8		
7	9	12.5	12.0	10.0	11.5		
7	12	13.0	12.0	11.5	12.2		
Strand mean		7.3	11.3	8.0		8.9	
9	0	3.0	12.0	11.5	8.8		
9	3	3.5	17.0	12.0	10.8		
9	6	5.0	10.0	9.0	8.0		
9	9	5.0	13.5	10.0	9.5		
9	12	14.0	18.5	13.5	15.3		
Strand mean		6.1	14.2	11.2		10.5	
7 and 9	0	3.00	11.75	9.25	8.00		
7 and 9	3	3.50	13.75	9.00	8.75		
7 and 9	6	4.75	10.25	7.25	7.42		
7 and 9	9	8.75	12.75	10.00	10.50		
7 and 9	12	13.50	15.25	12.50	13.75		
Combined mean		6.7	12.75	9.60			9.7

6. The decision lines are found from s_{error}^2 = 2.748, N = 60, and k = 30 (since there are 30 cells above containing means, one each for each of the two strand, five slack, and three gage sizes, or 2 × 5 × 3 = 30 combinations). Factor h_d from Fig. 15 is 17.72. Now

$$\text{Decision lines} = 9.7 \pm 17.72 \times 2.748/\sqrt{60}$$
$$= 9.7 \pm 6.3 = 3.4 \text{ to } 16.0$$

Any points falling outside these lines indicate arithmetic means of experimental effects that are significant at the 95% confidence level.

REFERENCE

1. L. S. Nelson, "Factors for the Analysis of Means," *Journal of Quality Technology*, Vol. 6, No. 4, October 1974, p. 1750181.

FURTHER READING

Davies, O. L., *Statistical Methods in Research and Production*, Hafner Press, New York, 1954.
Duncan, A. J., *Quality Control and Industrial Statistics*, Richard D. Irwin, Homewood, Ill., 1974.

Enrick, N. L., *Experimentation and Statistical Validation*, R. E. Krieger, Melbourne, Fla., 1983.

Enrick, N. L., *Manufacturing Analysis for Productivity and Quality/Cost Enhancement*, Industrial Press, New York, 1983.

Ott, E. R., *Process Quality Control: Troubleshooting and Interpretation of Data*, McGraw-Hill, New York, 1979.

15

PROCESS CONTROL

CHARLES A. CIANFRANI

Fischer & Porter Company
Warminster, Pennsylvania

I. INTRODUCTION

Process control is a vital element of virtually every industrial enterprise, since profitability, productivity, and product quality depend very fundamentally on effective total control of the process producing a product. The most intense applications of process control are found in the process industries, such as chemicals, drugs, food, pulp and paper, primary metals (both ferrous and nonferrous), fabricated metals, glass, and textiles, and in petroleum refining, water and wastewater management, and generation and control of electric power. Typical processes requiring control include the conversion of crude oil into gasoline, wood pulp into paper, coal or oil into electric power, and iron ore into steel.

Processing can be performed in either a continuous manner (a continuous process) such as in petroleum refining, or in a noncontinuous manner (a batch process) such as in heat treating. The types of properties that are typically controlled include temperature, pressure, flow, level, humidity, voltage, frequency, and analytical chemical properties such as pH and ionic concentration.

This chapter is directed at providing an understanding of the basic concepts of process control and how these concepts are applied in industrial environments. Such an understanding will enable the quality assurance practitioner to communicate effectively with plant personnel in their own language on day-to-day quality issues and to be intelligently involved in the selection of new process control equipment, since such equipment has a significant effect on product quality. The approach used in this chapter is qualitative and intuitive and does not rely on complex formulas or abstract theory.

II. PROCESS CONTROL: A HISTORICAL PERSPECTIVE

Process control originated along empirical lines, based on intuition and experience. A good historical example of rudimentary but effective process control is the heat treatment of metals accomplished by a blacksmith, who watched flame color, material color, smoke, and time to determine when the heat-treating task was completed. Since there were so many variables to watch, luck was a principal factor in such efforts.

As processes became larger in scale and more complex to meet volume and economic requirements, control was accomplished by using many people making individual judgments on a loosely coordinated basis (see Fig. 1). In the 1950s the indication of process status and control was consolidated into control rooms (Fig. 2), where a number of plant operators could maintain overall surveillance of the process from one location. Also in this time period control actions began to be dictated by electronic controllers rather than by operators. Consequently, process control operations were performed in a more consistent and uniform fashion.

In the 1960s and early 1970s process control continued to become more sophisticated and more centralized due to the improved capability of indicating and controlling instrumentation (see Fig. 3). More information was available about process phenomena and in a more usable form. Fewer operators were required and the results achieved became even more predictable. Also, process optimization (to increase throughput and lower costs) began to make a significant contribution to overall process operation. Although analog instruments and systems were predominant at this time, digital-based systems began to make their presence felt.

During the early 1970s the capabilities of digital-based process control systems began to make them more desirable than analog systems. Digital systems (see Fig. 4) were able to process more information faster and make this information available to an operator in a more usable form than were equivalent analog systems.

The next major evolutionary step occurred in the mid-1970s when distributed process control systems made their debut (see Fig. 5). In such systems

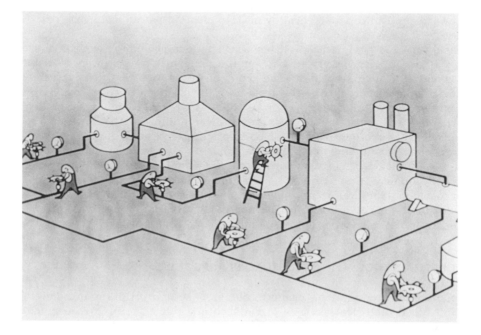

FIGURE 1   Early process control: Many people, many individual judgments.

FIGURE 2   During the 1950s, process control moved into control rooms.

FIGURE 3   In the 1960s and 1970s, more sophisticated and improved instrumentation was developed.

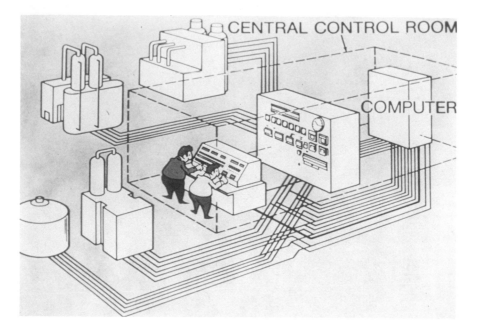

FIGURE 4   New digital systems in the early 1970s processed information faster and data were more usable to the operator.

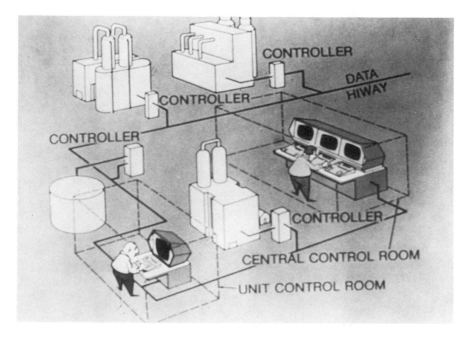

FIGURE 5   Distributed process control systems made their debut in the mid-1970s.

the control decisions were distributed into control rooms throughout the plant which were connected to a central control room where a computer and a chief operator could oversee the entire process. The distributed control approach combined the features, advantages, and benefits of all the previous approaches while eliminating most of the disadvantages.

Since the advent of distributed process control, advances have been made primarily in communications between field sensors and control rooms, in approaches used for interfacing the control system with operators (i.e., the human-machine interface), and in the basic speed and capability of the hardware elements of process control systems. Also, the power of the microprocessor and associated integrated-circuit chips has given rise to a plethora of process control system packages optimized for specific marketplace applications. All of the currently available sophistication, however, does not affect the validity of or the need to understand the basic concepts of process control that follow.

III. BASIC CONCEPTS OF PROCESS CONTROL

A. Simple Process

To illustrate the basics of process control, consider a simple process (see Fig. 6) composed of a source of raw feed liquid (A) which flows into a tank at a variable rate and must be heated so that it leaves the tank at pipe (B) as hot feed at temperature T. To heat the raw feed there is hot oil available (C) which flows through a heat exchanger.

The temperature of the feed liquid leaving the tank will be directly affected by the amount of hot oil passing through the heat exchanger. Therefore, the desired temperature T for the hot feed can be maintained by regulating the amount of hot oil C flowing through the heat exchanger. It is also desirable to assure that the level of feed in the tank does not exceed the top of the tank, and that the tank does not become empty.

To decide how to regulate the hot oil flow, and hence the temperature of the raw feed, it is necessary to know the temperature of the raw feed liquid. This can be accomplished in many ways. Most simply, a mercury thermometer could be held in the tank and read directly. A more appropriate approach would be to sense the temperature of the feed with a suitable *temperature sensor* (such as a thermocouple) and to display the value of the temperature on a chart recorder. Similarly, a float and a float-level recorder could be used to indicate liquid level. Finally, assume that (1) there are valves on the hot line (V_C) and on the output pipe of the tank (V_B), (2) the valves can be either fully open or fully closed, (3) initially the level of the tank is constant, and (4) the main concern is maintaining control of the temperature T at some desired value, say 150°C, which will be called the *set point*.

On-Off Control

Now, how could an operator go about maintaining the hot feed output from the tank (B) at a specific temperature T? The operator can fully open or fully close the two valves V_C and V_B, thereby regulating the amount of hot oil passing through the heat exchanger and the amount of hot feed flowing out of the tank. This form of control is called *two-position* or *on-off control*. The operator is comparing the indication of temperature on the chart recorder with a mental target of the set point and is opening valve V_C when the indicated temperature is below 150°C and closing V_C when the temperature is above 150°C.

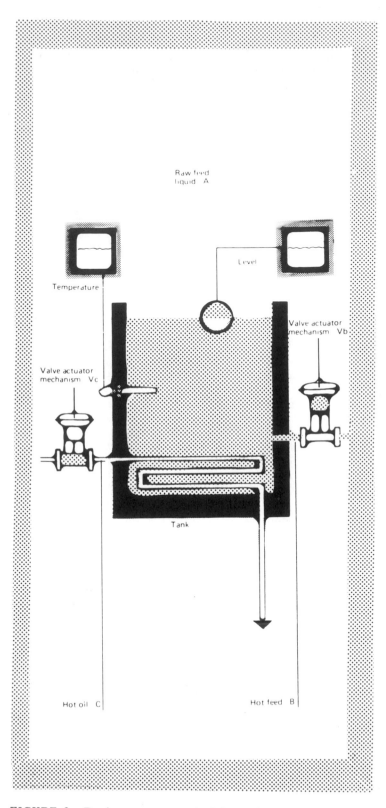

FIGURE 6   Basic process control in a simple process.

The indication of raw feed liquid temperature on the chart recorder would show oscillation about the set point of 150°C. The primary reason for this is that the heating effect of the hot oil is either completely supplied or completely withheld from the liquid in the tank. The amount of the oscillation above and below the set point depends on the *lags* of the process and the attention of the operator to the difference (or *error*) between the set point of 150°C and the temperature of the tank. The tank temperature in this example is known as the *process variable*, a control term that is used to identify a quantity in the process that is changing.

Proportional Control

It is obvious that although on-off control will provide a degree control over the process, something better is possible and desirable. If the process is viewed as a balance between energy in and energy out, it is reasonable to assume that smoother control of the output liquid will result if a steady flow of hot oil, C, is maintained, rather than alternating between full flow of hot oil and no flow of hot oil (i.e., on-off control). This control concept is analogous to taking a shower. It is more pleasant to have a steady stream of water at about 35°C than to alternate between water at 55°C and water at 10°C.

But what is the correct rate of hot oil flow? The correct rate of oil flow to hold the temperature of the output liquid at set point is obviously related to the rate of liquid flow into and out of the tank. Therefore, the on-off *control mode* must be modified. This can be accomplished by first establishing a steady flow value for hot oil that at average operating conditions tends to hold the process variable (the tank temperature) at the set point (i.e., 150°C). Once the flow value for the hot oil has been established, increases or decreases of the process variable from the set point (call this the *error*) can be used to cause corresponding increases or decreases in the hot oil flow.

The concept of taking corrective action in proportion to changes in the deviation of the set point from the process variable (i.e., changes in the error) is the concept of *proportional control*. To implement proportional control on a process, the control valves used must be of a type that can be positioned at any degree of flow from fully opened to fully closed. In addition, a mechanism to move the valve is required, such as an electric motor or a pneumatic valve positioner.

With such a system configuration (see Fig. 7) the operator can manually make gradual (proportional) adjustments to the hot oil valve as the temperature of the tank deviates from the set-point temperature. Control action (i.e., moving the hot oil control valve) should be relatively infrequent since a steady flow of hot oil will be maintained that is in close balance to the average needs of the process. The degree of sensitivity of valve change to error is called the *proportional gain*. The term that describes the new valve position where the process variable equals the set point is *manual reset*.

Proportional control is certainly much more effective than on-off control (and in practice costs more to implement), but it does have a serious deficiency. If there are frequent disturbances or process upsets, the process temperature hardly ever stays at set point. There is only so much proportional gain that can be applied before the process becomes unstable and frequent, and/or large changes in manual reset are not practical. Therefore, something still better than proportional control may be required.

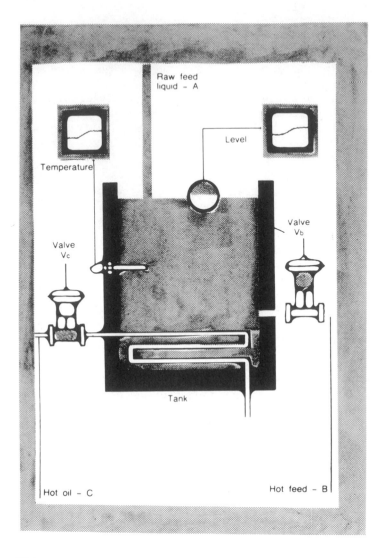

FIGURE 7   System configuration of proportional control on a process.

Integral Control

If the manual reset adjustment mentioned above could be made automatically, the offset error due to load changes would be eliminated. One approach to automatic adjustment of reset is to move the valve at a speed proportional to the deviation of the process variable from the set point. In other words, process control would be enhanced if a piece of instrumentation (such as a controller) would, through electronics, automatically move the valve faster if the deviation from set point became larger, and conversely move the valve more slowly if the deviation became smaller. When there exists no deviation from setpoint, no valve motion would occur.

Figure 8 illustrates what happens to the process illustrated in Fig. 6 when there is a change in the raw feed flow. Without any control, when the raw feed flow (A) increases, the temperature in the tank drops below the set point. With proportional control, the hot oil control valve opens and the process temperature rises to a level close to the set point but with a temperature offset. With automatic adjustment of the offset, the error is eliminated (after an initial overshoot of the set point).

The term used to describe the automatic adjustment of the reset is *integral control*. This name arises from the fact that the valve position is related to the integral of the error which has existed since time zero. When proportional and integral control are combined in the manner just described, the control form or control mode is called *two-mode* or *proportional-integral control*, commonly referred to as PI control.

Derivative Control

Finally, it seems reasonable to take one last step in addition to proportional control and integral control—taking control action based on the rate of change of an error signal. That is, the valve can be made to move proportionally in response to a changing deviation from the set point. This additional correction exists only when the error is *changing*. It disappears when the error stops changing, even though the size of the error may still be large. Such control action is called *derivative control*. Derivative control enhances process control because its contribution to control action is significant when the rate of change of the error signal is large and no contribution to control action is present when there is no rate of change of the error signal. Derivative control is illustrated in Fig. 9. When derivative control is combined with proportional control and integral control, the control form is called *three-mode* or *PID control*.

A Few More Basic Concepts of Process Control

There are a few additional process control terms that should be considered in conjunction with those described above: open-loop control, closed-loop control, and feedback. At times, control signals may be applied to a process based on information that is not directly obtained from the process variable; that is, the process is being controlled indirectly or inferentially. Under such conditions the process is considered to be operating under *open-loop control*. Another way of saying this is that the measured value *is not* compared directly with the set point. Experts in the process control field believe that a majority of the process control loops are typically operated in such an open-loop manner.

Conversely, a control loop is operating in a *closed-loop* manner when the results of the control manipulations are *compared* to the set point. The process by which the comparison against the set point takes place is called *feedback*.

PROPORTIONAL PLUS RESET CONTROL

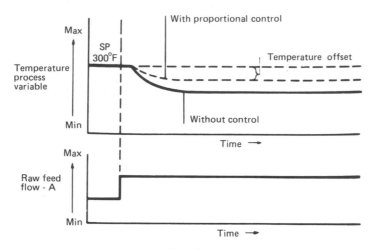

Response to load change proportional control only

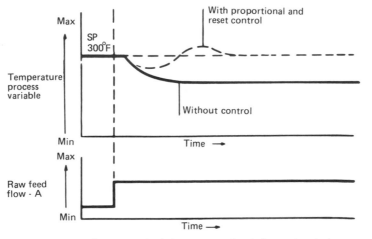

Response to load change proportional plus reset control

FIGURE 8   Process operation shown in Fig. 6.

The comparison against set point is very important. Unless the results of the control manipulations are compared against an objective (i.e., the set point), continuous human interaction will be required. With comparison to the set point occurring continuously, corrections can automatically be made as required. Feedback is therefore a most fundamental and necessary part of an effective process control system.

B. Simple Process Control System

Now that the basic concepts of process control have been presented, it is appropriate to consider the nature and function of a typical process control

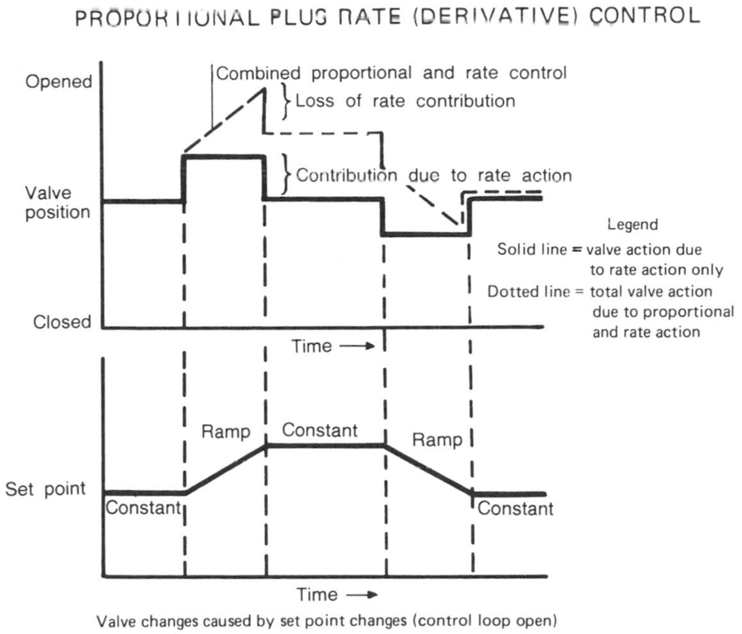

PROPORTIONAL PLUS RATE (DERIVATIVE) CONTROL

FIGURE 9   Schematic of derivative control.

system in an industrial environment. The key elements of a system to control
a process are sensors, controllers, and final control elements. Sensors—such
as temperature sensors (i.e., thermocouples) and level sensors—tell us what
is happening with the process. Temperature and level sensors are only a few
of the many kinds of sensors that can be used in a process control system.
There are sensors for the detection of pressure, humidity, flow, pH, conductivity, turbitity, speed, and many other physical and chemical phenomena.
The proper selection and application of sensors is a specialized art/science
that is a critical element of any process control system. Controllers take inputs from sensors and determine what can be done to assure that the process
behaves as expected. Controllers implement control actions, such as proportional, integral, and derivative control. Final control elements, such as valves,
are used to implement the instructions of the controllers. In other words, a
process control system includes *inputs* to controllers (from a thermocouple,
for example), the controllers, and *outputs* from controllers to final control
elements such as valves.

   Knowing and understanding a few control forms and how a controller works
however is not the same as understanding process control. There are additional factors to be considered. Processes have limits of controllability. Also,
control loops can interact. Control of one variable at the most desired set
point might preclude control of another variable at its optimum point. Also,
proper tuning of control loops is certainly an art. It is easy to see—after the
fact—why an integral action setting of x and a derivative action setting of y
are appropriate. When one must actually establish the controller settings on
line for a process, the "appropriate" settings are not nearly as obvious.

   The basics of process control were illustrated earlier by means of a simple
process that involved level, temperature, and flow control. The basics can

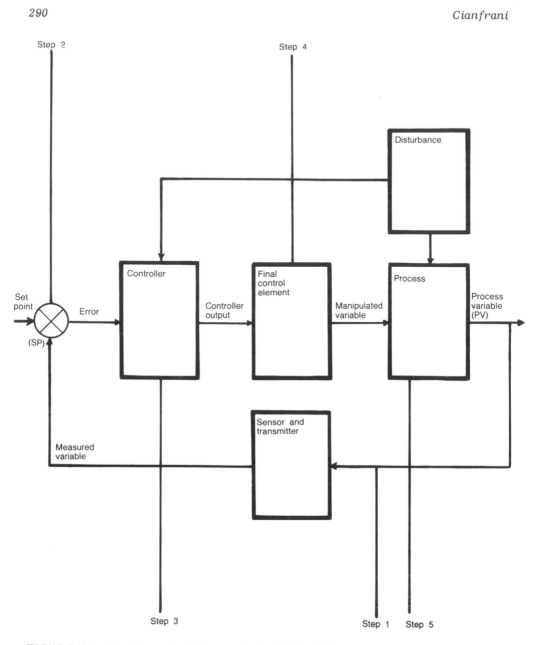

FIGURE 10   Simple control loop. Data fed back from the output modify the input to the process.

be illustrated further by looking at a block diagram of a process and the minimum equipment necessary to control it.

Figure 10 illustrates a simple control loop where information is fed back from the output of the process in a way that effectively modifies the input to the process to maintain process operation at the desired condition. Five steps are essential to achieving good process control for such a control loop.

1. The process variable that best represents the desired condition of the final product must be measured. This depends on the specific product. Measurements such as temperature, pressure, and flow are commonly used.
2. The process variable is compared with the desired value for that variable (i.e., the set point) and an error signal is generated.
3. The error signal is applied to the controller.
4. The controller determines the signal that must be applied to the final control element, such as a valve.
5. The process is continually manipulated in response to the output of the controller so that the difference between the process variable and the set point is as close to zero as the sensitivity of the system permits.

Another way of saying this is that the process control system must effectively *measure* what is to be controlled, *compare* the measured value with a set point (i.e., the desired value), and *correct* for any differences between the measured value and the desired value. The process of measuring, comparing, and correcting is the foundation of process control.

IV. CONCLUSION

The objective of this chapter was to provide an understanding of the basic concepts of process control. It has covered the key elements of a process control system, including sensors, controllers, and final control devices, and has illustrated how these elements can be configured to control a process. The basic control approaches or modes of control—on-off control, proportional control, integral control, and derivative control—were described and an intuitive explanation of the nature of each control form was presented. Throughout the chapter, common control terms were defined and explained. Overall, a foundation was established that will permit the quality practitioner to understand and appreciate the nature of process control systems and their contribution to optimum process operation.

There is a considerable body of knowledge that goes beyond the basics in every area discussed above. Selection and application of sensors is an area of specialization to which some engineers devote a lifetime. Development of basic and advanced control strategies and techniques for optimizing processes is similarly a segment of technology that provides full-time employment for many engineers. Tuning of controllers is an artform developed through many hours of exposure to actual operating conditions, coupled with a sound understanding of the theoretical bases of process control. The determination of acceptable cost-performance trade-offs must balance at least initial instrumentation investment, ongoing maintenance costs, process throughput, product quality, and system reliability. Finally, understanding the hardware and software used to achieve process control is becoming more and more difficult as the microprocessor continues to spawn new and increasingly exotic offerings from process control instrumentation suppliers.

The challenge confronting those who must interact with the world of process control is to learn and understand the basics, and to go beyond the basics with personal initiative to acquire the knowledge necessary to be able to communicate with specialists. It is not an easy challenge, but it can be an extremely interesting, intellectually satisfying, and professionally rewarding experience.

FURTHER READING

An Evolutionary Look at Process Control/1, Honeywell, Inc., Fort Washington, Pa.

Shinskey, F. G., *Process Control Systems*, 2nd ed., McGraw-Hill, New York.

Tucker, G. K., and D. M. Wills, *A Simplified Technique of Control System Engineering*, 3rd ed., Honeywell, Inc., Fort Washington, Pa.

16

RELIABILITY IMPROVEMENT

HAROLD S. BALABAN

Advanced Research and Development Group
Aeronautical Radio, Inc.
Annapolis, Maryland

I. INTRODUCTION

Failure of military equipment to perform as required is costly in terms of equipment readiness and maintenance and supply resources. In an effort to improve the reliability levels of sophisticated equipment, the military services have begun to incorporate long-term warranty provisions in procurement contracts. These warranty provisions are designed to motivate both the supplier and the user to produce, acquire, operate, maintain, and improve equipment to achieve a satisfactory level of field reliability. Reliability improvement warranty (RIW), the name used for such warranty provisions, is a commitment by the military equipment contractor to perform depot-type repair services at a preestablished price for a stated time. The basic approach has been used by the commercial airlines for a number of years and is considered to be a major factor in the high reliability levels experienced by airline equipment. Also adopted from airline practices is the concept of a guaranteed operational mean time between failures (MTBF), with the contractor guaranteeing that field MTBF values will equal or exceed contract-stipulated values. When such a guarantee is incorporated within an RIW, the term RIW/MTBF is used.

RIWs are normally negotiated in association with the production contract and apply to operational use of the production items. On the surface, an RIW can be viewed as simply a fixed-price maintenance agreement. Although such a view is not entirely incorrect, it is the motivation and implementation that differentiates an RIW from a repair contract and from a short-term warranty that protects against defective material.

In the 1970s, the RIW and RIW/MTBF concepts were applied to a number of military procurements. The success of these early applications provided the impetus for continued development and implementation. Today, there are well over 30 military programs in which RIW has been used or is under serious consideration. The concept is still evolving and recent applications have shown variations in coverage designed to meet the particular needs of the using service.

II. RIW GENESIS AND DEVELOPMENT

The achievement of satisfactory reliability and maintainability levels in military
operational systems has been a challenging problem for a number of years.
The potential for improved part and component R&M characteristics offered by
technology has been offset to a great extent by the demands for greater sophistication and performance.

During the 1960s, U.S. military agencies expended considerable effort in
developing approaches to achieving satisfactory field R&M performance. The
concept of formal R&M programs is now well established, as evidenced by
MIL-STD-785 for reliability and MIL-STD-470 for maintainability. Most large
military procurements now impose contractual requirements for such programs,
including specifications, predictions, design reviews, allocations, parts screening and burn-in, testing, and formal R&M demonstration procedures. A number of military standards, specifications, regulations, and handbooks form a
large body of R&M "how-to" documentation.

Although it is difficult to evaluate the success of the formal R&M program
approach quantitatively, continued use suggests that benefits have been realized. However, comparison of field results with predicted and test values
shows that reliability achievement has not been completely successful. Hirschberger and Dantowitz (1976) describe a comprehensive study comparing laboratory-demonstrated and field MTBF values for 95 distinct Navy Weapon Replaceable Assemblies (WRAs). Ground rules were established to provide consistent measurements in the laboratory and in the field; for example, field
failures due to identified mishandling were excluded. Figure 1 is a histogram
of the MTBF ratio for the 95 WRAs. Eighteen exhibited a field MTBF higher
than the MTBF observed in laboratory demonstration, while 77 exhibited a
lower field MTBF. By use of a geometric averaging technique, the average
ratio of laboratory-demonstrated MTBF to field MTBF was found to be 3.1:1.
Similar results were obtained for the ratio of predicted MTBF to field MTBF.

This phenomenon has prompted the military services continuously to seek
new approaches to assuring timely achievement of satisfactory field reliability.
In 1967, the U.S. Navy, through the Aviation Supply Office, contracted with
the Lear Siegler Company to provide a Failure Free Warranty (FFW) for the
2171P gyros then in use on A-4 and F-4 aircraft. Lear Siegler provided warranty repair services for 5 years on 800 of the 2500 gyros in the population.
Warranty pricing was based on a 30% improvement in MTBF, which was achieved.
The Navy's satisfaction with the initial contract resulted in a 5-year extension.
This FFW contract is considered the prototype of what is now known as RIW.

In the early 1970s additional small contracts incorporating RIW concepts
were awarded, including an Air Force contract to Lear Siegler for warranting
gyros in the F-111 aircraft and a Navy contract to the Abex Corporation for
warranting hydraulic pumps on the F-14 aircraft (Aviation Supply Office, 1973;
Markowitz, 1976).

Early in 1973 the U.S. Department of Defense (DoD), through the Defense
Advanced Research Projects Agency, contracted with ARINC Research Corporation to explore the potential of applying commercial airline warranty practices
to military avionics. It had been widely known that airline avionics of comparable functions in comparable operating environments were achieving reliability far superior to that of military avionics. In the DoD study, the airline
warranty approach was determined to be one of the significant reasons for
this disparity. It was concluded that the military could realize significant
avionics reliability and life-cycle cost benefits from properly constituted and

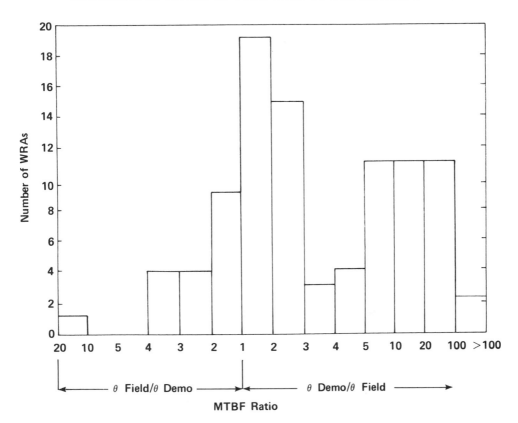

FIGURE 1   Histogram of ratios of field MTBF to demonstration MTBF.

applied warranties. The study was also one of the first to develop a life-cycle cost model for the quantitative evaluation of warranty (Balaban and Retterer, 1973).

The DoD's Electronics-X program was also under way during 1973, and a special study category devoted to warranties was established. The Electronics-X report, published early in 1974, concluded that long-term warranties could serve as a competitive alternative to military repair and recommended that they be applied to military electronics, (Gates et al., 1974).

The Electronics System Division of the U.S. Air Force applied the recommendations of these studies to the procurement of a standardized Air Force navigation equipment, now termed the ARN-118 TACAN. Up to 10,000 TACAN sets were to be purchased under either an RIW/MTBF with contractor depot maintenance or a logistic-support-cost commitment with Air Force depot maintenance. The procurement was restricted to the two contractors who successfully completed the Full Scale Development phase. After receiving competitive bids, the Air Force chose the RIW/MTBF alternative and selected Collins Radio as the equipment supplier. That Air Force TACAN RIW program was the first to employ the concept of guaranteed MTBF, together with a number of other innovative features, many of them adopted to balance government and contractor risks (Balaban and Nohmer, 1975).

At about the same time, the Army and Marine Corps became interested in applying RIW to commercially available navigation equipment and, under a formal two-step advertised procurement, Bendix Radio was awarded a contract to supply navigation radios for helicopter applications under an RIW and guaranteed MTBF (Mlinarchik, 1977).

Thus, during 1974 all U.S. military services were involved in warranty procurements in an attempt to secure reliable equipment at a reasonable cost. The DoD recognized the potential of this approach as well as the dangers of misapplication and misuse. In mid-1974 the Assistant Secretary of Defense (Installation and Logistics) promulgated a set of guidelines for RIW, including RIW application criteria, special funding requirements, and essential elements of the RIW contractual clause.

In mid-1974 the Air Force's Rome Air Development Center contracted with ARINC Research Corporation to develop a detailed set of guidelines on warranty application for Air Force electronic systems (Balaban and Retterer, 1975). In the same year the Air Force included RIW terms and conditions in the request for proposal for major avionic units of the Lightweight Air Combat Fighter aircraft (later to become the F-16). This major step showed industry that the Air Force was firmly in support of the RIW concept. Four NATO countries—Belgium, Denmark, Norway, and The Netherlands—also endorsed the RIW concept for the F-16 aircraft they were to purchase (Balaban et al., 1979).

Industry, on the other hand, had reservations about the RIW concept as applied to military systems. The umbrella industry organization known as CODSIA (Council of Defense and Space Industries Association) was the spokesman of industry concern and communicated its views in a number of letters (CODSIA, 1975). CODSIA's principal concern was the inability of contractors to reasonably price an RIW on equipment for which extensive field data were not available. The CODSIA letters established an important communication between government and industry for developing RIW approaches acceptable to both parties. The DoD and the military services certainly recognized the inherent risks of RIW. The DoD established a Tri-Service Reliability and Support Incentives Group to aid in developing and coordinating policy on RIW and other procurement approaches for reliability achievement.

By the mid-1970s, the RIW concept was well established and studies by a number of government and industry organizations were under way to evaluate and expand the approach (see Gándara and Rich, 1975; Weimer and Palatt, 1976; Gates et al., 1977; Balaban and Meth, 1978; Bilodeau, et al., 1979).

III. THE RIW PLAN

Specific terms and conditions of an RIW will depend on economic, procurement, logistic, equipment, and administrative aspects. Therefore, a standard set of specific terms and conditions applicable to all procurements does not exist. However, we can outline a basic RIW plan indicating the major ramifications and alternatives.

A. Warranty Statement

This is the basic provision of the RIW, which states that the contractor warrants that the equipment furnished under the contract will be free from defects in design, material, and workmanship; and will operate in its intended environment in accordance with contractual requirments for the period specified. The major distinction between this stated warranty and the usual one-year (public consumer) type is that the period covered by the former is of such duration that each delivered equipment is likely to fail one or more times during the warranty period. The seller therefore prices the warranty to cover expected repair costs, which, especially in a competitive procurement, must be consistent with stated or promised reliability levels.

B. Contractor Repair Obligation

Equipment that fails during the warranty period is returned by the government to a designated contractor repair facility, where the contractor is obligated to repair or replace the failed equipment at their expense. The contract may include a test procedure that the contractor must apply to repaired equipment to verify the repair to an on-site government representative upon request.

C. Exclusions

Certain failures not the fault of the contractor and which are completely beyond their control are normally excluded from warranty coverage. Examples include failures caused by fire, explosion, submersion, combat damage, and aircraft crash.

Two very difficult areas are mistreatment and system-induced failures (e.g., power transients). In many cases what caused the failure is not clear cut. If a contractor is experiencing more repair actions than anticipated, they will naturally look to broad exclusion terms to reduce profit erosion. Such broad exclusions create the possibility of continual arguments and litigation on warranty coverage. It is therefore recommended that exclusions be limited.

One approach used with respect to mistreatment was to define mistreatment as a possible occurrence only if obvious external physical damage or tampering was evident. Exclusions for system-induced failures or abnormal environmental stress are not recommended, since it is extremely difficult to prove such conditions existed.

Besides the advantages of minimizing disputes, this type of broad coverage forces the contractor to consider environmental extremes in their design and equipment modification strategy. For military warranty, the contractor is relieved from liability for special consequential or incidental damages.

D. Warranty Period

The period of coverage can be stated either in calendar years, operating hours, or both. The use of a calendar period is best from an administrative viewpoint and for planning for organic maintenance. In considering the period of coverage, the following factors are important:

1. The period should be long enough to provide strong contractor incentive for achieving and maintaining acceptance reliability. As a minimum, the period should be of such duration that at least several failures of each delivered equipment would be expected.
2. On a per-year basis, warranty costs decrease as the warranty period increased since nonrecurring costs are amortized over a longer period and contractor "learning" takes place.
3. An overlong warranty period (say, more than 4 years) may involve large uncertainties, forcing the bidder to price-in a large risk factor.

4. By providing for negotiated extensions to the initial warranty period, both the government and the contractor can extend the warranty, if deemed beneficial, at a price based on initial performance.

E. Unverified Failures

Some returned units will not exhibit failure when tested by the contractor. However, the contractor incurs costs in processing such units, and might feel justified in asking that they be paid for processing each unverified failure. This arrangement is not likely to motivate the contractor to minimize such occurrences through design, built-in test equipment (BITE), maintenance manuals, and training procedures. Even so, it is probably unfair to have the contractor absorb all unverified-failure costs. A compromise is to reimburse the contractor for all such returns that exceed a stated percentage within a reporting period. Values between 20 and 30% have been suggested for avionics. The contractor can use such a rate as a bound for pricing.

If the contractor feels that the combination of design, BITE, training, and manuals will lead to a lower percentage, they may choose a lower rate upon which to price for competitive reasons. In any case, there is continual incentive for the contractor to try to minimize the return of good items.

F. ECP Control

As the name implies, reliability improvement is the major feature of an RIW. By directly observing all field failures and being responsible for repair, the contractor can quickly identify failure patterns and institute appropriate corrective action through engineering change proposals (ECPs). ECPs, by terms of the warranty, are introduced at no cost to the government. Class I ECPs will generally follow normal MIL-STD-480 procedures necessary to configuration control, but because of the no-cost feature, should and can be expeditiously processed. Changes not affecting form, fit, and function can be introduced immediately, with proper notification to the resident government representative.

To assure a standard configuration at warranty expiration, the contractor should be required to incorporate all approved ECPs into returned units and to provide modification kits for the remaining unmodified units. If the warranty period is long enough to result in multiple returns of each unit, the number of unmodified units at warranty expiration will probably be small. If not, it may be advisable to negotiate for modification kits at warranty expiration so as not to inhibit ECT introduction.

G. Government Obligations

The government's major obligations under a warranty procurement include:

Testing all suspected failures on applicable test sets prior to return to the contractor
Utilizing approved shipping containers
Furnishing failure circumstance data
Minimizing buildup at the using activities

Meeting these obligations is beneficial to both the government and the contractor, and should not present undue difficulties for military maintenance personnel. However, in some programs there have been a number of instances in which the foregoing obligations have not been satisfactorily fulfilled. The military services have taken steps to correct deficiencies, such as by establishing better administrative and training procedures for RIW implementation.

H. Warranty Data Requirements

The contractor is normally required to maintain records and issue periodic reports necessary for assessing the effectiveness of the RIW, negotiating extensions, and making necessary contract price adjustments. Specific records to be maintained for each returned unit may include the following:

Date received by contractor
Serial number
Elapsed-time-indicator (ETI) reading
Condition of unit
Failure mode
Probable failure cause
Action taken for repair
Labor hours expended by labor category
Parts and material usage
Test results
Date stored or shipped

I. Miscellaneous

Briefly noted below are other terms and conditions that might be included within an RIW.

1. *Warranty labeling and seals*: The contractor should be required to install appropriate labeling and seals to indicate warranty coverage and minimize unauthorized tampering.
2. *Elapsed-time indicators*: If operate hours are the basis for warranty coverage, a requirement for reliable and accurate ETIs should be included.
3. *Lost unit adjustment*: A provision for adjusting the contract price for lost units, such as through aircraft crash, might be advisable for expensive units.
4. *Operate-hour adjustment*: If warranty coverage is on a calendar basis, provisions for adjusting the warranty price for deviations from a stipulated operate-hour factor used for pricing is advisable. Procedures for estimating total operate hours from ETI readings of returned units have been established (see Balaban, 1975).
5. *MTBF guarantee*: A major provision pioneered by the airlines requires that the contractor guarantee the equipment MTBF experienced in the operating environment. Failure to meet a guaranteed level requires the contractor to institute corrective action and provide loaner spares until the MTBF improves. Details of such a procedure are provided in Balaban (1975) and Balaban and Retterer (1975).
6. *Noncovered failures*: Since the government will generally not have a depot repair facility, provision for contractor repair of all returns is required, including those failures not covered under the warranty. This can be accomplished through a separate contract or through equitable adjustment in contract price for each such return.

J. Shipping

If the expense of shipping warranted equipment is small compared to the cost of repair, it is probably best for the government to bear all such shipping costs because the exact equipment deployment is usually unknown at the time of RIW pricing. Also, shipping through a government bill of lading provides government discounts and reduces or eliminates customs delays for equipment deployed overseas.

IV. LOGISTICS FLOW UNDER WARRANTY

The typical logistics flow process (Fig. 2) for a warranty repair is as follows:

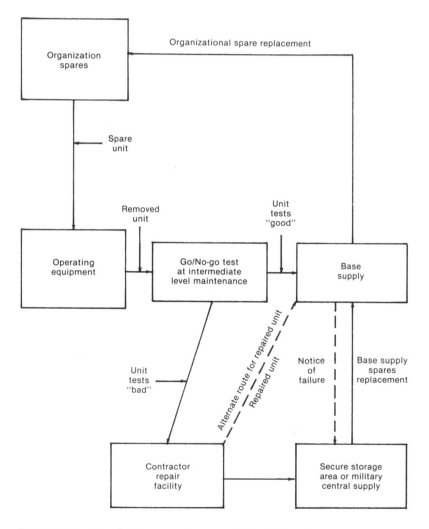

FIGURE 2   Typical warranty-repair logistics flow.

A suspected failure of a warranted unit is tested by military personnel at the using activity to verify the failure.

If the unit tests "good," it is put back into service or sent to supply as a ready-for-issue spare.

If the unit tests "bad," it is shipped with appropriate data to the contractor for repair.

The contractor receives the unit and verifies the failure and warranty coverage.

If the failure is not verified or is not covered by the warranty, this is corroborated by a government representative.

Covered failures are corrected at no additional cost to the government, and necessary data records are prepared.

The repaired unit is shipped back to the using activity, placed in a secure storage area or bonded storeroom maintained by the contractor, or sent to a central military supply depot.

In many respects this logistics flow process is similar to military depot repair or to contractor repair under a service contract. However, there are significant differences. Under military maintenance, modules rather than black boxes (e.g., a circuit card rather than a receiver unit) are sent back to a central depot facility; under warranty, the opposite is generally true. Return of black boxes can have a significant spares impact unless pipeline times are carefully controlled. In addition, RIW and RIW/MTBF contracts often have price adjustments or other controls associated with such factors as unverified failures ("test good"), field MTBF, utilization, lost units, ECPs, and batching of returns. If the government is to receive full value for the warranty and meet its contractual obligations, some new or modified administrative activities may be necessary. Generally, these have not been burdensome; however, to date there has been no major transition from warranty to organic maintenance for a large population of equipment. Transition must be carefully planned to ensure an orderly process and to preclude any reduction in operational availability.

V. INCENTIVES

The incentive feature of an RIW is clear. If a contractor can provide equipment that either fails less often than initially anticipated or can be repaired at lower cost than anticipated, their profit is increased. Therefore, with an RIW, the contractor has a direct profit incentive to provide equipment with good R&M characteristics. Under a normal procurement scenario, it might be said that R&M levels above minimum acceptable are not in the contractor's long-range profit interests. Although it is true that reliability must be *designed* into the system, it must also be recognized that an RIW provides a contractual framework in which the test-analyze-fix process can be extended to initial system operation for both reliability and maintainability. Such a process is basic for reliability and maintainability growth. It has been shown that providing the contractor with near-real-time information on field failures and depot maintenance facilitates R&M problem identification, correction, and growth.

Although there are well over 20 types of equipment procured under RIW or RIW/MTBF, only a few have accumulated enough data to permit testing whether the theoretical incentive features of such procurement concepts can be realized in practice. Figure 3 summarizes nine such types of equipment for

RIW Experience
Expected vs Field MTBF

Item	Service	Contract date	MTBF Expected	Field	MTBF Ratio Exp/Field
GYRO	Navy	1967	520	531	.98
GYRO	AF	1969	1300	1000	1.30
PUMP	Navy	1973	600	1100	.55
PUMP	AF	1975	5000	8500	.59
TACAN	AF	1975	800*	1650	.48
KLYSTRON	AF	1975	1000	3780	.26
INS	AF	1975	1090*	1125	.97
AHRS	AF	1975	1285*	1340	.96
OMEGA	AF	1976	700*	725	.97
*Guaranteed				Geo. Avg. =	.71

FIGURE 3   RIW experience: expected versus field MTBF.

which it is possible to compare observed field MTBF with expected or guaranteed values. It is seen that in eight of the nine programs, the observed field
MTBF met or exceeded expectations. Data presented in Fig. 1 for non-RIW
procurements show that only 20 of 111 types of equipment, or 18%, achieved
the expected reliability level. The geometric average of the ratio of expected
to field MTBF for the nine RIW-covered equipment types was 0.71 compared to
3.1 for non-RIW-covered equipment.

   Although this relatively small sample cannot be taken as final evidence that
with RIW or RIW/MTBF the military user can finally expect reliability to be at
levels originally intended, the results are certainly encouraging. In many
warranty programs there is strong evidence that contractors are paying significantly more attention to R&M than is normal under other procurement/
maintenance scenarios, again an indication that the theoretical incentives are,
indeed, real.

VI. ADVANTAGES, DISADVANTAGES, AND
APPLICABILITY OF RIW

The decision to include an RIW or RIW/MTBF in a procurement is a significant
one. Both the contractor and military customer may have misgivings, some
fully justified. For example, the military is concerned about dependence on a
commercial source for long-term repair and the supplier is concerned about
the risks of warranty pricing.

   In addition, structuring RIW and MTBF guarantee plans that are complete,
fair, and effective, and planning for their implementation, involve a great deal
of effort that should not be expended unless the RIW has a reasonably good

Factors	Standard Organic	R/W	RIW/MTBF
User risk in achieving objectives	High	Moderate	Low
Contractor pricing risk	Low	Moderate	High
Administration difficulty	Low	Moderate	High
Enforceability risk	N/A	Moderate	Moderate
Contractor reliability improvement motivation	Low	Moderate	High
Commitment time	N/A	Start of production	Start of production
Services provided	N/A	Depot maintenance plus no-cost ECPs	Depot maintenance, logistics assets if required, plus no-cost ECPs

FIGURE 4   Comparison of procurement methods.

chance of being successful. To provide some insight into the chances for success, three summary tables have been developed.

Figure 4 provides a comparative overview of the standard organic maintenance and RIW and RIW/MTBF plans with respect to some factors related to risk, motivation, and implementation. Figure 5 summarizes the major advantages and disadvantages of an RIW form of commitment with respect to procurement and operational factors. To assist in identifying those procurements for which significant warranty benefits can be realized, a number of application criteria are presented in Fig. 6. These criteria are generally qualitative and are intended to indicate the general feasibility of warranty application. If the criteria are satisfied, further detailed economic analysis is indicated. This table was initially developed for avionic units. See Cotton et al. (1979) for a similar table for ground electronics and Bilodeau et al. (1979) for applicability of RIW to dynamic systems.

The application criteria presented in Fig. 6 have been divided into three areas: procurement factors, equipment characteristics, and operational factors. The three areas are considered equally important with respect to accepting or rejecting the use of warranty. Each item presented is evaluated for the RIW and RIW/MTBF plans. For each criteria/plan combination, an importance factor is assigned as follows:

Major: Failure to meet any of the stated criteria could be grounds for not using the plan.
Secondary: Failure to meet a stated criterion will generally not be a sufficient basis for rejecting the plan, but a number of such failures could be.

Factor	Advantages	Disadvantages
Procurement considerations	Initial requirements for support equipment, data, training, module spares, R&M program elements, etc., are reduced, thus reducing the complexity of the procurement. Significant portion of support costs are known at the outset.	Close coordination with user, logistic, and legal activities is necessary until R/W contracting experience is acquired in developing appropriate terms and conditions, including any necessary escalation provisions. Contract price adjustments may be required periodically, and potential for legal disputes on liability is increased.
Reliability/ maintainability	Contractor and government have same goal of achieving good R&M characteristics. Growth can be achieved in faster and more cost-effective manner than with organic maintenance because of contractor incentives. Limited military maintenance will reduce maintenance-induced failure occurrences. More realistic contractor claims on operational reliability than for usual procurements.	Care has to be exercised to ensure that design for R&M and R&M ECP changes will be compatible with organic maintenance after transition from RIW.
Hardware acquisition costs	Will be reduced if formal R&M program requirements are relaxed.	Will be increased if the contractor expends additional effort in achieving good initial R&M, or because of risk protection.
Spares cost	Will be decreased because better reliability is achieved and control of depot-type repair turnaround time is exercised.	Could lead to increased costs because of sparing at the LRU rather than module level and because of possibly long pipeline time to and from the contractor.

Category	Advantages	Disadvantages
Maintenance personnel requirements	Reduced requirements for skilled base and depot maintenance personnel.	At transition to organic maintenance, a large increase in the number of skilled maintenance personnel may be required.
Support equipment	Limited requirements for initial base and depot support equipment. Purchase of such support equipment at transition will be a stabilized design. Support equipment support cost under RIW is also reduced.	In the event early and fast introduction of military maintenance is required, necessary test equipment may not be available.
Training and data	Initial requirements and costs are reduced. At transition, design will be stabilized, leading to better requirements definition.	Planning for a single, step-function organic maintenance takeover required. Training of cadre of military personnel during the RIW is recommended.
Logistic management and administration	Maintenance at the "box" level reduced management costs. Better R&M data will be available through warranty data records.	New or modified procedures need to be developed to support the warranty concept without adversely affecting the logistic management function. Ability to respond to an emergency situation may be impaired. Fast ECP evaluation necessary for most effective R&M growth.
Contractor	Long-term, stabilized work flow and parts demand. Good profit for good equipment. Increased chances for follow-on awards if RIW services are satisfactory and because of greater knowledge about equipment performance in operating environment.	Pricing risks are high. RIW implementation involves a greater-than-usual degree of good faith on both sides. Some problems may arise because of rigid government regulations or changes in government personnel.

FIGURE 5 Summary of RIW advantages and disadvantages.

Criteria	Importance Rating*	
	RIW	RIW/MTBF
Procurement		
The procurement is to be on a fixed-price basis.	1	1
Multi-year funding for warranty services is available.	1	1
The procurement is competitive.	2	2
Potential contractors have proven capability, experience, and cooperative attitude in providing warranty-type services.	2	2
The procurement quantity is large enough to make warranty economically attractive.	2	2
Analysis of warranty price versus organic repair costs is possible.	2	2
An escalation clause is included in the contract that is applicable to warranty or LSC costs.	3	3
The equipment will be in production over a substantial portion of the warranty period.	3	1
Equipment		
Equipment maturity is at an appropriate level.	1	1
Control of unauthorized maintenance can be exercised.	1	1
Unit is field-testable.	1	1
Unit can be properly marked or labeled to signify existence of warranty coverage.	1	1
Unit is amenable to R&M improvement and changes.	1	1
Unit is reasonably self-contained.	2	2
Unit can be readily transported to the contractor's facilities.	2	2
Unit has high level of ruggedization.	2	2
Unit maintenance is highly complex.	3	3
An elapsed-time indicator can be installed on the equipment	3	1

FIGURE 6   Warranty application criteria.

Criteria	Importance Rating*	
	RIW	RIW/MTBF
Operation		
Use environments known or predictable.	1	1
Equipment operational reliability and maintainability are predictable.	1	1
Equipment wartime or peacetime mission criticality is not of the highest level.	1	1
Equipment has a high operational utilization rate.	2	2
Warranty administration can be efficiently accomplished.	2	2
Duplication of an existing or planned government repair facility is not costly.	2	2
Unit reliability and usage levels are amenable to warranty maintenance.	2	2
Operating time is known or predictable.	2	2
Operational failure and usage information can be supplied to the contractor.	2	1
Backup warranty repair facilities are available.	3	3
Provision has been made for computing the equipment's MTSF.	N/A	1

*
 1 = Major, 2 = Secondary, 3 = Minor.

FIGURE 6   (Continued)

  Minor: Failure to meet one or more of these criteria is generally not considered serious but may require special considerations in structuring the warranty contract or administrative procedures.

VII. WARRANTY ECONOMIC ANALYSIS

A key part of the decision to use warranty is a comparative-cost analysis of the warranty versus user-supplied maintenance. Such analysis is generally performed on a life-cycle cost basis. Economic analysis can also be used in helping to structure contract terms and conditions for a cost-effective warranty, in selecting sources, and in negotiating final prices. The potential applications of warranty economic analysis are summarized in Fig. 7.

  Several life-cycle cost (LCC) models for warranty economic analysis have been developed (e.g., Balaban and Retterer, 1975, and Gates et al., 1977). Figure 8 lists the major cost categories of the RIW LCC model described in Balaban and Retterer (1975), which was patterned after the Air Force Logistic Support Cost (LSC) Model.

Life-Cycle Phase	Purpose of Economic Evaluation	Data Sources
Validation or Full-scale development	Investigate feasibility of RIW or other warranty form Develop terms and conditions for a preliminary warranty in R&D procurement package	Estimates from similar equipment and procurements, "standard" organic cost factors, R&M predictions
Preproduction and source selection	Develop final terms and conditions Evaluate economics of warranty vs procurement alternatives Select contractor on LCC basis	Contractor reports, contractor bid data, development/demonstration R&M test results, R&M predictions
Production/ operation	Determine if RIW should be extended Negotiate RIW extension prices Assess warranty from economic viewpoint	Field experience, contractor warranty reports, resident government representative reports

FIGURE 7   Summary of possible applications of warranty economic analysis.

Figure 9 presents the results of applying the warranty LCC model described in that reference to a typical procurement of an avionic equipment. A 10-year equipment life cycle is being considered and the analysis is made to compare discouted life-cycle cost for varying warranty periods with the cost of a total organic maintenance. Some additional details concerning this illustrative example are:

    Number of installed sets: 4750
    Spares to meet 95% sufficiency level
    Discount rate: 10%
    Set purchase price: organic maintenance—$4400
    Operate hours per month per installed set: 50

In Fig. 9 the horizontal or X-axis represents the warranty period being considered. The vertical axis represents the difference between life-cycle cost based on total organic maintenance and life-cycle cost based on a warranty of x years followed by organic maintenance for the remaining $(10 - x)$ years. For this example, all costs are discounted. Three different initial equipment MTBF values were considered: 235, 470, and 700 hours. For the 235-hour case, it is seen that a 3-year warranty provides the maximum saving (approximately $1.4 million) and the curve is relatively peaked. For the other two

Category	
Acquisition cost	The cost to purchase equipment to be installed in operating systems
Initial spares	The cost to purchase recoverable spare units/ modules for base and depot stock
Replenishment spares	The cost to purchase expendable or discard-at-failure modules to replace failed items
On-equipment maintenance	The labor, material, and transportation costs for intermediate and depot level maintenance
Support equipment	The cost to purchase intermediate and depot-level support equipment
Support of support equipment	The cost to operate and maintain the support equipment
Training	The cost to train government personnel in the maintenance and support of the equipment and the support equipment
Data	The cost to purchase documentation associated with operation, maintenance and support of the equipment and its support
Inventory management	The cost to provide inventory management functions for the equipment and its support
RIW price	The price paid to the contractor for providing the RIW
MTBF guarantee value	The value associated with the MTBF guarantee included with the RIW
Other costs	The costs associated with a particular procurement which are not covered by any of the other cost categories

FIGURE 8   Major cost categories for the RIW LCC model.

cases the sensitivity is not as great. For a 470-hour set, an RIW of from 3 to 8 years is appropriate from a LCC viewpoint, while the 700-hour-MTBF case yields the greatest saving over the 4-to-10-year period.

Other parameters, such as pipeline times, warranty pricing, and reliability-growth data inputs, might be varied to explore further the sensitivities related to warranty-period coverage. As an example of how RIW terms and conditions other than warranty period might be developed through the model, the pipeline-time input for spares stockage of the secure storage area or bonded storeroom is a direct function of the contractor turnaround time specified in the RIW. If warranty price can be related to the numerical turnaround-time value—by such means as detailed consideration of plant, test equipment, and personnel requirements, or by a more gross estimate—the trade-offs between turnaround time, spares, and warranty price as they affect total life-cycle

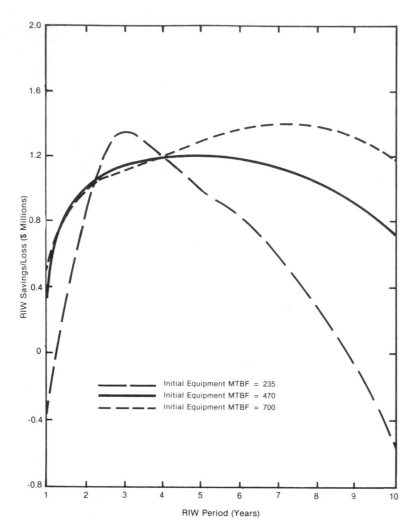

FIGURE 9   RIW life-cycle cost savings/loss for illustrative problem.

cost can be assessed. The capability of the LCC model to treat almost all relevant economic factors can be utilized to minimize the danger of suboptimization.

VIII. RISKS

While the military long-term warranty experience has been generally favorable,
available data and the number of programs have not been extensive enough
to permit firm conclusions on RIW effectiveness. Government and industry
have expressed concern over going too far too fast. There is a genuine fear
that RIW may have achieved fad status, that not enough thought is being
given to applicability and tailoring, and that the RIW concept itself may be in-
appropriate from the viewpoints of military self-sufficiency and industry risk.

Since the RIW concept is a major departure from current procurement and support practices, some degree of reluctance or rejection is to be expected. Industry concern has caused the Department of Defense and the military services to delay warranty implementation on some new acquisitions until applicability and risks can be further evaluated. The DoD has also issued guidelines for warranty implementation that place special emphasis on tailoring RIW terms so that rewards and risks to both industry and government are acceptable (Assistant Secretary of Defense, 1975). Some of the more frequently cited risks are:

1. Government risks
   a. *RIW price*: The government may pay too much for the warranty coverage.
   b. *Reduced self-sufficiency*: Long-term dependence on contractor support will reduce military self-sufficiency, especially if strikes or natural disasters occur at the contractor's facilities.
   c. *Administrative complexity*: The warranty concept introduces greater complexity into the military logistics system.
   d. *Transition*: The transition from RIW coverage to military maintenance introduces a number of administrative and logistics problems.
   e. *Equipment design*: The contractor may use the design that is most emenable to their warranty maintenance but is not the most appropriate for military repair following transition.
   f. *Contractor performance*: The contractor cannot or does not perform because of high repair costs, large losses, contract interpretation or loopholes, strikes, or natural disasters.
2. Contractor risks
   a. *Operational stresses*: Equipment may be subjected to unforeseen operational stresses.
   b. *Mishandling and tampering*: Military maintenance personnel may cause failures beyond contractor control.
   c. *Usage rate*: Increased equipment usage will increase failure exposure.
   d. *ECP processing*: Slow government processing of R&M ECPs will hamper the improvement process.
   e. *RIW price*: The contractor may bid too low a price because of competitive pressures, optimistic R&M estimates, or misinterpretation of provisions.

It is a formidable challenge to government and industry to ensure that the overall risk associated with a particular RIW application is acceptable to both parties. Fortunately, there are actions that can be taken to keep the risks within reasonable bounds, which can be categorized as follows:

Develop and use criteria for determining whether or not RIW is applicable.
Structure the procurement contract terms and conditions and implementation procedures to address high-risk factors.
Perform economic analyses in evaluating warranty potential and developing contractual and implementation procedures.

Figure 10 presents a number of approaches for risk reduction.

Risk Factor	Risk-Reduction Approach
Late notification of intent to use warranty	The intent to use warranty should be made known to the contractor as early as possible during engineering development so that he will have maximum opportunity to optimize his design.
Detailed government specification of item design	The use of functional specifications should be maximized to allow for design flexibility.
Application of RIW to advanced technology	Warranty may not be appropriate for completely revolutionary design. When applied to new technology, the program funding and schedule should allow for adequate reliability test effort. A cost-sharing RIW agreement could be considered.
Reliability-prediction uncertainty	The government should specify only a minimum acceptable level of reliability. Operational and environmental data should be provided to the contractor. Adequate time and funding for necessary reliability testing should be included in the contract.
Unpredictability of inflation rates for long-term agreements	The warranty price should be coupled with economic adjustment provisions to account for inflation.
Failure outside contractor control	Exclusions should be provided; they would normally include acts of God, fire, explosion, submersion, flood, combat damage, aircraft crash, and unauthorized tampering by government personnel. Exclusions for mishandling should be carefully worded.
Large number of unverified failures ("test goods") returned to contractor	Contractual provisions should be carefully tailored so that costs of processing good returns are equitably shared.
Item usage rate not precisely known	The contract should provide for a price adjustment for significant usage-rate variations or possibly have a cut-off on total operating time.
Data not supplied to contractor as required	Contract provisions should include government responsibilities for meeting data obligations in a timely manner. Contractor obligations for warranty performance may be related to receipt of applicable data
Uncertainty about shipping destinations of warranted items at time of bidding	If there is significant uncertainty about shipping costs, the government should assume these costs.

FIGURE 10   Contractor RIW risk factors and risk-reduction approaches.

Risk Factor	Risk-Reduction Approach
Effect on turnaround time of events that are out-side contractor's control (e.g., strike and uneven flow of failed units)	Relief from turnaround-time obligation should be included as part of the contract.
Time-consuming procedures for ECP approval	Warranty provisions should provide for expeditious approval of ECPs—perhaps by automatic approval unless notification is given within a certain time limit.

FIGURE 10   (Continued)

A. Risk Control

For effective implementation of the risk-reduction approaches, the RIW development process should entail the following government actions:

An early start on risk control
Consultation with military activities that have been involved with long-term warranties
Close coordination with logistics, using, and training commands
Continued contact with competing contractors
Early and continued coordination with procurement, legal, pricing, and contracting offices
Coordination with the cognizant government agency that will monitor the contractor's efforst

The contractor who is made aware of a potential RIW commitment for production equipment can also take action to control risks and maximize profit. The contractor must consider the field reliability of equipment as a major factor in pricing the warranty. An MTBF estimate that is too optimistic may cause severe monetary loss, while too pessimistic a value may result in loss of the contract to a lower-bidding competitor. Therefore, contractors must make efforts to design equipment with an MTBF that will keep them competitive, enable them to achieve a satisfactory profit, and be predictable. These requirements force contractors to view field reliability from a much different perspective than they did without RIW. Ideally, contractors will determine that allocating some "front-end" money to designing reliability into equipment will be their optimum strategy. To make such a decision they will probably have to spend some effort in the development or preproposal stages on reliability testing and analysis. They should also be concerned with the environment the equipment will encounter in the field, and obtaining such information may require some expenditure of resources.

Under an RIW, contractors are also concerned with the maintainability of their equipment, hoping to minimize the number of good units returned for warranty service (unverified failure, no trouble found) as well as the cost to perform a depot-type repair action. Again, it may be advisable to introduce more expensive design and manufacturing approaches that will improve their competitive and profit-making positions in the long run. From several RIW

procurements it is evident that contractors have made such expenditures with
the realization that acquisition price is no longer the only factor in cost-
related decisions.

IX. FUTURE RIW APPLICATIONS

In 5 years the number of programs containing long-term warranty commitments
has increased by a factor of 10. Experience has generally been favorable.
In most warranty programs that have yielded enough data for analysis, the
degree to which reliability/life-cycle cost goals have been attained is superior
to what has been observed in the past. Although there have been some difficulties in initial implementation, for the most part the military procurement,
operational, logistic, and maintenance systems seem capable of responding
positively to this procurement approach.
   It is still necessary to monitor current warranty programs carefully to
realize the maximum potential of this form of reliability and life-cycle cost control. RIW applicability and risk issues have not yet been fully resolved, and
for this reason the DoD had maintained a cautious posture.
   We cannot conclude at this time that planning to introduce the RIW concept
in a program will permit discontinuing current reliability and maintainability
program controls. Certainly, some adjustment may be in order—perhaps one
that will allow contractors more freedom in allocating funds for such control.
The need for adequate funding and time to obtain relevant R&M test data in
the development phase is critical for risk control on new-technology equipment
and can be the key to a successful RIW program. The future of RIW and RIW/
MTBF is promising if continued efforts are made to ensure that the concept is
properly applied and implemented. It is also necessary for the military services
to continue to support research in RIW and allied areas as technology, resources, and military demands change. The RIW concept that embodies the
suitable form of contractor incentive for R&M achievement will also be flexible
enough to encompass most foreseeable changes, provided that the appropriate
effort is made.

REFERENCES

1. Assistant Secretary of Defense (I&L), "Reliability Improvement War-
    ranty (RIW) Guidelines," memorandum dated September 16, 1975.
2. Aviation Supply Office, *Proceedings of the Failure-Free Warranty
    Seminar*, 1973.
3. Balaban, H., "Guaranteed MTBF for Military Procurement," *Proceed-
    ings of the 10th International Logistics Symposium (SOLE)*, 1975.
4. Balaban, H., D. Cuppett, and G. Harrison, "The F-16 RIW Program,"
    Proceedings of the 1979 Annual Reliability and Maintainability Symposium,
    1979.
5. Balaban, H., and M. Meth, "Contractor Risk Associated with Reliability
    Improvement Warranty," *Proceedings of the 1978 Annual Reliability and
    Maintainability Symposium*, 1978.
6. Balaban, H., and F. Nohmer, "Warranty Procurement: A Case History,"
    Proceedings of the 1975 Annual Reliability and Maintainability Symposium,
    1975.

7. Balaban, H., and B. Retterer, *The Use of Warranties for Defense Avionics Procurement*, ARINC Research Corporation Publication 1243, RADC Report TR-73-149, 1973.

8. Balaban, H., and B. Retterer, *Guidelines for Application of Warranties to Air Force Electronic Systems*, ARINC Research Corporation Publication 1451, 1975.

9. Bilodeau, A., F. Crum, W. Dumphy, and R. Kowalski, *The Application of Reliability Improvement Warranty to Dynamic Systems*, ARINC Research Corporation Publication 2025, 1979.

10. CODSIA, Comments on Warranties and RIW to the Honorable M. R. Currie, DDR&E, July 18, 1975; to Dr. Paul Arvis, U.S. Army Procurement Research Office, Fort Lee, Va., July 2, 1975; to Mr. M. D. Bruns, Chairman, Tri-Service Reliability and Support Incentives Group, OASD (I&L), December 30, 1975.

11. Cotton, S., F. Crum, et al., *Warranty-Guarantee Application Guidelines for Air Force Ground Electronic Equipment*, ARINC Research Corporation Publication 1996, 1979.

12. Gándara, A., and M. Rich, *Reliability Improvement Warranties for Military Procurement*, Rand Report R-7505, 1975.

13. Gates, R., B. Gourary, et al., *Electronics-X: A Study of Military Electronics with Particular Reference to Cost and Reliability*, 2 vols., Institute for Defense Analyses Report R-95, 1974.

14. Gates, R., R. Bicknell, and J. Bortz, "Quantitative Models Used in the RIW Decision Process," *Proceedings of the 1977 Reliability and Maintainability Symposium*, The Analytic Sciences Corporation, 1977.

15. Hirschberger, G., and A. Dantowitz, *Evaluation of Environmental Profiles for Reliability Demonstration*, Grumman Aerospace Corporation RADC Report TR-76-32, 1976.

16. Markowitz, O., "Aviation Supply Office FFW/RIW Case History 2, Abex Pump," *Proceedings of the 1976 Annual Reliability and Maintainability Symposium*, 1976.

17. Mlinarchik, R., "RIW Experiences at ECON," *Proceedings of the 1977 Annual Reliability and Maintainability Symposium*, 1977.

18. Weimer, C. D., and P. E. Palatt, *The Impact of Reliability Guarantees and Warranties on Electronics Subsystem Design and Development Programs*, Institute for Defense Analysis, IDA Study S-482, 1976.

17

EVOLUTION OF SOFTWARE QUALITY ASSURANCE

CARL C. BLAU, WILLIAM A. CHAPMAN,
and DONALD F. FAW

NCR Corporation
Dayton, Ohio

I. INTRODUCTION

The explosion of technology in the 1970s has caused the growth of several associated disciplines. What is presented here is a model describing the evolution of a relatively new discipline called software quality assurance (SQA). This evolution can be viewed as six states of SQA growth, which are dependent on management learning as well as technical factors. It is hoped that if the model has logically characterized the phases, some of the pain of the evolution can be avoided.

The first four phases of the model describe an evolution that characterizes most of the microcomputer industry today, while stages 5 and 6 are projections that suggest the philosophy for achieving maturity of the SQA function.

To test the validity of all six stages a survey was conducted in conjunction with the Computer Science Department of the University of Dayton with the guidance of Brother Neuendorf and several consultations with David Blazon and Mary Meadows of the NCR Corporation. The survey encompassed 51 large, medium-size, and small microcomputer manufacturers throughout the United States. The results of this summary are included herein.

Software quality assurance (SQA) is an interesting discipline to think about because it has so little form. It is a concept that is poorly defined and not at all well understood. It has been variously described as an audit, functional testing (inspection), checking for conformance to standards, statistical analysis, and mathematical modeling for reliability prediction. Clearly, this infant discipline has no generally agreed on definition and most practitioners have their own view of the subject.

The true nature of any abstract discipline in the business world is heavily determined by the way the people who control the function perceive it. Even if the quality assurance (QA) staff has a clear understanding of what SQA is or should be, the dominant question is: What does the president or general manager think it is? The evolution of SQA as described here is at least as dependent on the learning and perception of the senior managers in the company as it is the technical nature of the job. The thesis of this chapter is that SQA is an evolutionary function the exact nature of which at any given point in time is a function of the experiences and learning not only of the actual QA people but also of senior management, corporate staff groups, customers, and probably several others.

This evolution necessity is not confined to new or small organizations. As a matter of fact, it appears to have greater application in the large, established company, which often has defined ideas about product development and QA stemming from past experiences in what has become obsolete technology—the type of company that is experiencing a significant growth in software development because technological evolution is mandating a change in their product time.

II. STAGE 1: AUTONOMOUS DEVELOPMENT

Stage 1 of the evolution of the QA function is characterized by a total lack of QA (Fig. 1). It is worthwhile describing, though, because conditions at this time allow QA to come into being. Up until this time the company has been engaged in software development, either for internal use or in the product line, in a small way. The business has had relatively small dependence on software and the magnitude and complexity of the task has been small enough that the problems associated with it have not come to management attention. Management, as a matter of fact, views software development as a kind of mysterious process, largely trial and error, which adds intelligence to the product under development. As the amount of software development grows, either through the demands of internal users or the demands of the product technology, the first indication management gets of this increasing importance is that the complaints of users, either paying customer or internal, are becoming audible. The amount of money being spent for software development is becoming noticeable to management as well. The company is, at this point, involved in what Nolan (1979) called the initiation stage and just moving into Nolan's proliferation stage. As the company moves into the proliferation stage the volume of user complaints and the frequency with which the software development function comes to management's attention in conjunction with budget overruns and schedule slips directs management attention toward the software development function rather forcibly. As more time passes and the dependency of the business increases still more on the software development function, management becomes very alarmed that the problems appear to be getting worse instead of better. If this is an established company, it probably has a QA or QC function in place which is oriented toward manufacturing, and the leader of the existing QA function will be telling management that they should be getting active in this increasingly important aspect of the business. Management having a QA orientation from past experience will agree.

In terms of the survey, Fig. 1 (SQA evolution model) was distributed to 51 microcomputer manufacturers together with a questionnaire. Of the 20 responses received, three manufacturers indicated that their organizations could be characterized as stage 1. Two of the organizations had fewer than 10 developers, while one manufacturer indicated a development organization size of between 90 and 95 developers. It is interesting to note that three of the 20 respondents indicated that they were no longer in business, especially since the companies surveyed were selected on the basis of products they were delivering to the marketplace as recently as 18 months before.

IDENTIFYING THE STAGE

How can management determine what stage of development their SQA is in? The following portrayal can aid in making this assessment. Any one of the processes taken alone could be misleading but taken together these criteria provide a reliable image.

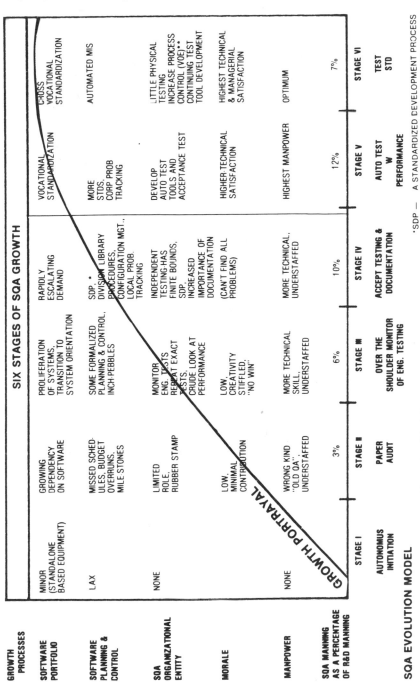

SQA EVOLUTION MODEL

Fig. 1 Software Quality Assurance Evolution Model.

III. STAGE 2: PAPER AUDIT

The SQA function comes into existence through the combined efforts of frustration on the part of general management and the desire of the existing QA manager to step up to what he or she perceives to be his or her responsibility. Unfortunately, management, neither general, QA, nor coprorate staff, have any idea what is involved in SQA—or, in fact, software development—on a serious scale. The understandable tendency is to go with what you have. Consequently, some deserving QA engineer is elevated to the position of project leader of SQA. Management still does not recognize the ultimate importance of the software development function or the SQA function, and it is permitted to evolve kind of with the tides rather than being planned from the top-down definition of needs. The development function is severely understaffed relative to the rapidly escalating demand for software development, and an understanding of the lead time necessary to acquire the appropriate people and make them productive has not been gained. These same conditions exist in the newly created SQA function. This condition is further to be expected at this stage since management primarily allowed the function to be created as a result of getting tired of last-minute surprises from the development group. At this stage management sees the SQA function primarily as an early-warning system to predict impending failure. Since this function is perceived to have a farily limited role to play, and since it will be understaffed, it will of necessity limit itself to a more-or-less paper review. The SQA function will concern itself with demanding published schedules, specification, and user documents.

The function will be staffed primarily with lower-level people: entry level or minimal experience. The function will do no or very limited functional testing, and if they do any at all they will be totally dependent on the development function for access to hardware, test beds, and training. Probably they will do no more than repeat the exact test routines the developer used except that it will be on a very limited sample basis. Management attitude will probably hold that it would be a wasteful duplication of expense to provide QA with the independent ability to prepare and execute tests. This phase also demonstrates a lack of system performance measures, a lack of training for professionals other than on-the-job training, and a primitive inaccurate error accounting system. Neither QA nor development will be aware of the value of and necessity for software configuariton management.

Development will view QA as a hindrance rather than a help. They will question the worth and contribution of the QA function, and given the capabilities of QA during this phase the challenge will have considerable basis in fact. Morale among the QA people will be poor because they will themselves realize that they are marginal contributors.

Throughout this period of time the development group is progressing deeper into Nolan's proliferation phase and the problems that originally motivated the creation of a QA group will have gotten worse instead of better. User complaints of improperly functioning software will have risen sharply, not because the software got worse (it stayed about the same), but because the amount in use has increased. The corresponding rate of software corrections and the subsequent compatibility problems resulting from a lack of configuration management will have begun to acquaint people with the importance of this function.

The SQA project leader will be telling management that he or she could detect and cause correction of many of the functional problems being experienced by the users if testing were actually being done. Of the 20 respondents, only one firm indicated that their organization was in stage 2, and this company had a development organization of fewer than 10 people. It should be recognized that the respondents were given only the model in Fig. 1 and the question-naire, not our characterization of the stages as presented herein. In response to the growing number of user complaints and out of a sense of frustration at being unable to "get a handle" on the software development function, manage-ment will agree to testing. SQA moves into its third stage, test monitoring.

IV. STAGE 3: TEST MONITORING

As the QA function moves into this phase it will see an increase in personnel but a shortage will still exist, possibly worse than in the previous stage. When management agreed to the change they did not give staffing much thought, but they expected that it would be done with no increase in personnel. Two other factors will conspire to cause the staffing to be inadequate. As the project leader is working up the inevitable defense of an increase in personnel, he or she will concentrate primarily on the number of calendar days and the number of people necessary to execute the tests. The leader's planning, through inexperience, will ignore or underestimate the amount of labor re-quired to *prepare* to execute the test. Since preparation effort for software testing is considerably higher than execution effort, the function will still be understaffed even though it gets larger. A second aspect of the problem will emerge for the first time, in that physical testing will probably require a gen-erally higher level of experience in the department than had previously been necessary, and some degree of specialized experience will also be needed. Neither of these things will exist initially, the need for them will not be recog-nized for some period of time, and after the need is recognized it will take some time to acquire the appropriate people and get them oriented.

Testing will be relatively primitive: manual stimulus with manual checking of response. Testing will be limited to subsystem or system-level testing. The need for some degree of formal training will be recognized and provided to the people in the department. Error accounting will still be a relatively primitive simple count of problems experienced, but the count will be more accurate and complete: partially because QA is now actually discovering a portion of the problems and reporting all of those and partially because development manage-ment will have learned the necessity of accurate error accounting for manage-ment and follow-up.

Toward the end of this phase, recognition may be given to the importance of performance measurement and a basic attempt will be made to do this by use of a stopwatch. Throughout the phase both development and QA have been gaining an understanding of the importance of configuration management, and this function will evolve to a fairly comprehensive level. Recognition of the need to allocate time in the schedule for testing will have been gained and ap-proximately 6% of the time will be allocated to QA and 15% to development. SQA will still be under fire from the development group relative to their over-all positive or negative impact on the project. However, development will now be confronted by the fact that QA is detecting problems after development in-dicated that the product was acceptable. Some of these problems will be trite in nature, even nit-picking, but some of them will be significant.

Morale in the SQA function will still be poor, even though visible contribu-tions are being made. This poor morale will have two contributing factors. The first is a direct result of the transition to the physical testing mode. Management now has an expectation that since the QA function is consuming a significant resource and has the responsibility to test the problems out of the product, they should do just that—not an unreasonable expectation at all. Unfortunately, with most software developments it is not humanly possible to achieve. The morale problem comes from the fact that the people realize that they have been given a task they cannot complete and they realize that management is unaware of it.

The second contributing factor to the low morale is the nature of the work itself. The function is staffed with professional programmer/analysts, most of whom have degrees. They are expected to sit down and develop an exhaustive (which they know is impossible) set of test cases at a level of painstaking detail (which does not excite many people) and then to apply these test cases to a system manually and manually verify the response. It takes very little time for them to realize that they are not designing software, they are not coding software, they are not learning a great deal at the technical level of their chosen profession, they are not enhancing their worth on the job market, and they are bored half out of their minds.

Management observes that QA is detecting problems, but significant problems are still finding their way into the users' hands. The problems the users are now finding are of a more subtle, harder-to-correct variety. In one sense removing the more straightforward problems in-house was a step backward; at least before, the users could be shown that development was able to remove problems with some dispatch. Now every one is in a state of frustration. It could be said that the culmination of this stage is the addition of a frustrated QA function to the frustrated users and frustrated management.

This phase of the evolution is unique in that some organizations get stuck here and never get beyond this point. Moving on to the next stage is an initially intimidating step and some organizations are just never able to take it. The tendency is to respond to increasing user and management frustration by trying to do better and better and more and more manual functional testing. The fact that manual testing has a very finite upper bound on productivity seems to take a long time to make itself visible. At some point during this phase an awareness grows that project and software documentation is of unanticipated importance. When this awareness reaches a certain level, it causes the phasing in of the next stage. Three of the 20 respondents indicated that they were in stage 3; one of the manufacturers had fewer than 10 developers, one had between 26 and 100, and the third had between 101 and 200.

V. STAGE 4: ACCEPTANCE TESTING AND DOCUMENTATION REVIEW

Management is coming to believe that many of their most frustrating problems are either caused or aggravated by lack of documentation or misunderstanding of requirements. They develop a set of requirements that demand the project planning be done in minute detail, including the definition of "inch-pebbles" instead of milestones prior to schedule commitments. User expectations must be rigorously defined and documented before the fact of actual development. At various and frequent points in the development cycle additional documents must be provided, such as subunit specs, test plans, interim progress reports, and test reports. Further, to ensure good communication among affected groups, several different groups must review and approve each of these documents. This phase of the evolution is described by most people as an avalanche of paper. Even though the philosophy is in the right direction, the probability

is that the pendulum is going to go too far. It creates immediate problems
with the developers. They perceive the introduction of this much documentation to be increasing their work load by 30% or more with no corresponding
adjustment of cost or schedule. Additionally, the development people turn a
little surly about restriction of their "creative freedom."

Naturally this step in the evolution of the developers' area has its effect in
the SQA area as well. A unique thing about SQA responsibilities during this
entire time is that they seem to be increasing monotonically. Each new crisis
and each new operational change in the development group seems to bring
about an increase in the responsibilities of the QA group, with none of the old
responsibilities ever being repealed. This stage in the development evolution
is no exception, in that QA has now gained the responsibility to review all
these newly defined documents the development group is responsible to create
and are required to create some additional documents themselves. Further,
there has been a growing trend for some time, which now peaks, to make QA
responsible for the correctness and completeness of the documents.

This phase results in an all-time low in the morale of the QA people. They
are now responsible for the quality of all development-performed tests, the
planning and execution of tests themselves, and now as an added tribute they
get to do the developers' proofreading. They have been assigned a massive
task which they cannot possibly contend with, and the nature of the task
is repetitive, boring, and does not even slightly resemble what they wanted
to do after finishing college.

There is an irony in the position that QA has come to occupy after all this
time. It probably has had the net effect of damaging the objectives of the
organization in a very subtle and probably unrecognized way. It may have
resulted in an actual reduction in the quality of the work coming out of development. The SQA physical testing effort is typically scheduled at the end of the
development cycle. The documentation validation is usually done in conjunction
with the testing. In effect, the QA activities have become an end-of-the-line
attempt at error detection. The fact that QA is there with that role has the
effect of generating a feeling of laxness on the part of developers relative to
their own efforts to eliminate problems prior to turning the software over to
QA. Over time this attitude grows to the point that developers recommend in
all seriousness that the product be turned over to QA untested.

It does not take a lot of insight to realize that problems must be found
earlier in the cycle. Even in those cases where earlier detection still does not
allow for correction on the original schedule, it at least affords management
some degree of maneuvering room. In any event, this approach results in
only a marginal improvement in quality.

When the QA group has evolved to the point described up to now, it has
reached its lowest ebb. Development is frustrated because QA perversely continues to find problems at the eleventh hour, to their considerable embarrassment. Management is frustrated to the point of flinching every time the QA
manager appears on the horizon. QA is frustrated because they perceive themselves to be responsible for all things all the time. Individual QA people are
miserable from continually being the bearers of bad tidings and being held in
contempt by their peers in development.

It appears that three alternatives are available at this point. Management
can abolish QA on the gorunds that even though they find problems, they miss
a lot of them too. The ones they do find, they find too late. The nature of
the job as it has evolved is such that it is very difficult to attract people to
the function and equally difficult to retain them. The second alternative seems

to be to continue with the same philosophy but to try to optimize it in some way. From remarks made earlier that does not seem too fruitful. The third alternative is to move on to phase 4 of the evolution, and this is the one that will be expanded on.

Prior to describing phase 4 of the evolution, it will be useful to establish several universal "truths":

1. Development people do not make good testers. They do not perceive themselves to be in the business of testing and they consider it an annoyance when they have to do it. It is often stated that developers are the most knowledgeable people about what they have developed and are therefore best qualified to do the testing. It is true that they are the technically most knowledgeable, but that is not the most important characteristic of a tester. As a matter of fact, that intimate technical knowledge can be an obstacle to good testing. Throughout the lengthy development process, the developer is constantly being conditioned to think positively. Good testers do not think positively; they think negatively.

2. There is also a kind of "familiarity breeds contempt" effect when testing is done by developers. Developers recognize a problem for what it is but are so intimately knowledgeable about the cause and the correction that they know it is only a 15-minute task to fix it. They therefore conclude that they can wait until next week to fix it, when they have nothing more interesting to work on. Before they realize it, there are so many minor problems that they have no chance to fix them all without slipping the schedule. This applies to the ones they remember, not the ones they have forgotton.

3. Software testing is not a one-shot proposition. Few programs ever written proved to be entirely acceptable in their original form. Exposure to a variety of users will always uncover problems that necessitate design changes and retesting. Even if error-free code could be generated, it would be necessary to do thorough testing to demonstrate that the code was, in fact, error free. Even then users, through experience, would require enhancements and alterations to their original specifications. The inevitable changes that occur to most software sooner or later cause areas of the program that were known to work at revision level 3 to no longer be working at revision level 7, despite everyone's assurances that none of the changes could possibly have affected the area in question.

4. Development people, when they do develop some automatic test capability, typically do not do a very good job. It certainly is not that they cannot. This is another function they do not perceive themselves as being responsible for. They typically will provide the minimum capability required in a form that requires great human interaction of highly trained persons because that approach will be the most expeditious. The usual result is that every tester will be a one-shot deal that has applicability to no other test task except the one on which they are currently working.

5. The effect this has on the organization as a whole is that it owns a series of entirely disjointed test capabilities which will be indecipherable to anyone except the primary users, and they will have lost their productivity at using the tester 3 months after they stop using it. In a short time the capability will be totally lost because it will be undocumented, and will require modification to be used for any other task then the one for which it was originally designed. The subsequent decision by the new developer in need of some test capability will be that it will be faster to design his or her own tester than to learn the old, undocumented tester and modify it to suit the current need. The impact of this mode of operation is even more severe on the

organization as a whole if a piece of software is turned over to a maintenance
programmer at some point in its life cycle. The maintenance programmer will
be totally ignorant of the tester, probably will be unaware of its existence,
and will also be unaware of some of the subtleties of the software from which
an automated tester could have protected him or her. Test software is a tangible asset and it needs to be managed by a group of people who recognize
that they have that responsibility.

6. The task of software testing must be structured so that the people
responsible for it are permitted to do it in a way that will provide them with
job satisfaction, technical growth and learning in their chosen profession,
and the respect of their peers.

7. In any environment where automated testing is the mode of operation,
it is elementary that those who control the test bed control the quality of the
test.

These "truths" provide the foundation for moving into a description of
phase 5 of the evolution, and the justification for the transition to phase 6.

The majority (10 of 20) of the respondents indicated that their facilities
had evolved to stage 4, in that acceptance testing was being performed by an
independent SQA organization which did not report to the development organization. The extent to which the respondents agreed with each of the individual growth processes of software portfolio, software planning and control,
SQA organizational entity, morale, personnel, and SQA staffing as a percentage of R&D manning identified in Fig. 1 is not specifically known, only that
the stage selected best described their company SQA activity. The extent to
which the microcomputer industry may or may not agree with any specific
characterization of a stage would have to be the subject of further survey and
study. The respondents were made up of mostly SQA middle-management
practitioners. Since the survey was directed to the director of quality assurance, the attitudes of senior management are not reflected in the survey results.

VI. STAGE 5: AUTOMATED TEST DEVELOPMENT
WITH PERFORMANCE MEASUREMENT

If the QA function has passed through the previous phases of the evolution,
the transition to this phase looks somewhat intimidating to them. At this point
they are still responsible for a very wide array of activities, and the addition
of the substantial task of developing automated testers with their available
resource looks impossible to absorb. As a matter of fact, it is impossible to
absorb. However, the SQA function that has passed through the previous
phases of evolution has almost certainly acquired some responsibilities as a
result of crises that should never have been assigned to them in the first place.
One example might be proofreading software documentation. This is a high-
labor-content job that should not be accepted by a function with 15% of the
total resources, and it should be reassigned where it belongs. The time has
now come where SQA must reevaluate all the tasks they have picked up over
the months or years, and divest themselves of those that they should not have
and never should have had. Some of the currently defined tasks must be replaced with the tester development function. If the organization is ever going
to pull itself out, it is essential that the development function be relieved of
the attitude that developed as a result of that end-of-the-line QA test. The
developers must be made to understand that they are responsible for the correct operation of the software they develop and for the accuracy of the documentation that describes it. Rather than depending on SQA to find problems

at the end of the cycle, the development group must develop an attitude of total indifference to the nature and content of any testing that SQA elects to do. This attitude of indifference must stem from the knowledge that they themselves have done a good, thorough job of testing prior to turning the software over to SQA.

From this point on, as the true testing responsibility is shifted to development, SQA begins to shift to a mode of developing software that can be described as stimulators, validators, exercisers, and so on. In the interest of future productivity the testers must be generalized as much as possible to extend their useful life and make them applicable to as many different test situations as possible. Software of this nature should be treated almost like product software, in the sense that it must be documented, controlled, and retained. It is a significant organizational asset.

This approach relieves the staff of a great deal of the hard work associated with the manual approach. It allows test repeatability with a minimum of time for subsequent testing. It affords technical growth for the people in the QA function. It results, over time, in a substantial improvement of morale through the changes in the nature of the work, and it makes the QA function much more attractive to job candidates. After a significant amount of test capability has been developed, the stage will be set for the move into the next phase of the evolution. As the level of automation has been phasing up, the amount of physical testing performed by QA has been diminishing, but both QA and development have been engaged in it. In some cases, due to the distrust generated in previous stages, QA has been repeating some of the development tests. The climate and capabilities exist to move into the next phase, which eliminates the redundancy, called test standardization.

When respondents were asked if they agree with stage 5 characterization, the majority of those that did respond to this question indicated concurrence, even though this required the highest resource investment. Four of the 20 respondents indicated that they did not agree with stage 5; however, none of these indicated an alternative as requested in the questionnaire, with the exception of one small manufacturer, who indicated that stage 4 would be the highest level achieved. Additionally, three of these four manufacturers did not have an independent SQA organization and had development organizations of fewer than 10 developers. The fourth organization was a very large corporation on the threshold of obtaining an independent design-proving function.

VII. STAGE 6: TEST STANDARDIZATION

The sixth stage of the evolution is characterized by QA being as thoroughly out of the business of physical testing as they will ever be. It will always be necessary for QA to be in a position to do physical testing if they so elect as an enforcement tool, but the bulk of the testing should be done by development. The development of automated test beds in turn makes possible and encourages the development of standard tests. The test application parameters described earlier can be devised to stimulate and stress the operating system in a known way. These parameters can then be placed in the library as a standard test that achieves certain known things agreed to by development and QA. Inherent in the design of the test systems or test strings is verifiable hard-copy output to attest to the fact that the test was completed successfully, whether it was executed by development or by QA.

The QA staff in this phase is fairly well sized to the job at hand. The qualifications of the people are significantly different from those in the second

or third stage. The function is now populated primarily with experienced
people. These people could have been developed from the low-level people
hired in earlier stages, transferred in from development, or hired at that level
of experience. The total number of people required is significantly lower than
would be required for a manual test approach of anywhere near comparable
thoroughness.

Having progressed through the previous stages of the evolution, the organization is able to detect and correct errors in the software with a high level
of efficiency. The organization is now ready to turn its attention to techniques
intended to prevent the errors from getting into the software in the first place.
Why didn't the organization move immediately to this approach rather than suffer the pain of the previous ones? First, it will always be necessary to do
physical testing, no matter how efficient an organization is at design and coding. No organization will ever be perfect or even close to it. Errors will be
made and they will have to be detected and corrected. Second, to some extent,
organizations will have to go through the learning process, or at least a portion
of it, as described here to understand what is desirable. It is the thesis of
this chapter, however, that avoidance of some of these problems is possible.

It should also be recognized that there are no clean partitions between the
phases as described here. Some things described are mutually exclusive because one thing builds from another. But some elements of all phases will be
seen in every phase. The phasing comes about as a function of the priorities
assigned to the various techniques by management.

The sixth phase concerns itself with the more abstract concepts of design
standards, coding standards, structure, and program parameters of that nature. The role of QA again undergoes a metamorphosis to an organization that
develops software whose objective is to analyze source files automatically for
compliance to these standards. QA does not ignore the approaches described
in the previous phases, but the body of automated test capabilities has grown
large enough and the number of standardized routines in existence comprehensive enough that the additions and modifications to the test capability required
by new development are no longer a full-time job. Morale remains high because
of the nature of the work. The overall productivity of the development function as a whole has the opportunity to improve significantly during this phase
because for the first time software is being written in a systematic way to
analyze code automatically for design quality. This allows specific training for
individual designers to point out and rectify weaknesses in the design they
are producing. A very comprehensive field performance reporting capability
has been evolving throughout the process, and it is possible to identify the
best programs as they perform in the field. These programs can then be analyzed in a systematic manner to determine what characteristics they have that
make them good. This provides for the obvious opportunity to learn as an
organization what the difference is between good and bad software.

The major management appeal of stage 6 is of course the lower SQA resource
investment; however, this does not imply that the overall corporate investment
will be less. To understand the rationale behind this, one must recognize that
no matter how nice the SQA auditor is, when rejecting defective software, the
manager is not endearing himself or herself to the development organization.
In many cases the penalty to the development organization is missed schedules,
budget overruns, poor performance appraisals, and poor morale. There is an
inherent tendency to view SQA as an overhead, no-value-added function.
Organizational pressures mount which tend to curtail SQA staff growth. The
development organizations argue if they had more personnel they could do it

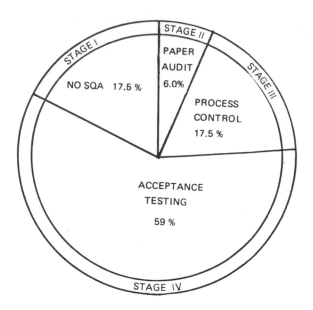

FIGURE 2   Microcomputer industry: current stage of SQA.

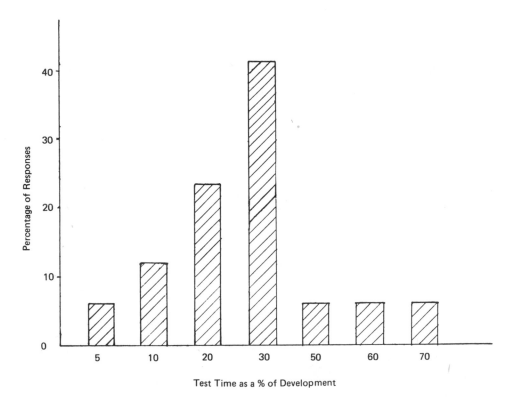

FIGURE 3   Test time as a percent of development.

right the first time. What is desired is "more developers and fewer inspectors." It is the authors' belief that in the long run, SQA organizations will not be able to sustain personnel levels beyond the 10 to 15% level.

Of the 13 manufacturers that did indicate separate SQA staffing levels, only one indicated a level greater than 15%, and this company had fewer than 10 developers. Three of the 13 (all large) corporations indicated a staffing level of 1%, while, paradoxically, maintaining that their SQA function performed independent acceptance testing. This seems strange given the labor-intensive investment inherent in an independent acceptance test approach.

If everything remained static from this point on, it would be possible to move to a stage 7, where QA would cease to exist. The organization has learned the required amount of documentation, it has learned how to detect software errors in-house efficiently, and it has learned how to specify design and coding standards which materially raise the probability that good software will be produced at first delivery. It has evolved a comprehensive software configuration management methodology and retrieves reasonably good data from the field on product performance. It appears that the organization has essentially arrived. Unfortunately, nothing ever remains static. Personnel changes will occur both within QA and within development. The success of some areas of operation will have resulted to some extent from the individual persons who have departed. New developments will come along that require modifications or enhancement of existing practices. The personnel turnover will necessitate a certain amount of retraining. One "universal truth" that will always remain is that development people are not in the business of testing and do not perceive themselves to be in that business. It is important to any development organization to have people around who do perceive themselves to be so directed, who demand to be shown rather than being told. For these reasons it seems unlikely that stage 7 can ever be implemented.

In summary, the majority of the respondents concurred with the model as presented; however, there appear to be inconsistencies between the SQA staffing levels reported and the stage of evolution at which the company claimed to be operating. A summary relative to the stage of evolution the respondents indicated they were in is shown in Fig. 2. With regard to software testing as a percentage of total development time, the majority of respondents indicated a test time of 30% or more of the total development time (Fig. 3).

REFERENCE

1. Nolan, R., "Managing the Crises in Data Processing," *Harvard Business Review*, March—April 1979, pp. 115—126.

18

SOFTWARE

H. K. BURBRIDGE

BFH Parametrics
Mountain View, California

I. INTRODUCTION

To attempt to treat the vast software subject in a single chapter is somewhat like attempting to bail the Atlantic Ocean with a teaspoon. The best that can be done is to furnish the reader with general information, some level of supporting detail for the general information, and a general overview of the process of coming to grips with software where it has its being. With this objective in mind, it has been assumed that readers will not be familiar with the intricacies of software. It follows that the overview will provide little of value to the software professional, but to the reader new to the field, the information presented ought to shed some light on a discipline as new as tomorrow. If nothing more than this is achieved, progress will have been made, for in no field of human endeavor has so much misinformation arisen. It has been said that software is incomprehensible to the average citizen, and phrases such as the "software mystique" are common. These concepts are not true—software is the outcome of logical processes, and there is no black magic being wrought by software practitioners.

The definition of software accepted by the U.S. General Accounting Office, which will be used as a point of departure for this chapter, divides software into three categories:

> Application software
> Operating systems software
> Utility software

Application software may be defined as a set of instructions, called program statements, or code, to do a specific job, such as payroll computation, inventory control, accounting, and many others. *Operating software* may be defined as a group of computer programs for monitoring and controlling the operation of a computer system while the application programs are running. *Utility software* is a term used to connote computer programs that perform various service functions, such as moving program and data files and accessing peripheral equipment. Simply stated, if one must have dealings with that

ubiquitous slave the digital computer, one must care for it and feed it so that
it will work effectively. Software is the food and drink of the digital computer.
The secret lies in maintaining the computer in a slave condition without becoming a slave to it. Since any consideration of software must include consideration of the digital computer, it is necessary to furnish some introduction
to that machine, at least in general terms.

First, and it bears repeating, the computer is a mindless beast. It knows
nothing more than human intelligence sees fit to tell it. Continuing the al-
legory, it is also a surly beast at times, and can be an implacable foe if one
does not take precautions with it. For example, assume that one must pay a
utility bill, one prepared by computer. A glance at the total shows that not
only is the total in error, but also on examination one knows that one has
paid the proper sum already. If one exercises the option of calling in about
it, or writing in even, one must prepare for frustration. Regardless of what
the human voice on the other end of the line may promise, the same old billing
will appear in your mail again, this time with a past due notice. The point?
Nothing will change; the computer will proceed as instructed until some human
agency elects to change instructions to the machine, ones which formally reflect that the account is paid. Unless this happens, the person complaining
is trapped in a mindless dialogue with a machine, to which no appeal is possible and which has no powers of adjudication. Dialogue with a computer involves discipline, for the machine is implacable. Depart one iota from the
dialogue it understands, and it will replay with a statement informing the
party instructing/querying it that the input is in improper form. It is un-
forgiving of human error of any sort, to the point where one almost becomes
convinced that one is dealing with a surly and churlish taskmaster. A more
serious aspect of transactions with a computer lies in the fact that the machine
cannot recognize the merit of any data fed to it. As long as these data are
in proper format, the machine will ingest them, process them, and provide an
output as instructed. This feature of computers gives rise to the watchword
of the software industry: "garbage in, garbage out."

With these prefatory remarks as introduction, a perfunctory examination of
the computer as a tool is in order; a "how it works/why it works" routine.
Automatic digital computer systems, regardless of size or complexity, merely
perform a series of arithmetic operations (additions, subtractions, multiplica-
tions, and divisions) using discrete quantities. Any problem that can be reduced to a sequence of arithmetic operations can be solved by a digital computer. The major advantages of an automatic digital computer are the speed
with which these arithmetic operations can be performed and the fact that an
automatic computer can be programmed to perform a long sequence of computations without the intervention of an operator. Digital computer systems are
used to solve complex scientific problems, to control complicated physical operations, to prepare payrolls, to maintain inventory records, and for countless
other applications in science, industry, and business. Problems that would
require several years of computation by a skilled human computer can be
solved in minutes by these modern electronic giants. However, the problem
must first be reduced to a form acceptable to the machine, and proper instructions must be prepared to guide the computer operations.

For purposes of analysis, a digital computer system can be divided into
four sections: (1) the arithmetic unit, in which arithmetic operations are
performed; (2) one or more storage units, in which information is stored; (3)
a control unit, which synchronizes the arithmetic operations and the transfer
of information; and (4) input-output equipment for feeding information into

and out of the computer. The relative size and complexity of each of these sections depend on the primary purpose for which the computer system is designed (Fig. 1).

In scientific computers designed to solve problems that require complex computations involving a relatively small amount of data, the arithmetic unit might be large and the storage unit small. In business applications, where the computations are not so complex but where large amounts of data must be stored, the situation is reversed. A general-purpose computer is a compromise in which the various sections are balanced to obtain maximum operating speeds for a wide variety of problems at minimum cost. Automatic features are justified if they can sufficiently increase the computer capacity or save enough labor hours in the preparation of problems to warrant the additional cost. A large, high-speed computer usually is not economical for an installation in which the work load cannot keep it busy. The tendency today is to channel information to highly efficient computers located at central data processing centers. This process is known as time sharing. Smaller computers, which are economical for less demanding applications, are being offered by several manufacturers.

To understand any automatic digital computer system, it is first necessary to understand the mathematical system employed by the computer. Because

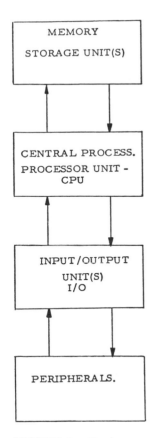

FIGURE 1   Basic computer system.

almost all electronic digital computers use some variation of binary notation, a review of the binary numbering system is in order.

II. NUMERIC CODING SYSTEMS

The decimal system of numerical notation, with which we are most familiar, uses 10 digits, 0, 1, 2, 3, 4, 5, 6, 7, 8, and 9. The actual value represented by each of these digits depends on its position or place in an expression. The first digit to the left of the decimal point indicates the number of units (10^0), the next digit indicates the number of tens (10^1), the next digit indicates the number of hundreds (10^2), the next digit indicates the number of thousands (10^3), and so on. Note that the digit in each position is the coefficient of some power of the base number 10, and the value of the expression is the sum of the values represented by the digits in all the positions.

By changing the base number, or radix, to 2, and applying the same basic rules, we have the binary system of positional notation. The binary system has only two digits, 0 and 1, which are used as coefficients of various powers of the base 2. The first digit to the left of the binary point indicates the number of units (2^0), the next digit indicates the number of twos (2^1), the next digit indicates the number of fours (2^2), the next digit indicates the number of eights (2^3), and so on, which must be added to obtain the value of the expression.

Statistical data are usually expressed in decimal notation, but because high-speed electronic circuits are readily adaptable to binary operation, almost all

TABLE 1   Several Common Methods for Binary Coding of Decimal Numbers

1 Decimal notation	2 Binary notation	3 Binary-coded- decimal notation		4 Excess-three notation	
00	00000	0000	0000	0011	0011
01	00001	0000	0001	0011	0100
02	00010	0000	0010	0011	0101
03	00011	0000	0011	0011	0110
04	00100	0000	0100	0011	0111
05	00101	0000	0101	0011	1000
06	00110	0000	0110	0011	1001
07	00111	0000	0111	0011	1010
08	01000	0000	1000	0011	1011
09	01001	0000	1001	0011	1100
10	01010	0001	0000	0100	0011
11	01011	0001	0001	0100	0100
12	01100	0001	0010	0100	0101
13	01101	0001	0011	0100	0110
14	01110	0001	0100	0100	0111
15	01111	0001	0101	0100	1000
16	10000	0001	0110	0100	1001
17	10001	0001	0111	0100	1010
18	10010	0001	1000	0100	1011
19	10011	0001	1001	0100	1100
20	10100	0010	0000	0101	0011

electronic computers employ binary coding. These two facts can be made compatible by using a system in which each decimal digit is represented by four
or more binary digits, not necessarily the binary numerical equivalent. Four
of the numerous ways of representing quantities from 0 through 20 are illustrated in Table 1.

In natural binary-coded-decimal notation, each decimal digit is represented
by the equivalent binary representation. In excess-three notation, each decimal digit is represented by the binary equivalent of the digit plus three. The
advantages of the excess-three coding system become apparent as it is applied
to the mathematical operation within a computer. In other coding systems,
arbitrary weights are assigned to each position. The value of the digit in any
column may be a fixed positive or negative quantity, or may vary according
to some pattern. In the floating-point system, all quantities are expressed
by a fixed number of significant digits and a scale factor. Obviously, it is
impossible to understand the logic of any computer system without first knowing the coding system it uses.

III. ARITHMETIC OPERATIONS

In positional notation using any base number, consecutive increases of one
unit are indicated by increasing by one the value of the coefficient of the zero
power of the base. When the quantity equals the base number, the coefficient
of the zero power of the base is again made zero, and 1 is added to the coefficient of the first power of the base. In a like manner, the sum of two
quantities is obtained by adding the coefficients in each position or column.
Each time the sum of the coefficients in any column equals or exceeds the base
number, one unit is carried over to be added with the coefficients of the next-
higher power of the base. For example, in binary notation (with equivalent
decimal notations in parentheses)

01	(1)	101	(5)	010011	(19)
+01	(+1)	+001	(+1)	+001101	(+13)
10	2	110	6	100000	32

The true complement of any quantity in positional notation is the quantity
which, when added to the first quantity, gives the least quantity containing
one more place. The base-minus-1s complement of any quantity is the quantity which, when added to the first quantity, gives the largest quantity containing the same number of places. In binary notation, 1 and 0 complement
each other. Table 2 illustrates the true complement and the base-minus-1s
(9s) complement of each decimal digit in ordinary decimal notation and in
binary-coded-decimal notation.

All of that binary arithmetic can get to be mind-boggling, but it suffices
to show that computers recognize 1s and 0s only. The secret lies in the arrangement of the 1s and 0s and their overall format. Software as defined is
nothing but data arranged in the 1s-and-0s patterns best suited to perform
computer operations. The arrangements, and they are many in number, are
called languages. Over the last few years languages have proliferated, to
the point where there are many that computers speak, and each language is
designed to facilitate a particular application or job that the machine is required to execute. Table 3 shows some of the languages in common use today.
What they all are is not germane to this discussion, but to select two examples

TABLE 2   Complement Notation for Decimal and Binary-Coded-Decimal
Numbers

	Decimal			Binary-coded decimal	
Digit	True complement	9s complement	Digit	True complement	9s complement
0	10	9	0000	1010	1001
1	9	8	0001	1001	1000
2	8	7	0010	1000	0111
3	7	6	0011	0111	0110
4	6	5	0100	0110	0101
5	5	4	0101	0101	0100
6	4	3	0110	0100	0011
7	3	2	0111	0011	0010
8	2	1	1000	0010	0001
9	1	0	1001	0001	0000

at random: COBOL is an acronym used to denote Common Business Oriented
Language. This is the language employed to produce the utilities bill, to
perform inventory control in the supermarket, and to carry out a host of
other general office tasks. FORTRAN (now in its fifth enhancement) is an
acronym denoting Formula Translation, and is one of the languages in wide
use for scientific programming, where mathematical problems of considerable
complexity are to be solved.

Note from Table 3 that the languages listed are ranked against the assembly
language, which is assigned a value of unity. This comes about from a number of causes. In the early days of software, one of the uses of it was to
create, often by perforated paper tape as a medium, instructions for running
numerically controlled machines performing the routine tasks of precision
grinding, turning, milling, drilling, shaping, and other machine shop functions. The language also handled assembly functions for routinized machine
assembly operations which tend toward known sequences of events. Machine/
assembly language thus became the arbitrary standard against which others
are now ranked. The ranking expresses the relative complexity of the language versus assembly language and furnishes a range of expansion factors.
Thus a highly complex programming task for which the language of choice is
FORTRAN V is five times more demanding than that of the basically simple
assembly language. This is of value when software must be costed.

Together with the language evolution came a bewildering set of terms in
use by the software creators. These terms are descriptors used in software
technology and are not to be confused with computer languages themselves.
To cite a few:

Architecture: The software systems engineer speaks of architecture
    rather than design. The term really means the three phases of effort
    used to evolve software. These are design, implementation, and inte-
    gration and test. When all three have been accomplished, a computer
    program is said to have been architected.
Application program: A set of instructions—called program statements or
    code—to perform a specific job.

TABLE 3 Comparison of Some Higher-
Order Languages to Assembly Language

Language	MOL/HOL Expansion[a]		
	Low	Average	High
Compass	—	0.65	—
Assembly	1	1	1
CMS-2	2.5	2.8	3.5
Microcode	2	3	3
COBOL	2.5	3	3.5
UNIX-C	—	3	—
OVIAL	3	4	5
Pascal	3	4	5
PRIDE	—	5	—
Corrall 66	—	5	—
FORTRAN	4	5.5	8
BASIC	—	6	—
FLOD	—	10	—
ALGOL	—	10	11
PL/1	7.5	10	13
Atlas	4.5	10	13.5
IFAM	—	13	—
APL	—	15	—

[a]MOL, machine operating language;
HOL, higher-order language.

Emulation: A hardware and software technique used to execute programs
developed for a different computer system.
Translation: A largely automated process of application software conversion in which the functional requirements and software design specifications are preserved. Called recoding when the process is largely manual.

There are thousands of other terms in use, and this has led to a number of
glossaries of terms being compiled and published. Some of these glossaries
are listed at the end of the chapter, but to give some idea of the magnitude
of the task, which is never-ending, consider the following: Data & Analysis
Center (a Division of ITT Research Institute), *A Bibliography of Software
Engineering Terms*, published in October 1979. This excellent work encom-
passes 147 pages of alphabetically arranged terms and their definitions.

All of the foregoing text has done little more than define briefly what software is all about, its relationship to the digital computer, and some of its

peculiarities as a product of human intelligence. What is needed now is at
least a cursory overview of software: what it does in the real world, how it
is architected, how it is fed and watered while it is in use, and how it is controlled. Control must include quality control, and in the software world this
poses special situations and problems not encountered in the world of hardware. One way to make the examination (and there are at least 10 ways of
doing it, perhaps more) is to use an example.

Let us postulate the case of a small business in the commercial products
world, a small plastics plant. The plant makes all manner of plastic items,
primarily as a feeder plant for the automotive industry. It provides extru-
sions, moldings, and pressings in a wide product line, including doorknobs,
tail and side lamp lenses, reflectors, stick-on side moldings, ashtray housings, simulated wood trim panels, and many others. Until 1981 the plant had
been labor intensive, employing some 100 people. Let us assume further that
2% of the employment mix is the management portion, 5% is general office and
sales staff, 5% is technical drafting and engineering, 2% is packaging and shipping, and the remaining 86% comprises the labor force, divided as 76% all-
product-oriented labor and 20% quality assurance. One can quarrel with the
figures, but as the plant is labor intensive, with a wide product line of "bits
and pieces," the inspection task demands a high staffing level. Considering
the case further, let us assume that the plant is suffering hard times, for
slaved to the automotive industry, with a high cost of labor and materials, it
is barely getting by. Management calls in a team of consultants, posing to
that team the question: How can we increase our profitability? The consultants study the plant processes and recommend that the plant work smart
rather than hard. They suggest that the main savings are to be effected by
adopting a labor-minimal posture, and this means a radical departure from the
established business practices of the company in question. The final recommendation is that most of the plant employees be terminated and that operations be conducted using automated machinery, controlled by a central computer. The implications are obvious, but to list a few of them, the recommendation implies:

Automation of the production lines with control-programmed machinery
The purchase of a computer and suitable software to control the entire
    production process
Automation of the inspection process, packaging, and readying for
    shipment
Automation of the office processes as far as possible, such as payroll,
    billing, records storage, and the like

To effect all this, the company decides to undertake the capital investment
and all the details concerned with that action. It decides, too, that a general-
purpose computer be purchased, one that will handle two major functions:
process control and business support. From what has been stated earlier,
it is obvious that the computer must speak at least two languages. This means
that it will require two different sets of software and handle them probably on
a time-shared basis. This presupposes that business operations can be handled
at times when the plant processes do not require direct control activity on the
part of that form of software.

Management must face a number of knotty problems, among which are:

Contracting for the software architecture (this can be done either with
    the supplier of the computer or by a software design house)

Purchasing the automated machinery for the production process, the inspection process, and the packaging process

Installing the new system and handling the changeover phase

Terminating the unskilled labor force and hiring personnel to care and
feed the computer, maintain the new machinery, and respond to the
outputs of the machine-produced office routines

There are, of course, many other problems to be handled, but such
changes can, have, and will happen; in fact, they are the wave of the future.
To return to software, it does not stretch the imagination very much to accept
the statement that almost any process that human beings can conceive can be
carried out by automation, a combination of software, and the machines that
it is architected to instruct. Just some of the processes handled very well by

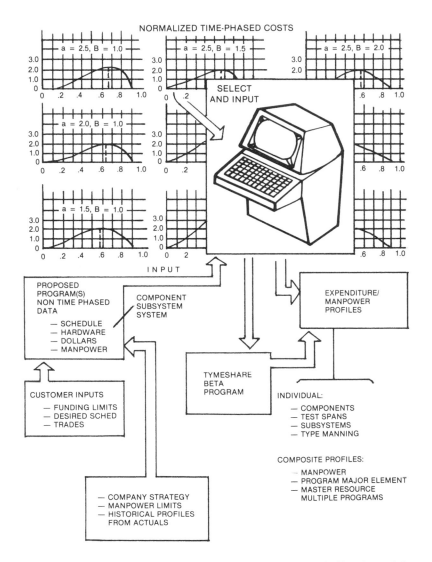

FIGURE 2 Profiling by multiple parametric or similar to pricing programs.

software are cost estimation and resource profiling as these affect production processes, and for that matter, design processes, too. A glance at Fig. 2 gives an insight into how that might be done. Most people in industry today are familiar with CADAM (computer-aided design and manufacture). In this process computer-aided design programs allow designers to both structure and test parts before manufacture. Similarly, computer-aided manufacture computers support employees and equipment during the manufacturing process.

IV. A PEOPLE PROBLEM

It is not within the province of this short chapter to comment on the social implications accompanying the rapid growth of software as a discipline. Suffice it to say that as software, allied with a digital computer, takes over ever-increasing numbers of production processes, trains of events of a social nature are set in motion. Processes that are presently labor intensive are becoming automated at an ever-increasing rate, and that raises the question of what to do with the jobless, whose employment has been preempted by the automation process. There are no easy answers to this question.

V. SOFTWARE PROBLEMS

In the software milieu, as in all other fields of endeavor, "there ain't no free lunch." Software, since it is created by human intelligence, has its fair share of problems. A partial list of these includes:

Dispelling the mystique which still surrounds software creation
Maintaining software current and the need for many and rapid
    enhancements
Coming to grips with workable, credible methods of costing software
    programs
Devising means for the control of software quality
Ensuring a continuing supply of well-trained system software engineers
    and software programmers
Standardizing regulations, both government and industry, applicable to
    the control of the software production process

These are problems on a macroscale, and again, there are no easy solutions.
    Returning for a moment to the postulation of the small plastics business, perhaps the most difficult decision facing management in that field is investment in a product that will control their entire line of business, but about which they know comparatively little. Again, an example may serve to shed light on some of the subordinate decisions to be faced.

VI. SOFTWARE QUALITY

Software, as a product line defined earlier, does not fail in the accepted sense. The quality manager is tasked with ensuring that quality is built into a product that does not wear out; that cannot easily be taken apart, piecewise, to replace deficiencies; and that quite often contains built-in diagnostics which either report on product state of health, or provide alternative methods of

TABLE 4   Typical Technical Specification Contents

1. Scope and purpose of computer program

2. Applicable computer hardware and interfaces

3. Technical requirements
   3.1 General design criteria
   3.2 Basic logic/mathematical models
   3.3 Input requirements
   3.4 Output reports
   3.5 Special instructions/restrictions/limitations

4. Verification requirements

5. Documentation requirements

TABLE 5   Basic Elements of a Software Configuration Control Program

1. Obtain authorization to use the completed computer program for production work.

2. Compile the computer program data package:
   a. Program description or abstract
   b. Source deck
   c. Technical reports, user's manual
   d. Sample input deck (for standard problems)
   e. Sample output (for standard problems)

3. Deliver data package to central computer file.

4. Verify that source deck is fully operational by running standard problems and checking results.

5. Place computer code under restricted access control and issue instructions to destroy all copies of source/decks/tapes and files other than central file master copy. Identify computer program by specific revision number.

6. Process all production use on master copy through central file.

7. Restrict any change to the computer code except through a documented change control process.

8. When authorized by management, provide a single copy of the production tape to the authorized programmer for revision, but do not allow production work on anything except the master copy.

9. After the revision is proven to be acceptable, obtain management authorization to replace the master copy with the revised master copy. Repeat steps 2 to 6.

10. Retain a history file of each master copy revision.

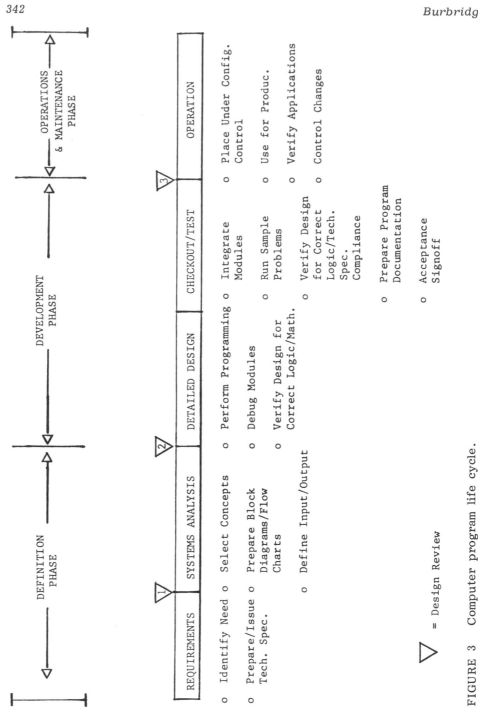

FIGURE 3   Computer program life cycle.

operation should some software subroutine not perform adequately. In the quality domain, no longer can the well-understood inspection aids, inspection instructions, tools of metrology, and standard skills be brought to bear. Software defects are often *subtle*, frequently cannot be perceived by visual inspection, and sometimes reveal themselves for no apparent reason. Permutations and combinations evolving from the statements above are legion, and space does not permit discussion of them here.

Obviously, the approach needed to solve these problems must be novel, and the software inspector must of necessity be a software professional, speaking many languages, skilled in diagnostics, and capable of rigorous discipline in software debugging, which requires intense concentration. Not the least of the problems besetting a company about to plunge into software is where to find trained personnel and how to pay the high cost that their employment demands. The life cycle of software, since it does not wear out in

TABLE 6   Variables That Affect Software Costs

Project size	Intensity of effort
Project type (management information system, radar, telemetry, etc.)	Changing requirements
	Programming language
Operational/customer environment	Compiler power and efficiency
Hardware constraints (system loading)	Development location (in-house or on-site)
Existing design	
Existing code	Project complexity
External interfaces (type and quantity)	Engineering requirements
	Programming requirements
Hierarchical design/functional flow structure	Configuration control
Number of functions performed	Documentation
Amount of code per function	Program management
Schedule constraints, lead times and overlaps	Design phase activities
	Implementation activities
Resource constraints	Test and Integration activities
ECN effects	Integration of independent projects
Economic trends	Verification and validation
Technology growth	Multiple test beds/installations
Fee, profit, and G&A	Government furnished software
Computer operation costs	Purchased software (e.g., subcontracts)
Overhead	
Organizational efficiency	Design-to-cost
Skills	Resource allocation with respect to time
Project familiarity	

the accepted sense, poses the problem of what is needed to maintain programs operational over some predetermined useful life span, and to provide the software with necessary enhancements so that it can accomplish its tasks, even though the scope of those tasks will probably change over time. While analogous to the operations and maintenance (O&M) phase of hardware programs, ongoing software programs require continual study and update with respect to daily operating conditions. This is the care and feeding process. As an illustration of "cradle-to-grave" software architecture, the process begins with a technical specification for the total software task. Table 4 illustrates a typical specification. Table 5 depicts the basic elements for configuration control of a software program. Finally, Fig. 3 represents the life cycle for a typical software/computer program.

VII. BOTTOM LINE

As with everything else in the workaday world, there has to be a bottom line for software programs. This is, of course, how much they cost, and in particular a method that will yield credible cost estimates for software programs, a priori. Today, cost estimates for software are usually prepared by use of a parametric cost estimating model. Several of these models are available and in wide use throughout industry and government. They explore the relationships existing among software descriptors and variables and the cost to obtain the software architecture contemplated. These models can be either of the closed form, parochial type, or the general-case type. Since the general-

TABLE 7   Software Model Configurations

---

1. Project magnitude (How big?)
   The amount of code to be produced.

2. Program application (What character?)
   The type of project, such as management information system, command and control, telemetry, communications, etc.

3. Level of new design and code (How much new work is needed?)
   The amount of design and code that cannot be taken from existing inventory.

4. Resources (Who will do the work?)
   The experience, skill, know-how, and cost of the assigned individuals or team, as applicable to the specified task.

5. Utilization (What hardware constraints?)
   The extent of processor loading relative to its speed and memory capacity.

6. Customer specifications and reliability requirements (Where and how used?)
   The level of requirements relating to testing, transportability, and end use of the product.

7. Development environment (What complicating factors exist?)
   The relative impact of unique project conditions on the normal time required to complete the job, measured with respect to the organization, resources, program application, and project size.

---

case model affords greater flexibility for program description and still provides credible cost estimates, this type of model seems to be preferred for the costing process. Such models consider the impact on cost of the variables listed in Table 6. In reality, the parametric software model requires categorical inputs of several sorts, and they may be grouped as shown in Table 7. The outcome is, of course, the necessary dollar resources to design, implement, test, and integrate the software of interest so that the final program may be brought on-stream.

VIII. CONCLUSION

Although this chapter does not answer "all the questions you always wanted to know about software, but were afraid to ask," it is hoped that the brief overview given will afford insight into the software overall process—the food and drink of the digital computer—and the computer itself as an indispensable tool of modern business and technology. As stated earlier, the computer can be a surly beast if not fed and cared for properly. Those who take the trouble to provide the computer with its preferred diet will find it to be docile, well behaved, and an indefatigable servant.

We end with some definitions which show that the software world is not without a sense of humor: The least unit of information recognized by a computer is a bit. A small group of adjacent bits when used by a computer (usually eight in number) is called a byte. Half a byte is called a nibble.

ACKNOWLEDGMENTS

J. A. Burgess, Manager, Quality Assurance, Westinghouse Electric Corp., Pittsburgh, Pa.: Computer Program Life Cycle; and RCA Corp., RCA PRICE Systems, Cherry Hill, N.J.: extracts from *RCA PRICE S3 Manual*.

BIBLIOGRAPHY

Gloss-Soler, S. A., *The DACS Glossary*, Data Analysis Center for Software, ITT Research Institute, October 1979.

Scientific American, September 1977 issue dedicated to computers and microelectronics, Scientific American, Inc., New York.

Sippl, C. J., *Microcomputer Handbook*, Petrocelli/Charter, New York.

Sippl, C. J., and C. P. Sippl, *Computer Dictionary*, 2nd ed., Howard W. Sams, Indianapolis, Ind., 1974.

Walter, Russ, *The Secret Guide to Computers*, Part 4, published by the author, 1978; one of a four-volume series, including Part 1: Basic; Part 2: Applications; and Part 3: Languages and a Commentary, with self-tests, more examples, and advanced language features.

Weik, M. H., *Standard Dictionary of Computers and Information Processing*, revised 2nd ed., Hayden, Rochelle Park, N.J., 1977.

19

ATTRIBUTES INSPECTION

JOHN J. HELDT

FLR Consulting Services
San Jose, California

I. INTRODUCTION

Attributes inspection can be described as "go" or "not go" inspection. The part, thing, or service is either good or bad. Although we would like for all of our products to be good the first time, it is easy to see that there is a cost trade-off between "perfection" and the replacement of a few bad parts at the consumer level.

For example, suppose that the cost of perfection (i.e., inspection of every part) is 10% of the total cost of product of a self-tapping screw made on an automatic screw machine. It would amount to a cost savings to the manufacturing firm to supply 105 screws for each 100 ordered, provided that they could sample inspect the process every so often at a cost of less than 1% of the product cost and that the sample inspection had a high probability of assuring 5 bad screws or fewer for every 100 made. In fact, the firm could split the savings with the customer who might be glad to exchange the slightly lower price for having the installer throw an occasional unthreaded (defective) screw into the salvage barrel.

Some poeple do not like to talk about "defectives"—they would rather think in terms of the good pieces or the "go" parts. But for this discussion, *defective* indicates that a part or assembly has one or more defects, while *defect* indicates the specific thing that is wrong with the defective part.

II. CONTROL OF PRODUCTION

One of the reasons for keeping records of a process is to find out how the process performs. When, on average, 2 of every 100 glass diodes are broken in the manufacturing process, it would be wise to produce 105 for every 100 ordered so as not to come up short when the order is filled. The 5 extra diodes per hundred was chosen because there is a high probability that if the diodes are drawn from stock in lots of 200 and if the true fraction defective (p') is 0.02, the lot will contain 5% or less broken diodes.

Figure 1 shows the p chart for this process, where the average fraction defective ($\bar{p}$) is equal to 0.02. The calculations for the upper control limit are

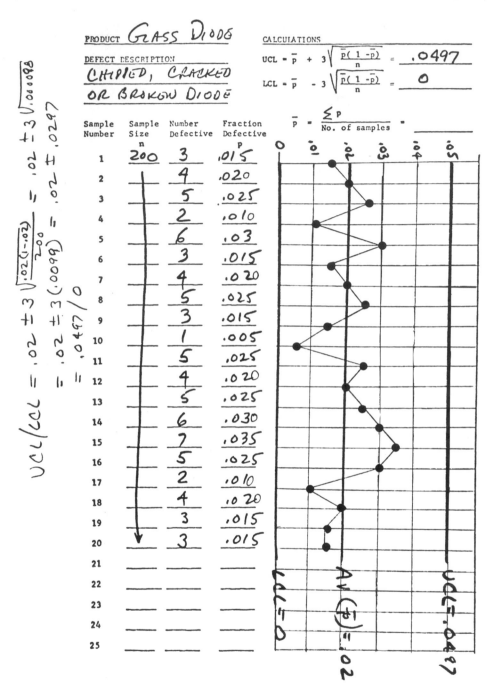

FIGURE 1   p chart showing 3 σ control limits.

shown at a value of 0.0497. This is the upper control limit for the process
when examining 200 per sample. From the calculations, the lower control
limit would be a negative number if the formula were followed with literal
exactness. But reason tells us that there can never be a negative number
of defectives; therefore, we use zero as our lower limit. For practical purposes, the average fraction defective, designated by $\bar{p}$, taken after 15 to
25 samples, is used as the best estimate of the true fraction defective designated as p'. When the true fraction defective is known for the diodes in
stock, the same limit calculations apply to lots drawn from that stock.

Another reason for keeping records of a process is to be able to see when
a process has gone out of control. This is the main reason for the calculation
of the upper and lower control limits. It is possible for the fraction defective
for a sample to exceed the upper control limit, but the probability is so remote
that it is wise to start looking for an assignable cause the first time a point on
the control graph is out of limits.

Since making it right the first time is always a quality aim, the control
chart can be used to judge progress. A decrease in the fraction defective,
which means that more items or services are being made right the first time,
can be spotted as a trend by observing that more than half the points on the
chart are below the centerline. Toward this end, some companies show the
upper control limit (UCL) at the 2σ point (i.e., at two-thirds of the excursion
indicated by the UCL) instead of the 3σ point, as shown in Fig. 1. Usually,
the average fraction defective (the centerline) is recomputed quarterly, especially if the average fraction defective has improved. In some cases the
chart is presented as a "yield" chart instead of a p chart. This means that
1 minus the fraction defective is shown instead of the fraction defective itself.

There is something to be said for each of the practical applications discussed above. Using tighter control limits means that the process comes under
scrutiny when there is only a 98% probability of a problem. Recomputing $\bar{p}$
quarterly is intended to consolidate the process improvement, thus imposing
tighter limits for the next quarter. Sometimes this can backfire. Poor product performance for a quarter can leave you with control limits for the next
quarter which mean very little.

A. The p Chart

The p chart is a process control chart that is recorded in terms of fraction
defective. It does not matter whether the fraction is expressed as a decimal
fraction, as in the example in Fig. 1, or as a percentage. It is wise to use
one or the other to avoid arithmetic errors. In application, a sample is taken
from production on a regular basis and inspected for defects. The sample is
numbered, the sample size is recorded, and the number of defects is tallied.

Depending on the process, the period between samples can be determined.
In the case of the glass diodes, for which the data are shown in Fig. 1, about
10,000 of the finished product are delivered daily, in rolls, with the ends of
the leads taped to hold the diodes in the roll but with the centers open for
visual inspection or testing. It was judged that two groups of samples per
day were sufficient to monitor the process. Thus a sample was taken around
midmorning and another was taken around midafternoon.

Since the inspection was going to be a simple visual accounting of all the
diodes that were cracked, chipped, or broken, a sample size of 200 was chosen.
It was deemed that the sample would be random (i.e., any individual part having an equal chance of being chosen) if the inspector took the next 200 out of

the tape machine. In this process the diodes are "counted" by measuring the length of the tape; therefore, the inspector simply snipped out the length of taped units that corresponded to 200 pieces twice each day.

Once the defective units were counted and entered into the record, the sample was returned to production, where it was added to the stock. For the example shown here, we assume that the inspector has inspected 200 samples, plotted them on a p chart, taken an average to find $\bar{p}$ and then calculated the upper and lower control limits. Once $\bar{p}$ is established, the formula used to calculate the limits is

$$\frac{UCL}{LCL} = \bar{p} \pm 3 \sqrt{\frac{\bar{p}(1 - \bar{p})}{n}}$$

When $\bar{p}$ is very small, the term $(1 - \bar{p})$ approaches 1; therefore, for practical purposes, whenever $\bar{p}$ is less than 0.1, the formula can be reduced to

$$\frac{UCL}{LCL} = \bar{p} \pm 3 \sqrt{\frac{\bar{p}}{n}}$$

Note that the term $\sqrt{\bar{p}(1 - \bar{p})/n}$ is multiplied by 3 and added to the average; therefore, this term is considered to be 3σ for the process when the sample size n is used.

Figure 2 shows a nomograph for finding this 3σ term for several values of the true fraction defective (p'). The true fraction defective is used in Fig. 2 because this is theoretical or "what if" calculation. Usually, the fraction defective $\bar{p}$ is considered to be an excellent estimate of the true fraction defective when based on 20 or more samples.

Figure 3 shows the same graph as shown in Fig. 1, except that the upper control limit is based on a 2σ value and the area from 1σ to 2σ is shaded to indicate "alert" when points fall in the shaded area. In theory, the probability of the process being in control when a point falls outside the 3σ limit is 0.00135, about once in 10,000 times. The probability of being in control when a point is outside the 2σ limits is 0.0227, a little more than 2%. Using the 1σ limit as the upper control limit gives a probability of 0.1587 that a point could be above the UCL with no change in the process. It is interesting to note that only one point above and one point below are in the shaded area. The four other points touching the ±1 sigma lines make the total 15% approximated, as postulated.

B. The np Chart

The np chart is a process control chart that is recorded in number of defectives. This is frequently used when the sample size is not always the same. Technically, the control limits should be calculated for each point on the graph, as shown in Fig. 4. Since this means a calculation each time a sample is checked, and that calculation is based on one sample only instead of the 15 to 25 samples that would give us more confidence in the limits, the upper control limits are usually calculated using an average sample size. When any individual point is outside the limits and the sample is greatly different from the average, this is usually noted on the chart since the difference in sample size may be the assignable cause that we would otherwise go looking for.

The formula for UCL/LCL is shown here:

$$\frac{UCL}{LCL} = n\bar{p} \pm 3 \sqrt{n\bar{p}(1 - \bar{p})}$$

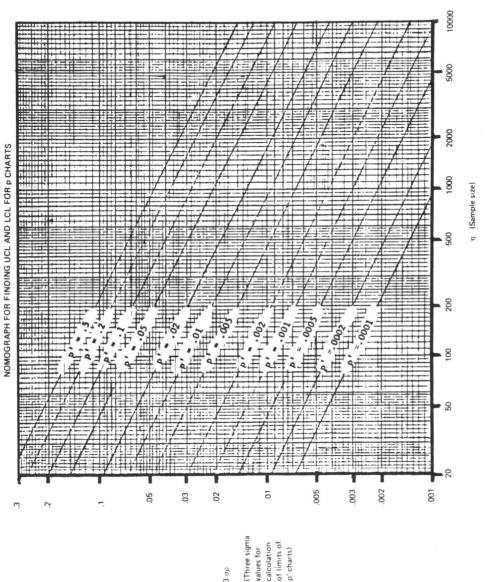

FIGURE 2   Nomograph for finding 3σ values for various values of the true fraction defective.

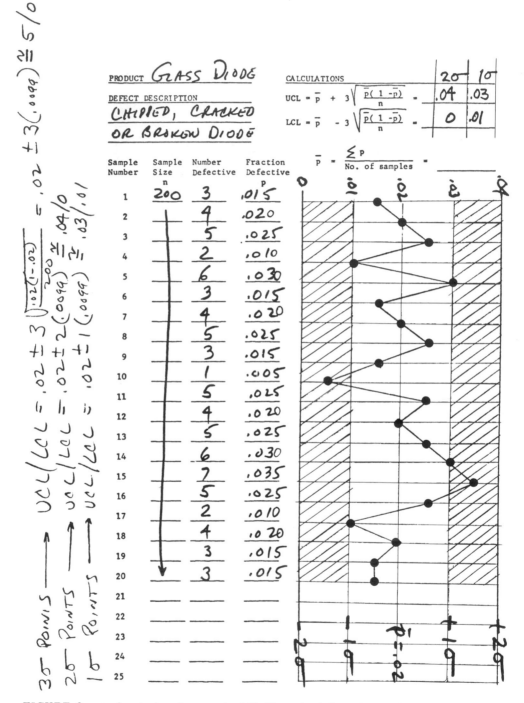

FIGURE 3   p chart showing control limits set at 2σ values with 1σ to 2σ areas crosshatched.

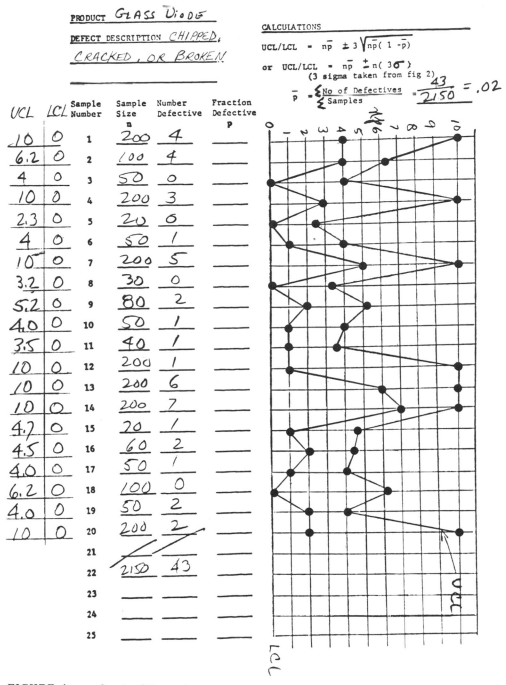

PRODUCT *GLASS DIODE*

DEFECT DESCRIPTION *CHIPPED,*
CRACKED, OR BROKEN

CALCULATIONS

UCL/LCL = $\overline{np} \pm 3 \sqrt{\overline{np}(1-\overline{p})}$

or UCL/LCL = $\overline{np} \pm n(3\sigma)$
  (3 sigma taken from fig 2)

$\overline{p} = \dfrac{\sum \text{No of Defectives}}{\sum \text{Samples}} = \dfrac{43}{2150} = .02$

UCL	LCL	Sample Number	Sample Size n	Number Defective	Fraction Defective p
10	0	1	200	4	—
6.2	0	2	100	4	—
4	0	3	50	0	—
10	0	4	200	3	—
2.3	0	5	20	0	—
4	0	6	50	1	—
10	0	7	200	5	—
3.2	0	8	30	0	—
5.2	0	9	80	2	—
4.0	0	10	50	1	—
3.5	0	11	40	1	—
10	0	12	200	1	—
10	0	13	200	6	—
10	0	14	200	7	—
4.7	0	15	20	1	—
4.5	0	16	60	2	—
4.0	0	17	50	1	—
6.2	0	18	100	0	—
4.0	0	19	50	2	—
10	0	20	200	2	—
		21			—
		22	2150	43	—
		23	—	—	—
		24	—	—	—
		25	—	—	—

FIGURE 4   p chart with variable sample size (np chart). Also shown is the variation in control limits.

Like the previous formula, this reduces to, $n\bar{p} \pm 3\sqrt{n\bar{p}}$, when $\bar{p}$ is very small (i.e., less than 0.1).

C. The 3σ Nomograph

The nomograph shown in Fig. 2 can be used for both p charts and np charts. In either event, the best estimate of the true fraction defective (p') is assumed to be the average fraction defective ($\bar{p}$). To use the nomography, find the sample size on the bottom line. Follow the vertical line for the sample size until it intersects the diagonal line corresponding to the best estimate of the true fraction defective. Follow the horizontal line from the point of the vertical line/diagonal line intersection to find the value of 3σ associated with that true fraction defective at that sample size.

For the p chart, add the 3σ value to the average fraction defective for the upper control limit and subtract it from the average fraction defective for the lower control limit. Remember, the lower limit is zero if the calculated lower control limit is a negative number.

For the np chart, find the 3σ value for the true fraction defective the same way. Then multiply this 3σ value by the sample size (n) and add to or subtract from the average number of defectives ($n\bar{p}$) to get the upper or lower control limits.

Interpolation between the lines of the 3σ nomograph gives an acceptable degree of accuracy for p or np charts. There is nothing magic about this nomograph; it merely reflects the ability of log-log paper to be used in taking square roots and in multiplying and dividing. To construct your own nomograph for other values, draw in the diagonal lines for those values of p' that you wish, on log-log paper. For the nomograph shown in Fig. 2, the 3σ value for each p' was calculated for n = 100 and n = 1000. Using these two points, the lines were extrapolated to the ends of the nomograph.

D. Other Charts

Two other types of attribute process control charts are "defects per unit" and "number of defects." An example of defects per unit would be when an auto agency keeps track of the number of defects on each truck that comes to them from the factory. Since each of these deficiencies must be corrected before the truck is delivered to the customer, the number of defects represents money to the dealership. For this reason, the incoming quality should be monitored in order to charge back to the factory for correcting the defects and to be immediately aware when the defects per unit get out of line. Defects per unit are symbolized as u and the upper and lower control limits are as follows:

$$\frac{UCL}{LCL} = \bar{u} \pm 3 \sqrt{\frac{u}{n}}$$

The subgroup size (n) should be held constant for this control chart.

An example of number of defects would be in monitoring the number of typographical errors on the front page of the newspaper. Since it is almost impossible to be perfect with regard to typos, a control chart would show us if we were improving and would tell us when extra care was needed (i.e., when we were out of control). The number of defects is symbolized by c and the formula for the upper and lower control limits is as follows:

$$\frac{UCL}{LCL} = \bar{c} \pm 3\sqrt{\bar{c}}$$

It is not intended here to be all-inclusive in this treatment of keeping records of processes, but rather, to illustrate the types of charts most frequently used and to show some of those that are used for special processes. With an understanding of the principles, it is a short step to the application of those principles to any other processes, universal or unique.

III. LOT ACCEPTANCE

Although it is feasible for a firm's managers to assure themselves that their process is in control using "go"/"not-go" data, customers would like to assure themselves that the material they buy does not exceed an agreed-upon level of defective parts. Since it would be self-defeating to the overall cost-savings plan to inspect each incoming part, the consumer usually selects a sample from the lot, examines it, and then accepts or rejects the lot based on the number of defects found. When a lot is rejected, it is subject to screening (inspection of each part), which means that the parts which are entered into stock under these circumstances contain no defects. This means that the quality of the product that a customer puts into stock on the average (average outgoing quality or AOQ) is better than the quality of the product as received by a factor depending on how many lots were rejected.

This leads to an interesting statement. When the incoming quality is very good, the average outgoing quality is very good. When the incoming quality is very bad, the average outgoing quality is very good—due to the screening of most of the lots. When the incoming quality is mediocre, the average outgoing quality is at its worst, with the most outgoing defects (limit) somewhere in this area. This average outgoing quality limit (AOQL) for any sample plan represents the maximum liability of the sample plan in the long run. The AOQL is discussed in Sec. IV.

There are three major distributions on which attribute probabilities are based.

A. The Hypergeometric Distribution

This distribution is considered to give the best probability when you know the exact number in the lot (N), and the exact number of defectives in that lot (D). From this we can determine the probability of finding d number of defectives in a sample of size n.

$$P_d = \frac{C\binom{N-D}{n-d}}{C\binom{N}{n}} \quad \text{where} \quad C\binom{D}{d} \text{ is a combination which equals } \frac{D!}{d!\,(D-d)!}$$

D! reads D factorial, which means that the number D is multiplied by D − 1, then d − 2, and so on, until D − the last number equals 1. This is illustrated by 5! (5 factorial) - 5 × 4 × 3 × 2 × 1 = 120.

The hypergeometric distribution is used mostly for probabilities in playing card games because the lot size is known (N = 52), the exact number of "defectives" are known (D = 4, for the number of aces, for instance), and the sample size is known (n = 5 for most poker hands or n = 13 for a bridge hand).

To illustrate the mathematics of the hypergeometric probabilities, the calculation is made for the probability of finding exactly 1 ace (d = 1) in a draw poker hand (n = 5) dealt from an ordinary deck (N = 52, D = 4).

$$P_1 = \frac{C\binom{52-4}{5-1}C\binom{4}{1}}{C\binom{52}{5}} = \frac{\frac{48!}{4! \cdot 44!} \cdot \frac{4!}{1! \cdot 3!}}{\frac{52}{5! \cdot 42!}} = \frac{48! \cdot 4! \cdot 5! \cdot 47!}{4! \cdot 44! \cdot 1! \cdot 3! \cdot 52!}$$

Note:

$$\frac{48!}{52!} = \frac{48 \cdot 47 \cdot 46 \cdot \ldots \cdot 3 \cdot 2 \cdot 1}{52 \cdot 51 \cdot 50 \cdot 49 \cdot 48 \cdot 47 \cdot 46 \cdot \ldots \cdot 3 \cdot 2 \cdot 1} = \frac{1}{52 \cdot 51 \cdot 50 \cdot 49}$$

$$\frac{47!}{44!} = \frac{47 \cdot 46 \cdot 45 \cdot 44 \cdot 43 \cdot 42 \cdot \ldots \cdot 3 \cdot 2 \cdot 1}{44 \cdot 43 \cdot 42 \cdot \ldots \cdot 3 \cdot 2 \cdot 1} = \frac{47 \cdot 46 \cdot 45}{1}$$

$$\frac{4!}{4!} = \frac{1}{1} \quad \text{and} \quad \frac{5!}{3!} = \frac{5 \cdot 4 \cdot 3 \cdot 2 \cdot 1}{3 \cdot 2 \cdot 1} = \frac{5 \cdot 4}{1}$$

From this you can see that

$$P_1 = \frac{47 \cdot 46 \cdot 45 \cdot 5 \cdot 4}{52 \cdot 51 \cdot 50 \cdot 49} = 0.2994736$$

which is a calculation that can easily be done on a hand-held calculator.

If you care to check it out, the probability of getting two aces in a five-card hand is about 4%, and the probability of getting no aces in a five-card hand is about 66%. From this you can see that getting three or four aces in a five-card draw are both very low in probability.

Hypergeometric probabilities are seldom used in attributes inspection or in attributes sampling plans except when the lots are small. Part of this is based on the difficulty of the mathematics involved. However, with the event of sophisticated hand-held calculators and computer subroutines, this distribution could become more important in the future.

B. The Binomial distribution

For the binomial calculations we do not need to know the size of the lot (N) or the number of defectives within the lot (D). All we need to know is the ratio of D to N. In other words, we can calculate the probability of finding exactly i defectives in a sample size of n, provided that we know that the true fraction defective p in the lot is fixed and constant at p'.

$$P_i = C\binom{n}{i}p'^{i} q'^{(n-1)} \quad \text{where } q' = 1 - p'$$

To illustrate the arithmetic of the binomial distribution, the probability of finding exactly 0, exactly 1, exactly 2, and exactly 3 defectives in a sample, n = 100, when the true fraction defective, p' = 0.02, is calculated.

$$P_o = C\binom{100}{0} 0.02^0 \cdot 0.98^{100} = \frac{100!}{0! \ 100!} \cdot 0.02^0 \cdot 0.98^{100} = 0.13262$$

$$P_1 = C\binom{100}{1} 0.02^1 \cdot 0.98^{99} = \frac{100!}{1! \, 99!} \cdot 0.02^1 \cdot 0.98^{99} - 0.27065$$

$$P_2 = C\binom{100}{1} 0.02^2 \cdot 0.98^{98} = \frac{100!}{2! \, 98!} \cdot 0.02^2 \cdot 0.98^{98} = 0.27341$$

The same methods can be used on the combination in the binomial distribution as are used on the combinations in the hypergeometric calculations. The Y^X feature on a hand-held calculator makes these calculations relatively simple. However, the binomial distribution is seldom used in calculations for attribute sampling plans and then only when the sample size is very small.

C. The Poisson Distribution

One reason for the infrequent use of the binomial distribution is the Poisson distribution. This was first given by S. D. Poisson over 150 years ago and can be used as a very close approximation of the binomial distribution. In addition to this close approximation and the relative ease of calculation, the Poisson distribution lends itself well to tabularization. The main discussion concerning acceptance of lots by attribute sampling will center around the table of the summation of terms of the Poisson distribution; however, a few calculations will be made here to demonstrate the arithmetic involved.

The Poisson distribution has only two variables. We can calculate the probability of finding exactly c number of defectives in a sample if we know the expected value (c'). The expected value c' is defined as np', where n is again the sample size and p' is the true fraction defective in a lot.

$$P_c = \frac{e^{-c'} \cdot c'^c}{c!}$$

where e is a constant, the base value for Naperian logarithms.

For a sample $n = 100$, with a true fraction defective $p' = 0.02$ (i.e., $c' = np' = np' = 100 \times 0.02 = 2$), the calculations are shown for the probability of finding exactly 0, 1, and 2 defects:

$$P_0 = \frac{e^{-2} \cdot 2^0}{0!} = \frac{0.13534 \cdot 1}{1} = 0.13534$$

$$P_1 = \frac{e^{-2} \cdot 2^1}{1!} = \frac{0.135434 \cdot 2}{1} = 0.27067$$

$$P_2 = \frac{e^{-2} \cdot 2^2}{2!} = \frac{0.13534 \cdot 4}{2} = 0.27067$$

Finding the e terms for the calculations above can be done either with the aid of an e table or by using a hand-held calculator with a natural logarithm capability. Taking the antilog (inverse ln) of 1 displays the numerical value of e; then the Y^X function can be used to raise it to the negative power desired.

Figure 5 shows how to go across the Poisson table to find the probabilities of 0, 1, 2, 3, and so on, defectives in a sample when the expected value is 2. It should be noted that the first three terms agree exactly with the three terms that we calculated above. Figure 6 illustrates the Poisson distribution for $c' = 3.4$.

0 _135_ P_0 = _.135_

1 _406_ P_1 = _.271_

2 _677_ P_2 = _.271_

3 _857_ P_3 = _.180_
          P_4 = _.090_
4 _947_
          P_5 = _.036_
5 _983_
          P_6 = _.012_
6 _995_
          P_7 = _.004_
7 _999_
          P_8 = _.001_
8 _1000_
          P_9 = _____

9 _____ P_{10} = _____

10 _____ P_{11} = _____

11 _____ P_{12} = _____

12 _____ P_{13} = _____

13 _____ P_{14} = _____

14 _____ P_{15} = _____

15 _____

16 _____

Expected Value	0	1	2	3	4	5	6	7	8
0.02	980	1.000							
0.04	961	999	1.000						
0.06	942	998	1.000						
0.08	923	997	1.000						
0.10	905	995	1.000						
0.15	861	990	999	1.000					
0.20	819	982	999	1.000					
0.25	779	974	998	1.000					
0.30	741	963	996	1.000					
0.35	705	951	994	1.000					
0.40	670	938	992	999	1.000				
0.45	638	925	989	999	1.000				
0.50	607	910	986	998	1.000				
0.60	549	878	977	997	1.000				
0.70	497	844	966	994	999	1.000			
0.80	449	809	953	991	999	1.000			
0.90	407	772	937	987	998	1.000			
1.00	368	736	920	981	996	999	1.000		
1.1	333	699	900	974	995	999	1.000		
1.2	301	663	879	966	992	998	1.000		
1.3	273	627	857	957	989	998	1.000		
1.4	247	592	833	946	986	997	999	1.000	
1.5	223	558	809	934	981	996	999	1.000	
1.6	202	525	783	921	976	994	999	1.000	
1.7	183	493	757	907	970	992	998	1.000	
1.8	165	463	731	891	964	990	997	999	1.000
1.9	150	434	704	875	956	987	997	999	1.000
2.0	135	406	677	857	947	983	995	999	1.000

FIGURE 5   Poisson distribution for an expected value c = 0.02.

Poisson Distribution for an <u>expected value</u>, c = 0.2

Example: If there are 2.0% red beads in a box what is
the probability of finding exactly 0 red
beads in a sample of 100? Exactly 1?, 2?,
3?, 4?, etc.

Note: n = 100, p' = .02, therefore the expected
value equals 2.

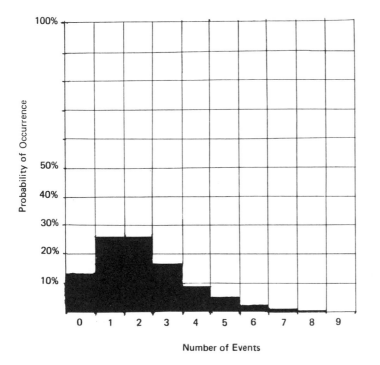

FIGURE 5 (Continued)

From Table		Subtract Last Term	
0	033	P_0 =	.033
1	147	P_1 =	.114
2	340	P_2 =	.193
3	558	P_3 =	.218
4	744	P_4 =	.186
5	871	P_5 =	.127
6	942	P_6 =	.071
7	977	P_7 =	.075
8	992	P_8 =	.015
9	997	P_9 =	.005
10	999	P_{10} =	.002
11	1000	P_{11} =	.001
12	____	P_{12} =	____
13	____	P_{13} =	____
14	____	P_{14} =	____
15	____	P_{15} =	____
16	____		

Expected Value	0	1	2	3	4	5	6	7	8	9	10	11
0.02	980	1.000										
0.04	961	999	1.000									
0.06	942	998	1.000									
0.08	923	997	1.000									
0.10	905	995	1.000									
0.15	861	990	999	1.000								
0.20	819	982	999	1.000								
0.25	779	974	998	1.000								
0.30	741	963	996	1.000								
0.35	705	951	994	1.000								
0.40	670	938	992	999	1.000							
0.45	638	925	989	999	1.000							
0.50	607	910	986	998	1.000							
0.60	549	878	977	997	1.000							
0.70	497	844	966	994	999	1.000						
0.80	449	809	953	991	999	1.000						
0.90	407	772	937	987	998	1.000						
1.00	368	736	920	981	996	999	1.000					
1.1	333	699	900	974	995	999	1.000					
1.2	301	663	879	966	992	998	1.000					
1.3	273	627	857	957	989	998	1.000					
1.4	247	592	833	946	986	997	999	1.000				
1.5	223	558	809	934	981	996	999	1.000				
1.6	202	525	783	921	976	994	999	1.000				
1.7	183	493	757	907	970	992	998	1.000				
1.8	165	463	731	891	964	990	997	999	1.000			
1.9	150	434	704	875	956	987	997	999	1.000			
2.0	135	406	677	857	947	983	995	999	1.000			
2.2	111	355	623	819	928	975	993	998	1.000			
2.4	091	308	570	779	904	964	988	997	999	1.000		
2.6	074	267	518	736	877	951	983	995	999	1.000		
2.8	061	231	469	692	848	935	976	992	998	999	1.000	
3.0	050	199	423	647	815	916	966	988	996	999	1.000	
3.2	041	171	380	603	781	895	955	983	994	998	1.000	
3.4	033	147	340	558	744	871	942	977	992	997	999	1.000

FIGURE 6 Poisson distribution for an expected value c = 3.4.

Poisson Distribution for an <u>expected value</u>, c = 3.4

Example: If you find 3.4 broken eggs per crate on
the average, what is the probability that
the next crate of eggs you open will have
0 broken eggs? What is your probability
of finding 1 or 2 or 3 or 4 or more?

Note: The <u>expected value</u> (c') in this case is 3.4.

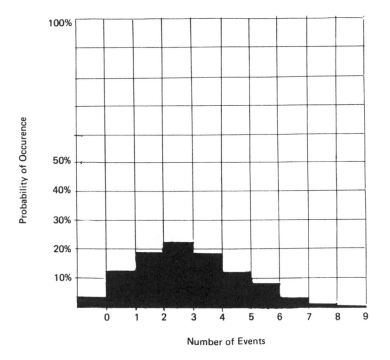

Number of Events

FIGURE 6   (Continued)

IV. SINGLE-SAMPLE PLANS

Single-sample plans are easy to understand and easy to use. When a lot of material is to be sampled, the inspector goes to a table and determines the sample size to be taken and the maximum number of defectives that is acceptable. MIL-STD-105D is frequently used. MIL-STD-105D has at least five different levels of inspection, not counting tightened and loosened. Double sampling is known to give the same level of confidence as single sampling with much less inspection on the average, but few people use it, either because they do not understand it or because they fail to see the advantage.

One sure way to feel more comfortable with any sample plan is to look at its operating characteristic (OC) curve. The OC curve will show you the true

Expected Value	0	1	2	3	4
0.02	980	1.000			
0.04	961	999	1.000		
0.06	942	998	1.000		
0.08	923	997	1.000		
0.10	905	995	1.000		
0.15	861	990	999	1.000	
0.20	819	982	999	1.000	
0.25	779	974	998	1.000	
0.30	741	963	996	1.000	
0.35	705	951	994	1.000	
0.40	670	938	992	999	1.000
0.45	638	925	989	999	1.000
0.50	607	910	986	998	1.000
0.60	549	878	977	997	1.000
0.70	497	844	966	994	999
0.80	449	809	953	991	999
0.90	407	772	937	987	998
1.00	368	736	920	981	996
1.1	333	699	900	974	995
1.2	301	663	879	966	992
1.3	273	627	857	957	989
1.4	247	592	833	946	986
1.5	223	558	809	934	981
1.6	202	525	783	921	976
1.7	183	493	757	907	970
1.8	165	463	731	891	964
1.9	150	434	704	875	956
2.0	135	406	677	857	947
2.2	111	355	623	819	928
2.4	091	308	570	779	904
2.6	074	267	518	736	877
2.8	061	231	469	692	848
3.0	050	199	423	647	815
3.2	041	171	380	603	781
3.4	033	147	340	558	744
3.6	027	126	303	515	706
3.8	022	107	269	473	668
4.0	018	092	238	433	629
4.5	011	061	174	343	532
5.0	007	040	125	265	440
5.5	005	027	089	202	358
6.0	002	017	062	151	285
6.5	002	010	043	112	224
7.0	001	007	030	082	173
7.5	001	005	021	059	133
8.0	000	003	014	042	100
8.5	000	002	009	030	074
9.0	000	001	006	021	055
9.5	000	001	004	015	040
10.0	000	000	003	010	029

Sample size (n) __80__

Accept number (c) __2__

Probability of Acceptance P_a	Expected Value np_1	True Fraction Defective p_1
95%	0.80	.01
70%	1.9	.024
50%	2.6	.033
30%	3.6	.045
10%	53	.066

FIGURE 7 Operating characteristic (OC) curve for single-sample plan, n - 80, c = 2.

fraction defective (p') associated with a probability of acceptance of 95%, which is generally called the acceptable quality level (AQL). The 5% probability of rejection of a lot as good as the AQL or better is called the alpha risk or the producer's risk because it represents the producer's chance of having a good lot rejected.

The OC curve also shows the true fraction defective associated with 10% probability of acceptance. This is generally called the lot tolerance percent defective (LTPD) and represents the worst quality normally associated with the sample plan. The 10% probability of acceptance is called the beta risk or the consumer's risk since it represents the consumer's chance of accepting a lot as bad or worse than the LTPD.

The OC curve also shows the point of indifference, which is the p' associated with 50% probability of acceptance. The average outgoing quality (AOQ) can also be derived from the OC curve. Multiply each probability of acceptance (P_a) by its associated p'. As mentioned earlier, P_a determines how often the lot is sent to stock without screening. When this is averaged with the percentage of lots that are screened, it is obvious that $P_a \cdot$p' is an excellent approximation of the AOQ. The AOQ can be plotted, and where it reaches its maximum (or limit) is called the average outgoing quality limit (AOQL). Figure 7 shows how the Poisson table is used to develop the OC curve for a single-sample plan, n = 80, c = 2. The AQL is at p' = 0.01, the LTPD at p' = 0.066, and the point of indifference is at p' = 0.033. Figure 8 shows the AOQ curve for the same sample plan where the limit is shown at AOQL = 0.017.

The P_a at which the AOQL is found varies with the accept number for the sample plan. For all sample plans where the accept number (c) is equal to 0.

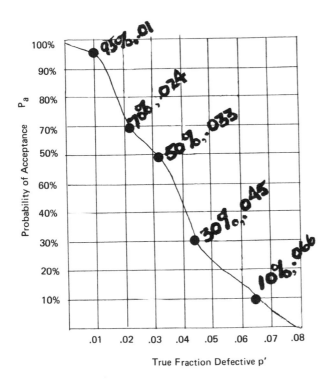

FIGURE 7   (Continued)

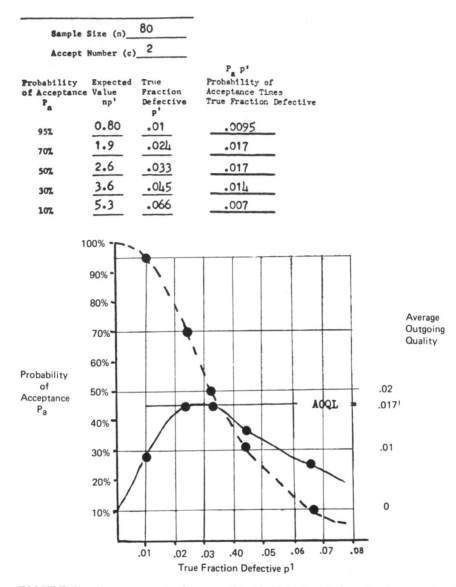

| Sample Size (n) | 80 | | |
| Accept Number (c) | 2 | | |

Probability of Acceptance P_a	Expected Value np'	True Fraction Defective p'	$P_a\ p'$ Probability of Acceptance Times True Fraction Defective
95%	0.80	.01	.0095
70%	1.9	.024	.017
50%	2.6	.033	.017
30%	3.6	.045	.014
10%	5.3	.066	.007

FIGURE 8   Average outgoing quality limit (AOQL) for single-sample plan, n = 80, c = 2.

the AOQL occurs when P_a = 37%. For c = 1, the AOQL is found when P_a = 49%. For c = 2, P_a = 62%. The P_a where the AOQL occurs can be found by finding the limit of the expected value (np') times the P_a for each value of c in the Poisson table. Figure 9 shows how this is done for c = 0, c = 2, and c = 6.

Figure 10 is a tabulation of each of the maximized values of $P_a \cdot$np'. This table works both ways. If the AOQL is desired for a sample plan where n = 200, c = 3, write the 200 in the blank next to 3 in the c column. Dividing the 1.93 in the AOQL generator column by 200 yields 0.00965 or approximately 0.01 as the AOQL for the sample plan. Dividing the AOQL generator by the desired AOQL will give the sample size for the acceptance number in that row for the sample plan associated with the desired AOQL.

Figure 11 is an OC curve approximator which is also useful in determining the AOQL. Three points are given for each accept number. Each point has

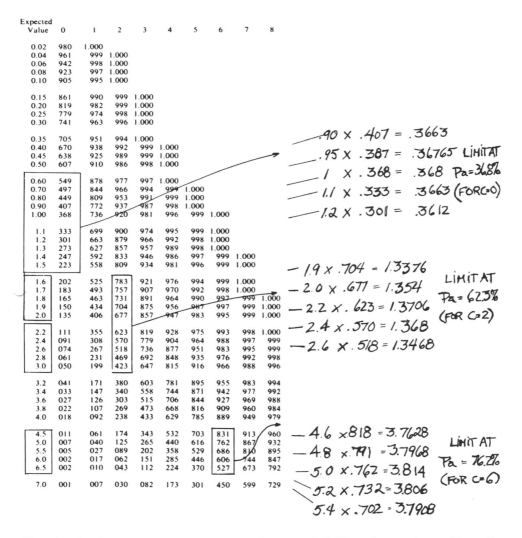

FIGURE 9 Development of the limit of the probability of acceptance times the expected value for selected points.

AOQL Generator (maximum value of $P_a \times np'$)	Desired AOQL ($P_a \times p'$)	Sample size (n) $n = \dfrac{P_a \times np'}{P_a \times p'}$	Acceptance number (c)
0.37	_____	_____	0
0.84	_____	_____	1
1.37	_____	_____	2
1.93	_____	_____	3
2.54	_____	_____	4
3.17	_____	_____	5
3.81	_____	_____	6
4.47	_____	_____	7
5.15	_____	_____	8
5.83	_____	_____	9
6.53	_____	_____	10
7.23	_____	_____	11
7.94	_____	_____	12
8.66	_____	_____	13
9.39	_____	_____	14
10.13	_____	_____	15
10.36	_____	_____	16
11.62	_____	_____	17
12.80	_____	_____	18

Reference: AOQL PLANS OPTIMIZE SAMPLING, Jan. 1977, "Quality."
Used with permission.

FIGURE 10   Average outgoing quality limit approximator.

P_a and np' listed; dividing np' by the sample size n gives p' for each P_a listed. With a little practice, these three points will serve very well for drawing the OC curve for any single-sample plan. Multiplying P_a by p' gives three points for plotting the AOQ curve, and in each case the midpoint of the three was chosen since at that value, $P_a \cdot p'$ gives the approximate AOQL for the sample plan. This is the same AOQL that is found for the same sample plan in MIL-STD-105D. The reason that it is referred to as "approximate" is that MIL-STD-105D requires that you adjust this AOQL by multiplying it by the factor $(1 - n/N)$, where N is the lot size and n is the sample size.

The use of the OC/AOQ approximator is shown in Figs. 12 and 13. Figure 12 compares three sample plans that have the same AQL. Nothing is to be said

n = ____		c = 0	
$P_a \times p'$	P_a	np'	p'
____	.95	.05	____
____	.37	1.0	____
____	.10	2.3	____

n = ____		c = 5	
$P_a \times p'$	P_a	np'	p'
____	.95	2.6	____
____	.72	4.4	____
____	.10	9.3	____

n = ____		c = 10	
$P_a \times p'$	P_a	np'	p'
____	.95	6.2	____
____	.82	8.0	____
____	.10	15.6	____

n = ____		c = 1	
$P_a \times p'$	P_a	np'	p'
____	.95	.35	____
____	.49	1.7	____
____	.10	3.9	____

n = ____		c = 6	
$P_a \times p'$	P_a	np'	p'
____	.95	3.2	____
____	.76	5.0	____
____	.10	10.5	____

n = ____		c = 11	
$P_a \times p'$	P_a	np'	p'
____	.95	6.9	____
____	.85	8.5	____
____	.10	16.4	____

n = ____		c = 2	
$P_a \times p'$	P_a	np'	p'
____	.95	.82	____
____	.62	2.2	____
____	.10	5.3	____

n = ____		c = 7	
$P_a \times p'$	P_a	np'	p'
____	.95	4.0	____
____	.77	5.8	____
____	.10	11.8	____

n = ____		c = 12	
$P_a \times p'$	P_a	np'	p'
____	.95	7.7	____
____	.84	9.5	____
____	.10	18.8	____

n = ____		c = 3	
$P_a \times p'$	P_a	np'	p'
____	.95	1.36	____
____	.65	3.0	____
____	.10	6.7	____

n = ____		c = 8	
$P_a \times p'$	P_a	np'	p'
____	.95	4.7	____
____	.78	6.6	____
____	.10	13.0	____

n = ____		c = 13	
$P_a \times p'$	P_a	np'	p'
____	.95	8.5	____
____	.83	10.5	____
____	.10	19.0	____

n = ____		c = 4	
$P_a \times p'$	P_a	np'	p'
____	.95	1.96	____
____	.71	3.6	____
____	.10	8.0	____

n = ____		c = 9	
$P_a \times p'$	P_a	np'	p'
____	.95	5.4	____
____	.81	7.2	____
____	.10	14.2	____

n = ____		c = 14	
$P_a \times p'$	P_a	np'	p'
____	.95	9.2	____
____	.85	11.0	____
____	.10	20.0	____

Reference: AOQL PLANS OPTIMIZE SAMPLING, Jan. 1977, "Quality."
Used with permission.

FIGURE 11   Operating characteristic curve and average outgoing quality curve approximator.

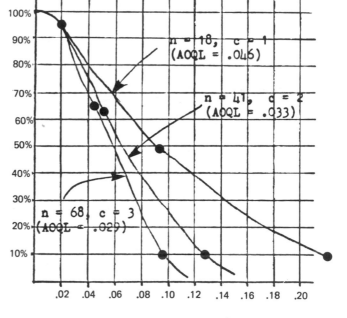

n = *18*   c = 1
P_a X p' P_a np'   p'
            .95   .35   *.0194*
.246 .49   1.7   *.294*
            .10   3.9   *.216*   —— *LTPD*
                                    AQL

n = *41*   c = 2
P_a X p' P_a np'   p'
            .95   .82   *.02*
.033 .62   2.2   *.054*
            .10   5.3   *.129*

n = *68*   c = 3
P_a X p' P_a np'   p'
            .95   1.36   *.02*
.029 .65   3.0   *.044*
            .10   6.7   *.093*

Calculations for
Operating Characteristic
Curves shown

FIGURE 12   Three single-sample plans, all with AQL = 0.02.

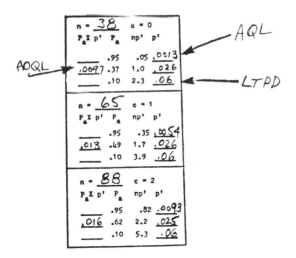

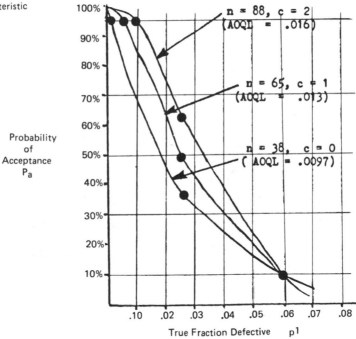

Calculations for
Operating Characteristic
Curves shown

Probability
of
Acceptance
P_a

True Fraction Defective p^1

FIGURE 13   Three single-sample plans, all with LTPD = 0.06.

against AQL plans; however, it is a wise practitioner who can look at the OC curves to choose the plan that is cost/quality-effective. The same statements apply to the LTPD plans compared in Fig. 13.

In any event, Figs. 12 and 13 serve to indicate the ease in using the tables in Fig. 11 to get a clear indication of the AQL, the LTPD, and the AOQL, with a minimum of calculation.

V. DOUBLE-SAMPLE PLANS

Double-sample plans offer one major advantage over single-sample plans. When the incoming quality is very good, the double-sample plan allows acceptance

Expected Value	0	1	2	3	4
0.02	980	1.000			
0.04	961	999	1.000		
0.06	942	998	1.000		
0.08	923	997	1.000		
0.10	905	995	1.000		
0.15	861	990	999	1.000	
0.20	819	982	999	1.000	
0.25	779	974	998	1.000	
0.30	741	963	996	1.000	
0.35	705	951	994	1.000	
0.40	670	938	992	999	1.000
0.45	638	925	989	999	1.000
0.50	607	910	986	998	1.000
0.60	549	878	977	997	1.000
0.70	497	844	966	994	999
0.80	449	809	953	991	999
0.90	407	772	937	987	998
1.00	368	736	920	981	996
1.1	333	699	900	974	995
1.2	301	663	879	966	992
1.3	273	627	857	957	989
1.4	247	592	833	946	986
1.5	223	558	809	934	981
1.6	202	525	783	921	976
1.7	183	493	757	907	970
1.8	165	463	731	891	964
1.9	150	434	704	875	956
2.0	135	406	677	857	947
2.2	111	355	623	819	928
2.4	091	308	570	779	904
2.6	074	267	518	736	877
2.8	061	231	469	692	848
3.0	050	199	423	647	815
3.2	041	171	380	603	781
3.4	033	147	340	558	744
3.6	027	126	303	515	706
3.8	022	107	269	473	668
4.0	018	092	238	433	629
4.5	011	061	174	343	532
5.0	007	040	125	265	440
5.5	005	027	089	202	358
6.0	002	017	062	151	285
6.5	002	010	043	112	224
7.0	001	007	030	082	173
7.5	001	005	021	059	133
8.0	000	003	014	042	100
8.5	000	002	009	030	074
9.0	000	001	006	021	055
9.5	000	001	004	015	040
10.0	000	000	003	010	029

.01 0.8 .809 .991 .186 94.6

.03 2.4 .308 .779 .471 117.7

.05 4.0 .092 .433 .391 107.3

.07 5.6 .024 .191 .167 93.4

.09 ____ ____ ____ ____ ____

FIGURE 14 Average total inspection for double-sample plan compared to equivalent single-sample plan.

based on the first sample. When the incoming quality is very bad, rejection can be based on the first sample. It is only when the quality level is in between that the decision is deferred until a second sample can be examined.

Figure 14 shows a comparison of the average total inspection required for a double-sample plan compared to its equivalent single-sample plan. The single-sample plan is n = 125, c = 2. The dashed line at 125 shows the average total inspection, since the single-sample plan will always require a sample of 125. The Poisson distribution is used to determine how often a second sample will be taken in the double-sample plan. In other words, what percentage of the time will the lot be neither accepted or rejected based on the first sample? The percentage between the accept number and one less than the reject number is taken from the Poisson table for several values of p'. This probability of a second sample is multiplied by the second sample size and added to the first sample size to get the average total inspection for each p'. As predicted, the ATI is lowest when the quality is very good or very bad and as postulated, never is as high as the constant single sample value. (*Note*: One minus the reject number was used to find the upper probability, since this is the last P_a before rejection.)

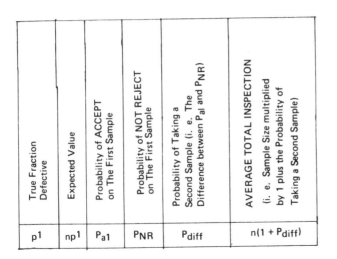

True Fraction Defective	Expected Value	Probability of ACCEPT on The First Sample	Probability of NOT REJECT on The First Sample	Probability of Taking a Second Sample (i. e. The Difference between P_{a1} and P_{NR})	AVERAGE TOTAL INSPECTION (i. e. Sample Size multiplied by 1 plus the Probability of Taking a Second Sample)
p^1	np^1	P_{a1}	P_{NR}	P_{diff}	$n(1 + P_{diff})$

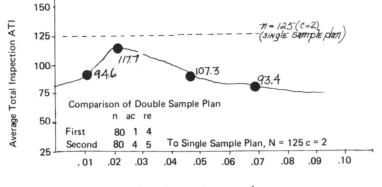

Comparison of Double Sample Plan

	n	ac	re
First	80	1	4
Second	80	4	5

To Single Sample Plan, N = 125 c = 2

True Fraction Defective p^1

FIGURE 14   (Continued)

Multiple sampling will not be discussed here, but multiple sampling offers the same advantages over double sampling as double sampling has over single samples.

The Poisson distribution is a convenient tool for use in determining the OC curve for double-sample plans. Some people think that this can be done by plotting the OC curve for the first sample and then plotting the OC curve for the single-sample plan represented by the total of both samples. Once this is done, you must decide whether to choose the tighter or looser plan as representative.

Figure 15 shows how to use the Poisson distribution to find the OC curve for a double-sample plan:

	n	Ac	Re
First	50	0	3
Second	50	3	4

Since the probability of acceptance is what is being looked for, all ways that the lot may be accepted must be examined.

Expected Value	0	1	2	3	4
0.02	980	1.000			
0.04	961	999	1.000		
0.06	942	998	1.000		
0.08	923	997	1.000		
0.10	905	995	1.000		
0.15	861	990	999	1.000	
0.20	819	982	999	1.000	
0.25	779	974	998	1.000	
0.30	741	963	996	1.000	
0.35	705	951	994	1.000	
0.40	670	938	992	999	1.000
0.45	638	925	989	999	1.000
0.50	607	910	986	998	1.000
0.60	549	878	977	997	1.000
0.70	497	844	966	994	999
0.80	449	809	953	991	999
0.90	407	772	937	987	998
1.00	368	736	920	981	996
1.1	333	699	900	974	995
1.2	301	663	879	966	992
1.3	273	627	857	957	989
1.4	247	592	833	946	986
1.5	223	558	809	934	981
1.6	202	525	783	921	976
1.7	183	493	757	907	970
1.8	165	463	731	891	964
1.9	150	434	704	875	956
2.0	135	406	677	857	947
2.2	111	355	623	819	928
2.4	091	308	570	779	904
2.6	074	267	518	736	877
2.8	061	231	469	692	848
3.0	050	199	423	647	815
3.2	041	171	380	603	781
3.4	033	147	340	558	744
3.6	027	126	303	515	706
3.8	022	107	269	473	668
4.0	018	092	238	433	629

$$p^1 = .01 \quad n = 50$$
$$np^1 = .50$$
$$0 \quad .607 \quad P_0 = .607$$
$$1 \quad .910 \quad P_1 = .303$$
$$2 \quad .986 \quad P_2 = .076$$
$$P_2 + P_1 + P_0 = .986$$
$$P_1 + P_0 = .910$$

$$p^1 = .04 \quad n = 50$$
$$np^1 = 2.0$$
$$0 \quad .135 \quad P_0 = .135$$
$$1 \quad .406 \quad P_1 = .271$$
$$2 \quad .677 \quad P_2 = .271$$
$$P_2 + P_1 + P_0 = .677$$
$$P_1 + P_0 = .406$$

$$p^1 = .08 \quad n = 50$$
$$np^1 = 4.0$$
$$0 \quad .018 \quad P_0 = .018$$
$$1 \quad .092 \quad P_1 = .074$$
$$2 \quad .238 \quad P_2 = .146$$
$$P_2 + P_1 + P_0 = .238$$
$$P_1 + P_0 = .092$$

FIGURE 15   Development of the approximate operating characteristic curve for a double-sample plan using the summation of Poisson terms

The lot may be accepted at once if there are 0 defectives in the first sample of 50. This is identified as P_0.

If there is 1 defective in the first sample of 50, the lot may be accepted if there are 0 or 1 or 2 defectives in the second sample of 50. (This is so since acceptance is allowed when there are 3 defectives in both lots.) This is written $P_1(P_0 + P_1 + P_2)$. Note that the probabilities are not identified as to sample since both samples have n = 50.

If there are 2 defectives in the first sample, the lot may be accepted if there are 0 or 1 defectives in the second sample. This is written $P_2(P_0 + P_1)$.

This concludes the probabilities of acceptance since if there are 3 defectives in the first sample, the lot is rejected.

The general P_a is written as follows:

$$P_a = P_0 + P_1(P_2 + P_1 + P_0) + P_2(P_1 + P_0)$$

Figure 15 shows how the Poisson distribution is used to find the required probabilities for three values of p' and the OC curve is constructed in the

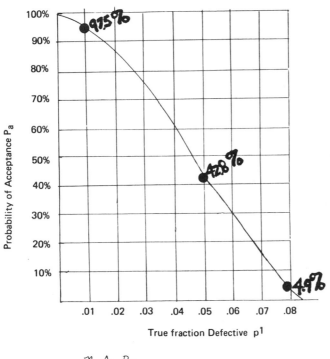

FIRST $\quad n,\ A_c\ R_E$
$\qquad\quad 50\ \ 0\ \ 3$

SECOND $\ 50\ \ 0\ \ 4$

$P_a\ =\ P_0\ +\ P_1\left(P_2 + P_1 + P_0\right) + P_2\left(P_1 + P_0\right) = \underline{\qquad}$

FOR p'=.01, .607 +.303 (.986)+.076(.910) =.975

FOR p'=.04, .135 +.271 (.677) +.271(.406) = .428

FOR p'=.08, .018 +.074 (.238) +.146(.092) = .049

FIGURE 15 (Continued)

Expected Value	0	1	2	3	4	5	6	7	8	9	10	11
0.02	980	1.000										
0.04	961	999	1.000									
0.06	942	998	1.000									
0.08	923	997	1.000									
0.10	905	995	1.000									
0.15	861	990	999	1.000								
0.20	819	982	999	1.000								
0.25	779	974	998	1.000								
0.30	741	963	996	1.000								
0.35	705	951	994	1.000								
0.40	670	938	992	999	1.000							
0.45	638	925	989	999	1.000							
0.50	607	910	986	998	1.000							
0.60	549	878	977	997	1.000							
0.70	497	844	966	994	999	1.000						
0.80	449	809	953	991	999	1.000						
0.90	407	772	937	987	998	1.000						
1.00	368	736	920	981	996	999	1.000					
1.1	333	699	900	974	995	999	1.000					
1.2	301	663	879	966	992	998	1.000					
1.3	273	627	857	957	989	998	1.000					
1.4	247	592	833	946	986	997	999	1.000				
1.5	223	558	809	934	981	996	999	1.000				
1.6	202	525	783	921	976	994	999	1.000				
1.7	183	493	757	907	970	992	998	1.000				
1.8	165	463	731	891	964	990	997	999	1.000			
1.9	150	434	704	875	956	987	997	999	1.000			
2.0	135	406	677	857	947	983	995	999	1.000			
2.2	111	355	623	819	928	975	993	998	1.000			
2.4	091	308	570	779	904	964	988	997	999	1.000		
2.6	074	267	518	736	877	951	983	995	999	1.000		
2.8	061	231	469	692	848	935	976	992	998	999	1.000	
3.0	050	199	423	647	815	916	966	988	996	999	1.000	
3.2	041	171	380	603	781	895	955	983	994	998	1.000	
3.4	033	147	340	558	744	871	942	977	992	997	999	1.000
3.6	027	126	303	515	706	844	927	969	988	996	999	1.000
3.8	022	107	269	473	668	816	909	960	984	994	998	999
4.0	018	092	238	433	629	785	889	949	979	992	997	999
4.5	011	061	174	343	532	703	831	913	960	983	993	998
5.0	007	040	125	265	440	616	762	867	932	968	986	995
5.5	005	027	089	202	358	529	686	810	895	946	975	989
6.0	002	017	062	151	285	446	606	744	847	916	957	980
6.5	002	010	043	112	224	370	527	673	792	876	933	966
7.0	001	007	030	082	173	301	450	599	729	830	901	947
7.5	001	005	021	059	133	242	379	525	662	777	863	921
8.0	000	003	014	042	100	191	313	453	593	717	816	888
8.5	000	002	009	030	074	150	256	386	523	653	763	849
9.0	000	001	006	021	055	116	207	324	456	587	706	803
9.5	000	001	004	015	040	089	165	269	392	522	645	752
10.0	000	000	003	010	029	067	130	220	333	458	583	697

SUMMATION OF POISSON TERMS

(Probability of finding c or less occurrences of an event that has an average number of occurrences as shown in the Expected Value Column at left.)

Decimal points are left out.

c numbers are shown at the top.

FIGURE 16   Summation of terms from the Poisson distribution.   (From E. C. Molina, *Poisson's Exponential Binomial Limit*, D. Van Nostrand Company, Princeton, N.J., 1947.)

conventional manner. Figure 16 shows the general summation of terms for the Poisson.

Construction of the OC curve for double-sample plans differs from single-sample-plan OC curve construction in that here, the various p' values are chosen and multiplied by n to find the expected value, which is used to determine the probabilities used to calculate P_a. Most authorities in the quality field refer to these as B-type probabilities compared to the A type (used for single-sample plans), where P_a is chosen first and p' is derived from the table.

VI. MIL-STD-105D

MIL-STD-105D, or ABC-STD-105D as it is sometimes called (ABC stands for America, Britain, and Canada), is so universal in application that it seems almost unpatriotic to think in terms of using any other sample plan. However, it bodes well to examine any sample plan that is in use, and if the same level of confidence can be had for less total work, or if a better plan can be substituted, this should be done.

MIL-Q-9858A, *Quality Program Requirements*, does not require the use of MIL-STD-105D. Paragraph 6.6 of that document states that any other sample plans shall be subject to government review and "shall provide valid confidence and quality levels." The tools and techniques presented here provide for intelligent comparisons of MIL-STD-105D sample plans and equivalent plans with less total inspection. Please note that MIL-STD-105 has been reproduced and appears in Appendix I.

FURTHER READING

Burr, I. W., *Statistical Quality Control Methods*, Marcel Dekker, New York, 1976.

Feigenbaum, A. V., *Total Quality Control*, 3rd ed., McGraw-Hill, New York, 1983.

Grant, E. L., and R. S. Leavenworth, *Statistical Quality Control*, 5th ed., McGraw-Hill, New York, 1980.

Hayes, G. E., *Quality Assurance: Management and Technology*, rev. ed., 4th printing, Charger Productions, 1980.

Heldt, J. J., *a.k.a. Sam Poisson*, Hitchcock Publishing Company, Wheaton, Ill., 1984.

20

VARIABLES INSPECTION

FRANK H. SQUIRES

Squires Associates
Los Angeles, California

I. INTRODUCTION

There are many books and manuals for the instruction of technicians, but few that give management a sufficiently clear idea of what the technicians are up to. It is not that management needs to go into the technical details, but management should have some insight into why the quality engineers select a particular technique instead of another.

The subject of inspection by attributes or by variables is particularly apt for this purpose. Let us start with a few definitions.

A. Definitions

Variability: The tendency to variation that affects every repetitive process.

Defect: A deviation from specification of a particular quality characteristic (e.g., length, depth, weight, etc.). The deviation may or may not have been caused by variability in the production process.

Defective: A discrete part or product suffering from one or more defects.

Deficiency: A "defect" in a production process causing the production of a proportion of defectives. The deficiency need not necessarily be a condition of the physical process; it may be an error in the planning.

Quality control: Originally referred to as statistical quality control. A body of procedures, including certain statistical techniques, originated by Walter A. Shewhart and colleagues in the 1920s and 1930s, and added to as the occasion required. Their purpose is best expressed by the title of Shewhart's classic text, *Economic Control of Quality of Manufactured Product*, first published in 1931.

Quality assurance: Any and all efforts made to assure that the products of a given company conform to applicable specifications and requirements. Most important, it includes the support of general management and of the operating departmental managers. A company's commitment to quality assurance is usually enshrined in a quality assurance manual, issued over the signature of the chief executive officer. The quality control department, with its procedures—statistical and otherwise—may be thought of as the executive or implemental arm of the quality assurance program.

Inspection by attributes: As defined by MIL-STD-105: "Inspection where-in the unit of product is classified simply as defective or nondefective with respect to a given requirement or set of requirements."

Inspection by variables: As defined by MIL-STD-414: "Inspection where-in a specified quality characteristic of a unit of product is measured on a continuous scale, such as pounds, inches, feet per second, etc., and the measurement is recorded."

B. Example of Inspection by Attributes

One hundred shafts have been submitted for inspection. We decide to inspect only for the diameter, the quality characteristic of primary interest; the survivors will then be inspected for secondary characteristics.

The diameter is specified as 0.500 in. plus or minus 0.002 in. We are concerned only to assure that the diameter of each shaft has the attribute of being not larger than 0.502 in. and not smaller than 0.498 in. We select a go/not-go snap gage having two stages, set at 0.502 and 0.498 in. A shaft will be acceptable if it passes through the first stage (0.502 in.) and not through the second stage (0.498 in.). Incidentally, inspection by attributes is popular with inspectors—indeed, with the trade as a whole—because of its relative simplicity. It is a laborious business to make and to record exact measurement, as in inspection by variables; the competence of the inspector is put to a sharper test than when inspecting by attributes.

The inspection is completed. The results are 85 acceptable, 15 defective. As for the defectives, we know only that the shafts are out of specification; whether they are larger than the high tolerance or smaller than the low tolerance, and by how much, are not known. We proceed with inspection of the secondary attributes and pass the acceptable pieces.

C. Example of Inspection by Variables

Now let us inspect the same 100 shafts by variables. In the selection of an instrument we must keep in mind that few of the shafts will measure exactly 0.498 or 0.499 in. etc. Many will fall in between these major graduations. The instrument must therefore read to the fourth decimal place; for this purpose we select a 1-in. micrometer with a vernier scale.

The shafts are measured; the result is still the same: 85 accept, 15 non-conforming. But now we have 100 measurements. We have the ability to look at the production process through the inspection measurements in the hope of identifying the deficiency that caused the production of 15 nonconforming pieces.

As a first step let us sum the 100 measurements and compute the average. We find the average diameter to be 0.5010 in. At this point we should inter-ject the advice that when inspectors are assigned to inspect by variables, it must be impressed on them that the nonconforming measurements must also be recorded. Otherwise, we would be unable to analyze the process as we are now about to do.

Since the average is on the high side and by such a substantial fraction of the total tolerance, we are almost certain to be right in assuming that it is no accident. This being an outside dimension, it is likely that *the machinist has followed a common practice* and has set up on the high side to avoid the

probability that defectives, if any, will not be smaller than the low tolerance limit. Undersize pieces are earnestly to be avoided since they must
be scrapped, an event likely to expose the machinist to sharp criticism. Oversize pieces can be reworked down to size, which is still not desirable but preferable. The saving of the rejected pieces by rework puts the event in the
category of "All's well that ends well." It is regrettable, but such attitudes
grow out of the anxiety felt by operators and managers on a tight schedule
when confronted by the loss of a substantial fraction of a quantity of urgently
needed parts—and the relief felt when it is discovered that the parts can be
"saved" by rework.

We have found the average of shaft diameters to be off on the high side of
the nominal dimension of 0.500 in. Let us compute the *range*, the difference
between the highest and lowest of the 100 measurements. Let it be 0.0055 in.
We are in more trouble since the total tolerance is only 0.004 in.

II. PROCESS VARIABILITY

We have collided with the great bugbear of repetitive production processes,
the *process variability*. We must check the *pattern of variability* before we
make any further assumptions about the behavior of the process. A frequency
distribution is constructed for this purpose from the 100 measurements. We
find the distribution of variables to be approximately normal (see Fig. 1(a)).
This means that the process has not been affected by "assignable" causes for
variation. For example, had there been two nodes, or a severe distortion of
the normally symmetrical shape, either would have indicated the existence of
an assignable cause for variation. Had this been the case, it would have been
brought to the attention of the machinist and his or her supervisor for correction. A second run would have been made, a sample inspected by variables,
and a frequency distribution plotted which, hopefully, would have been approximately normal.

In contrast with "assignable" causes for variation are "random" or "chance"
causes. These are attributable to the phenomenon of variability. They are
the causes that account for the symmetrical distribution of variables either
side of the average, densely clustered at the average and thinning out toward
the tails.

The standard deviation, a measure of dispersion, must be computed to enable us to make computations based on areas under the normal curve and to
get an estimate of probable future spread. Assume the computed standard
deviation to be 0.0010 in. The standard deviation must be multiplied by 6 to
get an *estimate* of the process "spread" on future runs. Observe that 6
standard deviations is in excess of the range of the 100 measurements, this
figure (0.0060 in.) being a computed estimate based on the sample of 100.

Figure 1(a) illustrates what actually happened as a consequence of the
well-intentioned action of the machinist. We will assume that when we discuss
it with the machine shop supervisor and the machinist, showing them Fig. 1(a)
and explaining it to them, they will agree that that was what was done. Had
it been an inside diameter, the same common practice would have followed in
reverse, the setup being made on the low side of the tolerance to avoid oversize holes, which cannot be reworked. Incidentally, the supervisor and machinist may be seeing a frequency distribution (and the story it so plainly
tells) for the first time. The first reaction tends to be one of skepticism.
Thought should be given in mass production plants to the instruction of inspectors and shop personnel in those statistical methods that apply to their work.

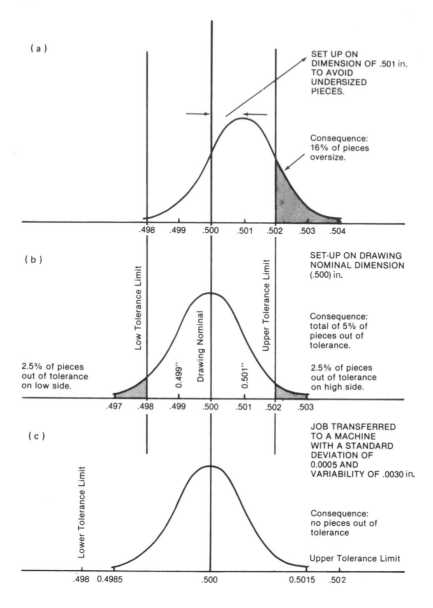

(a)

SET UP ON DIMENSION OF .501 in. TO AVOID UNDERSIZED PIECES.

Consequence: 16% of pieces oversize.

.498 .499 .500 .501 .502 .503 .504

(b)

SET-UP ON DRAWING NOMINAL DIMENSION (.500) in.

Low Tolerance Limit

Upper Tolerance Limit

Drawing Nominal

0.499"

0.501"

Consequence: total of 5% of pieces out of tolerance.

2.5% of pieces out of tolerance on low side.

2.5% of pieces out of tolerance on high side.

.497 .498 .499 .500 .501 .502 .503

(c)

JOB TRANSFERRED TO A MACHINE WITH A STANDARD DEVIATION OF 0.0005 AND VARIABILITY OF .0030 in.

Lower Tolerance Limit

Consequence: no pieces out of tolerance

Upper Tolerance Limit

.498 0.4985 .500 0.5015 .502

FIGURE 1   (a) Setup on dimension of 0.501 in. to avoid undersized pieces. (b) Setup on drawing nominal dimension (0.500 in.). (c) Job transferred to a machine with a standard deviation of 0.0005 in. and a variability of 0.0030 in. (d) Plating process centered on 10 millionths of an inch. (e) Plating process centered 3 standard deviations above the specified minimum of 10 millionths of an inch. (f) Plating process centered 2 standard deviations above the specified minimum of 10 millionths of an inch.

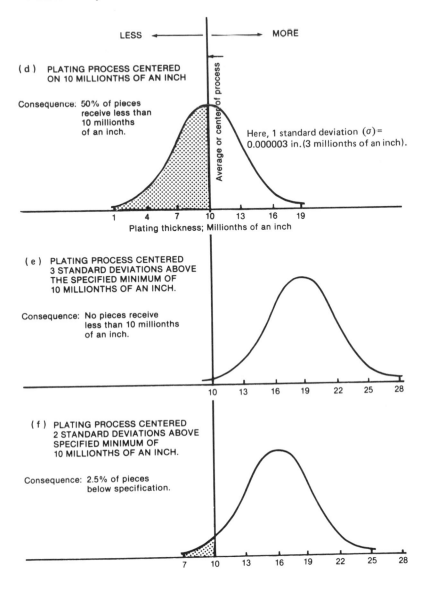

LESS ←——————— ——————→ MORE

(d) PLATING PROCESS CENTERED
ON 10 MILLIONTHS OF AN INCH

Consequence: 50% of pieces
receive less than
10 millionths
of an inch.

Average or center of process

Here, 1 standard deviation (σ) =
0.000003 in. (3 millionths of an inch).

1   4   7   10   13   16   19

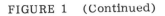
Plating thickness; Millionths of an inch

(e) PLATING PROCESS CENTERED
3 STANDARD DEVIATIONS ABOVE
THE SPECIFIED MINIMUM OF
10 MILLIONTHS OF AN INCH.

Consequence: No pieces receive
less than 10 millionths
of an inch.

10   13   16   19   22   25   28

(f) PLATING PROCESS CENTERED
2 STANDARD DEVIATIONS ABOVE
SPECIFIED MINIMUM OF
10 MILLIONTHS OF AN INCH.

Consequence: 2.5% of pieces
below specification.

7   10   13   16   19   22   25   28

FIGURE 1   (Continued)

Referring to Fig. 1(a), we see that the average of the distribution falls on the measurement 0.5010 in. because the machinist set it up that way. The pattern of variation, the natural "spread" of this particular machine performing this particular task, has moved as a whole to the high side. One "tail" sits on the low tolerance of 0.4980 in., while the other spreads beyond the high tolerance by 0.0020 in. (which in our example is 2 standard deviations).

Process variability exists in every repetitive production process. This variability produces a spread which moves up and down with the adjustments to the setup and should be known to all who work and manage mass production. The fact that it is not may account, in part, for the competitive success of Japan, where such information is available to all those affected by it.

We must find out what process variability means in numbers of defective pieces when the tail or tails of the distribution spread beyond either or both tolerance limits. A measurement in inches must be converted into the z number, the measurement expressed as so many standard deviations. In our case it is simple, since the measurement (0.0020 in. beyond the high tolerance limit) equals 2 standard deviations. Reference to a table of areas under the normal curve indicates that we should expect about 16% of pieces to be oversize, which, in fact, is what happened.

What would have happened had the setup been made right on the nominal dimension of 0.500 in? Referring to Fig. 1(b), we see that the average of the distribution has moved to the left and now coincides exactly with the nominal dimension of 0.500 in. The tails now reach beyond the upper and lower tolerance limits of 0.502 and 0.498 in. The area *under the curve and between the tolerance limits* is now 2 standard deviations either side of the average. Reference to the table of areas under the normal curve informs us that if the adjustment were made, about 95% of the pieces would be acceptable, with about 2.5% below the low tolerance and 2.5% above the high tolerance.

This is what can be learned about the process when inspection is made by variables. We learned that the setup had been deliberately displaced from the drawing nominal toward the high tolerance (although with the best of intentions), and that this machine was not the proper machine for the job because the variability (6 standard deviations) was in excess of the total tolerance on the diameter of the shaft.

III. A RATIONAL PRODUCTION POLICY

Every repetitive production process is afflicted with a natural spread. Therefore, any job should be assigned to a given process only when it is known that the process variability is *less than* the total allowable tolerance indicated on the blueprint.

Figure 1(c) indicates what would happen if the shafts were transferred to another machine. This piece of equipment had been subjected to statistical process analysis so that the process variability of 0.0030 in. (standard deviation of 0.0005 in. × 6) was known to be less than the total specified tolerance of 0.0040 in. *Caution*: Be sure to instruct the shop that the setup must be made on the drawing nominal dimension of 0.500 in.

The foregoing is not a plea for the universal use of inspection by variables. There are many occasions when inspection by attributes will be appropriate. When inspection by attributes has revealed a high proportion of defectives and there are outstanding orders for more of the same parts, the process should be investigated by variables inspection analysis. When an analyzed process and the job assigned to it are statistically matched (i.e., the variability of the process is known to be less than the total tolerance), the production run should be "controlled" by a control chart.

A. Investigation of Gold-Plating Process

To take another example, supplier ABC had secured a valuable contract from XYZ to gold plate large quantities of contacts. The contract specified that there should be not less than 0.000010 in. (10 millionths of an inch) of gold on each contact.

A preliminary run was made with the controls of the continuous plating process set at about 5% over the specified 10 millionths of an inch. Inspection by attributes revealed that a large proportion were well below the minimum of 10 millionths of an inch. No delivery was made. The customer complained bitterly; the completion of a complex device was being held up for lack of contacts.

In desperation the supplier boosted the setup to about 20 millionths of an inch. A sample inspected by attributes found the lot acceptable. They were shipped to the customer's satisfaction, but the supplier was in a panic. With appalling losses confronting management, a consultant was called in.

The consultant asked that a short run be made with the setup on 10 millionths of an inch. A sample of 100 pieces was inspected by variables. The mean of the 100 measurements was 10 millionths of an inch, which spoke well for the operator who made the setup. The standard deviation of the process was computed at 3 millionths of an inch, making the total "spread" of the process due to variability, 18 millionths of an inch. A frequency distribution indicated that the variation was approximately normal, so that the spread of 18 millionths of an inch had to be accepted as an inherent characteristic of the process in its condition at that time. Since the average of the distribution coincided with the specified "not-less-than" 10 millionths of an inch, the test lot was split down the middle, one half acceptable, the remaining half not (see Fig. 1(d)). This was to be expected given the nature and effect of variability in mass production processes.

The supplier's only apparent option was to make the setup 3 standard deviations above 10 millionths of an inch. Figure 1(e) indicates what would have happened had this been done. It should be pointed out that the normal distribution curve is asymptotic. The tails continue on to infinity on either side without dropping to the baseline. The area under ±3 standard deviations either side of the mean is actually 99.74% of the total. Nevertheless, the common practice has been followed of treating this area as 100%.

A conference was arranged between supplier and customer; the results indicated in Fig. 1(d) were studied and their validity was agreed upon. The final agreement was that the setup should be made 2 standard deviations above 10 millionths of an inch, whereby 2.5% of each lot would be below the specification down to 7 millionths of an inch. Figure 1(f) illustrates the situation. The price was adjusted, the method of sampling each lot by variables was agreed upon, and a suitable inspection form for recording the inspection results was drawn up, a copy to be shipped with each lot.

The supplier did more than breathe a vast sigh of relief. A seminar was arranged to instruct all concerned in the mysteries of variability: managers, sales personnel, producers, and inspectors. Something similar happened at the customer's plant.

B. Cadmium Plating

There is another situation that has to be watched carefully, the depositing of
not more than 3 ten-thousandths of an inch of cadmium on steel threads. I
have seen as much as 2 thousandths piled on by platers who thought that
"more was better." The single limit condition is always a problem in mass
production. A general manager might very well ask appropriate members of
the staff: Have we any single limit specifications, and what do we do about
quoting and producing them?

We seem to have spent most of this section on process variability and its
potential for disaster, but no single piece of information is of greater value
to corporations, managers, and operators engaged in mass production. Everybody knows that the purpose of inspection is to sort the good from the bad,
the acceptable from the unacceptable. "Inspection" is understood to mean
inspection by attributes, although the term is rarely used in the workshop.
Far too few know that inspection by variables is the key that may be used
to unlock the door to the phenomenon of variability and its awesome effects
on mass production.

IV. WHO'S RESPONSIBLE?

We have found that inspection by attributes revealed the unwelcome presence
of defectives, and that inspection by variables led us directly to the cause of
the defectives—i.e., process variability. This raises the question of who is at
"fault" for the presence of variability and its propensity for the production of
defectives?

Well, variability is the fault of the universe we inhabit, in which it seems
at times to be the only constant. So the question should read: Whose fault
is it that variability and its occasional dastardly behavior are not known and
allowed for?

Should the machinist know? Machinists acquire their skill during an apprenticeship and on the job. It is possible to learn a great deal on the job;
but one might work a lifetime on machines, constantly aggravated by out-of-
spec parts, and yet not arrive at the conclusion that the cause is, or might
be, an unremovable condition of the machine itself. It is part of the pride of
good machinists that they can make the machine do anything; when defectives
still occur they are more likely to blame themselves; the supervisor will blame
them, too!

Should the shop supervisor know? Should the production superintendent
know? A knowledge of variability has not, so far, been a required qualification for production supervision, although it can be seen that it would be a
great advantage.

Should the quality engineer know? Yes, if there is one. But he or she
cannot be effective unless it is the wish of management. Management cannot
utilize quality engineers with a knowledge of variability unless the managers
themselves are aware of it. General managers—without whose support nothing
can be expected to succeed—do not have to delve into statistical techniques.
They should know that variability is an ineradicable characteristic of repetitive production processes, and that the science of statistical quality control
was developed to measure it. We must conclude, therefore, that management
is responsible for the defectives attributable to variability.

Only the general manager has the authority to promulgate and enforce the
rational production policy mentioned earlier. This is a policy which would

dictate that a job be assigned to a repetitive production process only when it
is known that the total tolerance on the dimension is greater than the known
spread (6 standard deviations) of the process. The edict should designate a
planning manager with authority to deviate in an emergency (a suitable process
is not always available). Even then the quality engineers can assist the planning manager by a prediction of the percentage yield of acceptable parts to
be expected.

I bring up this matter of who is at fault for the incidence of defectives due
to variability because statements have been made in recent years by spokes-
persons for quality control that management is responsible for 60%, 70%, or
even 80% of defects. Whatever the exact figure may be in a given plant, it is
certain that some proportion of defects must be attributed to management.
Failure to deal with variability, or even to be uninformed on the subject, is
an example.

A. Effect of Schedule

What other management fault might there be? There is the schedule. Scheduling is typically over optimistic. The evidence is the frequency with which
the monthly schedule is not met. This happens in large and small production
and construction. Indeed, instances of large schedule slippages are quoted
on the airwaves all too often. I characterize overly optimistic scheduling as
"Sisyphustian" scheduling, in memory of the poor Greek demigod Sisyphus,
who offended Zeus; he was condemned to push an immense rock up a hill.
When he got to the top it rolled down to the bottom, he pushed it up, and down
it came again, and up and down and so on through all eternity. Poor Sisyphus
couldn't win, and neither can many a production manager who battles month
after month with schedules beyond the known resources of the company.

The rationale for such scheduling is that people work best when motivated
by a goal just out of reach. That may be; it is in line with the slogan: "The
difficult we do immediately. The impossible will take a little longer." One
often wishes that the merely difficult might be accomplished this week, or even
in the foreseeable future.

However, what are the effects of Sisyphustian scheduling on quality? Often
disastrous! It may be impossible to grasp what it is really like to be in work
areas where the schedule is slipping, unless one has been there and has had
some responsibility for the schedule. The supervisors are impatient with any
question about quality; indeed, they sometimes border on the manic. Operators are well aware of the tension in the air and raise no question about quality unless it be an error so gross that even a manic supervisor must agree that
it should be rejected. The expeditors from production control are on the backs
of everybody; if an inspector should pause for a moment to decide whether a
given part should or should not be rejected, one or more expeditors will pounce
upon him or her. It is an intimidating situation; the inspectors, unwilling to
be condemned as "nitpickers," become tolerant of the borderline case. No
single instance may be critical, but the accumulation of many dimensions just
over the borderline of the tolerance can spell disaster. Everyone is obsessed
with the schedule; it is not that anybody is against quality; they are all for
quantity. Whose "fault" is over optimistic scheduling? Management's.

Can the quality engineers do anything about the schedule? Yes, they can
and do disseminate the *statistics of schedule interruption*. For example, they
may report that the average percentage of lots of purchased material rejected
during the previous 3 months was, say, 8%. The average rejection rate in the

machine shop may have been 4%; on the assembly lines the average may have been, say, 7 defects per assembly, or more for the complex product, and so on. These figures should be factored into the schedule; too often they are not. The overly optimistic are sure that "things will be better this month!" The facts of schedule interruption are disregarded once again and will continue to be pushed aside until management steps in.

B. Effect of Technology

Although the situation is not quite that clearcut, *technology* is also a cause of defects that can be attributed to management. By "technology" I mean the propensity of designers to be constantly advancing the state of the art of design. This may necessitate an advance in the state of the art of production. For example, design changes may call for tolerances to the fourth decimal place when the shop is capable of holding dimensions to the third place, or to the fifth place when the current state of the art is the fourth place, and so on. Not only may new designs be beyond the capability of production, necessitating a frantic search for suppliers who may have the capability, but schedule and costs are thrown into confusion, with inevitable countereffects on quality.

General management cannot tell the designers to stand still, but their propensity for pushing the state of the art should be kept in mind. Many products are excellent for their purpose as they now exist. It would be most profitable to be able to make them in large numbers with the design as is. Engineering fervor could be directed toward the development of a substantially new design for the future market. Anyway, let management keep in mind that interruptions and confusion caused by schedule slippage and the constant interjection of design changes all tend to be detrimental to quality. Variability, schedule, and technology: all must be controlled.

FURTHER READING

Dodge, H. F., and H. G. Romig, *Sampling Inspection Tables*, 2nd ed., Wiley, New York, 1967.

Grant, E. L., and R. S. Leavenworth, *Statistical Quality Control*, 5th ed., McGraw-Hill, New York, 1980.

Ishikawa, K., *Guide to Quality Control*, Asian Productivity Organisation, Tokyo, 1976.

Juran, J. M., Editor-in-Chief, *Quality Control Handbook*, 3rd ed., McGraw-Hill, New York, 1974.

MIL-STD-105D, *Sampling Procedures and Tables for Inspection by Attributes*.

Peach, P., *Quality Control for Management*, Prentice-Hall, Englewood Cliffs, N.J., 1964.

Shewhart, W. A., *Economic Control of Quality of Manufactured Product*, D. Van Nostrand Company, Princeton, N.J., 1931.

Shewhart, W. A., in *Statistical Method from the Viewpoint of Quality Control*, W. E. Deming, ed., Lancaster Press, Lancaster, Pa., 1945 reprint.

21

MILITARY STANDARD 105D FOR THE LAYMAN

FRANK H. SQUIRES

Squires Associates
Los Angeles, California

I. INTRODUCTION

The official title of the standard MIL-STD-105D is *Sampling Procedures and Tables for Inspection by Attributes*. It is recommended that the copy of the standard included in the appendix to this chapter be referred to frequently. By reference during the discussion, the student, engineer, inspector, manager, or executive will become familiar with the standard and confident in its use.

Note the following comments and definitions.

1. The sampling plans were prepared for the military, but they are universally applicable. They are based on the laws of probability, which draw no distinction between military equipment and health supplies.
2. We will trust the statisticians who prepared them for the statistical validity and concentrate on their use as a ready-made tool of great value.
3. A quality characteristic may be thought of as an attribute or as a variable. Consider the diameter of a shaft. It is specified as 1.000 ± 0.002 in. As an attribute, the concern is whether the diameter lies between the limits of 0.998 and 1.002 in., or does not. Hence a go/not-go snap gage may be used. As a variable it would be required to measure the actual diameter, for example, 0.999 in., 1.001 in.
4. Inspection by attributes is appropriate for the acceptance of finished or partially finished items. Inspection by variables is appropriate when, in addition to deciding on acceptability of the lot, the production process from which the lot was drawn must be investigated. More on sampling inspection by variables can be found in MIL-STD-414.
5. MIL-STD-105D is also known as the international standard, ABC-105. In the early 1960s, statisticians from military procurement agencies of America, Britain, and Canada revised MIL-STD-105C for the

purpose of making available a common set of sampling plans. They produced the D revision for domestic use, and ABC-105 for international use.

6. The sampling plans in MIL-STD-105D are indexed to the AQL. The Dodge-Romig sampling plans are indexed to the LTPD and AOQL. The intent of the designers of MIL-STD-105D was to minimize the producer's risk. The intent of Dodge and Romig was to minimize the consumer's risk.

7. The producer's risk is the probability of the rejection of a good lot by sampling. "Good" means as good as, or better than, the AQL specified.

8. The consumer's risk is the probability of the acceptance of a bad lot by sampling. B means worse than the specified AQL. Both producer's risk and consumer's risk, terms originated by Dodge-Romig, are ineradicable features of every sampling plan. Expertise in the selection and use of sampling plans is manifested by knowledge of, and the ability to determine, the producer's and consumer's risks for any sampling plan.

9. In MIL-STD-105D: "The AQL is a designated value of percent defective (or defects per hundred units) that the consumer indicates shall be accepted most of the time by the acceptance sampling procedure."

10. A defective is a discrete item in which there are one or more non-conforming quality characteristics. A defect is a quality characteristic not in conformance with specification. Hence, when sampling by percent defective, we shall count defectives found in the sample. When inspecting by defects per 100 units, we shall count defects.

11. There are several preliminary steps which must be taken when the decision has been made to inspect by sampling. The lot size (Symbol N) is one of these steps that must be designated. It is specified by MIL-STD-105D that the lot "shall consist of product of a single type, grade, class, size, and composition, manufactured under essentially the same conditions and at essentially the same time."

12. The sample size (n) is number of units that must be drawn at random from the lot.

13. The acceptance number (c) is the permissible maximum number of defectives (or defects) that may be found in the sample to allow acceptance of the balance of the lot without further inspection.

14. The rejection number (d) is the smallest number of defectives (or defects) which, when found in the sample, is cause for the rejection of the balance of the lot. Since the majority of sampling is done with single-sampling plans, the rejection number is understood to be c + 1 and is not quoted. A sampling plan is typically defined by stating the sample size, n, and acceptance number, c. There are occasions when there is a difference of more than 1 between acceptance and rejection numbers; these will be pointed out in the anatomy of a sampling plan.

15. Degrees of severity of inspection are referred to as general inspection levels, designated by Roman numerals I, II, and III (see MIL-STD-105D, p. 9).

16. Further degrees of severity of inspection can be chosen from normal, tightened, and reduced sampling plans. This is a convenient time

to correct a common error. Inspection levels I and III are not reduced and tightened in relation to level II.

17. Special inspection levels include degrees of severity for use when
relatively small samples are necessary as, for example, when the
inspection is destructive. These are designated S-1 to S-4.

18. As the name implies, a simple sampling plan allows for the drawing
of one sample only, with one chance for acceptance or rejection.
Because of its simplicity, this is by far the most popular plan.

19. Double- and multiple-sampling plans allow the drawing of two or
seven samples, respectively, with a chance of acceptance (or rejection) on the first sample. In the long run there is a substantial
reduction in the amount of physical inspection that must be done to
decide for acceptance or rejection on a series of lots. Nevertheless,
there is too little of both done, the reason advanced being "administrative difficulty." This is a somewhat euphemistic way of saying
that it is too difficult to spell out to the inspectors what they have
to do. However, the benefits are such that it is worth a try.

20. Any given sampling plan may be defined as single, double, or multiple; normal, tightened, or reduced; inspection level I, II, or III;
or S-1 through S-4. Circumstances will dictate which combination
is appropriate, but all combinations are possible.

II. ANATOMY OF A SAMPLING PLAN

Assume that lots of 1000 of a given part are received with a delivery schedule
of one lot per week. These lots may be inspected 100% or sampled. Since
sampling will reduce the cost of inspection, why hesitate? Because to sample,
an AQL value must be selected. The AQL, a percent defective, is an indication of the percentage of nonconforming parts that can be tolerated in accepted
lots.

Who is to select the AQL? This is typically done by the statistical quality
control section of quality assurance, with assistance from design engineering.
Why the input from design? Because the part, or those quality characteristics
of the part to be inspected, must be classified. Classification of materials for
military use may be critical, major, or minor; these are defined on page 2 of
MIL-STD-105D. Assuming that the parts are for the commercial market, one
is not compelled to adopt the government's standard. However, classification
grades appropriate to the product must be developed and recorded in the organization's quality control manual.

III. MANAGEMENT SANCTION

It can be seen that lots accepted by sampling may include a number of nonconforming parts. This may be true even when the permissible number of nonconforming parts in the sample for acceptance is *zero*. It is essential that
management sanction the use of acceptance sampling; it should be detailed in
the quality assurance manual, which is authorized as a standard operating
procedure by the general manager's signature on the title page. This recommendation is made because although all managers are aware of the economy in
the cost of inspection and production effected by sampling, all are not aware

that the cost of the cost reduction is the probability of some nonconforming parts in accepted lots.

IV. SELECTION OF THE SAMPLING PLAN

It is agreed to sample. The part has been classified major (the alternatives being critical, major, minor, and superficial); the AQL selected is 1% defective; inspection level II, single, normal. If the customer were the military, it would be required to start at level II, unless otherwise agreed. It is not required in commercial work, but start at level II anyway because it is a good place to start. When it is found what kind of quality the supplier is sending in, sampling may go to reduced or tightened.

With a lot size of 1000, and an AQL of 1%, the sample-size code letter is required. Go to MIL-STD-105D (p. 9). The lot size of 1000 is in the group 501 to 1200. On that row and under column heading II is the code letter, J. Go to MIL-STD-105D (p. 10) to determine the sample size and acceptance number. On row J is the sample size, 80, and under the column headed 1.0 is the acceptance number, 2, and rejection number, 3.

V. INSPECTION

The first lot arrives; the inspector draws the sample of 80, inspects each individual part in the sample, finds 1 defective, and accepts the balance of the lot without further inspection. The sample, minus the defective, is returned to the lot. The quality of the accepted lot, as one may surmise, may be 1% defective or greater or less—the truth is that we do not know.

This is somewhat disturbing, but bear in mind that this is lot-by-lot inspection. Assume that when the next lot arrives it is sampled; 2 defectives are found and the lot is accepted.

The third lot arrives; 4 defectives are found and the lot is rejected. What to do? The lot may be returned to the supplier with instructions to screen the lot 100%. But again, a policy should be made. Screening in-house will cost more than anticipated, but there will be an excellent opportunity of finding out just what kind of quality is being supplied.

Screening reveals another 9 defectives. The quality (13 defectives in 1000) is running close to the required 1%.

The screened lot, minus the 13 defectives, is now 100% good. When this screened lot is added to the accumulating inventory it counteracts the quality of accepted lots that may have been worse than 1% defective. So it continues week by week; more lots are accepted than are rejected; rejected lots are screened and go into the inventory 100% good.

VI. AVERAGE OUTGOING QUALITY LIMIT (AOQL)

The accumulating inventory mix acquires an average outgoing quality (AOQ). This AOQ acquires a "limit," as rejected lots have been screened and defectives found in both the samples and screened lots have been replaced. Assuming that about 10 lots have been inspected, finding more acceptable than rejectable, what is the AOQL?

Go to MIL-STD-105D (p. 22). On row J and at its intersection with column 1.0 is the factor 1.7. The factor is converted to the AOQL by multiplying it by (1 − sample size/lot size), in this case 0.92. Hence the AOQL equals 1.57% defective. This is the worst value of the average outgoing quality provided that the screening of rejected lots has been done meticulously.

This procedure was originally developed by Dodge-Romig, and called for replacement of defectives found in samples and screened lots. However, in the 1967 reissue of the Dodge-Romig tables [1] there is a footnote on page 23 which states that lack of replacement makes too small a difference to be of any practical significance and may therefore be omitted when expedient.

A switch to tightened inspection will assure that the value of the AOQL will approximate the selected AQL. For this purpose go to MIL-STD-105D (p. 11) on row J and find the same sample size of 80, but under column 1.0 the acceptance number has been reduced from 2 to 1. The benefit is found on MIL-STD-105 D (p. 23), where on row J and under column 1.0 is the factor 1.1, which when multiplied by 0.92, is reduced to 1.012% defective. This is near enough to the selected AQL of 1%. In general, it will be found that when engaged in lot-by-lot inspection, the AOQL will approximate the selected AQL by using the tightened sampling plan.

VII. PRODUCER'S RISK

In the sampling plan N = 1,000, AQL = 1% defective, n = 80, c = 2, inspection level II, single, normal, there exists a probability that a good lot may be rejected. Assume the lot to be exactly 1% defective; then there will be 10 defectives in the lot of 1000. Hence it is possible that a random sample of 80 may pick up 3 or more defectives. The statistics are needed to determine the probability.

MIL-STD-105D (p. 46) is the family of operating characteristic curves for code letter J, sample size 80. The third curve from the left is marked 1.0. The horizontal axis is scaled for "submitted quality," the vertical axis for "probability of acceptance."

Enter the chart at 1 on the horizontal axis. Then follow the ordinate up to the point of intersection with curve 1.0 and from the point of intersection move left to the vertical axis. The vertical axis is intersected at 95. Since this indicates a 95% probability of acceptance, the probability of rejection is 5%. The numerical value of the producer's risk is symbolized as the alpha risk: hence 5% alpha risk.

Switching to the tightened plan assures that the AOQL will approximate the selected AQL of 1%. What happened to the producer's risk? Now refer to the tabulation below the curves. Observe that the column headings are for AQLs, normal inspection, while the numbers at the feet of the columns are for AQLs, tightened inspection. Hence the required curve is the one marked 0.65, since it is at the head of the column having 1.0 at its foot.

The intersection between curve 0.65 and the ordinate 1, when extended to the left, hits the vertical axis at 80% probability of acceptance; thus the alpha risk is 20%. Everything was equal except that the acceptance number was reduced from 2 to 1, yet it raised the probability of the rejection of a good lot from 5% to 20%. Which provides a general rule: All other things being equal, a reduction in the size of the acceptance number increases the probability of the rejection of good lots. An increase in the sample size, all other things remaining the same, would have the same effect.

VIII. TABULATION DIVISION

Observe on MIL-STD-105D (p. 46) the heavy line dividing the tabulation between columns 10 and 0.15. The column headings to the left of the dividing
line are for AQLs in percent defective; the column headings to the right of the
line are for AQLs in defects per 100 units.

The tabulation to the left of the line and the curves apply to AQLs in percent defective; the tabulation to the right of the line applies to plans based on
defects per 100 units only.

Observe in MIL-STD-105D that the tabulations are divided for code letters
A through J (pp. 20—46). The tabulations for code letters K through R
(pp. 48—60) are not divided; the curves and tabulation apply equally to AQL
percent and defects per 100-unit plans.

IX. CONSUMER'S RISK

The probability that the consumer may accept a lot worse than 1% defective
must now be confronted. Assume that the lot is as bad as 4% defective. There
will be 40 defectives in the lot, but there will still be 960 good pieces. The
sample of 80 might still pick up 2, or 1, or 0 defectives, thereby indicating
that we should accept the lot. What is the probability?

Again we appeal to the OC curve, MIL-STD-105D (p. 46). Enter the chart
at 4 on the horizontal axis, and follow the ordinate up to the point of intersection with the 1.0 curve. Then move to the left to the vertical axis. This
indicates that the probability is about 37%.

A. Dodge-Romig 5% and 10% Risks

It is customary, when specifying the consumer's risk, to indicate the quality
that may be accepted at a risk of 5% or 10%. What quality might be accepted
at a risk of 10%?

Enter the chart MIL-STD-105D (p. 46) at 10 on the vertical axis, continue
over to the point of intersection with the 1.0 curve, and drop to the horizontal
axis. This indicates a quality of 6.5% defective.

B. Caution Concerning OC Curves and Murphy's Law

OC curves indicate that certain events may occur; some are as startling as the
discovery that a 1% AQL plan may accept a lot as bad as 6.5% defective; Mur-
phy's law states that if an adverse event can occur, it will.

It is quite a common belief that one out of every 10 lots will be 6.5% defective. It will happen if, and only if, a lot as bad as 6.5% defective is submitted.
A supplier would have to be badly out of control for this to happen. But even
then there would be a 90% chance of rejection.

What would happen if sampling was done with the tightened plan of n = 80
and c = 1? Again, enter the chart at 10 on the vertical axis and move across
to the point of intersection with the 0.65 curve (tightened 1%). The quality
that might be accepted at 10% risk is now down to about 4.8% defective.

This change in the value of the quality that might be accepted at a risk of
10% (or any other stated risk) as a consequence of changing the acceptance
number provides us with another general rule. Any single change in the

specification of the sampling plan for a given set of conditions that "favors" the consumer (or supplier) will "disfavor" the supplier (or consumer).

By changing the acceptance number from 2 to 1, the producer "suffered" an increase in the likelihood of the rejection of good lots from 5% to 20%, whereas the consumer benefited by a reduction in the worst quality that might be accepted at 10% risk.

The worst quality that might be accepted at a stated risk is referred to by Dodge-Romig as the LTPD (lot tolerance percent defective) and by MIL-STD-105D as the LQ (limiting quality) MIL-STD-105D (p. 24). The term "worst quality" is favored because it means something to the layperson. The LTPD and LQ are esoteric terms which have to be laboriously explained. The numerical value of the risk is symbolized as the beta risk.

X. SAMPLING ECONOMICS

It is obvious that less inspection is being done, but how much less? Assume that 100 lots have been inspected. The inspectors would have handled 100,000 pieces if 100% inspection had been done. Assume that they were sampled at the normal condition and an alpha risk of 5% and that five lots had to be screened 100%. Then there would have been inspected a sample of 80 out of each of 95 lots (80 times 95 = 7600) and 5000 units would have been screened, for a total of 12,600. The ratio of the cost of 100% inspection to sampling (with this particular plan) is 100 to 12.6, say 100 to 13. It is the difference between employing 13 inspectors or 100. It is a salutary experience to apply this ratio or the applicable ratio to your own inspection force.

Had the tightened plan been used with an alpha risk of 20%, the ratio would have been 100 to 26.4, say 27, which is still a substantial saving in the cost of inspection.

A. Doubling Sampling

Consider that double sampling is to be used. The lot size is still 1000 and the AQL is 1% defective. The code letter is still J, the inspection level is II, and the plan will still be normal. Refer to MIL-STD-105D (p. 13). On row J are two samples of 50 each. On row J and under column 1.0 is the first pair of accept (Ac.) and reject (Re.) numbers. For the first sample of 50, they are 0 (zero) and 3. Hence, if the first sample of 50 drawn from the lot of 1000 should contain no defectives, the balance of the lot is accepted and the inspection is finished. If one or two defectives are found, the second sample of 50 is drawn. If the cumulative sum of defectives found in both samples does not exceed 3, the lot is accepted.

If three defectives (the acceptance number for the cumulative sum) is found in the first sample the recommendation of MIL-STD-105D is that the lot be rejected. However, hope springs eternal in the minds of inspectors as in other classes of the population, and the tendency is to draw the second sample in the hope that no defectives will be found, and the lot accepted. Generally, it is a vain hope.

The producer's risk and the consumer's risk are the same as for the single plan. The OC curves are true for single normal plans; they are approximately true for double and multiple plans.

B. Multiple Sampling

With the same requirements, let us find the conditions for multiple sampling. Refer to MIL-STD-105D (p. 16), where, on row J and under column 1.0 we find Ac. No. # and Re. No. 2, which means that even if no defectives are found in the first sample of 20, the lot cannot be accepted. However, the tables are saying that if two defectives are found in the first sample, it will save a lot of time to stop inspecting and reject the lot.

If 0 or 1 defective is found, the second sample of 20 is drawn and inspected. On this row the Ac. No. is 0, and the Re. No. is 3. Therefore, accept the lot if there are 0 defectives in the first two samples of 20 each. It is rare that inspection has to proceed to the seventh sample before a decision can be made.

Observe that with single sampling, 80 units had to be inspected before a decision could be made. With double sampling, it might have been made on the findings of a sample of 50. With multiple sampling the decision could be made on a sample of 40.

C. Benefits

Turn to MIL-STD-105 (p. 29). The key to the correct curve for any given double or multiple plan is the Ac. No. for the corresponding single plan. Hence the curve of interest is the second from the left on the top line. The Ac. No. of 2 is in the lower right corner. The vertical axes of the curves are scaled 1/4, 1/2, and 3/4 of the amount of sampling necessary with single sampling. To enter the curve on the horizontal axis take n times the proportion defective, where n is the single sample size: thus 80×0.01, which equals 0.8. There is an arrow at that point. Follow the arrow up to the points of intersection with both curves and extend to the left. It appears that with double sampling, and in the long run, the amount of physical inspection required will be about 80% of that required for single sampling; with multiple sampling, in the long run, the amount required will be about 67% of the volume of inspection required by single sampling. It is obviously worth the try to instruct the inspectors in the administrative details of double and multiple sampling.

D. Tightened and Reduced Sampling as Punishment and Reward

The tightened plan was reverted to assure that the AOQL would approximate the specified AQL. As the standard is administered by the military agency DCAS (Defense Contract Administrative Services), and assuming that a contractor is sampling lot by lot with a normal plan, the contractor may be switched to tightened if two out of five consecutive lots are rejected on normal sampling.

To get back on to normal, five consecutive lots must be found acceptable. The lots referred to must be lots receiving the original inspection; they cannot be reworked lots.

The switch to reduce in MIL-STD-105D requires that the following conditions be fulfilled:

The preceding 10 lots or more on normal inspection have been accepted on original inspection.
The total number of defectives (or defects) in the samples of the previous 10 lots shall be equal to, or less than, the number given in Table VIII, MIL-STD-105D (p. 28).

Production is at a steady rate.
Reduced inspection is considered desirable by the responsible authority.

What would the sum of defectives found in 10 previous samples have to be equal to or less than? Refer to MIL-STD-105D (p. 28). Since the previous 10 lots were acceptable, we would have inspected 10 lots of 80 each, for a total of 800. Hence enter the chart at row 800-1249. On that row and in column 1.0 is the number required; it is 4. It may fairly be said that it is almost as difficult to switch to reduced as for a camel to crawl through the eye of a needle. Indeed, it was the intention of the designers of the D revision that the quality would have to be better than the specified AQL to quality for the switch to reduced.

Refer to MIL-STD-105D (p. 12): On row J the sample size has been reduced to 32; under column 1.0 on row J we find Ac. No. 1 and Re. No. 3.

Why the gap between 1 and 3? Reduced inspection will continue as long as consecutive lots on original inspection are accepted. The first lot, in the sample of which 3 or more defectives are found, will be rejected and normal inspection must be resumed. If 2 defectives are found in a sample of 32, the lot is accepted, but return to normal.

There is no reason why a commercial producer should not impose the switching procedure on operations. Although the prime intent of inspection by attributes is to determine acceptability, inferences about the process may still be drawn. When two out of five consecutive lots are rejected by a normal sampling plan, it is an indication that the average quality level has fallen and that the process should be investigated. In the meantime, the sampling plan may be tightened up to protect the consumer. The switch to reduced sampling is a well-earned reward for exceptional quality work on the part of production.

XI. SMALL AQLs

Let it be assumed that quality control and design assign the AQL 0.065% because of the critical nature of a particular characteristic of the part. Lot size is 1000, the plan will be single, normal, inspection level II. MIL-STD-105D (p. 9) provides code letter J. MIL-STD-105D (p. 10), at the intersection of row J and column 0.065, contains an arrow pointing down. The arrow must be followed down to the first set of Ac. and Re. numbers (i.e., to 0 and 1 on row L).

It is a common error to retain the original sample size (of 80 in our sample). The entire plan must be adopted. Hence the sample size and Ac. No. will be 200 and 0. By the same token, the entire plan above the arrowhead must be adopted when it is necessary to follow an arrow up.

XII. PROTECTING THE CONSUMER FROM THE RISK OF SINGLE-LOT SAMPLING

There are many occasions when there is concern with one lot only. A 1% AQL sampling plan may accept a lot as bad as 6.5% defective at 10% beta risk. What can be done to improve the quality at 10% beta? The plan can be indexed to a selected "worst quality." Let the selected worst quality be 2%. Refer to MIL-STD-105D (p. 24). Observe the quality of 1.8% at the intersection of row K and column 0.10. This is near enough to 2%; it would provide a sample size of 125 and an acceptance number of 0; see MIL-STD-105D (p. 10).

It is desirable to find plans with an acceptance number greater than zero to minimize the probability of rejecting a good lot. Again referring to MIL-STD-105D (p. 24), the worst quality at 10% beta would be 2% exactly, with a sample size 200. This plan would require an acceptance number of 1; see MIL-STD-105D (p. 10).

Again, the quality 2.1% at the intersection of row M and column 0.40, MIL-STD-105D (p. 10), provides the acceptance number 3 at the intersection row M and column 0.40.

Thus there are three possible plans:

1.   1.8% worst quality, LTPD or L.Q. at 10% beta: n = 125, c = 0
2.   2.0% worst quality, LTPD or L.Q. at 10% beta: n = 100, c = 1
3.   2.1% worst quality, LTPD or L.Q. at 10% beta: n = 315, c = 3

Dodge-Romig developed their LTPD tables while working within Western Electric for Bell Laboratories, both a part of AT&T. They were concerned to assure a knowledge of the worst quality that might be accepted, and equally concerned to minimize as far as possible the probability that bad lots might be accepted.

Checking with Dodge-Romig, a plan for 2% LTPD at 10% beta is found on page 183 of the 1967 issue. Dodge-Romig offer six plans for lot sizes between 801 and 1000, the sample size getting increasingly larger from left to right. The smaller sample sizes may be used only when the process average is known. Since this is a single lot that is about to be inspected and since the process average is not known, we take the plan from the far right column. It is sample size 301, acceptance number 3.

This is close to the plan of 314 and 3 for an LTPD of 2.1% which we found in MIL-STD-105D. This example has demonstrated that although the plans in MIL-STD-105D are indexed for the AQL, they can be used to obtain a sampling plan for a situation in which the worst quality, or LTPD at a stated risk of acceptance, is specified.

XIII. DEFECTS PER HUNDRED UNITS (D/100u)

While anatomizing the percent defective sampling plan, we have proceeded as though each discrete unit of inspection had only the quality characteristic classified as "major." In practice, there might have been two, three, or four other characteristics which might have been classified "minor" and for which a 2.5% AQL plan might have been selected. The lot might then have been sampled for the major characteristic at 1% AQL; if it survived, the lot might then have been sampled at 2.5% AQL for the minor characteristics.

This raises the question: When is a part defective as far as the minor characteristics are concerned? When all three characteristics are out of specification? Yes, but the part is also defective if only one is out of specification.

If may be desired to "lump" the inspections into one plan. A proper regard for the quality would then prescribe that the applicable AQL would be 1%. In that case, each unit in the sample would be inspected for four characteristics, one major and three minor. A part would be considered defective if any one of the four was out of specification. Each individual piece in the sample would be in jeopardy four times. If the inspection of minor characteristics were conducted separately, each piece would be in jeopardy three times.

The inspection of more than one characteristic on each unit of a sample in percent defective sampling has the effect of increasing the sample size: that is, when two or more characteristics are inspected within one AQL.

It is customary procedure and is done every day. It emphasizes how precisely the inspection sampling instruction must be written, (e.g., "Inspect the following characteristics on each unit of the sample. Consider a piece defective if one or more are out of specification").

However, it is obvious that there must be a limit, although the limit of characteristics that may be examined on one unit of inspection in percent defective sampling remains a matter of debate. Consider characteristics of large products that may be classified minor or superficial, and of which there may be scores or hundreds. Examples of such products are airplanes, trucks, railroad cars, lumber, and foodstuffs.

Consider a lot of 12 planes submitted to the potential consumer for acceptance. Flying and safety characteristics will be meticulously inspected 100%. But there are many minor characteristics, upholstery for example, which must be inspected, for which a sampling plan would be appropriate.

Let there be 300 such minor characteristics on each plane. Each quality characteristic is a potential defect. How many potential defects are there in 100 units? 30,000.

What percentage of these may be out of specification? Zero percent would be preferred but since it is proposed to sample, a number must be chosen. Let it be 1%. Since 300 is 1% of 30,000, the sampling plan selected is 300D/100u.

Refer to MIL-STD-105D (p. 9) for the code letter. Let the plan be inspection level II, single, normal. Hence the code letter is B (rows 9 to 15, column II). Refer to MIL-STD-105D (p. 10) for sample size and acceptance number of defects (not defectives). Now a closer look must be taken at MIL-STD-105D (p. 10). Observe that the column headings run from 0.010 at the extreme left to 1000 at the extreme right.

From end to end, any one of the columns may be used for AQLs based on 100D/100u. But the columns are applicable to percent defective plans only from 0.010 to 10. Percent defective plans provided by MIL-STD-105D do not go higher than 10%. Reference to the column heading in MIL-STD-105D (p. 10) reveal that there is no heading 300. The custom is to use the next lower number in such a circumstance.

The plan 250D/100u will be used with sample size 3 and an acceptance number of 14 defects. Again, it is essential that the inspection instructions be precise (e.g., "Draw a sample of three from the lot of 12. Inspect the following 300 characteristics on each of the three units in the sample. Accept the lot if the total of defects is 14 or less; reject the lot if the total is 15 or more"). If we want a good job of inspection, we must write a good instruction.

As in the case of the example used for illustrating the AQL percent defective sampling plan, the plan for 250D/100u may be operated at any inspection level: normal, tightened, or reduced; single, double, or multiple. Look out for the asterisks and other symbols, and arrows pointing up and down, and read the footnotes on pages 9 through 21 of MIL-STD-105D.

REFERENCE

1. H. F. Dodge and H. G. Romig, *Sampling Inspection Tables*, 2nd ed., Wiley, New York, 1967.

FURTHER READING

Dodge, H. F., and H. G. Romig, *Sampling Inspection Tables*, 2nd ed.,
    Wiley, New York, 1967.
Grant, E. L., and R. S. Leavenworth, *Statistical Quality Control*, 5th ed.,
    McGraw-Hill, New York, 1980.
Ishakawa, K., *Guide to Quality Control*, Asian Productivity Organization,
    Tokyo, 1976.
Juran, J. M., Editor-in-Chief, *Quality Control Handbook*, 3rd ed., McGraw-
    Hill, New York, 1974.
MIL-STD-105D, *Sampling Procedures and Tables for Inspection by Attributes.*
Peach, P., *Quality Control for Management*, Prentice-Hall, Englewood Cliffs,
    N.J., 1964.
Shewhart, W. A., *Economic Control of Quality of Manufactured Product*,
    D. Van Nostrand Company, Princeton, N.J., 1931.
Shewhart, W. A., in *Statistical Method from the Viewpoint of Quality Control*,
    W. E. Deming, ed., Lancaster Press, Lancaster, Pa., 1945 reprint.

22

MILITARY/GOVERNMENT VENDOR SURVEILLANCE

FRANK SLIWAK

Consultant
Casselberry, Florida

I. INTRODUCTION

"The contractor is responsible for assuring that all supplies and services procured from his suppliers (subcontractors and vendors) conform to the contract
requirements." This mandate from MIL-Q-9858A directs the activities of every
company doing business with any department of the government when that
document is specified.

Supplier activity can be initiated after a positive make-or-buy decision has
been made. Management, with full knowledge of the capability of their manufacturing departments as well as available labor and machine loading time,
determines the specific action to be taken for each detail part on an approved
parts list. They decide which parts are to be manufactured at their existing
facilities. Applying good economic logic, they specify what has to be manufactured at outside facilities. These are the items that must be procured from
suppliers or vendors. This list is often stated as the make-or-buy list, and
it identifies the distribution of the work load within a company. The satisfactory performance of the total operation will result in the timely delivery of a
finished product to a satisfied customer for a profit.

To maintain an acceptable profit picture, the cooperation and support of
reliable suppliers is extremely important. Therefore, the selection of such
suppliers is a very significant responsibility for quality assurance. Capable
suppliers are identified in the CASE (Coordinated Aerospace Supplier Evaluation) Register, and/or individual contractor's approved suppliers listing.
These documents list the names of the company, their address, and their specialty, such as electronics, hydraulics, or mechanical. The reference companies may design and manufacture products, provide a special product, perform
specialty operations such as welding or machining, or do assembly functions
of specific items such as loading and soldering of printed circuit cards. There
are specialty companies that do plating, painting and heat treating, and so on.
There are also organizations that have the capability for performing additional
quality functions such as precision inspection, nondestructive testing, and
supplier surveillance. These and other elements are provided in the supplier
listings. To support industry, these documents—the CASE Register and

others—are updated periodically and the users have current information available to them. Scheduled and unscheduled surveys and audits supported by evaluations by major companies in the Untied States keep these listings as a reliable source of data. As a result, surveys of new suppliers need not always be performed because it is possible to use another company's evaluation. This saves time and money and assures a contractor that the supplier has a quality system. However, it is advisable that individual assessment be accomplished on small orders and positively before large contracts are awarded.

II. SURVEYS OF SUPPLIERS

A detailed on-site survey of a supplier facility and operation is mandatory when special criteria are identified in a large-dollar-volume contract. This may entail a design and development contract, or it may be a venture with a new supplier with numerous special capabilities and applications. Company policy should require that an evaluation of such suppliers be made by all involved disciplines before a decision to award a contract is made. Consequently, an assessment of the supplier's technical capabilities by engineering is the first requirement. Facilities, price schedule, and a thorough understanding of fiscal and production requirements are evaluated by materials and procurement. Another important factor for consideration is the potential suppliers conformance to the requirements of MIL-Q-9858A and other applicable specifications. This evaluation is conducted by quality assurance. Independent assessments of the supplier's total capability is the basis for the recommendation with justification for placing the contract with a specific organization.
      Evaluation of the following elements is necessary:

      Engineering ability
      Engineering experience
      Manufacturing capability
      Equipment
      Facilities
      Quality system and control
      Inspection and test facilities
      Equipment capability
      Knowledgeable personnel

The results of the evaluation can be:

      A: Company is good.
      B: Company is very good but they are overloaded with work and could not satisfy our schedule requirements.
      C: Company is very good and has personnel and facilities available to do the job on schedule.
      D: Company has good manufacturing capability and above-average engineering group. However, the quality system is weak and is not very effective.

Companies A, B, and C are acceptable, but their prices are very high. Company D has a very attractive price and compels management to give it consideration and may decide to award the contract to company D. However, a strong management team will support such a decision by approving the quality assurance recommendation of having a resident quality representative monitor this particular company. This is important. A contractor's representative can teach a supplier, work with a supplier, and help a supplier develop and implement a strong and effective quality system. This assistance, support, and control will provide a high-quality product at the right price and on time. This is a goal that not only helps a company stay in business but helps it grow.

III. SUPPLIER AUDITS

It is important to periodically evaluate a supplier's system and control. A quality audit performed two to four times a year helps to determine if the supplier's system is in control and how the product is being made. Are there design problems, material problems, manufacturing problems; how is the supplier checking the product? A prime concern must be the supplier's efforts toward defect prevention. If a supplier is not concerned about a fallout rate until it is too late, the next procurement can be at an increased price because someone has to pay for pieces above the NPA (normal parts allowance). The survey and/or audit must evaluate the following subsystems of a supplier's operation:

Raw material
Control of nonconforming material
Drawing and change control
Calibration
Vendor control of subcontractors
Receiving inspection
Inspection, test, and manufacturing areas
Packaging and shipping

There are many techniques and formats for conducting and documenting the findings of a survey and/or audit. But a realistic assessment with information is recommended. The manual in Figs. 1 to 9 can be used to document the results of the survey and follow-up audits. This format allows continued usage for a total of 17 separate evaluation periods (one survey and 16 audits), thereby retaining the entire history of a supplier in one file. The nine subsystems listed above have applicable questions designed to evaluate a particular aspect of the subsystem. These questions are numbered and each is assigned a maximum point total. For example, item 1 under subsystem 1 asks whether or not physical and chemical properties of materials are verified at periodic intervals. A possible point total of 10 is assigned (the first column immediately to the right of the question number). The supplier quality representative would then assess the supplier's compliance and in the right-hand column under "S," titled "actual points," assign the supplier a point from 0 to 10. Therefore, a supplier having excellent control for a 5-point item, will receive 5 points out of a possible 5 points; for average control, it may be 4 points, for minimum control, it may be 3 or 2 or fewer points. A grading system of this nature allows the person performing the survey or audit to present not only an evaluation but states how good or how bad the supplier is and provides space for specific detailed comments. These comments serve as a point

I T E M	CHARACTERISTICS AND COMMENTS	POINTS POSS.	S	ACTUAL POINTS			
				A	A	A	A
1	Are stated chemical and physical properties of materials verified at periodic intervals? Survey Comments_____	10		1	2	3	4
				5	6	7	8
				9	10	11	12
				13	14	15	16
2	Is there substantiating evidence (stamps or signature) to indicate that the certifications are checked against applicable specification? Check. Survey Comments_____	10		1	2	3	4
				5	6	7	8
				9	10	11	12
				13	14	15	16
3	Is the Raw Material segregated pending verification/ acceptance by Receiving Inspection? Check. Survey Comments_____	5		1	2	3	4
				5	6	7	8
				9	10	11	12
				13	14	15	16
4	Is it identified in a manner so as not to lose its identity when it is sub-divided? Check storage and machining area. Survey Comments_____	5		1	2	3	4
				5	6	7	8
				9	10	11	12
				13	14	15	16

FIGURE 1   Subsystem 1: raw material.

I T E M	CHARACTERISTICS AND COMMENTS	POINTS POSS.	ACTUAL POINTS				
			S	A	A	A	A
5	Is the material stored to prevent damage? Check storage. Survey Comments_____ _____ _____ _____ _____ _____	5		1 2 5 6 9 10 13 14	3 4 7 8 11 12 15 16		
6	Are material certifications filed for at least two years? Survey Comments_____ _____ _____ _____ _____ _____ _____	5		1 2 5 6 9 10 13 14	3 4 7 8 11 12 15 16		
	TOTAL	40					

FIGURE 1   (Continued)

I T E M	CHARACTERISTICS AND COMMENTS	POINTS POSS^r	ACTUAL POINTS				
			S	A	A	A	A
1	This sub-system covers parts as well as material, rework, deviations or scrap. The vendor shall establish and maintain an effective and positive system for controlling nonconforming items in-cluding <u>procedures</u> for the identification, segregation, presentation and disposition of reworked or repaired supplies. READ HIS PROCEDURES. Survey Comments_____	10		1 2 3 4 5 6 7 8 9 10 11 12 13 14 15 16			
2	Is all discrepant material properly identified (stamp, tag or other paperwork) when first discovered? Check. Survey Comments_____	10		1 2 3 4 5 6 7 8 9 10 11 12 13 14 15 16			
3	Are all defects correctly and sufficiently recorded, i.e., drawing number, nature of defect and number of pieces involved? Check records. Survey Comments_____	10		1 2 3 4 5 6 7 8 9 10 11 12 13 14 15 16			
4	Are there any historical records as to number of re-curring frequencies? Are rejection records analyzed to establish quality problem areas? Check records. Survey Comments_____	5		1 2 3 4 5 6 7 8 9 10 11 12 13 14 15 16			

FIGURE 2   Subsystem 2: control of nonconforming items.

I T E M	CHARACTERISTICS AND COMMENTS	POINTS POSS.	S	ACTUAL POINTS			
				A	A	A	A
5	Are the Corrective Action statements meaningful? Comments such as, "Operator Fault" or "It never happened before", etc. are not acceptable. Read a few randomly selected reports. Survey Comments_____ _____ _____ _____ _____	5		1 2 3 4 5 6 7 8 9 10 11 12 13 14 15 16			
6	Is there a "Hold Area" or metal cabinet available? Observe. Survey Comments_____ _____ _____ _____ _____ _____	5		1 2 3 4 5 6 7 8 9 10 11 12 13 14 15 16			
7	Are scrapped items identified and handled in accordance with existing scrap procedure? Check. Survey Comments_____ _____ _____ _____ _____ _____	5		1 2 3 4 5 6 7 8 9 10 11 12 13 14 15 16			
8	Is there an effective follow-up control by the assigned individual or group to assure that positive Corrective Action has been implemented and adhered to as indicated on C/A report? Check. Survey Comments_____ _____ _____ _____	10		1 2 3 4 5 6 7 8 9 10 11 12 13 14 15 16			

FIGURE 2 (Continued)

I T E M	CHARACTERISTICS AND COMMENTS	POINTS POSS	ACTUAL POINTS				
			S	A	A	A	A
9	Are records maintained for at least 2 years? Survey Comments_____ _____ _____ _____ _____ _____ _____	5		1 5 9 13	2 6 10 14	3 7 11 15	4 8 12 16
10	Are controls adequate on reworked items? Were the dis- crepant characteristics re-inspected after rework? Check records. Survey Comments_____ _____ _____ _____ _____ _____	10		1 5 9 13	2 6 10 14	3 7 11 15	4 8 12 16
	TOTAL	75					

FIGURE 2   (Continued)

I T E M	CHARACTERISTICS AND COMMENTS	POINTS POSS.	ACTUAL POINTS				
			S	A	A	A	A
1	Is there a procedure which shall assure that the latest applicable drawings and changes are used for fabrication, inspection, and testing? Check & review procedure. Survey Comments_____ _____ _____ _____ _____ _____	10		1 / 5 / 9 / 13	2 / 6 / 10 / 14	3 / 7 / 11 / 15	4 / 8 / 12 / 16
2	Are there any obsolete drawings filed with the current revisions? Check. Survey Comments_____ _____ _____ _____	5		1 / 5 / 9 / 13	2 / 6 / 10 / 14	3 / 7 / 11 / 15	4 / 8 / 12 / 16
3	Is there a rapid reference (card system or equivalent) reflecting the drawing number, revision and changes when applicable? Check. Survey Comments_____ _____ _____ _____	5		1 / 5 / 9 / 13	2 / 6 / 10 / 14	3 / 7 / 11 / 15	4 / 8 / 12 / 16
4	Are there any drawings bearing ink notation changes, minus the authorized signature? Check. Survey Comments_____ _____ _____ _____	5		1 / 5 / 9 / 13	2 / 6 / 10 / 14	3 / 7 / 11 / 15	4 / 8 / 12 / 16
	TOTAL	25					

FIGURE 3   Subsystem 3: drawings and change control.

I T E M	CHARACTERISTICS AND COMMENTS	POINTS POSS.	ACTUAL POINTS				
			S	A	A	A	A
1	This sub-system covers the following equipment: Electrical, Electronic, Tools and Gages. The vendor shall provide and maintain a written description of his calibration system (Recognized Standard Practices are acceptable) covering measuring and test equipment and measurement standards, their cycle and accuracies. READ HIS PROCEDURES. Survey Comments_____ ___ ____ _____ _____ ___ ____ __ ___ _____ _____ _____ ___ __ __	10		1 5 9 13	2 6 10 14	3 7 11 15	4 8 12 16
2	Is the equipment calibrated at established intervals? CHECK FILE CARDS. OBSERVE CALIBRATION DUE STICKERS IN SHOP. Survey Comments_____ ___ ____ _____ ___ __ ____ _____ _____ ____ _____ ___ __	10		1 5 9 13	2 6 10 14	3 7 11 15	4 8 12 16
3	Is the equipment calibrated against certified standards which are traceable to NBS? Survey Comments_____ _____ ___ ___ _____ __ ___ _____ _____ __ ____	10		1 5 9 13	2 6 10 14	3 7 11 15	4 8 12 16
4	Does the calibration record reflect actual findings and variations in value (in excess of instrument accuracy)? This is the only valid criteria that determines a reliable interval. Check his records. Survey Comments_____ ___ ____ ___ ___ _____ _____ _____ ___ _ ___ _____ __ __ ___	10		1 5 9 13	2 6 10 14	3 7 11 15	4 8 12 16

FIGURE 4   Subsystem 4: calibration.

I T E M	CHARACTERISTICS AND COMMENTS	POINTS POSS.	ACTUAL POINTS				
			S	A	A	A	A
5	Is obsolete equipment removed from active areas? Check. Survey Comments_____ _____ _____ _____	5		1 5 9 13	2 6 10 14	3 7 11 15	4 8 12 16
6	Certificates or Reports from other than the NBS shall attest to the fact that the Standards used in obtaining the results have been compared at planned intervals with NBS. Randomly select and read. Survey Comments_____ _____ _____ _____	5		1 5 9 13	2 6 10 14	3 7 11 15	4 8 12 16
7	WHEN APPLICABLE If there is a Standards Lab - Is the temperature controlled within $\pm$ 2°F? Recommend temperature is 23°C (73.4°F). Recommend relative humidity is 50% $\pm$ 2%. Check reading and records. Survey Comments_____ _____ _____	10		1 5 9 13	2 6 10 14	3 7 11 15	4 8 12 16
8	WHEN APPLICABLE Is the Instrument Repair Shop clean, dust-free and away from outside vibrations? Observe. Survey Comments_____ _____ _____	5		1 5 9 13	2 6 10 14	3 7 11 15	4 8 12 16

FIGURE 4   (Continued)

I T E M	CHARACTERISTICS AND COMMENTS	POINTS POSS.	ACTUAL POINTS				
			S	A	A	A	A
9	Perform a visual examination of several instruments (Elec. & Mech.) to check the general condition of equipment utilized. Survey Comments_____ _____ _____ _____	5		1 5 9 13	2 6 10 14	3 7 11 15	4 8 12 16
10	Is the percent full scale accuracy of the equipment in use appropriate in obtaining readings within component tolerance? Check. Survey Comments_____ _____ _____ _____	10		1 5 9 13	2 6 10 14	3 7 11 15	4 8 12 16
	TOTAL	80					

FIGURE 4   (Continued)

I T E M	CHARACTERISTICS AND COMMENTS	POINTS POSS	ACTUAL POINTS				
			S	A	A	A	A
1	Does the vendor's purchase order include quality requirements, applicable specification reference and/or other technical data as required? Review several P.O.'s. Survey Comments_____ _____ _____ _____ _____	10		1 5 9 13	2 6 10 14	3 7 11 15	4 8 12 16
2	Does vendor maintain any quality records or rating on his suppliers? Preferred sources are based on such evaluations. Ask to see his records. Survey Comments_____ _____ _____ _____ _____	5		1 5 9 13	2 6 10 14	3 7 11 15	4 8 12 16
	TOTAL	15					

FIGURE 5   Subsystem 5: vendor control of subcontractors.

I T E M	CHARACTERISTICS AND COMMENTS	POINTS POSS.	ACTUAL POINTS				
			S	A	A	A	A
1	Are all necessary specifications and drawings available in this area? Random check. Survey Comments_____ _____ _____ _____ _____ _____	10		1 5 9 13	2 6 10 14	3 7 11 15	4 8 12 16
2	Are all inspected items evidenced by stamp, tag or signature and clearly identified to indicate either conformance or rejection? Perform several checks Survey Comments_____ _____ _____ _____ _____	5		1 5 9 13	2 6 10 14	3 7 11 15	4 8 12 16
3	The vendor shall maintain physical separation of parts awaiting inspection or test, conforming material or parts, and rejections. Is access to untested hardware controlled? Survey Comments_____ _____ _____ _____ _____	5		1 5 9 13	2 6 10 14	3 7 11 15	4 8 12 16
4	The vendor shall maintain adequate historical records of all inspections and tests performed. The records must reflect the latest drawing, revision, and quantities approved/rejected, nature of rejection and/or test results Check files and work in-process. Survey Comments_____ _____ _____ _____	10		1 5 9 13	2 6 10 14	3 7 11 15	4 8 12 16

FIGURE 6   Subsystem 6: receiving inspection.

I T E M	CHARACTERISTICS AND COMMENTS	POINTS POSS.	ACTUAL POINTS				
			S	A	A	A	A
5	Is the inspection equipment calibrated and properly maintained? (Includes Hardness Tester). Survey Comments_____	10		1 5 9 13	2 6 10 14	3 7 11 15	4 8 12 16
6	Are all written guides (Procedure Sheets, Planning Sheets, etc.) implemented and adhered to? Spot Check. Survey Comments_____	10		1 5 9 13	2 6 10 14	3 7 11 15	4 8 12 16
	TOTAL	50					

FIGURE 6 (Continued)

I T E M	CHARACTERISTICS AND COMMENTS	POINTS POSS.	ACTUAL POINTS				
			S	A	A	A	A
1	Vendor shall maintain a positive system for identifying the inspection status of supplies. Identification may be accomplished by means of stamps, tags, routing cards, move tickets or other normal control devices. Check his system. Survey Comments_____ _____ _____ _____ _____	10		1 5 9 13	2 6 10 14	3 7 11 15	4 8 12 16
2	Are all necessary specifications, test procedures and drawings readily available? Check. Survey Comments_____ _____ _____ _____	10		1 5 9 13	2 6 10 14	3 7 11 15	4 8 12 16
3	Inspection and Testing documentation shall be prescribed by clear, complete, and current instructions with reference to the latest drawing revision and specification amendment. Read his instructions. Survey Comments_____ _____ _____ _____	10		1 5 9 13	2 6 10 14	3 7 11 15	4 8 12 16
4	When possible, are test values recorded in lieu of "OK" "Pass", or "Accept"? Check. Survey Comments_____ _____ _____	5		1 5 9 13	2 6 10 14	3 7 11 15	4 8 12 16

FIGURE 7   Subsystem 7: inspection, test, and manufacturing areas.

I T E M	CHARACTERISTICS AND COMMENTS	POINTS POSS.	S	ACTUAL POINTS			
				A	A	A	A
5	Is there an adequate inspection and test area? Observe. Survey Comments_____ _____ _____ _____ _____ _____ _____ _____ _____	5		1	2	3	4
				5	6	7	8
				9	10	11	12
				13	14	15	16
6	The vendor's operating data sheets (in-process and/or final) must not show evidence of deletions/additions without an authorized signature. All transactions must be in ink. Survey Comments_____ _____ _____ _____ _____	5		1	2	3	4
				5	6	7	8
				9	10	11	12
				13	14	15	16
7	Are there any travel sheets, cards or tags that are obliterated, etc. in use? Check. Survey Comments_____ _____ _____ _____ _____ _____ _____	5		1	2	3	4
				5	6	7	8
				9	10	11	12
				13	14	15	16
8	Test Procedures. Does the test technician have adequate procedures defining his function such as what equipment and attachments are needed, test tolerances, applicable specification and/or para., etc.? Survey Comments_____ _____ _____ _____ _____	10		1	2	3	4
				5	6	7	8
				9	10	11	12
				13	14	15	16
	TOTAL	60					

FIGURE 7   (Continued)

I T E M	CHARACTERISTICS AND COMMENTS	POINTS POSS.	ACTUAL POINTS				
			S	A	A	A	A
1	Does the area limit the entrance to authorized personnel only? Observe. Survey Comments_____ _____ _____ _____ _____	5		1 5 9 13	2 6 10 14	3 7 11 15	4 8 12 16
2	Are parts properly identified by means of stamping, tagging, or exterior marking of carton (drawing number, Etc.)? Are parts stored adequately to prevent damage, contamination, or deterioration? Check. Survey Comments_____ _____ _____ _____	10		1 5 9 13	2 6 10 14	3 7 11 15	4 8 12 16
3	This controlled area should house ONLY inspected/ accepted parts. Are there any discrepant parts held in this area? Check several locations. Survey Comments_____ _____ _____ _____	10		1 5 9 13	2 6 10 14	3 7 11 15	4 8 12 16

FIGURE 8   Subsystem 8: controlled stock area.

I T E M	CHARACTERISTICS AND COMMENTS	POINTS POSS	ACTUAL POINTS				
			S	A 1	A 2	A 3	A 4
4	AGE CONTROL Materials and articles having definite characteristics of quality degradation or drift with AGE and/or use, shall have each can or package marked to indicate the date of manufacture and expiration date at which the useful life will be expended. O-Rings are identified with a cure date (by quarters). The vendor shall ensure removal of such materials on a scheduled basis. Check stock. Survey Comments_____ _____ _____	10		1 / 5 / 9 / 13	2 / 6 / 10 / 14	3 / 7 / 11 / 15	4 / 8 / 12 / 16
5	Is there a semblance of order and cleanliness in this area? Observe. Survey Comments_____ _____ _____ _____	5		1 / 5 / 9 / 13	2 / 6 / 10 / 14	3 / 7 / 11 / 15	4 / 8 / 12 / 16
6	Are commercial parts properly segregated and identified from the military parts? Check. Survey Comments_____ _____ _____ _____ _____	5		1 / 5 / 9 / 13	2 / 6 / 10 / 14	3 / 7 / 11 / 15	4 / 8 / 12 / 16
	TOTAL	45					

FIGURE 8   (Continued)

I T E M	CHARACTERISTICS AND COMMENTS	POINTS POSS	ACTUAL POINTS				
			S	A	A	A	A
1	Is there a Shipping Inspector or delegated individual assigned with the responsibility to perform the duties of a Shipping Inspector? Observe and Question. Survey Comments _____ _____ _____ _____ _____	5		1 5 9 13	2 6 10 14	3 7 11 15	4 8 12 16
2	Does he check for final acceptance by inspection personnel. Verify that all required certs, records, etc. are enclosed in shipment prior to packing. Check. Survey Comments _____ _____ _____ _____ _____	10		1 5 9 13	2 6 10 14	3 7 11 15	4 8 12 16
3	Does the packaging assure maximum shipping protection for the criticality of vendor's product? Survey Comments_____ _____ _____ _____ _____ _____	10		1 5 9 13	2 6 10 14	3 7 11 15	4 8 12 16
4	Is there a specific hold area or table where the item awaiting packing is protected from any type of accidental damage? Observe or Question. Survey Comments_____ _____ _____ _____ _____	5		1 5 9 13	2 6 10 14	3 7 11 15	4 8 12 16
	TOTAL	30					

FIGURE 9   Subsystem 9: packing and shipping.

of reference for accurately and fairly evaluating a supplier's progress. This survey and audit concept permits a comparison of suppliers without inducing too much personal sentiment in the evaluation. When the audit is completed, the quality representative makes a rating of the supplier. This is based on the accumulated point total of all the subsystems. A particular supplier's rating might look something like this:

Subsystem	Possible points	Actual points
Raw material	40	30
Control of nonconforming items	75	60
Drawing and change control	25	25
Calibration	80	60
Vendor control of subcontractor	15	15
Receiving inspection	50	40
Inspection, test, and manufacturing areas	60	50
Controlled stock area	45	30
Packing and shipping	30	30
Total	420	340

$$\frac{\text{Actual points}}{\text{Possible points}} = \frac{340}{420} \times 100 = 80.1\%$$

Rating index	
Excellent	90–100%
Good	80–89%
Minimum	70–79%
Disapproved	69% or less

The supplier earned 340 out of a possible 420 points, which translates to 80.1% or a "good" rating, as shown by the rating index on the right. The vendor is officially approved. Any rating below 70% disqualifies the supplier. This recommended system for documenting the results of survey and audits provides excellent historical data that can be used in contract negotiations, supplier selections, and liability litigations.

IV. PREPARATION OF A CONTRACT

A contract or purchase order is constructed after it is determined what is wanted, how it shall be prepared, who is going to do it, how many are needed, where it will be delivered, what specifications and requirements are imposed, how much it will cost, and when it will be delivered or ready for delivery. Procurement or material generates the fine words in the contract, engineering stipulates the technical base, and quality imposes the special quality requirements. In imposing quality requirements, it should state: "The supplier has a quality system and must perform within the system criteria for the duration of the contract. The composite requirements are included in the contract." The contract received and approved by all management directors is then released to the supplier for approval. The same quality requirements are applicable to smaller (dollar volume) purchase orders that are generated by a purchase requisition for specific items (quality clauses Fig. 10).

	QUALITY ASSURANCE PROVISIONS
	APPROVED
	ISSUE DATE 6-26-79

PARAGRAPH NO.	APPLICABLE REQUIREMENTS
5	Certification of Materials: Shipments made against this Purchase Order must contain a statement of compliance by the Supplier's Quality Control activity, attesting that all materials used meet all applicable specifications which are to be listed on the certification, including cure date information for all synthetic and natural rubber material and parts used, and that physical/ chemical analysis for the materials used are on file and will be made available for MAI review. Certification to be furnished with each shipment.
6	Compliance required to Specifications: a) Quality per MIL-I-45208A & equip. calibration per MIL-C-45662A or b) Quality per MIL-Q-9858A & equip. calibration per MIL-C-45662A
7	All parts to be penetrant-inspected per MIL-I-6866.
8	Radiographic examinations per blue print requirements. NOTE: All radiographic plates become property of buyer and must be submitted with parts.

FIGURE 10

V. SOURCE INSPECTION

Major contractors impose customer source inspection for the same reason that the government requires source inspection. The principal reason is to assure themselves of a quality product. Other justifications for source inspection are:

1. Save time by not rerunning the test at the buyer's facility.
2. Eliminate the cost of duplicating inspection and test equipment at the expense of the supplier and contractor.
3. Subassemblies will be built up into assemblies and cannot be inspected at a lower tier at the buyer's facility.
4. The item or unit may be *drop-shipped*; that is, it will be transported directly to the user from the subcontractor and will never pass through the buyer's installation.

Besides being responsible for the quality of the product, source inspectors also verify the buildup process. Therefore, continuous surveillance of a supplier's operation is conducted by the resident representative, whose duties are normally to work with the supplier and assist them in their operation. A resident representative who is at a supplier facility works with a supplier on a day-to-day basis. The representative is responsible for monitoring the supplier's special processes, all inspection and tests, as well as periodically reviewing the planning documentation and test procedures and specifications. A part-time representative visits a supplier's facility periodically and maintains surveillance of activities on a scheduled basis. An itinerant, as he or she may be called, is still responsible for the supplier's compliance to contract requirements. Because of the limited unit quantities, or smaller dollar values, his or her total participation in daily quality activities is not required.

VI. INSPECTION REQUIREMENTS

Standardization of inspection criteria and methodology is the most positive way of eliminating product problems. Evaluation of a product is best accomplished by studying the item to determine what characteristics should be checked and to what level this inspection and/or test is to be made. Having identified the specific characteristics, they should be listed on an inspection data sheet (Fig. 11) with instructions: how it is to be checked, what equipment, tools, fixtures, and gages are to be used, to what acceptance quality level (AWL) they are to be checked. This tells you how to evaluate the lots of material. Lot identification and the results of the inspection and/or test are recorded on the inspection data sheet and you have a historical record for that item from a particular supplier. The data sheet is given to suppliers to duplicate the inspection test method and it also informs them of how parts will be checked and to what acceptance level the characteristics will be evaluated. Duplicating the same equipment and techniques by the supplier, the problems caused by differences in inspection and testing are reduced and occasionally eliminated. The inspection data sheet can also be used by the supplier quality representative when performing customer source inspection at the supplier's facility. Consequently, everyone is looking and checking the parts in the same manner using the same equipment, guidelines, and instructions.

INSPECTION DATA SHEET

Page ____ of ____

PART NO. ______________ INSPECTION STATION ________ DATE ________ REV. ____

PART NAME ______________ SUPPLIER ______________

MIL–STD–105D, Level II, Normal Degree unless otherwise specified.

0-AQL means 100% screening of stated characteristics.

PREPARED BY ______________

APPROVED ______________

Normal Description of Characteristics to be inspected to Specifications.	Dwg. Zone	INSPECTION METHOD	C/C	AQL	Date / RR No. / Lot Size / SAMPLE					

PROCESS AVERAGE								
		Quantity DEFECTIVE pcs. % DEFECTIVE Pcs.						
		Quantity DEFECTIVE Pcs. % DEFECTIVE Pcs.						
		Quantity DEFECTIVE Pcs. % DEFECTIVE Pcs.						
		Quantity DEFECTIVE Pcs. % DEFECTIVE Pcs.						
		Total Quantity DEFECTIVE Pcs. TOTAL % DEFECTIVE (when applicable)						

STATISTICAL COMMENT	REJECT DOCUMENT NO.						
	"D" Stamp lot rejected.						
	Acceptance Stamp for acceptance						
DISPOSITION CODE	Enter quantity and disposition code						

FIGURE 11 Inspection data sheet.

VII. SUPPLIERS' QUALITY ORGANIZATION

The person responsible for the quality operation has to be capable of managing the organization free of normal manufacturing interference and influences. Therefore, having the quality manager directly responsible to the president of the company identifies a positive attitude toward quality goals. The quality operation should be on an equal footing with finance, marketing, manufacturing, personnel, engineering, and product support. Keeping quality at the top management level will assure its effectiveness throughout the company. It will be free to influence such important contributors to quality as design, sales, services, training, and advertising. As it is with personnel and finance functions, it evolves into a support function for all operating arms of the business, helping them identify and achieve quality goals. While supporting the commitment of a *quality* product on *time* for the right *price*, it is capable of assuming total customer satisfaction with *quality first*.

VIII. QUALITY SYSTEM

The criteria for the quality operation and the methods for controlling the system are specified in the quality manual. The general outline of the manual must be in conformance with specifications MIL-Q-9858A, MIL-I-45208A, MIL-C-45662A, and other specifications, depending on the nature of the business. The manual identifies the operations and obligations of each department, the emphasis being on the quality assurance of processes and equipment from the time a purchase order is received to delivery of the finished product to the customer. An acceptable document specifies who is responsible, where the task will be accomplished, and by whom it will be performed. It is important to note that the quality manual should reflect a functioning system. If there are inconsistencies, the manual should be changed or the operation must be changed. Not complying with the methods and procedures specified in the manual can be a basis for supplier disqualification.

Major procurement for a complex subsystem or system may require by contract that a quality plan specifically identify how the quality system will function. This written plan must be approved by the customer and implemented without change for the duration of the contract. Any change requested by either a customer or a contractor must be approved before it can be implemented. Two major documents frequently supplement the quality plan. These are a standards of workmanship and a standard repair manual. The standards of workmanship satisfy both manufacturing and quality needs for a better understanding of levels of acceptance. Pictures of products identify nonacceptable, marginal, and acceptable examples. This is also supported by a paragraph describing the specific condition of the product. Examples of these situations clarify the condition and reduce the misunderstandings associated with a marginal product.

Timely disposition of minor nonconforming items has motivated companies to develop and implement as part of their documentation system a standard repair manual. Parts not manufactured to specification requirements can be made acceptable or usable by incorporating specific repair procedures. These procedures detail the methods permitted for product correction and must be acceptable to the customer, approved by the customer, and must be supported by official documentation. The data can become the basis for engineering changes or manufacturing process changes. However, it cannot be utilized in bypassing the controls and approval of the material review board or the requirements for positive corrective action.

IX. EMPLOYEE CERTIFICATION

Advances in technology and requirements for specialization have imposed greater needs for training of personnel to satisfy production requirements. Consequently, various programs have been developed to instruct employees to perform special tasks with specific techniques and equipment. This criterion has also been imposed on various inspection and test functions. Special equipment operated by specially trained personnel evaluate the products, making the training programs a very important element. Satisfactory completion of

special courses and an examination are the requirements. Successful completion is then acknowledged by an official certification of operators, assemblers,
inspectors, and testers. These controls assure the customer that knowledgeable personnel are performing these specialized tasks, which positively influence the level of quality of products delivered to them. Frequently, the requirement for examination and certification of personnel is specified in the
applicable specifications and individually identified as control requirements.

X. CONTROL OF NONCONFORMING MATERIAL

Material review, a system for control and processing of nonconforming material,
has been implemented in many companies for economic reasons. Items manufactured and not satisfying all the applicable specifications are not necessarily
scrap. Frequently, with minor repairs or rework, these items are usable and
may even be made conforming to the requirements. On other occasions, it may
not be in the best interest of customer and supplier to do anything to the
parts but to use them as is. This decision may be dictated by schedule, by
cost, or by application. This may be an isolated case, and additional cost and
effort coupled with lost time may not contribute much to the usability of the
item. Therefore, it becomes the decision of the material review board (customer representative, engineering, and quality usually make up the board) to
specify the ultimate usage of the item. To assist the material review board in
determining the disposition of the nonconforming material, corrective action—
reflecting what measures have been taken to prevent the problem from re-
occurring—must be documented and available for evaluation and decision making. Corrective action must be timely, effective, and positive. Superficial
fixes are not satisfactory. Therefore, it is important that all the causes be
identified and evaluated. The actions to remedy the problem are stated and
initiated. The responsible persons are notified of what must be done and how
it should be done. After it is completed, the corrective action is determined
to be satisfactory. It is extremely important that there be follow-up on the
action, to assure all parties that the same mistakes will not be repeated and
that corrective action has been implemented.

XI. SUPPLIER RELATIONS

Good relations with suppliers assure good products from suppliers. Good
communication—telling the supplier what is wanted—keeps them knowledgeable of the requirements, and cooperative. Toward this end, periodic audits
and supplier conferences are most beneficial. The periodic audit is an evaluation of the supplier's facility and an assessment of their program. Verifying
compliance to the supplier's written quality system and the contractor's requirements keep both parties informed of the current status and of the program
needs. Having the suppliers together for a day, in a supplier conference,
creates an opportunity for all types of information to be exchanged. In addition, this is an opportunity to find out why some people are not too cooperative and why others seem not to know the operational requirements. Developing a team spirit or partnership agreement helps to improve the level of quality.
    To improve supplier performance requires proper motivation on the part of
the contractor. Most companies today have a rating system. Notifying suppliers of their performance is the best technique for improving quality performance. Periodically, a written report of accomplishments either complimenting

SUPPLIER CONTROL EVALUATION PRODUCT: _____

SUPPLIER NAME _____ _____ YEAR ____ - _____

ATTENTION: _____ TITLE: _____

PERIOD		JAN	FEB	MAR	APR	MAY	JUN	JUL	AUG	SEP	OCT	NOV	DEC
TOTAL UNITS	RECEIVED												
	REJECTED												
	% REJECTED												
SAMPLE UNITS	INSPECTED												
	REJECTED												
	% REJECTED												

PERCENT REJECTED
• SAMPLE UNITS
▲- -▲ TOTAL UNITS

100
90
80
70
60
50
40
30
20
10

PERCENTAGE DISTRIBUTION OF UNIT DISPOSITIONS

	JAN	FEB	MAR	APR	MAY	JUN	JUL	AUG	SEP	OCT	NOV	DEC
RETURN TO VEND.												
REWORK												
ACCPT. AS IS												
SCRAP												

PERCENTAGE DISTRIBUTION OF DISCREPANCIES

	JAN	FEB	MAR	APR	MAY	JUN	JUL	AUG	SEP	OCT	NOV	DEC
FUNCTIONAL												
ASSY. INCOMP.												
FINISH												
NICKS, BURRS												
ELECTRICAL												
DIMENSIONAL												
IDENTIFICATION												
MISC.												
RATING:												
MANAGEMENT												
HARDWARE												

FIGURE 12 Supplier control evaluation.

the supplier for good performance or reprimanding a supplier for poor performance is a strong communication and motivation system (Fig. 12). Suppliers will take positive action to improve their operation if past performance is marginal. Suppliers will also strive to improve when they know the customer is keeping score. Suppliers recognize that a good performance rating can be a significant factor toward receiving additional business.

Many major corporations have implemented a program of recognition—an "outstanding supplier award." Public identification of an organization has stimulated many suppliers to perform well for a long period of time. It has been an incentive to the suppliers' personnel to encourage them to do better and produce a high-quality product. Suppliers have also recognized that they can be the recipient of additional business from customers who rate them high in performance. These suppliers know that they are in a position to get new business when other companies become aware of their outstanding performance in delivering high-quality products, on time.

23

COMMERCIAL VENDOR SURVEILLANCE

DAVID L. FIELD

Consultant
Lake Bluff, Illinois

I. INTRODUCTION

Modern procurement quality assurance is based on a systems approach to supplier selection and control. These systems include specification systems, supplier approval systems, supplier development systems, and supplier control systems. The objectives of these systems are to create conditions which are most often successful in achieving effective quality control.

It is important to recognize at the outset that none of the systems carries a 100% guarantee of success. But it is also important to recognize that each system increases the probability of achieving the desired level of quality. For example, a quality system evaluation that finds a good quality program in operation does not assure that good-quality product will always be shipped. Even the best of systems lets a clinker get through once in a while. On the other hand, a quality system evaluation that finds a bad quality program in operation usually is a good indicator that bad product quality is to be expected.

The value of a quality system evaluation lies in identifying system weaknesses that are likely to result in future problems. Once identified, these weaknesses can be corrected, compensated for, or avoided.

Facility surveys or evaluations that find a plant and its equipment in good order are not necessarily predictive of good-quality product. The best of facilities and equipment can be no better than the process design, the operators, the procedures, and the materials that interact with them. But, again, poor facilities and equipment that lacks process or machine capabilities commensurate with product requirements will almost always result in defective product. The value of a facility evaluation lies in making sure that product will not be manufactured on equipment that is inherently unable to meet specifications, or in a plant that lacks the capacity to produce the needed volume.

Product qualification testing provides evidence that the supplier is capable of manufacturing the product or, at least, was once able to make a few prototype units. It does not guarantee the supplier will always make good products, but if they cannot even make a few qualification samples, it would be foolhardy to trust them with a major production run.

These few examples illustrate the decision-making process of procurement quality control. In each case we can improve the odds substantially by learning our suppliers' strengths and weaknesses and by acting on that knowledge. Sampling inspection is based entirely on statistical probability concepts which provide specific decision rules.

The perfect procurement quality system has not yet been devised. The most successful ones usually use all of the foregoing program features. Each of these control systems has advantages, and each has a cost associated with it. Each will help identify and correct causes of quality problems but will not prevent all of them. The extent to which each of the procurement quality systems is applied should be evaluated carefully to make sure that they are cost-effective.

To ensure the quality of purchased material, it is essential that the material be manufactured under controlled conditions and be subjected to sufficient inspection and testing to demonstrate that it conforms to requirements. It is a universally accepted principle of quality that the only way one can "be sure that accepted product is good is to have the product made right in the first place" [1]. That holds true whether the product is made in-house or is purchased. In the case of purchased material, Burr [2] holds that "the least expensive and most desireable form of acceptance is to have producers who have installed statistical quality control."

The ultimate goal of a supplier surveillance system is to provide assurance that purchased material is satisfactory for its intended use and to achieve that assurance economically. To this end, maximum use should be made of supplier inspection and test data in the determination of fitness for use. Furthermore, no matter how thorough incoming inspection and testing may be, there are characteristics that cannot be evaluated. Some are characteristics that depend on the control of the manufacturing process, some must be evaluated by destructive testing, and some must be evaluated on test equipment using test technology far beyond a buyer's available resources.

Palmer and Paterson [3] have suggested some economies in verification inspection by the purchaser:

> "by transferring to the supplier the responsibility for providing the purchaser certified factual quality information of specified character and quantity . . . since it is possible to combine into one operation, the inspections which the manufacturer as a prudent supplier necessarily makes on his own behalf with those required for assurance purposes by the customer.

These economies based on certifications require that the supplier maintain adequate control over his manufacturing and testing operations to assure the accuracy and precision of the test results. Smith [4] points out that "it is virtually impossible for any supplier to certify his shipments without using sound methods for process quality control."

II. MAKE-OR-BUY DECISIONS

The determination of whether to make or buy materials, parts, subassemblies, and finished products involves complex evaluations of comparative advantages. Some of the factors to be considered are:

Comparative costs of manufacturing in-house or buying outside
Comparative quality of in-house and purchased materials

Comparative production schedules and lead times
Comparative value of alternative uses of in-house capital equipment
Comparative technological capabilities
Availability of alternative outside sources

III. PROCUREMENT SPECIFICATIONS

Procurement specifications often include product specifications, testing specifications, quality system specifications, sampling agreements, classification of
defects, and the like. It is important that these procurement specifications be
thoroughly reviewed by both parties prior to inclusion in the contract. It is
also important that a systematic change control system be applied to all these
specifications and to the contract itself.

A. Product Specifications

Product or material specifications should be stated in clear and unambiguous
terms and should conform to national standards in form and content to minimize
the chance of misinterpretation. These specifications may be controlled by
either the buyer or seller; however, any change in a specification must be
agreed to by both parties, and written modification of the contract or purchase
order should be made. When changes are not controlled in this manner, it is
not unusual to find a vendor on the critical path working overtime making
obsolete parts. Nor it is rare to find a buyer checking incoming materials to
an outdated specification.

B. Quality System Specifications

Although some companies have developed quality systems specifications for
their suppliers, many have none. Suppliers dealing with several customers
who impose quality system specifications are often troubled by conflicting requirements. To simplify and coordinate requirements, ASQC Std. C-1 [5] was
developed and adopted as ANSI Std. 21.8. This specification was specifically
designed for use in nongovernment procurements to provide a single standard
that can be used universally. "Conformance to this specification by a manufacturer will provide a system which will be acceptable to all but those industries which require detailed assurance of a specific type. It is recommended
for quality programs which are not required to meet government specifications"
[6]. Eight basic principles are universally found in the primary policies of
satisfactory quality systems, and it is the degree of conformance to these principles that is normally measured in the evaluation of any quality system.

Quality Management

The key to the management of quality lies in philosophy, objectives, and organizational structure. This philosophy forms the primary policy and should include the broad principles common to good quality control programs. The objectives should be clearly stated in specific terms and should provide operating
policies that guide the activity of the quality program. The organizational
structure should clearly define lines of authority and responsibility for quality
from top management down to the operating levels.

Design Information

Control of design and manufacturing information is the first step toward control of product. The control of engineering information and specifications consists of making sure that operating personnel are furnished with complete technical instructions for the manufacture and inspection of the product. This information consists of drawings, specifications, manufacturing instructions, special purchase order requirements, engineering change information, and any special information. A positive recall system is usually considered necessary to ensure against use of superseded or obsolete information.

Procurement

It is essential for the assurance of quality that procurement sources meet the standards for quality control imposed on the procuring agency. It would do little good for the consumer to specify rigid quality requirements for sources and then have those sources fail to use an equal amount of care in establishing subsources. Sources should be under continuous surveillance, and incoming material should be inspected to the extent necessary to assure that the requirements have been met.

Material

Control of the identity and the quality status of material in stores and in-process is essential. It is not enough that the right materials be procured and verified; they must be identified and controlled in a manner that will assure that they are also properly used. The entire quality program may be compromised if adequate controls are not maintained throughout procurement, storage, manufacturing, and inspection.

Manufacture

In-process inspection—utilizing the techniques of quality control—is one of the most satisfactory methods that has been devised for attaining quality of product during manufacture. Because many quality characteristics cannot be evaluated in the end product, it is imperative that they be achieved and verified during the production process.

Acceptance

Final inspection, testing, and packing are critical operations necessary to assure the acceptability of material. The specifications must form the basis for these activities. To the extent that in-process inspections are used to reduce or eliminate inspections of the final product, records of those inspections should be reviewed to verify conformance to requirements.

Measuring Instruments

Periodic inspection and calibration of certain tools, gages, testers, and some items of process control equipment are necessary for the control and verification of product quality. Controlled standards, periodically checked or referenced against national standards, will assure the compatibility of supplier and customer measurements. Inaccurate gages and testers can compromise the entire quality program, and may result in either rejection of good material or acceptance of defective material.

Quality Information

Records should be maintained for all inspections performed, and the data should be analyzed periodically and used as a basis for action. Quality data should be used to:

Improve the quality control operation by increasing or decreasing the amount of inspection

Improve the quality of product by the initiation of corrective action on processes or suppliers

Document certifications of product quality furnished to customers

Report quality results and trends to management

Unused or unusable data are evidence of poor management.

C. Sampling Agreements

When a buyer intends to use sampling inspection to determine the acceptability of purchased material, it is important that both seller and buyer agree on the sampling plans and the classification of defects to be used. It is important to note that sampling agreements are *not* agreements to accept any defective product. They are used to decide who will do (or pay for) the 100% inspection of lots that fail the sampling plan. Sampling inspection is nothing more than a statistical plan for arriving at a decision on the acceptability of an entire lot of material. There are risks for both the buyer and the seller when sampling inspection is used. These are the risks of a wrong decision: the producer's risk (the risk of having a good lot rejected) and the consumer's risk (the risk of accepting a bad lot).

An agreement to use a specific sampling plan is an agreement on the part of the buyer not to reject an entire lot without further inspection when the level of defectiveness in the sample is below a specified value. It also is an agreement by the seller to permit rejection and return of an entire lot without further inspection if the level of defectiveness in the sample is above a specified value. The buyer usually retains the right to inspect 100% at any time. Unless arrangements to the contrary are made, the buyer can always reject and return all defective units, regardless of the lot sampling results.

D. Vendor Approval

There are three major systems for establishing vendor approvals: (1) product qualification, (2) facility approval, and (3) process approval. A good procurement quality control program usually employs all three systems.

Product Qualification

When the product to be procured is an off-the-shelf item or vendor design, it is common to test samples carefully and evaluate the adequacy of design and conformance for the intended use. When the product to be procured is of the buyer's design, prototype units are usually manufactured and evaluated, followed by stringent inspection and testing of units from the first production run. Either of these two methods provides a sound initial qualification. Maintenance of qualification is established on the basis of inspection and testing of incoming lots.

Facility Approval

Another area that is often evaluated is the physical plant that will produce the product. A careful examination of the facility can establish whether adequate space, materials, machines, and personnel are available in sufficient quantity to support the intended production effort.

Process Approval

Process evaluation is concerned with the procedures and activities—the management—employed in arriving at an end product. It involves assumptions that certain methods of operation will lead to desirable results, and that such results can be most effectively obtained when activities are related to a set of goals and objectives [7].

> A process evaluation requires examination of the over-all program for evidence relating to (1) the setting of goals, (2) the existence of an adequate set of procedures for attaining these desired goals, (3) the implementation of the procedures, (4) the extent to which the goals are actually being met, and (5) the improvement of the procedures when a need is indicated. Caution must be exercised in process evaluations to avoid circular reasoning, since there may be a tendency to conclude that a program is effective merely because a set of procedures has been prescribed.

A typical quality program evaluation begins with a review of quality policy with supplier management, followed by an examination of operating practices, and concluding with a closing conference with supplier management. This is the pattern of many very successful supplier evaluations. Formal reports and appropriate follow-up action to obtain and verify necessary improvements in the quality system complete the action.

Within these broad limits, there are an infinite number of variations. Questionnaires, checklists, survey forms, rating systems, and other tools of the trade vary widely. Much has been written about the merits and demerits of various questionnaires and checklists, and interest in these "systems" is often far greater than they merit. More important is a basic understanding of the importance of the fundamental principles that must be observed to consistently manufacture equipment of high quality and reliability. Successful supplier evaluation programs invariably utilize professionals to evaluate supplier quality systems, and place major reliance on the evaluator's judgment rather than on a stereotyped "technique."

No two quality systems are the same. Each is the product of different environment, different personalities, and different problems. A model system in one plant might not work in another. Evaluation of a quality system is thus a review of a "one-of-a-kind" set of policies and practices. Effective application of the eight basic quality system requirements is what is measured during the survey, and the particular administrative method used in applying these principles is not of concern as long as these principles are applied in a manner that will assure the quality of product.

Throughout the evaluation, we must bear in mind the basic purposes of the evaluation: (1) to validate use of certified inspection and test records in lieu of performing inspections and tests, (2) to obtain quality system improvements, and (3) to prevent the development of quality problems. We must also remember that the quality system devised by the supplier is their own prerogative, not normally subject to customer control. Any system the supplier may elect to use which assures control of quality at a satisfactory level must be considered adequate.

The evaluation takes place in several distinct stages: first, the supplier's basic policies and procedures are reviewed and evaluated to determine whether they can reasonably be expected to assure control of quality; second, the supplier's operating methods are examined to see how well they agree with the stated policies and procedures and how adequately they do, in fact, assure the quality of product; third, the results of observations are evaluated and reported; and finally, the action taken as a result of the survey is evaluated. Excellent evaluative criteria for quality programs in the commercial area may be found in the ASQC *Procurement Quality Control Handbook* [6].

IV. SUPPLIER DEVELOPMENT

It will occasionally be found that no satisfactory supplier is available. None of the known sources qualify on the basis of product quality, plant capacity, or quality system. A program for developing one or more potential suppliers is needed. The first step in a development program is to establish the willingness of both parties to undertake a long-term commitment to one another. Development programs are often long and arduous and require considerable effort and expense on both sides. The changes needed may be physical improvement or expansion of the plant and its equipment, they may be policy and systems changes related to quality control, or they may involve redesign of products or processes. Supplier development is rarely a short-term project. It is not unusual for such programs to extend for several years. Sometimes new plants, new processes, or even new products are involved. The payoff can be handsome when a supplier works closely with customers and devises a facility or system that uniquely fills the customers' needs. The quality system evaluation can provide an agenda or blueprint for supplier development. It can also provide a measuring instrument for determining the degree of progress in reaching development goals [8].

> Show a positive attitude during the follow-up visit. Your vendor has told you he carried out certain corrective actions you agreed upon. You are there to verify that the corrective actions have been taken satisfactorily. If all corrective actions are acceptable and no additional problems become known, the vendor should qualify as an "Approved Supplier."

As industry progresses more and more toward complex products, we are faced with greater and greater reliance on the ability of our suppliers to completely control and measure the quality of product during the manufacturing process. As higher and higher quality and reliability requirements are imposed, it becomes increasingly more important that adequate quality systems control their manufacture. Supplier quality system evaluations on a continuing basis are essential for the assurance of quality and reliability.

V. SUPPLIER CONTROL

Once a supplier has been approved and begins regularly to provide materials, parts, assemblies, or services, it is important to make sure that the supplier continue to perform in a satisfactory manner. Inspection and testing of incoming shipments is the primary measurement of performance. The information thus obtained is used to develop performance ratings. Source inspection by visiting (or resident) inspectors is sometimes used in lieu of incoming inspection. Liaison visits often help maintain a smooth flow of acceptable materials by getting quick resolution of problems. Periodic quality system audits are useful in detecting changes in a vendor's organization, methods, or facilities that might affect product quality.

A. Source Inspection

Source inspection has unique advantages for both the buyer and the supplier. By having the customer's acceptance inspection take place in the supplier's plant, communication on problems is immediate, and since the problem material is present, there is no delay in initiating corrective action. No shipping costs have been incurred, no return shipment is needed, and the supplier can act promptly in replacing or repairing the nonconforming material. There are some dangers in source inspection; the supplier may relax final inspection and leave it to the customer's inspectors to find any problems. Or the source inspectors may become too closely associated with the supplier and may lose objectivity. Properly controlled, a source inspection activity can be cost-effective for both the supplier and the customer. It prevents shipment of unacceptable lots, permits immediate use of material when it is received—a shipping damage check is usually all that is needed—and permits drop-shipment direct to the buyer's customers.

B. Incoming Inspection

It is important to recognize that incoming inspection is one of the keystones of the supplier surveillance program. Incoming inspection provides a direct measurement of the effectiveness of the procurement quality program. A carefully planned inspection of a sample of each incoming lot of material provides objective evidence of the quality of that material, and the sampling plan provides a decision criterion for acceptance or rejection. The important thing about planning an inspection is to recognize that only important characteristics that bear on the fitness for use of the material should be checked in each lot. Plan what *not* to inspect. An initial qualification inspection might include checking all characteristics to make sure that the supplier has them all correct, but cut back to the important things for routine evaluation.

   The manner of recording inspection data from incoming (or source) inspections should also be carefully designed to aid in evaluating the supplier's performance and to provide clues to quality problems in a manner that facilitates rapid communication and corrective action. A quality history record that highlights repetitive defects and shows the quality of successive lots is very useful in seeing that chronic problems are recognized and subjected to corrective action procedures.

C. Supplier Ratings

Information from incoming or source inspection should be compiled and analyzed to determine how well suppliers are performing. Some form of index number is often used to compare vendors with one another and with a standard. A very simple rating system might simply determine the percent of incoming lots from a vendor that meet the acceptance criteria of the sampling plan. It will soon be seen with a rating system of this sort that some suppliers almost always ship acceptable product, many more usually furnish good material, and a few almost always ship substandard goods. There are many effective supplier rating systems described in the literature, and some of them integrate many factors into the index number. Some require computers to analyze the data and provide the complex calculations. The principle underlying all such plans, however, is concerned with identifying and recognizing the good guys, and with locating and penalizing the bad guys.

With the top performers, the objective is to increase business and to take advantage of their good control of quality by reducing or even eliminating inspection. The poor performers should either be developed or replaced.

D. Liaison Visits

Periodic liaison visits to and from suppliers help establish and maintain good communications. "Most of the so-called quality problems are really problems in communication. Nearly 90 percent of these problems stem from failure to pass along information in a form that can be understood at a time when it is needed" [9]. It is essential that quality problems be discussed and resolved on a regular basis. The supplier needs to know what kinds of problems the product can create for the buyer. Similarly, the buyer needs to know the supplier's problems so as to assess the potential effect on the buyer's products.

Operating with inadequate knowledge often results in assumptions that stray far from reality. Local "folk wisdom" develops from speculation about what "they" (the customer) will or will not accept; or, on the part of the customer, what "they" (the supplier) can or cannot supply. A concealed problem seldom gets resolved, but a shared problem usually is.

Juran, in contrasting the Japanese and American approaches to quality, points out [10]:

> The most fundamental of these differences is in the policy followed as to the basic relationship between vendor and buyer. At one extreme is the adversary concept: mutual doubt if not mistrust; reliance on contract provisions, documents, penalties and other elements of an arm's length relationship. At the other extreme is the teamwork concept: mutual trust and confidence, cooperation, joint commitment to the consumer, etc. This policy on basic relationship is of the utmost importance. It is decisive on such questions as extent of joint planning, mutual visits, technical assistance, exchange of data, etc.

Liaison visits should be used to develop teamwork and mutual respect between the buyer and seller. Openness and cooperation provide a sound foundation for quality improvement. An adversary relationship does not usually result in good quality.

E. Periodic Audits and Reevaluations

Supplier evaluations and audits have a limited period of validity. Each measures quality conditions at a moment in time. With the passage of time, these measurements become less and less valid. Management policies, organization structure, personnel, plant and equipment, processes, procedures, and other factors that affect quality are dynamic and change constantly.

Product audits which are essentially a repeat of the original product qualification testing are often used to make sure that the product has not changed. They also provide a check on both the supplier's inspection and test system and on the buyer's incoming inspection and test.

Process audits which review in detail all elements of the supplier's production methods provide a check on the stability of the manufacturing process as it affects a single product.

Quality systems reevaluations make sure that management policies, procedures, organization, and controls have not deteriorated. An example that comes to mind which illustrates the need for reevaluation is a case where a firm had an excellent quality system when evaluated. They had a long history of delivering nearly perfect product. Six months after the initial evaluation, the quality of product from that supplier dropped sharply. A reevaluation quickly established the cause of the decline in quality. The firm's new management had instituted a stringent cost-reduction program and the quality control department had been abolished.

VI. SUPPLIER CERTIFICATIONS

To achieve maximum economy in evaluating the quality of purchased material, purchasers often ask suppliers to certify the quality of each shipment. The certification is then used in lieu of incoming inspection and testing as a basis for acceptance of the material. When based on a program of quality system evaluation, establishment of a good track record as evidenced by consistently acceptable incoming inspection and test results, and when backed up by periodic validation inspection and testing, such a program provides adequate assurance of quality at a nominal cost.

Certifications may take many forms and will vary widely in validity. An implicit certification is present whenever a supplier ships material against a purchase order. The act of shipping material against a contract implies that the material is as required by that contract. Explicit certifications, however, are usually required when it is desired to use certification in lieu of inspection and testing. These vary in content and form from a simple statement of conformance to a detailed inspection and test report.

A. Certificates of Compliance

A certificate of compliance should identify the material it covers, should be specific as to the requirements being certified, should be traceable to specific data (inspection or test results) on which certification is based, and should be signed by a legally authorized representative of the company.

Certified copies of the supplier's inspection and test records provide an alternative to certificates of compliance. These provide the most reliable basis for acceptance, as they can be verified readily.

Verification of certifications is essential. Every certification should be examined carefully to make sure that it is complete and specific. Each value reported on certified inspection and test records should be compared with the specification. It is surprising how often a certification will prove that the material is not what is being certified.

When certificates of conformance are not accompanied by test data, it is a good idea occasionally to ask for the supporting data and to run independent tests to validate the supplier's results.

B. Validation of Certifications

Two types of validation are commonly used in evaluating certifications. The first is the routine comparison of the certification information to make sure that it covers the material received and that all the information is in agreement with the requirements. The second is a comparison of the supplier's inspection and test results with those obtained by independent checking by the buyer.

In the comparison of independent test results, it is important that the supplier's results vary by no more than the precision of the test method. The purpose of the independent testing is *not* to determine whether the material meets specification, but to determine whether the supplier's test data are valid.

"Because certification in its various forms contributes up to 80 percent to the assurance of product quality, it is an economical tool, without which we might be faced with the need for a substantial increase in inspection and testing requirements to obtain the same assurance" [11]. Close attention should be paid to the validity of certifications to maintain confidence in them. False or inaccurate certifications should be treated as the frauds that they actually are.

REFERENCES

1. E. L. Grant, *Statistical Quality Control*, McGraw-Hill, New York, 1952, p. 479.
2. I. W. Burr, *Engineering Statistics and Quality Control*, McGraw-Hill, New York, 1953, p. 357.
3. J. E. Palmer, and E. G. D. Paterson, "Acceptance Inspection of Purchased Material," *Quality Control Conference Papers*, 1951, American Society for Quality Control, Milwaukee, Wis., 1951, pp. 303–320.
4. W. H. Smith, "Problems of Receiving Inspection and the Assembly Line," *Quality Control Conference Papers*, 1951, American Society for Quality Control, Milwaukee, Wis., 1951.
5. American Society for Quality Control, *Specification of General Requirements for a Quality Program*, ASQC, Milwaukee, Wis., 1968.
6. American Society for Quality Control, Vendor-Vendee Technical Committee, *Procurement Quality Control—A Handbook of Recommended Practices*, 2nd ed., ASQC, Milwaukee, Wis., 1976.
7. A. F. Cone, D. L. Field, and J. LaPaz, "Evaluation of Contractor Quality Control Systems," 17th Midwest Quality Control Conference, Denver, Colo., October 26–27, 1962.
8. American Society for Quality Control, Vendor-Vendee Technical Committee, *How to Conduct A Supplier Survey*, ASQC, Milwaukee, Wis. 1977.
9. D. Turnbull, "Common Sense Could Be Called a Quality Program," *Quality Magazine*, April 1979, pp. 14–17.
10. J. M. Juran, "Japanese and Western Quality—A contrast," *Quality Magazine*, January 1979, pp. 8–12.
11. W. A. Sherman, "Certification—Tower of Babel?" *Industrial Quality Control*, August 1966, pp. 72–75.

FURTHER READING

Field, D. L., "Surveying and Evaluating Supplier Quality Systems," 17th American Society for Quality Control Conference, Chicago, 1963.

24

CONTRACT SURVEILLANCE

SPENCER HUTCHENS, JR.

Intertek Services Corporation
Rolling Hills, California

ROGER G. LANGEVIN

Argyle Associates, Inc.
New Canaan, Connecticut

I. WHY USE VENDOR SURVEILLANCE SERVICES?

The need for contract source inspection services continues to grow as the procurement process gets more and more complicated.

1. Procurement sources are becoming geographically more remote and dispersed.
2. Product technology continues to get more sophisticated.
3. Procurement material costs, operating expenses, and financial constraints continue to grow.
4. It is becoming increasingly difficult to secure and maintain appropriately qualified and skilled personnel.
5. Delivery schedules are getting tighter while lead times continue to grow.
6. Concern for product liability and warranty costs continues to get high priority.

The basic objective of vendor surveillance is to assure that the items being produced by the supplier conform to the buyer's specifications and standards. In-plant receiving inspection is sometimes sufficient to achieve this goal, but frequently is not. For many parts and assemblies, the only way to know that the item is up to standard is to have a buyer representative in the vendor's plant. That representative could accomplish the quality functions necessary.

In today's environment, many purchases are for items of extreme precision, high reliability, and complex design. Often in these cases it is very difficult, if not impossible, to uncover flaws by inspecting at time of receipt. Furthermore, if substandard products are detected by receiving inspection, the time delays and shipping costs incurred to return the items to the supplier can be a significant consideration. Surveillance at the supplier source helps to make possible defect prevention as opposed to defect detection.

A company engaged in the manufacture of a product for public consumption must assure that if the product is built to design specifications, it will perform as stated. The company must also take whatever steps are necessary to see that the specifications are met. Failure to do so could result in expensive litigation.

A substantial percentage of the components going into a manufacturer's products are provided by outside suppliers. In the electronics field, for example, a company's production may be limited solely to the assembly and installation of parts and subassemblies provided by subtier suppliers. In most other industries at least one-fourth or one-third of the total manufacturing cost is attributable to material purchased from vendors. Thus it is mandatory to be interested in the quality of items received from outside sources.

II. ADVANTAGE OF CONTRACTING FOR SERVICES

In most cases, the company uses its own employees and quality control personnel to handle the procurement control function. However, there is an increasing tendency to use vendor surveillance services. Such service organizations typically use people with extensive experience. These personnel have retired from quality assurance, quality engineering, quality control, or inspection positions in industry or government. Such specialists are not interested in going back to work on a full-time basis, but frequently they are available for short-term, temporary, or part-time assignments. An example of how they are effective would be when one would require their presence in a plant for one or two days a week for several weeks; or where an assignment involves working 4 hours per day for one month or one full week per month. Obviously, many other patterns of hours per day, days per week, and overall length of assignment are possible.

The depth and breadth of experience of these representatives makes them knowledgeable regarding many, and in some cases, all of the following skills:

Specifications preparation/interpretation
Conducting of quality surveys
Auditing
Process control
Sampling inspection
Receiving inspection
In-process inspection
Final inspection
First article inspection
Witnessing/conducting tests
Drawing and change control
Material review board actions
Packaging and shipping
Corrective action
Metrology
Precision measurement
Performance monitoring
Technical data/publications review
Reporting
Reliability
Maintainability
Configuration management

There are several advantages of contracting for vendor surveillance services:

1. Qualified people are available where services are needed, eliminating the cost of sending company personnel to the supplier's location

2. By using third-party inspection personnel, uninterrupted and continued operations are possible when company employees are not available for assignments away from the plant.

3. Use of contract personnel avoids the expenses of hiring, training, insurance, pension, holiday, vacation, and sick-leave costs. These would be required for company employees or new hires.

4. Contract inspection agencies can provide specialized talents and necessary skills which may not be available in-house. For example, a company may have a once-per-year requirement to source inspect certain materials or perform a quality audit or survey at a distant supplier. Another company might need help in designing and installing a complete vendor surveillance system.

5. A large experienced staff can effectively be provided "on call" at no cost until needed. This feature makes possible the expansion, and subsequent contraction, of the work force with a minimum of effort. Hiring new personnel and later effecting their release would generally be much more time consuming and expensive. Lean staffing, without its attendant risks, can be a reality and a feasible alternative.

6. Contract surveillance services provide an objective, third-party perspective to the buyer-vendor relationship. Although working for the buyer, the surveillance specialist does not have the built-in biases of the regular, full-time company employee.

7. The use of part-time or intermittent, short-term assignments (e.g., one day per week) on a cost-effective basis becomes quite feasible. This feature also permits the use of a person on a pilot or trial basis at minimal expense, to demonstrate his or her capability and available skills.

III. FINDING VENDOR SURVEILLANCE SOURCES

Sources for vendor surveillance services can be found in several ways. Probably the best source is through personal referrals. Talking with quality control personnel and other people in similar industrial situations will sometimes provide valuable references. Another avenue of investigation is through the reading of trade journals, including the advertisements therein. Another area to be considered is attendance at meetings and referrals from professional organizations such as the American Society for Quality Control and the National Association of Purchasing Management. Trade shows, conferences, and exhibits are also a possible source of relevant information. Contacts with other attendees regarding their experience in the use of surveillance services can be very helpful.

IV. EVALUATING AND SELECTING SOURCES

After identifying surveillance services, the task becomes one of choosing which is best qualified and equipped to meet the specific need. In evaluating and selecting sources a number of factors must be taken into account. Some of these are:

1. The experience and qualifications of the personnel in the organization.
    This aspect can usually be dealt with by reviewing their résumés and
    and credentials plus a telephone or personal interview. The selecting
    company will probably want to talk with representatives of the service
    organization who have been proposed to perform the required assign-
    ment. The financial and other details should probably be handled by
    purchasing, but the checkout of the ability to satisfactorily perform
    the source inspection, audit, survey, or other quality activity should
    be handled by a member of the buyer's quality organization.
2. The service organization's history, reputation, and base of customer
    relationships should be a consideration. This can be done by calling
    others who have used the organization's services.
3. Availability of personnel in the geographical area where needed must
    be considered. If a qualified person is not available in the area, it may
    be more economical to send someone from another location or from the
    company, provided that the person can be released without creating
    problems at the buyer's plant.
4. Responsiveness in meeting your needs, such as program/project re-
    quirements, scope, and timeliness of coverage, are important consider-
    ations. The ability to provide several candidates allows choosing the
    person who is best able to meet the specific need.
5. Financial and business references and other sources can be used to
    check financial posture and integrity.
6. Can the quality and accounting people easily deal with organization
    and reporting time, invoicing, and so on?
7. Adherence to code of ethics for all representatives.
8. Facilities and regional operational capabilities.

V. COST CONSIDERATIONS

In contracting for vendor surveillance, there should be a clear understanding
of rates, terms, and conditions between the company and the service organization. The scope and duration of the contract should be clearly defined.
Cost savings should be given full consideration and should be based on a comprehensive cost/benefit analysis. Finally, provision must be made for an adequate accounting system and related controls. The system must provide the
necessary data regarding time reporting, billing, and invoicing.

VI. PREPARATION FOR THE VENDOR SURVEILLANCE ASSIGNMENT

Following the selection of someone to represent its interests, the company must
take steps to assure that the representative is adequately prepared for the
assignment. An orientation session should be held in which the quality specialist is told the requirements of the assignment, what he or she is expected
to do, and introduced to the company's quality philosophy and policy. Beyond
that the person should be furnished applicable procedures, standards, specifications, or other guidelines. Reporting instructions (what, where, when, to
whom) should also be provided. The representative should be informed regarding tools, equipment, or other devices to be used, and given the authorization to perform the assigned tasks. If the foregoing are done properly,

the representative will be in a good position to meet the buyer's objectives for effective vendor surveillance and source inspection.

VII. EVALUATION OF PERFORMANCE

Just as it is important to check on goods purchased, so it is important to look into the value of vendor surveillance services provided. When a contract has been signed it is important to install and maintain operational controls to assure that what has been bought is delivered. The monitoring of the performance of the representative doing the surveillance should begin immediately after a reasonable orientation period. Performance appraisal should be based essentially on the same standards as those used to evaluate the efforts of full-time employees. As a general rule, most professional representatives furnished by supplier surveillance companies are more regular in attendance, more skill-ful and knowledgeable, more conscientious in the conduct of their duties, and able to work with less supervision than other workers. This is because most of them have successfully completed a career and are on a semiretired basis. They are proud of their past achievements and anxious to demonstrate that they are still quite capable of making a substantial contribution. In most cases, the financial reward they receive is secondary to the satisfaction of knowing that they are productive members of an organization.

However, it is far better to eliminate the substandard performance early in the assignment rather than put it off. Finding out too late about ineffective representation could have serious consequences. Results of performance evaluation should be fed back to the appropriate officials in the organization furnishing the surveillance service on a timely basis. Performance of an exceptional nature should also be noted in a routine manner and recognized accordingly. As noted above, many of those semiretired specialists are motivated by a desire to feel needed. Recognition of their achievements not only rewards them, but also further feeds their desire to do well.

VIII. CONCLUSION

There are times when outside quality assurance specialists can more effectively control the quality of materials, parts, components, and assemblies procured from suppliers. A number of reasons for this have been described: savings through avoidance of travel costs; obviating the need to lose valuable employees from in-plant activities; rapid expansion and contraction of the work force; availability of specializations not needed on a full-time basis; and third-party objectivity. As with other procurement, the contracting for quality surveillance services should focus on the economic value and degree of excellence being bought. For that reason a careful evaluation of organizations offering such services should be made before one is chosen. Once a selection has been made, the performance of the company and its representatives should be evaluated continually to assure that the service organization is accomplishing what was intended.

FURTHER READING

American Society for Quality Control, *How to Establish Effective Quality Control for the Small Supplier*, ASQC, Milwaukee, Wis.

American Society for Quality Control, *Procurement Quality Control—A Handbook of Recommended Practices*, 2nd ed., ASQC, Milwaukee, Wis., 1976.

Crosby, Phillip B., *Quality Without Tears*, McGraw-Hill Book Company, New York, 1984.

Feigenbaum, A. V., *Total Quality Control*, McGraw-Hill Book Company, 1961.

Juran, J. M., *Quality Control Handbook*, 3rd. ed., McGraw-Hill Book Co., New York, 1974.

25

QUALIFICATION TESTING

Philip Crosby Associates, Inc.
Winter Park, Florida

I. INTRODUCTION

Product qualification is a defect-prevention program and the last chance you
have to assure that the product or service, to be delivered to the customer, is
exactly like the requirement. The requirement can be in the form of drawings,
specifications, contracts, laws, or even forms and procedures, but in all cases,
it should meet the needs of both the customer and the company. The needs of
both the customer and the company must include not only quality and reliability requirements, but product safety and environmental considerations. These
considerations would include packaging of the product as well as handling,
use, and even misuse. Product qualification, therefore, covers a review and
test of all the requirements for the complete product or service cycle from the
market survey through product life. Life testing, to verify reliability, is an
extension of the product qualification and will be conducted throughout the
life of the product. Accelerated life testing should be conducted during product qualification to give preliminary assurance, prior to production, that the
product will meet its reliability predictions.

Although this chapter will primarily be concerned with product qualification,
services to customers must also be qualified and analogies to product qualification can be applied. Qualifying a service to its requirement will include review and testing of policies, procedures, forms, and systems. An insurance
company would be an example of this type of qualification. However, any service company or service function within a manufacturing company should follow the qualification procedure.

II. PURPOSE OF PRODUCT QUALIFICATION

Product qualification is a procedure that must establish the controls necessary
to assure the following:

1. Each product is subjected to specified qualification tests and inspections
   to assure that it conforms to every requirement defined in its marketing
   and engineering specifications.

445

2. A product is not delivered to a customer until it has passed all of its qualification tests and the related documentation is compatible: for example, marketing specification, engineering specification, qualification test specification, final acceptance test and shipping procedures, commercial specifications and advertising literature, and maintenance or installation manuals.

3. Requalification should be considered on a yearly basis (minimum) or after each major modification.

III. DEFINITIONS

The following are not intended to reflect the total definition of the terms but rather to stress that portion of the definition which is particularly pertinent to product qualification.

Qualification: inspection and test of a final product to assure that it meets all unit and customer requirements

Requalification: performing the original qualification procedure on a previously qualified product to assure that the product still meets the original or current requirements

Requirement: the mechanical, physical, chemical, electrical, and functional characteristics of the product

Marketing specification: the written requirements, produced and approved by the marketing department, reflecting the direct or anticipated product needs of the customer

Engineering specification: the written requirements, produced and approved by the engineering department, which reflect the requirements of the marketing specification, as well as additional unit requirements

Qualification specification: the written requirements, produced by the engineering department and approved by the quality department, which specify the unit actions necessary to prove that the product to be qualified meets all requirements in the marketing and engineering specifications

Qualification sample: a subassembly, component, system, or spare part built with the methods and techniques used in normal production of the product and inspected and tested to normal quality acceptance criteria

Process certification: an inspection and test report stating that a fabrication or assembly process meets the specified requirements

Test equipment certification: a written report stating that the test equipment meets all the specified requirements

Qualification test report: a clear and objective report, separating fact from opinion, which reflects the status of a product with respect to meeting all applicable requirements at a specific point in time

IV. APPLICATION

Qualification and requalification testing is concerned mainly with the design of the product and verification of processes. All functional requirements within all environments specified in the engineering specification will be tested. This activity should be part of the product plan.

In order to know how well samples tested conform to the design, the qualification procedure will include a formal acceptance test and inspection of tho production samples against the engineering drawings prior to qualification. The production samples tested should be made by normal manufacturing processes.

Due to the fact that products change during a period of production (e.g., design changes, vendor process changes, assembly and fabrication process changes, etc.), it is necessary that product "requalification" be considered a minimum of once a year or following any major redesign. Requalification should follow the same procedure used in the original qualification.

Qualification costs must be included in the budget and schedule of the development program with identifiable milestones.

V. POLICIES

To derive full benefits from a product qualification program and avoid misunderstandings in its application, there should be full agreement and commitment on the part of management to a quality policy. The quality policy must state simply that: "All employees of the company will perform exactly to the requirements, or officially change the requirements to what they and the customer really need."

Once the quality policy has been accepted by management, a product qualification policy should be issued to make it clear to all employees that management is very serious about meeting requirements. A sample policy is as follows:

POLICY GUIDE	POLICY	Number
	PRODUCT QUALIFICATION	Effective
		Cancels
Affects	Signature	Dated
SYSTEM	DIRECTOR-QUALITY	Page 1 of 1

INTENT

The intent of this policy is to establish the requirements for the qualification of all products manufactured or purchased for sale by this company.

APPLICATION

Each new product and associated documentation shall be subjected to specified tests and inspections at a planned stage in the product development cycle to assure that the production sample of the product conforms to every requirement defined in its marketing and engineering specifications.

Once a product has been qualified, the need to requalify by repeating some or all qualification tests shall be reviewed for each product every year and, in addition, after every major change. It is recognized that manufactured products will not continue to be identical with those that passed qualification tests.

A product shall not be delivered to or handed over to a customer until the company has complied with this policy.

RESPONSIBILITY

Performance of product qualification is a joint responsibility:

The company technical department is responsible for scheduling, budgeting, and performing product qualification, as well as formally issuing necessary specifications.

The company quality department is responsible for assuring that inspections and tests are performed according to specification by auditing these inspections and tests, as well as reporting the results.

The policy states the company's position with respect to product qualification and specifically assigns the quality and engineering departments the responsibility for applying the policy. This is important for two reasons:

1. Unless product qualification is budgeted for both time and money required, it will not occur.
2. The policy provides for the engineering department to be responsible for budgeting product qualification, providing the documentation, and performing the tests. Quality is responsible for monitoring or auditing the total operation and reporting the results. Regardless of which department actually performs these functions, there should be one department performing the test and another auditing and reporting the results. This approach will assure that assigned activities have been performed according to the written procedures.

In addition, a formal product qualification procedure should be written detailing the specific tasks to be completed in any product qualification. The following information would be included in this procedure.

A. Responsibilities for Product Qualification

The technical and quality departments have the prime responsibility for product qualification. Personnel in both of these departments must be assigned specific management responsibilities for each product designated for product qualification. The following assignments and actions will assure effective management of the program.

1. The general manager and the product line manager should approve qualification or requalification schedules established by the technical director.
2. The company technical director should:
   a. Appoint a technical program manager for each product to be qualified or requalified.
   b. Include the cost of qualification testing (and retesting necessitated by initial failures) as an identifiable item in the development budget. Charge all costs of the tests, including supply and refurbishing of test samples, to established cost centers.

    c. Include the necessary time for qualification testing in the development program.

    d. Include qualification testing as development milestones (minimum requirements: start of tests and publication of final qualification test report).

    e. Schedule all products requiring qualification or requalification. Issue a schedule in January for the current year.

3. The company technical program manager should:

    a. Define the product configuration to be tested.

    b. Approve the qualification test schedule.

    c. Ensure that samples for test are made by final manufacturing methods.

    d. Ensure that the required number of samples for test are made and delivered according to schedule.

    e. Ensure that personnel to carry out tests requiring expertise possessed by the technical department (e.g., functional tests) is available at the scheduled time.

    f. Ensure that functional test equipment is calibrated and available according to schedule.

    g. Ensure that the engineering specification defining the requirements that the product must meet has been written, approved by technical, marketing, and product line management and formally published according to schedule.

    h. Ensure that the qualification specification defining the qualification tests has been written, approved by the technical and quality departments, and formally published, according to schedule. This specification should include separate qualification of subassemblies or parts and packaging for shipping of product or spares.

    i. Approve (or formally disapprove) qualification test reports.

4. The company development program manager should correct the product design to overcome deficiencies revealed by failure of qualification tests.

5. The company quality manager should:

    a. Designate a quality program manager for each product to be qualified or requalified.

    b. Supply personnel to carry out tests and inspections (e.g., configuration checks, visual and mechanical inspections, verify certification of processes, qualification of vendor parts, test equipment certification and calibration).

    c. Approve qualification test reports.

6. The company quality program manager should:

    a. Take personal responsibility for ensuring that all aspects of the qualification are performed correctly according to schedule (including selection, inspection, and test of qualification samples) or that delinquencies are reported to the general manager.

    b. Advise the company comptroller of qualification testing in order that he or she may properly accumulate costs for reporting in conformance with comptroller's procedure concerning quality costs.

    c. Audit the measurable product qualification activities of the company technical director and technical program manager and report to the general manager unresolved deficiencies and omissions.

d. Provide the company technical program manager with assistance in drafting the qualification test specification, assuring that it is compatible with the engineering specification.
e. Approve or formally disapprove the qualification test specification.
f. Ensure that the qualification test log is filled in correctly and is retained for reference.
g. Report to company management monthly on the progress of the qualification tests against the schedule.
h. Prepare and submit interim and final qualification test reports to the general manager.
i. Issue a yearly summary of all product qualifications and re-qualifications listing products passing and those in-process with status.
j. Audit corrective action and retesting shown necessary by failure of tests and report results in the qualification test report.

Qualification Schedule

The unit technical director must as early as possible produce a qualification test schedule. This will give the planned dates for each key event in the qualification test program. It must be approved by the quality program manager and should be reviewed at each design review meeting. Figure 1 is an example of such a schedule.

Reporting Qualification Results

Qualification test log: Every event and failure occurring during the actual performance of the qualification tests must be recorded formally in a qualification test log. Overall control of the test log is the responsibility of the quality program manager.

Interim and final qualification or requalification test reports: The purpose of the qualification test reports is to give the general manager and his or her technical, marketing, and quality advisors a clear understanding of the status of the qualification testing. Special emphasis should be placed on those tests that have passed and failed. The report will give these managers confidence that the tests have been carried out correctly and have been reported objectively. The report should contain sufficient detail to meet these purposes, but should be as concise as possible. It must not assume that the reader has detailed knowledge of the product. Nor must understanding of the report depend on knowledge or reference to other documents (e.g., the qualification test specification). The report must be completely self-explanatory. If necessary, specially prepared summaries of other documents (but not the documents themselves) can be attached as appendices to the qualification test report.

Figure 2 illustrates the sections that should be included in a qualification test report. The title must state that the report was prepared by the unit quality program manager and be signed by the manager. The report must also be approved and signed by the unit technical program manager and must be approved by the company quality director and the technical director. Final qualification and requalification reports and all referenced documents should be filed as historical records for the life of the product.

Event	Planned start	Planned complete	Actual start	Actual complete	Responsible
1. First draft engineering specification written, approved, and issued					
2. First draft qualification test specification written, approved, and issued					
3. Qualification test samples made, selected, and delivered					
4. Configuration control inspection					
5. Visual and mechanical inspection					
6. Product safety review and risk analysis					
7. Review of environmental considerations					
8. Functional test (standard conditions)					
9. Functional test (marginal conditions)					
10. Dry heat test					
11. 1000-hr accelerated-life test					
12. Vibration					

FIGURE 1   Sample product qualification schedule.

Event	Planned start	Planned complete	Actual start	Actual complete	Responsible
13. Shock					
14. Altitude					
15. Salt spray					
16. Humidity					
17. Any other environmental conditions					

FIGURE 1   (Continued)

1.   Title; identification of item being qualification tested; date of report; identification as interim or final report.
2.   Approval signatures (unit's technical program manager, quality director, and the technical director).
3.   Distribution (unit and group management).
4.   Summary (this must clearly state that the product is qualified or that it is not qualified and state the reason).
5.   Contents of the report.
6.   Qualification test personnel (listing of unit personnel conducting product qualification).
7.   Test venue and date.
8.   Specification (engineering, qualification, and others).
9.   Identification of samples tested and the configuration tested.
10.   Assembly inspection and test status report of qualification samples (prior to qualification).
11.   List of certified test equipment used (range and accuracy and calibration date).
12.   Report on results of process certification at the time of qualification.
13.   Report on qualification of vendor parts, subassemblies, and components check.
14.   Report on results of product safety and risk analysis.
15.   Test log.
16.   Corrective action (planned and accomplished).
17.   Repeat of failed tests (history).
18.   Summary of test results and conclusion.

FIGURE 2   Sections of the final qualification test report.

VI. MANAGEMENT TRAINING IN PRODUCT QUALIFICATION

To derive full benefits from a product qualification program, all management and supervisory personnel should understand the reasons for qualification and their role in the program. Although the quality and technical departments have the prime responsibility for product qualification, all departments can contribute to the writing of the qualification test procedure. The manufacturing department has experience on past production problems, and the purchasing department must, for example, understand that only qualified components can be purchased.

For this reason, the quality, marketing, and technical departments should construct a training program to assure that all supervisors understand the total qualification program and how each function can contribute. The following typical questions should be answered in the training program, and a test similar to the following sample quiz should be given during training to assure understanding by attendees.

A. Instructor's Information

Typical Product Qualification Questions
(Handout) and Answers

1. *Where do I get the money?* Qualification testing is an intrinsic part of the development program. It must be a separately identifiable, costed and scheduled part of the development case.
2. *But I didn't budget money in my case; what do I do now?*
   a. This was a good argument before a product qualification policy was established.
   b. Determine essential requirements for the qualification test specification and see if critical portions can be done within present budget.
   c. Make sure that it is included in future new product plans.
3. *I haven't got the people to do product qualification this year.* Again this was a good excuse before a policy was issued. Qualification testing must be considered an important part of the overall development program. It must have its share of scarce resources. It is *not* just something you get to when everything else is in shape. This does not mean that one must have a gold-plated qualification test program and ignore other things.
4. *I do not have environmental test equipment to do product qualification.* This can be rented and products shipped to the rental location. Environmental testing is important, but it is only one aspect of qualification testing. What about the rest? What plans do we have to buy an environmental test chamber?
5. *My systems are large and complex. Product qualification as you have explained it is not practical.* Obviously, qualification testing of a complex system is different from that for a component. The required attitude is to determine how best it can be done, not say that it cannot. Some of the biggest problems have stemmed from inadequate qualification testing of major systems. One can develop methods for qualifying major subassemblies when the system is too large for a chamber.

Vincent

6. *My products have only limited sales. Product qualification, if I have to do it, will put me out of business.* Specify what is appropriate. If the margin is so poor, why develop the product?

7. *The qualification procedure says that new processes must also be qualified. This is not part of the development activity. Who should qualify new processes, and who should pay for them?* The main emphasis is on "products for sale." If a new process is required to develop the product, the qualification test of the product will cover the process. This is the responsibility of the developing house (and the technical department). Later, if the manufacturing department wants to introduce a new process, they must pay for the necessary requalification and charge this against cost reduction plans.

8. *I have too many new products to start qualification on them all at once. How do I decide which ones should be done first?* Do the most important first. But is it really true that you cannot do them all at once if you devise practical programs?

B. Quiz

1. Qualification testing is carried out to reveal weaknesses in design so that these can be eliminated before delivery to the customer.

   Answer: False.

   The purpose is to prove that the product conforms to the requirements. Qualification should be an assurance procedure that is exercised on a product that everyone feels will meet the requirements. However confident engineers are that the product will conform, there always seems to be a hidden weakness that must be corrected during qualification testing. Hence, an answer of true is not entirely wrong.

2. Qualification testing must be the responsibility of the technical department because only they really understand the product and they pay for the tests.

   Answer: False.

   Qualification testing is set up as a joint responsibility of the technical and quality functions. There is no other practical way of getting the products qualified other than by the cooperation of these two functions. Quality departments need the expertise of the technical department. Quality managers have to make sure that the programs happen and ensure that they are done in a disciplined manner and are reported objectively.

3. An important aspect of qualification testing is that it forces complete specification of the product.

   Answer: True.

   In many cases, there are subsystem specifications or partially complete system specifications or obsolete specifications but not a well documented up-to-date system specification. To write the qualification test procedure, there must be an engineering specification not to mention the maintenance manuals, customer literature, and specifications. During the writing of all these documents, the validity of the engineering specification is often questioned and the specification changed.

1. Even though the qualification tests are not complete, it is sometimes permissible to deliver some product to customers in order to meet promised delivery dates, provided that the quality manager approves.

   Answer: False.

   Even though it has been done, it is not permissible and is an indication that the program was improperly planned. If the product is shipped, management is taking a risk. Second, the quality manager does not determine when a deficient product will be shipped. This is a total management decision. Quality personnel are responsible for reporting the condition for a management decision. If there is not enough market to develop the product properly, to specify it properly and to qualification test it properly, you should not be developing that product.

5. The qualification test reports are not written to the general manager because they have to contain too much technical detail.

   Answer: False.

   The general manager wants to know if the product passed qualification— and must know to be able to make a decision as to whether the product can be released. Therefore, the report must be written in such a way that the general manager can understand it. If general managers cannot understand the qualification test report, it is an indication that the quality manager has not written a good report. When the quality manager has difficulty writing the report, this means that the qualification testing program has not been done in an organized way. If the program is done properly, writing the report is a very quick and easy job.

6. Qualification testing must be conducted on items made using production tools and processes.

   Answer: True.

   If you deviate, the unit is taking a risk. Handcrafted units, such as engineering model or breadboards, will not prove a production process or actual components to be used in production. Remember, product qualification not only proves the design but also the processes. Engineering testing during development is a prequalification. Product qualification can only be started when all drawings and specifications have been issued and development is complete. Qualification samples must come from pilot production.

7. A product that has passed all its qualification tests should give no problems in the future.

   Answer: False.

   In a complex piece of equipment, it is impossible to say that you will have no future failures. There are all kinds of possibilities of factors changing, over some of which quality people have absolutely no control. In the components business, products are requalified on a weekly basis to monitor the type of variability that creeps into metallurgical and chemical processes. A qualification test is a very useful thing, but it certainly does not assure that you are not going to have any problems in the future. In general, you could say that a qualified product will give you 90% assurance that the product will meet its requirements. You do not have a 50% chance that the product will even work if it has not been qualified.

8.   One product is usually sufficient.

Answer: False.

This can be statistically calculated, depending on the confidence and probability that managers feel they need. On large or expensive systems, one or two is usually sufficient and testing will not cause destruction of the sample. On smaller, less expensive products, several samples will be selected and can be tested to destruction. This gives an accurate measure of safety margins. This is also advisable to be done on subassemblies of larger systems.

26

RECOVERY COSTS

ROBERT W. GRENIER

Weil-McLain Co.
Michigan City, Indiana

A question often asked by manufacturing executives is: Can you recover dollars lost from supplier defective material other than base material cost, that is, labor, burden, and any additional labor and burden incurred while adding additional value in the manufacturing process?

The answer to that question is yes. A well-managed purchasing department assisted by quality assurance can and should. There may be times when some costs will be negotiated, but recovering costs to reduce bottom-line losses is a purchasing department responsibility.

Negative conditions in an economy are given as a reason for not recovering additional losses. A purchasing department should not be influenced by outside forces to perform in a consistent fashion regarding supplier recovery dollars. One will also find, generally, that reliable sources will react the same in the future as they have in the past.

The first premise that has to be made is that the purchasing department has the functional responsibility for procurement quality. Therefore, any associated supplier defective costs should be part of the purchasing department's expense budget. This budget becomes one main measurement of their annual activities. It is erroneous for general management to believe that major improvements can be made in reducing supplier defective costs if these dollars are in a quality department's budget. The latter function does not make the final choice of suppliers, nor do they negotiate the recovery of these lost dollars.

The object of a well-planned supplier assurance program is to improve customer acceptance of a product while reducing total unplanned losses in purchased material. How is this accomplished? The goal is met by reducing total gross supplier defective costs and increasing the recovery of these dollars. What is included in "gross defect dollars?" It consists of the base costs of the procured material and any associated labor and burden costs expended upon receipt, plus any additional lost labor with its associated burden if pieces are found defective after work has been performed. This would include removal and replacement of a defective item in an assembly area or at a customer site.

What role does supplier quality assurance have in the above if it does not have the main responsibility for procurement quality? Supplier quality has a responsibility in assisting purchasing in reducing unplanned supplier defects

and recovering the resultant defect costs. Let us examine how a supplier recovery system could help your company. Suppose that you have accepted a
position in the CJD Company as quality manager. CJD had no previous quality
systems in effect other than a basic inspection and sorting program.

In the initial systems review, one of the first things you should do is to
review the departmental expense budget for the past 12 months. If all the
defect costs of CJD are listed in your budget, one must be ready to sell the
"boss," hopefully the general manager, on the following concept. These costs
belong to the budgetary functions that have responsibility for performing an
action that will improve the situation. As far as make-or-buy decisions are
concerned, the quality department functionally does not design the parts,
does not buy the parts, does not make the parts, does not assemble the parts,
and does not service your product at customer sites. Your main activities are
to aid your industrial functionary counterparts in implementing prevention
activities and in their day-to-day product quality responsibilities. Hopefully,
your boss will understand, and in subsequent meetings with financial people,
the costs will be allocated to their proper responsibilities.

Once the action discussed above has been taken, one should analyze all
defect costs to find the various product quality levels. Special attention
should be given to the total supplier defective costs. Divide these total supplier costs by total sales for the given period of time (or dollar receipts) in
the same time frame to obtain supplier quality level percentage. Many prefer
to use dollar receipts because it divorces other financial costs which have no
impact on supplier costs such as marketing or direct design engineering costs.

After establishing supplier defective costs and related percentage, review
your in-house supplier control system. First, determine how your plant defective material is controlled. Many industries reject all the material at the
location where it is discovered. The defective material is then dispositioned
at this location, hopefully no later than 24 hours after rejection, by representatives of quality and other functions. Too often supplier defective material becomes intermixed with plant defective material. This material is susceptible to "gathering dust" if the control of a defect material system is not
procedurized and strictly enforced. Occasionally, this scattered and intermixed material and in-plant material is sent out to the scrap bins together.
The feedback date for the supplier defects and subsequent recovery costs are
lost.

The following system control methods are recommended. Once supplier
material has been determined to be defective, it should be properly identified
and immediately forwarded to a centrally located area for disposition. This
centrally located area should be under lock and key to prevent any defective
material from reentering the mainstream of acceptable material.

In some instances material will be found defective at a customer site. Many
companies may have a centrally located plant area where this material is returned for failure analysis evaluation. Customer and supplier representatives
then have the opportunity to review the status and reason for the defective
product. This review can enhance recovery opportunities.

Immediately after this initial review of customer returns, forward the vendor defective material to the "locked" area. By centrally locating all supplier
defective material in one area, proper control and ease of returning product
to supplier for corrective action and recovery of defect dollars are enhanced.

If disposition calls for "scrap" and/or "return to vendor," the purchasing
department representative should process the associated paperwork as quickly
as possible. The material should be on the way back to a supplier within 15

days of the date of discovery. Any longer will impede immediate corrective action on future deliveries.

When there is an urgency to meet production schedule, one may decide to have rework done in-house. An industrial engineer should then estimate the time and related costs of fixing the pieces. Armed with this information, the buyer can then contact the supplier, notifying them of the rejection and of the estimated cost of fixing the material. If these costs are reasonable, many suppliers will agree to your in-house rework on repair. It will often be cheaper than paying the costs of freight, paper processing, and the actual repair-rework or replacement costs at their facility.

If the disposition is "use as is," a design engineering representative should sign off, denoting acceptance of the deviation. The supplier should be notified for future corrective action procedures regardless of the "use as is," because it is truly a discrepancy.

During the continuing initial review of the defective material control systems, the reject form should be analyzed to make certain that it is not simply a common scrap ticket. The form should provide a clear description of the discrepancy and subsequent disposition of "use as is," "rework," "repair," and "scrap" (return to vendor). If the form is large enough, it can be used as the method for describing the defect and return notice for corrective action on subsequent material. The complete history is now on one sheet. If the form is simply a scrap ticket, the use as is and/or rework/repair defective material is never processed for corrective action by the supplier. There is no impact on correcting future shipments.

The rejection declaration should be precise and clear, avoiding such statements as "leaks," "porous," and "it doesn't fit." Say what the problem is and comment on dimensional or functional parameters.

Make sure that responsible personnel are properly trained in the internal material controls system of rejected material. This includes documentation procedures implemented by the material control department as well as the system for processing of forms on vendor defective material issued by the purchasing department.

The next step is to analyze rejects. During the initial review of the system one will find that the Pareto law of "significant few and trivial many" has a definite application. The analysis will show that a few of your suppliers are generating the majority of your defects. List those defects, with the associated costs of labor, material, and burden, in descending order of impact. Once this is done, forward it to the purchasing manager for his or her use in contacting the suppliers to improve their level of quality.

Even with a limited number of personnel, improvements can be made quickly by communicating solely with the major problem suppliers. Do not try to shotgun activities with all suppliers, as this will give you limited payback, and quality improvement of incoming material will be slow.

On a continuing monthly basis, the supplier quality assurance engineers, with their purchasing counterparts, should review the supplier's progress. As a matter of good business, in reviewing the corrective action timetable, always try to use the supplier's plan. Do not dictate an unreasonable time frame because it may be completely unachievable and destroy the desired corrective action efforts.

Another important step related to purchase material is the implementation of a procedure for dealing with new suppliers. A quality system survey should be conducted by representatives from purchasing and quality. After the initial contact by the purchasing department has been made, the agreement to the survey has been received, perform the survey as quickly as possible. A survey checklist is attached as a guide to what information could be analyzed (see Fig. 1).

Upon completion of a supplier system survey, the auditors should state whether or not the potential supplier is acceptable, conditional (i.e., certain system deficiencies must be corrected), or not acceptable. If a supplier is considered not acceptable, purchasing must send out inquiries to other reliable sources. A "good" purchasing department will buy only from reliable sources, regardless of economy. Reliable suppliers will also acknowledge their deficiencies, will try to correct their problems, and will accept the costs incurred by defective material.

When the quality system survey has concluded that a given supplier has the potential to furnish acceptable material, a preaward conference would be recommended. Why a preaward conference? It has been the author's experience that the majority of errors that a reliable supplier will make are traceable

1) Is the quality function a separate and distinct part of the suppliers organization?

2) The quality organization is comprised of:
   _____Inspectors _____Technicians ____Engineers

3) Are adequate written procedures established to define quality control operations and responsibilities?

4) Is there sufficient data available to confirm the quality control procedures are operational?

5) Does the supplier have an adequate drawing and change control program in effect?

6) Are adequate drawings and specifications available to manufacturing and inspection?

7) Are customer drawings and specifications utilized? Or does the supplier utilize own drawings and specifications which have been approved by the customer?

8) Is quality cost information reported and utilized by management?

9) Is classification of characteristics utilized and/or understood by by supplier personnel.

10) Are quality personnel trained or qualified for specific assignment?

Rank each question 0 to 5 based on observation of activity and stage of implementation. (N/A - not applicable)   Applicable
                                                                         Supplements

0 - required but not available   3 - average (operational)   _____
1 - available but non current   4 - above average
2 - minimal activity   implementation   _____
                                   5 - Outstanding for subject   _____

FIGURE 1   Survey checklist.

1) Is a tool calibration program in operation?

2) Is all information equipment identified and traceable to records?

3) Are records of calibration maintained and up to date?

4) Are master standards traceable to National Bureau of Standards?

5) Are personal tools calibrated the same as company tools?

6) Are tools, gages and test equipment adequately handled and protected to prevent damage.

7) Are metrology requirements periodically evaluated and new equipment added to upgrade capabilities.

1) Are adequate metallurgical laboratory facilities available and utilized? Source is_____

2) Are laboratory facilities and personnel adequate for the type of product produced?

3) Are laboratory procedures and instructions documented?

4) Are records of laboratory tests maintained and traceable to the products?

5) Laboratory capabilities include:
      physical test   microstructure
      chemistry   magnetic particle
      hardness   NDT (list)

1) Are quality requirements communicated to suppliers and subcontractors?

2) Are all incoming shipments submitted to inspection prior to storage or use?

3) Is each new job, issue change or initial shipment from a new source submitted to FACI?

FIGURE 1   (Continued)

4) Is raw material tested to determine conformance to
    specification?

5) Are incoming inspection instructions documented?

6) Are incoming inspection records maintained and
    up to date?

7) Is the validity of certifications verified periodically?

8) Are adequate gages and test equipment available to
    incoming inspection and is their calibration timely?

9) Is the acceptance status of each incoming shipment
    identified? How:
    Rough_____   Semi Finished_____   Finished_____

10) Is supplier quality performance evaluated and information
     fed back to suppliers?

1) Are work instructions documented and available on the job?

2) Is the required inspection tooling specified for each job
    and is it calibrated and available to the operator?

3) Is production tooling and gaging qualified prior to or at
    the time of first use?

4) Are inspection instructions documented and do they include
    specific characteristics and checking frequencies?

5) Are applicable drawings and specifications available at
    each work station where required?

6) Is each set-up qualified prior to running production?
    Arranged by: Operator____   Supervisor____   Inspector____

7) Do operators maintain a record of inspection and test that
    they perform?

8) Is acceptance criteria established for all products and
    processes?

9) Are special process controls utilized where applicable?

10) Are all units reviewed by inspection prior to storage or use?

11) Is material identity and acceptance status maintained?

12) Do inspection frequencies follow acceptable practices?

13) Have process capability studies been performed and is there
     evidence that capabilities are known?

FIGURE 1   (Continued)

1) Is all outgoing product submitted for final acceptance inspection?

2) Are inspection instructions documented and in use?

3) Are records of inspection and test maintained?

4) Is acceptance status clearly identified for all material accepted after inspection?

5) Are test procedures and acceptance criteria documented where applicable?

6) Are inspection and test records traceable to the product?

7) Are special identification, protection and packaging requirements documented and available to shipping?

8) Do final inspections and tests correlate with use or function of product?

1) Is non-conforming material adequately identified to prevent use or shipment?

2) Is rejected material promptly reported to management and action taken?

3) Do inspection and test records indicate the nature and number of observations as well as number of defects?

4) Are customer complaints recorded and is an appropriate corrective action initiated?

5) Is customer returned material evaluated to determine cause of rejection and plan corrective action?

6) Is customer advised of failure analysis findings and corrective action?

7) Are deviation requests and applicable authorizations documented?

8) Are records of rejections analyzed to segregate repetitive problems and plan corrective action?

9) Are records of corrective action maintained?

FIGURE 1   (Continued)

1)   Housekeeping

2)   Lighting in inspection

3)   Lighting in manufacturing

4)   Controlled operations

5)   Condition of information equipment

6)   Condition of manufacturing facilities

7)   Materials handling & storage

SUMMARY

Element	Potential	Score	Percent
Quality system	x5		
Calibration program	x5		
Metallurgical controls	x5		
Incoming material control	x5		
In process controls	x5		
Acceptance inspection	x5		
Information feedback	x5		
Rating	x5		

FIGURE 1   (Continued)

to lack of communication. This takes many forms: incomplete drawing information, misinformation on the part of the supplier as to a component's function
in your product, lack of packing and packaging information, and so on.

Purchasing, quality, design engineering, manufacturing, and the supplier's
sales, quality, and, at their option, representatives from the manufacturing
department should meet prior to the issuance of the purchase order. The
meeting agenda should be a detailed review of all proposed drawings. Clarify
any questions that the supplier may have and establish ground rules for quality acceptance criteria, manufacturing methods and processes, required packing and packaging protection, and the method of handling defective material.
At this time, recovery costs should be discussed and agreed to by both companies. Once this total agreement has been reached, the minutes of the meeting should be signed by representatives of your purchasing department and
the supplier's sales representatives as binding clauses to your future working
relationships.

In the continuing efforts to increase supplier recovery dollars, have the
purchasing manager provide the quality department with major purchase orders for present suppliers and any original quotes for potential suppliers.

TABLE 1

1978	Dollar Receipts	Supplier Gross Scrap	Percent Receipt	Dollar Receipts	Supplier Gross Scrap	Percent Receipts
Jan.	4,440,000	79,763	1.80	4,440,000	79,763	1.80
Feb.	5,100,000	65,750	1.29	9,540,000	145,513	1.53
March	6,838,000	127,464	1.86	16,378,000	272,977	1.67
April	5,072,000	107,733	2.12	21,450,000	380,710	1.77
May	5,770,000	82,630	1.43	27,220,000	463,340	1.70
June	6,532,000	118,874	1.82	33,752,000	582,214	1.73
July	3,857,000	82,846	2.15	37,609,000	665,060	1.77
Aug.	4,455,000	91,913	2.06	42,064,000	756,973	1.80
Sept.	7,900,000	135,858	1.72	49,964,000	892,821	1.79
Oct.	6,714,000	144,960	2.16	56,678,000	1,037,781	1.83
Nov.	6,471,000	158,870	2.45	63,149,000	1,196,660	1.89
Dec.	7,600,000	150,143	1.98	70,749,000	1,350,514	1.90

1979						
Jan.	4,300,000	29,984	0.70	75,049,000	1,380,497	1.83
Feb.						
March						
April						
May						
June						
July						
Aug.						
Sept.						
Oct.						
Nov.						
Dec.						

TABLE 1   (Continued)

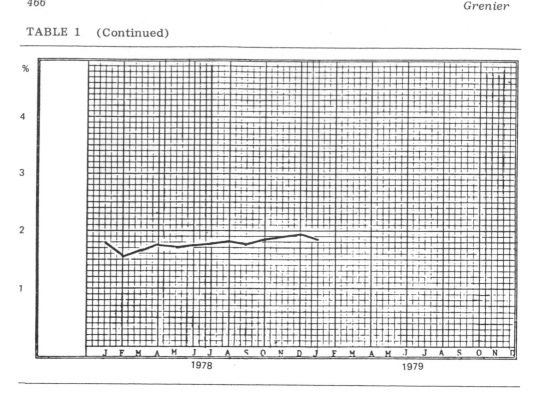

This should be done prior to issuance. The intent of this review is to assure that the proper and complete quality information is being forwarded to the supplier.

The next step in the implementation of your supplier quality system must deal with new-part acceptance. Upon receipt of the first lot of a new part number, regardless of supplier origin, a representative sample(s) should be submitted to a first article complete inspection (FACI). The FACI will confirm dimensionally, chemically, and metallurgically the conformance of the supplier's component to requirements. Under no circumstances should a piece be verified unless it is accompanied by the supplier's result, also denoting conformance to your requirements.

Once these systems are functioning, begin tracking "gross supplier defective dollars" on a separate chart. The base recommended is dollar receipts. Begin tracking these numbers for an ongoing 2-year period. As Table 1 shows, the first three columns list the month's receipts, the gross defective dollars, and the percentage of the first two columns. The next three columns are the year-to-date figures. At the bottom, track the year-to-date percentage on a 12-month moving average to show trend lines.

The second chart (Table 2) is the recovery portion of the gross unplanned loss dollars. As above, track ongoing costs for a 2-year span. The first monthly column reflects the gross supplier defective costs, the second column is the recovery dollars, and the third column is the percentage of the first two columns. The next three columns are the year-to-date figures. The graph below these numbers is the 12-month moving average trend line.

In the example, the recovery percentage year-to-date is almost identical to the previous year's total percent recovery. You will note that these reflect

TABLE 2

1978	Defect Scrap Dollars	Recovery Dollars	Percent Of Scrap	Scrap Dollars	Recovery Dollars	Percent Of Scrap
Jan.	79,763	49,016	61.5	79,653	49,016	61.5
Feb.	65,750	55,725	81.7	145,513	102,741	70.5
March	127,464	77,141	60.7	272,977	179,882	66.0
April	107,733	76,713	71.2	380,710	256,595	67.4
May	82,630	74,492	90.2	463,340	331,087	71.5
June	118, 874	91,786	77.3	582,214	422,873	72.6
July	82,846	62,277	75.2	665,060	485,150	72.9
Aug.	91,913	58,413	63.6	756,973	543,563	71.8
Sept.	135,848	92,494	68.1	892,821	636,057	71.2
Oct.	144,960	97,968	67.6	1,037,781	733,755	70.7
Nov.	158,879	126,135	79.4	1,196,660	859,890	71.9
Dec.	150,143	157,679	105.0	1,350,514	1,017,569	75.3
1979						
Jan.	29,983	22,942	76.5	1,380,497	1,040,511	75.4
Feb.						
March						
April						
May						
June						
July						
Aug.						
Sept.						
Oct.						
Nov.						
Dec.						

TABLE 2   (Continued)

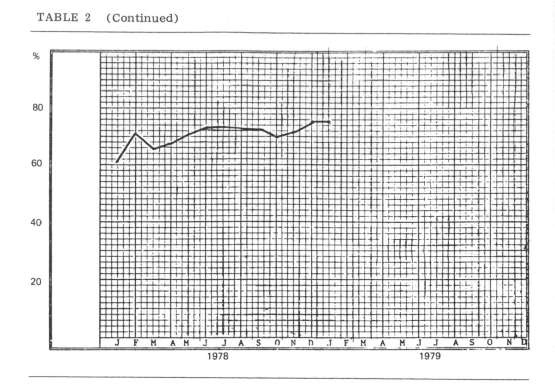

a 75% recovery rate. By measuring this way for several years, with the controls previously enumerated, an aggressive purchasing department, regardless
of economy, will show recoveries from 75 to 80% of their unplanned waste dollars. Once again, by earlier definition, the gross defect dollars reflect material, labor and burden costs, plus any additional lost labor and associated
burden if pieces are found defective after work has been performed. If you
do not include all three elements, you are losing dollars that are recoverable
for your operation.

In summation, what are some of the things that are done to maintain this
batting average?

1. A good purchasing department buys from reliable sources. Regardless
    of economy, reliable suppliers will acknowledge their mistakes and gen-
    erally accept the costs associated with defects.
2. In all cases return defective merchandise to a supplier. However, if
    you are going to repair an item in house due to the urgency of the
    pieces needed, write repair instructions and negotiate repair/rework
    costs with suppliers ahead of time. You will find that if you communi-
    cate with them what it will cost to fix the items in question, they will
    generally agree. Many times it will be cheaper for them to have you
    do it than to pay all the associated costs of transportation, delay,
    processing costs, and so on.
3. Return the defective item in a short period of time. Set your goal as
    2 weeks from date of rejection.
4. Set up a separate staging area for supplier defective material. For-
    ward in-house "return to vendor" material to this central staging area

for control   Do not leave material scattered all over.   Make certain that a procedure is written on handling defective material so that all functions know what are expected of them.

5. Be very definitive in the rejections. Do not simply write "defective" on your report. If possible, circle the defective area on the part by some means of identification.

In summation, experience has shown that a recovery factor of 75 to 80% of gross defect dollars is attainable. It is justifiable to charge lost labor and associated burden costs to the supplier. After all, isn't this true with your customers? Normally, you pay labor costs to fix your defective items found at a customer site. The same applies to your suppliers.

27

GEOMETRIC DIMENSIONS AND TOLERANCING

LOWELL W. FOSTER

Lowell W. Foster Associates, Inc.
Minneapolis, Minnesota

I. INTRODUCTION

Geometric dimensioning and tolerancing, or *geometrics* is a method of establishing controls for the geometry of a piece of hardware. It can be defined as "a means of dimensioning and tolerancing a drawing with respect to the actual function or relationship of part features which can be most economically produced." The language of geometrics conveys design requirements more clearly on the drawing. It provides a uniform communication to the manufacturing operations, and this melds all phases of the technical processes required to produce an electromechanical product.

It ensures that design requirements are clearly stated and thus carried out with less misunderstanding.
It assures interchangeability of mating parts at assembly.
It provides maximum tolerances to production.
It provides a uniform and universal drawing language.
Older methods of defining products no longer suffice on much of today's sophisticated design.
It is rapidly becoming the "spoken word" in engineering communication around the world.

Geometrics is an effective management tool. It facilitates communication between design, manufacturing, and all technical personnel involved. It further encourages valuable manufacturing and inspection techniques, and utilizes good standardization practices. It enhances the disciplined structure of engineering management by maximizing employee output in the technical areas and broadening its capabilities.
Geometrics should be used in the following situations:

When part features are critical to function or interchangeability
When datum references are necessary to ensure consistency between design, manufacture, and inspection operations
When functional gaging techniques are desirable
When standard interpretation is not already implied

Geometrics does not necessarily replace conventional or coordinate dimension-ing and tolerancing. One method supplements the other and should be used in combination for best advantage for the situation.

Geometrics can be successfully introduced in many ways: gradually, to replace confusing or archaic notes, or through a more expansive program to introduce the system as a new tool on a new project. Whichever method is chosen, do not expect broad success without a commitment to some form of education on the subject. This education can vary from introduction to shop personnel via shop meetings, pocket references, wall charts, bulletin boards, short classroom sessions, and so on, to in-depth seminars or courses for tech-nical and professional personnel.

Finally, geometrics, or geometric dimensioning and tolerancing, in its most modern form, is based on national and international standards. The American National Standards Institute, the top authority in the United States for volun-tary consensus standards, provides ANSI Y14.5-1973, *Dimensioning and Tol-erancing*. The International Standards Organization (ISO) provides ISO/1101, *Tolerances of Form and Position*.

II. GEOMETRICS SYMBOLS

Geometrics symbols (Fig. 1) can be used in place of notes on a drawing. Although the symbolic language must be learned, it has numerous advantages:

▱   FLATNESS

—   STRAIGHTNESS

◯   ROUNDNESS (CIRCULARITY)

⌀   CYLINDRICITY

⌒   PROFILE OF A LINE

⌓   PROFILE OF A SURFACE

⊥   PERPENDICULARITY (SQUARENESS)

∠   ANGULARITY

//   PARALLELISM

⟋   CIRCULAR RUNOUT

⟋   TOTAL RUNOUT *

⊕   POSITION

◎   CONCENTRICITY

⚌   SYMMETRY

---

*
Word TOTAL must be added beneath feature control symbol. Anticipated new symbol in future standards (ANSI, ISO), ⌓.

FIGURE 1   Geometric characteristics and symbols.

Symbols have a uniform meaning.

Symbols can be placed on the drawing more directly where the relationship applies.

Symbols can be drawn quickly and neatly with templates or conventional drawing tools.

Symbols adapt to computer-aided design or drafting.

Symbols are an international language.

Figure 2 compares a drawing using symbols versus notes, and Fig. 3 illustrates and defines briefly some additional symbols and terms.

Note: This chapter uses the U.S. customary or inch system as a basis. However, it must be clearly understood that the metric system base (the millimeter) can be used to no prejudice of the system; metric values of proper nomenclature are simply inserted in place of the inch value. With the gradual, yet steady, trend toward greater metric use, this option must be recognized.

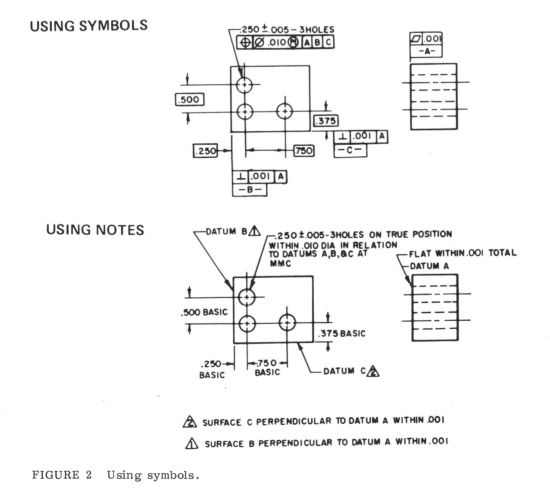

FIGURE 2   Using symbols.

OTHER SYMBOLS

Ⓜ   Maximum Material Condition   MMC

Ⓢ   Regardless of Feature Size   RFS

Ⓟ   Projected Tolerance Zone

⊕⌖   Datum Target

⌀   Diameter (cylindrical) Tolerance Zone

.XXX   Basic, Exact Dimension

-A-   Datum Identification Symbol

⊕ | ⌀ | .002 | Ⓜ | A   Feature Control Symbol (Frame)

TERMS

BASIC (BSC)	= Theoretically exact dimension.
DATUM	= Reference Points, Lines, Planes, Surfaces
FEATURE	= Component portion of a part, e.g., surface, hole, slot, etc.
LEAST MATERIAL CONDITION (LMC)	= Size opposite from MMC.
VIRTUAL CONDITION	= Collective effect of all tolerance variations on a feature.

FIGURE 3   Other symbols and terms.

III. FUNDAMENTAL PRINCIPLES

A. Maximum Material Condition Principle

Maximum material condition (MMC) provides the designer or drafter with a mechanism to calculate tolerances realistically and also provides advantages to production and inspection. By definition, maximum material condition is that condition of the part feature wherein it contains the maximum amount of material permitted by the stated size tolerance on the drawing (e.g., minimum hole size and maximum shaft size). Figure 4 illustrates the maximum material condition as it applies to representative mating parts.

The MMC principle is applicable only when (1) the feature controlled has some geometric relationship with another feature (e.g., a hole and an edge or surface, two or more holes in a pattern, a shaft and its axis, etc.), and (2) the feature, or features, is a "size" feature (e.g., a hole, pin, slot, etc.) which has a centerline, axis, or center plane. Note that the MMC principle is applicable in two orders of magnitude; that is, it has two separate and distinct meanings. One meaning is to indicate the "worst condition" (or other appropriate descriptors) that the part mating features will present to one another at assembly. The second and most important meaning is the principle or concept invoked by the symbol "circle M" (Ⓜ). This captures the subtlety of the effect of size deviation upon location. That is, as the part pin, for example, is produced at some size smaller than its MMC, that feature acquires an added form or positional tolerance in the amount of that departure from MMC. The part function is assured and more production tolerance is available, and if desired, functional gages can be utilized.

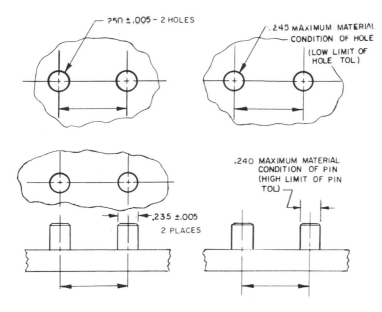

FIGURE 4   Maximum material condition principle.

B. Regardless of Feature Size

Another important principle is known as *regardless of feature size*. RFS, as
it is abbreviated in everyday jargon, simply means that the effect of the size
of the features, such as those shown in Fig. 4 (if, of course, RFS in invoked
on the drawing and not MMC) will *not* have an effect on the form or positional
tolerance. The stated form or positional tolerance is only to that amount
(maximum) regardless of the size to which the features are produced. Regardless of feature size means that the tolerance of form or position must be met
regardless of where the feature lies within its size tolerance.

As discussed later, the symbol "circle S" ($\circledS$) is stated on the drawing
when applied to positional tolerancing (i.e., according to Sec. IV, rule 2, or
as automatically invoked on *all* other geometrical tolerances (where applied to
a size feature relationship) according to rule 3.

As may be deduced, the RFS principle is usually applied to more-precision-
oriented parts, that is, where the effect of size departure from the MMC of
the controlled feature (or features) cannot be permitted to increase the form
or location tolerance.

IV. GENERAL RULES OF GEOMETRICS*

Also essential to a good understanding of geometrics are the general rules of
application. In addition to being very fundamental to the system, the general

---

*
  The symbols for maximum material condition (circle M) and regardless of
feature size (circle S) are also known as "modifiers"; that is, they are sometimes used to modify or change the implications of the following rules.

rules provide "handles" for the user. The general rules are self-explanatory as shown in Figs. 5 to 9 and described in the text.

A. Rule 1

Rule 1 deals with the relationship of size to form controls (see Fig. 5).

Interrelated Features

The form control provision of Rule 1, applies only to individual features and not to the interrelationship of features (see Fig. 6). Where such control of interrelated features is necessary, one of the following methods should be used to the extent dictated by the design requirements:

1. Specify a zero form tolerance at MMC for the features.
2. Indicate this control for the features involved by a note such as "PERFECT FORM AT MMC REQUIRED FOR INTERRELATED FEATURES."
3. Relate the dimensions to a datum reference frame.

Perfect Form at MMC Not Required

Where it is desired to permit a specified tolerance of form to exceed the boundary of perfect form at MMC, this may be done by adding to the drawing the suitable form tolerance and a note specifically exempting the pertinent size dimensions from the perfect form rule 1 requirement. A suitable note might be "PERFECT FORM AT MMC NOT REQUIRED."

B. Rule 2

Rule 2 deals with the symbology required to state MMC or RFS on positional tolerancing (see Fig. 7).

C. Rule 3

Rule 3 deals with the symbology required to state MMC or RFS, where appropriate, on form, attitude, and location controls (see Fig. 8).

D. Rule 4

Rule 4 deals with the symbology required to clarify geometric application to screw threads (see Fig. 9).

E. Rule 5

Rule 5 deals with the inference of virtual condition as it results from the interrelationship of size, form, attitude, and location tolerances. Rule 5 will not be clearly understood until good knowledge of the fundamentals of geometrics is acquired.

Although referenced in a feature control symbol at MMC, a datum feature of size controlled by a separate tolerance of location or form applies at its virtual condition. Where it is not intended for the virtual condition to apply, a zero tolerance at MMC should be specified for the appropriate datum features. Where no tolerance of location or form is specified for these features, a perfect form at MMC interrelationship is implied relative to each other as datums.

Unless otherwise specified, the limits of the dimension of an individual feature of size control the form of the feature as well as the size.

a) No element of the actual feature shall extend beyond a boundary of perfect form at MMC. This boundary is the true form implied by the drawing.

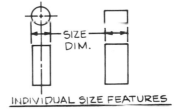

INDIVIDUAL SIZE FEATURES

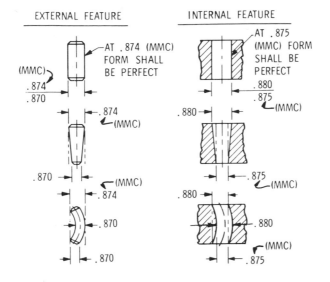

b) The actual size of the feature at any cross-section shall be within the LMC limit of size.

c) The form control provision of paragraph (a) does not apply to commercial stock such as bars, sheets, and tubing, where established industry standards prescribe straightness, flatness, and other conditions.

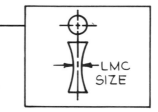

FIGURE 5   Rule 1

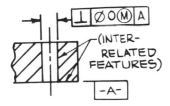

FIGURE 6   Interrelationship of features.

(Preferred Practice – Specify whether MMC or RFS).

For a tolerance of POSITION (formerly called true position), Ⓜ or Ⓢ shall be specified on the drawing with respect to the individual tolerance, datum reference(s), or both, as applicable.

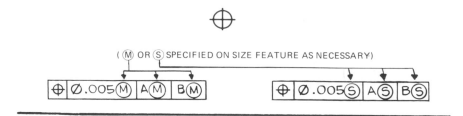

Alternate Practice   (MMC implied on ⊕ unless specified RFS).

For a tolerance of POSITION (formerly called true position), Ⓜ applies with respect to an individual tolerance, datum reference(s), or both, where no condition is specified. Ⓢ must be specified where it is required.

FIGURE 7   Rules 2 and 2a.

Virtual Condition

It is necessary to understand virtual condition as it applies to features. The following definition and the examples throughout the text will clarify its meaning. The virtual condition of a feature is a derived size generated from the collective effect of all profile variations permitted by the specified tolerances. It represents the most extreme condition of assembly at MMC. The virtual condition of a feature is thus the effective size of the profile that must be considered in determining the clearance between mating parts or features (see Fig. 10).

For other than a tolerance of position (formerly called true position), RFS applies with respect to an individual tolerance, datum reference(s), or both, where no condition is specified. Ⓜ must be specified on the drawing where it is required.

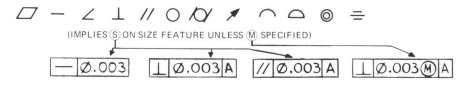

FIGURE 8   Rule 3.

Each tolerance of form or location and datum reference for a screw thread applies to the PITCH DIAMETER. Where design requirements necessitate an exception to this rule, a qualifying notation (such as MINOR DIA ($\varnothing$), MAJOR DIA ($\varnothing$), OD) shall be shown beneath the feature control symbol or datum identification symbol, as applicable.

MAJOR Ø   MAJOR Ø

For gears and splines, each form or location tolerance and datum reference shall designate the specific feature of the gear or spline to which it applies (e.g., MAJOR DIA ($\varnothing$), MINOR DIA ($\varnothing$), PITCH DIA ($\varnothing$), PD).

PD   PD

FIGURE 9   Rule 4.

Size + form or position error = shaft virtual condition

Size − form or position error = hole virtual condition

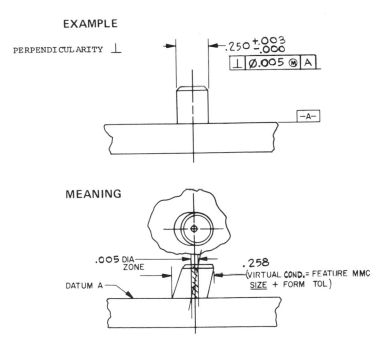

FIGURE 10   Virtual condition.

EACH DATUM REQUIRING IDENTIFICATION ON A DRAWING
IS ASSIGNED A DIFFERENT REFERENCE LETTER.

ANY LETTER EXCEPT I, O, OR Q MAY BE USED. DOUBLE
LETTERS MAY BE USED (AA, AB, ETC.) IF SINGLE LETTER
ALPHABET EXHAUSTED.

FIGURE 11   Datum identification symbol.

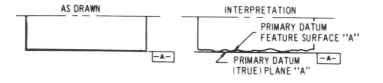

FIGURE 12   Establishing datum planes from datum surfaces.

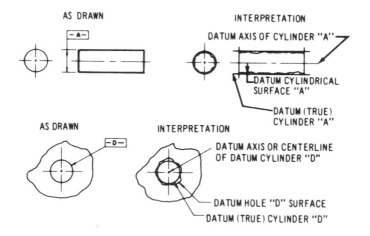

FIGURE 13   Establishing datum cylinders from datum features.

RELATIONSHIP OF DATUM PLANES AND
RELATED DIMENSION OR CENTER LINES:

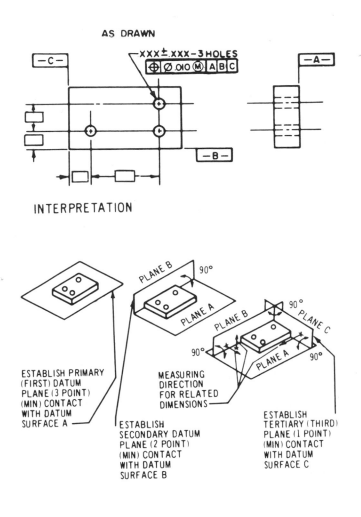

ALL DATUM PLANES (AS ESTABLISHED BY DATUM SURFACES) ON A PART
AND SHOWN AS INTERSECTING AT RIGHT ANGLES, ARE 90° BASIC BY
INTERPRETATION.

FIGURE 14   Three-plane concept.

Datums

The use of datums plays an important role in the application of geometrics. Datums provide a mechanism to capture design requirements (i.e., how the part mounts or the relationship of features) and ensure uniformity in fixturing, manufacturing, and inspecting the part.

Datums are points, lines, planes, cylinders, and so on, assumed to be exact for purposes of computation or reference and from which the location of features of a part may be established. Datums are established by, or are relative to, actual part features or surfaces. *Datum surfaces* and *datum features* are actual part surfaces or features used to establish datums and which include all the surface or feature irregularities and inaccuracies. The datum identification symbol is shown in Fig. 11.

Establishing Datums from Datum Surfaces and Datum Features

As seen in the foregoing definitions of datum, datum surfaces, and datum features, the datum as an exact entity is established by contact of the actual part feature with a simulated mating feature as represented by a surface plate, gage pin, precision collet, and so on. The datums are assumed to exist in associated processing equipment of high quality and thus simulate datum planes, cylinders, and so on, for purposes of verification. See Figs. 12 and 13 for examples of establishing datums from datum features and datum surfaces.

Three-Plane Concept

The three mutually perpendicular planes are fundamental to everyday life: to mathematics, geometry, machine movement, and engineering design. Without the three planes, engineering would be very hard pressed to define its product and inspection to measure it. The three planes have always existed; we have simply used them by intent in geometrics to identify and establish feature relationships. The three planes are, by geometric definition, mutually perpendicular. Figure 14 illustrates the establishment of the three datum planes and how the system invokes datum priority while reading the feature control symbol letter symbols left to right: that is, primary, secondary, and tertiary. datums (see Figs. 14 and 15).

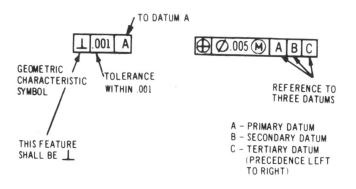

FIGURE 15   Feature control symbol.

V. APPLICATION OF TOLERANCES OF FORM, RUNOUT, AND LOCATION

The following series of illustrations and related text presents typical (and hypothetical) examples of the application of each control. The text explanation is minimized in favor of the pictorial illustrations. As described in the introductory paragraphs, a brief yet reasonably complete study of the major aspects of the subject is presented here. Should questions arise, or there is need for in-depth information, refer to one of the text references at the end of the chapter or the standard authority, ANSI Y14.5 (latest issue).

A. Application to Individual or Related Features

It is helpful in learning, or applying, geometrics to more clearly identify *certain* geometric characteristics for *certain* uses. That is, the more elementary controls (i.e., flatness, straightness, roundness, and cylindricity) are applied only to "individual" features, while perpendicularity, for example, is applied in a "related" feature requirement. Figures 5 and 6 explain the reasoning of each. An individual feature can be clearly identified as one that *does not* relate to a datum reference (i.e., there is no relationship other than to itself), although, of course, an individual feature can *be* a datum if desired. Related features always have datum relationships; it is their nature. Figure 16 will assist in identifying the characteristic types or categories as they are applicable to *individual* or *related* feature requirements.

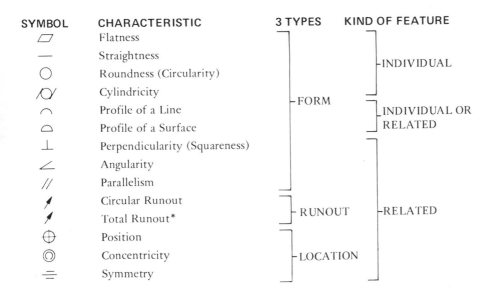

SYMBOL	CHARACTERISTIC	3 TYPES	KIND OF FEATURE
▱	Flatness		
—	Straightness		INDIVIDUAL
○	Roundness (Circularity)		
⌭	Cylindricity	FORM	
⌒	Profile of a Line		INDIVIDUAL OR
⌓	Profile of a Surface		RELATED
⊥	Perpendicularity (Squareness)		
∠	Angularity		
//	Parallelism		
⌁	Circular Runout	RUNOUT	RELATED
⌁	Total Runout*		
⊕	Position		
◎	Concentricity	LOCATION	
⌁	Symmetry		

---

* Word TOTAL required under feature control symbol.

FIGURE 16 Characteristics related to individual or related feature requirements.

B. Tolerances of Form and Runout

Tolerances of form and runout state the permissible variation of actual surfaces or features from the ideal as implied by the drawing. Form tolerances refer to flatness, straightness, roundness, cylindricity, parallelism, perpendicularity, angularity, profile of a surface, and profile of a line. Runout tolerance is a unique variation of form tolerance and is considered as a separate type of characteristic.

Form or runout tolerances should be specified for all features critical to the design requirements:

1. Where workshop practices cannot be relied on to provide the required accuracy
2. Where documents establishing suitable standards of workmanship cannot be prescribed
3. Where tolerances of size and location do not provide the necessary control

The following series of form and runout tolerance examples are presented for purposes of explanation of the basic principles. Symbolic notation of form and runout tolerances is, of course, recommended and emphasized throughout this section.

Tolerances of Form, Individual Features

Tolerances of form, applicable to individual features and where no datum is used, involve the following characteristics.

(FLATNESS)   (STRAIGHTNESS)   (ROUNDNESS)   (CYLINDRICITY)

These characteristics are used to specify form tolerances for *single surface, element*, or *size* features. No datum is involved because the "relationship" of the feature is to a perfect counterpart of itself (i.e., flatness relates to a *plane*, roundness relates to a *circle*, etc.). If a datum were to be used in such applications, the controlled feature would also be its own datum. This, of course, would be redundant, confusing, and incorrect and therefore is not done.

FLATNESS ▱

Flatness Tolerance

We may define *flatness* as the condition of a surface having all elements in one plane. *Flatness tolerance* specifies a tolerance zone confined by two parallel planes within which the entire surface must lie.

Flatness Tolerance Application

The accompanying figure shows how a flatness symbol is applied. The symbol is interpreted to read: "This surface shall be flat within 0.002 total tolerance zone over the entire surface." Note that the 0.002 tolerance zone is total variation. To be acceptable, the entire actual surface must fall within the parallel plane extremities of the 0.002 tolerance zone.

EXAMPLE

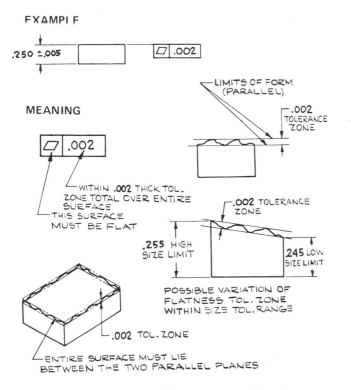

MEANING

FIGURE 17   Examples of flatness specifications.

A flatness tolerance is a form control of all elements of a surface as it compares to a simulated perfect geometric counterpart of itself. The perfect geometric counterpart of a flat surface is a plane. The tolerance zone is established as a width or thickness zone relative to this plane as established from the actual part surface.

Note (see Fig. 17) that the extremities or high points of the surface determine one limit or plane of the tolerance zone, with the other limit or plane being established 0.005 (the specified tolerance) parallel to it.

Since flatness tolerancing control is essentially a relationship of a feature to itself, no datum references are required or proper. Also, note that since flatness is a form tolerance controlling surface elements only, it is not applicable to RFS or MMC considerations*

In the absence of a flatness tolerance specification, the size tolerance and method of manufacture of a part will exercise some control over its flatness. However, when a flatness tolerance is specified, as applicable to a single surface, the flatness tolerance zone must be contained within the size tolerance

---

*Under special circumstances, where the flatness control is applicable to the total thickness of sheet metal, square rods, and so on, the methods described below for straightness on an RFS or MMC basis may be used (tolerance applicable to size feature and dimension).

limits*. It cannot be additive to the size tolerance. Where necessary, the terms "MUST NOT BE CONCAVE" or "MUST NOT BE CONVEX" may be added beneath the feature control symbol.

Straightness Tolerance

Straightness is a condition where an element of a surface or an axis is a straight line. A straightness tolerance specifies a tolerance zone within which an axis or all points of an element must lie.

Straightness Tolerance Application

A straightness tolerance is applied in the view where the elements to be controlled are represented by a straight line.

Straightness Tolerance—Surface Element Control. Straightness tolerance is typically used as a form control of individual surface elements such as those on cylindrical or conical surfaces. Since surfaces of this kind are made up of an infinite number of longitudinal elements, a straighness requirement applies to the entire surface as controlled in single line elements in the direction specified.

The accompanying figure illustrates straightness control of individual longitudinal surface elements on a cylindrical part. Note that the symbol is directed to the feature surface (or extension line), not to the dimension lines. The straightness tolerance must be less than the size tolerance.

All circular elements of the surface must be within the specified size tolerance and the boundary of perfect form at MMC. Also, each longitudinal element of the surface must lie in a tolerance zone defined by two parallel lines spaced apart by the amount of the prescribed tolerance where the two lines and the nominal axis of the part share a common plane.

Note: Since surface element control is specified, the tolerance zone applies uniformly whether the part is of bowed, waisted, or barreled shape (see Fig. 18).

Straightness Tolerance RFS and MMC. Where function of a size feature permits a collective result of size and form variation known as the virtual condition, the RFS or MMC principles may be used. In this instance, where the appropriate symbology and specifications are used, the part is not confined to the perfect form at MMC boundary. All sectional elements of the surface are to be within the specified size tolerance, but the total part surface may exceed the perfect form at MMC boundary to the extent of the straightness tolerance. This principle may be applied to individual size features such as pins, shafts, bars, and so on, where the longitudinal elements are to be specified with a straightness tolerance independent of, or in addition to, the size tolerance.

STRAIGHTNESS —

---

* Under special circumstances, a note specifically exempting the pertinent size dimension, such as "PERFECT FORM AT MMC NOT REQUIRED," may be specified.

EXAMPLE

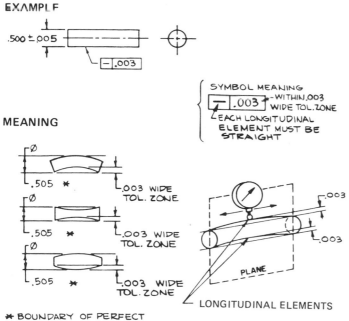

MEANING

★ BOUNDARY OF PERFECT
FORM AT MMC

FIGURE 18   Straightness control of individual longitudinal surface elements on a cylindrical part.

Straightness—RFS: Where a cylindrical feature is to be controlled on an RFS basis as in the following figure, the feature control symbol must be located with the size dimension or attached to the dimension line, and the diameter symbol must precede the straightness tolerance (see Fig. 19).

Straightness—MMC: Where a cylindrical feature has a functional relationship with another feature, such as a pin or shaft and a hole, the control of straightness on an MMC basis may be desirable. If the pin or shaft, for example, is to fit into a hole of a given diameter, the collective effect of the pin size and its straightness error must be considered in relationship to the hole size minimum (i.e., their virtual conditions must be considered relative to one another).

By stating the requirements on an MMC basis, the allowable straightness tolerance may increase an amount equal to the size departure from MMC. The feature control symbol must be located with the size dimension, or be attached to the dimension line; the diameter symbol must precede the straightness tolerance; and the MMC symbol must be inserted following the tolerance. In this manner maximum tolerance is achieved, part fit is guaranteed, and functional gaging techniques may be used (see Fig. 20).

ROUNDNESS ○
(CIRCULARITY)

Roundness Tolerance

Roundness is the condition on a surface of revolution where:

1. In the case of a cylinder or cone, all points of the surface intersected by any plane perpendicular to a common axis are equidistant from their axis.

EXAMPLE

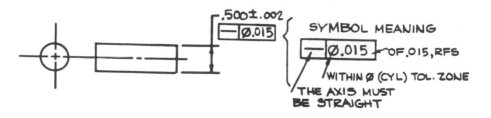

MEANING

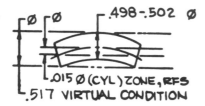

FIGURE 19   Straightness control of cylindrical feature on an RFS basis.

2. In the case of a sphere, all points of the surface intersected by any
    plane passing through a common center are equidistant from that center.

A roundness tolerance specifies a tolerance zone bounded by two concentric
circles within which each circular element of the surface must lie and applies
independently at any plane as described above.

EXAMPLE

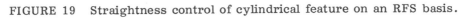

MEANING

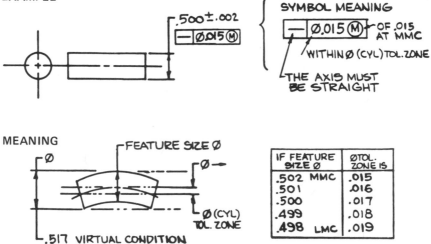

FIGURE 20   Straightness control on an MMC basis.

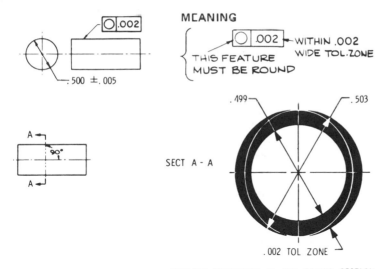

SURFACE PERIPHERY AT ANY CROSS SECTION
PERPENDICULAR TO THE AXIS MUST BE WITHIN
THE SPECIFIED TOLERANCE OF SIZE AND MUST
LIE BETWEEN TWO CONCENTRIC CIRCLES, ONE
HAVING A RADIUS .002 LARGER THAN THE OTHER

FIGURE 21   Roundness tolerancing can be used on any figure of revolution
or circular cross section.

Roundness Tolerance Application

Limits of size exercise control of roundness within the size tolerance. Often
this provides adequate control. However, where necessary to further refine
form control, roundness tolerancing can be used on any figure of revolution
or circular cross section (see Fig. 21).

CYLINDRICITY /○/

Cylindricity Tolerance

Cylindricity is the condition of a surface of revolution in which all points
(elements) of the surface are equidistant from a common axis. A cylindricity
tolerance specifies a tolerance zone bounded by two concentric cylinders within
which the surface must lie.

Cylindricity Tolerance Application

Limits of size exercise control of cylindricity within the size tolerance. This
control is often adequate. However, where more refined form control is required, cylindricity tolerancing can be used. Note that in cylindricity, unlike
roundness, the tolerance applies simultaneously to both circular and longitudinal
elements of the entire surface (see Fig. 22).

Tolerances of Form, Related Features

Tolerances of form used on related features which require a datum involve the
following characteristics:

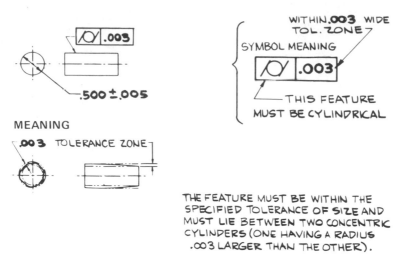

(PERPENDICULARITY)   (ANGULARITY)   (PARALLELISM)

These characteristics are used to describe form tolerances of *single surface,*
element, or *size* features and are always related to a *datum*

Tolerances of perpendicularity, angularity, and parallelism are also referred to as *attitude* (and sometimes *orientation*) tolerances. When applied to
flat surfaces, they invoke a control of "flatness" to that surface as well, to
the extent of the form tolerance specified. When perpendicularity is applied
to size features, rule 3 and RFS versus MMC considerations must be taken
into account.

PERPENDICULARITY ⊥
(SQUARENESS, NORMALITY)

Perpendicularity Tolerance

Perpendicularity is the condition of a surface, median plane, or axis which
is at exactly 90° to a datum plane or axis. A perpendicularity tolerance
specifies:

1. A tolerance zone defined by two parallel planes perpendicular to a
   datum plane within which
   a. The surface of a feature must lie
   b. The median plane of a feature must lie
2. A tolerance zone defined by two parallel planes perpendicular to a
   datum axis within which the axis of a feature must lie
3. A cylindrical tolerance zone perpendicular to a datum plane within
   which the axis of a feature must lie

4. A tolerance zone defined by two parallel, straight lines perpendicular to a datum plane or datum axis within which an element of the surface must lie

Perpendicularity Application

Figure 23 illustrates perpendicularity tolerance as applied to a surface. Figure 24 shows perpendicularity tolerance applied to a *size* feature. Note that the diameter symbol is used to indicate that a cylindrical tolerance zone is desired and that MMC has been specified.

Under "meaning" it can be noted that the tolerance of perpendicularity increases if the actual feature size departs from MMC. Functional gaging principles can be utilized as well in such an application and represents mating part assembly.

ANGULARITY ∠

Angularity Tolerance

Angularity is the condition of a surface, axis, or median plane which is at the specified angle (other than 90°) from a datum plane or axis. Angularity

EXAMPLE

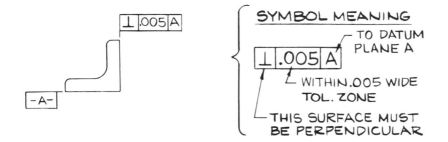

MEANING

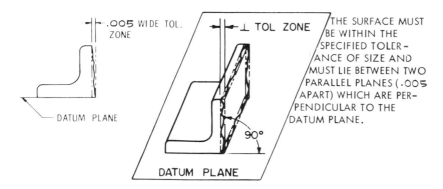

FIGURE 23 Perpendicularity tolerance as applied to a surface.

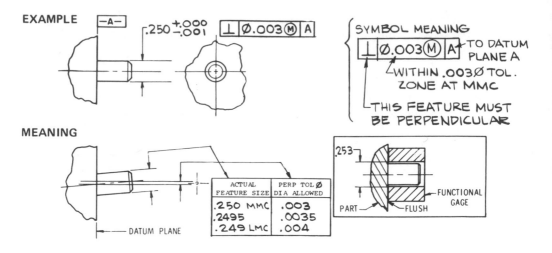

FIGURE 24   Perpendicularity tolerance applied to a surface.

tolerance is the distance between two parallel planes, inclined at the specified angle to a datum plane or axis, within which the toleranced surface, axis, or median plane must lie.

Angularity Application

Figure 25 shows a part with a surface angular requirement. Note that the symbol is interpreted as: "This surface must be at a 45° angle in relation to datum plane A within a 0.005-wide tolerance zone in relation to datum plane A."

The interpretation shows how the tolerance zone is established. Note that the angular tolerance zone is at 45° *basic* (exact) from the datum plane A. To be acceptable, the entire angular surface must fall within this tolerance zone. The angular surface must be contained within the limits of part size.

PARALLELISM //

Parallelism Tolerance

Parallelism is the condition of a surface or axis which is equidistant at all points from a datum plane or axis. A parallelism tolerance specifies.

1.   A tolerance zone defined by two planes or lines parallel to a datum plane (or axis) within which the axis or surface must lie
2.   A cylindrical tolerance zone parallel to a datum axis within which the axis of the considered feature must lie

Parallelism Application

Note that in our next illustration, Figure 26, the bottom surface has been selected as the datum and the top surface is to be parallel to datum plane A within 0.002. This figure illustrates the tolerance zone and the manner in which the surface must fall within the tolerance zone to be acceptable. Note that the tolerance zone is established parallel to the datum plane A. Note also

EXAMPLE

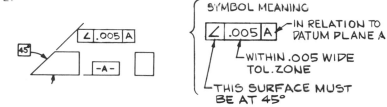

MEANING

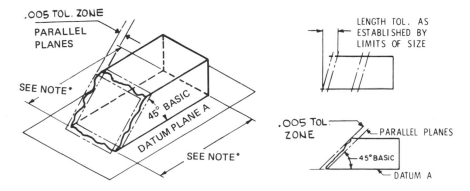

FIGURE 25   Illustration of a part with surface angular requirement.

EXAMPLE

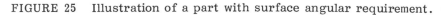

MEANING

FIGURE 26   Tolerance zone and the way the surface must fall within tolerance zone.

that the parallelism tolerance, when applied to a plane surface, controls flatness if a flatness tolerance is not specified (i.e., the implied flatness will be at least as good as the parallelism).

Figure 27 shows parallelism tolerance applied to a size feature with the datum feature also a size feature. MMC is applied to the feature controlled with the datum feature at RFS (rule 3).

Under "meaning" it can be noted that the tolerance of parallelism increases if the actual feature size departs from MMC. The feature must also meet location tolerances. It should be noted that the parallelism tolerance controls only the feature attitude, *not* location.

Tolerances of Form, Profile Tolerancing

Profile tolerancing is of two varieties and involves the following characteristics:

According to the design requirement, these characteristics may be applied to an individual feature, such as a single surface or element, or to related features, such as a single surface or element relative to a datum or datums.

(PROFILE OF A LINE)   (PROFILE OF A SURFACE)

Profile Tolerance

Profile tolerancing is a method used to specify a uniform amount of variation of a surface or line elements of a surface. A profile tolerance (either bilateral or unilateral) specifies a tolerance zone normal to the basic profile at all points

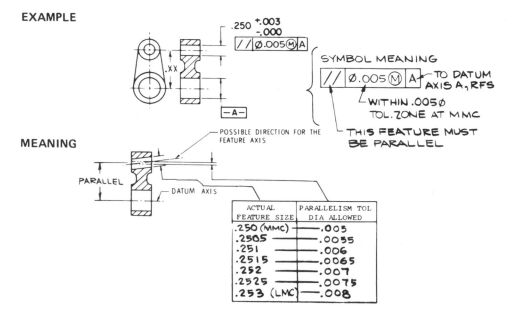

FIGURE 27   Parallelism tolerance applied to a size feature with the datum feature also a size feature.

of the profile, within which the specified part surface profile or line profile must lie.

Profile Tolerance Application

Profile tolerancing is an effective method for controlling lines, arcs, irregular surfaces, or other unusual part profiles. Profile tolerances are usually applied to surface features but may also be applied to a line (element on a feature surface). In either case, these requirements must be specified in association with the desired profile in a plane of projection (view) on the drawing as follows:

1. An *appropriate view* or section is drawn which shows the desired basic profile in true shape.
2. The profile is defined by basic dimensions. This dimensioning may be in the form of located radii and angles, or it may consist of coordinate dimensioning to points on the profile.
3. Depending on design requirements, the tolerance may be divided bilaterally to both sides of the true profile or applied unilaterally to either side of the true profile. Where an equally disposed bilateral tolerance is intended, it is only necessary to show the feature control symbol with a leader directed to the surface. For an unequally disposed or unilateral tolerance, phantom lines are drawn parallel to the ture profile to indicate clearly the tolerance zone inside or outside the true profile. One end of a dimension line is extended to the feature control symbol.

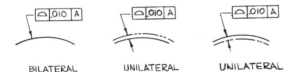

| BILATERAL | UNILATERAL | UNILATERAL |

Two Types of Profile Tolerance

In practice, a profile tolerance may be applied either to an entire surface or to individual line element profiles taken at various cross sections through the part. The two types or methods of controlling profile are:

Profile of a Surface. The tolerance zone established by profile of a surface tolerance is a three-dimensional zone or total control across the entire length and width or circumference of the feature; it may be applied to parts having a constant cross section or to parts having a surface of revolution. Usually, the profile of a surface requires datum references.

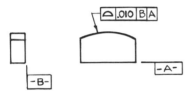

Profile of a Line. The tolerance zone established by the profile of a line tolerance is a two-dimensional zone extending along the length of the feature considered; it may apply to the profiles of parts having a varying cross section, such as a propeller, aircraft wing, nose cone, or to random cross sections of parts where it is not desired to control the entire surface as a single entity. The profile of a line may, or may not, require datum references.

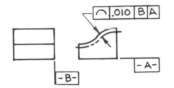

PROFILE OF A SURFACE ⌒

Figure 28 illustrates surface profile control and introduces a datum system.

PROFILE OF A LINE ⌒

Where line elements of a surface are to be specifically controlled or controlled as a refinement of size or surface profile control, the profile of a line characteristic may be used. Line profile control is applied in a manner similar to the application of surface profile.

Figure 29 illustrates line profile control as a refinement of size. As with surface profile, line profile must be shown in the drawing view in which it applies. The tolerance zone is established in the same way as the surface profile. However, its tolerance zone is disposed about *each element* of the surface. Therefore, the tolerance zone applies for the full length of each element of the surface (in the view in which it is shown), but only for the width or height at a cutting plane bisecting the element (see Fig. 29).

RUNOUT ↗ (CIRCULAR AND TOTAL)

Runout Tolerance

Runout is a composite tolerance used to control the functional relationship of one or more features of a part to a datum axis. Runout tolerance states how far an actual surface or feature is permitted to deviate from the desired form implied by the drawing during full rotation (360°) of the part on a datum axis.

Runout Application

Runout tolerancing is a method used to control the composite surface effect of one or more features of a part relative to a datum axis. Runout tolerance is applicable to rotating parts in which this composite surface control is based on the part function and design requirement. A runout tolerance always applies on an RFS basis; that is, size variation has no effect on the runout tolerance compliance.

Each feature considered must be within its individual runout tolerance when rotated 360° about the datum axis. The tolerance specified for a controlled surface is the total tolerance or full indicator movement (FIM) in terms of common inspection criteria. Former terms, full indicator reading (FIR), and total indicator reading (TIR) have the same meaning as FIM.

EXAMPLE

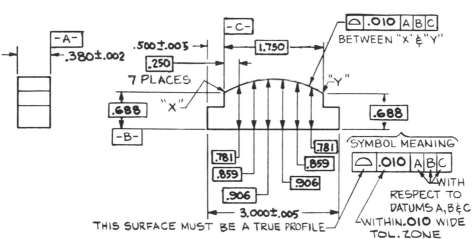

MEANING

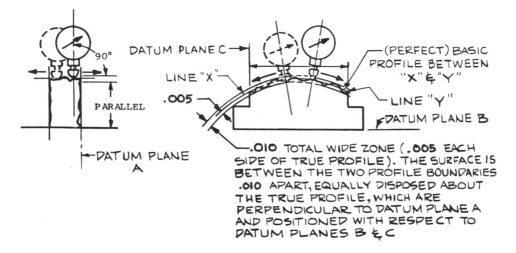

FIGURE 28   Illustration of surface profile control and introduction of a datum system.

A runout tolerance is a relationship between surfaces or features: therefore, a datum (or datums) is required. Runout tolerance may be applied as "circular" or "total," based on the part functional requirements. Figure 30 illustrates "circular" versus "total" runout application on a similar part.

EXAMPLE

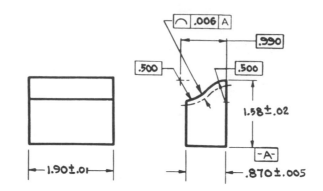

MEANING

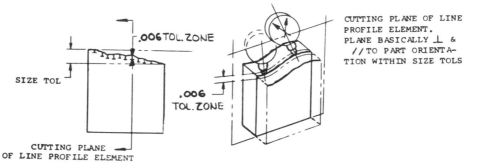

FIGURE 29   Line profile control as a refinement of size.

Figure 31 extends the principles of the previous examples. It is a shaft of multiple-diameters about a common datum axis C-D, with each feature, including the datum features, stating an individual runout tolerance. In addition to having both circular and total runout control, each datum feature has a cylindricity tolerance.

C. Coaxial Features: Selection of Proper Control

There are three methods of controlling interrelated coaxial features:

1. Runout tolerance (circular or total) (RFS)
2. Position tolerance (MMC)
3. Concentricity tolerance (RFS)

Any of these methods will provide effective control. However, it is important to select the most appropriate one both to meet the design requirements and to provide the most economical manufacturing conditions.

Following are recommendations to assist in selecting the proper control. If the need is to control only circular cross-sectional elements in a composite relationship to a datum axis RFS (e.g., multiple diameters on a shaft), or if the need is to control the total cylindrical or profile surface in composite relative

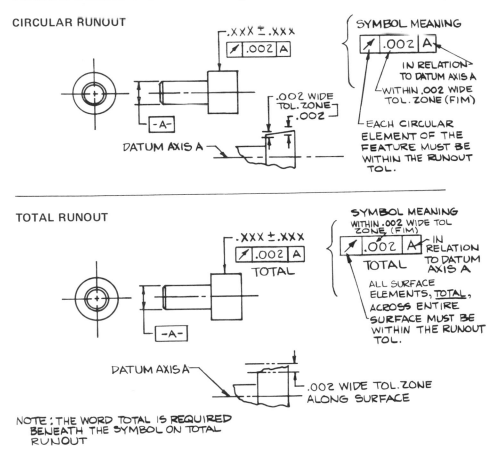

CIRCULAR RUNOUT

SYMBOL MEANING

IN RELATION TO DATUM AXIS A

WITHIN .002 WIDE TOL. ZONE (FIM)

EACH CIRCULAR ELEMENT OF THE FEATURE MUST BE WITHIN THE RUNOUT TOL.

.002 WIDE TOL. ZONE

DATUM AXIS A

TOTAL RUNOUT

SYMBOL MEANING

WITHIN .002 WIDE TOL ZONE (FIM)

IN RELATION TO DATUM AXIS A

ALL SURFACE ELEMENTS, TOTAL, ACROSS ENTIRE SURFACE MUST BE WITHIN THE RUNOUT TOL.

DATUM AXIS A

.002 WIDE TOL. ZONE ALONG SURFACE

NOTE: THE WORD TOTAL IS REQUIRED BENEATH THE SYMBOL ON TOTAL RUNOUT

FIGURE 30   Circular versus total runout application on a similar part.

to a datum axis RFS (e.g., multiple diameters on a shaft, bearing mounting diameters, etc.), use the most appropriate of the following:

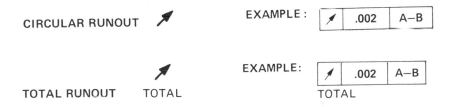

CIRCULAR RUNOUT   EXAMPLE: | ∕ | .002 | A—B |

TOTAL RUNOUT TOTAL   EXAMPLE: | ∕ | .002 | A—B |
TOTAL

If the need is to control the total cylindrical or profile surface and its axis in a composite location relative to the datum axis on an MMC basis (e.g., on mating parts to assure interchangeability or assemble ability), use

POSITION   EXAMPLE: | ⊕ | ⌀ .002 Ⓜ | A Ⓜ |

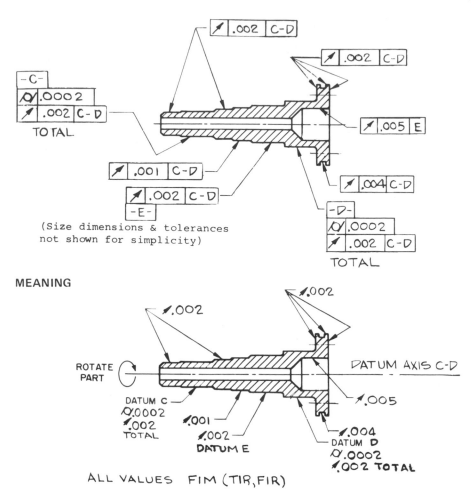

FIGURE 31   Extension of previous examples on a shaft of multiple-diameters about a common axis C-D.

If the need is to control the axis of one or more features in composite relative to a datum axis RFS (e.g., to control the balance of a rotating part), use

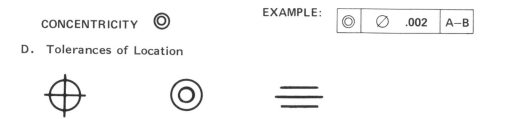

D. Tolerances of Location

Tolerances of location state the permissible variation in the specified location of a feature in relation to some other feature or datum. Tolerances of location refer to the geometric characteristics of position, concentricity, and symmetry.

Location tolerances involve features of size and relationships of centerlines, center planes, axes, and so on. At least two features, one of which is a size feature, are required before location tolerancing is valid. Where function or interchangeability of mating part features is involved, the MMC principle may be introduced to great advantage. Perhaps the most widely used and best example of the application of this principle is position tolerancing.

The use of the position concept in conjunction with the maximum material condition concept provides some of the major advantages of the geometric tolerancing system.

POSITION ⊕

Position Tolerance

Position is a term used to describe the perfect (exact) location of a point, line, or plane (normally the center) of a feature in relation to a datum reference or other feature. A position tolerance is the total permissible variation in the location of a feature about its true (or exact) position. For cylindrical features (holes and bosses) the position tolerance is the diameter (cylinder) of the tolerance zone within which the axis of the feature must lie, the center of the tolerance zone being at the exact position. For other features (slots, tabs, etc.) the position tolerance is the total width of the tolerance zone within which the center plane of the feature must lie, the center plane of the zone being at the exact position.

Position Theory

The top figure in Figure 32 shows a part with the hole pattern dimensioned and toleranced using the coordinate system. The bottom figure shows the same part dimensioned using the position system. Comparing the two approaches, the following differences are noted:

1. The derived tolerance zones for the hole centers result as square in the coordinate system and round in the position system.
2. The hole center location tolerance in the top figure is part of the co-ordinates (the 2.000 and 1.750 dimensions). In the bottom figure, however, the location tolerance is associated with the hole size dimension and is shown in the feature control symbol. The 2.000 and 1.750 co-ordinates are retained in the position application, but are stated as basic or exact values.

For this comparison, the 0.005 square coordinate tolerance zone has been converted to a 0.007 position tolerance zone. The two tolerance zones are superimposed on each other in the enlarged detail.

The black dots represent possible inspected centers of this hole on eight separate piece parts. It is seen that if the coordinate zone is applied, only three of the eight parts are acceptable. However, with the position zone applied, six of the eight parts appear immediately acceptable.

The position-diameter-shaped zone can be justified by recognizing that the 0.007 diagonal is unlimited in orientation. Also, a cylindrical hole should normally have a cylindrical tolerance zone.

A closer analysis of the representative black dots and their position with respect to the desired exact location clearly illustrates the fallacies of the coordinate system when applied to a part such as that illustrated. The dot in

COORDINATE SYSTEM

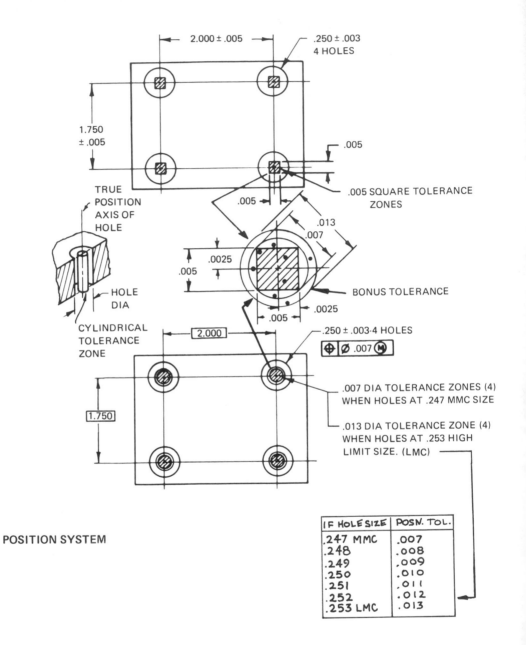

POSITION SYSTEM

IF HOLE SIZE	POSN. TOL.
.247 MMC	.007
.248	.008
.249	.009
.250	.010
.251	.011
.252	.012
.253 LMC	.013

FIGURE 32 Top figure shows a part with hole pattern dimensioned and toleranced using coordinate system. Bottom figure shows same part dimensioned using the geometric system.

the upper left diagonal corner of the square zone and the dot on the left outside the square zone are in reality at nearly the same distance from the desired exact center. However, in terms of the square coordinate zone, the hole on the left is unacceptable by a wide margin, whereas the upper left hole is acceptable.

In normal calculation of position tolerances, the tolerance is derived, of course, from the design requirement, not from converted coordinates. The maximum material sizes of the features (hole and mating component) are used to determine this tolerance. Therefore, the 0.007 position tolerance of the example would be based on the MMC size of the hole (0.247). As the hole size departs from MMC size, the position of the hole is permitted to shift off its "true position" beyond the original tolerance zone to the extent of that departure. The "bonus tolerance" of 0.013 illustrates the possible position tolerance should the hole be produced, for example, to its high limit size of 0.253. The tabulation in the lower part of the illustration shows the enlargement of the position tolerance zone as the hole size departs from MMC in production. Although only one hole has been considered in the explanation, the same reasoning applies to all the holes in the pattern relative to their respective "true positions."

Position tolerancing is ideally applied on mating parts in cases where fit, function, and interchangeability are the considerations. It provides greater production tolerances, ensures design requirements, and provides the advantages of functional inspection practices as desired.

Functional gaging techniques, familiar to a large segment of industry, are fundamentally based on the MMC position concept. It should be clearly understood, however, that functional gages are not mandatory in fulfilling MMC position requirements.

Some functional gaging principles are introduced in this chapter for the dual purpose of explaining the principles involved in positional tolerancing and for introducing the functional gaging technique as a valuable tool. A functional gage can often be considered as a representative mating part at its worst condition.

Position, although a locational tolerance, also includes form tolerance elements in composite. For example, as shown in the illustration, perpendicularity is invoked as part of the control to the extent of the tolerance zone, for the depth of the hole. Further, the holes in the pattern are also parallel to one another within the positional tolerance.

Mating Parts, Floating Fastener

Position tolerancing techniques are most effective and appropriate in mating part situations. The illustration following, in addition to demonstrating the calculations required, also emphasizes the importance of decisions at the design stage to recognize and initiate the position principles.

The mating parts shown in the illustration are to be interchangeable. Thus the calculation of their position tolerances should be based on the two parts and their interface with the fastener in terms of MMC sizes.

The two parts are to be assembled with four screws. The holes in the two parts are to line up sufficiently to pass the four screws at assembly. Since the four screws ("fasteners") are separate components, they are considered to have some "float" with respect to one another. The colloquial term "floating fastener application" has been used popularly to describe this situation.

The calculations are shown in the upper right corner of the illustration. Also note that, in this case, the same basic dimensions and position tolerances

are used on both parts. They are, of course, separate parts and are on
separate drawings. The calculations on the illustrated parts show a balanced
tolerance application in which the total permissible position tolerance of the
holes on the two parts is the same (i.e., 0.016). The total position tolerance
can, however, be distributed as desired. For example, if one part specifies
only 0.010 of the 0.016 tolerance available for each part, 0.006 may be added
to the calculated position tolerance of the mating part.

As seen from the illustration, part acceptance tolerances will increase as
the hole sizes in the parts are actually produced and vary in size as a departure from MMC. From the 0.016 diameter tolerance calculated, the tolerance
may increase to as much as 0.022, dependent on the actually produced hole
size.

A possible functional gage is also shown in the illustration. The 0.190 gage
pin diameters are determined by the MMC size of the hole, 0.206, minus the
stated position tolerance of 0.016. In this example, the same functional gage
can be used on both parts. Functional gages are, of course, not required
with position application, but they do provide an effective method of evaluation where desired.

Mating Parts, Fixed Fastener

When one of two mating parts has "fixed" features, such as the threaded
studs in Figure 33, the fixed fastener method is used in calculating position
tolerances. The term "fixed fastener" is a colloquialism popularly used to
describe this application. Both the term and the technique are applied to numerous other manufacturing situations, such as locating dowels, tapped holes,
and so on.

The advantages of the MMC principle as described for the floating fastener
application also apply here. However, with a fixed fastener application, the
difference between the MMC sizes of mating features must be divided between
the two features, since the total position tolerance must be shared by the two
mating features. In this example, the two mating features (actually four of
each in each pattern) are the studs and the clearance holes. The studs must
fit through the holes at assembly.

Again, it is seen that the clearance of the mating features as they relate
to each other at assembly determines the position tolerances. When one feature
is to be assembled within another on the basis of the MMC sizes and "worst"
condition of assembly, the clearance, or total tolerance, must be divided for
assignment to each of the mating part features. In this case, the derived
0.016 was divided equally, with 0.008-diameter position tolerance assigned to
each mating part feature (stud and hole). The total tolerance of 0.016 can be
distributed to the two parts as desired, as long as the total is 0.016 (e.g.,
0.010 + 0.006, 0.012 + 0.004, etc.). This decision is made at the design stage,
however, and must be fixed on the drawing before release to production.

As the part features of both parts are produced, any departure in size
from MMC will increase the calculated position by an amount equal to that departure. For example, the position tolerance of the upper part could possibly
increase up to 0.014, and that of the lower part up to 0.013 dependent on the
amount of departure from their MMC sizes. However, parts must actually be
produced and sizes established before the amount of increase in tolerance can
be determined.

Functional gages (shown below each part in the illustration) can be used
for checking, and although their use is not a requirement, they provide a
very effective method of evaluation if desired. Note that the functional gages

MATING PARTS — FLOATING FASTENER

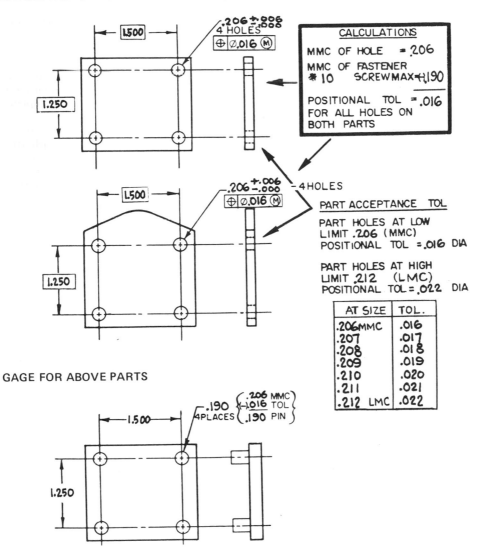

AT SIZE	TOL.
.206 MMC	.016
.207	.017
.208	.018
.209	.019
.210	.020
.211	.021
.212 LMC	.022

CALCULATIONS

MMC OF HOLE = .206

MMC OF FASTENER
#10 SCREW MAX = .190

POSITIONAL TOL = .016 FOR ALL HOLES ON BOTH PARTS

PART ACCEPTANCE TOL

PART HOLES AT LOW LIMIT .206 (MMC) POSITIONAL TOL = .016 DIA

PART HOLES AT HIGH LIMIT .212 (LMC) POSITIONAL TOL = .022 DIA

GAGE FOR ABOVE PARTS

FIGURE 33   Specifications on position when one of two mating parts has fixed fixtures.

resemble the mating parts; as a matter of fact, functional gages simulate mating parts at their worst condition.

Relation to Datums

Figure 34 shows a part where the datums are identified with the A, B, and C datum identification symbols and form tolerances are specified. Where part function, and thus the stated drawing requirements, are more critical, specified datums and greater geometric control are necessary.

In this figure it was necessary to control the accuracy of the datum surfaces in their specific relationship to each other. To accomplish this, identification of the specific surfaces as datum references was required. Further, since the hole position pattern was critical in its orientation to the surfaces, datum identification was required for this purpose. With specification of the datums, precedence of the datum surfaces is established.

Relation to Datum Targets

Where positional tolerancing relationships are to be related to specific points, lines, or areas as the functional requirement, or repeatability between manufacturing or inspection is of concern, datum targets may be used (see Fig. 35); see also Sec.V.E).

Noncylindrical Features and Coaxial Features

The principles of positional tolerancing covered in the foregoing sections can also be applied to noncylindrical and coaxial features. Calculation of tolerances, use of MMC or RFS principles, datums, and so on, are similar.

Figures 36 and 37 are examples of a noncylindrical and coaxial feature application of position tolerancing.

Position Tolerance Verification

Often position tolerancing is misunderstood, or even avoided, by concern for its verification or inspection. That is, X and Y measuring equipment is envisioned as a possibility, which would appear illogical to the diametrical (cylindrical) tolerance zones of the common position tolerance requirement. Of course, this is not so, as many methods can be used in verifying position tolerance. The fact of the matter is that positional tolerancing opens up many *new* and *more valid* methods, such as functional gaging without losing any past methods.

Position tolerancing can be effectively verified with any of the coordinate measuring tools or machines presently used in open setup inspection, comparators, and functional gaging. Some functional gage applications appear earlier in this position tolerancing section. Functional gaging is a recommended method where cost of the gage, production quantities, and so on, can be justified. It simulates part interface.

To illustrate one convenient method of inspecting a part with a coordinate measurement tool and making the translation to positional tolerance equivalents, Figure 38 is presented. The conversion illustrations in Figure 39 show representative coordinate results of an X and Y measurement process. By referring to the conversion table under the resulting differential value in X and Y, the translated positional value is derived. This, compared to the permissible position tolerance (and applying MMC principles when necessary), determines whether the hole is acceptable.

MATING PARTS — FIXED FASTENER

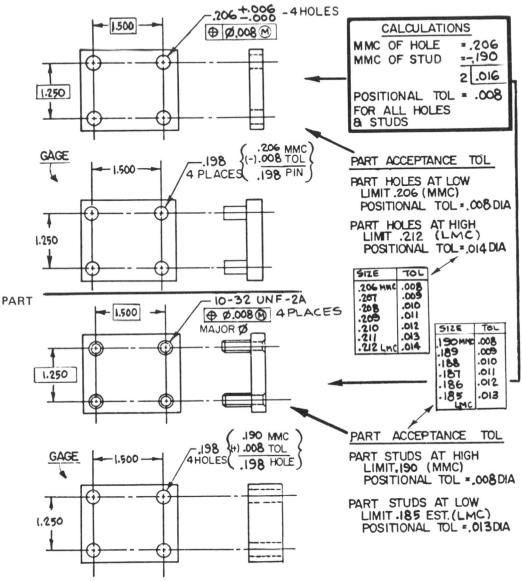

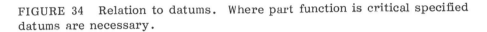

FIGURE 34   Relation to datums. Where part function is critical specified datums are necessary.

AS DRAWN

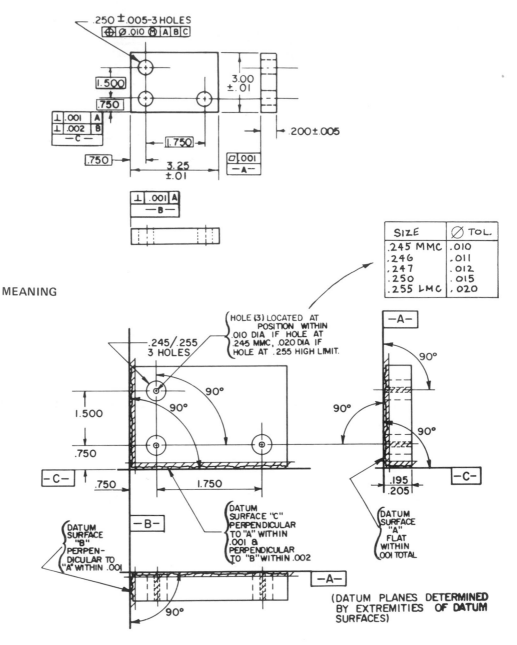

MEANING

SIZE	⌀ TOL.
.245 MMC	.010
.246	.011
.247	.012
.250	.015
.255 LMC	.020

FIGURE 35   Example of position tolerances as related to datum targets.

NONCYLINDRICAL PART FEATURES

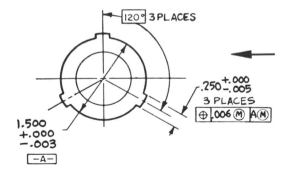

FIGURE 36   Example of positioning tolerance applied to noncylindrical part feature.

CONCENTRICITY ◎

Concentricity Tolerance

Concentricity is the condition where the axes of all cross-sectional elements of a feature's surface of revolution are common to the axis of a datum feature. Concentricity tolerance is the diameter of the cylindrical tolerance zone within which the axis of the feature(s) must lie; the axis of the tolerance zone must coincide with the axis of the datum feature(s).

Concentricity Application

Concentricity is a type of location tolerancing. It always involves two or more basically coaxial features of size and controls the amount by which the axes of the features may fail to coincide. Concentricity tolerance, due to its unique characteristic, is always used on an RFS basis. Where interrelated features are basically coaxial, we must first consider the possibility of using the more economical position or runout controls before considering concentricity (see also Sec. V.C).

The surface of a feature must be used to establish its axis. Therefore, all the irregularities or errors of form of a feature surface must be considered

COAXIAL FEATURES

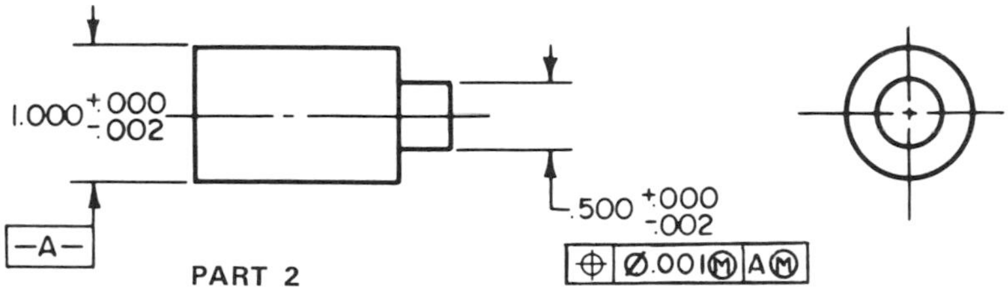

FIGURE 37   Example of position tolerance applied to coaxial features.

EXAMPLE

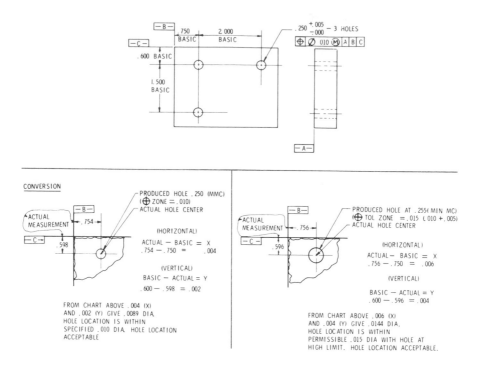

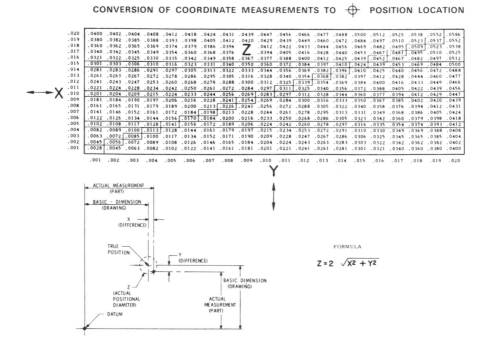

FIGURE 38   Illustration of one convenient method of inspecting a part with coordinate measuring tool.

FIGURE 39   Representative coordinate results of an X and Y measurement process.

in establishing the axis. For instance, the surface may be bowed, out of round, and so on, in addition to being offset from its datum feature. This usually involves a complex inspection analysis of the entire surface, and therefore requires a more time-consuming and costly procedure.

Concentricity requirements are required less frequently than position or runout requirements. However, where concentricity is required, it provides effective control over the more unique applications of coaxial relationships. For example, concentricity might be applied to the coaxiality requirements of a tape-drive pulley or of a capstan on a computer mechanism or a motor generator rotor. Often where balance is required, the out-of-roundness or lobing effect (or possible other form errors) may be permissible, although it may exceed the conventional FIM requirement. Hence any basically symmetrical form of revolution (hexagons, cones, etc.) or consistently symmetrical variation of such a form could satisfy a concentricity tolerance where a runout requirement may not (see Fig. 40).

SYMMETRY ⬌

Symmetry Tolerance

Symmetry is a condition in which a feature(s) is symmetrically disposed about the center plane of a datum feature. The tolerance governing the symmetry of a feature with respect to a datum is the distance between two parallel planes between which the median plane of the feature must lie, the parallel planes

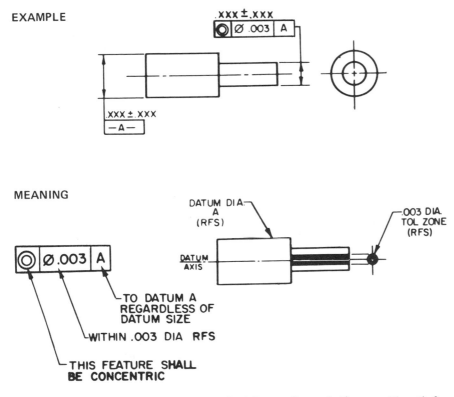

FIGURE 40   Any basically symmetrical form of revolution could satisfy a concentricity tolerance, a runout requirement may not.

being parallel to, and equally disposed about, the median plane, or axis, of the datum feature.

Symmetry Application

Like the two types of locational tolerance discussed previously, position and concentricity, symmetry deals with the location of actual features with respect to established center planes or axes. As its name implies, the purpose of any symmetry tolerance is to specify a symmetrical relationship for the toleranced feature, usually with the outside limits of the part for reasons of appearance, clearance, or fit to related or mating parts.

The accompanying figure shows a part using symmetry tolerancing on the slot; the part width is established as the datum. The requirement is to relate the slot location to the outside width of the part. To simplify explanation, size dimensions and tolerances of the slot and the datum width have been omitted.

Symmetry is a type of positional tolerancing. Where part features of a symmetrical shape are to be geometrically toleranced, it is recommended that the positional characteristic be used instead of symmetry. Symmetry is, however, a valid characteristic and may be applied, if desired, on an RFS basis only. In MMC applications of symmetrically shaped features, position tolerancing should be used (see Fig. 41).

EXAMPLE

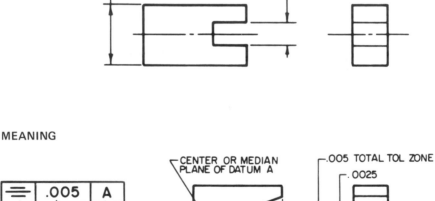

MEANING

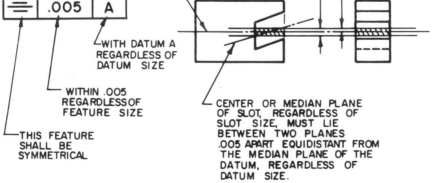

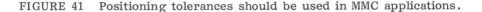
FIGURE 41   Positioning tolerances should be used in MMC applications.

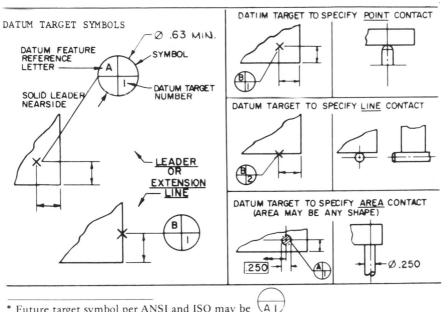

DATUM TARGET SYMBOLS

DATUM FEATURE REFERENCE LETTER

SOLID LEADER NEARSIDE

Ø .63 MIN.

SYMBOL

DATUM TARGET NUMBER

LEADER OR EXTENSION LINE

DATUM TARGET TO SPECIFY POINT CONTACT

DATUM TARGET TO SPECIFY LINE CONTACT

DATUM TARGET TO SPECIFY AREA CONTACT (AREA MAY BE ANY SHAPE)

.250

Ø.250

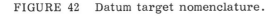

* Future target symbol per ANSI and ISO may be (A 1)

FIGURE 42 Datum target nomenclature.

AS DRAWN

DATUM PLANES ESTABLISHED FROM DATUM POINTS AND LINES ON IRREGULAR CONTOUR SURFACES :

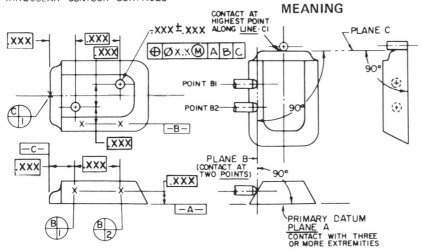

CONTACT AT HIGHEST POINT ALONG LINE-C1

MEANING

PLANE C

90°

POINT B1

POINT B2

90°

PLANE B (CONTACT AT TWO POINTS)

90°

PRIMARY DATUM PLANE A
CONTACT WITH THREE OR MORE EXTREMITIES

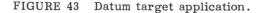

FIGURE 43 Datum target application.

E. Datum Targets

Where datum orientation is required on parts of irregular contour, such as castings, forgings, sheet metal, and so on, datum targets provide a valuable tool. Specified datum targets which serve as means of constructing special datum planes of orientation can be of three types: points, lines, or areas. Datum targets establish the necessary datum system framework and, in addition, ensure repeatable part location for manufacturing and inspection operations.

Datum targets are also used to indicate special, or more critical, design requirements where functional part feature relationships are to be indicated from specific points, lines, or areas on the part surface. Datum points and lines have been defined previously. A datum area is a datum established from a partial datum surface. On a drawing, a datum area is outlined with phantom lines and identified by diagonal slash lines. It may be of any shape.

The locations and/or sizes of datum points, lines, or areas are controlled by basic or untoleranced dimensions and imply exactness within standard tooling, gaging, or shop tolerances. Where necessary, toleranced locations or sizes may be used with datum target symbols.

Figures 42 and 43 illustrate the use of datum target symbols to establish datum planes and part orientation.

ACKNOWLEDGMENTS

Acknowledgment is given to Addison-Wesley Publishing Company, Inc., Reading, Massachusetts, for permission to extract certain material from the following texts: L. W. Foster, *Geometrics II: The Application of Geometric Tolerancing Techniques* (Using the Customary Inch System), February 1979; and L. W. Foster, *A. Pocket Guide to Geometrics II: Dimensioning and Tolerancing* (Reference ANSI Y14.5-1973), 1974.

BIBLIOGRAPHY

American National Standards Institute, *Dimensioning and Tolerancing*, ANSI Y14.5-1973.
Foster, L. W., *A Pocket Guide to Geometrics II: Dimensioning and Tolerancing*, Addison-Wesley, Reading, Mass., 1974.
Foster, L. W., *Geometrics II: The Application of Geometric Tolerancing Techniques*, Addison-Wesley, Reading, Mass., 1979.

FURTHER READING

American National Standards Institute, *Dimensioning and Tolerancing*, ASNI Y14.5M-1982.
Answerbook and Instructors Guide for Modern Geometric Dimensioning and Tolerancing, National Tooling and Machining Association, Fort Washington, Md.
Answerbook for Geometric Dimensioning and Tolerancing (Inch), Lowell W. Foster Associates, Inc., Minneapolis, Minn.
Answerbook for Geometric Dimensioning and Tolerancing (Metric), Lowell W. Foster Associates, Inc., Minneapolis, Minn.

Foster, L. W., *Geometrics, The Metric Application of Geometric Tolerancing*, Addison-Wesley, Reading, Mass.

Foster, L. W., *Geometrics II: The Application of Geometric Tolerancing (Using the Customary Inch System)*, Addison-Wesley, Reading, Mass., 1979.

Foster, L. W., *A Pocket Guide to Geometrics II: Dimensioning and Tolerancing*, Addison-Wesley, Reading, Mass., 1974.

Foster, L. W., *Symbols for Geometrics*, Addison-Wesley, Reading, Mass.

Foster, L. W., *A Workbook for Geometric Dimensioning and Tolerancing (Inch)*, Addison-Wesley, Reading, Mass.

Foster, L. W., *A Workbook for Geometric Dimensioning and Tolerancing (Metric)*, Addison-Wesley, Reading, Mass.

28

METROLOGY

GEORGE O. RICE

Rockwell International
Anaheim, California

I. INTRODUCTION

The subject of calibration of measuring and test equipment is one that is usually not treated (or only treated in a limited way) in a handbook on quality control. The increasing emphasis on this vital aspect of measurement by various governmental agencies, the implications of measurement error on safety and product liability, and the increasing awareness of the economics of measurement in business have all contributed to the need for including the subject in this handbook. This chapter, then, is intended to introduce the concept of calibration into the quality control program through an overview of the field and to relate the concepts involved to the various tasks of the quality control practitioner.

Although this chapter discusses the concepts of metrology standards, calibration, and so on, in an industrial setting, the conclusions are equally applicable to nonindustrial institutions, large and small. As will be seen, it is a fundamental tenet of this chapter that calibration of measuring and test equipment is both necessary and cost-effective. As in the more typical quality control functions, the costs associated with calibration depend on the protection desired; seen as a preventative measure, calibration costs are offset by the better decisions made in the research laboratory or production floor.

In the United States the term "metrology" entered the general use industrial vocabulary in its present sense probably about 30 years ago, although it had existed in less frequent use for some time prior to that. Even today, though, measurement specialists (metrologists) must take time to explain that metrology is neither the science of weather forecasting (meteorology) nor the science of the properties of metal (metallurgy). Metrology is, of course, important to both of these sciences, as it is to all science and industry.

Literally, *metrology* means "science of measurement" and is derived from two Greek words: *metro*, meaning "measure" or "measurement," and *logy*, meaning law or science. In its early use, and in its use in some areas of the world today, the word "metrology" has had a more restricted use than the very broad sense of its literal meaning, referring to measurements of the physical attributes of an artifact (e.g., length, mass, shape, etc.). However, in this chapter, as in most scientific and industrial institutions in the United States, the word "metrology" is used in its broadest sense, limited only by the context within which it occurs.

In the early years of its industrial use in the United States, "metrology" was normally used as the name of the organizational element responsible for the measurement references of the institution. Thus it was almost exclusively reserved as a name for the standards laboratory of academic, industrial, and governmental organizations (except the National Bureau of Standards). Today, it is not unusual (although by no means typical) for the word "metrology" to encompass all elements of an organization's calibration system, excluding only the end use of the measurement device.

Metrology, then, in the organizational sense, is the collection of people, equipment, facilities, methods, and procedures assembled to assure correctness or adequacy of measurements. Many institutions also append such related responsibilities as preventative and remedial service and, in some cases, inventory management tasks, such as accountability and utilization analysis. In this chapter we limit the organizational meaning of the term to responsibilities that pertain to correctness or adequacy of measurements.

Lord Kelvin stated: "[If] you can measure what you are speaking about and can express it in numbers, you know something about it; but when you cannot measure it, when you cannot express it in numbers, your knowledge is of a meager and unsatisfactory kind." All material objects and a good number of nonmaterial characteristics are measured in some way daily. People weigh themselves, the contents of canned goods are specified by volume or weight, gasoline is purchased by the gallon or liter, TV programming is based on the measurement of time, manufacturing plants measure parts that must be assembled or fitted together by other plants, aircraft and space vehicles must be assembled from thousands of parts which have been measured to a tolerance to assure that they will work together, and so on. Measurement in one form or another pervades all aspects of our lives. The existence of measurement capability at home, in the marketplace, in schools, in manufacturing, and in research is loosely connected within a country by a network referred to as the national measurement system. Informal measurements comprise the bulk of these and normally rely on judgment or experience as the means for validating (calibrating) their accuracy. Formal measurements, those in the marketplace and generally under the aegis of state or local weights and measures officials and those in industry, are by several orders of magnitude fewer in number but are of much more significance to the American economy [1].

To assure that measurements made at one place by one person yield (within a stated uncertainty) the same result as the same measurements made at other places by other persons, the national measurement system in the United States has evolved a hierarchy by means of which the uncertainty of measurement at each transfer is quantified. In regulated areas (i.e., principally weights and measures and industries under contract to or regulated by government) these conditions are usually well specified and adequately controlled. This hierarchical system provides a measurement capability which is highest at the National Bureau of Standards, from which the system flows outward and downward to various standardizing laboratories in industry and government, culminating in the marketplace (formally) or in the myriad of informal measurements made by most people daily [2].

The National Bureau of Standards (NBS) is this nation's custodian of the standards of measurement; it was established by an act of Congress in 1901, although the need for such a body had been seen by the framers of the Constitution. The two main campuses of the NBS are in Gaithersburg, Maryland, and Boulder, Colorado, where research in the phenomena of measurement and in the properties of materials and calibration of the reference standards submitted by laboratories from throughout the United States are carried out. The following is a generalization of the echelons of standards in the national measurement system:

National standards: including prototype and natural phenomena of SI (Système International, the worldwide organization of weight and measures standards) base units and reference and working standards for derived and other units

Metrology standards: reference standards of industrial or governmental laboratories

Calibration standards: working standards of industrial or governmental laboratories

Frequently, there are various levels within these echelons [3].

It is obvious that the NBS cannot calibrate all of the standards of every institution in the United States that calibrates measuring equipment. The system that has evolved over the years, however, has proven to be workable and includes the following features: NBS calibrates directly or by means of measurement assurance programs the reference-level standards of those organizations requiring the highest level of accuracy. These organizations calibrate their own working-level standards and the reference or working-level standards of other laboratories. In turn, working-level standards are used to calibrate the measuring and test equipment used to measure or test products.

Calibration is the comparison of a measurement device or system of a known relationship to national standards with another device or system of an unknown relationship in order to estimate the uncertainty in the latter. It may include adjustment and/or repair to minimize the uncertainty. Calibration, which begins with the measurements made at the NBS and culminates with those made in industrial calibration laboratories, is the process that assures consistency of measurements and provides the basis for interchangeability of parts and mass production.

The industrial standards laboratory is the custodian of a company's reference standards and provides a service similar to that which the NBS performs for the nation except on a far smaller scale and usually on a scope that is considerably less broad. In some cases the industrial standards laboratory is able to make some measurements as accurately as those made by the NBS. Reference standards maintained by the industrial metrology laboratories in the United Stated for calibration of working standards must have a known relationship to national standards. This may be accomplished by periodic calibrations by the NBS or, in some cases, the maintenance of "natural phenomena" (e.g., atomic frequency standards or freezing-point temperature references). The measurements made in industrial standards laboratories are intended to support calibration of the companies' measuring and test equipment. This equipment is used in research and development, in production, in inspection, in testing, and in diagnosis. Its accuracy must be sufficient for the purpose intended and, consequently, the first principle in calibration work is that the measurement requirement (i.e., the intent of the measurement) must be known.

Measurements made in manufacturing have a variety of purposes or intents, although one, the production of an item that complies with its specifications, is often thought to be their sole purpose. In most cases the other purposes support this general purpose. Others, though, may support continuing research and development, quality assurance, or other not specifically production-related purposes. Quite often the measuring or test equipment's accuracy (or other capability) may be different for each purpose. That is, equipment that is used solely to determine that a product is working or has a certain general characteristic may require less accuracy than equipment used to determine that the product is working within established limits or that the characteristic is within a specified tolerance.

Some companies locate the group responsible for metrology and calibration within the organization responsible for the quality program; others do not. Organizational location of the calibration function is no more important to the quality program than the location of other functions necessary or vital to the success of that program. What is important is that there be awareness of the different responsibilities and communication on all matters of mutual interest and concern.

A meaningful and effective quality program depends on an adequate system of measuring and test equipment calibration and control. Measurements made in production with uncalibrated equipment or (perhaps worse) with equipment inadequately calibrated can lead to erroneous decisions—either in accepting nonconforming material or in rejecting conforming material. A close, if not organizational relationship serves to minimize this potential for costly errors.

The remainder of this chapter explores the field of metrology: its concepts, its role in quality assurance, its role as a control system, and its management. In all these areas the intent is to provide an introduction of the field to the quality assurance practitioner and management, to allow meaningful communication and to provide an understanding of the metrology role within the company's quality control program.

II. CONCEPTS IN METROLOGY

A fundamental role of the metrology and calibration process is to assign accuracy or uncertainty statements to a measurement. *Accuracy* is the term used to describe the degree to which the measurement result reflects reality; accuracy is the statement made which defines how closely the measured value approximates the true value of a characteristic. Because the true value is unknowable, the accepted or specified value is normally used for this approximation. Most calibration work involves the determination or verification of the accuracy of a measuring instrument; most accuracy statements are given in percent, although higher-order accuracies are usually stated in parts per million (ppm).

Precision in measurement is the degree to which the result is repeatable under identical circumstances. In some respects, precision is a more important characteristic of a measurement than is accuracy. Measurements may be accurate and precise, accurate and imprecise, inaccurate and precise, and inaccurate and imprecise. The role of the metrology and calibration process is to quantify these measurement characteristics, to the extent required, by the design of experiments and careful consideration of all factors that could influence the results.

Error is an important consideration related to accuracy and is present in all measurements. The task of the metrologist, particularly in measurements that are at or near the state of the art, is to identify all contributions to

measurement error and to quantify those contributions. There are basically
two types of errors that may enter the measurement process: random and
systematic. The latter is typified by fixed bias and may sometimes be removable. The former is probabilistic and must be estimated statistically. Both
types of errors contribute to the total uncertainty of the measurement and to
the accuracy assignable.

The entire metrology and calibration process, at least in the industrial
sense, is intended to quantify measurement error contributions in respect to
the national standards of measurement. This "traceability of measurements"
has been a requirement for contractors doing business with the U.S. Department of Defense (DoD) for many years; it has received increased attention in
the last few years because of two unrelated developments. These are the creation of federal requirements concerning quality assurance and calibration by
agencies outside the DoD (e.g., FDA, NRC, OSHA, etc.) and the widespread
adoption of measurement assurance programs (MAPs) by the U.S. National
Bureau of Standards.

Traceability is a process intended to quantify a laboratory's measurement
uncertainty in relationship to the national standards; it is based on analyses
of error contributions present in each of the measurement transfers, from the
calibration of the laboratory's reference standards by the NBS, to the measurements made in the calibration transfers within the laboratory, and finally
to the measurements made on a product. Evidence of traceability is normally
required; it may be as simple as retention of certificates and reports of calibration or as complex as reproduction of the analyses demonstrating the uncertainties claimed for the measurements.

A laboratory that maintains its own reference standards (i.e., it relies on
no laboratory other than the NBS for calibration of its standards) must continuously monitor its own performance. Measurements on check standards,
intercomparisons of standards and participation in measurement assurance
programs sponsored by the NBS are means to quantify laboratory error sources
as well as to provide indications of the causes.

Measurement assurance, thought by some to relate only to methods used
in the metrology or calibration laboratory to secure calibrations by the NBS,
is one of the more important concepts in the measurement field. Although the
idea is not new, the application from the NBS to the industrial metrology and
calibration laboratory and ultimately to measurements made in factory operations has been given increased impetus in the last few years by the NBS and
by the National Conference of Standards Laboratories.

A feature of MAPs (which undoubtedly gave rise to the feeling that MAPs
affect only calibration laboratories) is that MAPs both provide NBS traceability
and quantify the participants' total uncertainty. Traditionally, calibrations
by the NBS determine the accuracy and precision of the measuring instrument.
MAPs, on the other hand, because the experiment involves measurements by
participants in their own laboratories, are able to include not only the accuracy
of the item, but also the contribution to error by the metrologist/technician,
by the laboratory environment, and by the practices/procedures of the laboratory [4].

Measurement assurance, in addition to being a concept of importance to
metrology and calibration laboratory managers, is one that should interest
quality assurance personnel involved in testing and measurement. Most factory
testing and measuring involves use of equipment whose accuracy has been determined thorugh calibration. Little, if any, consideration is given to errors
that may be contributed by the test operator, by his or her instructions or

procedures, or by the environments in which the equipment is operated.
Application of measurement assurance, including introduction of check fixtures
or standards and control charts, particularly when state-of-the-art measurements are being made or where the measurements made are of critical importance to the production process, can serve to reduce errors.

Periodic recalibration of measuring and test equipment is accepted by most
as necessary for measurement accuracy. A little more controversial is the
question of determining the basis of the period of recalibration. There are a
number of techniques in use to establish calibration intervals initially and to
adjust the intervals thereafter. These methods include the same interval for
all equipment in the user's inventory, the same interval for families of instruments [e.g., oscilloscopes, digital voltmeters (DVMs), gage blocks, etc.], and
the same interval for a given manufacturer and model number. Adjustments
of these initial intervals are then made for the entire inventory, for individual
families, or for manufacturer and model numbers, respectively, based on analyses or history. A study conducted for the NBS in connection with a review
of government laboratory practices identifies these and other methods [5].

One method establishes the initial interval of an instrument based on the
manufacturer model number. Adjustment of intervals is then made for the specific instrument based on its own performance. This method of interval adjustment is the only one known that considers the differences in production for
the instrument and differences in application and environmental factors when
the instrument is used [2].

The objective of adjusting the intervals between calibrations is to achieve
a predetermined quality level. Quality level, sometimes referred to as reliability, is the fraction of instruments returned for calibration which are found to
be within their specified tolerances. This information can also be used to
estimate the fraction of instruments in use which are in tolerance (see Table 1).

The existence of instruments in use which are (or have a possibility of
being) out of tolerance has given rise to considerable controversy over the
years. At issue is the effect that use of out-of-tolerance measuring equipment
has on the quality of products. On the one hand, logic suggests that an out-
of-specification product is more likely to be accepted by an out-of-tolerance
measuring instrument than by an in-tolerance measuring instrument. This
position may be summarized by the phrase "Bad instruments buy bad products."
The alternative view holds that the risk of accepting out-of-specification product (consumer or β risk) is probably less with out-of-tolerance instruments
than with in-tolerance instruments. Or, even if it is not, the risk of rejecting
in-specification product (producer or α risk) is so much greater than the β
risk that producers will take action long before the consumer is affected. The
controversy has led to several attempts by the DoD to revise its governing
specification for contractors' calibration control systems. The goal is to require that data resulting from calibration of measuring equipment found to be
out-of-tolerance be fed back to users. This "feedback" was to be used by
quality assurance to determine the need for corrective action and to alert customers to potential out-of-specification products already delivered.

Calculation of α and β risks under several assumptions of process capability
and measuring equipment accuracy indicates that measuring equipment that is
out of tolerance has only minimal impact on product quality. For example,
calculations with the following assumptions provide the risks displayed in
Table 1 [6].

   1.   Process capability is $\pm 2\sigma$.
   2.   Measuring equipment has accuracy ratios of 10:1, 4:1, and 2:1.

TABLE 1 Tabulation of α and β Risks[a]

Test equipment condition in use	Accuracy ratio					
	10:1		4:1		2:1	
In tolerance	0.32	0.24	1.18	0.02	3.84	0.01
Out of tolerance by 25%	0.31	0.22	1.15	0.06	3.90	0.05
Out of tolerance by 50%	0.31	0.21	1.16	0.08	11.55	0.13
Out of tolerance by 100%	0.39	0.18	1.19	0.23	8.88	0.28
Out of tolerance by 200%	0.56	0.11	1.87	0.38	9.19	0.20
Out of tolerance by 300%	0.82	0.10	4.79	0.39	95.5	0

[a] α Risk; in-specification product rejected as percent of products produced; β Risk; out-of-specification product accepted as percent of products produced.
Source: R. F. Schumacher, *Feedback of Out-of-Tolerance Data*, an internal study conducted by Rockwell International, Anaheim, Calif., 1981.

3. Measuring equipment inaccuracy (except for 10:1 case) is subtracted from product specification tolerances to create acceptance limits (i.e., a guardband is formed).
4. Measuring equipment is found to be in tolerance, or 25%, 50%, 100%, 200%, and 300% out of tolerance.

III. MEASUREMENT AND QUALITY ASSURANCE

Calibration of measuring equipment acts as a reference for all quality control decisions; measurements made with equipment whose capabilities (accuracy, stability, precision, etc.) are unknown or unproven will frequently lead to decisions that are incorrect. In many cases these incorrect decisions do not manifest themselves immediately; some never do. The problem is that without a known reference the reasons for subsequently observed anomalies (i.e., the causes) may never be determined certainly.

The effect of calibration on the quality control program begins with the establishment of the product's specifications. These specifications come from research and development laboratory measurements as well as from the physics and mathematics of the design. In other words, measurements made in the research and development laboratory contribute in some way to the product specifications, which, in production, the quality control function must assure are being achieved.

Measurements made in receiving inspection, in fabrication or process control, in subassembly testing, and in systems testing are all made with the intent of verifying that some characteristic of the product conforms to its specifications. The effect of calibration on the economic well-being of the institution are more vividly seen here. Erroneous decisions (rejection of products that actually conform to the specifications or acceptance of products that actually do not) are costly: costly in terms of money, in terms of wasted resources, and in terms of reputation.

Because measurements form the basis for most quality assurance decisions, particularly those pertaining to acceptance of products, equipment selected to make product measurements must be adequate for the purpose. Adequacy is usually interpreted to mean that the measuring equipment has an accuracy that is somewhat better than the tolerance of the characteristic being measured. A rule of thumb, adopted by many organizations, is that the accuracy of the measuring instrument should be one-tenth the tolerance of the characteristic to be measured. Many other organizations have adopted a one-fourth rule. (In most cases this accuracy ratio will be stated in reverse. That is, the rule of thumb will require an accuracy ratio of 10:1 or 4:1.)

The use of accuracy ratios provides a simple means for the determination of measuring equipment adequacy. In many cases the accuracy-ratio rule of thumb is all that is necessary to assure that the measuring equipment is adequate; in some cases, particularly in the standards laboratory but also in other testing situations where measurement capability is at or near the state of the art, such simplified approaches are not adequate. More sophisticated analyses involving statistical techniques must be employed. The use of accuracy ratios recognizes that all measurement processes have errors. But if the ratios meet the rule of thumb (i.e., 10:1 or 4:1) these errors are sufficiently small so as to be ignored. Some organizations believe that "sufficiently small" is when the accuracy ratio is at least 10:1, whereas others believe that an error is still "sufficiently small" when the accuracy ratio reaches as low as 4:1.

There are, however, a number of measurement situations in almost any modern production operation where for various reasons, some technical and some economic, an accuracy ratio of 10:1 (or even 4:1) is not possible or desirable. In those cases the error in the measurement contributed by the measuring equipment is no longer "sufficiently small" as to be ignored; some means of compensating for the error must be provided. There are various statistical methods of compensation, but the most widely used (probably because it is the easiest) is a direct subtraction of the measuring equipment error from the specified product tolerance.

An example should clarify the concept. Consider a product with a specified requirement of one characteristic of 10 ± 1V. This is a requirement for the product irrespective of how it is measured. If our rule for sufficiently small error is an accuracy ratio of at least 10:1, we must provide a measuring instrument capable of measuring 10 V to an accuracy of ±0.1 V. If we had such an instrument, we would use it to measure the 10 V, and if the measured value were between 9 and 11 V (inclusive), we would say that the product met this requirement. Suppose, however, that the best measuring instrument we had could measure 10 V only to an accuracy of ±0.2 V. In this case our accuracy ratio is only 5:1 and, by our rule, the error of the measuring instrument is large enough that it cannot be safely ignored. Using the direct subtraction method, the instrument's error of ±0.2 V is subtracted from the product's specified tolerance of ±1 V to create a new set of acceptance limits: ±0.8 V. Now, when this instrument is used to measure the 10 V, we would say that the product met the requirement if the measured value were between 9.2 and 10.8 V (inclusive). A product with a true value between 9 and 9.2 V or between 10.8 and 11 V might be rejected by this method even though it would comply with the product's specification. This is considered prudent because an instrument with a ±0.2 V uncertainty without the guardband has a high probability of rejecting a product with a true value greater which is within the limits specified (10 ± 1 V).

As noted previously, calculation of the α and β risks associated with selected accuracy ratios and for various out-of-tolerance conditions of the measuring equipment discloses that the α risk is far higher than the β risk. Selection of higher accuracy ratios, then, is not usually made because of potential product jeopardy, but rather because of the costs associated with rejecting a product that is actually acceptable: a decision based on economics.

Two very important tasks for the calibration function are implied by this example. One is that measuring equipment capability (i.e., accuracy, precision, etc.) must be determined. This may be accomplished in two ways. First, the equipment is initially evaluated by the metrology function to determine its basic capability. (In many cases this step is not performed; basic capability is assumed to be what the instrument manufacturer claims.) Second, the instrument is calibrated periodically, thus updating the determination of the instrument's capability.

The second task, which is shared by the quality assurance function, is the determination of the calibration requirements. The calibration requirements are derived from the product's specified tolerance and are not necessarily the same as the instrument's capability. Knowledge of the calibration requirements, if they are less than the instrument's capability, allows the calibration organization to make calibration decisions based on economics. If the calibration requirements exceed the instrument's capability, the quality assurance organization may suggest a product tolerance change, may select an instrument with improved capability, or may establish calibration requirements based on a different accuracy ratio. These decisions are partly technical and partly economic.

IV. CALIBRATION CONTROL SYSTEM

A typical calibration program may involve all or most of the following tasks: (1) evaluation of equipment to determine its capability, (2) identification of calibration requirements, (3) selection of standards to perform calibration, (4) selection of methods/procedures to carry out the measurements necessary for the calibration, (5) establishment of the initial interval and the rules for adjusting the interval thereafter, (6) establishment of a recall system to assure instruments due for calibration are returned, (7) implementation of a labeling system to visually identify the instrument's due date, and (8) use of a quality assurance program to evaluate the calibration system (process control, audit, corrective action, etc.).

Selection of the standards, methods, and procedures to carry out the calibration includes the decision relating to where the calibration will be performed. Some instruments may require use of a laboratory's highest level of standards and thus must be performed in the laboratory. Other instruments, however, may be calibrated in the using area by the transport of suitable standards to that area. Two methods are followed in this case. One, referred to as "in situ" calibration, requires external interface to the calibrated characteristics. When such interface exists, the instrument being calibrated remains in the specific location where it is used (e.g., in a rack-mounted configuration) and the calibration is performed. The second method, still performed in the using area, requires that the equipment be removed from its rack mounting to provide access to the measurement points used in calibration. Both of these methods have advantages over the more traditional method, which requires that the instrument be returned to a calibration laboratory. One advantage is that the calibration is performed with the environmental factors identical to the environmental factors present when the instrument is used. Another advantage is that the instrument does not have to be transported, thus reducing the potential for damage or movement-induced changes in the instrument. A major advantage is that the measuring system which includes the instrument being calibrated is not "down" while the instrument is being transported to and from a laboratory. However, instruments that cannot be adjusted from the front panel or instruments requiring large or unique standards must be returned to the standards laboratory for calibration. In addition, instruments that during calibration in the using area are found to be out-of-tolerance must also be returned to the laboratory for repair.

The recall system must be designed to assure that the calibration organization and the using organization are both aware in advance that an instrument will be due for calibration. Depending on the number of instruments being controlled and their geographic location differences, the system may be as simple as a card file or as sophisticated as a fully automated data processing system. The more sophisticated the system, the more that can be expected from it beyond the basic purpose of providing recall notification (e.g., history of previous calibrations, interval assignments, labor standards or actual costs, parts replaced, etc.).

Labeling of instruments to display their calibration due dates visually is a companion feature to the recall system. Labels indicate (by dates, color codes, or similar symbols) the date the instrument is due for its next calibration. This visual identification may be used by the quality assurance organization to assure that the instrument is not used beyond its due date.

Intervals are established in a variety of ways, as discussed previously. Principal objectives of an interval adjustment program include minimizing the potential for out-of-tolerance instruments in using areas, minimizing the costs of calibration, and assuring the required accuracy of instrumentation. The effectiveness of the interval adjustment programs can be estimated by measuring the average interval and its trend and by measuring the quality level.

Quality-level goals that vary from about 75% to above 95% have been established by different organizations. The relationship between intervals and quality levels is complicated by such factors as age of equipment in the inventory (new items are added to inventories), the makeup of the inventory (mechanical instrumentation, electronic test equipment, fixtures, etc.), and the accuracy assignments of instruments in the inventory. However, the quality level is one indicator of the effectiveness of the interval adjustment program. When combined with other indicators, such as the average interval, the minimum and maximum observed intervals, and a corrective-action system that is triggered by low intervals, the quality level is a sound method for evaluation of the total calibration control system.

V. MANAGEMENT

Organizationally, the calibration function may report to almost any company element. Philosophically, particularly if the laboratory includes the metrology functions of standards development and maintenance, the calibration function is most in tune with engineering and quality assurance. In an organizational sense there has long been a close link between the company element responsible for quality control and the element responsible for equipment calibration. In many companies this link is positive and direct; the calibration group reports to the executive responsible for quality control. In others, the calibration group maintains close liaison with its quality control counterpart. Is there a correct organization approach? That is, is there one organizational structure that is most effective and, consequently, recommends itself for all companies to consider? The answer is no. Very effective programs have been implemented in companies with the calibration group reporting to quality control, to engineering, to plant maintenance, to manufacturing, and to the firm's chief executive officer. The key is not found in organizational location; rather, it is found in the firm's policy or philosophy.

Most effective calibration programs not only display a top-management philosophy which emphasizes the importance of measurement control and reflects a close relationship with quality control; they also adopt and implement strong quality control programs within the calibration process itself. The most significant development in this regard in the last decade has been the emergence of a control system referred to as *measurement assurance*. Although understood by many as a means for economically and most effectively transferring measurement traceability to the industrial standards and calibration laboratories, measurement assurance is more than this. Actually, measurement assurance is a control system for measurements made throughout the institution: research, development, manufacturing, and so on.

Calibration, then, is intimately related to quality control. Without calibration the quality control decisions pertaining to the product are at best questionable. Without quality control in calibration, performance is subject to the same deterioration that affects other operations without quality control: increased errors, increased costs, and so on.

Productivity is an important topic in most institutions today, particularly in the United States. Improving productivity is cited as a necessity to the control of inflation, to the improvement of the standard of living, to the improvement of the balance of payments, to the increase of employment, and several other characteristics. The calibration function can contribute to productivity improvement, and the single most important area that is subject to managed improvement of productivity of calibration functions is (as it is for most other organizations) in the labor content. Reduction of the labor involved in the various calibration tasks can measurably contribute to a company's productivity improvement. The most promising way to reduce labor is to use (and increase the use of) computers and microprocessors. These may involve computers in data analyses or microprocessors in test automation. What is required is ingenuity coupled with a continuing concern for the adequacy of the measurement process. One study has shown that a particularly effective method to improve productivity is to identify and correct counterproductive practices [7].

The issues of importance to management of metrology and calibration laboratory include a capability in measurement adequate for the calibration tasks (a capability that includes equipment, personnel, facilities, and procedures), a budget sufficient to execute the responsibilities of calibration (including labor, expense, and equipment), and a well-defined mission statement for the calibration task. In many cases, the ability to forecast future measurement needs of the institution for periods in the mid to long term (i.e., 3 to 10 years) is an important asset of a metrology and calibration laboratory manager.

The capability of the laboratory to make the measurements required in carrying out its calibration tasks is a characteristic that must be assessed continuously. Coordination with the engineering and quality assurance organizations to provide the minimum capability when it is needed is an absolute requirement. This is of particular importance when the laboratory is operating at the state-of-the-art level or when new measurement requirements will push the laboratory toward the state of the art. Development of capabilities (including necessary coordination with the NBS) for state-of-the-art measurements may require several years; therefore, early planning is essential.

Budgets for the calibration tasks in some organizations are considered to be overhead, whereas in others they may be a combination of overhead and direct. Budgets should be based on an analysis of the tasks to be performed and should include labor budgets, expense budgets, and equipment (or capital) budgets. Budgeting methods (and the related budgeting difficulties) are normally unique to an institution. The principal requirements for a metrology and calibration laboratory manager in connection with budgeting are to understand his or her organization's budgeting system and to have a thorough grasp of his or her laboratory's tasks and their costs. Only in this way can the laboratory manager provide the forecasts essential to the approval of a budget that is adequate.

Control of the laboratory's costs (irrespective of the outcome of the budgeting process) is a measure of the manager's ability to balance the technical and economic needs of the calibration function. Control, of course, means meeting the established budgets for the tasks and identifying the tasks (and their costs) which change during the period of the budget to secure revisions to the budget (up or down). (It is just as important to identify budget decreases as budget increases for the financial well-being of the institution of which the calibration function is a part.)

Probably one of the most important steps that any laboratory manager can take in connection with assessing the adequacy of his or her measurement capabilities or with budgeting is the development of a well-defined mission statement. Such a statement should interrelate with and support the overall mission of the organization. Coupled with an objective evaluation of the laboratory's principal strengths and weaknesses, such a statement provides an excellent basis for organizational planning.

VI. CONCLUSION

Metrology and calibration laboratories are of significant importance to the quality assurance function whether or not the laboratories are organizationally a part of quality assurance. The principal role of such laboratories is to provide a measurement capability which is adequate for the institution. Whether the calibration function is organizationally within the quality assurance function or not, the need for continuing dialogue on matters of mutual interest cannot be overstated; a similar statement may be made in respect to the calibration function and engineering. In the final analysis, metrology is responsible for the integrity of measurement within our institutions, and measurements underlie the quality assurance program.

REFERENCES

1. R. C. Sangster, *Collected Executive Summaries: Studies of the National Measurement System, 1972–1975*, U.S. Department of Commerce, Washington, D.C., August 1976.
2. G. O. Rice, "Measurement Systems and the Standards Laboratory," Workshop Conference on the Management of Laboratory Instruments,

Cairo, Egypt, November 7–11, 1976. (Conference proceedings collected in a work titled *Management Systems for Laboratory Instrument Services*, Instrument Society of America, Research Triangle Park, N.C., 1980.)

3. D. A. Mack, "Instrumentation Calibration," Workshop Converence on the Management of Laboratory Instruments, Cairo, Egypt, November 7–11, 1976. (Conference proceedings collected in a work titled *Management Systems for Laboratory Instrument Services*, Instrument Society of America, Research Triangle Park, N.C., 1980.)

4. B. C. Belanger, "Measurement of Quality Control and the Use of NBS Measurement Assurance Program (MAP) Services," draft document (1980) to be published by U.S. Department of Commerce.

5. J. L. Vogt, *Optimizing Calibration Recall Intervals and Algorithms*, NBS Publication NBS-GCR-80-283, 1980.

6. R. F. Schumacher, "Feedback of Out-of-Tolerance Data," an internal study conducted by Rockwell International, Anaheim, Calif., 1981.

7. R. M. Ranftl, *R&D Productivity: An Investigation of Ways to Improve Productivity in Technology-Based Organizations*, Hughes Aircraft Co., Culver City, Calif., 1974, 1978.

29

INSPECTION EQUIPMENT

RONALD A. LAVOIE

Federal Products Corporation
Providence, Rhode Island

I. INTRODUCTION

This chapter describes the dimensional inspection equipment needed for the
various major inspection areas of a precision manufacturing operation. Although all the equipment listed would probably be needed in a large manufacturing operation, it will be apparent which items are vital even for a smaller-
scale operation. The major inspection areas are considered to be incoming inspection, post-process manufacturing inspection, automatic and semiautomatic
gaging, and the metrology laboratory.

The incoming inspection area inspects products from vendors as well as
the shop floor. It is an area that has to have a great deal of flexibility and be
capable of measuring a broad spectrum of dimensional characteristics. Post-
process gaging on the manufacturing floor usually involves dedicated gages.
Measurements are usually made by the machine operator shortly after a part is
removed from the machine. Automatic and semiautomatic gages perform measurements either off- or on-line with little, if any, operator involvement. Finally,
the metrology laboratory performs calibration functions on other gages as well
as specialized dimensional analysis work.

II. INCOMING INSPECTION

A. Surface Plate or Layout Inspection

Until the introduction of the coordinate measuring machine in the mid-1960s,
the surface plate "layout" technique was the primary means for measuring complex parts and fixtures. Today, surface plates are generally limited to measuring parts too large to place in a facility's coordinate measuring machine.
Sometimes surface plates must be used for accuracy requirements that are
greater than those possible with the coordinate measuring machine.

Typically, the accuracy potential of a surface plate is two to three times
greater than that of a coordinate measuring machine. However, surface plate
measuring techniques require highly skilled technicians and are 10 to 40 times
slower than measurements made on the coordinate measuring machine.

A typical surface plate setup consists of the following elements:

Surface Plate

A granite surface plate can vary in size from as small as 1 ft^2 to massive plates 10 ft by 20 ft and 3 ft thick. These plates are usually of quartz granite. The top surface of this granite is lapped flat to tolerances on the order of 50 μin. This lapped surface establishes a reference plane from which parts can be accurately fixtured and measured.

Height Transfer Stand

A height transfer stand and test indicator are used to indicate a critical surface on a part and to transfer that setting to the height micrometer (see Fig. 1). The reading on the height micrometer is the altitude from the surface plate to the critical surface on the part. Repeating this operation on another critical surface and subtracting the two readings will produce the distance between two surfaces on the part.

Height Standard

The height standard can be either mechanical or electronic. The mechanical version usually consists of a micrometer of 1-in. travel mounted on the top of a permanent stack of 1-in. steps usually 12 to 18 in. high. This height micrometer establishes a very accurate measurement standard which is perpendicular to the surface plate. Movement of the micrometer lead screw allows the positioning of the 1-in. steps anywhere within the 1-in. travel of the micrometer in 0.0001-in. increments.

Electronic versions of the height micrometer include a precision linear transducer which produces a digital readout of 0.0005 or 0.0001 in. resolution. These linear transducers are usually built into a height transfer stand, eliminating the need for a height micrometer. The accuracy of these systems varies substantially and is dependent on the mechanical rigidity and accuracy of the height transfer stand.

Gage Blocks

Gage blocks may also be stacked and placed vertically on the surface plate instead of on a height micrometer. This technique was popular before the advent of height micrometers. It is extremely slow and is used only when the inherent high accuracy of gage blocks is required.

Test Indicators

There are mechanical and electronic test indicators. Mechanical test indicators are still popular and are used where transfer accuracies of 0.0001 in. are adequate. Electronic indicators include an electronic transducer with a lever-type contact and an amplifier. Multiple ranges and optimum viewing angle of the amplifier display are its primary features. However, electronic test indicators are approximately 10 times more expensive than the mechanical test indicator.

Sine Plates

Sine plates in conjunction with gage blocks create very precise angles, on the order of 15 arc seconds. They are used to measure angles on a surface plate.

FIGURE 1   In a typical surface plate inspection operation, a height stand
and test indicator are used to transfer a reading from the workpiece to a
height standard. Proper orientation of the part is achieved by use of a sine
plate.

Simple and compound angle sine plates are available. The simple sine plate
creates an angle in one direction. The compound sine plate permits creation
of two angles oriented 90° to each other—a compound angle.

Fixturing

Surface plate inspection usually requires universal fixturing to facilitate
accurate positioning of a variety of parts. Typical fixturing consists of magnetic blocks and V blocks, right-angle knees, parallels, and a clamp.

B. Bench Inspection Station

Incoming inspection stations incorporate many inspection benches where hand
measurements are usually made. Surface plates are often a part of these

benches. Measurements that can be easily made with hand gages are performed here, and should not be made on expensive equipment such as coordinate measuring machines and optical comparators.

Length Measuring Devices

Micrometers

At least a 0- to 1-in. depth and a multianvil micrometer are usually available at these stations. A central station may also have the less frequently used, larger, special-application micrometers (see Fig. 2).

Calipers

Vernier calipers are the least expensive type available. They are used infrequently because they are difficult to read, resulting in reduced efficiency and errors of measurement. Dial calipers have more-or-less replaced the mechanical vernier caliper. They are easy to read, require less skill to operate, and produce fast, reliable readings. Electronic calipers with digital readouts are also available; however, they are twice as expensive as dial calipers.

Comparator Stand

A comparator stand and dial indicator afford rapid measurements of heights and diameters. The comparator stand is used for measuring large samples of

FIGURE 2   An inspector uses an inside micrometer to check a hole diameter. Other part dimensions will be checked using the dial calipers and micrometer.

the same dimension. With an electronic cartridge probe and amplifying system, it may be used for higher-accuracy requirements.

Bore Gaging

Pin Library

Pin gaging involves placing a series of pins at 0.001- or 0.0001-in. increments into a hole until one pin just fits and the next size does not. This is a coarse but effective means of measuring diameters. It is particularly useful in measuring the diameter of very small holes below the size practical for other types of bore-measuring devices.

Dial Bore Gages

Dial bore gages have the advantage of being adjustable over a broad range of measuring sizes, typically from ½ to 13 in. They do not require special masters. They may be mastered with gage blocks or a micrometer. This setting is then transferred to the measured hole without loss of accuracy.

Inside Micrometer

The inside micrometer covers a braod range of measuring diameters. It is, however, limited to holes at least 1 in. and larger. Accurate measurements with this device require careful manipulation of the micrometer to find the maximum diameter of the hole. It is only one-third as accurate as a dial bore gage.

Air and Electronic Plugs

Plugs are most often used in post-process production situations and are described more thoroughly in that section. However, plugs are useful in incoming inspection for the measurement of popular hole sizes. Standardization of hole sizes by the engineering department can make it practical to utilize this type of bore gaging. These gages are desirable because of their simplicity of operation, but they are limited to a specific diameter and usually require master setting rings.

Telescoping Gages

Telescoping gages are spring-loaded cylinders that expand to fill the hole they are measuring. They are then locked into position and their overall dimension measured with a micrometer. They are difficult to operate, requiring considerable skill, and arc limited to a 0.0005-in. accuracy.

Other Types

There are electronic and micrometer-type bore gages which do not require mastering. They read the inside diameter of a bore directly. Their high price has limited their use.

Miscellaneous

Simple measuring devices such as rules, protractors, and radius templates are commonly found in the bench inspection area.

C. Coordinate Measuring Machines

Since their introduction in the early 1960s, tens of thousands of coordinate measuring machines (CMMs) have been sold throughout the world. Today, practically every manufacturer of precision products has at least one CMM system. These machines measure most dimensions on complex parts 10 to 40 times faster than the former procedure of layout inspection. These systems are often used to inspect products produced by numerically controlled machining centers.

The more basic systems require only semiskilled operators, and their simplicity of operation, together with digital readouts, ensures reliable measurement results. They range in capacity from a 16 in. by 12 in. by 8 in. measuring cube to systems large enough to allow measurement of an auto body. Their accuracy potential is usually sufficient to satisfy the majority of production part inspection requirements.

Basic System

Basic coordinate measuring systems usually consist of air or ball-bearing ways which establish three axes: X, Y, and Z. The X axis establishes left-right motion; the Y axis, in-out motion; and the Z axis, vertical motion. Each of these axes has its own long-range linear transducer. The Z-axis shaft has a receiver at its lower end capable of accepting various measuring probes. A typical measurement involves placing a tapered probe into a hole and zeroing the three axes, then moving the tapered probe to a second hole. The digital display will indicate the distance between the holes.

Advanced Systems

Computer Assist

Many CMM systems have computers which are interfaced with the measuring system either as a stand-alone computer, a programmable calculator, or a microcomputer built within the digital display (see Fig. 3). These computing systems speed up the operation of the coordinate measuring machine and can reduce inspection time by at least 50% over noncomputer systems. The computers perform such functions as the following:

1. *Automatic axis alignment*: This compensates for misalignment of the part datums to the axes of the coordinate measuring machine.
2. *Coordinate conversion*: The conversion of rectangular coordinates to polar coordinate readout.
3. *Contour measurement*: The measurement of contours "on the fly," by simply sweeping the probe across a contoured surface.
4. *Centers of diameters and arcs*: Determining the center position of arcs and diameters by placing the probe at three equally spaced positions on the diameter of consideration.

It is not uncommon for a computer package to incorporate 30 features similar to those just described. They increase the efficiency of coordinate measuring machine operation and minimize the probability of an operator error.

Servomotor Drive

Servomotor drive of the axes of the CMM in conjunction with computer control allows for automatic inspection of parts. The operator simply loads the

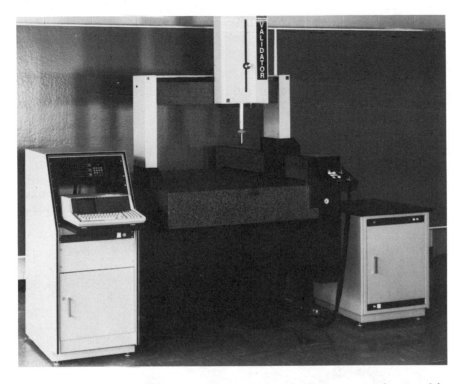

FIGURE 3   A direct computer-controlled coordinate measuring machine utilizing air bearings on all axes. (Courtesy of Brown & Sharpe Manufacturing
Company.)

part into the system, starts the operation, and the coordinate measuring machine performs all measurements automatically. These systems measure parts
very rapidly without operator fatigue or involvement. However, they do require the programming of the system for each particular part measured, and
this is advantageous only if you can amortize this programming time over a
substantial number of similar pieces.

Accessories

1. *Touch probes*: Touch probes will deflect when contacting a surface
   until a null point is detected, transmitting a signal to the computer.
   A touch probe has very little gaging force, and therefore does not
   impart any distorting forces to the coordinate measuring machine system, enhancing system accuracy. Also, it is commonly used with servomotor drive systems.
2. *Optical viewers*: Optical viewing devices placed on the end of the Z
   axis allow establishing reference and measuring points by means of
   optical techniques. A microscope viewer is particularly useful on fragile surfaces that will not allow mechanical contact. However, operation
   of a microscope produces considerable operator fatigue.
3. *TV viewers*: TV viewing systems can be operated in conjunction with
   a computer to automate completely the optical detection of edges and
   center of holes. Generally, these systems are limited to X and Y axis

measurement only. As imaging enhancing technology continues, these
systems should continue to receive greater acceptance.

D. Optical Comparators

Optical comparators are used to project the profile or image of a precision part
onto a large screen (see Fig. 4). The viewing screen displays an image that
is a precision magnification of the part. Most commonly, the part is magnified
10, 20, or 50 times its original size.

   The part is measured by comparing the image projected onto the screen to
a transparent overlay. Critical part parameters, such as contours and radi-
uses, are drawn on the overlay at the same magnification as that of the optical
comparator. The overlays are usually drawn with minimum and maximum tolerances. It is apparent at a glance whether or not the part meets the product
tolerance.

   Also, the staging area for the part is movable by means of lead screws
which are often monitored by linear, digital transducers. This allows precise

FIGURE 4   An optical comparator inspects the threaded portion of a splined
shaft. The system features a 30-in. screen plus digital readout of the horizontal and vertical position of the part. The machine can be interfaced with
instrumentation such as computers, printers, a vector positioner, and so on.
(Courtesy of Jones & Lamson Metrology Systems, Waterbury Farrel Division
of Textron, Inc.)

movement of the image on the screen, enabling measurements of characteristics such as hole diameter and hole-to-hole positions.

The optical comparator is particularly ideal for the measurement of contours and characteristics too fragile to probe mechanically. Typical applications are the measurements of threads, plastic parts, and air foil contours.

Basic System

The system consists of the following elements:

1. A collimated light source which projects a beam of light across the part to be measured.
2. A staging fixture which permits placement of the part such that it interrupts the collimated beam of light.
3. A lens system designed to amplify the shadow produced by the part: a precise amount, usually 10, 20, or 50 times the original part size.
4. A frosted-glass viewing screen from 10 to 50 in. in diameter on which the amplified shadow is viewed.

Optical comparators are available either as bench or free-standing systems. Bench systems are usually limited to 10- to 14-in. screens and use a vertical light beam. Free-standing systems usually incorporate larger screens 30 to 50 in. in diameter with a horizontal light source.

Advanced Systems

Servomotor Drives

Large optical comparators with 30- or 50-in. screens often have a screen displaced to one side. This allows the operator to stand directly in front of the screen without having the light source and part staging area between him or her and the screen. Servomotor drives on the part staging fixture allow the operator to move the image up and down and left to right as well as adjusting focus without having to leave the viewing area. Linear transducers built into the fixturing also permit remote monitoring of the part movement. These features provide twice the measuring efficiency and reliability.

Computer Assist

Computer features similar to those found in coordinate measuring machines have also been incorporated in optical comparator systems. As in the coordinate measuring machines, they improve operator efficiency and simplify system operation.

Edge Finder

The inclusion of an "optical eye" at the center of the screen eliminates the need to have an operator determine when a part "edge" has arrived at the screen center. This feature, in conjunction with servomotor drives and computer assist, completely automates optical comparators. The operator need only place the part onto the staging area and begin the measuring cycle. Each part measured this way requires considerable planning and programming. It is practical only when there are a sufficient number of parts to permit amortization of this initial programming effort.

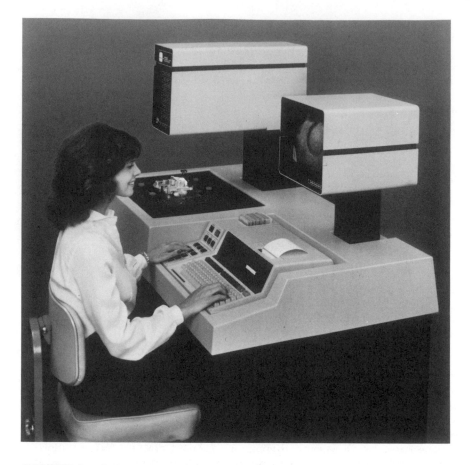

FIGURE 5   A new noncontact automatic gage with solid-state video imaging, a dedicated microprocessor control system, and computer analysis software. The gaging system is designed to provide accurate measurements of production-line parts, ranging from small electronic components to large cam shafts. (Courtesy of Optical Gaging Products, Inc.)

E. Automatic Video Gages

Automatic video gaging systems employ a TV camera, a light source, a part staging fixture, and a computer to automatically measure small (less than 5 in.) precision parts (see Fig. 5). Any characteristic that can be measured on an optical comparator can be measured on one of these devices. They are compact, bench-mounted systems incorporating operator interactive programming and are usually employed in medium-volume production-type measurement.

III. POST-PROCESS GAGING

A. Single-Dimension Gaging

Single-dimension gaging is often referred to as dedicated gaging. Such gages are used mostly in high-volume operations and measure the same characteristic for weeks on end. The dedicated nature of these gages means simplicity of setup and operation.

Inside Diameter/Outside Diameter Gaging

Indicating Snap Gages

Indicating snap gages are a quick, reliable way to measure outside diameters. Parts may be measured in or out of the machine (see Fig. 6). Snap gages are used to measure parts from 0 to 14 in. in diameter to an accuracy of 0.0001 in. Typically, this measuring range is covered by 7 to 14 models which are adjustable over a measuring range of 2 in. and 1 in, respectively.

Air Gaging

Air gaging systems employ the flow or back pressure of air to determine part size. A two-jet air plug consists of a body slightly smaller in diameter than the hole to be measured, with two air jets 180° apart (see Fig. 7). The flow of air from these jets is dependent on the size of the hole the plug is measuring. Larger clearance produces a greater flow or less back pressure. This principle is used to produce a variety of air gages to measure such characteristics as hole diameter, outside diameters, dimensional relationships such as taper, parallelism, squareness, bend, twist, and center distance.

Air gages are dedicated to measuring a particular characteristic. However, they allow you to measure many parts faster, more conveniently, and accurately than any other gaging method (see Fig. 8). Production workers do not require special training to use air gages. To check a hole, for instance, it is not necessary to develop skill in "rocking" the gage to find the true diameter. Merely insert the air plug in the hole and read the meter. It is as simple as that.

The noncontact characteristic of most air measuring units makes them particularly useful for checking soft, highly polished, thin-walled, or otherwise delicate material. Small gage heads and remote reading meters give air gages a distinct advantage in measuring multiple dimensions. Fixtures are smaller and remote meters permit placing contacts in positions that are inaccessible for other types of gages.

Air gages are readily adaptable to measuring parts in the machine. Their small gage heads make most dimensions accessible and the indicating meter can be located to make it clearly visible. A unique advantage is that the stream of air tends to clean the measuring area from coolant or oil, providing accurate measuring without first cleaning the part.

Electronic Plugs

Electronic plugs are used for measuring the inside diameter of holes (see Fig. 9). They operate in the same fashion as an air gage plug; however, they utilize mechanical contacts and an electronic transducer to measure size variations. Using only clean "electricity," the electronic plug is 50 times more energy efficient than air gaging, plus there is no risk of contamination and costly downtime due to "dirty" air.

Electronic plugs are 20 to 40% more expensive than comparable air gaging systems. However, they do not require an air supply. Electronic plugs are not sensitive to surface finish variations. Air gaging cannot be used on surface finishes greater than 50 μin. or in parts made of porous materials.

FIGURE 6 A snap gage measures an outside diameter of a part while still in the machine. (Courtesy of Federal Products Corporation.)

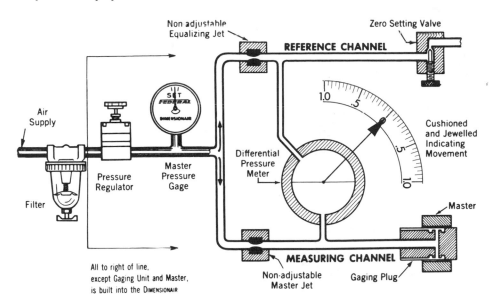

FIGURE 7   Basic components of a balanced air gaging system. With the balanced-type air system, the air from the supply line first passes through a regulator, then is divided into two channels. The air in one leg (the reference channel) escapes to the atmosphere through the adjustable zero restrictor, while the air in the opposite leg (the measuring channel) escapes to the atmosphere through the jets of the gage head. The two channels are bridged by an extremely precise indicating meter which responds immediately to any differential in air pressure between the two channels. This bridged system is similar to the familiar electrical Wheatstone bridge. (Courtesy of Federal Products Corporation.)

Bench-Type Inside Diameter/Outside Diameter Comparators.

These comparators are adjustable over a broad range of ID and OD sizes.
Typically, 3/4 to 9 in. on IDs and 3/8 to 9½ in. on ODs. Two- and three-point measurements for the detection of ovality and three-point out-of-round, respectively, are available with these devices. Measurements to 0.0001-in. accuracy are readily obtainable. The adjustable feature of these gages makes them particularly useful in applications where the dimensions checked change frequently.

Micrometers, Calipers, and Go/No Go Gaging

Applications where only one or two parts are being made at a time do not lend themselves to the types of gages previously discussed. The direct-reading nature of micrometers and calipers makes them ideally suited for applications of this type.

A go/no go ID gage consists of a minimum and a maximum size plug, representing the minimum and maximum tolerances of the ID. The operator should be able to introduce the minimum plug but not introduce the maximum plug. These gages have the advantage of being relatively inexpensive. However, they will determine only if the part is good or bad, and will not indicate trends.

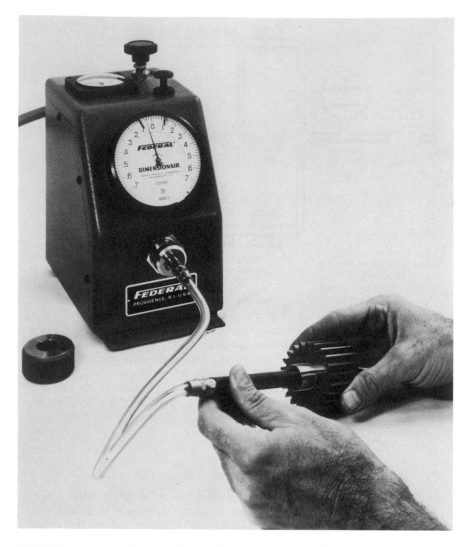

FIGURE 8 Ease of operation makes air gaging a fast accurate method for checking a particular characteristic. In this case (Dimensionair), an air plug is used to check the ID of a small gear. The master ring is shown next to the meter. (Courtesy of Federal Products Corporation.)

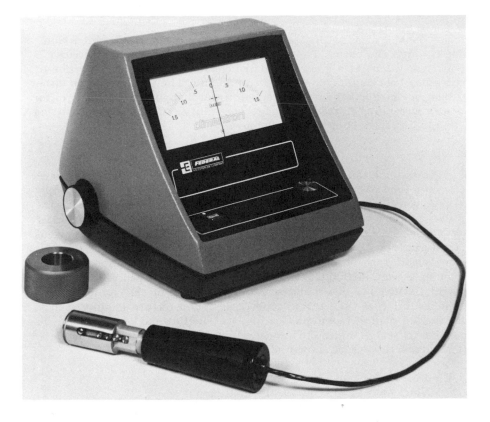

FIGURE 9   Fast, reliable bore measurement is possible with electronic plugs. (Courtesy of Federal Products Corporation.)

Depth Gages

Depth gages consist of a dial indicator, base, and a measuring point which
protrudes through the base. These instruments give accurate information
(0.0001-in. resolution) at a glance, and are convenient for the inspection of
slots, recesses, hole depths, keyways, and so on. They are available either
as hand-held devices or bench-type gages. Interchangeable points of different lengths and mounts increase the gage versatility. Gages with measuring
ranges of 0 to 3 in. are commonly available.

Fixture Gages

Fixture gages are specially designed gages for measuring one or more characteristics on a part. They are usually used in applications where general-
purpose gaging will not do the job. The fixture consists of mechanical components that support and locate the part to be measured. These mechanical
components orient the part such that indicating devices can measure various
part characteristics.

   Fixtures simplify measurements that would normally require specialized
skills or be extremely difficult to perform. The operator simply places the
part into the fixture and dial indicators or other types of electronic gaging
display the condition of the part. Properly designed fixture gaging is an
efficient, rugged gaging technique for high-production-part inspection. They
are expensive to design and build, and their use should be weighed against
the cost of alternative, more universal measuring systems.

IV. AUTOMATIC AND SEMIAUTOMATIC GAGES

An automatic and semiautomatic gage measures one or more characteristics on
a part and makes size decisions automatically (see Fig. 10). The part may be
fed by hand, by means of a cable hoist and a conveyor, or out of a hopper.
The gage may check 1, 2, or 50 dimensions. It may exercise corrective control or it may not. It may position, check, classify, segregate, record, mem-
orize, store, transfer, mark, or dispose. It can do any or all of these things
automatically, depending on need, but the gage is classified as an automatic
because precise size determination in millionths of an inch, if necessary, is
made and communicated automatically. Traditionally, a gage is called semiautomatic if there is some manual involvement, but the gage still does the deciding for the operator.

   An automatic gage can stand by itself as a final inspection device, and often
there is no machine control involved. With increasing frequency, automatic
gages are becoming part of the automated transfer line screening out bad
parts and applying corrective action when part size shifts toward or beyond tolerance. Automatic gages perform rather complicated measurements,
usually on high-precision parts that are impractical or impossible to obtain
any other way.

   A typical automatic gage consists of the following basic elements:

   A *part feed mechanism*, which moves the part through the gaging system
      and disposes of the part at the end of the measuring cycle.
   A *programmable controller*, which controls the processing of the part
      through the gaging system and its proper disposition.

FIGURE 10 Automatic gage for measuring large projectiles utilizes multi-
signal processing to classify parts as well as provide signals to machine operators when tolerances begin to approach reject area. In addition, the gage
interfaces with a main computer to provide a continuously updated record of
every measurement made and which machine produced the part measured. At
the end of each gaging cycle the processor automatically verifies that the
entire gage is up and running. (Courtesy of Federal Products Corporation.)

The *gaging station*, or stations, where the part is oriented and measured
via electronic or air transducers.

The *instrumentation system* that conditions the signals from the transducer
into a meaningful dimension.

The incorporation of microprocessors in instrumentation systems has increased
their capability. The more sophisticated systems contain all the electronic
signal-processing capability needed for virtually any complex measurement
application (see Fig. 11). The only difference between applications is the
instructions keyed into the system by the user through a built-in keyboard.
Besides signal-processing capability, these systems are capable of automatic
classification, tolerance limit setting, automatic zeroing to a master, and self-
diagnostics.

FIGURE 11   The Multi-Signal Processor (MSP) system is a total, universal
hardware package that can accommodate any number of gage applications,
even if each is entirely different. The only difference between applications
is the instruction set keyed into the MSP by the user through its built-in,
user-interactive, instructive "prompting" routine. The MSP can use input
signals in any combination that can be expressed as a mathematic equation,
simple or complex, using "plus," "minus," "multiply," "divide," "square,"
"square root," and "absolute value." (Courtesy of Federal Products
Corporation.)

V. METROLOGY LABORATORY

A. Calibration Functions

Calibration of high-accuracy standards such as master rings, gage blocks,
and so on, is often performed by outside, independent laboratories. Only
large companies have sufficient amounts of calibration to justify the purchase
and maintenance of high-accuracy calibration equipment. The accuracy potential of laboratory equipment can be realized only in a controlled environment.
Temperature, vibration, humidity, and cleanliness must be strictly controlled.
   Maximum accuracy potential can be obtained only by having: suitably calibrated masters; masters to be measured in good condition; high-quality, well-
designed instrumentation in good working order; well-trained operators; and
environment controls consistent with desired accuracy levels.

Master Ring and Disk Calibration

Master ring and disk calibration is performed on a horizontal master comparator (see Fig. 13). It utilizes stacked gage blocks as a master setting device

FIGURE 12   A precision measurement center is a precisely controlled environment for high-accuracy calibration of gage blocks, master rings, disks, and other precise measurement applications.

and compares these master readings with that of the rings or disks to be calibrated. These systems have a measuring range of 0.040 to 13.250 in. and a resolution of 0.000001 in.

Gage Block Calibration

Comparison

The most popular method of calibrating gage blocks is to compare the test block against a master block of known error (see Fig. 14). This method is most popular because it is the fastest method and produces adequate accuracy for most applications. A typical gage block comparator is adjustable to measure gage blocks from 0 to 4 in. The gage block comparator allows measurement of gage block error to 0.000001-in. resolution.

Interferometry

Grand master gage blocks are often calibrated by interferometry. This technique is recognized as being approximately twice as accurate as comparison checking of gage blocks; however, it is 10 times more time consuming.

Interferometric systems use light as their basic standard. Therefore, they do not require masters. Laboratories that use interferometric calibrators will

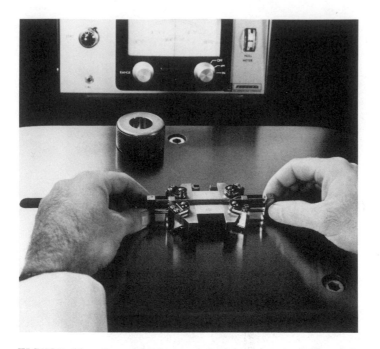

FIGURE 13   Gage blocks mounted in a nest are used to master a ring and disk comparator. (Courtesy of Federal Products Corporation.)

occasionally calibrate an audit package of gage blocks. This package is then checked by the National Bureau of Standards to assure that the laboratory's measuring system is operating at a satisfactory level of accuracy.

Threads and Plugs

Threads and plugs are usually checked in a comparator stand or a "super-micrometer" (see Fig. 15). Threads are usually checked in a supermicrometer using the three-wire method. The three-wire method utilizes thread wires which are a specific size, depending on the pitch of the thread. Measuring "over the wires" at a specific load in the supermicrometer will produce a dimension proportional to the pitch diameter of the thread. The thread profile is usually checked in an optical comparator to ensure that the thread has not experienced excessive wear.

Plugs are also checked in a supermicrometer using hardened and flat cylindrical anvils at specific loads. The load and the diameter of the cylindrical anvil varies depending on the diameter of the plug. Threads and plugs are checked to a resolution of 0.000010 in.

Dial Indicators and Electronic Transducers

Dial indicators and transducers can be checked by mounting them in a comparator stand and displacing the contact with gage blocks. Special calibration devices are available in applications where the volume will justify their initial cost. The special calibration device is significantly more efficient than the gage block method (see Fig. 16).

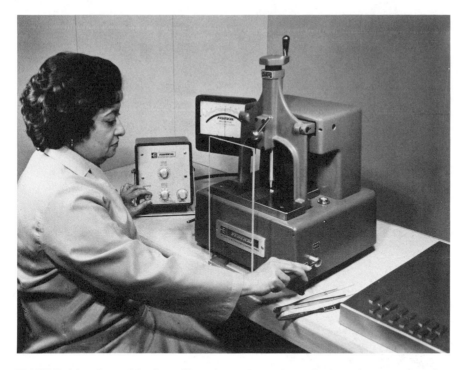

FIGURE 14 Gage block calibration takes place under tightest possible environmental controls. Above, a breath shield protects the measuring area from the warmth and humidity of the operator's breath. In the foreground gage blocks rest on a "soak plate" to achieve ambient temperature of the measuring environment. Utilizing a floating caliper design and true point-to-point measurement, this gage block comparator is guaranteed to calibrate within 0.000001 in. over its full range. (Courtesy of Federal Products Corporation.)

Surface Plate

Surface plates can be calibrated by auto collimation, laser interferometer, or electronic level. The auto collimation and laser interferometer involve the use of an accurate light beam reflected off a mirrored surface. The mirror is moved along the surface plate and variations in the topography of the surface plate cause this mirror angle to change and this angle is measured by the auto collimator or interferometer.

Auto collimation, the original method developed for the calibration of surface plates, has the liability of requiring two operators to perform the calibration. The laser interferometer system is often coupled to a programmable calculator so that the readings from the interferomter can be mathematically manipulated and then converted into a meaningful "map" of the surface plate.

The electronic level system consists of two electronic levels differentially coupled (see Fig. 17). One level remains at a reference point on the surface plate and the other level is moved along a straight edge. The electronic level system offers simplicity of operation and relatively low cost compared to a laser interferometer. Levels can be interfaced to a programmable calculator to produce these same type of information as a laser interferometer system.

FIGURE 15   A supermicrometer can be used to check threads and plugs.
(Courtesy of Pratt & Whitney Machine Tool Division.)

B. Dimensional Analysis

Calibration laboratories are often asked to perform other types of dimensional
analysis to assist in the diagnosing of manufacturing process problems.

Surface Finish and Profile

A profiling system analyzes, computes, displays, and records linear profile
and surface finish characteristics. A typical system consists of a probe, a
precision linear drive, and a control center. The control center usually includes a single- or dual-channel recorder, probe controls, digital displays,
and space for special function modules.

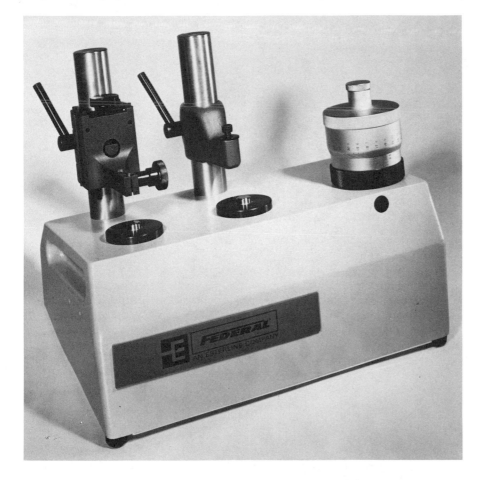

FIGURE 16   This universal calibrator allows precise monitoring of any type
of gaging system: dial indicators, air and electronic probes. A unique
micrometer and lever mechanism produces precise motion at either of two
calibrating stations. One station for high-magnification gages, such as electronic systems, provides minimum graduations in increments of 0.000010 in.
with a range of 0.100 in. For dial indicators or probes having ranges up
to 0.500 in., the second station offers high-definition calibration with graduation value of 0.00050 in. Repeat is one-fifth graduation. (Courtesy of
Federal Products Corporation.)

As the probe on the precision drive traverses the workpiece or test sample,
the signal generated is conditioned, amplified, displayed, and recorded. These
systems are capable of sensing displacements as small as 0.0000001 in. With
this exceptional accuracy, surface profile measurement systems are suitable
for a variety of laboratory and quality control tasks. They are especially useful for measuring deposits on thick- and thin-film microelectronic components.
General applications include surface measurements of inside and outside diameters, gear teeth profiles, grooves and flats. They immediately identify
such surface irregularities as belmouth, runout, taper, and waviness.

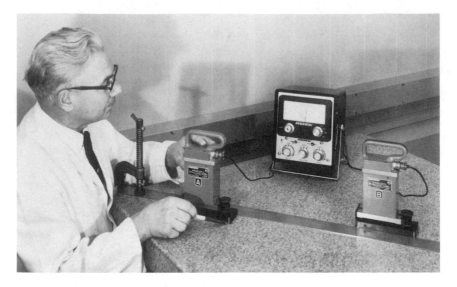

FIGURE 17   Electronic levels in surface plate calibration setup. (Courtesy of Federal Products Corporation.)

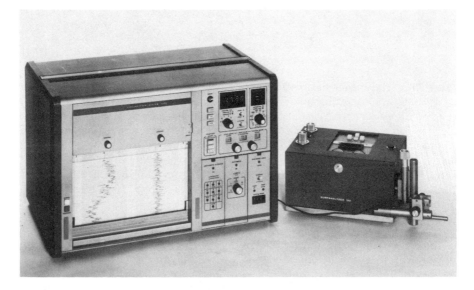

FIGURE 18   This surfanalyzer can be tailored to specific requirements by supplementing basic profile and roughness measurements with additional parameters such as roughness average, waviness, percent bearing area, and others. (Courtesy of Federal Products Corporation.)

Circular Geometry

Circular geometry gages are used to check roundness, concentricity, flatness, parallelism, and squareness of precision machined parts. Circular geometry systems consist of a precision spindle, one or more transducers, a signal conditioning system, and a data display and recording system (see Fig. 19).

Circular geometry gages are capable of measuring to an accuracy level of a few microinches. Systems are available to measure parts as small as 0.04 in. inside diameter to as large as 60 in. in diameter and up to 5000 lb. Circular geometry systems make practical the early detection of geometrical errors. They also provide the prime means for fast, effective troubleshooting to correct the problems that produced them. As each corrective measure is taken, the geometry system can quickly show the progress being made, drastically reducing the time required to arrive at an effective solution. The savings in downtime, the reduction of scrap, and functional improvement in critical parts that result from the ability of geometric analysis bring the unseen into sharp, unmistakable focus and can easily amortize the cost of the system in a matter of days.

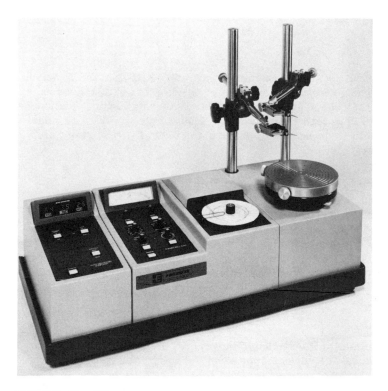

FIGURE 19 The geometry measurement system incorporates a rotary table supported by an air bearing spindle; an automatic centering computer that eliminates time-consuming mechanical centering of the workpiece; a digital readout of TIR from each gagehead as well as eccentricity and a polar chart recorder. (Courtesy of Federal Products Corporation.)

FIGURE 20   A universal measuring machine is a totally self-contained metrology center.   Linear and geometric accuracies of the highest order are combined with a spindle that has a guaranteed trueness of rotation to 5 millionths
of an inch (0.55 μm) TIR.   With the use of the small-angle divider, angular
determinations are made to an accuracy of ±0.5 arc second.   (Courtesy of
Moore Special Tool Co., Inc.)

Measuring Machines

Measuring machines of the type used in laboratories are usually high-accuracy
versions of coordinate measuring machines (see Fig. 20).   Their accuracies
are typically 10 times greater than that expected from a coordinate measuring
machine.   They are useful for the analysis of complex profiles and characteristics which would not normally lend themselves to single-purpose gaging.

FURTHER READING

Busch, T., *Fundamentals of Dimensional Metrology*, Delmar, Albany, N.Y.
Farago, F. T., *Handbook of Dimensional Measurement*, Industrial Press,
    New York.
Kennedy and Andrews, *Inspection and Gaging*, Industrial Press, New York.
Moore, W. R., *Foundations of Mechanical Accuracy*, Moore Special Tool
    Company, Bridgeport, Conn.
The Society of Manufacturing Engineers, *Handbook of Industrial Metrology*,
    Prentice-Hall, Englewood Cliffs, N.J.

30

COLOR MEASUREMENT

CAL S. McCAMY

Macbeth Division of Kollmorgen Corporation
Newburgh, New York

I. INTRODUCTION

It is very likely that human color vision evolved to a high degree because it was useful in the struggle for survival, but today we use color not only to judge the quality of foods and other natural products, but to satisfy our innate love of color for its own sake. Thus color is a valuable physical property often having more commercial importance than linear dimensions, area, volume, or mass. Good managers use good design, process control, and quality assurance as management tools to control physical variables, as part of the effort to maximize their return on investment. Color is managed in much the same way as other physical properties. The management of color demands an understanding of the nature of color, the way it is measured, and the methods of optimizing productivity that have been developed.

II. THE LANGUAGE OF COLOR

The normal human being can discriminate over 10 million different colors. Specifying colors in such a vast assortment is made possible by the fact that we perceive or can generate orderly relationships among colors.

The most generally recognized color-order system is that defined by A. H. Munsell in 1905. Munsell was a commercial artist who had suffered from the lack of a precise way of describing color. He devised a method and published it in his small booklet *A Color Notation* [1]. He observed that the colors of surfaces could be described by three attributes. The first of these he called *hue*. Hue designates the attribute of color we characterize by such names as red, yellow, green, blue, or purple. Munsell chose the hue names just given as the five principal hues. He then interpolated five hues between these. He designated them yellow-red, green-yellow, blue-green, purple-blue, and red-purple. We may blend paints or we may merely imagine colors starting with red and gradually becoming yellower until the color is yellow, then blending to green, blue, purple, and finally back to red. It is in the nature of human color vision that this hue series returns to its starting point; that is, we may

construct a hue circle. Munsell proposed to divide that circle into 100 equal
parts. Thus he assigned 10 such parts to each of the 10 hues he had named.

The second attribute of color is *value*. The value of a color merely describes how light or dark it is. Given two surfaces, an observer can decide
whether they are of the same lightness, or whether one is lighter or darker
than the other. Munsell proposed that we imagine a scale of lightness ranging from the blackest possible black to the lightest possible white and that we
divide that scale into 10 parts that appeared to be equal. This established
his value scale.

The third attribute of color was called *chroma*. Chroma is the difference
from gray. We may imagine a very pure red color having the same value as
a gray. We may then imagine the addition of very small amounts of the red to
the gray, causing a gradual departure from the gray. The more red that
would be added, the greater would be the departure. In this way we can
establish a chroma dimension. The chroma increases toward the pure chromatic color, red in the example given.

These three attributes of color may be regarded as the three dimensions of
a color space, as illustrated in Fig. 1. The space is represented by a cylindrical coordinate system. Value is shown along the vertical axis; hue is represented by the angular displacement around a circle, in much the same way
that the equator of the earth surrounds the earth; and chroma is measured
outward from the value axis. Black is at the bottom of this space and white
is at the top. All neutral colors (i.e., the various grays) are distributed
between black and white along the axis. The hues are arranged radially about
the axis and chroma increases laterally.

Munsell developed a notation for color. He used the notation H for hue,
V for value, and C for chroma. He indicated the value, to the necessary number of decimal places, on the scale of 10 mentioned earlier. The chroma scale
was visually divided so that vermilion (a bright red pigment consisting of mer-
curic sulfide) had a chroma of 10. The hue was designated either by the
scale of 100 for the whole circle or, more often, by the hue and the step on
a 10-step scale within the hue. The hues were symbolized by the initial letters
of the names of the hues: R, YR, Y, GY, G, BG, B, PB, P, and RP. His
notation for the red at the center of the 10 steps assigned to red was "5 R."
He annotated the hue, value, and chroma in the form H V/C. The notation

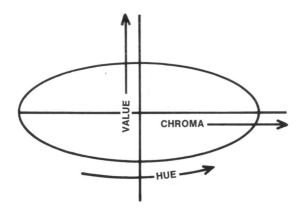

FIGURE 1   Diagram of the three-dimensional color space defined by Munsell
hue, value, and chroma.

"7.5R 4/8" meant that the hue was seven and a half units toward yellow in the hue region assigned to red, the value was four steps toward white from black, and the chroma was eight steps away from gray.

In 1918, Munsell founded the Munsell Color Company to provide physical standards in the form of painted-paper "chips." This operation, now a part of the Macbeth Division of Kollmorgen Corporation, is to this day the principal supplier of such standards to colorists in business, science, and industry. Each standard is identified by a Munsell notation made up of three symbols indicating Munsell hue, Munsell value, and Munsell chroma.

There have been a number of dictionaries of color that listed the names of colors and associated them with printed color patches. The colors were defined by exhibiting a sample. Very often, the names were taken from natural objects such as "rose," "peach," and "lemon yellow." Sometimes there was a reference to the pigment or dye used. Very many color names are of unknown origin and many have little apparent connection with the color.

The Inter-Society Color Council and the National Bureau of Standards developed a simplified language of color based on the Munsell system. The Munsell space was divided into regions bounded by specified values of hue, value, and chroma. Each of these was given a name. The names were the Munsell hue names, or such designators as pink, or brown, as appropriate. A standard set of adjectives was adopted. These included pale, dark, light, moderate, brilliant, strong, deep, and vivid. The National Bureau of Standards published *Color, Universal Language and Dictionary of Names*, NBS Special Publication 440 [2]. With this reference book, a standard name can be chosen for any Munsell notation. Conversely, the Munsell notation can be determined if the general color name is known. In addition, all of the major previous color dictionaries were consulted and the standard names were given for all the names previously listed. (The list is worth perusal for amusement's sake alone. We find "dream fluff," "happy day," "French nude," "Paris mud," "heart's desire," "pearly gates," "wafted feather," and "intimate mood," together with the more prosaic "battleship gray.")

To permit visualization of the 267 different colors for which standard names were chosen, the National Bureau of Standards has issued the ISCC-NBS Centroid Color Charts. These are color charts showing painted paper samples of the color at the centroid of each of the regions of Munsell space that has been given a standard color name. This publication is a supplement to NBS Special Publication 440, referred to as Standard Reference Sample 2107 [3].

The Munsell system provides the best known basis for visual color-tolerance standards. The ideal color is specified by the Munsell notation and the acceptable tolerances are then given in terms of deviations in hue, value, and chroma.

In some cases, a colored product may vary in hue only, in value only, or in chroma only. Such a variation is one-dimensional. In the case of a product varying in value only, we need only one standard representing the ideal color, one for the lighter limit, and one the darker limit. We may encounter products that vary in hue, value, and chroma but find that these variations are inter-related in such a way that the variation is essentially along a single line, possibly a curved line, in Munsell space. In such cases, it is still possible to use only three standards; one for the ideal, one for the variation in one direction, and one for the variation in the other direction. This is regarded as a one-dimensional color-tolerance set even though the colors representing the tolerances differ from the ideal in all three of the Munsell dimensions.

The colors of some products vary independently in two dimensions, such as hue and value. In such cases, the color tolerance set must include a desired color, two standards for the variation in one dimension and two standards for the variation in the second dimension. When there is a two-dimensional variation, it is generally advantageous to set the tolerances on the basis of the Munsell dimensions of hue, value, or chroma. These dimensions are visual in nature and are more readily communicated, visualized, and understood than dimensions made up of combinations of the Munsell dimensions.

When the color may vary in any way about the desired color, it is necessary to have a three-dimensional color-tolerance set. A three-dimensional color-tolerance set has the desired color, two tolerance standards for the variation in hue, two for value, and two for chroma. These colored standards are affixed to a card having openings so that any of the standards can be compared directly to the underlying surface.

III. LIGHT AND COLOR

When we compare colors, we must control the illumination if we are to make reliable and consistent judgments. Suppose that we compare two paints A and B in yellow light. We might find that they match and their color is kelly green. We might compare two other paints, C and D, and find that they match and they are peach-colored. Viewing the same four paints in white light we may find that A is blue, B is green, C is pink, and D is yellow. Although most people have a vague notion that colored things look different under different illuminants, it is not generally known that two colors can match under one illuminant and not match under another. When two colors match under one illuminant but fail to match under another, we say that they are a metameric match under the first illuminant, or we refer to them as metamers. The phenomenon of matching under one illuminant but not another is referred to as metamerism. If color judgments are to be consistent from time to time and place to place, they must be made under standard illumination.

In 1666, Sir Isaac Newton did a famous experiment that revealed the relationship between light and color. A beam of white light, in his case sunlight, was passed through a triangular prism. The beam was deviated to a different direction and at the same time dispersed into a spectrum. He observed that the spectrum had colors, which he called violet, indigo, blue, green, yellow, orange, and red, in that order. He observed that all these hues were components of white light. He then passed the colored spectrum light through a prism that deviated the light back in the original direction. When he did so, the components of the spectrum recombined to make white light. Thus he showed that white light could be separated into component colors and that the component colors could be recombined to make white light.

Suppose that we let the spectrum light fall on a white surface and we place colored glass in the beam. When red glass is placed in the beam, it transmits the red light, but absorbs the blue, green, and much of the yellow. When blue glass is placed in the beam, it absorbs the yellow light, but transmits the blue light. When green glass is placed in the beam, it absorbs the blue, yellow, and red light, but transmits the green light. When yellow glass is placed in the beam, it transmits the yellow and red, but absorbs the blue. On the basis of such observations, Newton concluded that the colors of objects are caused by the fact that the objects reflect or transmit more or less light of different parts of the spectrum.

Many years later, it was found that light is an electromagnetic wave phenomenon. A light beam is a series of waves of electric and magnetic fields, rippling through space. The distance from the top of one wave to the top of

the next is called the wavelength. In the light of the visible spectrum, the
wavelength increases from the shortest wavelength for violet light to the long
est wavelength for red light. It is this difference in wavelength that causes
the light of different colors to leave the prism at different angles. These
wavelengths are extremely short distances, so they are measured in nanometers. (About 25 million nanometers equals 1 in.) The visible spectrum has
wavelengths ranging from 360 nm at the violet end to 780 nm at the red end.
The human eye has little sensitivity outside the spectral region from 400 to
700 nm.

In 1931, the International Commission on Illumination* standardized illuminants to be used for viewing color. There were three. Illuminant A was an
incandescent lamp. That illuminant is quite well represented by an ordinary
household 100-W lamp operated at rated voltage. Illuminant B was direct
sunlight, and illuminant C was daylight, including the light from the sky.
The incandescent lamp was well specified and the sunlight and daylight were
produced by letting the light from that incandescent lamp pass through specified liquid filters. The nature of these three illuminants can be specified
by giving the amount of light in each small wavelength interval across the
spectrum. The incandescent lamp emitted very little blue light, but a lot
of light in the long-wavelength end of the spectrum. Sunlight was much
richer in blue light. Daylight has more blue light than light of longer
wavelengths.

Natural daylight varies considerably, from the reddish light of early
morning, to the nearly white light of noon, and reddish light at sunset.
Natural daylight also varies with cloud conditions, altitude, and other atmos-
pheric conditions from day to day, and even from minute to minute. Natural
daylight is not available at night nor in interior rooms of buildings. For
these reasons, in 1915, an illuminating engineer, Norman Macbeth, founded
a company to make equipment to provide artificial daylight for judging color.
It is an ongoing business to this day. A lighting booth has various kinds
of standard lighting in it and switches to select the desired kind. Most
booths today have artificial daylight, incandescent lamplight, and cool white
fluorescent light. All are important in business, science, industry, and art.
It is desirable to have colors match under all three kinds of light. The CIE
has adopted standard spectral power distributions for several phases of
daylight.

Sometimes we see objects so brightly colored that they appear to glow.
They appear to be reflecting more light than the amount of light shining on
them. This appearance is usually caused by fluorescence. Fluorescent
materials absorb energy in the ultraviolet or short-wavelength visible region
and then reemit it in the longer wavelengths in the visible spectrum. Viewing booths have ultraviolet lamps and a switch so that the ultraviolet can be
turned on or off. In this way, one can readily see whether or not a surface is noticeably fluorescent and the fluorescence can be appreciated as it
would be seen in natural daylight.

---

*
The International Commission on Illumination is generally referred to as
the CIE, from the initials of its name in French: Commission Internationale
de l'Éclairage.

IV. THE EYE

A light source may be characterized by the amount of light emitted in each
part of the spectrum. When the light is transmitted through a material or reflected from a surface, the selective nature of the transmission or reflection
determines the kind of light going to the eye. The color perceived depends,
of course, on the nature of the human visual system.

The human eye is insensitive to radiant energy in the ultraviolet region of
the spectrum at wavelengths shorter than about 350 nm. At these short wavelengths, the sensitivity of the eye begins to increase with increasing wavelength. It reaches a maximum at 555 nm, and then falls off until we reach the
red end of the visible spectrum. Beyond that is the infrared region, to which
our eyes are not sensitive. This relationship of sensitivity to wavelength is
called the human luminous efficiency function.

If we have three beams of light colored blue, green, and red, and we can
mix these three kinds of light in any desired proportion, we can obtain light
of any hue. The blue and green lights combine to give all the hues, from
blue through blue-green to green; green and red light combine to give the
hues from green to green-yellow to yellow to yellow-red or orange and finally,
to red. Red and blue combine to give all the various purples. Mixing the
third color with a mixture of the other two reduces the chroma. The three
colored lights may be mixed in the right proportions to make white light. This
process is called additive mixture because we start with darkness and add
light until eventually, when all three are mixed in ample proportions, we have
white light. Incidentally, the face of a color TV tube has numerous small
areas of phosphors, the phosphors being of three kinds, emitting blue, green,
and red light. Electron guns excite these dots in various proportions to produce all the desired colors.

In 1801, Thomas Young observed that if we can get all hues by mixing the
three primary colors of light, the human eye must contain three kinds of receptors. Researchers have now been able to identify three spectral sensitivity bands for the eye. Modern research has shown that there is very much
more to it than that, but the basic idea is right.

The facts of color mixture and this insight into the nature of color vision
suggest a method of measuring color. Suppose that we have a white screen,
divided by a black partition, so that we may illuminate the two halves of the
screen with different light sources. Let one half be illuminated by blue,
green, and red lights. Let us have some provision for adjusting the amounts
of these three independently and some means of knowing how much of each is
used. Let the other half of the screen be illuminated by light of some unknown
color. We have only to adjust the three colored lights until we obtain a visual
match. Then we record the amounts of the three lights required and we have
characterized the unknown color by three numbers. When this is done, we
find that there are some colors that cannot be matched with the given three
colored lights. However, in all cases, a match can be obtained if one of the
colored lights can be added to the other side of the screen. When we do that,
we regard that amount of light as a negative quantity. If this sort of experiment is set up in various places with different red, green, and blue sources,
we must expect to get different sets of three numbers for the same unknown
light source. If enough unknowns are measured on two instruments, a mathematical relationship can be found for predicting the values that will be obtained on one instrument once they are known for the other. This is known
as a transformation.

To provide a basis for obtaining the same numbers in all laboratories, in 1931 the International Commission on Illumination standardized three sensitivity curves that essentially represent the three sensitivities of the human eye. The actual sensitivity curves for the red, green, and blue receptors of the eye were mathematically transformed to eliminate negative values, and further transformed so that one of the three, the green one, matched the human luminous efficiency function. The three sensitivities were standardized by stating the amounts of the three required to match the light from the spectrum at each of a large number of wavelengths. The red sensitivity was called $\bar{x}$, the green was called $\bar{y}$, and the blue was called $\bar{z}$. The $\bar{x}$ curve has two lobes. These three curves are called CIE spectral tristimulus values or CIE color matching functions.

V. COLOR MEASUREMENT

Having these sensitivities standardized, it is possible for us to measure color and for various laboratories to obtain the same numbers. The principle is extremely simple.

Suppose that we have a standard light source, and the light is reflected from a surface to be measured. Let that light pass through one of four different filters to a photosensitive sensor. Let each filter and sensor combination be designed so that its spectral sensitivity is equivalent to one of the tristimulus value curves standardized by the CIE. (We need four instead of three filters because the $\bar{x}$ function has two lobes. The values measured with those two filters must be combined.) The three values resulting from measurements through these filters characterize the color of the reflecting surface. Such a device is called a filter colorimeter. This illustrates the fundamental principle of all color measurement.

This system is very simple, but it is not without its problems. Such devices have been built, but it is very difficult to design a light source and appropriate filters to produce a standard illuminant. Similarly, it is difficult to design filter and sensor combinations that closely approximate the desired sensitivity functions. Lamps, filters, and photosensors have notorious variation from one lot to the next, so even if an instrument can be designed and a production run is satisfactory, variation in components may make the next run unsatisfactory. The components may change with time.

We get around these problems by setting up a system to measure the amount of light reflected in each of a number of narrow wavelength intervals. A light source is used to illuminate the specimen to be measured. The light reflected (or transmitted) from the specimen is directed to a prism or grating that disperses the light into a spectrum. The amount of light reflected in each narrow wavelength interval is compared directly to the amount of light reflected from a standard white surface. In this way, the spectral emittance of the standard lamp does not have to match the CIE curve exactly. There are no filters in the receiver and the variation in spectral sensitivity of the photosensor is canceled out when we make such ratio measurements. A device that does this is called a spectrophotometer. The spectrophotometer provides a curve or table of values showing the percent of light reflected by the specimen in each wavelength interval in the spectrum. This percentage is called the spectral reflectance factor.

Once the spectral reflectance factor of the specimen is known, it is possible to compute the three values that would have been obtained with a perfect filter colorimeter. These three numbers are called tristimulus values and are given the symbols X, Y, and Z. This computation takes into account the nature of the illuminant in which we are interested, the spectral reflectance (or trans- mittance) factor of the specimen which was measured with a spectrophotometer, and the spectral sensitivity of the standard observer, as represented by CIE spectral tristimulus values $\bar{x}$, $\bar{y}$, and $\bar{z}$. These three tristimulus values X, Y, and Z represent the color of the specimen under the desired illuminant. Since $\bar{y}$ was transformed to match the sensitivity of the eye to light of various wave- lengths, the tristimulus value Y is a direct measure of the lightness of the color.

For many purposes, we are interested in the chromatic nature of the color, without regard for the lightness or value. To obtain a measure of the chroma- ticity, we compute three numbers x, y, z which represent the amount of the X in the total X + Y + Z, the amount of Y in the total X + Y + Z, and the amount of Z in the total of X + Y + Z. By the definition of these quantities, we see that the sum of x, y, and z is 1. If we know x and y, we can subtract their sum from 1 and find z; therefore, z is never computed and is never used. We compute x and y and call them chromaticities, or if we make a plot of the x and y, we call them chromaticity coordinates. Such a plot is shown in Fig. 2.

A plot of y with respect to x is called a CIE chromaticity diagram. On this diagram we may plot the colors of the light of each of the wavelengths in the spectrum. We find that the points plot along a horseshoe-shaped curved line. This is known as the spectrum locus. The chromaticity diagram has a very interesting property: If we have lights represented by two points on this diagram and we mix these two lights in all proportions, we find that the chro- maticities obtained lie along the straight line joining the two points. There- fore, the chromaticity diagram is a light mixture diagram.

It follows from this that if we join the two ends of the spectrum locus with a straight line, it will represent the colors obtained when we mix the light from the two ends of the visible spectrum. Below that line there are no colors, because these would represent mixtures of ultraviolet and infrared which are invisible to the eye. Having drawn that line, we encompass a closed region that includes every possible chromaticity. Light of any color must be made of some mixture of light of various wavelengths in the spectrum, and there- fore the chromaticities of all colors are inside that closed region.

We may plot the chromaticity of the illuminant on this diagram. The illumi- nant might be, for example, illuminant A, illuminant B, or illuminant C. That point also represents the chromaticity of a white surface reflecting light exactly like that coming from the illuminant. Therefore, that point is called the illu- minant point or the white point.

There is a triangular region at the bottom of the diagram defined by the illuminant point, the violet end of the spectrum locus, and the red end of the spectrum locus. The chromaticities in that triangle correspond to purple colors. It is important to note that purple does not appear in the spectrum. Purple is mostly a mixture of light from the two ends of the spectrum.

There have been studies of the exact relationship between Munsell hue, value, and chroma, and the CIE chromaticities. Diagrams and tables have been published showing this relationship, so if we know the CIE chromaticity coordinates and Y, we can determine the Munsell hue, value, and chroma [4].

In the early 1940s, David MacAdam performed a series of experiments on the repeatability of color matching. He used a visual colorimeter, presented a color, and asked observers to adjust the amounts of red, green, and blue

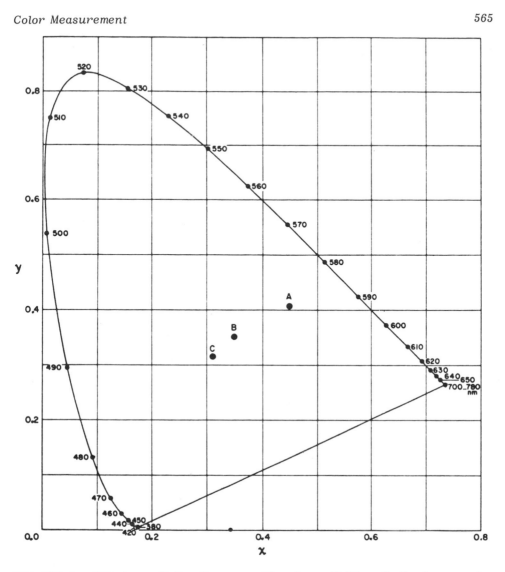

FIGURE 2   CIE chromaticity diagram. The chromaticities of all colors are in the area bounded above by the spectrum locus and below by the straight purple limit. The chromaticities of CIE illuminants A, B, and C are shown.

light to achieve a match. In some parts of the chromaticity diagram the data clustered very tightly. This meant that people could detect very small differences in chromaticity. In other parts of the chromaticity diagram the data spread quite widely, meaning that rather large chromaticity differences were imperceptible to those who were trying to make the match. The data systematically spread out more in one direction than in the perpendicular direction.

The data demonstrate that for color differences near zero, the chromaticity diagram is perceptually quite nonuniform. There have been numerous efforts to transform the diagram to make it uniform, but experiments have shown that no such transformation exists. We can at best make an approximation. Two approximations are in widespread use and have been recommended by the International Commission on Illumination. The need for a uniform space is particularly important for the evaluation of color differences. We would like a space in which the distance between two chromaticities is proportional to the perceived color difference.

Such color difference computations are made much simpler if we use a rectangular coordinate system. By a rectangular coordinate system, we mean a system such as length, width, and height. You may recall that the Munsell system is a cylindrical coordinate system. We have the central axis, which is the value scale, the hues are measured angularly around that axis, and chroma is measured outward from the axis. The CIE chromaticity diagram is also essentially cylindrical in nature if we imagine a Y axis perpendicular to the x, y-plane. We can perform the mathematical transformations to convert from the cylindrical coordinate systems to a rectangular system, and when we do, we usually convert to what is called an L,a,b system. L represents lightness; it is on the vertical scale with dark colors on the bottom and light colors at the top. That aspect is the same as it is in the Munsell system and the CIE chromaticity diagram. However, a and b are quite different from hue and chroma. Positive a represents redness; negative a represents greenness. Positive b represents yellowness; negative b represents blueness. All colors can be represented in this rectangular coordinate space. The modern form of this, recommended by the International Commission on Illumination, is CIELAB (pronounced "Sea-Lab") (see Fig. 3). This form of L,a,b space is distinguished from earlier forms by asterisks: L*,a*, and b*. Once we have transformed into that space, the distances between points representing colors are nearly proportional to the color differences as perceived by the eye [5].

It seems natural that the color of an object would depend on the spectral quality of the light in which it is seen, but most people do not realize that the color may depend on the direction of the illumination and the angle from which the object is observed. We speak of these conditions as geometric conditions. Satin, velvet, and crushed velore look the way they do because their appearance varies with the angles of illumination and angle of view. Polished wood can display a very considerable change in appearance as these angles are changed.

For these reasons it is necessary to standardize the geometric conditions of measurement. There are two general types of geometry, one being highly directional, the other being nondirectional. The highly directional mode can be of two types: Either we illuminate the sample at 45° to the perpendicular and view along the perpendicular, or we reverse that, illuminating along the perpendicular and viewing at 45° to the perpendicular. If we interchange the illuminating beam and viewing beam, ray for ray, we measure the same value of the reflectance factor, so these two methods of measurement are interchangeable.

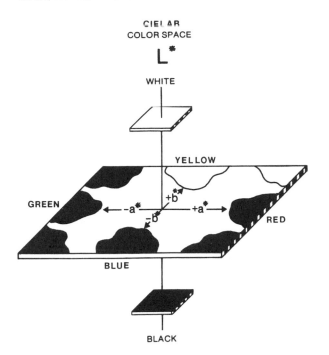

FIGURE 3   Diagram of an approximately uniform color space recommended by the International Commission on Illumination.   The three dimensions are L*, a*, and b*.   The abbreviated name of the space is CIELAB.

To measure reflectance factors with a nondirectional system, we use an integrating sphere, which is a hollow sphere painted flat white inside.   Again, we may proceed in either of two ways, which are interchangeable.   The first is to have the light enter the interior of the sphere and strike it on one side. The light striking the side of the sphere is reflected in all directions many times, so the interior of the sphere is uniformly bright.   The sphere illuminates a specimen through a port at the bottom of the sphere.   The specimen is then viewed and measurements are made through a port on the perpendicular or near the perpendicular to the surface of the specimen.   The alternative method is to illuminate the specimen along the perpendicular to the sample, let the sample reflect light to the sphere, let the sphere integrate the light reflected in all directions, and then view or measure the light reflected from the wall of the sphere.

VI. APPLIED COLORIMETRY

Now for the payoff. How is all this used to make a profit?

First, color science makes it possible to specify colors precisely in terms that are understood internationally.   A designer may toss a painted swatch on the table and say, "That's the color."   The swatch may be measured or compared to the Munsell book of color.   The Munsell or CIE notation can be used as a basis for communicating the color specification from place to place and recording the specification for future use.   This ability to communicate clearly and precisely is essential to efficient buying and selling in any business involving color.

The Munsell chips can be used to explore the range of variation that the designer considers tolerable. In setting tolerances, the designer must bear in mind that tight tolerances are expensive, because greater care must be exercised in producing the color and colors out of tolerance represent a loss. Single part items that need not match each other or anything else exactly can be assigned larger tolerances than items made of parts that must match or items that must match each other or some other thing. Munsell papers can be used to make color tolerance sets for use by inspectors. Careful management of the selection of tolerances optimizes return on investment by making the product no more precisely than is necessary to satisfy the manufacturing and marketing requirements.

Small businesses, those employing only simple operations with a few colors and those for which color is not a critical factor, may find a visual system of color specification and control entirely satisfactory. However, wherever color is a major concern and the business is of any size, it is likely that color measurement will more than pay for itself. Colorimetry is objective, repeatable, and much faster than visual interpolation. The measured values can be directly communicated from the spectrophotometer or colorimeter to computers, process controls, inventory control systems, and so on, to facilitate highly automated operations.

In "color businesses" such as paints, plastics, textiles, cosmetics, and packaging, it is necessary to manage the design, production, and marketing of many colors that are often changed. The methods used may be illustrated by following a color through the whole cycle in a textile firm.

A designer selects a color. A swatch of the color can be measured on a spectrophotometer. The spectral reflectance factor at each wavelength is transmitted directly to a computer. The computer computes a dye recipe that will produce that color. In fact, the computer may be designed to come as close as possible to matching the spectral curve at each wavelength. If that is done, the resulting product will match the designers sample under any illumination. If that is not needed, other design considerations, such as fastness and cost, may prevail. Obviously, the computer must be programmed to do all these things, and it must be supplied with the data resulting from the measurement of many dyed samples, fastness data, cost data, and so on. This procedure is known as colorant formulation. It is a key step in the successful management of color. It tells you how to make a desired color.

Once a formula has been computed, a batch of the colorant is mixed and a trial specimen is made. The trial is usually close but not quite on color. Colorants may have aged since the calibration data were taken, new shipments of colorants may be slightly different, the process of application of color may be a little different, or the substrate may not take color as before. The trial specimen is measured and the computer decides what would be the best way to correct the batch to make the color right. This procedure is known as batch correction. Many an amateur interior decorator has finally corrected the color of the paint but wound up with three times as much paint as was needed. This and other pitfalls must be avoided by well-designed batch correction systems. The entire profit may depend on wise batch correction or the decision to set a bad batch aside for use in some other way.

Once a good color is in production, the next concern is to see that production is uniform. This is called color process control. The color of the product is measured. If the process is continuous, as it is in the textile and paper

Industries, measurement must be made on-line; that is, equipment is positioned in place or scanned from place to place to measure the color of the product as it moves past, often at high speed. Piece goods are measured off-line. In either case, measured colors and measured color differences may be shown on video displays so that machine operators can control the process and similar displays may be made available in remote locations, such as the quality assurance department. Data may be displayed in the form of control charts, which are plots of color variation from the ideal, as functions of time. Usually, three plots are used to display the three dimensions of color. Tolerance limits are displayed as lines above and below the ideal line, so it is immediately obvious if tolerances are exceeded or there is a trend toward going out of tolerance. Alarms may be signaled if these conditions exist. In a few cases, the measured and computed data are automatically transmitted to mechanisms controlling conditions affecting the process, to control the process automatically. This procedure is called closed-loop operation. As of this writing, most processes are monitored but not controlled automatically. The profitability of modern process manufacturing industries depends on good process control and carefully chosen tolerances.

Incidentally, one should not overlook the fact that spectrophotometry and colorimetry are processes subject to the very kind of process control described above. Periodic measurements of stable colored standards are displayed on a control chart to reveal the condition of the measurement process in historic perspective. You cannot keep a production process in control with measuring instruments out of control.

By the time we have reached this stage, it would appear that little remains to be done in the way of color management. Not so; one of the most profitable techniques of color management comes in here. After all the good color design, colorant formulation, batch correction, and process control, suppose that there remains so much variation in the dyed fabric that your customers, who are apparel manufacturers, complain that the coat does not match the pants. You have done your best, but the variation of natural materials prevents you from achieving the uniformity demanded. Suppose, for simplicity, that a blue tends to range from greenish to purplish. The range is unacceptable. Maybe even half the range is unacceptable, but suppose that a third of the range would be all right. Measure the product and sort it into three lots that we might call "green," "blue," and "purple." Then organize order entry and shipping schedules so that a given customer and his or her subcontractors always receive material from the same lot. This technique is called shade sorting. The three-dimensional color space surrounding the centroid color is divided into shades, as many as necessary to achieve satisfactory uniformity within one shade designation. The customer gets matching goods and the manufacturer gets top price for all the product. That is color management.

REFERENCES

1. A. H. Munsell, *A Color Notation*, 14th ed., Munsell Color Co., Baltimore, Md.

2. *Color: Universal Language and Dictionary of Color Names*, NBS Special Publication 440, National Bureau of Standards, U.S. Government Printing Office, Washington, D.C., 1976.

3. *ISCC-NBS Centroid Color Charts*, Standard Reference Material 2107, National Bureau of Standards, U.S. Government Printing Office, Washington, D.C.

4. ASTM Standard D-1535-80, *Standard Method of Specifying Color by the Munsell System*, American Society for Testing and Materials, Philadelphia, Pa., 1982.
5. CIE Publication 15 (E-1.3.1) 1971, *Colorimetry*; CIE Supplement 2 to CIE Publication 15 (E-1.3.1) 1971, *Recommendations on Uniform Color Spaces—Color Difference Equations, Psychometric Color Terms*, 1978, Bureau Central de le CIE, 52, Boulevard Malesherbes, Paris, France.

FURTHER READING

Billmeyer, F. W., Jr., and M. Saltzman, *Principles of Color Technology*, 2nd ed., Wiley-Interscience, New York, 1981.
Committee on Colorimetry, Optical Society of America, *The Science of Color*, Optical Society of America, Washington, D.C., 1963.
Hunter, Richard S., *The Measurement of Appearance*, Wiley, New York, 1975.
Judd, D. B., and G. W. Wyszecki, *Color in Business, Science, and Industry*, 3rd. ed., Wiley, New York, 1975.
Wyszecki, G. W., and W. S. Stiles, *Color Science*, 2nd ed., Wiley, New York, 1982.

31

MICROSTRUCTURE ANALYSIS

JAMES A. NELSON

Buehler Limited
Lake Bluff, Illinois

I. INTRODUCTION

The rapid development of Western industrial technology has occurred in relatively recent times. To a large degree, this is the result of a growing understanding of materials and their application to solve engineering problems. Early human progress toward this end was very slow because we had first to discover new materials and then learn by empirical means how to utilize them. Without an established material science, developments had to be based on trial and error and were therefore very slow.

Metals have long captivated human curiosity because they possess unique properties that could be altered thermally and mechanically to meet various needs. The first accidental discovery of metals is believed to have occurred about 8000 B.C. in Eurasia. It could have been a meteorite laying on the ground as depicted in Fig. 1 or a bright nugget of gold found in a streambed. Metals were probably used first for jewelry, later as tools, utensils, and weapons.

Physical properties were the first method of characterizing metals. The enduring bright and lustrous appearance of gold was early appreciated by human beings, who discovered that it was harder than wood, but softer and less brittle than stone. When struck, it yielded rather than be fractured; when hammered repeatedly, it could be formed into thin sheets (leaf). By this tedious process, we learned to understand the physical properties of metals, natural alloys, and later our own contrived alloys. Even with this limited understanding of metals, based on physical properties, ancient civilization produced significant achievements, such as the lost wax casting process and the Damascus sword [1].

As history progressed, we learned that certain metals and alloys resisted weathering better than others, and that vegetable juices (acids) either darkened or brightened the polished surface of a particular metal or alloy. These natural acids were first used to decorate weapons and were an early application of primitive chemistry known as alchemy. Although alchemy was somewhat obsessed with the idea of producing gold from "base metals," it was nevertheless the forerunner of modern chemical analysis. As chemistry evolved, a more

FIGURE 1 Metal from heaven: discovery of meteoric iron by the ancient Egyptians. (Courtesy of Basic Incorporated, from an original drawing by Paul Calle.)

definite method of identifying materials was available, providing a more precise means of materials characterization.

Alchemists and philosophers had long speculated on the possibility of an internal structure in metals. This idea must have been inspired by orderly details they observed in wood and other materials. It was further encouraged by the observation of faint patterns on metallic surfaces, by the existance of treelike shapes (dendrites) in casting sinks, and by the faceted appearance of a coarse-grained metal fracture. Attempts to correlate the appearance of fractured surfaces to physical properties were common from A.D. 1500 to 1800. Founders of bronze bells, in the seventeenth century, believed a large grain fracture meant that more tin should be added; the color of a fracture was once used by iron makers to determine the metal's quality. These low-magnification observations were useful but not adequate to provide the information needed to understand the complex changes that occur in metallic alloys in various conditions of thermal and mechanical treatment. With the development of the scanning electron microscope (SEM), the study of fractures has again assumed significant proportions. The study of failure modes has been greatly aided by the scientific study of fractures.

The search for a discrete microstructure was pursued in both Great Britain and Europe. Most efforts to produce a satisfactory surface failed because the investigator did not adequately understand the characteristics of polished surfaces, or the abrasive processes that were used to achieve them. As a result, they succeeded, as C. S. Smith points out, in producing a burnished surface which did more to hide the microstructure than to reveal it.

It was not until Henry Sorby of Sheffield, England, applied careful preparation based on sound, proven principles that adequate surfaces were produced. Using simple but effective abrasive principles, which he had previously developed for rock analysis, Sorby achieved a polished surface which, when etched with a suitable acid, revealed clear microstructural detail. His success provided the basis for modern metallographic polishing and earned him the honorary title "Father of Metallography." He also adapted the transmitted light microscope to reflected light operation to produce the necessary brightfield illumination. Sorby also left various notes describing the microstructure he had observed. The name of some microstructures he observed remain to this day.

II. WHAT IS MICROSTRUCTURAL ANALYSIS?

Microstructural analysis is the technique by which the internal microstructure of metal or alloy is made visible for analysis. The surface of a metallic part, such as the welded pieces shown in Fig. 2a, cannot be directly examined to reveal the microstructure due to normal surface deformation and oxidation. To observe the internal microstructure, a part must be sectioned (cut) along a plane perpendicular to the area to be observed (Fig. 2a, dotted line). When the exposed and ground cut surfaces are etched (macroetched) with a solution consisting of equal parts of water and hydrochloric acid, coarse details such as the outline of the weld/parent-metal interface may be seen (Fig. 2b).

If the pieces are fully prepared, according to the sequence to be described later, fine microstructural details are revealed, as shown in Fig. 2c. In this photomicrograph at 50× magnification, the principal microstructural features may be seen. They are the parent metal, heat-affected zone (HAZ), and the weld metal. Also visible is a void in the fusion line which, if large enough, could be considered a significant defect.

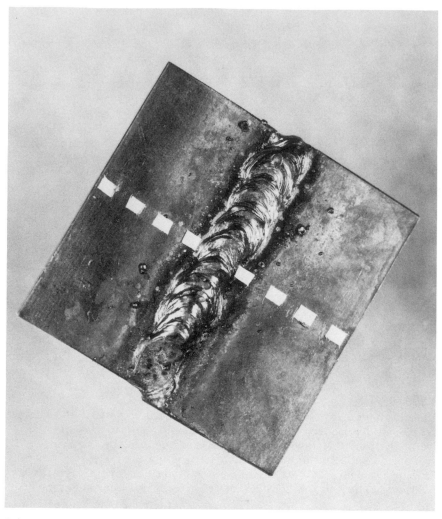

(a)

FIGURE 2   Metallographic sectioning of a weld: (a) surface appearance before sectioning, 75× (dashed line denotes plane of interest); (b) cross section showing plane of interest after grinding and macroetching; (c) polished
and microetched view of weldment at 50× magnification.

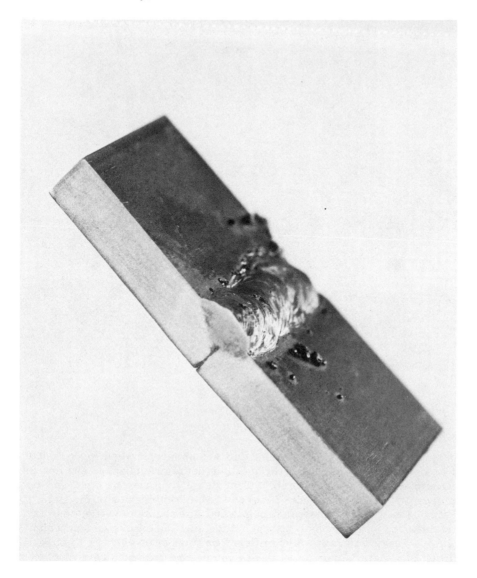

(b)

FIGURE 2   (Continued)

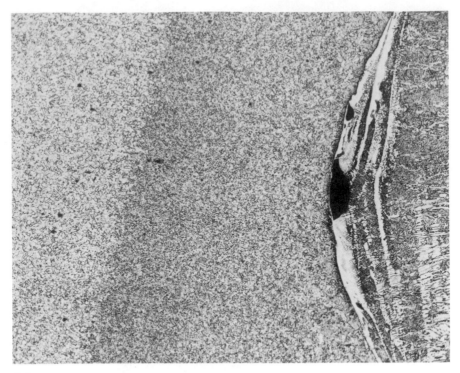

(c)

FIGURE 2   (Continued)

Microstructure consists of the details that are observed when we look at a
polished and etched surface of a material. The details we observe are not the
atomic structure which is considerably finer detail than may be observed by
light microscopy. What we actually observe are the boundaries of crystal
grains, various major alloy phases, precipitated intermetallic compounds, nonmetallic inclusions, and various inhomogeneities such as cracks and porosity.

The study of microstructure is significant because it enables us to observe
the condition of a material, or to compare two or more materials that display
different properties. Microstructure is the result of the chemistry plus the
thermal and mechanical treatments to which the material has been subjected.

Figure 3 shows the dendritic microstructure of an as-cast alloy, which is
characteristic of this condition. This microstructure is the result of an unequal distribution of chemical elements resulting from a particular rate of
cooling. Figure 4 shows a nickel-based alloy which has been modified by
thermal treatment to produce a homogeneous crystalline microstructure. Metallography is able to reveal such differences.

It must be remembered that a polished metallographic sample provides a
two-dimensional view of a three-dimensional microstructure. Figure 5a shows
a SEM view of flake graphite in gray iron. To show this three-dimensional
view, the matrix metal has been etched away, exposing the graphite flake. A
normal two-dimensional light microscope examination of a similar alloy would
appear like Fig. 5b. Although this seems to be a severe limitation, the information obtained is extremely valuable because it still provides an accurate

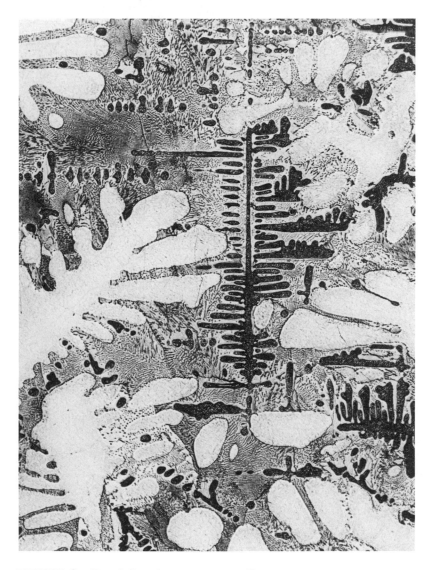

FIGURE 3   Dendrites in an as-cast alloy.

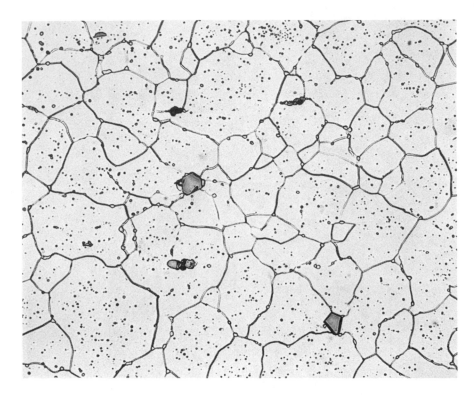

FIGURE 4   Crystalline microstructure of a nickel-based alloy. Magnification,
500×; etchant, 10% oxalic acid (electrolytic).

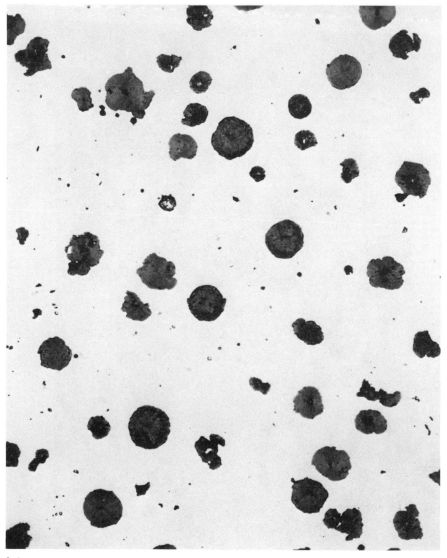

(a)

FIGURE 5   Comparison of ductile iron microstructures as revealed by (a) light microscopy and (b) scanning electron microscopy. (Courtesy of Foote Mineral Company.)

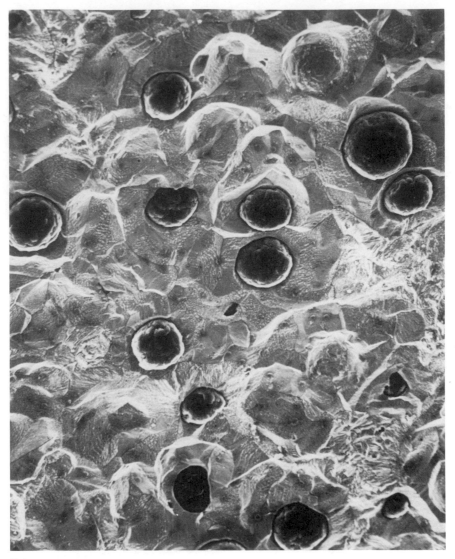

(b)

FIGURE 5   (Continued)

prediction of the three-dimensional condition. It must also be understood that microstructure alone cannot reveal precise qualitative information, but must be interpreted along with chemical analysis and physical properties, plus all known thermal and mechanical history. The role of metallography, therefore, is to provide a tool that permits the investigator to observe changes in microstructure which result from various processes. Using a reflected light microscope, he or she may observe obvious defects and microstructural constituents, surface phenomenon, and nonmetallic inclusions.

III. THE PRINCIPLES OF METALLOGRAPHIC PREPARATION

We have already observed that clear, usable microstructures were not revealed until adequate preparation techniques were devised. In his notes, Sorby commented: "Anything approaching to a burnished surface is fatal to good results."

A burnished surface may be defined as: "To make shiney by rubbing." This technique is employed by silversmiths to hide surface blemishes and produce a bright lustrous surface. Although a good metallographic polish (one capable of revealing the true microstructure) will nearly always be smooth and lustrous, this superficial appearance is no guarantee of success. There is more to a well-prepared metallographic sample than meets cursory observation. A burnished surface may be bright and lustrous, but it also consists of a layer of deformed metal which is incapable of revealing the true microstructure. In fact, we may observe what appears to be the true microstructure but which, in reality, could be a pseudomicrostructure, sometimes referred to as an artifact. The microstructure that is observed is not characteristic of the sample material and therefore cannot be used as a basis for analysis.

Conversely, metallographic preparation by careful abrasive polishing produces a surface that is free from harmful deformation. The true microstructure may be observed and useful information is easily obtained. Figure 6 illustrates the harmful effects produced by careless or excessively severe abrasive operations in the surface of gray iron, as seen in a cross-sectional view [2]. It is evident that various microstructural features are either distorted or obscured when incorrect preparation techniques are applied. For this reason, any preparation step that produces extensive mechanical deformation or fails to remove previously induced deformation is not acceptable. Similarly, any preparation technique that produces excessive surface heat is unacceptable.

To help understand the nature of the deformation, produced by abrasive action, Petzow [3] has provided a model (Fig. 7) which shows cross-sectionally the various components of a deformation groove produced by a coarse abrasive grain or other source of deformation. The dark upper ray, or spike, represents the area of severest deformation consisting of crystalline grains that have been distorted, or fractured, beyond recognition. This layer is permanently distorted and must be completely removed, together with the area of less severe plastic deformation directly beneath. Further down, elastically deformed layers have been affected but have recovered their original microstructure. While elastic deformation may seem to have no consequence, it is possible that subtle microstructural changes have been produced which are not characteristic of the true microstructure. In certain metals and alloys, elastic deformation may be sufficient to produce deformation bands or twins.

(a) Distorted Surface

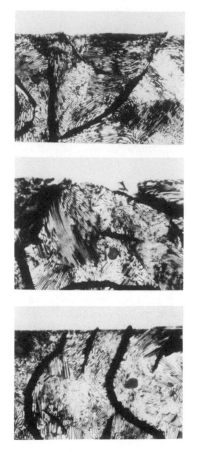

(b) Pitted Surface

(c) Well Prepared Surface

FIGURE 6   Effect of sample preparation quality on the microstructure. Apparent magnification, 10,000×.   (Courtesy of L. Samuels.)

To achieve a good metallographic polish by abrasive preparation, a systematic series of steps is required:

Sectioning
Rough grinding
Mounting
Fine grinding
Rough and final polishing

Each step must replace all abrasion damage produced by the previous steps with a lesser degree of abrasion until a satisfactory final polish is produced. In addition, each step must be performed with adequate lubrication and cooling to reduce the heat of friction. With rare exceptions, abrasive preparation for metallography is never performed without a coolant. In summary, sound metallographic preparation must produce a surface that is free of induced deformation, the surface must be flat, and the finish polish should be free of all scratches that could affect the analysis.

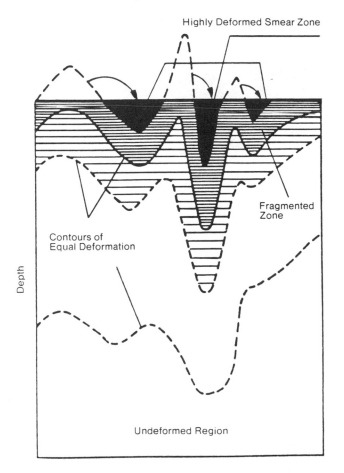

Highly Deformed Smear Zone

Fragmented
Zone

Contours of
Equal Deformation

Depth

Undeformed Region

FIGURE 7   Schematic model of mechanical deformation resulting from abrasive
preparation operations. (Courtesy of G. Petzow.)

IV. IMPLEMENTATION OF ABRASIVE PREPARATION

A. Sectioning

To obtain a manageable-size sample, a portion is cut from the bulk material.
Sectioning may be accomplished by various methods, including torch, band
saw, machining, or any other means of removing a portion of the material.
Small parts may require only one cut, and very small parts are often mounted
without any cutting. In this case, the desired plane of observation is reached
by careful grinding. Regardless of the method used to obtain a sample for
metallography, any gross mechanical deformation or heat effects must be kept
clear of the area of concern, so that the microstructure will not be altered.

Abrasive Wheel Sectioning

Abrasive wheel sectioning, using a cutter similar to that shown in Fig. 8, is
the most rapid, economical, and gentle method of sectioning rigid materials.
Metallographic cutters utilize a rotating abrasive disk consisting of abrasive
grains bonded by a rubber or resin-rubber matrix. Effective cutting is

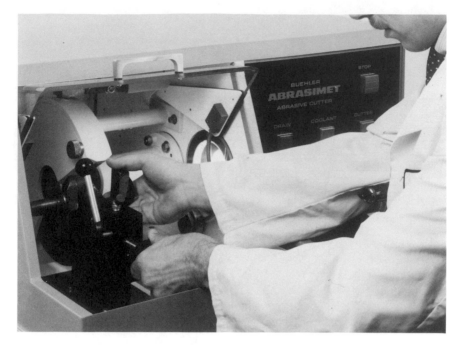

FIGURE 8   Abrasive cutter used to section rigid materials.

achieved by an intentional breakdown of the matrix bond which allows fresh
abrasive grains to be continually exposed. The sample material (workpiece)
must be held firmly in a clamping device and, depending on the specific design, the abrasive wheel pivots to make contact with the sample or the sample
is fed into the rotating wheel, which is in a fixed position. In either case,
the sample must be contacted by the abrasive wheel so that cutting will proceed at a rate that does not produce excessive heat.

The coolant flow must be adequate to cool the sample and, ideally, should
be aimed at the area of contact (the kerf) [4]. Cutters having a fixed coolant
nozzle provide a uniform application of coolant; that is, the volume of coolant
is applied equally to both sides of the abrasive wheel. When the cutter has
adjustable coolant nozzles, the operator must make sure they supply a uniform
flow. Failure to do so will create unequal heat dissipation, causing the abrasive wheel to wear irregularly. This results in an angled contact surface
(chisel-shaped) which will cause the abrasive wheel to turn from the normal
axis. The consequences of this condition are curved cuts and broken wheels.

Another prime requisite of good abrasive cutting is the wheel choice.
There are various compositions available, but some simple guidelines are as
follows:

Harder wheels for softer materials; softer wheels for harder samples
Alumina abrasive wheels for ferrous alloys and silicon carbide wheels for
    nonferrous metals and nonmetals
Diamond-rimmed wheels for cemented carbide and hard dense ceramics

Follow the manufacturer's recommendations and you will seldom go wrong.

Low-Speed-Saw Sectioning

The sectioning of delicate or heat-sensitive materials presents a unique problem that cannot be solved by conventional abrasive cutters. Parts such as thin metal diaphragms, thin-walled tubing, electronic parts, printed circuit boards, and biomedical components are materials that must be handled with special care. For these applications, the low-speed saw provides an excellent solution [5].

The low-speed saw (shown in Fig. 9) utilizes a diamond-rimmed metal wafering blade which does not break down freely like the abrasive wheel described previously. Diamond or cubic boron nitride (CBM) abrasive grains are embedded in a solid powdered metal matrix attached to a metal disk. The wafering blade, which is in a fixed position, rotates at a relatively slow speed (50 to 300 rpm) and makes contact with the sample material, which is held by a pivoting specimen arm which feeds the sample into the wafering blade by gentle gravity pressure, as shown in Fig. 9. A micrometer cross-feed enables the operator to locate the cutting plane precisely. As a result, cuts may be made at exact locations and thicknesses.

Although little preceptible heat is produced by the low-speed saw, use of a lubricant is nevertheless necessary to control heat that is concentrated at the point of contact between the abrasive and the workpiece. Lubricant is dragged by the blade to the sample, as the blade rotates through the lubricant contained in a tank at the base of the saw.

The unique features of the low-speed saw provide the conditions which are necessary to produce precision cuts without damage to the most delicate and heat-sensitive samples. Highly dissimilar materials, such as complex composites and extremely delicate composites such as solid-state electronic devices, may be sectioned at, or near, the plane of interest without inducing damage.

FIGURE 9   Use of a low-speed saw to section fragile or heat-sensitive materials.

The low-speed saw is therefore the answer to many sectioning problems which are beyond conventional cutting techniques.

B. Rough Grinding

Grinding with coarse abrasives (60 to 180 grit) is used primarily to correct poor surfaces or to obtain a particular plane for microscopic examination. Irregular surfaces may result from the use of torches or shop saws, and must be corrected before polishing proceeds. Rough grinding may also be used to remove heavy burrs, or burns, produced during previous cutting operations or heavy oxides resulting from heat treating that has been performed without a protective atmosphere.

Belt grinders are most commonly used because they are more convenient, economical, and utilize long-life, cloth-backed belts rather than less durable abrasive paper. Another advantage to belt grinding is the uniform material removal rate because the surface feet per minute (sfm) is identical at all contact positions. One disadvantage is the tendency of the belt to "whip," that is, to rise above the grinder table due to rotational centrifugal forces. As a result, the surface is not as flat as it is when using a disk grinder.

Disk grinders are used when extreme surface flatness and higher material removal rates are desired. Higher material removal rates are obtained because the effective sfm is significantly higher than is obtained with belt grinders. With the exception of special, high-performance composite abrasive disks, abrasive papers wear out more rapidly than belts that have a cloth backing.

Care must be observed during rough grinding to protect the sample from excessive exposure to heat and mechanical deformation. The operator must be protected from injury due to samples, or fragments, that might be hurled from the rapidly rotating belt or wheel. Some precautions to follow are:

Always wear safety glasses when grinding.
Do *not* use badly worn or torn abrasive disks or belts.
Avoid accidental contact, by any part of the body, with moving abrasive
    materials.
Use adequate coolant flow to reduce the surface heating of the sample.

C. Mounting

Metallographic sample preparation may be performed on unmounted samples if the edges are not important. However, they must be beveled to prevent snagging of the abrasive papers and cloths and prevent injury to the operator's fingers. To prevent these problems and provide a means of supporting highly irregular shaped samples, metallographic samples are normally encapsulated in a suitable plastic before further preparation. Mounting also minimizes rounding of sample edges and provides a safe, convenient means of holding the sample for both manual and automated preparation techniques.

Edge rounding is the tendency for polished edges of a sample to become a radius rather than be retained as a sharp edge. When this occurs, important microstructural details, such as surface layers, hardened cases, and corrosion products, may be distorted or unobservable. Figure 10 shows how edge rounding causes certain light rays to be reflected away from the rounded edge rather than return to the observer. If steps are taken to maintain edge flatness, nearly all light rays will be reflected back to the observer, thus revealing all the detail possible.

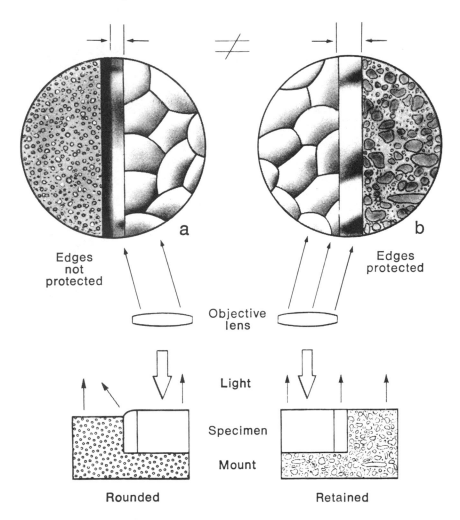

FIGURE 10   Effect of edge rounding on microstructural observations.

Resins used for mounting metallographic samples fall into two major categories: compression molding and room-temperature curing. Compression molding is more economical and convenient to use and is the best choice for mounting samples that will withstand the heat and pressure required. Room-temperature curing resins are favored when delicate or heat-sensitive samples are encapsulated. The choice of mounting techniques and specific resin systems will depend on the sample material and how soon the completely cured mount is needed for further preparation.

In compression molding, the sample is placed on the elevated, movable ram located within the cavity of a mold cylinder. After the ram and sample have been lowered into the cavity, a powdered resin is poured in, or a prepressed resin slug is placed into the cavity. The stationary, upper ram is secured to the open top end of the cylinder and pressure is applied to the resin and sample. As a result of the pressure applied by the press (Fig. 11), and heat by an external heater, the resin melts and forms a hard, solid mass that may be removed after a suitable curing time (about 7 to 10 minutes).

FIGURE 11   Using a mounting press to encapsulate a metallographic sample.

Room-temperature curing resins usually consist of two parts: a solid resin powder and liquid hardener, or a liquid resin and liquid catalyst. The sample is placed in a simple ring form on a smooth surface, each coated with a release agent that will prevent the sample from sticking to the mold and base. The mixed resin and hardener are simply poured into the mold and allowed to cure without pressure or externally applied heat. In some cases, heat may evolve due to an exothermic reaction during curing. This may help accelerate the curing process, or it may become the source of defects that will reduce the value of the mount. It is also possible to use carefully applied external heat to accelerate the curing process.

Completely cured mounts usually have sharp edges and protruding resin "flash." If these edge conditions are not corrected, the mount may snag the rotating polishing cloths during the later stages of preparation. The operator may also experience discomfort from the sharp edge that is in contact with his or her fingers. Rough grinding is used to chamfer the mount edges so that these problems will be avoided. Another minor problem occurs in cured mounts when the sample protrudes from the face of the cured mount. This occurs due to the different expansion and contraction characteristics of the sample and the encapsulant. If the embedded sample and the surrounding mounting material are not on the same plane when fine grinding is begun, it will be difficult to achieve a common plane by fine grinding. A light application of rough grinding is used to establish the common plane.

D. Fine Grinding

This is a series of grinding steps of decreasing coarseness which systematically reduces the level of abrasion so that subsequent cloth polishing will produce the desired final surface. Fine grinding is usually performed with 240-, 320-, 400-, and 600-grit abrasive papers in the form of stationary sheets or strips, or by using disks mounted on rotating polishing wheels.

Figure 12 illustrates the use of a manual fine grinder, a simple but efficient device. The various abrasive grits are positioned on separate platens so that

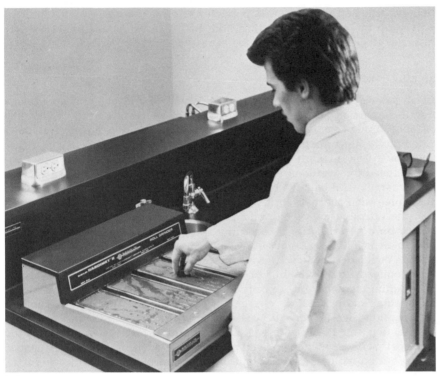

(a)

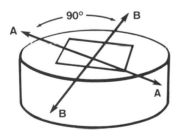

AA Direction of grinding in one grinding step
BB Direction of grinding in next step

(b)

FIGURE 12   Use of a manual fine grinder: (a) fine grinding performed on a roll grinder; (b) suggested directional motion for manual fine grinding.

the operator may proceed to the next step with only a brief water rinse. To determine the duration of each step, the operator rotates the sample 90° before the next step and is able to observe the progress by how completely the previous scratches have been removed. As in all metallographic sample cutting and grinding, lubrication (in this case water) is used to reduce friction at heat.

When fine grinding is performed on rotating wheels, less physical effort is required and an increase in sample production is usually achieved. Further increases in productivity may be realized by the use of semiautomatic devices which permit multiple samples to be prepared simultaneously. Larger and more modern high-volume sample preparation machines have also been developed which prepare up to 24 mounts at a time and utilize an advanced abrasive step which replaces the conventional multistep fine-grinding procedure.

E. Rough and Final Polishing

These two steps complete the basic polishing sequence and are similar because they are both performed on cloth-covered rotating wheels. In the earlier history of metallographic sample preparation, both steps were performed as separate napped cloth steps, using a coarser and a finer alumina abrasive. With the combination it was difficult to remove completely the deformation and scratches produced by previous abrasive steps and still maintain flatness and retain all microstructural constituents. This was a particular problem when polishing samples with microstructures of vastly differing chemistry and hardness. With the introduction of diamond abrasives to metallography, rough polishing took on a new meaning, becoming a key step that was distinctly different from final polishing. Deformation and scratches produced by previous abrasive steps could be completely removed and the resultant surface had a quality that reduced final polishing to a more cosmetic role.

Rough polishing, as presently practiced, employs one or more steps using a napless polishing cloth which is charged with a diamond abrasive in the range 30- to 3-μm particle size (1 μm = 0.0004 in.). A liquid extender is used to provide lubrication and to promote redistribution of the abrasive grain on the cloth. For most medium-hardness sample materials, such as non-heat-treated steels, a single step using 6-μm diamond abrasive on a napless cloth is sufficient. Additional steps are required as the hardness and complexity of the microstructure demands. There are no hard-and-fast rules that apply to such choices but, with experience, these decisions are more easily made.

Diamond is a necessity for rough polishing because it enables a metallographer to remove grinding deformation and scratches without producing edge rounding, microstructural relief, or pulled-out constituents. This is possible due to the extreme hardness of diamond and its durable cutting edges, which cut cleanly through hard and soft constituents. It is therefore desirable to spend more time in rough polishing, so that a minimum time is required for final polishing where polishing defects usually occur. Rough polishing is performed with high pressures and the sample should be rotated counter to the wheel rotation to avoid directional polishing effects, as illustrated in Fig. 13.

Final polishing is usually performed on a slightly napped cloth which has been premoistened with distilled water and charged with a very fine (0.3 to 0.05 μm) alumina abrasive slurry. Polishing times should be minimized to prevent edge rounding, relief, and pitting. The amount of moisture on the cloth is also a significant factor that affects the quality of final polishing. The cloth must be wet enough to prevent heating and deformation of the sample

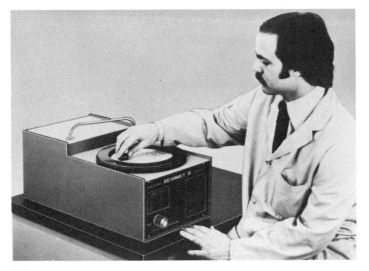

(a)

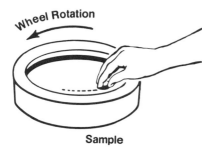

(b)

FIGURE 13   Use of a rotating wheel polisher/grinder to perform rough and final polishing: (a) rotating wheel polisher/grinder; (b) direction of polishing on a rotating wheel.

surface but dry enough to avoid the pitting of inclusions. An old rule of thumb said: "The cloth is correctly moistened when a sample lifted from cloth contact can be blown dry in 3 to 5 seconds with the operator's breath."

For more demanding applications, metallographers may choose to eliminate alumina and napped cloths entirely. In such cases, the final step would be 3-, 1-, or 0.25-μm diamond on a napless cloth. Although a very fine array of scratches will remain, their presence may be of less consequence than problems that may be created by excessive alumina polishing. This is often the case when the samples are intended for automatic image analyzers, where microstructural relief and pitting would produce erroneous results.

Later developments in abrasives give the metallographer better control over the results and the ability to prepare difficult materials with superior results [6]. Deagglomerated aluminas may be used to final-polish softer materials such as copper and aluminum alloys with fewer scratches and a less deformed surface. Conventional aluminas tend to leave excessive scratches, due to their natural tendency to agglomerate. These agglomerates act like coarser abrasive grains, producing scratches that are much larger than the actual abrasive grains should give. Deagglomerated aluminas consist of abrasive grains that are well separated and therefore produce a polished surface without coarse scratches.

Another help in solving final polishing problems is the colloidal silica polishing solutions, which is a chemically active colloidal suspension of silica particles. This solution may be used alone or in addition to alumina slurry. Colloidal silica is used to produce brilliant, scratch-free surfaces on a wide variety of materials, including copper, aluminum, stainless steel, lead, and others which tend to deform readily and produce unclear microstructures.

V. ANALYSIS OF POLISHED SAMPLES

A. Revealing the Microstructure

The as-polished surface produced by conventional abrasive techniques, other than the colloidal silica, are likely to have a very fine layer of deformation remaining. Although this may not obscure the microstructure, it could cause it to be less clearly defined, therefore more difficult to analyze. When residual scratches remain, or softer, more brittle constituents are slightly pitted, it is possible to restore the microstructure without a total repolish. One such technique is the etch-polish sequence, where the sample is lightly etched, then repolished on the final polishing wheel only enough to remove the etching effect.

This sequence may be repeated several times, if necessary, to remove residual deformation scratches and the effects of plucked constituents such as graphite in cast iron. Another technique, called "attack" polishing, utilizes an etchant which is applied directly to the final polishing wheel. The sample is simultaneously etched and polished and a better surface is produced because the remaining deformation is removed.

Metallographic etching is a separate post-polishing step that is used to reveal microstructural details which are not visible in the as-polished condition. Although nonmetallic inclusions, free graphite (cast irons) and numerous physical defects are visible without etching, far more information becomes available once the polished surface has been correctly etched. Although there are various etching techniques, the most common and useful type is chemical dissolution. This method employs a combination of solvent and chemical reagents, usually including one or more mineral acids which selectively attack various features of the microstructure, depending on their individual chemical and crystallographic properties. Specific features or constituents, such as grain boundaries, alloy phase boundaries, layer interfaces, and various precipitates, are delineated, depending on the specific etchant that is applied.

There are literally hundreds of etchants which have been devised by various investigators over the years, but a relatively few sample formulations are required to reveal the microstructures of most common alloys. Only proven, safe etching formulations should be selected and used according to printed directions and with accepted chemistry procedures. Etchants may be applied either by swabbing the sample surface, as shown in Fig. 14, or by total immersion into the etching solution, as recommended by the information source.

Certain corrosion-resistant alloys, such as stainless steel and various nickel-based superalloys may be difficult to etch by chemical dissolution. In such cases it may be necessary to employ electrolytic etching, where the

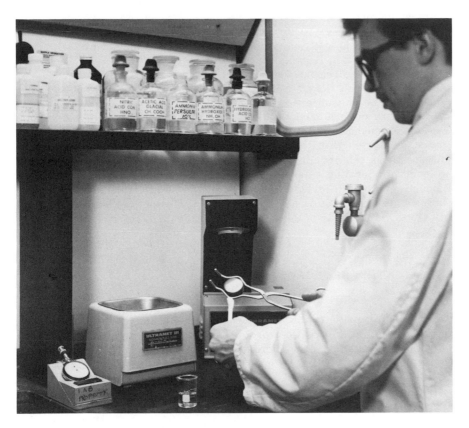

FIGURE 14   Etching a metallographic sample.

sample is made the anode in an electrolytic cell. Etching occurs when a low-voltage dc current is applied, causing a more energetic attack of the sample surface.

B. Microscopes

Microscopes are essential to make the microstructure visible to the investigator. Because the prepared metallographic sample has an opaque, polished surface, it is necessary to use a reflected light microscope rather than the transmitted light microscope used to view biological samples. Another basic requirement of a metallurgical microscope is the use of vertical illumination. Stereo microscopes, commonly used to observe unpolished and irregular surfaces, such as fractures, are not suitable for the examination of polished metallographic samples. In addition to the limited magnification range, they commonly employ oblique illumination, which gives a dark-field effect on polished samples. Dark-field illumination renders the microstructural details as bright lines in a dark background, rather than dark lines on a bright background which is characteristic of the desirable bright-field illumination.

Other types of illumination, such as polarized light and differential interference contrast, are useful adjuncts but are not the primary method of illumination used in metallographic analysis. Bright-field illumination is obtained through use of vertical illumination where the light path strikes the polished surface at a perpendicular angle and therefore returns on the same path to the observer or film plane via a special mirror. The need for bright-field illumination was recognized early by Henry Sorby who stated in his notes in 1885: "With oblique illumination, a polished surface looks black, but with direct [vertical] illumination it looks bright and metallic."

In addition to the requirement for vertical illumination, a metallurgical microscope must have a sufficient magnification range to resolve various microstructures that will be encountered. If photomicrographs are required, an integral or accessory camera must be available. Many metallurgical microscopes utilize an inverted specimen stage; the sample is placed polished face down onto an aperture stage plate. With this design, samples may be exchanged rapidly because the sample is self-leveling. When an erect stage microscope is used, a separate leveling operation must be performed. The sample is placed on a mound of modeling clay and leveled by pressing the sample with a leveling press. Microscopes that include all the essential features required for efficient microstructural analysis of metallurgical samples are referred to as metallographs.

VI. THE APPLICATION OF MICROSTRUCTURAL ANALYSIS

A correctly polished metallographic sample has no value unless the revealed microstructure is applied to practical problems. Figure 15 illustrates the wide range of information obtained from microstructural analysis. The actual utilization of microstructural information may be conveniently divided into three areas: materials characterization, process monitoring, and failure analysis.

A. Materials Characterization

Materials characterization was the goal of ancient philosophers and alchemists who wanted to understand the nature of matter. It was not until microstructural analysis became a practical reality that it was possible to develop new alloys by intention rather than by chance. When material properties became identified with specific microstructures, it was possible to evaluate visually the effects of chemical, thermal, and mechanical work variations. If, for example, a steel is rapidly quenched, it not only becomes hard but also has a characteristic needlelike microstructure. This visible condition therefore indicates that hardness has been achieved. Similarly, various other microstructures may be used as indicators of the success or failure of mechanical and thermal treatments.

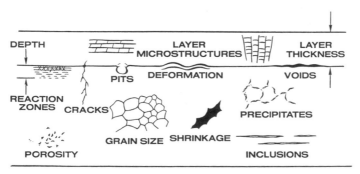

FIGURE 15   Microstructural details revealed by metallographic analysis.

Figure 16 lists some of the common microstructures which are found in iron-carbon alloys, together with an indication of how they tend to affect the alloy properties. Because two, or more, and often as many as five of these microstructures may be present at one time, this table cannot be used as a practical guide because they are interacting. The effects of the microstructure are best understood and most useful when considered in the light of a knowledge of chemical composition and thermal history.

Various reference books have been compiled to provide a guide to identify materials using photomicrographs of typical microstructures. It is significant to note that these visual guides are nearly always organized according to compositional families and subdivided by thermal treatment histories.

Microstructure	Identity	Impact
AUSTENITE	Soft phase which forms first—usually transforms into other phases—seen only in certain alloys	Soft and ductile—low low strength
FERRITE	Iron with elements in solid solution—soft matrix phase	Contributes ductility—little strength
GRAPHITE	Free carbon in any size and shape	Improves machinability and damping properties—reduces shrinkage—reduces strength severely depending on shape
CEMENTITE	Hard iron—carbon intermetallic phase	Imparts hardness, wear and corrosion resistance—severely reduces machinability
PEARLITE	Laminar phase—alternate layers of Ferrite and Cementite	Contributes strength without brittleness—
MARTENSITE	Hard structure produced by specific thermal treatment	Hardest transformation structure—brittle unless tempered
STEADITE	Iron-carbon-phosphorus eutectic—hard and brittle	Sometimes confused with Ledeburite—aids fluidity in molten state—brittleness in solid state
LEDEBURITE	Massive eutectic phase composed of Cementite and Austenite (Ledeburite transforms to Cementite and Pearlite on cooling.)	Produces high hardness and wear resistance—virtually unmachinable

FIGURE 16 Effect of microstructure on ferrous casting alloy properties.

B. Process Monitoring

Process monitoring through microstructural analysis is widely used to control the process of converting raw materials to finished products. One widely used application is the evaluation of nonmetallic inclusions in steels. This is important because the properties of steel components are directly affected by the type, size, and distribution of inclusion. A clever system of rating was devised by the Swedish Iron Makers Society and is known as the JK chart [7]. This elaborate method has been used as a manual method of assessment for many years, and variations are still used as part of newer automatic systems which employ television cameras and electronic analyzers (Fig. 17) [8].

Another useful application of microstructural analysis is to control heat-treating processes. It is well known that the hardenability of steel is directly dependent on the starting grain size, together with other properties. Various schemes for determining grain size, without microstructural analysis, have been devised but have met with only limited success. Microstructural analysis not only reveals the average grain size but also alerts the metallurgists to the presence of "abnormalities" that are not detectable by blind analysis but which are nevertheless significant to product quality.

The depth of surface hardening (case hardening) may be accurately measured by using an accessory measuring device placed on the microscope. A sample that has been polished and lightly etched is placed in a microhardness

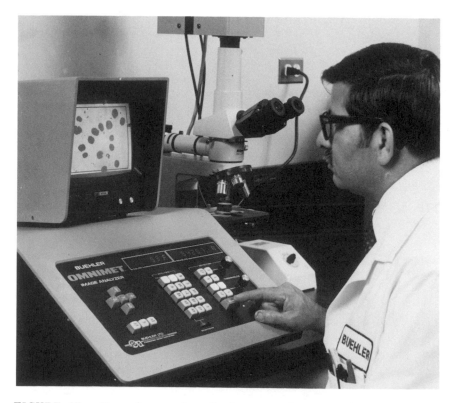

FIGURE 17   Use of an automatic image analyzer to determine percent graphite in ductile iron.

tester and very-light-load hardness indentations are made. A plot of the results provides an accurate view of the hardness profile.

Another highly useful application of microstructural analysis is to observe visual changes in materials due to mechanical and thermal processing. The success of such metalworking processes as rolling, forging, and stamping are highly dependent on the control of microstructure. This is dramatically illustrated by the phenomenon of grain growth and recrystallization which are directly affected by mechanical work and thermal treatment. Figure 18 illustrates this by a series of photomicrographs with brass as the test material.

C. Failure Analysis

Failure analysis is an extremely useful technique which makes effective use of microstructural information [9]. Application of this technique has advanced in recent years due to a better understanding of failure mechanisms and the availability of the scanning electron microscope. Metallography has long played a significant role in failure analysis, but the SEM and its related analytical accessories have provided an additional tool to the failure analyst. The strength of SEM microscopy and analysis lies in its ability to characterize surface information such as fracture faces. With its great depth of field and expended magnification, the scanning electron microscope is able to identify the actual mode of failure more rapidly and accurately.

Microstructural analysis, on the other hand, provides a below-the-surface view of the failure point of origin. By comparing a cross section of a failed area to an unfailed area, or a good part with a bad part, conclusions may

(a)

FIGURE 18   7/30 brass showing the effect of thermal and mechanical treatments. Original magnification, 300×; (a) 5% thickness reduction; (b) 25% thickness reduction; (c) 75% thickness reduction. All annealed at 350°C for 60 min.

(b)

(c)

FIGURE 18   (Continued)

often be reached without the aid of SEM or other more sophisticated analytical devices.

The value of failure analysis cannot be overemphasized [9]. It is not a test performed only after parts fail in service. Quality-conscious manufacturers employ failure analysis in a very positive way to test newly developed products before they are placed into service. Intentionally destructive tests that far exceed the actual service conditions are a valuable means of developing superior products and avoiding the hazards of product liability.

A manufacturer of heart pacemaker batteries, for example, destroys every fiftieth outer case to examine the microstructural or soundness of a critical weld. Failure of this weld would spell almost certain death for a person who depends on its reliability.

From a purely economic point of view, it makes good business sense to detect and identify the cause of product defects at the earliest possible time. If this is done, the manufacturer is able to prevent costly "value adding" to a product that is almost certain to be rejected at final inspection. If incoming raw material is of rejectable quality, why process this material further?

Microstructural analysis is extremely useful because it allows the user to get to the root causes of problems so that appropriate corrective action may be taken. Nondestructive tests are used to detect the presence of flaws but are, for the most part, limited to defects which are open to, or near, the surface. The greatest value of metallography lies in its ability to clearly characterize detected flaws and reveal their actual impact on the quality of the part.

REFERENCES

1. C. S. Smith, *A History of Metallography*, University of Chicago Press, Chicago, 1960.
2. L. E. Samuels, *Metallographic Polishing by Mechanical Methods*, Vol. 3, Pitman, Melbourne, 1971, p. 44.
3. G. Petzow, *Metallographic Etching*, Vol. 1, American Society for Metals, Metals Park, Ohio, 1978, pp. 9–11.
4. J. A. Nelson and R. M. Westrich, "Abrasive Cutting in Metallography," in *Metallographic Sample Preparation*, J. L. McCall and W. M. Mueller, eds., Plenum, New York, pp. 41–54.
5. The Low Speed Saw, *Metal Digest* (J. Nelson, ed., Buehler Ltd.), Vol. 22, 1983, p. 1.
6. J. A. Nelson, "New Abrasives for Metallography," in *Microstructural Science*, Volume II, Proceedings of the 15th Annual Technical Meeting, Institute of Metallographic Sciences, 1983, pp. 251–259.
7. G. F. Vander Voort, "Inclusion Measurement," in *Metallography Is a Quality Control Tool*, J. L. McCall and P. M. French, eds., Plenum, New York, 1980, pp. 1–88.
8. J. C. Oppenheim, "Introduction to Basic Quantitative Image Analysis," in *Microstructural Science*, G. Petzow, R. Paris, E. D. Albrecht, and J. L. McCall, eds., Elsevier, New York, 1981, pp. 163–170.
9. J. A. Nelson, "The Final Quality Tool: Failure Analysis," *Manufacturing Engineering*, November 1982, pp. 75–77.

FURTHER READING

American Society for Metals, *Metals Handbook, Eighth Edition*, Vol. 8, Metallographic Structures and Phase Diagrams, ASM, Metals Park, Ohio, 1973.

Petzow, G., *Metallographic Etching*, American Society for Metals, Metals Park, Ohio, 1982.

Samuels, L. E., *Metallographic Polishing by Mechanical Methods*, 3rd ed., American Society for Metals, Metals Park, Ohio, 1982.

Smith, C. S., *A History of Metallography*, University of Chicago Press, Chicago, 1960.

Van der Voort, G. F., *Metallography: Principles and Practices*, McGraw-Hill, New York, 1984.

32

TESTING LABORATORIES

KENNETH PACKER, RALPH DEAGHN, and the
STAFF of PACKER ENGINEERING

Packer Engineering
Naperville, Illinois

I. INTRODUCTION

The fundamental concept of quality may be thought of as "fitness for use."
This is a universal concept, applicable to all goods and services, and is judged
by the *user*, not by the manufacturer or supplier of the goods or services [1].
Fitness for use may be subdivided into categories as follows:

Proper design
Suitable materials
Acceptable manufacturing processes
Proper instructions on use

With a proper blending of design, material, and manufacturing, a system consisting of a number of components will have acceptable function and service
life. Additionally, the reliability of the system will satisfy the majority of the
users.

One of the functions of independent test laboratories is to assist manufacturers in assessing the degree of "fitness for use" or quality of their products.
Being independent, the laboratories are able to provide an unbiased view of
product quality, based on the combined perspectives of experts from many professional disciplines with the benefit of many years of industrial experience.

It has been estimated that there are approximately 3000 independent testing
laboratories in the United States which did $700,000,000 worth of business in
1979 [2]. Thus, with an average annual sales volume of $230,000, it can be
seen that the majority of these independent labs are small.

The services performed by independent laboratories cover a wide spectrum,
as illustrated by the following organization of services listed in the 1981 *Metal
Progress Testing and Inspection Buyers Guide and Directory* [3]

Calibration
Certification
Chemical analysis
Coating tests

Combustion tests
Consulting services
Corrosion resistance
Electromagnetic properties
Environmental tests
Failure analysis
Field service
Forming tests
Fire resistance (flammability) tests
Heat-treating tests
Industrial accident investigations
Legal assistance
Lubrication tests
Machining tests
Mechanical tests
Microscopic analysis
Nondestructive tests
Nuclear materials tests
On-site inspection services
Patent development and protection
Plating and coating tests
Product evaluation
Quality assurance/quality control
Radioactive materials testing
Repair of testing equipment
Research and development
Sample preparation
Special jigs and fixtures
Stress analysis
Thermal tests
Wear tests
Weld tests

It can be seen that independent test laboratories perform a wide variety of technical services. For the purpose of illustration, this chapter addresses services performed when there has been a problem which is suspected of being related to the quality of a component or its failure to perform its function.

The problem often starts with an accident or other incident suggesting the failure of a part. Once the part that has failed, causing the accident or "incident," has been identified, it is subjected to a rigorous process known as failure analysis. The result of the failure analysis will identify the reason for the failure with a high degree of reliability.

Accident reconstruction/failure analysis is essential to identify the true quality problem responsible so that proper steps may be taken to rectify or better control the design, the materials, or the manufacturing process. Several case studies illustrating successful use of the technique are given, and the concluding section considers what can be learned from accident reconstruction/failure analysis to prevent designing and manufacturing parts which are likely to fail prematurely in service.

II. ACCIDENT RECONSTRUCTION

Accident reconstruction is a systematic investigation of all the pertinent facts and available information surrounding an accident or incident. This includes the post-investigative procedures, witness statements of the accident during its occurrence, and any pre-accident information that would bring together the actual accident cause, sequence, and results.

Accident reconstruction is useful for many purposes. First, it may be necessary to determine the actual sequence of events or movements of various components which occurred during an accident so that the proper failure mode can be determined. Determining the accident cause establishes responsibility for the component that failed initially. This is useful in order to reexamine the design, operating procedures, and so on, to prevent recurrence of the problem or accident in the future. In some cases, the component might be acceptable, but misused. In those cases, additional instructions or warnings to the user must be provided.

A. Accident Matrix

The accident matrix is a means of ensuring that all the various components of an accident or incident are thoroughly investigated and documented. The matrix highlights any voids in the investigative procedures and indicates where additional information is necessary to reconstruct the accident properly. Figure 1 shows a typical accident matrix useful for this purpose. The vertical columns are labeled pre-accident, accident, and post-accident. The three horizontal rows are labeled man, machine, and environment. This 3 by 3 matrix covers all aspects needed to be examined in order to prepare a thorough, accurate, and reliable accident reconstruction.

Various bits of information about the man, machine, and environment obviously fall into one of the three time categories. After all the information obtained on any one of the three categories is listed, the matrix displays pertinent information on the incident at a glance.

Man

Man has always played a significant role in controlling the equipment, machinery, and vehicles that have been invented and devised to reduce his work burden or for recreational uses. Thus the physical and mental

	Pre-Accident	Accident	Post-Accident
Man			
Machine			
Environment			

FIGURE 1 Accident matrix.

health of the individual involved can be a significant consideration in the analysis and in the preparation of the accident reconstruction.

Behavior patterns preceding an accident, the mental state of the person involved, any factors that would have changed his or her behavior become important in determining the events leading up to an accident. In addition, the person's education and training are very important, since at times they help in evaluating his or her ability to operate the equipment or drive the vehicle involved in the accident. Special training related to the safety features of the equipment or vehicle and the person's attitude toward safety also determine his or her level of understanding and regard toward the equipment and/or vehicle he or she is operating. In evaluating the safety training given to the person, it helps to determine if it was sufficiently descriptive to provide him or her with an accurate assessment of the safe operating procedures that should be used with the machine.

Food and/or beverages that the person consumed prior to the accident may contribute to or modify his or her ability to handle the equipment properly. Work history is also significant since it assesses the person's normal behavioral patterns and perhaps his or her reasoning, which might have affected or caused the accident or incident.

Injuries, if any, incurred during the accident help to determine the forces that were working on the person. It also helps the accident reconstructionist to determine the direction of the person's movement during the incident. In a vehicle, this could determine in which direction the vehicle may have rolled over or the angle of impact with another object or another vehicle.

Eyewitness accounts of the accident are important in establishing the events occurring during the accident itself. Although the incident may have occurred so rapidly that the operator does not recall incremental movements, he or she may be able to give insight into the events leading up to the accident and even some events occurring during the accident itself. All of the person's statements become useful in determining if his or her recollection and statements correspond to the analysis and information derived from the other two categories.

Machine

The equipment involved in an accident or incident generally holds significant information that can be obtained from a macro and micro investigation of the unit after the incident. In addition, engineering detail drawings and assembly drawings and material specifications can be used to assess the initial "as-built" condition of the unit.

Operator's manuals or repair manuals give further information into the design of the unit and the control procedures and proper adjustments of moving parts. Usually, maintenance records are also available to lend insight into the care and maintenance given to the equipment. All these documents could in some manner be significant, depending on the type of failure or accident that occurred while the equipment was being used. Often, the operator and maintenance manuals of the equipment or vehicle can provide insight into its maintainability and reliability as well as the designer's approach to solving problems by guarding or warnings necessary for safe operation.

Most of the items that we have discussed with the machine have been pre-accident. They are the areas that will help define the machine's condition prior to the accident. A thorough post-accident examination of the machine is a valuable source of data for our accident matrix.

Hopefully, the machine will not have been modified or repaired since the accident. However, if the machine has been repaired and put back in service or moved from the accident site location, it is necessary to examine the parts or components that were removed from the unit and establish how they would have interacted with the machine during the accident. When investigating the machine after an accident, it is important to document the condition of the machine thoroughly before any components are removed, tested, or changed. This can be done by photographing the equipment from at least four different angles to give a general overall view to be augmented by close-up shots showing the interrelationships between the various components.

After or during the disassembly of a machine, it is necessary to document the condition and position of each component that may be pertinent in the investigation. To be safe, it is better to document all items found, even if during the initial investigation they do not appear to be related to the incident or accident. Later analysis of all the information may show contributory causes of other components in the system.

During this phase of the operation, one has to avoid "early blindness." Do not come to any conclusions during this portion of the investigation; they will influence you and, therefore, potentially alter your investigative techniques and/or procedures, leading to an incomplete examination of the unit.

Many assemblies may have to be disassembled after an accident or incident to determine their condition prior to or during the accident. Whenever a device is being disassembled, the previously mentioned documentation procedures should be used. Small, broken, or failed components within a major assembly could lead to its inability to perform as designed, and their orientation and failure within the assembly may be the clue as to how and why it failed. Analysis of individual failures is covered in Sec. III.

Environment

The environment is the category covering all other aspects of an accident or incident. Such aspects include the time of day, the weather at the accident scene, supervisory policies, training policies, lighting, job requirements, and skills required of the operator to operate the equipment or a vehicle.

In an automotive or aircraft accident, the weather and time of day play a significant role. The investigation should include data on any traffic control equipment, roadways, airways, and other pertinent surrounding conditions on which the operator would be dependent.

B. Documentation

To complete the accident matrix, many items will have to be documented with very precise measurements and/or detailed assessment of the failure modes. For a vehicle accident, it may be necessary to perform a detailed site survey with all the subtle changes in elevation and/or curvature that may become important to this accident reconstruction. The plot survey should document all damaged objects, skid marks, gouges, and so on, that would have been made by the vehicle(s) involved in the accident.

In an aircraft accident case, the damage done to the surrounding objects, houses, trees, crops, and so on, becomes important in determining the flight path of the aircraft, as well as the orientation of the aircraft before its impact. Thus, detailed plot surveys are a good method of detailing this type of information and preparing a workable document that can be usable at a later date.

Photography is recommended to document accurately both the site and the components involved in the accident. Photographs taken during any site survey or disassembly of equipment can be extremely helpful as later information is developed.

Scale models can sometimes be very useful in documenting information and helping in the determination of the sequence of events. They enable the investigator to visualize the sequence of events that must have occurred for the accident to happen. Scale drawings can be made to show the sequence of events in order to assess the accident properly.

In many cases it may be desirable to reconstruct the accident to obtain more information on the sequence of events. High-speed movies or videotapes may be used to document the movement of the various components involved. High-speed movies can take a $\frac{1}{2}$-second collision and spread it out over several minutes, enabling a very detailed study of the sequence of events.

If the accident scene was not properly documented at the time of the first investigation and only photographs were taken, photogrammetry can be used. This technique allows the derivation of heights and distances from two-dimensional photographs and helps in accurately positioning necessary objects.

Computer analysis of the data or computer modeling of the equipment is another way to determine the effect that static and dynamic forces have on the equipment in question. These outside forces may influence the accident, and knowing how the equipment will respond to them is extremely helpful. Nondestructive testing is used to compare the quality or integrity of components within the unit to similar components in other units to determine if the failure is due to a substandard-quality part.

C. Summary

The use of the accident matrix provides a technique for the investigator to list all the facts discovered into three categories: man, machine, and environment. In turn, it forces the investigator to categorize the data into pre-accident, during the accident, and post-accident categories. Thus some of the data that is difficult to get can be derived from information preceding and following an accident. The matrix allows the forming of logical conclusions and facilitates the best possible accident reconstruction that fits all the evidence at hand. It is also useful in substantiating information obtained in one segment of the matrix with that of another.

III. FAILURE ANALYSIS TECHNIQUES

The accident reconstruction previously discussed will usually need components which are suspected to have been casually related to the problem to be studied further. The field investigator or reconstructionist, after properly documenting all the pertinent details surrounding the suspected parts, will submit them to the laboratory for detailed study and analysis. It is also likely that the scope of the failure investigation will be directed along certain hypotheses due to the nature of the accident itself. This section emphasizes important routine and specialized techniques employed in a failure analysis. A number of tools utilized in the laboratory phase will be discussed in detail in a later section. Most of this discussion will center on the failure analysis of metallic components, since these are the predominant structural materials used in machines and systems. However, many of these techniques are applicable to other engineering materials, such as concrete, glass, and polymeric materials. Volume

10 of the *Metals Handbook* [4] is an excellent source book describing these
methods in detail.

A. Initial Inspection

It is critical to document thoroughly the as-received condition of any parts
before their character is changed by subsequent laboratory work. The primary technique required here is careful and exhaustive visual inspection,
aided by hand magnifiers or a stereoscopic microscope. Comprehensive photographic documentation, both of the overall artifact and macrophotography of
potentially significant areas of wear, distortion, corrosion, and so on, will
also help. Appropriate engineering drawings and material specifications should
be used for reference purposes. This phase of the analysis will serve to define areas for more detailed or destructive testing.

The direction of wear marks, distortions, and fractures will give significant
clues, not only of the type of loading, but also the direction and magnitude.
The time sequence of loading can also be deduced. The fracture patterns can
be interpreted to locate the point of crack initiation and the direction of propagation. In most cases, the fracture mode will tell whether the crack progressed over an extended period of time or whether failure was sudden.

At the completion of this phase of the examination, the failure analyst will
have a fairly good idea as to the failure mode. He or she will have formed
several possible hypotheses, which by critical subsequent tests can be narrowed down to a very small number of probabilities. In most cases the most
probable failure mode and cause can be confidently determined, provided that
the evidence is not too badly damaged.

B. Detailed Surface Analysis

Once the overall failure pattern has been determined, the process of the failure will usually leave distinct and telltale features on the surface of the part.
For instance, if impact with another object is the suspected cause, the direction of relative impact of those two parts may prove to be the definitive evidence. The impact will probably have transferred material from one object
to another, and the mutual smearing or cutting will exhibit directionality on a
microscopic level. Under the binocular microscope, the edges of the impact
mark will be pushed over in the direction of the applied force. Study of the
impact mark in the electron microscope will reveal metal removal similar to that
caused by a machining operation. While examining the part in the electron
microscope, any foreign material involved in the impact will be apparent and
with the energy dispersive analysis of x-rays (EDAX) attachment, these microscopic particles can be chemically analyzed and compared to the suspect object.

There are four primary modes of fracture. Each tells a great deal about
the type and duration of loads applied to the material.

Ductile

The simplest failure mode is ductile rupture, which results from a one-time
application of excessive force, causing complete separation immediately. The
ductility is often evidenced by stretching or necking down the material adjacent to the fracture and by a dull, silky fracture appearance. The fracture
will appear fresh but may have areas where oxidation is apparent. On the
microscopic level, such a fracture was formed as the excessive load created
voids around microscopic inclusions in the metal which grew as the loads

increased until they linked up at final separation. The failure mode is frequently referred to as microvoid coalescence. In the electron microscope, these microvoids appear to be an array of dimples on the surface, many times still retaining the initiating particle as if it were sitting in a teacup. Therefore, when this distinctive fracture mode is observed, it may be concluded that the loads exceeded the basic strength of the part.

Brittle

A second common fracture mode is brittle fracture, sometimes referred to as cleavage. Visual examination of a brittle fracture reveals little or no necking or ductility near the fracture plane. The fracture surface will exhibit numerous facets that will sparkle under bright light. (Laypeople frequently say that "the metal has crystallized." This is an erroneous statement because all metals are crystalline. The brittle fracture simply better exhibits the crystallinity.) In the electron microscope the fracture surface will exhibit a number of cleavage crack planes which are nearly parallel to one another. Each individual cleavage plane is relatively flat and represents the fracture across an individual metal grain. This fracture mechanism absorbs little energy and consequently propagates rapidly, approaching the speed of sound in that material. This mode of failure is usually sudden and catastrophic and can result in cracks running great distances if they are not arrested by tougher areas of the structure. Very tough materials will not undergo a brittle fracture. The material toughness which is the key material parameter in this failure mode is measured by the Charpy impact test (ASTM E-10) or linear elastic fracture toughness tests (ASTM E-399). As the toughness of the material decreases, the material fails by brittle fracture rather than by ductile fracture.

Intergranular

The third important failure mode is intergranular fracture, which is a separation of the material following a path between individual grains or crystals in the metal. There are two predominant reasons for intergranular separation. First, a brittle constituent—such as carbides resulting from improper heat treatment—may have formed in the grain boundaries of the material. If a material has a microstructure of tough grains and brittle grain boundaries, the easy fracture path is through the grain boundaries, and the resulting fracture will show numerous grain facets. The other common cause of intergranular fracture is due to environmental attack, commonly referred to as stress corrosion cracking, where the corrosive environment selectively attacks the grain boundaries and permits the grains to separate. Visually, both cleavage and intergranular fractures will appear brittle; however, the electron microscope will discriminate between fractures between the grains and fractures through the grains. The intergranular fracture will have an appearance similar to rock candy in the electron microscope. Standard optical metallography will also show whether fracture paths tend to progress through the grains or around the grains. Final determination of the failure cause in an intergranular fracture case will require knowledge of the source of stress, an evaluation of the corrosive environment and metallurgical quality. Certain classes of high-strength structural alloys are very susceptible to stress corrosion cracking, whereas simple metallurgical tests will show where a brittle grain boundary phase exists.

Fatigue

The fourth major classification of failure modes is metal fatigue, which accounts for a high percentage of failures in machinery. Fatigue is a progressive fracturing of the metal due to repetitive stressing because of such things as flexing or vibration. Again, this fracture mode leaves characteristic markings on the fracture surface. Visual examination will reveal a relatively smooth, polished appearance on the fracture surface with a number of beach marks which record the crack size at various times during its growth. When examined in the electron microscope, a number of very small ridges will be located; each one represents the increment of growth during one effective stress cycle. Fatigue progresses across the grains and this effect can be determined by standard optical metallography.

Fracture mechanics, which is an area of technology developed primarily by the aviation industry, has direct application for the failure analyst when studying fatigue problems. This technology allows the effect of crack size and cyclic stress to be compared to well-documented crack growth curves, which in turn provides information of the following sorts: (1) with a known or assumed flaw size, the cyclic stress acting on the part can be determined; (2) given the cyclic stress, the initiating flaw size can be determined; and (3) given a starting flaw size and starting stress cycle, the total fatigue life of the structure can be determined. Often the quality control executive is forced to determine the maximum permissible flaw sizes in the manufactured parts. Linear elastic fracture mechanics methods provide a rational basis for establishing necessary and cost-effective inspection measures.

Often, a field investigator will not be able to return the actual components to the laboratory for surface analysis. In such cases, surface replicating techniques are useful. Replicas have been successfully produced using two-part dental rubber such as that used for making dental impressions. This material is mixed and spread on the surface, where it cures in a matter of a few minutes. The material is readily strippable and will faithfully reproduce surface details, even when examined at magnifications greater than 100×.

A second technique utilizes cellulose acetate tape softened with a drop of acetone, which is pressed onto the surface and held with thumb pressure for a few minutes until it hardens. This material is also readily strippable from the surface, and although it is suited only for relatively small areas, the reproduction of fine details is excellent. Such material can be obtained at any scientific supply store and the technique can be learned readily to provide quite satisfactory replicas for laboratory study on the scanning electron microscope, the optical comparator, or by other means.

Once the mode of failure is determined, one or more of the causative agents may need further research or documentation. More often than not, the type of fracture, the metal quality, and the strength are relatively easy to determine. On the other hand, the environmental conditions and working stresses during operation are highly variable and unpredictable. Because of this, simulated service testing or field tests may be necessary to tell the complete story. A complete failure analysis will identify the type of failure and the factors that most significantly influence that failure mode. This information, when provided to the design engineering staff and the quality control department, will allow product improvement and optimum quality control measures.

IV. LABORATORY EQUIPMENT USED

Control of the mechanical and physical characteristics of metals and materials is important for the satisfactory performance of a part or mechanism. Generally, the physical strength of a material is the most important property; however, notch sensitivity, resistance to an agressive environment, thermal stability, and other factors are often even more important. Thus parts or components are produced to meet certain specifications or requirements. Often, the specification will be originated by the manufacturer or purchaser (company-type specification). Otherwise, a commonly used specification published by a technical society such as the ASTM (American Society for Testing and Materials) or a government agency is used. A specification is also necessary to ensure that the characterization of a material property is performed in a common, proper, and reproducible manner.

A. Testing Methods

Tensile Testing

The physical strength of a material (ultimate tensile strength) is determined by gradually applying a load to a metal coupon in a calibrated machine to determine the rupture load per unit of cross-sectional area (stress, expressed as pounds per square inch). Usually, the stress at which the material starts to deform permanently (yield strength) is determined during the same test. Other properties, such as the amount of elongation or reduction in the cross-sectional area, give indications of the material's ductility. ASTM E-8 is a typical and commonly used tensile testing specification.

Impact Testing

Impact testing measures the ability of a material to absorb a large amount of energy during a very short period of time. Although a material may be very strong (UTS), or have good ductility (percent elongation) in a tensile test, it may tend to snap or shatter like glass when subjected to shock loading. Notched bar impact testing of materials (ASTM E-23) is a commonly used impact testing method.

Impact testing utilizes a pendulum which is raised to a specific height and allowed to swing, striking the notched specimen at the bottom, then swinging through the rest of its arc. The energy absorbed by fracture of the specimen is measured by the loss in height of the arc after breaking the specimen. Often, impact tests are run at specific temperatures between −150° and 212°F to determine the fracture appearance transition temperature (FATT), at which the change in brittle (low energy) to ductile (high energy) behavior occurs.

Hardness Testing

Hardness testing measures the resistance of the metal to penetration. The Brinell hardness test (ASTM E-10) utilizes a 10-mm-diameter steel ball and a 3000-kg load (500 kg for soft nonferrous metals). The hardness of the material is obtained by measuring the diameter of the impression and converting it to the Brinell hardness number (BHN). The advantage of this test is that it correlates well with tensile strength and is good for nonhomogenous material such as castings, as it provides an averaging effect over a relatively large area.

The Rockwell hardness test (ASTM E-18) is a differential depth measurement test where the effective depth of penetration after application of two loads and the release of the second is proportional to the hardness. This test has many different scales for very hard to very soft materials, utilizing many different loads and indentor geometries. The Rockwell test is a very rapid, reliable test, and is particularly useful on very thin materials when the superficial scales are used. Rockwell hardness testing can also be performed on plastics (ASTM D-785).

The Vickers hardness test utilizes a square-based pyramidal diamond indentor with 136° face angles and different dead weights (usually 10 kg) to load the indentor into the material (ASTM E-92). Hardness is determined by measuring the length of the diagonals in the impression. Conversions of the Vickers hardness to another scale are at best approximations and require a specific conversion scale for the material being tested.

One common microhardness test is the Tukon (Knoop). This test measures hardness on a microscopic level and usually requires metallographic sample preparation. Microhardness can be used to measure hardness of very thin materials, special microscopic areas of interest, and can determine depth of case on heat-treated parts.

There are many different portable hardness testing methods and machines, including the King Brinell, Telle Brinell, and Equo-tip. Each of these machines/methods has many different advantages and disadvantages. As with conversion or interpretation of any hardness result, standardization and procedures should be verified for each case. Conversion can be made from one hardness scale to another or an approximate tensile strength obtained using ASTM E-140.

Metallography

Preparation of a metallurgical sample (ASTM E-3) involves removal of a small sample from the area of interest. The sample is then mounted in plastic and ground with successively finer grits until a polished, mirrorlike, surface is obtained. The sample is then etched with diluted acid or a combination of acids to bring out specific structural features when viewed in the microscope (at 50 to 1000×). Metallography can be used to determine structure, grain size, alloy content, inclusions content, carbon content, corrosion properties, rolling direction, and so on. Photographs are usually taken at magnification to record observations.

Material Characterization

For wear resistance, fatigue strength, fracture toughness, slow strain rate, and elevated temperature creep, there are many less common tests for specific materials (nonmetals) and/or very specific conditions (environment related). Many of these tests are referenced by common standards or may be commonly accepted in industry.

Fractography

A tremendous amount of information is contained on a fracture surface. It can be obtained by examination with the naked eye and a hand magnifier. Higher magnifications (up to 50×) can be achieved with a stereoscope. Specific fracture textures are usually viewed at magnifications of 100× and above with the scanning electron microscope (SEM). On fracture surfaces that

cannot be cut or are too large to handle the fracture, features can be replicated as discussed earlier.

Chemical Analysis

Checking the chemical composition of a material is commonly one of the first
tests run. Chemical testing is conventionally done with wet chemical or combustion methods on most materials. Infrared analysis is commonly performed
on plastics and rubbers. Very sophisticated and highly specialized instruments are available to check for elements at high levels of accuracy. An EDAX
(energy dispersive analysis of x-rays) unit is commonly attached to the SEM.
It is used to determine elemental species present and their homogeneity, and if
foreign materials are causing or participating in the problem.

Nondestructive Testing

Nondestructive testing (NDT) is usually used to detect cracking or defects
so that a failure may be prevented. It can also be used as a technique for
selecting sampling location on a failed part. Technicians and engineers are
usually qualified in accordance with ASNT SNT-TC-1A at level I, II, or III
or a similar specification.

Dye penetrant testing (PT) and magnetic particle testing (MT) are used
for surface defect detection (MT can be used for shallow, subsurface detection). Ultrasonic (UT) and radiography (RT) are usually used for internal
inspections.

Eddy current (ET) is both a surface and a subsurface test, as well as a
method for sorting materials or heat treatments. Acoustic emission is becoming more popular as a means for detecting crack propagation and preventing
failures.

Stress Measurements

Stress is commonly measured (indirectly) with strain gages. The strain gage
consists of a fine network of wires that is applied to the part. The gage
makes it possible to measure strain as a function of the change in the resistance of the wires. Brittle lacquer is commonly applied to a part and the part
loaded to crack the lacquer so that areas of high strain can be located for
gage application. X-ray diffraction is another common method, but is usually
limited in the size of part that it can accommodate.

Photoelastic methods measure strain by fringe changes under polarized
light. This type of test produces more qualitative than quantitative information.

Other Measurements

Other physical measurements, such as temperature, force, distance, velocity,
acceleration, pressure, and flow rate, can be determined and recorded by
electrical or other means. Actual measurements can be made on the item of
interest during use. These techniques are also used during simulation-type
testing.

B. Summary

The accuracy, exact nature, and applicability of the specific test method
should be well understood prior to its selection. Testing should be carried
out in accordance with an accepted standard or procedure to ensure that the

results are meaningful and comparable to other work. All instrumentation should be checked and calibrated in accordance with the appropriate standard or manufacturer's recommendations. For illustrative purposes, a list of many of today's available laboratory techniques follows.

I. *Visual*
   A. Direct observation
      1. Unaided eye
      2. Magnifier
      3. Binocular (stereo) microscope
      4. Metallurgical microscope (metallograph)
      5. Electron microscopes
         a. SEM (scanning electron microscope)
         b. TEM (transmission electron microscope)
         c. STEM (scanning/transmission electron microscope)
   B. Indirect
      1. Replication
         a. Dental
         b. Acetate
   C. Recording of visual observations
      1. Still photos
         a. Conventional
         b. Polaroid
         c. Infrared
      2. Movies
         a. Conventional
         b. High-speed
         c. Time lapse
      3. Videotape
II. *Dimensional*
   A. Rulers/scales
   B. Micrometers
   C. Vernier calipers
   D. Dial indicators
   E. Laser
   F. Feeler gages
   G. Hole gages
   H. Gage blocks
   I. Height gage
   J. Comparator
   K. Surface indicator (for contour and microfinish)
   L. Interferometer
   M. Microscope (with reticule eyepiece).
III. *Structural properties*
   A. Destructive
      1. Tensile testing (ASTM A-370 and E-6)
      2. Impact (ASTM E-23 and A-370)
      3. Fatigue (ASTM E-206)
         a. Servohydraulic, closed loop
         b. Krause tension-compression machine
      4. Fracture toughness (ASTM E-399)
         a. Compact tension
         b. Cantilever beam

        c.   Double cantilever
        d.   Precracked charpy
     5.   Creep testing
  B. Nondestructive
     1.   Hardness
        a.   Brinell (ASTM E-10)
        b.   Rockwell (ASTM E-18)
     2.   Microhardness (ASTM E-384)

IV. *Internal Structure*
  A. Destructive
     1.   Metallography (ASTM E-7)
        a.   Purposes
           (1)   Identification of phases present
           (2)   Case depth, plating thickness (ASTM B-487)
           (3)   Cleanliness (ASTM E-45)
           (4)   Grain size (ASTM E-112)
     2.   Macroetching (ASTM E-340)
        a.   Surface flaws
        b.   Flow lines
        c.   Dendritic solidification
  B. Nondestructive (NDT)
     1.   Radiographic (x-ray) (ASTM E-94)
     2.   Dye penetrant (ASTM E-165)
     3.   Magnetic particle (ASTM E-109)
     4.   Ultrasonic (ASTM E-114)
     5.   Acoustic emission

V. *Stress and Strain*
  A. Direct
     1.   Strain gaging (ASTM E-251)
     2.   Brittle lacquer
     3.   Extensometers
     4.   Stress-strain recording
        a.   Brush recorder
        b.   Magnetic tape
        c.   Light-beam oscillograph
        d.   X-Y records
  B. Indirect
     1.   Photoelasticity
     2.   Finite element analysis
     3.   Computer modeling

VI. *Chemical*
  A. Wet chemistry
  B. Spectrographic
     1.   Optical emission
     2.   X-ray spectrometers
     3.   Wavelength dispersive (WD) x-ray spectrometers
     4.   Energy dispersive (EDAX) x-ray spectrometers
     5.   Infrared Fourier transformer (IRFT) spectrometers
     6.   X-ray powder diffractometer
     7.   Mass spectroscopy
     8.   Electron spectroscopy
     9.   Auger spectroscopy
    10.   X-ray diffraction

       C. pH meter
       D. Chromatography
       E. Orsat analysis
       F. Atomic absorption
       G. Gas chromatograph
VII. *Force and pressure*
       A. Precision balance
       B. Electronic load cell
       C. Instrumented load bars and rings
       D. Proving rings
       E. Spring scale
       F. Pressure transducer
       G. Pressure gages
VIII. *Temperature*
       A. Thermometer
       B. Thermocouples
       C. Thermistor
       D. Optical pyrometer
       E. Tempil sticks
       F. Contact pyrometer
       G. Temperature dots
       H. Liquid crystals
IX. *Voltage and current*
       A. Precision galvanometer
       B. Standard cell
       C. Meters
       D. Oscilloscope
       E. X-Y recorder
       F. Light-beam oscillograph
       G. Amprobe
       H. Potentiometers
       I. Current transformers
X. *Time-related*
       A. Stopwatch
       B. Electronic stroboscope
       C. Oscilloscope
       D. Accelerometer
       E. X-Y recorder
       F. Frequency counter
       G. Movies/videotapes
XI. *Corrosion* (ASTM G-15)
       A. Weight loss (ASTM G-1)
       B. Intergranular attack (ASTM A-262)
       C. Pitting evaluation (ASTM G-16)
       D. Polarization (ASTM G-5)
       E. Stress corrosion
       F. Corrosion-fatigue
XII. *Support facilities*
       A. Machine shop
       B. Hoist (lift)
       C. Computer
       D. Darkroom

E. Library
F. Conference room
G. Heat-treating equipment

V. SELECTED CASE STUDIES

Following are cases involving the use of the services of an independent laboratory to solve quality problems and highlighting the methodology and equipment described earlier.

A. Diesel Engine Connecting-Rod Bearing Analysis

A major railroad experienced failure of diesel engine connecting rod bearings
when using replacement bearings. The bearings were analyzed and compared
to original-equipment bearings and found to be similar in chemistry, microstructure, and mechanical properties. Large differences were found in the
thickness of the leaded-tin-bronze overlay, which was shown to be related to
the variation in the performance of the bearings. The manufacturer producing
the bearings that failed prematurely failed to control the thickness of the
leaded-tin-bronze layer. In the case of the overlays that were too thick, the
high-intensity cyclic compressive stresses induced by the firing pressures
created shear stresses at a depth close to the bronze-steel boundary, which
generated fatigue cracks, ultimately causing a surface deterioration by spall-
ing, in less than 24 months. Control of the bronze thickness to limit the maximum cyclic shear stresses induced during operation made it possible to meet
the 30-month design limit.

B. Light Pole Failure

A 40-ft light pole that had been installed only 5 weeks earlier blew down in
heavy winds onto an automobile, crushing the roof. Inspection of the remaining light poles indicated that all had fatigue cracks at the junction between a
fillet weld joining the 40-ft-high square steel tubing into the base plate. An
analysis of the welding procedure, the tubing, and the base plate indicated
that all met the design specifications and all were acceptable by commercial
standards. The analysis showed that the design was inadequate for the cross
section of tubing used, the height, the weight and area of the luminary on
top, and the wind conditions in the area in which the poles were installed. A
design modification has been employed successfully as of the present time.

C. Press Bearings

A major manufacturer of large mechanical presses experienced costly warranty
claims due to the necessity for periodic replacement of the main and pitman
bearings in a 4000-ton press used to make automotive parts. The short life
of the bearings and journals was investigated by use of the scanning electron
microscope (SEM) and metallography, together with a complete analysis of the
materials, speed and loading factors, and lubrication practice. The SEM indicated a scoring-type destruction of the bearing surfaces, and metallographic
analysis of foreign particles found embedded in the bearings indicated their
source. The problem was found to be caused by foreign particles, generated

by fatigue cracks in the press structure, working their way into the bearings and scoring the surfaces. The bearing materials used were found to be satis factory, as were the design criteria used for the bearings themselves. A reconstruction of the press structure, followed by additional lubrication, has been shown to provide satisfactory performance.

D. Hospital Equipment

Equipment used for dispensing medication slowly over a period of several hours was found to have dispensed the entire contents of 250 milliliters of medication in less than an hour. An investigation of the equipment and possible misuse indicated the cause for this incident. The cause was the combination of three malfunctions, each of which had an extremely low probability of incidence, occurring at the same time, coupled with the failure of the hospital personnel responsible to detect the failure in time. Whereas the problem was analyzed after it had occurred, a methodical analysis during the development stage would have predicted the incident. The results of the investigation were design modifications that will prevent the recurrence of a similar incident, and improved operating procedures that will prevent it with existing units.

E. Parts Bin Safety Audit

An audit was performed on an automatic parts bin controlled by an operator sitting outside at a console. The original design of the parts bin did not allow for the possibility of a safety feature should the operator climb into the cabinet to clear a jam. The parts bin had the feature of restarting automatically once a jam was cleared, in which case it would proceed forward, unimpeded, possibly trapping the maintenance person inside if the power were not shut off in advance. Warning signs were designed to advise of proper safety precautions prior to maintenance. Additionally, a safety feature was recommended which would safeguard a person who might have disregarded the warnings.

VI. PREVENTION OF FAILURES

As described, independent laboratories can provide many services beyond the capabilities of the typical manufacturing firm. Generally, there are two occasions when a manufacturer should seek the services of an independent laboratory to assist with a quality problem: when an operating product line has experienced failures, and when concerns arise during the design/development or manufacturing stage which are beyond the expertise of the company. In either case, the laboratory can help provide a safer, more reliable, or more durable product, often at lower cost.

Whereas the preceding portion of the chapter has stressed the remedial aspects, there are a host of services that can be provided during the product development stages which will prevent the need for remedial action. For example, the lab can provide expert assistance with material selection to meet the design objectives of strength, corrosion resistance, wear resistance, and cost.

Overall, the expertise of the staff may be directed toward new products being designed and developed to provide an independent, thorough, methodical analysis, completely free of bias. In this way, the safety and reliability of the system may be predicted in advance, based on a study of the individual parts and their interrelationships, and problems may be solved before there are legal or warranty claims. But if the manufacturer did not have the foresight to consult with an independent lab before the product was put on the market and problems do develop in use, the lab may use the methods discussed to solve the problems in the quickest, least costly fashion.

The question "What will it cost?" is determined by several factors: equipment used, number of tests run, time spent, and so on. The cost of having nonroutine testing or analysis done by an outside lab is usually much less than the cost of setting up the equipment for one-time use. The lab's cost for specialized test equipment is spread out over many hours of use over the life of the equipment. The same thing is true of the trained personnel. The lab has people already adept at the test procedures, which obviously is more efficient than taking people away from their duties to learn a procedure to be used only a few times. The message here is that independent consulting firms have the personnel, the expertise, and the equipment ready to solve almost any quality problem more efficiently, quickly, and objectively than can be done in-house.

REFERENCES

1. J. M. Juran, *Quality Control Handbook*, 3rd ed., McGraw-Hill, New York, 1974.
2. D. Krashes, "Seeking the Quality Minded Laboratory," *Quality*, December 1980.
3. American Society for Metals, *Metal Progress Testing and Inspection Buyers Guide and Directory*, 2nd ed., ASM, Metals Park, Ohio, 1981.
4. American Society for Metals, *Metals Handbook*, 3rd ed., Vol. 10, ASM, ASM, Metals Park, Ohio.

33

ELECTRICAL PRODUCT DESIGN

RICHARD Y. MOSS

Hewlett-Packard Company
Palo Alto, California

I. INTRODUCTION

During the design of a new electronic product, the highest visibility is usually accorded to the obvious parameters of the product, such as size, price, or advances in the state of the art. Yet it is during this design period that the quality and reliability of the product are determined, and it is those characteristics which can, in the end, make or break it.

Analysis of the successes and failures of a variety of electronic products has led to two important observations:

1. About three-fourths of all the warranty repairs to the electronic products studied involved the replacement of electrical parts. Finding the causes and cures of these component failures is therefore the key to achieving major improvements in reliability.
2. Excessive failure rates in electronics are most often caused by a combination of inadequate design margins, excessive stress on components and materials, unnecessarily high component counts, and poorly controlled manufacturing processes.

High quality and reliability must be designed into a product from the start. It is never too early in the design cycle to begin improving the quality and reliability of the prospective product.

II. INVESTIGATION PHASE

The design of a new electronic product is an evolutionary process, which can be divided into two phases (Fig. 1). The first of these is called the investigation phase, during which a new product idea is studied for technical and market feasibility. Product specifications, development cost estimates, and schedule proposals are generated, and this almost always entails some development and testing of critical new circuits or of a new fabrication process. Two activities take place which have a significant bearing on the product's eventual reliability:

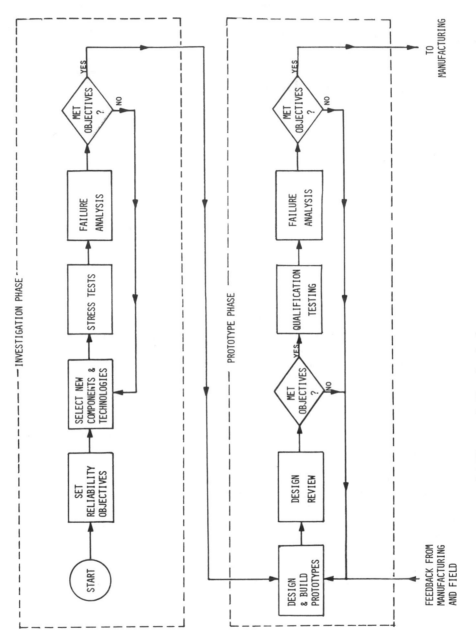

FIGURE 1   Product reliability evolution in design.

1. Setting of quality and reliability objectives
2. Selection and testing of new technologies and processes

A. Setting Objectives

The process of setting performance objectives for a new product exemplifies
the essence of the design engineering process: trying to find the optimum
trade-off between conflicting requirements in a rapidly changing technological
environment. Objectives need to be set in several areas: electrical and mechanical specifications, manufacturing cost, quality, and reliability. To be
effective, these objectives must be challenging but believable, and must be
objectively measurable. The types of quality and reliability objectives that
have been successfully used in electronic design projects fall into five general
classifications; of course, not all of them are necessarily applicable to any one
project.

Legal Requirements

The electrical design is obviously affected by safety (shock hazard) and electromagnetic compatibility (EMC) considerations, which are discussed in more
detail in the section on packaging. In addition, circuits that operate at high
voltages can generate ozone or x-rays which are harmful; high current or
high power circuits can become hot enough to cause a fire if they are not
properly protected, and an electronic product that fails at a critical moment
(particularly in medical electronics or process control) can result in a product
liability lawsuit which will be expensive and damaging to defend, even if the
defense is successful. Management's responsibility here is to state and enforce a clear policy that no product may be released to manufacturing or delivered to a user which is known to contain a preventable safety hazard or
which has not been thoroughly tested to verify that it is free of discoverable
hazards. One possible method of discovering potential problems is to do a
potential problem analysis of the foreseeable consequences of a failure or misapplication, and then attempt to design the product to be safe even under
those conditions [1]. Experience has shown that reducing the failure rate of
a product tends to reduce the total cost of liability by about the same percentage, so that the return on the extra engineering investment can be quite
large (see Chapter 13).

Reliability

High reliability, like any other performance feature, results when a challenging objective is set and met. One measure that is commonly used to specify
reliability is mean time between failures (MTBF), or its reciprocal, average
failure rate $\lambda(t)$. What is puzzling is that although many managers are familiar
with the bathtub curve (Fig. 2), which clearly shows that failure rate is a
variable with age, they fail to recognize that MTBF is also a variable, not a
constant. Thus if an attempt is made to measure the MTBF of a new design
using a short test duration, a pessimistic value corresponding to the infant
mortality region of the bathtub curve will be obtained. A better practice is
to specify the reliability, or probability of survival without failure of the product for a specified period of time and under specified conditions. Now it is
not possible to "play games" with the results by making the test longer or
shorter to influence the outcome. A still better practice is to keep an accurate

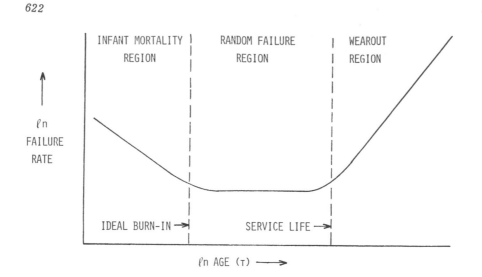

FIGURE 2   Failure-rate bathtub curve.

record of the actual times to failure as testing progresses, and then fit these
to a mathematical or statistical model [2]. This model can be used to expose
"infant mortality" or wear-out behavior in the product and hence to find the
causes of failure, as well as to predict more accurately the expected failure
costs and support needed.

Service Life

A second quantity which is often overlooked in specifying the life characteristics of an electronic product is the service life, that is, the useful life expectancy of the product before wear-out makes it uneconomical to repair and
maintain. While the marketing life of a particular design may be only a few
years due to rapid technological change, it is not unusual for the customer
to expect a service life of 10 to 20 years from a product. Designers of solid-
state electronics are often unaware that the components they use have wear-
out failure mechanisms and hence limited life expectancies. These wear-out
mechanisms must be eliminated or at least minimized wherever encountered, or
the components made easily replaceable where there is no alternative. (Light
bulbs are an example of a component with a rather short life, which are made
easily replaceable as a compensation.)

State of the Art

A popular rule of thumb in electronics is that it takes 5 years to develop a
complex fabrication process, such as those used in integrated circuits manufacturing, to the point that it is well understood and is producing the optimum
quality and reliability. Unfortunately, designers are not willing to wait that
long before starting to use a new technology, and in fact if it were not widely
used before that, the pressure to improve would be less and the mature state
would probably take even longer to achieve. At the other extreme, using an
obsolete process can increase costs as well as producing poor quality and reliability, so sticking to old processes is not the solution either. The optimum
strategy seems to be to take a calculated risk, where as much data as possible

is obtained by stress testing and failure analysis, the catastrophic problems solved, and a plan for longer-term improvements relentlessly pursued. It is obviously the job of management to be sure this happens.

Quality Costs

These are among the most effective kinds of objectives, since they are readily measurable and are related to other management objectives, such as expense control and profits. Ideally, an accounting system should be set up to collect all the quality costs, those related to appraisal and prevention, as well as failure and corrective action costs. If total quality costs cannot be determined, warranty cost as a percent of sales is a useful measure, as long as it is realized that this one item is only about 10 to 20% of the total quality cost. This measure has the advantage (or disadvantage) that it is the product of failure rate and repair cost, so some managers prefer to track each factor separately. In any case, it is reasonable to set a goal of 2:1 or 3:1 improvement on a new product, compared to previous levels. (This corresponds to 25 to 35% per year improvement, for a typical product life cycle of 3 to 5 years.) The first time that total quality costs are computed, they usually come as a shock to management, since it is not unusual to discover that they total 20 to 25% of the sales dollar in a company that thinks that their quality is pretty good, and where the obvious costs such as warranty and scrap total less than 5% of sales [3]. When it is further realized that from 25 to 50% of the payroll, facilities, and inventory are contributing to the cost of quality because they are employed in redesign, retest, troubleshooting, touchup and rework, rescheduling, servicing, and generally producing and fixing defects, it is easy to realize what huge gains in productivity and profit can be made by improving the quality and reliability of the goods and services provided. It is the responsibility of management to determine and control the total cost of quality, not just the "tip of the iceberg" items.

B. Technology Selection

Performance is normally a primary criterion for selecting a new technology or process. There are generally several alternatives, each with a different combination of performance, cost, and reliability attributes. A good strategy is first to eliminate the unreliable choices by stress testing and failure analysis, and then decide between the others, if more than one survives, on the basis of cost and performance. Usually, a new technology or process is not totally new, but rather evolves from the existing ones, so that something is known about the weaknesses and failure mechanisms to look for, and there will be a previous level of performance to compare to. An obvious but useful bit of advice is to select the component or technology which is least susceptible to the stresses that are expected in the product's defined environment; for example, it would not be smart to select a temperature-sensitive part to be used in a product aimed at wide-temperature-range applications. It is also worthwhile to remember that if the product is going to be manufactured for 3 to 5 years and have a service life of 10 years, the components used in it will have to be obtainable for the next 15 years. That means that the newest technologies, which have not yet been proven successful or promising enough to attract competing suppliers, and old technologies that are no longer competitive, should be minimized since they represent too big a risk in terms of future availability.

In the case of electronic components for general-purpose use, there are usually a bewildering array of alternatives, from which every designer will make a different choice. Standardization is the key to combating this, and one successful way to implement it is to set up panels or "sounding boards" consisting of designers, materials engineers, and reliability engineers to select and designate preferred parts for new designs. An additional benefit of standardization will be savings in both manufacturing and service inventories, better prices due to the higher volumes of the preferred parts, and a greatly enhanced ability to monitor the quality history of each part and each supplier because there are fewer to track.

C. Stress Testing

Stress testing *all* new component and technology types is vital to the prevention of disasters. The test philosophy at the Investigation phase should be to "*test to failure*," that is, to design the tests so that the stress level or duration is increased in predetermined steps until *multiple* failures occur and a *pattern* of failures is established. In the world of the reliability engineer, failures are information, and "testing for success" is a waste of time because no failures means no information. Although much can be learned from even a single failure, much more can be gained from the discovery of a repeatable pattern of failures. Even though the failures seem to occur randomly in time, nearly all have nonrandom causes which can be discovered and designed out.

Virtually all failure mechanisms are accelerated by increased stresses, which can be grouped into four classifications: electrical, thermal, chemical, and mechanical. Table 1 lists some examples of these four types, the most common failure mechanisms they activate, and some component types frequently affected. The most common electrical stresses are voltage and current. The product of the two is, of course, power which results in heat, but even by themselves these two can do quite a bit of damage. The most common voltage-induced failure is breakdown, either by exceeding the dielectric strength of an insulator or by avalanching a reverse-biased semiconductor junction. Heat tends to increase the susceptibility of most devices to voltage breakdown, and unless current is limited, damage or degradation is virtually certain. The source of the damaging voltage may be internal, such as a circuit operating too close to its specified maximum, or may be externally generated by ESD, surges, or operator error. A thin dielectric, such as the oxide layer in an integrated circuit, can be fatally damaged in less than a microsecond, so protection circuits must be capable of very fast response. There are several current-activated failure mechanisms, and again all of them are strongly accelerated by temperature. Electromigration is particularly insidious, since it is like the slow erosion of a riverbank by the rapid flow of water, and the longer the erosion continues, the weaker it becomes, so the failure rate has the "old-age wear-out" shape with time. Thin films such as are used to make the interconnections in state-of-the-art large-scale integrated circuits are particularly prone to electromigration, and it is becoming one of the most serious limitations to very large scale integrated circuit (VLSIC) technology. Current hogging has been around for a long time, but has become a more serious concern as switching power supplies have come into vogue. In this failure mode, the entire junction area does not switch on (or off) at once, but rather the current concentrates in a small part of the junction, leading to overheating of that small area, further concentration of the current in the hot spot, and so on, until failure results.

TABLE 1

Stress Type		Failure Mechanism	Component Type
Electrical	Voltage	Dielectric breakdown	Capacitor, high voltage insulation, MOS device
		Avalanche breakdown	Semiconductor junction
	Current	Electromigration, fusing	Thin films, integrated circuits
		Current hogging	Switching semiconductors
Thermal	Heat	Chemical reaction	Battery, electrolytic capacitor
		Ionic contamination	Semiconductor devices
		Intermetallic growth	Interconnections
Chemical	Moisture	Corrosion, dendrites	Thin films, plating
		Ionic contamination	Nonhermetic semiconductors
		Leakage resistance	High impedance and high voltage circuits
Mechanical	Temperature cycles	Differential expansion	Seals, power circuits, polymer encapsulation
		Condensation	Cavity packages
	Shock and vibration	Fatigue	Interconnections
		Loosening, movement	Mountings, adjustments
		Conducting particles	Cavity packages

Heat is the enemy of reliability. Chemists have long known that chemical reactions speed up exponentially with temperature, so electrical components that depend on chemical action, such as batteries or electrolytic capacitors, are greatly affected by temperature. Electronic designers are not always so aware, however, that elevated temperatures greatly increase failures due to increased leakage currents caused by increased mobility of ionic contaminants, and also can promote the growth of intermetallic compounds such as the famous "purple plague," which is a gold-aluminum compound which can cause failures inside a transistor or integrated circuit package. Finally, heat tends to accelerate most of the other failure mechanisms listed in Table 1, as we shall see as each is discussed. Consequently, elevated temperature is nearly always a component of accelerated stress testing, and is a major contributor to field failures of electronics.

Chemical stress, particularly when the chemicals are dissolved and transported by moisture, is a serious threat to reliability because the failure mechanisms are of the irreversible, old-age wear-out variety. Corrosion and growth of metal "whiskers" (dendrites) is a major reliability problem in severely contaminated environments such as around petroleum refineries, paper and wood pulp processing, close to salt water, or even just in a large metropolitan area. Copper, silver, and aluminum all corrode rapidly when exposed to more than a few parts per billion of chlorine or sulfur, especially if moisture and bias voltages are also present. Gold plating of connections and contacts has been the traditional answer, but gold is expensive and not effective in really severe environments; corrosion can occur through a tiny pore or scratch, or around the edge of the gold plating. Currently, tin-to-tin interconnection systems are being studied, and the results look promising in even the most severe environments, provided that the contact pressure is high enough to be essentially gastight at the point of contact. Finally, water containing any impurities at all is an electrical conductor, so leakage paths to high-impedance nodes or from high voltages must be controlled by encapsulation, long leakage paths, use of insulators such as Teflon which tend to inhibit the formation of moisture films, or by controlling humidity. Since there is no such thing as a truly waterproof plastic, polymer encapsulation is not a very good solution where humid environments must be tolerated. Plastic has the advantage that it does not corrode, but the disadvantage that water will diffuse into it over a period of days or weeks, carrying contaminating ions with it to attack the circuits inside.

Mechanical failures do occur in electronic parts, even solid-state ones with no moving parts. The biggest effect of temperature cycles is generally not the peak temperature or its duration, but the expansion and contraction of the various metals and plastics from which the components are constructed. The mismatch of their coefficients of expansion leads to tension, compression, and shear stresses on the interfaces between different materials, and this results in cracked seals, broken wire bonds, and even cracked IC chips. Components encapsulated in polymers, particularly high-power devices which heat and cool repeatedly, tend to fail the most often due to this phenomenon. Another effect of temperature cycles is to cause humidity cycles, particularly as temperature drops below the dew point and moisture condenses on or inside a component. Finally, there are the traditional failure mechanisms induced by shock and vibration: open circuits due to wear or cracking of repeatedly flexed interconnections, loosening and changes of settings of adjustable or critically aligned parts, and momentary short circuits caused by loose conducting particles such as tiny solder balls or wire scraps. Because of their transitory nature, these can be very difficult to find in failure analysis.

Calculating the acceleration factor (the ratio of failure rate at elevated stress to that at normal stress) of elevated-stress tests seems to be an obsession with many designers and reliability engineers, particularly when confronted with the necessity of doing stress tests for the first time. In many cases, calculating this acceleration factor is difficult or impossible, which leads to wildly speculative assumptions. If a calibrated acceleration factor is needed, the established method is to run tests at three or more different stress levels, determine a parameter of the failure distribution such as median life at each stress, and then try to model mathematically the behavior of this parameter versus stress. An example of this is shown in Fig. 3, which shows that the acceleration factor of temperature stress on this integrated circuit fits a mathematical model called the Arrhenius relationship, named after a famous Swedish chemist. In this model, median life is an exponential function of absolute temperature. Although it is useful to know that testing at 175°C decreases the median life by a factor of 26 compared to 125°C, the really important result of these tests was to discover that mobile charge migration was the dominant cause of failure, and then to design it out.

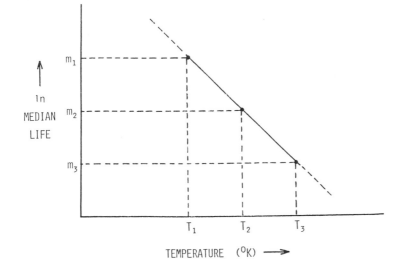

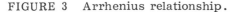

FIGURE 3   Arrhenius relationship.

There are two major pitfalls of elevated stress testing which must be avoided. One is the possibility of raising the stress so high that a new failure mechanism, one not found in real life, occurs because of a change of physical or mechanical state in the material. For example, it is not a valid accelerated test to raise the temperature of a component to the point where part of it, such as a solder connection, melts. The occurrence of this would usually be signaled on the mathematical model by a sudden change of slope. The second pitfall is more subtle, and could occur in the case where a part under test has two important failure mechanisms, one accelerated by the test stress and the other, not. As a result of the stress test, especially the calculations of the acceleration factor, one is tempted to divide the high failure rate (or multiply the low median life) at elevated stress by the acceleration factor and conclude that the reliability is very good, whereas in reality the undiscovered failure mechanism will dominate the statistics at normal stress and will produce an unacceptable poor reliability in the field. An example of this is shown in Fig. 4. There are two ways to avoid this pitfall; (1) by testing with a variety of stresses, particularly using multiple stresses simultaneously, so that you are less likely to overlook a failure mechanism; and (2) by avoiding extrapolations where the acceleration factor is large (e.g., 1000) and a small error in estimating its slope will produce a big error in estimating the reliability. To do this, more conservative testing requires larger sample sizes and longer tests, in order to get multiple failures and accurately establish an acceleration factor.

D. Failure Analysis

Failure analysis is a vital part of the design process, since it provides clues as to the cause of failure, so that the mechanism can be minimized or eliminated. There are two distinct parts to failure analysis: statistical analysis and the physical examination. Statistical analysis can provide important clues to the nature of the failure mechanism, as well as helping to determine the relative seriousness of the problem and the most economical cure. For example, a

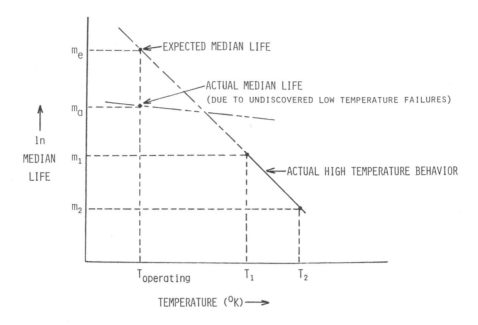

FIGURE 4   Pitfalls to accelerated testing.

failure mechanism that exhibits an "infant mortality" behavior might be most
economically eliminated by subjecting all the parts to an aging process such
as burn-in, while a failure mechanism that exhibits old-age wear-out behavior,
such as corrosion, metal migration, or mechanical fatigue, must be designed
out since aging will only make it worse. The statistical analysis should also
give a measure of the magnitude and cost of the problem, so that major efforts
are mounted only for major problems. Simple statistical techniques such as
graphs, histograms, and process control charts can be taught to workers at
nearly all levels of skill and education, and with the assistance of computer
programs even more complex procedures can be widely used. Teaching which
ones to use, writing the programs or procedures, and teaching their use is
best accomplished by a professional statistician. This fact, which has been
demonstrated by the success of American statisticians such as Joseph R. Juran
and W. Edwards Deming in Japan, will lead to a sharp increase in the demand
for statisticians and statistical training in American industries that wish to
improve their quality and reliability [4].

The physical examination part of a failure analysis provides the objective
evidence with which to identify the mechanism causing the failures, and hence
allows insight into ways to design it out, as well as better tests to detect that
particular type of failure. Most important, it allows the determination of who
is responsible for fixing the problem, not a trivial concern where both the supplier and the user are large, decentralized corporations, and each is pointing
a finger at the other. Physical failure analysis is not always successful in
finding the exact cause of failure, but the batting average is so high that the
problem can nearly always be solved. The failures caused by construction or
processing defects seem to be the ones which are most amenable to analysis in
the laboratory, while failures caused by momentary overstress or changes of
an unspecified parameter are the hardest to isolate. In such cases, the failure
analyst must also be a very good applications engineer, or else work closely

with one. It is also a very good idea in such cases to "prove" the analyst's
hypothesis by intentionally recreating identical failures. A small but suprio
ingly effective failure analysis laboratory can be created with a capital investment of less than $50,000 for equipment at an electronics manufacturing plant
or division operating at a yearly volume of twenty million dollars—or less—,
and can be kept very busy by a company or site electronic manufacturing at a
level of less than $20 million per year. As volume and experience grow, the
facility can be expanded to match the needs, since failure analysis is of immense value to production as well as product development. The analysis of
parts from qualification testing, incoming inspection, production failures, and
field returns is possible, and statistical analysis will help determine the
priorities [5].

III. PROTOTYPE PHASE

The second phase in a new product's evolution is the prototype phase. Often,
there are two or more iterations through this phase, during which the complete
product is designed and packaged, the performance characterized, and the
production documentation, such as schematics, material lists, and test procedures, produced. Events that affect the quality and reliability of the product happen all through the cycle, but for discussion purposes they can be
grouped into three topics: design rules, design review, and qualification
testing.

A. Design Rules

For some reason, design rules often exist for such activities as integrated
circuit or printed circuit layout, but seldom exist for electrical circuit design.
The growth rate in many electronics companies is such that 50% of the designers have less than 5 years' experience and are currently working on their
first design project. Typically, they learned the theory but not the practice
of design in school, and it is a foolish management that allows each of them to
learn the latter by trial and error when the errors are so costly. Design rules
should particularly address those areas where formal engineering education
stops short, such as:

1. *Thermal management*: Just because the vendor's data sheet says that
   the absolute maximum junction temperature of an integrated circuit is
   150°C (302°F) does not mean that it will operate reliably for 10 years
   at that temperature. The failure mechanisms that plague semiconductor
   devices are accelerated by a factor of 500 at 150°C compared to 85°C
   (185°F), so a device with a median life of 1000 years at 85°C will last
   only 2 years at 150°C. Teaching thermal management to the designers
   may well be the single most effective improvement measure that management can employ [6].
2. *Electrical derating and margin*: If a manufacturer of an electronic component is practicing statistical quality control (SQC), the data sheet
   specification limits of the components will probably be set at the 3σ
   points of the population. That means that only about 0.27% of the parts
   are likely to be outside the data sheet limits initally. However, the
   realities of life when employing commercial-grade components are that
   you are lucky if the data sheet limits reflect the 2σ points of the population. That means that about 5% of the parts can be expected to be

outside the data sheet limits initially, to say nothing of the effects of age and stress after the components are installed in the product. A consistent program of derating and extra margin in interpreting data sheet parameters of components will have a large payoff in product quality and reliability, second only to good thermal management.

3. *Regulatory compliance: Safety and EMC*: As mentioned previously, many countries have made compliance with their laws a requirement for selling products there, and the penalties include both fines and imprisonment. The frequency and cost of civil liability are also increasing, so it is essential that management develop and enforce a set of design rules that will assure safe and legal products.

4. *Process compatibility*: One of the quickest routes to disaster is to release a design that cannot be manufactured by the processes available. This is the area that is usually addressed by design rules for integrated circuit masks, printed circuit boards, and mechanical parts. A more subtle type of compatibility problem is the one where an electrical component is chosen that cannot be handled by automated equipment or cannot withstand the stresses of automated handling, soldering, washing, and test. Qualification testing of new components must include exposure to these process stresses, since a part damaged by the manufacturing process can have a tenfold-higher failure rate in the field.

5. *Standardization*: Although management is sometimes afraid that imposing restrictions on component choices may stifle creativity or limit performance, just the reverse is usually true. Most design engineers find that complete freedom really is the worst tyranny, since it takes much longer to evaluate all the choices and increases the risk of a bad choice. A well-managed standardization program can be a boon to engineering creativity and productivity rather than a hindrance. Letting the design engineers participate in the standardization process is a good way to minimize complaints and mistakes.

B. Design Review

It is shocking to see how seldom new product designs are subjected to a serious electrical design review. Perhaps managers are afraid they will bruise the sometimes delicate, sometimes inflated egos of their engineers. More likely, they (the managers) are afraid to expose their own ignorance. Whatever the excuse, it is not sufficient to justify the result. A design review, properly executed, is a valuable tool for assuring the quality and reliability of a new product. There should be a minimum of one design review during each phase of product development, and the following subjects should be examined:

1. *Design rule compliance*: Make sure that there are no misapplications, overstress, incompatible or nonstandard components, or violations of policy regarding safety and regulatory compliance.

2. *Compatability*: Is the design upward, downward, and laterally compatible with other products being developed or currently marketed? In this age of the computer, hardware and software incompatibilities are quickly evident to the customer, and both expensive and embarrassing to the manufacturer.

3. *Performance*: Are the latest reliability, electrical performance, and cost estimates converging on the product's final objectives? It is unwise but common human nature to assume that the problems in the

prototype version of the product will somehow magically disappear when a cleaned-up version is built. They will not, and you will probably gain some new problems as well.

An approach to design review, particularly of computer software, which has been gaining favor in some circles is called peer review. Here engineers of approximately equal organizational rank review each other's designs in an atmosphere presumably less threatening than a management review. There are undoubted benefits of such a system, but it should be a supplement rather than a substitute for a thorough review by a smart manager who knows how to ask the right questions, even if he or she does not know all the answers. As we shall see shortly, the best questions are often asked simply by testing the design.

C. Qualification Testing

Included under this heading are the physical tests made on the prototype hardware, and generally repeated on first production units. Three types of tests are performed: margin tests, life tests, and field trials. As mentioned previously, design margin plays a major role in determining the frequency of failure due to parameter shifts in components, and the margin tests are intended to be a check of that. A design standard should be established which sets the minimum ranges of environmental stress over which every product must operate satisfactorily, and still more severe ranges over which they must survive operation or storage, without damage. These ranges should be wider than in the real world, to provide a margin of error to compensate for the fact that the tests are performed on a very small sample, perhaps only one or two prototypes, and passing such a small number does not give much confidence about the whole population of product yet to be built. For example, available data seem to indicate that even in the most severe tropical climates, the temperature rarely exceeds 35°C (95°F) at 95% relative humidity, but to give reasonable confidence, the design margin should be tested by stressing a few prototypes to 40°C (104°F), 95% relative humidity.

A typical way of documenting a design standard is to organize it into several environmental classes, such as outdoor portable environment, industrial/commercial environment, and controlled environment. Military specification MIL-T-28800 is an example of a document that divides the electronic test equipment environments into seven classes with gradually decreasing severity [7]. Conditions for operating and nonoperating temperature, humidity, vibration, mechanical shock, altitude, and power fluctuations are specified for each class. While conducting these types of tests, it is a good idea to vary electrical parameters such as supply voltages, output loading, input signal levels, and timing to try to discover previously unsuspected interactions or marginal conditions. This same design standard can also set test conditions and performance requirements in the areas of electromagnetic compatibility (EMC), transient and electrostatic discharge (ESD) susceptibility, and electrical leakage currents (safety). The latter requirements will need to be reviewed and updated frequently, as a result of the growing body of international laws governing safety and EMC.

The complete series of tests typically requires several weeks to perform, even if several prototypes are available so that tests can be run in parallel. Specialized facilities are necessary to run the more technically difficult tests such as EMC, but many of the tests that are most valuable from the point of view of impact on quality and reliability can be run using inexpensive sources of heat, cold, moisture, and vibration. A test using an oven, a deep freeze, a humidifier, and a homemade shaker can uncover lots of problems to be designed out, and independent test labs can be employed to do EMC or safety certification tests where acquiring in-house facilities would be too expensive to justify.

Reliability verification tests (RVTs) differ from margin tests in several important ways. First, a much larger sample size and much longer duration are required, to be able to assign reasonable confidence bounds to the results. Sample sizes of 10 to 100 units are typical, as are durations of from 1000 to 4000 hr. Test conditions are tailored to the particular type of product being qualified and generally involve one or two accelerated stresses. A typical RVT will be run at elevated temperature and with maximum duty factor to achieve a high acceleration factor, and with sufficient units and hours to demonstrate the reliability goal with 80 or 90% confidence. There are many statistically designed test plans available to help management select the particular combination of units, duration, and confidence desired. A popular example is the sequential test plan found in MIL-STD-781, where the duration of the test is lengthened or shortened automatically as a function of how much better or worse the product is than the goal [8]. The unwary should be warned, however, that there are two serious limitations to this and similar plans:

1. An exponential life distribution is assumed; that is, it is assumed that the failure rate is constant and that there are no such things as infant mortality or wear-out. Experience tends to show that these are dangerous and unwarranted assumptions, especially in a new design that has not yet been "shaken down."
2. Constant-stress tests, with their beguilingly well-documented acceleration factors, can lead to a fool's paradise in which a serious failure mechanism is completely overlooked because it was not accelerated by the chosen stress.

A variation on these constant-stress life tests that is currently being tried and refined by both military and private industry involves the use of multiple, cyclical stresses. For example, the ambient temperature would be cycled between a low temperature (0°C) (32°F) and a high one (50°C) (122°F) at 1- to 4-hr intervals, while the ac power is simultaneously cycled on and off, and short intervals of vibration are occasionally introduced [9]. New products that have been subjected to 10,000 or more unit-hours of such testing and the resulting pattern failures designed out have enjoyed warranty failure rates dramatically less than those of similar products which had not been so tested, even when the comparison products were "mature" designs with several years of manufacturing history. Two key points have emerged from testing to date: (1) that the value of the testing is lost unless the pattern failures are designed out (so the earlier in the design cycle it is begun, the better); and (2) that temperature cycling below room temperature is at least as important as cycling above room temperature. There are several possible reasons for this, but the increase of humidity as the test chamber air is cooled is certainly a major factor—in fact, if the dew point is reached and moisture condenses on the product, problems will almost certainly be found in a new design.

Field trials are the third way in which a new product can be evaluated. In a large corporation, it may be possible to conduct the field trial inside, using the next bench or the next department as the test site. This is most successful when the new product is in final form, so that it is safe to use and the user need not be more sophisticated or better trained than the intended customer. Problems with the human interface, documentation, and abuse resistance of the product are often uncovered in this type of trial.

The design rules, design reviews, and qualification testing which are employed during the prototype phase of the design cycle are all vital to achieving a reliable product, but they are rarely enough. There are just too many degrees of freedom in a complex electronic product to be sure of getting it exactly right on the first try. The design nearly always continues to evolve after it is released to manufacturing, and management needs to assure that the evolution is toward a more reliable product, not just one that is cheaper to manufacture.

IV. MANUFACTURING PHASE

A. Transfer of Knowledge

The first problem to be solved is the transfer of knowledge from development engineering to production engineering. Good documentation is vital, but not all the important knowledge in the designers' heads is going to get put on paper, much less be absorbed by production. One attempted solution has been to transfer one or more design engineers to production together with the new design, as a sort of human repository of undocumented knowledge. An obvious problem with this approach is that although the designer is knowledgable about the design, he or she may not be similarly expert in the manufacturing process, and may even feel that this assignment is a dangerous detour in his or her career path. Another approach has been to assign a production engineer to the product at the start of the prototype phase, to absorb all that he or she can about the design, to see that it is thoroughly documented, and to try to steer the design so that "manufacturability" and compatibility with current manufacturing processes is assured. With today's fast-changing technology, the problem is that the manufacturing process is also evolving, and the designers find themselves trying to hit a moving target.

B. Process Control

A new buzzword in manufacturing management jargon is "concurrent design," in which a new product design is supposed to evolve in parallel with a new process design. It seems to me that this approach will be most successful where computer-aided design (CAD) is employed extensively, because every time the process is changed, the design rules must also change, and hence a complete design review and some changes may be needed. When it comes to producing a high-quality, high-reliability product, there is no substitute for a mature process that is under control and which has well-tested and documented design rules [10]. This is also the kind of process that can be automated successfully; automating a "flakey" design or process will only produce flakey products faster.

C. Stress Testing

Just as margin testing, stress testing, and failure analysis were vital to the design phases, the same kinds of testing on the larger sample sizes available in production can lead to further design improvements. Quality can be improved by performance testing of components, subassemblies, and finished

product, and reliability can be improved by incorporating stress into production tests to weed out weak but functioning parts and patterns of failure which
can be designed out. Multiple, cyclical stresses have been found to be more
effective than single or constant stresses, so production heat runs with temperature, power, and sometimes vibration cycles have evolved [11]. In an
experiment to demonstrate the greater effectiveness of cyclical stresses, 1300
production units of a tabletop digital computer were randomly divided into two
groups as they were produced, and their serial numbers recorded. One group
(A) of 650 was subjected to 48 hr of simultaneous temperature and power cycling, with temperature alternating between 0°C (32°F) and 40°C (104°F) once
every hour, and with the 120-V ac power turned off for 30 sec once each hour.
The units ran a digital self-test continuously, and results were monitored by
a computer system. The second group (B) of 650 was allowed to remain at
room temperature for 48 hr but was subjected to the same power cycling and
computer-monitored self-test as group A.

The results were dramatically different for the two groups. Of those in
group B (which ran at room temperature), 24% recorded some kind of failure
during the 48-hr heat run, whereas 55% of those in group A (which were temperature cycled) had a failure. All 1300 units were then thoroughly retested,
repaired or readjusted as needed, and shipped to users without any attempt
to segregate group A or B units. Failures or complaints from users were recorded as received through normal field service channels for the first 90 days
of use. Here group A had a much lower failure rate, about 12%, compared to
group B's 19%. Since the cost of a field service call is usually more than 20
times that of a product line repair on this type of product, the 7% improvement
in field failures repaid the 31% increase in factory repairs several times over,
including the cost and energy consumption of the temperature cycling facility.
Moreover, the increased level of factory repairs resulted in a study of the
causes, and as a pattern of failure emerged from the data, steps were taken
to design out the most frequent modes. Because design and production engineers could get trustworthy data and examine the failed units themselves,
they were able to take action much more quickly than when the failure reports
dribbled in from scattered and widely differing field sites. As these patterns
of failure are designed out of the product and process, both the factory and
field failure rates will improve further.

D. Design Control

It is important to stress that design control be maintained in production and
that the data from production and the user be fed back to the designers. One
reason is to try to avoid creating new problems with changes, but a more important one is to help the designers improve their design rules and practices.
A closed-loop system can produce a much more accurate result than an open-
loop one, whether it is an electronic system or a human system.

V. CONCLUSION

Reliability is not something that is added by inspection or a burn-in step in
manufacturing, or by requiring it in a specification, or by hiring reliability
engineers for the quality department. It is designed in, a little at a time, as
each part or process is chosen and incorporated into the design. Therefore,
every person who makes a design decision has a hand in determining that

design's reliability. Training and feedback are the tools to achieve improved reliability—training appropriate to each level in the organization, so that each person knows how to contribute, and feedback so that they can see the effects of their actions. Testing begun early in development and continued through manufacturing, with cyclical stresses that condense years into weeks or even days, provides the signals for the feedback loops. A failure should never be ignored or written off as random; it may occur at a random time or place, but it rarely has a random cause. Find the cause and you will probably be able to design it out.

The way to make sure that a reliable product evolves is for top management to get involved in setting reliability objectives, measuring the progress toward them, and making sure that everyone understands that they are the number 1 priority. The more actively management is involved and the more deeply it is committed, the better the results will be. In 1982, a Japanese-American joint venture company won the Deming prize, Japan's highest honor in the field of statistical quality control. Five years earlier, this same joint venture's quality and reliability were average by U.S. standards, and probably worse than average by Japanese standards. Every employee worked hard to make this improvement happen, but the unanimous opinion is that it happened because the company's president became the leader and champion of the effort.

REFERENCES

1. C. H. Kepner and B. B. Tregoe, *The Rational Manager*, McGraw-Hill, New York, 1955.
2. R. Y. Moss, "Modelling Variable Hazard Rate Life Data," *Proceedings, 28th Electronic Components Conference*, April 24—26, 1978, IEEE 78CH1349-O CHMT, pp. 16—22.
3. P. B. Crosby, *Quality Is Free*, McGraw-Hill, New York, 1979.
4. W. E. Deming, *On the Management of Statistical Techniques for Quality and Productivity*, 1981.
5. *Microcircuit Failure Analysis Techniques Procedural Guide*, Reliability Analysis Center RADC/RBRAC, 1981.
6. G. N. Morrison et al., *RADC Thermal Guide for Reliability Engineers*, RADC-TR-82-172, Hughes Aircraft Company, Culver City, Calif., June 1982.
7. MIL-T-28800, *Military Specification—General Specification for Test Equipment for Use with Electrical and Electronic Equipment*, Naval Electronic Systems Command.
8. MIL-STD-781, *Military Specification—Reliability Tests: Exponential Distribution*, Naval Air Systems Command.
9. R. A. Bailey and R. A. Gilbert, "Strife Testing," *Quality*, November 1982, pp. 53—55.
10. E. R. Ott, *Process Quality Control*, McGraw-Hill, New York, 1975.
11. A. E. Saari, R. E. Schafer, and S. J. VanDenBerg, *Stress Screening of Electronic Hardware*, RADC TR-82-87, Hughes Aircraft Company, Culver City, Calif., May 1982.

34

ELECTRICAL COMPONENTS

QUALITY ASSURANCE GROUP
ELECTRONICS DIVISION

Allen-Bradley Company
Milwaukee, Wisconsin

I. INTRODUCTION

The quality program presently in use at the Electronics Division of the Allen-Bradley Company is described in this chapter. Over the years the program has been successful in enabling the delivery of quality and high-reliability products to customers and although it is not yet fully in place, the company is now in the process of installing the next-generation system. Called the Total Quality Management System (TQMS), it is more advanced and uses the latest quality management techniques tailored specifically to product lines.

Quality and reliability assurance policy and procedure for the Electronics Division of Allen-Bradley Company are set forth in a manual available to customers, updated if contractually specified. Requirements beyond the manual are subject to negotiation. The manual itself is audited by the quality and reliability assurance manager, who must approve any revisions.

The manual has two purposes. One is to provide guidelines for an efficient, economical system to assure that quality and reliability requirements of the division's products are satisfied. The second is to provide a uniform means for inspection and testing to assure product conformity to drawings, specifications, standards, and/or contractual agreements. Included are quality organization, process flow, configuration change control, control of purchased material and of work in process, final test control, indication of inspection status, control of measuring equipment, nonconforming material control, and test facilities.

II. INSPECTION AND QUALITY CONTROL

Functional groups responsible for quality and reliability activities include the inspection department and the quality control department. Primary subgroups of the inspection department are new-part inspection, responsible for approval of all dies and tooling and specifying inspection requirements and procedures; the gaging section, responsible for designing, procuring, and maintaining mechanical measurement equipment; receiving inspection, responsible for acceptance purchased parts and material; and floor inspection, responsible for acceptance of parts made in the manufacturing departments.

The quality control department has responsibility for assuring conformity to design specifications and quality standards of all products manufactured in the division. This includes resistor quality control and variable resistor quality control, with quality responsibility in the respective product manufacturing, and finally, the calibration section, responsible for maintaining and calibrating measurement equipment used in the division.

Related functional groups include quality responsibility for microelectronic manufacturing, together with the quality and reliability assurance department and product safety department. The latter are corporate functions whose responsibilities are described in the product assurance policy.

The purpose of the configuration change control function is to assure that design information transmitted to manufacturing and other using activities is adequately controlled. It provides a formal system of controlling the release of engineering documents and changes to previously released documents, detailed in the engineering standards handbook. It also provides for classification and distribution of engineering documents. Quality and reliability assurance review all engineering documents pertaining to performance, reliability, and/or quality before those documents are released.

Control of purchased material establishes a system for purchased materials, parts, and/or devices. The policy provides that all purchased materials be processed through an inspection and/or test section. General inspection and/or test procedures include these elements: sampling tables and instructions for use, disposition of rejected lots of material, instructions on use of measuring equipment where applicable, instructions on use of forms and systems to expedite movement of material, and general quality standards applicable to similar material.

III. INSPECTION AND TEST PROCEDURE

Inspection and/or test procedures for each material, part, or device specify these elements: measurements of quality characteristics, measuring equipment to be used (where applicable), instructions on special inspection and/or test methods (where applicable), and the latest engineering drawing.

Selection of qualified suppliers requires purchasing department personnel to use the vendor rating reports issued by the inspection department as a consideration in selecting and/or eliminating vendors. Vendor surveys may also be a consideration.

Control of work in process establishes a system for acceptable manufactured parts and devices. All lots of manufactured material must be approved by quality control personnel before the lot can be moved from the manufacturing department that performed work on the material, unless inspection functions have been delegated to the manufacturing departments. General inspection procedures include the same elements outlined above.

Final test control establishes a system to assure that quality and reliability requirements of division products are satisfied before the products are stocked or shipped. All lots of division products must be approved by quality control department personnel before stocking or shipping. All lots must be sampled

per the plan specified in the appropriate policy and procedure or an equivalent sampling plan.

Test procedures for each device specify these elements: quality characteristic to be measured, measuring equipment to be used and instructions on usage
(where applicable), acceptable quality levels (where applicable), latest engineering drawings, and special environmental conditions. The manager of the
affected quality control department coordinates the recording of required test
data and assures that they are in a format acceptable to customer requirements
per contract.

IV. INDICATION OF INSPECTION

Indication of inspection status provides a method of identifying the status of
all products regardless of the degree of completion of the products. All personnel of the inspection department have an identifying punch, and as each
manufacturing operation is completed as specified on the routing card, the
card is punched if the material is acceptable and can be moved to the next
operation. Similarly, all personnel of the inspection department have a stamp
with the employee clock number and name. The stamp is used on the routing
card when all manufacturing operations are completed and the material is acceptable. All electronics quality control personnel have a stamp with the employee clock number as identification, and every accepted lot is stamped after
final inspection and/or test. Control of punches and stamps is the responsibility of the respective control office of the inspection and/or electronics quality control department.

Control of measuring equipment establishes methods to detect and correct
deficiencies in measuring standards, gages, and equipment. Certificates indicating the source and traceability of calibration, data of calibration, calibration results, and by whom certified are maintained for all primary standards.

The inspection department is responsible for assuring calibration of and
maintaining records of all physical size primary standards. The physics and
materials laboratory does the calibration for all electrical primary standards,
and the quality control department of the division for all electrical secondary
standards. They also are responsible for the calibration of all production test
equipment used by the manufacturing departments.

Calibration records for secondary standards, gages, and equipment include
identification number and location, calibration procedures and frequency, last
date of calibration and results, identity of the person performing the calibration, and a description of repairs or adjustments.

All calibration is traceable to the National Bureau of Standards. It is performed in a controlled environment if so specified on the procedure. The interval of calibration is determined by the amount of usage, stability, degree of
accuracy required, and recommendations of the supplier. There are documented calibration procedures for each type of standard, measuring gage,
or equipment. Each gage or piece of equipment is given an identifying number that cannot readily be removed. A sticker specifies the date of the
last and next calibration, and the identity of who calibrates must be attached
to each standard, gage, or equipment. Procedures for recall or pickup when
gages or equipment are due for calibration are maintained. All gages or
equipment must be calibrated after repair or adjustment. Personal gages of
inspection and electronics quality control department personnel are included
in the calibration program.

Nonconforming material control establishes a procedure to prevent unauthorized use of nonconforming material. It provides for handling and disposing of nonconforming material according to a specified policy and procedure. Nonconforming material is segregated from acceptable material to prevent inadvertent or unauthorized use. Segregation is accomplished by clearly marking the material as defective and removing it from the normal production areas.

V. WIDE-RANGING TEST FACILITIES

A wide range of test facilities are available, including analytical, microscopic, metallurgical, and performance testing. These capabilities are not part of the standard quality control procedures, but are available to support investigation or analysis of products, components, or materials.

Analytical facilities provide for many types of testing. Absorption spectrophotometry is used to determine the light-absorption properties of materials by wavelength. Atomic absorption provides rapid quantitative analysis of inorganic elements in solution. Differential thermal analysis measures heat change, identifies temperature of change, and analyzes phase change, such as melting and freezing curves of solids. Gas chromotography is used to separate and identify organic materials volatile enough to vaporize. Infrared spectroscopy identifies organic compounds.

Other analytical tests include optical emission spectrometry for quantitative analysis of impurity or additive concentrations of elements in materials and for semiquantitative survey of elements or quantitative analysis of low concentrations of elements in material. In addition, polarography is used to analyze minor or trace elements by electrochemical decomposition, and thermogravimetric analysis to measure the weight change of materials at different temperatures.

Microscopic analysis facilities include airborne particle concentration analysis, providing dust counts for clean room control; high-temperature microscopy, for examination at temperatures up to 1500°C; light microscopy, including macro- and microphotography, with magnification from 5 to 1500×; metallography and ceramography; microhardness testing; particle size, shape, and surface area analysis; and transmission electron microscopy, with magnification from 1500 to 200,000×.

The facilities in the physics laboratory include a dilameter to determine the coefficient of thermal expansion; an electron backscatter gage to determine plating or coating thickness (from 0.01 to more than 1.0 mil); an electron microprobe, for quantitative analysis of materials to determine chemical element distribution and concentration on a microscopic scale; infrared spectroscopy, to identify organic compounds; interferometry analysis, providing Tolansky optical interferometric measurement of film thickness in the range 50 to 30,000 Å; and nuclear spectroscopy, to measure the energy and intensity of gamma radiation emitted by artificial and natural radioscopes.

Other physical lab testing facilities include Radiflo-NDT, for leak checking of hermetically sealed electronic devices by pressurization with ^{85}Kr radioactive gas; a refractometer, for measurement of the optical index of refraction of solids and liquids; a thermal conductivity device, to measure thermal conductivity coefficient; ultrasonic testing-NDT for pulse-echo ultrasonic beam examination of solids, brazed, or welded materials for voids, cracks, or inhomogeneities; x-ray diffraction to identify inorganic compounds, crystal structures, and crystal orientation; x-ray emission-NDT for quantitative analysis of chemical elements in liquid or solid materials; and x-ray radiography-NDT, for inspection of materials for cracks or voids and inspection of encapsulation or sealed devices for proper assembly or mode of failure.

VI. INSPECTION EXAMPLE

An example of how the test facility and its equipment might be used is the analysis of conductive ink systems. The analytical labs utilize many types of scientific instrumentation to obtain complete chemical and physical characterization of the conductive ink systems used in the manufacture of thick-film networks. One instrument used for this characterization is the x-ray diffractometer. This instrument gives x-ray diffraction patterns that identify and quantify the crystallographic structure of the conductive components and glass matrix of unfired and fired inks. Such identification enables close control of ink chemistry and assures predictable and reproducible conductivity in the finished network.

VII. PROCESS FLOWCHART

The process flowchart (see Fig. 1) illustrates a typical example of the movement of product from purchased parts and raw materials through the inspection service groups, work-in-process inspections, various quality control patrol inspections and the laboratory and quality control service groups inspections, to final inspection and shipping or stocking.

The Electronics Division has learned that its quality and reliability assurance program makes a meaningful difference in the final product as shipped or stocked. It is, for example, generally acknowledged that the hot-molded carbon-composition fixed resistor is one of the most reliable electronic components ever made. In one application, it was reported by a customer that billions of operating hours have been recorded with zero failures in a satellite program. Such high reliability is important not only for military, space, or medical electronics applications, but also for many other industrial applications, where the cost of a failure either in the production line or in the field is too great a risk.

Hard data are provided from failure-rate life-test programs per military specification MIL-R39008B. These data are required to be taken and reported on every 6 months. This procedure is part of Allen-Bradley's own standard requirements. It is not practical to expect a user to duplicate the extensive quality assurance programs invested in by a major electronic component supplier. Instead, users should search out and ask for suppliers who are able to provide that kind of information as proof that the part really is what it is claimed to be.

Possibly the most valuable aspect of this reliability record is that it is not limited to specially selected parts for high-reliability military systems. When the same design, materials, machines, and processes are used to produce both industrial and military designation parts, the industrial users, with usage in the billions of parts, get the same kind of high-reliability performance.

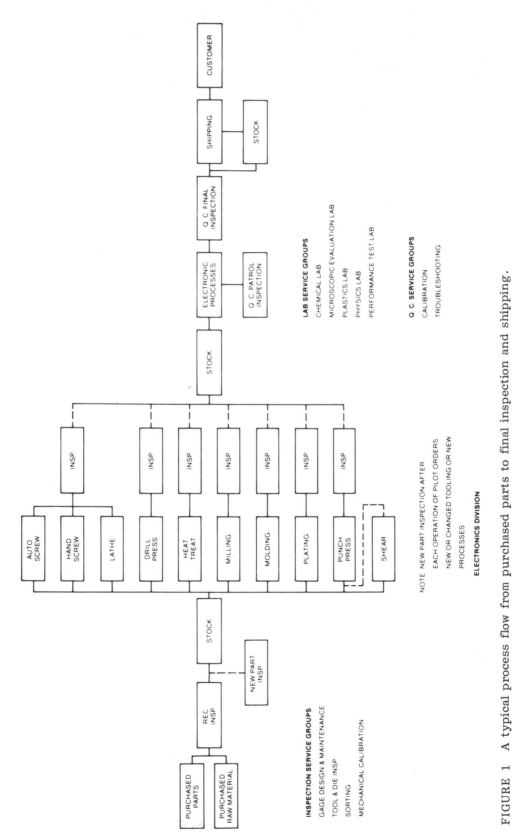

FIGURE 1 A typical process flow from purchased parts to final inspection and shipping.

Increasingly, attention is being focused on reliability for such industrial applications as telecommunications and microcomputer-controlled machines, where the value of the equipment is relatively high compared to that of the parts. With equipment lifetimes of 5, 10, and even 30 years being expected routinely, reliability becomes an even more crucial consideration for equipment designers.

35

ELECTRICAL ASSEMBLIES

DAVID PETTIGREW

Consultant
LaGrange, Illinois

I. INTRODUCTION

This chapter will describe the general concepts required to control the quality
and inherent reliability of electrical/electronic assemblies. An electronic assembly will be defined as an "individual" assembly, as opposed to a system. Examples would be a printed circuit board assembly or a switch. A switch is an
item composed of individual parts which functions as a single device. For
this reason most contractors require that the manufacturer implement an inspection system [1, 2] as opposed to a total quality system [3].

With the use of these primary concepts the reader should be able to establish a good set of ground rules—a foundation on which an effective, efficient,
and economical inspection system can be built. Each individual concept should
be explored for adaptation to an inspection system. The technical aspects
must be planned specifically for each device or homogeneous group of devices.

II. BASIC SUBSYSTEMS

There are, generally, 10 basic subsystems, or concepts, in any inspection
system. These can be expanded to meet individual or specific requirements.
These subsystems are:

1. Review the design requirements
2. Qualify the process
3. Evaluate receiving inspection
4. Evaluate process control
5. Evaluate finished-goods inspection
6. Establish reliability testing
7. Establish product audit
8. Establish systems audit
9. Evaluate quality costs
10. Evaluate total planning goals

This chapter will review and expand primarily on the first six subsystems and their application to the electronic assembly industry.

A. Review Design Requirements

Many electronic assembly companies have found that a formal design review board, composed of members of design engineering, quality control, manufacturing, purchasing, and sales, is of great value in eliminating—or at least reducing—potential problem areas. Other companies are less formal and may use a system that routes new and revised drawings and specifications to various departments for comments prior to release. Manufacturing process flow sheets and other such documents may be reviewed in the office rather than at meetings, with each responsible department signing off on the document prior to formal publication.

In a small shop, one or two people may have the entire responsibility, and little or no formal review will be necessary. In large organizations, certain project groups may want to discuss formally the total design. This type of design review will involve total quality operations, including process capability, cost, and reliability studies.

Following the design review, a preproduction prototype is assembled using hard tooling. This prototype is evaluated and the results are analyzed to determine the ability of the tooling, material, and personnel to meet design requirements.

Design review must concern itself with all aspects of customer satisfaction. The purpose of the design review should be to document procedures required to assemble, test, and inspect all new and/or redesigned assemblies. For those procedures quality control will require the aid of the manufacturing process flow schedule, operation by operation, from start to final assembly. A typical design review is shown in Table 1.

Design review in the electronic assemblies industry will normally require greater emphasis on receiving inspection, as most of the individual piece parts are typically purchased from outside vendors and assembled in the plant. It will be of the utmost importance to assure that only the smallest possible number of defective parts are accepted for stock. The goal is to assure that the proper equipment, technology, and personnel are available for the purpose of proper inspection.

TABLE 1   Design Review Flowchart: Customer Requirements

1. Review and interpret requirements	Sales department Quality control
2. Initial design	Design engineering
3. Design review	Engineering Quality control Manufacturing Purchasing Sales Tool design
4. Finalize design	Approve by all
5. Preproduction run	Analyze and test

B. Qualifying the Process

To properly qualify a process, it is necessary to understand what the process is. To understand the process, it is necessary to document its flow. The process flow document must define what is going to be done, and where it will be done. The best method to accomplish this is to start with an operational flowchart. At the start the idea must be that there will be no defects made. This simply means "doing it right the first time." The goal is to assure that each operation is performed in accordance with predetermined methods and specifications.

During the qualification process it will be desirable to have variables information. Variables inspection provides the most information from the least data, at the lowest overall cost. It is normal to overinspect at the onset of a new or a changed process. This overinspection will provide the additional data necessary to evaluate the process in a more complete manner.

Review the data with the flowchart to determine the real points of control that will be necessary. During the review look for ways to reduce overall costs. The initial qualification is where the price of the item may be determined. Try to eliminate or combine operations. Evaluate control points as the review proceeds and follow up closely on all points in the process. Remember to look for the good as well as the bad. In fact, look more closely at the good. The good indicates that something may be working well and may help in correcting other deficiencies. Perhaps the good is an indication that the proper discrimination is not being used, or there may be an operator who is continually adjusting to make the process work well. Or it may be that a portion of the operation is in fact superior to other portions. In any case investigate the total process to try to find improvements. Check every test and/or measurement for error and try to use different types of equipment in parallel as a test for similar results. Then test the significance of the results.

After the initial run it will be necessary to review the flowchart and sequence of operations for improvements and cost reduction. The flowchart may now be transformed into a formal specification that will not be changed except by formal agreement between responsible parties. When testing and documentation have been completed and necessary changes are implemented, the process should be capable of operating in control and within specifications. A typical qualification will incorporate the items shown in Table 2.

C. Evaluating Receiving Inspection

Normal acceptable quality level (AQL) sampling plans do not readily conform to the intent of receiving inspection in the electronic assembly industry for the following reasons:

Most piece parts will be purchased in a more or less finished condition. That is, the piece parts will be assembled directly into the product with little or no further work or finishing.
The majority of parts received will be purchased in lots or batches and must be dealt with as isolated lots rather than as items in a continuous process.

AQL sampling plans are not designed for isolated lots. MIL-STD-105 defines AQL as "the maximum percent defective (or maximum number of defects per hundred units) that can be considered satisfactory as a process average." (See MIL-STD-105, Appendix I.)

TABLE 2 Process Control: Typical Flowchart

Operation	Control[a]
1. Component preparation	O
2. Assemble stage 1	O
3. Assemble stage 2	O
4. Assemble stage 3	O
5. Assemble stage 4	O
6. Solder boards	O
7. Clean boards	O
8. Clip leads and touch-up	O
9. Preelectrical test	EVM
10. Assemble board in case	O
11. Solder leads to terminal	Ⓞ̲V
12. Seal and pot	O
13. Top off potting	O
14. Clean	O
15. Apply label	O
16. Print	O
17. Final clean	O
18. Visual inspection	O
19. Functional testing	Ⓞ̲VME
20. Ship or stock	O

[a]O, operator control; V, visual inspection;
M, mechanical inspection; E, electrical test;
Ⓞ̲, inspection function.

It does not say anything about individual lots or batches. It is important to remember that AQL plans do not guarantee the consumer (you) any set degree of protection. They do, however, guarantee the producer (your vendor) a good chance of having their product accepted even if it is significantly worse than the given AQL.

A number of sampling plans, including lot tolerance percent defective (LTPD), limiting quality (LQ), Dodge-Romig, and others, exist and can be adjusted to provide nearly any protection level short of zero percent defective. All of these plans require some trade-offs between supplier and purchaser protection and cost. Rather than use MIL-STD-105 just because it is "customary," the proper and appropriate sampling plan should be chosen. Under some conditions, 100% incoming inspection, or in a more recent development, mandatory statistical process control by the supplier, is required.

D. Evaluating Process Control

Quality control—or, more precisely, process control—is "the economic control of a process." Several methods of control must be explored, and the method used will depend primarily on the basic process. There are three basic processes in electronic assembly field.

1. *Machine-dominant processes*: A machine-dominant process is one in which the machine has the capability of running for extended periods with few or no adjustments necessary (a punch press operation, for example). First-article inspection would be the best type of control. A good rule of thumb is to have the process average as close to the nominal size as possible, with the spread not to exceed two-thirds of the specified tolerance. This rule will keep the process within the specifications, provided that the equipment is capable of operating in statistical control. This should have been determined during process capability studies conducted at the time of process qualification.

2. *Operator-dominant processes*: With operator-dominant processes, the control lies, as might be suspected, with the operator. Proper instruction, equipment, and procedures will enable the operator to build or assembly 100% acceptable product. A minimum amount of in-process inspection will be required to assure that procedures are followed and to assure that no outside influence will act on the decision of the operator. The in-process inspector will also assure that the procedures and instructions are correct and up to date.

3. *Material-dominant processes*: In the electronic assemblies industries, materials are primarily piece parts. The control of piece parts is receiving inspection. In some special cases it may become necessary to 100% inspect, or sort, the received parts. This type of sorting should usually be restricted to only one or two characteristics (parameters). These may be inspected automatically, and should be considered only when the state of the art is met or exceeded. Automatic testing is desirable whenever 100% inspection is performed. Hopefully, with good design review this operation was noted and the cost of sorting and rework estimated.

There is no single best system applicable to all processes. All methods must be investigated to produce the most efficient, effective, and economical control of the process. Look especially at the process flowchart for setup operations, high-quality or high-cost operations, and irreversible-type operations. These plus any natural opening in the process, such as part movement between operations and the stocking of subassemblies, are where control may be required.

E. Finished-Goods Review

Finished-goods review in the electronic assemblies industry is usually in the form of 100% functional testing at final inspection. This function may be performed either by production personnel or by quality control inspection personnel. The decision will depend largely on the complexity of the test and the documentation of the test results required. When the test is a simple attribute test or visual inspection, it is usually preferred that it be performed by production personnel. In this way corrective action on defects is usually faster and more palatable. When special documentation and/or complex test equipment is required, the testing is normally accomplished by technical personnel, who may document and analyze the results.

The purpose of final review should be to assure that all previous tests and operations have been performed satisfactorily and that the product will function

per design specifications. Malfunctions must be documented and feedback for
corrective action initiated in the most expedient manner possible. Whenever
practical, in-process inspection or operator inspection results should be part
of final goods review. Documentation of previous inspections and tests will
reduce the amount of time spent in final inspection.

Case Study

In the electronic assemblies industry many defect occurrences may be grouped
into homogeneous categories. For example, one manufacturer found a defect
rate of 11.5% in one family of switches. Upon investigation it was found that
the contacts were slightly loose in the plate holder. The contact was enlarged
in that area and the reject rate immediately rose to 13.2%. An analysis of the
product was conducted and the results analyzed. One type of switch displayed
fewer than 5% defectives. Continuing the investigation showed that one assembler was consistently assembling with fewer than 1% defective for the problem. A more complete investigation was performed with the one assembler who
consistently built good product. Upon watching and talking to that assembler,
it was noted that she was left-handed. While forcing the contacts into the
wiper plate she automatically gave them a clockwise twist, which compensated
for the contact problem. A slight modification of the contact forming tool and
the return of the original-size wiper plate dimensions reduced the defective
rate to less than 2% total. This operation was assumed to be parts dominant,
yet one operator made it an operator-dominant operation. In process control
you must keep all avenues open and assume nothing without facts to back up
your assumption.

F. Reliability Testing

Reliability testing has become a function with increasing importance. We are
all aware of the money-back guarantee. This may be all well and good in some
products; however, there are many items in the electronic assemblies industry
which definitely will not fit into the money-back category. One example would
be the switch that triggers the device used to open a parachute. It would be
extremely difficult to call a repairman to replace this item on the way down.
Anyone using the device would want a switch that is 100% reliable. Guarantees, no matter how good, seem to say: "We know that our product is not as
good as we would like it to be, but buy it anyway. We will repair or replace
any component that fails, at absolutely no charge to you."

Reliability testing conducted with well-planned forethought may devulge a
lot of information about the product or process. It can and will tell you where
to strengthen or redesign integral functions of your product and process.

Reliability testing in the electronic assemblies industry usually consists of
an accelerated-life test of a random sample of the product or its various components until failure. A point that must be considered in this type of test is
the effect of natural laws. If, for example, the assembly has moving parts,
excessive heat or wear generated by friction may occur. These natural phenomenon must be considered and accounted for. Government (MIL) specifications such as MIL-HDBK 217 can be used as a guide. A word of caution:
Most MIL specifications have been very carefully worded; do not try to interpret what they mean. If the meaning is not clear, obtain help either from a
government representative or from your customer.

G. Product Audits

Product audits on most electronic assemblies consist of field failure reports. These reports can be analyzed and evaluated to determine the reason for material returns. This may be a difficult task, as self-evaluation is often biased. But it is imperative that corrective action be taken to reduce returns and to improve the product.

H. Systems Audits

Systems audits are conducted on an informal basis in many organizations. They may consist of a paperwork analysis and may be performed either automatically through data processing, or be performed physically. The type of audit will depend largely on the facilities that the organization incorporates. A formal audit performed by a consulting firm can pay dividends in final product cost reduction. A good, professionally conducted audit should be performed at least once every 3 years. The cost should be offset by the results.

I. Total Planning Goals

Walter A. Shewhart has said: "A phenomenon will be said to be controlled when, through the use of past experience, we can predict, at least within limits, how the phenomenon may be expected to vary in the future. Here it is understood that prediction within limits means that we can state, at least approximately, the probability that the observed phenomenon will fall within the given limits."

The most important aspects of control in the electronic assemblies industry lie in two areas: 1. careful planning and 2. control of piece parts, whether purchased or manufactured. The final quality of your product will depend on how well your organization controls the individual piece parts and the processes used to assemble them.

REFERENCES

1. MIL-I-45208.
2. MIL-HDBK 51.
3. MIL-Q-9858.
4. MIL-STD-105.
5. MIL-HNDBK-217.

36

ELECTRONIC TESTING

JON TURINO

Logical Solutions, Inc.
Campbell, California

I. INTRODUCTION

One of the key elements in any quality program is the element of testing. Testing may be thought of primarily as the method by which we validate the correctness of the assembly operations that precede each testing step. A by-product of the electrical testing process is usually crucial information about where a failure lies in a defective assembly. This fault isolation information allows defective assemblies to be reworked and made into functioning assemblies. Another very valuable output of the testing process, if it is planned for and implemented properly, is definitive information about the nature of the failures that occur in an assembly. This information can be used by the quality organization to affect the assembly operations and thus eliminate recurring failures at their source.

Testing, as used throughout this chapter, refers primarily to electrical testing. Measurement of mechanical, visual, and similar physical parameters is normally thought of as part of the inspection process in the product manufacturing environment. Although inspection is indeed a form of testing, testing in industrial usage almost always refers to electrical (or mechanical) testing of some type. In this chapter we explore the purposes of electrical testing, the levels at which tests are performed, the methods for performing testing at the various levels, and the use of test data in improving product quality. Also covered are the use of quality data to formulate testing strategies and the impact of testability on testing.

II. PURPOSES OF TESTING

The main purpose of testing is the detection of faults within a device (such as a transistor), subassembly (such as a printed circuit board or chassis), subsystem, or system. Based on the results of the tests performed at each step in the manufacturing process, parts or assemblies are either rejected (at the component level) or reworked (at the subassembly, subsystem, or system level) so that only good items flow forward to the next stage of the manufacturing operation or get shipped to a customer.

Testing that results only in accept/reject decisions is referred to as go/ no go testing. Testing that results not only in accept/reject determinations but which also provides diagnostic information to allow for reworking of assemblies so that they become "go" assemblies is referred to as fault isolation testing. A small unit under test (UUT), such as a digital integrated circuit, which has no value added to it by the purchaser at time of receipt, is a prime candidate for go/no go testing. Bad parts are simply rejected back to the supplier. A large UUT, such as a printed circuit board or subsystem, which has had considerable value added to it during the manufacturing operation, is a prime candidate for fault isolation testing since it is usually more economical to repair such a unit than to replace it in its entirety and scrap it.

In general, the earlier in the manufacturing process that testing is performed, the less expensive is the task of performing it. Studies have proven that if a defective component is identified at component test, the cost to find the faulty part is about one-tenth the cost of finding that same faulty part once it has been assembled into the next assembly. So if it costs $0.50 to find a defective integrated circuit (IC) by testing the IC, it will probably cost $5 to find the same faulty part at the assembled printed circuit board level. As assemblies become larger and more complex, the cost of detecting and isolating faults continues to increase by an order of magnitude.

This order-of-magnitude ratio results primarily from the complexity of the tasks of procuring, fixturing, programming, and operating the test equipment as the levels of complexity of the UUT increase. It is much simpler to test a 40-pin large-scale-integration (LSI) microprocessor as a 40-pin device than it is to test that same device once it is surrounded by 100 or more other devices of similar complexity on a printed circuit board. Not only does it cost much more to write a test program for a 100-IC board than to write a program for a single device, it takes much more labor to isolate the defect. The cost of fault isolation is typically again an order or magnitude higher than the cost of go/ no go testing.

Thus one of the primary goals in developing a testing strategy as part of the quality process is to test as early in the process as possible since the earlier a fault is detected, the easier it is to detect. This "test earlier, test easier" philosophy is the key to improved testing productivity in an electronics manufacturing environment.

III. LEVELS AT WHICH TESTING CAN BE PERFORMED

Testing in the electronics manufacturing environment is typically performed at four discrete levels. These levels are:

1. Component or device test
2. Printed circuit board test
3. Subsystem or unit test
4. System or final test

The testing performed at each level can range from the very simple to the extremely complex, depending on the character of the UUT, the test specifications against which it must be tested, and the eventual use to which it will be put. A child's toy, expected to break or be discarded in a short time, may be subjected to minimal testing. A satellite, on the other hand, may be subjected to very thorough testing since the cost of sending the space shuttle out for a repair job is anything but trivial.

At the component test level, testing is performed to ensure that devices such as resistors, capacitors, diodes, transistors, and integrated circuits meet specifications and function properly before they are allowed to move to the stockroom or kitting areas. Parts that test "OK" should be identified as such, while parts that fail should be rejected to the vendor with an appropriate description of the reason for rejection.

At the board level, testing is performed to ensure that all the devices installed on the printed circuit board are the correct devices, that they have been installed correctly, and that they still function after being handled and soldered. This testing may be preceded by visual inspection operations or may include techniques designed to replace visual inspection operations (such as testing for solder splashes, open circuits, and incorrectly installed devices).

At the subsystem or unit level, testing is performed to ensure that all the subassemblies installed into the subsystem or unit function when assembled together. This is usually functional testing and may be preceded, again depending on the product, by testing or inspection of the back planes, harnesses, and power supplies, which might also be part of the subsystem or unit being tested.

At the final system-level test, testing is performed to ensure that the product meets its published specifications and operates properly before it is shipped to the customer. Functional testing or built-in testing is usually performed at this level. Also at this level—as well as at the preceding two levels—the fault isolation aspect of testing is a critical and high-cost element.

IV. METHODS OF TESTING

There are a great many methods available for testing at each level. At the device test level, simple go/no go functional testing may be performed with in-house-built equipment or inexpensive commercial equipment. More sophisticated ac and dc parametric testing equipment, either benchtop or large system, may also be employed. Testing can be performed on either a 100% basis or on an acceptable quality level (AQL) basis.

At printed circuit board test there are again many alternatives. In addition to in-house-built equipment or "hot mock-ups," there are commercial opens and shorts testers, in-circuit and static and dynamic functional testers, as well as the options for in-circuit emulation and signature analysis.

At the subsystem (unit) and system (final) test levels, most test equipment is either built in-house as dedicated or hot-mock-up equipment or system testing is performed with built-in software testing routines. There is a trend, much too slowly proceeding, toward commercial development of general-purpose subsystem and system testers which make use of machine vision and robotics which will significantly reduce the costs currently associated with testing at levels above the printed circuit board level. The primary categories of device test processes are:

Functional testing
Dc parametric testing
Ac parametric testing

Each of these test processes is designed to detect certain types of faults and the primary characteristics of each test method are illustrated in Figs. 1 (functional testing), 2 (dc parametric testing), and 3 (ac parametric testing). Any or all of these test methods may be applied to components with either bench-top or large systems. Obviously, the more exacting the test requirements, the more expensive the test equipment and test programs are likely to be.

Functional testing, illustrated in Fig. 1, is designed to verify that a device, when stimulated with a specified input pattern, outputs the expected response pattern. If the device indeed responds correctly, it is said to function. No tests are performed to determine whether or not the device performed its function within specified time limits or whether or not the device can success-fully interact with other devices which will later be connected to it.

Adding dc parametric testing, as illustrated in Fig. 2, helps to verify whether or not a device will interact properly with other components. Such parameters as input and output current, input and output voltage, and drive capability are measured.

Adding ac parametric testing, as shown in Fig. 3, provides even more in-formation about the device under test. Here we check for propagation delays, storage times, and rise and fall times. This type of testing is used to deter-mine whether or not the device will function in conjunction with other com-ponents within the specified timing requirements.

Any of these types of tests may be performed on devices either for char-acterization or for ongoing screening. During characterization, testing is designed to determine the minimum parameters under which all devices from multiple vendors will perform. During ongoing screening, testing is designed to ensure that incoming devices perform within the previously set limits.

At printed circuit board test, we again have many options. Each test method is designed to remove a certain set of fault types and has certain bene-fits and limitations associated with it. Each of the most common methods, and those benefits and limitations, is discussed briefly below.

A. Loaded Board Opens and Shorts Testing

Opens and shorts testing for loaded boards is a testing philosophy based on statistics that show that most printed circuit board (PCB) defects are due to problems related to open and short circuits. Most opens and shorts are a re-sult of the assembly and solder stages of the manufacturing operation.

Performing opens and shorts testing on loaded boards increases productivity and lowers costs by offloading simple faults from a more complex automatic test equipment (ATE) system. The fixturing is via a bed-of-nails fixture and it is typical to fixture the assembly to detect only shorts at this stage in the manu-facturing process. This is because 90% of the faults are typically short circuits and only 10% are opens. To fixture a PCB for both opens and shorts testing

FIGURE 1   Functional testing is performed to determine if specific inputs create the proper output.

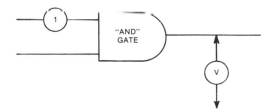

FIGURE 2 Dc parametric testing is performed to determine if devices will work properly when they are connected to other devices.

requires a test nail at the ends of every trace and is more costly than simple shorts testing, which requires only one "nail" per node.

The objective of loaded board opens and shorts testing is to isolate simple faults, for example, those points that are connected and should not be connected (90%), and those points that are not connected and should be connected (10%). The benefits of these tests include:

Isolation of process-induced shorts and opens at an early stage
Requires small programming effort
Requires low operator skill

The limitations include:

Little or no parametric capability
No functional test capability

B. In-Circuit Inspection Testing

In-circuit testing is the technique of testing each component on a printed wiring board on an individual basis, without regard to its intended circuit function. This testing philosophy is based on the following assumptions: (1) if all components are of the correct value, and they are all correctly installed, the PCB will function correctly; and (2) the majority of defects on PCBs are process induced.

In-circuit testers are very good at detecting and isolating manufacturing-induced faults on a PCB. They test digital ICs for their basic truth table functions and are able to make resistance, capacitance, and inductance measurements.

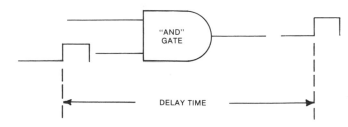

FIGURE 3 Ac parametric testing is performed to determine if the device will operate within specified time limits.

Electrical guarding is used during the power-off testing of discrete components on an assembled PCB. Guarding helps to reduce the effect of other components on the device under test (DUT). Due to the circuit configuration, it is often very difficult to get a good measurement due to parallel components and "sneak" paths to ground. There are some component configurations that cannot be effectively guarded. For example, parallel bypass capacitors on a power bus can be impossible to test and the failing component impossible to diagnose—especially if there are 20 or so of these devices on a bus and the fault is that of one or more of the capacitors is open.

The bed-of-nails fixture should contact each node. There is little need for making contact at each end of every trace, except on critical bus lines. The benefits of this type of testing include:

One-pass diagnostics
Easy to program
Easy board handling
Requires low operator skill

The limitations include:

Some components are untestable in-circuit
Tolerance of tester versus tolerance of UUT
Component interaction is not checked
Limited functional test capability

C. Static Functional Testing

Static functional testing involves testing a PCB as a functional entity rather than testing each component individually. Static functional testing involves sequencing the test vectors at rates lower than the normal operating speed of the UUT.

This technique assumes that if the assembly functions, all components must be of the correct value and installed correctly. It also assumes that process-induced problems cannot exist if the board functions properly. Fixturing of the UUT to the ATE is usually via the edge connector. Some static functional testers employ a limited bed-of-nails fixture for increased visibility to the UUT.

Input stimulus vectors are provided to sensitize faulty circuit paths and to exercise functions that the board will perform in the next assembly. If a fault occurs, the ATE prompts the operator with a sequence of node names that allows him or her to probe from the failing output along a bad circuit path until the fault is isolated. Some static functional ATE use a fault dictionary for fault isolation. With this technique, the operator is provided with a fault reference number to a list of known faults for that assembly. The operator then matches the fault reference number from the tester to the number of the fault description in the dictionary. The dictionary lists all possible sources of potential error for any given fault reference number. There is a separate dictionary which must be generated for each board.

The speed of test execution is usually limited by computer input/output rate for a go/no go analysis. For diagnostics, the limiting factor becomes the fault isolation time and number of operator probings required. For analog testing, the ATE is usually limited to the instrument conversion rate on the general-purpose instrumentation bus (GPIB). All tests are done at discrete stimulus/response setups, and this technique only requires a medium skill level for operation. The benefits of the testing include:

Verifies the functional integrity of the assembly
Usually provides higher next-assembly yields than methods discussed
   previously

The limitations include:

Does not test for timing-related faults
Slow test execution with long test patterns
Finds only one fault per pass

D. Dynamic Functional Testing

Functional testing, as described previously, involves testing assembled boards
as a functional entity rather than as individual components. Dynamic functional testing involves sequencing the test vectors at the equivalent (or higher)
operating speed of the unit under test. Dynamic testing is usually used for
the type of board which contains read-only memory (ROM), random access
memory (RAM), a microprocessor, and various peripheral devices.

Speeds in excess of 1 MHz are usually referred to as "dynamic" at the board
test level based on ATE manufacturers' definitions. "Real dynamic" usually
means that tests are performed at actual normal operating speeds of the unit
under test. The difference between the two definitions is one of technology
and terminology. Some devices cease to operate at speeds below about 800
kHz and dynamic testing is imperative. In addition, high test rates can reduce production test times. "Soft" failures, such as pattern sensitivities,
are more likely to be found with dynamic testing, regardless of whether it is
"ATE dynamic" or "real dynamic."

The internal architecture is similar to that of a static functional tester
except that memory behind each pin is used to store patterns for rapid broad-
side stimulus and response vectors. Signature analysis may be used to reduce large amounts of data to a single four- to eight-digit number and can
reduce the large amounts of response data from the unit under test which
must be analyzed by the ATE.

Bed-of-nails fixtures are not normally used due to high capacitive loading
and noise considerations. New fixtures are being introduced which work
around these problems, as new testers are introduced with high-speed functional and in-circuit capabilities on the same machine.

Dynamic functional testing is becoming more popular due to the difficulty
of finding certain types of soft failures and the need to approach true dynamic
testing conditions. There are, however, certain limitations on the ATE since
good design practice means using mature (i.e., slow) components in the design of an ATE system, while engineers are designing new products to be
tested using very high speed state-of-the-art technology. The benefits of
this type of testing include:

Verifies functional integrity of assembly
Verifies speed-related integrity of assembly
Fast test execution

The limitations include:

High cost of equipment
Finds only one fault per pass

E. In-Circuit Emulation

In-circuit emulation is a testing approach which is particularly useful in development applications. In-circuit emulation is sometimes used for production
and field service testing. This technique requires good software design and
usually requires a high level of skill for diagnostics.

This technique emulates the end-item operation via functional stimulus
programs which are input to the board from the microprocessor socket. Loop-
back board design can be employed to provide a good test of peripheral and
random logic. This technique also uses signature analysis to gather and analyze test data where the loop-back technique cannot be implemented.
The emulator provides a "captive" microprocessor of the same family as used
on the assembly, running at full speed, in a personality module. The PCB
under test can run its own programs or special diagnostic routines stored in
ROM. Test programs can then be structured for good repeatability of signatures. This technique has the advantage of allowing the transportation of
engineering programs to the testing functions provided that proper care has
been taken. The capital cost is relatively low, but usage requires careful
design attention.

Stimulus speeds to 20 MHz and above are possible. The maximum speed
for response data collection and analysis is currently about 10 MHz. Connection of the tester to the unit under test (UUT) requires a socket for the microprocessor. An RS-232-C serial I/O port can interface with host computers.
Large development systems are usually available with this type of tester for
added flexibility in program generation and editing. The benefits of this type
of testing include:

> Provides for full-speed operation
> Verifies functional and speed integrity
> Can use existing self-test programs
> Can be used in field service test

The limitations include:

> Minimal diagnostic capabilities
> Microprocessor must be removed during test
> Requires high skill level in production test

F. Dynamic Reference Testing

Dynamic reference testing is a technique whereby input stimulus is provided
to the UUT and a "known good" board, simultaneously. The outputs from the
two boards are exclusive-ORed and monitored for failures. This type of ATE
usually has automatic pattern generators, as well as the ability to use stored
patterns which are generated by the user.

Unlimited response vector lengths are theoretically possible because the
reference board acts like an infinite-length ROM for storage of diagnostic
nodal data. Pattern speeds to 10 MHz are attainable with this type of ATE,
and signature analysis techniques are used to verify that the known good
board still functions properly. The benefits of this type of testing include:

> Large numbers of test vectors can be applied at high speeds
> No LSI modeling required
> Verifies functional integrity

The limitations include:

> Requires manual test program generation
> Requires reference board for diagnostics

G. Signature Analysis

Signature analysis is not really a stand-alone test strategy unless the input stimulus vectors are provided from a source external to the unit under test. Signature analysis is often used as an adjunct to several testing methods, including in-circuit and functional, and serves basically as a data compression technique.

Data compression is achieved in the signature analyzer by probing a logic test node from which data are input for each and every circuit clock cycle that occurs within a circuit-controlled time window. Within the signature analyzer is a 16-bit feedback shift register into which the data are entered in either its true or complement logic state, according to previous data-dependent register feedback conditions. In all, there are 65,536 possible states to which the register can be set during a measurement window. These states are then encoded and displayed on four hexadecimal indicators and become a "signature." This signature is then a characteristic number representing time-dependent logic activity during a specified measurement interval for a particular circuit node. Any change in the behavior of this node will produce a different signature, indicating a possible circuit malfunction. A single logic state change on a node is all that is required to produce a meaningful signature. Because of the compression algorithm chosen, measurement intervals exceeding 65,536 clock cycles will still produce valid, repeatable signatures.

Serial data are shifted into the register along with a start, stop, and clock signal. The remainder uniquely defines nodal states and times as long as enough patterns have been circulated through the shift register. Input stimulus vectors can either be provided by on-board software or from an external source such as an ATE system or in-circuit emulator. The benefits of this type of testing include:

> Many thousands of tests can be applied at high speeds
> Fast program generation in many cases
> Large amounts of response data can be compressed
> Can be used for field service

The limitations include:

> Requires careful consideration in the design for testability
> Diagnostic resolution is poor in feedback loops and bus-structured boards

H. Dedicated Testers

A dedicated tester is typically a piece of in-house-built test equipment designed for the express purpose of testing one type of circuit board. These testers can be designed to test both digital and analog boards. The diagnostic capabilities are typically not as good as those developed by the ATE manufacturers. The ATE manufacturers have each invested millions of dollars into the research and development of ATE.

Dedicated testers are usually designed in-house by the test engineering department and may not have good documentation, procedures, and so on. They can, however, be tailored to a specific application, product, facility, or process. These testers are sometimes used when volumes are very high and many units are needed for throughput capabilities. Alternatively, dedicated testers are sometimes used when volumes are too low to justify commercial general-purpose ATE. The benefits of this type of testing include:

Tests can be tailored to the specific task
Can be inexpensive if designed properly

The limitations include:

Limited diagnostic capabilities
High skill levels are typically required
Can be very expensive if designed improperly

I. Hot-Mock-Up Testers

Another testing method used quite often is hot-mock-up. This technique is a form of a dedicated tester in that it is usually an in-house design and is dedicated to testing one type of circuit board. With this technique, a test system is configured using bits and pieces of the final product. All the components of the test system are known good, except the unit under test. The system exercises the unit under test and monitors responses.

Hot-mock-ups can be useful for quality assurance audit purposes and test program improvement, provided that good records are kept. The capital equipment cost is usually "buried" due to the fact that inventory surplus can be used to build the tester. The technique is highly labor intensive, in most cases, due to limited diagnostics. However, it does provide the ultimate in functional testing. The benefits of this type of testing include:

Requires little design effort
Inexpensive in terms of capital costs

The limitations include:

Little or no diagnostic capability
Requires high-skill-level operators
Usually has long test times

V. USING TEST DATA TO IMPROVE QUALITY

From the quality assurance standpoint, the most valuable output from any testing operation is the information on the quantity, types, and nature of the faults that were found at each level of test. With these data, it is possible to provide input to the manufacturing operations to effect changes that will preclude these faults in the future.

If, for example, the data from printed circuit board test show that fully 50% of the faults occurring at that test step are due to solder shorts, action can be taken to clean up the soldering process. It may be that a solder mask can be added to the board to eliminate 80% of the currently occurring faults. Or possibly there is a problem with the wave solder machine itself or with the solder or flux being used.

If functional system testing reveals that a large percentage of faults are due to functional or parametric failures of certain component types, those components can be prescreened, either at board test but preferably at component test, so that potentially faulty parts are detected as components and do not have to be isolated at system test.

Many ATE vendors offer networking and data communications systems to provide failure information data in real time. It is important, however, to make sure that these data are "real." A fixturing problem, for example, may lead to a daily report which indicates that out of 100 PC board failures, 92 were due to a defective resistor. In reality, the data that was automatically logged by the ATE system may reflect a fixturing problem rather than a rash of defective resistors.

The way to prevent contaminated data is to implement a data-gathering system that validates the ATE system diagnoses, either manually through rework reports or automatically through terminals connected into the networking system. The importance of noncontaminated data cannot be overstressed—if you have contaminated data, you are likely to be trying to solve nonexistent problems.

Using test data will allow major defect categories to be readily identified and systematically eliminated. The result will be more products of equal or higher quality out the door at less cost—improved productivity defined.

VI. FORMULATING TEST STRATEGIES USING QUALITY DATA

Developing a manufacturing test strategy without a data base is a formidable task. Experience, estimates, and outside consultants can help, but there is no better base on which to build and fine-tune a testing strategy than the quality assurance data from testing operations, which outline the numbers and types of faults likely to occur in a given operation. Without firm data, a test planner must make certain assumptions based on past experience and expected problems. This is satisfactory as long as the test strategy is not "cast in concrete" and can be changed as initial assumptions are verified or proven wrong. Regardless of where the data come from, there is an effective way, based on economics, to select a testing strategy. This method involves flowcharting the various testing options, creating a formula for each option, and cranking in the expected quantities, yields, and fault characteristics. Figure 4 shows the flow and formula for a typical board test operation, and Fig. 5

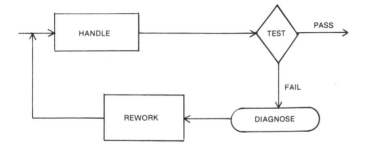

FIGURE 4   Printed circuit board test flow and formula.

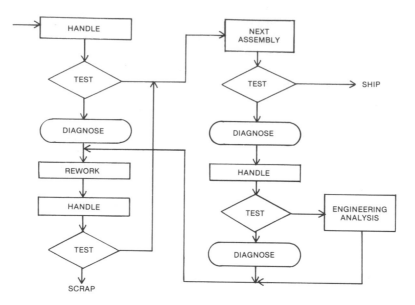

FIGURE 5   Expanded flowchart and formula.

illustrates the technique with system test, diagnosis, and failed board repair flows included.

By boiling down the choices to economic decisions, opinions are removed
and an objective judgment can be made. Further, this method allows for the
identification of major cost elements which can lead to further improvements
in the manufacturing process. The key elements include identifying which
types of test equipment remove which types of faults, estimating the total
distribution of faults at each level, and calculating the overall costs of each
given strategy.

Should there be special factors (e.g., human life considerations), certain
strategies may be eliminated immediately. Each of the remaining possible
strategies can be costed and then, one by one, each strategy can be "what-
ifed" to see if it might be fine-tuned itself. Remember, the objective is to
remove each type of fault as early in the process as possible, since this usually results in the lowest testing costs.

VII. THE IMPACT OF TESTABILITY ON TESTING

Perhaps the earliest place in the business cycle that testing costs can be
affected is in the design phase of a product. It is here that recurring
testing problems, just like recurring assembly faults, can be most effectively
eliminated.

The addition of a $0.05 resistor, as shown in Fig. 6, to allow initialization
of a circuit, can save perhaps $3000 in test programming costs and prevent
spending an average of $0.50 per circuit board in component costs due to
incorrect diagnoses and rework. More typical are recurring test cost reductions, primarily in the fault isolation areas, on the order of 5000 to 20,000%.

Another key testability consideration is to provide control of free-running
clock circuits on logic boards. If a company has made a $300,000 investment

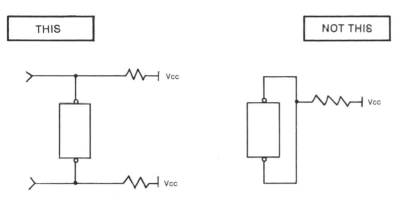

FIGURE 6 The addition of an inexpensive component to "initialize" a circuit (set it to a specific level or pattern) can often save a great deal of testing time.

in an ATE system, the last thing it needs is to have the brand-new 5-MHz system obsoleted immediately because a product design contains an uncontrollable free-running 10-MHz oscillator. Two NAND gates will solve this potential problem, as shown in Fig. 7.

It is, therefore, crucially important that testability, as well as producibility, manufacturability, reliability, serviceability, and all of the other -abilities be considered during the product development phase. This is the earliest place where quality and productivity may be improved.

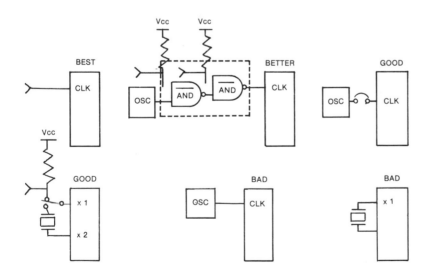

FIGURE 7 To provide useful testing, the ATE system clock (the circuit that controls the times at which events occur) must be able to control the clock on boards being tested. The addition of simple circuits permits the ATE clock to control the device-under-test clock.

VIII. CONCLUSION

Testing plays a critical role in the quality process. It is by testing that we determine that quality has indeed been designed and manufactured into the product. Testing is our validation that we "did it right." It is our data-gathering method for doing our jobs even more effectively. Each testing step is a critical data-gathering point and those data, noncontaminated, are our raw material for continuously improving the quality of our operations.

Indeed, quality assurance and quality control should not be looked upon as enforcers but as helpers. Quality data gathered through testing should be used as a management tool to improve processes rather than as a punitive weapon or a report card on manufacturing operations. With the real-time help available from testing, its role in the quality process cannot help but increase.

GLOSSARY

Analog: Circuitry whose inputs and outputs vary constantly in amplitude and frequency over time.

Automatic pattern generators: Hardware electronic circuits that are con-figured so that they continuously generate, without software or human intervention, test stimulus patterns for the unit under test.

Backplanes: The interconnection medium between multiple circuit cards. Sometimes called motherboards or card cages, these items typically con-tain power, ground, and signal-carrying circuitry but not active logic elements. The major defect categories that occur are short circuits and open circuits.

Bed-of-nails fixture: A vacuum, pneumatically, or mechanically operated interface between the test equipment and the unit under test that utilizes a grid of spring-loaded contacts to connect to all (or most, in some cases) of the electrical circuit nodes on the unit under test. The bed-of-nails fixture is used to gain control of the circuit under test and to achieve visibility into the circuit under test. The bed-of-nails fixture is most commonly used with in-circuit testers but may be used with functional testers to reduce test programming and unit under test troubleshooting times.

Broadside stimulus and response vectors: Patterns that are applied to and read from the unit under test at high speed in a parallel, or "broad-side," manner so that multiple pins change state, as contrasted with discrete stimulus and response, where pins are changed one at a time.

Conversion rate: The speed at which an electrical instrument can acquire, analyze, and present measurement information to a human being or a computer.

Digital ICs: Integrated circuits whose operation is characterized with (typically) two discretely defined logic states known as 1s and 0s. The circuitry in digital ICs is either on or off (thus the term *digital*) as con-trasted with analog ICs, whose inputs and outputs vary in both ampli-tude and frequency over time.

Discrete stimulus/response setups: The individual test stimulus and re-sponse measurement conditions applied to a unit under test. Discrete is used in this context to imply sequential operations, rather than con-tinuous operations, during the testing process.

Drive capability: The current sinking or sourcing ability of the device or unit under test (i.e., the ability of the device to force the inputs of the devices to which it is connected into the desired logic state).

Dynamic testing: A subset of functional testing characterized by applying stimulus patterns to the unit under test and measuring responses from the unit under test at speeds as close to the actual operating rate of the unit under test as possible. Also sometimes called "real-time" testing.

Edge connector: The interface between a printed circuit board and the circuitry to which it is connected. Usually constructed of gold-plated traces, but sometimes implemented with a dedicated connector, this interface is usually placed at or near one or more of the outside perimeters of the unit under test—thus the phrase "edge connector."

Electrical guarding: A stimulus/measurement technique used during in-circuit testing, implemented with an operational amplifier configuration in the tester, which attempts to isolate, or "guard out," the effects of other components which may be connected to the component under test and that would impair the accuracy of the desired measurement.

Fall time: The interval between the 90% and 10% signal swing points on the falling edge of a signal.

Family: As used in this context, family refers to "of the same parentage," in other words, processors whose architectures were derived from each other in an evolutionary or hereditary fashion. Examples are the Intel 8048 family or the Motorola 68000 family of devices.

Fault dictionary: A listing of possible faults ordered by failing test step and resulting test pattern, usually produced by a logic simulation software package.

Flowcharting: Making a drawing of the flow of a process.

Functional stimulus programs: The sets of software instructions or test patterns to be applied to the unit under test.

Functional testing: A testing technique used to verify the electrical performance of a unit under test. The underlying philosophy is that if an assembly functions, it must be correctly assembled with functioning components, all of the correct value, and not contain any defects. This philosophy is generally true. Some defect categories, specifically out-of-tolerance components and short circuits between buffer inputs and outputs, cannot readily be detected using functional testing.

General-purpose instrumentation bus (GPIB): A standard hardware and software protocol whose characteristics have been mandated by the Institute of Electrical and Electronic Engineers (IEEE). Using the GPIB allows many disparate instruments to be connected to form testing systems of all types.

Harnesses: Cable assemblies (i.e., sets of wires) which connect circuitry together.

Hexadecimal: A numbering system of the base 16. The numbers are 0 through 9 and A through F.

High-capacitive loading: A bed-of-nails fixture normally contains hundreds or thousands of wires that may be between 6 and 18 in. long. These long wires add capacitance in the fixture that the unit under test may not be able to drive either at all or at the desired operating speed.

In-circuit emulation: A testing technique where the control element on the unit under test (usually a microprocessor) is removed, either physically or electrically, and replaced by external hardware that provides stimulus and measurement capability in a manner similar to the element that has been removed and is being "emulated."

In-circuit testing: A testing technique that contacts every electrical node (connection) on the unit under test and verifies, to the best of its ability, that each component is the correct component, that it is correctly installed, and that there are no process-induced defects such as open circuits or short circuits. The underlying philosophy is that if the assembly has been done correctly, and all the parts are of the right value, the assembly will function. This philosophy is generally true. Some defect categories, specifically timing-related defects and functional interaction between components, cannot readily be detected using functional testing.

I/O rate: A phrase used to indicate that the maximum speed of the testing operation is limited by the product of computer input/output (I/O) speed and bus width, the number of software instructions that must be executed in order for the computer to set up the next set of stimulus and response conditions for a unit under test, and the number of unit-under-test pins whose states must be changed during each test step.

Large-scale integration (LSI): Devices containing in excess of 10,000 logic elements or gates on the same silicon chip.

Loop-back board design: The practice of providing some means for connected unit-under-test outputs to unit-under-test inputs (e.g., looping them back) so that testing can be performed without external edge connector circuitry.

Networking: The interconnection of multiple computer systems.

Node: An electrical connection between two components

Node names: The symbolic names given to circuit paths (e.g., Clock, Data, Power, Ground, etc.).

Noise considerations: The multiple long wires may lead to cross coupling of signals within the fixture, especially where fast rise and fall times characterize the logic behavior. Unwanted cross coupling is referred to as noise.

Parametric testing: The verification of specific unit-under-test characteristics such as voltage and current (dc parameters) and speed-related items such as rise time, fall time, and propagation delay (ac parameters).

Pattern sensitivities: Faults in circuitry that occur only when a set of stimulus vectors are applied in a specifically ordered sequence. The device under test may operate properly if, for example, a Fetch instruction is executed prior to a Jump instruction but may fail to operate properly if the order of the instructions (the test pattern) is reversed.

Peripheral and random logic: Logic devices and circuitry whose inputs and outputs do not connect directly to the address and data buses in a microprocessor- or microcomputer-based printed circuit board design. Peripheral logic includes things like communications controller devices, while random logic consists of things like AND and OR gates (e.g., SSI/MSI logic).

Personality module: An assembly of electronic parts that customizes the operation of and interface to the unit under test.

Propagation delay: The amount of time between the application of an input signal to a circuit and the effect of that input signal on the output of the circuit.

Rise time: The interval between the 10% and 90% signal swing points on the leading edge of a signal.

RS-232-C serial I/O port: A standard connection interface for computer peripheral equipment.

Signature analysis: A response-measuring technique wherein the logic activity on a unit-under-test circuit node is compressed into a four-

digit alphanumeric set of characters. The signatures originally taken
from a "known good" unit under test can be written down (or stored
in a computer) and referred to later when a defective unit under test
must be diagnosed.

Solder mask: A layer of protective coating applied to the solder side of
a printed circuit board to prevent solder from adhering to places where
it is not wanted.

Static testing: A subset of functional testing characterized by applying
stimulus patterns to the unit under test and measuring responses from
the unit under test at speeds well below the actual operating rate of the
unit under test.

Stimulus vectors: The electrical signals that are applied to a unit under
test to cause it to operate in a desired manner or to activate and propa-
gate faults within the circuit to the output pins of the edge connector
or other testing interface.

Storage times: A subset of propagation delay which refers to the amount
of time required to charge and discharge the capacitive elements in a
circuit.

Test nail: A spring-loaded pin which makes the actual contact to the unit-
under-test node when a bed-of-nails fixture is actuated. These "spring
probes" come in a wide variety of sizes, tip styles, and spring forces
for different testing applications.

Trace: The metallic circuit path on a printed circuit board which carries
signals from one component to another.

Truth tables: The sets of 1s and 0s typically applied to and expected from
a digital unit under test (IC or printed circuit board) arranged in an
array format.

BIBLIOGRAPHY

Turino, J., and H. F. Binnendyk, *Design to Test*, published by and copyright © 1982 Logical Solutions, Incorporated, Campbell, Calif.; sections
reproduced with permission.

Turino, J., *Test Strategy Development*, video course produced by and
copyright © 1981 Logical Solutions, Incorporated, Campbell, Calif., and
Workshop Material adapted from presentations in conjunction with
Cahners Publishing Company.

Design for Testability Seminar/Workshop, Logical Solutions, Incorporated,
Campbell, Calif., and Network Educational Services Limited, Buckingham,
England.

Electronic Test Engineering Course, produced for and presented at General
Electric Company, 1981, 1982, and *Fundamentals of Test Engineering*,
Copyright © 1981 Logical Solutions, Incorporated, Campbell, Calif.

FURTHER READING

Bateson, J., *In-Circuit Testing*, Van Nostrand Reinhold, New York
Davis, B., *The Economics of Board Testing*, published in the U.K.
How to Succeed in Test Engineering, Course Notes, Logical Solutions, Inc.
Turino, J., and H. F. Binnendyk, *Design to Test*, Logical Solutions, Inc.,
Campbell, Calif., 1982.

37

AUTOMATIC TEST EQUIPMENT

DOUGLAS A. BLAKESLEE

Eaton Corporation
Danbury, Connecticut

I. INTRODUCTION

The purpose of automatic test equipment (ATE) is, by the accepted definition, to evaluate electronic components, subsystems, and complete systems. Although there is electronic test equipment for a wide variety of products, ATE has come to mean automatic systems used in the manufacture and repair of electronic products.

The first ATE systems were designed for the military services as an aid to maintenance of complex weapons systems. The low skill levels of new recruits, coupled with increasing difficulty in retaining trained, experienced technicians, led the Department of Defense to invest heavily in ATE. The test systems were intended to be the electronic equivalent of a field engineer as an aid in repairing missiles, radar systems, fighter planes, and other military weapons. ATE captured the skills of the best engineers and, through step-by-step programs, diagnosed faults and led the repair technician through a sophisticated maintenance procedure.

Automatic test equipment for commercial purposes followed a different path. Semiconductor manufacturers, initially through in-house development, produced test equipment for use in their production lines. The objective of a selling price of pennies per unit dictated automated testing and sorting. Specialized test systems for each and every application proved very expensive. A merchant market developed in which manufacturers designed systems to cover as broad a spectrum of applications as possible. Most of the test equipment manufacturers were spin-offs from the semiconductor companies.

The manufacturers of electronic equipment found the need for a third form of ATE, the subsystem tester. Circuit boards, power supplies, and wiring frames are the three primary subsystems used in electronic equipment. Even if the components of an electronic device are known to meet specifications, errors of both omission and commission can occur during the assembly process. Experience has proven that finding errors and problems is far easier and less expensive in the subsystem stage of manufacture than when a complex product is completely assembled.

II. GENERATIONS OF ATE

Three generations of automatic test equipment have been developed so far.
The first generation consisted of hardware only. The individual tests to be
executed and the test programs were built into the equipment with minor programming changes accomplished by means of switches and patch panels or
through numerical control entered from paper tape or punched cards. Because the systems were entirely hardware, they were generic machines intended
for a preset set of tests on a given device or system. First-generation ATE
tended to be slow, cumbersone, and expensive. The onrush of electronic development in the late 1950s and early 1960s made first-generation machines
obsolete as soon as they were built. Because of their hardware design, they
could not be modified to meet new and more complex requirements.

The late 1950s saw the introduction of small computers called minicomputers.
These electronic processors had the ability to execute stored programs. (The
programs are called software.) A small computer grafted onto existing hardware became the second generation of ATE. Languages and formats were developed so that test programs could be developed on the computer and stored
in its memory or a peripheral storage device such as magnetic tape. Test
results from the hardware were fed to the computer for storage and analysis.
Second-generation ATE is characterized by the use of a computer as a programming and storage element.

The computer was often employed to control external power sources and
measurement instruments in an effort to enhance system capability. However,
it could not overcome the inherent lack of flexibility in the hardware. To
change to a new device or system required a major rebuilding of the system
hardware.

During the 1960s the third generation of ATE appeared. It was characterized by a concept that moved as much of the complexity from hardware to software. The elements of the system power sources, stimulus generators, measurement instruments, and interconnection matrices are all operated under software control. Thus, within the capabilities of the individual subsections, the
unit could test any device or system. A heavy burden was placed on the
computer which had to execute a program for each test and which needed
sufficient memory for long and complex test routines.

Minicomputer prices have dropped 10-fold for the processor and its per-
ipherals and 1000-fold for memory in a decade, a trend that continues. With
much of the hardware eliminated, ATE systems have become smaller, lighter,
and less expensive. In the process, the move to software produced systems
that are much easier to maintain because the power of the computer was employed to aid the maintenance procedure and because the amount of hardware
to be maintained was significantly reduced.

The characteristics of the fourth generation of ATE are apparent, although
no designs have been finished. The limitation of the third generation is that
a computer can execute only one instruction at a time. The next generation of
ATE will use distributed processing. Many tasks, including testing, creating
new tests, storing data, and so on, are ideally executed in parallel. Minicomputer functions are implemented in micro form as single semiconductor chips
called microprocessors or μPs. The cost of the microprocessors is so low that
using multiple units in parallel is far more cost-effective than the use of a
single minicomputer. The development of software programs and operating
systems to utilize the new miniature processors lags far behind the progress
on hardware.

II. ATE SYSTEM CLASSIFICATIONS

Automatic test systems are grouped into three broad categories by intended application: component test, circuit board test, and system test. They are also subdivided by the size and cost of the tester into two categories: small systems with price tags of $50,000 and under, and large mainframe systems which typically cost from $75,000 to over $2,000,000.

Within the component-test family there are a number of different systems intended for the various electronic component groups (see Table 1):

1. *Passive components*: test resistors, capacitors, inductors, and transformers.
2. *Discrete semiconductors*: include diodes, zeners, transistors, FETs, SCRs, triacs, PUTs, UJTs, and optical devices.
3. *Linear integrated circuits*: include operational amplifiers, voltage regulators, memory drivers, timers, audio circuits, data converters, and analog microprocessors.
4. *Digital integrated circuits*: divided into three primary subdivisions: memory, standard circuits, and microprocessors. There are general-purpose digital test systems as well as ATE intended for a particular subdivision such as memory circuits.
5. *Relay and power supply*: test subassemblies such as system components.

The characteristics of the various component ATE vary widely, which makes designing a universal test system very difficult. Passive-component test systems are typically limited to two- or three-terminal tests and can measure

TABLE 1 Applications for Automatic Test Systems

Testing Classes	Purpose	Approach
Passive component	Accept/reject sorting	Electrical parameters tested
Semiconductor component	Accept/reject sorting	Electrical parameters tested
Bare board, wiring	Accept/reject	Ohmic short, open; leakage current
In-circuit board test	Troubleshooting repair	Ohmic or impedance testing to models or electrical isolation
Functional board	Accept/reject troubleshooting repair	Parametric testing with physical isolation Comparison with known good board
Functional product	Accept/reject troubleshooting repair	Parametric testing at operating speed against design specification
Off-line maintenance	Accept/reject fault-isolate repair	Static, dynamic parametric testing against performance Specification and failure mode information

resistance, capacitance, and inductance. Discrete semiconductor testing requires a three-terminal tester with high voltage and high current capability, typically to 2000 V and 100 A. Precision power supplies, with both constant-current and constant-voltage capability, are needed for linear testing together with precision measurement circuitry and provision to connect to 128 terminals or more. Digital testing requires only low voltage and moderate current but needs complex pattern generators, multiphase clocking capability, connection paths to 256 terminals, and the ability to measure very short time intervals accurately. To support testing of linear/digital combination parts such as data converters and automotive engine controllers, linear test systems have been enhanced with slow-speed digital options. Some large digital test systems have had minor analog capability added. In general, however, full electronic component test capability requires at least four or five ATE systems.

Subassembly and board testing utilizes four types of ATE systems:

1. *Bare board and wiring verification*: tests the printed conductors on circuit boards and backplane or card-cage wiring. These testers measure resistance to locate open or shorted conductors.
2. *In-circuit testing*: includes simple resistance testing to find shorts and opens and the capability of testing each component on the board to assure that it has been installed properly and is functional.
3. *Functional test—comparison*: evaluates an unknown board by comparing its operating characteristics to known good boards.
4. *Functional test—operating*: operates the board in a way that emulates its use in the end product and tests its functions.

Wiring verification and in-circuit testers are inexpensive themselves but often require elaborate fixtures. Contact to the board under test is via a "bed of nails" containing up to 3000 individual contacts. The board is held in place by mechanical or vacuum pressure. Although some beds of nails can service more than one type of board, often an individual fixture is needed for each board to be tested. Similarly, a complex set of cables and connectors is needed for wiring verification of backplanes and card cages which often dwarf the test set.

There are specialized wiring verification testers manufactured which are intended only for cable assemblies and harnesses.

Functional testers evaluate a board from its connector, so complex bed-of-nails schemes are not needed. However, the board must be designed in such a way that all needed stimulus and measurement points are brought out to the connector; or a number of wires and clips are needed which connect to components on the board, a process that is time consuming and which can damage the board. Because of the limited number of connections to the board under test, the test operator is often provided with a hand probe which is used following instructions from the test system.

The current trend in high-volume electronic manufacturing is to use both in-circuit and functional testing. In-circuit testing is very effective at finding components inserted backward and shorts that could be difficult to locate during functional testing. Also, unskilled operators can be employed for in-circuit evaluation, as they just insert and remove boards. A functional test requires an operator with a high level of training and the tester itself is more expensive and complex. The functional test process moves much more quickly if circuit faults and defective components have been located and corrected. For manufacturers that cannot justify the cost of both in-circuit and functional board testers, ATE that performs in both modes is available, although it tends to be both expensive and complex.

To date no general-purpose ATE for final test at the systems level has been developed for the merchant market. Electronic products vary widely in final test requirements. A radio set is not similar to a large computer. Neither are tested in the same manner as for an electronic game or an automotive antiskid controller. System-level ATE is customed designed to test a particular item or product. The military, for example, will pruchase an ATE system for the Phoenix missile and for the avionic systems in the F16 fighter aircraft. ATE for final tests resemble functional board testers with enhanced power capability and specialized stimulus and measurement instrumentation added. The availability of a wide variety of power supplies and test instruments that can be used as modules in a system has aided in the design and construction of ATE for final-test applications.

IV. SYSTEMS SIZE

Small ATE systems, nicknamed "benchtops," are popular in incoming-inspection applications because of their low cost. Many of the small systems currently on the market are first-generation designs, although new versions using microprocessors are being introduced. The microprocessor-based small systems usually cost two to three times as much as the first-generation benchtops. Their high initial cost can easily be justified by their lower cost of programming and reduced operator setup time.

Benchtop systems are generally constructed as an integral unit with control keyboard, display, and storage device built in. Storage media are magnetic cards or magnetic tape in cartridge or cassette form. The miniature floppy disk drives now being developed will find application in small systems.

Small systems are designed to test a particular product family. Usually, they can evaluate between 70 and 90% of devices within the family. Tests and devices that require special conditioning, unusual stimulus, high power, or a high pin count cannot be run. The other disadvantage of benchtops is that they are slow, often many times slower than large mainframe systems.

Mainframe ATE is characterized by use of a general-purpose computer and mass-storage device plus provision for a large number of accessories and options. It has the capability to test all the devices in a family, and it can be expanded and reconfigured as requirements change.

V. APPLICATIONS FOR ATE

Manufacturers of electronic components use ATE to test and classify their products. Semiconductor components are tested in wafer form to eliminate defective devices before the assembly process, during assembly to assure that damaged devices are eliminated, and at the end of the production cycle to determine final classification of each part before marking. Component manufacturers also employ ATE in the engineering laboratory to characterize new designs and in the quality assurance department.

The manufacturers of electronic equipment use ATE for incoming inspection of components, circuit boards, and power supplies. Although this

TABLE 2   Typical Board-Test Results

No defects found	67%
Opens and shorts	16.5%
Missing or wrong parts	6.6%
Improper insertion	3.3%
Defective components	3.3%
Interactive functional failures	3.3%

inspection is the first step in the manufacturing process, the function is usually assigned as part of the quality assurance program. Once the circuit boards are assembled, they are tested on ATE for correct assembly (in-circuit testing) or functionality or both. ATE is also employed to verify cables, harnesses, and backplanes. Final tests may or may not use ATE. The current trend is to design a good deal of self-diagnostic capability into electronic products, which is a major aid in final tests. Military weapons systems almost always have ATE testing. Commercial practice has not reached this level of sophistication.

Incoming inspection and board test are often viewed as areas of trade-off. Firms with strong quality assurance programs emphasize incoming inspection. It makes no sense to use bad components, and a certain portion of each batch are known statistically to be bad. Manual inspection methods generally preclude 100% inspection. Automatic test equipment makes full inspection a realizable goal. The rule of 10s applies, where if it costs $0.05 to find a defective part at incoming inspection, it will cost $0.50 to find the same bad part at the board level and $5 at the system level. In organizations where manufacturing is dominant, there is a tendency to skip component testing and to attempt to find all faults at the board level. Unfortunately, board testers are not the best component test systems. Their function is to spot manufacturing defects and to check board functions. The typical defects found during in-circuit board testing are shown in Table 2.

Field service has traditionally been very labor intensive. As the use of electronics has become part of a wide variety of products, a severe shortage of trained technicians has developed. Thus the situation that gave impetus to the development of ATE in the military is occurring in the commercial sector. To improve the productivity of service personnel, a new class of ATE is being developed for board test afield. In addition, regional service centers are being established which have board and system test facilities similar to those of the factory.

VI. SYSTEM DESIGN

A block diagram of an automatic test system is shown in Fig. 1. The processor is typically a general-purpose minicomputer which acts as a system manager. It also interprets program instructions, controls system signal flow and timing, allocates system resources, provides mathematical capability, stores test results, and provides human-machine interface via terminals. In addition, depending on the design of the system, the computer may be active

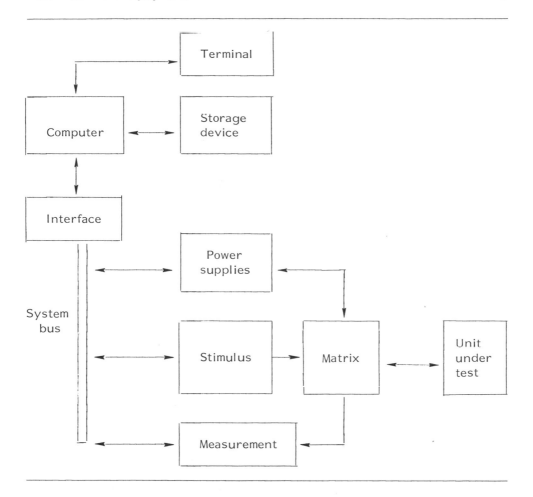

FIGURE 1   Generalized ATE system.

or passive in the execution of tests. It also can be used for automatic system calibration and for diagnostic maintenance aids.

The important computer characteristics are its speed, the amount of memory it can address, and how arithmetic functions are handled. Speed is important because the computer must handle many tasks, a requirement that limits the use of microprocessors in large systems because they are relatively slow. A memory-limited system can be difficult to use, so the amount of memory— especially the "free" memory left once the operating program is loaded—is important. Test systems must perform multiple arithmetic calculations. Multiplication and division are slow when done in software, so computers that feature hardware implementation of multiplication and division are preferred.

The computer will have provision for one or more terminals. As a rule, one terminal per test head or operator is desirable plus one terminal for system control. The terminals can be video display or printing type. Terminals communicate with the computer using the ASCII (American Standard for Communications Information Interchange) code in a direct-current loop or using the American Standard RS-232 interface. A line printer is employed where large volumes of test results are to be printed. It typically uses a parallel computer interface designed specifically for a given printer-computer combination.

A number of mass storage devices are used in ATE systems. They include:

1. *Hard disk*: a magnetic record that can store from 2.5 to 67 million bytes (1 byte is 8 bits) of information with fast access and high-speed data transfer.
2. *Floppy disk*: a flexible magnetic record that can store from 128,000 to 500,000 bytes of information. Access and transfer times are much slower than with a hard disk. Floppy disks must be handled carefully, as they are easily damaged by dust and fingerprints.
3. *Magnetic tape*: a tape employed in several forms, including reel to reel, cassett, and cartridge. The IBM-designed nine-channel tape format is often employed to back up disks in case they are damaged and to provide a transfer medium to separate computer systems.
4. *Paper tape*: a tape no longer used in new system designs except where computer memory is very limited (because the software required to run a paper tape unit is short and simple). Paper tape is also used as a common medium in older computers.

The terminals and mass storage devices are called I/O (input/output) devices for the computer. They are interconnected via a high-speed parallel bus. The structure of the bus varies from manufacturer to manufacturer and for different computer models. Most ATE systems are controlled by extending the computer bus through an interface which provides isolation and noise reduction. The details of the bus vary, but a bus generally features high-speed parallel operation where parts of the tester are treated as I/O devices; or direct memory access to the computer can be provided where parts of the tester are treated as memory addresses.

In component and board testers where test times are measured in milliseconds, a high-speed bus is required. The standard for interconnection of test instruments, IEEE-STD-488, is a relatively slow bus structure. A series of instruments and power supplies can be interconnected to a computer via 488 to form a custom ATE system. Its operation would be sufficient for system final test or where individual test times are long. 488 is also used to add and control extra instruments on component and board test systems where high-speed communication is not required.

Power supplies are a key element in automatic test systems. They vary widely in capability and accuracy. The power sources may be constant voltage, constant current, or both, called *V/I sources*. Most are programmable for voltage output and maximum current. The stability and forcing accuracy of the power sources are very important where precision measurements are to be made. Because long connecting cables are used which introduce both inductance and capacitance, power sources must be free of parasitic oscillations over a wide range of load conditions.

Power sources may be pulse types able to deliver high current for only short periods or units rated for continuous power. Discrete semiconductor test equipment usually employs pulse-type supplies, while linear IC and board testers have sources rated for continuous operation. V/I supplies can be employed as precision loads as well as sources by appropriate programming of voltage and current (positive voltage and negative current, for example). Precision power sources usually include measurement circuitry so that the current be forced into a lead and the voltage applied to the device or circuit under test can be checked.

Tests such as leakage current, breakdown voltage, and device gain can be performed using power supplies as the stimulus. Other sources of stimulus include audio, radio-frequency (RF), pulse, and digital-pattern generators. Specialized stimulus devices are required for unique devices; the stereo-signal and croma generators needed in testing entertainment/linear integrated circuits are examples. Basic stimulus generators are designed into automatic testers as system resources programmed via software as required. Others are offered as options.

When a special stimulus is needed which is beyond the capability of the ATE systems, additional test equipment may be employed, controlled by the system. Or conditioning, stimulus, and measurement circuits may be built for a particular device to be tested, called a test box, test package, or family board. Such units may be part of the mainframe or located at the device interface.

Basic dc and ac (audio-frequency) measurement capability is standard in most automatic test systems. A radio-frequency voltmeter is often an option, as is a counter for frequency, time, and period measurements. Where high resolution is needed, a counter with averaging capability is used.

System power, stimulus, and measurement resources are connected to the unit under test via a matrix. The size and complexity of the matrix varies widely, from two relays for polarity reversal in diode testers to several thousand switching paths for in-circuit board and cable testers. The important specifications for the matrix are its voltage and current capabilities and its frequency response. The matrix should have three or four leads per path to allow for remote voltage measurement. The matrix requires sufficient input paths for all system resources and accessories. The number of output paths needed is determined by the access points or pins at the unit under test.

At the output of the matrix is the interface to the unit under test. The interface may be a connector or adaptor socket. It often contains bypass capacitors to prevent oscillation of the unit under test. If special test or conditioning circuits are needed, they are usually located in the interface.

As the use of automatic test systems has grown, so have the requirements for programming and for data analysis. Most commercial ATE manufacturers have developed a form of test system manager; a computer system with provision for large-capacity storage on disk or magnetic tape. Although details of the test system managers vary widely from manufacturer to manufacturer, from 4 to 16 test systems can be connected to the manager. It can store large libraries of test programs and transmit individual programs to the testers on command. The testers pass test data and lot results to the manager, which has programs for data reduction and for sophisticated statistical analysis.

Some managers have programs for daily and weekly summary reports. An important feature of test system managers is the ability to support user programming in one or more high-level languages. This allows users to write their own analysis and report programs.

VII. SOFTWARE

The most important element in any automatic test system is the computer software. It determines how the system operates and the ease with which new test programs can be created. The cost of program generation is substantial, often several times the cost of the system itself.

The operating system used with the computer may be an original design by the tester manufacturer or one of the systems popular in minicomputers. A

custom-designed operating system is often more efficient and uses less computer memory space. However, it also usually lacks the flexibility of the general-purpose systems. Together with the operating system, the software for
ATE includes a master operating program (MOP) or executive program. This
software controls the tester, including such tasks as executing tests, communicating with terminals, data logging, and managing computer memory space.
The executive programs are extensive and require a major portion of the computer memory.

Some ATE systems use a standard language, such as BASIC, FORTRAN,
Pascal, or Atlas for program generation. Atlas has become a standard for
military and aerospace system ATE. Component and board testers usually have
a developed language roughly based on FORTRAN or BASIC, with enhancements and modifications to fit a particular requirement and set of hardware.
There is no standardization of semiconductor-device-tester languages. Each
manufacturer and usually each individual test set has a specialized language.
ATE also has sets of accessory software for system diagnostics, calibration,
operation of optional equipment, and specialized testing such as high-reliability
analysis.

VIII. PROGRAMMING

Automatic test systems for discrete components and simple integrated circuits
are usually preprogrammed by the manufacturer for all possible tests. Thus
programming in the true sense of the word is not needed. The user builds
test routines aided by the ATE system via *prompting* or *menu display*. In
the prompting approach, when a particular test is requested the tester responds with a series of questions that request forcing functions and limits.
The tester checks entries for appropriate responses and rejects errors. Menu
entry is similar. At each step the test system displays on a video screen all
the possible alternatives available at a given point in a test routine. The user
selects the desired step from the alternatives in the menu; then a new menu is
displayed with a new set of alternatives.

Test systems for complex integrated circuits and circuit boards allow programming where one or more instructions are contained per line. In some systems, generalized tests can be created without forcing functions or limits.
These generalized tests are called via software when needed. Forcing function
information is inserted before the test executes. In this way the programs for
each device can be quite simple. Other testers require that all tests must be
created for each device to be tested, which can be very laborious when many
similar types of devices are to be tested. For in-circuit board testing generalized software is available with the test systems where common components such
as diodes, gates, flip-flops, operational amplifiers and so on, are prewritten
in modules. Thus a good deal of the programming task can be reduced to calling the appropriate software module. Cable and backplane testers usually
have a self-programming feature where the pattern to be tested is "learned"
from a known good unit.

Manufacturers offer prewritten software for many of the popular integrated
circuits. They have also formed user groups where members contribute test
routines and in return receive copies of programs from others in the group.

A test routine for a complex device or board can take a month or more to
write. Because hundreds of instructions are involved, chances are high that
there will be one or more mistakes in the finished program. Corrections of

these mistakes requires a process called *debugging*. Modern ATE systems are equipped with hardware and software tools to aid in the debugging process. External access is provided to system resources, matrix connections, and control lines so that an oscilloscope or other test equipment can be employed to examine the dynamic performance of the system. Software aids include the ability to obtain a listing of the status of all system hardware at any point in a test routine. Such a list is valuable to show that all hardware was properly programmed at a given instant. An immediate execute mode of operation is also useful so that as changes are made in a routine, it can be executed to assure the desired result is achieved.

Computer-aided design techniques are increasingly being used to help in writing board- and system-test programs. A large-capacity computer can provide modeling and simulation techniques that dramatically reduce the time necessary to generate a complex program. Another trend is to use automatic test generation for semiconductor devices. In this approach all tests are pre-programmed. The specifications for all devices to be tested are stored in a library. The library can be within the system, in a central manager, or in another computer. To create a test routine, the user specifies the devices to be tested and the sorting priority desired. An efficient test routine is built automatically using the data in the library.

IX. MAINTENANCE

Early ATE systems often totally neglected calibration and maintenance requirements. Later generations have contained powerful software to aid in the maintenance process. The system as a whole is checked against an external or internal standard. Such diagnostic software provides an indication that the system is performing within specifications. If trouble is detected, specific diagnostics for a section of the unit can be run to pinpoint the problem to a particular circuit board or relay. Most ATE users do not attempt repair beyond changing boards and relays. Thus spare-boards kits are purchased with a test system. Manufacturers provide fast-turnaround board repair and a stock of spare boards at regional offices.

Modern ATE systems often contain a maintenance manual within the computer. Special programs tell the maintenance technician what tools and test equipment are required to perform a particular task, provide notes about proper procedures, and detail step by step how to proceed. The sophisticated programs check the technician's work as he or she proceeds.

The calibration standards for the ATE system should be removable as a unit, including the power supply, so that it can be sent to a laboratory for certification as a transfer standard. Traceability to the National Bureau of Standards is a requirement in some testing applications and a good procedure in all cases.

In systems that use manual calibration, the need for recalibration is indicated by diagnostic software. Additional software programs set up individual sections of the system for calibration. A technician then proceeds to make whatever manual adjustments are required. An important trend in ATE is to use automatic calibration. In one approach the system computer runs diagnostics continuously in the time spaces between test routines. Any errors that are found are corrected by inputs to digital-to-analog converters, which correct errors of scale or offset. The entire test system is recalibrated every few minutes. Another approach requires that the system be shut down once each shift. Extensive diagnostics are run and the error results found are stored in a software lookup table. When testing resumes, raw test results are adjusted by the values stored in the lookup table and corrected to eliminate errors. Thus the system is self-correcting by means of software for error of calibration over a range of ±10%. Typically, the hardware contains no adjustments at all.

38

MECHANICAL PRODUCT DESIGN

RICHARD Y. MOSS

Hewlett-Packard Company
Palo Alto, California

I. INTRODUCTION

That a good package is an essential ingredient of a reliable product is scarcely controversial, yet arriving at that goal is a process which is often fraught with conflict. Several possible reasons for this come to mind:

1. Package design is much more difficult than is generally recognized, since it involves poorly understood areas of design such as high-frequency shielding, heat transfer, mechanical engineering, and human factors.
2. The package design is often almost completely original, rather than being simply an original arrangement of standard parts, as much of the electrical design is.
3. The objectives and acceptance criteria for the package design are usually not clearly defined and recorded, and involve compromises between function and style, or engineering and art. Worse yet, it is often not clearly established who will have final approval authority over the package design, whereas there is seldom any argument over authority for approving the electrical design. The result is that upper management can get embroiled in deciding what color to paint it, while a crucial electrical design decision made at a much lower level goes unchallenged.
4. Whether or not a particular design is even feasible may well be a function of the availability of expensive tooling or a specific manufacturing process. Thus it is necessary to include the tooling and fabrication experts in the package design reviews. The management challenge is much greater when a whole committee must be pleased.

II. LEVELS OF PACKAGING

A. Component

Just as there are different levels of product complexity, ranging from components to systems, so there are different considerations at each level of packaging. At the component level, packaging tends to emphasize the protection of fragile or sensitive internal parts, and may even have to provide a special "environment," such as pressure or vacuum. Often, component packages must conform to industry standards, so the only freedom allowed the designer is in the choice of materials and manufacturing techniques.

The contribution of component packaging to reliability is crucial, as discussed at greater length in Chapter 33. Package-induced component failure modes such as overheating, electrical leakage due to contamination, corrosion, and mechanical fatigue due to cyclical thermal expansion dominate the failure statistics of electrical components. The rapid increase in the use of epoxy and silicone encapsulants, and reduced usage of corrosion-resistant but expensive precious-metal platings, have both contributed to this increase. Today's component packaging requires materials and process control expertise, and is definitely no place for amateurs.

B. Subassembly

The second level of packaging is the subassembly. The emphasis at this level is on the mounting and interconnection of components which are functionally grouped for convenience of testing and field maintenance, and to allow optional features to be added or removed easily. In electronic products, the subassembly level usually employs printed circuit technology to accomplish both the mounting and interconnection functions.

Reliability of the interconnections is of prime importance at this level of packaging, although the contribution to cooling and vibration resistance is more important than is usually recognized. The majority of small electrical components obtain more than 75% of their cooling by conducting the internal heat out the metal electrical leads to the printed circuit board, from which it is dissipated into the environment by air convection. Physical flexing, especially at resonance, of the printed circuit substrate (usually fiberglass-reinforced epoxy resin) is the major source of vibration damage to these small electrical components. Thus the design of the subassembly packaging is of major importance in product reliability.

C. Product

In many cases, the product is the highest level of packaging, and often has the greatest variety of demands placed on it. The product package provides the interface between the operator and the equipment and is supposed to protect each from the other. This means that there are legal considerations as well as practical: for example, compliance with regulations dealing with safety and electromagnetic compatibility (EMC). Another problem is that the product package is often the most original, least standardized level of packaging, and its appearance sets the "style" of the company's products. This tends to generate controversy, since decisions of "artistic taste" tend to get made (and changed) by upper management.

The interface functions of the package deserve additional discussion. The product package generally supports the control and display functions of the product, with digital and graphics displays becoming more popular daily. Most of the labeling and instructions which are required as a part of the product are mounted on, or are part of, the product package. Connectors and power cables generally are part of the package, and it may also provide cable strain relief. Finally, aids to transportation and mounting, such as handles, wheels, and mounting brackets, are usually considered part of the package design.

D. System

The highest level of assembly that will be discussed in this chapter is the system, which is often a collection of products interconnected so as to optimize the performance of a specific application. The function of the system level packaging is to "integrate" and interconnect products which may or may not be particularly compatible in appearance, and to provide system convenience features, such as a desk or console, aimed at a particular application. Improved efficiency, the reduction of operator errors and future expandability are benefits of a well-designed system package. Unfortunately, there are few roads—much less maps—in this part of the desert. The system design often ends up being the user's idea in one case, a particular designer's in another, and a "camel" design by a committee in a third.

Endless variety is possible, and production volumes are often so low that there is little incentive to employ extensive tooling or design standardization. Vertically integrated corporations can be the exception to this rule if they have the foresight and discipline to define a system packaging plan at the start, and then make the product packaging a modular subset of that. Obviously, management action is necessary to make that happen.

III. FUNCTIONS OF PACKAGING

The primary function of a package is that of a protective container: protection against the physical forces of gravity and acceleration, and a container to keep out (or in) heat, light, acoustic noise, foreign materials such as solids, liquids, and gasses, and to act as an insulator and shield against electrical signals. Each of these functions will be discussed in turn.

A. Withstanding Physical Forces

Physical forces usually result from the interaction of acceleration and mass, according to the simple equation $F = M \times A$ (force equals mass times acceleration). The acceleration may be the result of gravity, rotation, or complex motion such as occurs in vibration or physical shock. The application of force to a component, subassembly, or product will result in movement of some part; if this deformation is small, there may not be any malfunction; if it is large, failure will result. Many people are under the illusion that if the elastic limit of the material is not exceeded, no damage will result, but this is not always true. Buckling is an example of a common failure mode which can be initiated while stresses are below the elastic limit—for instance when a long, thin member with insufficient stiffness is compression loaded. High-cycle fatigue also occurs within the elastic range, after long periods of cyclical loading [1].

Plastic deformation and creep are examples of failure modes occurring when the elastic limit is exceeded. The difference is that plastic deformation either ceases after a short time or, if the stress is cyclical, ends in low-cycle fatigue. This is what happens when you break a piece of wire, such as a metal coat hanger or paper clip, by bending it back and forth past its elastic limit. Creep tends to continue as long as the stress is present, until the material fractures, either in shear or cleavage.

Another whole family of mechanical failure modes is loosely classed as wear, either adhesive or abrasive. Adhesive wear is probably the most common, and occurs when microwelds form and then shear, at the tiny points of contact that are the result of microscopic roughness of the load-bearing surfaces. Galling, scruffing, scoring, and seizing are all examples of adhesive wear. Abrasive wear is a self-descriptive term. It occurs when hard particles are present between two surfaces that are rubbing together, so that the surfaces are gouged or chipped away rapidly. If the particles come from the rubbing surfaces themselves, the term *fretting* may be applied. Similar failure modes are *pitting*, where high contact stresses result in cracking away of pieces of a surface, and *cavitation*, caused by pressure pulses in a fluid in contact with the surface. (This is the basis of ultrasonic cleaning [2, 3].)

The forces that activate all these failure modes generally come from the acceleration of gravity or motion. Vibratory motion is particularly destructive when it contains frequencies that excite resonance in a structure. (That is what caused the Tacoma Narrows bridge to collapse.) In resonance, the forces are increased as a function of the Q, or lack of damping, of the structure, so that the chances of exceeding the elastic limit are greatly increased. Examples of this type of failure are seen in electronic products where components are mounted and supported by their electrical leads, and fail by cracking and breakage of those leads when subjected to vibration. This can be avoided by mounting more massive components by their cases, and by supporting and rigidifying the PC assemblies so that damaging resonances are minimized. Thus vibration testing, including the search for resonances, is very important to assure the reliability of a new package. It is also obvious that the units tested must be exactly like the final design if the results are to be valid.

B. Heat Transfer

The next most important function of the package is the control of heat. Heat is transferred from a warm object to a cooler environment by a combination of three means: conduction, radiation, and convection. (Evaporative cooling will not be discussed here.) Conductive cooling occurs when there is direct contact between a source of heat and a cooler mass, or "sink." This is the primary means by which components transfer heat to the subassembly, and also contributes to the further transfer of heat from inside a product package to outside, as you will learn the hard way if you change from a good thermal conductor such as metal to a poor one such as plastic. The conductive heat flow is a function of the temperature difference, cross-sectional area, path length, and coefficient of thermal conductivity of the material; most metals and some ceramics are very good conductors of heat, whereas most plastics are poor conductors.

Radiation is the means by which heat escapes from a warm object to a cooler surrounding space without any contact. Radiation can take place in a vacuum and is a function of the emissivity of the hot surface (flat black paint has high emissivity, whereas a mirror is very low) and the temperature difference between the object and its surroundings. In most electronic products this temperature difference is only a few degrees, so radiation makes almost no contribution to the cooling.

Convection, the third means of cooling, requires the presence of a gaseous or liquid medium in which to set up convection currents. Convection is the main means by which the heat from electronic products is dissipated in the surrounding air; unfortunately, the rate of cooling is a function of the orientation (vertical versus horizontal) and dimensions of the hot surface, and of properties such as the density and velocity of the convective medium. This means that the temperature of a product which is cooled by air convection is affected by the altitude and humidity, the rate of airflow, and which "side" is up. Forced air convection is far more effective at cooling than is natural convection, provided that an air blockage (dirty filter) or fan failure does not occur. It is a good idea to provide some type of automatic thermal cutout or warning indicator in products where failure or blockage of the fan could result in damaging temperatures [4, 5].

C. Light

The function of the package as a container of light is most obvious in products with intense light sources, such as projectors or photocopiers; perhaps less obvious is the need to shield certain types of components from ambient light. Not only are traditional photographic materials light sensitive, but so are many devices with semiconductor junctions. Low-leakage diodes and transistors must nearly always be protected from light, to prevent photocurrents that can cause malfunction.

D. Acoustics

Vibrations that are coupled to the surrounding air result in acoustical noise, which is an annoyance in quiet environments and dangerous if it exceeds specified levels. It is becoming increasingly common for vibration-damping and noise-absorbent materials to be designed into new products and systems, and more and more companies are building their own sound-level-measurement facilities. One approach that has been employed successfully is to combine the functions of an electromagnetically shielded "screen room" with those of an acoustically quiet (anechoic) chamber, thus saving capital funds and floor space by combining two functions in one room. To do this, it is generally only necessary to make the dimensions, particularly the ceiling height, slightly larger than would be required for the screen room alone. This is simple and inexpensive to accomplish if planned in advance [6, 7].

E. Contaminant Barrier

An obvious function of the package is to keep contaminants out or, occassionally, in. At the component level, nearly all technologies must be protected from substances that cause leakage or corrosion, particularly those which easily dissolve in water. Water, in liquid or vapor form, and soluble compounds of chlorine or phosphorus are particularly troublesome around semiconductors and reactive metals such as aluminum, copper, or silver. The contamination problem has become more acute as component packaging has become more reliant on plastic encapsulation or polymer sealing, rather than on the more expensive hermetic seals using glass, ceramic, and metals with matched thermal expansion coefficients.

There are no plastics which are capable of making a moisture-impervious seal, so component technologies packaged in plastic must be limited to those insensitive to water and its attendant impurities. A promising approach to making plastic-encapsulated semiconductors reliable is the use of a moisture-impermeable passiviation, such as silicon nitride, on the semiconductor surface itself. Unfortunately, this process is not yet widespread.

At the subassembly, product, or system level it is less common to have a sealed package, so airborne contaminants usually circulate freely around and through the product. Splash-proof products are fairly common, but immersion-proof ones are not, particularly as they get larger. In addition to the difficulty of achieving a reliable seal on a large product, there is the problem of building the package strong enough to withstand the enormous pressure differences that occur at even moderate depths. The pressure at 10 ft depth in water is 624 lb/ft^2, and at 50 ft the pressure is over 3000 lb/ft^2. Most of us are not in the business of building submarines, so submersible products larger than a wristwatch or camera are generally impractical. Airborne dust and corrosives, particularly sulfur compounds, are a common problem in all sizes of package.

Corrosion failure of thin metal films, such as those used in electrical connectors, is a major cause of field failures. Gold plating has been the traditional solution to this problem, but the rising price of gold, coupled with the impossibility of covering all exposed metals with a sufficient thickness to resist the ever-increasing concentrations of corrosives in the environment, have prompted an intense search for substitute metals. No easy or inexpensive solutions have been found to date, so it is wise to continue to use good-quality connectors where they are required, and to minimize the number of connectors in a new design.

F. Electrical Insulation and Shielding

Another "protective container" function of the package is that of an electrical insulator and shield. Not only are the electrical signals inside the product a potential safety hazard, but with the trend toward increased density of electronics in our homes and everyday lives—television and video games, microwave ovens, digital calculators and home computers, and citizen's band radios, to name a few—the management of the electromagnetic "environment" has become an urgent problem. The regulatory agencies of most industrialized nations are leaping into the breach, proposing sweeping regulations with tenuous basis in theory and no practical means of compliance or enforcement. Even if the technical considerations are separated from the economic and political, the trend is inexorably toward more regulation.

Management's best strategy is to establish an organization within the company to become expert in these regulated areas, to keep everyone informed of current and proposed rules, and to try to persuade the regulatory agencies to act reasonably. A list of important regulatory agencies is shown in Table 1.

Taking safety considerations first, there are six categories of hazard to be prevented:

1. *Electrical shock*: Preventive measures include insulation, shielding and grounding, interlocks, fuses, circuit breakers and ground current interrupters, current limiters, cover panels requiring special tools for removal, proper size and location of enclosure openings, automatic discharge of energy-storage devices, strain relief and elimination of sharp radii in wiring, and warning labels.
2. *Mechanical hazards*: Preventive measures include elimination of sharp edges, protective grilles over rotating parts such as fans (adequate to keep out hair as well as fingers), designs with wide bases and low centers of gravity to prevent tipover, and shields against explosion or implosion of breakable components such as cathode ray tubes.
3. *Fire and burns*: Preventive measures include the use of nonflammable materials, designs that limit the maximum temperatures of exposed

TABLE 1   World Product Regulatory Agencies

Abbreviation	Country	Name
ANSI	United States	American National Standards Institute
BRH	United States	Bureau of Radiological Health
BSI	United Kingdom	British Standards Institute
CEBEC	Belgium	Belgian National Safety Agency
CEE	International	International Commission of Rules for the Approval of Electrical Equipment
CENELEC	Europe	European Committee for Electrotechnical Standardization
CPSC	United States	Consumer Product Safety Commission
CSA	Canada	Canadian Standards Association
DEMKO	Denmark	Danish Electrical Material Control Organization
EI	Finland	Finnish Electrical Inspectorate
EIA	United States	Electronic Industries Association
FDA	United States	Food and Drug Administration
FEMCO	Finland	Finnish Electrical Approval Agency
IEC	International	International Electrotechnical Commission
IEEE	United States	Institute of Electrical and Electronic Engineers
IMQ	Italy	Instituto Italiano del Marchio de Qualità
KEMA	Netherlands	Keuring van Elektrotechnisch Materialen
MITI	Japan	Ministry of International Trade and Industry
NEMKO	Norway	Norges Elektriske Materiall Kontroll
NFPA	United States	National Fire Protection Association
OSHA	United States	Occupational Safety and Health Administration
OVE	Austria	Osterreichischer Verband für Elektrotechnik
SAA	Australia	Standards Association of Australia
SEC	Australia	State Electricity Commission of Victoria
SEMKO	Sweden	Svenska Elektriska Material Kontrollanstalter
SEV	Switzerland	Schweizer Electrotechnische Vereinigung
UL	United States	Underwriters Laboratories
UTE	France	Union Technique de L'Électricité
VDE	Germany	Verband Deutscher Elektrotechniker

surfaces, and packages that will contain burning or molten material resulting from an internal failure, rather than allowing it to run out an opening.

4. *Radiation*: Intense, ultraviolet, or laser light or objectionable sound must be contained or eliminated, and hazards such as x-ray or micro-wave radiation must be carefully controlled.

5. *Hazardous chemicals and materials*: The best bet is not to use such materials. Where they are an intrinsic part of the component, such as acid electrolyte in a battery, they should be packaged so as to be leakproof, and labeled to prevent the package from being opened.

6. *Labeling*: The risk is that the warning or instructional labels will be missing, illegible, or not readily visible, and thus fail to perform their intended function. Labels must last as long as the product, which is many years in most cases, and must be kept simple and few.

The second area of regulatory agency interest is electromagnetic compatibility (EMC). The agencies are generally interested only in the interference that the product generates, but a customer is also interested in the susceptibility of the product to electromagnetic interference (EMI), since he or she does not want the product to malfunction when in the proximity of an uncontrollable source of EMI, such as lightning, or an allowed one, such as a radio or TV transmitter.

The measures necessary to control interference generation and susceptibility are generally the same: shielding by enclosure in high-conductivity metals, avoidance of slot radiators by using conductive gaskets at joints and round holes with diameter much less than the shortest wavelength to be attenuated, shielded cables and connectors, and electrical filter circuits on unshielded connectors such as the ac power receptacle [8]. In the case of low-frequency magnetic field containment, the shielding metal must have a high magnetic permeability, such as certain steels or special alloys, and wiring must either be coaxial or twisted pair, so that external magnetic fields are either minimized or canceled.

Electrostatic discharge (ESD) is a common electrical phenomenon that is not yet widely regulated, but is nonetheless serious. History is full of examples of catastrophies caused by a static spark in the presence of a flammable or explosive material such as textile dust, gunpowder, rocket fuel, petroleum fumes, anesthetics, or hydrogen gas, to name only a few. More recently, it has been realized that EDS is responsible for a significant fraction, probably 5 to 30%, of all the electronic component failures in production and field use. Several degrees of failure can be described: In the most severe cases the energy of a static discharge can cause immediate, catastrophic failure of a semiconductor device or other sensitive component. A second, more subtle kind of failure results when a discharge, too low in voltage to generate a visible spark or to be felt by a human being, degrades a part so that its probability of failing later is greatly increased. This is probably the most common situation, where the initial damage occurs during the manufacture of components and subassemblies, but it is the product or system that subsequently fails. The third type of failure is a "soft" failure, or error, which most often plagues digital computer systems. Here it is usually the EMI generated by the static discharge that changes the contents of a computer memory, resulting in loss of data, expensive reprocessing because results are not correct, or even disruption of a computer-controlled process.

The prevention of ESD problems is simple in principle, and affects the package in two ways:

1. Products and systems must be designed to withstand ESD at the worst-case levels encountered in the field. This generally means that the package must be a "Faraday cage" (a complete, conducting box), and all wiring that enters or leaves the enclosure must incorporate protective circuitry.
2. All ESD-sensitive components and assemblies must be stored and transported in static-protective containers. The best protective container is, again, a Faraday cage. Conductive (carbon-loaded) plastic, metallized plastic, and metal foil are examples of such containers that are readily available [9].

G. Maintenance Accessibility

The last, but not least, function of the package is the role that it plays in maintenance. Probably everyone has had a personal experience with a product that was unserviceable because of poor access or lack of adjustability. This problem most often occurs where the subassembly is tested and calibrated separately at the factory but must be serviced while installed in the product or system. Not only must there be easy access to test points and adjustments, but also subassemblies or components with the highest probability of maintenance should be the easiest to access or remove. This is especially true of air filters in front of cooling fans; the product can fail due to overheating if the filters are not easy to see and clean. In planning the partitioning of components into subassemblies, items requiring frequent replacement should be mounted so that they can be individually replaced; if they are mounted on a larger assembly which must also be replaced, the only result is to raise the average repair cost.

IV. THE DESIGN PROCESS

A. Objectives

Setting objectives is just as important in package design as it is in electrical design. The objectives should be written down and approved at the appropriate management levels, not just informally discussed or understood. There are five major factors to be considered in setting objectives for the package design:

Legal Requirements

Creating a safe product which complies with the regulatory agency requirements in the countries and market sectors chosen is certainly top priority. Although it is a legitimate management decision to exclude a certain country or market segment—and hence to avoid compliance with that country's regulations—it is often difficult to implement that decision. Products have a way of being resold to a third party who may not observe the restrictions, or transferred from the country of purchase to one where the product is not legal. It is far safer to meet or exceed all the regulations that apply to that type of product, as long as they are not mutually contradictory. This may cost extra in design or even in manufacture, but it may well be cheaper in the long run, because of reduced liability.

Customer's Expectations

The customer has a right to expect a product which is of high quality, reliability, and serviceability. In package design, that translates into a package that meets all its specifications, is long-lived, and has good accessibility for maintenance or repair. Quantifying these objectives is difficult: Quality might be specified as the percentage with no defects, reliability would be measured by the survival under various accelerated test conditions or the survival percentage in warranty, and serviceability could be measured in terms of the average time to perform certain benchmark repairs.

Environment

The objective would be to meet the stated quality and reliability goals over a wide range of environmental stresses, such as temperature, humidity, altitude, vibration, and contaminants. Not only must the package itself survive, but also its supporting functions must be performed successfully; adequate cooling for the electronics must be provided even at maximum altitude and temperature, for example.

State of the Art

As is the case with electrical design, we often wish to gain performance or reduce cost with state-of-the-art technology. But it is also usually true that the newest technique is not the most reliable until after several years of evolution. Jumping into a new packaging technology too soon can cost an unaffordable price in redesign, retooling, and warranty replacements, but so can the use of an obsolete approach. A successful strategy from a quality viewpoint is to be neither the first nor the last to adopt the newest technology, but be the best. Setting tough but realistic objectives for design, tooling and fabrication costs, schedules, and yields is a good way to start.

Quality Costs

The bottom line is, after all, profit or loss. Scrap, rework, inspection, and replacements all reduce profits, so setting objectives for these is appropriate. Over the long haul, warranty costs will tend to be the most painful, because they represent a dissatisfied customer who has an increased probability of taking his or her business elsewhere next time. Studies at two large corporations have shown that the result is a multiplication of the effect of warranty costs on profit; each 1% of the sales dollar spent on warranty is associated with a 5 to 6% reduction in pretax profits.

B. Project Management

Since most package designs are a team effort in parallel with other design activities, such as electrical or software design, the management challenge is to promote communication between the separate parts of the project, and to keep them all on schedule and aimed at the same target. The bigger the project, the more meetings there have to be [10]; in this situation, it is particularly important that there be planning of the purpose of each meeting, and that each participant comes fully prepared. As the project moves toward completion, there will be more conflicting details to be resolved, and larger expenditures to be authorized. The project manager whould be sure to review all the appropriate data in the following six categories.

Product Design

In package design, more can be accomplished using models and mock-ups than is the case in electrical design. One reason is that three-dimensional objects are difficult to visualize correctly from two-dimensional drawings, so this is a much safer means to get reactions to subjective factors such as styling and color, to assess human factors such as convenience and placement of elements, and to study accessibility for maintenance, subassembly mounting and interconnection problems, and even some aspects of cooling, such as provision for airflow.

Computer-aided design (CAD) and computer-aided artwork (CAA) are valuable in this area, as well as allowing the use of design rule and tolerance checking programs to catch errors early, greatly reducing the number of iterations before an error-free design is achieved.

Stress Analysis

The effects of the four horsemen of stress—electrical, mechanical, thermal, and chemical—must be tested and reviewed repeatedly during the evolution of the package design. Especially important is the margin between maximum stresses to be encountered and the minimum strength of the design. Usually, designers know, or think they know, this margin; it is important to document this information and then verify it by testing. This raises the delicate issue of designers whose ego would be bruised by the implication that you do not believe or trust them, and hence must verify a design's quality by testing. If you are the type who would fly on an airplane that had never before been tested, go ahead and release a product that has not been tested. Otherwise, plan on stress tests for each stage in the evolution.

Stress Testing

There are two distinctly different types of stress testing: step-stress testing to determine the design margin, and stress-accelerated life tests to verify reliability. Thermal mapping, environmental testing, and abuse testing are all ways of verifying that the design has sufficient margin and confirms the designer's expectations. In step-stress testing it is important to continue to increase the stress until a consistent pattern of failures emerge, since this tells much more about the design than a test with no failures, and the position of the threshold of failure is a sensitive barometer of change. A design where the failure threshold is 50% above the ratings inspires much more confidence than one where the margin is only 5%, or one where the margin has deteriorated since the previous test.

Stress-accelerated life tests generally subject the design to a fixed stress, or combination of stresses, and it is the duration of the test that is increased until a consistent pattern of failures emerges. (The stresses may be applied cyclically, but the limits and rates are fixed.) Early in the design, the intent is to find the dominant failure mechanisms and attempt to design them out; at the end, the intent of the test may well be to establish, with a specified confidence, that a minimum reliability has been achieved.

Regulatory Conformity

Since creating a safe and legally conforming product is the top priority, it follows that review of the results of tests of this is an important project management function. If achieving reliability without testing is difficult to imagine,

then convincing the regulatory agencies (or, in the worst case, the jury),
that you have a safe and conforming product is impossible. It is also nearly
impossible to achieve such a design as an afterthought, or in a hurry. Product safety and electromagnetic compatibility must be part of the design from
the start, and must be verified by testing.

Manufacturability

There are many activities related to the eventual manufacture of the new design which must be planned and initiated long in advance of the start of production, and many of them depend on the design team for their initiation, if
not completion. Tooling must be designed and built, and items fabricated with
that tooling tested as outlined above. Documentation (drawings, material lists,
etc.) must be completed and reviewed, and long-lead materials ordered, received, and incoming acceptance tests performed. (It is especially important
to perform incoming tests on new materials or those from new vendors.)

In addition to tooling, new or reassigned capital equipment needed for fabricating, finishing, or testing the new design must be budgeted, purchased,
and installed. With the sophisticated computer-controlled or numerically controlled machine tools often needed in the fabrication of package designs, it is
important they the accuracy and calibration be checked when the equipment
is first installed, and regularly thereafter. Last, but certainly not least, it
is generally necessary to provide training for the manufacturing personnel in
the peculiar or critical aspects of assembly and test procedures. Since these
concerns are generally known only to the designers in the beginning, it is the
responsibility of management to make sure that they get communicated and
documented.

Marketability

You may well ask how marketing affects the quality and reliability of a package design. The answer is: in several ways. If the product is announced,
shown to customers, or introduced at an industry show before it has completed
its design and testing, the result can be a temptation to skip some tests or
ship product before the tests are completed and all the major problems solved.
This certainly affects the quality of the product. Also, if operation and service manuals are not finished, if sales and service personnel are not trained
and inventories of spares and special test equipment available, the customer's
expectations will not be satisfied, and a fiasco can result. The excitement
generated by receiving a new product soon fades, but the bad taste of poor
performance lives on and on.

V. CONCLUSION

Successful package design requires strong management skills as well as or-
iginality and competence in a broad variety of engineering skills. This usually
results in a team approach to design, so a high degree of cooperation and coordination is required. The traditional pitfalls of subjective judgment, controversy, and the resulting redesign can be avoided by careful planning and
by defining goals so that objective decisions are made at each project check-
point. The levels of management approval that should be obtained are roughly
parallel to the hierarchy of levels of packaging; that is, the system and product levels require the highest levels of management approval, and the components the lowest (unless components are the final product, or course). When

it comes to quality and reliability, however, none of the levels of packaging can be considered to be less important than the others. A weakness at any level can result in a system or product failure; the chain is truly only as strong as its weakest link.

REFERENCES

1. P. H. Wirshing and J. E. Kempert, "A Fresh Look at Fatigue," *Machine Design*, May 20, 1976, pp. 120–123.
2. C. Lipson, "Basic Course in Failure Analysis—Lesson 1: How Parts Can Fail," *Machine Design*, October 16, 1969, pp. 146–149.
3. A. D. S. Carter, *Mechanical Reliability*, Wiley, New York, 1972.
4. A. W. Scott, *Cooling of Electronic Equipment*, Wiley, New York, 1974.
5. D. S. Steinberg, *Cooling Techniques for Electronic Equipment*, Wiley, New York, 1980.
6. L. L. Beranek, *Noise and Vibration Control*, McGraw-Hill, New York, 1971.
7. A. P. G. Peterson and E. E. Gross, Jr., *Handbook of Noise Measurement*, 7th ed., General Radio Company, 1974.
8. H. W. Ott, *Noise Reduction Techniques in Electronic Systems*, Wiley, New York, 1976.
9. *Electrostatic Discharge Training Manual*, Navsea SE 003-AA-TRN-010, Naval Sea Systems Command, September 1980.
10. F. P. Brooks, Jr., *The Mythical Man-Month*, Addison-Wesley, Reading, Mass., 1975.

39

HARDNESS TESTING

ANTHONY DeBELLIS

Acco Industries, Inc.
Bridgeport, Connecticut

I. INDENTATION HARDNESS TESTING

The most commonly used indentation hardness tests are the Brinell, Rockwell, Rockwell superficial, and microhardness tests (Knoop and Vickers). Briefly, the Brinell test is used for testing forgings and castings, especially cast iron. The Rockwell test is used for testing ferrous and nonferrous materials, hardened and tempered steel, case-hardened steel, sheet materials in the heavier gages, and cemented carbides. The Rockwell superficial test is also used for ferrous and nonferrous materials where lighter loads are required, such as testing thin case-hardened surfaces, as well as nitrided cases, decarburized surfaces, and sheet material in thin gages. Microhardness tests (Knoop and Vickers) are used for very small and thin parts as well as for case depth determinations. A description of these test methods follows.

II. THE BRINELL TEST

The Brinell method consists of indenting a test specimen with a steel ball (usually 10 mm) with a load which is usually 3000 kg but reduced to 500 kg for soft metals. The full load is applied for 10 to 15 sec in the case of iron and steel, and for at least 30 sec in the case of other metals. After the load is removed, the diameter of the indentation is measured. The Brinell hardness number is calculated by dividing the load applied by the surface area of the indentation:

$$\text{Brinell hardness number (HB)} = \frac{P}{\pi(D/2)\left[D - \sqrt{D^2 - d^2}\right]}$$

where

P = load (kg)

D = diameter of ball (mm)

d = diameter of indentation (mm)

The indentation diameter is the average of two readings at right angles and the Brinell hardness number is determined by referring to tables similar to Table 1.

Hardened steel cannot be tested with a hardened steel ball by the Brinell method because the ball will flatten during penetration and a permanent deformation will take place. However, a hardened steel ball is satisfactory in testing softer metals. A significant error will be introduced in the Brinell number for values over 450 when high-grade hardened steel balls are used.

Carbide balls are recommended for Brinell testing of materials up to 630. Because of the difference in elastic properties between the steel and carbide balls, the type of ball used might be specifically reported where Brinell hardness values exceed 200. Brinell hardness numbers determined with a steel ball are designated HBS (e.g., 450 HBS) and with a carbide ball HBW (e.g., 450 HBW).

A. Test Surface Preparation

The surface on which the Brinell indentation is to be made must be filed, ground, machined, or polished with emery paper (3/0 emery paper is suitable) so that the indentation diameter is clearly enough defined to permit its meas-

TABLE 1

Dia. of Indentation	500 KGM Load	1500 KGM Load	3000 KGM Load	Dia. of Indentation	500 KGM Load	1500 KGM Load	3000 KGM Load	Dia. of Indentation	500 KGM Load	1500 KGM Load	3000 KGM Load
2.00	158	473	945	3.50	50.3	151	302	5.00	23.8	71.5	143
2.05	150	450	899	3.55	48.9	147	293	5.05	23.3	70.0	140
2.10	143	428	856	3.60	47.5	143	285	5.10	22.8	68.5	137
2.15	136	409	817	3.65	46.1	139	277	5.15	22.3	67.0	134
2.20	130	390	780	3.70	44.9	135	269	5.20	21.8	65.5	131
2.25	124	373	745	3.75	43.6	131	262	5.25	21.4	64.0	128
2.30	119	356	712	3.80	42.4	128	255	5.30	20.9	63.0	126
2.35	114	341	682	3.85	41.3	124	248	5.35	20.5	61.5	123
2.40	109	327	653	3.90	40.2	121	241	5.40	20.1	60.5	121
2.45	104	314	627	3.95	39.1	118	235	5.45	19.7	59.0	118
2.50	100	301	601	4.00	38.1	115	229	5.50	19.3	58.0	116
2.55	96.3	289	578	4.05	37.1	112	223	5.55	18.9	57.0	114
2.60	92.6	278	555	4.10	36.2	109	217	5.60	18.6	55.5	111
2.65	89.0	267	534	4.15	35.3	106	212	5.65	18.2	54.5	109
2.70	85.7	257	514	4.20	34.4	104	207	5.70	17.8	53.5	107
2.75	82.6	248	495	4.25	33.6	101	201	5.75	17.5	52.5	105
2.80	79.6	239	477	4.30	32.8	98.5	197	5.80	17.2	51.5	103
2.85	76.8	231	461	4.35	32.0	96.0	192	5.85	16.8	50.5	101
2.90	74.1	222	444	4.40	31.2	93.5	187	5.90	16.5	49.6	99.2
2.95	71.5	215	429	4.45	30.5	91.5	183	5.95	16.2	48.7	97.3
3.00	69.1	208	415	4.50	29.8	89.5	179	6.00	15.9	47.8	95.5
3.05	66.8	201	401	4.55	29.1	87.0	174	6.05	15.6	46.9	93.7
3.10	64.6	194	388	4.60	28.4	85.0	170	6.10	15.3	46.0	92.0
3.15	62.5	188	375	4.65	27.8	83.5	167	6.15	15.1	45.2	90.3
3.20	60.5	182	363	4.70	27.1	81.5	163	6.20	14.8	44.4	88.7
3.25	58.6	176	352	4.75	26.5	79.5	159	6.25	14.5	43.6	87.1
3.30	56.8	171	341	4.80	25.9	78.0	156	6.30	14.2	42.8	85.5
3.35	55.1	166	331	4.85	25.4	76.0	152	6.35	14.0	42.0	84.0
3.40	53.4	161	321	4.90	24.8	74.5	149	6.40	13.7	41.3	82.5
3.45	51.8	156	311	4.95	24.3	73.0	146	6.45	13.5	40.5	81.0

urement. There should be no interference from tool marks. The surface should be representative of the material and not decarburized, case-hardened, or otherwise superficially hardened to any considerable extent.

B. Indentation Measurement

The diameter of the indentation is measured by a microscope to the nearest 0.01 mm (0.0004 in.). The error in reading the microscope should not exceed 0.01 mm, to keep the error in the Brinell number less than 1%. A stage micrometer is usually provided with the microscope and should be used frequently to check its calibration.

Brinell indentations may exhibit different surface characteristics. When some metals are tested there is a ridge around the impression extending above the original surface of the test piece; at other times the edge of the impression is below the original surface. In some cases there is no difference whatever. The first phenomenon is called a "ridging" type of impression and the second a "sinking" type. Cold-worked alloys generally have the former, and annealed metals the latter type of impression.

The definition of the Brinell number relates it to the surface area of the indentation. To determine this, it is necessary to measure the diameter of the indentation, assuming that this is the diameter of the indentation with which the ball was in actual contact. But in view of ridging- and sinking-type impressions, there is a question as to the exact part of the visible indentation with which actual contact was made. In the case of ridging-type impressions the diameter of the indentation is greater than the true value, whereas with sinking-type impressions, the reverse is true. No way is known of making certain that the correct diameter is measured, and the judgment and experience of the operator introduce a personal factor into the test.

In some materials, the brink of the indentation is poorly defined, especially when hardened steels (even with polished surfaces) are tested; the use of carbide balls produces a more distinct indentation.

Brinell indentations made on some materials are far from round; those on materials which have been subjected to considerable rolling are elliptical in shape, whereas those on heat-treated steels are quite round. For indentations that are not circular, an average value of the Brinell number may be obtained by measuring the diameter in four directions approximately 45° apart.

C. Spacing of Indentations

For accurate results, indentations should not be made too close to the edge of a piece. Lack of sufficient supporting material on one side will cause the resulting indentation to be large and unsymmetrical. The error in Brinell number is negligible if the distance from the center of the indentation is not less than $2\frac{1}{2}$ times the diameter of the indentation from any edge of the test piece.

Indentations cannot be made too close to one another. Under such conditions, the material may be cold-worked by the first indentation, or there may not be sufficient supporting material for the second indentation. The latter condition would produce too large an indentation, whereas the former may produce too small an indentation. The distance between centers of adjacent indentations should be at least three times the diameter of the indentation in order to have the error in the Brinell number of the order of less than 1%.

D. Selecting the Load

The standard loads for Brinell testing are 3000, 1500, and 500 kg. The load should be selected to keep the ratio of the diameter of the indentation to the diameter of the ball (d/D) greater than 0.24 and less than 0.60. When a ratio is less than 0.24, the resulting indentation is so small that errors in determining the diameter become a large proportion of the total diameter. Further, the test loses sensitivity and small differences in hardness values are not differentiated. For a ratio greater than 0.60, the test becomes supersensitive.

To meet these requirements for a given load the hardness must fall within the following ranges:

    3000 kg: BHN 96 to 600
    1500 kg: BHN 48 to 300
    500 kg: BHN 16 to 100

E. General Precautions

When indentations are made on a curved surface with the 10-mm-diameter ball, the radius of the test specimen should not be less than 1 in.

Indentations should not be made within $2\frac{1}{2}$ times the diameter of indentation from each other or from the edge of the specimen.

The load should be applied normal to the specimen and perpendicular to within 2°.

The thickness of the piece being tested should be such that no bulge or marking showing the effect of the load appears on the side of the test piece opposite the indentation.

The surface finish on which the indentation is to be made should be such that the indentation diameter is clearly defined.

III. THE ROCKWELL TEST

The Rockwell test is the most commonly used of all indentation hardness tests. The test can be made within 5 to 10 sec depending on the size and hardness of the specimen. The hardness number is indicated directly on either a dial gage or digital readout.

A. Principle of Test

As shown in Fig. 1, the Rockwell test consists of measuring the additional depth to which a steel ball or Brale diamond penetrator is forced by a heavy (major) load beyond the depth of a previously applied light (minor) load.

The minor load is applied first and a reference or set position is established on the dial gage of the Rockwell tester. Then the major load is applied without moving the piece being tested, the major load is removed, and the Rockwell hardness number is automatically indicated on a dial gage or digital readout.

The Brale diamond penetrator is used for testing material such as hardened steels and cemented carbides. The steel ball penetrators, available with 1/16-, 1/8-, 1/4-, and 1/2-in. diameter, are used when testing materials such as steel, copper alloys, aluminum, and plastics, to name a few.

Rockwell testing falls into two categories: regular Rockwell testing (e.g., HRC and HRB scales) and Rockwell superficial testing (e.g., HR 30N and

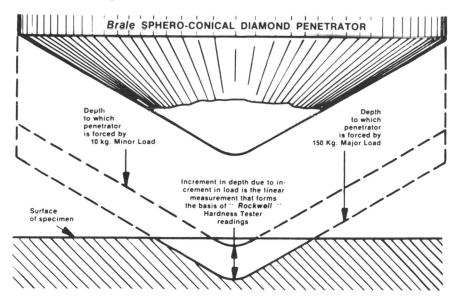

FIGURE 1   Spheroconical diamond penetrator.

HR 30T scales). The dial gage divisions on all Rockwell testers are such
that high Rockwell hardness numbers represent hard materials and low numbers represent soft materials.

Regular Rockwell Testing

In regular Rockwell testing the minor load is 10 kg and the major load can be
either 60, 100, or 150 kg. No Rockwell hardness number is given by a number
alone. It must always be prefixed by a letter signifying the value of the major
load and type of penetrator. A letter has been assigned for every possible
combination of load and penetrator, as shown in Table 2.

One Rockwell number represents a penetration of 0.002 mm (0.000080 in.).
Therefore, a reading of 60 HRC indicates penetration from minor to major load
of $(100 - 60) \times 0.002$ mm = 0.080 mm or 0.0032 in. A reading of 80 HRB indicates a penetration of $(130 - 80) \times 0.002 = 0.100$ mm or 0.004 in.

Superficial Rockwell Testing

In superficial Rockwell testing the minor load is 3 kg and the major load can
be either 15, 30, or 45 kg. No Rockwell superficial hardness number is given
by a number alone. It must always be prefixed by the major load and a letter
for the type of penetrator. A scale designation has been assigned for every
possible combination of load and penetrator, as shown in Table 3.

One Rockwell superficial number represents a penetration of 0.001 mm or
0.000040 in. Therefore, a reading of 80 HR30N indicates penetration from
minor to major load of $(100 - 80) \times 0.001 = 0.020$ mm or 0.0008 in.

B. Scale Selection

In many instances Rockwell hardness tolerances are specified or are indicated
on drawings. At times, however, you must select the Rockwell scale for a

TABLE 2   Regular Tester

Scale Symbol	Penetrator	Load in Kilograms-force
B	1/16″ ball	100
C	*Brale*	150
A	*Brale*	60
D	*Brale*	100
E	1/8″ ball	100
F	1/16″ ball	60
G	1/16″ ball	150
H	1/8″ ball	60
K	1/8″ ball	150
L	1/4″ ball	60
M	1/4″ ball	100
P	1/4″ ball	150
R	1/2″ ball	60
S	1/2″ ball	100
V	1/2″ ball	150

given test specimen or part. Knowledge of the factors governing the choice of the proper Rockwell scale is valuable in this situation, as the choice is not only between the regular hardness tester and superficial hardness tester, with three different major loads for each, but also between the Brale diamond penetrator and the 1/16-, 1/8-, 1/4-, and 1/2-in.-diameter steel ball penetrators or a combination of 30 different scales.

In the event that no specification exists or there is doubt about the suitability of a specified scale, an analysis should be made of the controlling

TABLE 3   Superficial Tester

Scale Symbol	Penetrator	Load in Kilograms-force
15N	N *Brale*	15
30N	N *Brale*	30
45N	N *Brale*	45
15T	1/16″ ball	15
30T	1/16″ ball	30
45T	1/16″ ball	45
15W	1/8″ ball	15
30W	1/8″ ball	30
45W	1/8″ ball	45
15X	1/4″ ball	15
30X	1/4″ ball	30
45X	1/4″ ball	45
15Y	1/2″ ball	15
30Y	1/2″ ball	30
45Y	1/2″ ball	45

factors important in the selection of the proper scale (e.g., type of material and thickness of specimen).

C. Type of Material

ASTM Standard E18 lists all regular Rockwell scales and typical materials for which these scales are applicable. This list (reprinted in Table 4) provides an excellent starting point. Table 4 includes only the Regular Rockwell scales; however, this information can be a helpful guide even when one of the superficial scales may be required. For example, note that the C, A, and D scales—all with the diamond penetrator—are used on hard materials such as steel and tungsten carbide. Any material in this hardness category would be tested with the diamond penetrator. The choice to be made is whether the C, A, D, 45N, 30N, or 15N scale is applicable. In any event, the possible scales have been reduced to six. The next step is to find the scale—whether it be regular or superficial—that will guarantee accuracy, sensitivity, and repeatability.

TABLE 4 Typical Scale Applications

Scale Symbol	Typical Applications of Scales
B	Copper alloys, soft steels, aluminum alloys, malleable iron, etc.
C	Steel, hard cast irons, pearlitic malleable iron, titanium, deep casehardened steel and other materials harder than B 100
A	Cemented carbides, thin steel and shallow case-hardened steel
D	Thin steel and medium casehardened steel and pearlitic malleable iron
E	Cast iron, aluminum and magnesium alloys, bearing metals
F	Annealed copper alloys, thin soft sheet metals
G	Phosphor bronze, beryllium copper, malleable irons. Upper limit G 92 to avoid possible flattening of ball
H	Aluminum, zinc lead
K	
L	
M	Bearing metals and other very soft or thin
P	materials. Use smallest ball and heaviest load that
R	do not give anvil effect
S	
V	

D. Thickness of Specimen

The material immediately surrounding a Rockwell test is cold-worked. The extent of the area cold-worked depends on the type of material and previous work hardening of the test material. The depth of material affected has been found to be on the order of 10 times the depth of the indentation. Therefore, unless the thickness of the material being tested is at least approximately 10 times the depth of the indentation, an accurate Rockwell test cannot be expected. This "minimum thickness" ratio of 10:1 should be regarded only as an approximation.

The depth of penetration for any Rockwell test can be calculated, but in actual practice this is not necessary, as "minimum thickness" charts are available. These minimum thickness values (Table 5) do follow the 10:1 ratio in some ranges, but are actually based on experimentation on varying thicknesses of low-carbon steels and on hardened and tempered strip steel.

TABLE 5   Minimum Specimen
Thickness

Any greater thickness & hardness can be safely tested on indicated scale	Rockwell Superficial Hardness Tester			Rockwell Hardness Tester		
	15 N 15 Kg.	30 N 30 Kg.	45 N 45 Kg.	A 60 Kg.	D 100 Kg.	C 150 Kg.
Thickness in inches	Diamond "N" "Brale" Penetrator			Diamond "Brale" Penetrator		
.006	92	–		–	–	–
.008	90	–	–	–	–	–
.010	88	–	–	–	–	–
.012	83	82	77	–	–	–
.014	76	80	74	–	–	–
.016	68	74	72	86	–	–
.018	X	66	68	84	–	–
.020	X	57	63	82	77	–
.022	X	47	58	78	75	69
.024	X	X	51	76	72	67
.026	X	X	37	71	68	65
.028	X	X	20	67	63	62
.030	X	X	X	60	58	57
.032	X	X	X	X	51	52
.034	X	X	X	X	43	45
.036	X	X	X	X	X	37
.038	X	X	X	X	X	28
.040	X	X	X	X	X	20

Any greater thickness & hardness can be safely tested on indicated scale	Rockwell Superficial Hardness Tester			Rockwell Hardness Tester		
	15T 15 Kg	30T 30 Kg.	45T 45 Kg.	F 60 Kg.	B 100 Kg.	G 150 Kg.
Thickness in inches	1/16" Ball Penetrator			1/16" Ball Penetrator		
.005	93	–	–	–	–	–
.010	90	87	–	–	–	–
.015	78	77	77	–	–	–
.020	X	58	62	100	–	–
.025	X	X	26	92	92	90
.030	X	X	X	67	68	69
.035	X	X	X	X	44	46
.040	X	X	X	X	20	22

A typical example of the use of these tables should be helpful. Consider a requirement to check the hardness of a strip of steel 0.014 in. thick, of approximate hardness 63 HRC. According to Table 5, the material must be approximately 0.028 in. for an accurate Rockwell C scale test. Therefore, this specimen should not be tested on the C scale. A handy tabulation to make at this point is the approximate converted hardness on the other Rockwell scales equivalent to 63 HRC. These values, taken from Wilson Conversion Chart No. 52, are 73 HRD, 83 HRA, 70 HR45N, 80 HR30N, and 91 HR15N. Referring once again to Table 4, for hardened 0.014-in. material, there are only three Rockwell scales to choose from: 45N, 30N, and 15N. The 45N scale is not suitable, as the material should be at least 74 HR45N. On the 30W scale, 0.014-in. material must be at least 80 HR30N—the material in question is 80 HR30N. On the 15N scale, the material must be at least 76 HR15N. This material is 91.5 HR15N. Therefore, either the 30N or the 15N scale may be used. After all limiting factors have been eliminated, and a choice exists between two or more scales, the scale applying the heavier load should be used. The heavier load will produce a larger indentation, covering a greater portion of the material, and a Rockwell hardness number more representative of the material as a whole will be obtained. In addition, the heavier the load, the greater the sensitivity of the scale.

The foregoing approach would also apply in determining which scale should be used to measure the hardness of the case for a case of known approximate depth and hardness. Minimum-thickness charts as well as the 10:1 ratio serve only as guides. After determining the Rockwell scale, based on minimum thickness values, an actual test should be made and the underside directly beneath the area of test examined to determine if the material was disturbed or if a bulge exists. If so, the material was not sufficiently thick for the applied load, resulting in a condition known as the "anvil effect," and the Rockwell scall applying the next lighter load should be used. On softer materials the high stress concentration due to insufficient thickness will result in flow of the material.

When either anvil effect or flow exists, the Rockwell hardness number obtained may not be a true value. The use of several specimens piled one on top of the other is not recommended. The slippage between the contact surfaces of the several specimens makes a true value impossible to obtain.

E. Spacing of Indentation

An indentation hardness test cold-works the surrounding material, and if another indentation is placed within this cold-worked area, the Rockwell hardness test will be affected. Usually, the readings will be higher than on the virgin material.

If the indentation is placed too close to the edge of a specimen, the material will yield and the Rockwell hardness number decreased accordingly. Experience has shown that the distance from the center of the indentation to the edge of the specimen must be at least $2\frac{1}{2}$ diameters to assure an accurate test.

The distance from center to center of indentations must be at least three diameters. Usually, the softer the material, the more critical the spacing, but if a distance of three diameters is maintained, the indentations will be far enough apart for most materials.

F. Support for Test Piece

An important requirement of The Rockwell test is that the surface being tested be normal (at right angles) to the penetrator and that the piece being tested not move or slip as the major load is applied. The depth of indentation is measured by the movement of the plunger rod holding the penetrator; therefore, any slipping or moving of the piece will be followed by the plunger rod and the motion transferred to the dial gage, causing an error. As one point of hardness represents a depth of only 0.000080 in., a movement of only 0.001 in. could cause an error of over 10 Rockwell numbers. The support itself must be of sufficient rigidity to prevent its permanent deformation in use.

Sheet metal, small pieces, or pieces that do not have flat undersurfaces are tested on an anvil having a small, elevated, flat bearing surface. Pieces that are not flat should have the convex side on the bearing surface.

IV. MICROHARDNESS TESTING

The term *microhardness* usually refers to indentation tests made with loads up to 1000 g. The indenter is either the Vickers or the Knoop diamond indenter. The size of the indentation, which is extremely shallow, is such that it must be precisely determined with a microscope with good resolving power. It is very important that the surface being tested be lapped flat and be free from scratches. For tests with loads of 100 g or lighter, a metallographic finish is necessary. (See Chapter 31.)

The microhardness test is generally used for testing the following:

Small precision parts
Surface layers
Thin materials and small-diameter wires
Exploration of small areas
Hardness of constituents
Hardness near the edge of cutting tools
Dental materials

A. Knoop Scale

The Knoop hardness number is the applied load divided by the unrecovered projected area of the indentation. The Knoop indenter (Fig. 2) is a diamond ground to pyramidal form that produces a diamond-shaped indentation having an approximate ratio between long and short diagonals of 7:1. The pyramid shape has an included longitudinal angle of 172°30' and included transverse angle of 130°0'. The depth of indentation is about one-thirtieth of its length. The Knoop hardness number is the load divided by the projected area. Both hard and brittle materials may be tested with the Knoop indenter.

The Knoop hardness number (HK) is the ratio of the load applied to the indenter, P (kgf) to the projected area A (mm^2). By formula,

$$HK = \frac{P}{A} = \frac{P}{C\ell^2}$$

where

P = applied load (kg)

A = unrecovered projected area of indentation (mm^2)

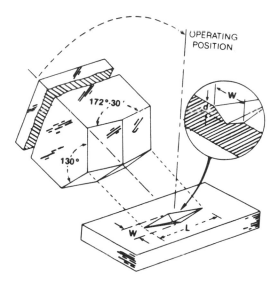

FIGURE 2   Knoop indenter.

ℓ = measured length of long diagonal (mm)

C = 0.07028 = constant of indenter, relating projected area of the indentation to the square of the length of the long diagonal

The Knoop hardness number calculated from this equation can be found in ASTM Standard 384.

B. Vickers Scale

The Vickers hardness number is the applied load divided by the surface area of the indentation. The Vickers indenter is a diamond ground in the form of a square-based pyramid with an angle of 136° between faces (Fig. 3).

With the Vickers indenter, the depth of indentation is about one-seventh of the diagonal length. For certain types of investigation, there are advantages to such a shape. The diamond pyramid hardness (DPH) number (HV) is the ratio of the load applied to the indenter, P (kgf), to the surface area of the indentation (mm^2), or

$$HV = \frac{2P \sin(\theta/2)}{d^2}$$

where

P = applied load (kg)

d = mean diagonal of the indentation (mm)

θ = angle between opposite faces of the diamond = 136°

The Vickers hardness number calculated from this equation can be found in ASTM Standard E384.

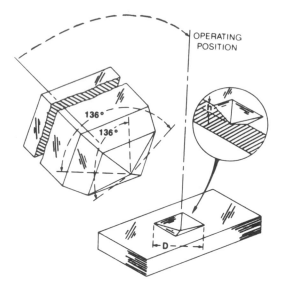

FIGURE 3   Diamond pyramid indenter.

C. Knoop Versus Vickers

Figure 4 is a comparison of indentation made with Knoop and Vickers under loads of 3000, 1000, 500, and 100 g on steel of approximate hardness 550 HV (1000-g load). For a given load, the Vickers indenter penetrates about twice as far into the specimen as the Knoop indenter, and the diagonal will be about one-third of the length of the Knoop indentation. Thus the Vickers test is less sensitive to surface conditions than the Knoop test, and for equal loads the Vickers indentation, because of its shorter length, is more sensitive to errors in measuring the indentation.

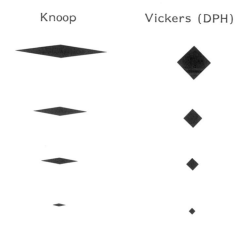

FIGURE 4   Indentation comparison. Knoop and diamond pyramid indentations under loads of 3000, 1000, 500, and 100 g. (Not to actual size.)

D. Surface Preparation

To permit accurate measurement of the length of the Knoop indentation or diagonals of the Vickers indentations, the indentations must be clearly defined. A sharp indentation is in fact the criterion for surface preparation, and as a rule the lighter the test load, the higher the degree of surface finish required.

In many instances the piece to be tested for microhardness will also be used for metallographic examination, in which case mounting, polishing, and even etching are justified. More often than not, however, mounting is not necessary and only a simple polishing is required.

Many standard fixtures are available for supporting the majority of parts normally tested for microhardness. At the start of any testing work a piece should be placed on one of these fixtures and a test made. If the indentation is clearly defined, no polishing is required. If the indentation is not clearly defined, the test surface should be polished with varying grades of emery paper until the indentation is sharp. If even 4/0 emery paper is not successful, polishing with diamond paste and a felt bob is recommended. When testing at loads below 100 g it may be necessary to go to a metallographic finish. (Refer to ASTM Designation E3.)

E. Optical Equipment

Optical equipment used in microhardness testers for measuring the indentation must focus both ends of the indentation at the same time as well as be rigid and free from vibration. Lighting also plays an important role. Complete specifications of measurement, including the mode of illumination, are necessary in microhardness testing techniques. Polarized light, for example, results in definitely larger measurements than does unpolarized light. Apparently, this is caused by the reversal of the defraction pattern; that is, the indentation appears brighter than the background. In recording data, the magnification should be reported.

Dry objectives having the highest resolving power available are generally used, but oil immersion objectives may be necessary under some conditions. For dry lenses, with the highest numerical aperture that can be used, an accuracy of ± 0.5 µm is possible. Also, the same observer can compare differences between two specimens to ± 0.2 µm accuracy. It should, however, be added that considerable experience and care are necessary to obtain this accuracy.

F. Hardness Number Depends on Load

Prior to the advent of the microhardness tester, it had been assumed that the Vickers indenter (as well as other indenters giving geometrically similar indentations) produced a hardness number which was independent of the indenting load. Speaking very generally, this can be accepted for loads of approximately 1000 g and up. However, microhardness testing, when performed with loads of less than 500 g with the Knoop and 100 g with the Vickers indenter, is a function of the magnitude of the test load. In most instances, microhardness values, particularly Knoop values, decrease with increasing load, as Fig. 5 illustrates.

Some observers have noticed, however, an initial increase in microhardness values with increasing load. This is followed by a range in which the hardness becomes independent of the load or decreases continuously to a constant

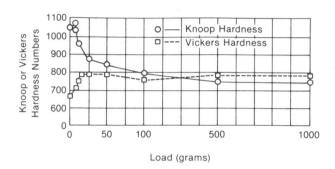

FIGURE 5   Hardness values as function of test load.

value. This effect occurs with a wide range of materials, from those as
soft as copper to fully hardened martensitic steel.

The apparent increase in hardness with decrease in load (in properly prepared surfaces, of course) is caused primarily by an error in the determination of the size of the indentation and in the elastic recovery of the indentation. As the size of the indentation decreases, a change in hardness will result. It may be related to the stress-strain curve of the material and the
relationship between the size of the indentation and the constituents of the
material.

From a practical standpoint, however, load dependence does not have to
be a problem. The choice of load depends on the size and depth of indentation which is considered to be most desirable. Generally, the indentation is
made as large as practicable to obtain the greatest accuracy possible. As
long as a single load is used throughout a study, the load dependence takes
on less significance. Using different loads in any particular investigation
alters the hardness numbers as measured. The lighter the load, the more
significant the change. As a general rule, any comparison of Knoop hardness

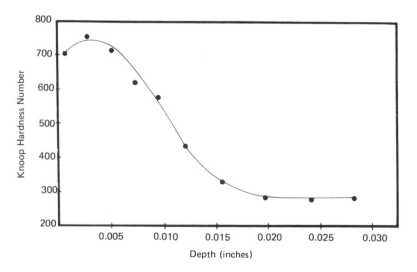

FIGURE 6   Knoop hardness gradient through carburized case with 1-kg
load.

FIGURE 7 Photomicrograph of hardness gradient through carburized case.

numbers with loads under a value of 500 g and Vickers hardness numbers
under a value of 100 g is incorrect unless the load dependence of the hardness is clearly pointed out. Indicate the load use when listing Knoop or
Vickers numbers.

G. Case Depth Determinations

The microhardness test is extremely useful in determining "effective" case
depth. Effective case depth is the distance normal to the surface of the
hardened case where the hardness is a specified value. This hardness is
usually 50 HRC. The microhardness test, usually the Knoop test, is the most
accurate and repeatable method of determining the effective case depth by
means of a hardness traverse. As illustrated in Fig. 6, the hardness gradient is determined from a small distance from the surface inward on a cross-
sectioned and polished specimen. 50 HRC converts to 542 HK, and therefore,
for the example illustrated, the effective case depth is approximately 0.009 in.
(Fig. 7).

40

TENSILE TESTING

JOSEPH J. CIEPLAK

Acco Industries, Inc.
Bridgeport, Connecticut

I. INTRODUCTION

The basic principles of tension and compression testing have changed hardly at all since 1865, when the Riehle brothers of Philadelphia designed and manufactured the first tensile testing machine (Fig. 1). A known load is applied to a sample of the material being tested, and the deformation of the material under that load is measured. Throughout the test, the deformation, or elongation, is measured to determine the relative relationship of the deformation to the load.

A thicker sample of the same material requires a larger breaking load than that required by a smaller sample. It is therefore necessary to normalize the load and deformation into parameters that do not depend on sample size (Fig. 2). To do this, we convert load into stress by dividing the load applied by the area over which the load acts. The resulting units are called stress, and, in the English system, are expressed as pounds per square. In most cases, the load is normalized by testing specimens of specific length, width, and thickness.

To normalize deformation, we determine the change in length of the sample under a specified load and divide that result by its original length. The resulting parameter is called strain, and in the English system is indicated as inches per inch. Both of these definitions are properly referred to as engineering stress and engineering strain, as they do not take into account the necking down which occurs as a sample is stretched toward breaking.

II. LOAD-DEFORMATION CURVE

The normal result of a tension or compression test is a plot of load versus deformation on graph paper. This plot is called a stress-strain curve, or more accurately a load-deformation curve, and it is this graph which gives us the basic information used to calculate all our results.

In a typical stress-strain curve for metals, load is plotted on the left-hand vertical axis, and elongation is plotted on the horizontal bottom axis.

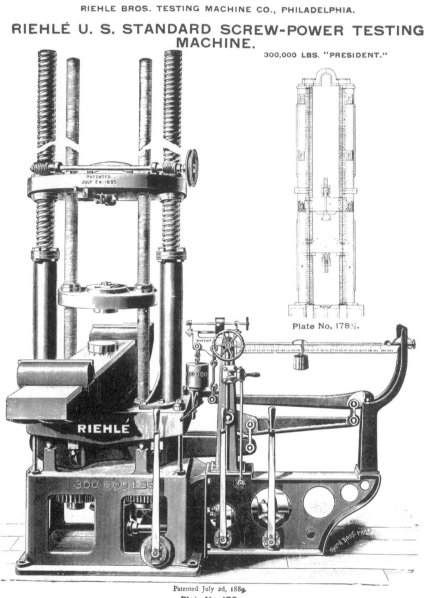

RIEHLE BROS. TESTING MACHINE CO., PHILADELPHIA.

RIEHLÉ U. S. STANDARD SCREW-POWER TESTING MACHINE.

300,000 LBS. "PRESIDENT."

Plate No. 178½.

Patented July 2d, 1889.
Plate No. 178.

Plate 178½ is a sketch showing columns A, B, and the upper grip head D, that are substituted, when ordered, for the outer heavy screw columns and upper head shown in Plate 178. The columns can be extended in sections any desired height. E, F, G, H, are slots in the columns through which heavy steel bars are passed supporting the upper grip head D. I is a tie head.

FIGURE 1   The Riehle Brothers' original tensile test machine.

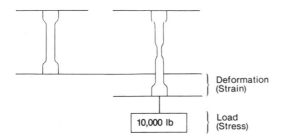

FIGURE 2   A load applied to a sample is called *stress*. The resulting deformation of the sample is called *strain*. *Engineering* stress and strain do not include the effects of sample neck-down.

A typical load-deformation curve is shown in Fig. 3. The first portion of the curve between the zero point and point A is the elastic portion. In this region there is a direct and uniform relationship between the amount of load applied and the resulting elongation, represented by a straight line. These results are indicative of most metals. Other materials, such as plastic or rubber, do not normally exhibit a straight-line relationship anywhere on the curve. Up until point A, which is called the proportional limit, the test could be aborted and the sample would return to its original length with no permanent change having resulted from the test. Once the test has gone through the proportional limit, the material generally has undergone permanent deformation and no longer will be able to return to its original condition.

Points B and C are graphically determined yield points which represent the stress value at which the material being tested exhibits a specific limiting

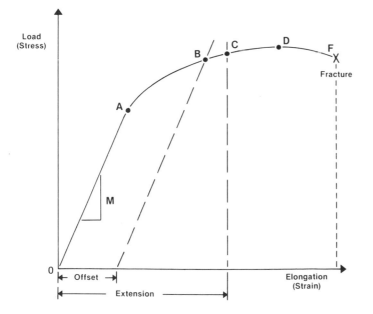

FIGURE 3   A typical load-deformation (stress/strain) curve.

permanent deformation. This yield stress is generally regarded as the stress beyond which the material cannot be used in normal circumstances. Farther along the graph, point D represents the highest load or the highest stress seen by the sample during the testing process. This point is called the ultimate strength. All loading done after this point will be at a lower level as the sample "necks down" (i.e., its cross-sectional area decreases as the elongation begins to increase rapidly). Point F is the fracture point at which the sample breaks and the test is concluded.

Once the graph has been drawn by the recording device connected to the tensile tester, the operator must graphically obtain the desired results. The slope of the line, up to point A, represents the completely elastic relationship of the stress to the resulting strain. For metals, this is called Young's modulus and is obtained by dividing a specific change in stress by the corresponding change in strain. The Young's modulus of many metals can be expressed in millions of pounds per square inch.

Points B and C represent two different methods of determining the yield strength of the material. The choice of method depends on the material being tested and its normal characteristics. In the *offset* method, a particular strain offset is chosen, often 0.2% of the gage length, and a parallel line is then drawn 0.2% to the right of the zero starting point until it intersects the stress-strain curve. This point, B, is then considered the yield strength by the offset method. Similarly, the yield strength by the *extension-under-load method* is determined by moving a predetermined distance to the right of the zero point, often a 0.5% elongation, and then drawing a perpendicular line upward until it intersects with the stress-strain curve. This point, C, is then considered the yield point by the extension-under-load method. In both cases, the particular offset or extension being used is an integral part of the testing results and must be recorded in order for the results to be reproducible by other laboratories.

If we were testing other materials, we might be looking for different results. For instance, Young's modulus would be meaningless for rubber material, as there would be no straight-line portion of the curve. If we were testing a plastic material, we would be concerned with the tensile strength at the breaking point and the percent elongation at particular points during the loading process and at the breakpoint. Another calculation sometimes necessary for plastic testing is tensile energy absorbed (TEA). This result is obtained by integrating the area under the curve from the zero point to the fracture point. Although the tensile test itself is basically a simple test, the analysis of the results becomes the important task.

III. APPLICATIONS

Although a simple test, the tensile test provides information which can be used for many purposes. For example, in those cases where material is being made as part of a continuous process, specimens may be taken at specific intervals from the production line and tested on a universal testing machine (UTM) to determine the properties of the material being produced. If the test results show incorrect properties or a lack of homogeneity in the material, the laboratory can feed this information back to the manufacturing people to have the process adjusted to bring it to within the appropriate specifications.

Some products, such as steel, reinforced fiberglass, and wood composites, are sold with a guarantee that they conform to certain strength specifications.

In these cases a tensile machine is used to qualify the products sold, and a copy of the results obtained from the test is often supplied with the material as proof of conformance.

Occasionally, it becomes necessary to verify certain materials to determine their mechanical properties before their use in a manufacturing process. In these circumstances, samples of an unknown or questionable material are tested in a tensile machine to ensure that they meet specifications.

Design engineers often choose a material to be used in a finished product by considering its structural characteristics, its formability, or its fatigue-resisting characteristics. In these cases, the design engineering group will compile information concerning tensile results and will probably specify tests to be run on the material they are considering for use in a critical application. In the never-ending search for stronger, lighter-weight, and less costly material, the universal testing machine is used routinely to compile research information for analysis by material scientists.

IV. UNIVERSAL TESTING MACHINE COMPONENTS

In its simplest form, a universal testing machine system (Fig. 4) includes a load frame where the test is actually performed. The load frame must, of course, be rugged enough for the application. Some means of control over the load frame is necessary. This control can be as simple as a hand wheel on a valve or as complex as a computer to control the loading and unloading process and the rates at which these are done. Generally, a recorder is used to record permanently the results of the test.

Grips or some other accessory device are used to interface between the sample being tested and the load frame itself. The action and use of the grips is often one of the most critical and least understood parts of the test. Many people who have been in the tensile testing industry for long periods of time consider the use and choice of grips to be an art, patiently and painstakingly learned through experience.

We also need a load-measuring device, such as a load cell, a pressure transducer, or a mechanical beam, to provide information concerning the load applied.

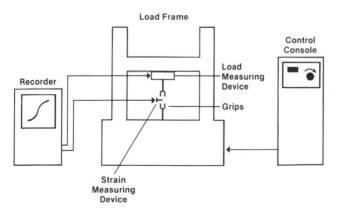

FIGURE 4   Block diagram of a universal testing machine. Either tension or compression can be applied to the sample.

Additionally, in most instances we require information concerning the amount of elongation or deformation the sample has undergone. For these cases we use a strain measuring device such as an LVDT extensometer, a crosshead motion transmitter, a deflectometer, or even an infrared extensometer.

V. FACTORS IN SELECTING A UTM

A great variety of factors determines the appropriate choice of a universal testing machine, including type of testing, load capacity, testing speeds, maximum elongation, data compilation, operator skill, location, and cost.

1. *Type of testing*: Foremost among the questions that arise is whether the machine will be used for a single purpose, such as repeated testing of 0.505-in. test bars, or whether the machine will be used where versatility is required, such as in a professional testing lab, where testing may be performed on anything from aluminum foil and paper to concrete beams and reinforcing bars.

2. *Load capacity*: All the specimens to be tested must be reviewed and a determination made as to the highest load capacity required. In many cases it is possible to reduce the dimensions of the specimen if for some reason a higher-capacity machine is not available. Universal testing machines are generally purchased with the maximum capacity of the load frame as the determining factor, and with ranging modules or auxiliary load cells to provide testing capacities at intermediate positions below the maximum capacity of the load frame. For instance, a 60,000-lb load frame can easily be provided with full-scale ranges of 60,000, 30,000, 12,000, and 6000 lb. The use of auxiliary load cells would provide even lower-capacity full-scale ranges.

3. *Testing speeds*: Rubber generally requires testing at 20 in./min, while most metals require testing at much slower speeds, such as 0.2 in./min. You must determine beforehand the testing speed requirements of your samples and use a testing machine with the appropriate speed ranges.

4. *Maximum elongation*: Metals that elongate only a few percentage points do not require large travel of the crosshead. A 6-in. hydraulic ram provides sufficient movement. However, materials such as plastic and rubber may elongate 600 or 700% and require large crosshead travel. In these cases, a screw-powered load frame is required. Many labs also have special testing conditions that must be considered. For example, a wider-than-normal load frame may be necessary for those applications in which furnaces or ovens will be used in the test procedures. Some compression tests require the ability to apply loads offset from the centerline of the specimen. The testing machine being considered must have the ability to operate correctly under offset loading conditions.

5. *Data Compilation*: If no permanent copy is required, a simple dial gage or digital display is all that is necessary. If permanent records must be kept, either a recording device or a printing device is necessary to supply copies of these results. If data are to be fed to a computer terminal, sophisticated data acquisition equipment is required. In situations where process control is being performed by the tensile test, it is necessary that high production rates be maintained. In these cases it would be wise to use a single-purpose machine set up specifically for the material being tested. The loss of versatility is more than made up for by the increase in efficiency. If, however, we are discussing a research lab situation, the speed at which testing is performed is not nearly as critical as the ability to perform a great variety of test functions.

6. *Operator skill*: The degree of machine control and data acquisition capability of the testing system affect the operator's skill requirements In general, the more the machine does, the higher the skill level of the operator must be.

7. *Location*: The physical size of the tester must be accommodated by the space available. This is especially important for testers that are unusually high or which require a pit to be located beneath the load frame. Second, unusually high- or low-temperature conditions and environmental conditions, such as humidity, dust, and oil, must be considered, especially as the equipment becomes more sophisticated and uses more electronic components. Third, the electrical power available to the machine is also critical, again, especially as the tester becomes more sophisticated. Testing systems that use microprocessor control generally require a clean, isolated source of power and no fluctuations in either voltage or current. Induction motors, for example, will cause erroneous results and possible loss of memory to nearby electronic equipment. A power failure, even one lasting only seconds, will abort the test being performed and will probably cause loss of memory and in some computer systems, possibly loss of software.

8. *Cost*: The initial price of the equipment is only one cost element to be considered. Maintenance cost, personnel cost, and the cost of lost opportunity are other very real costs.

VI. CONTROLS

Controls for universal testing machines can either be fixed to the load frame or mounted on a separate console. The load-indicating module displays the load being applied at any point in time. An electronic module adjusts the signal coming from the load cell so that it is properly zeroed under start-test conditions. Another module controls the operating functions of the machine. A sweep dial indicates the speed of the ram. Other controls and pushbuttons turn the machine on or off, choose tension or compression modes, and adjust the speed. The signal conditioning module takes the signal from the LVDT extensometer, demodulates it, and sends it to an X-Y recorder.

Depending on the type of testing being done, it may be necessary for the universal testing machine to have some type of machine control ability. For example, the tester may be required to hold a particular load or a particular position or a particular strain. Additionally, you may want to perform a test that cycles between various loads, positions, or strain conditions. It may also be necessary to control the rate of load application or the rate of strain application.

This type of machine control is available from most microprocessor systems or by specific modules that can be added to the tester's console. Microprocessor-controlled equipment can simplify many machine control functions which formerly were time consuming and complicated to run.

The advent of computer and microprocessor control systems now makes it possible to eliminate much of the tedious deskwork and calculations that are usually necessary to transcribe the raw data into usable information. Without computer assistance, it is not uncommon for an operator to take 5 min to perform the test and another 10 to 15 min to perform the calculations. Many tensile testing systems are now available with data acquisition capabilities to perform a variety of calculations automatically to arrive at final results. Additionally, some systems contain enough memory to hold data from prior tests and

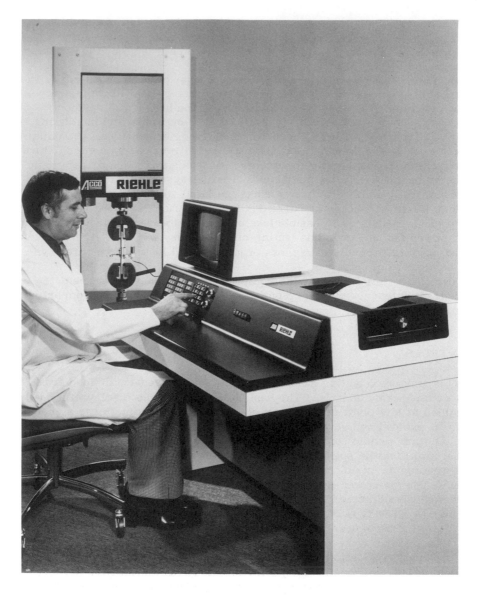

FIGURE 5   A modern, computer-controlled universal testing machine.

intermix it with data from the current test in progress in order to determine average, mean, and standard deviation characteristics. Yield load, yield strength, modulus, ultimate strength, percent elongation, break load, break stress, creep, relaxation, energy under the curve, and mean and standard deviation are all examples of data acquisition requirements that can now be performed routinely and efficiently by microprocessor- and computer-based systems.

Microprocessor-controlled data acquisition systems can be either preprogrammed or user programmable. Either version allows the operator to control the load frame, measure load and strain, analyze the results obtained, compute appropriate parameters, output the information to a CRT screen, a recorder, or a peripheral computer device, and record the information. Preprogrammed units (Fig. 5) require less operator skill and are generally less expensive to purchase, but they may not have the versatility of programmable units.

Preprogrammed units will use PROM (programmable read-only memory) chips and other microprocessor components to store the program and secure it from inadvertent loss or change, but PROM chips also keep the user from modifying the program at will. Programming entries and testing parameters are entered into the computer's memory through the front keyboard panel, and the test is then performed according to these choices.

Programmable control systems generally require either a programmer to program the control and data acquisition functions, which would be stored on disk or magnetic tape, or purchase of manufacturer-supplied software to run the appropriate tests. Programmable controls offer more power and versatility to the user but generally require a higher skill level, a larger investment, and a more controlled environment than do preprogrammed controllers.

While the test is running, the computer system will display the resulting data on the CRT screen. Upon completion of the test, the CRT screen (and printer and recorder if supplied) will display the finished data in the form requested.

VII. COMPUTER LIMITATIONS

A word of caution: As powerful as computer control is, it is no better than the information it receives and the programs it follows. Every computer-controlled program must follow an algorithm established by the programmer. This algorithm approximates as closely as possible the answers that would be obtained by a skilled operator doing manual calculations. The strength of the computer is that it does the computations in the same way every time; the answer is always the same given the same information.

However, there are certain limitations. For example, if we ask the computer to calculate the Young's modulus, it must take a particular stress value and divide it by a particular strain value over the straight-line portion of the graph, the region between zero and A shown in Fig. 3. An operator would look at that line and by eye, be able to tell within reason where the straight-line portion lies.

The computer must use other methods to determine the straight-line portion of the graph. We can program the computer to compare each value that it sees with a prior value and then determine whether the line is still straight, but we have to tell it how far off the line can be before it is no longer straight. If we make our parameters too tight, the computer will read each bump or glitch in the graph as the end of the straight-line portion and will make an erroneous determination of Young's modulus. If we make our algorithm parameters too loose, the computer may make an erroneous late decision on Young's modulus.

Often, the algorithm tells the computer to begin taking data at a certain percent of the load range, to end taking data at a higher percent of the load range, and to consider all data in between those two points as a straight line. This method works very well provided that the data are linear between those two positions. Essentially, the choice of the correct program is dependent on the characteristics of the material being tested, and it is not always self-evident in what ways the program characteristics and the material characteristics interact.

VIII. ACCESSORIES

Auxiliary load cells provide full-scale testing at loads below the capacity of the original tester. Many recording devices, such as an X-Y recorder, are available for plotting stress-strain curves. Strip-chart recorders plot stress or strain versus time. Strain and elongation measuring devices include LVDT-type extensometers, deflectometers, crosshead motion transmitters, infrared extensometers, and optical encoders. Extensometers, for example, use knife edges to establish a fixed gage length in the unstressed state. As the load is applied, the bottom knife edge follows the deformation of the sample and mechanically transmits the deformation to a coil, which translates this mechanical movement into an electrical voltage. The electrical voltage is sent to a signal demodulator, where the signal is conditioned for plotting on a recorder.

Grips are used to hold the sample during the testing procedure. It is important that the grips attach themselves firmly to the sample and that no movement in the grips themselves occurs during the critical part of the testing process. It is also important to prevent the grip inserts from breaking or otherwise deforming the sample so as to cause premature failure and therefore, erroneous data.

For heavy load applications, suspended grips are not normally acceptable because the loads are too great and will spring the housings. Open-front grip housings are quite rugged, as they must withstand high loads during the testing process. A rack-and-pinion arrangement is often used to open and close the wedge grips, which are located in the center of the open-front grip housings. The wedge grips are interchangeable depending on the size and type of sample being tested. Flat grips are used for flat samples, and vee grips are used for round samples. Some grip housings also provide hydraulic means of opening and closing the grips.

Closed grip housings require inserting grips through the top or bottom of the crosshead when they are changed or repositioned. This type of housing is the most cumbersome to use but is able to withstand the greatest loads.

41

HEAT TREATING

DAN D. ASHCRAFT

Oklahoma State University
Stillwater, Oklahoma

I. INTRODUCTION

According to the American Society for Metals (ASM), heat treatment is defined as "heating and cooling a solid metal or alloy in such a way as to obtain desired conditions or properties." Such a broad, generic definition requires further explanation to provide meaning and be technologically useful. Heat treatment can be applied to a number of commercial metals with a variety of results. Rather than delving into the science of metals, the focus of this chapter will be on the practical side of this area of physical metallurgy. Furthermore, discussion will be limited to changes in mechanical properties (i.e., strength, hardness, ductility, toughness, etc.) brought about by the effects of heat treatment.

Most applications of engineering metals, as dictated by the design requirements, are based on the economics of selection and processing techniques available. Seldom does a single metal or alloy have all the attributes needed to satisfy the engineering specifications, even though it is possible to enhance a desirable mechanical property by heat treating. Sometimes there are competing requirements. The necessity of changing mechanical properties to fit the performance criteria often results in a compromise of properties. For instance, strength and hardness are usually gained at the expense of ductility. Also, there are those situations requiring the opposite effect in a material; specifically, the reduction on mechanical properties. This occurs frequently in the processing of metals, where it becomes necessary intentionally to decrease strength and increase ductility to accommodate further processing.

Classically, there are three methods by which metallic properties can be altered. The first technique is to control the chemical composition of the metal by adding and deleting certain chemical elements. The second technique is to change the shape of the metal mechanically by plastically deforming the metal; that is, to apply sufficient pressure under controlled conditions to cause a permanent change in shape. Finally, the thermal technique of heat treatment can also have a pronounced affect on mechanical properties of metals. Not only does the temperature itself have an affect, but of equal importance is the control of the thermal cycle. It is the combination of the rate of heating to a

TABLE 1   Common Mechanical Properties

Property	Definition	Measurement units[a]	Alterable by heat treating
Strength (ultimate tensile)	Ratio of maximum load to original cross-sectional area	Psi MPa	Yes
Hardness	Resistance of a metal to plastic deformation, usually by indentation	HB HRC	Yes
Ductility	Ability of material to deform plastically without fracturing	% e % RA	Yes
Toughness	Ability of a metal to absorb energy and deform plastically before fracturing	lbf-ft N-m	Yes
Stiffness	Ability of a metal or shape to resist elastic deflection (modulus of elasticity)	Psi GPa	No

[a]Psi, pounds per square inch (tensile test); MPa, megapascal (tensile test); HB, hardness Brinell (Brinell hardness test); HRC, hardness Rockwell C scale (Rockwell hardness test); % e, percent elongation (tensile test); % RA, percent reduction of area (tensile test); lbf-ft, pounds force-foot (impact test); N-m, newton-meter (impact test); GPa, gigapascal (tensile test).
Source: American Society for Metals, *Metals Handbook*, Vol. 1, Properties and Selection, ASM, Metals Park, Ohio.

certain temperature, the holding time at temperature, and the cooling rate that will determine the resulting properties. Table 1 indicates which mechanical properties can be affected by heat treatment.

To better understand the process of heat treating of metals and their alloys, a brief introduction will describe metals and the principles behind the internal phenomena that bring about the changes in mechanical properties. Following this will be a presentation of common heat treatment processes used for both ferrous and nonferrous metals. Although it is far from the intent of this chapter to be an exhaustive treatise, it will provide the necessary terminology and basic understanding of heat treatment. The concepts addressed here, as well as those beyond this chapter, are covered in many excellent references on heat treating; some of which are at the end of this chapter.

II. STRUCTURE OF METALS

Most commercial engineering metals are not single-element, pure metals, but are commonly alloys, containing two or more elements. In some alloys the presence of an element or elements is intentional. In others they are by-products of the ore extracting and processing operations. Although the cost for complete removal is prohibitive, by-products are kept to a minimum to reduce deleterious effects.

In the transition of a metal from the liquid to the solid state, clusters of metal atoms arrange themselves into a regular and repeated geometric pattern of a crystalline nature. As solidification continues, more atoms are added and this arrangement grows three dimensionally until it abuts an adjacent lattice or exhausts the surrounding liquid. Material properties are largely dependent on the arrangement of this lattice structure. Commercially used metals (Fig. 1) are aggregates of small, irregularly shaped, randomly oriented crystals called grains. The grain size depends on the number of original nucleation sites present during solidification and can subsequently be altered by plastic deformation and heat treatment.

Grains grow at such a rapid pace during solidification that perfect alignment of all atoms in the lattice structure is prevented. This occurs within individual grains as well as at the boundary between adjacent grains. The resulting crystal imperfections are important in two areas. First, in the deformation of metals, these imperfections can be moved when sufficient stress is applied, allowing metals to deform plastically. This capitalizes on the ability of metals to shift their atomic bonds without rupture or cleavage. Planes of

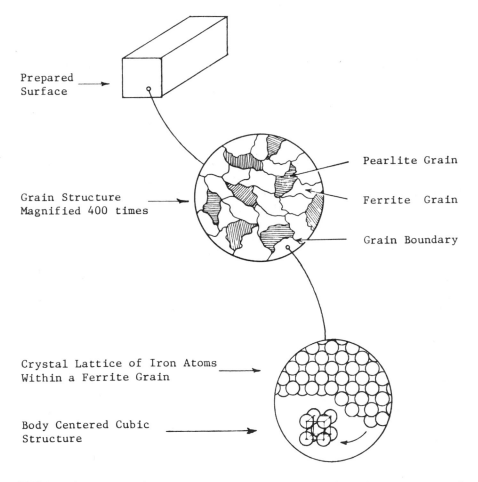

Prepared Surface

Grain Structure Magnified 400 times

Pearlite Grain

Ferrite Grain

Grain Boundary

Crystal Lattice of Iron Atoms Within a Ferrite Grain

Body Centered Cubic Structure

FIGURE 1 Schematic representation of an annealed 1040 steel at the microscopic and atomic levels.

high atomic density, or packing, slide past one another in a compressed ripple effect. Commonly referred to as slip, this phenomenon makes possible many manufacturing operations, such as forging, extrusion, drawing, forming, and cutting. To improve the mechanical properties of strength and hardness, it is only necessary to impede the movement of dislocations or other crystal imperfections. This can be accomplished by alloying with certain-sized elements, which restricts dislocation movement or sufficiently distorts the lattice structure. Higher stress levels are required for plastic deformation, thus improving strength and hardness. Cold working or heat treating can also distort the atomic structure to such a degree as to alter mechanical properties.

The second area where imperfections are helpful is in solid-state diffusion or migration of atoms. At elevated temperatures, as in heat treating, atoms are more dynamic and vibrate so actively that they can move from one lattice position to another. This is all the more facilitated by vacancies or other types of imperfections and is responsible for transformations that occur within metallic structures.

Commercial uses of alloyed metals are so numerous and varied that it is necessary to use general terms to describe their metallic structures in order to discuss their heat treatment and the resultant transformations. The basic structure—that which is physically distinct and mechanically separable—is called a phase. The first of two possibilities are the homogeneous phases, consisting basically of compounds and solid solutions. Chemical compounds are unique substances, the characteristics of which can be used to enhance mechanical properties. Solid solution types consist of alloying atoms randomly substituting for atoms in the lattice structure (substitutional solid solutions) or fitting in the spaces between the solvent atoms (interstitial solid solutions). Both solid solutions and uniformly distributed compounds cause distortion of the lattice structure in the area surrounding the solute atoms, with a resulting change in properties.

The structure known as a mixture constitutes the second phase possibility. Mixtures consist of any combination of two or more homogeneous phases. The dominant and most continuous phase determines a material's properties. Heat treatment makes it possible to alter these phases.

III. HEAT TREATMENT PRINCIPLES

Changing mechanical properties of a metal by altering its metallurgical structure is the main function of heat treatment. Since this involves controlled heating and cooling of the metal, it is important to understand the solid-state transformations or changes that occur during this cycle. The key to successful heat treatment is knowing what phases are present for a given material at a certain temperature and, after a prescribed cooling cycle, being able to predict properties based on resulting structures.

Some metals, notably iron and its alloys, can change lattice structures readily. This polymorphic phenomenon has a pronounced affect of the heat treatability of these materials. A metal thus changing from one lattice structure to another is said to undergo a phase transformation. Other metals, such as aluminum, do not change lattice types.

A. Stages of Heat Treatment

Three stages of heat effect can be considered to occur during a heating cycle. A single-phase solid solution will be used to illustrate these stages. The first is a low-temperature process called recovery. Assuming that the metal was previously cold worked, the lattice would be distorted and grains elongated. As the metal heats up, thermal energy begins to relax the strained lattice. The bonds between metal atoms, which were stretched and held into that position by internal stress, are now relieved and elastic recovery has been established. During this springback of the elastically displaced atoms there is only a slight change in strength and hardness. If no previous distortion of lattice exists while heating through this region, no alteration in microstructure takes place.

The next stage, recrystallization, occurs as heating continues beyond the recovery range. At the grain boundaries a strain-free lattice begins to form from the plastically distorted lattice. These small grains are typical of those formed upon solidification and have the same composition and lattice as the original structure. More minute grains form within the boundaries of each original grain until all the distorted lattice has recrystallized. The temperature at which this begins is dependent on the amount of prior cold working; the more severe the deformation, the more residual energy that is present, and a lower temperature will initiate the process.

Further heating, or holding for long periods after recrystallization, results in grain growth. Some of the new grains just formed will begin to enlarge in size by absorbing other less inclined grains. Since mechanical properties are closely linked with grain size, it is important to control the grain growth. As a rule the smaller grains provide increased strength, hardness, and toughness. When compared to a cold-formed metal, a recrystallized metal is soft, has the lowest strength, and is the most ductile—prerequisites for further plastic deformation. In most cases, after recrystallization grain size will be refined, but the constituents of the grains can vary dramatically with cooling rate.

The final stage of any heat treatment involves the cooling of the metal. The rate of cooling will determine the grain structure, and subsequently, the mechanical properties. Some metals respond by an increase in mechanical properties when cooled rapidly, whereas others may show a decrease. Very slow cooling produces another effect. Rates of cooling between these can result in a variety of structures. Few metals exhibit the same response to heat treatment, the resulting change in properties being dependent on the metal treated. Discussing the heat treatment of specific classes of metals will clarify this concept.

IV. HEAT TREATMENT OF FERROUS METALS

Iron-based, or ferrous, metals constitute the largest tonnage of metals heat treated. Included in this category are plain carbon steels, alloy steels, cast irons, tool steels, stainless steels, and heat-resistant alloys. To simplify this topic, only plain carbon steels are discussed here in any detail. Plain carbon is a qualifier for steels used to designate those which have only carbon as a major alloying ingredient. The other categories are discussed in a number of references at the end of the chapter.

It is important to note that the fundamental heat treatment principles apply regardless of which type of ferrous metal is treated. The main emphasis is the control of heat treatment parameters and the special precautions necessary to produce a satisfactory outcome. Various steels respond differently to heat treatment cycles, the major cause being their distinctive chemical compositions. Knowing at what temperatures certain phase(s) exist and when phase changes

can occur, as a result of a particular cooling rate, is indispensable to heat
treating. Two types of transformation diagrams have been developed which
provide this information graphically: the equilibrium diagram and the isothermal transformation diagram.

A. Iron Carbon Equilibrium Diagram

The classical iron carbon equilibrium diagram, a portion of which is shown in
Fig. 2, is used to illustrate the phase(s) in a plain carbon steel. The phase(s)
present, at a given temperature, is dependent on the carbon content of the
steel when the metal is held at that temperature long enough for equilibrium.
Equilibrium is a solid-state condition of stability or balance among atoms so
that there is no driving force for change. Detailed discussions of this diagram
are contained in the references. However, to apply the basic heat treatment
concepts, it will be necessary to have a brief exposure to the transformations
that take place within this diagram.

The fact that steel can exist in many phases is among its most important
characteristics. For the purpose of discussing heat treating of steels, compositions of less than 2% carbon at temperatures below 2000°F will encompass
the most frequently encountered phases (Fig. 2). In this area there are regions separated by critical temperature lines which indicate that a change of
phase will occur when a line is passed or crossed.

AISI 1040 (American Iron and Steel Institute designation for plain steel
with 0.4% carbon) will serve as an example. Since the grain structure of this

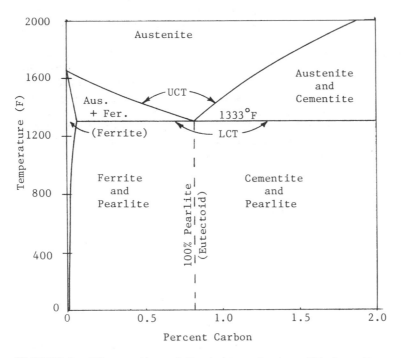

FIGURE 2   The portion of the iron-carbon equilibrium diagram applicable to
heat treatment of plain carbon steels. UCT and LCT indicate upper and lower
critical temperatures.

metal determines many of its mechanical properties, it will be a major focus of this discussion. The heating cycle will be used to illustrate the constituents present and the phase changes that occur at different temperatures. A typical heat treatment cycle begins with the steel at room temperature. A carbon steel, with less than 0.8% C, when slowly cooled to room temperature after solidification, exists as a two-phase structure of ferrite and pearlite (Fig. 1). The relative amount of each depends on the carbon content: The further the percentage is below 0.8%, the more ferrite; the closer the percentage is to 0.8%, the more pearlite. Ferrite is a solid solution whose body-centered-cubic (BCC) structure has virtually no solubility of carbon. As a result it is the softest, the lowest strength, and the most ductile phase of steel. The pearlite grain, on the other hand, is a mixture composed of ferrite and cementite that forms during the eutectoid reaction at 1333°F. This transformation generates a laminated grain consisting of alternating layers, or platelets, of ferrite and cementite. Cementite, an iron carbide compound, is very hard and wear resistant, constituting the hardest phase in the iron carbon equilibrium diagram. Because of the laminar cementite, the pearlite grain structure is much stronger, less ductile, and harder than ferrite.

Heat treating the 1040 steel, which can now be considered a polycrystalline aggregate of ferrite and pearlite grains, begins by heating to the lower critical temperature (Fig. 2). At this point the pearlite grains begin to transform. Cementite becomes unstable at about 1350°F and starts to dissociate. Simultaneously, the laminar ferrite allotopically transforms by shifting its BCC structure into a new face-centered-cubic (FCC) structure called austenite. Austenite has the ability to absorb interstitially more carbon than ferrite, as much as 2%. Acting somewhat like a sponge, austenite absorbs all the carbon atoms dissolving from cementite until the supply of carbide is exhausted. The microstructure is now the original ferrite grains and the newly formed austenite grains. Interestingly, the reaction is a form of recrystallization and the grain size of the old pearlite grain has been reduced in size, composed now of several small austenite grains.

As the temperature rises further, the remaining ferrite grains begin to transform to austenite. Again the transformation takes place primarily at the grain boundary, and the ferrite grain is refined into smaller austenite grains. When the upper critical temperature is reached, the resultant 100% austenitic grain structure undergoes an important reaction. The previously pearlitic austenite is high in carbon, 0.8%, and the austenite from the old ferrite is very low. If the temperature is raised 100°F above upper critical and held there, the carbon atoms will diffuse or migrate from areas of high concentration to areas of low concentration. The resulting microstructure will be more homogeneous with respect to carbon distribution and more likely to have uniform properties, particularly when cooled quickly.

Austenite is a key structure in steels. Not only is it desirable for hot forging due to the ease with which FCC plastically deforms, but austenite signals completion of the first and second stages of heat treatment: those of solution treating and homogenization. When a steel has been completely austenitized it is ready for the final stage of heat treatment, that of cooling. A metal incompletely austenized will not reach full potential when cooled, particularly when a single-phase structure is desired as a final structure. Thus metals are held at austenizing temperatures for an hour per inch of the largest cross section to ensure complete transformation.

B. Isothermal Transformation Diagram

The rate at which austenite is cooled determines the final structure of the metal and thus its resulting properties. The diagram most useful in determining the correct rate of cooling is called an isothermal transformation diagram or more commonly a time-temperature transformation (TTT) diagram. Figure 3 illustrates schematically the transformation products as a function of the cooling rate of austenite for a specific steel. Although developed by studying isothermal cooling effects, the diagrams can be superimposed with continuous cooling curves, resulting in a conservative estimate of transformation products. This is normally sufficient for most engineering applications. When more stringent requirements prevail the continuous cooling diagrams are used.

C. Common Heat Treatment Processes

The majority of heat treatment processes require the same first and second stages, differing only in temperature and soaking time, depending on alloy composition. These processes include full annealing, normalizing, and hardening. The exceptions are those restricted to heating temperatures below critical transformation ranges, such as in stress relieving and tempering.

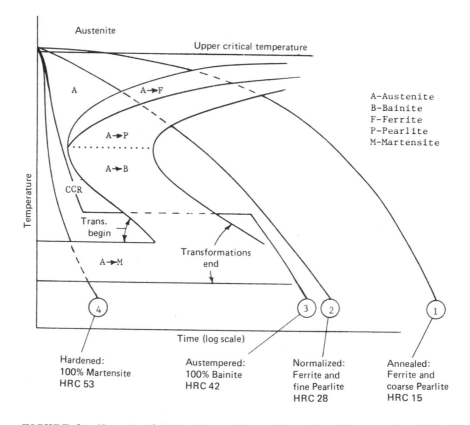

FIGURE 3 Hypothetical isothermal transformation diagram for AISI 1040 steel superimposed with cooling curves, 1 through 4, illustrating typical heat treatments. Dashed lines indicate transformations.

Annealing

The term *annealing* generally refers to the heat treatment cycle that will impart softness and ductility to a metal in any other previous condition (i.e., cold worked or hardened). When the term is used without qualification it is considered to mean full annealing. The process involves fully austenitizing the metal and cooling slowly at 50 to 100°F per hour (curve 1, Fig. 3), usually controlled by cooling in the heat-treating oven or furnace.

It is important when austenitizing that metals be heated slowly and uniformly. With rapid heating a temperature gradient can exist; the outside reaches the critical temperature while the inside is still below it. This condition can promote stress at the surface that could cause warpage. Another deleterious outcome of large thermal gradients is that the higher temperature outside will be austenitic for a longer period. There is a possibility that grain growth will occur in this region.

After annealing, the microstructure, representing steel in its lowest-strength condition, consists of recrystallized ferrite and pearlite grains. Typical uses for annealing are for improved machinability, for further processing requiring plastic deformation, or for completely removing any internal stresses present from operations, such as casting, welding, forging, and so on.

Stress Relieving

Generally considered as a special category of annealing, stress relieving is a heat treatment for reducing the internal stress. After various manufacturing operations requiring plastic deformation, residual stresses are produced. Even castings or weldments can have induced internal stresses due to the nonuniform cooling normally involved. If these locked-in stresses remain in a material, they can cause premature failure, cracking, or excessive distortion during processing or while in service, rendering the part unfit for use.

The process of stress relief is one of subcritical heat treating; that is, the workpiece is heated to a temperature below the lower transformation or recrystallization temperature. The exact temperature depends on the amount of prior cold working and chemical content. For plain carbon steel the temperature range of not greater than 1200°F is generally satisfactory. However, should this temperature exceed the recovery range, the metal will begin to recrystallize. Although the stress will certainly be relieved, other desirable mechanical properties may be reduced. The idea is to reduce only the internal stress without sacrificing strength, hardness, or other properties intentionally induced.

The actual process of stress relieving consists first of heating to the required temperature. The workpiece is held at temperature until uniformly heated; it is then removed from the furnace and allowed to cool in still air or simply furnace cooled. As a rule, parts are placed in a warm furnace and heated to temperature rather than having cold parts thrust into a hot furnace. The nonuniform heating can cause distortion, and the higher the heating temperature, the more important it is to control the heating rate.

Normalizing

Similarly to annealing, parts to be normalized are fully austenitized and held at temperature until homogeneous. But instead of the slow furnace cool of annealing, the part is removed from the furnace and cooled by ambient air (normal cooling) at a slightly quicker rate, 200°F per hour (curve 2, Fig. 3).

The faster cooling generates smaller-grained ferrite and more abundant pearlite upon transformation from austenite. Additionally, the cementite and ferrite platlets are closer together, resulting in a finer pearlite than that of the coarse-grained annealed pearlite. This contributes greatly to the increased strength and hardness of normalized steels compared to those annealed. It is important to point out that some high alloy/medium carbon steels may respond to air cooling by substantially hardening. Normalizing, with its subsequently refined grain size and corresponding increases in mechanical properties, is often a final heat treatment. Normalizing can also be used to improve the machinability characteristics, particularly in low-carbon steels, which when annealed are often too soft and gummy.

Hardening

One of the most interesting and useful characteristics of steel is its ability to attain extreme hardness and high strength under controlled conditions. Three conditions are essential for successful hardening. The first condition is that sufficient carbon, the hardening element, be present. Steels with carbon contents of 0.3% or above show appreciable response to hardening heat treatment, reaching a high hardness of Rockwell C65 at about 0.8% carbon without significant improvement in hardness as content increases.

The second condition, as in all heat treatements, is to heat to the correct temperature range and hold to form a homogeneous fully austenitic steel. The final condition is that the steel be cooled at the required rate to prevent the formation of other softer transformation products (i.e., ferrite and pearlite). If an austenitized steel is cooled very rapidly by being plunged into a cold quenching medium, such as water, the normal equilibrium transformation reactions do not have enough time to take place. The carbon normally expelled when slowly cooled does not precipitate out of solution with the iron and form carbides. Instead, the FCC lattice of austenite shifts so abruptly that the carbon is trapped. The FCC iron tries to transform to a BCC structure, but because of the excess carbon atoms present interstitially, a highly strained body-centered tetragonal (BCT) system is formed. This so distorts the atomic lattice structure that very high hardness ensues. The hardness is a function of how severely distorted or strained the lattice becomes as a result of the amount of carbon present in the BCT. This supersaturated solid solution of carbon in BCT iron is called martensite. Martensite does not all form at the same temperature. Transformation begins at a temperature dependent on the chemical composition of the steel and ends several hundred degrees lower. The main objective of quench hardening is to form a fully martensitic structure. The minimum cooling rate that will accomplish this is called the critical cooling rate (CCR). The controlling factor in determining the CCR is again the chemical composition of the steel. The I-T diagrams shown in Figs. 4 and 5 illustrate this effect. Note that the nose or extreme left-hand portion of the curve is shifted farther to the right in the alloy (4340) than in the plain carbon (1050).

Hardenability

Hardenability is defined as the ability of a steel to be hardened uniformly from the surface of the part to the center. For a given cooling rate, the part size can influence the transformation products. Since the mass effect of large sections causes them to take longer to cool than do thin sections, the result may be softer structures at the center. Alloy ingredients added to steels

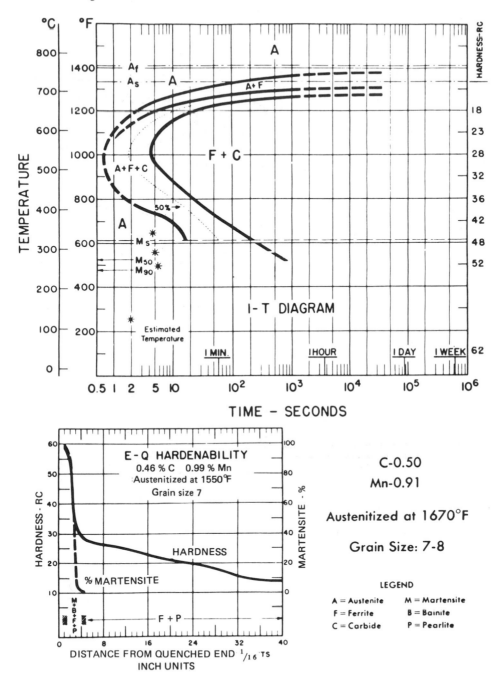

FIGURE 4   Isothermal transformation (I-T) diagram and end quench (E-Q) hardenability chart for AISI 1050 plain carbon steel. (By permission, from *Atlas of Isothermal Transformation and Cooling Transformation Diagrams*. Copyright: American Society for Metals, 1977.)

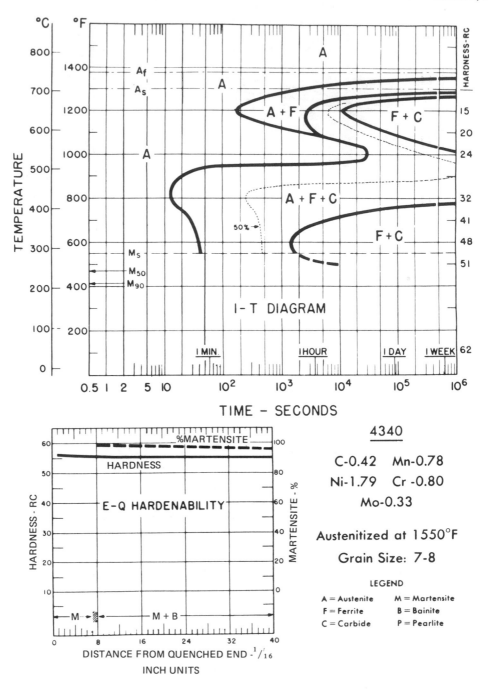

FIGURE 5   Isothermal transformation (I-T) diagram and end quench (E-Q) hardenability chart for AISI 4340 alloy steel. (By permission, from *Atlas of Isothermal Transformation and Cooling Transformation Diagrams*. Copyright: American Society for Metals, 1977.)

enhance response to heat treatment and tend to make the material easier to heat treat, particularly when thicker-cross-sectioned parts require through hardening. By essentially moving the nose of the TTT curve to the right, the cooling rate at the center may be sufficient for full hardness via improved hardenability. Another aspect of this concept is that a slower cooling rate can produce the same result in an alloyed steel as a faster rate in plain carbon. Therefore, slower quenching mediums, such as oil, may be used. If sufficient alloy content is present, the CCR may slow to a point requiring only air cooling while still producing a very hard structure of martensite uniformly throughout its thickness. Metals with this characteristic are said to have high or good hardenability.

Hardenability is commonly measured by the end quench test. A comparison of the end quench (E-Q) hardenability curves of Figs. 4 and 5 shows that both steels have high hardness, HRC 60 to 55. This is due to the fact that the hardness of a critically quenched, fully martensitic steel is primarily a function of carbon content. But the hardness drops abruptly in the 1050, indicating low hardenability, whereas the 4340 maintains this hardness and thus has high hardenability, the depth to which the hardness exists being largely a function of alloy content.

Tempering

With its high hardness, martensite is correspondingly brittle, usually not a desirable mechanical property. It is therefore common practice to remove or reduce the brittleness to a degree by the process of tempering. By reheating a quenched hardened steel to a temperature some point below the lower transformation, additional adjustments in mechanical properties are possible. As a martensitic steel is heated, the lattice structure, which is very distorted as it tightly grips the carbon, begins to release some carbon from solid solution and relaxes. This decomposition of martensite is a function of temperature and holding time. Basically, the higher the temperature and the longer the time, the more pronounced the effect.

When, depending on material design requirements, it may be desirable to maintain high hardness and wear resistance while reducing brittleness, a low tempering temperature, 200 to 400°F, would be chosen. At the other extreme, if improvement in toughness were required, a higher tempering temperature, 1200°F, would sacrifice the high hardness for better impact properties. Tempering between these two extremes represents a compromise of hardness and strength for ductility and toughness, as illustrated in Fig. 6.

Austempering

An intermediate transformation product known as bainite is the last member of the "ite" family. Full bainitic structure can be formed only by an interrupted quenching process. Austenitized steel is cooled critically, generally into a liquid salt bath, to a temperature above the martensite start temperature. It is then held there isothermally until the complete austenite-to-bainite transformation occurs and then cooled normally to room temperature (curve 3, Fig. 3). Metals cooled in this fashion must be of small cross section to be cooled critically. When such a transformation results in 100% bainite the heat treatment process is called austempering. While having similar strength and hardness of equivalent steels that were quench hardened, an austempered steel will exhibit increased ductility and a significant increase in toughness; very

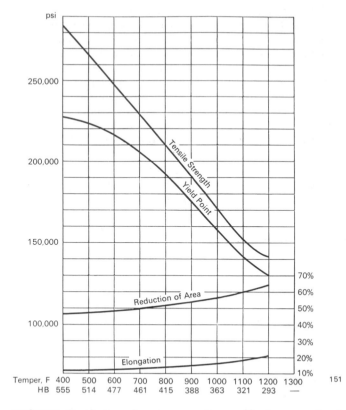

FIGURE 6   Tempering temperature effect on mechanical properties of an oil quenched 4340. (From *Modern Steels and Their Properties*, Bethlehem Steel Corp.)

good for lawn mower blades, shovels, and so on. Another advantage of austempering is that it is a complete heat treatment, whereas quench hardening is normally followed by secondary treatment tempering.

Surface Heat Treatment

In some cases it is desirable to increase the mechanical properties at the surface of a metal only. Two techniques make it possible to treat the surface of steels. First, when the carbon content in a steel is below that necessary for substantial hardening it can be increased by one of several carburizing processes. Parts to be carburized are austenitized in the presence of a carbonaceous medium, causing carbon diffusion into the surface. With sufficient carbon at the surface, quenching will harden the case while the core, with insufficient carbon, remains softer. It should be pointed out that carburizing is a reversible reaction. Therefore, in heat treatment processes at elevated temperatures, the furnace atmosphere must be controlled to prevent surface decarburizing and scaling. Other surface alloying processes are used to diffuse a variety of elements into the surface of steels.

   In the second technique, called selective hardening, a hardenable steel (steel with enough carbon to quench harden) is heated on the surface only and rapidly cooled, forming a hard martensite case. The two common processes are known as flame and induction hardening, which refer to the method used

to heat the surface. The main advantage of selective hardening is that it is
a much faster process and more easily automated than surface alloying. Currently, laser and electron-beam technologies are being used to provide finer
control and are particularly well suited to selectively harden parts having
complex geometry.

V. HEAT TREATMENT OF NONFERROUS METALS

Whereas ferrous alloys are used for more engineering application than nonferrous metals, nonferrous metals have a wider variety of useful characteristics and properties. Most widely used of the nonferrous group for structural applications are the aluminum alloys. Among their important properties
is their light weight, coupled with the ability to improve their mechanical
properties. These attributes often make aluminum alloys useful as a substitute
for the lower-strength steels.

Mechanical properties of aluminum alloys can be enhanced by some of the
same mechanisms used for steel. For most commercial uses the pure form of a
metal lacks the required mechanical properties. Three mechanisms exist for
altering properties of aluminum: alloying, strain hardening, and heat treatment. The first of these is the most common form of aluminum. Alloyed aluminum can be further enhanced, with respect to mechanical properties, by the
other two mechanisms, which categorize aluminum alloys as either non-heat-
treatable or heat-treatable alloys.

A. Non-heat-treatable Aluminum Alloys

Beyond the initial alloy strengthening, the non-heat-treatable aluminum can
be strain hardened. In fact, cold working is the only method possible for
increasing the strength and hardness of these alloys, as they do not respond
to strengthening heat treatments. Table 1 shows the increases in mechanical
properties of typical aluminum alloys that have been work hardened. Notice
the temper heading. This temper designation, one of four such developed by
the Aluminum Association, does not have the same connotation as tempering
heat treatment used for steels. With respect to aluminum alloys it refers to
additional operations performed on the alloy beyond the initial alloying process.
In this case the series suffix "H" indicates degrees of strain hardening (e.g.,
3003 H14).

B. Heat-Treatable Aluminum Alloys

The heat-treatable aluminum alloys can be subjected to thermal processing,
which will enhance mechanical properties. This is possible because the elements used in the alloys of this series exhibit increased ability to absorb more
alloying elements at high temperatures and a decrease in this solubility at lower
temperatures—prime prerequisites for precipitation hardening. The process
involves heating to elevated temperature until alloy ingredients dissolve into
solution and become homogeneously distributed among the aluminum atoms.
After solution heat treatment the alloy is rapidly cooled, generally water
quenched, trapping the elements. The metal is soft and ductile and easily
workable immediately after cooling. However, the unstable supersaturated
structure soon begins to precipitate naturally. The alloying elements come
out of solution in the form of fine compounds which are uniformly distributed.

The subsequent distortion of the lattice structure improves strength and hardness of these alloys. This natural aging begins to strengthen rapidly within the first hour and reaches a maximum in 4 to 5 days, depending on the alloy. The aging process can be accelerated by heating above room temperature. Referred to as artificial aging, this technique is quicker but does not attain as high a strength. Heat-treatable alloys can also be cold worked if done immediately after solution treating, and appreciable increases in strength and hardness result when naturally or artificially aged. Typical mechanical properties are shown in Table 2.

Two additional heat treatments, annealing and stress relief, can be employed regardless of whether the aluminum alloy is categorized as heat treatable or not. Annealing of aluminum or its alloys requires heating to the recrystallization range, which will produce a smaller strain-free grain structure. This softening is particularly important when cold forming, where the reduction is so severe that the metal becomes hard and brittle. The cooling rate after recrystallization is generally slow. The compounds that precipitate during this cooling generally coalesce into large groups and do not impart substantial strengthening to the alloy that is commonly produced by finely dispersed precipitate.

When a manufacturing process induces deleterious stresses on an aluminum alloy it is often recommended that stress relief treatment be employed. The alloy is heated to below its recrystallization temperature, allowed to soak, and then cooled at any rate that will not reintroduce stress. No appreciable loss in strength will occur and harmful stresses will be reduced.

TABLE 2   Representative Mechanical Properties of Typical Wrought Aluminum Alloys

Alloy	Non-heat-treatable						Heat-treatable					
	1100		3003		5005		2024		6061		7075	
Temper[a]	0	H18	0	H14	0	H18	0	T4	0	T4	0	T6
Tensile strength (ksi)	13	24	16	22	18	29	27	69	18	35	33	83
Yield strength (ksi)	5	22	6	14	6	28	11	57	8	21	15	73
Elongation (% in 2 in.)	35	9	30	8	30	6	20	10	25	22	17	11
Hardness (BHN)	23	44	28	40	30	51	47	125	30	65	60	150

[a] O, annealed; H14, strain hardened, half hard; H18, strain hardened, full hard; T4, solution treated, naturally aged; T6, solution treated, artificially aged.

Source: Aluminum Standards, Aluminum Association, Inc., Washington, D.C., 1979.

C. Heat Treatment of Copper Alloys

Another, but no less important category of nonferrous metals is that of the copper alloys. Copper has as its most useful properties high electrical and thermal conductivity. Coupled with high ductility for formability and corrosion resistance for longer environmental life, copper is suitable for a number of commercial applications. When strength and hardness of copper are less than required, they can be increased only by cold working, as unalloyed copper does not respond to strengthening heat treatments.

Copper is commonly alloyed with a variety of different elements to meet necessary design requirements. Classified commercially as brasses and bronzes, these copper alloys can be further modified, with respect to mechanical properties, by either plastic deformation (cold working) or heat treatment or both. Each copper alloy has a response to heat treatment unique to its chemical composition.

Brasses

Brass is a copper alloy with zinc as the major alloying element. Brasses can vary in zinc content up to 45% and are commonly called red or yellow, depending on their color. Strength and hardness of brasses increase as a result of solid solution strengthening up to about 40% zinc. Beyond this amount strength and ductility deteriorate owing to the presence of a brittle second-phase structure which has the possibility for heat treatment, although it is rarely performed. The majority of brasses are of the single-phase type and therefore are not strengthenable by heat treatment. The common strengthening procedure is cold working. To soften such a work-hardened brass, an annealing heat treatment is required. This is particularily useful when drastic reductions in cross section, requiring repeated deformations, are needed.

As described previously, distortion of grain structure from cold working sets up a severely strained atomic structure. These residual stresses are relieved in the first stage of annealing. Brasses, especially yellow, are susceptible to the phenomenon of stress-corrosion cracking. This occurs where a stressed metal exhibits an accelerated corrosion at a local surface stress concentration. The localized corrosion causes the formation of a crack which is further propagated by the existing stress, often ending in a premature failure.

By heating to stress-relieving temperatures, but below the recrystallization point, the material will retain cold-worked mechanical properties without stress-corrosion cracking. If reduction in strength and hardness is desired, the recrystallization stage of annealing must be reached. Cooling rate from these temperatures has no effect on these single-phase brasses.

Bronzes

Bronze is a generic name applied to most other alloys of copper, the exception being the copper-zinc brasses. The name implies a better class of alloy than brass with respect to strength and corrosion resistance. Among the numerous bronzes the most common commercially used are those where copper is alloyed with tin, aluminum, silicon, or beryllium.

Tin bronze has higher strength and hardness and wear resistance due to the presence of a relatively brittle copper-tin compound which forms upon solidification. Stress relieving and annealing are the most common heat treatments for tin bronze.

Aluminum bronze, unlike tin bronze, can be quench hardened for superior strength, hardness, and wear resistance. The resulting microstructures are similar to that found in steel. When tempered, aluminum bronze will be additionally strengthened, owing to a small amount of precipitation hardening.

Silicon bronze, similar to tin bronze, can only be annealed or stress relieved, as it does not respond to quench hardening. However, silicon bronze has the distinction of being the strongest of the work-hardenable copper alloys, with comparable mechanical properties to mild steel and corrosion resistance of copper.

Beryllium bronze (also called beryllium copper) enjoys commercial importance due in part to acquired strengths as high as those of alloy steel. This most dramatic improvement in mechnaical properties, coupled with good conductivity and corrosion resistance, make beryllium bronze widely used in electric contacts, switches, and so on, where high hardness, fatigue strength, and wear resistance are needed. These enhanced properties are obtained by precipita- that used in aluminum alloys (see Section V.B).

All copper alloys can be obtained from the mill or supplier in the desired form and condition (e.g., strip, bar; solution annealed, hardened; etc.). Of particular importance is specifying the condition particularly when additional fabrication is necessary, such as the punch press operations of piercing, blanking, and forming. The ease with which these operations are performed is related to their preforming properties and should be matched accordingly.

The precipitation hardening of beryllium bronze is a two-stage thermal treatment. The solution heat treatment can and should be supplied by the mill. The end user then need only perform the hardening heat treatment after forming to desired configuration. The age hardening is accomplished simply by heating to the recommended low temperature, causing a fine dispersion of precipitated beryllium-copper compounds. When severely deforming beryllium bronze for special operations, such as deep drawing, it may be necessary to soften and restore preforming properties. This would normally be accomplished by annealing; however, if beryllium bronze is fully annealed, it will not respond to precipation hardening. Therefore, the work should be solution annealed by heating to above the recommended critical temperatures for a sufficient time to allow complete decomposition of precipitate followed by critical quenching. This will produce a workable product by preventing the precipitate from forming. The ease of prehardened fabrication and advantage of age hardening to high strengths make beryllium bronze one of the more commercially important copper alloys.

VI. QUALITY IN HEAT TREATMENT

Heat treatment parameters must be considered and properly orchestrated to produce the desired effect of the heat treatment cycle. Obviously, the process must be carefully controlled using the proper equipment, correct and accurate temperatures, suitable quenching mediums, and prescribed procedures for consistently satisfactory performance. In assuring the quality of heat-treated parts, process control requires being able to determine when parts do not meet engineering specifications. A number of destructive and nondestructive tests are available to ascertain the change in mechanical properties due to heat treatment. Among these tools are hardness testing and metallographic analysis.

Hardness testing after heat treatement can indicate if a part is within hardness specifications. Hardness of a metal generally reflects the microstructure present. The Rockwell and the Brinell hardness tests can be performed with relative ease and speed, therefore lending themselves well to process control.

If parts are not within tolerance, the cause should be investigated. Hardness testing, eddy current testing, and other such testing techniques will indicate only when an out-of-tolerance condition exists, not why it exists. Clues to the cause(s) are often revealed in the microstructure and can be examined metallographically. This involved process prepares the surface of a sample part for microscopical viewing and subsequent interpretation. Grain structures are clearly visible, making it possible to determine what phases are present. For example, incorrect phases in a quench-hardened steel (e.g., ferrite and pearlite together with the desired martensite) may reveal improper heat treatment and indicate a possible cause to investigate.

VII. CONCLUSION

The focus of this chapter has been to introduce the concept of heat treatment as a common manufacturing process which can drastically modify metallic properties and thus extend the usefulness of engineering metals. For the process to be effective, it must be correlated with other manufacturing processes, so that economical use of metals can be optimized.

Heat treatment was defined as controlled heating and cooling of metals purposefully to obtain desirable mechanical properties. Several manufacturing operations involve incidental heating and cooling cycles in their processing (i.e., casting, hot forging, and welding) but are not considered to be heat treating. Only when thermal treatment is for the express purpose of predictably altering mechanical properties is it considered heat treating. However, this is not to say that the heat effect and rate of cooling will not alter mechanical properties with these other operations.

In review, there are several keys or factors to successful heat treatment of metals. First, the content of the alloy to be treated must be known as well as its prior processing history. Cold working, hot working, or heat treating can affect the metal's response to a particular heat treatment. Also, the quality of the chemical content must be controlled as well as the cleanliness, freedom from segregation, and grain size. Next, the required heating temperature and rating of heating needs to be determined. The proper elevated temperature is crucial in modifying mechanical properties. After reaching the desired temperature a soaking period is necessary so that the heat affects the microstructure equally. The metal is held at temperature until uniformly homogeneous or until the desired conditon is obtained. It is important to note that furnace atmospheres be controlled, so that deterioration of the part surface is reduced. The final stage, and perhaps the most crucial, is the cooling rate. When metals are heated to above their critical temperatures and cooled at rates varying from drastic water quenching to milder furnace cooling, a variety of mechanical properties are possible.

It is recommended that quality professionals and others interested in heat treatment consult the list at the end of this chapter. The one single source for comprehensive and in-depth information regarding heat treatment and process control is the American Society for Metals. Many other useful references are also listed, ranging from theoretical to the practical. Major manufacturers and suppliers of commercial metals can also be excellent sources of information.

FURTHER READING

Aluminum Association, Inc., *Publications Guide*, AAI, Washington, D.C.

American Society for Metals, *Metals Handbook, Ninth Edition*, Vol. 4; *Heat Treating*, ASM, Metals Park, Ohio, 1982.

American Society for Metals, *Heat Treater's Guide*, ASM, Metals Park, Ohio, 1982.

American Society for Metals, *Principles of Heat Treatment of Steel*, ASM, Metals Park, Ohio, 1980.

Avner, S. H., *Introduction to Physical Metallurgy*, McGraw-Hill, New York, 1974.

Bethlehem Steel Corp., *Modern Steels and Their Properties*, Handbook 3310, Bethlehem, Pa.

Climax Molybdenum Co., *Literature on Molybdenum Bearing Steels*, Greenwich, Conn.

Flinn, R. A., and P. K. Trojan, *Engineering Materials and Their Applications*, Houghton Mifflin, Boston, 1981.

Machine Design, Materials Reference Issue, Penton/IPC, Inc., Cleveland, Ohio, 1983.

MIL H-6875F, *Process for Heat Treatment of Steel*, and MIL H-6088F, *Heat Treatment of Aluminum Alloys*, Naval Publications and Forms Center, Philadelphia, Pa.

Republic Steel Corp., *Alloying Elements and Their Effects*, Cleveland, Ohio, 1976.

United States Steel, *The Making, Shaping and Treating Steel, Eighth Edition*, Pittsburgh, Pa., 1964.

42

GRINDING TECHNOLOGY

WILLIAM SCHLEICHER

Hitchcock Publishing Co.
Wheaton, Illinois

I. INTRODUCTION

From the time when prehistoric man first rubbed two stones together to make
a tool or a weapon, abrasives have accompanied humanity's long, slow march
into our modern civilization. The abrasive process, as well as stones used
as hammers and chipping devices, are among our earliest tools. The early
stones evolved into grinding wheels; sandpaper developed later into abrasive
belt machining. Machines were invented to drive grinding wheels and belts
and became essential to the manufacture of everything from pots and pans
to the precise parts used in space-age products. The next time the dentist
drills into your teeth with a diamond-mounted wheel revolving at over
100,000 rpm, you can appreciate how far we have come from the time the
caveman rubbed two stones together.

In this brief overview of the grinding process, we discuss the grinding
wheel (i.e., abrasives, bonds, etc.), extremes of the grinding operation,
rough and finish grinding, grinding machines, rules of thumb for greater
efficiency, and abrasive belt grinding.

II. THE GRINDING WHEEL

A. Types of Abrasives

Silicon Carbide

In 1891, Edward Acheson fused a mixture of powdered coke, a form of carbon,
and clay. The resulting few crystals were silicon carbide, a hitherto unknown
substance. Today, the raw materials of silicon carbide are silicon dioxide and
finely ground petroleum coke. Two types of silicon are produced, green and
black. The green is slightly more pure than the black and is more friable;
that is, the abrasive grain is more easily fractured on impact. Think of friable and semifriable in terms of not too tough, semitough, tough, and extra
tough. By controlling the crushing of the grain after it comes from the furnace, various shapes can be produced: sharp for general grinding and polishing, a rounded or block type for foundry and heavy-duty snagging.

743

Aluminum Oxide

At about the same time as Dr. Acheson's work, Charles B. Jackson fused beauxite, an impure aluminum ore, in an arc furnace, crushed the resulting dense mass into abrasive particles, and called it aluminum oxide.

There are four types of aluminum oxide grains: friable, semifriable, tough, and extra tough. Friable wheels are pure white aluminum oxide grain, cool cutting, and are used in vitrified wheels for toolroom grinding. By adding chromium oxide, pink or "ruby" wheels result, while the addition of vanadium oxide gives a green wheel. Variations in the crushing process produces grains in a large variety of shapes and sizes for different applications.

Aluminum oxide is softer than silicon carbide, but it is a much better-wearing tool on high- and medium-carbon steels; silicon carbide is superior on chilled cast iron, copper, aluminum, and other nonferrous metals. Silicon carbide deals effectively with the glass-hard scale on cast iron, but is inferior on steel, whether scaly or not.

Sintered Aluminum

Another abrasive, of recent origin, is sintered alumina, which is made by ceramic firing, not by electric fusion. Its fine crystal size and controlled grain size make it useful in heavy grinding of stainless steel billets.

Diamonds

Diamonds come in two types, man-made and natural. They are used to true and dress grinding wheels, which they cut with perfect ease; when dispersed in graded grain sizes in various bonding materials, they act as grinding wheels for cutting especially resistant substances: glass, stone, ceramics, and cemented carbides.

Superabrasives

Like man-made diamonds, cubic boron nitride (CBN) wheels are produced under tremendous pressure and heat, just as nature produces diamonds. CBN is a man-made substance and must not be confused with man-made diamonds. It is referred to as a superabrasive and there is a tendency to lump man-made diamonds with CBN. It is useful in grinding many materials, whereas diamonds have very few applications in steel grinding. Diamonds, being carbon, burn up in air at about 1000°F. CBN is quite a bit softer than diamond, but harder than all other materials. The relative Knoop hardnesses are:

Diamond	7000
Cubic boron nitride	4700
Silicon carbide	2480
Aluminum oxide	2100

Alumina Zirconia

These grains are made by cofusing aluminum oxide with zirconium oxide and cooling the molten material rapidly. They are very tough for snagging and heavy grinding.

B. Grain Size

The lumps of abrasive, as they come from the furnace, are reduced to manageable size in jaw crushers, then further reduced through steel rollers to sizes suitable for grinding wheels. Uniformity of size is vitally important, and screening them is done mechanically; they are characterised as coarse, medium, fine, and very fine. The range is from 8 (coarse) to 240 (very fine).* Finer sizes are classified as flour and are separated by more sophisticated means.

C. Grade

The strength with which the bond holds the grains is known as the grade or hardness of the wheel and can be varied through wide limits. The hardness of the wheel does not relate to the hardness of either the abrasive or the bond, only to the resistance the bond offers against letting the abrasive be torn out of the wheel.

D. Structure

This is the relationship of abrasive grain to bonding material and the relationship of these two elements to the spaces or void that separate them. The precise relationship of these three elements can be controlled so that the grinding wheels can be made dense or open,† or in varying degrees of density or openness to suit grinding conditions.

Bond

The grains are held together by one of six kinds of bonds: vitrified, or ceramic, which is used in more than half of the wheels made; silicate (of soda); resinoid (synthetic resin); shellac; rubber; and oxichloride (of magnesium). Each grain is supported in the wheel by a post‡ of bond and joined to other grains by a network of it. New bonds are constantly being tested. Generally speaking, the bond itself has little or no cutting action.

Diamond and cubic boron nitride (superabrasive) wheels in resinoid and vitrified bonds are produced in the same manner as other types of wheels, except that the abrasive, or diamond, section of the wheel is only a fraction of an inch deep on the working face. Metal bonds are frequently used. In certain types of CBN wheels an electroplating process bonds a single layer of superabrasive to the wheel.

---

* Aluminum oxide grains range in screened sizes from 4 (coarse) to 240 (very fine); silicon carbide ranges from 8 to 240. Screening machines have bronze and silk screen cloths made to very close tolerances. For example, a No. 20 grain will pass through a screen with 16 meshes per linear inch and will be retained on a 24-mesh screen, which accommodates a finer grain than a No. 20.

† Wheels for surface grinding will have grain embedded wider apart in the wheel bond to provide adequate chip clearance between the grain, hence, open; wheels for crankshaft grinding will have grain lying closer together and will thus be denser.

‡ The thousands of grains embedded in the bond do not touch. Each grain is held in place and connected to the next grain by a piece of the bond, thus making a network of bonds and grains. The bond surrounding each grain is called a "post." The size of the posts of bond supporting each grain is a measure of the hardness of the grade. The larger the posts, the harder the grade.

E. Standard Marking System

Grinding wheels are identified by a standard identification system of six numbers and a prefix; the prefix identifies the manufacturer; 1, the type of abrasive; 2, abrasive grain size; 3, grade; 4, structure; 5, bond; and 6, manufacturer's record (optional).

It can readily be appreciated that the combinations of grain, size, grade, bonds, and so on, permit an unlimited variety of combinations to meet grinding conditions. Because of the unlimited combinations it is often said that grinding is an art rather than a science. The larger companies have abrasive engineers whose specialty is abrasive machining. The wheel manufacturers' engineers should be consulted for most efficient wheel selections to meet specific requirements.

F. Shapes of Wheels

Shapes include the common round wheel; formed wheels having specially formed faces; segments for larger surface grinding areas; cone and plug wheels to reach hard-to-reach spots; mounted wheels used in tool and die shops; disk wheels for grinding on the side of the wheel; reinforced wheels composed of layers of glass cloth and abrasive bond mix.

III. THE GRINDING OPERATIONS

The grinding operations extend from one extreme to the other: from heavy stock removal in steel mills and foundries, to producing parts to microinch finish and tolerance, leaving the middle to the metal cutting tool; however, advanced manufacturing practice finds many applications for grinding in this middle land. Grinding in this huge middle land has become known as abrasive machining, although many professionals consider all grinding abrasive machining.

A. Rough Grinding

Semifinished steel consists of blooms, billets, and slabs that have been hot rolled from steel ingots and allowed to cool. Before the steel can be subjected to further operations it must be conditioned by removing surface defects (i.e., ingot cracks, scabs, seams, cinder patches, and other defects). At one time large scabs were removed with hammer and chisel, then with pneumatic hammer and machine clippers. Scarfing and an oxygen-fuel torch that melts the steel and "blows off" the molten surface of the steel were introduced next. These all gave way to the grinding wheel. Swing frame and grinding and semiautomatic and automatic billet grinding machines were born for conditioning.

Foundry and forge grinding has advanced with improved casting technology. Automated and semiautomated casting practices have taken over for better control, reliability, and faster production. Important developments permit castings to be of closer dimensions, sometimes permitting grinding to be performed on cast parts without a prior metal-cutting operation; thus many parts can be ground in the rough. This grinding from the rough on some parts falls into the area of abrasive machining mentioned earlier. A floor stand and portable grinders remove risers, gates, and flashings, all of which have been cast smaller. These are also removed by swing-frame, cutoff, and swing-frame cutoff machines, as well as automatic snag grinding systems. With these systems the operator can load, grind, and unload an average casting in 10 to 15 sec.

Wheels for foundry service are almost always of the organic resinoid bond types. Compromises must be made in selecting snagging wheels for foundry work. A large selection is generally undesirable. Weld grinding relies heavily on portable grinders ranging in speeds up to 17,000 sfpm. A typical specification would be aluminum oxide 12 to 16 grit, medium hard, resinoid bond. Portable grinders, either straight or vertical, are used.

With the development of the resinoid-bonded wheel, cutting-off operations were encouraged. One might question whether cutting off, which is precise and delivers a fine finish, should be covered under rough grinding, but inasmuch as steel bars come into the shop and are often cut into blanks by a hacksaw or the faster cutting-off grinding, it might be classified as rough grinding. The purist will point out that abrasive cutting delivers such a respected finish to the cutoff part that further finishing operations are eliminated. For ferrous materials, aluminum oxide wheels are used; for nonmetallics, including concrete, brick, and plastics, silicon carbide are the wheel of choice. However, rubber wheels are used for a very fine finish. Two other types of bonds are resinoid and rubber-resinoid.

B. Finish Grinding

At the other end from rough grinding lies finish grinding, honing, lapping, and superfinishing. The latter three are processes for securing greater accuracy and smoothness in a metal surface than is possible to achieve with abrasive wheels.

Honing

The finish developed by honing is the result of reciprocation of the rotating honing head in the hole. Honing is generally used for inside-diameter work, although honing machines are used for torus-shaped parts such as ball tracks of ball bearings. The honing head is an abrasive stone.

Lapping

This is an abrading process for refining the surface finish and geometrical accuracy of flat, cylindrical, and spherical surfaces. It removes surface waves, tool marks, grinding fuzz, slight distortions, and minor defects. Most lapping is done with a loose abrasive in a vehicle which rolls between the work and the lap, which in such a case is a softer material, usually cast iron. In this form of lapping the work and lap are not positively driven but rather guided in contact with each other so that fresh points of contact are made by constantly changing relative movement. The vehicle with which the abrasive is mixed can be oil, grease, or soap and water. Various abrasives are used; for instance, aluminum oxide is used in the range of 9.5-μm up to 22.5-μm particles.

Superfinishing

Whereas honing finishes the internal surfaces of workpieces and lapping finishes flat surfaces, superfinishing performs the same function on the outside diameter of workpieces. An abrasive stick is applied under mild pressure to a rotary workpiece. At the same time the abrasive stick is reciprocated across the workpiece. The stone is curved to correspond to the curve of the work. The process produces a finish of from 1 to 60 µin. Vitrified stones are generally used.

As in all things, functional lines must not be too finely drawn. A certain amount of overlapping exists in all three finishing processes.

IV. COSTS

A few words about costs—a subject where angels fear to tread—may not be amiss at this point. For many years producing tolerances of 0.0001 in. or less involved higher costs. Today, such tolerances are common. Grinding machines are more rigid, have more horsepower, and perform with less vibration. As tolerances become even tighter and microinch finishes become necessary, costs go up, especially on production runs. Yet technology has advanced to a point where honing, lapping, and superfinishing—for many years final choices for microinch finishes—are at home on production work. Also, many grinding machines today will deliver the finish and tolerances that were formerly the sole province of honing, superfinishing, and lapping. Today, machine builders and practitioners will challenge the statement that costs go up when tighter tolerances and better finishes are required. The variables of material, finish and tolerance required, number of parts needed, size and shape of parts, and so on, all influence the selection of the most efficient and cost-effective method. However, it is best to stop and inquire of design engineers whether their tight tolerances and fine finishes are essential.

Whenever an operation can be eliminated from the manufacturing cycle, costs are reduced. Thus many parts that are currently milled or broached, and then ground to close tolerance and finish, should be considered for grinding without a previous operation. Removal of $\frac{1}{4}$ in. of stock on a disk grinder is not unusual. Operations and technology must constantly be examined with a view toward greater efficiency and productivity at lower cost as long as quality requirements are not compromised.

Many metal removal operations now being performed by conventional cutting tools can become more cost-effective if performed on grinding machines. Major cost reductions result from the following:

1. Sharpening of cutting tools is eliminated; the abrasive wheel sharpens itself. As dull abrasive particles are torn away during the grinding process, new and sharp grits take their places.
2. Setup time and fixturing are reduced.
3. Many parts are ground at one time on disk grinders or on through-feed centerless grinders.
4. Inspection is automatic, with in-process size control.

V. THE GRINDING MACHINES

Various grinding machines can be discussed only in broadest outlines. The technical expertise of engineers and manufacturing personnel comes into play in selecting the right machine for the job. Cost, productivity, and quality play a part in the selection. In the majority of cases the work selects its own machine; however, technical developments are such that no piece part, whether it be machined on a metal-cutting or a grinding machine, should ever be free of the question: Is this the best way to machine this part?

The *horizontal spindle reciprocating table* is the common surface grinder, ranging from small toolroom grinders to large 250-hp machines with tables long enough to accommodate long and large workpieces.

With *vertical spindle rotary table grinders* parts are either clamped or held by magnetic chucks on circular rotating grinders. The horizontal spindle is stationary. Many parts are ground simultaneously with high production rates. These machines may have more than one spindle and more than one table.

Traveling table face grinders have a horizontal spindle. The wheel is composed of abrasive segments, used for large workpieces (i.e., shear blades, mold blocks, knife grinding, etc.).

Vertical spindle reciprocating table grinders are for grinding wide parts with high stock removal rates. Table widths on standard models are up to 42 in. wide. For wide work, wheels are of the segmented type to allow sufficient coolant to reach the work. Machines may utilize 325 hp.

Vertical disk grinders permit loading of parts into individual work-holding stations which index automatically into the grinding zone. During grinding, the individual work-holding stations rotate with parts in the direction opposite to the rotation of the grinding disk.

Disk grinding uses the faces of bonded abrasive disks fastened to steel plates. On double-disk machines the abrasive disks are opposed and the work-pieces, held in place by a work-holding fixture, are fed through and between the two revolving disks. This permits both sides of a piece part to be ground to exact parallelism and thickness. Extremely fine finishes are possible. Production rates are high.

Centerless grinding originated as a method of grinding long bars that were too long to be accommodated on standard cylindrical grinding machines. At the same time it established itself among short cylindrical parts, piston pins and the like, and spread quickly to the entire class now handled by the through-feed technique. Any type of small circular parts are accommodated. The piece part lies between two wheels, a grinding wheel and a regulating wheel, or feed wheel, of smaller diameter. To prevent the piece part from falling between the wheels, a blade between the wheels holds it in place. A large variety of parts, long or short, can be centerless ground. It is also used for lapping of cylindrical pieces.

Cylindrical grinding imparts final size and finish to cylindrical parts such as shafts. There are four essential elements of cylindrical grinding: the work rotates, the grinding wheel rotates, the wheel is fed toward and away from the work, and either one or the other of the rotating elements is traversed with respect to the other.

Angular head grinding is performed on shafts with multiple diameters and shoulders. The wheel grinds the shaft diameter and shoulder simultaneously, entering the work at an angle.

Internal grinding finishes inside diameters of holes as small as 0.040 in. and up to several inches. In addition, it can grind front faces, tapers, and recessed and inside faces. It is much more versatile than merely grinding inside diameters. The spindle is horizontal, and the work is held in chucks.

Jig grinding is used primarily in tool and die work for precise finishing of small holes in large workpieces that cannot be chucked. The spindle is vertical and the workpiece is fixtured on a table. As in internal grinding, jig grinding will grind tapered holes, contoured profiles, and hemispherical shapes.

Tool and cutter grinding is used for the sharpening of metal-cutting tools. In sharpening carbide inserts, diamond wheels are the choice. A wide range of grinders sharpen everything from simple single-point tools to complex end mills.

Form grinding, or profile grinding, grinds a specific form in a piecepart. A template of the shape and size desired in the part guides the grinding wheel in transferring the form of the template into the workpiece. A large comparator-like viewing screen, which shows the relation of the template to the workpiece, permits the operator to advance the grinding wheel incrementally until the part is completed.

In *crushform grinding*, the profile desired on the workpiece is ground or machined unto a metal roll which is then brought into contact with the grinding wheel, transferring the profile of the metal roll to the grinding wheel. Rolls are sometimes diamond-impregnated for longer life. It is used for cylindrical, surface, and centerless thread grinding. The grinding wheel, having thus been formed to the desired shapes, transfers these shapes to the piecepart.

Creep-feed grinding is a grinding development within recent memory, having had its start in Europe, where it is used extensively and effectively. It is also used in Japan. This country lags in its use. It is a moot point whether it should be listed under machines or grinding techniques. The advantage of creep-feed grinding lies in its ability to take a rough forging and grind it to desired size, form, and finish without a previous metal-cutting operation. It achieves the desired end result in one or at most several passes of the grinding wheel. The amount of stock removed in one pass is considerable and generally requires a slow table speed, although speeds up to 60 in./min are not unusual. The process is used primarily for grinding forms and slots and is thus a form of crushform grinding with the form having been crushed into the grinding wheel. Difficult-to-machine materials, such as the tough nickel-based alloys used in turbine blades, are accommodated by creep-feed grinding. The root sections of turbine blades with tolerances of 0.0002 in. are ground by this method.

In addition to the types of machines mentioned, there are machines of specific types of work: roll grinding for grinding large rolls in steel mills, thread, gear, cam and camshaft, springs, and other types of special application machines.

Technology in grinding machines has not lagged behind developments in other metal removal machines. One internal grinder is programmed on a card which is inserted in a slot in the machine and operations are performed without adjustments, thereby permitting jobs to be periodically retrieved and quickly machined. Sizing of the wheel and dressing are programmed and performed automatically in many modern machines. Computer controls are used extensively where all functions of table, wheel, speeds and feeds, and so on, as well as dressing and sizing are programmed. Tolerances and finishes are measured continuously, wheel wear is compensated for to assure that the final workpiece will conform to specified size and finish.

VI. OTHER IMPORTANT CONSIDERATIONS

A. Grinding Fluids

The basic functions of grinding fluids are very similar to those of cutting fluids, being either oils or water-soluble products. They are used to keep the temperature of the work uniform; reduce friction between work and wheel;

wash away chips, metal particles, abrasive and other foreign matter; prevent loading of the wheel face, which reduces the cutting action of the abrasive; and assist in attaining required surface finish.

Filtration of the grinding fluids is a necessity in grinding. Filtration units separate contaminants from the coolant (i.e., abrasive grains torn loose during grinding, metal particles, and other contaminants). Coolants are filtered in the system and returned clean to the machine. There are many types of coolant cleaning systems, ranging for individual units attached to each machine, the most popular, to large centrally located systems serving hundreds of machines.

B. Dressing and Truing

Because abrasives become dull before they are torn away from the bond, or because they dull due to a chemical reaction of heat and metal, they must be dressed so that fresh, sharp abrasives are presented to the work. In truing, the form of the wheel is kept to size, and at the same time dressed, by a diamond which traverses the form of the wheel, thereby both dressing the wheel and maintaining its form or squareness. Sometimes a diamond roller of the exact form as the wheel is used for form grinding. The variations, types of dressers, and purposes for their uses is too wide for complete discussion here. However, dressing is vital in any grinding operation.

C. Safety

At any time safe operation of grinding wheels is good business. Because they are breakable they should not be tossed around like baseballs. They should be handled with care. Storage should be provided in a manner to prevent chipping or breaking. Manufacturers' recommendations should be followed carefully. The basic publication of safety is *American National Safety Code for the Use, Care, and Protection of Abrasive Wheels*, B7.1.

D. Factors Influencing Wheel Selection

Hard materials are better ground with finer-grit-size wheels; soft materials, with coarse grit sizes. Aluminum oxide wheels are used for high-tensile-strength materials, such as steel and high-grade cast iron; silicon carbide is best for low-tensile, nonferrous, and nonmetallic materials. CBN resists chemical attacks by iron, cobalt, and nickel at high temperatures. Diamonds are for carbides and dressing and truing. The finer the finish required, the finer the grit size necessary.

Where stock is to be removed without regard for finish or geometry, resinoid-bonded wheels are the choice; for precise geometry, vitrified wheels are used. Large contact areas require coarse-grit wheels, smaller contact sizes use finer-grit wheels. Large areas of contact produce low unit pressures, and consequently soft-grade wheels are desirable; when contact areas are small, unit pressures are high and hard-grade wheels are recommended.

VII. ABRASIVE BELT GRINDING

Machining with abrasive belts or coated abrasives permits very fast metal removal on large and small workpieces. With abrasive belts it is possible to remove a cubic inch of hardened tool steel in 10 sec. Abrasive grains are deposited electrostatically to a flexible and prepared backing. The grains are oriented on the belt so that the long axis of the grain is positioned on the backing for maximum cutting efficiency. Aluminum oxide, silicon carbide, alumina zirconia, flint, garnet, and emery grains are used.

Various bonding agents hold the abrasive together on the belt: glue bond, modified glue bond, resin glue bond, resin-over-resin bond, and waterproof bond. Machines are for cylindrical and some centerless grinding, although the largest applications lie in surface grinding. Rough and finish grinding is performed at high speeds with high rates of stock removal. This is a grinding operation not to be slighted. Different machines designed for coated abrasives can accommodate sizes from as small as 1 in. to belt widths of several feet for the surfacing of steel sheets and furniture (i.e., tabletops and desktops). Machines range from small $100 table models to special equipment costing $2.5 million.

BIBLIOGRAPHY

Farago, F. T., *Abrasive Machining Methods*, Industrial Press, New York, 1976.

G. Lewis and W. Schleicher, *The Grinding Wheel*, Grinding Wheel Institute, Cleveland, Ohio, 1978.

McKee, R. L., *Machining with Abrasives*, Van Nostrand Reinhold, New York, 1981.

Grinding Technology, a collection of articles by the editors of *Manufacturing Engineering*, Society of Manufacturing Engineers, Detroit, Mich., 1982.

FURTHER READING

Bhateja, C., and R. Lindsay, eds., *Grinding, Theory, Techniques and Troubleshooting*, Society of Manufacturing Engineers, Detroit, Mich., 1982.

Farago, F. T., *Abrasive Methods Engineering*, Industrial Press, New York, 1976.

The Grinding Wheel Institute, *Abrasive Machining*, Cleveland, Ohio, 1984.

G. Lewis and W. Schleicher, *The Grinding Wheel*, 3rd ed., Grinding Wheel Institute, Cleveland, Ohio, 1978.

McKee, R. L., *Machining with Abrasives*, Van Nostrand Reinhold, New York, 1981.

43

FOUNDRY TECHNOLOGY

PAUL J. MIKELONIS

General Casting Corporation
Brookfield, Wisconsin

I. INTRODUCTION

Metal casting is the most direct method of producing a desired shape and is accomplished by pouring a molten metal into a form that retains the metal as it solidifies. The form containing the shape or casting configuration is usually produced from sand that has been bonded with clay, water, and other additives, to give it strength for handling and also for holding the molten metal. Forms (molds) can also be produced from other materials, such as graphite, rubber, plaster, metal, or refractory mixtures of alumina, silicates, gypsum, and so on. Sands can be bonded with materials such as sodium silicate, furfurals, phenolics, cement, thermosetting resins, or oils (linseed, cottonseed, or fish oils are used). Since the major tonnage of castings are produced from clay-bonded sand molds and ferrous metals (which include gray cast iron, steel, ductile cast iron, malleable cast iron), the practices in this chapter will relate to these materials and processes. A great many of the practices are adaptable to all metal-casting operations.

The metal-casting industry is the fifth largest industry in the United States in dollar value added by manufacturing. Metal casting or founding dates back to 3100 B.C. as verified by cast bronze sculpture and statuary found by archeological teams in Asia and Africa. The Chinese were casting iron in a variety of shapes several hundred years before the birth of Christ. The area that is now called Tanzania, in eastern Africa, shows evidence of irons and even a form of steel being melted and cast somewhere around A.D. 800. Between A.D. 1000 and 1500 metal casting evolved from an expression of art form to the casting of military hardware, print type, and even some engineering shapes.

With over 20 million tons of ferrous and nonferrous castings produced in a year, every other manufacturing industry is touched in some manner by metal castings as a component of the product they produce, the product itself, or in the equipment or machines used in production.

The intricacies and multitudinous variables that enter into a metal-casting operation can be appreciated by looking at a generalized flowchart of a foundry operation in Fig. 1. The variety of materials and processes that enter into the

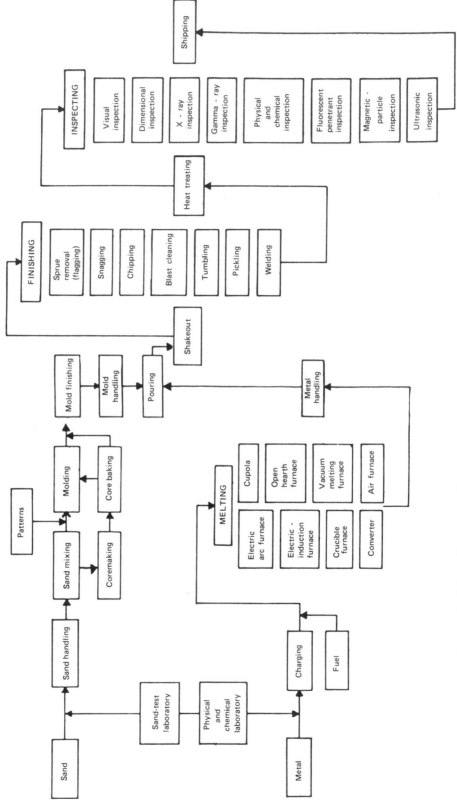

FIGURE 1 Flowchart of a typical foundry operation.

foundry work require a great deal of process control to produce a cast product that will fulfill the casting users' requirements and specifications.

The assurance of quality through control of processes and quality control procedures in metal casting is a growing science. In the early days of metal castings, when primarily art castings were being produced, a single artisan performed all the work. Artisans would create a pattern, produce the mold, melt the metal, pour the molten metal into the mold, and then clean the casting to a level of quality that would meet their level of perfection. Since the means of inspection were only sensory appraisal techniques, the approach to quality was relatively simple.

A great number of foundries were in operation in the United States by 1900. In 1897, E. H. Putnam, publisher of the magazine *The Trades Man*, in commenting on the quality of casting production stated: "Without abating quantity, quality must be worked up to the highest degree and when this is reached, the hard work is just begun, for any abatement of vigilance will be followed by a corresponding decline in quality." Since liability suits on product failure were evident as early as 1875, the evaluation of casting material quality was adopted and standardized at the start of the century. Material specifications for pig iron and other foundry materials appeared in 1907. By 1915, inspection procedures for assessing casting quality were advocated together with defect reporting and analysis by forward-looking foundrymen, who contended that properly organized inspection departments were necessary for the success of the metal-casting industry.

In 1942 an industry paper by H. H. Fairfield entitled "Statistical Methods as an Aid to Foundry Operations" was a first study and report on quality control techniques in the foundry. The American Foundryman's Society published its handbook *Statistical Quality Control for Foundries* in 1952. The use of control methods, including procedures to know the costs of quality, are more prevalent as castings customers become more sophisticated in their purchases and as castings producers realize the need to generate integrity in their castings.

As foundries have progressed from assessing defects to plotting their results in some form, various forms of analysis are used to define sources of defects and levels of quality. As a first approach to decision making, because it is the most economical one, previous experience is first explored to determine a course of corrective action. In this sense, quality assurance is attained through the art of experience judgment. This action must be based on statistical evaluation of current as well as previous quality levels, and thus the quality assurance discipline becomes more successful in a remedial way to sell the art.

II. DESIGNING A QUALITY ORGANIZATION

A. The Quality Assurance Manual

A formal quality assurance program cannot be adequately installed or disciplined, once in operation, without documenting what and how it is all about. The balance of this section contains much information that should be part of the quality manual. Staffing, responsibilities, process procedures, process auditing, materials control, and inspection procedures should be covered in writing.

B. Staffing

The staffing of a foundry for a quality assurance program will be a function of the size of the physical plant, the size and number of castings produced, and the complexity or criticality of these castings. Since a percentage of employees involved in the program compared to total employees in the plant is not necessarily a good guide when the foregoing variables are considered, it is best to use dollars expended in the quality program as a percentage of sales dollars for a guide. This type of association permits better control of personnel and facilities with a direct comparison of the value of the work performed as reflected by the plant financial statement. A good guide for this is the manual *Quality Costs—What and How* published by the American Society for Quality Control.

A review of singular and multiplant manning will give the reader an opportunity to appraise his or her facilities for personnel needs. One must think in terms of the prevention and appraisal aspects of process and quality control to best estimate staffing requirements.

A 100-melt-ton-per-day operation (producing 50 tons of good castings) producing relatively intricate cored castings in gray iron would need the following personnel based on a one-shift operation. For the prevention aspects of the program:

Quality assurance manager	1
Process engineer	1
Process control observer	1

For the appraisal aspects of the program:

Chief inspector	1
Inspection supervisor	1
Line inspector	3
Audit inspector	1
Layout inspector	1
Laboratory technician	1

Some personnel would be required who would spend only part of their time in each of the foregoing functions; these would be:

Technical director	1
Plant metallurgist	1
Quality assurance supervisor	1
Process control supervisor	1
Laboratory supervisor	1
Clerk and secretary	1

In this example we have 11 full-time employees plus 6 part-time employees who will be spending 10 to 30% of their time on quality assurance. A semiautomatic, intricately cored casting operation would then be utilizing the equivalent of 14 people or 4.7% of a possible 300 total employment.

In the case of multiplant operations, plant staffing would remain as above and a corporate staff would consist of:

Director of quality assurance	1
Staff quality assurance engineer	1
Staff quality assurance technician	1

These personnel would aid and audit the plant programs as well as provide direction to conform to the corporate philosophy on quality.

An organization chart for personnel at the plant level is shown in Fig. 2. At the corporate level in the multiplant operation, the director of quality assurance would report directly to the president, and the staff personnel would report to the director.

Responsibilities of the full-time plant quality assurance personnel are defined as follows:

1. *Quality Assurance Manager*
   a. Establishes and monitors process control procedures
   b. Initiates scrap reduction projects
   c. Maintains quality records and customer specifications
   d. Maintains plant quality assurance manual
   e. Establishes and maintains incoming materials control
   f. Maintains instrument surveillance for accuracy and calibration
2. *Process Control Supervisor*
   a. Aids line supervisors in writing process control procedures
   b. Supervises process control observer
3. *Process Engineer*
   a. Defines process procedures in conjunction with line supervisors
   b. Documents process procedures
4. *Process Control Observer*
   a. Observes and audits compliance of process procedures to documented procedures
   b. Aids line foremen in detecting process deviations
   c. Aids in associating casting defects with process deviations

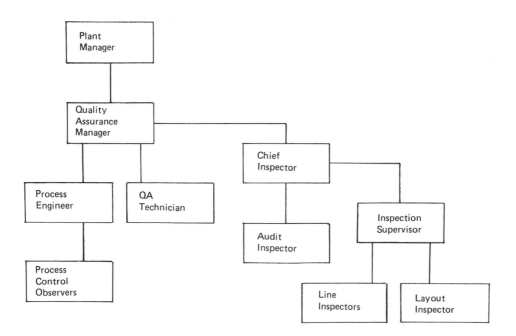

FIGURE 2 Plant-level quality organizational chart.

   5. *Chief Inspector*
       a. Supervises all sensory inspection procedures
       b. Supervises all nondestructive evaluations of castings
       c. Aids in defining and documenting defects for correction
       d. Acts as foundry-customer liason on casting problems
   6. *Audit Inspectors*
       a. Audit casting quality beyond line inspection

III. PURCHASED MATERIAL CONTROL

All materials used in the foundry should be purchased to materials specifications mutually agreed on by the materials supplier and the foundry. Materials
received should be accepted on the supplier's inspection and test results or
the foundry's inspection test results.

   Base materials such as sand, metal, and alloys should be easily controlled,
as standard specifications and testing have been available and used for many

TABLE 1   Material Specification Sources

Material	Specification source[a]
Sand	AFS, supplier
Sand additive carbonaceous	Supplier
Sand additive clay	SFSA, supplier
Sand binders	Supplier
Sand castings	Supplier
Resin-coated sand	AFS, supplier
Chaplets	Supplier
Pig iron	ASTM, supplier
Scrap charge metals	ISIS, supplier
Primary melting alloys	AA, supplier
Secondary melting alloys	AA, supplier
Ladle alloys	ASTM, supplier
Ladle fluxes	Supplier
Melting fluxes	Supplier
Abrasive shot	SAE, SFSA, supplier
Abrasive grinding wheels	Supplier

[a]AFS, American Foundrymen's Society; SFSA, Steel
Founders Society of America; ASTM, American Society
for Testing Materials; ISIS, Institute of Scrap Iron
and Steel; AA, Aluminum Association; SAE, Society
of Automotive Engineers.

DATE:	NO. M2
CHANGE NO. 3	PAGES 1 of 1

MATERIAL: Purchased steel scrap
Cut structural and plate scrap, 2 feet and under

DESCRIPTION: This is clean steel, such as plate structural shapes, shearings, punchings, and crop ends.

USE: Used as a low carbon, low silicon, free from alloys charge material for steel, gray iron, and ductile iron.

REQUIRED SPECIFICATIONS:

1.   CHEMISTRY -

Carbon	0.10—0.40%
Silicon	0.10—0.30%
Manganese	0.30—0.90%
Phosphorus	0.04% maximum
Sulfur	0.04% maximum

Free of all other alloys, except in residual percentages.

2.   SIZE: Dimensions shall be a maximum of 24" long × 12" wide, and not less than 1/4" thick, with a minimum weight of one pound. Not more than 5%, by weight, of material less than one pound unit weight, will be acceptable in any one shipment.

3.   GENERAL: All material shall be free of all attachments, dirt, excessive rust or corrosion. There shall be no nonferrous materials or foreign material of any kind.

SAMPLING & ACCEPTANCE: Incoming material shall be visually inspected by authorized personnel from the melting department before unloading commences who will acknowledge acceptance of the material by signing the weigh ticket.

Where a material does not meet the required specifications, terms for acceptance or rejection will be negotiated between foundry plant personnel and the seller.

Chemical analysis may be performed on any suspect material, using ASTM standard analytical methods.

FIGURE 3   A typical purchase specification for scrap metal.

DATE:	NO. S1

CHANGE NO. 2	PAGES 1 of 1

MATERIAL: Lake sand

DESCRIPTION: A subangular sand from dunes and bottom deposits in the
Great Lakes area. This material may be relatively free of
AFS clay, but may have up to 8.0% non-silica materials.
Screen distribution is usually on three screens, peaking on
the 70 screen. AFS grain fineness can be 45 to 70.

USE: This sand is used primarily in the manufacture of cores in the oil,
furan, or resin coated mixes.

REQUIRED SPECIFICATIONS:

1. SCREEN ANALYSIS

Screen Number	Minimum %	Maximum %
30	0.0	1.0
40	4.0	7.0
50	25.0	35.0
70	45.0	55.0
100	15.0	20.0
140	0.0	2.0
GFN	48	52

2. PHYSICAL AND CHEMICAL PROPERTIES:
   a. Acid Demand Value   = 35 maximum
   b. AFS clay   = 1.0% maximum
   c. Moisture as rec'd.   = 0.5% maximum
   d. Sand temp. as rec'd. = 100°F maximum

SAMPLING & ACCEPTANCE: Incoming sand shall be tested at a frequency
designated by the purchasing plant. Where
vendor reliability has been established, acceptance shall be based on the supplier's laboratory
report.

All tests will conform to the latest standard
testing procedures as outlined in the AFS Sand
Handbook.

REJECTION: All material failing to meet specifications will be subject to
rejection.

FIGURE 4   A typical purchase specification for core sand.

DATE:	NO. C51
CHANGE NO. 6	PAGES 1 of 1
MATERIAL: Core oil	

DESCRIPTION: A material formulated from drying oils, resins, and solvents in proportions at the discretion of the supplier to their chemical properties ranges. The composition is not a part of the specification.

USE: Used as a binder in the production of core sands.

REQUIRED SPECIFICATIONS:

1. The oil will be suitable for producing oil sand core mixes used in cores at curing temperatures of 400°F to 460°F for a time of 3.0 to 6.0 hours, dependent on core configuration.
2. The oil will be homogeneous and free from all contaminants including water, dirt, and sediment. It shall not separate during storage and must be compatible with cereal binders, iron oxide and other core sand additives.
3. TECHNICAL PROPERTIES
   a. Non-volatiles (calculated)   = 80—85%
   b. Specific gravity @ 60°F   = 0.945—0.947
   c. Viscosity @ 100°F   = 270 ssu
   d. Baked tensile strength (400°F baking temperature) of standard core sand mix.

Baking Time	Tensile in PSI
30 min.	105
45 min.	310
60 min.	300
90 min.	275
120 min.	255
180 min.	255

   Test procedures will be those found in the latest edition of the AFS Foundry Sand Handbook.
4. The oil must fulfill all foundry production requirements as well as meet technical properties.

SAMPLING & ACCEPTANCE: Acceptance shall be based on suppliers' test results where suppliers' reliability has been established. If the material does not meet the properties and requirements specifications, it shall be subject to rejection as agreed on by plant personnel and the foundry Purchasing Department.

FIGURE 5   A typical purchase specification for core binder oil.

years. Other materials such as sand binders and additives have been caught up in a rapidly changing product technology and close cooperation between the producers and users is vital in designing acceptance tests and specifications.

A. Material Specifications

Specifications for foundry materials have been developed by a number of organizations involved in standards writing. Materials that are common to both ferrous and nonferrous casting operations are listed in Table 1 with the availability of specifications. Typical material specifications are shown in Figs. 3 to 5.

B. Purchasing to Suppliers' Test Results

The reasons for purchasing to suppliers' test results include situations where costly and sophisticated testing is required, where a supplier has established himself as qualified and reliable, or where a foundry is too small to have all the required test equipment and personnel to operate the equipment. The test results should be sent prior to or with the material to define acceptance or rejection of the material prior to use in the foundry. One person in the foundry should be responsible for receiving and taking action on the material test results as well as maintaining a file of the test records for a period of a year after the material is used. A time-versus-data plot for purchased material is useful to maintain a record of the supplier's performance on material properties.

C. Receiving Inspection and Testing of Materials

Where the size of the plant will justify it, a receiving inspector, reporting to the quality assurance manager, can be charged with inspecting, sampling, and having material tests performed. These control procedures can be performed with guidance from the department general supervisor whose materials are involved. The sampling and tests that are to be used should be established in conjunction with the supplier. If sampling and testing differ from those of suppliers, the results can be questionable. Test procedures are sometimes provided by the national standards writing bodies noted previously; if this is the case, both supplier and foundry should use the standard tests.

D. Auditing Supplier's Facilities

The need to visit suppliers and audit supplier quality programs is an important part of a total quality effort. In establishing new suppliers as well as visiting current suppliers, a determination is made to qualify the source for reliability. An audit sheet can be used to assure compliance of all important controls. Noting items such as incoming materials control, record keeping, instrument inspection and calibration, identification and routing of defective material, documentation of test results, and use of a formal quality program will aid in establishing supplier integrity.

IV. PROCESS CONTROL

Foundry process control is an effort expended to prevent the production and use of nonconforming materials, cores, core equipment, molds, mold equipment,

Process Check	Location	Time	Comments/Action

Sand Preparation

1. Sand mix posted

2. Additives added in proper sequence

3. Muller mixing at proper cycle times

4. Sand tests taken from muller and stations as required

5. All sand tests are documented

6. Sand test equipment cleaned and calibrated regularly

Process audit for sand preparation, core sand or mold sand.

FIGURE 6   Process audit.

metal, and so on, to aid in producing a reliable and usable casting. Process control in the metal-casting industry, through inspection and auditing in the various processing areas, is a more economically sound means of producing good-quality castings than any attempts to inspect quality into the final cast product. Both process audits (Fig. 6) and job instruction sheets (Fig. 7) can be instrumental in defining the working of a process control system.

A. Control of Core-making Processes

All core-sand mixes will have process write-ups giving the material quantities, sequence of material additions, and mixing instructions regarding times and other special instructions. Required properties and frequency of testing of the core sand should also be stated. Instructions for disposal of sand or cores not meeting minimum required properties should also be given in the process write-ups.

Core coatings will have a process write-up stating mixing instructions, required test properties, and frequency of testing. Posting of test results at the coating workstations permits easy auditing.

Equipment for producing cores, after being accepted initially as accurate and usable, should be inspected prior to and after production runs. In the case of long-running production work, the inspection of equipment prior to each production shift will reduce the chance of poor-quality cores being produced.

The core maker, core inspector, and process control observer should be part of a system to inspect all cores for correct surface contour, soundness, proper curing, and dimensional accuracy. Intricate cores may need fixtures for gaging. Using assembly fixtures for multicomponent core assemblies will assure dimensional accuracy.

Customer _____ Part No. _____

Original Issue Date _____

Material Specification _____

Mechanical Properties _____ Hardness Range _____

Chemical Requirements _____

Molding

Flask _____

Chaplets: Cope: Size _____ No. _____ Drag: Size _____ No. _____

Ram-up Core _____ Chills _____ Nail Up Core _____ Vents ____

Exothermic Riser Sleeve: Size _____ No. _____

Other Requirements _____

Core

Cores/Casting _____ Type: Shell _____ Oil _____ Insocure _____

Production By: Bench _____ Small Blower _____ Shell _____ U180 _____

              Hot Box _____ Sand Composition _____

Blow Pressure _____ Invest Time _____ Cure Time _____ Box Temp __°F

Venting _____ Core Weight _____

Pour and Shift

Metal Temperature: Max. _____ Min. _____ Pour Time _____

Mold Weights: No. _____ Size _____ Shakeout Time ____

Riser Hot Top _____ Other Requirements _____

Cleaning and Heat Treating

Grinding _____ Gauging _____ Straightening _____

Heat Treat Cycle _____

Pieces/Tray _____

Inspection

% Hardness Tested _____ Test Location _____

Ultrasonic _____ Eddy Current _____

FIGURE 7 Job instruction sheet.

B. Control of Molding Processes

Molding sand mixes are documented just as the core-sand mixes in the preceding section. Since most molding and mixing operations perform a number of sand properties tests, plotting of test results at that station can be an aid to tracking results and anticipating necessary changes as trends develop.

Good, well-maintained pattern equipment is an essential starting point for producing good molds. Inspection of patterns prior to startup of production for proper contour, cuts or gouges, properly anchored gates and risers, and so on as listed in Fig. 8, can be used to check molding equipment by process control observers, molding supervisors, or the molders.

Molds containing cores or complicated core assemblies should have core-setting fixtures to help establish good dimensional control and also avoid some core-related casting defects.

Closing and handling of molds on storage lines is also important. Unnecessary abuse of the molds can result in casting surface defects.

C. Control of Melting, Pouring, and Shakeout Processes

Quality metal starts with control and inspection of charge materials used to produce the metal. Once the correct material is available and used, the accurate weighing and placing of the charge materials in the melt unit must be followed. Most metals do not offer a great latitude in the chemistry of the metal's composition, so charge materials should be purchased to a specified chemical analysis which may be certified by the supplier or accepted on the basis of user test results.

Good melting control is dependent on measuring and controlling metallurgical qualities, metal temperature, metal chemistry, and even gas content of the metal as the melting process progresses. Many forms of process control equipment and tests, such as molten metal pyrometers, spectrometers, thermal analysis equipment, chill tests, and microstructure examination, are means of assessing metal quality. Use of these means to get data for making melting adjustments, where necessary, to meet required specifications, adds to the metal quality.

Batch melting, compared to continuous melting methods, affords a better opportunity to make adjustments prior to pouring. However, the judicious and programmed use of metal testing in continuous melting can be useful in reducing property ranges and improving quality.

Many metals require ladle additives such as alloys, inoculants, degassers, or slag coagulants. Too often, the mechanics of adding these additives is ignored. Each material has an optimum addition rate and time as well as point of entry into the molten metal. These procedures should be documented and followed to assure the proper response of the metal to the additive.

Once the metal is ready for pouring, the handling and postmelting treatment of the metal require disciplined control. Metal temperature control is important to both ferrous and nonferrous metals. Many casting defects, ranging from gas porosity to surface inclusions, can be related directly to metal temperature control in handling and pouring the molten metal. Maintaining a documented system of job cards that identify the proper metal temperature pouring range as well as optimum pouring times for the given mold becomes the basis for a process control audit on pouring practices.

Mold shakeout control after pouring off the molds is another process area requiring documentation of job requirements as to time from pour to shakeout and possibly special handling instructions. Because all metals are section

Molding	Performed	NA
1. Check pattern equipment for condition		
2. Check mold procedure		
3. Check that peen boards and core setting gauges are used		
4. Check scrap trend against molding (ramoff, drops, etc.)		
5. Proper cope off procedure (one of 1st five molds)		
6. Check core fit and defective cores		
7. Correct number, size and quality of cores, chills and chaplets		
8. Correct diameter and condition of down sprue		
9. Flask is opened and closed properly		
10. Tight flasks are clamped properly		
11. Proper length of closing pins		
12. Proper mold vents and size		
13. Proper blow out procedure		
14. Check that mold hardness is taken regularly		
15. Check for defective or worn equipment		
16. Check for loose or worn pins and bushings		
17. Proper push off procedure		
18. Correct sand or facing used		
19. Correct number of flask bars and gaggers		
20. Check for cracked molds		
21. Proper codes and test bars		
22. Check molds for cleanliness		
23. Inspect interior of mold		

FIGURE 8   Mold process inspection list.

sensitive to some degree, metallurgical control which can affect mechanical properties is also a function of the optimum time that castings remain in the mold prior to shakeout. Observance of this discipline is another step in meeting the required customer specification.

D. Control of Cleaning and Heat-Treating Processes

The cleaning department has the prime function of preparing the raw castings to a condition and configuration suitable for the customer's processing or use. Cleaning operations define the physical appearance of the casting, and the user's incoming inspection makes its initial judgment of casting acceptance based on its sensory qualities. The control of abrasive shot blasting, grinding, and chipping affects the surface finish, cosmetic appearance, and dimensions of the castings. The use of a job process card to guide the work performed on the casting and serve as an audit inspection guide is worthwhile documentation. A photograph of the casting referencing critical cleaning areas can be attached to the process card for further direction.

Heat treatment is required for many ferrous as well as nonferrous metals. Correct heat treating requires adherence to proper time-at-temperature cycles. Heat treatment results can be affected by the amount and geometry of loading the castings into the heat treatment furnace. Improper loading can result in missing the required metallurgical or mechanical properties, warpage or distortion of the castings, and wasting of heat energy. The job process card showing loading characteristics and optimum load weight for a given furnace will serve to identify proper control of heat treatment. Temperature and time at temperature should also be part of the job process card information. Castings that have been heat treated should be qualified by some means, such as hardness inspection or microstructure evaluation, (see also Chapter 31) on a sampling basis. Heat treatment lots are identified and associated with the sample inspection and documented accordingly.

V. INSPECTION

Inspection is the act of evaluating some characteristic of the casting as compared to a standard to determine if the part conforms to a specification. The level of inspection required will be derived from historical data on the same or similar castings, performance of the part regarding machining by the customer, service life, and the producing foundry's process capabilities. Specifications may not cover all the characteristics pertinent to the casting being inspected, and evaluation requires that a preliminary judgment be made if the casting is fit for its intended use. Obviously, the customer makes the final judgment. Use of an actual casting for a go/no go standard can be a supplementary aid to an inspection job process card. The use of this actual standard reduces questionable judgment calls that may be made on marginal quality castings and helps to preserve the marketability of the casting.

A. Sensory Inspection Characteristics

An inspection of sensory characteristics, which includes all surface-related items such as discontinuities, inclusions, and not-to-contour surface, can be performed at many processing points in the cleaning room. Work areas such as shakeout, gate and riser removal, abrasive cleaning, grinding, and chipping can be informal inspection stations where nonconforming castings can be removed from the main flow of work. In all cases, though, the inspection department still makes the final decision on casting integrity prior to shipment.

B. Internal Sensory Inspection Characteristics

Castings such as cylinder heads, compressor housings, valve bodies, and so on, that have complex internal configurations may require optical aids to assess internal surface quality. Dental mirrors, fiber optics, and special viewing lights allow for a more critical appraisal of surface conditions.

C. Dimensional Inspection Characteristics

Inspection for conformance to dimensional specifications can be accomplished by use of a checking fixture that accepts the contour of the casting or picks up certain gage points. When high production is obtained from a given pattern, a complete dimensional layout should be performed at a frequency to assure that customer-required dimensions are maintained to the drawing tolerance. A number of items will determine the frequency of layout inspection required: material used for the pattern equipment, molding process, type of molding, and number of molds produced.

D. Gaging Inspection

Assurance that castings will be compatible with machining fixtures and with other components in assembly can best be determined by using gaging fixtures. Gages may range from simple contour form such as are used to define the opening in a manifold to more sophisticated forms as used for complicated castings such as heads, blocks, or housings. The latter type of fixture may not only define contours, but assess machining fixture points to the extent that they are machined to a given dimension.

E. Hardness Inspection

The mechanical hardness test is probably the most extensively used means of evaluating casting quality since hardness relates to mechanical properties as well as the microstructure. Because of this test's wide usage, some extra time must be spent in describing the test and some of the problems that may occur in using it.

The hardness test measures a metal's resistance to permanent deformation by a certain sized or shaped indenter under a given load. The most common of these tests are the Brinell and the Rockwell test. Other tests for hardness include the Vickers, Knoop, and the sclerescope. (See also Chapter 39.)

The Brinell hardness test is performed by applying a constant load, usually 3000 kg, on a hardened steel ball, called the indenter, that is 10 mm in diameter. ASTM Standard E10 describes the complete testing procedure, as well as the calibrating and standardizing methods for Brinell test equipment. Loads of 500 or 1500 kg can be used for softer materials or thin sections, where cracking may occur. If the hardness is expected to be over 400 HB (2.90 mm or less), a tungsten carbide ball should be used rather than a hardened steel ball.

The quality and reliability of Brinell testing can be adversely affected by both the operator and the machine. Operator-induced problems that can contribute to inaccurate results are:

1. Ground surface on test piece is too rough.
2. Surface of test piece is on an angle.
3. Hardness indentation is too close to the edge of the casting.
4. Test piece temperature is much higher than room temperature (should be less than 50° differential).
5. Measuring scope tipped when reading indentation diameter.

An example of the influence of these five factors on accuracy is shown in Table 2, where sections of a standard steel bar were taken and the different conditions tested by five inspectors.

Machine-induced conditions can also result in erroneous readings, including:

1. Indenter ball flattened.
2. Machine does not hold pressure.
3. Machine pressure readings are in error.

Hardness test results should be compared on lots of castings rather than on individual castings when differences occur. It is found that the frequency distribution and average of hardness readings will be quite comparative despite differences on individual readings.

Another widely used quality test procedure is the Rockwell hardness test. This test develops a number based on an indentor's penetration depth under a relatively light load beyond which it has been driven by a heavy load. The light load of 10 kg is applied followed by the major load, which is applied and removed with a direct reading being obtained on the indicator dial of the Rockwell test machine. A number of different scales are used, the B and C scales being the most common for metals. The B scale uses a 1/16-in.-diameter

TABLE 2   Hardness Measurement Variations Due to Differences in Test Accuracy

Inspector	#1	#2	#3	#4	#5
Indentation Diameter mm					
4.70 mm					xxxxx
4.65 mm		x			
4.60 mm	xx	xx	xx	xxxxx	xxxxx
4.55 mm	xx	xx	xxxxxx		
4.50 mm	xxxxxxxxxxxx	xxxxxx	xxxxx	xxxxxxxxxx	xxxxxxxxx
4.45 mm	xxx	xxxx	xxxx	x	
4.40 mm	xxxxxx	xxxx	xxxxx	xxxxxxxx	xxxx
4.35 mm	x	xxx	xxx		
4.30 mm	x	xxxx	x	xxxx	xxxx
$\bar{X}$ =	4.485	4.448	4.468	4.459	4.511

hardened steel ball (penetrator) and a major load of 100 kg. The C scale uses a 120° diamond cone penetrator requiring a 150-kg major load.

The same precautions used to assure reliable readings in the Brinell hardness test are also common to the Rockwell hardness test. The quality of the surface finish, angled or nonparallel surfaces, rounded surfaces, and surface scale are critical items to be controlled for accurate test results.

F. Sampling Plans

Acceptance inspection by the foundry in assessing product quality or by the user in incoming inspection can be advantageously accomplished by use of sampling plans. Assuming that inspectors follow a prescribed plan for sampling and the inspection is performed accurately to conformance requirements, some economy is gained. Destructive testing is sometimes used on the samples, adding to the assurance of the lot being acceptable. Good sampling is dependent on randomness and avoidance of any bias in selecting the samples. Any bias such as previewing the lot and selecting castings as to good and bad quality levels, avoiding inconvenient pieces or always sampling from the same location in a container, will void a good sampling plan. Good supervision and auditing are necessary to avoid these problems by assuring that the agreed-on sampling plan is being followed.

Many casting producers and consumers use sampling plans without realizing that there is a necessary discipline in executing the plan and that there are risks, such as rejecting usable lots and accepting poor-quality lots. It is recommended that people responsible for supervising inspection sampling utilize standard sampling plans such as MIL-STD-105D or MIL-STD-414. These two standards define sampling for inspection by attribute (casting is good or bad) and by variable (a specific quality characteristic is measured).

It is not too unusual for foundries to use a normal acceptable quality level (AQL) of 1.5%. This is the maximum percent defective that can be considered satisfactory as a process average for acceptance of casting lots for a defect or a group of defects. This tells the supplier that the plan will regularly accept the lots provided that the process average level (of defectives) shown is less than $1\frac{1}{2}$ per 100. Thus the AQL relates to an average for a number of lots rather than a single lot regarding the expectations of nonconformance. For a more thorough understanding of these sampling plans, see Appendix 1.

A 100% inspection plan is used for critical castings, large castings, or small lots. In the case of small castings, consideration should be given to determine if the service application justifies a 100% inspection where large lots are involved.

With any type of sampling plans where a great number of characteristics are to be inspected on a single casting, human failing is reduced if one person checks one characteristic per casting at a time, rather than checking all characteristics in one operation.

VI. TESTING

The determination of a casting's quality and reliability is performed by testing. Testing entails means other than the immediate sensory determination of a casting's fitness for use. Mechanical and electronic aids have been technologically developed. These testing and evaluation tools include x-ray and gamma-ray radiography, ultrasonic and sonic testing, eddy current testing, magnetic particle testing, and liquid penetrant testing together with older, established procedures such as hardness and leak testing. All these test methods are used to determine one or more of a castings properties such as soundness, surface or subsurface condition, mechanical properties, or a metallurgical property, which in turn reflects the quality and reliability of the casting being tested.

Advances have been made in other forms of testing and the near future will see expanded use in casting applications. Methods such as acoustic and optical holography, acoustic emission, infrared testing, and sophisticated forms of radiography will be available for qualifying casting integrity. An aid to selecting test methods is shown in Table 3.

A. Internal Soundness

The internal soundness of castings can be determined to any degree of accuracy by only two methods: radiography or ultrasonics. Radiography is a means of providing a two-dimensional picture of the intensity distribution of radiation that has passed from a source through the casting onto a film. The solid material attenuates the intensity of the radiation, and internal discontinuities or changes in material section size will attenuate the radiation at varying intensity to produce a shadow image on the film. X-rays have been used successfully on castings since the Coolidge x-ray tube was de-developed in 1912. Present-day equipment usually consists of a high-voltage power supply or transformer and the x-ray tube, and x-ray type photographic film specifically selected for the application.

Gamma rays (for radiography) are a form of electromagnetic radiation just like x-rays, but differ in wavelength. Gamma rays are emitted from radioactive atomic nuclei. The most common gamma-ray sources are cobalt-60 and iridium-192, although other sources, such as thalium-170, cesium-137, and radium, are available. Gamma-ray testing equipment consists of the radioisotope encapsulated in a lead-shielded storage safe. A cable or pneumatic drive handling system is used to move the radioisotope from its storage safe to the radiographic position.

Radiography can be used to detect a variety of discontinuities and flawed conditions in castings that may not be visible externally. Such conditions as cold shuts, cracks, gas porosity, shrinkage, misruns, unfused chaplets, core shifts, nonmetallic inclusions, and segregation can be detected and a film record obtained. To correctly assess the film record for casting condition, standard reference radiographs are used.

Radiographic inspection has a number of advantages and limitations compared to other testing methods. The advantages are:

1. Provides a record of the inspection.
2. Is nondestructive in nature.
3. Reveals the internal nature of the casting to determine its serviceability.
4. Can be relatively inexpensive for small castings, where the internal quality and soundness is vital.

The limitations of radiography are as follows:

1. Can be relatively costly for large, intricately shaped castings requiring a large number of film exposures.

TABLE 3   Nondestructive Test Comparison

Methods	Flaws Detected	Advantages	Limitations
Eddy-current	Cracks, seams and microstructure	Moderate cost, portable, readily automated	Conductive metals only, shallow penetration, geometry sensitive, reference standards of help
Magnetic particle	Cracks, seams, voids inclusions porosity	Simple, inexpensive, senses shallow surface flaws	Ferromagnetic materials only, operator dependent, can give irrelevant indications
Liquid penetrant	Cracks, laps, seams, porosity	Inexpensive, portable, easy to use	Operator dependent, irrelevant indications can occur, flaw must be open to accessible surface
Ultrasonic	Cracks, voids porosity, laps,	Excellent penetration, good sensitivity, requires access to one side only	Requires mechanical coupling to surface, manual method is slow, operator dependent
X-ray radiography	Porosity, voids inclusions, cracks	Detects internal flaws, portable, gives permanent record, can be used on all metals	Costly compared to other methods, possible health hazard, may be insensitive to some laminar flaws

2. Laminar-type discontinuities may not be discovered.
3. Equipment, facilities, and operation costs may be high if few radiographs are to be taken.

The use of ultrasonics to detect internal discontinuities is common for castings. Sound waves traveling through a casting will be reflected at any interface, such as a flaw. These reflected waves are analyzed for the distance they have traversed to isolate and determine the extent of an internal defect. Gray cast irons, however, may be difficult to interpret because of the free graphite in the metal which scatters the ultrasonic energy, thus diffusing the sound beam.

The advantages of ultrasonic testing for flaw detection are:

1. Economical for single shapes for production lots.
2. Castings can be tested from one side only.
3. Has good sensitivity in detecting small flaws.
4. Has good comparative accuracy in defining the size and depth of flaws.
5. Allows for automated procedures on a go/no go basis.

Limitations of ultrasonic testing are:

1. An experienced operator is needed to perform the inspection competently.
2. This is a small-area-coverage technique, and large castings require a great deal of time.
3. Requires good coupling of transducer and casting, which is sometimes difficult.
4. For metals such as cast iron, expert interpretation of readouts is necessary.

B. Surface Discontinuities

Flaws that are at the surface or slightly subsurface may sometimes be visible but are often not discernible. To detect this type of discontinuity, several techniques are available. These include magnetic particle for ferromagnetic materials, liquid penetrant, or eddy current testing.

Magnetic particle inspection is based on inducing a magnetic field into the ferromagnetic material. The flux will be interrupted by any break (such as a crack) in the field. The magnetism at the surface is increased by the field bypassing the defect. On applying a fine magnetic powder, dry or suspended in a liquid, the powder will build up around the discontinuity and define it. When the defect is at right angles to the magnetic field, good definition is obtained. Magnetic fields can be induced by using permanent magnets, electric currents, or electromagnetic yokes, coils, or prods. This method can be used for large or small castings, although it may be a slow procedure for small castings.

Liquid penetrant inspection is used to define discontinuities of a porous nature that are internal but open up to the surface of the casting. Color contrasting and fluorescent dyes are used in the liquid penetrant to enhance the visibility of the penetrant drawn through the flaw by capillary action, onto a developer that is placed on the surface of the casting.

Eddy current techniques can be used to detect surface or slightly subsurface defects such as cold shuts, cracks, inclusions, and porous areas. By using a source of magnetic field which induces eddy currents, a sensor picks up changes in the magnetic field caused by the eddy currents. These changes in the magnetic field are then read on a meter where the reading is proportional to the magnetic field change, or on a display where the readings are proprotional to the phase magnitude or modulation of the magnetic field. This method of detecting flaws is not as reliable as the ultrasonic procedure. However, for the surface cracks or seams, the eddy current procedure can be used at a relatively fast testing rate.

C. Mechanical Properties

The most common mechanical-properties tests are those for determining strength and hardness. The use of separately cast test bars that represent the metal in the casting has been the standard specification procedure for obtaining data on mechanical properties. In the last few years, as liability problems have increased, there has been a growing trend to section tensile specimens from a casting at some critical section to determine actual properties in the casting. This trend will continue and standard specifications will probably be written accordingly.

Strength can be determined through measurement of other properties, such as hardness, acoustical resonant frequency, ultrasonic energy velocity, and electrical or magnetic properties. These various properties are influenced by the metallurgical makeup of the metal, which in turn can be associated with the strength of the metal.

Hardness has an established relationship with the metal's tensile strength and is referenced for some metals in a number of ASTM and SAE material specifications.

The acoustical property *resonant frequency* can be used to determine certain mechanical properties. By creating mechanical energy that causes vibrations in a test piece and measuring the amplitude of these mechanical vibrations, it is found that the amplitude is at a maximum level of the resonant frequency of the cast iron under test. It was found that an empirical relationship exists between the resonant frequency and the tensile strength in cast irons.

High-frequency energy, where sound waves have a frequency greater than 20,000 Hz, has been useful in defining graphite form in cast irons, which in turn relates to tensile strength. An example of the relationship of velocity to tensile strength of cast irons is shown in Fig. 9.

Eddy current testing of ferromagnetic materials using induced electric currents can also be used to determine the mechanical properties of metal castings. Test equipment usually consists of an amplifier, cathode ray display, and two sets of coils, one for encircling a standard piece and a second to encircle the unknown piece. A correlation exists between the magnetic properties of the metal and the metallic matrix, which in turn relates to hardness and tensile strength.

D. Metallurgical Properties

Many factors such as the chemical makeup of the metal, postmelt treatment of the molten metal, cooling rate of the casting as related to design and shakeout time, and heat treatment affect metallurgical quality. In most metals, the metallurgical quality is predictable, depending on the known control of the foregoing factors. However, with metals such as gray cast iron and its section sensitivity, ductile and compacted graphite cast iron and its control through

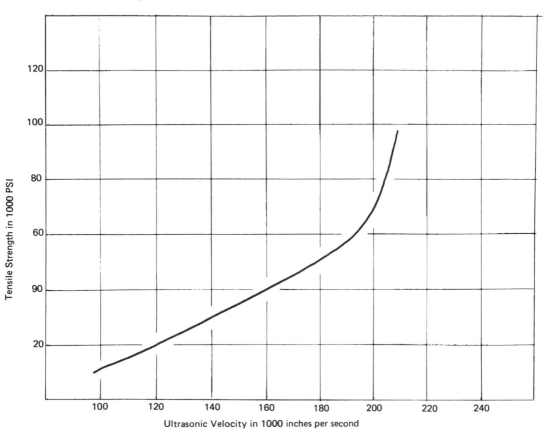

FIGURE 9   Tensile strength versus sound velocity in cast iron.

ladle or mold treatment, assurance of quality can be gained only through micro-structural tests. These tests are performed on separate cast specimens, lugs attached to the casting, or sections of the casting itself. Steel microstructural control is quite predictable, depending on its chemistry and heat treatment control.

VII.   QUALITY AUDIT SYSTEMS

Quality audit systems are designed to supplement normal process control pro-cedures and to act as an early warning system to assure production of quality castings. These systems can also act as an aid to supervisors in maintaining a high level of quality for the work performed in their specific process area. Materials, processes, and product are covered in the quality audit with a great deal of emphasis placed on "appraisal" and "prevention" to assure materials and processes conformance and thus to minimize product nonconformance.

The manning of a quality audit system may be handled in several ways. In a single plant operation the process control observer would be responsible for the audits of materials and processes, while the audit inspector would be responsible for the casting (product) quality audit. In a very small plant the quality assurance manager would be responsible for all audits. In multiplant operations the director of quality assurance and his staff would have the responsibility for performing quality audits. It is not unusual in multiplant operations to have plant audit teams exchange audits with other plants. Frequency of the audits, which can cover the entire plant or only certain processing areas, should be determined by the quality of performance.

A. Materials

Material audits cover materials produced in metal-casting operations and also purchased materials. Audit points should include:

1. Do purchase orders adequately define material requirements including standard specifications, if available?
2. Are purchased materials tested in-house at a frequency that is properly defined?
3. Are materials purchased on suppliers' tests properly accepted or rejected on test results? Are tests on file for review?
4. Are materials properly segregated and identified? Are they used on a first-in first-out basis? Are they stored per the manufacturer's specified environmental conditions?

B. Processes

A good process control system requires that job process cards be maintained. This documentation becomes the basis for a quality audit of processes. Audits of the various process areas should be cognizant of the following items:

1. *Core-making*
   a. Are core boxes and associated equipment maintained properly?
   b. Is core sand mixed and prepared to documented recipes?
   c. Are cores made to proper contours and free of defects?
   d. Are stored cores inspected and properly identified as fit to use?
2. *Molding*
   a. Are patterns, flasks, and associated equipment accurate and properly maintained?
   b. Is molding sand prepared to documented recipes and delivered to the molding floor to stated specifications?
   c. Is molding performed to stated standards?
   d. Is the closing and handling of molds performed with care?
3. *Melting, Metal Handling, Mold Shakeout*
   a. Is the melt charge makeup properly weighed and delivered to the melt unit?
   b. Is the melt unit operated properly regarding energy input, time of melting, fluxing, and tapping from the melt unit?
   c. Is the molten metal qualified for chemical and metallurgical properties before being dispatched to pouring stations?
   d. Does the metal get the proper ladle treatment?
   e. Is the molten metal of the proper temperature for pouring, and is it poured at the required rate?
   f. Are molds shaken out at the required time and the castings properly handled to avoid damage?

4. *Cleaning, Heat Treatment, Inspection*
   a. Are the castings cleaned to the specified contour?
   b. When required, are castings heat treated to the specified time and temperature cycle and so identified?
   c. Are castings appraised for sensory characteristics throughout the cleaning process to avoid shipment of defective castings?
   d. Are castings inspected to customer requirements as identified on job inspection process cards?
   e. Are critical inspection tests such as leak and soundness documented and castings marked as inspected?

Product quality audits of the castings can be performed in the shipping area from shipments ready for the customer. Sample lots taken at some given AQL should be selected with randomness and audit inspected for all customer-specified characteristics such as hardness, dimensions, soundness, or microstructure. Frequency of inspection audits should be determined by the foundry's past performance on the given job, as judged by tabulation of customer complaints and returned nonconforming castings.

VIII. STATISTICAL APPLICATIONS FOR METAL-CASTING QUALITY PROGRAMS

There are a great number of statistical techniques available as aids in controlling metal-casting processes, assessing material or process capability, tabulating defects and process problems, solving defects where multivariable effects are present, and data gathering and appraisal. With the use of low-cost computer time sharing, minicomputers, and programmable calculators much of the work can be performed quickly. However, a great deal of basic and even advanced statistical work can be performed by hand calculations or with the help of a hand-held calculator.

Effective quality control starts with knowing what you are doing in all your processes. This requires the collecting of accurate process data in statistical fashion to properly appraise the process capabilities. Typically, any bias in accumulating data can be detrimental to data evaluation. Randomization of data collection is necessary to avoid conclusions that are slanted and possibly erroneous.

A. Control Charts

Control charts are produced by plotting a series of observations which form a pattern. In a foundry, the observations are measurements taken of conditions within the process being studied. By applying statistical tests, control limits for the process can be established. Any fluctuation of the observations beyond the control limits indicate that the pattern is unnatural and the process is out of control. Combining past job experience and knowledge with the information on control charts can provide confidence as well as answers to many production problems.

Two types of control charts are used in foundry operations. One is the average and range of X-bar and R chart and the other is the p chart or proportion chart.

The average and range chart is a very sensitive control chart for tracking performance and identifying causes for unnatural fluctuations. The use of this chart is extensive regarding sand and metal properties variations. A

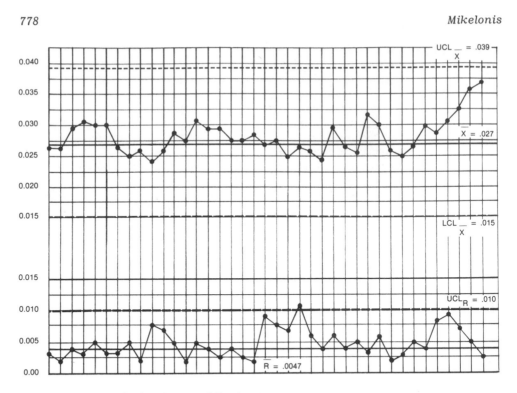

FIGURE 10   Typical X-bar and R chart.

typical application of this form of plotting is shown in Fig. 10. This chart is
used as an aid in controlling the final sulfur content of steel through monitoring the sulfur content of incoming steel scrap. The sulfur analysis is taken
on each of five loads of scrap steel received daily and the daily average, $\overline{X}$, is
plotted together with the range, R, of the daily sulfur analyses. During the
end of the month a definite upward trend is noted. Five consecutive readings
above or below the median line indicates a possible continuing trend. The
range, R, shows the daily range to be low, and therefore the scrap steel shipments as a group are indicating similar, but higher, sulfur contents. Action
should be taken to maintain control. Getting another form of steel scrap or
going to another supplier might be in order.

   The p, or proportion, chart represents the proportion of defective pieces
as a percentage of the total. Thus where we check for only bad and good
pieces, we are performing an attributes measurement. The p charts are frequently used in foundry applications to assess performance of various production items. An example of a p chart is shown in Fig. 11. In this case a pipe
core for an aluminum manifold was being checked for cracks prior to leaving
the core room for the molding area. The investigation of the results over the
upper control limits indicated that a substitute machine operator had not been
instructed on procedures for removing the core from the core box and storing
the cores properly in storage racks, resulting in an unusually high number
of defective pieces.

   Data that have been developed for the control charts can also be presented
in other forms. The frequency distribution plot and the normal probability

NO.	Number Defective	Fraction Defective	CRACK					Remarks
Plant	ABC Co.							
Department No.	CORE		Part Name _pipe core_ Part No. 32684 B					
Machine No.	B4		Oper. No. & Description _core making - blower machine_					
Pcs. per Hr.	100		Reasons for Reject					
Subgroup Size								
Sample Size	20							
1	2	0.10	2					
2	0	0	0					
3	1	0.05	1					
4	0	0	0					
5	1	0.05	1					
6	1	0.05	1					
7	3	0.15	3					
8	0	0	0					
9	0	0	0					
10	1	0.05	1					
11	1	0.05	1					
12	2	0.10	2					
13	0	0	0					
14	0	0	0					
15	0	0	0					
16	1	0.05	1					
17	0	0.0	0					
18	2	0.10	2					
19	1	0.05	1					
20	0	0	0					
21	4	0.20	4					
22	3	0.15	3					
23	5	0.25	5					
24	6	0.30	6					
25	1	0.05	1					

FIGURE 11   p Data sheet and p chart.

Plant   A BC   co.

Department No.	Part Name _pipe core_	Part No. 32684 B
Machine No. B 4	Oper. No. & Description core making – blower machine	
Pcs. per Hr. 100	Subgroup Size	Sample Size 20

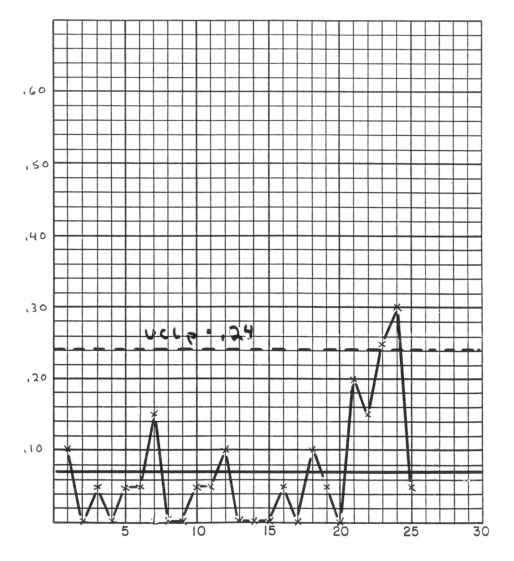

FIGURE 11   (continued)

plot oan be developed from the base data. Both of these plotting techniques
can be useful tools to determine job or process capabilities.

The grouped frequency distribution (graphically displayed as a bar chart)
represents a set of observations showing the frequency of occurrence of the
values of the variable in ordered classes. A good example of this formal plotting is shown, using Brinell hardness readings, in Fig. 12. The plotted data
show the Brinell reading hardness spread from 163 to 241 with the majority of
single readings at 217. There is a skewing of the readings to the left on the
lower hardness end, although the overall distribution appears relatively normal.
This frequency distribution not only gives us information about the population
of castings being inspected but can be used in other ways. This plot should
be compared with plots for the same castings produced at different times to
determine if changes have occurred in the hardness distribution. If there
are changes, it may be necessary to check the processes that affect hardness,
to see if they are in control. Comparing the plot with plots for other Brinell
test operators on similar lots of castings can also indicate if operators are
showing any bias or if the test procedure is properly followed.

Another technique utilizing data as compiled for frequency distribution
studies or control chart plotting is called a normal probability plot. This type
of plot can be useful in process capability studies. The following study demonstrates the use of a frequency distribution and a normal probability plot to

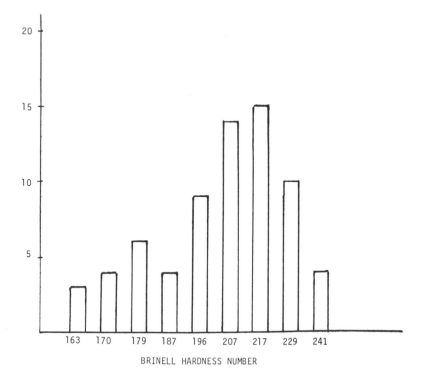

FIGURE 12   Frequency distribution of casting hardness.

evaluate dimensional control and possible action to improve this control in a large (700-lb) casting. The study was undertaken to determine what the variation in wall thickness would be in the cope and drag (top and bottom walls as cast) of the casting. Since a very large body core formed the inside cavity of the casting a number of variables are under consideration: dimensional accuracy of the core, tightness of core prints, possible core movement in the mold, mold wall movement, and possibly others. The frequency plot in Fig. 13 shows that wall thickness varied from 0.48 to 0.75 in. in the cope, while the variation was 0.56 to 0.72 in. in the drag. This told us that the large core tended to be pushed upward (thinner walls on the cope side) as a result of molten metal pressure as the casting was being poured. By tightening up the core prints and placing reinforcing bars in the cope flask to minimize core and mold wall movement, wall thickness became more equal and the variation reduced.

The data taken from the cope and drag wall measurements were used to develop a probability plot. Table 4 shows the readings given in 0.02-in. increments.

The midpoint percentage is plotted against the wall thickness on normal probability paper as shown in Fig. 14. The best-fit line is placed through the plotted points. The process average is at the intersection of the 50% line and is shown to be 0.625. The 3σ upper limit is at the intersection of the rightmost vertical line and the best-fit line and is found to be 0.81. The 3σ low limit is at the intersection of the leftmost vertical line and the best-fit line and reads 0.44. The process capability is the upper 3σ limit minus the lower 3σ limit or 0.37. The standard deviation is the process capability divided by 6 or 0.062.

TABLE 4   Casting Wall Thickness Measurements

Dimension	No. of readings	Cumulative readings	Cumulative %	Mid-point %
0.49–0.50	1	1	0.8	0.4
0.51–0.52	6	7	5.2	3.0
0.53–0.54	8	15	11.2	8.2
0.55–0.56	6	21	15.7	13.3
0.57–0.58	10	31	23.1	19.4
0.59–0.60	16	47	35.1	29.1
0.61–0.62	19	66	49.3	42.2
0.63–0.64	19	85	63.4	56.3
0.65–0.66	19	104	77.6	70.5
0.67–0.68	12	116	86.6	82.1
0.69–0.70	14	130	97.0	91.8
0.71–0.72	2	132	98.5	97.7
0.73–0.74	1	133	99.3	98.9
0.75–0.76	1	134	100.0	99.6

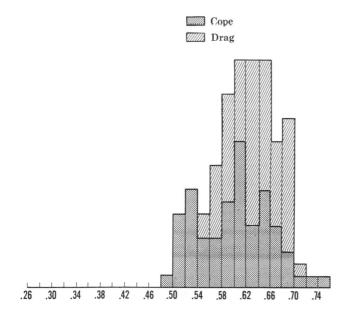

FIGURE 13   Frequency distribution of wall thickness.

Other information can be determined from the plot, such as prediction of percentages above and below a given value, comparison with specification values, and obviously a determination of process or machine capability under the conditions studied.

The techniques mentioned in this section on control charts can be used in many areas of foundry processing, utilizing the data that have been gathered through routine testing and checking of sands, cores, molds, metal, and castings. Proper and thorough analysis of the plots, whether control charts, frequency distribution studies, or probability plots, will provide statistically sound information for decision making. A number of references listed at the end of this chapter should be studied to enhance one's knowledge in these areas.

B. Defect Studies

Statistical techniques for defect studies are used extensively. Among those used are the ones covered in the section on control charts. The control charts of metal and sand properties data can be associated with defects having a direct relation to those properties. Using attribute control charts by job, by defect, or by defect for the individual job is useful in recognizing the occurrence of trends. Distribution studies of defect types in Pareto chart form indicate where the effort to reduce defects should be stressed. It usually shows that four or five defects are the major contributors to the overall defect total and by concentrating the defect reduction effort on these few will net the greatest economic gain. Probability plotting will determine the expected results for material or machine performance, and this can relate to defect occurrence if the process related to material or machine is "out of control."

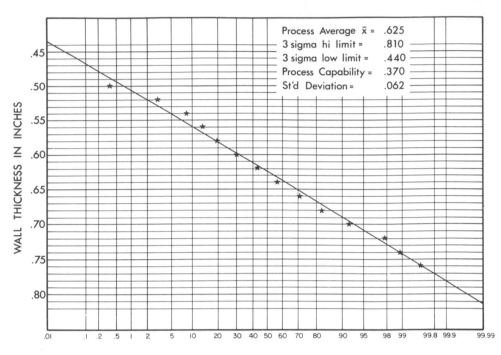

FIGURE 14   Process capability study.

   In any study, casting defects should not be rated on a go/no go basis.
Defects occur at some level of severity, and to judge properly the effects
of the variables in the casting process, defects should be rated to a given
severity level or number. For example, by rating from 0 or perfect to 5 or
exceedingly bad, judgment on the effect of a process change can be evaluated
and statistical procedures more easily applied. When working with small castings, visual standards can be selected to allow sensory judgment of the defect.
By selecting the standards to represent quality between the six standard ratings of 0, 1, 2, 3, 4, and 5, judging of test castings can be performed by comparing with the standards as better or worse than the standard and a whole
number assigned as to defect severity.
   Defect records should be informative enough to provide clues to the
source of the problem.   If the casting has more than one type of defect,
record all visible defects since one defect may be associated with another and
point out some process deficiency. On a single-type defect study, the location
of the defect should be recorded. A heavy concentration of the same defect in
a given area of the casting can lead to the cause of the problem.
   Once the cause is found, it should be tested to see if it is controllable and
actually is the root cause for the defect. If you cannot create the defect by
varying the cause, you do not have the root cause, and further study is required. A number of causes and effects, like a series of chain links, must be
studied until the controllable cause is established. Most defects are a result of
a multivariance effect resulting in the need for the study above.
   It is also true that a great deal of defect solving can be accomplished by
using past experiences in similar situations as a guide for corrective action.
Certainly, this is the most economical and the most expedient approach to defect

solving. When this fails, the use of statistical methods should be advocated. Most foundries generate and collect a substantial amount of data in their processes. This data can be used in statistical studies and the results used to solve problems.

C. Problem Solving

Many years ago, Frederick Taylor advocated a scientific approach to problem solving and decision making. At the time Taylor professed his philosophy, quality control techniques were virtually unknown and tools such as calculators and computers were nonexistent. However, even with all the progress made in statistical aids and equipment, a review of Taylor's precepts is in order.

1. Properly identify the problem. Probably the most difficult step and as some unknown author once stated, "If you can't define the problem in one sentence, you don't know the problem."
2. Gather all the needed facts and evaluate them.
3. Determine the various solutions and recommend the most likely solution.
4. Once the solution has been proven, act on it.

The first three steps can be performed by using various statistical and analytical techniques, some of which we will demonstrate. These methods will speed up the decision-making process and verify any conclusions reached.

Many problems in metal casting relate to a decision in a material or process change, the relationship of process variables to the quality of the product, or perhaps deciding which of two materials or methods will produce the best product after limited testing is performed. Several test procedures can be used to establish the better of two items. One of these procedures is the t test, a statistical test to determine if a significant difference exists between the averages of two methods. The data obtained from the two methods is considered as coming from a normal population and that variances of the two methods are considered equal. An example of the t test is shown in Table 6. Values are shown in Table 7. This is a foundry experiment where the effects of two gating systems on surface inclusions were studied. The castings from the two methods were rated as to defect severity in the manner described earlier in this chapter.

From Table 7, we substitute the known quantities in the equation

$$\sigma^2 = \frac{\Sigma(X_A^2) - [(\Sigma X_A)^2/n_1] + \Sigma(X_B^2) - [(\Sigma X_B)^2/n_2]}{n_1 + n_2 - 2}$$

$$= \frac{71 - [(29)^2/15] + 117 - [(39)^2/15]}{(15 + 15 - 2)}$$

$$= 1.09 \quad \text{or} \quad \sigma = 1.04$$

testing for t gives us

$$t = \frac{\bar{X}_A - \bar{X}_B}{\sigma} \quad \frac{n_A \times n_B}{n_A + n_B}$$

$$= \frac{1.93 - 2.60}{1.04} \quad \frac{15 \times 15}{15 + 15} = 1.76 \text{ with 28 degrees of freedom}$$

TABLE 6   Results of the Defect
Severity Using Gating Systems A
and B*

Gating system A			Gating system B		
2	1	0	2	2	1
1	2	2	3	3	3
3	2	2	3	3	2
2	3	3	2	5	1
4	1	1	4	2	3

*
 0, perfect; 1, very slight; 2, slight;
3, poor; 4, very bad; 5, horrible.

TABLE 7 Squaring the Defect Severity Ratings of Table 6 (X_A^2 and X_B^2)

Gating system A	X_A^2	Gating system B	X_B^2
2	4	2	4
1	1	3	9
3	9	3	9
2	4	2	4
4	16	4	16
1	1	2	4
2	4	3	9
2	4	3	9
3	9	5	25
1	1	2	4
0	0	1	1
2	4	3	9
2	4	2	4
3	9	1	1
1	1	3	9
$\Sigma\ X_A = 29$	$\Sigma\ X_A^2 = 71$	$\Sigma\ X_B = 39$	$\Sigma\ X_B^2 = 117$

$$\bar{X}_A = \frac{29}{15} = 1.93 \qquad\qquad \bar{X}_B = \frac{39}{15} = 2.60$$

TABLE 8   Factors for t Tests

Degrees of Freedom	$t_1\%$		
	5	1	0.1
1	12.71	63.66	636.62
2	4.30	9.93	31.60
3	3.18	5.84	12.94
4	2.78	4.60	8.61
5	2.57	4.03	6.86
6	2.45	3.71	5.96
7	2.37	3.50	5.41
8	2.31	3.36	5.04
9	2.26	3.25	4.78
10	2.23	3.17	4.59
11	2.20	3.11	4.44
12	2.18	3.06	4.32
13	2.16	3.01	4.22
14	2.15	2.98	4.14
15	2.13	2.95	4.07
16	2.12	2.92	4.02
17	2.11	2.90	3.97
18	2.10	2.88	3.92
19	2.09	2.86	3.88
20	2.09	2.85	3.85
21	2.08	2.83	3.82
22	2.07	2.82	3.79
23	2.07	2.81	3.77
24	2.06	2.80	3.75
25	2.06	2.79	3.73
27	2.05	2.77	3.69
28	2.05	2.76	3.67
29	2.04	2.76	3.66
30	2.04	2.75	3.65

Checking Table 8, we see that t at 1.76 is not significant, and no real difference exists between the results of the two gating systems.

Another procedure that can be used to provide a measure of significance between sets of results from two methods is called the endpoint count. The simplest form of this significance testing would require (from the previous example) six castings produced with gating A and six castings produced with gating B. Again, we are to determine the effects of the gating system on the surface inclusion defect. The 12 molds are produced, 6 of each gating system, and then poured in a randomized manner to avoid any bias regarding the other processing variables. After the castings are cleaned up, they are ranked with regard to the inclusion defect from the worst to the best casting and the results set up as in Table 9.

The castings above the upper line (before a change of rank as related to gating system occurs) and below the lower line constitute an end count of five. The balance of the castings overlap between the two gating systems in regard to defect severity. The end count determines the significance of the difference between the two methods:

End count less than 7; there is no difference.
End count 7 to 9 would indicate a significant difference.
End count 10 or more indicates a proven difference.

Since the end count in this exercise was 5, it is concluded that neither gating system, A or B, has a significant effect on the inclusion defect.

Other tests of significance are available. For example, the F or variance ratio test can be used where three or more groups of data are compared. The

TABLE 9   Example of an End Point Test

	Rank	Gating system A	Gating system B	End count
Worst	12	×		
	11	×		= 4
	10	×		
	9	×		
	8		×	
	7		×	
	6		×	
	5		×	
	4	×		
	3		×	
	2	×		
Best	1		×	= 1
				—
				5

sophistication of statistical methods for appraising control of processes, finding causes for lack of control, defect solving, and so on, goes well beyond the scope of the information presented in this section of the chapter. It is not advisable to attempt using all the available methods until the basic ones are mastered well. Certainly, if one starts a statistical program with control charts, they should be set up with good data, plotted accurately and analyzed carefully. Just this one technique can be tremendously valuable in attaining process control that will be economically advantageous. After all the possibilities are exhausted in control chart applications, time can be spent in learning and using other statistical aids. A number of reference books are presented below to aid in designing your program.

BIBLIOGRAPHY

American Foundrymen's Society, *Statistical Methods as an Aid to Foundry Operations*, Transactions of the American Foundrymen's Society, Des Plaines, Ill., 1942.

American Foundrymen's Society, *Statistical Quality Control for Foundries*, AFS, Des Plaines, Ill., 1952.

American Foundrymen's Society, *AFS Metalcasters Reference and Guide*, AFS, Des Plaines, Ill., 1972.

American Society for Quality Control, *Quality Costs—What and How*, 2nd ed., ASQC, Milwaukee, Wis., 1971.

American Society for Quality Control, *Guide for Reducing Quality Costs*, ASQC, Milwaukee, Wis., 1977.

American Society for Testing Materials, *Manual on Presentation of Data and Control Chart Analysis*, STP 15D, ASTM, Philadelphia, 1976.

Boyde, D. W. Sr., Milwaukee, Wis., personal communication.

Department of Defense, MIL-STD-105D and MIL-STD-414, U.S. Government Printing Office, Washington, D.C., 1963 and 1957.

Freund, J., and I. Miller, *Probability and Statistics for Engineers*, 2nd ed., Prentice-Hall, Englewood Cliffs, N.J., 1977.

Grant, E. L., and R. Leavenworth, *Statistical Quality Control*, 4th ed., McGraw-Hill, New York, 1972.

National Aeronautics and Space Administration, *Nondestructive Testing*, NASA SP-5113, U.S. Government Printing Office, Washington, D.C., 1973.

Rowe, C A., Milwaukee, Wis., personal communication.

Western Electric Company, *Statistical Quality Control Handbook*, 2nd ed., WEC, New York, 1958.

FURTHER READING

American Foundrymen's Society, *Iron Castings Handbook*, 3rd ed., AFS, Des Plaines, Ill., 1981.

American Foundrymen's Society, *Metalcasters Reference and Guide*, AFS, Des Plaines, Ill.

American Foundrymen's Society, *Metal Casting and Molding Processes*, AFS, Des Plaines, Ill.

American Foundrymen's Society, *Steel Castings Handbook*, AFS, Des Plaines, Ill.

Sanders and Gould, *History Cast in Metal*, American Foundrymen's Society, Des Plaines, Ill.

Taylor, Flemings, and Wulff, *Foundry Engineering*, 2nd ed., American Foundrymen's Society, Des Plaines, Ill., 1959.

44

TEXTILES

NORBERT L. ENRICK

Kent State University
Kent, Ohio

I. INTRODUCTION

In recent years, there has been a considerable degree of acceptance of quality control principles and applications by textile managements, as evidenced by the installation of control laboratories and quality control programs. The impetus, spurring this development, is not merely the fact that a quality-controlled yarn or fabric is a more salable product. Rather, it is the unexpected but well-documented observation that enhanced quality is usually accompanied by a remarkable lowering of production costs.

II. QUALITY AND COST BENEFITS

The results of a sound quality control program, in terms of quality and cost, may be viewed in the following major categories of accomplishments:

1. Reduced off-standard output, as regards "seconds," "allowances," and other deficiencies, in yarn, fabric, or cut-and-sewn items. As quality improves, profit increases, since fewer losses from off-standard merchandise, sold at a discount, are experienced.
2. Reduced waste. In several processes, such as carding and combing, there exists a problem of removing short "nonspinnable" fibers, leaf, and trash while minimizing the concomitant removal of good fiber. Quality-controlled stock, being a more uniform stock, can be carded and combed more efficiently. As a result, the waste removed will contain a maximum of undesirable components, with a minimum of good fibers mingled with the waste.
3. Fewer yarn and thread breaks in spinning, weaving, knitting, and sewing, thus enhancing productivity. Inefficient waste removal in carding and combing, combined with nonuniform stock, permits short fibers, trash, thin spots, doubled-over and bunched fibers to continue into subsequent processes. When a break occurs as a result of these

imperfections, there is then idle machinery until the operator can service the machine. Moreover, the higher the rate of breaks at various
types of machines, the more labor costs will be incurred.

4. Improved operator morale as a result of generally better running conditions from process to process throughout the mill.
5. Savings in raw stock. When processing equipment is maintained in excellent condition, and proper attention is given to uniform blending
   and drafting, it is not unusual to permit processing of somewhat less
   expensive raw stock than otherwise needed, and yet come out with a
   premium fabric. Although a premium fabric may bring only a few cents
   a yard more than a standard quality fabric, such profit improvements
   are important when it is considered that a mill sells many millions of
   yards per year. Similarly, with regard to raw stock, only a few cents
   may be saved per pound. Yet this saving will be significant if it is
   realized that in general raw materials costs represent from 70 to 90%
   of all direct costs of spinning the ordinary cotton yarn.
6. Consistent sales, even in times of poor business conditions in the industry, because of the firm's superior quality reputation.
7. As an overall result, a general improvement in management of production and sales, and a stronger competitive position of the mill.

Thus the old-fashioned axiom that "higher quality means higher costs" is
being proved untrue in the mill that keeps proper quality controls. We thus
observe how the manufacturer using quality controls ends up with a product
of higher quality and lower costs than a competitor who neglects controls and
permits costs, machine efficiencies, and quality to deteriorate.

Moreover, in a fabric or yarn, it is usually not feasible to segregate the
good yarn from the bad in any one long length of material, so it may be said
with emphasis that you cannot inspect quality into a fabric; you must spin it
into the yarn and weave it into the cloth.

Although the principles and benefits of quality control are applicable to all
types of production, whether cotton, wool, man-mades, or blends are used,
the so-called cotton system for cotton, synthetics, and blends is still the
dominant system and specific references will usually refer to illustrations from
this system.

III. NATURE OF PROCESSING

To discuss textile quality control in detail, it is first desirable to consider
briefly the nature of the production process to be controlled. Figure 1 shows
a representative setup used to process man-made fibers and cotton, from raw
stock to spun yarn. In the picking stage, stock is formed into a sheet of some
50 yards of fiber which is rolled and known as a lap. The form of this and
subsequent stock is depicted in Fig. 2.

The carding process, in which the stock is cleansed of trash, short fibers,
and other imperfections, yields the next product, a strand of loosely held fibers known as sliver. When cotton or man-mades are processed on the cotton
system, the "i" in sliver is pronounced as in "diver;" on the other hand, for
woolen sliver it is pronounced as in "liver." The strand is usually coiled into
a can.

Because card sliver is very uneven, it is subjected to one or two drawing
processes, in which reliance is had on blending for an evening-out effect. For

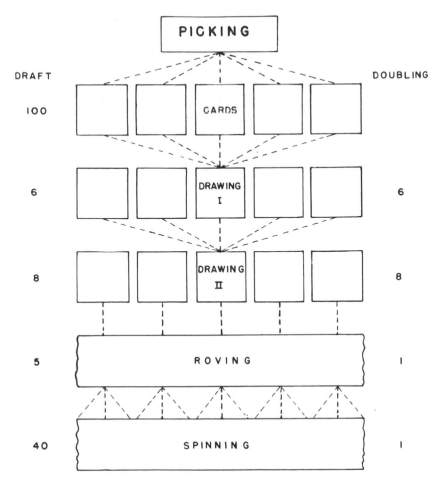

TOTAL DOUBLINGS = 6 X 8 = 48

TOTAL DRAFT = 100 X 6 X 8 X 5 X 40 = 960,000

FIGURE 1 Schematic of yarn processing. Each department, from pickers to spinning, contains several output positions or "deliveries." Flow of stock from department to department, among machines and deliveries, is more or less at random.

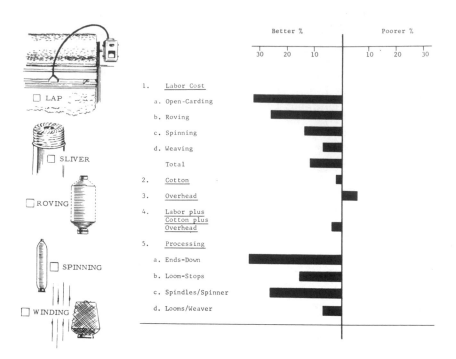

FIGURE 2   Typical products. Picking process produces a rolled-up sheet of fibers known as a "lap," followed by sliver coiled into cans at the carding, drawing, and combing processes. Roving bobbins are a coarse-strand fore-runner of yarn bobbins. Yarn, in turn, may be twisted and wound in various forms, suitable for knitting or weaving.

example, if six strands of sliver are fed into a set of drawing rolls, which will then attenuate or "draft" the combined stock by a factor of 6, so that the weight per yard of the sliver produced equals the weight per yard of each individual strand fed, it may be expected that

$$V_{sliver\ produced} = \frac{V_{sliver\ fed}}{\sqrt{number\ of\ strands\ fed}}$$

where V represents the variation coefficient of the sliver. For two drawing processes, there would be 6 × 6 or 36 strands fed. Assuming a V of 4% for the card sliver being fed, we would expect the sliver coming off the second drawing process to have a V of $4/\sqrt{36}$ or 1.5%. A small empirical allowance, to take into account drafting and other machinery imperfections, would raise the expected value to a V of about 1.8%. If, in actual processing and testing, this 1.8% is significantly exceeded, this signals the existence of a findable cause of trouble in the processing. It is noteworthy that the adoption of drawings as a means of blending strands was made long before the statistical

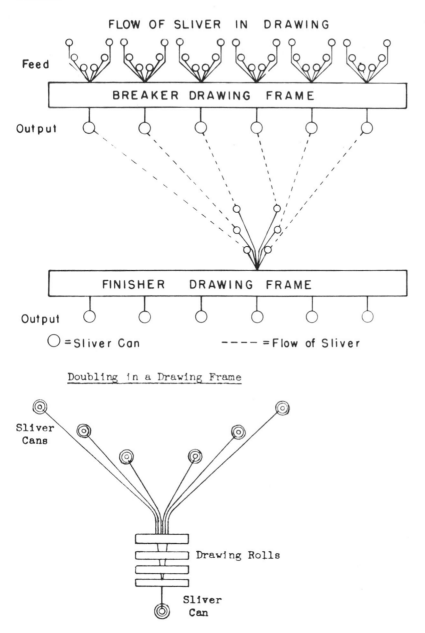

FLOW OF SLIVER IN DRAWING

Doubling in a Drawing Frame

FIGURE 3 Schematic of drawing. Two processes of drawing, breaker (I) and finisher (II) are used, with a blending of six strands of sliver at each. For simplicity, only one of the six feeding positions in drawing II are shown. The blending is known as "doubling."

thoughts pertaining to the standard error of the mean—of which drawing is a physical demonstration—and entered the realm of production engineering. Yet the ideas occurred in inchoate form (see, e.g., Ref. 1). Figure 3 illustrates the two drawing processes discussed.

The evened-out strand of finished drawing sliver is now ready for attenuation through drafting. A first such process, known as "roving," may attenuate a sliver of 50 grains per linear yard to a strand of roving consisting of 5 grains per linear yard, as the result of a draft of 50 to 5, or 50/5 or 10. A further drafting, by a factor of 10 to 30, will result in yarns of various degrees of fineness. Yarn, in turn, may be wound, twisted, and packaged in various ways, resulting in knitting and weaving yarns, roping, braided materials, and sewing thread.

IV. ELECTRONIC EVALUATION

The development of electronic instruments for testing the evenness of textile strands has greatly aided in understanding the nature of variations in processing. The principle of these instruments, such as the Uster evenness tester, is to pass the strand through a pair of electronic sensing plates and to chart the fluctuations in density of the material on an automatic recorder. Examples of various man-made fiber yarns are given in Fig. 4.

A further interesting use of the instrument is to check the inch-to-inch variations in linear density of stock, as sliver is spun into roving and yarn, and the yarn is then twisted into two-ply (two strands) and three-ply (three strands). Figure 5 illustrates a typical set of mill results.

The relatively even finished sliver becomes a somewhat uneven strand of roving, followed by a quite variable yarn. The term "20's yarn" refers to the fact that 20 lengths of 840 yards each of this yarn weigh 1 lb. The twisting processes, in which first two and then three yarns are blended or "plied" together, results in an evening-out action, quite similar to the effect of the previously discussed two drawing processes. The electronic evaluation can be used to demonstrate the soundness of the various blending processes in a mill, and the corresponding validity of the statistical formula presented above.

The increase in variations in the roving and yarn-spinning processes (sections B and C of the graph) tends to support the view that drafting without blending increases relative variability of stock. Yet a statistical analysis shows this explanation to be only partially correct. For a full analysis, the behavior of fibers in a yarn cross section must be considered, as will be shown next.

V. CONTROL OF FIBER VARIATIONS

Variations in the number of fibers per cross section, as illustrated in Fig. 6, result in "short-term" or inch-to-inch" variation. Control of this unevenness of strands is important, since high uniformity does not only mean better-quality yarns and fabrics, but also fewer strand breaks in processing. A thin spot, with relatively few fibers in the cross section, may break under the tensions of drafting and package winding; while on the other hand, a thick spot may clog up in various small openings of drafting and package-winding sections of machinery, again causing a break.

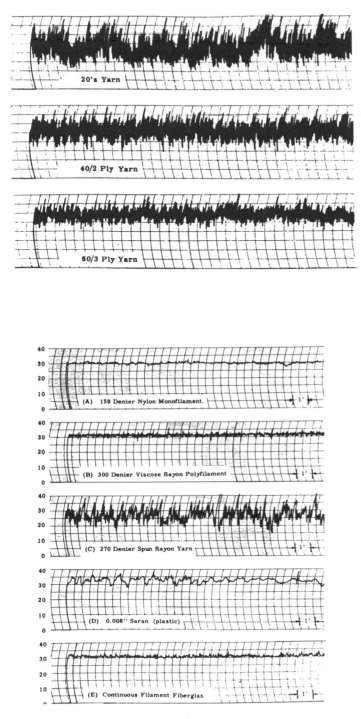

FIGURE 4   Inch-to-inch variations in linear density of various man-made fiber yarns. Spun rayon yarn, which is processed on cotton spinning equipment, shows variations of a pattern that would also be expected for cotton yarn.

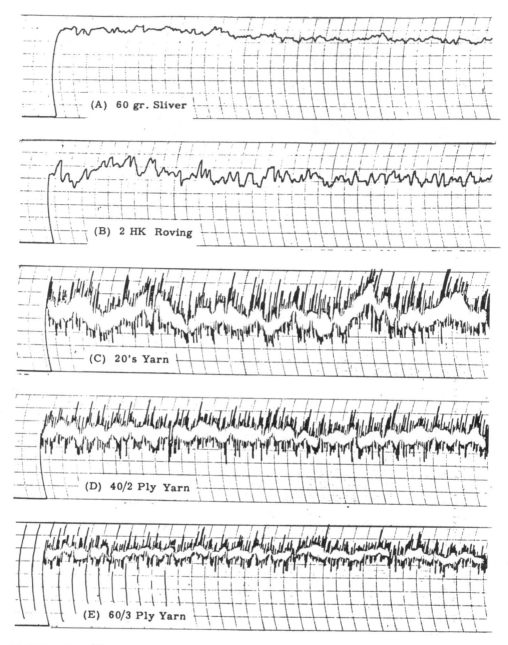

FIGURE 5   Effects of drafting and blending on evenness of strands of textile
material.   The even sliver (section A) is the result of blending in two processes
of drawing; increased unevenness results from the drafting in roving frames
and yarn spinning (sections B and C).   Twisting of plied yarn, being a blending operation, reduces variability of stock (sections D and E).

FIGURE 6   Schematic of cross section of a small segment of spun yarn. In actuality, fibers will not all be lined up straight, but the number of fibers per inch, or smaller segment, will vary in a more-or-less random manner. A yarn with fewer fibers per average cross section (i.e., a finer yarn) will exhibit relatively higher variability on an electronic evenness tester.

Suppose now that we have set the drafting rolls on a spinning frame to yield a yarn with an average of 36 fibers per inch of cross section. The rolls will produce these 36 inches per length, but with a certain amount of random fluctuation. At best, we might expect that the pattern of variation per cross section might be described by a Poisson distribution. For the expected standard deviation, σ_{fibers}, we would thus write

$$\sigma_{fibers} = \sqrt{\text{fibers per cross section}}$$
$$= \sqrt{36}$$
$$= 6 \quad \text{number of fibers per cross section}$$

It is customary and convenient, for purposes of ready comparison among various finenesses of strands, to express standard deviation data in terms of variation coefficient. As a result, the standard deviation of six fibers per cross section, expected for the 36-fiber yarn, is converted to

$$V_{fibers} = \frac{\sigma_{fibers}}{\text{average fibers per cross section}}$$
$$= \frac{\sigma}{\overline{X}}$$
$$= \frac{6}{36}$$
$$= \frac{1}{6} \text{ or } 0.167 \text{ or } 16.7\%$$

It is apparent, therefore, that as the fineness of a strand decreases, so will the number of fibers per cross section, and thus the corresponding variation coefficient. The results, in sections A to C of Fig. 5, are therefore to be expected, and will be reflected in increasing values of the variation coefficient, such as read directly from the meters of the automatic integrator that is usually attached to a Uster evenness tester.

Drafting, by reducing the fibers per cross section, thus increases expected variation. In addition, the effects of drafting roll imperfections, settings, amount of draft, and counterbalancing effects of doublings (together with drafting in the drawing process) will exert their influence. By careful consideration of these factors, which operate in a manner described schematically

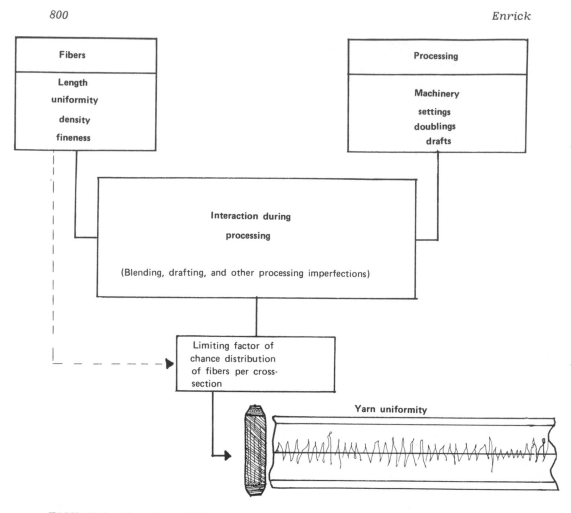

FIGURE 7   Relation of fiber properties, processing conditions, and chance
fluctuations in their effect on yarn uniformity. Although the number of fibers
per cross section sets a limit beyond which a randomly drafting pair of rolls
cannot achieve evenness, yet attention to fiber characteristics, machine settings, and control will yield the optimal degree of economically feasible yarn
uniformity.

in Fig. 7, improvements in engineering design and manufacture of processing
machinery, as well as improvements in processing settings and control of uniformity have been achieved. The net result has been that the superior mill
utilizes far fewer processing stages, requiring fewer blending operations, and
running the stock more than twice the speeds considered feasible some time
ago.

For example, assume that the actual observed variation coefficient (on the
Uster automatic integrator) had been 25% on the aforementioned yarn, for
which the expected value of expected coefficient had been determined at 16.7%.
Management is now enabled to evaluate this excess of observed over expected
unevenness from various viewpoints, involving these comparisons:

1. Variation fed from prior process
2. Variation obtained on various machines on the same yarn
3. Variation of other yarns (with more and fewer fibers per average cross section)
4. Variation observed in other mills

Actually, such examinations should occur for each processing stage. Then, as individual causes for undue variation are found (such as given in Tables 1 to 6) and corrected, variability will improve correspondingly from process to process.

TABLE 1

Within-Lap Variation

1. Opening line feed is irregular, or stock is improperly opened (clumpy).

2. Blending reserve level varies excessively or driving belt slips.

3. Out-of-roundness of calender rolls and gears, fluted rolls, beaters and beater bearings, screens and screen bearings, or loggerhead bearings.

4. Lap pins bent and vibrating.

5. Evener motion insensitive due to belt slippage, lint or grease clog-up, or excessive play in mechanical linkages.

6. Fluted roll wear or wear of fluted roll drives.

7. Screen surface uneven or clogged.

8. Fan speeds improper, causing uneven, excessive or inadequate air passages, such as turbulent air flow at screens, excessive air pressure in waste box.

9. Improperly set or choked dampers.

Lap-to-Lap Variation on Picker

Excessive variation in lap weight, from lap-to-lap on the same picker, may be due to excessive or inadequate weight adjustments by the operator; or due to unsatisfactory lap weighing scales, which do not give fine enough readings to permit proper picker adjustments based on actual lap weights. Lack of instruments showing moisture content and providing for compensating devices, such as moisture-regain counter-weights for lap scales, may cause excess variation in true weight from lap-to-lap. Variation in lap length, causing faulty weight values.

Overall Variation

Excessive overall variation indicates differences in actual draft between pickers. This resultant variation in lap weights between pickers, added to the lap-to-lap variation within pickers, and the variation within laps, yields overall variation. The latter is fed into the cards and drawing.

Source: N. L. Enrick, *Industrial Engineering Manual for the Textile Industry*, R. E. Krieger, Melbourne, Fla., 1978.

TABLE 2   Causes of Excessive Variation in the Carding Process

1. Excessive Within-Card Variation

    a.   Worn doffer bearings.

    b.   Untrue calender rolls.

    c.   Worn feed-roll bearings.

    d.   Undue slippage of lap from lap roll to feed roll.

    e.   Defective or chattering gears in bonnet.

    f.   Unsatisfactory clothing.

    g.   Excessive variation in the lap.

2. Excessive Overall Variation

Excessive overall variation indicates differences in actual draft between cards, caused by one or more of the following causes:

    a.   A difference among lap rolls on different cards, (1/8-inch or more).

    b.   Differences in settings among card grinders' sections.

    c.   Wrong gears in drafting train, particularly tension gears.

    d.   Differences in age and wear among card sections, thereby demanding differences in tightness of settings.

    e.   Differences in trumpet sizes (especially if cast iron).

    f.   Differences in average lap weight off different pickers which are then transferred into the cards.

Source: N. L. Enrick, *Industrial Engineering Manual for the Textile Industry*, R. E. Krieger, Melbourne, Fla., 1978.

TABLE 3   Causes of Excess Variation in the Drawing Process

1. Excessive Within-Delivery or Within-Frame Variation:

    a.   Weight hooks elongated, bent and rubbing the steel rolls.

    b.   Adjustable weight hangers too long and resting on the weight-release bars.

    c.   Weight linkage binding and weights resting on bolt ends.

    d.   Worn or broken roll stands.

    e.   Scored roll necks.

    f.   Bent rolls (due to driving gears off and on).

    g.   Damaged gears (chattering or broken teeth).

    h.   Flattened top rolls with worn coverings.

    i.   Gears not meshed properly.

TABLE 3 (continued)

2. Excessive overall variation:

Excessive overall variation indicates differences in actual draft between frames, caused by one or more of the following:

    a. Variation transferred from card groups that run at different average level and feed in the channeling (rather than random) flow of drawing.

    b. Different draft or crown gears in use on some stock.

    c. Differences in trumpet sizes among different frames. (Note: If different trumpets are used on one frame, excess within-frame variation results.)

    d. Differences in tension gears among different frames.

    e. Differences in actual draft among different make, year, or wear of frames, not compensated by gearing.

    f. Differences in weighting used on frames.

Source: N. L. Enrick, *Industrial Engineering Manual for the Textile Industry*, R. E. Krieger, Melbourne, Fla., 1978.

TABLE 4 Causes of Excessive Variation in the Combing Process

1. Within-Delivery or Within-Machine Variation

    a. Non-standard drafts, such as between lap roll and feed roll or between detaching roll and calendar roll.

    b. Rolls, eccentric or sticking.

    c. Nipper knives bent or misaligned.

    d. Needles broken or bent.

    e. Timing of top combs or detaching rolls off-standard.

    f. Gears damaged (chattering or broken teeth), or not meshed properly.

    g. Roll stands worn or broken, roll necks scored.

    h. Weight linkage binding, or elongated and bent weight hooks.

2. Overall Variation

Excessive overall variation indicates differences in waste extraction or actual draft between frames, caused by one or more of the following:

    a. Variation transferred from lap-winder or ribbon lappers run at different average level and feeding in channeled (rather than random) flow to combing.

    b. Differences in draft or tension gears, or trumpet sizes.

    c. Differences in noils removed.

Source: N. L. Enrick, *Industrial Engineering Manual for the Textile Industry*, R. E. Krieger, Melbourne, Fla., 1978.

TABLE 5   Causes of Excessive Variation in the Process Producing Roving

1. Excessive Within-Delivery or Within-Frame Variation:

   a. Builder motion belt slippage.

   b. Roll defects, such as: fluted, marks caused by the flutes of steel rolls; channeled, a groove is formed by constantly running the stock over the same surface; flattened, by leaving the weights on while not running; rough surface, due to uneven wear or loosening of some of the surface of the cover; loosened cots, due to adhesive releasing the cloth, leather, cork or synthetic or to leather stretching; and variable diameters, due to poor cloth or leather or to poor buffing or due to uneven wear on the frame.

   c. Torsional roll vibration.

   d. Clogged or chipped flutes.

   e. Faulty gearing; worn, damaged or improperly meshed gears.

   f. Worn roll bearings or scored journals.

   g. Stretching of sliver fed due to uneven tension.

   h. Differences in twist in sliver fed.

   i. Differences in roll settings within frame.

   j. Faulty weighting device or weights not properly applied.

   k. Worn or broken roll stand; waste collected in roll stand.

   l. Variations in bobbin diameter.

   m. Bent flyers or rough spots on flyers.

   n. Differences in tensions between spindles.

   o. Irregular or clogged aprons.

   p. Slack chains.

2. Excessive Overall Variation:

   a. Variation transferred from drawing through channeling rather than random flow of stock.

   b. Use of different gears (lay, tension, draft or twist) between frames on the same stock.

   c. Differences of roll diameters or roll settings between frames.

   d. Differences in models and makes of frames.

   e. Differences in roll coverings between frames.

   f. Differences in weighting between frames.

   g. Differences in draft distribution between frames.

Source: N. L. Enrick, *Industrial Engineering Manual for the Textile Industry*, R. E. Krieger, Melbourne, Fla., 1978.

TABLE 6   Causes of Excessive Variation in the Spinning Process

1. Within-Delivery Variation

   a. Skewers, skewer bearings or bobbin suspension holders defective or clogged with waste.

   b. Stretched roving from roving frame, misplaced roving bars or faulty roving trumpets.

   c. Rolls worn, run-out, misaligned, improperly set or weighted, or improperly covered (static-producing).

   d. Drafting aprons worn, grooved, seamy, or slipping.

   e. Bearings worn, misaligned.

   f. Gears defective or not meshing properly.

   g. Lifter rods worn or sliding.

   h. Spindles improperly lubricated; running on worn bearings; bent or otherwise out of balance.

   i. Rings worn or out of alignment with spindles.

   j. Travelers worn or of improper weight.

2. Within-Machine Variation

   a. Differences in roving twist, tension, or size from different frames.

   b. Differences in trumpet sizes.

   c. Unequal tape tensions and slippage.

   d. Cylinder misaligned, or bearings misaligned.

   e. Differences in roll weightings; or bent, damaged or otherwise faulty weight hooks or saddles.

   f. Differences in gearing between the sides of the frame.

   g. Unequal roll wear, or ring wear.

3. Room-Overall Variation

   a. Differences in actual draft or contraction among frames.

   b. Differences in overall frame conditions, or in model and make.

   c. Differences in roll weightings or roll settings.

   d. Differences in roving size from different frames, channeled into spinning frame groups.

Source: N. L. Enrick, *Industrial Engineering Manual for the Textile Industry*, R. E. Krieger, Melbroune, Fla., 1978.

VI. LABORATORY TESTING PROGRAM

Control of inch-to-inch variations in linear density, while of special value and interest, is nevertheless only one of the many testing and control activities that occur in the cost-conscious mill. A typical laboratory testing program covers a wide range of tests, inspections, checks, and controls, as illustrated for the mill in Fig. 8, for spinning and weaving. A generalized control program covering the four important processing systems is given in Fig. 9.

When one considers the 30,000 to 100,000 output positions in the typical mill—an individual spinning frame has some 400 spindles—the staggering task of controlling quality, productivity, machine efficiency, waste, and maintenance is readily visualized. A comprehensive documentation of the sampling procedures, test and inspection details, control chart methodology, and management control activity that are a necessity for a competitive mill today, with applications from all processing systems and fibers, was recently published [2]. To be effective, such a program must not contain any loopholes. For example, it is of little value to have perfect drafting rolls operating on precision ball bearings with minimal eccentricity, when in a prior process there was improper carding or unbalanced blending of stock.

An illustration of the transfer of quality problems from process to process is afforded by Fig. 10, for stock weight from drawing through spinning, as depicted by a set of control charts. Drawing sliver is weighed in terms of grains per yard, while roving and yarn are measured in reciprocal terms of "hank roving" and "yarn count," reflecting the number of 840-length yards of stock needed to make 1 lb. Notice how the heavy sliver was soon reflected in equally heavy roving and then yarn (under a reciprocal system, a low hank or count value means "heavier"). The charts have an interesting history, having been constructed from a mill's laboratory log book. Management doubted the usefulness of "going to the trouble of making control charts." Such charts were then constructed from the existing records and the following point was made:

> If the charts had been used *during production*, the tendency for the processing to "go heavy" would have been noted on the seventh day of the month. Corrective action—such as changing one tooth on the drawing crown gear—would have avoided the unsatisfactory product that followed and passed into roving, yarn, and then fabric over the subsequent several days. The losses, in terms of expensive raw stock used to produce heavier-than-specified cloth—avoidable by a quick change in gearing—exceeded many thousand times the cost of maintaining such a control chart for a year.

It is thus desirable to supplement the laboratory testing program with control charts. Where such charts aid in process engineering, they are usually maintained in the laboratory, but where they aid operators during production or else will provide incentives for greater operator care and proficiency, they are best kept right on the production floor. The time spent on such activities has been shown to be well rewarded in terms of cost savings and quality improvements during processing.

Test and Purpose		Opening Line	4 Pickers	120 Cards	12 Breakers	16 Finishers	14 Roving	160 Spinning	Yarn Prep.	1260 Looms	Cloth Room
Routine Sizing Control yarn and cloth, weights and variation	Freq.		Weekly	Weekly	Weekly	Daily	Daily	Daily	--	--	Weekly
	Number		8 Laps	10 Cards	1 Del/Fr.	1 Del/Fr.	7 Frs.	4 Frs.	--	--	All Styles
	Hrs/Wk		0.5	0.5	1.0	6.0	6.0	3.0	--	--	2.0
Speeds Maintain production and quality standards	Freq.	5 Wks.	5 Wks.	Weekly	5 Wks.	5 Wks.	5 Wks.	5 Wks.	5 Wks.	Weekly	5 Wks.
	Number	1 line	4 Pickers	10 Cards	12 Frs.	16 Frs.	14	160	10	126	Folders
	Hrs/Wk.	0.1	0.1	0.5	0.1	0.1	0.1	0.5	0.2	0.5	0.2
Roll Runout Assure good drafting	Freq.				20 Wks.	10 Wks.	10 Wks.	10 Wks.			
	Number				72 Del.	80 Del.	14 Frs.	160 Frs.			
	Hrs/Wk.				0.2	0.5	0.2	1.0			
Uster Evenness Assure uniform yarn	Freq.		Weekly	Weekly	Weekly	Weekly	Weekly	Weekly			
	Number		4 Laps	10 Cards	3 Frs.	3 Frs.	3 Frs.	12 Frs.			
	Hrs/Wk.		2.0	1.5	0.5	0.5	0.5	2.0			
Roving Traverse Minimize wear on rolls	Freq.						5 Wks.	Weekly			
	Number						7 Frs.	12 Frs.			
	Hrs/Wk.						0.1	1.0			
Idle Deliveries Maintain production efficiency	Freq.				Weekly	Weekly	Weekly	2 Wks.			
	Number				72 Del.	80 Del.	1764 Spdl.	47,232			
	Hrs/Wk.				0.1	0.1	0.5	2.0			
Feeding Percentage and Delivery Rate	Freq.	5 Weeks	5 Weeks								
	Number	1 Line	4								
	Hrs/Wk.	0.2	0.2								
Settings Check (Card Settings and Spooler Snick Plate)	Freq.			Weekly					5 Weeks		
	Number			1 Card					10/Spool		
	Hrs/Wk.			0.5					0.2		
Flat Strips, Nep Count and Trumpet Size	Freq.			5 Weeks							
	Number			10 Cards							
	Hrs/Wk.			1.0							
Spoon and Trumpet Knock-off Check	Freq.				2 Weeks	2 Weeks					
	Number				72 Del.	80 Del.					
	Hrs/Wk.				1.0	1.0					
Ply Twist	Freq.								5 Weeks		
	Number								1 Twister		
	Hrs/Wk.								0.1		
Slasher Temperature, Stretch, Size Pick-up Analysis and Moisture Regain	Freq.								Weekly		
	Number								1 Slasher		
	Hrs/Wk.								5.0		
Cloth Analysis and Strength	Freq.										Weekly
	Number										1 Style
	Hrs/Wk.										3.0
Check of Yardage Clocks, fold length and width	Freq.										Weekly
	Number										2 Folders
	Hrs/Wk.										1.0
Quill Check	Freq.									Weekly	
	Number									126 Looms	
	Hrs/Wk.									1.0	
Finished Grading Check	Freq.										Weekly
	Number										2 Graders
	Hrs/Wk.										2.0
Relative Humidity Check	Freq.		Weekly	Weekly	Weekly	Weekly	Weekly	Weekly		Weekly	Weekly
	Number										
	Hrs/Wk.		0.1	0.2	0.1	0.1	0.1	0.5		1.0	0.1

FIGURE 8   Typical laboratory testing program. Some 20 different types of tests, applied to the 10 processing stages, from cotton opening and picking in the mill, to spinning and cloth room, are crucial. The program shown is a recommended minimal schedule. Many mills find it profitable to have further types of tests.

OVER-ALL DESIGN OF YARN MILL QUALITY CONTROL			
CATEGORY OF TESTING	COTTON SYSTEM Cotton, Cut-Staple Synthetics and blends	FILAMENT SYSTEM Synthetics	WOOLEN SYSTEM Wool, Synthetic Blends	WORSTED SYSTEM Wool, Synthetic Blends
RAW STOCK	Length Grade Strength Fineness Maturity Damage Variations	Denier Condition Strength Filaments Dye Index Variations	Length Grade Crimp Fineness Variations	Length Grade Crimp Fineness Oil Content Neps Variations
	PURPOSE: Check quality of raw stock and allocate stock to the most suitable yarns and fabrics.			
MACHINERY SPEEDS	Opening- Spinning Winding Twisting	Winding- Twisting	Dusting- Spinning Winding Twisting	Drawing- Spinning Winding Twisting
	PURPOSE: Assure that machine speeds stay set for best quality and production throughout the mill.			
MACHINE SETTINGS	Beaters Combs Rolls Pins Traverses Spacings	Tensions Traverses Spacings Alignments Rolls	Tapes Tensions Rolls Pans Alignments	Pins Combs Rolls Traverses Spacings Alignments
	PURPOSE: Check that all machine settings are maintained at standard so as to yield optimum performance.			
USTER EVENNESS	Pickers through Spinning	Winding through Twisting	Roping through Spinning	Sliver through Yarn
	PURPOSE: Assure even sliver, roving and yarn of high quality and good processing performance.			
OTHER CHECKS	SIZING: Maintain standard yarn weights. RUN-OUT: Minimize defects from vibrating (run-out) rolls. PACKAGES: Maintain standard package sizes and handling. ENDS-DOWN: Check on running conditions of stock. PRODUCTION: Control efficiency of production. WASTE: Minimize avoidable waste of spinnable fibers.			

FIGURE 9   Generalized testing program, as applicable to the four principal spinning systems, using man-made filament and staple as well as natural fibers. Only the principal categories of testing are shown, essential to high quality and low cost.

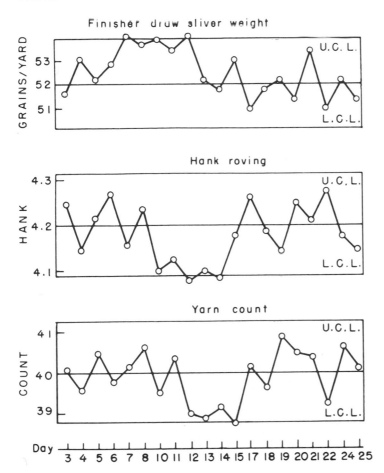

FIGURE 10   Process-to-process control charts, drawing through yarn.   Upper and lower control limits (UCL and LCL) are shown.   Control is applied to the most important test, stock weight, from the finisher drawing process on.   Because of reciprocal weighing systems, in terms of "hank" and "count," representing "number of 840-yard lengths per pound," a low hank or yarn count means that the stock is heavy.   Drawing sliver is weighed directly, in grains per linear yard.

VII.   CONCLUSION

Quality control means initial expenditures for testing equipment and salaries for inspection and testing personnel.   It is therefore only natural that the

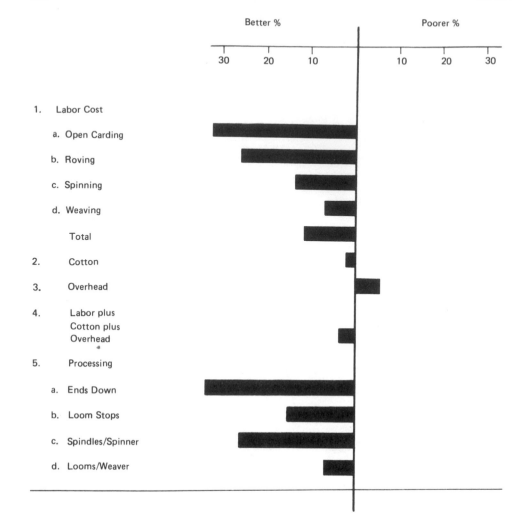

FIGURE 11   Cost comparison. Both mills produce print cloth for the same market. Yet the "excellent" mill has lower costs as a result of quality control. Because of quality control, there is a slightly higher overhead. Note also the improvements in processing attained. The data shown are taken from Table 7.

question is raised: Does this expenditure pay for itself? To evaluate this question, a group of mills recently asked this author to study labor costs, overhead, and processing conditions among their print-cloth processing set-ups. From this survey, two mills designated by "very good" and "excellent" are depicted in Fig. 11, supplemented by the data in Table 7.

TABLE 7   Cost Comparison of Excellent Mill Versus Very Good Mill
(See Also Fig. 11 for Visual Portrayal)

	Higher %	Lower %	Better %	Poorer %
1. Labor Cost				
a. Open-carding		32	32	
b. Roving		27	27	
c. Spinning		13	13	
d. Weaving		8	8	
Total		11	11	
2. Cotton		2	2	
3. Overhead	6*			6*
4. Labor plus Cotton plus Overhead		3**	3**	
5. Processing				
a. Ends-down		33	33	
b. Loom-stops		15	15	
c. Spindles/spinner	28		28	
d. Looms/weaver	8		8	

*
 This represents the cost of quality control and related additional overhead in the "excellent" mill.
**This is the overall competitive cost advantage, not considering the additional benefits of better quality.

     The excellent mill had 6% higher overhead cost, as a result of quality control and related industrial engineering activities. Yet it was rewarded many times by lower labor costs, since stock of better quality needs less tending. Moreover, yarn breaks, known as "ends-down" in the trade, as well as loom stops from yarn breaks, were decreased. Assignment of spindles and looms to operators could be increased, since spinners and weavers were required to do less piecing up of broken "ends" of textile strands.

The principles of quality control as a management philosophy, methodology, and tool, toward overall improvement of operations, quality and costwise, demonstrated in many industries are thus also found to hold in textile production: A quality-controlled fabric is a less costly, yet better and more salable fabric.

REFERENCES

1. E. Leigh, *The Science of Modern Cotton Spinning*, 2nd ed., Palmer & Howe, London, 1873.
2. N. L. Enrick, *Management Control Manual for the Textile Industry*, R. E. Krieger, Melbourne, Fla., 1979.

FURTHER READING

Association of Textile Industrial Engineers, *Industrial Engineering Manual for the Textile Industry*, R. E. Krieger, Melbourne, Fla., 1978.
Enrick, N. L., *Management Control Manual for the Textile Industry*, R. E. Krieger, Melbourne, Fla., 1980.

45

QUALITY IN FINANCIAL SERVICES

CHARLES A. AUBREY, II

*Continental Illinois National Bank and Trust Company of Chicago
Chicago, Illinois*

I. INTRODUCTION

Quality control as a well-developed body of theory and techniques has existed
for a long time in product manufacturing industries. It is only relatively recently that financial institutions, along with other service industries, have
begun to flirt with the formal application of quality control along the lines defined by the manufacturing model. There are several reasons for this. First,
there are obvious dissimilarities between the process of producing physical
products and handling financial transactions which complicate the wholesale
use of quality control tools in banking. Second, the basic nature of our business, with its pervasive tradition of responsibility in handling other people's
money, always requires extensive controls which inherently tend to yield high
quality. Still, any organized attempt to develop a program to enhance quality
in a bank will inevitably take on some of the characteristics of classical "quality
control," including the formal structure of the quality control unit itself, as
well as activities such as setting quality standards, measuring conformance to
standards, and reporting to management.

Before going any further, it would be useful to nail down what we mean by
quality. Frequently, the term expresses a general, almost abstract characteristic of excellence; it evokes the sense of an intangible, immeasurable attribute.
(So when business analysts slip into the jargon of their trade and say that
something is qualitative rather than quantitative, they are suggesting that it
is less concrete, less susceptible to measurement.) Since the heart of a meaningful quality assurance program has to be an effective system for measuring
quality, our definition of quality should be rooted in measurable terms. A recent National Science Foundation study developed an approach to measuring
quality in banks. The study articulated a definition of quality which expresses
its essence aptly: "Quality is the degree to which a product or service conforms to a set of predetermined standards related to the characteristics that
determine its value in the marketplace and its performance of the function for
which it was designed." What this means is that customer needs and expectations need to be determined regarding each product and service. These needs,
then, should be reflected in standards—quality standards which are simply the

product or service's basic characteristics. Finally then, the product or service should continuously conform to the standards, and if it does, customers will be satisfied and continue to buy the product or service.

To carry out quality control a system must be established to set standards or objectives, monitor the standards or give feedback, and be able to influence the system or make changes when the standards are not met. Quality assurance is an activity of overseeing the system, particularly if quality control is in a decentralized environment, to assure that quality control is functioning properly.

II. DETERMINING YOUR CURRENT QUALITY COMMITMENT AND LEVEL AND DEVELOPING A PLAN

To help establish its conceptual footing, and a plan, one must know where they are. Several weeks of meetings with various management, staff, and salespeople in various departments are needed to get a feeling for the current climate relative to quality in the bank. Particular attention should be focused on perceptions of what quality is and what special activities are currently being pursued to measure, sustain, and improve quality. A sample of senior and middle line and staff people in both sales and operations should be surveyed. To provide a degree of structure to the discussions, responses to the following interview questions could be sought.

1. During this year's planning process, were formal objectives regarding service quality prepared?
2. Have these objectives been met? If so, how has this been determined?
3. Do you intend to make any changes during the remainder of this year which will improve service quality performance?
4. Do you intend to incorporate quality objectives in the next year's plan? If so, have you formulated any of these yet?
5. Do you have formalized service quality policies and procedures written and implemented?
6. What specific standards do you actually use to evaluate your current service quality performance?
7. Do you have a method or system to apply the standards? If so, are you satisfied with the results?
8. Do you generate a quality performance report(s) on a periodic basis comparing actual quality performance against your standards?
9. Do you have quality control mechanisms in effect to provide feedback to those areas which have made errors? If yes, how does the system work?
10. Do you communicate your quality performance to your seniors? If so, through what media and to what extent?
11. Are you aware of departmental or corporate standards used to measure your service quality performance?
12. Do you feel that top management is committed to high quality? Does this help or hurt your efforts toward quality performance?
13. What can and should be done to increase commitment to quality assurance at all levels?

14. Do you have any suggestions or guidelines which should be incorporated into a corporate policies bulletin on service quality?

15. What would you estimate to be the current cost of quality assurance within your area? In other words, what percent of your total expenses and total manpower is associated with quality assurance and error correction?

16. Are your current resources limiting your level of quality? Do you require additional expense or personnel to improve your level of service quality performance to a higher level than your current performance? If yes, how many more personnel would you require, and what additional expenses would you incur?

17. In your opinion, what is the relationship between quality and productivity?

18. Do you feel that your customers perceive the same relationship?

19. What is your perception of what our customers think about Continental's service quality performance and employee awareness of the importance of the customer?

20. In your opinion, do you think our bank employees have an appropriate customer awareness or sensitivity attitude? If no, why not, and what can be done to improve this attitude?

21. Do your training programs include customer sensitivity or awareness training? If so, how is this being accomplished?

A. Operating Management Perceptions and Practices

What follows is a summary of the oral responses provided by the management people in a major money center bank,* who offered their comments on what their units were doing to assure quality and their observations about quality in general.

Performance Measures

Most operating units capture some data on performance which affects quality. Some common measures are number of errors, holdover, and turnaround time. (Table 1 displays various types of data which, according to the respondents, are collected in their respective units.)

Performance Quality Objectives

While the majority of managers affirmed the existence of objectives relating to quality—and asserted that they were being met—there seemed to be a generally low level of awareness of just what the objectives were. The responses indicated a lack of regular reports comparing actual to standard performance along quality dimensions, and where such reports existed, they seldom got visibility above the division manager level but stayed within the unit of origin. None of the respondents indicated a knowledge of department or corporate quality objectives, although there was a universal feeling that senior management is committed to high quality.

---

*
Continental Bank, Chicago, Ill.

TABLE 1 Summary Chart of Quality Activities

Division/unit	Processing Quality											Customer Service Quality						
	Quality performance reports	Errors (number)	Errors and adjustment (cost)	Holdover (number)	Holdover (cost)	Turnaround time	Systems downtime	Customer profile	Quality surveys	Rates of quality	Standards for quality	Customer service reports	Investigations and inquiries	Investigations vs. inquiries	Aging	Errors	Holdover	Customer service section
Bond: Bond operations	×			×								×	×		×		×	×
General banking services																		
International services	×	×	×			×				×		×		×	×	×		×
Collections	×	×	×	×				×			×	×		×	×			×
Credit information	×		×							×				×	×			
Paying and receiving	×		×									×					×	
Precious metals																		
Customer service	×		×	×	×							×	×	×	×	×	×	×
Signature	×			×	×							×		×	×	×	×	×
Letters of Credit	×	×		×			×			×		×		×	×	×	×	×
Loan support/processing	×	×					×			×	×							
Loan review	×	×								×		×						
Domestic wire transfer	×		×			×												
Support services	×			×		×			×			×			×		×	
Safekeeping/special services												×			×	×	×	
FX operations												×	×		×	×	×	

	1	2	3	4	5	6	7	8	9	10	11	12	13	14	15	16	17	18	19	20
Personal Banking																				
Facilities operations	×		×	×	×		×		×	×			×	×		×			×	
Charge card Operations													×	×		×			×	
Consumer credit operations													×	×		×				
Mortgage servicing													×	×		×				
Real estate: Real estate operations													×	×		×				
Trust: Trust operations	×	×				×	×			×			×		×	×			×	
OMS																				
operations																				
Balance control	×	×	×		×	×		×					×		×	×	×	×	×	
Bookkeeping	×	×	×		×	×		×		×										
Document processing	×	×	×		×	×		×		×										
Proof transit	×	×	×		×	×		×		×	×									
Remittance banking	×	×						×		×	×		×	×					×	×
General services																				
Properties development						×														
Properties management									×					×						
General duties									×	×	×			×						
Distribution services									×	×	×									
Printing and graphic services	×	×		×					×	×	×									
Redords management/storage/filing	×	×								×	×									
Systems																				
Systems development	×				×	×		×	×	×										
Systems operations	×	×			×	×	×	×	×	×										

Attitudes Toward Quality

Most of the people interviewed believed that their unit's quality was very good. There was general agreement that improvement in quality would be in-itiated most effectively by increased emphasis on quality by the corporate office and department heads, with continual reinforcement up and down the line at all levels. The one area of weakness in performance which was widely recognized was in the level of customer relations skills exhibited by the work force generally. The pervasive view was that our people do not display ade-quate sensitivity to customers. The solutions posed most often were better training, continuous efforts to promote awareness, and managerial attention. Very few units, according to the respondents, have formal training in cus-tomer service skills, including human relations training or awareness programs.

Recurring Comments

A number of comments surfaced repeatedly in the discussions with operating management and staff. Here is a sampling:

1. The bank needs a centralized inquiry and complaint tracking system to monitor problems by type or information requested, type of prob-lem, customer, and product.
2. Automated systems support is critical to maintaining high quality.
3. The quality of the work force is deteriorating with obvious implica-tions for our overall quality.
4. Our supervisory training should emphasize quality together with the other aspects of production.
5. Customer service personnel too frequently are assigned based on technical knowledge rather than interpersonal skills.
6. The performance appraisal process should provide for evaluation of the quality aspects of performance and this should be reflected in the reward system.
7. Communication between units needs to be improved.
8. Salespeople need to be thoroughly trained in all aspects to our products and services and understand operation constraints which limit what they can reasonably offer customers.
9. We need better means of assessing customer perceptions of our service.
10. We should pay particular attention to new accounts, which are particularly vulnerable to quality problems.
11. The impact of poor quality on customers is especially critical today in view of the increasing assertiveness of our customers.

B. Administrative Perceptions of Quality

A number of interviews were conducted with key administrative people in each line department to get a flavor of how administrators view our quality. Since the quality of our services is a vital part of their marketability, it is important that our quality be high and that our salespeople have confidence in that qual-ity. The interviews with select administrators suggest that there is considera-ble perceived room for improvement.

Although the respondents generally viewed the quality of the sales force as very good, some commented that with rapid staff growth to accommodate busi-ness expansion, we have experienced a temporary dilution in experience.

The activity that came in for the sharpest criticism was the operating support provided to commercial services. Errors and lack of timeliness in service delivery and response were cited as the chief lapses in quality. The most frequent complaint made by the respondents was that errors occurred too frequently and took too long to correct. There was a general feeling that customers would tolerate errors if they were corrected promptly. However, this kind of response to problems was believed to be untypical.

It was felt that because of inadequate communication processes, improper information, or faulty procedures, it is difficult to get customer problems to the right area for handling. Further, because of the frequent impact of multiple units on particular transactions, there are sometimes jurisdictional dealys during which no one area or person will assume responsibility for fixing a problem. Even when the problem is ultimately resolved, the quality of the final communication with the customer is not uniform or reliable. The fundamental problem is perceived to be a lack of sensitivity to the customer's needs, an absence of customer awareness.

C. Customer Perceptions of Quality

Although the perceptions of Continental's quality held by operating management and administrative people offer a vital perspective, the most important set of perceptions is that held by our customers and potential customers. There is no comprehensive study available which tells us how our customers perceive our quality. The corporation has done some research among select groups of customers and potential customers which has included, among other data, findings relating to quality. The most notable examples are the annual studies done by Greenwich Research Associates concentrating on corporate and correspondent banking. (There is also a Greenwich study on corporate trust, but for the sake of brevity in this summary, we will omit it here.)

The Greenwich studies contain a great deal of data without attempting to make an overall ranking of banks by significant characteristics. To get a feeling for a particular characteristic such as service quality, numerous questions which relate to service quality must be reviewed.

Corporate executives evaluate banks on their ability to meet their needs by the flexibility of service (credit and noncredit) provided (1), the quality of the account officers (2), and the strength of the bank's interest in their company (3). The strength of the bank's operating capabilities is ranked 9. Executives cite the reasons that banks become more important to them is the amount of domestic credit provided (1), the level of cash management services (2), and the caliber of account officers (3). On the other hand, banks become less important due to lack of account officer attention (1), too many operating errors (2), and below-average caliber of account officers (3).

As can generally be observed, the scope and depth of services offered by a bank are the prime considerations of corporate executives in choosing, continuing, and enhancing bank relationships, with account officer capabilities second. The decision to reduce or discontinue bank relationships is generally based on the lack of account officer capabilities, weaknesses in bank operations, or high error rates.

Generally, Continental ranks fourth in account officer quality and fifth in the quality of operations among other commercial banks. (The quality characteristics of an account officer include timeliness of response, performance, experience, knowledge, and time assigned to an account. Operating quality includes speed and accuracy of the service and speed of error correction.)

Correspondent bankers evaluate and select banks similarly to corporate executives; the top three criteria are the same: flexibility of services to meet needs, the caliber of account officers, and the bank's interest in the correspondent. Operating capabilities, which were ranked ninth by corporate executives, are ranked fifth by bank executives. Once a bank is corresponding, the relationship is evaluated in terms of accuracy of the services (1), quality of cash letter services (2), and flexibility of services (3). Correspondent banks become more important and are utilized more due to fast cash letter services (1), more account officer attention (2), and more overline support (3). They become less important and service is discontinued due to inadequate service from calling officers (1), decline in the need for correspondent services (2), and too many operational errors (3).

Although the scope and depth of services and the caliber of account officers are most important in the evaluation and selection of a correspondent, operating quality, accuracy, and speed are the major factors used to determine whether to continue and increase service usage. Account officer attention and service usage and flexibility are less important than operating quality once a correspondent is selected. Bankers are also more sensitive to quality in services than to the price they pay for those services.

Continental's account officers are generally fifth compared to all other banks and are ranked second regionally. (These perceptions are based on follow-up, knowledge, ease of interaction, and knowledge of the customer.) Generally, Continental's operating quality ranks third compared to the other banks providing correspondent services. (The relevant quality characteristics include error rates, corrective action, speed, accuracy, and response to inquiries.)

Another example of research which yields data on quality are the "shopping" studies performed regularly by Personal Banking. These studies utilize "shopping" by trained researchers posing as customers and documenting their perceptions of products and services, with particular attention paid to the customer relations skills of personal bankers, tellers, and receptionists. Continental's performance is then compared with the results of similar studies at several other Loop banks. (The most recent study included data on First National Bank, Harris, and Central National.) Continental's performance generally has been equal or marginally superior to the other banks studied. Also, there has been definite improvement in our performance over the last several surveys.

The Greenwich research and the Personal Banking "shopping" studies are only two examples of a variety of surveys which are periodically done to measure customer and noncustomer perceptions of Continental services. The overall impression that is created by looking at the results of the various studies is that Continental is viewed favorably as a quality bank. However, it is also clear that quality is a vital dimension of how customers and potential customers evaluate us, along with other banks, so enhancing our position in the marketplace demands that we pay continued and increased attention to quality.

D. A Quality Assurance Program

It is apparent that Continental is a quality bank. This is supported by the perceptions of our customers and the unmistakable record of years of increasing profits. However, there is room for improvement. While there is justifiable pride among our staff members in our overall quality, there is also a general recognition that we can do better. We need to generate a more visible, emphatic commitment to quality at all levels of management. This commitment

should be embodied in demanding objectives and reinforced in our reward system. It should be made unequivocably clear to all our employees that quality
really matters. Finally, we should do much more to increase an awareness of
the customer throughout our staff and polish the customer relations skills of
our sales and service people.

A new unit is being formed to provide a focal point for the corporation's
efforts to maintain and enhance quality. The quality assurance division will
fulfill this mission in a cooperative effort with management by pursuing these
objectives:

Mission

It is the mission of the quality assurance division to assist management at all
levels throughout the Continental Illinois Corporation to maintain a consistently
high quality of service in all our activities and assist in creating and maintaining an appropriate awareness on the part of every employee of the importance
of quality and the customer.

Quality Assurance Objectives

Objective 1: Develop, organize, and staff the quality assurance division.
Objective 2: Help management of various units establish or update quality
assurance objectives, policies, procedures, and performance standards.
Objective 3: Develop, then help management implement, a comprehensive
quality control, monitoring, and reporting system.
Objective 4: Develop and implement a quality-cost measurement system.
Objective 5: Develop and implement a communications and motivational
program to enhance employee awareness of the importance of the customer and to ensure a high quality of customer service throughout the
corporation.
Objective 6: Design and employ customer feedback programs to measure
customer perceptions of service and product quality.
Objective 7: Continually review quality assurance and customer awareness
programs and trends in banking and other service industries.

III. QUALITY STANDARDS AND MEASURES

Quality characteristics or standards, and their corresponding measures, should
be developed during new product development. But most financial institutions
will already be delivering hundreds of mature products which have already gone
through the new product development stage. Therefore, it will be necessary
to develop quality characteristics or standards and their corresponding measures for the products that are already being delivered to customers. This will
be the most significant task in most institutions. After these are established,
the task will be to shift to the process as it relates to new product development.

In the financial service industry—which is very labor intensive—the process
for developing quality characteristics for products and services should be
handled through a group participative process. The people processing the
product know it best and know the problems that can occur and where they can
occur. The approach that has worked in numerous financial institutions is a
series of four 2-hour group meetings which take place with those people under
a first-line supervisor. Either all the people may be involved under the first-
line supervisor or under the supervisor and selected key people. This par-
ticipatory group process takes approximately 8 hours of time for each section

under a supervisor, and approximately an additional and equal number of
hours for the quality control analyst or engineer who will facilitate the process.

A. Quality Awareness and Understanding

The first of the four two-hour sessions is devoted to defining quality, to discussing what quality is, how it can be measured, the benefits of measuring
quality, and how quality once it is measured can be analyzed and therefore
controlled and improved. The second part of this session is devoted to developing functional flowcharts for each product that is being processed by the
section. It is not unusual to have from one to six products being provided
by an individual section. In most cases they are not providing the total processing of a product but only part of the process to deliver that service. The
flowcharts start with all sources of input to the section, identify all the major
functions or changes of state which take place during the processing, and end
with the identification of where the finished service goes, be it to the customer
or another area of the bank. These flowcharts are thoroughly discussed so
that all members understand the charts and the process they represent.

At the conclusion of the first session each member is given a copy of the
functional flowcharts that were developed and the concept of a deviation is
explained. A deviation is anything that goes wrong in the process. The flowchart is like a blueprint diagram: If everything goes right and the service
has matched the blueprint, the service is delivered correctly, but when something deviates from this blueprint it is called a deviation. The people in the
group are then charged or given a homework assignment to develop all the deviations that could possibly take place in the functional flowchart. It is important to note here that they are not asked to identify only the deviations
that do take place, but those that do take place as well as those that *could*
take place during the process.

B. Brainstorming the Process

Ideally, the next 2-hour meeting is scheduled for the following day. Depending on the work load and the scheduling for the area in which the process is
taking place, the process sometimes may take place every other day or one
2-hour meeting a week in successive weeks, but we have found that the closer
that the meetings can be to each other, the better the results of the process.
In the second meeting the people come back together in the group, having
individually generated a list of all the deviations which they believe can go
wrong in the process. The second session starts out with a controlled brainstorming method in which each person responds in turn one at a time, going
clockwise or counterclockwise around the table, identifying one deviation which
they have identified. This process may take place and continue for 15 to 20
min, at which point a break should be taken for people to collect their thoughts,
to rest, and possibly to think about and jot down some new ideas on deviations.

While the process is taking place and the people are in turn giving their
possible deviations, a person is recording these on flipcharts and they are
numbered. When the flowchart was completed in the previous session, each of
the functions as well as the input and the output points were given unique
numbers so that when deviations were identified, the person who identified
the deviation also made an attempt at indicating at what point on the flowchart
that deviation was introduced into the system or where it took place. It is not
unusual for this controlled brainstorming to take up the entire 2 hours, and

in some cases an extension of an hour or sometimes 2 hours is needed to complete the brainstorming of all possible deviations. At this point, the participants are given the list of defects to take home with them and to review. They are specifically charged with reviewing the list, to determine whether there are duplicates, to assure that they understand each of the deviations, and to be sure that there are no additional deviations which have not been identified which need to be recorded. The next day when they return this list will be discussed.

C. Selecting the Key Defects

The third session, which is hopefully the following day, begins with a discussion of the list of deviations that have been identified on the previous day. The group in a discussion format will combine like deviations, add any new deviations, and discuss those that anyone has any doubts about. At this point we want a complete list that is concise, accurate, and understandable.

Next the group is asked to rank or vote on those deviations which are key quality determinates. Key quality determinates are those deviations which meet one of two tests. The first test is: Does it affect the customer significantly if it takes place? The second test is: If it happens, does it consume a large amount of resources to correct? For example, it may take a relatively high proportion of time to reprocess, or an interest penalty may be incurred if a transaction is not handled properly.

The voting process consists of 15 cards handed out to each member. Each member then reviews the list of deviations and selects the 15 which they feel, based on the two tests, are most important. The second step is to rank them from 1 to 15, a weight of 15 being the most important and a ranking of 1 being the least important. The cards are then collected and compiled. The deviations which have recieved votes are ranked from highest weight to lowest weight. These reflect the group's consensus as to the key deviations. The key deviations are those for which quality measures and quality standards will be developed. All quality deviations identified are not measured, only the principal ones. If we were to try to monitor and measure several hundred items in each area, the reporting and inspection process would be unwieldy. We would in fact be making everything important—and if everything is important, nothing is important. Therefore, we will concentrate on the key deviations for the remainder of the process.

At the end of this session the group is introduced to the concept of measurement. Most measures take the form of a ratio or the number of deviations which could occur that have been identified over the volume processed. We call these ratios quality measures. A second method, which is used less often, is called a frequency. A frequency is simply the number of occurrences that took place or the number of deviations that happened during a specific time period—a week, a month, a day. So in effect they are implicitly a ratio, the number of deviations over a time period, whether it be days, weeks, or months. This type of quality measure is discouraged but is useful in some situations. It is important to note here that as we take deviations and convert them into measures, we no longer use the term *deviation*, which was indicative of something going wrong in the process. We now call them *defects*. We call them defects because when we began measuring their occurrence, they will be quality standards which will not be met and will therefore be classified as defects. After the group has been introduced to the concept of measurement, a list of the key deviations in descending order is given to the group and the group is charged with developing measures for these items for the following session, which hopefully will take place on the following day.

D. Developing Quality Measures

The fourth session begins with a group using the controlled brainstorming technique of listing all the measures which they have developed for all the defects. This process continues with a break every 15 to 20 min until all possible measures have been exhausted for the list of key deviations. At the conclusion of the listing process, discussion takes place to be sure that everyone understands each of the measures that have been identified, to be sure that there are measures for every one of the key defects, and to make sure that there are no duplicates. Wherever appropriate, if additional measures can be generated, those are added to the list.

The last step in the measurement process is to vote on measures when there is more than one possible measure for each defect identified. If there is more than one measure, the group votes on which measure they feel is the most effective measure for that defect. The last thing that is accomplished in this session is to go back to the functional flowchart developed in the first session and indicate the earliest point that each measure can be implemented so that we can catch it as early as possible in the process. For example, if a defect occurs in the first step or function of the process, it would be most desirable to be able to catch it in the second step or before the second step rather than to catch it in the tenth step or the tenth function. If we catch it in the tenth step, we may have to go back and redo 1 through 9 before proceeding to step 10. If we can catch it at or before the second step, there would be a minimum of reprocessing and less possibility that the defect would escape to the customer.

The next step in the process is to take the total list of defects, the flowchart, the key defects, and the measures and present them to the area management. The quality control engineer and the supervisor present these items to the next level of management for their approval, modification, or additions. Upon approval by the appropriate level of management, the measures are implemented. It is now the responsibility of the quality control engineer or analyst working with the supervisor to implement the measures that have been approved in the appropriate point in the process. The flowchart is used as a starting point, but the analyst and the supervisor assess whether that in fact is the earliest point in the process or if an earlier point can be established. It is also the responsibility of the quality control analyst to access the best way to collect data. The possibilities range from collecting data through automation, which may or may not be in place, all the way through manual sampling. The analyst designs check sheets, reporting forms, and sampling plans, and works to coordinate automation as necessary to gather the data needed for the measures as efficiently and effectively as possible.

E. Quality Standards

Once the measures have been implemented, monitoring (primarily sampling) begins. Several days to weeks of data are collected, depending on the amount of volume, and closely monitored each day by the supervisor and analyst. This is to assure understanding on the part of those checkers and inspectors who are collecting and reporting. Control charts are constructed to determine the process capability of the system. The mean quality level for each measure and 1 and 2 standard deviation points, once determined, are considered the system's process capabilities.

The process capability is now the basis for setting the quality standard or objective for each measure. This process tells us empirically where we are, but more important, we need to know how our customers feel about the quality level of the service they are receiving. The methods of receiving input from customers are various and range from very simple to complex. These methods will be discussed later but are an important ingredient in determining the standards.

Let us suppose that a process has the capability of 0.005% of checks misfiled. Most managers would agree that five checks misfiled out of 100,000 is reasonable for their operation or from a consumer's point of view. However, when actually surveyed, consumers expected even better quality. If their expectations are close to the standard, a goal or objective could be set slightly better than the process capability to motivate better performance and assure customer satisfaction. If their expectation were much greater than the process capability, two avenues are possible. A breakthrough or quality improvement project would have to be initiated to improve the quality level dramatically, or we would continue at the same quality level with a significantly increased standard and possibly improve significantly but more likely not—and lose customers.

At the other extreme, a checking account statement delivery process could have a capability of 10 working days after cutoff. Many managers and consumers would agree that this sounds too long. Survey data revealed that this is an adequate quality level for customers. Therefore, it would have been inprudent to waste resources to improve the quality level further. It is important from a motivational standpoint that standards are both challenging and achievable. If they are not doable, employees will give up. If they do not allow the employee to stretch, their potential will be minimized. As can be seen, customers' expectations and needs are extremely important in setting quality standards in mature financial services.

F. Measuring Quality and Setting Quality Standards for New Services

Setting standards for new services is a more difficult task but takes the same form as for mature products. Once the need for a new product has been determined—and this should include extensive market research with potential customer surveys—the marketing, operating, quality, and product management people together write the service characteristics or quality specifications. Operations and quality control then identify the existing processes that will provide the service and model or engineer the new process that will have to be created and their prospective quality level. If the process capability is adequate or at least close to the specifications, the new service should go ahead and these standards used to launch the service. If the process capability is far apart, a breakthrough or quality improvement project will be necessary prior to launch. If far apart and a breakthrough seems unlikely or there are no resources to carry out an improvement project, the new services should not be introduced.

G. Examples of Quality Measures and Objectives

A service characteristic of commercial credits which is very high on our customer's list of importance is the amount of credit they receive (see Table 2). A measurement of this service characteristic could be the percent of credit

TABLE 2   General Examples of Quality Measures

Measure	Example
Operations	
Accuracy	Number of errors/number of items
	Number of adjustments/number of items
	Number of audit adjustments/number of items
	Number items out of balance/number of items
	Dollar errors and adjustments/total expense
Reliability	On-line system downtime/time on the system
	On-line system downtime during critical period/time of critical period
Timeliness	Elapsed time from receipt to processing
	Amount of volume held over by age
	Amount of volume held over/total volume
	Dollar amount held over/dollar total received
Credit	
Amount of credit	Dollar credit received/dollar credit requested
	Credit requests approved/credit requests received
	Credit requests denied/credit requests received
Speed of credit	Elapsed time from credit request receipt to decision
	Elapsed time from credit decision to disbursement
Effective calling	Number of visits/number of visits expected
	Maximum number of calls per day
	Time spent per call
	Business gained/number of calls made
Effective lending	Number of charged-off loans/number of loans outstanding
	Amount of charged-off loans/amount of loans outstanding
Experience and knowledge	Number of officers turned over/number of officers
	Number of backup officers/account
	Number of officers trained/number of officers
	Number of officers with number of years experience/number of officers
Securities	
Performance	Dollar amount return/dollar principal
	Dollar amount growth/dollar base
	Research indicated return/actual return
Speed	Elapsed time for settlement
Teller	
Speed	Number of customers in the queue
	Amount of time in the queue
Timeliness	Time per transaction
	Turnaround time for no-wait or mail transactions

TABLE 2 (continued)

Measure	Example
Accuracy	Teller differences Amount charged off/amount handled
Customer service	
Timeliness	Elapsed time from receipt of customer inquiry or problem to answer or resolution
General	Number of customer inquiries or problems/number of customers Number of customer inquiries or problems/volume of service Business load/number of customers
Personnel: Effectiveness	Number of candidates rejected/number of candidates sent on interviews Number of days that jobs have been unfilled
Staff project	
Timeliness	Number of project hours actual/number of project hours estimated
Effectiveness	Dissatisfied users/projects completed

granted divided by credit requests. Specific objectives or standards for this quality measure could be 100% for customers who consider the organization their lead or first-tier bank, 90% for second tier, or 80% for third tier. Not supplying adequate credit to customers who consider the organization their primary lender (assuming credit worthiness) could cause these customers to develop new bank relationships and cost a loss of both current and future business. Not attempting to supply increased credit to customers for which we are a second- or third-tier bank would effectively keep us from becoming their primary bank. On the other hand, if resources are limited, we may want to design our objectives or standards to keep our position stable if we have an appropriate customer mix and are profitable.

In an operating area a service characteristic of a checking account (demand deposit) is deposit credits. A quality measure for the deposit characteristic could be the number of misposted deposits over the total number of deposits posted. A specific standard would be 1 for every 3000 deposits. If this ratio is not met or exceeded, customers could become dissatisfied with the service and switch banks. Each misposted deposit could result in an investigation and possible compensation to the customer for the loss of funds. If this ratio is not met, it would signal management of a problem and an effort would be launched to discover the cause of the excessive quality deviations.

A third example is the customer service or investigation process with which everyone throughout the bank is familiar. An important characteristic of this function, since it is usually a result of a quality deviation in another service, is timeliness of the response. This could be measured by the number of working days from receipt to final communication with the customer on the problem.

Three days from receipt to response could be our standard or objective.
Three or fewer would be meeting the quality objective and more than 3 days
would mean a quality deviation or lack of quality. If repeated, this poor quality could mean a loss of business. In addition, failure to meet this objective
continually could mean that there are inefficiencies in the investigation process
or an excess volume of inquiries. Before this problem can be solved it must
be identified, and quality measures and standards provide the identification
process. Once solved, the quality objective can be met, and if the problem
was an inefficiency, a cost saving would be realized, and if it was due to an
excess volume, the characteristic that was failing and causing the high volume
could be put back on target.

These are just a few examples of those quality measures that can be developed by identifying the key service characteristics which the customer
values in each service. Setting an objective or standard of quality performance can be based on common sense or statistics, but the important aspect is
planning, being aware of the level of quality today and determining where you
want to be tomorrow, then *monitoring* and *controlling* in relation to that plan
and rewarding for results.

IV. CUSTOMER PERCEPTION OF QUALITY

"Customers expect more today. We want to get the dope on how we are doing
right now, what is actually happening in the trenches." This colorful comment
made by AT&T's customer services director, Robert Gryb, expresses a keen
concern for the customer that is currently being shared by an overwhelming
number of service industries. This renewed recognition of the powerful role
played by the customer is a result of increased regulation and competition confronting almost all industries today. Consequently, methods to measure a person's interpretation of what he or she sees, feels, and hears, otherwise referred to as "customer perception," have also received acute attention as instrumental tools for determining customer satisfaction. However, just as no
two persons' perceptions are exactly alike, neither are the techniques used to
measure customers' attitudes and beliefs. Rather, there are a variety of techniques available, each having unique characteristics that qualify it for specific
research objectives.

A. Mail Surveys

For instance, mail surveys are conducted among samples of usually hard-to-get
respondents with self-administered questionnaires that are shorter than other
forms of surveys. The questionnaire is generally mailed with an introductory
letter and self-addressed stamped envelope to increase convenience of return.
Mail surveys are advantageous because they are usually less expensive than
telephone or personal interviewing and do not require a large field staff. The
anonymity of mail interviewing allows respondents to be more frank in their
answers, especially on sensitive financial issues. Also, certain sections of the
population may be more easily reached by mail than by other techniques, so
that a geographically dispersed clientele can be contacted.

On the other hand, sequence bias, in which the respondent modifies his or
her answers after having read all the questions first, puts a severe limitation
on the mail survey. Moreover, mail surveys suffer from a dilemma whereby
those who do return their questionnaires tend to be better educated and have

greater interest in the topic. There is never a guarantee that the survey was not filled out by someone other than the intended respondent. Even when these mail questionnaires are returned, they come in so slow and scattered that mail survey completion time is the worst of any technique. Finally, nonresponse bias proposes the problem of what to do about those who did not return the questionnaire. In view of printing and postage costs and the possible need for follow-up mailing, the cost per return can actually be high if the nonresponse rate is large.

On the contrary, Chemical Bank has experienced a healthy 25% response rate utilizing the mail survey method. Questionnaires designed to evaluate the bank's branch services are inserted in customers' monthly statements based on the rationale that "when you open your statement, you are thinking about banking." Mail surveys are sent to half the customers of each of Chemical's 250 branches to identify such problems as unresponsive tellers, lengthy waiting time, and inconvenient hours.

B. Electronic Surveys

Candid responses have also been gathered by four "pushbutton questionnaires" installed on a rotating basis in each of the 100 offices of Lloyd's Bank California. The instant feedback machines require only 30 sec of a customer's time to answer 11 questions anonymously, including the rating of attention received from branch management, accuracy of servicing accounts, and the courtesy, efficiency, and speed of tellers. The tabulated information is quickly printed out, so that management can take immediate action to identify problem areas and improve service. According to executive vice-president Carl Wiese, this pushbutton procedure "shows our customers that we value their opinions and comments enough to provide a quick, easy, private way for them to tell us how we're doing."

Customers are not the only ones questioned about their perceptions of banking services, though. In a Public Opinion Survey done at California First Bank, management perceptions of what the bank's image is to the public is measured by beginning all questions with the inquiry: "How did customers answer the following?" The notion of management employees trying to wear the customers' shoes temporarily works well to point out any discrepancies between actual customer attitudes and the perceived beliefs that employees have as to how their customers view the bank and its services.

C. Panel Survey

In addition, customer attitudes toward the American Telephone and Telegraph Company are being detected by a questionnaire completed by a panel of 2200 customers. Begun in 1972, the customer feedback program is called Public Overview and is conducted by the National Family Opinion Inc. To form the panel, AT&T takes the national census and tries to find 2200 people who represent roughly the same sort of distribution as in the population at large. The panel is reconstituted every 4 years, while one-fourth of the panel must be replaced every year due to deaths, disappearances, and moving. Panel members are not paid, yet AT&T does drop them birthday and Christmas gifts.

Three major attitude indexes are studies: overall quality of service, overall cost, and company image. Just recently, general questions about the company were added, including whether or not AT&T is perceived as a polluter. Curiously enough, panel members have not necessarily had current contact with the phone company, so that their opinions are based on such outside factors as rate cases and publicity.

Results clearly indicate that customer attitude toward employees has been deteriorating since the Public Overview program was initiated. To counteract this distressing trend, Bell System managers have worked into their public speeches declarations of AT&T's increasing emphasis on employee courtesy and service.

D. Handout Surveys

One of the most ambitious programs to measure customer perception is the annual customer service audit conducted at J. L. Hudson Co., which operates fashion shops and restaurants in Detroit. Initially, a questionnaire touching all aspects of store life is handed out to customers at point of sale. After these forms are mailed back by customers, they are cataloged on a computer and reviewed by a task force composed of top executives in all areas of store management. The task force has a weekly 3-hour meeting and works like a Senate Investigating Committee, examining every facet of operations before brainstorming with a list of recommendations derived from the criticisms contained in the customer audits. To ensure speedy implementations of the task force's suggestions, a point value for service based on the audits is built into each executive's annual performance review. Goals for the improvement of service are also built into the company's annual business plans.

To gain feedback, another merchandise retailing store chain, Zayre, distributes questionnaires printed in five different languages in their "Zayre Cares" pamphlets, which outline available customer services such as layaway and exchange plans. In much the same way, at Rich's retail store in Atlanta, question cards are cautiously put in customers' packages and shopping bags. For as vice-president for consumer affirst, Ken Rich warns: "We must do this spasmodically. If you do this for very long it becomes old hat to customers and they no longer respond, or their answers are rote. We usually do it for about 6 to 8 weeks at a shot, and get almost 200 responses a week. When interest lags, we discontinue the program."

Not to be excluded, the restaurant industry is also making an ardent effort to gather customer feedback and pinpoint problems by use of the comment card or "table top questionnaire" which is available at tables, counters, and cash registers in a majority of restaurants. Normally, there are no customer incentives to respond to these cards, yet most customers indicate that prepaid postage and easily accessible cards are sufficient reasons to respond. Comment cards have a limited place in the perception research process because customers who voluntarily fill in the cards are not often indicative of the typical guest. Therefore, the question cards are generally best utilized as inner comparison devices for tracking significant operating changes which might accompany a change in management or the menu. Nevertheless, customer comment cards, which can either be mailed back, given to an employee, or dropped in a collection box near an exit door, have frequently been used to take definitive follow-up action. Such follow-up action begins with the operations vice-president, who must analyze and tabulate results from the cards and formulate some conclusions and decisions. A customer card summary is then distributed to top management, regional managers, and unit managers. An unusual example of action taken as a result of analysis of comment cards took place at Win Schuler's restaurant and is reported by Hans Schuler himself: "A unique onion soup was mentioned on many comment cards as being 'too thick.' The thickness of the soup was considered to be a factor that made the soup a 'signature' item. Instead of changing the recipe, the decision was made to expand the menu description and train the waitress to inform the customer of the consistency of this unique product."

E. Action Lines

Similarly, the First Arizona Bank has developed an Action Line program which uses customer comment forms in all their branch offices in order to measure customer satisfaction. The form's design immediately identifies the nature of the comment; either compliment, suggestion, or special problem. It also solicits such detailed information from the customer as purpose of the visit to the bank, services used, and waiting time for service. When collected and reviewed in volume, these data reveal problem areas experienced by different branches.

F. Telephone Surveys

Customer attitudinal measurement can also be accurately measured by the telephone interview. Telephone calls are made to a random sample of clients in designated geographic areas, with each call lasting about 10 to 15 min. An appealing aspect of the telephone interview is that a high number of respondents can be obtained with a minimum of effort, making it an extremely economical and efficient technique. Quality control can be kept at a nearly perfect level, since interviews are conducted from one centralized location and a field supervisor is able to listen in on any interview to assure that it is being correctly conducted. Quality control can be further enhanced by employing a professional interviewing staff and using the WATS lines to call into any area of the country. Once the calls are put through, 80 to 90% of the customers contacted will agree to complete the interview. As with mail surveys, people are more likely to answer candidly because of the element of anonymity.

Unfortunately, the telephone interview cannot be as long as in-home interviews, and people who do not have telephones are excluded, permitting a chance for bias. However, it should be noted that only 5% of American households are phoneless, and probably such people would not be bank customers anyway.

With only 5% of American households without a phone, AT&T has become "The Biggest Company on Earth" and has developed TELSAM (telephone service attitude measurement), a customer feedback project that conducts 1 million telephone interviews annually to round up opinion from its 55 million customers. Female homemakers do most of the day interviewing, and college students work there at night with as many as 45 employees asking customers about their latest encounters with the Bell System at any one time. Normally, an interviewer will ask the customer to rate the promptness of an operator or give the degree of courtesy shown by a repairman. All this critical information is collected at a TELSAM site in either Pennsylvania or Denver, each being run by separate research firms. After that, all the customer data are pumped into a central computer, from which monthly reports are made and sent to the Bell System management for review and possible action. Demonstrably, it was discovered through the TELSAM project that customers favored a more personalized telephone approach in which operators answer with their own names when they pick up a call. Immediately, operators adopted the new personalized procedure to heighten customer satisfaction.

G. Interviews

The banking arena has also tuned into the telephone interview as a vital vehicle for finding out about customer perception. The Middle Market Banking
Study, done by an outside marketing service for Mellon Bank, relied on the
flexible telephone technique to question 500 financial executives of randomly
selected firms in the Pittsburgh area which have annual sales between $3
million and $50 million. Questions asked during the interview were based solely
on primary commercial banking relationships and covered such areas as degree
of satisfaction with primary banks, factors considered most important in the
choice of a commercial banking institution, and rating of primary banks in
terms of these key factors. Respondents' responses were grouped geographically into both Pittsburgh's county market and suburban market for tabulation.
Data were presented for the total sample in terms of industry groups (e.g.,
manufacturing, wholesale trade, etc.) and sales volume ranges. Where appri-
ate, recap tables were provided to facilitate review.

In addition to the mail and telephone interviews, customer perception can
be measured by the personal interview. Respondents are randomly selected
for interviews either in their homes or offices, so that the interviewer must
secure in advance the respondent's permission to participate in the interview.
This type of interview can generally be more lengthy because there are fewer
pressures on the part of the respondent to terminate if the respondent has
already invited the interviewer into his or her home or office. In such a face-
to-face situation, the interviewer has the ability to probe more effectively and
incorporate any body language into the respondent's comments, adding another
measure of quality in those areas of questioning where it is applicable. When
visual support for the perceptions being researched is helpful or necessary,
the interviewer can show the respondent samples of the product and easily use
data collection devices such as rating scales and card-sorting techniques.

On the negative side, the personal interview is one of the most costly techniques because of travel expenses and the high number of visits that are
needed. Sampling bias is becoming harder to control since some interviewers
refuse to conduct in-home interviews in transition neighborhoods. Such com-
munities, however, still contain many senior citizens who may not have high
assets but concentrate what they have in savings deposits and thus are of
some importance to bankers. Worse yet, the face-to-face element of the personal interview can intimidate the respondent and prevent candid participation.
Because supervisors are unable to overhear the actual face-to-face interview
being conducted, they are less able to be aware of the interviewers' effectiveness in dealing with the respondent.

Fortunately, Greenwich Research Associates have overcome the problems
plaguing the personal interview and have effectively employed this method to
discover current perceptions in large corporate banking. This survey's sample
is based primarily on corporations listed in the Fortune Double 500 Directory
and supplemented by lists of leading U.S. corporations published in other
business magazines. The total universe includes 1861 of the nation's largest
corporations, of which 1140 are chosen to complete the interviews, representing all large corporations' sales rank and industry groups.

Care is taken to interview only corporate executives who have direct responsibility for banking decisions. An initial request for an interview is directed to the vice-president of finance or to the treasurer. Each executive
then receives a letter of introduction and explanation of the survey. These
executives are encouraged to include their assistants in the interview or in a

separately conducted one, as they tend to be specialists in day-to-day bank relations, cash management, and operations. Next, each executive is telephoned for an appointment at the time and place of his choice. Afterward, a letter confirming the appointment is sent out with an enclosed worksheet dealing with questions on domestic borrowings, cash balances, noncredit services, and so on. The worksheet, by covering dollar volume and "use" tables, increases response accuracy, eases the work of the executive in accumulating information, and shortens the personal interview time.

These personal interviews, conducted by trained business managers, cover a company's dealings with its banks and its overall banking policies to evaluate the strengths and weaknesses of each bank as seen by its large corporate customers. Every major bank in every region of the country is evaluated. To accomplish this, each executive is shown a list of 70 banks and is asked a series of questions concerning solicitations for each bank. Second, all executives are asked to list on a self-administered form the banks they use most for domestic and international banking.

The questionnaire for this large-scale research has six different versions to expand the scope of the research. Each company's financial officer is asked to evaluate his bank's calling officers, top management, credit and pricing policies, operational capabilities, and service usage. At the onset of the interview, the respondent is given a card deck with labeled cards to which he or she is asked to refer for certain questions. These cards contain descriptive lists of banking services, banking advantages, and so on, which are individually coded so that a respondent's verbal answer can be easily tabulated by the interviewer on a corresponding form.

After completion of the over 1000 interviews, data are compiled by Greenwich Research in an annual report sold to banking institutions throughout the country. Specific reports included in this research, such as the Competitive Situation Report, the Penetration Report, and the Special Action Report, are used by various divisions of banks to identify trends and improve services.

The personal interview technique was also chosen by the Bank Research Associates in their attempt to measure accurately banking customers' perceptions of automated services and bank machines. With this method, sophisticated scaler techniques could be utilized in 300 randomly selected in-home interviews conducted during 1976 in a large midwestern metropolitan city. Data collection tools for the interviews consisted of demographic questions relating to age, income, and the like; open-ended questions on bank machines; and stimuli statements on individual cards relating to specific attributed of banking machines.

H. Q-Sorts

To clarify this unique "Q-sort" methodology, the respondent was given a deck of 29 cards containing a single statement on each card and was asked to make comparative preferences by sorting the cards along a 6-point scale ranging from strongly disagree (1) to strongly agree (6). The scale was printed on a board placed before the respondent (without numerical values) and contained an even number of positions to force a determination of whether there was agreement or disagreement with the statement. The stimulus for the sort was: "In my opinion a bank machine should . . ." Statements following this stimulus included "give me a printed statement describing my transactions, be found in all major grocery stores, and be the way most banking will be done in the future."

The data generated from the Q-sort technique allowed an analysis by statements through rankings of percentages and intensity of agreement. A frequency distribution was constructed for each statement for the "agree" side
(4, 5, or 6), each slot was totaled, and means and percentages were computed
and ranked. Similar statistics were developed for the "disagree" side. To
furnish insight into the intensity of the respondents' feelings, an agree potency index (API) was created and ranked so that the perceptual intensity of
the various statements could be determined. This empirical investigation is
still being continued on an ongoing basis to identify and monitor changes in
the consumer's perceptions of banking services.

I. Semantic Differential

Another scaler technique that is commonly called on for personal interviews
and even mail surveys is the semantic differential. The semantic differential
measures the meaning that a concept might have for people by using three
major scales or dimensions: evaluative scales, which measure favorable and
unfavorable dimensions; potency scales, which measure strong and weak dimensions; and activity scales, which measure fast and slow dimensions. The
subject is asked to rate the concept (bank) on a series of 7- or 5-point scales.
These scales are bipolar, in that the endpoints on the scale represent extreme
opposite opinions. An example would be:

Pleasant employees ——— ——— ——— ——— ——— Unpleasant employees

When incorporating the semantic differential into a research study there are
basically two separate groups that can act as subjects. First, the study can
utilize only noncustomers (potential customers) of each bank to perform the
ratings. If noncustomers are utilized, the scales should be constructed in a
balance format: that is, an even number of both favorable and unfavorable
points around a center or neutral point of each dimension.

The second option available is using only present customers of each bank to
rate their own bank. Because customers of a bank will often tend to see only
the favorable aspects of their bank and suppress the negative views they may
have, an unbalanced scale should be used with a larger number of points on the
scale at the positive side. An unbalanced scale, where there are four favorable,
one neutral, and two unfavorable points, eliminates "end piling" at a single
point on the scale. If both customers' and noncustomers' perceptions are obtained for a single bank, they should be presented as separate graphic profiles.

Both the Q-sort and the semantic differential are important research tools
for intercept interviewing. Here persons are selected at random to be interviewed on location at shopping centers, coming out of bank offices, or at other
public areas where a fairly typical cross section of the prime audience sought
can be found. The participants are approached by an interviewer, who asks
their cooperation by answering a few questions. The moderator then takes the
participant to a nearby location away from the mainstream of traffic to conduct
a structured interview using a preapproved questionnaire. Because of a high
number of people located in the area, a number of interviews can readily be
obtained within a short period of time, which controls interview expense. Better yet, the homogeneity of the participants can be automatically controlled by
the selection of the site. Most assuredly, then, if a bank wants to interview
its customers on some particular aspect of service, intercepting them as they
leave the bank building would give a 100% homogeneous group of customers.

At the other end of the continuum is the fact that most of the participants are in a hurry and will not tolerate lengthy discussions. In some cases, such as outside a bank's office, it becomes apparent who the interviewing is being done for, and the anonymity of the sponsoring firm is lost. Or the respondent, if aware of the sponsor, may be inclined to respond more positively toward the participating sponsor while on his or her home ground.

J. Focus Groups

This "home ground" bias is eliminated with the focus group interview, another research tool conducted on "neutral ground" in the office of a professional research service. Focus groups usually range in size from 8 to 12 persons who are assembled together with a qualified group leader for discussion of some specific aspect of banking. The group interview sessions can last from 1 to 2 hours with participants being selected by the research service using current demographic data. The primary role of the moderator is to encourage a good give-and-take among participants about the subject at hand, making sure that no one controls the group discussion. At the end of the session a detailed written report is drawn up by the leader and submiteed to the bank.

The interaction of group members can be particularly beneficial because it tends to relax each respondent, providing a better source of information than in a one-on-one situation. The more natural environment brings out people's views, thoughts, and positive and negative feelings toward the subject. The profile of these participants can be tightly structured so that the group can be all women, all people who are heavy users of charge cards, and so on. This homogeneous group composition provides an opportunity to gain attitudes of a very specific, prime-prospect kind of consumer within the marketplace. Body language and voice inflection expressed in the focus discussions add an extra dimension for interpretation of respondents' comments by the moderator and even by the client when sessions are videotaped. Focus group interviews are especially useful for gathering information and input on major issues that can later be incorporated into a questionnaire for a quantitative study.

Quantitative research is not provided by focus discussions—only qualitative data can be extracted because with such a small sample the reactions of participants in the group cannot be projected to the entire marketplace. It can also be difficult to assemble special interest groups, particularly professionals with demanding schedules.

Nonetheless, this focus group approach has become a major adjunct to the research efforts at the Farmers and Mechanics Savings Bank in Minneapolis. There, participants are paid a mere $5, making the total cost $300 per session, including the final report submitted by the moderator. Given the meager payment, motivation for the participants seems to be the opportunity to influence the bank and be made to feel important.

Introduction of a Bank by Phone service, the first such program of its kind in the country, and a project particularly important in a unit banking state such as Minnesota, emerged successfully only after focus group discussions in which participants explained that the preliminary version was too complicated and would not be understood by the average bank customer. Further refinements were made and currently, the only "problem" with the Bank by Phone service is its overwhelming popularity.

Ralph Klapperich, F&M's marketing vice-president, who is able to observe session responses firsthand through a two-way mirror, insists that the focus interview has features that no other research method can offer, "It is a two-way

communication and because it is unstructured and somewhat open-ended, it is
a device for getting closer to your customers, which can only benefit both the
institution and the public."

Win Barnes, vice-president of Shell Motorist Club, could not agree more
with Mr. Klapperich. Barnes, who is also manager of the direct mail division
for Shell Oil Company, sees the focus group interview as a diagnostic tool that
"is not for the timid. These poeple tell you exactly how they feel." Consequently, through a series of focus discussions held in three major cities across
the country, Shell learned that their customers did not rank the club's benefits in the same order of importance that the Sehll management thought they
would. Ironically enough, some of the benefits Shell executives thought to be
most important turned out to be least important, and vice versa.

A more aggressive stance on customer input has also been adopted by a
Minneapolis retail store called Dayton's. At Dayton's, focus interviews are
conducted under the guise of "consumer advisory panels." The panel consists
of twenty customers selected randomly from charge account lists or recommended
by former panel members. A monthly luncheon is held in which a different
consumer topic is discussed each time. Panel members may be asked to shop
in a specified department and then compare with other stores, or asked their
opinions on advertisements. The store manager, Reuel Nygoard, admits that
suggestions from the panel have resulted in the addition of a swim shop, together with other changes in customer service.

In a far-fetched fashion, employee meetings may be considered as a vehicle
for focus discussions and a chance to learn about customers' perceptions. In
the opinion of Unicare Food Services' president, Ed Lump: "Sometimes the
best way to find out how customers feel is to probe employees in a general
meeting or private conference; at times customers will say things to them they
will not say to management."

K. Shopper Surveys

Unknowingly, employees can provide further insights into customer perception
through shopper surveys that enable specific customer service to be audited
by an outside agency. In a shopper survey, trained surveyors pose as inquir-
ing or transacting customers to evaluate employees on "customer contact performance." These shoppers measure, in the case of the banking business, the
customer contact performance of tellers, receptionists, and new accounts' personnel on the basis of their work performance, their customer relations' skills,
product knowledge, cross-sales efforts, and closing comments. Once field
work is completed, the questionnaires listing all rating criteria mentioned above
are edited and turned over for data processing. Two types of ratings are
applied to measure customer contact performance. The first is a percentage of
positive answers to specific points being shopped. An example would be: "Was
there a line?" The second type of measurement asks shoppers to evaluate performance on a 5-point rating scale, where one is the highest rating. This
scaling technique measures attitudinal differences that could not be handled
by an absolute "yes-no" answer. A typical case would be receptionist measurement for helpfulness, with the overall CINB response being a 1.94.

The final report is based on the computer printouts and illustrates performance findings with table charts. Uniform, measurable standards of performance
for customer contact people are established. Such a summary of results pin-
points areas of strengths and weaknesses so that corrective actions can be
taken. As with the Chicago Loop Shopping Survey, many banks participate in

a shopper survey together, not only to gain input about the performance of their own customer contact people, but also to obtain the merged performance data of other banks for comparison purposes.

L. Inquiries and Complaints

Comparisons are curcial because customers are demanding much more today. Consequently, close attention must be given to customer complaints and in quiries, which have become so highly sophisticated that the enlightened airlines industry no longer views complaints as negative problems but rather as "suggestions in disguise." No matter what the viewpoint, registered complaints sound out customers' perceptions only too loud and clear.

That is why the essential features of any complaint-handling program should include prompt acknowledgment of complaints, clear assignment of responsibility for handling and investigating the complaint, and prompt close-out of the complaint, with a 2-week target where practicable. The major goal of such a program is to convince customers of the company's genuine concern and desire to be responsive to any problems they may encounter.

At Manufacturers Hanover Trust, a computerized customer inquiry reporting system controls, tracks, and analyzes communications received by respondent, corporate, and brokerage customers. The most significant aspect of the new system is that it distinguishes between controllable and noncontrollable branch and consumer credit incidents. Attitude-, efficiency-, or performance-related problems are controllable ones that bank personnel can correct. Noncontrollable incidents are those outside the direct control of branch personnel, such as central bookkeeping and data processing.

Wells Fargo Bank in California has also computerized their procedures for complaint handling. All written complaints are routed through a customer relations center. When it receives a complaint, the center simultaneously enters it into the computer and forwards it to the administrative office of the department in question. The center allows the department 2 days to acknowledge to the customer receipt of the complaint, and 10 days to solve the problem or to notify the customer that progress is being made. Meanwhile, progress toward resolution is updated daily on the computer system. Data on complaint correspondence is maintained by an extensive system of codes identifying the source and type of correspondence, its status, and each action taken. Once the complaint has been resolved and a solution has been communicated to the customer, the responding department forwards a copy of its response to the center, which checks to make sure that a solution really was found and tries to determine whether some changes in bank policies are warranted. The center prepares quarterly reports on the complaints received, broken down by the product or service involved. For senior management, the center also prepares year-to-date summaries that highlight trends to identify particular problem areas.

M. Hotlines

The hotline is yet another recent tool which a number of firms have instituted to facilitate communications, which of course includes the registering of complaints. A hotline provides a direct two-way communication link whereby a company can gage the customer's overall impression of the firm or solicit advice on service attributes.

What's more, the First National Bank of Oregon is turning its own hotline, known as the Savers' Hotline into a source of personal information for its customers. The Savers' Hotline was initiated in the summer of 1979 to help consumers understand changes in the regular savings rate and in time deposit requirements, which were authorized by the Federal Reserve Board. It was available to all Oregonians, free of charge, from June 23 to August 3, from 7 a.m. to 7 p.m., 7 days a week.

During the 6 weeks the hotline was in operation, approximately 750 calls were received, with Mondays tending to be busiest. Interestingly enough, about one-fourth of the calls came from branch personnel who were unable to answer branch customers' questions sufficiently, so sought out the knowledgable hotline staff, made up of management training employees.

Since it was the first time the $3.4 billion deposit bank, which is Oregon's largest and oldest bank, ever tried anything like the hotline, they admit: "We weren't fully aware of what type of response we would get. But it was less than we had reasonably anticipated . . . . We would have been more pleased with a higher response, but the hotline was introduced as a trial— strictly on a test basis."

Even with the low response rate, the personal source of information provided by the hotline was appreciated by a number of people. According to Paul Haist, manager of the bank's public relations department: "Most people expected to hear a recording and were grateful to speak with a live, breathing person."

Other industries, such as Shell Oil Company and Zayre, have integrated well-advertised toll-free 800 hotlines into their operations so that customers may call in complaints or just inquire about something. Corrective action programs at Whirlpool and Chrysler have established hotlines to help customers reach responsible company officials with their inquiries or complaints. Otherwise, if customer complaints are ignored or shunted to low-level personnel who are neither trained nor measured on their response to angry complainants, consumer mistrust and outright hostility can result. Admittedly, the hotline is an expensive addition to the service program, but most companies that have them regard them as good investments, especially if they can turn irritated customers into sources of perception information.

Perception information from the customer is exactly what interviews, focus groups, surveys, comment cards, complaint bureaus, and hotlines are trying to capture. Granted, there is no one technique that is most appropriate for every research project, yet it appears that the mail survey is the most popular method utilized to gain customer feedback. Very simply, it is an easy and inexpensive procedure. The most efficient research tool is the telephone interview. This flexible method does not succumb to the notoriously poor response rate characteristic of the mail survey. More important, the quality control that can be maintained with the telephone interview is superior.

Still, these two techniques are not without their weaknesses. Both rely soly on quantitative data, ignoring any qualitative measure derived from body language or visual supports. The personal interview, however, is able to extract more in-depth information. At the same time, it should be noted that while the personal interview may include the added dimension of body language, it also involves a face-to-face encounter that tends to suppress candid responses.

In today's marketplace, though, candid responses are rarely discouraged, as 1980 consumers voice their positive and negative opinions at full volume. Such an up-front and demanding character currently assumed by customers has forced companies to take more expedient or even immediate corrective actions to improve their products and services. In this never-ending attempt to improve services, no single follow-up trend stands out except the factor of timeliness as managements strive to fulfill customers' desires and needs.

46

NUCLEAR QUALITY

LEWIS E. ZWISSLER

Management Analysis Company
San Diego, California

I. INTRODUCTION

Inasmuch as this chapter is included as a part of a handbook in which the various aspects of quality assurance and quality control are discussed in detail, the discussion will be limited to the requirements for quality assurance programs established by law and the implementing procedural requirements imposed by the Nuclear Regulatory Commission. The methodology and specific ways in which the requirements may be implemented are given elsewhere in this manual.

It is emphasized that the various documents setting forth Nuclear Regulatory Commission requirements are changing constantly and it is necessary to assure that the particular issue governing a specific case is consulted. For example, a construction permit may be issued in 1972 and include requirements in force as of that date. Some time later in the construction phase, say 1979, later issues are published. Licensees must decide whether they wish to comply with the later issue, and if so, include the change in their safety analysis reports. In some instances, it is mandatory to update the requirements, as in the case of changed requirements resulting from the Three Mile Island incident. The reader is cautioned to be aware of this situation and to keep abreast of the current environment in the nuclear power generation industry.

It is impossible to provide a detailed discussion of the entire content of the requirements for all applications of nuclear activities in the short chapter of this manual. A general idea of the scope and complexity of activities related to the assurance of quality is presented, and suitable references are given to enable the reader to pursue the subject further. The practice of quality assurance in the nuclear industry has resulted in the evolution of a body of technology peculiar unto itself [1].

II. HISTORY OF LEGISLATION GOVERNING DEVELOPMENT AND USE OF ATOMIC ENERGY

The nuclear industry began with the demonstration of the first self-sustaining nuclear reaction under the west stands of the stadium at the University of

Chicago. The immediate result of this event was the application of the technology to the production of the first nuclear bomb, popularly called the atom
bomb, which was dropped over Hiroshima, Japan.

It was apparent to the physicists, however, that the greatest potential for
the new discovery was in the production of power for peaceful and military
uses. Prophesies of abundant cheap, safe, and limitless energy became the
order of the day. Forecasts of a utopian civilization were commonplace.

It became apparent very shortly that the dangers of military uses of atomic
energy could potentially lead to mass destruction that might, in fact, leave
the earth an uninhabitable planet. The seriousness of this possibility lead to
negotiations among the United States, Great Britain, and Canada, resulting in
the issuance of the statement entitled "Agreed Declaration on Atomic Energy"
on November 15, 1945 [2], wherein the parties agreed to participate in an exchange of scientific literature for peaceful ends and to make available to the
world the basic scientific information essential to the development of atomic
energy. It was anticipated that this would lead to an era of reciprocal trust
among all nations and permit development of atomic energy for peaceful purposes within a climate of confidence throughout the world.

Included also was a proposal to establish a commission under the United
Nations with the objective of preparing recommendations for eliminating the
use of atomic energy for destructive purposes and promoting the use for industrial and humanitarian purposes. This proposal was approved on January
24, 1946, by the unanimous vote of the plenary session of the UN and the
United Nations Atomic Energy Commission (UNAEC) was created.

Subsequently, Bernard Baruch, U.S. Ambassador to the UN, proposed the
formation of International Atomic Development Authority, but after more than
2 years of bitter debate regarding primarily the right to inspect domestic installations in all countries and the nuclear disarmament, UNAEC reached an
impasse on May 17, 1948, and recommended dissolution.

Subsequently, the USSR exploded its first A-bomb in August 1949 and the
United Kingdom followed in October 1952. The UNAEC was dissolved by the
UN General Assembly on January 11, 1952.

In the meantime, the U.S. Congress passed the Atomic Energy Act of 1946
(Public Law 79-585), commonly called the McMahon Act, establishing the civilian
U.S. Atomic Energy Commission (AEC) with broad statutory responsibility for
atomic energy in the United States effective January 1, 1947. The AEC was
the successor to the Manhattan District, U.S. War Department, which had
developed the A-bomb [3].

President Eisenhower, expressing his concern and that of the United States
generally, presented his famous speech "Atoms of Peace" to the UN General
Assembly on December 8, 1953, asking that a way be provided to bring the
benefits of peaceful uses of atomic energy to all people of the world despite
the deadlock with the USSR over the question of disarmament. Congress passed
the Atomic Energy Act on August 30, 1954, superseding previous legislation and
establishing the Joint Committee on Atomic Energy with representatives from
both houses of Congress to oversee the activities of the AEC.

This act combined the regulatory and promotional activities in one agency,
the Atomic Energy Commission, which was directed to:

1. Maximize contribution of atomic energy (AE) to national defense and
    security
    a. Procure adequate stocks of uranium materials
    b. Production of AE materials, notably fissionable

  c. Development, fabrication, and storage of nuclear weapons
  d. Development of military reactor applications
  e. Control of classified AE materials
  f. Technical support of U.S. efforts toward achieving international
    control of AE
 2. Maximize contribution of AE to scientific and industrial progress
  a. Conduct and sponsor basic research in AE sciences
  b. Development of peaceful uses
    (1) Reactors for power generation
    (2) Other civilian reactors
    (3) Applications of radioisotopes and radiation
    (4) Peaceful use of AE nuclear explosives
  c. Dissemination of scientific information
  d. International cooperation
  e. Education and training
 3. Protect the public (exclusive of defense)
  a. Licensing and regulation
  b. Research on biological effects of radiation, improve radiation
    standards
  c. Monitor fallout

The act encouraged engaging in significant international cooperation and giving substantial assistance to other nations, subject to bilateral agreements approved by the Congress. Twenty-four countries had entered into agreements by July 1955. A draft of the International Atomic Energy Agency (IAEA) charter was submitted to the 84 UN members on August 22, 1955. The Conference on the Statute of the IAEA was concluded on October 26, 1956, ready for signature. The statute entered into force July 29, 1957, which is normally considered the birthdate of the IAEA. Of the 87 states invited to sign, 80 entered into the agreements. The statute, briefly stated, is: "To further peaceful uses of Atomic Energy throughout the world, and to do so in such a manner that the agency's assistance is not misused for any military purposes." The agency is therefore authorized by the signatories to implement a program for international control of atomic energy.

The latest legislative action by the U.S. Congress was taken when the Energy Reorganization Act of 1974 (Public Law 93-438) (88 Stat. 1233; 42 USC 5801) was passed and implemented by Executive Order 11834 effective January 19, 1975. This action was taken primarily to separate the regulatory and promotional activities into two independent agencies: the Nuclear Regulatory Commission (NRC) for regulation and the Department of Energy (DoE) for promotion of all forms of energy. The Act abolished the Atomic Energy Commission and transferred to the Nuclear Regulatory Commission all the licensing and related regulatory functions assigned to the AEC by the Atomic Energy Act of 1954. The functions included the Atomic Safety and Licensing Board Panel and the Atomic Safety and Licensing Appeal Panel.

The principal NRC offices are located in the Washington, D.C. area. There are five regional offices, responsible for carrying out investigations and inspections, located as follows:

Region I: King of Prussia, Pennsylvania
Region II: Atlanta, Georgia
Region III: Glen Ellyn, Illinois
Region IV: Arlington, Texas
Region V: Walnut Creek, California

III. UNITED STATES NUCLEAR REGULATORY COMMISSION RULES AND REGULATIONS [5]

The Rules and Regulations of the United States Nuclear Regulatory Commission are contained in Title 10, Code of Federal Regulations—Energy. There are a total of 34 separate parts, covering the full scope of the responsibilities and authorities. The code is administered by the commissioners.

The commission is composed fo five commissioners appointed by the president with the approval of the Senate. The president designates the chairman. The NRC means that the commission and all offices, employees, and representatives authorized to act in any case or matter. The organizational structure and reporting relationships are shown in the organization chart (Fig. 1) and Table 1. The Office of Inspection and Enforcement has the greatest impact on quality assurance and quality control.

The NRC Rules and Regulations are contained in Title 10 of the Code of Federal Regulations [5]. They are designed to protect the health and safety of the public and have the force of law. Herein is the basic difference between the government inspection and enforcement actions of the NRC and those of the Defense Contract Administration Service (DCAS). In the latter activity the government is buying materials and services and the DCAS inspector is enforcing a contractual relationship. There is some latitude in permitting waivers and deviations from contractual requirements with the concurrence of the contracting officer. The NRC inspection, on the other hand, has no authority, in theory, to permit variations from the rules and regulations, as they are in fact the law of the land.

The scope of 10CFR is too vast to cover here and the reader is referred to Ref. 5, with a caution to note that the rules and regulations are constantly changing and that the latest supplements should be consulted. The main impact on quality assurance is in the activities of the Office of Standards Development and the Office of Inspection and Enforcement.

A. Office of Standards Development

The Office of Standards Development develops and recommends standards (e.g., technical regulations and regulatory guides) that NRC needs to regulate nuclear facilities and commercial uses of nuclear materials. These standards deal with radiological health and safety and environmental protection, materials and plant protection (safeguards), and antitrust review in accordance with the Atomic Energy Act of 1954, as amended, and the Energy Reorganization Act of 1974, as amended. The office also coordinates NRC participation in national and international standards activities. There are two divisions:

1. The Division of Engineering Standards develops standards for nuclear safety in the design, construction, and operation of nuclear reactors and nuclear power plants, other production and utilization facilities, and facilities for the storage, processing, and use of nuclear materials; and for materials safety activities, including the production, use, and transportation of radioactive products; provides technical assistance to NRC staff regarding research, resolution of generic issues, and the development, evaluation, and application of standards to specific safety problems associated with nuclear reactors, nuclear power plants, and fuel cycle facilities, transportation of nuclear materials, and the production and use of radioactive products; and in its assigned areas of responsibility maintains liaison with and provides technical input to other federal agencies, the American National Standards Institute (ANSI),

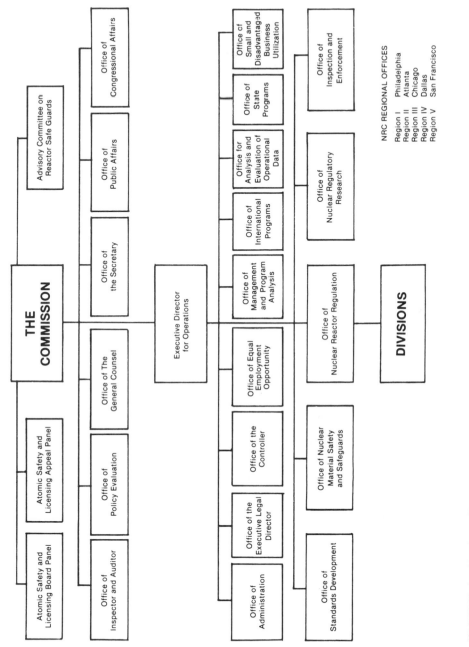

FIGURE 1 Nuclear Regulatory Commission.

TABLE 1   The Commission

Panels, boards, and committees
  Atomic Safety and Licensing Board Panel
  Atomic Safety and Licensing Appeal Panel
  Advisory Committee on Reactor Safeguards
  Other committees, boards, and panels

Commission staff
  Office of Inspector and Auditor
  Office of Policy Evaluation
  Office of the General Counsel
  Office of the Secretary
  Office of Public Affairs
  Office of Congressional Affairs

Executive director
  Office of the Executive Director for Operations

Staff offices
  Office of Administration
  Office of the Executive Legal Director
  Office of the Controller
  Office of Equal Employment Opportunity
  Office of Planning and Analysis
  Office of International Programs
  Office of State Programs
  Office of Management Information and Program Control

Program offices
  Office of Nuclear Material Safety and Safeguards
  Office of Nuclear Reactor Regulation
  Office of Nuclear Regulatory Research
  Office of Standards Development
  Office of Inspection and Envorcement

professional societies, international agencies (in coordination with the Office of International Programs), and other organizations.

2. The Division of Siting, Health and Safeguards Standards develops standards for the protection of licensees' employees, the public, and the environment from the effects of NRC-licensed activities in matters involving radiological protection, environmental effects, and safeguarding of nuclear materials and facilities; provides advice and technical assistance to NRC staff regarding research, resolution of generic issues, and the development, evaluation, and application of standards to specific licensing or other regulatory problems associated with nuclear materials or facilities; and on matters pertaining to its areas of responsibility maintains liaison with and provides technical input to other federal agencies, state agencies, ANSI, professional societies, international agencies (in coordination with the Office of International Programs), public interest groups, and other organizations.

B. Office of Inspection and Enforcement

The Office of Inspection and Enforcement develops policies and administers programs for inspecting licensees to ascertain whether they are complying with

NRC regulations, rules, orders, and license provisions, and to determine whether these licensees are taking appropriate actions to protect nuclear mate rials and facilities, the environment, and the health and safety of the public; inspecting applicants for licenses, as a basis for recommending issuance or denial of a limited work authorization, construction permit, or an operating license; inspecting suppliers of safety-related services, components, and equipment to determine whether they have established quality assurance pro- grams that meet NRC criteria; investigating incidents, accidents, allegations, and unusual circumstances, including those involving loss, theft, or diversion of special nuclear materials*; enforcing commission orders, regulations, rules, and license provisions; recommending changes in licenses and standards, based on the results of inspections, investigations, and enforcement actions; and notifying licensees regarding generic problems so as to achieve appropriate precautionary or corrective action. Headquarters divisions are responsible for developing the inspection program, assuring the technical adequacy of enforcement cases and investigations, preparing notifications to appropriate parties, providing technical management and support for NRC response to incidents, and monitoring and appraising the performance of regional offices. NRC's five regional offices are responsible for carrying out inspections and investigations. There are the following organizational components:

1. The Division of Fuel Facilities and Materials Safety is responsible for those inspection and enforcement functions that pertain to radiological and environmental protection at reactors and fuel facilities and handling of licensed materials, and for criticality control at fuel facilities.
2. The Division of Safeguards Inspection is responsible for those inspec- tion and enforcement functions that pertain to protection of nuclear materials and reactors.
3. The Division of Reactor Construction Inspection is responsible for those inspection and enforcement functions that pertain to reactor construction.
4. The Division of Reactor Operations Inspection is responsible for those inspection and enforcement functions that pertain to reactor operations.
5. The Executive Officer for Operations Support is responsible for develop- ing requirements for enforcement and investigations; managing assigned investigations; assuring consistency of the enforcement program among the various offices; developing the program for response to incidents; and providing centralized administrative support.
6. The Executive Officer for Management and Analysis is responsible for budgets, financial control, computer services, management information systems, planning, personnel management, contract administration, technology and inspection training, and management studies and analyses.
7. Each regional office reports to the director, Office of Inspection and Enforcement, and performs the following functions within its assigned geographical area: inspects applicants, licensees, and others subject to NRC jurisdiction; investigates incidents, accidents, allegations, and

---

*
Special nuclear material is defined in 10CFR Part 70 as "plutonium, uranium-233, uranium enriched in the isotope 233 or in the isotope 235, and any other material which the Commission . . . determines . . . but does not include source material . . . ."

other unusual circumstances involving matters subject to NRC jurisdiction; evaluates licensee event reports, and provides response, as
appropriate; recommends changes in NRC programs, based on the results of inspections and investigations; and takes enforcement action,
to the extent delegated; or recommends enforcement actions to the
appropriate headquarters division of the office.

IV. PART 10CFR 50, DOMESTIC LICENSING OF PRODUCTION AND UTILIZATION FACILITIES

A production facility is one used for the formation of plutonium (Pu) or ura-
nium-233 (U-233) or for the separation of isotopes of these elements, and any
facility for processing irradiated materials. Laboratory-scale facilities used
for experimental or analytical purposes only and certain others meeting special
requirements are exempted. A utilization facility is any nuclear reactor other
than one used primarily for the formation of Pu or U-233. There are specific
requirements for exemption or licensing certain facilities and it is suggested
that Part 50 be consulted for more detailed information.

There are two classes of licenses. Class 104 is required for medical therapy
and research and development facilities. Class 103 covers commercial and industrial facilities. In general, the definitions, procedures, and other information regarding applications and granting of licenses are covered in the main
body of Part 50. There are 15 appendices, which provide specific requirements
for design, siting, and operation of nuclear power plants. Inasmuch as the
subject is very complex, there is some overlap in the subject matter, so certain
design requirements are found in the body of Part 50. A careful study is required to achieve a full understanding of the subject.

An applicant desiring a license (Class 103) may submit an application for a
construction permit without having a final approved design when sufficient
information is available in the form of a preliminary safety analysis report
(PSAR), environmental report, and financial and other data [5, para. 50.33–
50.35] to support the request. As the design is finalized, a final safety analysis report (FSAR) is submitted with a request to amend the construction
permit to an operating license. It is permissible to combine these two documents into a single application if all required information is available at the
time the application is filed.

The construction permit and amendments to issue an operating license receive a public hearing conducted by the Atomic Safety Licensing Board (ASLB)
[5, Part 1, paragraph 1.11], consisting of three members selected from the
Atomic Safety and Licensing Board Panel appointed by the commission. The
Atomic Safety and Licensing Appeal Board (ASLAB) is appointed and functions
in a similar manner in those cases where the commission determines that a review of ASLB or other presiding officers initial decisions is needed.

An additional review is performed by the Advisory Committee on Reactor
Safety (ACRS) [5, Part 1, paragraph 1.20]. In addition, the ACRS provides
support to the Department of Energy (DoE) with regard to its nuclear activities
and facilities, as well as initiating reviews of specific generic matters or nuclear
facility safety-related items.

Upon determination that an applicant has met all the standards, requirements, and regulations and that all other interested agencies and bodies have

been notified, the commission will issue a license or construction permit containing such conditions and limitations as are deemed appropriate and necessary. Note that similar but not identical procedures and requirements exist for Class 104 licenses.

The PSAR must include the principal design criteria for the proposed facility. The appendices to Part 50 contain specific general design criteria for nuclear power plants (Appendix A) and many other guides and information which must be considered in the design construction and operation.

There is a tremendous amount of work involved in preparing the SARs. The regulations require that they include the principal design criteria for the proposed facility. These include the structures, systems, and components to provide reasonable assurance that the facility can be operated without undue risk to the health and safety of the workers and the public. The information required fills several volumes and many conceptual drawings. It may take years to prepare, and costs run into the millions of dollars. This is understandable when we realize that a 1250-million-watt nuclear power plant may cost $1 billion or more and take 10 or more years to bring on-line after project approval is obtained.

The general design criteria establish the minimum requirements for the principal design criteria for water-cooled nuclear power plants and are considered generally applicable to other kinds of nuclear power units. There are 64 criteria included in Appendix A. Criterion 1 is quoted here, as it relates specifically to the general quality assurance requirements.

> Criterion 1: Quality standards and records. Structures, systems, and components important to safety shall be designed, fabricated, erected, and tested to quality standards commensurate with the importance of the safety functions to be performed. Where generally recognized codes and standards are used, they shall be identified and evaluated to determine their applicability, adequacy and sufficiency and shall be supplemented or modified as necessary to assure a quality product in keeping with the required safety function. A quality assurance program shall be established and implemented in order to provide adequate assurance that these structures, systems, and components will satisfactorily perform their safety functions. Appropriate records of the design, fabrication, erection and testing of structures, systems, and components important to safety shall be maintained by or under the control of the nuclear power unit licensee throughout the life of the unit.

Other criteria establish requirements for design to permit periodic inspection and testing the operability and functional performance of components and systems.

V. PART 10CFR50, APPENDIX B

Appendix B is entitled "Quality Assurance Criteria for Nuclear Power Plants and Fuel Reprocessing Plants." This document is the fundamental statement governing quality assurance for the nuclear power industry. It is impossible to distill the essence of the document in a summary, so it is included here in its entirety:

Title 10—Code of Federal Regulations—Part 50
Appendix B
Quality Assurance Criteria for Nuclear Power
Plants and Fuel Reprocessing Plants

Introduction

Every applicant for a construction permit is required by the provisions of
Section 50.34 to include in its preliminary safety analysis report a description of the quality assurance program to be applied to the design, fabrication, construction, and testing of the structures, systems, and components
of the facility. Every applicant for an operating license is required to include, in its final safety analysis report, information pertaining to the
managerial and administrative controls to be used to assure safe operation.
Nuclear power plants and fuel reprocessing plants* include structures,
systems and components that prevent or mitigate the consequences of
postulated accidents that could cause undue risk to the health and safety
of the public. This appendix establishes quality assurance requirements
for the design, construction, and operation of those structures, systems,
and components. The pertinent requirements of this Appendix apply to
all activities affecting the safety-related functions of those structures,
systems and components; these activities include designing, purchasing,
fabricating, handling, shipping, storing, cleaning, erecting, installing,
inspecting, testing, operating, maintaining, repairing, refueling, and
modifying.

As used in this appendix, "quality assurance" comprises all those
planned and systematic actions necessary to provide adequate confidence
that a structure, system, or component will perform satisfactorily in service. Quality assurance includes quality control, which comprises those
quality assurance actions related to the physical characteristics of a material, structure, component, or system which provide a means to control
the quality of the material, structure, component, or system to predetermined requirements.

I. ORGANIZATION

The applicant† shall be responsible for the establishment and execution of
the quality assurance program. The applicant may delegate to others, such
as contractors, agents, or consultants, the work of establishing and executing the quality assurance program, or any part thereof, but shall retain
responsibility therefor. The authority and duties of persons and organizations performing activities affecting the safety-related functions or
structures, systems, and components shall be clearly established and delineated in writing. These activities include both the performing functions and
attaining quality objectives and the quality assurance functions. The

---

*Amended 36 FR 18301.
†While the term "applicant" is used in these criteria, the requirements are,
of course, applicable after such a person has received a license to construct
and operate a nuclear power plant or a fuel reprocessing plant. These criteria will also be used for guidance in evaluating the adequacy of quality
assurance programs in use by holders of construction permits and operating
licenses.

quality assurance functions are those of (a) assuring that an appropriate quality assurance program is established and effectively executed and (b) verifying, such as by checking, auditing, and inspection, that activities affecting the safety-related functions have been correctly performed. The persons and organizations performing quality assurance functions shall have sufficient authority and organization freedom to identify quality problems; to initiate, recommend, or provide solutions; and to verify implementation of solutions. Such persons and organizations performing quality assurance functions shall report to a management level such that this required authority and organization freedom, including sufficient independence from cost and schedule when opposed to safety considerations, are provided. Because of the many variables involved, such as the number of personnel, the type of activity being performed, and the location or locations where activities are performed, the organizational structure for executing the quality assurance program may take various forms provided that the persons and organizations assigned the quality assurance functions have this required authority and organizational freedom. Irrespective of the organizational structure, the individual(s) assigned the responsibility for assuring effective execution of any portion of the quality assurance program at any location where activities subject to this Appendix are being performed shall have direct access to such levels of management as may be necessary to perform this function.

II. QUALITY ASSURANCE PROGRAM

The applicant shall establish at the earliest practicable time, consistent with the schedule for accomplishing the activities, a quality assurance program which complies with the requirements of this appendix. This program shall be documented by written policies, procedures, or instruction and shall be carried out throughout plant life in accordance with those policies, procedures, or instructions. The applicant shall identify the structures, systems, and components to be covered by the quality assurance program and the major organizations participating in the program, together with the designated functions of these organizations. The quality assurance program shall provide control over activities affecting the quality of the identified structures, systems, and components, to an extent consistent with their importance to safety. Activities affecting quality shall be accomplished under suitably controlled conditions. Controlled conditions include the use of appropriate equipment; suitable environmental conditions for accomplishing the activity, such as adequate cleanness; and assurance that all prerequisites for the given activity have been satisfied. The program shall take into account the need for special controls, processes, test equipment, tools, and skills to attain the required quality, and the need for verification of quality by inspection and test. The program shall provide for indoctrination and training of personnel performing activities affecting quality as necessary to assure that suitable proficiency is achieved and maintained. The applicant shall regularly review status and adequacy of the quality assurance program. Management of organizations participating in the quality assurance program shall regularly review the status and adequacy of that part of the quality assurance program which they are executing.

III. DESIGN CONTROL

Measures shall be established to assure that applicable regulatory requirements and the design basis, as defined in Section 50.2 and as specified in
the license application, for those structures, systems, and components to
which this appendix applies are correctly translated into specifications,
drawings, procedures, and instructions. These measures shall include provisions to assure that appropriate quality standards are specified and included in design documents and that deviations from such standards are
controlled. Measures shall also be established for the selection and review
for suitability of application of materials, parts, equipment, processes that
are essential to the safety-related functions of the structures, systems
and components.

Measures shall be established for the identification and control of design
interfaces and for coordination among participating design organizations.
These measures shall include the establishment of procedures among participating design organizations for the review, approval, release, distribution and revision of documents involving design interfaces.

The design control measures shall provide for verifying or checking the
adequacy of design, such as by the performance of design reviews, by the
use of alternate or simplified calculational methods, or by the performance
of a suitable testing program. The verifying or checking process shall be
performed by individuals or groups other than those who performed the
original design, but who may be from the same organization. Where a test
program is used to verify the adequacy of a specific design feature in lieu
of other verifying or checking processes, it shall include suitable qualification testing of a prototype unit under the most adverse design conditions.
Design control measures shall be applied to items such as the following:
reactor physics, stress, thermal, hydraulic, and accident, analyses; compatibility of materials; accessibility for inservice inspection, maintenance,
and repair, and delineation of acceptance criteria for inspections and tests.

Design changes, including field changes, shall be subject to design control measures commensurate with those applied to the original design and
be approved by the organization that performed the original design unless
the applicant designates another responsible organization.

IV. PROCUREMENT DOCUMENT CONTROL

Measures shall be established to assure that applicable regulatory requirements, design bases, and other requirements which are necessary to assure
adequate quality are suitably included or referenced in the documents for
procurement of material, equipment, and services, whether purchased by
the applicant or by its contractors or subcontractors. To the extent necessary, procurement documents shall require contractors or subcontractors
to provide a quality assurance program consistent with the pertinent provisions of this appendix.

V. INSTRUCTIONS, PROCEDURES, AND DRAWINGS

Activities affecting quality shall be prescribed by documented instructions,
procedures, or drawings, or a type appropriate to the circumstances and
shall be accomplished in accordance with these instructions, procedures,
or drawings. Instructions, procedures, or drawings shall include appropriate quantitative or qualitative acceptance criteria for determining that important activities have been satisfactorily accomplished.

VI. DOCUMENT CONTROL

Measures shall be established to control the issuance of documents, such as instructions, procedures, and drawings, including changes thereto, which prescribe all activities affecting quality. These measures shall assure that documents, including changes, are reviewed for adequacy and approved for release by authorized personnel and are distributed to and used at the location where the prescribed activity is performed. Changes to documents shall be reviewed and approved by the same organizations that performed the original review and approval unless the applicant designates another responsible organization.

VII. CONTROL OF PURCHASED MATERIAL, EQUIPMENT, AND SERVICES

Measures shall be established to assure that purchased material, equipment, and services, whether purchased directly or through contractors and subcontractors, conform to the procurement documents. These measures shall include provisions, as appropriate, for source evaluation and selection, objective evidence of quality furnished by the contractor or subcontractor, inspection at the contractor or subcontractor source, and examination of products upon delivery. Documentary evidence that material and equipment conform to the procurement requirements shall be available at the nuclear power plant or fuel reprocessing plant* site prior to installation or use of such material and equipment. This documentary evidence shall be retained at the nuclear power or fuel reprocessing plant* site and shall be sufficient to identify the specific requirements, such as codes, standards, or specifications, met by the purchased material and equipment. The effectiveness of the control of quality by contractors and subcontractors shall be assessed by the applicant or designee at intervals consistent with the importance, complexity, and quantity of the product or services.

VIII. IDENTIFICATION AND CONTROL OF MATERIALS, PARTS, AND COMPONENTS

Measures shall be established for the identification and control of materials, parts, and components, including partially fabricated assemblies. These measures shall assure that identification of the item is maintained by heat number, part number, serial number, or other appropriate means, either on the item or on records traceable to the item, as required throughout fabrication, erection, installation, and use of the item. These identification and control measures shall be designed to prevent the use of incorrect or defective material, parts, and components.

IX. CONTROL OF SPECIAL PROCESSES

Measures shall be established to assure that special processes, including welding, heat treating, and nondestructive testing, are controlled and accomplished by qualified personnel using qualified procedures in accordance with applicable codes, standards, specifications, criteria, and other special requirements.

---

*Amended 36 FR 18301.

X. INSPECTION

A program for inspection of activities affecting quality shall be established and executed by or for the organization performing the activity to verify conformance with the documented instructions, procedures, and drawings for accomplishing the activity. Such inspection shall be performed by individuals other than those who performed the activity being inspected. Examinations, measurements, or tests of material or products processed shall be performed for each work operation where necessary to assure quality. If inspection of processed material or products is impossible or disadvantageous, indirect control by monitoring processing methods, equipment, and personnel shall be provided. Both inspection and process monitoring shall be provided when control is inadequate without both. If mandatory inspection hold points, which require witnessing or inspecting by the applicant's designated respresentative and beyond which work shall not proceed without the consent of its designated representative are required, the specific hold points shall be indicated in appropriate documents.

XI. TEST CONTROL

A test program shall be established to assure that all testing required to demonstrate that structures, systems, and components will perform satisfactorily in service is identified and performed in accordance with written test procedures which incorporate the requirements and acceptance limits contained in applicable design documents. The test program shall include, as appropriate, proof tests to installation, preoperational tests, and operational tests during nuclear power plant or fuel reprocessing plant* operation, of structures, systems and components. Test procedures shall include provisions for assuring that all prerequisites for the given test have been met, that adequate test instrumentation is available and used, and that the test is performed under suitable environmental conditions. Test results shall be documented and evaluated to assure that test requirements have been satisfied.

XII. CONTROL OF MEASURING AND TEST EQUIPMENT

Measures shall be established to assure that tools, gages, instruments, and other measuring and testing devices used in activities affecting quality are properly controlled, calibrated, and adjusted at specified periods to maintain accuracy within necessary limits.

XIII. HANDLING, STORAGE, AND SHIPPING

Measures shall be established to control the handling, storage, shipping, cleaning, and preservation of material and equipment in accordance with work and inspection instructions to prevent damage or deterioration. When necessary for particular products, special protective environments, such as inert gas atmosphere, specific moisture content levels, and temperature levels, shall be specified and provided.

---

*Amended 36 FR 18301.

XIV. INSPECTION, TEST, AND OPERATING STATUS

Measures shall be established to indicate, by the use of markings such as stamps, tags, labels, routing cards, or other suitable means, the status of inspections and tests performed upon individual items of the nuclear power plant or fuel reprocessing plant.* These measures shall provide for the identification of items which have satisfactorily passed required inspections and tests, where necessary to preclude inadvertent bypassing of such inspections and tests. Measures shall also be established for indicating the operating status of structure, systems, and components for the nuclear power plant or fuel reprocessing plant,† such as by tagging valves and switches, to prevent inadvertent operation.

XV. NONCONFORMING MATERIALS, PARTS, OR COMPONENTS

Measures shall be established to control materials, parts, or components which do not conform to requirements in order to prevent their inadvertent use or installation. These measures shall include, as appropriate, procedures for identification, documentation, segregation, disposition, and notification to affected organizations. Nonconforming items shall be reviewed and accepted, rejected, repaired, or reworked in accordance with documented procedures.

XVI. CORRECTIVE ACTION

Measures shall be established to assure that conditions adverse to quality, such as failures, malfunctions, deficiencies, deviations, defective material and equipment, and nonconformances are promptly identified and corrected. In the case of significant conditions adverse to quality, the measures shall assure that the cause of the conditions is determined and corrective action taken to preclude repetition. The identification of the significant condition adverse to quality, the cause of the condition, and the corrective action taken shall be documented and reported to appropriate levels of management.

XVII. QUALITY ASSURANCE RECORDS

Sufficient records shall be maintained to furnish evidence of activities affecting quality. The records shall include at least the following: Operating logs and the results of reviews, inspections, tests, audits, monitoring of work performance, and material analyses. The records shall also include closely-related data such as qualifications of personnel, procedures, and equipment. Inspection and test records shall, as a minimum, identify the inspector or data recorder, the type of observation, the results, the acceptability, and the action taken in connection with any deficiencies noted. Records shall be identifiable and retrievable. Consistent with applicable regulatory requirements, the applicant shall establish requirements concerning record retention, such as duration, location, and assigned responsibility.

---

*Amended 36 FR 18301.
†Ibid.

XVIII. AUDITS

A comprehensive system of planned and periodic audits shall be carried
out to verify compliance with all aspects of the quality assurance program
and to determine the effectiveness of the program. The audits shall be
performed in accordance with the written procedures or check lists by appropriately trained personnel not having direct responsibilities in the areas
being audited. Audit results shall be documented and reviewed by management having responsibility in the area audited. Follow-up action, including
re-audit of deficient areas, shall be taken where indicated.

The various parts are known familiarly as the "18 Criteria" and define fully
the quality assurance program requirements for the nuclear power industry.
There are other requirements for licenses to use special nuclear material, but
in general they are not as all inclusive as Appendix B. The discussion of
quality assurance here is based on the nuclear power industry since it incorporated the most complete set of requirements.

VI. SAFETY ANALYSIS REPORTS

Referring to the definition of quality assurance in Appendix B, "quality assurance comprises all those planned and systematic actions necessary to provide
adequate confidence that a structure, system or component will perform satisfactorily in service. Quality assurance includes quality control, which comprises those quality assurance actions related to the physical characteristics
of a material, structure, component or system which provide a means to control the quality of the material, component or system to predetermined requirements," it is often difficult to segregate quality assurance from other requirements. In fact, the definition provides a broad umbrella over all activities.
This situation is clarified to some degree by the requirements for the quality
assurance program (Appendix B) and the contents of the safety analysis report (SAR).

Regulatory Guide 1.70 [6] defines the format and contents of the SAR.
The quality assurance (QA) program and specific guidelines for implementation
are covered in Chapter 17 of Regulatory Guide 1.70. The description of the
QA program must include all activities during design construction, preopera-
tion, and operation at the earliest practical time consistent with the schedule
for accomplishing the activity.

In addition, the NRC has issued regulatory guides and documents containing guidance on acceptable methods of implementing portions of the QA program. These are popularly called the "Rainbow Series" because of the colors
of the covers, green for the construction phase (Wash 1309) [7], gray for the
design and procurement phase (Wash 1238) [8], and orange for the operation
phase (Wash 1284) [9].

The SAR may indicate that this guidance is to be followed specifically, or
if not followed, a description of alternative methods that will be used and the
manner in which they will be implemented. In particular, in all cases it is required that the organizational element responsible for implementation of various provisions must be identified. That is whether it be the applicant, the
architect-engineer, the nuclear steam system supplier, the constructor, or
the construction manager.

Those documents contain a number of draft standards. As they become
approved by the American National Standards Institute (ANSI) as American

National Standards, they may be endorsed by regulatory guides. The applicability of each guide versus the draft standard is addressed in each guide or may be covered in amendments to the Standard Format as they are issued.

VII. REGULATORY GUIDES AND THE STANDARD REVIEW PLAN

The Atomic Energy Commission recognized, very early, that additional information beyond that included in the Federal Code was needed to clarify the intent of the staff in judging whether the SAR satisfied requirements. Further guidance was published in June 1966 [11].

The AEC Regulatory staff found that the initial submittal of SARs did not provide sufficient information and it was necessary to make specific requests for additional data. To resolve this problem, in 1970 the commission instituted a series of Safety Guides which stated solutions to specific issues that were acceptable to the staff and the Advisory Committee on Reactor Safeguards. Then in 1971 a new series of Information Guides was initiated to list information frequently omitted from applications.

Finally, in February 1972, the AEC issued a standard [12] covering the information and the standard format for the SAR. This has since been superseded by a series designated as the Regulatory Guides, including the standard as Regulatory Guide 1.70 (usually written Reg. Guide 1.70).

The Regulatory Guide series, as of this writing, consists of 282 individual guides with 26 additional ones under consideration and issued for public comment. They are divided into 10 general divisions as shown in Fig. 2.

To standardize the regulatory staff requirements, a series of standard review plans were developed for guidance of the staff. These were combined into a Standard Review Plan published in September 1975 [13]. The primary purpose of the plan is to improve the quality of and uniformity of staff reviews and to present a well-defined base from which to evaluate proposed changes in the scope and requirements of the reviews. Specific areas of review are identified and the associated acceptance criteria to guide the staff in their review. In some cases, branch technical positions are stated as acceptable methods for satisfying the acceptance criteria. Conformance to the standard format is not mandatory; however, if not followed, the staff review time may take longer since they may take longer to locate the information.

In summary, the quality assurance requirements mandated by law to safeguard the health and safety of the public are contained in Title 10 Code of Federal Regulations. These are further augmented by the Regulatory Guides and the many national consensus standards referenced in the guides.

VIII. NUCLEAR STANDARDS

There are many codes and standards adopted by industry as consensus standards that are applicable to the nuclear industry. The primary governing body for the preparation, balloting, acceptance, and publication is the American National Standards Institute (ANSI). The standards are designated by the ANSI number, date of issue, and title: for example, ANSI-N45.2-1977, *Quality Assurance Program Requirements for Nuclear Facilities*.

The standards are prepared by organizations, usually technical societies, who are certified by ANSI as standard preparing agencies. The American

Division		Number Active	Number Under Consideration
1	Power Reactors	144	0
2	Research and Test Reactors	5	1
3	Fuels and Materials Facilities	25	6
4	Environmental and Siting	12	4
5	Materials and Plant Protection	52	6
6	Products	7	1
7	Transportation	6	3
8	Occupational Health	21	3
9	Antitrust Review	3	1
10	General Guides	7	1
		282	26

FIGURE 2   U.S. Nuclear Regulatory Commission rules and regulations regulatory guides.

Society of Mechanical Engineers is the responsible body for preparing and maintaining the primary document governing quality assurance program requirements, ANSI-45.2, noted above. In addition, there are several, so-called daughter standards containing supplementary requirements for various activities. The daughter standards are listed in Table 2, together with the Regulatory Guides that endorse their application.

The AMSE Quality Assurance Committee has been engaged in preparing a single Quality Assurance Standard incorporating many of the daughter standards. This document, ANSI-NQA-1, was published in 1979. A list of the standards included is given in Table 3.

The NRC has not endorsed ANSI-NQA-1 at this writing but is expected to do so when it achieves general industry acceptance. It is anticipated that this will occur in the near future.

The ASME Boiler and Pressure Vessel Code (BPVC), Section III, states the quality assurance program requirements for work covered by the code. Many governmental agencies have adopted the code and impose the code by law on the construction and installation of pressure vessels and power plant components. To become certified, a manufacturer or installer must develop a documented quality assurance program meeting the requirements of the code and apply for an ASME survey. An ASME survey team reviews the quality assurance manual describing the program and its implementation. After a successful survey the ASME issues a certificate authorizing performance of code work. The certified manufacturer or installer is then said to be an "N" stamp holder. The certificate must be renewed every 3 years by passing a resurvey by ASME.

The quality assurance requirements for owners, manufacturers, and installers of nuclear facility components and parts are included in article NCA-4000 of Section III, ASME-BPVC, entitled "Quality Assurance." The code

TABLE 2   ANSI-N45.2 and Daughter Standards N45.2.X and Endorsing
NRC Regulatory Guides[a]

		Endorsing reg. guide
N45.2-1977	Quality Assurance Program Requirements for Nuclear Facilities	1.28
N45.2.1-1973	Cleaning of Fluid Systems and Associated Components During Construction Phase of Nuclear Power Plants	1.37
N45.2.2-1978	Packaging, Shipping, Receiving, Storage and Handling of Items for Nuclear Power Plants (under Construction Phase)	1.38
N45.2.3-1973	Housekeeping During the Construction of Nuclear Power Plants	1.39
N45.2.3(a)-1978	Addenda to N45.2.3-1973	
N45.2.4-1977 IEEE-336-1977	Installation, Inspection and Testing Requirements for Instrumentation and Electric Equipment During the Construction of Nuclear Power Generating Stations	1.30
N45.2.5-1978	Supplementary Quality Assurance Requirements for Installation, Inspection and Testing of Structural Concrete and Structural Steel During the Construction Phase of Nuclear Power Plants	1.94
N45.2.6-1978	Qualifications of Inspection, Examination and Testing Personnel for the Construction Phase of Nuclear Power Plants	1.58
N45.2.8-1975	Supplementary QUALITY Assurance Requirements for Installation, Inspection and Testing of Mechanical Equipment and Systems for the Construction Phase of Nuclear Power Plants	1.116
N45.2.9-1979	Requirements for Collection, Storage and Maintenance of Quality Assurance Records for Nuclear Power Plants	1.88
N45.2.10-1973	Quality Assurance Terms and Definitions	1.74
N45.2.11-1974	Quality Assurance Requirements for the Design of Nuclear Power Plants	1.64
N45.2.12-1977	Requirements for Auditing of Quality Assurance Programs for Nuclear Power Plants	−
N45.2.13-1976	Quality Assurance Requirements for Control of Procurement of Items and Services for Nuclear Power Plants	1.123

TABLE 2   (continued)

		Endorsing reg. guide
N45.2.14 IEEE-P-467 (draft; not published)	Quality Assurance Program Requirements for the Design and Manufacture of Class 1E Instrumentation and Electrical Equipment for Nuclear Power Generating Station	−
N45.2.15 (draft; not published)	Hoisting, Rigging and Transporting of Items for Nuclear Power Plants	−
IEEE 498-1975 (N45.2.16)	Requirements for the Calibration and Control of Measuring and Test Equipment Used in the Construction and Maintenance of Nuclear Power Generating Stations	−
N45.2.20 (draft; not published)	Supplementary Quality Assurance Requirements for Subsurface Investigations Prior to the Construction Phase of Nuclear Power Plants	−
N45.2.23-1978	Qualification of Quality Assurance Program Audit Personnel for Nuclear Facilities	−

[a]Standards may be obtained from the following:

>   ANSI-45.2 documents
>   ASME Order Department, 345 East 47th Street, New York, NY
>   10017 (for all published standards)
>   *Note*: Prices lower for ASME members.
>   IEEE documents
>   IEEE Standards Department, 345 East 47th Street, New York, NY
>   10017
>   Regulatory guides
>   U.S. Nuclear Regulatory Commission, Washington, DC   20555
>   Attention: Director of Standards Development.

TABLE 3 N45.2.XX—Incorporated in NQA-1

N45.2.6	Qualification of Inspection, Examination and Testing Personnel for Nuclear Power Plants
N45.2.9	Requirements for the Collection, Storage and Maintenance of Quality Assurance Records for Nuclear Power Plants
N45.2.10	Quality Assurance Terms and Definitions
N45.2.11	Quality Assurance Requirements for the Design of Nuclear Power Plants
N45.2.12	Requirements for Auditing of Quality Assurance Programs for Nuclear Power Plants
N45.2.13	Quality Assurance Requirements for Control of Procurement of Items and Services for Nuclear Power Plants
N45.2.23	Qualification for Quality Assurance Program Audit Personnel for Nuclear Power Plants

covers all pressure retaining components, such as pressure vessels, piping, pumps, and valves. In addition, the requirements for component supports, core supports, and concrete reactor vessels and containments are included. The requirements of NCA-4000 parallel very closely 10CFR50 Appendix B.

The code also includes the requirements for the Material Manufacturer's and Material Suppliers' Quality System Program in article NCA-3800. A material manufacturer is defined as an organization which certifies that the material is in compliance with the requirements of the basic material specification.

The code covers quality requirements in addition to the quality program. Section V, Nondestructive Examination, covers examination methods for detecting surface and internal discontinuities in materials, welds, and fabricated parts and components. Included are methods for radiography, ultrasonic, liquid penetrant, magnetic particle, eddy current, visual, and leak testing examinations. They are invoked to the extent they are referenced and required by other code sections. Personnel performing nondestructive examination are required to be qualified in accordance with SNT-TC-1A [14] when specified by the referencing section, or an alternate system specifically accepted by the referencing code section. Otherwise, qualification requirements may be in accordance with the manufacturer's established procedures. The referencing code section may also require examinations to be performed to a written procedure demonstrated to the satisfaction of the authorized inspector.

Section IX, Welding and Brazing Qualifications, relates to the qualification of welders, welding operators, and brazers and brazing operators and the procedures used in welding or brazing according to the ASME code. There are two controls involved. The first is that of performance qualification, which is designed to assure that the welder or brazor has the skill to deposit sound weld metal. The second, procedure specification and qualification, is to determine that the weldment is capable of having the required properties for its intended application.

Section XI, Rules for Inservice Inspection of Nuclear Power Plant Components, sets forth the rules for examination, testing, and inspection of components and systems in a nuclear power plant. They constitute the requirements to maintain the plant and to return it to service in a safe and expeditious manner after a plant outage.

Compliance with the rules is mandatory and the authorized nuclear inspector must verify that the program has been completed prior to permitting the plant to return to service. The owner must provide access in the design and arrangement of the plant to permit the conduct of the examinations and tests. Plans, schedules, and procedures for conducting the inservice inspection program must be filed with the enforcement and regulatory authorities having jurisdiction at the plant. In addition, results of examination and tests must be documented together with required corrective actions taken or to be taken.

IX. NATIONAL BOARD OF BOILER AND PRESSURE VESSEL INSPECTORS

The ASME assures enforcement of the code by requiring a manufacturer or installer to retain the services of a qualified person from the National Board of Boiler and Pressure Vessel Inspectors. This person is called an authorized nuclear inspector (ANI). He or she is required to witness operations which he considers critical to the process and to review all documentary evidence that substantiates that the operations were performed in accordance with code requirements. Upon acceptance of all owrk, the ANI applies the "N" stamp to the finished product and documents authorizing their use.

The ANI is responsible for maintaining a continual inspection and surveillance of the implementation of the QA program to ensure that it meets the code. The ANI must also approve any changes to the ASME-approved QA manual. The ANI exercises a very powerful influence, inasmuch as he or she has the authority and responsibility to accept or reject work completed or in-process and to approve or disapprove the implementation of the QA program.

There are many codes and standards prepared by various organizations which are used in specifying the quality requirements for nuclear manufacturing, installation, and operation. These include the Institute of Electrical and Electronic Engineers (IEEE), American Concrete Institute (ACI), American Iron and Steel Institute (AISI), American Institute of Chemical Engineers (AICHE), American Welding Society (AWS), American Society of Civil Engineers (ASCE), and many others. The applicable codes and standards are invoked by the engineering design documents, which define the design, or by the technical specifications, which govern the operation of a nuclear power plant. The quality assurance program provides the implementing procedures to assure that the requirements are met.

X. VENDOR QUALITY ASSURANCE

The design, manufacturing, and construction of a nuclear power plant involve a large number of participating organizations. It is vitally important that each of these conform to the applicable quality requirements. Criteria IV, 10CFR50 Appendix B, Procurement Document Control, specifies that the measures shall be established to assure that applicable regulatory and other requirements necessary to assure adequate quality are included or referenced in the procurement documents. Contractors or subcontractors are required to provide a quality assurance program consistent with the pertinent provisions of 10CRF50 Appendix B.

Criterion VII, 10CFR50 Appendix B, Control of Purchased Material, Equipment and Services, requires measures to be established to assure that purchased material, equipment, and services conform to the procurement documents. They may include, as appropriate, source evaluation and selection, objective evidence of the quality furnished, and inspection at source or upon delivery. In addition, documentary evidence of conformance must be at the site prior to installation or use. The effectiveness of the control of quality by contractors and subcontractors is assessed at intervals consistent with the complexity, quantity, and importance of the product or services.

The requirements above impose a significant effort on the quality assurance function. It is necessary to participate in the design activity to review specifications to assure that the essential quality requirements are included in the design documents. These and other provisions for implementing source surveillance, inspection, and audit must be included in the procurement documents.

The process of vendor evaluation and selection must include a determination that a vendor is qualified to perform the procurement documents and has an acceptable quality assurance program. This usually entails a review of the quality assurance manual and an on-site review to assure that the program is being implemented.

The quality assurance plan for a procurement includes witness points where the buyer desires to witness an operation, hold points beyond which work cannot proceed until inspection acceptance of work is accomplished, and final acceptance prior to shipment. In addition, provision for surveillance and audit to determine the effectiveness of the quality assurance program is included.

XI. THIRD-PARTY-SUPPLIER EVALUATION

There have been many efforts on the part of industry and the NRC to relieve the burden of performing evaluation of vendor's quality assurance programs. It is obvious that if every purchaser performs a survey on every vendor, a great proliferation of surveys results. Vendors have been swamped by surveys from multiple buyers, all directed at the same objective.

The Coordinating Agency for Supplier Evaluation (CASE), an outgrowth of the coordinated aerospace supplier evaluation, has implemented a program to reduce the number of surveys that a utility licensee must have performed to satisfy Appendix B. CASE is a voluntary association of utilities, architect engineers, constructors, and other organizations whose members interchange the results of surveys of suppliers to the nuclear industry. There are two classes of membership: sustaining, which requires the performance of a stipulated number of audits each year, and participating, eligible to receive the CASE Register of Approved Suppliers, published on a quaterly basis. The sustaining members perform audits on other members to assure that acceptable audit procedures are being followed.

The CASE register has been endorsed by the NRC as evidence that an acceptable survey has been performed by a CASE member. Any member desiring to utilize a CASE survey as evidence of an acceptable quality assurance program of a vendor must obtain the results of the survey from CASE headquarters, review the survey to assure themselves that the audit results are acceptable, and maintain them in file as objective evidence of the survey. The CASE program is maintained by the Aerojet Liquid Rocket Company, Sacramento, California [15]. The NRC is currently engaged in a pilot program with ASME to determine the acceptability of the ASME "N" stamp program as evidence that a manufacturer or installer has an approved quality assurance program.

A. Reporting of Defects and Noncompliance

The NRC issued 10CFR Part 21, effective January 6, 1978, to implement the requirements of Section 206 of the Energy Reorganization Act of 1974. Any responsible officer of a firm constructing, owning, operating, or supplying the components of any facility or activity regulated by the act who obtains information reasonably indicating a failure to comply with the act or any applicable rule, regulation order, or license of the NRC relating to substantial safety hazards, or becomes aware of a defect which could create a substantial safety hazard, is required by Part 21 to notify the NRC. Failure to do so is punishable by a fine not to exceed $5000 per day, to a maximum of $25,000.

Each person or firm is required to post a copy of Part 21, Section 206, of the Energy Reorganization Act, and procedures for complying with the regulation. They shall assure that each procurement document, when applicable, include that the provisions of 10CFR Part 21 apply.

The regulation governing the reporting of unplanned events that have or could have an impact on safety-related items is stated in 10CFR 50.55 (e). The reports are termed licensee event reports and the NRC publishes a summary report distribution to all licensees and other interested parties.

The regulation states that the holder of a construction permit shall notify the NRC of each deficiency found in design and construction which if it remained uncorrected could adversely affect the safety of operations of the nuclear power plant throughout its expected lifetime. These deficiencies are characterized as significant: breakdown in any portion of the quality assurance program; deficiency in the final design as stated in the criteria of the SAR; deficiency in construction or damage to structure, system, or components; or deviation from performance specifications as stated in the SAR which could affect the ability to perform its intended safety function. The holder of the construction permit must notify the NRC of a reportable deficiency within 24 hours and file a written report within 30 days.

XII. DEPARTMENT OF ENERGY

The Department of Energy was created by the Energy Reorganization Act of 1974 and was given the authority to promote the use of all forms of energy. The prior agencies, the Atomic Energy Commission and the Energy Research and Development Administration, initiated the development of standards for application to nuclear research and development entitled RDT standards. These were named for the Division of Reactor Development and Technology and the designation has been maintained through the various organizational changes.

The standard for quality assurance programs RDT-F2-2 was designed to provide requirements peculiar to R&D programs advancing the state of the art. The standard is structured into eight sections related to the various phases of a project. Section 1 is introductory and related to organization and is always invoked. The other sections may be invoked to cover distinct and independent phases of a project, such as design only, development testing, procurement, and so on.

TABLE 4   NE(RDT) Standards Categories (Formerly RDT Standards)

A. Operation

    1. Coolant, coolant control
    2. Radiation control, safety

C. Instrumentation and controls

    1.   Instrumentation practices
    2.   Test equipment
    3.   Control, data centers
    4.   Flow measurement
    5.   Level measurement
    6.   Pressure measurement
    7.   Temperature measurement
    8.   Miscellaneous sensors, transmitters
    9.   Readout devices
    10. Signal conditioners
    11. Controllers
    12. Analytical instrumentation
    13. Computers
    14. Radiation measurement, monitoring
    15. Neutron flux measurement
    16. Reactor protection
    17. Miscellaneous components, materials
    18. Electric insulators

E. Equipment: mechanical, fluid

    1.   Valves
    2.   Reactor vessels
    3.   Pumps
    4.   Heat transfer equipment
    5.   Pressurizers
    6.   Reactor internal structures, core components, control rod drives
    7.   Piping
    8.   Special mechanisms
    9.   Air handling
    10. Vessels, tanks
    11. Liquid purification, treatment
    12. Shielded casks, carriers
    13. Reactor fuels, materials, assemblies
    14. Seals, static and dynamic
    15. Systems, multiple components
    16. Irradiation, experiment and test components
    17. Process equipment

F. Programs, procedures, methods

    1. Program administration, miscellaneous
    2. Quality assurance
    3. Testing
    4. Maintenance

TABLE 4   (continued)

 5.   Cleaning, marking, packaging
 6.   Fabrication
 7.   Identification
 8.   Construction, installation
 9.   Design
10.   Fire protection methods
11.   Chemical and physical analysis, experimental data handling

M. Materials

 1.   Welding rods, electrodes
 2.   Fittings, flanges, forgings
 3.   Pipe, tubing
 4.   Castings
 5.   Plate, sheet, strip
 6.   Bolting, bolting materials
 7.   Bar, rod, wire, extruded shapes
 8.   Springs
 9.   Metallic seals
10.   Ingots
11.   Seals, gaskets, packings
12.   Thermal insulation
13.   Liquids
14.   Gases
15.   Paints, protective coatings
16.   Adsorbents, adsorbent filter materials
17.   Miscellaneous

P. Electrical
 1.   Wire, cable
 2.   Power systems and equipment
 3.   Electrical penetrations
 4.   Heating equipment
 5.   Motors, drives

S. Structures, buildings

A subsidiary program document, RDT-F2-4, covers the requirements for
the quality verification program. This standard is used for procurement or
manufacture of simple components where inspection programs are adequate to
verify conformance to requirements.

The total scope of RDT standards covers the broad range of program and
product requirements. There are seven categories including a total of 70
standards. Table 4 lists the categories and the standards included in each
type.

At the start of the RDT standards program, the standards were given a
"T" designation (i.e., F2-2T) and were considered tentative until proven by
use, so they could be eliminated in the event that they could be replaced by
a national consensus standard. These standards are used by the Department
of Energy to govern the quality requirements of their programs. There are

rarely, if ever, encountered in the commercial nuclear industry. They may, however, be encountered by suppliers furnishing material or services to proj ects such as the Fast Flux Test Facility (FFTF) and the Liquid Metal Fast Breeder Reactor (LMFBR).

XIII. ASQC MATRIX OF NUCLEAR QUALITY ASSURANCE PROGRAM REQUIREMENTS

The original Matrix of Nuclear Quality Assurance Program Requirements was prepared by the Interface Subcommittee of the Nuclear Power Technical Committee-ASQC in April 1973. Subsequent expansion and changes led to a revised matrix published as the second edition [16].

The matrix lists 71 quality assurance program elements extracted from the various quality assurance criteria contained in 10CFR50 Appendix B. The elements are compared with similar statements or corresponding elements in other quality program documents. The documents compared in the matrix are listed in Table 5. The scope of the matrix is limited to the phases of design, procurement, manufacturing, and construction. The operations phase has explicitly been omitted.

The matrix can be used as a cross index to a given quality element and a particular standard or code. It is also very helpful in the preparation of a quality assurance program to assure that all quality elements are included and how existing quality programs need to be altered to meet nuclear requirements.

TABLE 5   Quality Assurance Programs
Listed in ASQC Matrix of Nuclear Quality
Assurance Program Requirements

ASME-NA-4000	(1976 Summer Addenda)
ASME-NA-3700	(1975 Summer Addenda)
RDT F2-2	
MIL-Q-9858A	
ANSI 45.2, Revision 1	
ANSI 45.2.1	Reg. Guide 1.37
ANSI 45.2.2	Reg. Guide 1.38
ANSI 45.2.3	Reg. Guide 1.39
ANSI 45.2.4	Reg. Guide 1.30
ANSI 45.2.5	Reg. Guide 1.94
ANSI 45.2.8	
ANSI 45.2.9	Reg. Guide 1.88
ANSI 45.2.11	Reg. Guide 1.64
ANSI 45.2.12	
ANSI 45.2.13	

The Energy Division of the ASQC is in the process of updating the matrix to the latest requirements, including the International Atomic Energy Agency standards. It is always advisable to consult the latest changes of the various documents referenced in the matrix.

XIV. CONCLUSION

It is patently impossible to condense in a short discussion all the facts and ramifications of the quality assurance requirements applicable to the nuclear indistry. The basic document is, of course, the Rules and Regulations of the Nuclear Regulatory Commission contained in Title 10, Code of Federal Regulations. Evolving from this document is a plethora of regulatory guides, national codes and standards, and other documents which influence the nuclear quality assurance programs. The foregoing material is not intended to be an all-inclusive review but to give the initiate or one interested in the nature of quality assurance in the nuclear industry an introduction to the subject which together with the references will serve as a starting point for further study.

A significant difference exists in the implementation of the quality assurance program in the government-regulated nuclear industry and the Department of Defense procurement of materials and services. The NRC regulations have the force of law and the NRC does not have the prerogative of permitting departures from SAR commitments, designs, and specifications. This is specifically different from the DoD contract representatives, who can agree to accept material departing from design requirements provided that it can be demonstrated as capable of performing its intended function. In theory, at least, this means that the nuclear power plant must meet exactly the requirements of the design. As a result, the construction must meet all requirements and the construction forces cannot accept the normal compromises acceptable in commercial work. The necessity of completely documenting that acceptable work has been completed adds another unusual burden to construction.

The rigor of the nuclear quality assurance program is of the same order of magnitude as that required of the aerospace industry and is sometimes even more demanding, as in the nuclear steam supply system. The law and regulations apply to safety-related structures, systems, and components that prevent or mitigate the consequences of postulated accidents that could cause undue risk to the health and safety of the public. The balance of the plant may be subject to a quality assurance program in accordance with the desires of the owner. Such a program may be imposed to improve the reliability and availability of the operating plant.

REFERENCES

1. B. W. Marguglio, *Quality Systems in the Nuclear Industry*, Special Publication 616, American Society for Testing and Materials, Philadelphia, 1977.
2. P. C. Szasz, *The Law and Practices of the IAEA*, Legal Series 7, IAEA, Vienna, 1970.
3. J. F. Hogerton, *The Atomic Energy Deskbook*, Rheinhold, New York, 1963.
4. U.S. Nuclear Regulatory Commission, Annual Report, 1978.

5. United States Nuclear Regulatory Commission, Rules and Regulations, *Title 10, Code of Federal Regulations—Energy* (commonly abbreviated as 10CFR, followed by the particular part, i.e., 10CFR50, part 50). Copies may be obtained from the Superintendent of Documents, U.S. Government Printing Office, CIB-SSOS, UCP, Washington, D.C. 20401.

6. Regulatory Guide 1.70, Revision 3, *Standard Format and Content of Safety Dnalysis Reports for Nuclear Power Plants* (LWR Edition), November 1978.

7. WASH 1309, *Guidance of Quality Assurance Requirements During the Construction Phase of Nuclear Power Plants.*

8. WASH 1283, *Guidance on Quality Assurance Requirements During Design and Procurement Phase of Nuclear Power Plants.*

9. WASH 1284, *Guidance on Quality Assurance Requirements During the Operations Phase of Nuclear Power Plants.*

10. NUREG-75/087, *Standard Review Plan for the Review of Safety Analysis Reports for Nuclear Power Plants* (LWR Edition), March 1979.

11. Atomic Energy Commission, *Guide to the Organization and Contents of the Safety Analysis Reports*, une 30, 1966.

12. Atomic Energy Commission, *Standard Format and Content for Safety Analysis Reports for Nuclear Power Plants*, October 1972.

13. NUREG-75/087, *Standard Review Plan for the Review of Safety Analysis Reports for Nuclear Power Plants* (LWR Edition), September 1975.

14. SNT-TC-1A, *Recommended Practice for Nondestructive Testing Personnel Qualification and Certification*, American Society for Nondestructive Testing, Columbus, Ohio, 1975.

15. G. F. Dakin, *CASE*, Case Data Center, Dept. 8210, Bldg. 2002, Aerojet Liquid Rocket Company, P.O. Box 13222, Sacramento, CA 95813.

16. American Society for Quality Control, *Matrix of Nuclear Quality Assurance Program Requirements*, 2nd ed., ASQC, Milwaukee, Wis., 1976.

FURTHER READING

Lester, R. H., N. L. Enrick, and H. E. Mottley, Jr., *Quality Control for Profit*, 2nd ed., Marcel Dekker, New York, 1985.

Spectral Magazine, Special Issue on Three Mile Island, IEEE, New York, November 1979.

47

QUALITY IN THE SERVICE INDUSTRIES

NORBERT L. ENRICK

Kent State University
Kent, Ohio

I. INTRODUCTION

Modern methods of quality control were developed and matured in *manufacturing industries*. These involve the processing and fabrication of materials into finished durable and nondurable goods. By contrast, *nonmanufacturing industries* are broken down into two major categories: (1) mining, agriculture, and construction; and (2) service. Since mining, agriculture, and construction are similar to manufacturing in that material is processed into finished product, it is not surprising that quality control methods for these operations are quite parallel to those used in manufacturing. Service, however, is a relatively distinct nonmanufacturing activity: Work is performed for someone else. For example, a person receives health care, or a manufacturer receives marketing, promotion, and distribution of its products by a service firm.

II. A VIEW OF SERVICE BUSINESS FIRMS

Service business firms differ considerably among each other, but may yet be presented in terms of broad classifications, such as whether they are primarily personal, automated, or mixed in the type of functions performed, as suggested in Fig. 1. the amount of skilled and unskilled labor involved, and the degree of clerical and technical or professional effort required, permit further sub-classifications. Distinctions are valid only in broad and general terms. For example, health care may involve primarily professionals (doctors, nurses, pharmacists) or clerical workers (patients' appointments, patient and medication records, billing), but there will also be skilled labor (the plumbing and electrical repair crews, for example) and unskilled services (such as janitorial). Figure 1 is thus intended as a general view only.

III. ORGANIZATION OF SERVICE FIRMS

Entities concerned primarily with service, such as in communication; transportation, distribution, and marketing; financial; or government functions

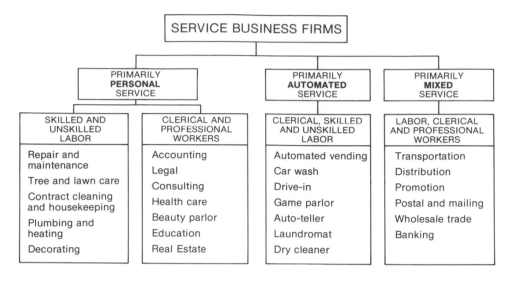

FIGURE 1   Service businesses by type: automated versus personal.

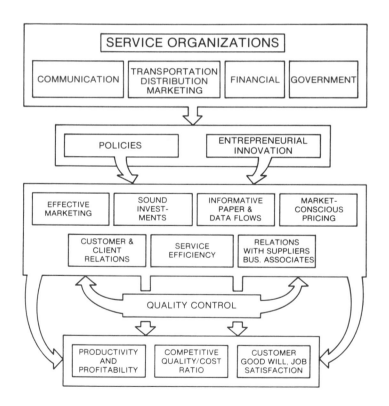

FIGURE 2   Policies and innovative entrepreneurship of service organizations.
Quality assures good performance and aids in achieving productivity, competitive quality/cost ratios, and customer satisfaction.

have in common the need to develop policies. These policies revolve about strategies and plans to achieve effective marketing, to make sound investments, to arrange for the flow of paperwork and data that yields relevant, essential information, and to achieve market-conscious pricing. The latter activity will often be in need of differentiation to take account of varying market segments. Beyond these aspects, policies must be conscious of the value of good customer and client relations, the growth potential involved in service efficiency, and the need for good relations with suppliers, business associates, and others.

Competitively alert firms are those who combine policymaking with a heavy emphasis on entrepreneurial innovation. It is the effect of such innovation on service, resulting in higher productivity, better quality/cost ratios, and enhanced customer goodwill that may distinguish two banks or two fast-food chains. Quality control, as emphasized in Fig. 2, is the organizational tool for assuring that innovations work as intended (or are successively revised until entrepreneurial goals are accomplished).

The feedback mechanism inherent in innovation policymaking is explored further in Fig. 3. Market demand analysis, consideration of economic, political, and social trends, and cognizance of technological developments and opportunities should result in policies, strategies, and plans regarding quality of

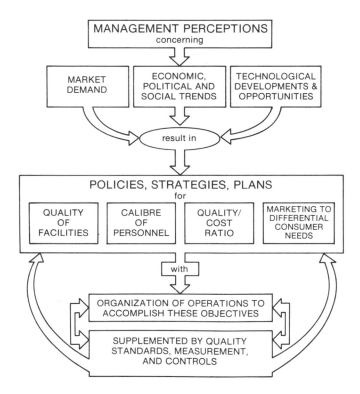

FIGURE 3   Growth of service quality. Policies, strategies, and plans are based on management perceptions of customer needs, and lead to goals and standards. These objectives, in turn, are assured through proper controls, including quality control.

facilities, caliber of personnel, the quality/cost ratio to be achieved, and the meeting of customer needs in distinct market segments. Organization of the operations must be designed to accomplish these objectives. For each part of the activities involved there must be quality standards, means to measure these standards, and controls for conformance. Where control programs show that standards cannot be achieved, revision of standards or of operations may be required. Where management perceptions of future needs are valid, and are followed up effectively with strategies and quality controls, a growth in the quality and efficiency of service will accrue over time—thus giving the more alert organization an ever-increasing edge over competition.

In practice, these principles will lead to the need for compromise: A good mix must be found between internal organization that optimizes productivity and externally oriented service relating to customer needs. It is gratifying to note that the move to centralized computer installations, dictated by internal productivity requirements, is giving way to decentralization as mini- and micro-computers are installed. This technological development permits the establishment of multitudes of smaller processing points, more specifically adapted to the needs of market segments and specifically identified customer groups. Support services can then be aligned to markets.

IV. SERVICE QUALITY CONCERNS

Quality control, started to enhance the quality/cost ratio achieved in production, has more recently been finding increasing acceptance in the service fields. The quality concerns and the control applications are, in fact, quite parallel. A few examples will demonstrate.

1. *Defects per unit*: In weaving, for example, we might be concerned with the number of slubs, spots, and missing picks per 100 yards of fabric. This is a production matter. In a mail-order house, management may be concerned with the number of order-filling mistakes per 100 shipments. This is a service problem. In both instances, a sampling plan or control chart, based on the defects-per-unit concept, is applicable.

2. *Percent defective*: In the manufacture of thermostats, a sample is checked to determine the percent of units that fail to live through 10,000 actuations. In a telephone operation, a sample may be taken to ascertain the percent of "information" calls that received discourteous, erroneous, or otherwise deficient responses. In both cases a control chart for percent defective (fraction defective) aids management in distinguishing significant from chance variations of sampling.

3. *Variables*: In manufacturing, deviations of observed measurements (dimensional, temperature, weight) from standards and tolerances are evaluated through sampling and testing. In a hotel, the room-to-room uniformity of temperature (such as at 74 ± 2°F) may be checked periodically. A control chart for variables, for either case, aids in long-range control.

4. *Reliability*: Product reliability is the probability that an item will function properly for a given time under the expected future conditions of use. Service reliability may similarly be measured in terms of the probability that a certain type of repair will result in failure-free operation for a guaranteed period of time.

It should be clear that many aspects of service quality are tied to product quality. As a result, the reliability of a computer installation in servicing a banking operation is, in turn, dependent on the reliability that was built in by the manufacturer of the equipment.

V. SERVICE QUALITY DESIGN

The well-recognized principle in manufacturing quality control that all such activities begin with the design of the product applies in a parallel manner to service. The supplier must identify the user's needs, the cost factors involved, and the particular choice of service factors that will satisfy the needs. Human beings have a wide spectrum of needs. As a result, a good deal of product diversification in manufacturing finds its counterpart in service businesses. Examples are found in restaurant menus, styling options in a beauty parlor, or the variety of treatments available in a hospital. But diversification has its limits. It is not practical or economical to offer too wide a range of choices. Thus simplicity is required by providing merely a range of key lines of service, or by establishing service modules that can be combined in various ways to meet particular needs. Time, well-being, and continuity are the main ingredients that go into the determination of quality of many service functions.

A. Service Time Standards

The quality of a service represents the sum of all those individual characteristics that define the nature of the service. A minimal standard requires that the customer seeking service is being accommodated. An important feature of most services, however, is the time spent by the customer in obtaining the service. The *service time* is thus an important quality characteristic. It refers to the time required, from the origin of demand for service to its point of completion, in terms of reasonably meeting the demand. In this connection one must also consider the concept of *service transaction*: the sum of one or more individual services, with each individual service followed by subsequent service in an essentially uninterrupted flow.

Service is generally classified in terms of duration (such as the time to wait for a telephone dial tone) and the frequency (such as how often, on the average, the phone is used to dial out). These two taxonomies are combined graphically in Fig. 4. In some instances (such as postal services) time values apply primarily to objects (the mail in the system), while others (such as grooming services) involve personal waiting. Queues or waiting lines will occur most often in the lower left rectangle, where frequency or "persistence" of service demand is low and service duration is relatively short. Service businesses in this group are usually smaller, such as branches or franchise operations. They are thus also highly competitive, since many other installations will offer the same type of service. Customer waiting time is thus a parameter that cannot be neglected. It is for these reasons that one often sees a grocery store manager at the cash register, or executives managing vending stands at Disney World: to effectively meet peak demand periods and not alienate or lose customers, it behooves everyone to chip in with his or her service time. In fact, this flexibility is an axiom of service management. But it is a limited tool, and long-range standards can be met only through queueing analysis.

Standards are usually twofold: (1) the average time allowed for a service transaction, and (2) the average time that the customer waits until service is initiated. The service time distribution (usually following a negative exponential distribution) and the arrival rate distribution (usually the arrivals of customers follow the Poisson distribution) must be considered. The latter will be superimposed on a time-series function, with variations in hourly, day-of-the-week, and seasonal terms. Queueing theory is complex, but its application

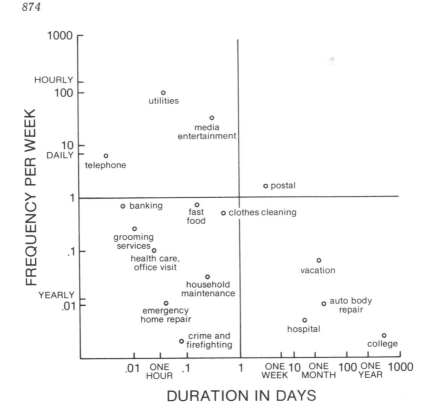

FIGURE 4   Duration and frequency relations of service. The rectangle represented by the lower left-hand part generally represents smaller firms with
relatively infrequent, short-duration services. (Adapted from J. R. Troxell,
"Service Time Quality Standards," *Quality Progress*, Vol. 14, No. 9, September
1981, pp. 35–36.)

will permit a balancing of service costs (increasing with the number of service
channels provided) with customer losses (decreasing with number of service
channels). Quality and cost factors are thus balanced. A way of dealing with
the problem of excess channels and thus excess personnel during slack periods
is to offer special inducements during slow hours or seasons, such as in terms
of price or extra service. Inducements to the public to make appointments is
a further device often used to reduce fluctuations in arrival rates of customers
and service damand.

Typically, telephone companies will have standards for the maximum wait of
a customer for a dial tone, while many fast-food outlets have standards for the
wait-plus-service span per demand. The need to serve within time constraints,
while avoiding costly and undue service facility idleness, is considered in terms
of an economic balance.

B. Standards for Well-Being

Consideration of the consumer's well-being is a further ingredient of quality
standards for service. The person installing a washing machine in the home
should arrive within the time span promised, perform the work promptly and

efficiently, and display a cheerful and yet unobtrusive (no mud-tracking or other annoyances) manner. Positive aspects of service including the following:

1. *The personal approach*: The customer is important, his or her personal needs should be heard, and every effort made to satisfy the customer. At the very least this will make the customer feel good and incline him or her to continue calling on the service organization.

2. *A tasteful atmosphere*: A dentist's office with interesting magazines and a tension-relieving fish tank, for example, will do much to relieve patient anxiety, particularly when children are brought by parents. A travel bureau whose decor and decorations do not invite a longing for distant places is hardly doing its best to promote exotic trips.

3. *Information*: Not leaving the bad news to be experienced later. The customer has a right to know the advantages and drawbacks of alternative services offered.

4. *Care*: The plane is late, but the airline provides a reasonable estimate of when it will arrive. The passenger can then plan and adjust accordingly. People in charge of providing service can often be unduly callous. Take, for example, this sign recently seen at a computer installation: "We're down. Our estimate of your intelligence will be enhanced if you do not ask when we'll be back on the air." Aside from the arrogance displayed, this sign conveys a lack of care on the part of the service provider for the needs of the user to do his or her own time-cognizant planning.

5. *Safety*: Standards to assure that the customer, while eating at a restaurant, or using the facilities of a hotel, or being conveyed on a carrier, will be safe are a mandatory ingredient of all service systems. Codes prescribing safe conditions have been on the statute books of most countries for many hundreds of years. The sword of extensive liability suits, forged in the past two decades, is an additional spur to safety precautions.

6. *Nonabandonment*: A lawyer fails to follow through on the probating and other duties of settling an estate. A travel agent arranges a tour and then the principal carrier goes into bankruptcy. A hotel room is reserved but does not become available. All these are cases of discontinuity of service or outright abandonment. One aspect of good standards for service quality is to assure continuity of service. The availability of "loaners" by a car dealer's service facility is part of this quality. Making appointments, providing for peak loads with appropriate forecasts, and doing the necessary management planning are parts of a continuity program in service.

VI. CONFORMANCE TO DESIGN

Good features and standards of service have little value unless management supplements these specifications with effective controls that assure conformance during actual operations. It is convenient to view controls as *internal* or *external*, as will be discussed.

A. Internal Controls

These relate to quality assurance of those features of operations which are not directly visible to the customer. When a telephone company maintains close controls of components used in the maintenance of the communication system, it will further the reliability of operations, but the clientele is never aware of the manifold activities involved. Similarly, the user of electricity is unaware of the efforts that go into assuring the supply and quality of coal used in the generating operation. Neither does a patient know much of the procedures that must be enforced to guarantee supersterility in an orthopedic operating room.

Ultimately, of course, every aspect of internal control will be experienced by the consumer, in quality, cost, or convenience terms. Thus telephone service interruptions may indicate inadequate maintenance, high utility costs may reflect poor purchasing and inspection practices, and failure to have sterility in an operating room may produce infections. In banking, as a further illustration, the quality of check imprints is quite important. Otherwise, if controls are not maintained, customers will be inconvenienced when wrong accounts are credited or debited, and costs increase as clerical and administrative effort goes into correction of these errors. A restaurant's efforts to maintain sanitary conditions in food preparation are taken for granted by the diner, but if there is a failure, devastating results can ensue.

An interesting case of internal failure occurred some time ago when the supervisor of a gas utility would maintain BTU content below standard, jacking it up whenever the inspector from the regulatory authorities would arrive. The failure was exposed quite accidentally when the inspector happened to read a dissertation by a student who had used his own independent sample for an analysis of variations and for the purpose of calculating suggested control limits. It should be clear that (1) fraud is usually self-defeating in the long run, and (2) controls should be so designed (including random, unexpected sampling) that fraud will be exposed quickly.

In conclusion, it should be noted that every service business involves an internal system, with activities rarely observed by its clientele. It is important that these systems be well designed, with good standards for performance, and assurance that specifications are met in practice.

B. External Controls

Here we are concerned with those qualities of service which are experienced directly by the customer. Common to all needs is the provision for cleanliness and freedom from failure, such as a clean room in a hotel, with heating and cooling system operational. But many aspects of service are relatively intangible, such as the friendliness, willingness, and concern of the servers.

Many service organizations, such as hotels and restaurants, have questionnaires for customers that inquire about service in terms of friendliness, courtesy, and cleanliness, as well as convenience and general acceptability. It is quite common, when offering a training seminar, to inquire of the participants with regard to their satisfaction with the topics, their presentation, and their relevance to actual needs.

C. Quality Costs

As in the manufacturing industries, service organizations are faced with the problems of costs of quality. Although such costs can be determined, few businesses make the effort to find out what percent of effort is involved, since thus far there is little known regarding the relation of these costs to sales. Some methods that have been used are as follows:

Comparison of costs, quality of service, and volume of business among comparable parts of a business, such as among branches

Attempts to compare competitors' efforts with one's own cost, quality, and sales results

Some cost control efforts can be self-defeating. For example, it used to be fashionable in manufacturing industries to hold indirect labor costs to a fixed percentage of direct labor. This accounting approach can be self-defeating when additional cost expenditures for indirect labor—such as better maintenance and improved control of quality—will result in the saving of materials and the avoidance of rejects, rework, and customer complaints. The experience in manufacturing has its parallels in service, when, for example, failure to have auxiliary personnel results in long waits for customers, or in a running out of vital supplies, or in other failures at the point of delivery.

External quality is thus the more visible part of the efforts of a service organization. Its effective functioning requires assurance at all times, but the accomplishments at the external level are very much dependent on well-functioning internal controls.

VII. ORGANIZATIONAL ASPECTS

The quality control department so prevalent in manufacturing industries is something you will not find when you ask for it among most service firms. In the service industries, the concept of a staff of professionals concerned primarily with quality is thus far finding little acceptance. Instead, such quality control as exists is part of the concern of the managers, supervisors, and operating personnel in performing all of their functions. Excellent levels of service are often accomplished.

A hospital, for example, usually does not have a quality control department, but there will be staff people concerned with quality, costs, and performance. Moreover, a provision of "incident reports" serves to isolate instances in which standards and procedures have either not worked or have been violated. A review of these reports, discussion with the persons involved, and consideration of the implication of the findings, will in turn result in a consideration of changes in procedures or personnel, as may be indicated. In other instances, a review of sales volumes, complaints, service quality questionnaires, and other evidences of quality of performance, with comparisons among selling units, branches, or other similar parts of the organization, serve as vital feedback for control and corrective action.

In conclusion, service organizations do not have the well-defined quality control functions common to manufacturing, but quality must nevertheless be recognized as that important ingredient which assures continuity, success, and profitability of the service facility.

VIII. DATA PROCESSING QUALITY

Most service organizations, because of the large number of customers served and the multitudes of individual transactions that are generated internally and externally, must rely on extensive computer processing to abstract meaningful information. Data are needed for decision support as well as for control of quality and costs.

In establishing an effective information system with proper controls to prevent the potential for error, an integrated approach, as shown in Fig. 5, will be of value. After consideration of the various points of data processing, where transfers, translations, and reproduction of information occurs, the relevant operational controls must consider the following:

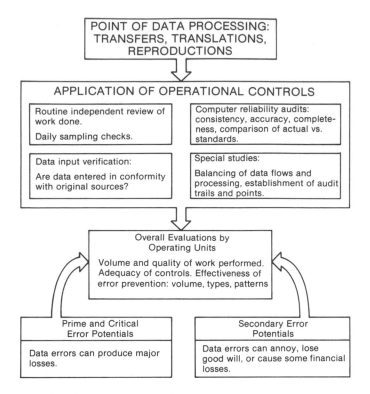

FIGURE 5   Data processing points requiring operational controls. Emphasis varies with potentials for major versus minor, secondary errors.

Routine independent review of work done, usually on the basis of sampling checks performed daily.

Audits of the reliability of computer operations: consistency, accuracy, completeness, and comparisons of actual results versus standards. The quality of programs is reflected in these measures.

Verification of data inputs, particularly with regard to conformity with the original sources and the transactions they represent.

Special studies to assure balancing of data flows and processing, and to establish audit trails and points for expenditures, income, and costs.

Individual operating units can now be subjected to overall evaluation by comparing volume and quality of work. Adequacy of controls, effectiveness of error prevention as regards volumes, types, and patterns, and related matters can thus be subjected to managerial evaluation and corrective review. In turn, cognizance must be had of prime and critical errors with potential for major losses, as against secondary, less significant cources of error. It is all too well known that the alternative to control is crisis management, such as when a major error threatens large losses or an excess of minor failures accumulates into a major problem.

IX. IMPROVEMENT OF QUALITY

The particular nature of the service industry, with multitudes of service points and masses of customers, presents a challenge as regards offering quality and assuring that this is maintained. Entrepreneurial innovation and creativity can aid considerably in improving quality. Some recent trends are noted below.

1. *Centralization*: A fast-food chain or an ordinary chain of restaurants, for example, will usually find it profitable to do a large part of processing in centralized facilities. In this manner the inspection of incoming food, the control of processing, and surveillance of cost and quality are under uniform, single management.

2. *Deemphasis on franchising*: At one time it was economical and efficient to lease or sell franchises for various types of service businesses. Usually, close control was attained over the franchisee's performance, by periodic inspection visits and maintenance of stringent quality requirements. In recent years, however, court decisions have tended to favor the individual franchisee who has failed to comply with contractual requirements. As a result, guarantee of uniform service quality throughout the franchiser's territory is under greater central control by moving toward ownership, such as by buying out the franchisee.

3. *Strategic analyses*: Special analyses using operations research techniques can be made to improve the internal service apparatus. For example, where service includes delivery operations, a strategic analysis of the number of vehicles available, the customer needs, routing alternatives, and frequency factors may lead to a reduction in costs while reducing the "wait" time. Banking operations, involving the complexities of check cashing, multitudes of debits and credits, statements issuance, and the like, can benefit from analyses to speed up check cashing (thus increasing money funds available) and to reduce lack of clarity or errors in customer statements (thus minimizing inquiries and resultant administrative and clerical costs).

Quality improvement depends to a large extent on the interest of top management, the atmosphere of free inquiry and encouragement of creativity throughout the firm, and the motivation and ingenuity of the staff to develop and implement cost-saving and service-enhancing functions.

X. MOTIVATION

Principles and practices of employee motivation in manufacturing apply also to the service industries. The following factors stand out:

1. Service employees, through their direct contact with customers, can directly contribute to goodwill, increased sales, and growth of clientele of the firm. Incentives, financial or otherwise, for employees to accomplish their best, supplemented by education and training courses, are an important factor.

2. Customer contact gives employees direct information on consumer reactions to the services offered. A means must be found whereby this information can be accumulated and reviewed periodically.

3. Customer questionnaires, as previously discussed, together with disguised inspection visits (the employee should not know that the "customer" is an inspector), permit management to identify the superior employee.

Motivation to perform well has been accomplished successfully in the vast majority of service organizations. Incentives range from expressions of approval and appreciation by management to monetary incentives and the potential for advancement. Most people like to do well in their job performance, and it is management's task to create the proper atmosphere to facilitate good work and to recognize and reward performance.

XI. QUALITY CIRCLES

Installation of quality circles (QCs) in service organizations represents an important means of tapping the creativity, interest, and motivation of individual employees toward quality improvement and cost reductions. An illustrative case is provided by the Human Resources Development (HRD) group at Henry Ford Hospital. Established in 1980, with the aim of involving first-level employees, the circles were designed to look into means for improving the quality of goods and services produced, reduce operating expenses, enhance the quality of work life, and concomitantly achieve optimal levels of patient care. The initial plan involved a cautious approach of just six departments: occupational therapy, dietetics, environmental housekeeping, general stores and distribution, computer services, and the satellite clinic business office.

A. Task Assignment

One first-line supervisor from each area served as the quality circle leader, with subsequent leader orientation meetings to prepare them for training. This orientation was done through a quality circle consultant. Emphasis was placed on open communication among participants and nonparticipants, management's continuing support for the quality circle process at all levels, and voluntary commitment to the program by all members of the quality circle. Information meetings showed the way in which quality circles bring about benefits to the individual and hospital. This approach generated considerable employee interest. However, it was also necessary to stress member responsibilities and to develop criteria for the principal types of problems likely to require QC solutions.

B. Criteria

Circle meetings were scheduled on a weekly basis. Guidelines or criteria relating to problem solutions were set:

  Problems tackled must be related to the work of the members.
  Problems must affect product or service quality to deserve attention.
  Cost reduction and work environment issues are relevant topics.
  Patient care and patient satisfaction are paramount concerns.
  Projects, at least initially, should be of a nature that permits a reasonable
    expectation of completion within 3 to 6 months.

While the scope of a QC program might eventually be expanded, it is important to begin with clearly defined criteria for the scope of activities to be covered. Once a good working relationship has been established, so that individual QC members are aware of their potentials, responsibilities, and limitations, more formidable tasks may be considered.

C. Projects

Once the criteria have been set, the QC looks for projects to be tackled. Usually, there are many problems that deserve attention. In the case of Henry Ford Hospital, the QC tackled these initial projects:

Dietetics dining service: Improving speed of service, reducing waste of materials, eliminating safety hazards, creating a more pleasant atmosphere.

General stores facility: Rearrangement of storage methods and procedures, smoothing of work and materials flow, with resultant enhanced productivity.

Environmental housekeeping: Curtailment of waste of cleaning materials and improved utilization of disposable items (such as paper towels, bags, and the like).

Staffing: Implementation of a rotation system to enhance personal growth and development of staff and to permit greater flexibility in scheduling.

Billing: Improved procedures that (1) reduce customer inquiries, (2) reduced requests for additional information from insurors, and (3) reduced billing errors.

The only area in which early gains could not be identified within a relatively short time was computer services.

Quality circles, the invention of the Japanese, building on American concepts of statistical quality control, have their important place in manufacturing as well as service industries. They are a means of involving first-line and other employees, soliciting their creative input, and thereby enhancing not just the quality of work life and employee morale, but contributing to cost savings and quality gains. It is difficult to conceive of a medium-sized or large organization that can be effective without quality circles. QCs are also of considerable value in smaller firms, but in some instances management can achieve close relations with the workers, with interactions that produce results akin to those found more formally in quality circles.

XII. CONCLUSION

Quality control in the service industries means (1) design, often involving a high degree of creativity and entrepreneurial innovation, aiming at optimal service; (2) control to assure that actual operations conform to designs, based on standards and specifications, and involving review of relevant operating and inspection data; and (3) motivation of employees in tangible form (such as quality incentives and rewards) and intangible ways (such as via quality circles). Opportunities for quality improvement exist widely among service businesses. Future competitiveness will be assured only to those who take a serious interest in quality design, quality control, and quality-of-service motivation, with emphasis on innovation and improvement.

FURTHER READING

Chase, R. B., "Where Does the Customer Fit in a Service Operation?" *Harvard Business Review*, Vol. No. 5, November–December 1978, pp. 137–141.

Enrick, N. L., "Quality Circles in Health Care," *Journal of Neurological and Orthopaedic Surgery*, Vol. 3, No. 1, April 1982, pp. 67–68.

Jenkins, W. B., "Quality Management," *Journal of Systems Management*, Vol. 33, No. 5, May 1982, pp. 24–27.

Main, J., "Towards Service Without a Snarl," *Fortune*, Vol. 103, No. 6, March 23, 1981, pp. 50–56.

Ruback, K., "The Implementation of Quality Circles at Henry Ford Hospital," *Quality Circles Digest*, Vol. 1, No. 1, Fall 1981, pp. 23–28.

Shaw, J. C., and R. Capoor, "Quality and Productivity: Mutually Exclusive or Interdependent in Service Organizations?" *Management Review*, Vol. 68, No. 3, March 1979, pp. 25–38.

Thomas, D. R. E., "Strategy in Different Service Businesses," *Harvard Business Review*, Vol. 56, No. 4, July–August 1978, pp. 158–164.

Troxell, J. R., "Service Time Quality Standards," *Quality Progress*, Vol. 14, No. 9, September 1981, pp. 35–37.

48

QUALITY IN WOOD PRODUCTS

DARRELL WARD
Consultant

West Chicago, Illinois

I. FIRST IMPRESSIONS

Industrial woodworking machinery found in any sizable furniture plant is totally different from machinery that one sees in a home workshop or a small custom cabinet shop. It performs the same functions but in a more efficient fashion, often performing several functions in one pass with much less manual effort.

Machining of lumber is done first to make "dimension" or rough oversize blanks in the rough mill long before any recognizable parts appear. The rough mill breaks down the properly conditioned lumber; chops out the major defects to get usable lengths; planes by hit-or-miss thickness settings, just enough to expose the grain pattern and remaining defects; ripsaws to clean up rough edges of wide boards and make strips for slim parts or panels; planes solid panels that make exposed wood parts such as tops; rerips other solid dimension or panel stock for legs, arms, backs, turning squares, rails, stiles, or any other parts that will show when the unit is finished.

Parts processing in the machine room produces recognizable shapes, profiles, contoured surfaces, and molded edges. The finish machining completed in that department generally brings parts to final shape. It also prepares the precision joints for assembly.

Every machine room* operation is a step in quality assurance, often dependent on a setup person's skill and the operator's judgment until later inspection of dimensional tolerance and surface condition at other stations.

---

*The colloquial expression "room" is commonly interchangeable with "department" and "mill," sometimes used jointly with the latter as in "millroom." Millroom or "machine room" generally refers to the area of finish machining to distinguish it from the rough mill. "Room" refers to a specific area of activity, not necessarily a space enclosed by walls. However, certain "rooms," such as the sanding room and the finishing room, actually should be separated to avoid product contamination and air pollution.

The sanding room follows machining. This department, which may be an entire floor in many multistory plants, removes tool marks, and smoothes and polishes the wood surfaces prior to assembly and finishing of complete units.

Sanding is usually not feasible after assembly. But frequent scuff sanding with fine abrasive paper may be required at several points between the main sanding room and the finishing room.

Parts and subassemblies are joined in the cabinet room with any of several kinds of adhesives, each formulated for particular applications and working properties. Parts are pressed or clamped before anything is disturbed. Frequently, mechanical fasteners are applied to retain assemblies so that they can be freed from the clamps without joints being disturbed. This method keeps production moving. Some joinery is designed to depend solely on special types of mechanical fasteners without glue.

A final inspection, patching, repair, and white goods cleanup readies assembled units for the finishing room. Countless numbers of finishing systems formulated by coating suppliers, many requiring two dozen or more steps in process, are applied to obtain the desired effect that was planned by the designer in cooperation with the sales and marketing staff.

As will be pointed out in more detailed discussion of each department in the sections that follow, quality assurance (QA) factors embrace the entire spectrum of processing unpredictable wood materials, from rough mill to final inspection, including the warehousing of materials, parts, subassemblies, and unfinished units if that should become necessary prior to finishing and shipping merchandise to a customer.

This introduction only highlights the major departmental divisions in a typical furniture manufacturing plant, simply to give the reader an overview of basic operations. The sections that follow provide three further levels of perception. The first level consists of more specific detail on the many operations within each department and the machines generally required. The second level explains several principal operations and workstation functions where quality assurance must be applied, else the function performed will inhibit or reduce final product quality. The third level suggests QA measures that can be applied in key areas, most of which have been observed in various plants around the country. Some of the suggestions are refined from more primitive versions; some are totally new to many woodworkers.

Because of space limitations, there is no attempt in this chapter to cover quality control as a statistical tool. Neither is every kind of quality assurance measure cited, for the same reason. However, there are enough to put the woodworking newcomer on the right track.

II. THE ROUGH MILL

This is the department where boards begin to be processed. First, however, the lumber must have been produced at a sawmill, green, and later conditioned in a dry kiln after drying down to a moisture content (MC) of about 6 to 8% for furniture processing (10 to 12% for millwork). The rough mill then breaks down the boards to make rough dimension.

Dimension material is made in units and in multiples of the required lengths and widths, slightly oversize to allow further machining and sanding that produce final shapes and finished dimensions. Many subsequent processing steps are necessary before dimension pieces are converted into parts for the end product.

Rough mill equipment and processing sequences vary considerably between different plants. If many long pieces of standard narrow widths are wanted, as for moldings or other slim stock, full-length raw boards are ripsawed into strips first. Then a number of "chopsaw" stations crosscut the strips to remove unwanted defects and produce required lengths.

When short pieces of a few standard lengths and many different widths are required, as for most furniture parts, long rough boards are processed in a different sequence to get the best yield. They are crosscut first for the standard lengths. Large defects that spoil more than half the width are usually removed at the first "cutoff station."

Rough planing may be required to expose more of the surface defects to the ripsaw operators. But rough planing is not intended for heavy stock removal to make perfectly clean, flat surfaces. It is only a hit-or-miss operation.

"Thicknessing" and fine surfacing are achieved on a "surfacer" or sharp knife precision planer at a later stage. Some rough mills include an automatic double-edge jointer to give the ripsawyers a smoother and straighter edge for their first cut.

Several ripsaw stations make narrow widths from the short, wide boards and remove most of the defects left by the cutoff operator. The more astute rough mills include small, fast-action chopsaws, designated as "salvage saws," which remove the smaller defects left by the ripsawyers and thus save the shortest usable lengths. Reject pieces from all the machine operations are thrown to the waste conveyor that carries unusable "offal" or waste and scrap to a wood hog, a machine that reduces waste and scrap to chips and splinters.

Minimum standards established by engineering for the product being manufactured determine when widths and lengths are too small for any local application. Some plants have worked out unique schemes for fingerjointing short lengths to make long parts or for edge gluing and blocking narrow widths to produce turning squares and glue blocks.

Note that there is a great difference between rejects and defects, more so in furniture than in any other major wood industry. Many wood characteristics that are technically defects, compared with straight-grained wood or "clear" lumber, are often acceptable "character markings" in some design applications.

That is one of numerous reasons why personal judgment prevails where engineers sometimes fear to tread. Any woodworking plant manager will tell you that the initial breakdown (cutoff) operator "can make or break the plant" with respect to material costs and yield. His judgment on what to save for later reject decisions and what should be thrown out as scrap at his station is crucial both to material yield and product quality.

When crosscutting is done first, some very desirable long, clear lengths that lie on either side of a knot can be wasted if the breakdown operator decides to remove the defect instead of leaving it for the ripsaws.

The ripsawyer's judgment is crucial, too, because if he cuts through the center of a knot so that it appears in the edges of both adjoining pieces, the one cut could double the number of rejects in the parts just made. This assumes, of course, that alternate cuts for usable widths either side of the knot could have left the knot contained within a single piece for possible salvage. If it is partially included in the edges of both pieces, he makes two rejects instead of one.

A. QA Considerations

How large should a defect be to justify cutting a huge chunk all the way across
a wide board? When can the cutoff operator leave a defect and save material
by letting a ripsaw cut one narrow strip from a board that makes several long,
clear parts such as sofa rails? When should a saw cut, either rip or crosscut,
be made right through the center of a knot or other defect? Such decisions
at initial breakdown can change from day to day with different cuttings for
different kinds of products.

Determining what is a defect in the raw material is often more esthetic or
cosmetic than an engineering calculation or mechanical fact. Size and color of
knots that are structurally sound may be very desirable one day or for one
type of product but totally unusable in the next day's cutting for another type
of product, perhaps only because of the difference in species of wood being
cut. A knotty pine design, for example, demands a nice scattering of sound
knots. But the same style of furniture in maple may not allow anything less
perfect than pin knots or bird's eyes, and sometimes not even those.

Imperfections once considered objectionable often become character marks
as designers and manufacturers shrewdly adapt those natural patterns of
interesting defects into new designs.

Knotty pine eventually became so popular that a premium grade will now
specify so many of such and such kinds of knots per foot of board length and
width. A piece can be rejected if it does not contain enough knots or if they
are not more or less evenly scattered.

The ripsawyer has decision-making responsibilities that sometimes outnum-
ber those of the breakdown operator. Although the ripsawyer works with
boards already cut to various nominal lengths, he must decide in many instances which widths are best to make for each length.

How much material should he take on the first edging or trim cut to
straighten the piece and (usually) make an edge suitable for gluing into a
panel? If he takes too little there can be some stain showing, perhaps a
"wane" edge that makes a reject. If he takes too much, he wastes material
and may drastically reduce gross yield.

Should he make many pieces the same narrow width or make all pieces as
wide as possible between defects? An order for rail stock may demand as
many as possible of a given width. An order for panel stock normally will
prefer an assortment of nonuniform widths.

What should he do about making the last cut come as close to the remaining
rough edge as possible when he is trying to get good yield? Usually, the last
strip is not usable if it is less than 1 in. wide. When he cuts nicely to both
sides of a knot, should he throw away the strip that contains the knot in the
middle?

All of these questions may have different answers in different plants or in
the same plant when it is making a different product on different days. Literally speaking, a cutting is not a cutting is not a cutting. . . .

III. STANDARD SAMPLES

Standard samples offer one QA solution to the situation; however, it may vary
with different products. Standard samples show which defects are acceptable
and which are true rejects even when these evaluations are different for different products. The procedure of using standard samples can save arguments
and time-consuming decisions.

The standard samples should be limited to exactly the types of parts or pieces that are normally produced at the workstation or within the department where they are to be used. They should be selected from factory runs, as they occur, to show typical variations in sample parts that have acceptable defects. Each piece selected must at least meet a minimum acceptable quality level (MAQL). When parts are of similar shapes but quite different in standards for two different product lines, it may be best to have different displays of samples according to which product is being run.

For each type of defect that is acceptable, there should be an equivalent sample that is not acceptable. Workers should be able to look at the sample display and see exactly where the MAQL cutoff point is. Once the two sets of samples are collected, you can make a display board for mounting all the related samples in one group.

Ideally, the board can be painted in a flat color that will contrast with the parts displayed. A horizontal stripe should be painted across the board. Let the stripe represent a line that separates MAQL borderline parts from actual rejects, acceptable defects above the line and rejects below. Lettering on the board need not be elaborate to explain the point. Some plants are bluntly concise with lettering above the line: "Save it!" and below the line: "Toss it."

We suggest putting the MAQL line one-quarter up from the bottom because there can be many variations of acceptable defects. You will need more room for them. Anything of poorer quality than the near misses will be more obvious and need not be displayed below the line.

With little experience, any worker can pull a questionable piece and compare it directly with the sample board parts to determine if the piece is acceptable. This is simple enough, but there is another step toward quality assurance: incentive to make the comparison.

People tend to work rapidly at a steady pace while concentrating on their work under production pressure. They may argue: "If I have to check every piece, my piece count will drop!" True if there is an unnecessary waste of time for perfection. But the objective in establishing an MAQL proves that perfection is not expected. If it were, there would be no need for the standard samples. The idea is not to have people carelessly passing along parts that obviously will not be acceptable, while saving all parts that are.

The way many plants handle this situation, assuming that there is an incentive system, is to discount all unacceptable parts from the total quantity produced for the day. Usually, this can be traced to specific operations or machines. If so, the workers who generate waste are penalized against their total number of pieces for the day. If they run, say 1200 parts and 150 are not above the MAQL, their piecework count is scored at only 1050.

If there is a group or work center activity in which workers are not easily singled out for the specific operations they perform or how much they contribute toward the whole area output, the group is put on a group incentive. This worked quite well in the finishing department of one plant where it was impossible to pinpoint individual errors or neglect. When the whole group was credited for better-than-standard output and got an incentive over base pay at the end of a period, they learned to work as a team instead of individuals. The group quickly became very self-policing. If anyone overstayed break periods, for example, or caused rejects that lowered the piecework count, fellow workers goaded the person more than a supervisor would. If shirkers did not correct their attitude quickly, the other workers requested that the supervisor shift the shirker to another department.

Parts in process, controlled by standard sampling, can be even more important than some flaws in finishing. Suppose that an unacceptable piece is

made and passed along for assembly, where it may go unnoticed. The reject
then becomes part of the finished product, which may be repaired but could
be bad enough to throw out the whole unit. Many minor flaws generated on
the finishing line can often be repaired. But a bad part cannot always be
removed easily after it is assembled with others. In that case, a single part,
perhaps worth only a few cents, can cause the loss of many labor hours and
many dollars in manufacturing costs put into the unit after the one bad piece
was passed along.

Carelessness or reluctance by a worker to make certain that parts are acceptable when they leave that worker's station simply reenacts the fable of a
kingdom being lost for the sake of a horseshoe nail. The story might well be
part of an informal indoctrination when standard samples are first introduced
to a work center or department.

If a plant has tried standard sampling and it failed after it became "old
hat," it is very likely that the problem lies in substandard supervision or
poorly motivated leadership of some kind. A new start with fresh samples on
a new board, a full indoctrination in what it means and how it is expected to
be used, plus a direct tie-in to piecework incentive credit only for acceptable
parts may do the trick. If this approach does not work, management had
better do some in-depth investigation.

Standard samples are of particular value at several key stations in the
rough mill: initial breakdown at the cutoff saws, at the ripsaws, and at the
sorting tables. If there is a salvage saw, this should be included.

In some plants, the layout is such that two or more stations can view the
same sample board if it is placed in the proper location. The salvage saws,
for example, might be operated by people who also attend a sorting table or
who are positioned close by that operation.

Many large furniture plants have a line of ripsaws too long for anyone to
view a sample board from one end to the other. In that case, more than one
board can be displayed. The value in quality assurance is far greater than
the bit of trouble required to make up as many sample boards as will serve
the purpose.

Standard samples of parts in process to show MAQL parts versus rejects
are valuable at layup tables for gluing and panel making. They can serve at
many different cutting and shaping machine stations in the machine room, the
sanding room, the cabinet room, and especially in the finishing room.

Woodworking is particularly sensitive to the fact that when you deal with
quality assurance you are in a misty area of human psychology more than basic
engineering. This is especially true of a plant that produces a wide variety
of products for different market levels. No one likes to take pride in making
a "cheap" product, so people need a better understanding of management objectives and why their contribution is valuable. Even low-priced furniture
and some promotional goods have their quality standards and must be substantially built. There will be a definable MAQL even though the design, cost of
materials, or simplicity of finish meet the requirements of the low-end market.

Standard samples can apply across all quality levels, and when the MAQL,
high or low, is more consistent, the market responds accordingly. The QA
manager's responsibility is cut out for him by the company he keeps . . . or
the one that keeps him! First define the objectives. Then make them easy to
achieve. Standard sampling is one means for speaking loudly and clearly in
a field that sadly needs more and better communications to instruct and train
the (usually) lower-paid workers.

IV. MAKING PANELS

Thin, large area parts are called panels. They need not be perfectly flat but do represent a plane even if ornamentally contoured, as in a raised or recessed panel door. Except for contemporary styles, panel components traditionally are surrounded by framing or supported by structural members. In contemporary casegoods and wall units, panels usually are of 3/4-in. or thicker material and are self-supporting, like bookcase end panels.

A panel may be made from a single board or from several narrow strips of lumber edge-glued together. A panel shaped with a wide cove or concave slope around its edges is framed to make a raised panel. A flat panel of thin material becomes a recessed panel when it is fitted into grooves of thicker frame members. Sometimes a frame is concealed inside a case, serving as a structural unit only to support a thin panel that is exposed outside. This arrangement is called "panel-on-frame" construction.

Furniture "casegoods" have "end panels" on both ends, regardless of how long or deep the boxlike structure happens to be. The ends are to the right and left while you stand facing the front. Case backs and tops are panels named for their application. Case tops generally are given more special attention than other surfaces. For cases that stand against the wall, backs often are simply unfinished utility panels of thin man-made board merely to close the case against dust and pests.

Panels are made of single-piece man-made board materials, such as hardboard, particleboard, or fiberboard. They are also made up in multilayers as laminated wood or plywood with a core of common lumber or of any man-made board. More expensive and fancier veneers are used for the exposed faces in both types of construction.

Veneer means any thin material less than 1/4 in. thick. Some are cut as thin as 1/100 in. Material thicker than 1/4 in. is considered either a board or solid panel because it can be self-supporting in common widths.

Solid wood panels for exposed parts and for furniture-type plywood cores start in the rough mill, after boards are ripsawed. The lengths of the pieces were established by initial breakdown, thickness by the rough planer, widths by the ripsaws. The sorting and inspection functions after the ripsaw output include making up pallet loads of pieces all the same length and thickness but of random widths. It is not desirable to have all the same width for most applications. Pieces are stacked in layers of the approximate width of rough panel size when they go to the panel gluing operation.

Pieces of the same length and thickness are glued together along the edges to make wide panels. Some of those panels become plywood core stock. Thin panels of better quality are set aside for reripping to make other parts, such as rails and stiles. Thicker panels are ripped into turning squares.

Structural parts that do not show may be cut from panels of acceptable defects. Parts to be exposed in finished merchandise are cut from panels made of selected stock. The visible glue lines from the edge-gluing operation are not considered defects in most furniture and will appear at random in finished panels, turnings, and other exposed parts, such as arms, legs, and seat rails or table aprons.

A. Quality Considerations

What should go into a panel? The material should be of the same length, thickness, and species if the panel is to be recut to make exposed parts. An exception is made in medium- and low-priced furniture when any compatible species with relatively bland grain are used together as "mixed hardwoods." Generally, that term implies a mix of diffuse-porous species, such as soft maple, poplar, birch, basswood, beech, sycamore, and similar woods that have insignificant grain pattern or color.

Species of more interesting grain pattern and color, such as oak, pecan, hickory, mahogany, walnut, and several others, are separated from the mixed hardwoods because they command a better price for veneers and exposed solids. Hard maple and cherry are two of the diffuse-porous species that are premium materials for hardness and durability and are therefore not included in mixed hardwoods.

Product specifications may or may not require that all exposed panels be made of clear stock or acceptable pattern-enhancing defects. It should be borne in mind constantly in woodworking, more than most other industries, that defects do not necessarily mean rejects. Several kinds of defects are not only incorporated in a design as desirable appearance factors, but some even sell at a premium.

Core stock for plywood can contain almost anything that is structurally sound (i.e., no loose knots, honeycomb, warp, collapse, serious checking, or pockets of mold and fungi). Sound knots, stain, or uneven color between heartwood and sapwood make no difference in the structural properties of core stock.

Regardless of later application, in core stock or exposed parts, all edge-glued panels should be laid up with alternate pieces flipped so that when you look at the end grain the growth rings of the tree alternate up and down, not all in the same orientation. This is because a board of any width tends to cup or warp like a trough when growth rings try to flatten out as the wood dries.

If alternate pieces are reversed, any slight cupping of the narrow panel pieces with later changes in moisture content will result in slight waviness. This is the main reason for ripsawing wide boards into narrow pieces and gluing them back together to make wide panels. If panel pieces are edge-glued with growth rings all laid in the same orientation, the panel may later curl, like a section of a drum or barrel. A simple but sometimes overlooked QA practice is to keep workers constantly alert to an alternating pattern of end grain as panel parts are laid up, frequently checking before clamping or pressing.

B. Edge Gluing

Panels are edge-glued with several varieties of both thermoplastic and thermosetting formulations, sometimes a mixture of both to obtain some of the advantages of each. Many different methods are used for clamping or pressing the parts together while the adhesive sets, dries, or cures, as the case may be.

A thermoplastic cold-setting assembly glue, commonly a polyvinyl acetate (PVA) emulsion, called "white glue" in the shop, is used with bar clamps that reach across the width of the panel and pull all the pieces together, edgewise. The bond is made by coalescence as moisture evaporates from the resin emulsion, commonly within 20 min to an hour.

Casein is an old favorite organic adhesive derived from milk. It makes an excellent cold-setting bond, but mixing it properly is rather tedious. It also takes longer to cure than modern synthetics, at least several hours if not overnight at room temperature but much faster with heat. It has excellent moisture resistance and is still used for interior beam laminating and for applying door skins to interior flush doors.

True thermosetting resins are catalyzed and converted rapidly to a nearly impervious substance with the application of heat. When used for their obvious advantages of high moisture resistance and stability, hot clamping or pressing is required. Heat may be transferred in the clamps or press by several means: steam, recirculating heated oil, electric resistance heater elements, and electronic or "high-frequency" curing systems that work on the principle of a microwave oven.

The most common and economical adhesive for hot pressing is urea-formaldehyde (UF). This resin cures to a permanently hard and rather brittle substance with high moisture resistance. It requires highly elevated temperatures when clamp or press time is a matter of minutes and seconds. It may cure at room temperature over a period of many hours or a few days, but this is not practical for most production plants.

A disadvantage of UF is lack of viscous body. Without additives, it has no gap-filling properties. Therefore, joints must be perfectly machined and precisely mated when pressed or clamped. Otherwise, a defect known as a starved joint occurs. Gap filling is improved by adding limited quantities of ground walnut shell flour as an extender that also gives it body.

There are modifications of UF that include other resins. This makes a glue line that may have some of the properties of each. That can be a decided advantage or disadvantage for different products and working conditions. Solids content, additives, fillers, modifiers, ratio of catalyst to resin, and moisture content all affect the working characteristics in process and physical properties of the end product.

Good QA practice suggests either using adhesives premixed by the supplier or keeping close watch over correct proportioning and mixing locally, exactly to the manufacturer's specifications.

C. Making Plywood

"Furniture plywood" traditionally is a five-ply construction with a rather thick, edge-glued lumber core panel of poplar that serves as a substrate. A crossband of thick poplar veneer is laid on both faces with grain at right angles to the core.

There also are man-made crossband materials that eliminate any concern for grain direction. A fancy face veneer is laid parallel in grain direction to the core but on top of the crossband. Only one expensive face may be applied when that is the only exposed face in a finished product. However, a lower-cost backing sheet of similar physical properties must be laid on the reverse face to make a "balanced" panel that resists warping. Fancy veneers are applied to both faces if both are to be exposed in the finished product.

"Telegraphing" is a surface defect that crossband helps reduce or prevent. If you lay up a thin face veneer directly on edge-glued core stock, every glue line will eventually show through the veneer. When the core absorbs moisture, the glue lines swell and little ridges show in the face veneer's finished surface. If the core dries out too much, as with wintertime heat and insufficient moisture in the air, each glue line of the core shrinks. This then telegraphs through the surface as little grooves.

Modern furniture plywood can be three-ply construction. The core materials used in this case are any of the man-made boards, sanded to proper thickness and surface texture. Single veneer faces are bonded directly to the core panel. Crossband generally is not necessary because there is no grain direction in the man-made core material.

One of the advantages of using a monolithic man-made board for core stock is that there are no glue lines to telegraph. You can apply face veneers directly to the board without crossband in most instances. Another advantage of board core over lumber core is that it requires less machining and handling to make large panels, and the panels tend to remain flat.

However, glue lines are not the only source of telegraphing from defects on the substrate surface. Large dust particles, chips, or any foreign matter that contaminate the glue or fall on the surface during layup will telegraph through face veneers. Therefore, good QA practice in panel making demands a clean and orderly work area, especially around the glue spreader and veneer-handling area, to avoid inclusions during layup.

D. Good-Quality Gluing

How much adhesive is required for a good bond? This varies with the species of wood, the moisture content of both wood and glue, operating temperatures, and glue characteristics. The glue supplier recommends what is best for the application. The objective is to get good "wetting" and penetration into both faces of a joint. Double gluing or coating both parts ahead of assembly is the best method. Applying adhesive to only one face is not the best practice, although necessary in some procedures.

The "spread rate" or quantity of glue per square foot must be enough to coat and penetrate both parts while leaving enough, ideally, to form a film of about 1 mil (one-thousandth of an inch) throughout the glue line.

Suppliers specify spread rate in pounds per hundred square feet of surface, which when viewed from the edge, appears as a line: the "glue line." That is fine for large panel surface calculations, but correct spread rate for edge joints and assembly of small parts is not easily measured. It requires an experienced eye, but that experience is quick to develop.

If glue is spread properly and clamped or pressed sufficiently to make good surface contact (about 100 psi), there will be some squeeze-out along the outside of the glue lines. Too much squeeze-out will drip or run. This indicates that glue is being wasted, sometimes a rather costly insurance. Not enough squeeze-out leaves edges obviously not well filled in the glue line. The correct squeeze-out makes a continuous, small bead 1/16 to 1/8 in. along all of a glue line.

Two important factors engineered into adhesive formulations are "open assembly time" and "closed assembly time." Good glue spread, joint surface wetting, and squeeze-out are not simple or irrelevant matters. That is why open and closed assembly times are engineered for the user's working conditions and shop practices.

First, moisture content must be correct in the adhesive and in the wood throughout the gluing procedure. Then glue-coated surfaces may remain exposed to the air for the specified open assembly time that is allowed for parts to be brought together. But they should be exposed no longer than specified; otherwise, precure may occur. When that happens the joint cannot be closed fully and will never develop full strength.

Closed assembly time is the time allowed for parts to be brought together loosely. This allows time for surface wetting of uncoated layers and for the film to start gelling prior to heavy clamping. Clamping too soon produces too much squeeze-out and does not leave enough film in the glue line to make the bond.

Good QA practice requires checking of supplier specifications against shop practices to see if optimum results actually are being obtained. Similar

adhesives from different suppliers and different batches from the same
supplier must also be checked for compliance with specifications and shop
procedures.

E. Veneering and Panel Pressing

Glue spreaders, layup tables, and presses are the major equipment items
required for making laminated panels and plywood. Spreaders, also called
"distributors," are a variation of roll coaters. Some glue spreaders are made
with one contact roll for applying adhesive to only one surface of parts,
sheets, or panels. Others are built like old-fashioned clothes wringers, with
top and bottom rolls that coat both surfaces in one pass.

When a layup is for three-plying, the core panel is run through the double
spreader to be coated on top and bottom. The panel is then laid down on top
of one face veneer and covered by another.

When five-plying, only the crossbands are run through the spreader for
coating both surfaces. A layup then starts with a face veneer on the table.
A crossband, wetted on both faces, is laid on top of the veneer and the thick
core panel is laid on top of the crossband. A second crossband, also gener-
ously wetted with glue on both faces, is placed on top of the core and covered
by another face veneer. Thus only two members of the five-layer package are
coated with glue by the spreader.

Double gluing is not as feasible in veneering as in edge-gluing and joint
assembly. So to have good spread and proper wetting of all components, glue
spreaders are equipped with rubber rolls that are grooved in a variety of
patterns according to the adhesive and working conditions.

Glue rolls do not lay down a smooth coating as do paint rollers. Instead,
they lay down closely spaced beads that spread out under stacking pressure
to wet both contacting surfaces before heavy pressure is applied.

Roll groove patterns are designed to get good distribution with many different kinds of adhesives at their required spread rates. Adjustments must
be made in the adhesive mix, settings of the contact rolls, and doctor rolls or
blades, as well as pressure against the panel surface for different adhesives
and sometimes for different species of wood. Different adhesives may require
a different roll grooving. One set of rolls cannot apply all adhesives equally
well.

These and other factors magnify the technical problems in bonding panel
layups because of the large surface areas processed. Entire surfaces, whether
for small panels like nightstand tops or for large wall panels, must be evenly
spread with the correct amount of adhesive.

Moisture content must be correct, especially for hot pressing. Too little
moisture will result in delamination from starved joints. Too much will cause
a "blow" or a pocket of steam that can leave an internal bubble. Sometimes it
will blast through the thin veneer.

Many veneers bleed through if the glue has too much moisture. This condition can wet and seal the exposed face, causing a mottled, uneven color
when a finish is applied later. Sanding will not eliminate this undesirable condition unless the veneer is sanded off and totally replaced.

There are so many QA variables introduced through selection of adhesive,
gluing procedures, open assembly time, closed assembly time, clamping time,
and working temperature that to get perfect results in panel making without
outside help would require an operator or supervisor with a major in wood
technology and a minor in chemistry.

Fortunately, suppliers offset these problems with well-experienced and technically competent representatives backed up by research lab scientists. The QA function then becomes more of a responsibility for making certain that instructions are followed to the letter and sloppy methods are not allowed to develop in shop practices.

V. FINISH MACHINING

Finish machining, performed in the "machine room," includes all the secondary operations for making parts. Raw material for these operations enters processing in such forms as dimension blanks, turning squares, and panel stock produced in the rough mill. The tools that perform final machining functions are of two major types: sawblades that make sawdust and knife edge tools that make shavings or chips. Boring tools, drill bits, shaper cutters, and router bits may be loosely included with cutterheads used in jointers, planers, automatic lathes, profilers, and double-end tenoners as tools with knife cutting edges that make shavings or chips instead of sawdust. Several combination or multifunction machines may use any or all tool types: sawblade, knifelike end cutters, and rotary side cutters that make straight or spiral shear cuts.

"Abrasive machining" performs stock removal and final shaping of parts by abrasive methods that produce "sander dust," which is not like sawdust, chips, or shavings. Abrasive machining is like grinding. It may use either soft or hard abrasive-filled wheels. It is also done with coated abrasives bonded to several cloth and paper backings in the form of sheets, pads, and belts. A backing form, pressure pad, contact roll, or platen forces the abrasive to cut into the wood surface. However, with few exceptions other than abrasive planing, most abrasive operations occur in the "sanding room."

A. Machine Setups

Initial setups prior to a production cutting are normally the work of special setup mechanics in large plant or skilled machine operators, lead men, and supervisors in smaller plants. Setups require precision gages and measuring instruments for adjustments and for checking parts after trial cuts. Tolerances of approximately 1 mm are usual for key dimensions, but virtually zero tolerance is demanded for shaped edges and the grinding of tools that cut such edge patterns.

Precision-ground steel templates are used sometimes for checking panel thickness and nearly always for checking patterns of shaped edges on tops or important moldings. The setup man and inspector hold the template firmly against the shaped edge and if any daylight is seen anywhere along the pattern profile, the pattern machined in the trial part is considered unacceptable. Setup adjustments may clear the trouble, but sometimes the cutting tool may require regrinding.

B. Problems in Quality

Several quality problems that can occur in the machine room seem quite mysterious to the uninitiated. Most relate to moisture. A change in dimensions, for example, may have nothing to do with how well a part is machined. It may occur simply because of moisture movement. Such changes definitely will occur if the wood is not properly conditioned before machining. Fuzzy surfaces may

result from slightly dull tools but usually are traced to moisture. There can
be too much moisture in the wood, making it "stringy" or impossible to machine well. But fuzzing that occurs after a well-machined part has been sitting
around for a few days is caused by moisture picked up from the air. Chipping,
tearing, and flaking of wood surfaces while machining may result from too little
moisture in the wood or dull tools.

Surface "glazing" at any machine operation is caused by dull cutters or
those ground with incorrect bevel and/or relief angle. Fairly sharp cutters
may glaze when taking a "bite" too shallow. Wood cells are mostly cellulose,
a plastic substance that will crush and look glossy if not cut incisively with
razor-sharp tools.

Glazing is not always visible. When the cells are partly crushed rather
than cleanly sliced, the burnishing action of the tool at the point of contact
may seal the cells without making a noticeable change in appearance. Glazed
surfaces inhibit good penetration of adhesives for a good glue bond. A less-
smooth-looking but clean sawcut surface often makes a better bond than a
knife-cut surface from a planer or jointer if the knives are not maintained
with razor-sharp edges. Glazed surfaces will show lighter in color after finishing because they also prevent even penetration of stains and other coatings.

C. Show and Tell

Standard samples can be used to good advantage in the machine room for
detecting problems in the material, the machine, the tools, and in the plant
environment. Make up samples of parts that have been distorted by moisture
changes after correct machining. This can be done with one set of samples by
using pieces that were known to have had 12 to 15% moisture content (MC)
when they went through the rough mill. Make others from good blanks known
to be in the range 6 to 8% MC, perfectly machined, but left standing around
the shop (not an air-conditioned office) for several days when the relative
humidity is high.

Use a micrometer or precision dial caliper to check dimensions on both kinds
of parts immediately after machining. Mark on the parts the readings taken
at that time. Take new readings after about a week of room exposure. Mark
those on the parts and note the differences. Use a smudge of chalk on finger-
tips rubbed over a small surface area of both kinds of parts at the end of the
exposure period. Note differences in surface texture and write up observations on that factor.

Make other samples that show several varieties of glazing, fuzzy surfaces,
flaky surfaces, and any other defects that occur periodically. Have all the
parts put through finishing at the same time but without going through the
sanding room. Have them sealed and finished as is.

Be sure that each part has been previously marked with an identifying
code. Cross-reference the code to the source of the identified problem before
it goes to the finishing room. After finishing, some parts may look better
than expected, others much worse. A complete set of such parts mounted on
a sample board can serve as a constant reminder for older workers or education for new people.

Good machine operators do not make mistakes purposely. Mistakes often
are made from lack of experience that develops a discriminating eye. They
also occur with unreasonable pressure to meet production schedules.

Alertness to what is happening before things get out of hand, full awareness of quality levels required, and a sense of pride in producing that quality

at a reasonable output rate are vital to finish machining where final shapes, surfaces, joints, and tolerances are established.

VI. SANDING

Sanding is achieved with several different abrasive minerals, natural and synthetic, in different grit sizes as coated abrasives, bonded either to paper or cloth backing. Cut sheets of lightweight paper backing with medium or fine grits are known as "cabinet paper." Long sheets cut from continuous rolls are bonded together at the ends to make endless belts.

Belts may range in width from less than 1 in. to more than 60 in. The term "wide belt" applies to 12 in. and wider. Lengths can be whatever a user requires, from small portable tool belts up to wide sanding machines that stand 8 ft tall or higher.

Abrasive grit sizes range from around 600 and finer to a coarse, large grain 1/24 in. in diameter. Reference to a 600-grit size means particles that are approximately 1/600 in. in diameter. Coarser grits are used for fast stock removal, while the finer grits are used for smoothing and polishing. Direct wood polishing seldom uses grits finer than 200, often only 150. Finer abrasives are used, however, for rubbing and polishing finish coatings.

Other forms of abrasive are used in furniture manufacturing. One is an abrasive-filled, nonwoven nylon that comes in pads or sheets, used primarily for fast-cut rubbing or polishing of finish coatings, not usually on raw wood. Another form of abrasive, foam-filled, looks like a grinding wheel. It is used for smoothing and polishing long strips of moldings or the shaped edges of tops. The rim of the wheel is first shaped to mate with the molding; then it retains that shape as it wears down.

A. Abrasive Planing

A generic term coined by the author before the process was introduced in the early 1960s, abrasive planing is a method for heavy stock removal on boards and panels to make the surfaces flat and bring the material to a required thickness. Tolerances commonly range from holding plus or minus 0.005 in. across panels 4 and 5 ft wide by 8 or 10 ft long.

Abrasive planing is not usually part of the sanding room. Its purpose is for thicknessing core stock to make plywood and laminated panels, also for planing solid wood parts, boards, and panels to uniform thickness to be smoothed later. The machine may be physically located in the rough mill or machine room, but we include it here as a form of sanding.

B. Rough Sanding

While abrasive planing is designed for heavy stock removal up to 1/8 in. and more, rough sanding is for light stock removal of 1/16 in. or less. Rough sanding with 60- to 80-grit abrasives accomplishes some leveling of the surface, but its primary purpose is to remove tool marks, chatter, glazing, or other surface imperfections left after machining.

Rough sanding must cut through all those surface imperfections before fine sanding can proceed satisfactorily. Rough sanding is the first step toward good surface quality after planing to thickness, surfacing, molding, shaping, profiling, routing, bandsawing, or other final machining of a part.

C. Finish Sanding

Smoothing or "finish sanding" is not a well-defined step but a gradation of sanding steps performed with a series of progressively finer grits. The process will start around 80 to 100 grit and progress up to 120 or 150 grit. Different species, densities, and conditions of wood respond differently to the various grit sizes and mineral types. Generally, softer woods require finer grits and dense hardwoods, such as oak, require coarser grits to obtain an apparently similar surface.

Finish sanding should remove all previously visible scratch pattern prior to polishing if the merchandise is to be best quality. This is one cost-cutting area for low-end manufacturers because sanding is tedious and costly for perfect results. But any deficiency in sanding shows immediately after a finish is applied.

D. Wood Polishing

Wood polishing is the last sanding operation prior to finishing. It may begin with grit sizes around 150 and progress to finer grits. Abrasive-impregnated nonwoven nylon in pads, "flap wheels," and large cylinder rolls are used for final polishing on many items. Some polishing requires portable power tools. In many areas it is done by hand where tool pads or belts cannot reach.

Polishing is done to bring the surface or parts to final smoothness while leaving the pores of the wood still open, uniformly receptive to any coating that may be applied. Parts not well sanded and polished will show a profusion of scratch pattern left by earlier sanding, all emphasized the moment a pigmented filler or stain penetrates the surface.

Sanding and polishing are typically part of white goods preparation, repair, and inspection for finishing. Extensive fine sanding is mandatory for assemblies that show any smudges from handling. It is necessary for all units that have had time to absorb moisture and raise fuzzy grain before they are sealed.

E. Sanding Samples

Most people in the sanding room are trained to recognize what makes a good part or a satisfactory surface. Several stages of critical sanding are done with special inspection lamps to check surface quality before parts may leave the area. Nevertheless, sample boards that show good and bad sanding results at the major stages in process can be invaluable for training and as reference standards. Sample boards provide exact guidelines for sanding department personnel and new trainees. Samples enable people to compare scratch patterns and different degrees of polish.

Some parts do not require the same degree of polish as others and samples illustrate the MAQL for different kinds of parts. Make a set of samples from duplicates of the same part, each gathered after the major stages in sanding and polishing. Send all of them directly to finishing. When those samples are mounted, each identified with its last operation, no better visual example can be given. Everyone can see immediately why sanding and polishing are always considered the beginning of a good finish.

VII. ASSEMBLY GLUING

The main assembly department of most furniture plants is called the "cabinet room" because that is where cabinets or casegoods go through final assembly. Subassemblies and glued components may be put together in other areas to have additional machining and sanding performed before they join panels, frames, and other parts in the cabinet room.

A basic principle of good assembly gluing is the application of a uniform, thin film of adhesive with good penetration of all adjoining surfaces in contact. This is not possible without excellent machining of parts to make well-fitted joints. Some plants allow "a dab of glue in a dowel hole" plus a metal pin or staple "just to hold until the glue cures."

This leaves uncertainty as to whether the joint is held by the glue or the fastener. A better-quality joint is produced by a special fastener designed for that purpose with no glue at all.

Top-quality furniture work with well-machined and properly fitted joints can be tested in a simple manner. Assemble all the parts without glue or fasteners. If the knockup holds together firmly and *looks* properly assembled, it *will be* when you add the correct amount of adhesive or proper fastener to make the assembly permanent.

One reason why assembly workers may cheat on the glue is because in final assembly of presanded parts, not much squeeze-out, if any, can be permitted. Spillover on exposed surfaces will result in holdout that prevents penetration of finish coatings applied later. The glue can be chipped off when dry, but some will have penetrated the wood cells. It is better to remove the glue quickly with a damp rag, let the surface dry, then scuff-sand the raised grain.

Spillover need not be readily visible before it will cause serious problems. Even invisible areas of slight glue penetration become so serious that some plants build darkened inspection booths illuminated by ultraviolet light. An additive pigment in the glue formulation makes otherwise undetectable spots glow in the dark with bright colors. If any glue-stained spots do appear at this inspection point, the piece must be repaired in the area or sent back to the cabinet room for rework or parts replacement. The cabinet room does not want kickbacks from the inspector. This encourages assembly workers to lean more in favor of too little rather than too much glue.

Joints may not be fitted perfectly or the method of spreading glue may not produce a completely even coating on all adjoining surfaces. When these conditions prevail, that joint and perhaps the entire assembly may be unreliable. Less obvious problems include incorrect moisture in the wood, improper clamping of parts, dust or other foreign matter picked up in the glue line, perhaps a bad batch of adhesive, or improper mixing if done locally.

Assembly is one area where a display of standard samples will not cover all contingencies. Joinery is an art combined with highly complex technology. But fortunately, all major adhesive suppliers have troubleshooters to solve problems for plant managers when there are no wood technologists or experienced QA managers present.

Yet a sample board is not a bad idea for daily reference, as well as training. Samples can be made up to show the results of a starved joint, excess squeeze-out, also holdout on a part after it goes through finishing. The latter will show quickly where good coating penetration was impossible.

Depending on the type of plant and kinds of product or materials handled, a little imagination can be applied to many displays of MAQL parts and rejects.

For example, a display might show a mitered frame corner joint with three samples. One should show a good joint. A second might show the corner tips not matched. A third could illustrate the result if a joint was not perfectly square when it was clamped.

While there can be many possible applications of assembly samples, it is better to be extremely selective and use them only when problems and rejects occur repetitively, or when training is particularly difficult. If a department is inundated with reference samples, people may tend to ignore them.

VIII. FINISHING

Finishing is a technology too extensive for adequate discussion in an introduction to woodworking. But a few highlights may enable a newcomer to recognize a finishing department when he or she first sees one and next, after knowing what is happening in that department, be able to appreciate some differences in the inumerable finishes that may be applied.

Coating material suppliers, like adhesive suppliers, are technicians who do the research and develop finishing systems to satisfy the designer and manufacturer. They then set up the complete system in a plant and provide step-by-step instructions which, if followed implicitly, will make the end product look exactly like the R&D samples that were approved.

Finishing systems vary widely in coating formulations, sequence of application, and methods employed by different plants. The ideal system for one plant or product may not be suitable for another.

A. Materials to Build a Finish

The most common material used in furniture finishing is conventional lacquer, essentially cellulose dissolved in a complex blend of solvents. Cellulose is plentiful in nature and is found in wood cells, corn and cane stalks, cotton, and many other organic fibrous materials. Man-made resins extracted from petroleum and other sources have led to more complex coatings with improved properties. There are numerous combinations of alkyds, ureas, urethanes, epoxies, polyesters, acrylics, vinyls and other synthetics used in modern formulations.

But simple lacquers are still favored for their clarity and appearance of "depth." Depth is the optical effect obtained from three properties of the dried coating. One is the refractive index of the resin or its light-bending characteristic as through a lens or prism. Another is the amount of penetration into the wood cells below the surface film. The third is thickness. But even when a film is only 1 mil (0.001 in.) thick, it can give the illusion that you are looking much deeper if it penetrates well into natural wood cells which, within themselves, are translucent or semitransparent.

Good lacquer finishes, especially on exotic and fine hardwood species with well-prepared surfaces, produce a three-dimensional effect not easily reproduced or imitated. This is because the brilliance and depth of a good lacquer finish are easily recognized by a trained eye, often "felt" without analytical examination by a layperson, who simply admires fine wood merchandise. The appearance of depth in natural wood finishes has a certain "live feeling" to it that distinguishes it from a kind of dullness and unnatural flatness associated with printed grain patterns.

A lacquer finish is usually built by spraying a thin, barely wet coating on a prepared surface, letting the solvents evaporate to leave a thin film. Successive applications obtain a higher build. Lacquer coatings are unique in that each successive application "bites" into the one below. Freshly applied solvent partially redissolves the surface of the previous coating, which blends with the next. In this manner, any number of applications will add thickness while building into one heavier, monolithic film. Build is a relative measure of the film thickness or the sum of several coatings that make a complete finish, whether lacquer or other materials are combined.

Wet coatings generally are "flashed" at room temperature or in a slightly warm tunnel to let the higher volatiles evaporate. The still "tacky" coating can then be "baked" in a moderate oven to remove all slower-moving volatiles that leave the all-solids film. This forced drying puts product through the plant faster than slower air drying and assists in maintaining more uniform control over product quality. It also helps eliminate or greatly reduce problems caused by ambient moisture when a coating is air-dried.

"Blushing" is a problem with fast-drying lacquers in a high-humidity environment. Moisture picked up from surrounding air by the wood, also carried in the spray mist, can make a lacquer coating cloudy. This is because the solvents evaporate faster than the moisture that is entrapped in the film. Blushing is minimized on high-humidity days by adding retarder, a slower-drying solvent that delays flash time to allow the moisture to evaporate with the solvents.

Minor blushing may disappear after thorough drying. Sometimes it can be corrected by respraying the surface with thinner and letting it dry more slowly. Blushing may also disappear when put through an oven for forced drying. But extreme blushing may only blister when baked. That will require "stripping" and refinishing.

Hot spraying, a method that employs a heater between supply pot and spraygun, has two advantages. It helps prevent blushing caused by condensation of moisture on a cold surface. It also enables the operator to apply a higher-solids or thicker-viscosity material, thinned by heat rather than added solvent. High-solids materials spray easier when heated and obtain a greater film build in one coat without sagging.

Basic lacquers are not durable enough to withstand much abuse, moisture, heat, household chemicals, or abrasion. Lacquers are thermoplastic and will melt at elevated temperatures. However, lacquer may be modified with other resin additives, some being thermosetting resins, thus changing the working properties and durability of the film.

Synthetics generally are blended with catalysts and other ingredients to make conversion varnish, a thermosetting compound. It "cures" to a much greater hardness and resistance than natural varnish. But modern synthetics, especially those in the "superfinish" category, are more difficult to handle than lacquer. They cannot be so easily stripped off to refinish a mistake. Unless caught before cured, most synthetics can be removed only be sanding, a process that also might remove some expensive face veneers. Synthetics are formulated to offset this objection by making them cure very slowly, if at all, before they are exposed to heat. As long as they are still "tacky" they can be stripped, when necessary for repairs.

Thermosetting resins that cure or polymerize when a catalyst is added have a shorter shelf life than lacquers. Catalyzed materials will gel in a sealed container if left standing long enough. Synthetics often are furnished by the supplier with catalyst to be added only when they are ready to apply. Once the catalyst is added, the solids-to-solvent balance must be maintained in a mixer pot at the workstation, either manually or by automatic devices, to compensate for solvent loss and retain working viscosity. Material in a pressure pot that feeds directly to a spraygun in a closed system requires less attention.

All reusable containers, hose, and spraygun must be thoroughly cleaned at the end of a shift, sometimes more frequently; otherwise, the entire system will be fouled with gummy or solidified plastic.

B. Finishing Methods

There are many different methods for applying a finish according to product, plant facilities, and coatings selected for the job. The most popular method in furniture manufacturing is conventional air spraying. This becomes more sophisticated by adding heat between supply reservoir and spraygun.

Moving up another step is airless spraying, accomplished by tremendous hydraulic pressure in the coating material instead of atomization by air. Airless spraying works on the principle of injector jets rather than the carburetor. Airless spraying can lay on heavier coatings with less solvent and less overspray wasted in a cloud of mist.

The next step up is heated airless. This takes advantage of the best of two worlds. Coatings are thinned by heat rather than solvent, so still less solvent can be used. Moreover, when high-solids materials are thinned by heat, without adding solvent to obtain good spraying viscosity, each coat can be applied with a heavier build without sagging.

A much higher technology method is electrostatic finishing, which is not spraying at all in the elementary sense for the original electrostatic method. Some do incorporate the spraygun principle, but the process was first developed with disk atomization. A very slow trickle of coating fluid is introduced near the center of a large, whirling disk that revolves like a high-speed phonograph record. As the fluid is whirled by centrifugal force toward the rim, its flow is accelerated until, at the sharp edge, it flies off into space as a fine, almost invisible mist.

This tricky method of atomizing is incidental to the main principle, which is to charge the coating with a high potential of several thousand volts. The atomizing disk is at high potential while the product being finished is grounded by the conveyor. This makes the highly charged mist particles rush to the product surfaces and cling firmly by electrostatic attraction. Mist particles tend to wrap around the product surfaces instead of shooting past like a cloud.

The method was used for metal finishing for several years before a way was found to make the surface of wood parts conductive. This is now done routinely by dipping wood parts in a tank of fast-drying solvent that contains a hygroscopic compound. When the solvent evaporates the residual compound is invisible with respect to the wood color and grain, but it attracts moisture from the air to the wood surface. Although oven-dried wood is a good insulator, moist wood is conductive. It can be grounded to attract the mist particles. After the first coating is applied and dried, later research showed that parts can simply be passed through a chamber of high humidity or fine water mist just ahead of the electrostatic applicator. This way, any number of coatings can be applied.

Roll coating is a method that simply employs the same principle as a paint roller used for wall painting. But the machine is a precisely engineered industrial distributor of the coating material from a transfer or contact roll that simulates offset printing. Viscosity control, recirculation of coating material,

roll adjustments, and pressure of offset roll against work surfaces are precision engineered and react to sensitive adjustments. The method is most
economical for material utilization. There is no waste from overspray, although
there may be a good bit of solvent evaporation. Waterborne materials have
virtually no loss. A minimum film build can be achieved while completely covering a surface, but the method is limited mostly to flat panel stock.

An extension of that method does include actual printing by offset from
engraved cylinders. Multistage grain printing on top of roll coated base coats
can reproduce by rotogravure the finest wood grain patterns and colors on a
low-cost substrate. The same finishing line may or may not complete a panel's
finish with sealer and top coats.

A less common but vital method for coating mostly flat panel is curtain
coating. It also can be used for some kinds of moldings. It, too, is a high
speed and very economical method of getting all the coverage possible from a
gallon of coating.

There are different kinds of machines for curtain coating. One works with
a precision, knife-controlled slit along the length of a reservoir of material
under pressure. Another works like a waterfall pouring over the lip of a long
vat. Both systems essentially maintain a continuous thin curtain between head
and catch pan across the width of an interrupted conveyor. Material is re-
circulated by pumps so that none is wasted. As in roll coating, solvent must
be added to compensate for evaporation and maintain viscosity.

Parts or panels riding on the conveyor pass through the unbroken curtain
of fluid. Hydraulic pressure, viscosity, solids content, and conveyor speed
are regulated for the type and thickness of coating desired. Flat panels work
best. Thick edges cannot be coated very well. Contoured parts, such as wide
moldings, can be curtain-coated but will have uneven build. The coater must
be protected from drafts because the fluid curtain may waver or break.

C. Finishing Samples

Furniture finishing probably was the first area in which sample boards were
used. They are more complex than the sample boards or chips you may find
in a local paint store. A portion of the raw wood being finished is masked
off as each step in the entire finishing system is applied. This produces a
sequence of steps, perhaps a dozen or more, progressing from raw wood to
final top coat. Coating suppliers often use such samples to show the entire
sequence of steps plus a larger area of final top-coat appearance.

The QA method used in many furniture plants employs larger samples and
more of them. Such samples may range from about 6 to 8 in. square up to
more than 2 ft square when the matched pattern of a fancy face veneer is
rather large and must be fully controlled for density and color over fancy
grain patterns.

Typical "high-end" furniture finishes may require two dozen or more steps,
counting the several coatings, the drying, and the manual treatments before
and/or after drying. Sample panels often are made available at key stations
where processing affects color hue and shade, transparency, wood grain, and
other appearance factors. The samples must be large enough to compare visually, in proper light, with tops, fronts, and end panels of casegoods as well
as fine tabletops and desktops. Some plants control finishing quality well
enough to match a piece to a room grouping even if the customer bought only
two or three pieces several years earlier. Office furniture manufacturers often
have to satisfy this need in the higher-priced lines as an office is expanded.

Beyond coating applications in the finishing room, itself, a plant should have sample panels showing the exact surface texture and sheen the finish must have after it goes through the rubbing department.

D. Conclusion

There are other, less-familiar methods of commercial finishing and QA factors not covered in this introductory chapter on woodworking. The subject of finishing reaches into several disciplines, such as chemistry, surface preparation of different products, moisture control in the product material and plant atmosphere, and specially engineered equipment of many kinds designed for application and control of coatings. Then there is the art and craftsmanship necessary for any skilled workers to bring out the ultimate appearance potential within the coating system employed.

FURTHER READING

Coleman, D. G , *Woodworking Fact Book*, former Chief of the Division of Research, Information and Education, Forest Products Laboratory, Robert Speller & Sons, Publishers, New York.

Constantine, A., Jr., *Know Your Woods*, rev. ed., Scribner, New York, 1975.

Feirer, J. L., *The Woodworker's Reference Guide and Sourcebook*, Scribner, New York.

49

QUALITY IN THE FOOD INDUSTRY

BEN. A. MURRAY

Ben Murray Associates
New York City, New York

The control of quality in the food business has some unique problems. Every person consumes food, so most people consider themselves experts on the quality of food. This is carried through into the management of all food companies, and it is up to the quality manager to carefully put food quality control on an objective, measurable basis in all areas possible. The second problem with the food industry is that it is sometimes considered good to have variation in quality of the food product. For instance, this is supposed to give certain foods a homemade appearance, but this philosophy leads to nonuniformity in all parts of food quality control and must be recognized, and if variations are desired, the variations themselves must be carefully controlled.

Quality is like water in that both always flow downhill, not upward. The only way to prevent the downhill flow is to either have a dam or to have a pump to pump the quality back uphill. A system like that listed below is a dam to the quality in a food company, and the professional quality manager is the pump who must always be lifting the standards and systems back to their proper levels. For quality managers to do their jobs properly in the food industry, they must measure, report, and insist on corrective action in the 10 areas described below.

I. QUALITY ORGANIZATION

Food processing plants vary tremendously in quality assurance and quality control systems. Many small food processors have only one technically trained person and this person organizes and manages all technical activities from new product development to quality control, to dealing with the federal government on regulatory matters. In large modern food-processing companies, specialized quality groups have been organized and practice detailed quality assurance and quality control.

It is very important to organize the quality system in a food-processing plant so that the measurement activities (which is really what quality control is all about) are conducted properly and accurately, are reported to the proper management levels, and are used to produce proper corrective action. If quality control is permitted to be part of the production management, there may be a tendency to ignore signs of upcoming problems and to fail to take corrective action. Although some production supervisors certainly are quality minded, an organization that puts quality control under production sooner or later will find conflicts of interest. It is very important and must be stressed over and over that food quality control must not report to production.

In most modern food-processing companies, food quality control reports directly to the plant manager. The plant manager can, of course, always overrule the quality control manager and has the perogative to ship inferior material if desired. Of course, such an organization requires that standards and specifications have been set for all materials, finished products, and so on, and this will be covered in later paragraphs. Again, in the food-processing organization, whether the quality control department consists of one person or many, they must be required to report matters exactly the way they are. It is extremely important that reports be written and circulated promptly to all interested parties. Problems that are not written down are not corrected. In some of the modern quality control areas, in particular, statistical quality control, the plant management will have to take results on faith, as it is doubtful if they will wish to become expert in this type of technical activity. Statistical quality control is a readily used form of quality control in many industries and is used to determine if food-processing lines are under control. It also tells line operators when to take action to put processes back in control which have temporarily fallen out.

II. PEOPLE IN FOOD-PROCESSING QUALITY

There are many extremely competent people involved in food quality control who have little formal training. However, if you are organizing for the future, you will find it very desirable to hire people with training in one of the biological or chemical sciences. Many different disciplines must be involved in food-processing quality control, such as chemistry, microbiology, entomology, statistics, and many other areas. A certain familiarity with all of the above is necessary so that proper measurement techniques can be used to both solve problems with quality and, even more important, prevent problems from happening. Although employees without formal training can be very valuable, it is wise to build on their skills using formal technical training to develop a competent food quality control system. Probably the best background is a degree in food technology.

III. FOOD LABORATORIES

Food laboratories deal not only with chemical testing and microbiological testing, but also with the area called organoleptical (dealing with the senses, such as taste). Many of the chemical testing areas are covered in detail in manuals such as the *Official Methods of Analysis of the Association of Official Analytical Chemists*, or other texts developed by container companies and food departments of larger universities. Other areas, such as food tasting, smelling, and comparing with other products, have also been covered in some detail by many

authors. It is very important that organoleptical testing be carefully controlled to remove personal bias from the tests. Most of these tests should be
performed on a "blind" basis; that is, the control sample should not be identified. If the control sample is examined together with one or two test samples
and it cannot be identified, the tester may be certain that there are no outstanding differences. Sometimes, rather extreme methods must be taken so
that control or raw samples cannot be identified. Different-colored lights,
removal of all labels and packages, addition of foreign colors, and so on, may
be used so that the standard is not obvious.

Frequently, it is desirable to set up check laboratories within a food quality control system. The most important testing will be done at the plant level
as close to the time of production as possible. If raw materials that are improper can be detected before their use in the processing, it will obviously be
much more satisfactory. The same is true with finished product testing. If
an improper finished product can be detected soon after its production, the
processing line can be stopped or altered so that a minimum amount of defective material is produced. Some of this testing is frequently done right
out on the processing line and some of it will be done in a plant laboratory.
However, it is possible that testing techniques can drift away from the
standard method, and therefore it is very important to occasionally run companion samples in another laboratory. This laboratory can be in a corporate
or divisional laboratory away from the production facilities or it can be a
private independent laboratory. In any case, the sample should be tested
first in the plant location and then sent with the results to the check laboratory. The results from the two laboratories are compared to see if they are
reasonably in agreement. Please note that this testing is not done as a way
of releasing or rejecting the actual material reported by the sample. It is a
means of testing the system and that only. Probably the actual production
material will have been shipped and used long before the test samples are retested and the results compared. However, if the results do not agree between the two laboratories, an immediate investigation should take place to see
why. Usually, deviations can be found and corrected long before they become
important to the finished product. This testing technique should be used on
chemical, microbiological, and organoleptical tests.

IV. SPECIFICATIONS AND SYSTEMS

Exact specifications must be drawn up in a food-processing plant for raw
materials, sanitation controls, finished products, in-process controls, and
many other areas. Frequently, we find that raw materials do not have
precise specifications. It is only fair to all suppliers and receivers that
the specifications are written down so that all concerned have a contract to
supply and to receive proper materials. These specifications should include
testing methods and permissible variations. Provisions for rejection of raw
materials that do not meet the specifications should be included. Also, speci-
cations should be written down and agreed upon for the finished products.
If the specifications cannot be defined in chemical or microbiological terms,
color photographs, drawings, physical measurements, and so on, can be used
as ways to describe what the finished product should be like. Shelf life,
storage conditions, and other areas should be included in the finished product
specification program.

V. INGREDIENT TESTING

Food-processing plants vary, from those that actually collect raw materials
from the farmers' fields, to those who only assemble other ingredients which
have been processed and partially assembled along the production chain. The
same principles apply, however, in any of these situations. In the first case,
ingredient testing starts with the maturity and quality of the raw materials
while they are growing in the field. For instance, peas are carefully tested
all during the final stages of ripening until they are harvested at the optimum
time to ensure top quality in addition to top yields. If the processing gets
behind schedule because of weather or other reasons, and the tester measurements show that the raw materials will not produce the proper grade of finished
product, whole fields may be skipped so that only the peas of the proper maturity are harvested. (These skipped fields are salvaged later for use as seed
peas or perhaps dried peas.)

In the case of raw materials or ingredients which have been purchased, it is
very important that the food processor test these ingredients upon receipt. At
this point, the specification requirement again becomes very important. Even
before unloading a lot of ingredients, inspections should be made of the delivery
vehicle to be certain that the ingredients are not contaminated with insects,
rodents, or foreign materials or odors. If the delivery appears to be contaminated, it should be rejected at this time and not accepted for storage or use.
If the delivery appears satisfactory, it is then unloaded but kept in a hold
area until samples can be examined either by the receiving department or by
a quality control laboratory. Inspection may only be visual to ensure that the
materials appear to be the right color and odor, or it may proceed to a quite
complex chemical or microbiological testing. It should be stressed, however,
that this is one of the most critical of the steps in the quality control chain in
food processing. It is possible to make defective finished products from excellent raw materials, but it is not possible to make good finished products
from defective raw materials. In other words, the level of quality can only
go down from the level of the ingredients; it can never go up. After raw
materials are accepted, tested, and then released for production, control tags
should be added so that the progress of the ingredients can be tracked throughout the food manufacture. If it becomes necessary to locate exactly where ingredients were used, this must be possible. Occasionally, regulatory agencies
will arrive and ask for records showing usage of certain lots of raw materials,
and if no records are available, the entire plant's production may be embargoed.
It is also possible that a finished product may turn out to be defective, and
the quality control department will need to know exactly which lots of ingredients were used in this finished product. Therefore, some sort of tagging system must be in effect to maintain the identity of all lots of ingredients.

VI. IN-PROCESS CONTROL

Critical control points are determined and carefully documented for each part
of the processing line. As we discussed in the area of ingredient testing, it
is very important to maintain the level of quality all the way from the raw
materials through to the finished product. Since the level of quality can be
reduced at several points along the processing line, these points must be carefully measured and test readings documented. If problems occur later, the
problem point can then be identified and corrected. Hopefully, corrections
will be made at critical control points before large quantities of defective

finished products are made. It is very important, though, to determine just exactly what these critical control points are so that a quality control system may be set up. For instance, on a frozen-food processing line, the temperature of the gravy as it enters the pot pie or dinner must be carefully controlled and documented, as this temperature is critical to prevent microbiological growth. If the temperature gets too high, off-flavors can result, but if it drops too low, bacteria may survive and spoil the product. Of course, weights of individual components of frozen foods are also extremely critical, as these are prescribed by federal regulations and each dinner must have the proper amount. So, in addition to weights, certain temperatures, certain quantities of thickening agents, and so on, must be controlled during the process to ensure that when the product arrives at the end of the processing line, it is completely satisfactory.

VII. FINISHED PRODUCT TESTING

Finished product testing varies again from chemical and microbiological testing to taste testing. At varying periods of time, products that have been labeled as containing certain quantities of nutrients must be tested to verify that the label statements are correct. These laboratory tests must be carefully documented and retained for several years to prove label compliance. Also, the finished product should be tested with the appropriate chemical tests to ensure that (1) all ingredients have been added, (2) proper processing has taken place, and (3) foreign materials have not found their way into the finished product. Microbiological testing must be included in the case of frozen foods and, of course, the incubation and testing of canned goods is necessary to prove that the cans have been sterilized and that the lot is safe for shipment. Frequently, some of the products are compared in taste testing with either control samples or with competitors' samples which have been sampled in the field and sent back to the food-processing unit. We must caution you that the age of the competitors' samples should be approximately the same as yours if the test is to be valid. Frequently, it is not possible to know the age of products purchased in the grocery store, but it is important not to test fresh product from your plant against product which may be several years old from competitors.

Shelf-life testing is usually done so that products may be removed from the field before they become unsatisfactory to the consumer. Accelerated shelf-life tests—usually at elevated temperatures—can be performed in a reasonably short time. These tests can provide good estimates of product life in years at room temperatures. The finished product is your last chance to assure that processing steps have been performed properly and that customer satisfaction and regulatory agency requirements have been met. It is essential that you have documented tests at this point to prove what the quality of the product was, including weights at the time it was manufactured and shipped to the field.

VIII. DISTRIBUTION CHAIN QUALITY

Various food-processing methods produce products of different shelf life, ranging from 2 days in the case of fresh bread to 4 or 5 years in the case of certain canned goods. Every product must be looked at and tested in the field to make certain that products do not deteriorate to the point where they will be unsafe or even just unsatisfactory to the final consumer. Some food products are stored dry, some in the frozen state, some canned in tin or plastic pouches, and some are merely kept at room temperature and used within a relatively short period of time. It is important that the food processor understand the quality of the finished products and how this quality will change in the distribution chain. In dry storage warehouses in the south of the United States, for instance, temperatures of 125°F may be fairly common in the summertime. In northern areas in the wintertime, below-freezing temperatures can drastically change the texture of various canned products. The storage of products next to others that have strong odors can completely change the acceptability of your finished products. Food products are made for the consumer to use, and therefore the quality at that time is the most important factor, and the food processor must be an expert in his product until it is actually consumed in the home or institution.

IX. REGULATORY ASPECTS OF FOOD PROCESSING

Food products are carefully controlled not only by the federal government but by state and local regulatory agencies. Of course, safety is paramount, but proper weights, labeling, pricing, and so on, are also watched with increasing frequency in the marketplace. The quality control of food products requires that all laws and regulations be carefully studied before production. Prevention is the governing word, and it is important to abide by all laws and regulations because, in addition to the possibility of seizure and loss of the finished product, food manufacturers may be criminally liable for shipping misbranded, misprocessed materials on the open market.

After the food regulations have been determined, it is very important to test and document those tests to prove that your products did meet all regulations at the time of processing and shipping. As mentioned in Section VIII, the quality of food can change due to other factors after it leaves your control. Therefore, it is very important to prove that while a product was in your control, you took all reasonable precautions to manufacture, test, and report on the product's quality. Many food-processing companies, both large and small, use consultants who are familiar with all of the legal details involved in food processing. Also, trade associations, such as the National Food Processors Association, may be the only way that small food processors can keep up with constantly changing food laws. Some of the state and local laws may conflict with federal laws, and these conflicts should be studied *before* food products are produced.

X. QUALITY IMPROVEMENT IN FOOD PLANTS

During the last few years, a program called "quality improvement" has been used in some food-processing plants to involve all of the plant personnel in quality assurance. This program has turned out to be a very efficient system for preventing problems from affecting product quality. Programs have been developed for all sizes of food-processing plants and involve everyone from office worker, truck driver, process worker, and sanitation personnel in producing uniform, high-quality food products. Additionally, these systems have proved to be an excellent way of reducing costs while producing and controlling high product quality. The cost of quality, which is a way of using present accounting systems to sort costs caused by errors, is a good way of measuring the improvement of a food-processing plant. Since products that are properly made from raw material receipt through the distribution chain have both uniform quality and lowest possible costs, the cost of quality is a good indicator of an efficient, productive food-processing company.

Basically, quality improvement involves organizing the individual manufacturing units into a team. The team concentrates on the most costly and repetitive problems and then organizes itself to solve those problems. The cost of quality is used to chart the progress of the program. Each member of the management team, from president and general manager down to each individual supervisor, is indoctrinated in the quality improvement concept. They are trained to accept the fact that almost all errors are caused by management, not the workers. After each supervisor understands this, the workers are asked to submit ideas that will help them or the company perform perfect work. The overall thrust of the program is to prevent errors from happening, rather than catching them after they occur. The individual worker's ideas are based on "nothing being too unimportant," and this simple approach usually produces ideas that are very good just because they are very simple. The progress in individual departments is charted so that all workers are kept aware of their progress. All progress is charted in dollars if at all possible, to emphasize how costly mistakes can be. Finally, after about a year in the typical program, the production unit tries to have as close to a perfect day as possible. During the preparation for the "zero-defects day," great strides are often made in eliminating apparent small problems so that they will not occur on ZD day. This examination of the entire manufacturing process ends up with a ZD day, which always results in the most efficient, most productive day in the history of the unit. This happens because everyone in the unit, from general manager to cleanup workers wants it to happen. After this day, the unit recycles its program to see if they can do even better the next year.

Many other parts of this program are not detailed here. Obviously, it is very important to recognize workers who strive for perfection every day, and the whole program is put on a positive tone by publicizing people who suggest ways to eliminate errors. Usually, the combination of a quality improvement program together with classical food quality control procedures as listed in the first nine sections of this chapter results in the most desirable quality control program for a food unit.

XI. CONCLUSION

The basic principles listed above apply to all types of food plants. Control is the guiding word, and prevention is the goal in every food unit. Plants that are not actively controlled should be considered actively out of control. Errors that are not prevented will probably happen over and over. It costs less to produce good-quality products the first time than to do it over again and again. Quality control, in addition to being an economic consideration, is a necessity from the regulatory point of view and from an honest professional desire to give the customer good, wholesome, safe products every time. Quality control, when it is done properly, does not cost anything, but actually returns money, goodwill, and safety to each company.

FURTHER READING

Crosby, P. B., *The Art of Getting Your Own Sweet Way*, McGraw-Hill, New York, 1975.

Crosby, P. B., *Quality Is Free*, McGraw-Hill, New York, 1979.

Murray, B. A., *"Balanced Quality Control,"* Food Industries Quality Control European Symposium, Madrid, 1973.

Official Methods of Analysis of the Association of Official Analytical Chemists, 12th ed., 1975.

Laboratory Manual for Food Canners and Processors, Vols. 1 and 2, National Canners Association, AVI, Westport, Conn., 1968.

Amerine, M., R. Pangborn, and E. B. Roessier, *Principles of Sensory Evaluation of Food*, Academic Press, New York, 1965.

Kramer and Twigg, *Fundamentals of Quality Control for the Food Industry*, Vols. 1 and 2, AVI, Westport, Conn., 1970.

Puri, S. C., D. Ennis, K. Mullen, *Statistical Quality Control for Food and Agricultural Scientists*, G. K. Hall, Boston, 1979.

A Complete Course in Canning, The Canning Trade, Inc., 1975.

Waste Measurement, Waste Management Guidelines; ITT-CBC Quality Department, 1976.

Incoming Material Inspection Program, ITT-CBC Quality Department, 1977.

Crosby, P. B., *Cutting the Cost of Quality*, ©Industrial Education Institute, Farnsworth, Boston, 1967.

Fourteen Steps to Quality Improvement (Quality Improvement Through Defect Prevention), ITT-CBC Quality Department, 1974.

Allan and Murray, "Identifying and Removing Causes of Error in a Food Manufacturing Plant," *Food Technology*, 1972.

Allan and Murray, "Identifying and Removing Causes of Error in a Food Manufacturing Plant," *Food Technology*, 1973.

Murray, B. A., *Making Quality Improvement Work*, Quality Improvement, Inc., 1980.

APPENDIX

MIL-STD-105D
29 April 1963

SUPERSEDING
MIL-STD-105C
18 July 1961

MILITARY STANDARD

SAMPLING PROCEDURES AND TABLES
FOR INSPECTION BY ATTRIBUTES

MIL-STD-105D
29 APRIL 1963

DEPARTMENT OF DEFENSE
Washington 25, D.C.

SAMPLING PROCEDURES AND TABLES FOR INSPECTION BY ATTRIBUTES

MIL-STD-105D   29 APRIL 1963

1. This standard has been approved by the Department of Defense and
is mandatory for use by the Departments of the Army, the Navy, the Air
Force and the Defense Supply Agency. This revision supersedes MIL-STD-
105C, dated 18 July 1961.

2. This publication provides sampling procedures and reference tables
for use in planning and conducting inspection by attributes. This
publication was developed by a working group representing the military
services of Canada, the United Kingdom and the United States of America
with the assistance and cooperation of American and European
organizations for quality control. The international designation of this
document is ABC-STD-105. When revision or cancellation of this standard
is proposed, the departmental custodians will inform their respective
Departmental Standardization Office so that appropriate action may be
taken respecting the international agreement concerned.

3. The U.S. Army Munitions Command is designated as preparing
activity for this standard. Recommended corrections, additions, or
deletions should be addressed to the Commanding Officer, U.S. Army CBR
Engineering Office, Attn: SMUCE-ED-S, Army Chemical Center, Maryland.

CONTENTS

SAMPLING PROCEDURES AND TABLES
FOR INSPECTION BY ATTRIBUTES

1. SCOPE

1.1 PURPOSE. This publication establishes sampling plans and procedures for inspection by attributes. When specified by the responsible authority, this publication shall be referenced in the specification, contract, inspection instructions, or other documents and the provisions set forth herein shall govern. The "responsible authority" shall be designated in one of the above documents.

1.2 APPLICATION. Sampling plans designated in this publication are applicable, but not limited, to inspection of the following:

a. End items.

b. Components and raw materials.

c. Operations.

d. Materials in process.

e. Supplies in storage.

g. Data or records.

h. Administrative procedures.

These plans are intended primarily to be used for a continuing series of lots or batches. The plans may also be used for the inspection of isolated lots or batches, but, in this latter case, the user is cautioned to consult the operating characteristic curves to find a plan which will yield the desired protection (see 11.6).

1.3 INSPECTION. Inspection is the process of measuring, examining, testing, or otherwise comparing the unit of product (see 1.5) with the requirements.

1.4 INSPECTION BY ATTRIBUTES. Inspection by attributes is inspection whereby either the unit of product is classified simply as defective or nondefective, or the number of defects in the unit of product is counted, with respect to a given requirement or set of requirements.

1.5 UNIT OF PRODUCT. The unit of product is the thing inspected in order to determine its classification as defective or nondefective or to count the number of defects. It may be a single article, a pair, a set, a length, an area, an operation, a volume, a component of an end product, or the end product itself. The unit of product may or may not be the same as the unit of purchase, supply, production, or shipment.

2. CLASSIFICATION OF DEFECTS AND DEFECTIVES

2.1 METHOD OF CLASSIFYING DEFECTS. A classification of defects is the enumeration of possible defects of the unit of product classified according to their seriousness. A defect is any nonconformance of the unit of product with specified requirements. Defects will normally be grouped into one or more of the following classes; however, defects may be grouped into other classes, or into subclasses within these classes.

2.1.1 CRITICAL DEFECT. A critical defect is a defect that judgment and experience indicate is likely to result in hazardous or unsafe conditions for individuals using, maintaining, or depending upon the product; or a defect that judgment and experience indicate is likely to prevent performance of the tactical function of a major end item such as a ship, aircraft, tank, missile or space vehicle. NOTE: For a special provision relating to critical defects, see 6.3.

2.1.2 MAJOR DEFECT. A major defect is a defect, other than critical, that is likely to result in failure, or to reduce materially the usability of the unit of product for its intended purpose.

2.1.3 MINOR DEFECT. A minor defect is a defect that is not likely to reduce materially the usability of the unit of product for its intended purpose, or is a departure from established standards having little bearing on the effective use or operation of the unit.

2.2 METHOD OF CLASSIFYING DEFECTIVES. A defective is a unit of product which contains one or more defects. Defectives will usually be classified as follows:

2.2.1 CRITICAL DEFECTIVE. A critical defective contains one or more critical defects and may also contain major and or minor defects. NOTE: For a special provision relating to critical defectives, see 6.3.

2.2.2 MAJOR DEFECTIVE. A major defective contains one or more major defects, and may also contain minor defects but contains no critical defect.

2.2.3 MINOR DEFECTIVE. A minor defective contains one or more minor defects but contains no critical or major defect.

3. PERCENT DEFECTIVE AND DEFECTS PER HUNDRED UNITS

3.1 EXPRESSION OF NONCONFORMANCE. The extent of nonconformance of product shall be expressed either in terms of percent defective or in terms of defects per hundred units.

3.2 PERCENT DEFECTIVE. The percent defective of any given quantity of units of product is one hundred times the number of defective units of product contained therein divided by the total number of units of product, i.e.:

$$\text{Percent defective} = \frac{\text{Number of defects}}{\text{Number of units inspected}} \times 100$$

3.3 DEFECTS PER HUNDRED UNITS. The number of defects per hundred units of any given quantity of units of product is one hundred times the number of defects contained therein (one or more defects being possible in any unit of product) divided by the total number of units of product, i.e.:

$$\text{Defects per hundred units} = \frac{\text{Number of defectives}}{\text{Number of units inspected}} \times 100$$

2

4. ACCEPTABLE QUALITY LEVEL (AQL)

4.1 USE. The AQL, together with the Sample Size Code Letter, is used for indexing the sampling plans provided herein.

4.2 DEFINITION. The AQL is the maximum percent defective (or the maximum number of defects per hundred units) that, for purposes of sampling inspection, can be considered satisfactory as a process average (see 11.2).

4.3 NOTE ON THE MEANING OF AQL. When a consumer designates some specific value of AQL for a certain defect or group of defects, he indicates to the supplier that his (the consumer's) acceptance sampling plan will accept the great majority of the lots or batches that the supplier submits, provided the process average level of percent defective (or defects per hundred units) in these lots or batches be no greater than the designated value of AQL. Thus, the AQL is a designated value of percent defective (or defects per hundred units) that the consumer indicates will be accepted most of the time by the acceptance sampling procedure to be used. The sampling plans provided herein are so arranged that the probability of acceptance at the designated AQL value depends upon the sample size, being generally higher for large samples than for small ones, for a given AQL. The AQL alone does not describe the protection to the consumer for individual lots or batches but more directly relates to what might be expected from a series of lots or batches, provided the steps indicated in this publication are taken. It is necessary to refer to the operating characteristic curve of the plan, to determine what protection the consumer will have.

4.4 LIMITATION. The designation of an AQL shall not imply that the supplier has the right to supply knowingly any defective unit of product.

4.5 SPECIFYING AQLs. The AQL to be used will be designated in the contract or by the responsible authority. Different AQLs may be designated for groups of defects considered collectively, or for individual defects. An AQL for a group of defects may be designated in addition to AQLs for individual defects, or subgroups, within that group. AQL values of 10.0 or less may be expressed either in percent defective or in defects per hundred units; those over 10.0 shall be expressed in defects per hundred units only.

4.6 PREFERRED AQLs. The values of AQL given in these tables are known as preferred AQLs. If, for any product, an AQL be designated other than a preferred AQL, these tables are not applicable.

5. SUBMISSION OF PRODUCT

5.1 LOT OR BATCH. The term lot or batch shall mean "inspection lot" or "inspection batch," i.e., a collection of units of product from which a sample is to be drawn and inspected to determine conformance with the acceptability criteria, and may differ from a collection of units designated as a lot or batch for other purposes (e.g., production, shipment, etc.).

5.2 FORMATION OF LOTS OR BATCHES. The product shall be assembled into identifiable lots, sublots, batches, or in such other manner as may be prescribed (see 5.4). Each lot or batch shall, as far as is practicable, consist of

5.   SUBMISSION OF PRODUCT (continued)

units of product of a single type, grade, class, size, and composition, manufactured under essentially the same conditions, and at essentially the same time.

5.3 LOT OR BATCH SIZE.
The lot or batch size is the number of units of product in a lot or batch.

5.4 PRESENTATION OF LOTS OR BATCHES.
The formation of the lots or batches, lot or batch size, and the manner in which each lot or batch is to be presented and identified by the supplier shall be designated or approved by the responsible authority. As necessary, the supplier shall provide adequate and suitable storage space for each lot or batch, equipment needed for proper identification and presentation, and personnel for all handling of product required for drawing of samples.

6.   ACCEPTANCE AND REJECTION

6.1 ACCEPTABILITY OF LOTS OR BATCHES.
Acceptability of a lot or batch will be determined by the use of a sampling plan or plans associated with the designated AQL or AQLs.

6.2 DEFECTIVE UNITS.
The right is reserved to reject any unit of product found defective during inspection whether that unit of product forms part of a sample or not, and whether the lot or batch as a whole is accepted or rejected. Rejected units may be repaired or corrected and resubmitted for inspection with the approval of, and in the manner specified by, the responsible authority.

6.3 SPECIAL RESERVATION FOR CRITICAL DEFECTS.
The supplier may be required at the discretion of the responsible authority to inspect every unit of the lot or batch for critical defects. The right is reserved to inspect every unit submitted by the supplier for critical defects, and to reject the lot or batch immediately, when a critical defect is found. The right is reserved also to sample, for critical defects, every lot or batch submitted by the supplier and to reject any lot or batch if a sample drawn therefrom is found to contain one or more critical defects.

6.4 RESUBMITTED LOTS OR BATCHES.
Lots or batches found unacceptable shall be resubmitted for reinspection only after all units are re-examined or retested and all defective units are removed or defects corrected. The responsible authority shall determine whether normal or tightened inspection shall be used, and whether reinspection shall include all types or classes of defects or for the particular types or classes of defects which caused initial rejection.

7.   DRAWING OF SAMPLES

7.1 SAMPLE.
A sample consists of one or more units of product drawn from a lot or batch, the units of the sample being selected at random without regard to their quality. The number of units of product in the sample is the sample size.

7.2 REPRESENTATIVE SAMPLING.
When appropriate, the number of units in the sample shall be selected in proportion to the size of sublots or subbatches, or parts of the lot or batch, identified by some rational criterion.

7. DRAWING OF SAMPLES (continued)

When representative sampling is used, the units from each part of the lot or batch shall be selected at random.

7.3 TIME OF SAMPLING. Samples may be drawn after all the units comprising the lot or batch have been assembled, or samples may be drawn during assembly of the lot or batch.

7.4 DOUBLE OR MULTIPLE SAMPLING. When double or multiple sampling is to be used, each sample shall be selected over the entire lot or batch.

8. NORMAL, TIGHTENED AND REDUCED INSPECTION

8.1 INITIATION OF INSPECTION. Normal inspection will be used at the start of inspection unless otherwise directed by the responsible authority.

8.2 CONTINUATION OF INSPECTION. Normal, tightened or reduced inspection shall continue unchanged for each class of defects or defectives on successive lots or batches except where the switching procedures given below require change. The switching procedures given below require a change. The switching procedures shall be applied to each class of defects or defectives independently.

8.3 SWITCHING PROCEDURES.

8.3.1 NORMAL TO TIGHTENED. When normal inspection is in effect, tightened inspection shall be instituted when 2 out of 5 consecutive lots or batches have been rejected on original inspection (i.e., ignoring resubmitted lots or batches for this procedure).

8.3.2 TIGHTENED TO NORMAL. When tightened inspection is in effect, normal inspection shall be instituted when 5 consecutive lots or batches have been considered acceptable on original inspection.

8.3.3 NORMAL TO REDUCED. When normal inspection is in effect, reduced inspection shall be instituted providing that all of the following conditions are satisfied:

a. The preceding 10 lots or batches (or more, as indicated by the note to Table VIII) have been on normal inspection and none has been rejected on original inspection; and

b. The total number of defectives (or defects) in the samples from the preceding 10 lots or batches (or such other number as was used for condition "a" above) is equal to or less than the applicable number given in Table VIII. If double or multiple sampling is in use, all samples inspected should be included, not "first" samples only; and

c. Production is at a steady rate; and

d. Reduced inspection is considered desirable by the responsible authority.

8.3.4 REDUCED TO NORMAL. When reduced inspection is in effect, normal inspection shall be instituted if any of the following occur on original inspection:

a. A lot or batch is rejected; or

b. A lot or batch is considered acceptable under the procedures of 10.1.4; or

c. Production becomes irregular or delayed; or

d. Other conditions warrant that normal inspection shall be instituted.

8.4 DISCONTINUATION OF INSPECTION. In the event that 10 consecutive lots or batches remain on tightened inspection (or such other number as may be designated by the responsible authority), inspection under the provisions of this document should be discontinued pending action to improve the quality of submitted material.

9. SAMPLING PLANS

9.1 SAMPLING PLAN. A sampling plan indicates the number of units of product from each lot or batch which are to be inspected (sample size or series of sample sizes) and the criteria for determining the acceptability of the lot or batch (acceptance and rejection numbers).

9.2 INSPECTION LEVEL. The inspection level determines the relationship between the lot or batch size and the sample size. The inspection level to be used for any particular requirement will be prescribed by the responsible authority. Three inspection levels: I, II, and III, are given in Table I for general use. Unless otherwise specified, Inspection Level II will be used. However, Inspection Level I may be specified when less discrimination is needed, or Level III may be specified for greater discrimination. Four additional special levels: S-1, S-2, S-3 and S-4, are given in the same table and may be used where relatively small sample sizes are necessary and large sampling risks can or must be tolerated.

NOTE: In the designation of inspection levels S-1 to S-4, care must be exercised to avoid AQLs inconsistent with these inspection levels.

9.3 CODE LETTERS. Sample sizes are designated by code letters. Table I shall be used to find the applicable code letter for the particular lot or batch size and the prescribed inspection level.

9.4 OBTAINING SAMPLING PLAN. The AQL and the code letter shall be used to obtain the sampling plan from Tables II, III or IV. When no sampling plan is available for a given combination of AQL and code letter, the tables direct the user to a different letter. The sample size to be used is given by the new code letter not by the original letter. If this procedure leads to different sample sizes for different classes of defects, the code letter corresponding to the largest sample size derived may be used for all classes of defects when designated or approved by the responsible authority. As an alternative to a single sampling plan with an acceptance number of 0, the plan with an acceptance number of 1 with its correspondingly larger sample size for a designated AQL (where available), may be used when designated or approved by the responsible authority.

9.5 TYPES OF SAMPLING PLANS. Three types of sampling plans: Single, Double and Multiple, are given in Tables II, III and IV, respectively. When several types of plans are available for a given AQL and code letter, any one may be used. A decision as to type of plan, either single, double, or multiple, when available for a given AQL and code letter, will usually be based upon the comparison between the administrative difficulty and the average sample sizes of the available plans. The average sample size of multiple plans is less than for double (except in the case corresponding to single acceptance number 1) and both of these are always less than a single sample size. Usually the administrative difficulty for single sampling and the cost per unit of the sample are less than for double or multiple.

10. DETERMINATION OF ACCEPTABILITY

10.1 PERCENT DEFECTIVE INSPECTION.
To determine acceptability of a lot or batch under percent defective inspection, the applicable sampling plan shall be used in accordance with 10.1.1, 10.1.2, 10.1.3, 10.1.4, and 10.1.5.

10.1.1 SINGLE SAMPLING PLAN.
The number of sample units inspected shall be equal to the sample size given by the plan. If the number of defectives found in the sample is equal to or less than the acceptance number, the lot or batch shall be considered acceptable. If the number of defectives is equal to or greater than the rejection number, the lot or batch shall be rejected.

10.1.2 DOUBLE SAMPLING PLAN.
The number of sample units inspected shall be equal to the first sample size given by the plan. If the number of defectives found in the first sample is equal to or less than the first acceptance number, the lot or batch shall be considered acceptable. If the number of defectives found in the first sample is equal to or greater than the first rejection number, the lot or batch shall be rejected. If the number of defectives found in the first sample is between the first acceptance and rejection numbers, a second sample of the size given by the plan shall be inspected. The number of defectives found in the first and second samples shall be accumulated. If the cumulative number of defectives is equal to or less than the second acceptance number, the lot or batch shall be considered acceptable. If the cumulative number of defectives is equal to or greater than the second rejection number, the lot or batch shall be rejected.

10.1.3 MULTIPLE SAMPLE PLAN.
Under multiple sampling, the procedure shall be similar to that specified in 10.1.2, except that the number of successive samples required to reach a decision may be more than two.

10.1.4 SPECIAL PROCEDURE FOR REDUCED INSPECTION.
Under reduced inspection, the sampling procedure may terminate without either acceptance or rejection criteria having been met. In these circumstances, the lot or batch will be considered acceptable, but normal inspection will be reinstated starting with the next lot or batch (see 8.3.4 (b)).

10.2 DEFECTS PER HUNDRED UNITS INSPECTION.
To determine the acceptability of a lot or batch under Defects per Hundred Units inspection, the procedure specified for Percent Defective inspection above shall be used, except that the word "defects" shall be substituted for "defectives."

11. SUPPLEMENTARY INFORMATION

11.1 OPERATING CHARACTERISTIC CURVES.
The operating characteristic curves for normal inspection, shown in Table X (pages 30-62), indicate the percentage of lots or batches which may be expected to be accepted under the various sampling plans for a given process quality. The curves shown are for single sampling; curves for double and multiple sampling are matched as closely as practicable. The O.C. curves shown for AQLs greater than 10.0 are based on the Poisson distribution and are applicable for defects per hundred units inspection; those for AQLs of 10.0 or less and sample sizes of 80 or less are based on the binomial distribution and are applicable for percent defective inspection; those for

11. SUPPLEMENTARY INFORMATION (continued)

AQLs of 10.0 or less and sample sizes larger than 80 are based on the Poisson distribution and are applicable either for defects per hundred units inspection, or for percent defective inspection (the Poisson distribution being an adequate approximation to the binomial distribution under these conditions). Tabulated values, corresponding to selected values of probabilities of acceptance (P_a, in percent) are given for each of the curves shown, and, in addition, for tightened inspection, and for defects per hundred units for AQLs of 10.0 or less and sample sizes of 80 or less.

11.2 PROCESS AVERAGE. The process average is the average percent defective or average number of defects per hundred units (whichever is applicable) of product submitted by the supplier for original inspection. Original inspection is the first inspection of a particular quantity of product as distinguished from the inspection of product which has been resubmitted after prior rejection.

11.3 AVERAGE OUTGOING QUALITY (AOQ). The AOQ is the average quality of outgoing product including all accepted lots or batches, plus all rejected lots or batches after the rejected lots or batches have been effectively 100 percent inspected and all defectives replaced by nondefectives.

11.4 AVERAGE OUTGOING QUALITY LIMIT (AOQL). The AOQL is the maximum of the AOQs for all possible incoming qualities for a given acceptance sampling plan. AOQL values are given in Table V-A for each of the single sampling plans for normal inspection and in Table V-B for each of the single sampling plans for tightened inspection.

11.5 AVERAGE SAMPLE SIZE CURVES. Average sample size curves for double and multiple sampling are in Table IX. These show the average sample sizes which may be expected to occur under the various sampling plans for a given process quality. The curves assume no curtailment of inspection and are approximate to the extent that they are based upon the Poisson distribution, and that the sample sizes for double and multiple sampling are assumed to be 0.631n and 0.25n respectively, where n is the equivalent single sample size.

11.6 LIMITING QUALITY PROTECTION. The sampling plans and associated procedures given in this publication were designed for use where the units of product are produced in a continuing series of lots or batches over a period of time. However, if the lot or batch is of an isolated nature, it is desirable to limit the selection of sampling plans to those, associated with a designated AQL value, that provide not less than a specified limiting quality protection. Sampling plans for this purpose can be selected by choosing a Limiting Quality (LQ) and a consumer's risk to be associated with it. Tables VI and VII give values of LQ for the commonly used consumer's risks of 10 percent and 5 percent respectively. If a different value of consumer's risk is required, the O.C. curves and their tabulated values may be used. The concept of LQ may also be useful in specifying the AQL and Inspection Levels for a series of lots or batches, thus fixing minimum sample size where there is some reason for avoiding (with more than a given consumer's risk) more than a limiting proportion of defectives (or defects) in any single lot or batch.

TABLE I — Sample size code letters

(See 9.2 and 9.3)

Lot or batch size	Special inspection levels				General inspection levels		
	S-1	S-2	S-3	S-4	I	II	III
2 to 8	A	A	A	A	A	A	B
9 to 15	A	A	A	A	A	B	C
16 to 25	A	A	B	B	B	C	D
26 to 50	A	B	B	C	C	D	E
51 to 90	B	B	C	C	C	E	F
91 to 150	B	B	C	D	D	F	G
151 to 280	B	C	D	E	E	G	H
281 to 500	B	C	D	E	F	H	J
501 to 1200	C	C	E	F	G	J	K
1201 to 3200	C	D	E	G	H	K	L
3201 to 10000	C	D	F	G	J	L	M
10001 to 35000	C	D	F	H	K	M	N
35001 to 150000	D	E	G	J	L	N	P
150001 to 500000	D	E	G	J	M	P	Q
500001 and over	D	E	H	K	N	Q	R

Code Letter

9

TABLE II-A — Single sampling plans for normal inspection (Master table)

(See 9.4 and 9.5)

Acceptable Quality Levels (normal inspection)

Sample size code letter	Sample size	0.010		0.015		0.025		0.040		0.065		0.10		0.15		0.25		0.40		0.65		1.0		1.5		2.5		4.0		6.5		10		15		25		40		65		100		150	
		Ac	Re	Ac	Re	Ac	Re	Ac	Re	Ac	Re	Ac	Re	Ac	Re	Ac	Re	Ac	Re	Ac	Re	Ac	Re	Ac	Re	Ac	Re	Ac	Re	Ac	Re	Ac	Re	Ac	Re	Ac	Re	Ac	Re	Ac	Re	Ac	Re	Ac	Re
A	2	↓		↓		↓		↓		↓		↓		↓		↓		↓		↓		↓		↓		↓		↓		↓		↓		0	1	1	2	2	3	3	4	5	6	7	8
B	3	↓		↓		↓		↓		↓		↓		↓		↓		↓		↓		↓		↓		↓		↓		↓		0	1	1	2	2	3	3	4	5	6	7	8	10	11
C	5	↓		↓		↓		↓		↓		↓		↓		↓		↓		↓		↓		↓		↓		↓		0	1	1	2	2	3	3	4	5	6	7	8	10	11	14	15
D	8	↓		↓		↓		↓		↓		↓		↓		↓		↓		↓		↓		↓		↓		0	1	1	2	2	3	3	4	5	6	7	8	10	11	14	15	21	22
E	13	↓		↓		↓		↓		↓		↓		↓		↓		↓		↓		↓		↓		0	1	1	2	2	3	3	4	5	6	7	8	10	11	14	15	21	22	30	31
F	20	↓		↓		↓		↓		↓		↓		↓		↓		↓		↓		↓		0	1	1	2	2	3	3	4	5	6	7	8	10	11	14	15	21	22	↑		↑	
G	32	↓		↓		↓		↓		↓		↓		↓		↓		↓		↓		0	1	1	2	2	3	3	4	5	6	7	8	10	11	14	15	21	22	↑		↑		↑	
H	50	↓		↓		↓		↓		↓		↓		↓		↓		↓		0	1	1	2	2	3	3	4	5	6	7	8	10	11	14	15	21	22	↑		↑		↑		↑	
J	80	↓		↓		↓		↓		↓		↓		↓		↓		0	1	1	2	2	3	3	4	5	6	7	8	10	11	14	15	21	22	↑		↑		↑		↑		↑	
K	125	↓		↓		↓		↓		↓		↓		↓		0	1	1	2	2	3	3	4	5	6	7	8	10	11	14	15	21	22	↑		↑		↑		↑		↑		↑	
L	200	↓		↓		↓		↓		↓		↓		0	1	1	2	2	3	3	4	5	6	7	8	10	11	14	15	21	22	↑		↑		↑		↑		↑		↑		↑	
M	315	↓		↓		↓		↓		↓		0	1	1	2	2	3	3	4	5	6	7	8	10	11	14	15	21	22	↑		↑		↑		↑		↑		↑		↑		↑	
N	500	↓		↓		↓		↓		0	1	1	2	2	3	3	4	5	6	7	8	10	11	14	15	21	22	↑		↑		↑		↑		↑		↑		↑		↑		↑	
P	800	↓		↓		↓		0	1	1	2	2	3	3	4	5	6	7	8	10	11	14	15	21	22	↑		↑		↑		↑		↑		↑		↑		↑		↑		↑	
Q	1250	↓		↓		0	1	1	2	2	3	3	4	5	6	7	8	10	11	14	15	21	22	↑		↑		↑		↑		↑		↑		↑		↑		↑		↑		↑	
R	2000	↓		0	1	1	2	2	3	3	4	5	6	7	8	10	11	14	15	21	22	↑		↑		↑		↑		↑		↑		↑		↑		↑		↑		↑		↑	

↓ = Use first sampling plan below arrow. If sample size equals, or exceeds, lot or batch size, do 100 percent inspection.
↑ = Use first sampling plan above arrow
Ac = Acceptance number
Re = Rejection number

SINGLE NORMAL

10

TABLE II-B — Single sampling plans for tightened inspection (Master table)

(See 9.4 and 9.5)

Acceptable Quality Levels (tightened inspection)

Each AQL column gives **Ac** (acceptance number) and **Re** (rejection number). ↓ = Use first sampling plan below arrow. ↑ = Use first sampling plan above arrow.

Sample size code letter	Sample size	0.010	0.015	0.025	0.040	0.065	0.10	0.15	0.25	0.40	0.65	1.0	1.5	2.5	4.0	6.5	10	15	25	40	65	100	150
A	2	↓	↓	↓	↓	↓	↓	↓	↓	↓	↓	↓	↓	↓	↓	↓	↓	↓	0 1	1 2	2 3	3 4	5 6
B	3	↓	↓	↓	↓	↓	↓	↓	↓	↓	↓	↓	↓	↓	↓	↓	↓	0 1	1 2	2 3	3 4	5 6	8 9
C	5	↓	↓	↓	↓	↓	↓	↓	↓	↓	↓	↓	↓	↓	↓	↓	0 1	1 2	2 3	3 4	5 6	8 9	12 13
D	8	↓	↓	↓	↓	↓	↓	↓	↓	↓	↓	↓	↓	↓	↓	0 1	1 2	2 3	3 4	5 6	8 9	12 13	18 19
E	13	↓	↓	↓	↓	↓	↓	↓	↓	↓	↓	↓	↓	↓	0 1	1 2	2 3	3 4	5 6	8 9	12 13	18 19	27 28
F	20	↓	↓	↓	↓	↓	↓	↓	↓	↓	↓	↓	↓	0 1	1 2	2 3	3 4	5 6	8 9	12 13	18 19	27 28	↑
G	32	↓	↓	↓	↓	↓	↓	↓	↓	↓	↓	↓	0 1	1 2	2 3	3 4	5 6	8 9	12 13	18 19	27 28	↑	↑
H	50	↓	↓	↓	↓	↓	↓	↓	↓	↓	↓	0 1	1 2	2 3	3 4	5 6	8 9	12 13	18 19	27 28	↑	↑	↑
J	80	↓	↓	↓	↓	↓	↓	↓	↓	↓	0 1	1 2	2 3	3 4	5 6	8 9	12 13	18 19	27 28	↑	↑	↑	↑
K	125	↓	↓	↓	↓	↓	↓	↓	↓	0 1	1 2	2 3	3 4	5 6	8 9	12 13	18 19	27 28	↑	↑	↑	↑	↑
L	200	↓	↓	↓	↓	↓	↓	↓	0 1	1 2	2 3	3 4	5 6	8 9	12 13	18 19	27 28	↑	↑	↑	↑	↑	↑
M	315	↓	↓	↓	↓	↓	↓	0 1	1 2	2 3	3 4	5 6	8 9	12 13	18 19	27 28	↑	↑	↑	↑	↑	↑	↑
N	500	↓	↓	↓	↓	↓	0 1	1 2	2 3	3 4	5 6	8 9	12 13	18 19	27 28	↑	↑	↑	↑	↑	↑	↑	↑
P	800	↓	↓	↓	↓	0 1	1 2	2 3	3 4	5 6	8 9	12 13	18 19	27 28	↑	↑	↑	↑	↑	↑	↑	↑	↑
Q	1250	↓	↓	↓	0 1	1 2	2 3	3 4	5 6	8 9	12 13	18 19	27 28	↑	↑	↑	↑	↑	↑	↑	↑	↑	↑
R	2000	↓	↓	0 1	1 2	2 3	3 4	5 6	8 9	12 13	18 19	27 28	↑	↑	↑	↑	↑	↑	↑	↑	↑	↑	↑
S	3150	↓	0 1	1 2	2 3	3 4	5 6	8 9	12 13	18 19	27 28	↑	↑	↑	↑	↑	↑	↑	↑	↑	↑	↑	↑

↓ = Use first sampling plan below arrow. If sample size equals or exceeds lot or batch size, do 100 percent inspection.

↓ = Use first sampling plan below arrow.

↑ = Use first sampling plan above arrow.

Ac = Acceptance number

Re = Rejection number

SINGLE TIGHTENED

TABLE II-C — Single sampling plans for reduced inspection (Master table)

(See 9.4 and 9.5)

Acceptable Quality Levels (reduced inspection)†

Sample size code letter	Sample size	0.010		0.015		0.025		0.040		0.065		0.10		0.15		0.25		0.40		0.65		1.0		1.5		2.5		4.0		6.5		10		15		25		40		65		100		150	
		Ac	Re	Ac	Re	Ac	Re	Ac	Re	Ac	Re	Ac	Re	Ac	Re	Ac	Re	Ac	Re	Ac	Re	Ac	Re	Ac	Re	Ac	Re	Ac	Re	Ac	Re	Ac	Re	Ac	Re	Ac	Re	Ac	Re	Ac	Re	Ac	Re
A	2	↓		↓		↓		↓		↓		↓		↓		↓		↓		↓		↓		↓		↓		↓		↓		0	1	0	2	1	2	2	3	3	4	5	6	7	8
B	2	↓		↓		↓		↓		↓		↓		↓		↓		↓		↓		↓		↓		↓		↓		0	1	0	2	1	3	1	3	2	4	3	5	5	6	7	8
C	2	↓		↓		↓		↓		↓		↓		↓		↓		↓		↓		↓		↓		↓		0	1	0	2	1	3	1	4	1	4	2	5	3	6	5	8	7	10
D	3	↓		↓		↓		↓		↓		↓		↓		↓		↓		↓		↓		↓		0	1	0	2	1	3	1	4	2	5	2	5	3	6	5	8	7	10	10	13
E	5	↓		↓		↓		↓		↓		↓		↓		↓		↓		↓		↓		0	1	0	2	1	3	1	4	2	5	3	6	3	6	5	8	7	10	10	13	14	17
F	8	↓		↓		↓		↓		↓		↓		↓		↓		↓		↓		0	1	0	2	1	3	1	4	2	5	3	6	5	8	5	8	7	10	10	13	↑		↑	
G	13	↓		↓		↓		↓		↓		↓		↓		↓		↓		0	1	0	2	1	3	1	4	2	5	3	6	5	8	7	10	7	10	10	13	↑		↑		↑	
H	20	↓		↓		↓		↓		↓		↓		↓		↓		0	1	0	2	1	3	1	4	2	5	3	6	5	8	7	10	10	13	10	13	↑		↑		↑		↑	
J	32	↓		↓		↓		↓		↓		↓		↓		0	1	0	2	1	3	1	4	2	5	3	6	5	8	7	10	10	13	↑		↑		↑		↑		↑		↑	
K	50	↓		↓		↓		↓		↓		↓		0	1	0	2	1	3	1	4	2	5	3	6	5	8	7	10	10	13	↑		↑		↑		↑		↑		↑		↑	
L	80	↓		↓		↓		↓		↓		0	1	0	2	1	3	1	4	2	5	3	6	5	8	7	10	10	13	↑		↑		↑		↑		↑		↑		↑		↑	
M	125	↓		↓		↓		↓		0	1	0	2	1	3	1	4	2	5	3	6	5	8	7	10	10	13	↑		↑		↑		↑		↑		↑		↑		↑		↑	
N	200	↓		↓		↓		0	1	0	2	1	3	1	4	2	5	3	6	5	8	7	10	10	13	↑		↑		↑		↑		↑		↑		↑		↑		↑		↑	
P	315	↓		↓		0	1	0	2	1	3	1	4	2	5	3	6	5	8	7	10	10	13	↑		↑		↑		↑		↑		↑		↑		↑		↑		↑		↑	
Q	500	↓		0	1	0	2	1	3	1	4	2	5	3	6	5	8	7	10	10	13	↑		↑		↑		↑		↑		↑		↑		↑		↑		↑		↑		↑	
R	800	0	1	0	2	1	3	1	4	2	5	3	6	5	8	7	10	10	13	↑		↑		↑		↑		↑		↑		↑		↑		↑		↑		↑		↑		↑	

↓ = Use first sampling plan below arrow. If sample size equals or exceeds lot or batch size, do 100 percent inspection.

↑ = Use first sampling plan above.

Ac = Acceptance number

Re = Rejection number

† = If the acceptance number has been exceeded, but the rejection number has not been reached, accept the lot, but reinstate normal inspection (see 10.1.4).

SINGLE REDUCED

12

TABLE III-A — Double sampling plans for normal inspection (Master table)

(See 9.4 and 9.5)

Acceptable Quality Levels (normal inspection)

*In each Acceptable Quality Level cell below, the two numbers shown are "Ac Re" (Acceptance number / Rejection number). ↓ = Use first sampling plan below arrow. ↑ = Use first sampling plan above arrow. * = Use corresponding single sampling plan.*

Sample size code letter	Smpl	Sample size	Cumulative sample size	0.010	0.015	0.025	0.040	0.065	0.10	0.15	0.25	0.40	0.65	1.0	1.5	2.5	4.0	6.5	10	15	25	40	65	100	150
A				↓	↓	↓	↓	↓	↓	↓	↓	↓	↓	↓	↓	↓	↓	↓	↓	*	↓	↓	↓	↓	↓
B	1st	2	2	↓	↓	↓	↓	↓	↓	↓	↓	↓	↓	↓	↓	↓	↓	↓	*	0 2	0 3	1 4	2 5	3 7	5 9
	2nd	2	4	↓	↓	↓	↓	↓	↓	↓	↓	↓	↓	↓	↓	↓	↓	↓	*	1 2	3 4	4 5	6 7	8 9	12 13
C	1st	3	3	↓	↓	↓	↓	↓	↓	↓	↓	↓	↓	↓	↓	↓	↓	*	0 2	0 3	1 4	2 5	3 7	5 9	7 11
	2nd	3	6	↓	↓	↓	↓	↓	↓	↓	↓	↓	↓	↓	↓	↓	↓	*	1 2	3 4	4 5	6 7	8 9	12 13	18 19
D	1st	5	5	↓	↓	↓	↓	↓	↓	↓	↓	↓	↓	↓	↓	↓	*	0 2	0 3	1 4	2 5	3 7	5 9	7 11	11 16
	2nd	5	10	↓	↓	↓	↓	↓	↓	↓	↓	↓	↓	↓	↓	↓	*	1 2	3 4	4 5	6 7	8 9	12 13	18 19	26 27
E	1st	8	8	↓	↓	↓	↓	↓	↓	↓	↓	↓	↓	↓	↓	*	0 2	0 3	1 4	2 5	3 7	5 9	7 11	11 16	17 22
	2nd	8	16	↓	↓	↓	↓	↓	↓	↓	↓	↓	↓	↓	↓	*	1 2	3 4	4 5	6 7	8 9	12 13	18 19	26 27	37 38
F	1st	13	13	↓	↓	↓	↓	↓	↓	↓	↓	↓	↓	↓	*	0 2	0 3	1 4	2 5	3 7	5 9	7 11	11 16	17 22	↑
	2nd	13	26	↓	↓	↓	↓	↓	↓	↓	↓	↓	↓	↓	*	1 2	3 4	4 5	6 7	8 9	12 13	18 19	26 27	37 38	↑
G	1st	20	20	↓	↓	↓	↓	↓	↓	↓	↓	↓	↓	*	0 2	0 3	1 4	2 5	3 7	5 9	7 11	11 16	17 22	↑	↑
	2nd	20	40	↓	↓	↓	↓	↓	↓	↓	↓	↓	↓	*	1 2	3 4	4 5	6 7	8 9	12 13	18 19	26 27	37 38	↑	↑
H	1st	32	32	↓	↓	↓	↓	↓	↓	↓	↓	↓	*	0 2	0 3	1 4	2 5	3 7	5 9	7 11	11 16	17 22	↑	↑	↑
	2nd	32	64	↓	↓	↓	↓	↓	↓	↓	↓	↓	*	1 2	3 4	4 5	6 7	8 9	12 13	18 19	26 27	37 38	↑	↑	↑
J	1st	50	50	↓	↓	↓	↓	↓	↓	↓	↓	*	0 2	0 3	1 4	2 5	3 7	5 9	7 11	11 16	17 22	↑	↑	↑	↑
	2nd	50	100	↓	↓	↓	↓	↓	↓	↓	↓	*	1 2	3 4	4 5	6 7	8 9	12 13	18 19	26 27	37 38	↑	↑	↑	↑
K	1st	80	80	↓	↓	↓	↓	↓	↓	↓	*	0 2	0 3	1 4	2 5	3 7	5 9	7 11	11 16	17 22	↑	↑	↑	↑	↑
	2nd	80	160	↓	↓	↓	↓	↓	↓	↓	*	1 2	3 4	4 5	6 7	8 9	12 13	18 19	26 27	37 38	↑	↑	↑	↑	↑
L	1st	125	125	↓	↓	↓	↓	↓	↓	*	0 2	0 3	1 4	2 5	3 7	5 9	7 11	11 16	17 22	↑	↑	↑	↑	↑	↑
	2nd	125	250	↓	↓	↓	↓	↓	↓	*	1 2	3 4	4 5	6 7	8 9	12 13	18 19	26 27	37 38	↑	↑	↑	↑	↑	↑
M	1st	200	200	↓	↓	↓	↓	↓	*	0 2	0 3	1 4	2 5	3 7	5 9	7 11	11 16	17 22	↑	↑	↑	↑	↑	↑	↑
	2nd	200	400	↓	↓	↓	↓	↓	*	1 2	3 4	4 5	6 7	8 9	12 13	18 19	26 27	37 38	↑	↑	↑	↑	↑	↑	↑
N	1st	315	315	↓	↓	↓	↓	*	0 2	0 3	1 4	2 5	3 7	5 9	7 11	11 16	17 22	↑	↑	↑	↑	↑	↑	↑	↑
	2nd	315	630	↓	↓	↓	↓	*	1 2	3 4	4 5	6 7	8 9	12 13	18 19	26 27	37 38	↑	↑	↑	↑	↑	↑	↑	↑
P	1st	500	500	↓	↓	↓	*	0 2	0 3	1 4	2 5	3 7	5 9	7 11	11 16	17 22	↑	↑	↑	↑	↑	↑	↑	↑	↑
	2nd	500	1000	↓	↓	↓	*	1 2	3 4	4 5	6 7	8 9	12 13	18 19	26 27	37 38	↑	↑	↑	↑	↑	↑	↑	↑	↑
Q	1st	800	800	↓	↓	*	0 2	0 3	1 4	2 5	3 7	5 9	7 11	11 16	17 22	↑	↑	↑	↑	↑	↑	↑	↑	↑	↑
	2nd	800	1600	↓	↓	*	1 2	3 4	4 5	6 7	8 9	12 13	18 19	26 27	37 38	↑	↑	↑	↑	↑	↑	↑	↑	↑	↑
R	1st	1250	1250	↓	*	0 2	0 3	1 4	2 5	3 7	5 9	7 11	11 16	17 22	↑	↑	↑	↑	↑	↑	↑	↑	↑	↑	↑
	2nd	1250	2500	↓	*	1 2	3 4	4 5	6 7	8 9	12 13	18 19	26 27	37 38	↑	↑	↑	↑	↑	↑	↑	↑	↑	↑	↑

↓ = Use first sampling plan below arrow. If sample size equals or exceeds lot or batch size, do 100 percent inspection.
↑ = Use first sampling plan above arrow.
Ac = Acceptance number
Re = Rejection number
* = Use corresponding single sampling plan (or alternatively, use double sampling plan below, where available).

DOUBLE NORMAL

TABLE III-B — Double sampling plans for tightened inspection (Master table)

(See 9.4 and 9.5)

Acceptable Quality Levels (tightened inspection)†

Each AQL cell below is given as "Ac Re" (Acceptance number / Rejection number). Cells shown blank contain directional arrows per the legend; ***** = use corresponding single sampling plan.

Code	Smpl	Sample size	Cumulative sample size	0.010	0.015	0.025	0.040	0.065	0.10	0.15	0.25	0.40	0.65	1.0	1.5	2.5	4.0	6.5	10	15	25	40	65	100	150
A	1st																				↑	*	*	*	*
	2nd																								
B	1st	2	2															*			0 2	0 3	1 4	2 5	3 7
	2nd	2	4																		1 2	3 4	4 5	6 7	11 12
C	1st	3	3														*			0 2	0 3	1 4	2 5	3 7	6 10
	2nd	3	6																	1 2	3 4	4 5	6 7	11 12	15 16
D	1st	5	5													*			0 2	0 3	1 4	2 5	3 7	6 10	9 14
	2nd	5	10																1 2	3 4	4 5	6 7	11 12	15 16	23 24
E	1st	8	8												*			0 2	0 3	1 4	2 5	3 7	6 10	9 14	15 20
	2nd	8	16															1 2	3 4	4 5	6 7	11 12	15 16	23 24	34 35
F	1st	13	13											*			0 2	0 3	1 4	2 5	3 7	6 10	9 14		
	2nd	13	26														1 2	3 4	4 5	6 7	11 12	15 16	23 24		
G	1st	20	20										*			0 2	0 3	1 4	2 5	3 7	6 10	9 14			
	2nd	20	40													1 2	3 4	4 5	6 7	11 12	15 16	23 24			
H	1st	32	32									*			0 2	0 3	1 4	2 5	3 7	6 10	9 14				
	2nd	32	64												1 2	3 4	4 5	6 7	11 12	15 16	23 24				
J	1st	50	50								*			0 2	0 3	1 4	2 5	3 7	6 10	9 14					
	2nd	50	100											1 2	3 4	4 5	6 7	11 12	15 16	23 24					
K	1st	80	80							*			0 2	0 3	1 4	2 5	3 7	6 10	9 14						
	2nd	80	160										1 2	3 4	4 5	6 7	11 12	15 16	23 24						
L	1st	125	125						*			0 2	0 3	1 4	2 5	3 7	6 10	9 14							
	2nd	125	250									1 2	3 4	4 5	6 7	11 12	15 16	23 24							
M	1st	200	200					*			0 2	0 3	1 4	2 5	3 7	6 10	9 14								
	2nd	200	400								1 2	3 4	4 5	6 7	11 12	15 16	23 24								
N	1st	315	315				*			0 2	0 3	1 4	2 5	3 7	6 10	9 14									
	2nd	315	630							1 2	3 4	4 5	6 7	11 12	15 16	23 24									
P	1st	500	500			*			0 2	0 3	1 4	2 5	3 7	6 10	9 14										
	2nd	500	1000						1 2	3 4	4 5	6 7	11 12	15 16	23 24										
Q	1st	800	800		*			0 2	0 3	1 4	2 5	3 7	6 10	9 14											
	2nd	800	1600					1 2	3 4	4 5	6 7	11 12	15 16	23 24											
R	1st	1250	1250	*			0 2	0 3	1 4	2 5	3 7	6 10	9 14												
	2nd	1250	2500				1 2	3 4	4 5	6 7	11 12	15 16	23 24												
S	1st	2000	2000			0 2																			
	2nd	2000	4000			1 2																			

↓ = Use first sampling plan below arrow. If sample size equals or exceeds lot or batch size, do 100 percent inspection.
↑ = Use first sampling plan above arrow.
* = Use corresponding single sampling plan (or alternatively, use double sampling plan below, where available).
Ac = Acceptance number
Re = Rejection number

DOUBLE TIGHTENED

TABLE III-C — Double sampling plans for reduced inspection (Master table)

(See 9.4 and 9.5)

Acceptable Quality Levels (reduced inspection)†

In the grid below, each Acceptable Quality Level (AQL) cell gives the acceptance/rejection pair "Ac Re" for the indicated sample. Cells outside the numeric band contain directional arrows (→ / ←) and asterisks (*) as described in the legend; these are left blank here. Each code letter has a first-sample (1st) and second-sample (2nd) row.

Code	Smpl	Sample size	Cumulative	0.010	0.015	0.025	0.040	0.065	0.10	0.15	0.25	0.40	0.65	1.0	1.5	2.5	4.0	6.5	10	15	25	40	65	100	150
A																									
B																										
C																										
D	1st	2	2															0 2	0 3	0 4	0 4	1 5	2 7	3 8	5 10
D	2nd	2	4															0 2	0 4	1 5	3 6	4 7	6 9	8 12	12 16
E	1st	3	3														0 2	0 3	0 4	0 4	1 5	2 7	3 8	5 10	7 12
E	2nd	3	6														0 2	0 4	1 5	3 6	4 7	6 9	8 12	12 16	18 22
F	1st	5	5													0 2	0 3	0 4	0 4	1 5	2 7	3 8	5 10	7 12	
F	2nd	5	10													0 2	0 4	1 5	3 6	4 7	6 9	8 12	12 16	18 22	
G	1st	8	8												0 2	0 3	0 4	0 4	1 5	2 7	3 8	5 10	7 12		
G	2nd	8	16												0 2	0 4	1 5	3 6	4 7	6 9	8 12	12 16	18 22		
H	1st	13	13											0 2	0 3	0 4	0 4	1 5	2 7	3 8	5 10	7 12			
H	2nd	13	26											0 2	0 4	1 5	3 6	4 7	6 9	8 12	12 16	18 22			
J	1st	20	20										0 2	0 3	0 4	0 4	1 5	2 7	3 8	5 10	7 12				
J	2nd	20	40										0 2	0 4	1 5	3 6	4 7	6 9	8 12	12 16	18 22				
K	1st	32	32									0 2	0 3	0 4	0 4	1 5	2 7	3 8	5 10	7 12					
K	2nd	32	64									0 2	0 4	1 5	3 6	4 7	6 9	8 12	12 16	18 22					
L	1st	50	50								0 2	0 3	0 4	0 4	1 5	2 7	3 8	5 10	7 12						
L	2nd	50	100								0 2	0 4	1 5	3 6	4 7	6 9	8 12	12 16	18 22						
M	1st	80	80							0 2	0 3	0 4	0 4	1 5	2 7	3 8	5 10	7 12							
M	2nd	80	160							0 2	0 4	1 5	3 6	4 7	6 9	8 12	12 16	18 22							
N	1st	125	125						0 2	0 3	0 4	0 4	1 5	2 7	3 8	5 10	7 12								
N	2nd	125	250						0 2	0 4	1 5	3 6	4 7	6 9	8 12	12 16	18 22								
P	1st	200	200					0 2	0 3	0 4	0 4	1 5	2 7	3 8	5 10	7 12									
P	2nd	200	400					0 2	0 4	1 5	3 6	4 7	6 9	8 12	12 16	18 22									
Q	1st	315	315				0 2	0 3	0 4	0 4	1 5	2 7	3 8	5 10	7 12										
Q	2nd	315	630				0 2	0 4	1 5	3 6	4 7	6 9	8 12	12 16	18 22										
R	1st	500	500			0 2	0 3	0 4	0 4	1 5	2 7	3 8	5 10	7 12											
R	2nd	500	1000			0 2	0 4	1 5	3 6	4 7	6 9	8 12	12 16	18 22											

◊ = Use first sampling plan below arrow. If sample size equals or exceeds lot or batch size, do 100 percent inspection.

◁ = Use first sampling plan above arrow.

† = If, after the second sample, the acceptance number has been exceeded, but the rejection number has not been reached, accept the lot, but reinstate normal normal inspection (see 10.1.4).

* = Use corresponding single sampling plan (or alternatively, use double sampling plan below, where available).

Ac = Acceptance number

Re = Rejection number

DOUBLE REDUCED

TABLE IV-A — Multiple sampling plans for normal inspection (Master table)

(See 9.4 and 9.5)

Sample size code letter	Smpl	Sample size	Cumulative sample size	0.010 Ac Re	0.015 Ac Re	0.025 Ac Re	0.040 Ac Re	0.065 Ac Re	0.10 Ac Re	0.15 Ac Re	0.25 Ac Re	0.40 Ac Re	0.65 Ac Re	1.0 Ac Re	1.5 Ac Re	2.5 Ac Re	4.0 Ac Re	6.5 Ac Re	10 Ac Re	15 Ac Re	25 Ac Re	40 Ac Re	65 Ac Re	100 Ac Re	150 Ac Re	250 Ac Re	400 Ac Re	650 Ac Re	1000 Ac Re
A				↓	↓	↓	↓	↓	↓	↓	↓	↓	↓	↓	↓	↓	↑	*	↓	↓	*	*	*	*	*	*	*	*	*
B																	*	↑		‡	‡	‡	‡	‡	‡	‡	‡	‡	‡
C																*	↓	↓	‡	‡	‡	‡	‡	‡	‡	‡	‡	‡	↑
D	1st	2	2	↓	↓	↓	↓	↓	↓	↓	↓	↓	↓	↓	*	↑	↓	# 2	# 2	# 3	# 4	0 4	0 5	1 7	2 9	4 12	6 16	↑	↑
	2nd	2	3															# 2	0 3	0 3	1 5	1 6	3 8	4 10	7 14	11 19	17 27		
	3rd	2	6															0 2	0 3	1 4	2 6	3 8	6 10	8 13	13 19	19 27	29 39		
	4th	2	8															0 3	1 4	2 5	3 7	5 10	8 13	12 17	19 25	27 34	40 49		
	5th	2	10															1 3	2 4	3 6	5 8	7 11	11 15	17 20	25 29	36 40	53 58		
	6th	2	12															1 3	3 5	4 6	7 9	10 12	14 17	21 23	31 33	45 47	66 68		
	7th	2	14															2 3	4 5	6 7	9 10	13 14	18 19	25 26	37 38	53 54	77 78		
E	1st	3	3	↓	↓	↓	↓	↓	↓	↓	↓	↓	↓	*	↑	↓	# 2	# 2	# 3	# 4	0 4	0 5	1 7	2 9	4 12	6 16	↑	↑	↑
	2nd	3	6														# 2	0 3	0 3	1 5	1 6	3 8	4 10	7 14	11 19	17 27			
	3rd	3	9														0 2	0 3	1 4	2 6	3 8	6 10	8 13	13 19	19 27	29 39			
	4th	3	12														0 3	1 4	2 5	3 7	5 10	8 13	12 17	19 25	27 34	40 49			
	5th	3	15														1 3	2 4	3 6	5 8	7 11	11 15	17 20	25 29	36 40	53 58			
	6th	3	18														1 3	3 5	4 6	7 9	10 12	14 17	21 23	31 33	45 47	65 68			
	7th	3	21														2 3	4 5	6 7	9 10	13 14	18 19	25 26	37 38	53 54	77 78			
F	1st	5	5	↓	↓	↓	↓	↓	↓	↓	↓	↓	*	↑	↓	# 2	# 2	# 3	# 4	0 4	0 5	1 7	2 9	↑	↑	↑	↑	↑	↑
	2nd	5	10													# 2	0 3	0 3	1 5	1 6	3 8	4 10	7 14						
	3rd	5	15													0 2	0 3	1 4	2 6	3 8	6 10	8 13	13 19						
	4th	5	20													0 3	1 4	2 5	3 7	5 10	8 13	12 17	19 25						
	5th	5	25													1 3	2 4	3 6	5 8	7 11	11 15	17 20	25 29						
	6th	5	30													1 3	3 5	4 6	7 9	10 12	14 17	21 23	31 33						
	7th	5	35													2 3	4 5	6 7	9 10	13 14	18 19	25 26	37 38						
G	1st	8	8	↓	↓	↓	↓	↓	↓	↓	↓	*	↑	↓	# 2	# 2	# 3	# 4	0 4	0 5	1 7	2 9	↑	↑	↑	↑	↑	↑	↑
	2nd	8	16												# 2	0 3	0 3	1 5	1 6	3 8	4 10	7 14							
	3rd	8	24												0 2	0 3	1 4	2 6	3 8	6 10	8 13	13 19							
	4th	8	32												0 3	1 4	2 5	3 7	5 10	8 13	12 17	19 25							
	5th	8	40												1 3	2 4	3 6	5 8	7 11	11 15	17 20	25 29							
	6th	8	48												1 3	3 5	4 6	7 9	10 12	14 17	21 23	31 33							
	7th	8	56												2 3	4 5	6 7	9 10	13 14	18 19	25 26	37 38							
H	1st	13	13	↓	↓	↓	↓	↓	↓	↓	*	↑	↓	# 2	# 2	# 3	# 4	0 4	0 5	1 7	2 9	↑	↑	↑	↑	↑	↑	↑	↑
	2nd	13	26											# 2	0 3	0 3	1 5	1 6	3 8	4 10	7 14								
	3rd	13	39											0 2	0 3	1 4	2 6	3 8	6 10	8 13	13 19								
	4th	13	52											0 3	1 4	2 5	3 7	5 10	8 13	12 17	19 25								
	5th	13	63											1 3	2 4	3 6	5 8	7 11	11 15	17 20	25 29								
	6th	13	78											1 3	3 5	4 6	7 9	10 12	14 17	21 23	31 33								
	7th	13	91											2 3	4 5	6 7	9 10	13 14	18 19	25 26	37 38								
J	1st	20	20	↓	↓	↓	↓	↓	↓	*	↑	↓	# 2	# 2	# 3	# 4	0 4	0 5	1 7	2 9	↑	↑	↑	↑	↑	↑	↑	↑	↑
	2nd	20	40										# 2	0 3	0 3	1 5	1 6	3 8	4 10	7 14									
	3rd	20	60										0 2	0 3	1 4	2 6	3 8	6 10	8 13	13 19									
	4th	20	80										0 3	1 4	2 5	3 7	5 10	8 13	12 17	19 25									
	5th	20	100										1 3	2 4	3 6	5 8	7 11	11 15	17 20	25 29									
	6th	20	120										1 3	3 5	4 6	7 9	10 12	14 17	21 23	31 33									
	7th	20	140										2 3	4 5	6 7	9 10	13 14	18 19	25 26	37 38									

Acceptable Quality Levels (reduced inspection)

↓ = Use first sampling plan below arrow. If sample size equals, or exceeds, lot or batch size, do 100 percent inspection.
↑ = Use first sampling plan above arrow (refer to preceding page, when necessary).
Ac = Acceptance number
Re = Rejection number
# = Acceptance not permitted at this sample size.
‡ = Use corresponding double sampling plan (or alternatively, use multiple sampling plan below, where available).
* = Use corresponding single sampling plan (or alternatively, use multiple sampling plan below, where available).

TABLE IV-A — Multiple sampling plans for normal inspection (Master table)
(Continued)

(See 9.4 and 9.5)

MULTIPLE NORMAL

17

TABLE IV-B — Multiple sampling plans for tightened inspection (Master table)

(See 9.4 and 9.5)

Acceptable Quality Levels

The table is a master table of multiple sampling plans for tightened inspection. The leftmost columns identify each plan; the body is organised by Acceptable Quality Level (AQL), each with an **Ac** (accept) and **Re** (reject) column. Arrows indicate "use the first sampling plan below (or above) the arrow," a dot (•) indicates use of the corresponding single sampling plan (or double sampling plan), and **#** indicates acceptance not permitted at that stage.

Left index columns:

Sample size code letter	Smpl	Sample size	Cumulative sample size
A			
B			
C			
D	1st	2	2
	2nd	2	4
	3rd	2	6
	4th	2	8
	5th	2	10
	6th	2	12
	7th	2	14
E	1st	3	3
	2nd	3	6
	3rd	3	9
	4th	3	12
	5th	3	15
	6th	3	18
	7th	3	21
F	1st	5	5
	2nd	5	10
	3rd	5	15
	4th	5	20
	5th	5	25
	6th	5	30
	7th	5	35
G	1st	8	8
	2nd	8	16
	3rd	8	24
	4th	8	32
	5th	8	40
	6th	8	48
	7th	8	56
H	1st	13	13
	2nd	13	26
	3rd	13	39
	4th	13	52
	5th	13	65
	6th	13	78
	7th	13	91
J	1st	20	20
	2nd	20	40
	3rd	20	60
	4th	20	80
	5th	20	100
	6th	20	120
	7th	20	140
K	1st	32	32
	2nd	32	64
	3rd	32	96
	4th	32	128
	5th	32	160
	6th	32	192
	7th	32	224

Representative readable Ac/Re entries (7 stages, 1st–7th):

Code D

AQL	Ac (1st–7th)	Re (1st–7th)
10	# # 0 0 1 1 2	2 2 2 3 3 3 3
15	# 0 0 1 2 3 4	2 3 3 4 4 5 5
100	0 3 7 10 14 18 21	6 9 12 15 17 20 22
150	1 6 11 16 22 27 32	8 12 17 22 25 29 33
250	3 10 17 24 32 40 48	10 17 24 31 37 43 49
400	6 16 26 37 49 61 72	15 25 36 46 55 64 73

Code E

AQL	Ac (1st–7th)	Re (1st–7th)
65	0 3 7 10 14 18 21	6 9 12 15 17 20 22
100	1 6 11 16 22 27 32	8 12 17 22 25 29 33
150	3 10 17 24 32 40 48	10 17 24 31 37 43 49

Code F

AQL	Ac (1st–7th)	Re (1st–7th)
40	0 3 7 10 14 18 21	6 9 12 15 17 20 22
65	1 6 11 16 22 27 32	8 12 17 22 25 29 33
100	3 10 17 24 32 40 48	10 17 24 31 37 43 49

Code G

AQL	Ac (1st–7th)	Re (1st–7th)
25	0 3 7 10 14 18 21	6 9 12 15 17 20 22
40	1 6 11 16 22 27 32	8 12 17 22 25 29 33
65	3 10 17 24 32 40 48	10 17 24 31 37 43 49

(The full master table continues across the AQL columns 0.010, 0.015, 0.025, 0.040, 0.065, 0.10, 0.15, 0.25, 0.40, 0.65, 1.0, 1.5, 2.5, 4.0, 6.5, 10, 15, 25, 40, 65, 100, 150, 250, 400, 650, 1000 — each with Ac and Re sub-columns — with arrows directing to the appropriate plan above or below where numeric entries are not shown.)

MULTIPLE TIGHTENED

18

TABLE IV-B — Multiple sampling plans for tightened inspection (Master table)
(Continued)

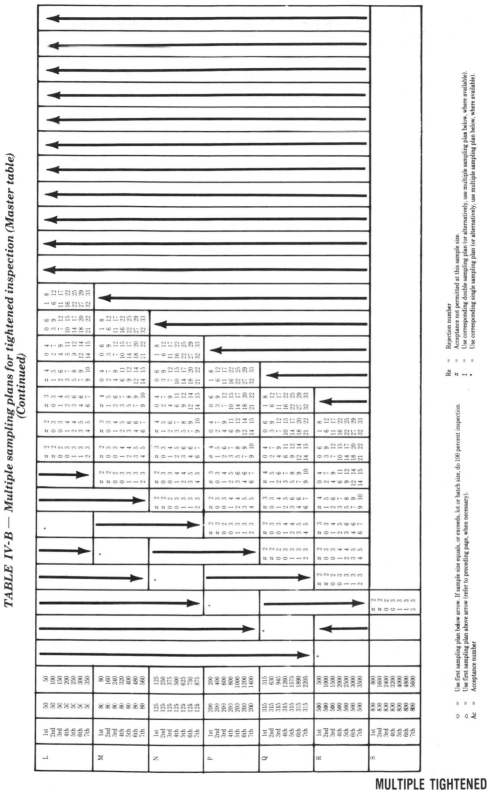

Re = Rejection number
# = Acceptance not permitted at this sample size.
↓ = Use corresponding double sampling plan (or alternatively, use multiple sampling plan below, where available).
↑ = Use corresponding single sampling plan (or alternatively, use multiple sampling plan below, where available).

◊ = Use first sampling plan below arrow. If sample size equals, or exceeds, lot or batch size, do 100 percent inspection.
◊ = Use first sampling plan above arrow (refer to preceding page, when necessary).
Ac = Acceptance number

MULTIPLE TIGHTENED

TABLE IV-C — Multiple sampling plans for reduced inspection (Master table)

(See 9.4 and 9.5)

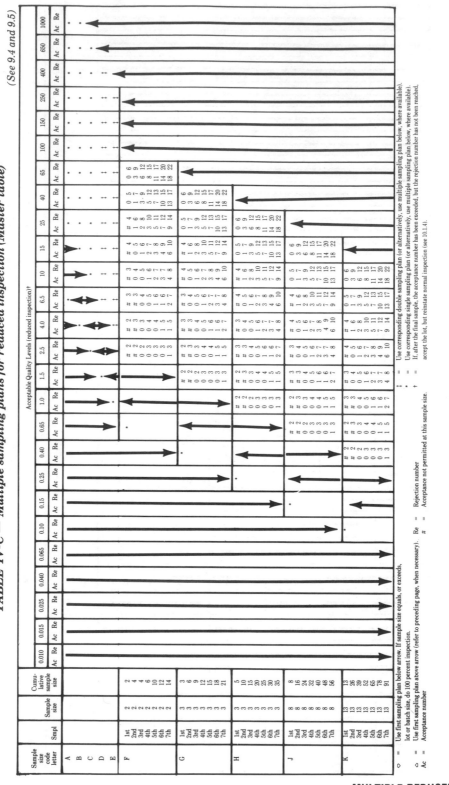

◊ = Use first sampling plan below arrow. If sample size equals, or exceeds, lot or batch size, do 100 percent inspection.

⇩ = Use first sampling plan above arrow (refer to preceding page, when necessary).

Ac = Acceptance number

Re = Rejection number

= Acceptance not permitted at this sample size.

† = Use corresponding double sampling plan (or alternatively, use multiple sampling plan below, where available).

= = Use corresponding single sampling plan (or alternatively, use multiple sampling plan below, where available).

+ = If, after the final sample, the acceptance number has been exceeded, but the rejection number has not been reached, accept the lot, but reinstate normal inspection (see 10.1.4).

MULTIPLE REDUCED

TABLE IV-C — Multiple sampling plans for reduced inspection (Master table)
(Continued)

(See 9.4 and 9.5)

Sample size code letter	Smpl	Sample size	Cumulative sample size	Acceptable Quality Levels (reduced inspection)†
L	1st	20	20	(AQL 4.0) Ac 0 / Re 5 · · · (AQL 6.5) Ac 0 / Re 6 · · · (10–1000) ←
	2nd	20	40	(4.0) 1 / 9 · · · (6.5) 3 / 9
	3rd	20	60	(4.0) 3 / 12 · · · (6.5) 6 / 12
	4th	20	80	(4.0) 5 / 13 · · · (6.5) 8 / 15
	5th	20	100	(4.0) 7 / 15 · · · (6.5) 11 / 17
	6th	20	120	(4.0) 10 / 17 · · · (6.5) 14 / 20
	7th	20	140	(4.0) 13 / 17 · · · (6.5) 18 / 22
M	1st	32	32	(2.5) 0 / 5 · · · (4.0) 0 / 6 · · · (6.5) ←
	2nd	32	64	(2.5) 1 / 9 · · · (4.0) 3 / 9
	3rd	32	96	(2.5) 3 / 12 · · · (4.0) 6 / 12
	4th	32	128	(2.5) 5 / 13 · · · (4.0) 8 / 15
	5th	32	160	(2.5) 7 / 15 · · · (4.0) 11 / 17
	6th	32	192	(2.5) 10 / 17 · · · (4.0) 14 / 20
	7th	32	224	(2.5) 13 / 17 · · · (4.0) 18 / 22
N	1st	50	50	(1.5) 0 / 5 · · · (2.5) 0 / 6
	2nd	50	100	(1.5) 1 / 9 · · · (2.5) 3 / 9
	3rd	50	150	(1.5) 3 / 12 · · · (2.5) 6 / 12
	4th	50	200	(1.5) 5 / 13 · · · (2.5) 8 / 15
	5th	50	250	(1.5) 7 / 15 · · · (2.5) 11 / 17
	6th	50	300	(1.5) 10 / 17 · · · (2.5) 14 / 20
	7th	50	350	(1.5) 13 / 17 · · · (2.5) 18 / 22
P	1st	80	80	(1.0) 0 / 5 · · · (1.5) 0 / 6
	2nd	80	160	(1.0) 1 / 9 · · · (1.5) 3 / 9
	3rd	80	240	(1.0) 3 / 12 · · · (1.5) 6 / 12
	4th	80	320	(1.0) 5 / 13 · · · (1.5) 8 / 15
	5th	80	400	(1.0) 7 / 15 · · · (1.5) 11 / 17
	6th	80	480	(1.0) 10 / 17 · · · (1.5) 14 / 20
	7th	80	560	(1.0) 13 / 17 · · · (1.5) 18 / 22
Q	1st	125	125	(0.65) 0 / 5 · · · (1.0) 0 / 6
	2nd	125	250	(0.65) 1 / 9 · · · (1.0) 3 / 9
	3rd	125	375	(0.65) 3 / 12 · · · (1.0) 6 / 12
	4th	125	500	(0.65) 5 / 13 · · · (1.0) 8 / 15
	5th	125	625	(0.65) 7 / 15 · · · (1.0) 11 / 17
	6th	125	750	(0.65) 10 / 17 · · · (1.0) 14 / 20
	7th	125	875	(0.65) 13 / 17 · · · (1.0) 18 / 22
R	1st	200	200	(0.40) 0 / 5 · · · (0.65) 0 / 6
	2nd	200	400	(0.40) 1 / 9 · · · (0.65) 3 / 9
	3rd	200	600	(0.40) 3 / 12 · · · (0.65) 6 / 12
	4th	200	800	(0.40) 5 / 13 · · · (0.65) 8 / 15
	5th	200	1000	(0.40) 7 / 15 · · · (0.65) 11 / 17
	6th	200	1200	(0.40) 10 / 17 · · · (0.65) 14 / 20
	7th	200	1400	(0.40) 13 / 17 · · · (0.65) 18 / 22

(AQL header columns, left to right: 0.010, 0.015, 0.025, 0.040, 0.065, 0.10, 0.15, 0.25, 0.40, 0.65, 1.0, 1.5, 2.5, 4.0, 6.5, 10, 15, 25, 40, 65, 100, 150, 250, 400, 650, 1000 — each with Ac and Re sub-columns. Columns outside each code letter's numeric band are shown with arrows (↓, ↑, ←, →) and dots (·).)

↓ = Use first sampling plan below arrow. If sample size equals, or exceeds, lot or batch size, do 100 percent inspection.
↑ = Use first sampling plan above arrow (refer to preceding page, when necessary).
Ac = Acceptance number
Re = Rejection number
\# = Acceptance not permitted at this sample size.
* = Use corresponding single sampling plan (or alternatively, use multiple sampling plan below where available).
† = If, after the final sample, the acceptance number has been exceeded, but the rejection number has not been reached, accept the lot, but reinstate normal inspection (see 10.1.4).

MULTIPLE REDUCED

AOQL NORMAL

TABLE V-A — *Average Outgoing Quality Limit Factors for Normal Inspection (Single sampling)*

(See 11.4)

Acceptable Quality Level

Code letter	Sample size	0.010	0.015	0.025	0.040	0.065	0.10	0.15	0.25	0.40	0.65	1.0	1.5	2.5	4.0	6.5	10	15	25	40	65	100	150
A	2								42	69									42	69	97	160	220
B	3							28	46	65								28	46	65	110	150	220
C	5															18	17	27	39	63	90	130	190
D	8														12	11	17	24	40	56	82	120	180
E	13													7.4	6.5	11	15	24	34	50	72	110	170
F	20												4.6	4.2	6.9	9.7	16	22	33	47	73		
G	32											2.8	2.6	4.3	6.1	9.9	14	21	29	46			
H	50										1.8	1.7	2.7	3.9	6.3	9.0	13	19	29				
J	80									1.2	1.1	1.7	2.4	4.0	5.6	8.2	12	18					
K	125								0.74	0.67	1.1	1.6	2.5	3.6	5.2	7.5	12						
L	200							0.46	0.42	0.69	0.97	1.6	2.2	3.3	4.7	7.3							
M	315						0.29	0.27	0.44	0.62	1.00	1.4	2.1	3.0	4.7								
N	500					0.18	0.17	0.27	0.39	0.63	0.90	1.3	1.9	2.9									
P	800				0.12	0.11	0.17	0.24	0.40	0.56	0.82	1.2	1.8										
Q	1250			0.074	0.067	0.11	0.16	0.25	0.36	0.52	0.75	1.2											
R	2000	0.029	0.046	0.042	0.069	0.097	0.16	0.22	0.33	0.47	0.73												

Note: For the exact AOQL, the above values must be multiplied by $\left(1 - \dfrac{\text{Sample size}}{\text{Lot or Batch size}} \right)$ (see 11.4)

TABLE V-B — Average Outgoing Quality Limit Factors for Tightened Inspection (Single sampling)

Code letter	Sample size	0.010	0.015	0.025	0.040	0.065	0.10	0.15	0.25	0.40	0.65	1.0	1.5	2.5	4.0	6.5	10	15	25	40	65	100	150
A	2																			42	69	97	160
B	3															12			28	46	65	110	170
C	5														7.4			17	27	39	63	100	160
D	8													4.6			11	17	24	40	64	98	160
E	13												2.8			6.5	11	15	24	40	61	98	150
F	20											1.8			4.2	6.9	9.7	16	26	40	62		
G	32										1.2			2.6	4.3	6.1	9.9	16	25	39			
H	50									0.74			1.7	2.7	3.9	6.3	10	16	25				
J	80								0.46			1.1	1.7	2.4	4.0	6.4	9.9	16					
K	125						0.18	0.29			0.67	1.1	1.6	2.5	4.1	6.4	9.9						
L	200					0.12				0.42	0.69	0.97	1.6	2.6	4.0	6.2							
M	315				0.074				0.27	0.44	0.62	1.0	1.6	2.5	3.9								
N	500							0.17	0.27	0.39	0.63	1.0	1.6	2.5									
P	800			0.046			0.11	0.17	0.24	0.40	0.64	0.99	1.6										
Q	1250		0.029			0.067	0.11	0.16	0.25	0.41	0.64	0.99											
R	2000	0.018			0.042		0.097	0.16	0.26	0.40	0.62												
S	3150			0.027		0.069																	

Acceptable Quality Level

Note: For the exact AOQL, the above values must be multiplied by $\left(1 - \dfrac{\text{Sample size}}{\text{Lot or Batch size}}\right)$ (see 11.4)

AOQL TIGHTENED

TABLE VI-A — Limiting Quality (in percent defective) for which P_a = 10 Percent (for Normal Inspection, Single sampling)

(See 11.6)

Code letter	Sample size	Acceptable Quality Level															
		0.010	0.015	0.025	0.040	0.065	0.10	0.15	0.25	0.40	0.65	1.0	1.5	2.5	4.0	6.5	10
A	2															68	
B	3														54		
C	5													37			58
D	8												25			41	54
E	13											16			27	36	44
F	20										11			18	25	30	42
G	32									6.9			12	16	20	27	34
H	50								4.5			7.6	10	13	18	22	29
J	80							2.8			4.8	6.5	8.2	11	14	19	24
K	125						1.8			3.1	4.3	5.4	7.4	9.4	12	16	23
L	200					1.2			2.0	2.7	3.3	4.6	5.9	7.7	10	14	
M	315				0.73			1.2	1.7	2.1	2.9	3.7	4.9	6.4	9.0		
N	500			0.46			0.78	1.1	1.3	1.9	2.4	3.1	4.0	5.6			
P	800		0.29			0.49	0.67	0.84	1.2	1.5	1.9	2.5	3.5				
Q	1250	0.18			0.31	0.43	0.53	0.74	0.94	1.2	1.6	2.3					
R	2000			0.20	0.27	0.33	0.46	0.59	0.77	1.0	1.4						

LQ (DEFECTIVES) 10%

24

TABLE VI-B — Limiting Quality (in defects per hundred units) for which P_a = 10 Percent
(for Normal Inspection, Single sampling)

(See 11.6)

Acceptable Quality Level

Code letter	Sample size	0.010	0.015	0.025	0.040	0.065	0.10	0.15	0.25	0.40	0.65	1.0	1.5	2.5	4.0	6.5	10	15	25	40	65	100	150
A	2															120			200	270	330	460	590
B	3														77			130	180	220	310	390	510
C	5													46			78	110	130	190	240	310	400
D	8												29			49	67	84	120	150	190	250	350
E	13											18			30	41	51	71	91	120	160	220	300
F	20										12			20	27	33	46	59	77	100	140		
G	32									7.2			12	17	21	29	37	48	63	88			
H	50								4.6			7.8	11	13	19	24	31	40	56				
J	80							2.9			4.9	6.7	8.4	12	15	19	25	35					
K	125						1.8			3.1	4.3	5.4	7.4	9.4	12	16	23						
L	200					1.2			2.0	2.7	3.3	4.6	5.9	7.7	10	14							
M	315				0.73			1.2	1.7	2.1	2.9	3.7	4.9	6.4	9.0								
N	500			0.46			0.78	1.1	1.3	1.9	2.4	3.1	4.0	5.6									
P	800		0.29			0.49	0.67	0.84	1.2	1.5	1.9	2.5	3.5										
Q	1250	0.18			0.31	0.43	0.53	0.74	0.94	1.2	1.6	2.3											
R	2000			0.20	0.27	0.33	0.46	0.59	0.77	1.0	1.4												

LQ (DEFECTS) 10.0%

TABLE VII-A — Limiting Quality (in percent defective) for which P_a = 5 Percent (for Normal Inspection, Single sampling)

(See 11.6)

Code letter	Sample size	Acceptable Quality Level														
		0.010	0.015	0.025	0.040	0.065	0.10	0.15	0.25	0.40	0.65	1.0	1.5	2.5	4.0	6.5	10
A	2															78	
B	3														63		
C	5													45			66
D	8												31			47	60
E	13											21			32	41	50
F	20										14			22	28	34	46
G	32									8.9			14	18	23	30	37
H	50								5.8			9.1	12	15	20	25	32
J	80							3.7			5.8	7.7	9.4	13	16	20	26
K	125						2.4			3.8	5.0	6.2	8.4	11	14	18	24
L	200					1.5			2.4	3.2	3.9	5.3	6.6	8.5	11	15	
M	315				0.95			1.5	2.0	2.5	3.3	4.2	5.4	7.0	9.6		
N	500			0.60			0.95	1.3	1.6	2.1	2.6	3.4	4.4	6.1			
P	800		0.38			0.59	0.79	0.97	1.3	1.6	2.1	2.7	3.8				
Q	1250	0.24			0.38	0.50	0.62	0.84	1.1	1.4	1.8	2.4					
R	2000			0.24	0.32	0.39	0.53	0.66	0.85	1.1	1.5						

LQ (DEFECTIVES) 5%

TABLE VII-B — Limiting Quality (in defects per hundred units) for which P_a = 5 Percent
(for Normal Inspection, Single sampling)

(See 11.6)

Code letter	Sample size	0.010	0.015	0.025	0.040	0.065	0.10	0.15	0.25	0.40	0.65	1.0	1.5	2.5	4.0	6.5	10	15	25	40	65	100	150
A	2															150			240	320	390	530	660
B	3														100			160	210	260	350	440	570
C	5													60			95	130	160	210	260	340	440
D	8												38			59	79	97	130	160	210	270	380
E	13											23			37	48	60	81	100	130	170	230	310
F	20										15			24	32	39	53	66	85	110	150		
G	32									9.4			15	20	24	33	41	53	68	95			
H	50								6.0			9.5	13	16	21	26	34	44	61				
J	80							3.8			5.9	7.9	9.7	13	16	21	27	38					
K	125						2.4			3.8	5.0	6.2	8.4	11	14	18	24						
L	200					1.5			2.4	3.2	3.9	5.3	6.6	8.5	11	15							
M	315				0.95			1.5	2.0	2.5	3.3	4.2	5.4	7.0	9.6								
N	500			0.60			0.95	1.3	1.6	2.1	2.6	3.4	4.4	6.1									
P	800		0.38			0.59	0.79	0.97	1.3	1.6	2.1	2.7	3.8										
Q	1250	0.24			0.38	0.50	0.62	0.84	1.1	1.4	1.8	2.4											
R	2000			0.24	0.32	0.39	0.53	0.66	0.85	1.1	1.5												

Acceptable Quality Level

LQ (DEFECTS) 5.0%

27

TABLE VIII — Limit Numbers for Reduced Inspection

(See 8.3.3)

LIMIT NUMBERS

Number of sample units from last 10 lots or batches	Acceptable Quality Level																					
	0.010	0.015	0.025	0.040	0.065	0.10	0.15	0.25	0.40	0.65	1.0	1.5	2.5	4.0	6.5	10	15	25	40	65	100	150
20-29	*	*	*	*	*	*	*	*	*	*	*	*	*	*	*	0	0	2	4	8	14	22
30-49	*	*	*	*	*	*	*	*	*	*	*	*	*	*	0	0	1	3	7	13	22	36
50-79	*	*	*	*	*	*	*	*	*	*	*	*	*	0	0	2	3	7	14	25	40	63
80-129	*	*	*	*	*	*	*	*	*	*	*	*	0	0	2	4	7	14	24	42	68	105
130-199	*	*	*	*	*	*	*	*	*	*	*	0	0	2	4	7	13	25	42	72	115	177
200-319	*	*	*	*	*	*	*	*	*	*	0	0	2	4	8	14	22	40	68	115	181	277
320-499	*	*	*	*	*	*	*	*	*	0	0	1	4	8	14	24	39	68	113	189		
500-799	*	*	*	*	*	*	*	*	0	0	2	3	7	14	25	40	63	110	181			
800-1249	*	*	*	*	*	*	*	0	0	2	4	7	14	24	42	68	105	181				
1250-1999	*	*	*	*	*	*	0	0	2	4	7	13	24	40	69	110	169					
2000-3149	*	*	*	*	*	0	0	2	4	8	14	22	40	68	115	181						
3150-4999	*	*	*	*	0	0	1	4	8	14	24	38	67	111	186							
5000-7999	*	*	*	0	0	2	3	7	14	25	40	63	110	181								
8000-12499	*	*	0	0	2	4	7	14	24	42	68	105	181									
12500-19999	*	0	0	2	4	7	13	24	40	69	110	169										
20000-31499	0	0	2	4	8	14	22	40	68	115	181											
31500-49999	0	1	4	8	14	24	38	67	111	186												
500000 & Over	2	3	7	14	25	40	63	110	181	301												

*Denotes that the number of sample units from the last ten lots or batches is not sufficient for reduced inspection for this AQL. In this instance more than ten lots or batches may be used for the calculation, provided that the lots or batches used are the most recent ones in sequence, that they have all been on normal inspection, and that none has been rejected while on original inspection.

TABLE IX — Average sample size curves for double and multiple sampling (normal and tightened inspection)

(See 11.5)

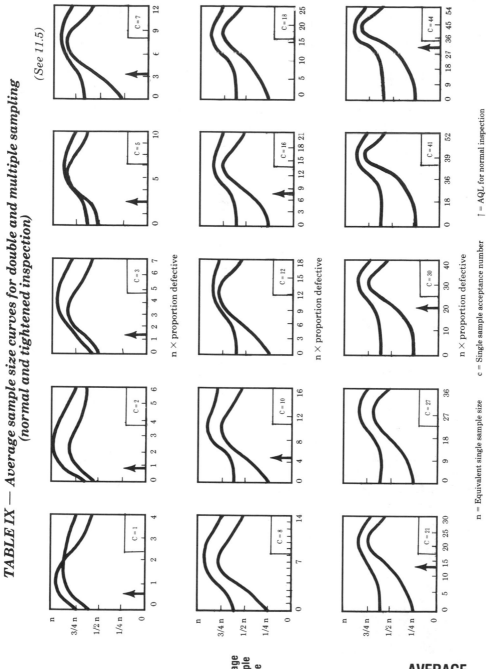

n = Equivalent single sample size

c = Single sample acceptance number

↑ = AQL for normal inspection

29

TABLE X-A — Tables for sample size code letter: A

CHART A — OPERATING CHARACTERISTIC CURVES FOR SINGLE SAMPLING PLANS
(Curves for double and multiple sampling are matched as closely as practicable)

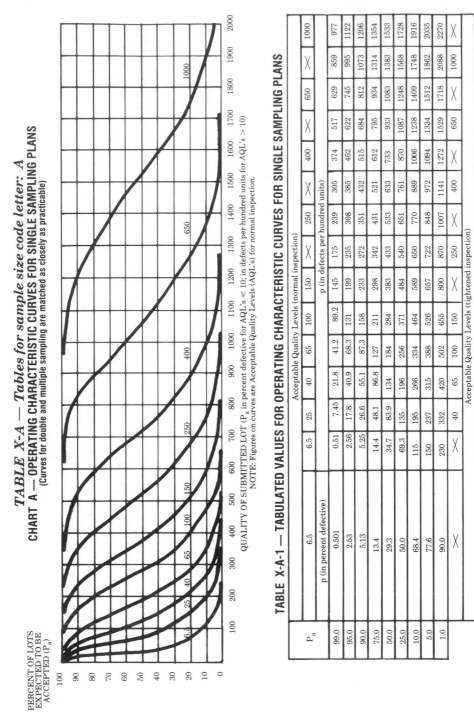

PERCENT OF LOTS EXPECTED TO BE ACCEPTED (P_a)

QUALITY OF SUBMITTED LOT (P_a in percent defective for AQL's ≤ 10; in defects per hundred units for AQL's > 10)

NOTE: Figures on curves are Acceptable Quality Levels (AQL's) for normal inspection.

TABLE X-A-1 — TABULATED VALUES FOR OPERATING CHARACTERISTIC CURVES FOR SINGLE SAMPLING PLANS

Acceptable Quality Levels (normal inspection)

P_a	6.5	25	40	65	100	150	X	250	X	400	X	650	X	1000
	p (in percent defective)	p (in defects per hundred units)												
99.0	0.501	7.45	21.8	41.2	89.2	145	175	239	305	374	517	629	859	977
95.0	2.53	17.8	40.9	68.3	131	199	235	308	385	462	622	745	995	1122
90.0	5.13	26.6	55.1	87.3	158	233	272	351	432	515	684	812	1073	1206
75.0	13.4	48.1	86.8	127	211	298	342	431	521	612	795	934	1314	1354
50.0	29.3	83.9	134	184	284	383	433	533	633	733	933	1083	1383	1533
25.0	50.0	135	196	256	371	484	540	651	761	870	1087	1248	1568	1728
10.0	68.4	195	266	334	464	589	650	770	889	1006	1238	1409	1748	1916
5.0	77.6	237	315	388	526	657	722	848	972	1094	1334	1512	1862	2035
1.0	90.0	332	420	502	655	800	870	1007	1141	1272	1529	1718	2088	2270
	X	40	65	100	150	250		400		650		1000		X

Acceptable Quality Levels (tightened inspection)

Note: Binominal distribution used for percent defective computations; Poisson for defects per hundred units.

TABLE X-A-2 — SAMPLING PLANS FOR SAMPLE SIZE CODE LETTER: A

Type of sampling plan	Cumulative sample size	Less than 6.5	6.5 Ac	6.5 Re	↓ Ac	↓ Re	10 Ac	10 Re	15 Ac	15 Re	25 Ac	25 Re	40 Ac	40 Re	65 Ac	65 Re	100 Ac	100 Re	150 Ac	150 Re	↓ Ac	↓ Re	250 Ac	250 Re	↓ Ac	↓ Re	400 Ac	400 Re	↓ Ac	↓ Re	650 Ac	650 Re	↓ Ac	↓ Re	1000 Ac	1000 Re	Cumulative sample size
	2																																				2
Single	2	▽	0	1	Use Letter D		Use Letter C		Use Letter B		1	2	2	3	3	4	5	6	7	8	8	9	10	11	12	13	14	15	18	19	21	22	27	28	30	31	2
Double		▽	*		Use Letter D		Use Letter C		Use Letter B		(*)		(*)		(*)		(*)		(*)		(*)		(*)		(*)		(*)		(*)		(*)		(*)		(*)		
Multiple		▽			•		•		•		•		•		•		•		•		•		•		•		•		•		•		•		•		

Acceptable Quality Levels (normal inspection)

	Less than 10	10	15	25	40	65	100	150	250	400	650	1000

Acceptable Quality Levels (tightened inspection)

A

▽ = Use next subsequent sample size code letter for which acceptance and rejection numbers are available.

Ac = Acceptance number.

Re = Rejection number.

• = Use single sampling plan above (or alternatively use letter: D).

(*) = Use single sampling (or alternatively use letter B).

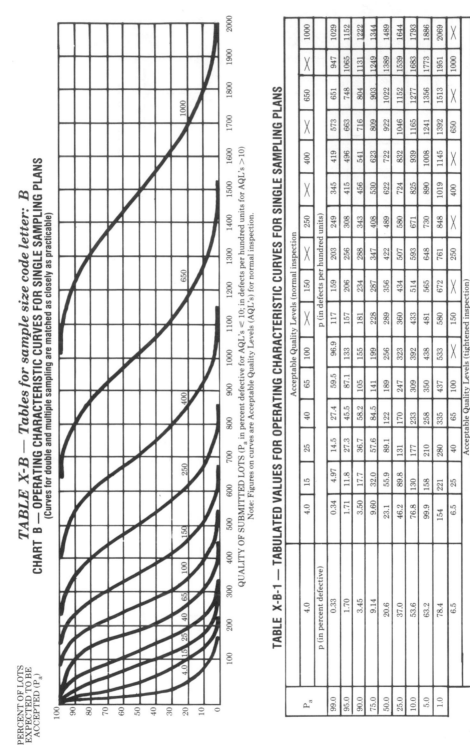

TABLE X-B — Tables for sample size code letter: B

CHART B — OPERATING CHARACTERISTIC CURVES FOR SINGLE SAMPLING PLANS
(Curves for double and multiple sampling are matched as closely as practicable)

QUALITY OF SUBMITTED LOTS (P_a in percent defective for AQL's ≤ 10; in defects per hundred units for AQL's >10)

Note: Figures on curves are Acceptable Quality Levels (AQL's) for normal inspection.

TABLE X-B-1 — TABULATED VALUES FOR OPERATING CHARACTERISTIC CURVES FOR SINGLE SAMPLING PLANS

P_a	4.0	15	25	40	65	100	X	150	X	250	X	400	X	650	X	1000
	p (in percent defective)							p (in defects per hundred units)								
99.0	0.33	4.97	14.5	27.4	59.5	96.9	117	159	203	249	345	419	573	651	947	1029
95.0	1.70	11.8	27.3	45.5	87.1	133	157	206	256	308	415	496	663	748	1065	1152
90.0	3.45	17.7	36.7	58.2	105	155	181	234	288	343	456	541	716	804	1131	1222
75.0	9.14	32.0	57.6	84.5	141	199	228	287	347	408	530	623	809	903	1249	1344
50.0	20.6	55.9	89.1	122	189	256	289	356	422	489	622	722	922	1022	1389	1489
25.0	37.0	89.8	131	170	247	323	360	434	507	580	724	832	1046	1152	1539	1644
10.0	53.6	130	177	233	309	392	433	514	593	671	825	939	1165	1277	1683	1793
5.0	63.2	158	210	258	350	438	481	565	648	730	890	1008	1241	1356	1773	1886
1.0	78.4	221	280	335	437	533	580	672	761	848	1019	1145	1392	1513	1951	2069
	6.5	25	40	65	100	150	X	250	X	400	X	650	X	1000	X	

Acceptable Quality Levels (tightened inspection)

Notes: Binomial distribution used for percent defective computation; Poisson for defects per hundred units.

TABLE X-B-2 — SAMPLING PLANS FOR SAMPLE SIZE CODE LETTER: B

Acceptable Quality Levels (normal inspection)

Type of sampling plan	Cumulative sample size	Less than 4.0	4.0 Ac Re	6.5 Ac Re	10 Ac Re	15 Ac Re	25 Ac Re	40 Ac Re	65 Ac Re	100 Ac Re	150 Ac Re	250 Ac Re	400 Ac Re	650 Ac Re	1000 Ac Re
Single	3	▽	0 1	Use ↑	Use ↑	1 2	2 3	3 4	5 6	7 8	10 11	14 15	21 22	30 31	44 45
Double	2	▽	*	Use ↑ Letter A	Use ↑ Letter	0 2	0 3	1 4	2 5	3 7	5 9	7 11	11 16	17 22	25 31
Double	4			Letter A	Letter D	Letter C	1 2	3 4	4 5	6 7	8 9	12 13	18 19	26 27	37 38	56 57
Multiple		▽	*			‡	‡	‡	‡	‡	‡	‡	‡	‡	‡

Cumulative sample size: Single = 3; Double = 2, 4.

Acceptable Quality Levels (tightened inspection)

Less than 6.5	6.5	10	15	25	40	65	100	150	250	400	650	1000
▽	X	X	X	X	X	X	X	X	X	X	X	X

▽ = Use next subsequent sample size code letter for which acceptance and rejection numbers are available.

Ac = Acceptance number.

Re = Rejection number.

* = Use single sampling plan above (or alternatively use letter E).

‡ = Use double sampling plan above (or alternatively use letter D).

B

33

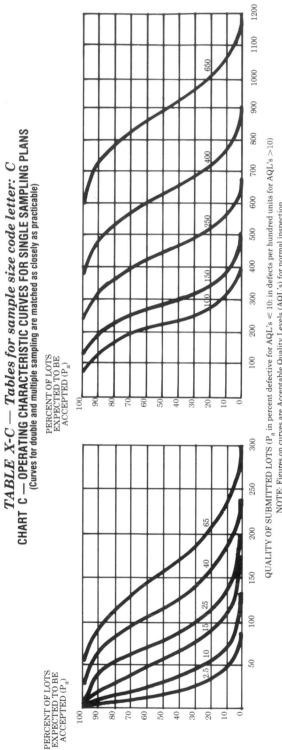

TABLE X-C — *Tables for sample size code letter: C*
CHART C — OPERATING CHARACTERISTIC CURVES FOR SINGLE SAMPLING PLANS
(Curves for double and multiple sampling are matched as closely as practicable)

PERCENT OF LOTS
EXPECTED TO BE
ACCEPTED (P_a)

PERCENT OF LOTS
EXPECTED TO BE
ACCEPTED (P_a)

QUALITY OF SUBMITTED LOTS (P_a in percent defective for AQL's ≤ 10; in defects per hundred units for AQL's >10)

NOTE: Figures on curves are Acceptable Quality Levels (AQL's) for normal inspection

TABLE X-C-1 — TABULATED VALUES FOR OPERATING CHARACTERISTIC CURVES FOR SINGLE SAMPLING PLANS

P_a	Acceptable Quality Levels (normal inspection)																
	2.5	10	2.5	10	15	25	40	65	100	150	250	400	650
	p (in percent defective)							p (in defects per hundred units)									
99.0	0.20	3.28	0.20	2.89	8.72	16.5	35.7	58.1	70.1	95.4	122	150	207	251	344	391	568	618
95.0	1.02	7.63	1.03	7.10	16.4	27.3	52.3	79.6	93.9	93.9	123	154	185	249	298	398	449	639	691
90.0	2.09	11.2	2.10	10.6	22.0	34.9	63.0	93.1	109	140	173	206	273	325	429	482	679	733
75.0	5.59	19.4	5.76	19.2	34.5	50.7	84.4	119	137	172	208	245	318	374	485	542	749	806
50.0	12.9	31.4	13.9	33.6	53.5	73.4	113	153	173	213	253	293	373	433	553	613	833	893
25.0	24.2	45.4	27.7	53.9	78.4	102	148	194	216	260	304	348	435	499	627	691	923	987
10.0	36.9	58.4	46.1	77.8	106	134	186	235	260	308	356	403	495	564	699	766	1010	1076
5.0	45.1	65.8	59.9	94.9	126	155	210	263	289	339	389	438	534	605	745	814	1064	1131
1.0	60.2	77.8	92.1	133	168	201	262	320	348	403	456	509	612	687	835	908	1171	1241
	4.0	✕	4.0	15	25	40	65	100	150	250	400	650	250	✕	400	✕	650	✕
									Acceptable Quality Levels (tightened inspection)									

Note: Binominal distribution used for percent defective computation; Poisson for defects per hundred units.

TABLE X-C-2 — SAMPLING PLANS FOR SAMPLE SIZE CODE LETTER: C

Each cell under an AQL column gives the acceptance (Ac) and rejection (Re) numbers.

Acceptable Quality Levels (normal inspection)

Type of sampling plan	Cumulative sample size	Less than 2.5	2.5 (Ac Re)	4.0	✕	6.5	10 (Ac Re)	15 (Ac Re)	25 (Ac Re)	40 (Ac Re)	65 (Ac Re)	✕ (Ac Re)	100 (Ac Re)	✕ (Ac Re)	150 (Ac Re)	✕ (Ac Re)	250 (Ac Re)	✕ (Ac Re)	400 (Ac Re)	✕ (Ac Re)
Single	5	▽	0 1	Use Letter B	Use Letter E	Use Letter D	1 2	2 3	3 4	5 6	7 8	8 9	10 11	12 13	14 15	18 19	21 22	27 28	30 31	41 42
Double	3	▽	*	Use Letter			0 2	0 3	1 4	2 5	3 7	3 7	5 9	6 10	7 11	9 14	11 16	15 20	17 22	23 29
Double	6						1 2	3 4	4 5	6 7	8 9	11 12	12 13	15 16	18 19	23 24	26 27	34 35	37 38	52 53
Multiple		▽	*				‡	‡	‡	‡	‡	‡	‡	‡	‡	‡	‡	‡	‡	‡

Acceptable Quality Levels (tightened inspection): Less than 4.0, 4.0, ✕, 6.5, 10, 15, 25, 40, 65, 100, 150, 250, 400, 650

▽ = Use next subsequent sample size code letter for which acceptance and rejection numbers are available.
Ac = Acceptance number.
Re = Rejection number.
* = Use single sampling plan above (or alternatively use letter F).
‡ = Use double sampling plan above (or alternatively use letter D).

C

35

TABLE X-D — Tables for sample size code letter: D
CHART D — OPERATING CHARACTERISTIC CURVES FOR SINGLE SAMPLING PLANS
(Curves for double and multiple sampling are matched as closely as practicable)

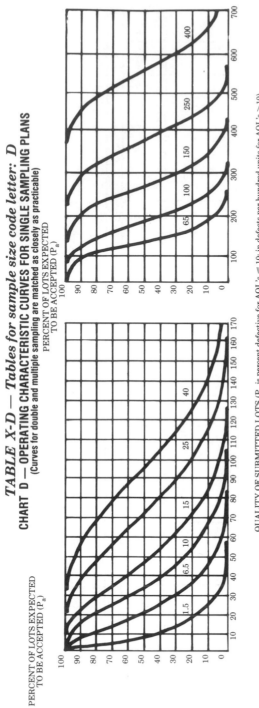

QUALITY OF SUBMITTED LOTS (P_a is percent defective for AQL's ≤ 10; in defects per hundred units for AQL's >10)

NOTE: Figures on curves are Acceptable Quality Levels (AQL's) for normal inspection.

TABLE X-D-1 — TABULATED VALUES FOR OPERATING CHARACTERISTIC CURVES FOR SINGLE SAMPLING PLANS

P_a	Acceptable Quality Levels (normal inspection)																		
	1.5	6.5	10	1.5	6.5	10	15	25	40	65	100		150		250		400	
	p(in percent defective)									p (in defects per hundred units)									
99.0	0.13	2.00	6.00	0.13	1.86	5.45	10.3	22.3	36.3	43.8	59.6	76.2	93.5	×	129	157	×	215	244	×	355	386
95.0	0.64	2.64	11.1	0.64	4.44	10.2	17.1	32.7	49.8	58.7	77.1	96.1	116	156	186	249	281	399	432
90.0	1.31	6.88	14.7	1.31	6.65	13.8	21.8	39.4	58.2	67.9	87.8	108	129	171	203	268	301	424	458
75.0	3.53	12.1	22.1	3.60	12.0	21.6	31.7	52.7	74.5	85.5	108	130	153	199	234	303	339	468	504
50.0	8.30	20.1	32.1	8.66	21.0	33.4	45.9	70.9	95.9	108	133	158	183	233	271	346	383	521	558
25.0	15.9	30.3	43.3	17.3	33.7	49.0	63.9	92.8	121	135	163	190	218	272	312	392	432	577	617
10.0	25.0	40.6	53.9	28.8	48.6	66.5	83.5	116	147	162	193	222	252	309	352	437	478	631	672
5.0	31.2	47.1	59.9	37.5	59.3	78.7	96.9	131	164	180	212	243	274	334	378	465	509	665	707
1.0	43.8	58.8	70.7	57.6	83.0	105	126	164	200	218	252	285	318	382	429	522	568	732	776
	2.5	10	×	2.5	10	15	25	40	65	100	×	150	×	250	×	400	
	Acceptable Quality Levels (tightened inspection)																		

36

TABLE X-D-2 — SAMPLING PLANS FOR SAMPLE SIZE CODE LETTER: D

Type of sampling plan	Cumulative sample size	Less than 1.5	1.5	2.5	X	4.0	6.5	10	15	25	40	X	65	X	100	X	150	X	250	X
		Ac Re	Ac Re	Ac Re	Ac Re	Ac Re	Ac Re	Ac Re	Ac Re	Ac Re	Ac Re	Ac Re	Ac Re	Ac Re	Ac Re	Ac Re	Ac Re	Ac Re	Ac Re	Ac Re
Single	8	▽	0 1	Use Letter C	Use Letter F	Use Letter E	1 2	2 3	3 4	5 6	7 8	8 9	10 11	12 13	14 15	18 19	21 22	27 28	30 31	41 42
Double	5	▽	*				0 2	0 3	1 4	2 5	3 7	3 7	5 9	6 10	7 11	9 14	11 16	15 20	17 22	23 29
	10						1 2	3 4	4 5	6 7	8 9	11 12	12 13	15 16	18 19	23 24	26 27	34 35	37 38	52 53
Multiple	2	▽	*				# 2	# 2	# 3	# 4	0 4	0 4	0 5	0 6	1 7	1 8	2 9	3 10	4 12	6 15
	4						# 2	0 3	0 3	1 5	1 6	2 7	3 8	3 9	4 10	6 12	7 14	10 17	11 19	16 25
	6						0 2	0 3	1 4	2 6	3 8	4 9	6 10	7 12	8 13	11 17	13 19	17 24	19 27	26 36
	8						0 3	1 4	2 5	3 7	5 10	6 11	8 13	10 15	12 17	16 22	19 25	24 31	27 34	37 46
	10						1 3	2 4	3 6	5 8	7 11	9 12	11 15	14 17	17 20	22 25	25 29	32 37	36 40	49 55
	12						1 3	3 5	4 6	7 9	10 12	12 14	14 17	18 20	21 23	27 29	31 33	40 43	45 47	61 64
	14						2 3	4 5	6 7	9 10	13 14	14 15	18 19	21 22	25 26	32 33	37 38	48 49	53 54	72 73
		Less than 2.5	2.5	X	4.0	6.5	10	15	25	40	X	65	X	100	X	150	X	250	X	400

Acceptable Quality Levels (normal inspection) — top header; Acceptable Quality Levels (tightened inspection) — bottom row.

D

△ = Use next preceding sample size code for which acceptance and rejection numbers are available.
▽ = Use next subsequent sample size code for which acceptance and rejection numbers are available.
Ac = Acceptance number
Re = Rejection number
* = Use single sampling plan above (or alternatively use letter J)
\# = Acceptance not permitted at this sample size.

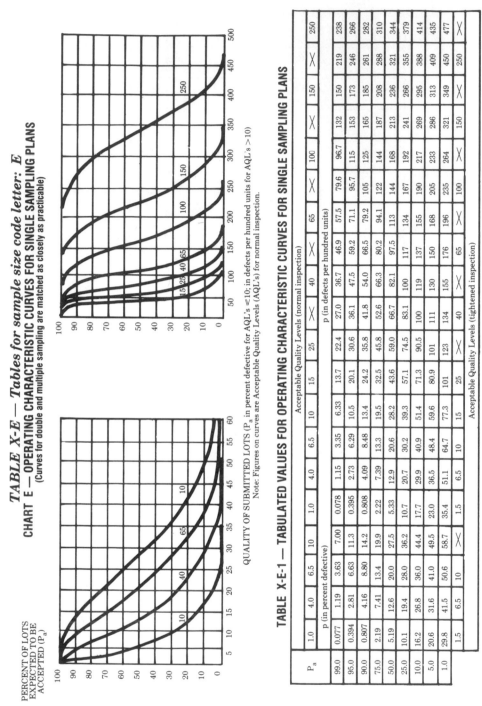

TABLE X-E — Tables for sample size code letter: E

CHART E — OPERATING CHARACTERISTIC CURVES FOR SINGLE SAMPLING PLANS
(Curves for double and multiple sampling are matched as closely as practicable)

QUALITY OF SUBMITTED LOTS (P$_a$ in percent defective for AQL's ≤10; in defects per hundred units for AQL's >10)

Note: Figures on curves are Acceptable Quality Levels (AQL's) for normal inspection.

TABLE X-E-1 — TABULATED VALUES FOR OPERATING CHARACTERISTIC CURVES FOR SINGLE SAMPLING PLANS

Acceptable Quality Levels (normal inspection)

P$_a$	1.0	4.0	6.5	10		15		25		40		65		100		150		250
	p (in percent defective)					p (in defects per hundred units)												
99.0	0.077	1.19	3.63	7.00		6.33	13.7	22.4	27.0	36.9	46.9	57.5	79.6	96.7	132	150	219	238
95.0	0.394	2.81	6.63	11.3		10.5	20.1	30.6	36.1	47.5	59.2	71.1	95.7	115	153	173	246	266
90.0	0.807	4.16	8.80	14.2		13.4	24.2	35.8	41.8	54.0	66.5	79.2	105	125	165	185	261	282
75.0	2.19	7.41	13.4	19.9		19.5	32.5	45.8	52.6	66.3	80.2	94.1	122	144	187	208	288	310
50.0	5.19	12.6	20.0	27.5		28.2	43.6	59.0	66.7	82.1	97.5	113	144	168	213	236	321	344
25.0	10.1	19.4	28.0	36.2		39.3	57.1	74.5	83.1	100	117	134	167	192	241	266	355	379
10.0	16.2	26.8	36.0	44.4		51.4	71.3	90.5	100	119	137	155	190	217	269	295	388	414
5.0	20.6	31.6	41.0	49.5		59.6	80.9	101	111	130	150	168	205	233	286	313	409	435
1.0	29.8	41.5	50.6	58.7		77.3	101	123	134	155	176	196	235	264	321	349	450	477
	1.5	6.5	10	X		15	25	40	65	100	150	250						

Acceptable Quality Levels (tightened inspection)

Note: Binomial distribution used for percent defective computations; Poisson for defects per hundred units.

TABLE X-E-2 — SAMPLING PLANS FOR SAMPLE SIZE CODE LETTER: E

Acceptable Quality Levels (normal inspection). Each cell shows **Ac Re** (acceptance number, rejection number).

Type of sampling plan	Cum. sample size	<1.0	1.0	1.5	2.5	4.0	6.5	10	15	25	40	65	100	150	250	>250	Cum. sample size
Single	13	▽	0 1	Use	Use	1 2	2 3	3 4	5 6	7 8	10 11	14 15	21 22	30 31	44 45	△	13
Double	8	▽	*	Use Letter D	Use Letter G	0 2	0 3	1 4	2 5	3 7	5 9	7 11	11 16	17 22	25 31	△	8
	16					1 2	3 4	4 5	6 7	8 9	12 13	18 19	26 27	37 38	46 47		16
Multiple	3	▽	*	Use Letter D	Use Letter F	# 2	# 2	# 3	# 4	0 4	0 5	1 7	2 9	4 12	6 16	△	3
	6					# 2	0 3	0 4	1 5	1 6	3 8	4 10	7 14	11 19	17 27		6
	9					0 3	0 3	1 5	2 6	3 8	6 10	8 13	13 19	19 27	29 39		9
	12					0 3	1 4	2 6	3 7	5 10	8 13	12 17	19 25	27 34	40 49		12
	15					1 3	2 4	3 6	5 8	7 11	11 15	17 20	25 29	36 40	53 58		15
	18					1 3	3 5	4 6	7 9	10 12	14 17	21 23	31 33	45 47	65 68		18
	21					2 3	4 5	6 7	9 10	13 14	18 19	25 26	37 38	53 54	77 78		21

Acceptable Quality Levels (tightened inspection):
Less than 1.5 | 1.5 | X | 2.5 | 4.0 | 6.5 | 10 | 15 | 25 | 40 | 65 | 100 | 150 | 250 | X | Higher than 250

△ = Use next preceding sample size code letter for which acceptance and rejection numbers are available.
▽ = Use next subsequent sample size code letter for which acceptance and rejection numbers are available.
Ac = Acceptance number.
Re = Rejection number.
* = Use single sampling plan above (alternatively use letter H).
# = Acceptance not permitted at this sample size.

E

TABLE X-F — Tables for sample size code letter: F
CHART F — OPERATING CHARACTERISTIC CURVES FOR SINGLE SAMPLING PLANS
(Curves for double and multiple sampling are matched as closely as practicable)

PERCENT OF LOTS EXPECTED TO BE ACCEPTED (P_a)

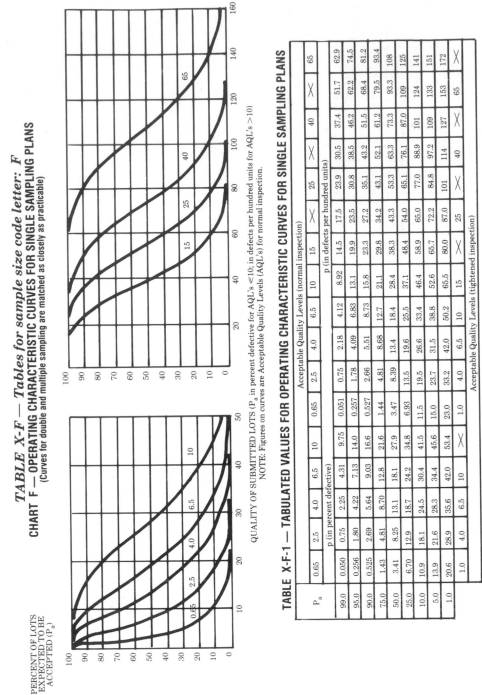

QUALITY OF SUBMITTED LOTS (P_a in percent defective for AQL's ≤10: in defects per hundred units for AQL's >10)
NOTE: Figures on curves are Acceptable Quality Levels (AQL's) for normal inspection.

TABLE X-F-1 — TABULATED VALUES FOR OPERATING CHARACTERISTIC CURVES FOR SINGLE SAMPLING PLANS

Acceptable Quality Levels (normal inspection) — p (in percent defective)

P_a	0.65	2.5	4.0	6.5	10
99.0	0.050	0.75	2.25	4.31	9.75
95.0	0.256	1.80	4.22	7.13	14.0
90.0	0.525	2.69	5.64	9.03	16.6
75.0	1.43	4.81	8.70	12.8	21.6
50.0	3.41	8.25	13.1	18.1	27.9
25.0	6.70	12.9	18.7	24.2	34.8
10.0	10.9	18.1	24.5	30.4	41.5
5.0	13.9	21.6	28.3	34.4	45.6
1.0	20.6	28.9	35.6	42.0	53.4
Tightened	1.0	4.0	6.5	10	✕

Acceptable Quality Levels (tightened inspection)

Acceptable Quality Levels (normal inspection) — p (in defects per hundred units)

P_a	0.65	2.5	4.0	6.5	10	15	✕	25	✕	40	✕	65
99.0	0.051	0.75	2.18	4.12	8.92	14.5	17.5	23.9	30.5	37.4	51.7	62.9
95.0	0.256	1.78	4.09	6.83	13.1	19.9	23.5	30.8	38.5	46.2	62.2	74.5
90.0	0.527	2.66	5.51	8.73	15.8	23.3	27.2	35.1	43.2	51.5	68.4	81.2
75.0	1.44	4.81	8.68	12.7	21.1	29.8	34.2	43.1	52.1	61.2	79.5	93.4
50.0	3.47	8.39	13.4	18.4	28.4	38.3	43.3	53.3	63.3	73.3	93.3	108
25.0	6.93	13.5	19.6	25.5	37.1	48.4	54.0	65.1	76.1	87.0	109	125
10.0	11.5	19.5	26.6	33.4	46.4	58.9	65.0	77.0	88.9	101	124	141
5.0	15.0	23.7	31.5	38.8	52.6	65.7	72.2	84.8	97.2	109	133	151
1.0	23.0	33.2	42.0	50.2	65.5	80.0	87.0	101	114	127	153	172
Tightened	1.0	4.0	6.5	10	15	25	✕	40	✕	65	✕	

Acceptable Quality Levels (tightened inspection)

Note: Binomial distribution used for percent defective computations; Poisson for defects per hundred units.

TABLE X-F-2 — SAMPLING PLANS FOR SAMPLE SIZE CODE LETTER: F

Acceptable Quality Levels (normal inspection) — top label of each column
Acceptable Quality Levels (tightened inspection) — bottom label of each column

Each AQL column header is shown as **normal / tightened**; each data cell is given as **Ac Re**. A "✕" indicates that plan is not available at that AQL.

Type of sampling plan	Cumulative sample size	Less than 0.65 / Less than 1.0	0.65 / 1.0	1.0 / ✕	✕ / 1.5	1.5 / 2.5	2.5 / 4.0	4.0 / 6.5	6.5 / 10	10 / 15	15 / ✕	✕ / 25	25 / ✕	✕ / 40	40 / ✕	✕ / 65	65 / ✕	Higher than 65
Single	20	▽	0 1	Use Letter E	Use Letter H	Use Letter G	1 2	2 3	3 4	5 6	7 8	8 9	10 11	12 13	14 15	18 19	21 22	△
Double	13	▽	*	Use Letter E	Use Letter H	Use Letter G	0 2	0 3	1 4	2 5	3 7	3 7	5 9	6 10	7 11	9 14	11 16	△
	26						1 2	3 4	4 5	6 7	8 9	11 12	12 13	15 16	18 19	23 24	26 27	
Multiple	5	▽	*				# 2	# 2	# 3	# 4	0 4	0 4	0 5	0 6	1 7	1 8	2 9	△
	10						# 2	0 3	0 3	1 5	1 6	2 7	3 8	3 9	4 10	6 12	7 14	
	15						0 2	0 3	1 4	2 6	3 8	4 9	6 10	7 12	8 13	11 17	13 19	
	20						0 3	1 4	2 5	3 7	5 10	6 11	8 13	10 15	12 17	16 22	19 25	
	25						1 3	2 4	3 6	5 8	7 11	9 12	11 15	14 17	17 20	22 25	25 29	
	30						1 3	3 5	4 6	7 9	10 12	12 14	14 17	18 20	21 23	27 29	31 33	
	35						2 3	4 5	6 7	9 10	13 14	14 15	18 19	21 22	25 26	32 33	37 38	

Cumulative sample size (right column): Single 20; Double 13, 26; Multiple 5, 10, 15, 20, 25, 30, 35.

△ = Use next preceding sample size code for which acceptance and rejection numbers are available.

▽ = Use next subsequent sample size code for which acceptance and rejection numbers are available.

Ac = Acceptance number

Re = Rejection number

* = Use single sampling plan above (or alternatively use letter J)

= Acceptance not permitted at this sample size.

F

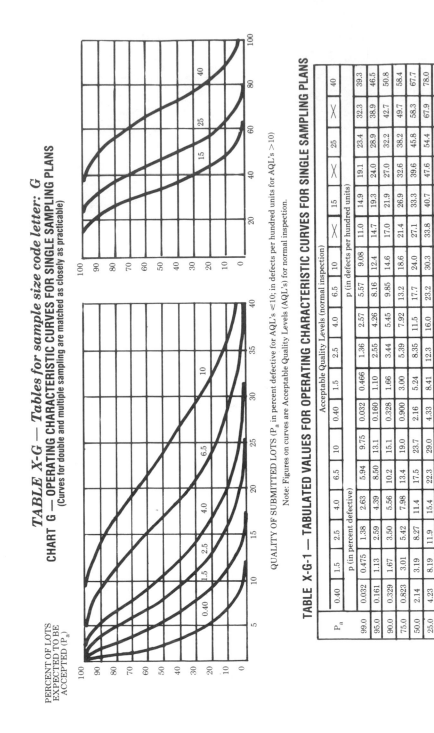

TABLE X-G — Tables for sample size code letter: G
CHART G — OPERATING CHARACTERISTIC CURVES FOR SINGLE SAMPLING PLANS
(Curves for double and multiple sampling are matched as closely as practicable)

PERCENT OF LOTS EXPECTED TO BE ACCEPTED (P_a)

QUALITY OF SUBMITTED LOTS (P_a in percent defective for AQL's ≤10; in defects per hundred units for AQL's >10)

Note: Figures on curves are Acceptable Quality Levels (AQL's) for normal inspection.

TABLE X-G-1 — TABULATED VALUES FOR OPERATING CHARACTERISTIC CURVES FOR SINGLE SAMPLING PLANS

Acceptable Quality Levels (normal inspection)

p (in percent defective)

P_a	0.40	1.5	2.5	4.0	6.5	10
99.0	0.032	0.475	1.38	2.63	5.94	9.75
95.0	0.161	1.13	2.59	4.39	8.50	13.1
90.0	0.329	1.67	3.50	5.56	10.2	15.1
75.0	0.823	3.01	5.42	7.98	13.4	19.0
50.0	2.14	5.19	8.27	11.4	17.5	23.7
25.0	4.23	8.19	11.9	15.4	22.3	29.0
10.0	6.94	11.6	15.8	19.7	27.1	34.1
5.0	8.94	14.0	18.4	22.5	30.1	37.2
1.0	13.5	19.0	23.7	28.0	35.9	43.3
(tightened)	0.65	2.5	4.0	6.5	10	15

p (in defects per hundred units)

P_a	0.40	1.5	2.5	4.0	6.5	10	15	✕	25	✕	40	✕
99.0	0.032	0.466	1.36	2.57	5.57	9.08	11.0	14.9	19.1	23.4	32.3	39.3
95.0	0.161	1.10	2.55	4.26	8.16	12.4	14.7	19.3	24.0	28.9	38.9	46.5
90.0	0.329	1.66	3.44	5.45	9.85	14.6	17.0	21.9	27.0	32.2	42.7	50.8
75.0	0.900	3.00	5.39	7.92	13.2	18.6	21.4	26.9	32.6	38.2	49.7	58.4
50.0	2.16	5.24	8.35	11.5	17.7	24.0	27.1	33.3	39.6	45.8	58.3	67.7
25.0	4.33	8.41	12.3	16.0	23.2	30.3	33.8	40.7	47.6	54.4	67.9	78.0
10.0	7.19	12.2	16.6	20.9	29.0	36.8	40.6	48.1	55.6	62.9	77.4	88.1
5.0	9.36	14.8	19.7	24.2	32.9	41.1	45.1	53.0	60.8	68.4	83.4	94.5
1.0	14.4	20.7	26.3	31.4	41.0	50.0	54.4	63.0	71.3	79.5	95.6	107
(tightened)	0.65	2.5	4.0	6.5	10	15	✕	25	✕	40		

Acceptable Quality Levels (tightened inspection)

Note: Binominal distribution used for percent defective computations; Poisson for defects per hundred units.

TABLE X-G-2 — SAMPLING PLANS FOR SAMPLE SIZE CODE LETTER: G

Acceptable Quality Levels (normal inspection) — values shown as "Ac Re"

Type of sampling plan	Cumulative sample size	0.40	0.65	✕	1.0	1.5	2.5	4.0	6.5	10	✕	15	✕	25	✕	40	Higher than 40
Single	32	0 1	Use Letter F	Use Letter J	Use Letter H	1 2	2 3	3 4	5 6	7 8	8 9	10 11	12 13	14 15	18 19	21 22	△
Double	20	*				0 2	0 3	1 4	2 5	3 7	3 7	5 9	10	7 11	9 14	11 16	△
Double	40					1 2	3 4	4 5	6 7	8 9	11 12	12 13	15 16	18 19	23 24	26 27	
Multiple	8	*				# 2	# 2	# 3	# 4	0 4	0 4	0 5	0 6	1 7	1 8	2 9	△
Multiple	16					# 2	0 3	0 3	1 5	1 6	2 7	3 8	3 9	4 10	6 12	7 14	
Multiple	24					0 2	0 3	1 4	2 6	3 8	4 9	6 10	7 12	8 13	11 17	13 19	
Multiple	32					0 3	1 4	2 5	3 7	5 10	6 11	8 13	10 15	12 17	16 22	19 25	
Multiple	40					1 3	2 4	3 6	5 8	7 11	9 12	11 15	14 17	17 20	22 25	25 29	
Multiple	48					1 3	3 5	4 6	7 9	10 12	12 14	14 17	18 20	21 23	27 29	31 33	
Multiple	56					2 3	4 5	6 7	9 10	13 14	14 15	18 19	21 22	25 26	32 33	37 38	
AQL (tightened inspection)		Less than 0.65	0.65	✕	1.0	1.5	2.5	4.0	6.5	10	15	✕	25	✕	40	✕	Higher than 40

G

Legend:

△ = Use next preceding sample size code for which acceptance and rejection numbers are available.

▽ = Use next subsequent sample size code for which acceptance and rejection numbers are available.

Ac = Acceptance number

Re = Rejection number

* = Use single sampling plan above (or alternatively use letter K)

\# = Acceptance not permitted at this sample size.

TABLE X-H — Tables for sample size code letter: H

CHART H — OPERATING CHARACTERISTIC CURVES FOR SINGLE SAMPLING PLANS
(Curves for double and multiple sampling are matched as closely as practicable)

PERCENT OF LOTS EXPECTED TO BE ACCEPTED (P_a)

QUALITY OF SUBMITTED LOTS (P_a in percent defective for AQL's ≤10; in defects per hundred units for AQL's >10)

NOTE: Figures on curves are Acceptable Quality Levels (AQL's) for normal inspection.

TABLE X-H-1 — TABULATED VALUES FOR OPERATING CHARACTERISTIC CURVES FOR SINGLE SAMPLING PLANS

Acceptable Quality Levels (normal inspection)

P_a	0.25	1.0	1.5	2.5	4.0	6.5	X	10	0.25	1.0	1.5	2.5	4.0	6.5	X	10	X	15	X	25
	p (in percent defective)								p (in defects per hundred units)											
99.0	0.020	0.306	0.888	1.69	3.66	6.06	7.41	11.1	0.020	0.298	0.872	1.65	3.57	5.81	7.01	9.54	12.2	15.0	20.7	25.1
95.0	0.103	0.712	1.66	2.77	5.34	8.20	9.74	12.9	0.103	0.710	1.64	2.73	5.23	7.96	9.39	12.3	15.4	18.5	24.9	29.8
90.0	0.210	1.07	2.23	3.54	6.42	9.53	11.2	14.5	0.210	1.06	2.20	3.49	6.30	9.31	10.9	14.0	17.3	20.6	27.3	32.5
75.0	0.574	1.92	3.46	5.09	8.51	12.0	13.8	17.5	0.576	1.92	3.45	5.07	8.44	11.9	13.7	17.2	20.8	24.5	31.8	37.4
50.0	1.38	3.33	5.31	7.30	11.3	15.2	17.2	21.2	1.39	3.36	5.35	7.34	11.3	15.3	17.3	21.6	25.3	29.3	37.3	43.3
25.0	2.74	5.30	7.70	10.0	14.5	18.8	21.0	25.2	2.77	5.39	7.84	10.2	14.8	19.4	21.6	26.0	30.4	34.8	43.5	49.9
10.0	4.50	7.56	10.3	12.9	17.8	22.4	24.7	29.1	4.61	7.78	10.6	13.4	18.6	23.5	26.0	30.8	35.6	40.3	49.5	56.4
5.0	5.82	9.13	12.1	14.8	19.9	24.7	27.0	31.6	5.99	9.49	12.6	15.5	21.0	26.3	28.9	33.9	38.9	43.8	53.4	60.5
1.0	8.80	12.5	15.9	18.8	24.3	29.2	31.7	36.3	9.21	13.3	16.8	20.1	26.2	32.0	34.8	40.3	45.6	50.9	61.1	68.7
	0.40	1.5	2.5	4.0	6.5	X	10	X	0.40	1.5	2.5	4.0	6.5	X	10	X	15	X	25	X

Acceptable Quality Levels (tightened inspection)

Note: Binomial distribution used for percent defective computations. Poisson for defects per hundred units.

TABLE X-H-2 — SAMPLING PLANS FOR SAMPLE SIZE CODE LETTER: H

Type of sampling plan	Cumulative sample size	Less than 0.25	0.25	0.40	×	0.65	1.0	1.5	2.5	4.0	6.5	×	10	×	15	×	25	Higher than 25	Cumulative sample size
		Acceptable Quality Levels (normal inspection)																	
		Ac Re	Ac Re	Ac Re	Ac Re	Ac Re	Ac Re	Ac Re	Ac Re	Ac Re	Ac Re	Ac Re	Ac Re	Ac Re	Ac Re	Ac Re	Ac Re	Ac Re	
Single	50	▽	0 1	Use Letter G	Use Letter K	Use Letter J	1 2	2 3	3 4	5 6	7 8	8 9	10 11	12 13	14 15	18 19	21 22	△	50
Double	32	▽	*				0 2	0 3	1 4	2 5	3 7	3 7	5 9	6 10	7 11	9 14	11 16	△	32
	64		*				1 2	3 4	4 5	6 7	8 9	11 12	12 13	15 16	18 19	23 24	26 27		64
Multiple	13	▽	*				# 2	# 2	# 3	# 4	0 4	0 4	0 5	0 6	1 7	1 8	2 9	△	13
	26						# 2	0 3	0 3	1 5	1 6	2 7	3 8	3 9	4 10	6 12	7 14		26
	39						0 2	0 3	1 4	2 6	3 8	4 9	6 10	7 12	8 13	11 17	13 19		39
	52						0 3	1 4	2 5	3 7	5 10	6 11	8 13	10 15	12 17	16 22	19 25		52
	65						1 3	2 4	3 6	5 8	7 11	9 12	11 15	14 17	17 20	22 25	25 29		65
	78						1 3	3 5	4 6	7 9	10 12	12 14	14 17	18 20	21 23	27 29	31 33		78
	91						2 3	4 5	6 7	9 10	13 14	14 15	18 19	21 22	25 26	32 33	37 38		91
		Less than 0.40	0.40	×	0.65	1.0	1.5	2.5	4.0	6.5	×	10	×	15	×	25	×	Higher than 25	
		Acceptable Quality Levels (tightened inspection)																	

△ = Use next preceding sample size code for which acceptance and rejection numbers are available.
▽ = Use next subsequent sample size code for which acceptance and rejection numbers are available.
Ac = Acceptance number
Re = Rejection number
* = Use single sampling plan above (or alternatively use letter L)
\# = Acceptance not permitted at this sample size.

H

TABLE X-J — Tables for sample size code letter: J

CHART J — OPERATING CHARACTERISTIC CURVES FOR SINGLE SAMPLING PLANS
(Curves for double and multiple sampling are matched as closely as practicable)

PERCENT OF LOTS EXPECTED TO BE ACCEPTED (P_a) — vertical axis (100, 90, 80, 70, 60, 50, 40, 30, 20, 10, 0)

QUALITY OF SUBMITTED LOTS (P_a in percent defective for AQL's ≤10; in defects per hundred units for AQL's >10) — horizontal axis (1–40)

Curves labeled: 0, 0.65, 1.0, 1.5, 2.5, 4.0, 6.5, 10, 15

NOTE: Figures on curves are Acceptable Quality Levels (AQL's) for normal inspection.

TABLE X-J-1 — TABULATED VALUES FOR OPERATING CHARACTERISTIC CURVES FOR SINGLE SAMPLING PLANS

Acceptable Quality Levels (normal inspection)

p (in percent defective)

P_a	0.15	0.65	1.0	1.5	2.5	4.0	X	6.5	X	10
99.0	0.013	0.188	0.550	1.05	2.30	3.72	4.50	6.13	7.88	9.75
95.0	0.064	0.444	1.03	1.73	3.32	5.06	5.98	7.91	9.89	11.9
90.0	0.132	0.666	1.38	2.20	3.98	5.91	6.91	8.95	11.0	13.2
75.0	0.359	1.202	2.16	3.18	5.30	7.50	8.62	10.9	13.2	15.5
50.0	0.863	2.09	3.33	4.57	7.06	9.55	10.8	13.3	15.8	18.3
25.0	1.72	3.33	4.84	6.31	9.14	11.9	13.3	16.0	18.6	21.3
10.0	2.84	4.78	6.52	8.16	11.3	14.2	15.7	18.6	21.4	24.2
5.0	3.68	5.80	7.66	9.39	12.7	15.8	17.3	20.3	23.2	26.0
1.0	5.59	8.00	10.1	12.0	15.6	18.9	20.5	23.6	26.5	29.5
(tightened)	0.25	1.0	1.5	2.5	4.0	X	6.5	10	10	X

p (in defects per hundred units)

P_a	0.15	0.65	1.0	1.5	2.5	4.0	X	6.5	X	10	X	15
99.0	0.013	0.186	0.545	1.03	2.23	3.63	4.38	5.96	7.62	9.35	12.9	15.7
95.0	0.064	0.444	1.02	1.71	3.27	4.98	5.87	7.71	9.61	11.6	15.6	18.6
90.0	0.131	0.665	1.38	2.18	3.94	5.82	6.79	8.78	10.8	12.9	17.1	20.3
75.0	0.360	1.20	2.16	3.17	5.27	7.45	8.55	10.8	13.0	15.3	19.9	23.4
50.0	0.866	2.10	3.34	4.59	7.09	9.59	10.8	13.3	15.8	18.3	23.3	27.1
25.0	1.73	3.37	4.90	6.39	9.28	12.1	13.5	16.3	19.0	21.8	27.2	31.2
10.0	2.88	4.86	6.65	8.35	11.6	14.7	16.2	19.3	22.2	25.2	30.9	35.2
5.0	3.75	5.93	7.87	9.69	13.1	16.4	18.0	21.2	24.3	27.4	33.4	37.8
1.0	5.76	8.30	10.5	12.6	16.5	20.0	21.8	25.2	28.5	31.8	38.2	42.9
(tightened)	0.25	1.0	1.5	2.5	4.0	6.5	6.5	X	10	10	15	X

Acceptable Quality Levels (tightened inspection)

Note: All values given in above table based on Poisson distribution as an approximation to the Binominal

TABLE X-J-2 — SAMPLING PLANS FOR SAMPLE SIZE CODE LETTER: J

Acceptable Quality Levels (normal inspection)

Type of sampling plan	Cumulative sample size	<0.15 Ac Re	0.15 Ac Re	0.25 Ac Re	0.40 Ac Re	0.65 Ac Re	1.0 Ac Re	1.5 Ac Re	2.5 Ac Re	4.0 Ac Re	6.5 Ac Re	10 Ac Re	15 Ac Re	Higher than 15 Ac Re*
Single	80	▽	0 1	Use Letter H	Use Letter H	1 2	2 3	3 4	5 6	7 8	10 11	14 15	21 22	△
Double	50	▽	*	Use Letter H	Use Letter H	0 2	0 3	1 4	2 5	3 7	5 9	7 11	11 16	△
	100			Use Letter K	Use Letter L	1 2	3 4	4 5	6 7	8 9	12 13	18 19	26 27	
Multiple	20	▽	*			# 2	# 2	# 3	# 4	0 4	0 5	0 6	2 9	△
	40					# 2	0 3	0 3	1 5	1 6	3 8	3 9	7 14	
	60					0 2	0 3	1 4	2 6	3 8	6 10	7 12	13 19	
	80					0 3	1 4	2 5	3 7	5 10	8 13	10 15	19 25	
	100					1 3	2 4	3 6	5 8	7 11	11 15	14 17	25 29	
	120					1 3	3 5	4 6	7 9	10 12	14 17	18 20	31 33	
	140					2 3	4 5	6 7	9 10	13 14	18 19	21 22	37 38	

Acceptable Quality Levels (tightened inspection)

Less than 0.25	0.25	0.40	0.65	1.0	1.5	2.5	4.0	6.5	10	15	Higher than 15

△ = Use next subsequent sample size code for which acceptance and rejection numbers are available.

▽ = Use next preceding sample size code for which acceptance and rejection numbers are available.

Ac = Acceptance number

Re = Rejection number

* = Use single sampling plan above (or alternatively, use letter M)

\# = Acceptance not permitted at this sample size.

J

47

TABLE X-K — Tables for sample size code letter: K

CHART K — OPERATING CHARACTERISTIC CURVES FOR SINGLE SAMPLING PLANS
(Curves for double and multiple sampling are matched as closely as practicable)

PERCENT OF LOTS EXPECTED TO BE ACCEPTED (P_a)

QUALITY OF SUBMITTED LOTS (P_a in percent defective for AQL's ≤ 10; in defects per hundred units for AQL's >10)

NOTE: Figures on curves are Acceptable Quality Levels (AQL's) for normal inspection)

TABLE X-K-1 — TABULATED VALUES FOR OPERATING CHARACTERISTIC CURVES FOR SINGLE SAMPLING PLANS

P_a	Acceptable Quality Levels (normal inspection)												
	0.10	0.40	0.65	1.0	1.5	2.5	✕	4.0	✕	6.5	✕	10
	p (in percent defective or defects per hundred units											
99.0	0.0081	0.119	0.349	0.658	1.43	2.33	2.81	3.82	4.88	5.98	8.28	10.1
95.0	0.0410	0.284	0.654	1.09	2.09	3.19	3.76	4.94	6.15	7.40	9.95	11.9
90.0	0.0840	0.426	0.882	1.40	2.52	3.73	4.35	5.62	6.92	8.24	10.9	13.0
75.0	0.230	0.769	0.382	2.03	3.38	4.77	5.47	6.90	8.34	9.79	12.7	14.9
50.0	0.554	1.34	2.14	2.94	4.54	6.14	6.94	8.53	10.1	11.7	14.9	17.3
25.0	1.11	2.15	3.14	4.09	5.94	7.75	8.64	10.4	12.2	13.9	17.4	20.0
10.0	1.84	3.11	4.26	5.35	7.42	9.42	10.4	12.3	14.2	16.1	19.8	22.5
5.0	2.40	3.80	5.04	6.20	8.41	10.5	11.5	13.6	15.6	17.5	21.4	24.2
1.0	3.68	5.31	6.73	8.04	10.5	12.8	18.3	16.1	18.3	20.4	24.5	27.5
	0.15	0.65	1.0	1.5	2.5	✕	4.0	✕	6.5	✕	10	
	Acceptable Quality Levels (tightened inspection)												

Note: All values given in above table based on Poisson distribution as an approximation to the Binominal

TABLE X-K-2 — SAMPLING PLANS FOR SAMPLE SIZE CODE LETTER: K

Type of sampling plan	Cumulative sample size	Less than 0.10	0.10	0.15	><	0.25	0.40	0.65	1.0	1.5	2.5	><	4.0	><	6.5	><	10	Higher than 10	Cumulative sample size
		Ac Re	Ac Re	Ac Re	Ac Re	Ac Re	Ac Re	Ac Re	Ac Re	Ac Re	Ac Re	Ac Re	Ac Re	Ac Re	Ac Re	Ac Re	Ac Re	Ac Re	
Single	125	▽	0 1	Use Letter J	Use Letter M	Use Letter L	1 2	2 3	3 4	5 6	7 8	8 9	10 11	12 13	14 15	18 19	21 22	△	125
Double	80	▽	*				0 2	0 3	1 4	2 5	3 7	3 7	5 9	6 10	7 11	9 14	11 16	△	80
	160		*				1 2	3 4	4 5	6 7	8 9	11 12	12 13	15 16	18 19	23 24	26 27		160
Multiple	32	▽	*				# 2	# 2	# 3	# 4	0 4	0 4	0 5	0 6	1 7	1 8	2 9	△	32
	64						# 2	0 3	0 3	1 5	1 6	2 7	3 8	3 9	4 10	6 12	7 14		64
	96						0 2	0 3	1 4	2 6	3 8	4 9	6 10	7 12	8 13	11 17	13 19		96
	128						0 3	1 4	2 5	3 7	5 10	6 11	8 13	10 15	12 17	16 22	19 25		128
	160						1 3	2 4	3 6	5 8	7 11	9 12	11 15	14 17	17 20	22 25	25 29		160
	192						1 3	3 5	4 6	7 9	10 12	12 14	14 17	18 20	21 23	27 29	31 33		192
	224						2 3	4 5	6 7	9 10	13 14	14 15	18 19	21 22	25 26	32 33	37 38		224
Acceptable Quality Levels (tightened inspection)		Less than 0.15	0.15	><	0.25	0.40	0.65	1.0	1.5	2.5	><	4.0	><	6.5	><	10	><	Higher than 10	

The AQL columns above are Acceptable Quality Levels (normal inspection); the last row gives Acceptable Quality Levels (tightened inspection).

K

△ = Use next preceding sample size code for which acceptance and rejection numbers are available.

▽ = Use next subsequent sample size code for which acceptance and rejection numbers are available.

Ac = Acceptance number

Re = Rejection number

* = Use single sampling plan above (or alternatively use letter N)

\# = Acceptance not permitted at this sample size.

TABLE X-L — Tables for sample size code letter: L
CHART L — OPERATING CHARACTERISTIC CURVES FOR SINGLE SAMPLING PLANS
(Curves for double and multiple sampling are matched as closely as practicable)

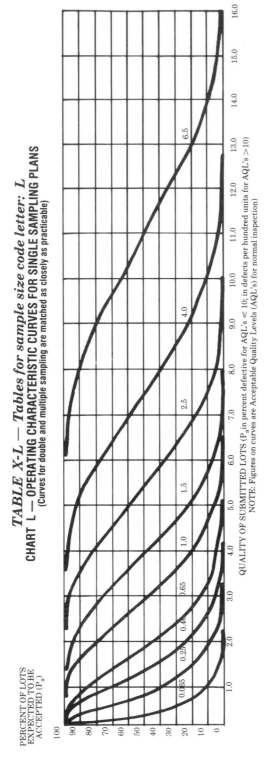

PERCENT OF LOTS EXPECTED TO BE ACCEPTED (P_a)

QUALITY OF SUBMITTED LOTS (P_a in percent defective for AQL's ≤ 10; in defects per hundred units for AQL's >10)
NOTE: Figures on curves are Acceptable Quality Levels (AQL's) for normal inspection)

TABLE X-L-1 — TABULATED VALUES FOR OPERATING CHARACTERISTIC CURVES FOR SINGLE SAMPLING PLANS

P_a	Acceptable Quality Levels (normal inspection)											
	0.065	0.25	0.40	0.65	1.0	1.5	X	2.5	X	4.0	X	6.5
	p (in percent defective or defects per hundred units)											
99.0	0.0051	0.075	0.218	0.412	0.893	1.45	1.75	2.39	3.05	3.74	5.17	6.29
95.0	0.0256	0.178	0.409	0.683	1.31	1.99	2.35	3.09	3.85	4.62	6.22	7.45
90.0	0.0525	0.266	0.551	0.873	1.58	2.33	2.72	3.51	4.32	5.15	6.84	8.12
75.0	0.144	0.481	0.864	1.27	2.11	2.98	3.42	4.31	5.21	6.12	7.95	9.34
50.0	0.347	0.839	1.34	1.84	2.84	3.84	4.33	5.33	6.33	7.33	9.33	10.8
25.0	0.693	1.35	1.96	2.56	3.71	4.84	5.40	6.51	7.61	8.70	10.9	12.5
10.0	1.15	1.95	2.66	3.34	4.64	5.89	6.50	7.70	8.89	10.1	12.4	14.1
5.0	1.50	2.37	3.15	3.88	5.26	6.57	7.22	8.48	9.72	10.9	13.3	15.1
1.0	2.30	3.32	4.20	5.02	6.55	8.00	8.70	10.1	11.4	12.7	15.3	17.2
	0.10	0.40	0.65	1.0	1.5		2.5		4.0		6.5	
	Acceptable Quality Levels (tightened inspection)											

Note: All values given in above table based on Poisson distribution as an approximation to the Binominal

TABLE X-L-2 — SAMPLING PLANS FOR SAMPLE SIZE CODE LETTER: L

Values shown for each Acceptable Quality Level are "Ac Re" (Acceptance number, Rejection number). ⤬ denotes an arrow column.

Acceptable Quality Levels (normal inspection)

Type of sampling plan	Cumulative sample size	Less than 0.065	0.065	0.10	⤬	0.15	0.25	0.40	0.65	1.0	1.5	⤬	2.5	⤬	4.0	⤬	6.5	Higher than 6.5
Single	200	▽	0 1	Use Letter K	Use Letter N	Use Letter M	1 2	2 3	3 4	5 6	7 8	8 9	10 11	12 13	14 15	18 19	21 22	△
Double	125	▽	*	Letter	Letter	Letter	0 2	0 3	1 4	2 5	3 7	3 7	5 9	6 10	7 11	9 14	11 16	△
Double	250			K	N	M	1 2	3 4	4 5	6 7	8 9	11 12	12 13	15 16	18 19	23 24	26 27	
Multiple	50	▽	*				# 2	# 2	# 3	# 4	0 4	0 4	0 5	0 6	1 7	1 8	2 9	△
Multiple	100						# 2	0 3	0 3	1 5	1 6	2 7	3 8	3 9	4 10	6 12	7 14	
Multiple	150						0 2	0 3	1 4	2 6	3 8	4 9	6 10	7 12	8 13	11 17	13 19	
Multiple	200						0 3	1 4	2 5	3 7	5 10	6 11	8 13	10 15	12 17	16 22	19 25	
Multiple	250						1 3	2 4	3 6	5 8	7 11	9 12	11 15	14 17	17 20	22 25	25 29	
Multiple	300						1 3	3 5	4 6	7 9	10 12	12 14	14 17	18 20	21 23	27 29	31 33	
Multiple	350						2 3	4 5	6 7	9 10	13 14	14 15	18 19	21 22	25 26	32 33	37 38	

Acceptable Quality Levels (tightened inspection)

	Less than 0.10	0.10	⤬	0.15	0.25	0.40	0.65	1.0	1.5	⤬	2.5	⤬	4.0	⤬	6.5	Higher than 6.5

Legend

△ = Use next preceding sample size code for which acceptance and rejection numbers are available.

▽ = Use next subsequent sample size code for which acceptance and rejection numbers are available.

Ac = Acceptance number

Re = Rejection number

* = Use single sampling plan above (or alternatively use letter P)

= Acceptance not permitted at this sample size.

51

TABLE X-M — Tables for sample size code letter: M
CHART M — OPERATING CHARACTERISTIC CURVES FOR SINGLE SAMPLING PLANS
(Curves for double and multiple sampling are matched as closely as practicable)

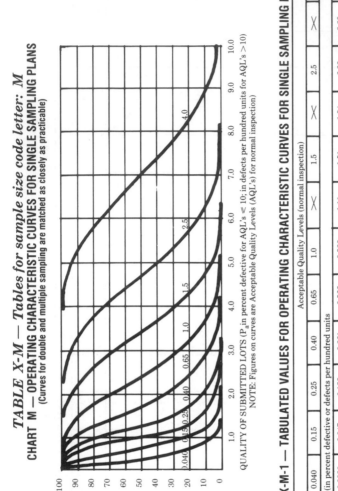

QUALITY OF SUBMITTED LOTS (P_a in percent defective for AQL's ≤ 10; in defects per hundred units for AQL's >10)

NOTE: Figures on curves are Acceptable Quality Levels (AQL's) for normal inspection)

TABLE X-M-1 — TABULATED VALUES FOR OPERATING CHARACTERISTIC CURVES FOR SINGLE SAMPLING PLANS

P_a	Acceptable Quality Levels (normal inspection)											
	0.040	0.15	0.25	0.40	0.65	1.0	✕	1.5	✕	2.5	✕	4.0
	p (in percent defective or defects per hundred units											
99.0	0.0032	0.047	0.138	0.261	0.566	0.922	1.11	1.51	1.94	2.38	3.28	3.99
95.0	0.0163	0.112	0.259	0.433	0.829	1.26	1.49	1.96	2.44	2.94	3.95	4.73
90.0	0.0333	0.168	0.349	0.533	1.00	1.48	1.72	2.23	2.75	3.27	4.34	5.16
75.0	0.0914	0.305	0.580	0.804	1.34	1.89	2.17	2.74	3.31	3.89	5.05	5.93
50.0	0.220	0.532	0.848	1.17	1.80	2.43	2.75	3.39	4.02	4.66	5.93	6.88
25.0	0.440	0.854	1.24	1.62	2.36	3.07	3.43	4.13	4.83	5.52	6.90	7.92
10.0	0.731	1.23	1.69	2.12	2.94	3.74	4.13	4.89	5.65	6.39	7.86	8.95
5.0	0.951	1.51	2.00	2.46	3.34	4.17	4.58	5.38	6.17	6.95	8.47	9.60
1.0	1.46	2.11	2.67	3.19	4.16	5.08	5.53	6.40	7.25	8.08	9.71	10.9
	0.065	0.25	0.40	0.65	1.0	✕	1.5	✕	2.5	✕	4.0	✕
	Acceptable Quality Levels (tightened inspection)											

Note: All values given in above table based on Poisson distribution as an approximation to the Binominal

52

TABLE X-M-2 — SAMPLING PLANS FOR SAMPLE SIZE CODE LETTER: M

Acceptable Quality Levels (normal inspection) — cell values shown as Ac/Re (Acceptance number / Rejection number)

Type of sampling plan	Cumulative sample size	Less than 0.040	0.040	0.065	✕	0.10	0.15	0.25	0.40	0.65	1.0	✕	1.5	✕	2.5	✕	4.0	Higher than 4.0	Cumulative sample size
Single	315	▽	0/1	Use Letter L	Use Letter P	Use Letter N	1/2	2/3	3/4	5/6	7/8	8/9	10/11	12/13	14/15	18/19	21/22	△	315
Double	200	▽	*	Use Letter L	Use Letter P	Use Letter N	0/2	0/3	1/4	2/5	3/7	3/7	5/9	6/10	7/11	9/14	11/16	△	200
	400						1/2	3/4	4/5	6/7	8/9	11/12	12/13	15/16	18/19	23/24	26/27		400
Multiple	80	▽	*	Use Letter L	Use Letter P	Use Letter N	# 2	# 2	# 3	# 4	0/4	0/4	0/5	0/6	1/7	1/8	2/9	△	80
	160						# 2	0/3	0/3	1/5	1/6	2/7	3/8	3/9	4/10	6/12	7/14		160
	240						0/2	0/3	1/4	2/6	3/8	4/9	6/10	7/12	8/13	11/17	13/19		240
	320						0/3	1/4	2/5	3/7	5/10	6/11	8/13	10/15	12/17	16/22	19/25		320
	400						1/3	2/4	3/6	5/8	7/11	9/12	11/15	14/17	17/20	22/25	25/29		400
	480						1/3	3/5	4/6	7/9	10/12	12/14	14/17	18/20	21/23	27/29	31/33		480
	560						2/3	4/5	6/7	9/10	13/14	14/15	18/19	21/22	25/26	32/33	37/38		560
Acceptable Quality Levels (tightened inspection)		Less than 0.065	0.065	0.10	0.15	✕	0.25	0.40	0.65	1.0	1.5	✕	2.5	✕	4.0	✕	Higher than 4.0	✕	

M

△ = Use next preceding sample size code for which acceptance and rejection numbers are available.

▽ = Use next subsequent sample size code for which acceptance and rejection numbers are available.

Ac = Acceptance number

Re = Rejection number

* = Use single sampling plan above (or alternatively use letter Q)

\# = Acceptance not permitted at this sample size.

TABLE X-N — Tables for sample size code letter: N
CHART N — OPERATING CHARACTERISTIC CURVES FOR SINGLE SAMPLING PLANS
(Curves for double and multiple sampling are matched as closely as practicable)

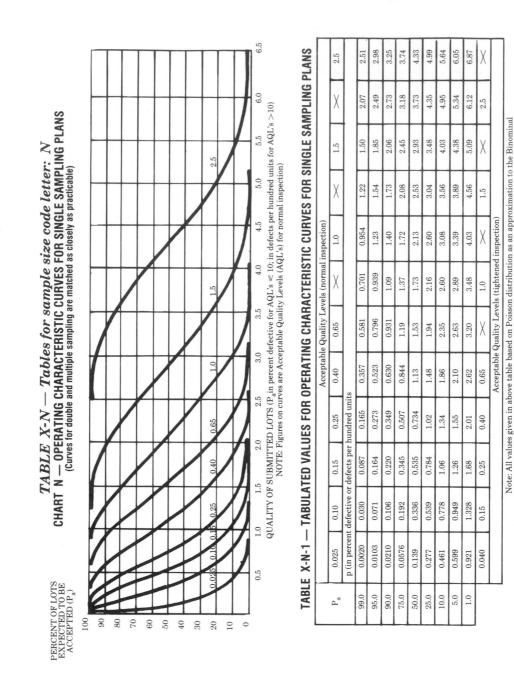

PERCENT OF LOTS EXPECTED TO BE ACCEPTED (P_a)

QUALITY OF SUBMITTED LOTS (P_a in percent defective for AQL's $\leq$ 10; in defects per hundred units for AQL's $>$10)

NOTE: Figures on curves are Acceptable Quality Levels (AQL's) for normal inspection

TABLE X-N-1 — TABULATED VALUES FOR OPERATING CHARACTERISTIC CURVES FOR SINGLE SAMPLING PLANS

P_a	\multicolumn{12}{c}{Acceptable Quality Levels (normal inspection)}
	0.025	0.10	0.15	0.25	0.40	0.65	✕	1.0	✕	1.5	✕	2.5
	\multicolumn{12}{c}{p (in percent defective or defects per hundred units)}
99.0	0.0020	0.030	0.087	0.165	0.357	0.581	0.701	0.954	1.22	1.50	2.07	2.51
95.0	0.0103	0.071	0.164	0.273	0.523	0.796	0.939	1.23	1.54	1.85	2.49	2.98
90.0	0.0210	0.106	0.220	0.349	0.630	0.931	1.09	1.40	1.73	2.06	2.73	3.25
75.0	0.0576	0.192	0.345	0.507	0.844	1.19	1.37	1.72	2.08	2.45	3.18	3.74
50.0	0.139	0.336	0.535	0.734	1.13	1.53	1.73	2.13	2.53	2.93	3.73	4.33
25.0	0.277	0.539	0.784	1.02	1.48	1.94	2.16	2.60	3.04	3.48	4.35	4.99
10.0	0.461	0.778	1.06	1.34	1.86	2.35	2.60	3.08	3.56	4.03	4.95	5.64
5.0	0.599	0.949	1.26	1.55	2.10	2.63	2.89	3.39	3.89	4.38	5.34	6.05
1.0	0.921	1.328	1.68	2.01	2.62	3.20	3.48	4.03	4.56	5.09	6.12	6.87
	0.040	0.15	0.25	0.40	0.65	1.0	✕	1.5	✕	2.5	✕	✕
	\multicolumn{12}{c}{Acceptable Quality Levels (tightened inspection)}

Note: All values given in above table based on Poisson distribution as an approximation to the Binominal

TABLE X-N-2 — SAMPLING PLANS FOR SAMPLE SIZE CODE LETTER: N

Acceptable Quality Levels (normal inspection)

Type of sampling plan	Cumulative sample size	Less than 0.025	0.025	0.040	0.065	⋈	0.10	0.15	0.25	0.40	0.65	⋈	1.0	⋈	1.5	⋈	2.5	Higher than 2.5	Cumulative sample size
		Ac Re	Ac Re	Ac Re	Ac Re	Ac Re	Ac Re	Ac Re	Ac Re	Ac Re	Ac Re	Ac Re	Ac Re	Ac Re	Ac Re	Ac Re	Ac Re	Ac Re	
Single	500	▽	0 1	Use Letter M	Use Letter Q	Use Letter P	1 2	2 3	3 4	5 6	7 8	8 9	10 11	12 13	14 15	18 19	21 22	△	500
Double	315	▽	*	(Letter)	(Letter)	(Letter)	0 2	0 3	1 4	2 5	3 7	3 7	5 9	6 10	7 11	9 14	11 16	△	315
	630						1 2	3 4	4 5	6 7	8 9	11 12	12 13	15 16	18 19	23 24	26 27		630
Multiple	125	▽	*				# 2	# 2	# 3	# 4	0 4	0 4	0 5	0 6	1 7	1 8	2 9	△	125
	250						# 2	0 3	0 3	1 5	1 6	2 7	3 8	3 9	4 10	6 12	7 14		250
	375						0 2	0 3	1 4	2 6	3 8	4 9	6 10	7 12	8 13	11 17	13 19		375
	500						0 3	1 4	2 5	3 7	5 10	6 11	8 13	10 15	12 17	16 22	19 25		500
	625						1 3	2 4	3 6	5 8	7 11	9 12	11 15	14 17	17 20	22 25	25 29		625
	750						1 3	3 5	4 6	7 9	10 12	12 14	14 17	18 20	21 23	27 29	31 33		750
	875						2 3	4 5	6 7	9 10	13 14	14 15	18 19	21 22	25 26	33 33	37 38		875
		Less than 0.040	0.040	⋈	0.065	⋈	0.10	0.15	0.25	0.40	0.65	⋈	1.0	⋈	1.5	⋈	2.5	Higher than 2.5	

Acceptable Quality Levels (tightened inspection)

N

△ = Use next preceding sample size code for which acceptance and rejection numbers are available.

▽ = Use next subsequent sample size code for which acceptance and rejection numbers are available.

Ac = Acceptance number

Re = Rejection number

* = Use single sampling plan above (or alternatively use letter R)

\# = Acceptance not permitted at this sample size.

TABLE X-P — Tables for sample size code letter: P
CHART P — OPERATING CHARACTERISTIC CURVES FOR SINGLE SAMPLING PLANS
(Curves for double and multiple sampling are matched as closely as practicable)

PERCENT OF LOTS EXPECTED TO BE ACCEPTED (P_a)

Curve labels: 0.015, 0.065, 0.10, 0.15, 0.25, 0.40, 0.65, 1.0, 1.5

QUALITY OF SUBMITTED LOTS (P_a in percent defective for AQL's ≤ 10; in defects per hundred units for AQL's >10)

NOTE: Figures on curves are Acceptable Quality Levels (AQL's) for normal inspection)

TABLE X-P-1 — TABULATED VALUES FOR OPERATING CHARACTERISTIC CURVES FOR SINGLE SAMPLING PLANS

P_a	Acceptable Quality Levels (normal inspection)											
	0.015	0.065	0.10	0.15	0.25	0.40	X	0.65	X	1.0	X	1.5
	p (in percent defective or defects per hundred units)											
99.0	0.0013	0.0186	0.055	0.103	0.223	0.363	0.438	0.596	0.762	0.935	1.29	1.57
95.0	0.0064	0.0444	0.102	0.171	0.327	0.498	0.587	0.771	0.961	1.16	1.56	1.86
90.0	0.0131	0.0665	0.138	0.218	0.394	0.582	0.679	0.878	1.08	1.29	1.71	2.03
75.0	0.0360	0.120	0.216	0.317	0.527	0.745	0.855	1.08	1.30	1.53	1.99	2.34
50.0	0.0866	0.210	0.334	0.459	0.709	0.959	1.08	1.33	1.58	1.83	2.33	2.71
25.0	0.173	0.337	0.490	0.639	0.928	1.21	1.35	1.63	1.90	2.18	2.72	3.12
10.0	0.288	0.486	0.665	0.835	1.16	1.47	1.62	1.93	2.22	2.52	3.09	3.52
5.0	0.375	0.593	0.787	0.969	1.31	1.64	1.80	2.12	2.43	2.74	3.34	3.78
1.0	0.576	0.830	1.05	1.26	1.64	2.00	2.18	2.52	2.85	3.18	3.82	4.29
	0.025	0.10	0.15	0.25	0.40	0.65	0.65	1.0	1.0	X	1.5	X
	Acceptable Quality Levels (tightened inspection)											

Note: All values given in above table based on Poisson distribution as an approximation to the Binominal

TABLE X-P-2 — SAMPLING PLANS FOR SAMPLE SIZE CODE LETTER: P

Type of sampling plan	Cumulative sample size	Acceptable Quality Levels (normal inspection)																Higher than 1.5	Cumulative sample size
		0.010	0.015	0.025	×	0.040	0.065	0.10	0.15	0.25	0.40	×	0.65	×	1.0	×	1.5		
		Ac Re	Ac Re	Ac Re	Ac Re	Ac Re	Ac Re	Ac Re	Ac Re	Ac Re	Ac Re	Ac Re	Ac Re	Ac Re	Ac Re	Ac Re	Ac Re	Ac Re	
Single	800	▽	0 1				1 2	2 3	3 4	5 6	7 8	8 9	10 11	12 13	14 15	18 19	21 22	△	800
Double	500	▽	*	Use Letter N	Use Letter R	Use Letter Q	0 2	0 3	1 4	2 5	3 7	3 7	5 9	6 10	7 11	9 14	11 16	△	500
	1000						1 2	3 4	4 5	6 7	8 9	11 12	12 13	15 16	18 19	23 24	26 27		1000
Multiple	200	▽	*				# 2	# 2	# 3	# 4	0 4	0 4	0 5	0 6	1 7	1 8	2 9	△	200
	400						# 2	0 3	0 3	1 5	1 6	2 7	3 8	3 9	4 10	6 12	7 14		400
	600						0 2	0 3	1 4	2 6	3 8	4 9	6 10	7 12	8 13	11 17	13 19		600
	800						0 3	1 4	2 5	3 7	5 10	6 11	8 13	10 15	12 17	16 22	19 25		800
	1000						1 3	2 4	3 6	5 8	7 11	9 12	11 15	14 17	17 20	22 25	25 29		1000
	1200						1 3	3 5	4 6	7 9	10 12	12 14	14 17	18 20	21 23	27 29	31 33		1200
	1400						2 3	4 5	6 7	9 10	13 14	14 15	18 19	21 22	25 26	32 33	37 38		1400
		Less than 0.025	0.025	×	0.040	0.065	0.10	0.15	0.25	0.40	×	0.65	×	1.0	×	1.5	×	Higher than 1.5	
		Acceptable Quality Levels (tightened inspection)																	

△ = Use next preceding sample size code for which acceptance and rejection numbers are available.
▽ = Use next subsequent sample size code for which acceptance and rejection numbers are available.
Ac = Acceptance number
Re = Rejection number
* = Use single sampling plan above.
\# = Acceptance not permitted at this sample size.

TABLE X-Q — Tables for sample size code letter: Q
CHART Q — OPERATING CHARACTERISTIC CURVES FOR SINGLE SAMPLING PLANS
(Curves for double and multiple sampling are matched as closely as practicable)

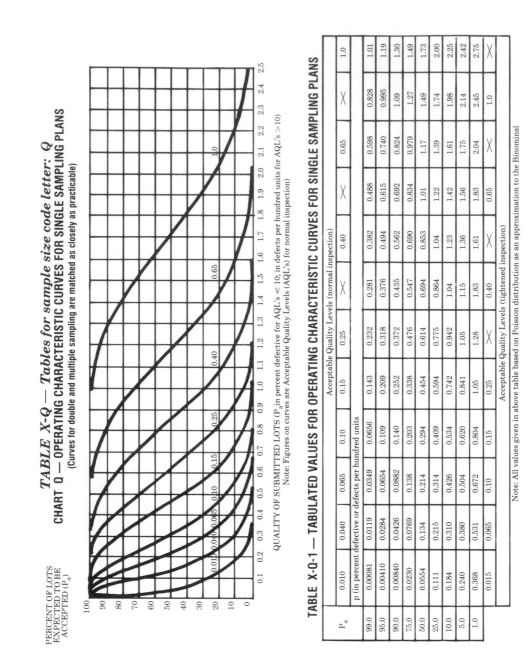

PERCENT OF LOTS EXPECTED TO BE ACCEPTED (P_a)

QUALITY OF SUBMITTED LOTS (P_a in percent defective for AQL's ≤ 10; in defects per hundred units for AQL's >10)
Note: Figures on curves are Acceptable Quality Levels (AQL's) for normal inspection

TABLE X-Q-1 — TABULATED VALUES FOR OPERATING CHARACTERISTIC CURVES FOR SINGLE SAMPLING PLANS

P_a	Acceptable Quality Levels (normal inspection)											
	0.010	0.040	0.065	0.10	0.15	0.25	X	0.40	X	0.65	X	1.0
	p (in percent defective or defects per hundred units)											
99.0	0.00081	0.0119	0.0349	0.0656	0.143	0.232	0.281	0.382	0.488	0.598	0.828	1.01
95.0	0.00410	0.0284	0.0654	0.109	0.209	0.318	0.376	0.494	0.615	0.740	0.995	1.19
90.0	0.00840	0.0426	0.0882	0.140	0.252	0.372	0.435	0.562	0.692	0.824	1.09	1.30
75.0	0.0230	0.0769	0.138	0.203	0.338	0.476	0.547	0.690	0.834	0.979	1.27	1.49
50.0	0.0554	0.134	0.214	0.294	0.454	0.614	0.694	0.853	1.01	1.17	1.49	1.73
25.0	0.111	0.215	0.314	0.409	0.594	0.775	0.864	1.04	1.22	1.39	1.74	2.00
10.0	0.184	0.310	0.426	0.534	0.742	0.942	1.04	1.23	1.42	1.61	1.98	2.25
5.0	0.240	0.380	0.504	0.620	0.841	1.05	1.15	1.36	1.56	1.75	2.14	2.42
1.0	0.368	0.531	0.672	0.804	1.05	1.28	1.83	1.61	1.83	2.04	2.45	2.75
	0.015	0.065	0.10	0.15	0.25	X	0.40	X	0.65	X	1.0	X
	Acceptable Quality Levels (tightened inspection)											

Note: All values given in above table based on Poisson distribution as an approximation to the Binominal

TABLE X-Q-2 — SAMPLING PLANS FOR SAMPLE SIZE CODE LETTER: Q

Acceptable Quality Levels (normal inspection)

Type of sampling plan	Cumulative sample size	0.010 / 0.015	0.025	0.040	0.065	0.10	0.15	0.25	0.40	X	0.65	X	1.0	Higher than 1.0
		Ac Re	Ac Re	Ac Re	Ac Re	Ac Re	Ac Re	Ac Re	Ac Re	Ac Re	Ac Re	Ac Re	Ac Re	Ac Fe
Single	1250	Use Letter · 0 1	1 2	2 3	3 4	5 6	7 8	10 11	12 13	14 15	18 19	21 22		△
Double	800	Use Letter · 0 2	0 3	1 4	2 5	3 7	5 9	6 10	7 11	9 14	11 16			△
	1600	Use Letter · 1 2	3 4	4 5	6 7	8 9	11 12	12 13	15 16	18 19	23 24	26 27		
Multiple	315	# 2 · # 2	# 2	# 3	# 4	0 4	0 4	0 5	0 6	1 7	1 8	2 9		
	630	# 2 · 0 3	0 3	0 3	1 5	1 6	2 7	3 8	3 9	4 10	6 12	7 14		
	945	0 2 · 0 3	1 4	2 6	3 8	4 9	6 10	7 12	8 13	11 17	13 19			
	1260	0 3 · 1 4	2 5	3 7	5 10	6 11	8 13	10 15	11 17	12 17	16 22	19 25		
	1575	1 3 · 2 4	3 6	5 8	7 11	9 12	11 15	14 17	14 17	17 20	22 25	25 29		
	1890	1 3 · 3 5	4 6	6 9	9 12	12 14	14 17	18 20	18 19	21 23	27 29	31 33		
	2205	2 3 · 4 5	6 7	9 10	13 14	14 15	18 19	21 22	21 22	25 26	32 33	37 38		

Left-margin reference cells (lower AQL columns 0.010–0.040): Single — "Use Letter"; Double — "Use Letter", * , P, S, R; Multiple — R, P, S, * .

Acceptable Quality Levels (tightened inspection)

0.010	0.015	0.025	0.040	0.065	0.10	0.15	0.25	0.40	0.65	X	1.0	X	Higher than 1.0

Cumulative sample sizes (top/right): 1250; 800; 1600; 315; 630; 945; 1260; 1575; 1890; 2205.

Q

△ = Use next preceding sample size code for which acceptance and rejection numbers are available.
* = Use single sampling plan above.
\# = Acceptance not permitted at this sample size.
Ac = Acceptance number
Re = Rejection number
* = Use single sampling plan above.

59

60

TABLE X-R — Tables for sample size code letter: R
CHART R — OPERATING CHARACTERISTIC CURVES FOR SINGLE SAMPLING PLANS
(Curves for double and multiple sampling are matched as closely as practicable)

PERCENT OF LOTS EXPECTED TO BE ACCEPTED (P_a)

QUALITY OF SUBMITTED LOTS (P_a in percent defective for AQL's ≤10; in defects per hundred units for AQL's >10)
NOTE: Figures on curves are Acceptable Quality Levels (AQL's) for normal inspection.

TABLE X-R-1 — TABULATED VALUES FOR OPERATING CHARACTERISTIC CURVES FOR SINGLE SAMPLING PLANS

P_a	Acceptable Quality Levels (normal inspection)										
	0.025	0.040	0.065	0.10	0.15	0.25	⋈	0.40	⋈	0.65	⋈
	p (in percent defective or defects per hundred units)										
99.0	0.0074	0.0218	0.0412	0.0892	0.145	0.239	0.175	0.374	0.305	0.517	0.629
95.0	0.0178	0.0409	0.0683	0.131	0.199	0.309	0.235	0.462	0.385	0.622	0.745
90.0	0.0266	0.0551	0.0873	0.158	0.233	0.351	0.272	0.515	0.432	0.684	0.812
75.0	0.0481	0.0868	0.127	0.211	0.298	0.431	0.312	0.612	0.521	0.795	0.934
50.0	0.0839	0.134	0.184	0.284	0.384	0.533	0.433	0.733	0.633	0.933	1.08
25.0	0.135	0.196	0.256	0.371	0.484	0.651	0.540	0.870	0.761	1.09	1.25
10.0	0.195	0.266	0.334	0.464	0.589	0.770	0.650	1.01	0.889	1.24	1.41
5.0	0.237	0.315	0.388	0.526	0.657	0.848	0.722	1.09	0.972	1.33	1.51
1.0	0.332	0.420	0.502	0.655	0.800	1.02	0.870	1.27	1.14	1.53	1.72
		0.040	0.065	0.10	0.15	⋈	0.25	⋈	0.40	⋈	0.65
	Acceptable Quality Levels (tightened inspection)										

Note: All values given in above table based on Poisson distribution as an approximation to the Binominal

TABLE X-R-2 — SAMPLING PLANS FOR SAMPLE SIZE CODE LETTER: R

R

Acceptable Quality Levels (normal inspection)

Ac = Acceptance number Re = Rejection number (↓/↑ arrow = use first sampling plan shown by the direction of the arrow)

Single sampling plan (cumulative sample size 2000)

AQL	0.010	0.015	0.025	0.040	0.065	0.10	0.15	0.25	0.40	0.65	Higher than 0.65
Ac Re	0 1	↓	1 2	2 3	3 4	5 6	7 8	10 11	14 15	21 22	△

Double sampling plan (cumulative sample size 1250, then 2500)

AQL	0.010	0.015	0.025	0.040	0.065	0.10	0.15	0.25	0.40	0.65	Higher than 0.65
First (1250) Ac Re	*	↓	0 2	0 3	1 4	2 5	3 7	5 9	7 11	11 16	△
Second (2500) Ac Re			1 2	3 4	4 5	6 7	8 9	12 13	18 19	26 27	△

Multiple sampling plan (cumulative 500, 1000, 1500, 2000, 2500, 3000, 3500)

Cumulative sample size	0.025 Ac Re	0.040 Ac Re	0.065 Ac Re	0.10 Ac Re	0.15 Ac Re	0.25 Ac Re	0.40 Ac Re	0.65 Ac Re
500	# 2	# 2	# 3	# 4	0 4	0 5	1 7	2 9
1000	# 2	0 3	0 3	1 5	1 6	3 8	4 10	7 14
1500	0 2	0 3	1 4	2 6	3 8	6 10	8 13	13 19
2000	0 3	1 4	2 5	3 7	5 10	8 13	12 17	19 25
2500	1 3	2 4	3 6	5 8	7 11	11 15	17 20	25 29
3000	1 3	3 5	4 6	7 9	10 12	14 17	21 23	31 33
3500	2 3	4 5	6 7	9 10	13 14	18 19	25 26	37 38

(For AQL 0.010 and 0.015 the double and multiple plans use * / ↓; Higher than 0.65 = △.)

Acceptable Quality Levels (tightened inspection)

The lower AQL scale (tightened inspection): 0.010, 0.015, 0.040, 0.065, 0.10, 0.15, 0.25, 0.40, 0.65.

Single sampling plan (2000)

AQL	0.015	0.025	0.040	0.065	0.10	0.15	0.25	0.40	0.65
Ac Re	↓	0 1	1 2	2 3	3 4	5 6	8 9	12 13	18 19

Double sampling plan (tightened, 0.65 column verified)

0.65 First (1250)	0.65 Second (2500)
9 14	23 24

Multiple sampling plan (tightened, 0.65 column)

Cumulative	0.65 Ac Re
500	1 8
1000	6 12
1500	11 17
2000	16 22
2500	22 25
3000	29 31
3500	33 37

Notes on small AQL (tightened): Double/Multiple use **Use Letter Q** (0.010), **Use Letter P** (0.015), **Use Letter S** (0.025).

△ = Use next preceding sample size code letter for which acceptance and rejection numbers are available.

Ac = Acceptance number.

Re = Rejection number.

* = Use single sampling plan above.

\# = Acceptance not permitted at this sample size.

61

TABLE X-S — Tables for sample size code letter: S

Type of sampling plan	Cumu-lative sample size	Acceptable Quality Level (normal inspection) ✕	
		Ac	Re
Single	3150	1	2
Double	2000	0	2
	4000	1	2
Multiple	800	#	2
	1600	#	2
	2400	0	2
	3200	0	3
	4000	1	3
	4800	1	3
	5600	2	3
		0.025	
		Acceptable Quality Level (tightened inspection)	

Ac = Acceptance number
Re = Rejection number
\# = Acceptance not permitted at this sample size.

S

INDEX OF TERMS WITH SPECIAL MEANINGS

INDEX